CONSUMER PRICE INDEX MANUAL

Concepts and Methods | 2020

International Labour Organization

eurostat

United Nations

OECD

WORLD BANK GROUP

Cataloging-in-Publication Data
IMF Library

Names: International Labour Office. | International Monetary Fund. | Organisation for Economic Co-operation and Development. | European Union. | United Nations. | World Bank.
Title: Consumer price index manual : concepts and methods.
Description: Washington, DC : International Monetary Fund, [2020]. | Includes bibliographical references.
Identifiers: ISBN 978-1-48435-484-1 (Paper)
978-1-51354-299-7 (ePub)
978-1-51354-298-0 (PDF)
Subjects: LCSH: Consumer price indexes—Methodology. | Price indexes.
Classification: LCC HB225.C66 2020

Eurostat Catalogue number: OA-04-20-634-EN-C (Paper)
Eurostat Catalogue number: OA-04-20-634-EN-N (PDF)

Please send orders to:
International Monetary Fund, Publication Services
P.O. Box 92780, Washington, D.C. 20090, U.S.A.
Tel.: (202) 623-7430 Fax: (202) 623-7201
E-mail: publications@imf.org
Internet: www.elibrary.imf.org
www.bookstore.imf.org

CONTENTS

Box

Figures

Tables

FOREWORD

The *Consumer Price Index Manual: Concepts and Methods* contains comprehensive information and explanations on compiling a consumer price index (CPI). The Manual provides an overview of the methods and practices national statistical offices (NSOs) should consider when making decisions on how to deal with the various problems in the compilation of a CPI.

The chapters cover many topics. They elaborate on the different practices currently in use, propose alternatives whenever possible, and discuss the advantages and disadvantages of each alternative. Given the comprehensive nature of this Manual, it will satisfy the needs of many users.

This publication on the practice of compiling CPIs is an update of *Consumer Price Index Manual: Theory and Practice*, published in 2004. Through the mechanism of the Intersecretariat Working Group on Price Statistics (IWGPS), the update has been managed by the International Monetary Fund (IMF) and jointly published by the organizations of the IWGPS: the Statistical Office of the European Union (Eurostat), the International Labour Organization (ILO), the IMF, the Organisation for Economic Co-operation and Development (OECD), the United Nations Economic Commission for Europe (UNECE), and the World Bank.

The primary purpose of the Manual is to assist countries in producing CPIs that reflect internationally recommended methods and practices. It draws upon a wide range of experience and expertise to describe practical and suitable methods to guide countries in their efforts to improve the quality and international comparability of their CPIs and to meet user needs. The Manual is intended for statistical offices (or other compiling agencies) as a reference to compile the CPI and for training purposes. CPI users, such as employers, workers, policymakers, and researchers, are also targeted. The Manual will not only inform them about the different methods that are employed in collecting data and compiling such indices but will also provide them with information on the limitations of CPIs, so that the results may be interpreted correctly.

The 2004 Manual included extensive theoretical chapters. The theoretical chapters are omitted in the updated version of the Manual, which focuses on providing guidance on best practices for CPI compilation concepts and methods. A companion publication will be released separately that focuses on the theoretical foundations of CPIs. This publication, labeled *Consumer Price Index Theory*, provides an overview of the conceptual and theoretical issues that drive the methods and practices.

Mariana Kotzeva
Director General
Eurostat

Rafael Diez de Medina
Chief Statistician/Director, Department of Statistics
International Labour Office

Louis Marc Ducharme
Chief Statistician and Data Officer, Director, Statistics Department
International Monetary Fund

Paul Schreyer
Chief Statistician, Director, Statistics and Data Directorate
Organisation for Economic Co-operation and Development

Lidia Bratanova
Director, Statistical Division
United Nations Economic Commission for Europe

Haishan Fu
Director, Development Data Group
World Bank Group

PREFACE

The *Consumer Price Index Manual: Concepts and Methods*, herewith referred to simply as the Manual, is an update of the 2004 publication *Consumer Price Index Manual: Theory and Practice*. Since 2004, methods and best practices, as well as user needs, have continued to evolve. Countries have expressed the need for a manual that better reflects current best practices and includes more practical compilation advice. The Manual was prepared under the auspices of the Intersecretariat Working Group on Price Statistics (IWGPS), which consists of six organizations: the Statistical Office of the European Union (Eurostat), the International Labour Organization (ILO), the International Monetary Fund (IMF), the Organisation for Economic Co-operation and Development (OECD), the United Nations Economic Commission for Europe (UNECE), and the World Bank. The Manual is published jointly by the six organizations.

The IWGPS, together with experts from a number of national statistical offices (NSOs) and academia, has collaborated since 2015 on updating this Manual. The sponsoring organizations endorse the principles and recommendations contained in it as good practice for statistical agencies in compiling their consumer price indices (CPIs). Because of practical and resource constraints, some of the current recommendations may not be immediately attainable by all NSOs, and they should therefore serve as guidelines or targets for agencies as they revise their CPIs and improve their CPI programs. There are not always clear-cut solutions to specific conceptual and practical problems such as sample design, choice of index formula, adjustment of prices for quality changes, and the treatment of new products. NSOs must therefore rely on the underlying economic and statistical principles laid out in this Manual to arrive at practical solutions.

The Consumer Price Index

The CPI is an index that measures the rate at which the prices of consumption goods and services are changing from one period to another. The prices are collected from shops or other retail outlets. The usual method of calculation is to take an average of the period-to-period price changes for the different products, using as weights the average amounts that households spend on them. CPIs are official statistics that are usually produced by NSOs, ministries of labor, or central banks.[1] They are published as quickly as possible, generally within four weeks after the reference period.

The Manual is intended for the benefit of agencies that compile CPIs, as well as users of CPI data. It explains in some detail the methods that are recommended for use to calculate a CPI. A separate companion publication, *Consumer Price Index Theory,* explains the underlying economic and statistical theory on which the methods are based.

A CPI is a measure of price changes of the goods and services purchased by households in their role as consumers. It is also widely used as a proxy measure of inflation for the economy as a whole, partly because of the frequency and timeliness with which it is produced. It has become a key statistic for purposes of economic policymaking, especially monetary policy. It is often specified in legislation and in a wide variety of contracts as the appropriate measure for adjusting payments (such as wages, rents, interest, social security, other benefits, and pensions) for the effects of inflation. It can therefore have substantial and wide-ranging financial implications for governments and businesses, as well as for households.

This Manual provides guidelines for NSOs or other agencies responsible for constructing a CPI, bearing in mind that the resources available for this purpose are limited. Calculating a CPI cannot be reduced to a simple set of rules or standard set of procedures that can be mechanically followed in all circumstances. While there are certain general principles that may be universally applicable, the procedures followed in practice, whether they concern the collection or processing of the prices or the methods of aggregation, must take account of particular circumstances. These include the main use of the index, the nature of the markets and pricing practices within the country, and the resources available to the national statistical office (NSO). NSOs have to make choices. The Manual explains the underlying economic and statistical concepts and principles needed to enable NSOs to make their choices in efficient and cost-effective ways and to be aware of the full implications of their choices.

The Manual draws upon the experience of many NSOs throughout the world. The procedures they use are not static but continue to evolve and improve in response to several factors. First, research continually refines and strengthens the economic and statistical theory underpinning CPIs. For example, clearer insights have recently been obtained on the relative strengths and weaknesses of the various formulas and methods used to process the

[1] For simplicity, the Manual refers in general to NSOs as the statistical agencies responsible for compiling the CPI.

basic price data collected for CPI purposes. Second, recent advances in information and communications technology, such as the availability and the technical capabilities to make effective use of large-scale administrative data sets, have affected CPI methods. Both of these theoretical and data developments can impinge on all the stages in compiling a CPI. New technology can affect the methods used to collect prices and transmit them to the NSO. It can also improve the processing and checking, including the methods used to adjust prices for changes in the quality of the goods and services covered. Finally, improved formulae help in calculating more accurate and reliable higher-level indices, including the overall CPI itself.

International Standards for Consumer Price Indices

The objectives of the international standards for CPI compilation are to provide guidelines on best practices that can be used by countries when developing or revising a CPI and to promote the quality and international comparability of national CPIs.

In many countries, CPIs were first compiled mainly to be able to adjust wages to compensate for the loss of purchasing power caused by inflation. Consequently, the responsibility for compiling CPIs was often entrusted to ministries, or departments, of labor. The International Conference of Labour Statisticians (ICLS), convened by the Governing Body of the ILO, therefore provided the natural forum in which to discuss CPI methodology and develop guidelines.

The first international standards for CPIs were promulgated in 1925 by the Second ICLS. The first set of standards referred to "cost of living" indices rather than CPIs. A distinction is now drawn between two different types of indices. A CPI can be defined simply as measuring the change in the cost of purchasing a given "basket" of consumption goods and services, whereas a cost of living index is defined as measuring the change in the cost of maintaining a given standard of living, or level of utility. For this reason, the Tenth ICLS in 1962 decided to adopt the more general term "consumer price index," which should be understood to embrace both concepts. There need not be a conflict between the two. As explained in the Manual, the best practice methods are likely to be very similar, whichever approach is adopted.

The international standards for calculating CPIs have been revised four times, in 1947, 1962, 1987, and 2003 in the form of resolutions adopted by the ICLS. The 1987 standards on CPI were followed by a manual on methods (Turvey and others 1989), which provided guidance to countries on the practical application of the 1987 standards. The 1989 manual on methods was revised, expanded, and published in 2004.

The 51st Session of the United Nations Statistical Commission endorsed this Manual as an international statistical standard on March 4, 2020 and urged all countries to use this Manual in the compilation of their national CPIs.

The Background to the Present Update

Since 2004, substantial progress has been made in developing new data sources, price collection methods, and related index calculation methods. This update incorporates these developments and reflects experience gained improving CPI compilation methods. Finally, evolving user needs and the need for greater international comparability contributed to the necessity for updating the 2004 Manual.

In response to the various developments in CPI compilation methods and the emergence of new data sources, the need to update the 2004 Manual was recognized and agreed in 2014. A formal recommendation to revise the manual was made at the meeting of the UNECE Expert Group on Consumer Price Indices, Geneva, May 2014, jointly organized with the ILO. The participants of this meeting noted a need for clearer, more prescriptive recommendations where research, methodological development, and practical experience support such recommendations and guidelines.

Following the 2014 meeting in Geneva, the IWGPS endorsed the need to update the Manual and selected the IMF as lead agency to manage the update. The overall objective of this update was to develop a more concise manual that provided more practical advice wherever possible. The updated material takes into account experiences gained on the applicability and usefulness of the 2004 Manual; incorporates relevant developments in methods and practices as well as theory and research over the last decade; updates material on data sources, data collection methods, and related calculation methods to reflect developments since 2004; reflects recent developments in user needs; and harmonizes the CPI concepts in line with the *System of National Accounts 2008*.

The Organization of the Update

The six international organizations listed at the beginning of this preface, concerned with the measurement of inflation, have collaborated on the update of this Manual. They have provided, and continue to provide, technical assistance on CPIs to countries at all levels of development. They joined forces to establish the IWGPS to develop international standards and recommendations on price statistics, document best practice guidelines, and support their implementation.

The responsibilities of the IMF, as lead agency within the IWGPS for this update, were to:

- Appoint the various experts on price indices who participated in the updating process, as members of the Technical Expert Group (TEG/CPI), providing substantive advice on the content of the Manual and serving as authors
- Provide the financial and other resources needed
- Arrange meetings of the TEG/CPI, prepare the agendas, and write the reports of the meetings
- Arrange for the publication and dissemination of the Manual

The drafting and updating have entailed meetings and discussions over a five-year period, during which CPI experts from NSOs, international and regional organizations, and academia have participated. The updated Manual owes much to their collective advice and expertise.

The experts participating in the TEG/CPI were invited in their personal capacity as experts and not as representatives, or delegates, of the NSOs or other agencies in which they might be employed. Participants were able to give their expert opinions without in any way committing the offices from which they came.

The update of the Manual involved multiple activities:

- The development of the Manual outline and the recruitment of experts to draft the various chapters
- The review of the draft chapters by the members of the TEG/CPI, the IWGPS, other experts, and CPI compilers
- The posting of the draft chapters on a special website for comment by CPI compilers and data users
- Discussions by the TEG-CPI to finalize each of the chapters
- Agreement by the IWGPS on the adequacy of the content and quality of the chapters for having a global consultation of countries' views
- Formal global consultation by the United Nations Statistics Division
- Inclusion of comments and suggestions from the global consultation
- Final copyediting of the whole Manual
- Endorsement by the 51st Session of the United Nations Statistical Commission

Electronic versions of the Manual are available on the IMF website (www.imf.org/cpi) and the IMF eLibrary (r.imfe.li/cpi-manual). The IWGPS will issue guidance notes that will amend and update specific chapters to address and clarify particular issues as needed. This is especially true for emerging discussions and recommendations to be made by international groups reviewing the CPI, such as the ICLS, the United Nations City Group on Price Indices (the "Ottawa Group"), and the UNECE Expert Group on Consumer Price Indices.

Comments and suggestions on the Manual are welcomed by the IWGPS and should be sent to the International Monetary Fund (email: STARECPIM@imf.org). They will be considered for any future revisions.

ACKNOWLEDGMENTS

The organizations of the Intersecretariat Working Group on Price Statistics (IWGPS) wish to thank all those involved in the drafting and production of the *Consumer Price Index Manual: Concepts and Methods*. Particular thanks go to Brian Graf, the editor, and Margarida Martins, who coordinated work on the Manual. Their efforts greatly enhanced the quality of the Manual. Nada Hamadeh, IWGPS Chair, also deserves special thanks for her efforts to ensure a timely completion of this update.

The current Manual represents an update of the 2004 Manual published by the International Labour Organization (ILO). Individual authors were recruited to review and update each chapter. Some chapters required extensive updating and rewriting, while others needed only minimal updating from the 2004 version of the manual. Two new chapters have been added on scanner data and updating Consumer Price Index (CPI) weights.

The IWGPS established the Technical Expert Group on the CPI (TEG-CPI) for updating the Manual. Members of the TEG-CPI were as follows: Maria Mantcheva, IMF (Retired), Co-chair of the TEG-CPI; Brian Graf, IMF, Co-chair of the TEG-CPI and editor; Margarida Martins, IMF, Secretariat; Badria Al-Aadi, NCSI (Oman); Paul Armknecht, IMF (Retired) and U.S. Bureau of Labor Statistics (Retired); W. Erwin Diewert, University of British Columbia (Canada); David Fenwick, UK ONS (Retired); Claude Lamboray, Eurostat and STATEC (Luxembourg); Yunita Rusanti, BPS-Statistics Indonesia; Raphael Posse, INEGI (Mexico); Mick Silver, IMF (Retired); Valentina Stoevska, ILO; and Jan Walschots, Statistics Netherlands (Retired).

The Manual benefited from the experience of several experts responsible for updating the individual chapters. The authors included: Paul Armknecht, IMF (Retired); Corinne Becker, Swiss FSO; David Fenwick, UK ONS (Retired); Jan de Haan, Statistics Netherlands; Brian Graf, IMF, editor of the Manual; Claude Lamboray, Eurostat; Maria Mantcheva, IMF (Retired); Valentina Stoevska, ILO; Marcel van Kints, ABS; Mick Silver, IMF (Retired); and Jan Walschots, Statistics Netherlands (Retired).

The Manual has also benefited from valuable contributions by many other experts who served as primary reviewers for individual chapters, including: Badria Al-Aadi, NCSI (Oman); Carsten Boldsen, UNECE; Rob Cage, Bureau of Labor Statistics (United States); Barra Casey, CSO (Ireland); Ronald Johnson, Expert (external reviewer); Patrick Kelly, Statistics South Africa; Brent Moulton, Expert (external reviewer); Ragnhild Nygaard, Statistics Norway; Niall O'Hanlon, IMF; Federico Polidoro, ISTAT (Italy); Rafael Posse, INEGI (Mexico); Yunita Rusanti (BPS-Statistics Indonesia); and V. Thuy, GSO (Vietnam).

Finally, the Manual benefited from a comprehensive review and feedback from members of the IWGPS. These include: Carsten Boldsen, UNECE; Yuri Dikhanov, World Bank; Robert Dippelsman, IMF; Louis Marc Ducharme, IMF; Claudia Dziobek, IMF; Anne-Sophie Fraisse, OECD; Nada Hamadeh, IWGPS Chair, World Bank; Francette Koechlin, OECD; Paul Konijn, Eurostat; Claude Lamboray, Eurostat; Jarko Pasanen, Eurostat; Pierre-Alain Pionnier, OECD; Valentina Stoevska, ILO; Gabriel Quiros-Romero, IMF; James Tebrake, IMF; and Peter van de Ven, OECD.

The IMF acted as the Secretariat of the TEG-CPI.

The TEG/CPI officially met twice: March 7–9, 2016 (Washington, DC) and January 18–20, 2017 (Vienna). Informal meetings were held on the sidelines of the meetings of the UNECE Expert Group on CPIs in 2016 and 2018. The Manual also benefited from detailed chapter-by-chapter discussions of the IWGPS members during October 29–30, 2018 (Paris) and January 9–10, 2020.

Gemma Diaz from the IMF Communications Department provided extensive editorial and production support for the final version of this Manual.

ACRONYMS AND ABBREVIATIONS

2008 SNA	System of National Accounts 2008
API	Application Programming Interface
CADC	Computer-Assisted Data Collection
COGI	Cost of Goods Index
COICOP	Classification of Individual Consumption According to Purpose
COLI	Cost of Living Index
CPI	Consumer Price Index
DQAF	Data Quality Assessment Framework
DQRS	Data Quality Reference Sites
DSBB	Dissemination Standards Bulletin Board
EAN	European Article Number
EFQM	European Foundation for Quality Management
e-GDDS	Enhanced General Data Dissemination System
EU	European Union
EUROSTAT	Statistical Office of the European Union
FISIM	Financial Intermediation Services Indirectly Measured
G20	Group of Twenty
GDP	Gross Domestic Product
GEKS	Gini, Eltetö, Köves, and Szulc
GK	Geary–Khamis Method
GSBPM	Generic Statistical Business Process Model
GST	Goods and Services Tax
GTIN	Global Trade Item Number
HBS	Household Budget Survey
HFCE	Household Final Consumption Expenditure
HFMCE	Household Final Monetary Consumption Expenditure
HGMC	Hedonic Geometric Mean Characteristics
HGMI	Hedonic Geometric Mean Imputation
HICP	Harmonised Index of Consumer Prices
ICP	International Comparison Program
ILO	International Labour Organization
IMF	International Monetary Fund
IWGPS	Intersecretariat Working Group on Price Statistics
L-T	Long Term
MMM	Matched-Model Method
MSE	Mean Square Error
N.A.	Not Available
NPISH	Nonprofit Institutions Serving Household
NSDP	National Summary Data Page
NSO	National Statistical Office
OECD	Organisation for Economic Co-operation and Development
OLS	Ordinary Least Squares
OOH	Owner-Occupied Housing
PPI	Production Price Index
PPP	Purchasing Power Parities
PPS	Probability Proportional to Size
R&D	Research and Development
SDDS	Special Data Dissemination Standard
SKU	Stock Keeping Unit
SPD	Structured Product Descriptions
SRS	Simple Random Sampling
S-T	Short Term
TDH	Time Dummy Hedonic
TPD	Time Product Dummy

TQM	Total Quality Management
UN	United Nations
UNECE	United Nations Economic Commission for Europe
UPC	Universal Product Code
VAT	Value-Added Tax
VIF	Variance Inflation Factors

INTRODUCTION, OVERVIEW, AND BASIC STEPS FOR THE CONSUMER PRICE INDEX DEVELOPMENT

1

Introduction

1.1 Chapter 1 provides a self-contained overview of the uses and the basic steps for compiling the consumer price index (CPI). More than just a summary of the chapters to follow, Chapter 1 guides the reader through the compilation process and highlights best practices that are explained in greater detail in subsequent chapters. The flow of the chapter follows the different steps needed to develop and maintain a CPI program that better reflects the standards and best practices set out in the Manual.

1.2 Both compilers and data users will benefit from reading Chapter 1. This chapter provides a primer on the methods used to compile the CPI and explains why one method is preferred over another. The chapter aims to provide a clear, easily understood summary of best practices and compilation methods without being overly technical.

Developing the Consumer Price Index

1.3 CPIs measure changes over time in the general level of prices of goods and services that households acquire (use or pay for) for the purpose of consumption. In many countries, they were originally introduced to provide a measure of the changes in the living costs faced by workers, so that wage increases could be related to changing levels of prices. However, over the years, CPIs have widened their scope and now are widely used as a macroeconomic indicator of inflation, as a tool by governments and central banks for monetary policy and for monitoring price stability, and as deflators in the national accounts. With the globalization of trade and production and the liberalization of the markets, national governments, central banks, and international organizations place great importance on the quality and accuracy of national CPIs, and their international comparability.

1.4 Different conceptual frameworks can be used to address fundamental issues relating to the nature of the index. For example, different concepts are used if the CPI intends to measure the change in the cost of a fixed-weight basket of goods and services or whether the target is to measure the change in the cost of living, that is, the cost of maintaining a given standard of living, taking into account the fact that when prices change consumers change their expenditure patterns. The use and conceptual basis of the index will determine the method of construction.

1.5 The method of construction also allows (or should allow) CPIs to be adapted for a wide range of specific uses. For example, they can be adapted to calculate specific inflation rates for social groups such as pensioners or low-income households. Their product coverage can be adapted to show what the rate of inflation is in particular sectors, such as energy or food, or excluding particular products, such as alcohol and tobacco. They can shed light on the effect of tax changes or government-regulated price changes on the rate of inflation. They can be compiled on a regional basis, showing different inflation rates within different parts of a country or between urban and rural areas.

1.6 CPIs are now considered as one of the most important economic and social indicators produced by national statistical offices (NSOs)[1] throughout the world. Against this background, the challenge of NSOs is fourfold: to identify user needs; to conceptualize user needs with regard to economic concepts; to translate the underlying concept into statistical measurement terms following the fundamental principles of price index measurement; and to construct the indices so defined and evaluate them against purpose.

Overview of the Consumer Price Index Uses and Needs

1.7 A CPI can be used for a variety of purposes, the most common ones being: the indexation of wages, rents, contracts, and social security payments; the deflation of household final consumption expenditure in the national accounts; and the use as a general macroeconomic indicator, especially for inflation targeting and for setting interest rates. Elements of a CPI are also often used in the calculation of purchasing power parities and extrapolating purchasing power parities between benchmark years as required in the International Comparison Program (ICP).[2]

1.8 Given the many uses of CPIs, it is unlikely that one index can perform equally well in all applications. Some countries therefore construct several CPI variants for specific purposes. Each index should be properly defined and named to avoid confusion, and a "headline" CPI measure should be explicitly identified. Where only one CPI is published, it is the main use that should determine its type and scope. If there are several major uses, compromises may have to be made with regard to how it is constructed. The purpose of a CPI should guide all aspects of its construction. CPI producers need to know how their index is being used

[1] NSO is used to describe the compiling agency in this Manual regardless of the institutional setting in a country.

[2] See Chapter 4, *Consumer Price Index Theory*, and Appendix 5, International Comparison Program.

to ensure that it fulfills its purpose. In this connection, user consultation is important.

1.9 This section reviews the various uses of a CPI before examining some of the issues confronted by the index compiler relating to the scope of the index and the practical measurement and compilation decisions which must be made.

The Different Uses of a Consumer Price Index

1.10 CPIs have three main uses:

- *Indexation*

  A CPI may be used for wage or contract indexation of any specific group, whether of a population acquiring products, or of a subset of products themselves. In either case, it should represent the coverage of the group concerned. For instance, it can be argued that the weights of a CPI used for indexation of pensions should cover only the expenditure of the pensioner population. The product and outlet list could also be more appropriately targeted, if the data exist. This means, for example, that a CPI used for indexing pensions may use weights relating to pensioner households and may exclude products which may be thought largely irrelevant to this group of households such as educational items. Similarly, for domestic indexation, the CPI should cover only expenditure of the resident population (see Section on Geographical Coverage and Chapter 2 for more information). More generally, it must be decided whether the CPI should be, in principle, a cost of living index (COLI) or a cost of goods index—these two very different concepts are discussed in the following text.

  For certain specific types of indexation, such as for rents, users may prefer to use just the subindex for rents. In such cases, the subindex should be of a statistical quality sufficient for that purpose.

- *National accounts deflation*

  This use requires consistency between the price data used for the CPI and the expenditure data used in the national accounts. Both data sets should cover the same set of goods and services and use the same concepts and same classification, in principle the Classification of Individual Consumption According to Purpose (COICOP). For example, the national accounts require the valuation of goods produced for own consumption, whereas this is sometimes excluded from the CPI either as a matter of principle or for pragmatic reasons. This applies mainly to the valuation of the services of owner-occupied housing and the consumption of own-produced food.

- *Inflation measurement*

  It can be argued that central banks ideally need a timely index relating to total inflation, not just consumer inflation. But NSOs generally are unable to construct such indices, in part because of the measurement issues relating to government consumption. In the absence of such an index, most central banks rely on a CPI, using the domestic concept (as described in the next section and in Chapter 2), but measured on as wide a basis as possible, with regard to both products and geographical coverage. The same applies to the use of the CPI as a general macroeconomic indicator.

Overview of the Consumer Price Index Concepts

Type of Index Number Formula

1.11 Experts generally agree that the ideal type of index for a CPI would be a "superlative" index such as the Fisher index, which will be discussed in the following text and in Chapter 8. Superlative indices make equal use of the prices and quantities (that is, the expenditure weights) in both periods being compared (the reference period and the current period). Current period expenditure weights are usually not known, so in practice nearly all CPIs rely on weights relating to a weight reference period some time earlier. An exception to this are actual transactions that can be captured at the points of purchase through the use of scanner data (as discussed in Chapter 10).

1.12 Some countries aim to produce a COLI. But such an index is in fact a type of superlative index and suffers from the same practical defect as mentioned previously, and it is not possible to compile in real time.

1.13 Many countries state in their published metadata that they use a Laspeyres index or a "Laspeyres-type" index for their national CPI which, in practice, is not the case. It is important, nevertheless, for NSOs to state publicly what type of index is being calculated in their CPI. A true Laspeyres index uses quantity data which relate to exactly the same period as the price reference period. In practice, however, this is difficult to obtain and rarely the case. Most NSOs have a price reference period which is later than the period to which the quantity data or weights relate. Also, the weights usually will span, say, a year rather than a month (or quarter). This is because one of the main sources of weights data is a household budget survey (HBS), as discussed in Chapter 3, which, ideally, run for 12 consecutive months. The HBS generally produces usable results a year or more after the end of a survey period.

Index Formula at Lower (Elementary Aggregate) Level

1.14 The first stage in the calculation of CPIs is the calculation of elementary price indices, which are then aggregated to obtain higher-level price indices. Expenditure weights are not usually available below the elementary aggregate level. The three most widely known elementary index formulas are the Carli, the Dutot, and the Jevons. These are all based on unweighted averages of prices or price relatives, and each is associated with a number of assumptions which will have an impact on measured inflation. The Carli (a simple arithmetic average of price relatives) and Dutot (the ratio of simple arithmetic averages of prices) formulas have a number of problems associated with their use—particularly the chained Carli, which is discouraged as it is particularly associated with having a known, and potentially substantial, upward bias. The Jevons formula (the ratio of simple geometric averages or the geometric average of price relatives) is increasingly used as it avoids many of the problems associated with the arithmetic versions. It should be noted that an arithmetic average is always greater than or equal to a geometric average and that the difference will be greater, the greater the variance in the price relatives. The choice of formula becomes more important the greater the diversity of price movements which is one argument for ensuring that elementary aggregates are as homogeneous as possible. This topic is discussed in more detail in Chapter 8.

Index Formula at Higher Level

1.15 The higher-level indices are calculated simply as weighted averages of the elementary price indices. The weights typically remain fixed for a sequence of at least 12 months. Some NSOs revise the CPI weights at the beginning of each year to try to approximate as closely as possible the current consumption patterns, but many countries continue to use the same weights for several years. At a minimum, weights should be updated every five years. The use of fixed weights has a considerable practical advantage that the index can make repeated use of the same weights. This saves time and resources. Revising the weights can be both time-consuming and costly if it requires a new HBS to be carried out. However, the longer the period between weight updates, the less relevant and representative the CPI becomes. Many NSOs are moving toward annual or biannual weight updates.

1.16 In Chapters 2–4 of *Consumer Price Index Theory,* the superlative indices Walsh, Fisher, and Törnqvist show up as being "best" in all the approaches to index number theory. These three indices give very similar results so that for any practical reason it will not make any difference which one is chosen as the preferred theoretical target index because they most closely approximate a COLI. The theoretical target index is a matter of choice and affects the choice of formula used to calculate the index. In practice, an NSO may prefer to designate a basket index that uses the actual basket in the earlier of the two periods as its target index on grounds of simplicity and practicality. As noted previously, it is not possible to compile a superlative index in real time. In other words, the Laspeyres index may be the theoretical target index because NSOs produce a CPI that lies between a COLI and a cost of goods index.

Acquisition, Use, or Payment Approach

1.17 A CPI is based on the measurement of the change in prices of the goods and services included in the basket. The vast majority of goods (but not necessarily of total values) are priced in the retail outlets selling them. It should be noted that most often the prices recorded are the labeled prices, which are assumed to be the prices actually paid by consumers. It is also generally assumed that payment for the goods is made at the time of purchase—indeed the consumer would regard the two events as identical. However, payment can be in cash or on credit, including credit cards for which the due date of payment may be several weeks after the actual purchase.

1.18 The time factor is important also in other ways. A consumer may decide to buy a larger than normal quantity of a particular good if there is a special price reduction. The product may then be stored at home and "consumed" (that is, used) over a relatively long period. Cans of food, for example, offered cheaply for a limited period, may be stored at home without deterioration for months, and consumed at the usual frequency.

1.19 Another issue concerns the definition of "usage." A bottle of milk will typically be consumed within a few days of purchase. Consumption is likely to take place in the month for which the CPI is calculated. But a semidurable good such as a shirt will be worn many times over a period of probably several years. Durable goods such as televisions and refrigerators may be used for a decade or more. The question arises as to which CPI month (or months) should the purchase be allocated.

1.20 With services, these questions can be even more complex. Take, for example, the purchase of a season ticket for a bus service. This may be a single payment for a pass which gives ("free") unlimited bus transport for a year. It can be seen that although this example is clearly a service (the use of bus transport over a period of time), it has much in common with the purchase of a durable or semidurable good such as a television or shirt which provides a type of service over a long period. A service such as a medical operation can also be regarded as durable, since it is likely to give long-term health benefits to the patient.

1.21 CPI theory devotes much thought to these issues, which can have important implications not only for how a CPI is compiled but also for the results. Three different approaches can be identified:

- The *acquisitions approach* relates to when the good or service is acquired, irrespective of when it is actually used or consumed. The time of acquisition of a good is the moment at which the legal ownership of the good passes to the consumer. This is usually the point at which the purchaser incurs a liability to pay. On the other hand, with a service there is no change in ownership; it is "acquired" at the time the producer provides it (for example, a single bus journey or airline flights). A CPI based on this approach measures the change in the cost of acquiring a product. The timing of the recorded prices should be consistent with the way in which the value would be recorded in the expenditure data used for the CPI weights.
- The *use approach* relates to the period over which the product is consumed or used. A CPI based on this approach measures the change in the cost of using the product over time; in other words, the cost of the good is distributed over its useful life. Expenditures on durable goods and services are liable to fluctuate depending on the expected duration of their useful life.
- The *payments approach* relates to the period of time when the actual period-to-period payments for the product are made. This can differ from the period when it is acquired and when it is used. When payments are not made in cash, there may be a long period before the purchase is paid for, whether by credit card or other methods. The time at which these debits are made is irrelevant for the recording of the price. The price to be recorded is the price payable at the time of acquisition (though sometimes the method of payment may itself affect the price).

1.22 NSOs need to have a clear policy on which of these approaches is used in their CPI. In practice, the choice between the three approaches is an issue relating to durable goods and its impact is likely to affect the weight given to owner-occupier housing costs. Each of these approaches is discussed in Chapter 10 of *Consumer Price Index Theory*. In countries where food expenditures and other expenditures on nondurables, semidurables, and services account for a significant share of the CPI basket and where credit financing is rarely used, the acquisition, use, and payment approaches will give very similar results and hence the CPI can satisfy many uses equally well. This is the principal reason why most countries use, either implicitly or explicitly, the acquisitions approach to define what constitutes consumption expenditure.

Geographical Coverage

1.23 There are two distinct aspects to the question of the geographical coverage of a CPI. The first relates to the country as a whole (domestic versus national coverage), the second to its regions.

The National versus Domestic Concept

1.24 A CPI can have "national" or "domestic" coverage.

- *National* coverage means that the CPI should cover the expenditure made by resident households (at purchasers' prices)[3] of the country, regardless of where the expenditure takes place. The national concept is appropriate when the CPI is being used for indexation of incomes and cost of living measures. The weights for expenditure abroad can be included in the HBS, but measuring prices paid abroad poses problems. The national concept thus poses a measurement problem for collecting prices abroad.
- *Domestic* coverage means that the CPI would cover all the expenditure made within the economic territory of the country, including the household final consumption expenditure made by foreign visitors. It is appropriate where the CPI is used for national inflation analysis and monetary policy. Many countries carry out surveys of the expenditures of foreign visitors, for example, via International Passenger Surveys conducted at major border crossings and airports by NSO staff. This is particularly important for those countries which have a large number of foreign tourists, or a high level of cross-border shoppers. Foreign visitors will generally have very different expenditure patterns from those of resident households (for example, they will spend more on hotels and restaurants) and to omit them could introduce serious distortions into a CPI aiming to follow the domestic concept, especially if the main purpose of the index is to measure the inflation trends in the economy.

1.25 For the national concept, internet purchases from foreign websites or websites of retailers based abroad should be included in the CPI. So should purchases made abroad more generally, including such items as fees for foreign boarding schools, even if the item, in this case education, is consumed outside the country. Where such purchases are made in the foreign currency, they should be converted to the domestic currency at the relevant exchange rate. Clearly, it would be impracticable to collect prices directly in foreign countries on a continuous basis, although surveys of prices done in order to compute purchasing power parity may provide an occasional benchmark. Where the regular collection of the relevant prices is not practical, it may be possible to obtain a reasonable proxy for price movements using published subindices of the other countries' CPIs.

1.26 Under the domestic concept, the treatment of internet purchases requires a broader approach, especially given its growing importance. Most NSOs which have examined the issue have concluded that internet purchases from home whether from domestic or foreign websites, should be included in the CPI. Care must be taken to convert foreign purchases to the national currency as differences in exchange rates will affect the price paid (for more information on this topic, see Chapters 2 and 11). Chapter 2 provides more information on the domestic versus national concepts, while Chapter 3 provides more detail on the application of these concepts with regard to developing weights.

Regional Coverage

1.27 Concerning the regional coverage of the CPI, the general rule is that a national CPI should cover expenditures and prices throughout the country. However, comprehensive coverage is not always necessary, especially if regional CPIs are not published and the sampling program ensures that the index is representative of the whole country. In such situations, CPI compilers should collect evidence from time to time on the trends in prices in different regions over periods which cover differences in seasonal variations, to ensure that the sample remains representative. Any region which shows price trends significantly different from the others should be covered by the CPI if its inclusion is likely to have a significant effect on the national CPI and will improve representativeness. But there is little point in spending scarce resources collecting prices in sparsely populated regions if that would have little or no impact on the national CPI. When carrying out these sensitivity tests, regional weights can often be an issue. In this case, population may sometimes be used as a proxy for regional consumer expenditure. However, where regional CPIs are aggregated to compute the national CPI, weights should be based on regional expenditure rather than population data.

1.28 Another difficulty regarding regional CPIs is related to the national versus domestic concept. It can sometimes be the case that a household lives in one region but does most of its shopping in an adjacent region, particularly when a household lives close to a regional "border." The question of whether the expenditure weights and the prices should be allocated to the region of expenditure or the region of residence is usually dictated by practical issues. As with the national concept discussed previously, if the region of expenditure is used (equivalent to expenditure abroad by a domestic resident) some method must be found for estimating the proportions of expenditure made by "visiting" consumers in the various regions so that this can be reflected in the price indices.

1.29 Finally, the question often arises as to whether a CPI can be limited to urban areas or if rural areas should also be covered, as in many countries a significant part of population resides in rural areas. Having a rural CPI is important for poverty analysis. Again, in principle, the whole territory should be covered, but clearly, the impact on the national

[3] The *System of National Accounts 2008* (*2008 SNA*, paragraph 6.69) formally defines purchasers' prices. According to the *2008 SNA*, the purchaser's price is the amount paid by the purchaser, excluding any value-added tax or similar tax deductible by the purchaser, in order to take delivery of a unit of a good or service at the time and place required by the purchaser. The purchaser's price of a good includes any transport charges paid separately by the purchaser to take delivery at the required time and place.

CPI of including rural areas where relatively few monetary transactions take place will often argue against their inclusion on grounds of cost. The view taken will depend, at least in part, on the size and treatment of own-account production. If own-account production is included in the CPI, the weights should include a valuation of the physical quantities of such products, often derived from the HBS. The prices will normally be the same as those used for actual transactions for the same goods sold in the same locality.

1.30 Where the weights derived from an HBS are available for rural as well as urban households it is generally better to use the weights for urban and rural households combined, even if price collection is limited to urban areas, as this will normally improve the representativeness of the index. But, where feasible, price statisticians should undertake pilot calculations to test whether this is the case.

Reference Population for the Consumer Price Index

1.31 The group of households included in the scope of a CPI is referred to as the "reference population." According to the *2008 SNA*, households are made up of private households and institutional households. *Private households* are defined as groups of persons who share the same living accommodation, who pool some or all of their resources and consume select goods and services collectively. Members of the same household do not necessarily have to belong to the same family, as long as there is some sharing of resources and consumption. *Institutional households* consist of persons living permanently, or for a very long period of time, in institutions other than private households. These include religious institutions, hospitals, the military, prisons, or retirement homes. Persons who enter such institutions only for short periods of time should be treated as members of the individual households to which they normally belong (the *2008 SNA* defines household, private, and institutional household in paragraphs 4.149–4.154). Temporary foreign workers may live together in special housing blocks, which may also be treated as institutional households in the population census.

1.32 Expenditure on accommodation and living costs, such as lodging fees and charges for meals, imposed by the institution, as well as personal expenditure by the individual on, for example, clothes and toiletries, should be included in the CPI. However, care should be taken to ensure there is no double counting where, for instance, a family rather than an individual pays the accommodation costs charged to a patient in a hospital. A data source like the HBS should be designed to pick up the amount spent on such charges just once and the standard convention is to record it against the household which incurs the costs. In the previous example, the accommodation costs should be included under the expenditure of the family, and not the individual. If individuals spend their own money on clothes and other incidental expenditure, then the HBS should record this expenditure as being incurred by the individuals. In practice, many HBSs do not cover institutional households and, where this expenditure is considered to be significant, estimates will need to be made from, for example, special surveys of people living in institutions or by reference to the expenditure patterns of similar people, say, the same sex, age, and socioeconomic group, living in noninstitutional households.

1.33 In considering the practical issues relating to the inclusion of institutional households in a CPI, two questions need to be asked. First, is the expenditure pattern of institutional residents likely to be significantly different from household residents? Second, even if the answer is yes, would their exclusion from the CPI be likely to significantly affect the national (or regional) CPI? To answer these questions, some research should be carried out on a sample basis.

1.34 Some countries exclude certain household types from the CPI, such as the very wealthy or the very poor. Such exclusions may be on theoretical grounds (for example, using the argument that the expenditure of the wealthy, who are relatively few in number, should not be allowed to affect a CPI which may be used for indexation of wages of ordinary workers) or on practical grounds (for example, using the argument that wealthy households tend to have low response rates to HBSs, and their inclusion can lower the quality of expenditure weights). Such exclusions make the CPI inconsistent with the national accounts coverage. For a CPI which is used for indexation of wages, the exclusion of pensioners and wealthy households may be justified on conceptual grounds. For example, it may be considered that such households are likely to spend their money on atypical products and including them would distort the relevant overall average. It is also argued by some that pensioner households should be excluded in principle from an index used for the escalation or indexation of state pensions because of the circularity involved (the level of state pension influences expenditure patterns which are then used in the up-rating calculation) while others would argue that it is logical that indexation should be based on an index reflecting the expenditure of pensioner households and their specific inflation experience. Note that if wealthy households are excluded, the CPI basket should not include products likely to be bought only by the excluded group, nor should outlets specializing in such products be included in the sample. Conversely, if the wealthy are included, some "luxury" products and outlets should also be included in the sample. For the analysis of national inflation, it is considered that the more comprehensive the CPI, the better.

Democratic versus Plutocratic Weights

1.35 A "democratic" CPI uses weights based on the average proportionate share that households in the whole population have spent on the item. Hence, the share of a specific item in the basket is calculated for each household. The weight for the item is the sum of the household shares divided by the number of households. Many households may purchase the item, but also, a number of households will not make such purchases. The average share is thus based on the experience of each individual household, whether they have purchased the item or not. Each household share is equally weighted in deriving the average. The alternative "plutocratic" CPI calculates the item shares as the total expenditure on the item by all households divided by the total expenditures of all items purchased by households. This latter method gives more weight to the high-spending households. It is argued that a democratic index is more suitable for showing the impact of inflation on the average household but is very rarely compiled by NSOs. There is a consensus that a plutocratic index is the appropriate index to use for national accounts deflation and for a general measure of inflation.

1.36 Many countries publish a range of CPIs relating to subsectors of the population such as all households, low-income households, or pensioner households, but a CPI based on democratic weights is very rare.

Product Exclusions

1.37 In its role as an indicator of total consumer inflation, the CPI should in principle cover all types of goods and services which are consumed in the national retail market. In practice, some types of products may be excluded for policy reasons while other exclusions are unavoidable in practice. These may include: goods sold illegally, such as narcotics; black market sales of mobile phones and other goods; gambling; and prostitution. In most of these cases, except perhaps for legal lotteries, there will be no expenditure data from the HBS and prices are difficult if not impossible to collect. Thus, in principle, estimates of weights and prices will need to be made for the purpose of producing deflators, even if the expenditure is not covered in the CPI. Solutions will need to be found to the practical measurement issues. For instance, if a CPI covers gambling, it is not the gross stakes which should be included in the weight, but the net stakes, which is broadly equivalent to the margin taken by the gambling operator. As it is not likely that the net stakes can be measured, one solution may be to distribute the weight for gambling across other subclasses in COICOP class 09.4.6 (recreational and sporting services).

1.38 The treatment of *second-hand goods* is often found to be problematic. As far as transactions within the household sector are concerned, sales will balance purchases, so the weights will be zero, and they may be excluded from the CPI. But in many countries, there are significant sales of imported second-hand goods from dealers and other third parties, such as cars and clothing. Where sales of imported second-hand goods sold by dealers or other third parties are significant relative to sales of new goods of the same product, such sales should be included, in both weights and prices (as described in Chapter 11).

1.39 CPI compilers sometimes face proposals from governments or pressure groups to exclude certain categories of products for nonstatistical reasons. Common examples are alcohol and tobacco in some countries where their consumption is socially discouraged or they can only be purchased illegally. While it is acceptable to produce a variant of the CPI excluding such products, the all-items CPI should include them, where practical, to ensure that the index presents a true and accurate picture of national inflation.

1.40 Chapter 2 covers in some depth the treatment of other excluded or partly excluded products, including taxes and licenses, subscriptions, insurance, gambling, financial transactions, hire purchase, and interest payments.

Imputed Transactions and Imputed Prices

1.41 A distinction can usefully be made between imputed transactions and actual transactions where a price is imputed. In the category of actual transactions, a prescribed medicine would be provided free as part of a national health service. There is a "transaction" in the sense that a product changes hands but at "zero" price so that it does not constitute a monetary transaction. The conventions for a CPI constructed for the purposes of indexation or the measurement of inflation as a macroeconomic indicator exclude from coverage this category of nonmonetary transaction, so no price should be imputed.

1.42 A CPI should measure the prices of final consumption by a household. In principle, the first category, imputed transactions where households do not incur a liability but bear the costs of acquiring the good or service in another way, should be included in a CPI used for deflation in the national accounts compilation and, in principle, can be included in a CPI compiled for other purposes. Perhaps the most important example is the consumption of own-account production products such as food and owner-occupied housing services. Here, there is no actual transaction at all, and thus no price. If the transaction is to be valued, a price has to be imputed. This would usually be done by reference to actual purchases of the same product in, say, nearby markets. But even when this is done for the purpose of national accounts compilation, it is not necessarily appropriate to include production for own consumption in a general-purpose CPI or in a CPI used for indexation. Indices used as a general measure of inflation or for indexation should be based on a narrow definition of consumption that includes only monetary expenditure. From the point of view of measuring inflation and also for the purposes of income indexation, the most common view is that it is best to omit production for own consumption on pragmatic grounds. Furthermore, goods and services purchased by households which are then used as inputs into own-account production are normally treated as if they themselves were consumption goods and services, and therefore are included in the CPI. Some countries may find it useful to produce two versions of the CPI: one including and the other excluding own-account production. This topic is further discussed in Chapter 11.

Deciding on the Index Coverage and Classification Structure

1.43 Classification is a central theme in the compilation of the CPI. Choosing a classification system is the first step in compiling the CPI because its subaggregates must be defined in such a way that the expenditure weights and prices will relate precisely to the coverage of the subaggregates. The classification is also important because it establishes the framework to define and draw the boundaries for the inclusion of the representative items in the index (and sometimes the outlets). Finally, the classification system helps in defining which level of the hierarchy will be suitable for publication.

1.44 In years past, countries used their own distinct systems for classifying the range of products covered by their CPI. Most countries have now, however, moved to the international standard classification COICOP.

1.45 COICOP was first developed for the *1968 SNA* to provide the structure for classifying household final consumption expenditure. The various components of household final consumption expenditure are often used as the basis for the weights in the CPI. The 2003 International Labour Organization (ILO) Resolution on CPIs requires that national CPI classifications should be reconcilable with COICOP at least at its higher aggregation levels. Most countries have adopted COICOP in their economic statistics (for example, in the CPI, national accounts, ICP, and HBSs), with a clear advantage for integration of data sets and enhanced analytical capabilities.

Classification Systems: The General Case

1.46 In its broadest sense a classification is a procedure in which individual items are organized into categories (classes) and subcategories (subclasses) based on information on one or more characteristics inherent to the items. A classification structure will usually have these same items (or elements) arranged in a hierarchically ordered system based on category–subcategory relationships where the subcategory has the same description as the associated category in addition to one or more descriptions. For example, an apple is a subclass of fruit. So any apple is a fruit, but not every fruit is an apple. A product needs to have a more detailed description to be an "apple" and not just a "fruit."

1.47 In principle, a classification system can be based on any attribute of the objects being classified. Normally, organizing a population of items into categories must leave no two categories with any item in common; in other words, the categories must be mutually exclusive. Also, the categories must collectively include all of the items which are in the population—the categories must be exhaustive. For example, in the case of the CPI, its classification should include the entire universe of goods and services that are covered by the index (for example, fresh food purchased in a store by a consumer is part of the CPI, while heavy machinery such as a tractor is not) and no product should be included in two different categories in the structure.

The Consumer Price Index Classification System

1.48 COICOP, as its name implies, is founded on the principle of "purpose" (see Box 1.1). It is a purpose-type classification because throughout the aggregation program the products are grouped according to the purpose (or function) they usually fulfill such as transport, nourishment, shelter, and so on. Most national CPIs aim at measuring the change of the cost of a basket of goods and services, which is consumed for the purpose of satisfying certain needs. A purpose-based classification would therefore appear to be the logical classification system for a CPI.

1.49 The official COICOP is a five-digit classification. NSOs will expand the COICOP to six and seven digits to obtain more detail for their use. At the higher level of the classification, the products are grouped according to the purpose. Households will select various goods and services in order to satisfy their consumption objectives (that is, renting an apartment for the provision of shelter or eating an apple for the purpose of nourishment). These goods and services are disaggregated further into various groups and may not be based solely on the principle of purpose but also according to product type. For example, oranges and apples are included in the "Fruit" category. The more detailed breakdown is often a product-type classification because these items share a similar production process and are certainly sold at fruit stands or the same location in the supermarket.

Box 1.1 Classification of Individual Consumption According to Purpose (COICOP)

The COICOP classification structure has been updated and the new version, COICOP 2018, was endorsed by the United Nations Statistical Commission in March 2018. COICOP 2018 replaces COICOP 1999 as the official standard classification for the CPI.

While a number of countries have begun to implement COICOP 2018, many others will implement the updated classification in the coming years during a future CPI update. Because many countries continue to use COICOP 1999, the Manual presents some examples using COICOP 2018 and others using COICOP 1999.

Chapter 2 summarizes the key changes made to COICOP. The detailed classification structures for both COICOP 2018 and COICOP 1999 are included as appendices to the Manual.

Deriving the Weighting Pattern

1.50 A CPI measures changes in the cost of a representative basket of goods and services. This involves weighting aggregated prices for different categories of goods and services so that each takes an appropriate share to reflect the budgets of the households covered by the index. For instance, if most people spend far more on fresh vegetables than on electricity, then a price rise for fresh vegetables must have more effect on overall price rises than a similar-sized increase for electricity. Therefore, at the lowest level, each elementary aggregate should receive a weight equal to the ratio of expenditure by the covered households on items represented by that aggregate to total expenditure by covered households on all items within the scope of the CPI. Chapter 3 discusses the derivation and sources of the expenditure weights and provides detailed guidance on specific issues.

1.51 The 2003 ILO Resolution on CPIs makes the obvious but important point that the weights follow directly from the scope of the index as well as from the choice between the "acquisition," "use," or "payment" approach, as described in paragraph 1.22. It also states that there are two main sources of information: HBSs and national accounts, and that the weights should be reviewed and updated at least every five years. Additionally, new sources of weight information are being developed such as actual expenditures on various types of transactions based on scanner data and other electronic formats. Such sources are being evaluated and exploited for use in development of weights now and in the future.

1.52 The use of expenditure weights is consistent in concept with a CPI based on the acquisition, payment, and user cost approaches although the treatment of major durable goods and housing can present a problem, particularly the costs of owner-occupied housing. The use of weights in a CPI based on total consumption expenditure is often referred to as plutocratic weights because this concept gives more weight to the expenditure patterns of high-spending households (which will also tend to be those with higher incomes). Paragraph 1.36 provides more details on plutocratic weights.

1.53 The goods and services consumed by the households can in principle be acquired in four ways: (1) purchase in monetary transactions; (2) from own production; (3) as payment in kind; and (4) as transfers or gifts from other economic units, including social transfers in kind provided by government and nonprofit institutions serving households.

1.54 The weights are determined by the scope of the CPI and should be derived on the basis of the relevant coverage and types of consumption and with reference to SNA concepts. But it should be noted that there are several delineations of consumption used, as described in Chapter 2. The broadest possible scope for goods and services would cover all four of the previous categories. It would include all social transfers in kind in the form of education, health and housing, and other goods or services provided free of charge or at nominal prices. The total acquisition of goods and services thus described is equivalent to household actual final consumption in the SNA. For the CPI as a general measure of inflation, the more relevant would be to include only goods and services purchased in monetary transactions by the households. Only monetary transactions generate prices that can be observed for the CPI, but this then leaves outstanding the issue of owner-occupier housing services which is considered in detail in Chapter 11.

1.55 It is against this background that a CPI often follows the concept of household final consumption expenditure, as laid down in the *2008 SNA*. This approach is often recommended for a CPI being used as a macroeconomic indicator, restricted to the appropriate reference population, or "Index Households," where the CPI is being used as a compensation index. This compensation index might, for example, exclude the very rich.

1.56 Household final consumption expenditure includes nonmonetary transactions (such as for owner-occupier housing or consumption of own production of food). The concept of "household final monetary consumption expenditure," used in the European Union Harmonised Index of Consumer Prices defines both the goods and services to be covered, and the price concept to be used, and refers only to monetary transactions. Household final monetary consumption expenditure is a useful concept but many countries prefer to also include some nonmonetary transactions (in particular owner-occupier housing) in their CPI, sometimes using imputed costs thus moving the coverage of the index closer to household final consumption expenditure. Chapter 2 provides more details on the different types of consumption.

1.57 The conceptual issues relating to the construction of weights are discussed in detail in Chapter 3.

Weighting Structure

1.58 The weighting structure should follow the aggregation structure of the CPI. For instance, if this structure is based on COICOP, then this is the structure which should be used for the weights.

1.59 Additional subdivisions can be introduced where there is further stratification of the sample to include geographical location, outlet type, or a more detailed product level classification. Thus, the weighting structure will depend on the sample design for price collection and compilation and in particular the need for more detailed weights which may be generated by additional sample stratification. In general, NSOs will collect some prices centrally and adopt up to four levels of sampling stratification for local price collection: locations; outlets within locations; items within different sections of expenditure; and varieties. The sampling of varieties is normally conducted in the field by price collectors and does not normally involve explicit weights (see Chapter 5). Stratification is frequently used to increase sampling and operational efficiency, especially where the retail market is heterogeneous (see Chapter 5). Some levels are the following:

- *Central shops weights* to represent a small number of large supermarket chains or chain stores which have uniform prices across branches and prices are provided by the shops' headquarters.
- *Stratum weights*. For some types of expenditure, purchasing patterns may differ markedly by region or type of outlet, and in these cases, stratification will improve the accuracy of item indices. For example, each locally collected item in the index could be allocated to one of the different stratum types to allow the best available information about purchasing patterns to be incorporated in the index calculation. Depending on the structure of the retail market, the stratum types could be: region and outlet type; region only; outlet-type only; and no stratification. The assignment of stratum type will depend on the information available for constructing the weights for each item and the number of prices collected per item. In principle, all locally collected items might be stratified by both region and outlet type, but if the weights data are unreliable or nonexistent at this level of detail, then the item may be allocated to another stratum type. Allocation also partly depends on which outlet types are specified for the collection of prices and the number of prices collected. If the rules for the choice of outlets did not specify that both a chain and an independent outlet should be chosen for an item, there may be too few prices collected in one of these outlet types to make stratification by outlet type meaningful. In some instances, there may be no stratification because research has shown that stratification has little effect.

  The weight of an elementary aggregate (that is, the stratum weight) should reflect the expenditure on the entire elementary aggregate and not the weights of the outlets and items that have been chosen to represent it. For instance, if spaghetti is chosen as the representative product under the elementary aggregate with the heading of pasta products, then the weight of this category should reflect expenditures for all pasta products and not solely the "lower" weight of spaghetti; that is, the weight of the pasta category will be represented entirely by spaghetti. Similarly, if an expenditure category is divided into two elementary aggregates according to outlet type, say, open markets and supermarkets, with corresponding market shares of food sales, 70 percent and 30 percent, respectively, then the same rule as mentioned previously should apply. For instance, suppose a single store is selected as the representative outlet for a particular food item sold in supermarkets in a country where two supermarket chains have equal sales, then the sales from the sampled store will account for the total value of the expenditure weight of 30 percent; the weight of the elementary aggregate for this food item sold in supermarkets should not be 15 percent (0.30×0.50), that is, a weight based only on the sales of the selected supermarket.
- *Product or item weights* (in the current context the terms can be interchangeable). Some products or items may be intended only to represent themselves; others represent a subclass of expenditure within a section. For instance,

within electrical appliances, an electric cooker may represent only itself and not any other kinds of electrical appliances. However, other products or items will represent price changes for a set of products or items, which are not all priced, so for these the weight reflects total expenditure on all products or items in the set. For example, a screwdriver may be one of several items representing all spending on small tools within home improvement and maintenance materials, and there are other items within the section representing all spending on paint, timber, fittings, and so on.

- *Upper-level or section weights.* It is common practice to give each section an integer weight in parts per thousand or per hundred so that the sum of the section weights is 1,000 or 100. It is likely that most of these weights will be based on the HBS results. The main exceptions will be some housing sections, including (where applicable) mortgage interest payments and depreciation, where weights are estimated from other sources (see Chapter 11), and for certain other sections (for example, tobacco, confectionary, soft drinks, and alcoholic drinks) where the HBS may be thought to under-record expenditure and better data are available elsewhere. Many countries also use national accounts household final consumption expenditure estimates where available at the COICOP group or class level and the HBS expenditure distribution at the lower levels. This is also an area where scanner data can be used to more accurately reflect the expenditure distribution.

Implicit Weights Within Elementary Aggregates

1.60 An unweighted formula (for example, Jevons or Dutot—see paragraphs 1.145–1.151 on elementary price indices) is usually used when aggregating the elementary aggregate price relatives of the sample of products at the elementary aggregate level. This practice is usually justified on the grounds that the required information such as market shares is simply not available to a sufficient level of precision. However, if broad-based estimates of market shares are available, then these can be used as implicit weights for determining the sample of price observations to enhance the accuracy of the elementary price index. Some possible sources for this information are transaction shares from scanner data, trade publications, market reports, and consultation with industry experts.

1.61 The sample of price observations based on implicit weights can be updated independently and more frequently than the weights of the elementary aggregate; however, the price statistician will need to ensure that the weights are both coherent and consistent within the elementary aggregate. It is best to review them at the time of updating the basket.

Weights for Products for Which Prices Are Not Collected

1.62 As it is not feasible to collect a full set of prices from every outlet, including market stalls and street vendors, and from every provider of a service, all prices have to be sampled. This means that in practice there will be some products which consumers spend money on for which prices will not be collected (see Chapter 4). However, the expenditures for these products need to be included in the expenditure weights. There are two ways of doing this: (1) including the weight in a related elementary aggregate (this may involve the creation of a "miscellaneous" category), or (2) having the weight of the product for which no representative prices exist equal to zero, which essentially redistributes the weight to other elementary aggregates.

1.63 In general, the prices for the product for which prices are not collected will be expected to exhibit a similar movement to the other products in the elementary aggregate and the first of the previous two methods should be used. The second method may be used where the elementary aggregate is heterogeneous, or the associated price index is not considered very reliable. Because of the negligible size of the weight value involved, the consequence on the overall index will also be negligible whichever method is used.

Data Sources

1.64 Depending on the population coverage, weights for a CPI are derived either from expenditure data based on estimates drawn from a sample covered in the HBS or from national accounts estimates of household final consumption expenditure. It should be emphasized, however, that expenditure estimates in the national accounts are usually partially based on HBS information, although they may differ with regard to coverage, and that in some countries these are not available or not compiled at a detailed level. The two sources are not entirely independent. Note also that national accounts data may also be used when the HBS is conducted too infrequently to ensure the reliability of the CPI or when the expenditure weights need to be updated more often than the periodicity of the HBS. Nevertheless, an HBS will still have to be conducted eventually because it is an important source for benchmarking the components of household final consumption expenditure of the national accounts. Other sources for the weights are also available and are usually complementary to these two main sources. These include administrative data sources or retail trade statistics data. These are discussed in Chapter 3.

1.65 When various sources of information are used for generating the weights in a CPI, the compiler should take the time to check the data to ensure that the results are consistent and plausible with what is expected or investigate further if necessary.

Household Budget Surveys

1.66 When using the HBS as the basis for developing CPI weights, the sample size (number of households) should be sufficient to ensure that the expenditure data yielded produce statistically reliable and representative weights at the elementary aggregate level. In some countries, the acceptable statistical quality is based on the coefficient of variation (the ratio of the standard deviation to the mean). For those expenditure weights that are unable to meet the minimum requirement of reliability, three options should be considered:

- If reliable expenditure data are not available for an elementary aggregate, they can be combined with another related elementary aggregate to form a new broader elementary aggregate (for example, "wheat bread" could be combined with "rye bread" to form a new category called "bread"). This approach will often lead to a more reliable elementary aggregate but may require an adjustment to the existing structure of the CPI.

- If annual HBS data are available, then expenditures could be averaged over more than one year thus improving the statistical reliability of the data, with regard to standard errors, but to the detriment of timeliness. It should also be noted that averaging may not improve the statistical quality of the expenditure estimates if a particular category of household expenditure is rapidly growing or declining. Averaging is useful if the particular expenditure category under consideration shows a lot of variability over several HBSs but no clear trend. This is an area where statisticians will have to use their judgment. The basket reference period should not be arbitrarily chosen and periods of less than a year should be avoided because of seasonal influences on consumption patterns. Furthermore, some countries exclude, from multiyear averages, years which are exceptional, for example, as a result of particularly poor harvests leading to high prices and distorted expenditure weights.
- Leave the CPI structure unchanged and simply accept that the weight for the particular elementary aggregate concerned is less than ideal. Whether this is an acceptable position to take will depend on the weight of the elementary aggregate and on its importance, particularly to analysts. For example, it would be a difficult position to sustain if the elementary aggregate has a large weight and is presented as a published subindex.

1.67 It should be noted that in normal circumstances weights can tolerate a certain degree of imprecision before having a significant effect on the overall CPI, particularly at the higher levels of aggregation, or main divisions of the CPI. But this is less so at lower levels. For instance, an index described as "fruits and vegetables" where the true weight for fruit is 40 percent and the weight of vegetables is 60 percent, but with a biased estimate of the expenditure weights, fruits account for 60 percent of the index and vegetables the remaining 40 percent. The biased weights affect the relative importance of both fruits and vegetables in the basket, giving too much weight to fruit and too little weight to vegetables. Consequently, the price index for "fruits and vegetables" will be also biased. To minimize the potential for such occurrences, it is recommended that the compiler always strives to get the best possible estimates for the expenditure weights.

1.68 An annual HBS is optimal for a CPI because as well as avoiding one-off setup costs, it permits the annual updating of the weights, hence reducing the substitution bias associated with out-of-date weights in a fixed-basket index like the CPI. Furthermore, it provides the opportunity for using multiyear weights to reduce the sampling error and, where considered appropriate, minimize the sampling variance associated with unusual expenditure patterns in a particular year (for instance, abnormal circumstances affecting consumer behavior such as political events, natural disasters, or oil shocks). But obtaining reliable consumption estimates is challenging and there is a persistent trade-off between data quality and survey cost.

National Accounts

1.69 The use of national accounts weights ensures consistency and comparability between the CPI and national accounts definitions and classification systems for household consumption, which is an advantage when compiling a CPI as a macroeconomic indicator and for use as a deflator.

1.70 National accounts have two inherent advantages:

- The household final consumption expenditure aggregate of national accounts may be derived mainly from the HBS, but national accountants will often use other sources of information before finalizing their results, especially in cases where the accuracy of the HBS is in doubt such as where underreporting is present. National accounts go through an additional quality assurance process and reestimation should increase the reliability of the weights.[4]
- Even if the HBS is updated infrequently, CPI weights can still be updated at regular intervals from national accounts data for higher-level aggregates at the division or group level.

1.71 However, there are two inherent disadvantages with national accounts data:

- They are generally only available at the national level, so deconstruction of the national accounts data to provide a finer level of detail or to produce regional expenditure weights may be necessary using other available sources of information. Other data sources include HBSs, retail surveys, aggregated transaction from scanner data, and administrative data such as statistics on excise duty. National accounts data can be used to derive weights at the more aggregate level, and HBS data can then be applied to derive weights at the lower levels of the aggregation program. If the expenditure data from the HBS are not viewed as sufficiently detailed to ensure a minimum of acceptable accuracy, or if a demand exists for indices of a finer breakdown (for example, there is a need for a price index for apples but only expenditures for all fruit can be derived from the HBS), then other potential data sources can be used for disaggregating the expenditures, including surveys of retail sales from establishments, point-of-sales surveys and aggregated scanner data, surveys of production, export and import data, and administrative data. Note that some of these sources may also be used for stratifying expenditures according to sales volumes by retail outlet type and by region.
- National accountants apply an element of discretion and judgment when making operational decisions relating to the construction of national accounts. Some of the details of these decisions are not always readily available to users. Consequently, compilers of the CPI should consult with their national accounts counterparts regularly before using their data for weights in order to ensure that they are consistent with the objectives of the CPI.

Designing the Sample

1.72 Chapter 4 gives advice both on sample selection, that is, how to construct a sample, and on estimation procedures, that is, how to estimate the CPI from the sample

[4]This assumes the national accounts have independent expenditure side estimates, and household final consumption expenditure is not estimated as a residual.

of prices collected. This Manual recognizes that in practice nonprobability sampling sometimes needs to be carried out. Similarly, although the 2003 ILO Resolution states that probability sampling techniques are to be preferred, it goes on to say that "where appropriate sampling frames are lacking and it is too costly to obtain them, samples of outlets and products have to be obtained from non-probability methods" and that "statisticians should use available information and apply their best judgement to ensure that representative samples are selected."

1.73 To construct a perfectly accurate CPI, the price statistician would need to record the price of every variety of every good and service purchased by the consumer. This would mean collecting a full set of prices from every outlet, including market stalls and street vendors, and from every provider of a service, including public utilities such as water and electricity, private transport including shared minibuses and the hire of rickshaws, modern forms of communication, such as mobile telephones, and the provision of domestic service. As this is not feasible in practice, most prices have to be sampled and this involves local price collection in a selection of outlets in a sample of locations chosen to be representative of the country as a whole and at selected times on selected days.

1.74 The exceptions to selecting a sample of prices as described in the previous one are prices which can be collected from a central source, such as a public utility provider, national retail chain headquarters, or a government department. For many of these items, all prices will be taken and no sampling will be involved. For example, the service provider may give the NSO a full price list or tariff from which all the prices can easily be extracted. This may be the case where sampling would not make sense or would be unreliable because the number of prices is very small. For instance, no sampling would be involved if an electricity tariff consisted of a standard standing charge for service provision and a standard charge per kilowatt of electricity used, which was the same for all customers regardless of location and only varied with total usage (with heavy users getting a discount after a certain threshold). In this case, the tariff prices would be collected and applied to a typical cross-section of users and varying quantities of electricity. Sampling would be used to choose a cross-section of users.

Approaches to Drawing Samples

1.75 The focus of this section is on sampling procedures for local price collection in outlets, including options relating to probability and nonprobability sampling. There is a section in Chapter 5 which specifically addresses the special challenges of sampling prices in markets and prices charged by street traders. Chapter 5 also addresses the associated issue of price bargaining and discusses the issue of volatile prices.

1.76 As only a sample of prices will be recorded in the course of local price collection, there is inevitably some sampling error in measuring the CPI. The sampling procedures should aim to minimize this sampling error, maximize sampling efficiency (that is, obtain the maximum sampling precision for minimum fieldwork and processing costs) and reduce bias as much as possible. The sample design should allow publication of subindices at all levels which have been decided upon, such as regional indices or separate subindices for urban and rural areas. As well as cost, a limiting factor in sample design is the time taken in collecting prices. Practical considerations that will need to be considered include the availability of price collectors and transportation issues.

1.77 In general, NSOs adopt four levels of sampling for local price collection: locations; outlets within locations; items within different sections of the expenditure classification; and product varieties. Stratification is also frequently used to increase sampling efficiency, especially where the retail market is heterogeneous. Often a combination of probability sampling and nonprobability sampling is used.

1.78 When using probability sampling, the units in the sample are selected so that each has a known nonzero probability of selection. For instance, locations could be randomly selected from local administrative areas with probability according to total population,[5] the population representing a proxy for the retail turnover in the area. Within a location, outlets could be randomly selected from a business register, with probability according to their individual turnover or sales or by floor area measured by an enumerator listing and visiting each shop. Sample selection based on probability according to size increases sampling efficiency. Also, as the aim is to have a sample which is representative of retail turnover, the prices subsequently collected on the previous basis would then not need to be rebalanced by reweighting if the assumption holds that those population and floor areas are good proxies for turnover. Alternatively, each location and outlet could be given an equal chance of selection in the sample, regardless of the total proportion of the retail market that they account for, but then reweighting would be necessary.

1.79 In practice, sample selection is never straightforward, and compromises must be made for good practical reasons even when a sampling frame exists. Administrative boundaries may not coincide well with statistical targets. For instance, choosing administrative areas using probability according to population could ignore the inconvenience of administrative boundaries that straddle the border between a commercial district and a residential area so that, contrary to the intention, the commercial district has no chance of being selected as it contains no houses. Also, a visit to the location may indicate that it is impractical for the collection of prices, for example, because of a physical barrier such as a railway or river bisecting the area and causing difficulties of access. Similarly, very rarely do NSOs have readily available sampling frames which reliably list all retail outlets, particularly recent openings, and even fewer will have lists that cover all market stalls in all types of markets, or mobile street vendors. The relative advantages and disadvantages of random and purposive sampling should be examined at each stage of the sample selection. It is recommended that the NSO should first decide on the ideal sampling solution and then modify this to take into account practical constraints.

1.80 The ultimate goal should be:

- *An overall sample which is representative of the total population of goods and services being offered for sale*

[5] A more appropriate alternative might be number of workers employed or aggregated retail turnover in the location if this is known. This may be the case where most shopping is done in town centers but with most people living in residential areas in the suburbs.

and purchased. The sample chosen should be representative of price levels and, most particularly, price movements. All variations of items and outlet types should be considered for each product and chosen to reflect typical consumer purchasing habits.

- *A variance or mean square error which is as low as possible*. Samples should be reasonably optimized. At the very least, a basic analysis of sampling variance should be conducted, even if an overall estimate of the precision of the CPI cannot be made.
- *Optimization*. The entire set of sample prices should be optimized to meet the publication needs of the CPI, taking into account user requirements, practical data collection considerations, and cost.

Collecting and Editing the Prices

1.81 Chapter 5 provides an overview of the most appropriate survey methods for the collection of prices while Chapter 10 discusses the detailed approaches that can be used for scanner data. In large part, the considerations are the same as for sample design and will depend on local circumstance. For instance, the methods should consider: the purchasing habits of consumers and the extent to which they use licensed and unlicensed markets and internet purchases; the structure of the retail market including the balance between markets, small independent shops, and large retail chains; the extent of public ownership and price control; the diversity of goods and services being sold; the pricing structures used, including tariffs; and whether bargaining is common. The availability of central records of prices charged also has an important bearing. The 2003 ILO Resolution emphasizes the importance of well-trained price collectors who adhere to the standard procedures.

1.82 There are two basic price collection methods:

- *Local price collection* where prices are obtained from outlets located around the country. This will include licensed and unlicensed markets and street vendors as well as shops. Normally the price collector will need to visit the outlet to observe the prices although the prices for some items may be collected by other means, including telephone and price lists.
- *Central price collection* is often used where prices can be collected by the head office without the need for fieldwork. This may also include centrally regulated or centrally fixed prices which can be obtained from the regulatory authorities, although in these cases checks will need to be made to ensure that the goods and services in question are actually available and sold at the stated price. It is not unusual to find goods subject to price control being sold at a different "unofficial" price. Central price collection can be further broken down into:
  - *Prices which are combined with prices collected locally*. For instance, this may occur when a supermarket chain provides centrally determined price lists or actual transaction data, from scanners, eliminating the need for the price collector to visit a shop in person.
  - *Prices which are used on their own to compute centrally constructed indices*. Most tariffs fall into this category.

1.83 Goods and services that normally are paid according to a tariff can pose problems when their structures are modified over time, compromising the principle of unchanged consumption. Examples include public transport fares, electricity, main water supply, physicians, hospital services, and telecommunications. For utilities, the payment may consist of a standard rate per unit of consumption sometimes in combination with a fixed charge. A solution to this problem is to define representative services or bundles of services (for example, categories of consumers and specific services consumed). For these, it is important that the prices experienced by a representative range of customers and tariffs are observed and that customer profiles are kept constant over time. More detailed advice is given in Chapter 11 on selected special cases.

1.84 The focus in the next paragraphs is on locally collected prices. It begins by reviewing the principles behind collecting prices for a CPI and then considers the practical collection issues and how these should be managed. A working assumption has been made that the index being compiled is an acquisition index (see Chapter 4). It is also assumed that prices are being collected for a monthly price index with prices therefore being collected, in general, every month. Some countries produce only a quarterly CPI, while others produce a weekly index, especially for fresh food. The concepts and procedures discussed will apply to price collection practices, whatever the frequency of index publication.

The Principles of Price Collection

1.85 Except in a small number of cases, such as the treatment of owner-occupied housing costs, a CPI is usually designed to measure the change in the actual transaction prices of goods and services bought by consumers. However, collectors cannot normally observe individual transactions as they occur, so they must usually observe the price marked on or assigned to the product and assume that these are the transaction prices. Many countries are also improving the collection of actual transaction prices through the use of electronic technologies such as scanner data and internet purchases. An exception to observation and electronic capture is bargaining, where a price might not even be displayed, and this case is discussed in detail in Chapter 5. Special procedures apply when outlets in which items are being priced close down, or the items which the price collector was pricing at a particular outlet are no longer sold by that outlet. These procedures are covered in Chapters 4 and 7.

The Principle of a Fixed Basket

1.86 Underlying all of what follows in this section is an important principle: the necessity to compare prices on a like-to-like basis from one period to the next. This has two consequences:

- Where the price collector has the role of selecting what variety of a product to price in a particular outlet, a consideration should be whether that variety will be available to price over a reasonably long period (tight specifications are of no use if the described variety cannot be found in the outlets). This is in addition to being typical of what is sold to customers.

- The price collector should record additional information needed to ensure the unique identification of the variety priced so that:
  - The same variety continues to be priced in the case of price collection being carried out by a different person.
  - The identification of quality change can be evaluated when the variety disappears and is replaced by a different one allowing an adjustment for quality change to be made.

Variety Specifications

1.87 There are no firm rules, especially regarding the use of looser or tighter variety specifications: each country may choose its preferred methods—and stick to them. However, there are a number of considerations in deciding on variety specifications:

- Tight specifications leave less discretion to the price collector, so the reliability and training of collectors are factors to consider when deciding whether to use loose or tight specifications.
- Particular care should be taken to ensure that the specification is very detailed for heterogeneous items where there is scope for significant difference between one variety and another, and for items which by nature are highly specified. Cars and hi-tech goods fall into the latter category.
- Tight specifications also allow for the calculation of meaningful average prices:
  - Average prices are useful in identifying outliers and assessing the accuracy of the reported prices.
  - Average prices allow comparisons of price levels, including between, for example, regions or urban and rural areas.

1.88 Responsibility for specifying the items to be priced should normally rest with the head office. Specifications should be reviewed on a regular basis to determine whether they continue to be relevant. A revision of specifications could be implied by: (1) a large number of missing price quotations; (2) a large number of substitutions; or (3) a wide variation in the distribution of collected price levels.

1.89 Some countries find structured product descriptions (SPDs) from the ICP helpful for specifying items to be priced in a CPI. As well as providing a ready-made framework for detailed item specifications the use of SPDs has the additional advantage of facilitating greater integration between the two price collection exercises leading, among other things, to savings in collection costs from using the same price quotes in both the CPI and ICP.

Data Editing

1.90 Once the price information has been collected and recorded it has to be edited. Data editing is the process of ensuring correct and usable data for calculation of price indices for elementary aggregates. Data editing is sometimes referred to as input editing. There are three steps in this process:

- The detection of possible errors and outliers
- The verification and correction of data
- Output review

The detection of errors in the collection and recording of price information must occur as soon as possible after the information is collected. Detection is usually achieved by examining price movements and checking those that exceed some predefined limits or appear to be unrealistic based on an analysis of all available information. Statistical outputs should sufficiently portray the reality of the economy, and with an output review, the compiler ensures the indices reflect reality.

1.91 It should be noted that while price collectors should examine every price they collect, subjecting every collected price to the same level of examination by collection supervisors and index compilers is not considered necessary and generally is not feasible. It is recommended that, to improve cost-effectiveness, some form of significance rating should be applied to determine how much time and effort should be expended on editing individual prices.

- In general, prices from elementary aggregates with relatively small price samples should receive more attention from the index compiler. This is because the weights of the elementary aggregates are broadly equal. Each individual price movement from these elementary aggregates will have potentially a much more significant influence on the index calculations than any individual price movement from an elementary aggregate with a large number of price quotes.
- Price samples from elementary aggregates with high expenditure weights should be examined critically as the high expenditure weight will make all price movements within the sample significant to the index calculation.
- The highest risk is associated with elementary aggregates with relatively large weights but few price quotes and with complex index construction. This situation is associated with utilities and other services which account for relatively large expenditures and where there may be only one or a handful of suppliers and prices are based on complex tariffs. Petrol prices could be another example.

1.92 There are two main categories of checking and identifying possible data errors and outliers, as further described in Chapter 5:

- Nonstatistical checking
- Statistical checking

1.93 Some of the editing techniques discussed in Chapter 5 work best when applied to large quantities of data. The best results will therefore be obtained if conducted at the location where many prices are available to any analyst. This will generally be regional offices or, more probably, in the head office. However, the techniques can be adapted and still be applied to prices held by a small collection center as a way of quickly and efficiently detecting extreme prices. Abnormal prices such as sale prices, or price movements, such as sale recovery prices, may be excluded from automated procedures for the detection of outliers, in particular the setting of upper and lower bounds, but should nevertheless be checked, for instance by reference to previous price history. For seasonal items, such as fresh food and clothing, abnormal price movements will be normal. These price movements should not be excluded from the outlier detection procedures. It is important that an appropriate method is used to validate these prices. Chapter 5 provides more details on the different data validation methods.

Maintaining and Updating the Sample

1.94 One strategy to deal with the changing universe of products would be to resample, or reselect, at regular intervals the complete set of items to be priced. For example, with a monthly index, a new set of items could be selected each January. Each set of items would be priced until the following January. Each January, both sets would be priced in order to establish a link between each set of 12 monthly changes. Resampling each year would be consistent with a strategy of updating the expenditure weights each year. For example, the Harmonised Index of Consumer Prices and many national CPIs in the European Union Member States resample items annually.

1.95 Although resampling may be preferable to maintaining an unchanged sample or selection, it may not be practical for those countries that update weights infrequently. When the CPI is updated every five years, for example, systematically resampling the entire set of products each year would be difficult to manage and costly to implement. Moreover, it does not provide a complete solution to the problem of the changing universe of products, as it does not capture price changes that occur at the moment when new products or new varieties or models are first introduced. Many producers deliberately use the time when products are first marketed to make significant price changes.

1.96 A more practical way in which to keep the sample up to date is to rotate it gradually by dropping certain items and introducing new ones. Items may be dropped for two reasons:

- The product is believed by the price collector or head office to be no longer representative. It appears to account for a steadily diminishing share of the total expenditures within the basic categories in question.
- The product may simply disappear from the market altogether. For example, it may have become obsolete as a result of changing technology or unfashionable because of changing tastes, although it could disappear for other reasons.

1.97 At the same time, new products or new qualities of existing products appear on the market. At some point, it becomes necessary to include them in the list of items priced. This raises the general question of the treatment of quality change and the treatment of new products.

Missing Products and Adjusting for Changes in Quality

1.98 A CPI should reflect the change in the cost of buying a fixed basket of goods and services of constant quality. In practice, this represents a challenge as products can permanently disappear or be replaced with new versions of a different quality or specification, and new products can also become available.

1.99 Chapter 6 discusses the nature of "quality" and methods for adjusting prices for quality change. It provides detailed guidance both on implicit methods of quality adjustment, such as the overlap method and class mean imputation, and on explicit methods, including expert judgment, and the hedonic approach. Chapter 7 delves more deeply into the issue of item substitution, particularly on methods of incorporating new products into the index.

1.100 The 2003 ILO Resolution advises that when a product disappears "clear and precise rules should be developed for selecting the replacement product." It lists three selection strategies: the most similar; the most popular; and the most likely to be available in the future. On quality adjustment, this resolution states that "when a quality change is detected, an adjustment must be made to the price, so that the index reflects as near as possible the pure price change." It guards against the automatic assumption that "all price change is a reflection of the change in quality." It does not recommend particular explicit or implicit methods of quality adjustment but does state that "the methods used should as far as possible be based on objective criteria."

Missing Products

1.101 In order to measure price change from one period to the next, the price statistician tracks, for each elementary aggregate, the prices of a fixed sample of items. The detailed characteristics of the products, that is, the varieties of goods and services selected for pricing, are recorded to assist the price collector in fulfilling the aim of pricing exactly the same product in the same outlet in the same location so that the CPI compares "like-to-like" in subsequent periods. Also, the recording of detailed characteristics, especially price-determining features, can help when needing to make adjustments to the recorded price due to changes in specification and hence quality. In practice, the particular product being priced in a specific outlet may become unavailable—for example, the product is discontinued, may be in temporary short supply, or may be a seasonal product which disappears when out of season. These situations are discussed in Chapters 6 and 7 of this Manual, and in Chapter 9 of *Consumer Price Index Theory*. In all other cases, the price statisticians need to estimate the price of any missing product that they believe will return to the market within a reasonable time, or, if they believe it will not return, find a suitable replacement. If the price statisticians believe that the product will not return, the replacement should be either (1) as similar as possible to the previous one, or (2) the most popular "similar" product in the shop, or (3) the similar product that most likely will be available for future pricing. Unlike approach (1) which leaves the sample "static" with the risk that it will be increasingly out of date and difficult to collect prices for, approaches (2) and (3) have the advantage of introducing an element of sample replenishment. This is where quality adjustment becomes an issue. The price index should reflect only pure price changes—the price index should not reflect any portion of the price difference that is due to increases or decreases in quality between the missing item and its replacement. A value needs to be placed on any change in specification between the old and replacement item and a quality adjustment applied accordingly. This approach to quality adjustment applies to any replacement strategy, but is particularly relevant where sample replenishment takes place.

1.102 Three situations that regularly occur are the following:

- Substitution procedures where an item, product, or outlet disappears, including the introduction of new items
- The imputation of a price when a product is temporarily out of stock (excluding seasonal goods)
- Quality adjustment where a change of product involves changes in its price-determining characteristics

Substitution Procedures

1.103 In a dynamic retailing environment, there is a continuous turnover both in outlets and in products.

Outlets

1.104 If an outlet goes out of business or refuses to participate in the price collection survey, it should be replaced with the same sort of outlet (for example, a market stall should be replaced with a market stall, or a single shop with a single shop) in the same location and conducting the same type of business (in other words selling the same types of goods). For example, if the previous shop was a butcher selling refrigerated meat, then another butcher selling refrigerated meat should replace it. If probability sampling was used to select the original outlet, the sampling frame should be revisited and a replacement outlet selected from the same stratum. Regardless of how the replacement is found, the original outlet's sampled items should be assigned to the replacement outlet for price observation.

1.105 If an outlet changes location, a decision on whether the price collector should follow the outlet to its new location needs to consider both sampling and operational issues:

- *Sampling issues*. The principle of maintaining a like-for-like comparison holds. In practice, the balance of the sample needs to be maintained to ensure that it continues to be representative. Stratification is frequently used to increase sampling efficiency and ensure that the sample is representative. This means that when an outlet changes its location, reference needs to be made to the stratification and selection procedures used in the initial sample selection. For instance, assume that shopping locations were initially selected from local administrative areas, stratified by an urban/rural split and outlet type, and then outlets randomly selected from those outlets within the chosen local administrative areas. Then the relocating outlet can be followed to its new location if it continues to fall in precisely the same stratum. However, if the outlet moves away from the original shopping location, for example, from an urban shopping district to a rural area outside the city or to another urban district within the city, or if it relocates within the same shopping location but becomes part of a multiple chain, then it has moved to another stratum and a suitable replacement for it should be found from within the original stratum, in order to maintain the sample balance.
- *Operational issues*. As mentioned in Chapter 5 there may sometimes be operational reasons for departing from the sample generated by the standard selection procedures. For instance, efficient scheduling of price collection and the availability of price collectors may make following the outlet to its new location impractical, even though it has stayed in the same stratum. Similarly, a visit to the new location may indicate that it is impractical for the collection of prices, for example, because of a physical barrier such as a railway or river bisecting the area and causing difficulties of access.

Products

1.106 If a chosen product is temporarily missing and no price is recorded, a note to this effect should be made by the price collector. For a product temporarily missing, a price has to be imputed. Nonseasonal items and varieties should be replaced if missing more than a predefined period of time. For example, if it is out of stock for three consecutive months, then the collector should be instructed to choose a replacement which matches as closely as possible the product description unless it is decided to take the opportunity of a disappearing good to update the sample. Where a product is permanently unavailable for pricing, procedures need to be in place for determining a replacement and then impute a new base price if the replacement is of a different quality. Methods for imputing a missing price are discussed in the following text.

1.107 As the issues relating to temporarily and permanently missing products differ—and their treatment is different—it is important for the price collector to establish whether the unavailability of a product is likely to be temporary or permanent. A price may be considered as temporarily missing if the same product is likely to return to the market within a reasonable time period. This includes seasonal items for which special procedures apply (see Chapter 11). Permanent unavailability, on the other hand, occurs when a variety is withdrawn from the market with no prospect of returning in the same form. Products may be temporarily missing, for example, due to supply shortages caused by factors such as the seller underestimating demand, strikes by factory or transportation workers, or supply problems with imported products. In these cases, the price collector, although not able to observe a price in the current period, may have obtained information (for example, from the shopkeeper) to suggest that the same variety will become available again at some, perhaps unknown, time in the future.

1.108 The previous discussion does not cover seasonal products, that is, where a product or item may disappear, because it is a seasonal product and it may be expected to reappear when it is next in season. The case of seasonal products is covered in detail in Chapter 11. Imputation procedures are fairly similar for both temporarily missing and seasonal products.

Temporarily (Nonseasonal) Missing Products

1.109 If it is believed that a missing product will be available again in a reasonable time, then the price statistician has three options:

- *Omit the variety for which the price is missing* so that a like-for-like comparison is maintained using matched pairs. The elementary index uses only those observations for which the price collector obtained prices of exactly the same variety in the current and previous periods. In this approach, the price change for the deleted product, which was recorded up to the point immediately before its disappearance will be disregarded from that point on.

This may cause problems, for example, if it unbalances the sample.

- *Carryforward the last observed price.* Carrying forward the last observed price is only recommended in the case of fixed or regulated prices. Although this provides price continuity in the periods when observations cannot be made, it is likely that short-term movements in the index are biased, since the subindices in question will show no change when prices are not available. If prices in general are rising, the bias will be downward, whereas if prices are falling, the bias will be upward. Carryforward is not recommended, particularly when there is high inflation or when period-to-period movements (as opposed to annual movements) in the price index are important. The carry-forward method is appropriate only if there is reason to believe that the price has not changed. Typically, it will be difficult for the price statistician to validate the belief that the price has not changed, unless the price is fixed or regulated.
- *Imputation.* The best solution by far is to impute a price. Imputation makes use of the best available information to provide an unbiased estimate of price movement. The principal methods for imputing prices are shown in more detail in Chapter 6. There are essentially two choices:
  - *Impute the missing price by reference to the average price change for the prices that are available in the elementary aggregate (overall mean imputation).* This assumes that the price change of the missing product, if it had been available in the shop, would have been equal to the average change in prices in the elementary aggregate. This may be a reasonable assumption if the elementary aggregate is fairly homogeneous. This method of imputation is equivalent to the "omit" method (see first bullet point), no matter whether a Jevons, Carli, or Dutot method of aggregation is used at the elementary aggregate level. In a given month this approach provides similar results to the "omit" method described in the first bullet previously; however, across time, the two approaches will not produce the same results if the index is compiled using the short-term formulation. This is because the imputed prices are used to compile the index from month to month.
  - *Impute the missing price by reference to the average price change for the prices of "comparable" varieties from another similar outlet (class mean imputation).* This represents a more precise match between the missing product and the products supplying an imputed price. It is normally preferable to impute using the average price change in the elementary aggregate unless the imputations are unreliable because of small sample sizes.

1.110 A detailed discussion on imputation methods is presented in Chapter 6.

Permanently Missing Products

1.111 When the situation arises where a product permanently disappears or is replaced by a new version with a different specification, normally two actions are required by the price statistician:

- Selecting a replacement product for pricing
- Quality adjusting the price if there are differences in quality between the outgoing product and its replacement

Each is considered in turn.

The Selection of a Replacement Product for Pricing

1.112 In practically every period for which a price index is compiled, some varieties of a product become permanently missing, not just in particular outlets but also because they are no longer produced or imported. If no action is taken, the sample of prices will diminish. Permanently missing varieties are problematic not just because of the potential impact on how representative the sample is, but also because it will lead to estimation of price change with samples that do not match from period to period; that is, the composition of the matched pairs changes. In addition, the index number for the latest month will be less reliable than that for the previous month because of the smaller sample size.

1.113 The price statistician's task is to maintain the sample size by finding replacements for the specific varieties when they are no longer available and are not expected to return within a reasonable time. One of two alternative strategies can be adopted (replace with the most similar product and sample replenishment). Under both options it is important to identify any differences in quality between the original and replacement varieties as it is crucial to ascertain whether there is a quality difference, and, if there is, to estimate its value and calculate a quality-adjusted price.

1.114 *Replace with the most similar product.* This reduces the role of quality adjustment, as the more similar a product is, the less is the required quality adjustment (see paragraphs 1.118–1.131) but contributes to the deterioration in the representativeness of the sample where a product starts disappearing from the shops because it is being replaced by something new and sales are declining. Finding the replacement that is most similar to the original variety requires knowledge about characteristics of the previous variety. Good practice in price collection involves maintaining up-to-date descriptions of the variety's characteristics. The ICP developed SPDs for most item categories: these provide a framework to list the various characteristics—prioritized in order of their importance—of the varieties for each category.[6] Such descriptions of characteristics can be used to match the characteristics between the old variety and various replacements so that critical characteristics are matched and less important characteristics can be noted. Critical characteristics are those that impact or contribute to determining the price, such as type of product (canned tuna fish), brand (StarKist), size (150 milliliter), and packaging (tin, in water). Less important characteristics are those that do not affect the price, such as color of the label on the package or the location in the shop where the product is displayed. The salient considerations can be incorporated

[6]See the ICP 2003–2006 Handbook on the World Bank ICP website at https://www.worldbank.org/en/programs/icp/brief/handbooks-and-operational-guides.

into a decision-making framework for identifying a similar product, as follows:

- There is a basic match of the main characteristics, particularly those which determine price.
- Consumers perceive them as similar even though some characteristics may be different. This may be the variety in the shop that buyers are most likely to buy in place of the original.
- They are used for the same purpose and in similar situations. For food this may include a consideration of whether the brand is one for everyday consumption or only for special occasions.

1.115 Under the "replace with a similar product" strategy, an updated version of a product (that is, the one that the supplier lists as the replacement), is the logical starting point for the replacement for its predecessor. In most instances this would be the one that is the most similar to the original variety, so the price statistician can compare "like-to-almost-like." In instances where the most similar variety is also one that is likely to soon disappear, the price collector should select the variety that is most popular within the outlet for the product class. Although this strategy is less likely to yield a replacement that is sufficiently similar to permit direct price comparison, it will reduce the likelihood of the replacement disappearing in the near future and will keep the need for quality adjustment to a minimum.

1.116 *Sample replenishment*—replace the missing product or variety with the currently most representative one by going through a process of resampling. The extent to which a sample remains representative is highly dependent on the rules used for item replenishment when a particular variety or product disappears from the shelf of a particular outlet. Compared with the option of replacement with the most similar product, sample replenishment has the benefit of maintaining the current representativeness of the sample. If disappearing products are always replaced with similar products, the sample will gradually become less relevant to market reality. Sample replenishment also increases the chances of the replacement being available on the shop shelf for pricing. The problem of a deteriorating sample increases with the rate of turnover in varieties and products and with the rate of product development.

Adjusting the Price for Differences in Quality

1.117 When a product disappears or is replaced with a new version of a different quality or specification, then one of the following methods of introducing the price of the replacement is adopted:

- Comparable replacement
- Direct (explicit) quality adjustment
- Implicit quality adjustment (imputation)

In all cases, a nominal price in the base month is needed for the new or replacement product—this nominal base price is used until the next rebasing.

1.118 The price collector should record the specifications (the price-determining characteristics) of the new variety so that the head office can determine if the replacement is of similar quality to the original variety. The price collector should determine if the outlet is likely to continue selling the replacement. If it is also expected to be discontinued in the near future, then a different variety should be selected—either another that is similar to the first, or the most popular variety within the product line. As will be seen, there are several different methods for both the explicit and the implicit types of quality adjustment, but there are some common themes in the methods of each of these two main types. Explicit methods estimate the impact on price of changes in characteristics or features of the product. Implicit methods estimate the impact on price indirectly by reference to price differences between different varieties.

Comparable Replacements

1.119 If the selected replacement product is regarded as comparable, then the observed price change is treated as a pure price change. But the price statistician should gather and examine all the available evidence, if possible taking advice from market experts where necessary, before coming to such a conclusion. Even in cases where a replacement product is believed to be of comparable quality, care should be taken, since experience suggests that most goods tend to undergo steady improvements, especially hi-tech and electrical goods.

Direct or Explicit Quality-Adjustment Methods

1.120 There are a number of direct or explicit methods for determining the price associated with a change in quality. But quality adjustment is not an exact science, and different evaluations can yield different results. The point is that even if the evaluation methods used are somewhat imprecise in the measurement of the quality difference, it is important to make an adjustment. If quality differences are not removed, the price index will reflect the quality change in addition to pure price change and is likely to have an upward bias because quality usually increases.

1.121 Chapter 6 provides a flowchart of the decisions needed for making quality adjustments. The most common ways of making an explicit quality adjustment in practice are as follows:

- *Package size adjustment.* The value of a change in package size is assumed to be proportional to the relative change in the package size.
- *Expert judgment.* The price collector determines the value either through direct knowledge or in consultation with personnel in the shop where the product is sold. Alternatively, NSO staff, who may be knowledgeable about the product, can estimate a value. Reliance on an individual's knowledge concerning the products depends, however, on the individual obtaining sufficient market information and is also liable to subjectivity. The judgment needs to be properly informed.
- *Reference to the producer cost.* The production cost from the producer can be used in the case of an improvement to an existing product, although a judgment then needs to be made on whether to apply an adjustment factor. For example, the adjustment might consist of the normal retail markup to reflect wholesalers' and retailers' costs and profits. In the context of a COLI, a downward adjustment may be appropriate to account for the fact that the new "standard" feature will not increase the utility to all

purchasers, for example, some may not welcome air conditioning in a car because of the extra running costs. Compilers of the producer price index often attempt to gather information on production costs from manufacturers for quality-adjustment purposes. However, producers may be unwilling to provide information on their marginal costs for reasons of confidentiality. There are a number of potential problems with using the producer cost method. In particular, it is not necessarily the case that the cost of production, with an adjustment factor along the lines described previously, gives a good indication of the selling price.[7]

- *The former "option" price.* In the case where an optional feature has become standard, the former price charged for the optional feature can be used as the explicit quality-adjustment value but again, consideration will need to be given to whether a scaling-down factor should be applied—in this case possibly a downward adjustment to reflect the reduced production costs of making a feature "standard" and also, in the cost of living context, that the utility gain is less than the increase in price. Some of the concerns relating to using producers' costs (see the previous bullet point) apply, the main difficulty being that it is likely that the market valuation of the options will have changed once they become standard, indeed, it is often because of changing market circumstances that producers make former options standard.
- *Hedonic regression.* Another way to obtain a value of the quality difference is to use hedonic regression to estimate the value of changes in a product's characteristics. See Chapter 6 and also the *Handbook on Hedonic Price Indexes and Quality Adjustments in Price Indexes* published by the Organisation for Economic Co-operation and Development for more information.[8] Hedonic methods require large databases with a wide range of product characteristics. Such databases are seldom available in NSOs (though for some products scanner data from large stores may be a viable source in some countries) and can involve substantial development and maintenance costs. In addition, hedonic models need to be reestimated periodically. Hedonic methods should be applied only where they add significantly to the statistical integrity of the index. This is most likely to be the case with hi-tech high-turnover goods.

1.122 In explicit methods, the monetary value of the quality difference is determined directly using one of the previous methods and then applied to a previous period's observed price for the "old" item. This will yield an estimate of what the replacement item would have cost in the previous period.

1.123 Assume that the NSO was able to determine that, based on the differences in characteristics, the value of the quality difference between Brand C and Replacement 1 was \$25 in period 1. The price statistician can add this amount to the price of Brand C in period 1 to obtain an adjusted price.

Implicit Quality Adjustment

1.124 If the replacement product is of a different quality or specification and no information is available to quantify the difference, then assumptions have to be made about what proportion of the price difference is accounted for by differences in quality. Implicit quality adjustment creates an imputed "quality-adjusted" price based on price changes from similar varieties of the product. The precise nature of the imputation depends on the index formula that is used. A basic assumption underlying the most commonly used implicit quality-adjustment methods is that the difference in quality between varieties simultaneously available in the market is equal to the difference in price between the varieties or models.[9] Thus, when a product disappears from the shelf, an underlying assumption is made when imputing a price that a price differential continues to reflect a difference in quality. The different methods of imputation available to the index compiler are described in paragraphs 1.127–1.131.

1.125 Most countries construct some form of a fixed-base price index. If price movements are estimated using long-term price relatives from the base period, then the base price may be adjusted proportionately for the estimated quality difference. If price movements are estimated using short-term relatives from the previous period, then an imputation adjustment can be implicitly made by estimating the missing variety's price in the current month from the average price change in its elementary aggregate. The price change of the omitted observation is equal to the change in its elementary aggregate.

Overlap Pricing

1.126 This method requires knowledge of the prices of the two varieties in the same time period—the overlap period. If the old and new varieties are available at the same time because the price collector either knows in advance that the old variety will disappear soon and selects and prices a replacement, or the outlet is able to accurately give the price of the replacement in a previous period when the old variety was priced, then the price difference between the two is taken to be the value of the quality difference. The rationale is that it cannot be due to price change because price change occurs only over time. The price index uses the old variety in the overlap period and the new variety in the next period and the price differential between the old and new varieties

[7] In constructing a CPI, consumer valuations of products should be decisive, and the cost of production is irrelevant in this context. In "equilibrium" situations, the cost of production (using a "normal" cost of capital in the producer's user cost formula) should give a close approximation to the selling price (and hence the consumer's valuation of the product). But it is in disequilibrium situations, involving new products, that research and development has to be amortized using monopolistic prices where new products and obsolescence of old products is likely to occur that the assumptions of equilibrium break down.

[8] Jack Triplett. "Handbook on Hedonic Indexes and Quality Adjustments in Price Indexes: Special Application to Information Technology Products." STI Working Paper 2004/9, Statistical Analysis of Science, Technology and Industry; OECD Publications, Rue André-Pascal, 75775 Paris, Cedex 16, France. http://www.oecd.org/dataoecd/37/31/33789552.pdf.

[9] For the argument to be valid it has to be assumed that the consumers are rational and well informed about available alternative choices. It also has to be assumed that the market is "in a state of equilibrium," that is in a state that would persist indefinitely if all given conditions remained unchanged. In practice, these assumptions may be adequate or inadequate to varying degrees in different product areas. Equilibrium conditions may be disrupted by temporary imbalances between supply and demand, such as stock clearances, bad harvests, or scarce, much-demanded new models.

never affects the index. In this case, the market has determined the value of the quality adjustment.

Overall Mean Imputation

1.127 Overall mean or nonclass mean imputation (also referred to as "linking," "splicing," or bridge overlap method in the context of the European Union's Harmonised Index of Consumer Prices) imputes an overlap price for the old variety in the current period by reference to the price changes between the previous and current periods of similar varieties or items. The latter are used to impute a price change for the old variety, which can then be used to obtain the imputed price. The ratio of the imputed price for the old variety and the price of the new variety in the current period is the estimated quality adjustment.

1.128 An estimate of the price of the missing variety can still be made even though the price of the replacement variety may not be known for the previous pricing period using the overall mean price change for the elementary aggregate.

1.129 The overall mean procedure assumes that the pure price change from the replaced item to the replacement item is the same as that for the composite of all other goods in the same group. It is used frequently because of its simplicity, but there can be an inherent bias built into the methodology, particularly when major model changes are occurring. The direction and extent of this bias is a matter for debate but depends on whether the actual quality-adjusted change in price is bigger or smaller than the measured price changes of the items used in the imputation. Major price changes can frequently occur at the time new varieties or models of a product are introduced. This is quite common, for example, with new vehicles, household appliances, electronic equipment, and clothing items. As the new varieties are introduced there may still be a substantial supply of the old varieties which are showing little price change or may actually be declining in price. In consequence, using the old varieties' price changes to impute the price changes for new ones will underestimate the actual price change for the new varieties and cause a downward bias in the price index. The use of the overall mean imputation procedure, in which all observations in the elementary aggregate are used, is not recommended for such cases. It is also possible, and can be argued (but less convincingly), that the use of the overall mean leads to an upward bias because the price changes associated with models that are unchanged in quality will be further along the evolutionary cycle and therefore will be rising less rapidly. An alternative imputation procedure, called "class mean" imputation, avoids some of the problems associated with bias.

Class Mean Imputation

1.130 Class mean imputation is similar in procedure to the overall mean imputation, but uses only the price changes of "comparable" replacements to impute the overlap price, the replacements being limited to those that have exactly the same price-determining characteristics, or those items with replacements that have been declared comparable after review or have already been quality-adjusted through one of the "explicit" methods. For example, when the arrival of a new model of a particular brand of motor vehicle forces price collectors to find replacements, some of the replacements will be of comparable quality, others can be made comparable with explicit quality adjustments, but the remaining ones will need imputed prices. Class mean imputation calculates imputed price relatives using only the prices of comparable and, where appropriate, explicitly quality-adjusted varieties or models. In general, it does not use the prices for the varieties or models that were not replaced, because these are likely to be different from those of new models. The prices of old models tend to fall as they become obsolete, while the new models (represented by the replacements) tend to have a higher price before falling. This may not be relevant in developing countries where new products appear in the retail market relatively late at a "mature" price. Using class mean imputation adds complexity but reduces two types of bias referred to earlier: bias from ignoring quality change altogether and treating all price movements as price change, and bias from overadjusting for quality change by treating some pure price change as quality change.[10]

New Products

1.131 An entirely new product, in contrast to a new variety of an existing product, is essentially a replacement of a previously popular product and represents a good or service that:

- Was not included and could not be included in the price index during the initial selection of the current market basket and which is now available for possible inclusion in the index
- Cannot be easily linked to the service flow or production technology of existing goods and services; that is, it represents a distinct departure from previously available products insofar as it is a step change with regard to technology or utility to the consumer
- Has a recognizable and generally accepted new benefit to consumers as a result of becoming available

1.132 The last two cases help to distinguish an entirely new product—referred to as a *revolutionary* product—from an existing product whose features and, in consequence, "quality" has changed—an *evolutionary* product. A revolutionary product is an entirely new good or service that is not closely tied to a previously available product. A revolutionary product tends to be a good or service that is expected to satisfy some need in a new way and is unlikely to fit neatly into an existing CPI item category. As an example, when mobile telephones were first introduced, they provided a significantly new service. While on the one hand, they provided an extension of an existing flow of service (telecommunication), on the other hand, they provided a dimension of service that was new (the opportunity to make "mobile" calls away from a fixed telephone) and a distinct product from existing landline telephone services (it was a step change in technology). It is therefore an example of a revolutionary product. More recent examples of revolutionary products are broadcasting (streaming) services for television and smartphones, downloads of games, and electronic storage of data (the "cloud"). Examples of evolutionary products would be

[10]Clothing items usually require additional procedures to control substitutions depending on the season of the year (for example, autumn/winter versus spring/summer clothing).

new models of household appliances such as refrigerators and washing machines where improvements in quality are introduced from time to time. Evolutionary products can also be newly added brands of currently available products such as a new type of canned fish or electronic appliance which differs from those currently available. For example, a current brand of canned fish may consist of certain types of fish (mackerel, salmon, or tuna) and then a new variety for one of the canned fish is introduced which is packed in water rather than oil.

1.133 The focus is on keeping the basket of goods and services that are priced up to date and relevant. It covers both truly and completely new products, that is, those which are *revolutionary*, as well as those which are *evolutionary* and also goods or services previously provided free and thus previously excluded from the CPI. It does not deal directly with substitution and quality change when a good or service unexpectedly disappears. This is the subject of Chapter 7.

Planning for the Introduction of New Products

1.134 There are three sets of circumstances in which new goods and services are included in the CPI:

- *As "replacements" for products which no longer exist.* This is normally associated with evolutionary products. Producers often discontinue old versions of their products and introduce new versions that are quite similar but may be of a different quality at a different price. Note that "quality change" includes changes in technical specifications as well as more clearly visible outward changes in design. This can happen frequently and is usually unplanned for in a CPI, although not necessarily unexpected. It is often associated with forced replacements when collectors go to price a product only to find that it is no longer sold. In the CPI, collection procedures usually instruct price collectors to replace the old versions (models) with:
  - *The most similar model.* For example, when the old model of washing machine is discontinued, the price collector is instructed to replace it with another model which has similar (though probably not identical) specifications and to record any changes in characteristics (specifications) to aid the evaluation of potential quality differences.
  - Alternatively, replacements can be products that are currently the *most popular* with consumers. This represents a deliberate attempt to refresh the CPI basket when a replacement has to be made. For example, the current varieties of canned fish may include tuna. Producers may have introduced a new variety that contains tuna packed in water rather than oil, and consumers are now shifting their buying patterns to purchase more of the new variety. There is no external factor forcing the consumer to change to the new product.

1.135 In some instances, when a model ceases to be produced, the manufacturer will indicate which model is the replacement and the CPI collection procedures instruct the price collector to start collecting the price of this replacement. This also normally contributes to the replenishment of the sample, as manufacturers usually introduce more up-to-date features into new models. However, the representativeness of the new model, as measured by its popularity, will only be determined over time.

1.136 Further discussion of the methods for introducing into the CPI basket replacements for products which no longer exist and disappear from the shop shelves is presented in Chapter 7.

- As a *supplement* to the sample by adding a new variety or making a targeted replacement to drop an old variety and add a new one. This represents a more proactive approach to product substitution. Again, it is normally associated with evolutionary products. The CPI collection procedures instruct price collectors to replace the old, less popular variety of canned tuna fish in oil, with the new, more frequently bought tuna packed in water even though the former remains available. This is different from the standard reactive approach of replacing the old disappearing variety with the new one because the old variety still exists and may not be discontinued although may be increasingly difficult to find (and less popular/lower turnover shares). The new variety is supplementary to the old variety and begins to gain market share while the old variety declines in market share. This more proactive approach requires the price statistician to monitor the market for the entry of new varieties and to get a sense of their popularity with consumers, for example, by noticing the changing proportions of shelf space occupied by the different varieties or by talking to the shopkeeper. The head office can also help by gathering sales information from other sources.
- As a *planned introduction of a revolutionary product* which consumers begin to buy so that the product has an increasing share of the market. The appearance of revolutionary products in the marketplace and consumer reaction to them, as measured by sales, are less predictable than for evolutionary products. Revolutionary products also tend to have different price trends from other products in the sample and can therefore exert an influence on the CPI disproportionate to actual sales. For these reasons, revolutionary products are important, represent a significant challenge, and warrant special attention, requiring the price statistician to be particularly attentive and proactive.

1.137 The previous circumstances can be managed either in a planned way, as part of a regular process of updating the CPI basket, including chain linking (covered in Chapter 9) or in an ad hoc way when the need arises, or the circumstances warrant action to be taken.

Timing of the Introduction of New Products

1.138 The timing of introduction of new products can vary by the type of product and may be dictated by the method of incorporation into the index. For revolutionary products, it can be particularly critical to the accuracy of the index as there is a greater potential for introducing bias if these products are ignored. This is less likely to be the case for evolutionary goods.

1.139 Chapter 7 presents two alternative strategies that can be adopted when choosing a forced replacement, already mentioned in the previous paragraphs—replacing with the most similar product or replacing the missing item or variety with the currently most representative one. The strategy of replacement with the most popular is more likely to maintain the relevance of the sample by going through a process of resampling and identifying an appropriate replacement product. In order to make a properly judged decision on which strategy to follow and to inform the choice of replacement product and timing of introduction, the NSO needs to be aware of current consumer market trends, including what new products are becoming popular and what supplementary products are being introduced. It also needs to monitor product turnover, which can be an indication of the rate of product development associated with evolutionary products, and can vary between different categories of products. This information can be obtained from data gathered by price collectors and their supervisors, commodity experts in the NSO (for instance, working on the CPI or the producer price index) or from trade journals, products identified through scanner data, and consumer reports.

1.140 Evolutionary products should be included in the sample as soon as it is clear that consumers are shifting to these new products from the old versions. A frequent updating of the basket reduces the need for the ad hoc introduction of evolutionary products.

1.141 Revolutionary products usually first appear in the marketplace at a high initial price to cover development costs and to exploit the novelty value to the consumer. The prices generally start to decline as they become more established and competing varieties enter the market resulting in increased supply. The timing of introduction into the CPI basket is a critical issue—if introduced too late it will not only reduce the representativity of the CPI basket but could also give too much weight to any price decline associated with obsolescence of the product it is replacing when it nears the end of its life cycle but is still in the CPI basket. For revolutionary products the timing of their introduction into the CPI is important. In practice, often they are not introduced until they can be included in a new basket at the time of a CPI revision. This can lead to out-of-date and unrepresentative baskets if the revisions are carried out infrequently or with a long time lag, for instance as a result of delays in processing HBS data. But the price statistician is also confronted with uncertainty; it is not always clear how the retail market will react in the longer term to the introduction of a revolutionary product—some will be highly successful, achieving significant sales volumes and market stability in a relatively short time, while others may achieve high sales at an early stage which are not maintained.

1.142 Methods of introduction which overcome the problem of lack of timeliness include sample supplementation, targeted replacement procedures, and reinitiating (or rotating) the sample for the elementary aggregate or COICOP class. These methods are discussed in detail in Chapter 7 and, sample reinitiation apart, are generally applicable to evolutionary products. For revolutionary products, a new elementary aggregate must often be created. Frequent updating of the CPI basket reduces the potential problems and the introduction of revolutionary new products at the time of a basket update has a number of operational advantages: namely, the old weights do not need to be rescaled if a new product class is introduced when an old basket which does not include the new product class is still being used. Because it is not known exactly which other expenditures are being reduced relatively as the new product is purchased, this rescaling of weights is somewhat arbitrary and may lead to credibility issues.

Calculating the Consumer Price Index

1.143 The calculation of CPIs usually proceeds in two stages. First, price indices are estimated for the elementary expenditure aggregates, or simply elementary aggregates. Then these elementary price indices are averaged to obtain higher-level indices using the relative expenditure values of the elementary aggregates as weights.

Elementary Price Indices

1.144 The weights used in the CPI are generally derived from the HBS at levels that are typically for an item grouping such as cheese, butter, or milk. There is no identification of the specific variety of the product and an associated weight. NSOs select a sample of individual varieties to represent each item, but there are often no weights available at the variety level. The NSOs then use some method of averaging to produce an average price or an average price change to use in deriving the item or elementary index. This level of computation is usually referred to as an elementary aggregate because it is the first level at which an index is compiled for aggregation to higher levels of the CPI.

1.145 When weights are not available, the choice of the averaging method can be very important. Chapter 6 of *Consumer Price Index Theory* shows that the larger the variation in the individual prices, the larger the difference among the standard averaging methods. Both arithmetic and geometric averaging can be used, but as demonstrated in Chapter 8 of this Manual and Chapter 6 of *Consumer Price Index Theory*, geometric average formulas are recommended.

Arithmetic Average

1.146 The two methods used historically by NSOs to calculate the elementary indices are the ratio of average prices, known as the Dutot index, or the average of price relatives, known as the Carli index. Each of these formulas can be calculated using either the long-term price relative formula (comparing current to base period prices) or the short-term price relative formula (comparing current to previous period prices). The short-term versions of these formulas calculate a long-term relative change by chaining together the short-term price relatives. Appendix 6 illustrates the mathematical formulas for the Dutot and Carli indices. Chapter 8 provides details on the use of these formulas.

1.147 As shown in Chapter 8, it should be noted that the chained Carli produces different results than those for the fixed-base Carli using the average of long-term price relatives. The chained Carli price index has a definite upward bias. This chained version of the Carli index should not be used by NSOs for calculating elementary-level indices in the CPI.

Geometric Averages

1.148 With the introduction of the *CPI Manual* in 2004, a major emphasis was placed on using geometric averaging when weights are not available for the individual prices in the CPI elementary indices. The geometric price index is known as the Jevons price index and is calculated either as the ratio of the geometric average prices or as the geometric average of the price relatives. The Jevons formula can be found in Appendix 6, and Chapter 8 provides more detail on using the Jevons.

1.149 The Jevons index generally provides different estimates than both the Dutot or the Carli. Whether using the long-term price relative method or the short-term relative method Jevons indices yield the same index numbers as shown in Chapter 8. The same property holds true for the long-term and short-term Dutot indices. This property does not hold true for the Carli index. The chained short-term Carli index is always equal to or greater than the long-term Carli index.

1.150 Chapter 6 strongly encourages the use of the Jevons price index for calculating elementary indices where weights are unavailable. It notes that the Dutot price index should only be used in cases where the sample of transactions is homogeneous with respect to base price levels or price trends. It strongly discourages the use of the short-term Carli price index because of its known upward bias. The short-term method for the Jevons index will easily accommodate replacement varieties or adjustments for quality changes. As mentioned earlier, the NSO will only need to collect prices for the current and previous periods to enter in the system. If the long-term method is used, quality adjustments will involve changing the base price of the transaction for the value of the quality change as shown in Chapter 8.

Choice of Higher-Level Index Number Formula

1.151 The NSO has to decide on the kind of index number to use. The extensive references dealing with index theory in the bibliography of this Manual reflect the fact that there is a very large literature on this subject. Many kinds of mathematical formulas have been proposed over the past two centuries. While there may be no single formula that would be preferred in all circumstances, most economists and compilers of CPIs seem to agree that, in principle, the index formula should belong to a small class of indices called superlative indices. A superlative index may be expected to provide an approximation to a COLI. A characteristic feature of a superlative index is that it treats the prices and quantities in both periods being compared symmetrically. Different superlative indices tend to have similar properties, yield similar results, and behave in very similar ways. Because of their properties of symmetry, a superlative index is also likely to be seen as desirable even when the CPI is not meant to be a COLI.

1.152 When a monthly or quarterly CPI is first published, however, it is invariably the case that there is not sufficient information on the quantities and expenditures in the current period to make it possible to calculate a symmetric, or superlative, index. In cases where the prices and quantities are available, care must be taken to use index methods that do not result in biased estimates (for example, chain drift). Such methods are discussed in detail in Chapters 2–4 of *Consumer Price Index Theory*. While it is necessary to resort to second-best alternatives in practice, being able to make a rational choice between the various possibilities means having a clear idea of the target index that would be preferred in principle. The target index can influence practical matters such as whether the weights used in the index should be price updated.

1.153 A comprehensive, detailed, rigorous, and up-to-date discussion of the relevant index number theory is provided in Chapters 2–10 of *Consumer Price Index Theory*. Most of the standard indices used to compile CPIs (Laspeyres, Lowe, and Young) have known biases. The next paragraphs include summaries of the different formulas that can be used. Chapter 8 provides more details on these formulas that can be used to calculate the CPI.

Price Indices Based on Baskets of Goods and Services

1.154 The purpose of an index number may be explained as comparing the values of households' expenditures on consumer goods and services in two time periods. Knowing that expenditures have increased by 5 percent is not very informative if one does not know how much of this change is attributable to changes in the prices of the goods and services, and how much to changes in the quantities purchased. The purpose of an index number is to decompose proportionate or percentage changes in value aggregates into their overall components of price and quantity change. A CPI is intended to measure the price component of the change in households' consumption expenditures. One way to do this is to measure the change in the value of an aggregate, holding the quantities constant.

Lowe Indices

1.155 One very wide, and popular, class of price indices is obtained by defining the index as the relative change, between the periods compared, in the total cost of purchasing a given set of quantities, generally described as a "basket." The meaning of such an index is easy to grasp and to explain to users. This class of index is called a Lowe index, after the index number pioneer who first proposed it in 1823 (see Chapter 2 of *Consumer Price Index Theory*). Most NSOs make use of some kind of Lowe index in practice. The Lowe index formula can be found in Appendix 6 and is described in more detail in Chapter 8. Lowe indices are widely used for CPI purposes.

1.156 In principle, any set of quantities could serve as the basket. The basket does not have to be restricted to the quantities purchased in one or other of the two periods compared, or indeed any actual period of time. The quantities could, for example, be arithmetic or geometric averages of the quantities in the two periods. For practical reasons, the basket of quantities used for CPI purposes usually has to be based on a survey of household consumption expenditures conducted in an earlier period than either of the two periods whose prices are compared. For example, a monthly CPI may run from January 2018 onward, with January 2018 = 100, but the quantities may be derived from an annual expenditure survey made in 2015 or 2016, or even spanning both years. As it takes a long time to collect and process expenditure data, there is usually a considerable time lag before such data can be introduced into the calculation of CPIs. The basket may also refer to a year, whereas the index may be compiled monthly or quarterly.

1.157 The index can be written, and calculated, in two ways: either as the ratio of two value aggregates, or as an arithmetic weighted average of the price ratios, or *price relatives*, p_i^t/p_i^0 (where p_i^t refers to the price of the item in the current period and p_i^0 refers to the price of the item in the reference period) for the individual products using the hybrid expenditure shares s_i^{0b} as weights. The expenditures are described as hybrid because the prices and quantities belong to two different time periods, 0 and *b*, respectively. The hybrid weight may be obtained by updating the actual expenditure shares in period *b*, namely, $p_i^b q_i^b / \Sigma\, p_i^b q_i^b$, for the price changes occurring between periods *b* and 0 by multiplying them by the relative prices, p_i^0/p_i^b.

Laspeyres and Paasche Indices

1.158 Any set of quantities could be used in a Lowe index, but there are two special cases which figure very prominently in the literature and are of considerable importance from a theoretical point of view. When the quantities are those of the price reference period, the Laspeyres index is obtained. When quantities are those of the other period, the Paasche index is obtained. Appendix 6 provides the mathematical formulas for the Laspeyres and Paasche indices.

Young Index

1.159 Instead of holding constant the quantities of period *b*, an NSO may calculate a CPI as an arithmetic weighted average of the individual price relatives, holding constant the expenditure shares of period *b*. The resulting index is called a *Young* index, again after another index number pioneer. The Young index formula can be found in Appendix 6 and is described in more detail in Chapter 8.

1.160 Whether to price update or not, and the resulting choice of index, is discussed in more detail in Chapter 9 (see also Chapter 3 of *Consumer Price Index Theory*).

Short-Term Price Index Formulas

1.161 Many countries use a modified version of the Lowe or Young index that compiles the index based on short-term price changes rather than the long-term price changes. This modified method can be compiled in two ways. Using the first approach, index compilation involves a two-step estimation process that breaks down the price movements into short-term, period-to-period changes that are used to bring forward the index from the previous period. In the second approach, elementary-level indices are compiled based on chained short-term price changes and the calculation of upper-level indices uses the base period weights. There is no preference as to which approach is preferred. Countries can decide which approach should be applied. The use of the short-term formula makes it easier for NSOs to introduce replacement items in the sample if the ones they have been tracking are no longer available. The short-term approach also enables the NSOs to make quality adjustments as improvement (or deterioration) is made to the sampled varieties. The NSO only needs to collect the current and previous prices for the item in order to introduce it into the index. In using the long-term method, the base price will need to be adjusted for the changes in the quality of the items in the sample. Chapter 8 provides the formulas for different approaches for the modified versions of the Lowe and Young indices.

Geometric Young, Laspeyres, and Paasche Indices

1.162 In the geometric version of the Young index, a weighted geometric average is taken of the elementary aggregate price relatives using the expenditure shares of period *b* as weights. The geometric Laspeyres is the special case in which $b = 0$; that is, the expenditure shares are those of the price reference period 0. Similarly, the geometric Paasche uses the expenditure shares of period *t*. It should be noted that these geometric indices cannot be expressed as the ratios of value aggregates in which the quantities are fixed. They are not basket indices, and there are no counterpart Lowe indices.

1.163 The geometric Young and Laspeyres indices have the same information requirements as their arithmetic counterparts. They can be produced on a timely basis. Thus, these geometric indices must be treated as serious practical possibilities for purposes of CPI calculations. As explained in Chapter 8, the geometric indices are less likely to be subject to different types of index number biases than their arithmetic counterparts. Their main disadvantage may be that, because they are not fixed-basket indices, they are not so easy to explain or justify to users.

Symmetric Indices

1.164 The standard price index methods used in most countries today, that is, the Lowe and Young indices, date back 90 years to those proposed by W. C. Mitchell (1927) and G. H. Knibbs (1924). Index number theory has advanced substantially, particularly in the past 30 years, to provide better information on what the target index number formula should be. Various approaches have been used to evaluate index number formulas and derive those best suited for inflation measures. The research presented in *Consumer Price Index Theory* has resulted in improvements for fixed-basket formulas and identified target indices that are symmetric averages of standard formulas. The target indices are the Fisher, Törnqvist, and Walsh price indices, discussed in detail in Chapter 8. However, these usually cannot be produced in final form except with a lag because they require both current and past weight information. Thus, most NSOs use the fixed-basket indices where the weight data are derived from some past period. An exception can occur in countries where scanner data are available and symmetric indices can be produced in real time using the methods presented in Chapter 10.

1.165 A symmetric index is one that makes equal use of the prices and quantities in both the periods compared and treats them in a symmetric manner. There are three symmetric indices that are widely used in economic statistics; these three indices are also superlative indices, the Fisher, Walsh, and Törnqvist. The formulas for each are provided in Appendix 6, and Chapter 8 provides details on using each of these index formulas.

1.166 Different formulas are used at different stages of aggregation. At the elementary or first stage, where prices are first combined to form an index, many countries will not use weights. At the second and higher levels, weights are applied, but these weights generally relate to some period in the past that becomes less representative with the passage of time. When compared to the target indices (Fisher, Walsh, or Törnqvist), it becomes apparent that the indices produced in practice are of substantially lower quality than the target indices. This Manual discusses these issues thoroughly and provides approaches that countries can implement over time to move closer to the target measures.

Updating the Weights and Linking of Series

1.167 Chapter 4 notes that over time the CPI weights and basket become less representative of the consumer market. The weights and basket should be updated at least once every five years to maintain their relevance. Many countries strive to conduct an HBS on a five-year cycle to use for updating the CPI basket and provide detailed information on household expenditures for use in the national accounts. From the HBS consumption estimates, NSOs will identify the most important items to use in the new CPI basket as discussed in Chapter 3. Deriving the new basket involves adding items that have gained importance since the previous HBS and deleting those that are no longer important based on their shares in the HBS.

Introducing New Weights and the Consumer Price Index Basket

1.168 The new basket is then used to review the sample of items and outlets to ensure that the samples are representative of products being purchased by consumers and the places in which they are purchased. The new weights and sample are used to start a new CPI with updated weight and price reference periods. Typically, the weight reference period precedes the price reference period. The NSO must decide how the new weights and sample will be introduced in the CPI. It also must decide on the price reference period, if it will differ from the weight reference period.

1.169 If the price reference period and weight reference period are the same (Laspeyres), then the new sample is used to compile the CPI directly. If the two periods differ, most likely with the weight period preceding the price reference period, there are two main options for updating the CPI weights. One approach is to price update the weights to the price reference period (Lowe index) to keep the implied quantities fixed at the weight reference period levels. The second approach is to keep the expenditure shares fixed (Young index).

1.170 Chapter 9 examines the different approaches to price updating the weights (paragraphs 9.6–9.10) and discusses the recent research on price updating (paragraphs 9.11–9.18). A key issue in the decision is whether there has been substantial price change between the weight reference period and the price reference period when the weights are introduced into the CPI. Generally, if there is a substantial price change between the price and weight reference periods, the weights should not be price updated. As noted previously, price updating the weights assumes that the quantities have remained fixed. If prices have changed substantially, this assumption is less likely to be true. It would be more realistic to assume the expenditure shares have remained fixed, in which case the price change is offset by a compensating quantity change.

1.171 For infrequently updated CPIs, a single year is preferred as the price reference period. Where a single month (or quarter) is used, the prices of some seasonal products will be unavailable or unusually high or low and many unusual or imputed prices may have to be used for the price reference period. For countries with infrequent weight updates, it is preferable that the price reference period is a whole year in which seasonal prices would be appropriately represented. In some months there will be no sales of, for example, seasonal fruit, but an average price for the whole year would still be available for the price reference period.

1.172 The index reference period should be one year. Using a single month or quarter to serve as the index reference period (= 100), can result in distorted index changes because of the unusual or imputed prices in that period.

1.173 Chained CPIs weights are updated on an annual basis. Because annual updating allows for a relatively small lag between the weight and price reference periods, a single month is used as the price reference period. There is a continuing flow of price data that may include imputations, and a relatively small number of changes in specifications or products; the major exercise is to introduce the new weights into the flow of price data and link this to the existing chain.

1.174 For infrequently rebased CPIs, the use of a single month as the price reference period is not advised; however, it is often the case that the country's resources only allow for a price reference period of less than a full year. NSOs should strive to maximize the number of months used as the price reference period, with the goal of using a full year.

1.175 A primary shortcoming of using a short reference period for infrequently rebased CPIs is that out-of-season items in the price reference period will have no observed or economically meaningful price. The decision as to which month to use for the price reference month should consider when seasonal items with relatively high weights are in season. If these items are not in season, an imputed price will have to be used and consideration should be given to the validity of imputation methods for out-of-season items in this context. For example, if the carryforward method (which is discouraged) is used and the reference month uses an imputed price for the out-of-season item, the index may be unduly low. As mentioned previously, the two-stage Laspeyres aggregation is preferred since it avoids the need for long-term price comparisons with this one-month price reference period.

1.176 A primary shortcoming of using a longer price reference period are the resources needed to collect a full year of prices for all items included in the CPI basket. Some countries struggle with the resources to collect prices for two baskets (old and new) simultaneously. To minimize the burden, some countries have begun looking at preliminary expenditure data on a quarterly basis during the HBS collection period and to identify any new items that may be introduced into the basket. Once new products have been identified, prices can be collected.

Linking Previous Consumer Price Index to the New Price Index Reference Period

1.177 The NSO may choose to start the new series using the new price reference period as the new index reference period. In Chapter 9 the recommendation is that when new weights are introduced there should be an overlap period for the two indices so that they can be linked together. The overlap period is used to develop adjustment factors that may be applied to the old series to bring it to the same level as the new series. The linking of the old and new index series creates a continuous time series of data, which users need.

1.178 At minimum, a single common period is required as an overlap period between the indices. While a single overlap period can be used when the CPI is updated annually, this is not the preferred method when the index is updated less frequently. In the case of infrequent updates, an annual overlap is preferred. Some NSOs update the CPI weights each year so that the time lapse between the weight reference period and the link month is short. The single period link could be used in these instances. Chapter 9 provides a detailed discussion of annual weight updates.

1.179 Most NSOs will establish a new index reference period using an annual average from a previous year. The simplest and easiest method for users is to link the series with data for the month preceding the introduction of the new series (link month). This involves re-referencing the old series at each level to the annual average index for the new price reference period. However, there will be a discontinuity between the index level for the new index and that for the re-referenced index level for the old series in the link month. This reflects the difference in price trends between the old and new series as the new weights are being introduced. There are three steps involved to link this difference:

- Re-reference the old index series to the new index reference period
- Compile the new index series in the link month using the new weight structure
- Link the new series to the old series by using forward linking factors or, if using the short-term price relative method, start the new series indices at the level of the old series in the link month

1.180 If the NSO or users want to continue the old CPI series for future periods in time, they can produce a set of forward linking factors to use in future months as the new CPI is released. The forward linking factor raises the level of the new CPI series to that of the old series thus keeping the series on the old reference period.

Organization and Management

1.181 The production of the CPI is a complex operation involving extensive fieldwork by data collectors; processing, review, and editing of the collected data; compilation of indices; and their dissemination to the public. The whole process requires careful planning and management to ensure that the data products conform to good management and statistical practice. Appropriate management procedures for the CPI are described in Chapter 13.

1.182 Price collectors should be well trained to ensure that they understand the importance of selecting the right products for pricing. Inevitably, price collectors are bound to use their own discretion to a considerable extent. As already explained, one issue of crucial importance to the quality and reliability of a CPI is how to deal with the slowly evolving set of products with which a price collector is confronted. Products may disappear and have to be replaced by others, but it may also be appropriate to drop some products before they disappear altogether if they have become unrepresentative. Price collectors need to be provided with appropriate training and very clear instructions and documentation about how to proceed. Clear instructions are also needed to ensure that price collectors collect the right prices when there are sales, special offers, or other exceptional circumstances.

1.183 The price data collected must also be subjected to careful checking and editing. Many checks can be carried out automatically, using standard statistical control methods. It may also be useful to send out auditors to accompany price collectors and monitor their work. The various possible checks and controls are explained in detail in Chapter 13.

1.184 The head office staff also need to be trained on index methods and procedures for review of collected data, imputation of missing data, quality-adjustment procedures when needed, as well as index compilation and dissemination processes. Improvements in information technology should obviously be fully exploited. New and more efficient computers and database applications are continuously being developed. As resources permit, new technologies and organization improvements should be implemented.

1.185 Staff training and process reviews are an essential part of continuous quality improvement. Staff should receive regular training in their discipline and should be invited to operational reviews where all team members can raise concerns and, where appropriate, tackle specific issues through individual or group training.

Publication and Dissemination

1.186 As noted previously and in Chapter 2, the CPI is an important statistic whose movements can influence the central bank's monetary policy, fiscal policy, and the national budget; affect stock markets; influence wage rates and social security payments; and so on. There must be public confidence in its reliability, and in the competence and integrity of those responsible for its compilation. The methods used to compile it must therefore be fully documented, transparent, and open to public scrutiny. Many countries have an official CPI advisory group consisting of both experts and users. The role of such a group is not just to advise the NSO on technical matters, but also to promote public confidence in the index.

1.187 Users of the index also attach great importance to having the index published as soon as possible after the end of each month or quarter, preferably within two or three weeks. There are also many users who do not wish the index to be revised once it has been published. Thus, there is likely to be some trade-off between the timeliness and the quality of the index.

1.188 Publication should be understood to mean the dissemination of the results in any form. Most countries do not release their CPI in print, or hard copy. NSOs now tend to release the CPI electronically and make it available through the internet on their website.

1.189 As explained in Chapter 14, good publication policy goes beyond timeliness, confidence, and transparency. The results should be made available to all users, in both the public and the private sectors, at the same time and according to a publication schedule announced in advance. There should be no discrimination among users in the timing of the release of the results. The results should not be subject to governmental scrutiny as a condition for their release and should be seen to be free from political or other pressures.

1.190 There are many decisions to be taken about the degree of detail in the published data and the different ways in which the results may be presented. Users need to be consulted about these questions. These issues are discussed in more detail in Chapter 14; however, it is recommended to provide users with detailed data that are presented in a long time series. Detailed indices should include detailed item and area indices.

Special Cases

1.191 Certain products and issues have proven to be challenging for compilers with regard to both developing weights and collecting prices. Chapter 11 focuses on selected special cases and provides detailed advice for some of the more problematic products and issues compilers face. These include the treatment of seasonal items, housing, internet purchases, second-hand goods, own-account production, tariffs, transport services, health, education, social protection, and financial services.

1.192 Wherever possible, the chapter identifies the preferred approach for the treatment of each special case; however, currently there is no preferred approach for the treatment of owner-occupied housing services. The section on housing in Chapter 11 identifies the different possible methods for the treatment of owner-occupied housing and describes the advantages and disadvantages of each method.

Errors and Biases

1.193 The CPI, like all other statistics, may be subject to general error that may occur during any stage of the estimation process but also errors that are unique to the CPI (for example, substitution bias and quality change bias). Chapter 12 describes not only the different types and sources of potential errors, but also potential biases and their sources. Finally, Chapter 12 provides insight into how to address these errors and biases.

Annex 1.1

Formula Notations

$I^{0:t}$	Index
$I_{EA}^{0:t}$	Elementary index
$I_{C}^{0:t}$	Carli index
$I_{D}^{0:t}$	Dutot index
$I_{J}^{0:t}$	Jevons index
$I_{Jc}^{0:t}$	Chained Jevons index
$I_{Dc}^{0:t}$	Chained Dutot index
$I_{Cc}^{0:t}$	Chained Carli index
$I_{L}^{0:t}$	Laspeyres index
$I_{Lo}^{0:t}$	Lowe index
$I_{Y}^{0:t}$	Young index
$I_{ge}^{0:t}$	Geometric index
$I_{GL}^{0:t}$	Geometric Laspeyres index
$I_{GLo}^{0:t}$	Geometric Lowe index
$I_{GY}^{0:t}$	Geometric Young index
$I_{MY}^{0:t}$	Modified Young index
$I_{MLo}^{0:t}$	Modified Lowe index
$I_{HR}^{0:t}$	Harmonic mean price relatives
$I_{RH}^{0:t}$	Harmonic mean prices
$I_{LM}^{0:t}$	Llyod-Moulton index
$\ln p$	Log of price
n	Sample size
N	Population size
p	Price
$\hat{p}$	Quality adjusted price
P	Price relative
p_i^0	Base price observed for variety i
p_i^t	Price in current period for variety i
p_i^{t-1}	Price in previous period for variety i
q	Quantity
s_i^t	Percentage shares in period t
t	Current period
$t-1$	Previous period
T	End of index link
w	Weight
w_i^b	Weight of the item in the weight reference period
$w_i^{b(t)}$	Weight price updated from the weight reference to period t
$w_{agg}^{b(t)}$	Aggregate weight price updated from the weight reference period to period t

USES, CONCEPTS, SCOPE, AND CLASSIFICATIONS OF CONSUMER PRICE INDICES

2

Introduction

2.1 Chapter 2 begins with an overview describing the uses of the consumer price index (CPI). The primary uses drive the decisions regarding the concepts and scope for the index. As described in this chapter, countries face the reality of having to compile and disseminate a general-purpose index that tries to meet a variety of user needs. *The System of National Accounts 2008* (*2008 SNA*) provides the general framework for the concepts used to compile the CPI. The chapter explores each of these concepts in detail and how they are applied to the CPI. The chapter concludes with a discussion of the recommended classification for the CPI. The Classification of Individual Consumption According to Purpose (COICOP) serves as the internationally recommended classification system for developing weights and compiling CPIs. The previous version of COICOP, adopted in 1999, was updated and has been released as COICOP 2018. The classification section highlights the key changes between COICOP 2018 and the previous version, and identifies some important issues for consideration as countries begin implementing the new classification system.

Consumer Price Index Uses

2.2 The CPI represents a key indicator of economic performance in most countries. This section will focus on why CPIs are compiled and their uses.

A Range of Possible Consumer Price Indices

2.3 As noted in Chapter 1, compilers have to consider the needs of users in deciding on the group of households and the range of consumption goods and services covered by a CPI. As the prices of different goods and services do not all change at the same rate, or even move in the same direction, changing the coverage of the index will change the results obtained. Thus, there can be no single, unique CPI that meets all needs, and a range of possible CPIs could be defined.

2.4 While there may be interest in a broadly defined CPI, covering all the goods and services consumed by all households, there are many other options for defining CPIs that cover specific sets of goods and services, which may be more useful for particular analytic or policy purposes. When only a single CPI is compiled and published, there is a risk that it may be used for purposes for which it is not appropriate. More than one CPI could be published to meet different analytic or policy needs but each index must be clearly defined and explained by metadata. Otherwise, the publication of more than one CPI can be confusing to users who may view consumer inflation as a pervasive phenomenon affecting all households similarly. The coexistence of alternative measures could undermine their credibility for many users. Additionally, given budgetary constraints, many national statistical offices (NSOs) cannot compile more than one index. They face the reality of having to compile a single general-purpose index.

2.5 This section describes the most important uses for CPIs and indicates how the coverage of a CPI can be affected by the use for which it is intended. The question of the appropriate coverage of a CPI must be addressed before defining the appropriate methodology to be used. As described in the following text, whether the theoretical basis of a CPI is intended to be a cost of living index (COLI), a cost of goods index, or a general-purpose index, it is necessary to determine exactly what kinds of goods and services and what types of households are meant to be covered. This can only be decided based on the main uses of the index, which will drive decisions on the concepts and methods used.

2.6 Where only one CPI is published, it is the main use that should determine its type and scope. If there are several major uses, compromises may have to be made about how it is constructed. The purpose of a CPI should influence all aspects of its construction. CPI producers need to know how the index is being used if they are to ensure that it is fit for purpose. In this connection user, consultation is important.

Consumer Price Indices and General Inflation

2.7 Measures of the general rate of inflation in the economy are needed for various purposes:

- Controlling inflation is usually one of the main objectives of government economic policy, although responsibility for controlling inflation may be delegated to the central bank. A measure of general inflation is needed to set targets and to assess the degree of success achieved by the government or central bank in meeting anti-inflation targets.
- A measure of general inflation is also needed for both business and national accounting purposes, particularly for current purchasing power accounting.
- The concept of a relative price change is important in economics. It is convenient therefore to be able to measure the actual changes in the prices of individual goods or services relative to some measure of general inflation. There is also a need to measure neutral holding (or capital) gains and losses on assets, including monetary assets and liabilities.

2.8 A CPI is not a measure of general inflation, as it only measures changes in the prices of consumer goods and services purchased by households. A CPI does not cover capital goods, such as houses, or the goods and services consumed by enterprises or the government. Any analysis of inflation pressures in the economy must also take into account other price movements, such as changes in the prices of imports and exports, the prices of industrial inputs and outputs, and also asset prices.

2.9 However, even though the CPI does not measure general inflation, its movements may be expected to be highly correlated with those of a more general measure, because household consumption expenditure represents a large proportion of total final expenditure. In particular, the CPI should provide a reliable indicator of whether inflation is increasing or decreasing and also of possible turning points in the rate of inflation. This information is highly valuable even if the CPI may be systematically understating or overstating the general rate of inflation.

Use of the Consumer Price Index for Monetary and Economic Policy Purposes

2.10 The CPI is a key macroeconomic indicator and widely used for assessing economic policy, for monetary policy purposes, and for macroeconomic planning. It is also commonly used by governments and central banks to set inflation targets. As part of this, some countries produce measures of "core" or "underlying" inflation, based on the CPI or selected subindices of the CPI. In a few countries, the central bank produces measures of core inflation. Central banks require access to detailed weight, index, and price data for these calculations, and the NSO should provide these data. Central banks calculate core inflation using a variety of different methods that require access to these detailed data. For those NSOs that compile core inflation, the most common method used is known as the exclusion method. Under this method, the weights and prices of those items deemed volatile (that is, susceptible to short-term shocks) are excluded from the index. The items excluded can include items such as fresh fruit, vegetables, fish, meat, fuel, and so on. The NSO should work closely with the central bank to define the volatile items. The list of volatile items should be reviewed and updated as needed on a regular basis. When publishing the core inflation measure, the NSO or central bank should fully explain the methods used and define the purpose and uses for these data to avoid confusing users.

2.11 For monetary policy purposes, flash estimates of the CPI may be produced, which are released before the official CPI and give early warnings or signals about the development of consumer price inflation. More information on related or alternative measures can be found in Chapter 14.

Indexation

2.12 With indexation, the monetary values of certain payments, or stocks, are increased or decreased in proportion to the change in the value of a specified price index. Indexation, most commonly applied to monetary flows such as wages, pensions, social security benefits, rents, interest, or taxes, may also be applied to the capital values of certain monetary assets and liabilities. Under conditions of high inflation, the use of indexation may become widespread throughout the economy.

2.13 The objective of indexation of money incomes may be either to maintain the purchasing power of those incomes with respect to certain kinds of goods and services or to preserve the standard of living or economic well-being of the recipients of the incomes. These two objectives are not quite the same, especially over the longer term. Maintaining purchasing power may be interpreted as changing money income in proportion to the change in the monetary value of a fixed basket of goods and services purchased with that income. Maintaining the purchasing power of income over a fixed set of goods and services does not imply that the standard of living of the recipients of the income is unchanged.

2.14 When the indexation applies to monetary assets or liabilities, it may be designed to preserve the real value of the asset or liability relative to other assets or relative to the values of specified flows of goods and services.

The Type of Index Used for Indexation

2.15 When income flows such as wages or social security benefits are index-linked, it is necessary to consider the implications of choosing between a COLI and a price index that measures the changes in the cost of purchasing a fixed basket of goods and services, a type of index described here as a Lowe index. The widely used Laspeyres and Paasche indices are examples of Lowe indices. The Laspeyres index uses a typical basket purchased in the earlier of the two periods compared, while the Paasche uses a basket typical of the later period. In contrast, a COLI compares the cost of two baskets that may not be exactly the same, but which bring the same satisfaction or utility to the consumer.

2.16 Indexation using a Laspeyres price index will tend to overcompensate the income recipients for changes in their cost of living. Increasing incomes in proportion to the change in the cost of a basket purchased in the past ensure that the income recipients have the opportunity to continue purchasing that same basket if they wish to do so. They would then be at least as well off as before. However, by adjusting their pattern of expenditures to take account of changes in the *relative* prices of the goods and services they buy, they would be able to improve their standard of living or economic well-being because they can substitute goods and services that have become relatively cheaper for ones that have become relatively dearer. In addition, they may be able to start to purchase completely new kinds of goods that provide new kinds of benefits that were not available in the earlier period. Such new goods and services tend to lower a COLI when they first appear even though no price can actually be observed to fall, as there was no previous price.

Indexation of Wages and Pensions

2.17 As noted in Chapter 1, the indexation of wages was the main objective behind the original compilation of CPIs, although there has always been a general interest in measuring inflation. If the indexation of wages and pensions is the main justification for a CPI, it has direct implications for the coverage of the index. First, it suggests that the index should be confined to expenditure made by households whose principal source of income is either wages or pensions. Second, it may suggest that expenditure on certain types of goods and services, such as luxury items, may be excluded from the index. See also paragraph 1.35 in Chapter 1.

Indexation of Social Security Benefits

2.18 It has become common practice in many countries to index the rates at which social security benefits are payable. There are many kinds of benefits, including retirement pensions, unemployment benefits, sickness benefits, or child allowances. When indexing benefits of this kind is the main reason for compiling the CPI, it may suggest restricting the coverage of the index to certain types of households and goods and services. Some kinds of goods and services could then be excluded from the index based on political decisions that certain goods and services are deemed undesirable—for example, expenditure on alcoholic beverages and tobacco.

2.19 Alternatively, separate CPIs for different categories of households could be compiled. For example, an index may be compiled covering the basket of goods and services purchased by households whose principal source of income is a social security pension.

2.20 As already noted, publishing more than one CPI may be confusing if inflation is viewed as affecting everyone in the same way. Such confusion can be avoided by providing a detailed explanation of the purpose and use of each alternative index (as explained in Chapter 14). It is not difficult to explain that price changes are not the same for different categories of expenditure. In practice, some countries publish more than one index.

2.21 The main reason why it may not be justifiable to publish more than one index is that the movements in the different indices may be virtually the same, especially in the short term. In such cases, the costs of compiling and publishing separate indices may not be worthwhile. In practice, differences in the patterns of expenditure between different groups of households may not be large enough to yield significantly different CPIs.

2.22 Finally, it should be noted that the deliberate exclusion of certain types of goods and services by political decision on the grounds that the households toward whom the index is targeted ought not to be purchasing such goods or services or ought not to be compensated for increases in the prices of such goods and services, cannot be recommended because it exposes the index to political manipulation. For example, suppose it is decided that certain products such as tobacco or alcoholic beverages should be excluded from a CPI. There is a possibility that, when taxes on products are increased, these products may be deliberately selected for higher taxes with the knowledge that the resulting price increases would not be reflected in the CPI. Such practices are not unknown.

Indexation of Interest, Rents, and Other Contractual Payments

2.23 It is common for payments of both rents and interest, especially mortgage rates, to be indexed to the CPI. Governments may issue bonds with an interest rate specifically linked to the CPI. The interest payable in any given period may be equal to the fixed rate of interest plus the percentage change in the CPI. Payments of housing rents may also be linked to the CPI.

2.24 Creditors receiving interest payments do not consist only of households. In any case, the purpose of indexing interest is not to maintain the standard of living of the creditors but rather to maintain their real wealth by compensating them for the neutral holding, or capital losses on their loans incurred as a result of general inflation. A CPI may not be the ideal index for this purpose but may be used in the absence of another more suitable index.

2.25 Many other forms of contractual payments may be linked to the CPI. For example, legal obligations to pay alimony or for the support of children may be linked to the CPI. Payments of insurance premiums may be linked either to the all-items CPI or to a subindex relating to some specific types of expenditure, such as the costs of repairs.

Taxation

2.26 Movements in a CPI may be used to affect the amounts payable in taxation in several ways. For example, liability for income tax may be affected by linking personal allowances that are deductible from taxable income to changes in the CPI. Under a system of progressive taxation, the various thresholds at which higher rates of personal income tax become effective may be changed in proportion to changes in the CPI. Liability for capital gains tax may be reduced by basing it on real, rather than nominal, capital gains by reducing the percentage increase in the value of the asset by the percentage change in the CPI over the same period. In general, there are various ways in which some form of indexation may be introduced into tax legislation.

Deflation: Changing Current Values to Volume Measures

2.27 Price indices, such as the CPI, can be used to remove the effect of changes in prices from current value data or to convert nominal data into data in volume terms (*2008 SNA*, paragraph 2.146). In general, changes in current value aggregates of output or expenditure can be decomposed into changes in price and volume components. Deflation separates the price effect from the volume changes. While aggregates of income may not, strictly speaking, be broken into price and volume components, they may be calculated in constant purchasing power or to maintain a constant standard of living, which is described as being in real terms. Converting nominal data into data in real terms provides a consistent and meaningful measure across time.[1]

Measures of Real Consumption and Income

2.28 Price indices can be used to deflate final consumption expenditure at current prices or money income to derive measures of consumption expenditure in volume terms (also known as real consumption) and real income. Real measures involve volume comparisons over time (or space). There are two different approaches to such comparisons which are analogous to the distinction between a Lowe, or basket, index and a COLI.

[1]The SNA distinguishes between volume and real measures. For example, the *2008 SNA*, in paragraph 15.181, notes that many flows in the SNA, such as cash transfers, do not have price and quantity dimensions of their own and cannot, therefore, be decomposed in the same way as flows related to goods and services. While such flows cannot be measured in volume terms, they can nevertheless be measured "in real terms" by deflating their values with price indices in order to measure their real purchasing power over some selected basket of goods and services that serves as the numeraire.

2.29 The first approach defines the change in the consumption expenditure as the change in the total value of the goods and services actually consumed, measured at the fixed prices of some chosen period. This is equivalent to deflating the change in the current value of the goods and services consumed by an appropriately weighted Lowe price index. The change in real income can be measured by deflating the change in total money income by the same price index.

2.30 The alternative approach defines the change in consumption expenditure in volume as the change in economic well-being derived from the goods and services actually consumed. This may be estimated by deflating the change in the current value of consumption expenditure by using a COLI (see paragraphs 2.84–2.91). Real income may be similarly obtained by deflating money income by the same COLI.

2.31 The two approaches cannot lead to the same results if the pure price index and the COLI diverge. The choice between the two approaches to the measurement of consumption expenditure in volume and real income will not be pursued further here, as the issues involved are essentially the same as those already considered in the parallel discussion of the choice between a Lowe, or basket, price index and a COLI (see paragraphs 2.82–2.91).

Consistency between Price Indices and Expenditure Series

2.32 The data collected on prices and the data collected on household expenditure must be mutually consistent when measuring the volume of consumption. This requires that both sets of data cover the same set of goods and services and use the same concepts and classifications. Problems may arise in practice because the price indices and the expenditure series are often compiled independently of each other by different departments of an NSO or even by different agencies.

National Accounts

2.33 The CPI is mainly used in the national accounts to derive volume measures of household final consumption expenditure (HFCE). HFCE at current prices should be deflated at the most detailed level as possible using the respective CPIs (*2008 SNA*, paragraph 15.140). In addition, and in the absence of other indicators, the CPI is often used to derive volume measures of other national accounts aggregates, but this use of the CPI is neither ideal nor encouraged.

Purchasing Power Parities

2.34 Many countries participate in regular international programs enabling purchasing power parities (PPPs) to be calculated for household actual consumption expenditure. The calculation of PPPs requires the prices of individual consumer goods and services to be compared directly between different countries. Real expenditures and real incomes can then be compared between countries in much the same way as between different time periods in the same country.

2.35 It is not proposed to examine PPP methodology here but simply to note that PPPs create another demand for basic price data. When such data are being collected, it is important to recognize that they can be used for PPPs as well as CPIs. PPPs are essentially international deflators that are analogous to the intertemporal deflators needed for the national accounts of a single country. Thus, while the processing and aggregation of the basic data for CPI purposes should be determined by the needs of the CPI itself, it is appropriate to take into account the requirements of these other kinds of price indices at the data collection stage. There may be important economies of scale obtained by using a single collection process to meet the needs of several different types of indices.

2.36 The International Comparison Program (ICP) represents one of the largest efforts to develop PPPs. Given limited staff and budgetary resources, there is a need for careful consideration to identify potential synergies between the ICP and CPI. These possible synergies are the topic of an ongoing task force under the auspices of the ICP. The objective of this task force is to develop guidelines for countries to maximize limited resources for the collection of price data needed for both programs, while ensuring that the reliability and representativity of the CPI is not adversely affected. Appendix 4 provides detail on the ICP which is managed by the World Bank.

2.37 Thus, operationally as well as conceptually, the CPI needs to be placed in the context of a wider set of interrelated price indices. The compilation of CPIs predates the compilation of national accounts by many years in some countries, so the CPI may have originated as a free-standing index. However, the CPI should no longer be treated as an isolated index whose compilation and methodology can proceed quite independently of other statistics.

Use of the Consumer Price Index for Accounting under Inflation

2.38 When there is inflation, both business and national accounts have to introduce adjustments that are not needed when the price level is stable. This is a complex subject that cannot be pursued in any depth here. Two methods of accounting are commonly used, and they are summarized in paragraphs 2.39 and 2.40. Both require price indices for their implementation.

Current Purchasing Power Accounts

2.39 Current purchasing power accounts are accounts in which the monetary values of the flows in earlier time periods are scaled up in proportion to the increase in some general index of inflation between the earlier period and the current period. In principle, the index used should be a general price index covering other flows in addition to HFCE, but in practice, the CPI is often used by default in the absence of a more suitable general index.

Current Cost Accounting

2.40 Current cost accounting (*2008 SNA*, paragraphs 1.65–1.67) is an accounting method in which the cost of using goods and assets in production is calculated using current prices of those goods and assets as distinct from the prices at which the assets were purchased or otherwise acquired in the past (historic costs). The current cost of using a good or asset takes account not only of changes in the general price level but also of changes in the relative price of that type of asset since it was acquired. In principle, the price indices that are used to adjust the original prices paid for the goods and assets should be specific price indices relating to that particular type of good or asset, and such indices are calculated and used in this way in some countries. However, when there are no such indices available, the all-items CPI, or some subindex of the CPI, have been used for this purpose.

Consumer Price Indices and International Comparisons of Inflation

2.41 CPIs are also commonly used to make international comparisons of inflation rates. An important example of their use for this purpose is provided by the European Union (EU). Since the mid-1990s, EU member countries have compiled Harmonised Indices of Consumer Prices (HICP) that are used as an aggregate measure of inflation for the euro area and to compare consumer price inflation across member countries, and for monetary and economic policy purposes of the EU.

2.42 Another example would be the Group of Twenty (G20) CPI compiled by the Organisation for Economic Co-operation and Development. One of the outcomes of the G20 Data Gaps Initiative was the compilation of aggregates for the G20 countries. Using the headline[2] (all-items) indices, the G20 aggregate provides a measure of inflation for the G20 countries. For more information on the G20 CPI, see *Methodology Notes: Compilation of a G-20 Consumer Price Index* available on the Organisation for Economic Co-operation and Development website.[3]

2.43 Finally, CPIs are used for purposes of international comparisons by a range of international organizations, including the Food and Agriculture Organization, the International Labor Organization, the International Monetary Fund, Organisation for Economic Co-operation and Development, World Bank, and others.

Popularity of Consumer Price Indices for Economic Analysis

2.44 The CPI is a high-profile statistic. CPIs seem to have acquired a unique status among economic statistics in most countries. Changes in the CPI tend to receive significant publicity and often make headline news. There are several factors which help to explain this:

- All households experience the phenomenon the CPI intends to measure. The general public faces changes in the prices of consumer goods and services, and the direct impact those changes have on their living standards. Wages, pensions, and social security benefits may be adjusted according to changes in the CPI, which also will have a direct impact on households' income. Interest in CPIs is not confined to the press and politicians.
- Countries disseminate the CPI frequently, usually each month, so that the rate of consumer inflation can be closely monitored. The CPI is also a timely statistic that is released very soon after the end of the period to which it refers.
- The CPI is a statistic with a long history, as noted in Chapter 1. People have been familiar with it over this period of time.
- Although price changes for certain kinds of consumer products are difficult to measure because of quality changes, price changes for other kinds of goods and services, such as capital goods and government services, especially public services, tend to be even more difficult to measure.
- Most countries have deliberately adopted a policy of not revising the index once it has been published. This makes it more attractive for many purposes, especially those with financial consequences such as indexation. The lack of revisions may create a somewhat spurious impression of certainty, but it also seems to enhance the credibility and acceptability of the index.

2.45 The widespread use of the CPI for purposes other than those for which it was designed can be explained not only by the various factors listed in paragraph 2.44 but also with the fact that no satisfactory alternative or more comprehensive measures of inflation are available monthly in most countries. For example, the CPI may be used as a proxy for a more general measure of inflation in business accounting, even though it may be clear that, conceptually, the CPI is not the ideal index for this purpose. Similarly, the fact that the CPI is not subject to revision, together with its frequency and timeliness, may explain its popularity for indexation purposes in business or legal contracts in contexts where it also may not be very appropriate conceptually. These practices may be defended on the grounds that the alternative to using the CPI may be to make no adjustment for inflation. Although the CPI may not be the ideal measure, it is much better to use it than to make no adjustment.

2.46 Although the CPI is often used as a proxy for a general measure of inflation, this does not justify extending its coverage to include elements that go beyond household final consumption. If broader indices of inflation are needed, they should be developed in addition to the CPI, leaving the CPI intact. Some countries are in fact developing additional and more comprehensive measures of inflation within the SNA framework.

Inflation Perceptions

2.47 While countries strive to compile and disseminate a CPI that provides a reliable measure of price change, many data users, especially individual households, perceive the headline inflation rate to be incorrect. This perception negatively affects the credibility of the index and user confidence. NSOs should make every effort to improve these perceptions.

2.48 Individual consumers may regard the headline measure of inflation as wrong because they do not fully appreciate CPI concepts and compilation methods. First, the CPI represents a composite of all households, reflecting the average total expenditure of all households on the goods and services included in the basket, and not the expenditure of any single household. Second, the index represents a weighted average change over time in the prices paid by consumers. This means that some prices are increasing while others are decreasing. The impact of the price change of each item included in the basket is determined by the weight of that item.

2.49 To build user confidence and enhance credibility, NSOs should enhance transparency and provide more

[2] For the EU and Turkey, the HICP is used in the aggregation, while for all other countries, the national CPI is used.
[3] http://www.oecd.org/sdd/prices-ppp/CPI-G20-methodology.pdf.

details on the concepts and methods used to compile the CPI (that is, metadata). Index compilation methods should be explained in detail and made available to all users on the NSO website and in hardcopy as needed. In addition, NSOs can provide better explanations to frequently asked questions. Many NSO websites include a frequently asked questions section to respond to questions regarding concepts and methods used or to avoid common misperceptions. Finally, detailed data should be disseminated on the NSO website. More detailed data provide more information to all users to better understand the source(s) of price change. Chapter 14 provides more information on the need to provide more detailed data and metadata.

The Need for Independence and Integrity of Consumer Price Indices

2.50 Because of the widespread use of CPIs for various types of indexation, movements in the CPI can have major financial ramifications throughout the economy. The implications for the government alone can be considerable, given that the CPI can affect interest payments and taxation receipts, as well as the government's wage and social security outlays.

2.51 When financial interests are involved, there is always a risk that both political and nonpolitical pressure groups may try to exert an influence on the methodology used to compile the CPI. The CPI, in common with other official statistics, must be protected from such pressures. Partly for this reason, many countries establish an advisory committee to ensure that the CPI is not subject to inappropriate outside influence or pressure. The advisory committee may include representatives of a cross-section of interested parties, as well as independent experts able to offer professional advice. To enhance user confidence and transparency, details on the methodology used to compile CPIs should be made available to the general public.

Concepts and Scope of the Consumer Price Index

2.52 As noted previously in paragraphs 2.38–2.43 and in Chapter 1, the primary uses of the CPI will determine the concepts and scope used to compile the index. This section provides a more detailed look at the different concepts used to compile the CPI, as well as scope and coverage issues.

Concepts

2.53 While this chapter does not provide a detailed overview of SNA definitions and concepts, it should be noted that the SNA serves as the conceptual basis, or framework, for the CPI. Definitions for expenditure, consumption, households, and other concepts are derived from the SNA.

2.54 Households may acquire goods and services[4] for purposes of final consumption in four main ways: (1) they may purchase them in monetary transactions; (2) they may produce them themselves for their own consumption; (3) they may receive them as payments in kind through barter transactions, particularly as remuneration in kind for work done; and (4) they may receive them as free gifts, or transfers, from other economic units, including social transfers in kind provided by government. The treatment of household production activities is addressed in paragraphs 2.154–2.168.

2.55 The broadest concept of final consumption for CPI purposes would be a price index embracing all four categories of consumption goods and services listed previously. This set of consumption goods and services may be described as total acquisitions. Total acquisitions are equivalent to the total household actual final consumption as defined in the SNA (*2008 SNA*, paragraph 9.81). The *2008 SNA* distinguishes between *household actual final consumption* and *HFCE*, as explained in paragraphs 2.56–2.59.

2.56 According to the SNA (*2008 SNA*, paragraph 9.56), HFCE includes the expenditure incurred by resident households on consumption goods or services. These include purchases of consumer goods and services, as well as the estimated (imputed)[5] value of barter transactions, goods and services received in kind, and goods and services produced and consumed by the same household (production for own consumption).

2.57 *Household actual final consumption*, as defined in the *2008 SNA* (*2008 SNA*, paragraph 9.81) consists of the consumption goods and services acquired by individual households. The total value of household actual final consumption includes the sum of these three components: (1) the value of households' expenditures on consumption goods or services, including expenditures on nonmarket goods or services sold at prices that are reduced or not economically significant,[6] (2) the value of the expenditures incurred by government units on individual consumption goods or services provided to households as social transfers in kind, and (3) the value of the expenditures incurred by nonprofit institution serving households (NPISHs) on individual consumption goods or services provided to households as social transfers in kind.

2.58 Household actual final consumption is a broader concept than HFCE, and the difference between the two concepts is linked to the concepts of acquisitions and expenditure, as explained in paragraphs 2.59–2.61.

Expenditure

2.59 *Expenditure* on goods and services is the value of the amount that buyers pay, or agree to pay, to sellers in exchange for goods or services that sellers provide to them or to other institutional units designated by the buyers (*2008 SNA*, paragraph 9.32). In other words, expenditure is made by the economic units who pay for the goods and services that bear the costs. However, many of the goods and services consumed by households are financed and paid for by government units or nonprofit institutions. They are mostly services such as education, health, housing, and transport.

[4]The *2008 SNA* defines goods and services in paragraphs 6.14–6.21.

[5]The term "imputation" is used in the SNA (*2008 SNA*, paragraph 3.75) with a specific narrow meaning: it is preferable to reserve that term for the kind of situation that involves not only estimating a value but also constructing a transaction. In this manual, the term "imputation" has a broader meaning.

[6]Prices are said to be economically significant when they have a significant influence on the amounts the producers are willing to supply and on the amounts purchasers wish to buy (*2008 SNA*, paragraph 6.95).

Household Actual Final Consumption

Value of Expenditures on Consumption Goods or Services, Including Payments for Nonmarket Goods or Services Sold at Nonsignificant Economic Prices (9.56)	Value of Expenditures Incurred by Government Units or NPISH on Individual Consumption Goods or Services Provided to Households as Social Transfers in Kind (9.81)

Household Final Consumption Expenditure (HFCE)

Value of Expenditures on Consumption Goods or Services, Including Payments for Nonmarket Goods or Services Sold at Nonsignificant Economic Prices (9.56)

Purchases of Consumer Goods and Services (monetary transactions)	Purchases of Consumer Goods and Services (barter transactions)	Goods and Services Provided by Employers to Their Employees in Remuneration for Work Done	Consumer Goods and Services Produced and Consumed by the Same Household

Household Final Monetary Consumption Expenditure (HFMCE)

Purchases of Consumer Goods and Services (monetary transactions)

Individual goods and services provided free of charge, or at prices that are not economically significant, to individual households by governments or nonprofit institutions are described as social transfers in kind[7] (social transfers in kind do not include collective services provided by governments to the community as a whole, such as public administration and defense).

2.60 The expenditure on social transfers in kind is incurred by the governments or nonprofit institutions that pay for them, and not by the households that consume them. It could be decided that the CPI should be confined to final consumption expenditure incurred by households, in which case free social transfers in kind would be excluded from the scope of the index. Even if they were to be included, they can be ignored in practice when they are considered to be provided free, on the grounds that households incur zero expenditure on them. Of course, their prices are not zero from the perspective of the units that finance the social transfers, but the relevant prices for a CPI are those payable by the households.

2.61 Social transfers cannot be ignored, however, when governments and nonprofit institutions decide to introduce (or eliminate) charges for them, a practice that has become increasingly common in many countries. For example, if the CPI is intended to measure the change in the total value of a basket of consumption goods and services that includes social transfers, increases in their prices to households from zero to some positive amount increase the cost of the basket and should be captured by a CPI. The CPI should reflect the full extent of the price change in the period the price increases from zero to some positive amount. With a zero price, the good or service is generally excluded from the CPI; however, when the price changes from zero to some positive amount, it becomes a newly significant good or service and can be treated in the same way as other new goods or services are introduced. Chapter 7 provides an overview of the different methods for including new goods or services in the CPI. Alternatively, if the price decreases from some positive amount to zero, this also must be reflected in the CPI. The question remains how to deal with the weight for that item. One option may be to use a zero price and adjust the weights during the next update. Another option may be to redistribute the weight to the other items within the class. Finally, it may be decided that the best approach would be to redistribute the weight broadly over all items. The treatment of health, education, and social protection services in the CPI is further discussed in Chapter 11.

Acquisitions and Uses

2.62 It has been customary in the literature on CPIs to draw a distinction between acquisitions of goods and services by households and their subsequent use (consumption) to satisfy their households' needs (the *2008 SNA* defines acquisitions in paragraphs 9.36–9.38 and consumption of goods and services in paragraphs 9.39–9.41). Consumption goods are typically acquired at one point of time and used at some other point of time, often much later, or they may be used repeatedly, or even continuously, over an extended period of time. The times of acquisition and use nevertheless coincide for many services, although there are other kinds of services that provide lasting benefits and are not used up at the time they are provided. This is further explained in paragraphs 2.63–2.67.

2.63 Acquisition of a good refers to the moment at which ownership of a good transfers to the consumer. In a market setting, it is the moment at which the consumer incurs a liability to pay, either in cash, credit, or in kind. Acquisition of a service cannot be determined as easily because the provision of a service does not involve an exchange of ownership. Instead, it typically leads to some improvement in the condition of the consumer. Consumers acquire a service at the same time that the producer provides it and the consumer accepts a liability to pay. In a market situation, therefore, the time of acquisition for both goods and services refers to the time at which the liability to pay is incurred. The distinction between time of acquisition and time of use is particularly important for durable goods and certain kinds of services.

[7]The *2008 SNA* refers to social transfers in kind in paragraphs 6.234 and 6.235.

2.64 A "nondurable" good would be better described as a single-use good (durable goods are defined in paragraph 9.42 of the *2008 SNA*). For example, food and drink are used once only to satisfy hunger or thirst. Heating oil, coal, or firewood can be burnt once only, but they are nevertheless extremely durable physically and can be stored indefinitely. Households may hold substantial stocks of so-called nondurables, such as many foodstuffs and fuel, especially in periods of political or economic uncertainty.

2.65 Conversely, the distinguishing feature of consumer durables, such as furniture, household equipment, or vehicles, is that they are durable under use. They can be used repeatedly or continuously to satisfy consumers' needs over a long period of time, possibly many years. For this reason, a durable is often described as providing a flow of "services" to the consumer over the period it is used. Some durables last much longer than others, the less durable ones being described as "semidurables" in COICOP, for example, clothing. Dwellings are not classified as consumer durables in COICOP. They are treated as fixed assets and not consumption goods, and therefore fall outside the scope of COICOP and the CPI. However, the housing services produced and consumed by owner-occupiers are included in COICOP and classified in the same way as the housing services consumed by tenants. More information on the treatment of housing is available in Chapter 11.

2.66 Consumers may continue to benefit, and derive utility, from some services long after they were provided because they bring about substantial, long-lasting, or even permanent improvements in the condition of the consumers. The quality of life of individuals receiving medical treatments such as hip replacements or cataract surgery, for example, is substantially and permanently improved. Similarly, consumers of educational services can benefit from them over their entire lifetimes.

2.67 For some analytical purposes, it may be appropriate to treat certain kinds of services, such as education and health, as the service equivalents of durable goods. Expenditure on such services can be viewed as investments that augment the stock of human capital. Another characteristic that education and health services share with durable goods is that they are often so expensive that their purchase has to be financed by borrowing or by running down other assets.

Monetary and Nonmonetary Transactions

2.68 A distinction may also be drawn between monetary and nonmonetary transactions depending if the payment made or liability incurred is stated in units of currency. A monetary transaction occurs when a household pays in cash, by check or credit card, or otherwise incurs a liability to pay, in exchange for the acquisition of a good or service. Nonmonetary transactions occur when households do not incur a liability but bear the costs of acquiring the goods or services in some other way.

2.69 Households may incur nonmonetary transactions when household members receive goods and services from their employers as remuneration in kind (*2008 SNA*, paragraphs 9.51 and 9.52). The employees pay for the goods and services with their own labor rather than cash. Consumption goods and services received as remuneration in kind can, in principle, be included in a CPI using the estimated prices that would be payable for them on the market.

2.70 Another important category of nonmonetary transaction occurs when households consume goods and services that they have produced themselves (*2008 SNA*, paragraphs 9.53–9.55). The households incur the costs, while the expenditure is deemed to occur when the goods and services are consumed. Own-account production of this kind includes the production of housing services by owner-occupiers. The treatment of goods and services produced for own consumption raises important conceptual issues that are discussed in more detail in paragraphs 2.154–2.157 and in Chapter 11.

2.71 The narrowest concept of consumption that could be used for CPI purposes is one based on monetary transactions only. As noted previously, HFCE includes barter transactions, goods and services received in kind, and production for own consumption. A concept of consumption based only on monetary transactions excludes many of the goods and services actually acquired and consumed by households. On the other hand, only monetary transactions generate the prices needed for CPI purposes. The prices of the goods and services acquired through nonmonetary transactions cannot be directly observed and have to be imputed or estimated on the basis of the prices observed in monetary transactions. Imputed or estimated prices do not generate more price information. Instead, they affect the weighting, increasing the weight of the prices used to value nonmonetary transactions for which prices have to be imputed or estimated.

2.72 If the main reason for compiling a CPI is the measurement of inflation or as an input into monetary policy decisions, the scope of the index should be restricted to monetary transactions only, especially since nonmonetary transactions do not generate any demand for money. The HICP, used to measure inflation within the EU, is confined to household final monetary consumption expenditure (HFMCE) (see Appendix 1).

Domestic and National Concept of Expenditure

2.73 The concept of residence is based on the center of predominant economic interest of the institutional unit (that is, household, in the case of the CPI), and not on nationality or legal criteria. The SNA states that the most commonly used concept of economic territory is the geographic territory administrated by a government, although it may be larger or smaller than this (as in a currency or economic unit, or a region in a country). The economic territory also includes the territorial enclaves in the rest of the world (embassies, consulates, military bases, scientific stations, and so on). As a general rule, institutional units are considered resident in a certain economic territory if they are engaged in activities and transactions on a significant scale for one year or more. According to the SNA, the residence of individual persons is determined by that of the household of which they form part and not by their place of work, and all members of the same household have the same residence as the household itself. If members of a household work and reside abroad so long that they acquire a center of economic interest abroad, they cease to be members of their original household (*2008 SNA*, paragraphs 4.10–4.15).

2.74 Therefore, according to the *2008 SNA* (*2008 SNA*, paragraph 9.79), HFCE refers to the expenditure incurred by resident households, whether that expenditure is incurred within the economic territory or abroad. Additionally, nonresident households may make expenditure inside the economic territory of a country. Depending on the residence principle, there are two important concepts related to CPI coverage: the domestic and national concept.

2.75 The *national concept,* which aligns with the HFCE concept as defined in the *2008 SNA*, includes expenditure made by resident households, whether it takes place on the economic territory or elsewhere. This means that the expenditure of resident households at home should be adjusted by adding the expenditure of resident households abroad (imports) and deducting the expenditure of nonresident households in the home territory (exports).

2.76 The *domestic concept* is not based on the residence of households, rather on the territory where the consumption or expenditure occurs. It covers the consumption expenditure made by all households on the economic territory of a country, including the expenditure of nonresidents of the country and excluding the expenditure of residents abroad.

2.77 Decisions about the choice of the concept used depend on the main use of a CPI. For inflation analysis and monetary policy purposes, it is the price change within a country which is of interest. An index of inflation is needed that covers all "domestic" consumption expenditure that takes place within the geographical boundaries of the country, whether made by residents or nonresidents.

2.78 When CPIs are used for escalating the incomes of residents, it may be appropriate to adopt the "national" concept which covers all the expenditure of residents, whether inside or outside the country. Household budget surveys (HBSs) can cover all these types of expenditure. For example, the prices paid for airline tickets and package holidays bought within the domestic territory should be covered. It can be difficult, however, to obtain price data for the goods and services purchased by residents when abroad, although in some cases subindices of the partner countries' CPIs might be used.

2.79 The treatment of purchases made online requires special consideration. In principle, the domestic and national concepts could provide guidance on how to treat the expenditure made on goods and services, including digital downloads, purchased online. In many cases, however, internet-based outlets may be based (registered) abroad and this expenditure would be considered cross-border shopping. For those countries following the national concept, the approach is clear. Strictly speaking, under the domestic concept, this expenditure would not be included because it would be defined as expenditure abroad; in practice, this requires a broader interpretation. The nature of internet purchases, therefore, requires a different way of thinking and special consideration, especially with regard to the domestic concept. Additionally, internet purchases continue to grow in importance.

2.80 Many countries have carefully considered how to include the expenditure (and prices) made on goods and services via the internet. For the purchase of goods, the expenditure and prices should be reflected in the country where the goods are delivered.

2.81 Services purchased on the internet can be more problematic for CPI compilation because there are both tangible and digital services. Tangible services would include the traditional services such as transportation, hotels, entrance to cultural/sporting events, or education. Digital services would include telecommunications, broadcasting (for example, streaming or downloading music, movies, or television content) and other services (for example, software). If the service is consumed in the economic territory where the household is resident, it should be included in the CPI; however, if the service is consumed outside of the economic territory of the country, it would be excluded. For example, if a household reserves a hotel room that will be used and paid for in another country, it would be considered out of scope. For digital services, because the service is being consumed within the economic territory of a country, the expenditure and prices should be included in the country where the household resides. More details on the treatment of internet purchases can be found in Chapter 11.

Basket Indices and Cost of Living Indices

2.82 A fundamental conceptual distinction may be drawn between a *basket index* and a *COLI.* In a CPI context, a basket index is an index that measures the change between two time periods in the total expenditure needed to purchase a given set, or basket, of consumption goods and services. It is called a "Lowe index" in this Manual. A COLI is an index that measures the change in the minimum cost of maintaining a given standard of living. Both indices therefore have very similar objectives in that they aim to measure the change in the total expenditure needed to purchase *either* the same basket *or* two baskets whose composition may differ somewhat but between which the household is indifferent.

Basket Indices

2.83 CPIs are often calculated as either Lowe or Young indices in practice. Their properties and behavior are described in detail throughout this Manual. The operational target for most CPIs is to measure the change over time in the total value of a specified basket of consumption goods and services purchased, or acquired, by a specified group of households in a specified period of time. The meaning of such an index is clear. It is necessary to ensure that the selected basket is relevant to the needs of users and also kept up to date. The basket may be changed at regular intervals and does not have to remain fixed over long periods of time. The determination of the basket is considered in more detail in Chapter 3.

Cost of Living Indices

2.84 The economic approach to index number theory treats the quantities consumed as being dependent on the prices. Households are treated as price takers who are assumed to react to changes in *relative* prices by adjusting the *relative* quantities they consume. A basket index that works with a fixed set of quantities fails to allow for the fact that there is a systematic tendency for consumers to substitute items that have become relatively cheaper for those that have become relatively more expensive. A COLI based on the economic approach does take this substitution effect into account. It measures the change in the minimum expenditure needed to maintain a given standard of living when utility-maximizing households adjust their patterns of purchases in response to changes in relative prices. In contrast to a basket index, the baskets in the two periods in a COLI will generally not be quite the same in the two periods because of these substitutions.

2.85 The properties and behavior of COLIs are explained in some detail in Chapter 4 of the publication *Consumer Price Index Theory*. A summary explanation has already been given in Chapter 1. The maximum scope of a COLI would be the entire set of consumption goods and services consumed by the designated households from which they derive utility. It includes the goods and services received free as social transfers in kind from governments or NPISH. Because COLIs measure the change in the cost of maintaining a given standard of living or level of utility, they lend themselves to a uses rather than an acquisitions approach (see also paragraphs 2.62–2.67), as utility is derived not by acquiring a consumer good or service but by using it to satisfy personal needs and wants.

2.86 Economic well-being may be interpreted to mean not only economic welfare, that is, the utility linked to economic activities such as production, consumption, and working, but also the general well-being associated with other factors such as security from attack by others. It may not be possible to draw a clear distinction between economic and noneconomic factors, but it is clear that total economic well-being is only partly dependent on the amount of goods and services consumed.

2.87 *Conditional and unconditional COLIs.* In principle, the scope of a COLI is influenced by whether it is intended to be a conditional or unconditional COLI. The *total welfare* of a household depends on a string of noneconomic factors such as the climate, the state of the physical, social, and political environment, the risk of being attacked either by criminals or from abroad, the incidence of diseases, and so on, as well as by the quantities of goods and services consumed. An *unconditional COLI* measures the change in the cost to a household of maintaining a given level of total economic well-being allowing the noneconomic factors to vary as well as the prices of consumption goods and services. If changes in the noneconomic factors lower economic well-being, then some compensating increase in the level of consumption will be needed in order to maintain the same level of total economic well-being. For example, if there is an adverse change in the weather, that requires more fuel to be consumed to maintain the same level of comfort as before. The cost of the *increased quantities* of fuel consumed drives up the unconditional COLI, irrespective of what has happened to prices. There are countless other events that can impact on an unconditional COLI, from natural disasters such as earthquakes to man-made disasters such as climate change or acts of terrorism.

2.88 While there may be interest in an unconditional COLI for certain analytical and policy purposes, it is deliberately defined to measure the effects of many other factors besides prices. If the objective is to measure the effects of price changes only, the nonprice factors must be held constant. Given that a COLI is meant to serve as a CPI its scope must be restricted to exclude the effects of events other than price changes. A *conditional* COLI is defined as the ratio of the minimum expenditure needed to maintain a given level of utility, or standard of living, in response to price changes, assuming that all the other factors affecting economic well-being remain constant. It is conditional not only on a particular standard of living and set of preferences but also on a particular state of the nonprice factors affecting economic well-being. COLIs, in this Manual, are to be understood as *conditional* COLIs.

2.89 A conditional COLI should not be viewed as second best. An unconditional COLI is a more comprehensive COLI than a conditional COLI, but it is not a more comprehensive *price* index than a conditional index. An unconditional index does not include more price information than a conditional index and it does not give more insight into the impact of price changes on households' economic well-being. On the contrary, the impact of the price changes is diluted and obscured as more variables impacting on economic well-being are included within the scope of the index.

2.90 Lowe indices, including Laspeyres and Paasche, are also conditional, being dependent on the choice of the basket. The fact that the value of a basket index varies in predictable ways according to the choice of basket has generated much of the large body of literature available on index number theory. Conceptually, Lowe indices and conditional COLIs have much in common. A Lowe index measures the change in the cost of a specified basket of goods and services, whereas a conditional COLI measures the change in the cost of maintaining the level of utility associated with some specified basket of goods and services, other things being equal.

2.91 In practice, it is not possible to compile a true COLI. Some countries construct the CPI for indexation purposes and employ methods to approximate a COLI. Similarly, other countries construct their CPI with the primary purpose of measuring inflation, in which case a cost of goods index would be the target index. The selection of a cost of goods index or a COLI as target for the CPI has consequences concerning the scope of the index and the way different goods or services are included in the index. In practice, most countries compile a general-purpose index that strives to meet both compensation and inflation measurement needs in a single index.

Consumer Price Index Scope

Households and Outlets Included in the Scope of a Consumer Price Index

Population Coverage

2.92 The group of households included in the scope of a CPI is referred to as the "reference households," or the "reference population." In this context, scope refers to the households intended to be represented in the CPI; on the other hand, coverage refers to the actual households represented by the index.

2.93 According to the SNA, households are an institutional sector made up of private households and institutional households. *Private households* are defined as groups of persons who share the same living accommodation, who pool some or all of their resources and consume selected goods and services collectively. Members of the same household do not necessarily have to belong to the same family, as long as there is some sharing of resources and consumption. *Institutional households* consist of persons living permanently, or for a very long period of time, in institutions. These include religious institutions, hospitals, the military, prisons, or retirement homes. Persons who enter such institutions only for short periods of time should be treated as members of the individual households to which they normally belong (the *2008 SNA* defines household, private, and institutional household in paragraphs 4.149–4.154).

2.94 Following the SNA definition of HFCE (*2008 SNA*, paragraph 9.56) both private and institutional households are considered in the scope of the CPI, and in principle should be covered. For example, the EU's HICP coverage of households includes institutional households, consistent with the SNA definition (for more information, see Appendix 1). Nevertheless, in many countries, the consumption expenditure of institutional households may be of negligible importance, or it may be problematic to collect suitable expenditure data from institutional households. For these reasons, it may be decided to exclude the consumption expenditure of institutional households from the actual coverage of the CPI. It may also be the case that the compensation (indexing wages and salaries) of only private households is one of the main purposes of the CPI, which may also justify disregarding the consumption expenditure of institutional households.

2.95 In almost all countries, the CPI scope includes as many private households as possible and is not confined to those belonging to a specific socioeconomic group. In some countries, however, extremely wealthy households are excluded for various reasons. Their expenditure may be considered to be very atypical, while their expenditure data, as collected in an HBS, may be unreliable, as the response rates for wealthy households in an HBS are usually quite low. In addition, it may be too costly to collect prices for some of the consumer goods and services purchased exclusively by the wealthy. Other countries may decide to exclude other kinds of households. Such exclusions affect the expenditure weights to the extent that the patterns of expenditure of the excluded groups differ from those of the rest of the population. As far as possible, countries should define the scope to include all households regardless of size, location, or income.

2.96 In addition to a single wide-ranging official (headline) CPI relevant to the country as a whole, more and more countries publish a range of alternative indices relating to subsectors of the population (for example, low-income households or retirees).

Geographical Coverage

2.97 Geographical coverage refers either to the geographical coverage of expenditure or the coverage of price collection. Ideally, these two should coincide, whether the CPI intends to be a national or a regional index. In general, for the geographical coverage of expenditure, the index should include expenditure made by all households, urban and rural, throughout the country.

2.98 In many countries, prices are collected in urban areas only because their movements are considered to be representative of the price movements in rural areas. In these cases, if national weights are applied, the resulting index can be considered a national CPI. If price movements in urban and rural areas differ significantly and price collection is restricted to urban areas because of resource constraints, then urban weights should be applied, and the resulting index must be considered as an urban and not a national CPI. Most countries tend to use weights covering urban and rural households, although in the majority of cases, price collection takes place in urban areas only. Of course, the borderline between urban and rural is inevitably arbitrary and varies from country to country. For example, in one country, urban price collection is interpreted to include villages with as few as 2,000 residents, while in others this threshold may be higher.

2.99 Decisions about geographical coverage with regard to urban versus rural coverage depend on the population distribution and the extent to which expenditure patterns and the movements of prices tend to differ between urban and rural areas.

2.100 When compiling regional indices, the concept of residence (as described in 2.73) applies to the region in which a household is resident. It is possible to draw a distinction between the expenditure within a region and the expenditure of the residents of that region, analogous to the distinction between the "domestic" and "national" concepts of expenditure at the country level. The same issues arise for regional indices as were discussed in the previous section for national indices. The principles applying to cross-border shopping between regions are the same as for international cross-border shopping (for a description of cross-border internet purchases, see the section on internet purchases in Chapter 11), but data availability is generally different. if the scope of the regional index is defined to include the purchases by regional residents when in other regions (and exclude purchases by consumers that are not residents of the region), although price data for the other regions should be readily available, it is unlikely that expenditure data will be available with the necessary split between expenditure within, and expenditure outside, the region of residence.

2.101 When compiling a regional index, care must be taken to treat cross-border purchases in the same way in all regions. Otherwise double counting, or omission, of expenditure may occur when regional data are aggregated. Where regional indices are aggregated to give a national index, the weights should be based on regional expenditure data rather than on population data, as discussed in Chapter 3.

2.102 Many countries try to satisfy the differing needs of their many CPI users by deriving a family of indices with different coverage, headed by a single wide-ranging official (headline) CPI which is relevant to the country as a whole. In some large countries, regional indices are more widely used than the national CPI, particularly where the indices are used for indexing wages and salaries. Thus, in addition to the headline CPI, which has the widest coverage possible, alternative indices are published which may relate to: (1) subsectors of the population; (2) geographical regions; and (3) specific product groups. Subindices of the overall (official all-items) CPI should be published at a level as detailed as possible, since many users are interested in the price change of specific product groups.

Outlet Coverage

2.103 The coverage of outlets is dictated by the purchasing behavior of the reference households. In principle, the prices relevant to CPIs are the prices paid by households. In practice, however, it is necessary to rely mainly on the prices at which products are offered for sale in retail shops or other outlets (including online outlets). All the outlets from which the reference population makes purchases are in the scope of the CPI and should be included in the sampling frame from which the outlets are selected.

2.104 Examples of outlets are: (1) retail shops (from very small permanent stalls to multinational chain stores); (2) market stalls and street vendors; (3) online and web-based retail outlets; (4) establishments providing household services (for example, electricians, plumbers, or window cleaners); (5) leisure and entertainment providers; (6) health and education services providers; (7) communication and transport providers; (8) public utilities; and (9) government agencies and departments.

2.105 Given the growing importance of online and web-based retailers, there is a significant need for NSOs to carefully review and augment outlet sampling frames to include online and web-based retailers. Collecting prices from online and web-based retailers raises a number of different issues that are addressed in more detail in Chapter 11.

2.106 In practice, prices are collected from only a sample of outlets and the samples may change, either because outlets open and close or because there is a deliberate periodic rotation of the sample. When the prices in the outlets newly included in the sample are different from those in the previous outlets, it is necessary to decide whether the price differences are apparent or genuine price changes. If they are assumed to be apparent, the difference between the price recorded previously in an old outlet and the new price in the new outlet is not treated as a price change for CPI purposes, the difference being treated as attributable to quality difference. As explained in more detail in Chapter 6, if this assumption is correct, the price changes recorded in the new outlets can simply be linked to those previously recorded in the old outlets without introducing any bias into the index. The switch from the old to the new outlets does not have any impact on the CPI.

2.107 If the price differences between the old and the new outlets are deemed to be genuine price changes, however, the simple linking just described can lead to bias. When households change the price they pay for a product by changing outlets, the price changes should be captured by the CPI. As explained in more detail in Chapter 6, it seems that most NSOs assume that the price differences are not genuine and simply link the new price series to the old. This procedure, although widely used, assumes that markets are always perfect, and that genuine price variation never occurs. This unrealistic and questionable assumption may lead to an upward bias. Such bias is described as *outlet rotation bias*.

2.108 The differences between old and new outlets becomes even more pronounced when the outlet sample expands to include web-based outlets. In principle, web-based outlets provide some greater utility to the consumer with regard to choice, convenience, and service; however, in practice, it is difficult to quantify the value of this added utility. While concrete guidance cannot be provided at this time, accounting for the differences when consumers switch from old to new outlets will be considered as part of the research agenda included in Appendix 6 of this Manual.

2.109 Outlet replacement and the treatment of price differences between the old and new outlets are discussed in Chapter 7. Methods for selecting a sample of outlets from which to collect prices are discussed in detail in Chapter 4.

Price Coverage

2.110 A CPI should reflect the experience of the consumers to whom it relates and should therefore record what consumers actually pay for the goods and services included in the scope of the index. The expenditure and prices recorded should be purchaser's prices (*2008 SNA*, paragraphs 6.64–6.68). Purchaser's prices refer to those prices paid by consumers to acquire ownership of goods or services. Purchaser's prices include any taxes (not deductible by the purchaser) and service charges on the products, and taking account of all discounts, subsidies, and most rebates, even if discriminatory or conditional. It may be virtually impossible, however, to take account of all discounts and rebates in practice. Sensible practical compromises are needed, for which recommendations and examples are given in Chapter 5.

2.111 When households pay the full market prices for products and are then subsequently reimbursed by governments, social security programs, or NPISH for some of the amounts paid, CPIs should record the market prices less the amounts reimbursed. This kind of arrangement is common for educational and medical expenditure (health, education, and social protection are addressed in Chapter 11).

2.112 *Taxes and subsidies.* All taxes on products, such as sales taxes, excise taxes, and value-added tax (VAT), are part of the purchasers' prices paid by consumers which should be used for CPI purposes. Similarly, subsidies[8] should be taken into account, being treated as negative taxes on products. For information on the treatment of taxes and subsidies on the national accounts, see *2008 SNA*, paragraphs 7.71–7.106.

2.113 For some analytical and policy purposes, it may be useful to estimate a CPI that measures price movements excluding the effects of changes in taxes and subsidies. For monetary policymakers, the price increases resulting from changes in taxes on products or subsidies are not part of an underlying inflation process but are attributable to their own use of these economic levers. Similarly, when a CPI is used for escalation purposes, any increase in a CPI resulting from increases in taxes on products leads to an increase in wages and benefits linked to the CPI, despite the fact that the aim of the tax increase might have been to reduce consumers' purchasing power. Alternatively, an increase in subsidies might be intended to stimulate consumption, but the resulting lower prices could be offset by a smaller increase in indexed wages and benefits.

2.114 *Net price indices.* Net price indices in which taxes on consumer goods or services are deducted and subsidies are added to the purchasers' prices may be compiled. Such indices do not, however, necessarily show how prices would have moved if there were no taxes or changes in taxes. It is notoriously difficult to estimate the true incidence of taxes on products: that is, the extent to which taxes or subsidies, or changes therein, are passed on to consumers. It is also difficult to account for the secondary effects of changes in taxes. In order to estimate the secondary effects, input–output analysis can be used to work out the cumulative impact

[8] The SNA defines subsidies as current unrequited payments that government units make to enterprises on the basis of the level of their production activities or the quantities or values of the goods or services that they produce, sell, or import. Subsidies are not payable to final consumers; current transfers that governments make directly to households as consumers are treated as social benefits (*2008 SNA*, paragraphs 7.98–7.99). The use of the term "subsidies" is broader than the use in the SNA.

of taxes and subsidies through all the various stages of production. For example, some of the taxes on vehicle fuel will enter the price of transport services which in turn will enter the prices of transported products, some of which will enter the prices paid for consumer products by retailers and hence the prices which they charge to consumers. A more practicable alternative is therefore simply to confine the taxes and subsidies for which correction is made to those levied at the final stage of sale at retail; that is, primarily to VAT, sales, and excise taxes. Estimating prices less these taxes only, or corrected for changes in these taxes only, is more feasible. In the case of a percentage sales tax or VAT, the calculation is simple, but in the case of excise taxes, it would be necessary to ascertain the percentage markup by the retailer, since the excise tax will also be marked up by this percentage. However, in practice, it is not possible to determine the percentage markup by the retailer.

Price Variation

2.115 Price variation occurs when exactly the same good or service sells at different prices at the same moment of time. Different outlets may sell exactly the same product at different prices, or the same product may be sold from a single outlet to different categories of purchasers at different prices.

2.116 If markets were "perfect" in an economic sense, identical products would all sell at the same price. If more than one price was quoted, all purchases would be made at the lowest price. This suggests that some products sold at different prices may not be identical but must be qualitatively different in some way. When the price differences are, in fact, attributable to quality differences, the price differences are only apparent, not genuine. In such cases, a change in the average price resulting from a shift in the pattern of quantities sold at different prices would reflect a change in the average quality of the products sold. This would affect the volume and not the price index.

2.117 If NSOs do not have enough information about the characteristics of goods and services selling at different prices, they have to decide whether to assume the observed price differences are genuine or only apparent. The default procedure most commonly adopted in these circumstances is to assume that the price differences are not genuine. This assumption is typically made for both CPI and national accounts purposes.

2.118 However, markets are seldom perfect. One reason for the coexistence of different prices for identical products may be that the sellers are able to practice price discrimination. Another reason may simply be that households lack information and may buy at higher prices out of ignorance. Also, outlets may provide different levels of service which would be reflected in the prices paid by consumers. Finally, markets may be temporarily out of equilibrium as a result of shocks or the appearance of new products. It must be recognized, therefore, that genuine price differences do occur for a number of different reasons.

Price Discrimination

2.119 Economic theory shows that price discrimination tends to increase profits. Different households may pay different prices for identical products because of market imperfections. Price differences may persist because households may not be aware of them, or they may have imperfect information because the costs of searching for the retail outlets selling at the lowest prices may be too high. Even when households are aware of the price differences, it may be too inconvenient or costly to visit the outlets selling at the lowest prices. Another reason for the persistence of price differences is that many service producers deliberately practice price discrimination by charging different households different prices for identical services (for example, by charging lower prices or fees to pensioners or people with low incomes). As services cannot be retraded, price discrimination is extremely common, or even prevalent, among service producers. Household expenditure is nevertheless recorded at the prices actually paid, as this is the appropriate value of the transaction.

2.120 Apparent price differences between the same goods or services are often not genuine price differences as they may be due to differences in quality, including differences in the terms or conditions of sale. For example, lower prices are often charged for bulk purchases of goods or off-peak purchases of services. Such expenditure is recorded at the prices actually paid; that is, after deducting from the standard or list prices or charges any discounts for bulk or off-peak purchases.

2.121 Price discrimination can cause problems in the compilation of price indices. Suppose, for example, that a service supplier discriminates by age by charging senior citizens, aged 60 years or more, price p_2 and everyone else price p_1, where $p_1 > p_2$. Suppose, further, that the supplier then decides to redefine senior citizens as those aged 70 years or more, while otherwise keeping prices unchanged. In this case, although neither p_1 nor p_2 changes, the price paid by individuals aged 60–70 years changes and the average price paid by all households increases.

2.122 The example in paragraph 2.121 illustrates a point of principle. Although neither of the stated prices, p_1 and p_2, at which the services are on offer changes, the price paid by certain households changes if they are obliged to switch from p_2 to p_1. From the perspective of the households, price changes have occurred and a CPI should, in principle, record a change. When prices are collected from sellers and not from households, such price changes can be missed if price collectors do not pay attention to the conditions of sale.

Price Variation between Outlets

2.123 The existence of different prices in different outlets raises similar issues. Genuine price differences are almost bound to occur when there are market imperfections, if only because households are not perfectly informed. When new outlets sell at lower prices than existing ones, there may be a time lag during which exactly the same item sells at different prices in different outlets because of consumer ignorance or inertia.

2.124 Households may choose to switch their purchases from one outlet to another or even be obliged to switch because the universe of outlets is continually changing, some outlets closing down while new outlets open up. When households switch, the effect on the CPI depends on whether the price differences are genuine. When the price differences are genuine, a switch between outlets changes the average prices paid by households. Such price changes ought to be captured by CPIs. On the other hand, if the price differences reflected quality differences, a switch would change the average quality of the products purchased, and hence affect volume, not price.

2.125 Most of the prices collected for CPI purposes are offer prices. Offer prices may not in all cases correspond to the actual transaction prices paid by households. In these circumstances, the effects of switches in the pattern of households' purchases between outlets may remain unobserved in practice. When the price differences reflect quality differences, the failure to detect such switches does not introduce any bias into the CPI. In this case, buying at a lower price means buying a lower-quality product, which does not affect the accuracy of the price index. However, when the price differences are genuine, the failure to detect switches will tend to introduce an upward bias in the index, assuming households tend to switch toward outlets selling at lower prices. This potential bias is described as *outlet substitution bias*.

Expenditure and Other Payments Generally Outside the Scope of Consumer Price Indices

2.126 Given that, conceptually, most CPIs are designed to measure changes in the prices of consumption goods and services, it follows that purchases of items that are not goods and services fall outside the intended scope of a CPI: for example, purchases of bonds, shares, or other financial assets. Similarly, payments that are not purchases because nothing is received in exchange fall outside the index: for example, payments of income taxes or social security contributions.

2.127 The implementation of these principles is not always straightforward, as the distinction between an expenditure on a good or service and other payments may not always be clear in practice. A number of conceptually difficult cases, including some borderline cases of a possibly controversial nature, are examined in paragraphs 2.128 and 2.129.

Transfers

2.128 *Transfers.* A transfer is a transaction in which one unit provides a good, service, or asset to another without receiving any good, service, or asset in return (*2008 SNA*, paragraph 8.10), that is, transactions in which there is no counterpart. Transfers are unrequited. As no good or service of any kind is acquired by the household when it makes a transfer, the transfer must be outside the scope of a CPI. The challenge is to determine whether or not certain kinds of transactions are in fact transfers, an issue common to both CPIs and national accounts.

2.129 *Social security contributions and taxes on income and wealth.* As households do not receive any specific, individual good or service in return for the payment of social security contributions, they are treated as transfers (*2008 SNA*, paragraph 8.16) that are outside the scope of CPIs. Similarly, all payments of taxes based on income or wealth (the ownership of assets) are outside the scope of a CPI since they are unrequited compulsory transfers to government (*2008 SNA*, paragraph 8.15). Property taxes on dwellings (commonly levied as local authority taxes or rates) are outside the scope. It may be noted, however, that unrequited compulsory transfers could be incorporated within an unconditional COLI or within a more broadly defined conditional COLI that allows for changes in some other factors besides changes in the prices of consumption goods and services.

2.130 *Licenses.* Households have to pay to obtain various kinds of licenses and it is often not clear whether they are simply taxes under another name or whether the government agency issuing the license provides some kind of service in exchange, for example, by exercising some supervisory, regulatory, or control function. In the latter case, they could be regarded as purchases of services (*2008 SNA*, paragraphs 8.64c and 9.70).

2.131 Payments by households for licenses to own or use certain goods or facilities are, by convention, classified as consumption expenditure, not transfers, and are thus included within the scope of a CPI. For example, license fees for radios, televisions, driving, firearms, and so on, as well as fees for passports are included. On the other hand, licenses or fees for owning or using vehicles, boats, and aircraft, and for hunting, shooting, and fishing are conventionally classified as current taxes and are therefore outside the scope of CPIs. Many countries, however, do include taxes for private vehicle use as they regard them as taxes on consumption for CPI purposes. As the actual circumstances under which licenses are issued, and the conditions attaching to them, can vary significantly from country to country, NSOs may wish to deviate from the proposed conventions in some instance. However, in general, it seems appropriate to make use of conventions internationally agreed by the relevant experts and to be consistent with the SNA.

2.132 *Gifts and subscriptions.* Gifts are transfers, by definition (*2008 SNA*, paragraph 3.82), and thus outside the scope of a CPI. Payments of subscriptions or donations to charitable organizations for which no easily identifiable services are received in return are also transfers (*2008 SNA*, paragraph 8.132). On the other hand, payments of subscriptions to clubs and societies, including charities, which provide their members with some kind of service (for example, regular meetings or magazines) can be regarded as HFCE and included in a CPI.

2.133 *Tips and gratuities.* Noncompulsory tips or gratuities are considered gifts and are outside the scope of a CPI. There may be cases, however, where gratuities are compulsory, and in these cases, the payment should be included in the expenditure on, and the price of, the good or service in questions. For example, where restaurants include a compulsory service charge on the bill, this would be included in a CPI.[9] In cases where payment of a tip or gratuity is customary, although not compulsory, it could be argued that because payment of a tip is expected, it should be included in both the expenditure and the price; however, on practical grounds, these tips and gratuities are often excluded because the amount given is discretionary and it is not possible to define a single amount or percentage that should be added.

[9]The SNA states that commissions, gratuities, and tips received by employees should be treated as payments for services rendered by the enterprise employing the worker, and so should also be included in the output and gross value added of the employing enterprise when they are paid directly to the employee by a third party (*2008 SNA*, paragraph 7.44). Therefore, the prices considered for final uses include the tips paid.

Insurance

2.134 *Insurance.* There are two main types of insurance: life and nonlife insurance (*2008 SNA*, paragraph 17.6). In both cases the premiums have two components: the net premium, described as the payment for the insurance, and the service charge payable to the insurance enterprise for arranging the insurance (that is, a fee charged for calculating the risks, determining the premiums, administering the collection and investment of premiums, and the payment of claims).

2.135 The service charge is not directly observable by the policyholders or insurance companies. It is an integral part of the gross premium that is not separately identified in practice. As a payment for a service it falls within the scope of a CPI, but it is difficult to estimate.

2.136 In the case of nonlife insurance, the net premium is essentially a transfer that goes into a pool covering the collective risks of policyholders as a whole. As a transfer, it falls outside the scope of a CPI. In the case of life insurance, the net premium is essentially a form of financial investment. It constitutes the purchase of a financial asset, which is also outside the scope of a CPI.

2.137 Finally, it may be noted that when insurance is arranged through a broker or agent separate from the insurance company, the fees charged by the brokers or agents for their services are included within the scope of the CPI, over and above the service charges made by the insurers.

Gambling

2.138 *Gambling.* The amounts paid for lottery tickets or placed in bets also consist of two elements that are usually not separately identified—the payment of an implicit service charge (part of consumption expenditure) and a current transfer that enters the pool out of which the winnings are paid (*2008 SNA*, paragraph 8.136). Only the implicit or explicit service charges payable to the organizers of the gambling and taxes fall within the scope of a CPI. The service charges are usually calculated at an aggregate level as the difference between payables (stakes) and receivables (winnings).

Transactions in Financial Assets

2.139 *Transaction in financial assets.* Financial assets are not consumption goods or services (*2008 SNA*, paragraph 11.8). The creation of financial assets and liabilities, or their extinction (for example, by lending, borrowing, and repayments), are financial transactions that are quite different from expenditure on goods and services and take place independently of them. The purchase of a financial asset is not expenditure on consumption, being a form of financial investment.

2.140 Some financial assets, notably securities in the form of bills, bonds, and shares, are tradable and have market prices (*2008 SNA*, paragraph 11.64). They have their own separate price indices, such as stock market price indices. Many of the financial assets owned by households are acquired indirectly through the medium of pension programs and life insurance. Excluding the service charges, pension contributions by households are similar to payments for life insurance premiums. They are essentially forms of investment and are thus excluded from CPIs. In contrast, the explicit or implicit fees paid by households for the services rendered by financial auxiliaries such as brokers, banks, insurers (life and nonlife), pension fund managers, financial advisors, accountants, and so on are within the scope of a CPI. Payments of such fees are simply purchases of services. For more detailed information, see the section on Financial Services in Chapter 11.

2.141 *Purchases and sales of foreign currency.* Foreign currency is a financial asset. Purchases and sales of foreign currency are therefore outside the scope of CPIs. Changes in the prices payable, or receivable, for foreign currencies resulting from changes in exchange rates are not included in CPIs. In contrast, the service charges made by foreign-exchange dealers are included within the scope of CPIs when households acquire foreign currency for personal use. These charges include not only explicit commission charges but also the differences between the buying or selling rates offered by the dealers and the average of the two rates (*2008 SNA*, paragraph 11.34).

2.142 Transactions in financial assets do not change wealth and there is no consumption involved. A transaction of a financial asset merely rearranges the individual's asset portfolio by exchanging one type of asset for another. For example, when a loan is made, the lender exchanges cash for a financial claim over the debtor. Similarly, the borrower acquires cash counterbalanced by the creation of an equal liability. Such transactions are irrelevant for CPI purposes.

2.143 In general, when a household borrows from financial institutions, including moneylenders, the borrowed funds may be used for a variety of purposes including the purchase of assets such as dwellings or financial assets (for example, bonds or shares), as well as the purchase of expensive goods and services. Similarly, the credit extended to the holder of a credit card can be used for a variety of purposes. In itself, the creation of a financial asset and liability by new borrowing has no impact on a CPI. There is no good or service acquired, no expenditure, and no price.

2.144 Hire purchase (see 2.147) and mortgage loans must be treated consistently with other loans. The fact that certain loans are conditional on the borrower using the funds for a particular purpose does not affect the treatment of the loan itself. Moreover, conditional loans are by no means confined to the purchase of durable goods on "hire purchase." Conditional personal loans may be made for other purposes, such as large expenditure on education or health. In each case, the contracting of the loan is a separate transaction from the expenditure on the good or service and must be distinguished from the latter. The two transactions may involve different parties and may take place at quite different times.

2.145 Although the provision of finance is a separate transaction from the purchase of a good or service for which it is used, it may affect the price paid. Each case needs to be carefully considered. For example, suppose the seller agrees to defer payment for one year. The seller appears to make an interest-free loan for a year, but this is not the economic reality. The seller makes a loan, but it is not interest-free. Nor is the amount lent equal to the "full" price. Implicitly, the purchaser issues a short-term bill to the seller to be redeemed one year later and uses the cash received from the seller to pay for the good. However, the present value of a bill at the time it is issued is its redemption value discounted by one year's interest. The amount payable by the purchaser at the time the purchase of the good actually takes place is the present discounted price of the bill and not the full redemption price to be paid one year later. It is this discounted price that should be recorded for CPI purposes. The difference between the discounted price and the redemption price is, of course, the interest that the purchaser implicitly pays on the bill over the course of the year. This way of recording corresponds to the way in which bills and bonds are actually valued on financial markets and also to the way in which they are recorded in both business and economic accounts (*2008 SNA*, paragraph 17.266). Deferring payments in the manner just described is equivalent to a price reduction and should be recognized as such in CPIs. The implicit interest payment is not part of the price. Instead, it reduces the price. This example shows that in certain circumstances the market rate of interest can affect the price payable but it depends on the exact circumstances of the credit arrangement agreed between the seller and the purchaser. Each individual case needs to be carefully considered on its merits.

2.146 This case needs to be clearly distinguished from hire purchase, considered in 2.147, when the purchaser actually pays the full price and borrows an amount equal to the full price while contracting to make explicit interest payments in addition to repaying the amount borrowed.

2.147 *Hire purchase*. Under a hire purchase agreement, a buyer leases a good over a period of time and does not acquire ownership until the full amount of the contract is paid (*2008 SNA*, paragraph 9.73). In the case of a durable good bought on hire purchase, it is necessary to distinguish the de facto, or economic, ownership of the good from the legal ownership. The time of acquisition is the time the hire purchase contract is signed and the purchaser takes possession of the durable. From then onward, it is the purchaser who uses it and derives the benefit from its use. The purchasing household becomes the de facto owner at the time the good is acquired, even though legal ownership may not pass to the household until the loan is fully repaid.

2.148 By convention, the purchasing household is treated as buying the good at the time possession is taken and paying the full amount in cash at that point. At the same time, the purchaser borrows, either from the seller or some financial institution specified by the seller, a sum sufficient to cover the purchase price and the subsequent interest payments. The difference between the cash price and the total sum of all the payments to be made is equal to the total interest payable. The relevant price for CPI purposes is the cash price payable at the time the purchase takes place whether or not the purchase is facilitated by some form of borrowing. The treatment of hire purchase is the same as that of financial leases whereby fixed assets, such as aircraft, used for purposes of production are purchased by a financial institution and leased to the producer for most or all of the service life of the asset (*2008 SNA*, paragraph 17.304). This is essentially a method of financing the acquisition of an asset by means of a loan and needs to be distinguished from operational leasing, such as hiring out cars for periods of time (*2008 SNA*, paragraph 17.301). The treatment of hire purchase and financial leasing outlined here is followed in both business and economic accounting.

2.149 *Interest payments*. The treatment of interest payments on the various kinds of debt that households may have incurred raises both conceptual and practical difficulties. Nominal interest is a composite payment covering four main elements whose mix may vary considerably. The first component is the pure interest charge, which is the interest that would be charged if there were perfect capital markets and perfect information. The second component is a risk premium that depends on the creditworthiness of the individual borrower and can be regarded as a built-in insurance charge against the risk of the debtor defaulting. The third component is a service charge incurred when households borrow from financial institutions that make a business of lending money. Finally, when there is inflation, the real value of a loan fixed in monetary terms (that is, its purchasing power over goods and services) declines with the rate of inflation. However, creditors offset the real holding, or capital, losses they expect to incur by charging appropriately high rates of nominal interest. For this reason, nominal interest rates vary directly with the expected rate of general inflation, a universally familiar phenomenon under inflation conditions. In these circumstances, the main component of nominal interest may therefore be the built-in payment of compensation from the debtor to the creditor to offset the latter's real holding loss. When there is very high inflation it may account for almost all of the nominal interest charged.

2.150 The treatment of the first component, the pure interest charge, is somewhat controversial but this component may account for only a small part of the nominal interest charged. The treatment of the second component, insurance against the risk of default, is also somewhat controversial because it can be difficult to measure in practice.

2.151 The third component, the payment of compensation for the creditor's real holding loss, is clearly outside the scope of a CPI. It is essentially a financial transaction. It may account for most of nominal interest under inflation conditions.

2.152 The fourth component constitutes the purchase of a service from financial institutions whose business is to make funds available to borrowers. It is known as the financial service indirectly measured and clearly falls within the scope of a CPI. It is included in COICOP (COICOP 2018, class 12.2.1). The service charge is not confined to loans made by "financial intermediaries," institutions that borrow funds in order to lend them to others. Financial institutions that lend out of their own resources provide the same kind of services to borrowers as financial intermediaries. When sellers lend out of their own funds, they are treated as implicitly setting up their own financial institution that operates separately from their principal activity. The rates of interest of financial institutions also include service charges.

2.153 It is clear that interest payments should not be treated as if they were just pure interest or even pure interest plus a risk premium. It is very difficult to disentangle the various components of interest. It may be practically impossible to make realistic and reliable estimates of the service charges embodied in most interest payments. Moreover, for CPI purposes it is necessary to estimate not only the values of the service charges but changes in the prices of the services over time. Given the complexity of interest flows and the fact that the different flows need to be treated differently, payments of nominal interest should not be included in a CPI, especially in inflation conditions.

Household Production

2.154 *Household production.* Households can engage in various kinds of productive activities that may be either aimed at the market or intended to produce goods or services for own consumption (*2008 SNA*, paragraphs 1.41 and 1.42).

2.155 Households may engage in business or commercial activities such as farming, retail trading, construction, and the provision of professional or financial services. Goods and services that are used up in the process of producing other goods and services for sale on the market constitute intermediate consumption (*2008 SNA*, paragraph 6.213). They are not part of the final consumption of households. The prices of intermediate goods and services purchased by households are not to be included in CPIs. In practice, it is sometimes difficult to draw a clear distinction between intermediate and final consumption, as the same goods and services may be used for either purpose.

2.156 Households do not in fact consume directly all the goods and services they acquire for purposes of consumption. Instead, they use them as inputs into the production of other goods or services which are then used to satisfy their needs and wants. For example, basic foodstuffs such as flour, cooking oils, raw meat, and vegetables may be processed into bread, cakes, or meals with the assistance of other inputs including fuels, the services provided by consumer durables, such as fridges and cookers, and labor of members of the household. Inputs of materials, equipment, and labor are used to clean, maintain, and repair dwellings. Inputs of seeds, fertilizers, insecticides, equipment, and labor are used to produce vegetables, flowers, and so on.

2.157 The practical alternative, if the output is not intended for sale, is to treat the goods and services acquired by households on the market for use as inputs into the various kinds of household production activities as if they were themselves final consumer goods and services. They provide utility indirectly assuming that they are used exclusively to produce goods and services that are directly consumed by households. This is the practical solution that is generally adopted not only in CPIs but also in national accounts where household expenditure on such items is classified as final consumption. Although this seems a simple and conceptually acceptable solution, exceptions may be made for specific kinds of household production that are particularly important and whose outputs can readily be identified.

2.158 *Subsistence agriculture.* In the national accounts, an attempt is made to record the value of the agricultural output produced for own consumption. In some countries, subsistence agriculture may account for a large part of the production and consumption of agricultural produce. The national accounts require such outputs to be valued at their market prices (*2008 SNA*, paragraphs 24.47–24.49). For an index used for monetary policy purposes or as a general macroeconomic measure of inflation, it is not appropriate to follow this procedure for CPI purposes.

2.159 A CPI may record either the actual input prices or the imputed output prices, but not both. If the imputed output prices for subsistence agriculture are included in a CPI, the prices of the purchased inputs should be excluded. This could remove from the index most of the market transactions made by such households. Expenditure on inputs may constitute the principal contact that the households have with the market and through which they experience the effects of inflation. It therefore seems preferable to record the actual prices of the inputs and not the imputed prices of the outputs in CPIs.

2.160 *Housing services produced for own consumption.* There is no unique recommendation for the treatment of owner-occupied housing services in the CPI, as described in Chapter 11. There is no general consensus on what constitutes best practice. Conceptually, the production of housing services for own consumption by owner-occupiers is no different from other types of own-account production taking place within households. The distinctive feature of the production of housing services for own consumption, as compared with other kinds of household production, is that it requires the use of an extremely large fixed asset in the form of the dwelling. In economics, and also national accounting (*2008 SNA*, paragraphs 6.34 and 6.117), a dwelling is regarded as a fixed asset so that the purchase of a dwelling is classified as gross fixed capital formation and not as the acquisition of a durable consumer good.

2.161 It is important to note that there are two quite distinct service flows involved in owner-occupied housing services. One consists of the flow of *capital services* provided by the dwelling which are consumed as *inputs* into the production of housing services. The other consists of the flow of *housing services* produced as *outputs* which are consumed by members of the household. The two flows are not the same. The value of the output will be greater than that of the input. The capital services are defined and measured in exactly the same way as the capital services provided by other kinds of fixed assets, such as equipment or structures other than dwellings. As explained in more detail in Chapter 11, the value of the capital services is equal to the user cost and consists primarily of two elements, depreciation and interest, or capital costs. Capital costs are incurred whether or not the dwelling is purchased by borrowing on a mortgage. When the dwelling is purchased out of own funds, the interest costs represent the opportunity cost of the capital tied up in the dwelling, that is, the forgone interest that could have been earned by investing elsewhere.

2.162 There are three main options for the treatment of own-account production and consumption of owner-occupied housing services in CPIs. One is to price the output of housing services consumed by owner-occupiers. The second is to price the inputs, including the inputs of capital services. The third is to include the price of the dwelling. If housing services are to be treated consistently with other forms of production for own consumption by households, the input approach should be adopted. The production and consumption of housing services by owner-occupiers may, however, be considered to be so important as to merit special treatment.

2.163 If it is decided to price the outputs, the prices may be estimated using the market rents payable on rented accommodation of the same type. This is described as the rental equivalence approach. One practical problem is that there may be no accommodation of the same type that is rented on the market. For example, there may be no rental market for rural dwellings in developing countries where most of the housing may actually be constructed by the households themselves. Another problem is to ensure that the market rents do not include other services, such as electricity or heating, that are additional to the housing services. An additional challenge is that market rents, like the rentals charged when durables are leased, have to cover the operating expenses of the renting agencies as well as the costs of the housing services themselves and also provide some profit to the owners. Finally, rented accommodation is inherently different from owner-occupied housing in that it may provide the tenants with more flexibility and mobility. The transaction costs involved in moving from one house to another may be much less for tenants than for owners.

2.164 In principle, if the *output* approach is adopted, then the prices of the inputs into the production of housing services for own consumption, such as expenditure on repairs, maintenance, and insurance, should not be included. Otherwise, there would be double counting.

2.165 The alternative is to price the inputs into the production of housing services for own consumption in the same way that other forms of production for own consumption within households are treated. In addition to intermediate consumption, such as expenditure on repairs, maintenance, and insurance, the costs of the capital services must be estimated and their prices included in the CPI. The technicalities of estimating the values of the flow of capital services are dealt with in Chapter 10 of the publication *Consumer Price Index Theory*. As in the case of other types of production for own consumption by households, it is not appropriate to include the estimated costs of labor provided by the owners.

2.166 Whether the input or the output approach is adopted, it can be challenging to estimate the relevant prices. The practical difficulties experienced may sometimes be so great as to lead compilers and users to query the reliability of the results. There is also some reluctance to use imputed prices in CPIs, whether the prices refer to the inputs or the outputs. It has therefore been suggested that the attempt to measure the prices of housing service flows should be abandoned. Instead, it may be preferred to include the prices of the dwellings in the CPI. In most cases, these are observable market prices, although many dwellings, especially in rural areas in developing countries, are also built by their owners, in which cases their prices still have to be estimated on the basis of their costs of production. Ultimately, it may be useful for CPI compilers to rely on owner-occupied dwelling services estimated in the national accounts.

2.167 Including the prices of dwellings in CPIs should involve a significant change in the scope of the index. A dwelling is clearly an asset and its acquisition is gross fixed capital formation and not HFCE. While the same argument applies to durables, there is a substantial difference of degree between a durable consumption goods and a dwelling as reflected by the considerable differences in their prices and their service lives. In principle, therefore, extending the scope of a CPI to include dwellings implies extending the scope of the index to include gross fixed capital formation.

2.168 The advantage of including dwellings in the CPI is that it does not require estimates of either the input or output service flows, but conceptually it deviates significantly from the concept of a CPI as traditionally understood. In the case of both durable consumption goods and dwellings, the options are either to record the acquisitions of the assets in the CPIs at their market prices or to record the estimated prices of the service flows, but not both. Just as no service flows from durables are included in CPIs at present because their acquisitions were included; similarly if the prices of dwellings are included in CPIs, the service flows would have to be excluded. As explained in Chapter 11, the acquisitions approach may give insufficient weight to durables and dwellings over the long term because it does not take account of the capital costs incurred by the owners of the assets.

Treatment of Some Specific Household Expenditure

2.169 Some of the expenditure made by households may not be on goods and services for household consumption and would therefore fall outside the scope of a CPI. One major category consists of the business expenditure made by households.

Fees of Agents and Brokers

2.170 *Fees of agents and brokers*. The *2008 SNA* classifies expenses associated with the transfer of real estate (including real estate agents' commissions) as part of gross fixed capital formation (*2008 SNA*, paragraphs 10.48–10.52). Although harmonization is desirable, in some countries some CPI concepts do not precisely follow the national accounts concepts.

2.171 When a house is purchased for own use by an owner-occupier, it can be argued that the transfer costs associated with purchase (and sale) should be treated as consumption expenditure. The fees paid to an agent to buy or sell houses are included in many national CPIs, provided that the house is to be occupied by the owner and not rented to a third party.

Undesirable, Informal, or Illegal Goods and Services

2.172 *Nonobserved economy: informal or illegal production of goods and services* (*2008 SNA*, paragraphs 6.39–6.48). As described in 2.56, HFCE includes the expenditure incurred by resident households on consumption goods and services, and therefore these fall within the scope of a CPI, irrespective of whether their production, distribution, or consumption is informal or illegal. Particular kinds of goods or services must not be excluded from the CPI because their consumption is socially discouraged, or their production informal or illegal. Such exclusions could be quite arbitrary and undermine the objectivity and credibility of the CPI. In the case where certain goods or services have been excluded from the index, these exclusions should be clearly documented and explained.

2.173 First, it should be noted that some goods and services might be deemed to be undesirable at sometimes and desirable at others, or *vice versa*. Similarly, some goods or services may be deemed to be undesirable in some countries but not in others at the same point of time. The concept of an undesirable good or service is inherently subjective and somewhat arbitrary and volatile.

2.174 Second, if it is accepted that some goods and services may be excluded on the grounds that they are undesirable, the index is thereby exposed to actual or attempted manipulation by pressure groups.

2.175 Third, attempts to exclude certain goods or services by pressure groups may be based on a misunderstanding of the implications of so doing. For example, if the CPI is used for escalating incomes, it may be felt that households ought not be compensated for increases in the prices of certain undesirable products. However, excluding them does not imply lowering the index. A priori excluding some items is just as likely to increase the CPI as reduce it, depending on whether the price change for the item in question is below or above the average for other goods and services. For example, if it is decided to exclude tobacco from a CPI and the price increase for tobacco products is below average, excluding tobacco actually increases the real income of smokers.

2.176 While goods and services that households consume should not, in principle, be excluded from a CPI because they are acquired in the informal economy or even illegally, it may be impossible to obtain the requisite data on the expenditure or the prices, especially on illegal goods and services. They may well be excluded in practice.

Luxury Goods and Services

2.177 *Luxury goods and services.* When a CPI is used as an index of general inflation, it ought to include all households regardless of their socioeconomic group and also all consumer goods and services regardless of how expensive they are. Similarly, the scope of an index used for purposes of escalating incomes should include all the goods and services purchased by the reference households, irrespective of whether any of these goods and services are considered to be luxuries or otherwise unnecessary.

2.178 If the reference households are confined to a selected group of households, the index will effectively exclude all those items that are purchased exclusively by households that are not in the group. For example, excluding the wealthiest 5 percent of households will, in practice, exclude many luxury items from the scope of the index. As already noted, such households may be excluded for various reasons, including the unreliability of their expenditure data and the fact that collecting prices for some items purchased exclusively by a relatively small minority of households may not be cost-effective. However, once the group of reference households has been decided and defined, judgments should not be made about whether to exclude certain part of their expenditure that is considered to be nonessential or on luxuries.

Second-Hand Goods

2.179 *Second-hand goods.* Markets for used or second-hand goods exist for most durable goods. HFCE includes expenditure on second-hand goods and these are therefore within the scope of a CPI. Household sales of durables constitute negative expenditure, and the weights for second-hand goods are based on household net expenditure (that is, total purchases less sales). The total expenditure on a particular type of second-hand good is a function of the rate at which it is bought and sold (that is, a higher turnover rate or number of transactions gives a higher total expenditure). A higher turnover does not, however, increase the rate at which any individual good can be used for purposes of consumption or the flow of services that may be obtained from the good.

2.180 Households may buy second-hand goods through any of the following routes:

- Directly from another household—the selling household will record the proceeds of the sale as receipts. Net expenditure (that is, expenditure less receipts) is zero, so no weight is attached to purchases and sales from one household to another.
- From another household via a dealer—in principle, household expenditure on the services of the dealers is given by the values of their margins (the difference between their buying and selling prices). These intermediation services should be included in CPIs. They should be treated in the same way as the fees charged by financial intermediaries. The margins may be extremely difficult to estimate in practice. Care should be taken to include trade-ins either as purchases by the dealers or receipts of households.
- Directly from another sector (for example, from a corporation or from abroad)—the weight would be household purchases of the second-hand goods from other sectors less sales to other sectors.
- From another sector (for example, corporation or from abroad) via a dealer—the appropriate weight is given by household purchases from dealers less any household sales to dealers plus the aggregate of dealers' margins on the goods that they buy from and resell to households.

2.181 In some countries, many of the durables purchased by households, especially vehicles, may be imports of second-hand goods from other countries. The prices and expenditure on these goods enter the CPI in the same way as those for newly produced goods. Similarly, in some countries, there may be significant net purchases of second-hand vehicles by households from the corporations' sector.

Imputed Expenditure on Goods and Services

2.182 *Imputed expenditure on goods and services.* As explained in paragraphs 2.59–2.67, many of the goods and services acquired and used by households for their final consumption are not purchased in monetary transactions but are acquired through barter or as remuneration in kind, or are produced by households for their own consumption. It is possible to estimate what households would have paid if they had purchased these goods and services in monetary transactions or, alternatively, what it cost to produce them. In other words, values may be imputed for nonmonetary transactions.

2.183 The extent to which it is desirable to include imputed expenditure within the scope of a CPI depends partly on the main purpose of the index. If the CPI is intended to be a measure of consumer inflation, it can be argued that only monetary transactions should be included. Inflation is a monetary phenomenon measured by changes in prices recorded in monetary transactions. Transactions include the buying and selling of a good or service. Monetary transactions occur when a seller exchanges ownership of a good or service in exchange for some form of monetary payment. Even when the main use of a CPI is for indexation purposes, it can be argued that it should only reflect changes in the monetary prices actually paid by the reference population. For example, consistent with the objective of monitoring inflation in the EU, the aim of the HICP compiled by Eurostat is to measure inflation faced by consumers. The concept of HFMCE used in the HICP defines both the goods and services to be covered, and the price concept to be used (that is, prices net of reimbursements, subsidies, and discounts). HFMCE refers only to monetary transactions and includes neither consumption of own production (for example, agricultural goods or owner-occupied housing services), nor consumption of goods and services received as income in kind.

2.184 *Discounts, rebates, loyalty programs, and "free" products*. CPIs should take into account the effects of rebates, loyalty programs, and money-off vouchers. Given that a CPI is meant to cover all the reference households, whether in the country as a whole or in a particular region, discounts should be included even if they are available only to certain households or to consumers satisfying certain payment criteria.

2.185 It may be difficult to record discriminatory or conditional discounts for practical reasons. When only one selected group of households can enjoy a certain discount on a specific product, the original stratum for that product is split into two new strata, each experiencing different price changes and each requiring a weight. So, unless weight reference period expenditure for all possible strata are known, it is not possible to record discriminatory discounts correctly. Similarly, with conditional discounts (for example, discounts on utility bills for prompt payment), it can be difficult to record the effect of the introduction of such offers unless data are available on the proportion of customers taking advantage of the offer. These kinds of practical problems also arise when there is price discrimination and the sellers change the criteria that define the groups to whom different prices are charged, thereby obliging some households to pay more or less than before without changing the prices. These cases are discussed further in Chapter 5.

2.186 Although it is desirable to record all price changes, it is also important to ensure that the qualities of the goods or services for which prices are collected do not change in the process. While discounted prices may be collected during general sales or discount seasons, care should be taken to ensure that the quality of the products being priced has not deteriorated.

2.187 The borderline between discounts and rebates can be hazy and is perhaps best drawn according to timing. In other words, a discount takes effect at the time of purchase, whereas a rebate takes effect some time later. Under this classification, money-off vouchers are discounts and, as with the conditional discounts mentioned in paragraph 2.185, can only be taken into account in a CPI if they relate to a single product and if the take-up rate is known at the time of CPI compilation. Since this is highly unlikely, the effect of money-off vouchers is usually excluded from a CPI. It should be noted that the discount is recorded only when the voucher is used, not when the voucher is first made available to the consumer.

2.188 Rebates may be made in respect of a single product (for example, air miles), or may be more general (for example, supermarket loyalty programs where a $10 voucher is awarded for every $200 spent). As with discounts discussed previously, such rebates can only be recorded as price falls if they relate to single products and can be weighted according to take-up. Bonus products provided "free" to the consumer, either by larger pack sizes or offers such as "two packs for the price of one," should be treated as price reductions, although they may be ignored in practice when the offers are only temporary and quickly reversed. When permanent changes to pack sizes occur, quality adjustments should be made (see Chapter 6).

2.189 Given the practical difficulties in correctly recording all these types of price decreases, it is usual to reflect discounts and rebates only if widely available. More and more countries include discounts associated with loyalty cards because most shoppers obtain and use the loyalty card, effectively meeting the criteria that the discount or rebate should be widely available. Discounts during seasonal sales may be recorded provided that the quality of the goods does not change.

2.190 As noted in Chapter 10, scanner data more effectively reflect discounts, sales, and promotions.

Consumer Price Index Classifications

2.191 The classification system upon which any CPI is built provides the structure essential for many stages of CPI compilation. Most obviously, it provides the weighting and aggregation structure, but it also provides the basis for stratification of products in the sampling frame, at least down to a certain level of detail, and it dictates the range of subindices available for publication.

2.192 The international standard for classification of individual final consumption expenditure is the *Classification of Individual Consumption According to Purpose* (COICOP). COICOP is part of a set of classifications of expenditure according to purpose, also known as *functional* classifications, and have formed an integrated part of the SNA since 1968 (*2008 SNA*, paragraphs 29.9–29.20). COICOP covers the individual final consumption expenditure incurred by three institutional sectors: households, NPISHs, and general government. Individual final consumption expenditure is that which benefits individual persons or households.

2.193 A few countries continue to use a country-specific classification system and have not adopted COICOP. To enhance international comparison, these countries should provide bridge tables to map their national classification systems to COICOP.

2.194 While part of the SNA, COICOP is intended for use in several other statistical areas. In addition to CPIs, COICOP is also used for HBS, analysis of living standards, and for compilation of PPPs.

2.195 COICOP was revised in 2018 to reflect changes in consumption patterns and the emergence of new goods and services since the previous version, introduced in 1999. The updated version, referred to as COICOP 2018, consists of 15 divisions:

- Divisions 01–13 covering the final consumption expenditure of households
- Division 14 covering the final consumption expenditure of NPISHs
- Division 15 covering the individual consumption expenditure of general government

2.196 COICOP 2018 has four levels of detail organized in a hierarchical structure—divisions, groups, classes, and subclasses:

- Division (two-digit level), for example, 03 Clothing and footwear
- Group (three-digit level), for example, 03.1 Clothing

- Class (four-digit level), for example, 03.1.2 Garments
- Subclass (five-digit level), for example, 03.1.2.1 Garments for men or boys

2.197 Divisions 01–13, which cover households, include 63 groups, 186 classes, and 338 subclasses. The full COICOP 2018 structure can be found in Appendix 3.

2.198 *Classifying according to purpose.* COICOP groups HFCE on individual goods and services according to the purpose they are deemed to fulfill, such as nourishing the body, preventing and curing illness, acquiring knowledge, or traveling from one place to another. The principle of classifying according to purpose means that where similar or related products exist in either physical or virtual forms (for example, books, music, videos, or games) the product should be categorized in a unique class based on the predominant purpose. For example, the purchase of electronic or virtual books (for example, eBooks or audiobooks) should be classified in the same class or subclass as paper books because they are used for the same purpose. Similarly, software and apps may provide the household with a specific service. If the payment is actually not for the software but for an associated service, which is provided with the help of the software or the app, the expenditure should be classified under the corresponding service. As a general rule, expenditure on second-hand goods are classified together with the new goods since they are used for the same purpose. One exception is the recording of motor cars, where the subclass level allows a separate recording of new motor cars and second-hand motor cars (COICOP 2018 Subclass 07.1.1.2).

2.199 *Multipurpose goods and services.* While most goods and services can be assigned to a single purpose, some goods and services could plausibly be assigned to more than one purpose. Examples include motor fuel which may be used to power vehicles classified as transport as well as recreational vehicles; bicycles which may be purchased for transport or recreational purposes; or sports footwear which may be used for sports or for leisure wear. In cases where goods and services can be used for different purposes, they should be assigned to the division considered to represent the primary or predominant purpose.

2.200 *Disaggregation of COICOP.* The detail provided by COICOP, even at its most detailed level, may not be sufficient for the required analysis or to meet country-specific needs. In such cases, classes or subclasses can be further subdivided as needed. There are clear advantages in maintaining the basic structure of COICOP to facilitate comparison between countries, over time and between different statistical domains such as CPIs, household expenditure statistics, and national accounts aggregates. It is recommended that additional detailed categories created to meet specific needs still can be aggregated into the existing COICOP Class or Subclass.

2.201 *Type of product.* COICOP classes and subclasses are divided into services (S), nondurables (ND), semidurables (SD), and durables (D). This additional classification facilitates other analytical applications. For example, an estimate may be required of the stock of consumer durables held by households, in which case the goods in those COICOP classes that are identified as "durables" provide the basic elements for such estimates. As explained earlier in paragraphs 2.64 and 2.65 the distinction between nondurable goods and durable goods is based on whether the goods can be used only once or whether they can be used repeatedly or continuously over a period of more than one year. Semidurable goods differ from durable goods in that their expected lifetime of use, though more than one year, is often significantly shorter and their purchasers' value is substantially less.

2.202 Although a systematic separation between goods and services is applied, some classes and subclasses contain both because it is difficult for practical reasons to break them down into goods and services. Such classes and subclasses are usually assigned an S, as the service component is considered to be predominant. Similarly, there are classes that contain either both nondurable and semidurable goods or both semidurable and durable goods. Such classes and subclasses are assigned an ND, SD, or D according to which type of good is considered to be predominant.

2.203 *Bundled goods and services.* Single expenditure outlays (that is, where there is no itemized price information for the individual goods or services) may sometimes comprise a bundle of goods and services that serve different purposes. Examples include telecommunication (for example, payment of one price for multiple services that include mobile phone, internet, television, and landline telephone); package tours which include payment for transport, accommodation, and catering services; education services that include payment for transport, accommodation, and educational materials; inpatient hospital services that include payments for medical treatment, accommodation, and catering; and transport services that include meals and accommodation in the ticket price (for example, passenger air transport). Single outlays covering two or more purposes and not separately invoiced should be classified according to the predominant product or service of the bundle.

Key Changes from COICOP 1999 to COICOP 2018

2.204 COICOP 2018 reflects changes in consumption patterns and the emergence of new goods and services. The main changes from COICOP 1999 and COICOP 2018 include the following.

Introduction of a New Subclass Level

2.205 COICOP 2018 introduces an additional fifth-digit level denominated subclass that was not part of COICOP 1999. The introduction of these new subclasses facilitates further harmonization of data collection and aggregation, improving comparability of the resulting statistics. It also improves the correspondence with the Central Product Classification to more easily reconcile with production data.

Restructuring of Division 06 Health

2.206 Division 06 is restructured to allow for a better alignment of COICOP with the International Classification for Health Accounts and its family of classifications.

Restructuring between Division 08 Information and Communication, and Division 09 Recreation, Sport, and Culture, and Renaming of the Divisions

2.207 To better reflect household use of information and communication technology, a number of goods and services have been moved from Division 09 to Division 08. Division

08 has been renamed *Information and Communication* (formerly *Communication*) and Division 09 was renamed *Recreation, Sport, and Culture* (formerly *Recreation and Culture*) to better reflect the coverage of the divisions.

Division 12 Insurance and Financial Services, and Division 13 Personal Care, Social Protection, and Miscellaneous Goods and Services

2.208 Personal care, social protection, and miscellaneous goods were included in Division 12 of COICOP 1999; Division 12 of COICOP 1999 has been divided into two divisions in COICOP 2018—Division 12 *Insurance and Financial Services*, and Division 13 *Personal Care, Social Protection, and Miscellaneous Goods and Services*. This change creates two, more homogeneous divisions.

2.209 In addition to the previously mentioned major changes, a number of changes were introduced at the more detailed levels for most divisions.

Implementing COICOP 2018

2.210 Implementation of COICOP 2018 must be done with care to avoid confusing data users and to prevent any loss in user confidence that could result from this confusion. NSOs should coordinate the implementation of COICOP 2018 simultaneously across programs (for example, national accounts and CPI). To further minimize any impact on data users, the introduction of COICOP 2018 should coincide with a routine update of the CPI.

Key Recommendations

- Consult with key data users to identify and define uses for CPI data. This ensures that the data compiled remain relevant. It is important that NSOs consult with data users on a routine and regular basis.
- When the CPI is used for inflation analysis and monetary policy purposes, the domestic concept should be used.
- When the CPI is used only for escalating the incomes of residents, it may be appropriate to adopt the national concept.
- The weights and prices in the CPI should be based on the purchaser's price. Purchaser's prices refer to those prices paid by consumers to acquire ownership of goods or services and include any taxes and service charges on the products, and taking account of all discounts, subsidies and most rebates, even if discriminatory or conditional.
- NSOs are encouraged to provide central banks with detailed weight, item, and price data in anonymized forms so that they may calculate different measures of core inflation or for analytical purposes.
- Geographic coverage of expenditure should include all expenditure of households regardless of income, size, or location (urban and rural).
- Geographic coverage of price collection should be as broad as possible.
- It is critical to communicate and explain changes adopted when implementing COICOP 2018. The introduction of COICOP 2018 should coincide with a routine CPI update.

Annex 2.1

Use of Price Statistics in the National Accounts—Supply and Use

Uses											
	Domestic Production	Intermediate					Final Consumption		Fixed Capital Formation		
		Agriculture	Mining and Manufacturing	Construction	Wholesale and Retail Trade	Other Services	Households	Government	Construction	Equipment	Exports
	Agriculture	APPI	APPI	APPI	APPI	APPI	CPI	PPI	—	—	XPI/PPI
	Mining and Manufacturing	PPI	PPI	PPI	PPI	PPI	CPI	PPI	—	PPI	XPI/PPI
	Construction	CPPI	CPPI	CPPI	CPPI	CPPI	CPI	PPI	CPPI	—	XPI/CPPI
Supply	Wholesale and Retail Trade	(a)	(a)	(a)	(a)	(a)	(a)	(a)	(a)	(a)	(a)
	Other Services	SPPI	SPPI	SPPI	SPPI	SPPI	CPI	SPPI	SPPI		XPI
Imports		MPI	MPI	MPI	MPI	MPI	CPI	MPI	MPI	MPI	
Labor		LCI	LCI	LCI	LCI	LCI	LCI	—	—	—	—

APPI, Agriculture producer price index (output); MPI, Import price index; CPI, Consumer price index; PPI, Producer price index; CPPI, Construction producer price index (output); SPPI, Services producer price index; LCI, Labor cost index; XPI, Export price index.

(a) Margins—these are combined with prices and goods—not observed separately.

EXPENDITURE WEIGHTS AND THEIR SOURCES 3

Introduction

3.1 A consumer price index (CPI) is usually calculated as a weighted average of the relative price changes of the goods and services covered by the index. The weights attached to each good or service reflect their relative importance as measured by their shares in the total consumption of all households. The weight determines the impact that its price change will have on the overall index. The weights should be made publicly available for the information of data users, to ensure public confidence in the index and enhance transparency. The International Monetary Fund maintains a CPI database that includes detailed weight data.[1]

3.2 Because the weights assigned to the different goods and services in the basket influence changes in the CPI, the accuracy and reliability of CPI estimates depend upon the quality of the weights used. Therefore, it is necessary to have weights that reflect, as closely as possible, current consumer expenditure patterns.

3.3 Chapter 3 discusses what the CPI weights should represent and how they can be derived. First, this chapter provides an overview of the conceptual basis of the weights to clarify what expenditure should be included when developing weights. Next, the main data sources for the weights are introduced and the practical steps that must be completed when deriving weights are discussed. Finally, some special cases are discussed at the end of this chapter.

Conceptual Basis of the Weights

3.4 The expenditure weights used in a CPI have to be consistent with the conceptual framework of the index as discussed in Chapter 2. Expenditure data can be obtained from different data sources with household budget surveys (HBSs) being the most common. When exploiting these data sources, the scope and the concept of the index will determine which goods and services should be covered in the CPI weights. If countries compile supplementary or alternative CPIs to meet multiple user needs, separate weighting structures would then be estimated, reflecting the different concepts or intended uses of the index. The main conceptual aspects that must be considered when deriving weights are discussed in paragraphs 3.5–3.18.

Geographical Coverage: National versus Domestic Concept

3.5 The geographical coverage of a CPI may follow either the "national" concept or the "domestic" concept. The national concept measures price changes experienced by resident households, regardless of whether expenditure is made within the country or abroad. Under the domestic concept, the scope of the CPI (with regard to both prices and weights) considers the economic territory and includes expenditure of both residents and nonresidents.

3.6 An HBS generally identifies all relevant expenditures made by resident households and may make a distinction between expenditure made within the economic territory and abroad. If the main purpose of the index is to measure price changes experienced by resident households, the weights should, in principle, include their expenditure abroad. If, however, the aim is to include the expenditure made by foreign visitors, thus reflecting all purchases of consumer goods and services made by resident or nonresident households within the country, sources other than the HBS must be used. An HBS does not cover expenditure made by nonresident households.

3.7 For practical reasons, even if the weights cover the expenditure made both at home and abroad, prices may be collected only for those goods and services acquired within the economic territory of the country. Such an approach assumes that the price changes of the goods and services acquired abroad are similar to the price changes for the same goods and services acquired at home. Alternatively, it may be possible to use CPI subindices compiled by the respective countries to measure the price changes of the goods and services acquired abroad.

3.8 In principle, the weights should represent the whole country and all regions should be covered. Separate expenditure weights can also be derived for each region, in which case the expenditures must be sufficiently representative at the regional level. This is especially important if the expenditure pattern differs between regions. For instance, it is common that the consumption habits vary between urban and rural areas. The same principle applies to harmonized CPIs, covering a group of countries, where each country can be regarded as a "region" with its own national weights.

3.9 The discussion of national and domestic concepts applies to regional subdivisions. It can sometimes be the case that a household lives in one region but does most of its purchases in an adjacent region, particularly if it lives close to a regional border. Practical issues dictate whether the expenditure weights (and the prices) should be allocated to the region of expenditure or the region of residence. In any case, treatment should be consistent across all regions to avoid missing or double counting parts of household expenditure.

Population Coverage

3.10 The target or reference populations will be defined based on the main purpose and use of the index, as described

[1] http://data.imf.org/.

in Chapter 2. In principle, all types of households should be covered, irrespective of their income or other socioeconomic factors. If any income groups, types of households, or geographic areas are excluded, for example, for cost or practical considerations, this should be explicitly stated in the index metadata. In some countries, the wealthiest households are excluded because their expenditure may be atypical or the HBS information may be less reliable. Other countries may exclude the expenditures of the very poor for the same reason. Another practice is to compile a CPI which excludes both extremes of the income distribution. If the primary use of the CPI is for adjusting incomes of a certain subgroup of the population for increases in the cost of living, then such subgroup may be the appropriate target population.

3.11 The weights may or may not include the expenditure made by people living in institutional households. Institutional households refer to people living permanently in an institution or who may be expected to reside in an institution for a very long time, as described in Chapter 2. Many countries exclude expenditure of such households in their CPI because of the difficulty of obtaining reliable expenditure information, or because the expenditure associated with such households is unlikely to be significant in comparison with private households. The choice to include or exclude the expenditure made by institutional households may depend on the main source for the weights. While weights primarily based on national accounts household final consumption expenditure (HFCE) data may include consumption of institutional households, the weights primarily based on an HBS would exclude consumption expenditures of institutional households. In considering the practical challenges relating to the inclusion of institutional households in a CPI, two questions need to be asked. First, is the expenditure pattern of institutional households likely to be significantly different from private households? Second, even if the answer is yes, would their exclusion from the CPI be likely to significantly affect the national CPI?

Monetary and Nonmonetary Transactions

3.12 A portion of HFCE consists of nonmonetary transactions, such as expenditure on goods and services produced for own account and remuneration in kind. Furthermore, as described in Chapter 2, the broader concept of household actual final consumption includes goods and services provided without charge or subsidized by governments and nonprofit institutions serving households. Depending on the main use of the CPI, a decision must be made whether to include nonmonetary transactions in the weights or if it is more appropriate to limit the scope of the index to monetary transactions only. Production for own consumption is treated by some countries as within the scope of the CPI, and in other countries as out of scope. In some countries, own-account production constitutes a significant portion of HFCE. It can be argued that while it is part of gross domestic product and should therefore be included to improve consistency with national accounts, and especially for producing deflators, it is not necessarily appropriate for a CPI used as a general measure of inflation or for indexation where the narrowest concept of consumption, based on monetary transactions, is used. If the CPI includes own-account production, the weights should include a valuation of the physical quantities of such products, the latter often derived from the HBS.

Expenditures That Are Out of Scope

3.13 In its role as a measure of total consumer inflation, the CPI should, in principle, cover all types of goods and services that are consumed by the reference population. Some types of products may be excluded for practical reasons. These may include products that are illegal, black market sales, gambling, or prostitution. Some products may also be excluded because of policy reasons. For instance, it can be decided to exclude certain categories of goods or services for purposes of compiling alternative aggregations or for analysis (for example, exclude tobacco from an index that is used for a specific purpose). Whenever certain in-scope goods or services have been excluded from the index, this should be clearly documented and explained to users.

3.14 Only household consumption expenditure is relevant for the construction of CPI weights. As explained in Chapter 2, expenditure on assets such as works of art, financial investment (as distinct from financial services), payments of social security contributions, fines or income taxes, interest payments, or repayments of debts are not considered to be household consumption expenditure and should be excluded from the coverage of the weights and the index.

3.15 Business-related expenditure is explicitly excluded from the scope of a CPI. Consequently, this expenditure must also be excluded from the CPI weights. Households may own unincorporated or informal enterprises, whereby expenditure for some products is used partly for business purposes and partly for final consumption. In principle, only the portion used for final consumption should be included in the CPI weights.

Democratic and Plutocratic Weights

3.16 The use of aggregated expenditure to derive CPI weights reflects the principle that each household contributes to the weights with an amount proportional to its expenditure. This is referred to as plutocratic weighting and means that the expenditure patterns of high-spending households have more influence on the index. The use of plutocratic weights is generally considered more appropriate particularly for CPIs which have been constructed to be a general measure of inflation, for national accounts deflation, and as the basis for monetary policymaking. In principle, it is also possible to derive democratic weights, where each household is given equal weight. While democratic weights may be considered appropriate for an index used to reflect the consumer inflation experience of the "typical" or "average" household, they are rarely used in practice. If all households have similar expenditure patterns, the democratic and plutocratic approaches lead to similar results. However, most often the expenditure pattern depends on the total level of expenditure of a household. There can be significant differences between both approaches, especially if the distribution of household expenditure is unequal. Table 3.1 presents an example. The lower-spending household (household 1) spends in relative terms more on food than the higher-spending household (household 2). Consequently, the weight for food is higher in the democratic approach than in the plutocratic approach.

Table 3.1 Example of Plutocratic versus Democratic Weights

	Expenditures for Household 1		Expenditures for Household 2		Expenditures for Households 1 & 2	Plutocratic Weights	Democratic Weights
	Value	Share (percent)	Value	Share (percent)	Value	Weights (percent)	Weights (percent)
	(a)	(b)	(c)	(d)	(e)	(f)	(g)
Food	10	33	20	20	30	23	27
Other Goods and Services	20	67	80	80	100	77	73
Total	30	100	100	100	130	100	100

3.17 In Table 3.1, plutocratic weights are calculated first by summing the expenditure made by each household in each group. Expenditure on food is summed (10 + 20) to derive the total expenditure on food (30). The same is done for expenditure on other goods and services (20 + 80) to derive total expenditure on other goods and services (100). The total expenditure for each group is then summed to derive total expenditure on all items (30 + 100 = 130). Plutocratic weights reflect the relative importance of each group (30/130 = 23 percent and 100/130 = 77 percent). For the democratic weights, an average of the individual shares for each household is calculated and used for the weight. The democratic weight for food equals the average of the shares for each household ([33 + 20]/2 = 27 percent). The same calculation is made for other goods and services ([67 + 80]/2 = 73 percent).

3.18 For analytical purposes, additional weighting structures may be derived to measure the inflation experience of different subgroups of households. Such an analysis is typically conducted by classifying households according to a sociodemographic variable such as income, age, or educational level. Depending on the objective of the analysis, either democratic or plutocratic weights could be derived for the different household groups.

The Weighting Structure of the Consumer Price Index

3.19 The calculation of a CPI usually proceeds in two stages. In the first stage, elementary indices are estimated for each of the elementary aggregates. In the second stage, a weighted average is taken of these elementary indices using the expenditure shares of the elementary aggregates as weights. Elementary aggregates are usually the smallest groups of goods and services for which expenditure data are available. They may cover the whole country or separate regions within the country. Likewise, elementary aggregates may be developed for different types of outlets. The nature of the elementary aggregates depends on data needs and the availability of expenditure data. Elementary aggregates may therefore be defined differently in different countries. Other types of weights (for example, nonexpenditure weights representing market shares), if available, may be used within the elementary aggregate.

3.20 The weights are usually classified according to the Classification of Individual Consumption According to Purpose (COICOP), also used in the national accounts and the HBS. Some countries develop a more detailed product classification that refines the products defined at the subclass level. These product categories are not part of COICOP, but in many cases, more detailed breakdowns of COICOP subclasses are needed for CPI purposes to better reflect country-specific circumstances and needs. For example, a country may develop a more detailed weighting structure for "Rice" to include specific types of rice (for example, basmati rice or long-grain rice).

3.21 The weights for the COICOP groups, classes, and subclasses are their shares in the total consumption expenditures of the reference population. The data sources used to derive these shares are discussed in the following text. In addition, the weight for a subclass can be further stratified by region, by outlet or outlet type, or by a combination of both region and outlet. The elementary aggregate weights are the stratum weights according to expenditure class or subclass, region, and type of outlet. If no breakdown by region or outlet is used, the subclass becomes the elementary aggregate.

3.22 The weight of an elementary aggregate should reflect the expenditure on the entire elementary aggregate and not the weights of the outlets and varieties that have been chosen to represent it. For instance, the weight for the subclass "Rice" should be based on the total expenditure made on rice, although the rice varieties selected for regular price collection only represent a fraction of this expenditure. Likewise, if an expenditure category is divided into two elementary aggregates according to outlet type (for example, open markets and supermarkets, with corresponding market shares of food sales, 60 percent and 40 percent, respectively), these proportions would be used to estimate the stratum weights, whatever the importance of the specific outlets eventually sampled.

3.23 The methods used to calculate the elementary price indices from the individual price observations collected within each elementary aggregate are explained in Chapter 8. Working upward from the elementary price indices, all indices above the elementary aggregate level are described as higher-level indices that can be calculated from the elementary price indices using the weights of the elementary expenditure aggregates. The aggregation structure is consistent, so that the weight at each level above the elementary aggregate is always equal to the sum of its components. The price index at each higher level of aggregation can be calculated using the weights and price indices for its components, that is, the lower-level or elementary price indices.

Regional Weights

3.24 Weights stratified by region may be used in the CPI, depending on the size and structure of the country, data availability, resources, and the purpose of the index.

Introducing regional weights creates more homogeneous entities which are likely to experience similar price movements and have similar consumption patterns. It may be necessary to distinguish different regions because CPIs for individual provinces or states may be required for administrative or political purposes. In addition, in federal countries, indirect taxes and hence price developments may differ between the provinces or states.

3.25 In some countries, there may be large differences between urban and rural areas with regard to consumption patterns and price developments. A common practice is to introduce a stratification level that distinguishes between urban and rural areas. This approach assumes that data sources are available to derive expenditure weights separately for urban and rural areas. Moreover, prices must be collected in both rural and urban areas to compile the respective stratum indices.

3.26 If the weights derived from the HBS are available for rural and urban households and if price collection is limited to urban areas, one approach is to combine the weights for urban and rural households. This approach enhances the representativity of the index because the weights represent all households, both urban and rural. In this case, the prices faced by rural households will implicitly be imputed by those collected in urban areas. This can be an acceptable assumption if most of the monetary transactions made by households living in the rural areas take place in urban areas and if the relative changes in prices in rural and urban areas follow the same general trend. Alternatively, if prices are only collected in urban areas, it could also be decided to restrict expenditure weights to urban households and compile an accurate urban CPI.

3.27 Within a given COICOP subclass, the regional weight represents the consumption expenditure in the region in proportion to the expenditure in the whole country for that subclass. For example, if 60 percent of the total expenditure on fresh fruits occurs in the North region and 40 percent in the South region, then these proportions can be used to derive the regional elementary aggregate weights. If at the country level, the expenditure share for fresh fruits is 5 percent, this share can then be split between the regions so that 5 percent × 60 percent = 3 percent of the total national expenditure relates to fresh fruits in the North and 5 percent × 40 percent = 2 percent to fresh fruits in the South.

3.28 Regional weights may typically be obtained from the HBS if the sample design of the HBS is representative at the regional level and supports the development of reliable regional weights. When reliable estimates are not available from an HBS, population statistics are sometimes used to split household expenditure across regions; however, this approach is not preferred as it assumes that expenditures per capita or per household are the same in all regions. For instance, there are usually large differences between urban and rural populations in the level and pattern of items consumed. Finally, national accounts data, if compiled by the expenditure approach and available at the regional level, can also be used to estimate regional weights.

3.29 In practice, there are different strategies to derive regional weights depending on the availability and the quality of data sources. To develop a national weighting structure based on regional weights, first estimate household expenditure by region. Each of the regional expenditure values can then be summed up to obtain the expenditures at the national level. Alternatively, expenditures are first estimated at the country level before being distributed across different regions.

3.30 Consistency should be ensured between the product and the regional dimensions. In the example in Table 3.2, expenditure is estimated for three products in two regions (Table 3.2A). The expenditure share of each stratum in the national index corresponds to the stratum expenditure divided by the national total (Table 3.2B). According to this example, region 1 has a total weight of 38.8 percent. At the same time, product 1 has a weight of 24.5 percent at the national level.

3.31 If detailed product expenditures are only available at the national level, the regional product expenditures must be estimated. This can be done by using shares derived from the total expenditures that are made within a region. Table 3.2C assumes that product expenditures at the country level are available, and only total expenditure by region is known. In Table 3.2D the product expenditures for the country are then disaggregated by region, using a weight

Table 3.2 Deriving Expenditure Weights by Region

Table 3.2A Expenditure by Product and Region

	Region 1	Region 2	Country
Product 1	400	800	1,200
Product 2	500	1,000	1,500
Product 3	1,000	1,200	2,200
Total	**1,900**	**3,000**	**4,900**

Table 3.2B Regional Product Shares

	Region 1 (percent)	Region 2 (percent)	Country (percent)
Product 1	400/4,900 = 8.2	16.3	24.5
Product 2	10.2	20.4	30.6
Product 3	20.4	24.5	44.9
Total	**38.8**	**61.2**	**100.0**

Table 3.2C Expenditure by Region (Regional Product Expenditures Not Available)

	Region 1	Region 2	Country
Product 1	N.A.	N.A.	1,200
Product 2	N.A.	N.A.	1,500
Product 3	N.A.	N.A.	2,200
Total	**1,900**	**3,000**	**4,900**

Table 3.2D Product Expenditures for the Country Disaggregated by Region

	Region 1	Region 2	Country
Product 1	1,200 × 1,900/4,900 = 465	1,200 × 3,000/4,900 = 735	1,200
Product 2	1,500 × 1,900/4,900 = 582	1,500 × 3,000/4,900 = 918	1,500
Product 3	2,200 × 1,900/4,900 = 853	2,200 × 3,000/4,900 = 1,347	2,200
Total	**1,900**	**3,000**	**4,900**

Table 3.2E Regional Product Shares (estimated)

	Region 1 (percent)	Region 2 (percent)	Country (percent)
Product 1	465/4,900 = 9.5	15.0	24.5
Product 2	11.9	18.7	30.6
Product 3	17.4	27.5	44.9
Total	**38.8**	**61.2**	**100.0**

N.A. = Not available

All totals are shown in bold.

of 1,900/4,900 = 38.8 percent for region 1 and a weight of 3,000/4,900 = 61.2 percent for region 2. The regional product shares in Table 3.2E obtained with this method differ slightly from those in Table 3.2B. Ideally, the sample size by region will support expenditure estimates by product within each region, as shown in Tables 3.2A and 3.2B.

Outlet-Type Weights

3.32 Prices are collected from a variety of outlets and outlet types. In addition to the regional dimension, the subclass could also be stratified by outlet or by outlet type. This can be especially useful if price levels and price changes differ significantly across outlets. Information about the sale or market share of the outlets may be used to form elementary aggregate weights specific to a given outlet type. In some countries, the HBS directly collects expenditure data by type of outlet which can then be used to estimate these stratum weights. The use of HBS data ensures consistency between the product weights and outlet-type weights. Other potential sources to derive outlet or outlet-type weights include point-of-purchase surveys, scanner data, business registers, or retail trade statistics. It may only be possible to develop outlet or outlet-type weights for a broader category of products so that the same proportions have to be used to disaggregate the expenditures on the different items within product groups. One should bear in mind that these additional data sources may not be completely aligned with the scope and the coverage of the CPI and may have their own limitations. It may, therefore, be necessary to make further adjustments to the data extracted from such sources.

3.33 In the example in Table 3.3, outlet types 1 and 2 have market shares of 60 percent and 40 percent, respectively, and this same breakdown holds for both regions and for all three products. If a division is made according to the type of outlet and region, then each item within a given region comprises two elementary aggregates: one for outlet type 1 and one for outlet type 2. In this example, the weight for the elementary aggregate for product 1 in region 1 sold in outlet type 1 would then be 8.2 percent × 60 percent = 4.9 percent. This same calculation would be used to develop weights for outlet type 2.

Data Sources

3.34 The HBS serves as the primary data source for CPI weights for most countries. These are household-based surveys that collect data on households' expenditure and consumption of goods and services. Alternatively, national accounts data can serve as a data source. While national accounts data rely to some extent on expenditure data from the HBS, other data sources can be used to supplement the HBS data. Apart from the HBS, many other data sources can and should be used to improve the accuracy of the CPI weights. Such complementary data sources can be used in a number of ways, including (1) validating and correcting HBS estimates; (2) disaggregating the higher-level expenditures to develop a more detailed weighting structure; and (3) estimating expenditures for certain product categories.

Table 3.3 Deriving Expenditure Weights by Region and by Outlet Type

	Region 1 (percent)		Region 2 (percent)		Country (percent)
	Outlet Type 1	Outlet Type 2	Outlet Type 1	Outlet Type 2	
Product 1	8.2		16.3		**24.5**
	4.9	3.3	9.8	6.5	
Product 2	10.2		20.4		**30.6**
	6.1	4.1	12.2	8.2	
Product 3	20.4		24.5		**44.9**
	12.2	8.2	14.7	9.8	
Total	**38.8**		**61.2**		**100.0**

Household Budget Surveys

3.35 In most countries, the HBS serves as the primary data source for deriving expenditure shares for the goods and services covered by the CPI. As the HBS may have been designed to serve more than one purpose, the survey design should meet the requirements for the CPI. Ensuring that CPI specific needs are met requires close coordination between the CPI and HBS staff. The classifications used for HBS and CPI should be consistent and preferably based on COICOP.

3.36 Data for a normal year should be used as the basis for developing CPI weights. Given that many HBSs are conducted infrequently, this can be challenging to manage in practice. If possible, an average of multiple years could be used, but this can only be done if the HBS is conducted continuously. In the absence of a continuous HBS, alternative data sources would be needed to develop weights. This issue of relying on a normal year to develop weights supports the need for more frequent weight updates.

3.37 The main requirements for the CPI include ensuring that the survey broadly represents the CPI reference population, and that all types of final consumption expenditure made by households are covered. The HBS sample size (number of households) should ensure that the expenditure data yielded are suitable to develop statistically reliable weights for the CPI at the elementary aggregate level. The HBS item list should be designed so that the information obtained maps directly into the CPI classification system. Ideally, the survey should also collect the data needed for deriving net weights for second-hand goods (see paragraphs 3.89–3.92). The interview and recording periods should be appropriately distributed over time to ensure that annual estimates can be obtained taking into account possible seasonal patterns.

3.38 The expenditure values used to derive weights should be consistent with the conceptual approach (acquisition, use, or payment) adopted for the CPI (for additional information on this topic, see Chapters 2 and 11). For some services, the moment when the service is consumed and acquired can differ from the moment when the service is paid for. The approach used in the HBS for determining the timing of consumption should be the same as the one used in the CPI. For most goods, the moments of acquisition, payment, and consumption coincide. Sometimes, the HBS focuses on the consumption of food products, which includes food purchased by the household, but also own production of food or food received for free. For durable goods, there is no difference between the acquisition approach and the payment approach if the purchase has not been financed with a loan. Once acquired, the use of such goods can span over several years. The HBS may collect different types of information regarding durable goods.

3.39 Theoretically, the HBS provides information on the regional breakdown of expenditure used to develop reliable regional weights. For this purpose, the regional dimension must be appropriately incorporated in the sampling design of the HBS. Depending on its design, the HBS may also provide information on the types of outlets and the brands purchased. In particular, it can be possible to identify internet purchases. Disaggregation of expenditure by type of outlet can be useful not only to construct elementary aggregates at a more detailed level but also to improve the sample design for outlets and items for price collection.

3.40 Like the HBS, national food surveys are special surveys with the primary emphasis on collecting information on family expenditure for food products. These surveys provide a very detailed breakdown of food expenditure that can be used to derive the weights for detailed elementary aggregates.

3.41 The detailed expenditure obtained from the HBS can be subject to measurement errors. There is often under or overreporting on luxury goods and services, as well as on certain types of products such as alcoholic beverages and tobacco. Moreover, the respondent household may not correctly remember the details of all the expenditure that took place during a given recall period. Therefore, HBS estimates should be reviewed and evaluated for completeness of coverage by comparing with secondary source data.

3.42 Given that the HBS in many countries is based on probability sampling methods, statistical quality indicators (for example, standard error and coefficient of variation) for the weights can be calculated. The analysis of these indicators can provide the index compiler with information on the structure of the elementary aggregates. If an analysis of the HBS data shows, for example, that the expenditure data for oranges are of poor statistical quality, then alternative data sources could be used to improve the reliability of the weights or a more broadly defined elementary aggregate such as citrus fruit could be considered instead. In a similar way, suppose that the HBS provides an unreliable expenditure estimate for an item at a detailed local level. It may then be preferable to derive an estimate based on the expenditure share of that item within a broader geographical area. To find the best compromise between lowering the variance of the item expenditure estimate and biasing it toward the spending pattern of the broader geographical area, a composite share can be computed that averages the initial direct share with the share obtained for the broader geographical area.

3.43 The frequency of updating the CPI weights depends on how often an HBS is conducted. For the purposes of the CPI, it is desirable for the HBS to be conducted at least every five years. This will allow countries to revise and update their expenditure weights every five years (or more frequently). Some countries conduct continuous HBSs with gradually rotating samples. However, a program of annual surveys with samples large enough to provide the type of estimates required for CPI weights can be very costly. For this reason, some countries conduct large-scale surveys at five-year intervals, perhaps supplemented with a smaller annual sample. Other countries distribute a large sample over several years. The average of the results over several successive years of smaller-scale surveys may provide a set of satisfactory annual estimates. The weights derived as the average of two or three years will also smooth any erratic consumer behavior over a shorter period, for example, because of events such as droughts or floods, civil strife, oil price shocks, or exceptionally mild or cold winters.

National Accounts Data

3.44 National accounts can be an alternative source for deriving CPI expenditure weights, if reliable estimates for HFCE are available. The practical advantage is that HFCE is updated every year, whereas an HBS may only be conducted on a less frequent basis. However, national accounts may only be available at the national level and the use of other available data sources would be needed to develop more detailed or regional expenditure weights.

3.45 The index compiler must understand the differences in scope and definition of consumption before using national accounts data for CPI weights. If the CPI is restricted to monetary transactions, then only a subset of HFCE must be used, excluding its nonmonetary components. Additionally, the CPI may adopt a different treatment for expenditure on types of goods and services, such as owner-occupied housing, or even a different scope, especially concerning institutional households.

3.46 National accounts data may be used to improve HBS weights for products that are underreported in the HBS. Note that national accounts' estimates for HFCE are usually based on data from the HBS as well as a wide range of other sources such as domestic production, retail sales, tax information, and import and export data.

3.47 In practice, weights for the main product groups can be obtained from the national accounts down to a certain level of disaggregation. Each of these weights can then be disaggregated by applying the detailed HBS expenditure groups to the national accounts consumption groups. The combination of national accounts and HBS data ensures consistency between the CPI and the national accounts data on HFCE at the level of the main consumption groups. The use of national accounts data also facilitates more frequent weight updates. For instance, CPI weights can be updated at regular intervals using national accounts data for the higher-level aggregates. The updated expenditure is then distributed using the shares obtained from the HBS or other sources that may only be updated less frequently.

3.48 CPI compilers should consult with their national accounts counterparts regularly before using national accounts data for weights to ensure that they are consistent with the objectives and uses of the CPI. In some cases, national accountants need to apply an element of discretion and judgment when making operational decisions related to the construction of some national accounts aggregates. Moreover, the preliminary national accounts estimates are in general revised several times before the final estimates are available. The most recent available data may not be sufficiently stable for CPI purposes. There is a trade-off between timeliness and quality.

Other Data Sources

Administrative Data Sources

3.49 For some product categories, one option is to estimate expenditures from administrative data sources instead of relying on survey data. For instance, expenditure on medical products can often be obtained from relevant bodies in charge of the national health systems. In some countries, tax data for certain products such as alcohol or tobacco lead to more accurate estimates of expenditure than HBS data which suffers from underreporting. It can be also difficult for households to properly report explicit charges paid for financial services in an HBS. Moreover, the derivation of weights for insurance services requires special consideration (see paragraphs 3.87 and 3.88). Therefore, it may be preferable to use regulatory data sources to derive expenditure estimates for financial services and insurance. Administrative data sources are not always perfectly comparable with CPI coverage and may suffer from their own errors. For instance, tax revenue on tobacco also covers sales made to nonresident households whereas the CPI may only be limited to resident households. Most of the administrative data sources are also used in the national accounts which, as noted previously, can serve as a data source for weights.

Retail Trade Statistics

3.50 Statistics on retail sales by region and type of outlet may be available for broad groups of products. One disadvantage of using these data is that some of the sales may be to groups outside the reference population, including corporations or the government. The corresponding purchases do not form part of household final consumption. Some sales may also be to nonresidents, who may be part of the reference population. Furthermore, for regional sales data, it needs to be kept in mind that sales may include purchases made by households living in other regions.

Population Censuses

3.51 Population censuses provide data on the geographical distribution of the population and households, as well as on the regional differences in household size and composition. Combined with estimates of regional levels of household expenditure, these data can be used to estimate regional expenditure weights, especially when such estimates are not available from an HBS with a satisfactory degree of precision. In the absence of any expenditure statistics, population statistics might be used as the basis for regional weights. However, such an approach should be avoided because it assumes that expenditure per capita or per household is the same in all regions and ignores the fact that there are usually large differences between the urban and rural populations in the level and patterns of consumption.

Scanner Data

3.52 Scanner data can also be used to derive and update weights in a more frequent and timely manner. These data are based on electronic data records that are stored in the databases of sellers. Such scanner data sets include the quantities sold and the corresponding value aggregates. The limitations of this information should, however, be borne in mind. The first one is that scanner data cannot be connected to a specific type of household, whereas the data from the HBS can. Moreover, scanner data may only have limited outlet coverage. Finally, scanner data may not be fully consistent with the scope of the CPI, as no distinction can be made between sales to businesses, government, or households.

3.53 Scanner data can also be a good source for deriving detailed weighting structures especially at the lower levels of the index hierarchy. For instance, a detailed product and outlet stratification can be introduced by disaggregating the expenditure for a broader product category that was obtained from the primary data source. The use of scanner data to construct weights is further discussed in Chapter 10.

Market Intelligence and Trade Associations

3.54 If the product categories are sufficiently important, additional data sources might be consulted. A survey may be conducted with a small selection of outlets to obtain general information on the breakdown of sales for a specific product category. Existing market information can also be an option. Associations of importers or distributors, other industry groups, or marketing agencies and boards are likely to have some general information on the breakdown of sales for specific products.

Tourism Expenditure Surveys

3.55 If the CPI follows the domestic concept, the expenditure of nonresident households within the national territory must be included in the weights. In countries where tourism is important, tourism expenditure surveys can be conducted to estimate nonresident household expenditures that can be added to the expenditure made in the country by resident households obtained through the HBS. Nonresident visitors will generally have very different expenditure patterns from those of residents (for example, they will spend more on hotels and restaurants).

Point-of-Purchase Surveys

3.56 Point-of-purchase surveys provide data that can be used to estimate weights for different types of outlets and can be used to develop a sample frame of outlets where households make purchases. For products purchased, households are asked about the amounts spent in each outlet where purchases have been made. Given that household surveys are costly and that there is overlap between the HBS and point-of-purchase surveys, it is possible to combine the two into an integrated survey that collects expenditure and outlet data at detailed levels.

3.57 A simpler version of this survey may be conducted to obtain weights for groups of products by outlet type. As an alternative, in the absence of this type of survey, national retail sales statistics by outlet type from a survey of outlets could be used to estimate a breakdown of sales by outlet type.

Deriving the Weights in Practice

3.58 Once the reference population and the coverage of goods and services have been decided, the weights need to be derived. The weights are calculated as the proportions of the total consumption expenditure of all goods and services included in the index basket for the reference population during the reference period. The reliability of the CPI weights will obviously depend, to a large extent, on the reliability of the household expenditure data. In practice, the derivation of weights involves a series of steps.

Arrange the Data According to the Classification and Coverage of the CPI

3.59 The detailed expenditure items identified in the HBS, or other data sources, must be mapped to the CPI expenditure classes. If HBS classes do not match CPI expenditure classes, the HBS results must be transformed to match the CPI classes. This can be done by aggregating or disaggregating the relevant HBS headings over the relevant CPI expenditure subclasses. Such transformation is achieved much more easily and more reliably if the coding list for expenditure items in the HBS is coordinated with the corresponding list of items used for collecting price observations for the CPI. As noted previously, both the HBS and CPI should use the same classification system (ideally COICOP).

3.60 The HBS expenditure data may include payments that are outside the scope of the CPI. For example, payments of income taxes or social security contributions, life insurance premiums, remittances, gifts and other transfers, investments, savings, and debt repayments should not be considered because they are not consumption expenditure. These should be excluded from the total used to calculate the expenditure shares that serve as the basis to estimate the CPI weights.

Correcting for Over- and Underreporting by Combining Different Data Sources

3.61 The results from the HBS need to be carefully examined and adjusted to take account of under or overreporting of consumption expenditure on different types of products. This is a relevant problem affecting HBS data. Evidence suggests that the understatement of expenditures can be significant for certain goods and services in the HBS if their consumption is socially discouraged, such as tobacco and alcoholic beverages. Expenditures on durable goods also tend to be underreported. Some products, such as vehicles or other major durable goods, are purchased infrequently. When purchased, the amount spent on such products can be considerable. As the HBS is a sample survey, estimates are subject to sampling errors, which may be relatively large for such infrequent expenditures. For major durable goods, HBS estimates should be compared with other sources such as import statistics or administrative data.

3.62 Other expenditures are not reported because the purchases were small, and easily forgotten by the respondent. Therefore, to the extent possible, results from the HBS should be compared and combined with other data sources when constructing CPI weights, especially when the HBS sample is small.

3.63 The usual strategy to correct for over or underreporting is to use supplementary information from other relevant data sources such as tax data, administrative data, other independent surveys, or HFCE from the national accounts, and to apply correction factors. For instance, assume that tax revenue data indicate that annual sales for cigarettes may be twice as high as the total annual expenditure estimated from the HBS. The CPI weight is thus obtained by increasing the HBS expenditure on cigarettes by two to better reflect the sales data.

3.64 In countries with reliable and detailed national accounts data, the commodity-flow method can be used to adjust data considered less reliable from the HBS. The use of the commodity-flow method within the Supply and Use Table framework, as described in the *System of National Accounts*, enables data drawn from different primary sources to be reconciled and balanced against each other. The commodity-flow method may be used to improve estimates of HFCE derived from the HBS by adjusting them to account for additional information provided by statistics on sales, production, and imports and exports of consumer goods and services.

3.65 The Supply and Use Tables form an integrated framework where supplies of different kinds of goods and services originating from domestic industries and imports are allocated between various intermediate or final uses, including HFCE. The product balance for any product recognizes that the sum of output at basic prices plus imports plus trade and transport margins plus taxes on products less subsidies on products is equal to the sum of intermediate consumption, final consumption, and capital formation, all expressed at purchasers' prices, plus exports (*System of National Accounts 2008* [*2008 SNA*], paragraph 14.5). The HFCE estimates obtained can be compared with the corresponding estimates from the HBS to provide conversion factors to adjust HBS expenditure data for under or overreporting.

3.66 There are some practical limitations to applying the commodity-flow method. Often the balance can only be established for a category of products broader than the product categories used in the CPI classification. Moreover, data are usually compiled at the national level and no detailed regional breakdown is available. Finally, the HBS may not be the only inaccurate data source for a particular product and the estimates of other components of the product balance can also be unreliable.

Adjusting Household Budget Surveys

3.67 Even if expenditure data obtained from the HBS results are considered accurate, adjustments might still be needed to account for any significant changes in expenditure patterns between the period when the survey was conducted and the period when the new weights are introduced. Adjustments will typically be made for products belonging to fast-evolving markets and which are significantly losing or gaining importance during this period. It is possible that expenditure on some products may not be available from the HBS because the products appeared on the market after the survey had been completed. Additional data sources must then be accessed to estimate expenditure for new products. Expenditure should also be reviewed if there are known changes that have occurred following administrative decisions, such as changes in taxation, that entered into force only after the HBS was conducted.

Treatment of Expenditure for Unimportant or Difficult-to-Measure Products

3.68 The HBS, which in most cases is the main source for deriving the detailed weights, usually includes observations on a much larger variety of goods and services than it is practical to collect prices for in the CPI. Some products may have a weight which for all practical purposes is negligible. The prices of products with very small weights may not be worth collecting if their contribution to the CPI is very small. In practice, a cutoff threshold can be defined to select the products to be included in the CPI basket (see Chapter 4 for a description of different sampling techniques).

3.69 Among the consumption expenditure, there are also likely to be a few products for which the prices, or price changes, cannot be directly or satisfactorily measured, such as gambling. It may be difficult if not impossible to compile a reliable price index for such products. A decision must then be made on how to treat the expenditure allocated to such difficult-to-measure products.

3.70 Even if the product weight is small or if there are measurement problems, the product is still included in the scope of the CPI. For those products with relatively low weights, it is not efficient to collect prices; however, the CPI should cover these expenditures. Some price change should be explicitly or implicitly assumed or imputed. In practice, there are different options:

- The weight of the product is combined with one or several related products. For instance, if the weight for "cheese" is small, it can be combined with the weight for "milk." This means that the elementary aggregate is now weighted using expenditures on milk and cheese although only prices for milk will be collected. This option assumes that the price index for cheese would change in the same manner as the observed price index for milk. In practice, the weights for the products could be kept separated but price changes must be explicitly imputed. To continue using the previous example, the price index attached to the weight for cheese would simply be identical to the price index for milk. This is the preferred approach.
- An alternative approach is to set the weight for which no representative prices exist equal to zero. This option removes the item from the scope of the CPI and is equivalent to the assumption that the price of the excluded product would have moved in the same way as the all-items CPI for all the products actually included in the index. This approach is, in general, not recommended.

3.71 Table 3.4 shows examples of different options for the treatment of unimportant expenditures. In the example, the expenditure for product 3 is not relevant. One option is to add this expenditure to item 1. Alternatively, it may be added to products 1 and 2 proportionally to the weights of these two products. Finally, it can be removed, which implies that the total expenditure for the three products is now reduced. In general, the last option should be avoided, and expenditures should be allocated to products with similar price behavior. Because of the negligible size of the weight value involved, the consequence on the overall index will in general be negligible whichever method is used.

Table 3.4 Treatment of Products for Which No Prices Are Collected

	Initial Expenditures	Allocate to Item 1	Allocate to Items 1 and 2	Remove Expenditure
Product 1	7	8	7.7	7
Product 2	3	3	3.3	3
Product 3 (minor item)	**1**	**0**	**0**	**0**
Total	**11**	**11**	**11**	**10**

Weight Reference Period

3.72 The weight reference period refers to the time period to which the expenditure data used to estimate weights were collected. For a fixed-basket CPI which keeps weights constant over several periods, the weight reference period is typically a 12-month period, such as a calendar year. A month or quarter is too short to be used as a weight reference period, since any month or quarter is likely to be affected by accidental or seasonal influences. This is especially important in countries where the composition and size of expenditure can fluctuate significantly throughout the year. In some countries, data for a single year may not be adequate because of unusual economic conditions or due to insufficient sample size. In these cases, an average of more than one year of expenditure data may be used to calculate the weights.

3.73 As the CPI is sensitive to the selection of the weight reference period, it might be preferable to choose a "normal" consumption period as the basis for weights and to avoid periods in which there are special factors of a temporary nature at work. To achieve this, it may be necessary to adjust some of the values to normalize them and to overcome any irregularities in the data. One option might be to smooth particularly erratic observations, for example, by taking an average of HBS data over more than one year. All available information concerning the nature of consumption in a weight reference period should be taken into consideration.

3.74 During periods of high inflation, multiple year weights may be calculated by averaging value shares rather than averaging actual value levels. Averaging value levels will give too much weight to the data for the most recent year. Another option is to update the values for each year to a common period and then to compute a simple arithmetic average of adjusted yearly data.

3.75 As the weight reference period usually precedes the price reference period, the expenditure weights may be price updated to take account of the relative price changes from the weight reference period to the price reference period. The technique of price-updating expenditure data or CPI weights from a past period does not make weights reflect current expenditure patterns. New CPI weights can only be derived if new expenditure data are available. Price updating of weights is discussed in more detail in Chapter 9.

Frequency of Weight Updates

3.76 The expenditure weights should be updated at regular intervals, as often as possible, but at least every five years. The decision of when to update the weights often depends on the availability of appropriate data sources. Rather than waiting for the weights to become outdated before deciding to update them, the recommended approach is to plan for regular scheduled updates subject to the available data sources. In general, there is a lag between the weight reference period and the moment that the weights are introduced in the CPI. The overall principle is to minimize the implementation lag so that the weights used in the CPI are as up to date as possible. New weights should be introduced in a timely manner, as soon as the required source data are available. For instance, expenditure weights referring to year y – 2 could be introduced with the January index of year y.

3.77 If weights are kept fixed over longer time periods, the index will be unresponsive to substitution effects or changes in consumer preferences. In the short term, consumers may change consumption patterns in response to shifts in relative prices, mostly between products included in the same class or subclass. In the medium or long term, consumption patterns are also influenced by factors other than price changes. Most importantly, under rising incomes, changes in the level and distribution of household income will cause a shift in demand for goods and services toward goods and services with higher income elasticities. Demographic factors such as aging of the population and technological changes are examples of other factors that affect spending behavior in the longer term. Furthermore, new products will be introduced, and existing ones may be modified or become obsolete. As a result of both relative price changes and long-term effects, the weights may become out of date and less representative of current consumption patterns. As shown in Chapter 2 of the publication *Consumer Price Index Theory*, the bias in a fixed-basket index is likely to increase with the age of the weights. At some point, it therefore becomes desirable to use the weights of a more recent period to ensure that the index is weighting appropriately the price changes currently faced by consumers.

3.78 If data sources such as the HBS are available only at irregular or infrequent intervals, the frequency of weight revision may necessarily be linked to the availability of results from the HBS. When the weights are to be fixed for several years, the objective should be to adopt weights that are not likely to change much in the future, rather than precisely reflect the activity of a particular period that may be abnormal in some way. Even if weights are updated only every five years, it is desirable to review the weights in between to ensure that they remain sufficiently reliable and representative. The review, which may be limited to weights at the elementary index level and their major components, should examine whether there are indications that important changes may have taken place in the consumption pattern since the weight reference period.

3.79 To reduce upper-level substitution bias, it would be preferable to update the weights more often such as every three years, every two years, or even every year; however, this depends on the availability of data to develop new weights. Any bias which may follow from using a Lowe index (see Chapters 1 and 8 for information on price index formulas) with a fixed basket of goods and services will not have time to accumulate to a significant magnitude. Also, by updating the weights more frequently, there is the opportunity to introduce newly significant goods and services in a timely manner. At the same moment, the sample of outlets and varieties to be priced can be updated simultaneously, although the sample should be maintained in between two weight updates. Countries that are experiencing significant economic changes, and thus more rapid changes in the consumption pattern, should consider updating their weights more frequently.

3.80 The benefits of updating weights more often should be assessed and compared to the additional costs of such an exercise. If feasible, empirical studies can be conducted on historical data to assess the impact of updating weights more frequently, of choosing different weight reference periods, and of minimizing the time lag between the weight reference period and the price reference period. The resulting indices can then be compared to specific target indices.

3.81 An intermediate solution is to update weights only at the higher level, for example using national accounts data, which can then be disaggregated down to the lower levels using shares from the HBS, which has not been updated. Partial weight updates are further discussed and illustrated in Chapter 9.

3.82 Frequent updating of weights and chaining can lead to chain drift. For a Laspeyres or a Lowe index, the drift can be upward if there are systematic fluctuations in consumption and prices. Suppose that the prices for petroleum products went down between the old and the new weight reference period, causing an increase in the quantities consumed and expenditure for these products. If petroleum prices subsequently rise after the new weights are introduced, the aggregate CPI will rise more rapidly than before since these products now have more importance. At the level of broad product categories, expenditure data analyzed over longer periods often follow trends. Chaining can have a downward impact if, for instance, there is a gradual shift from one product to another product for which prices are rising slower. A direct CPI compiled with unchanged weights is often found to be higher than the chained index compiled, for instance, with annually updated weights. Chain drift is more problematic with high-frequency updating of weights and chaining at the level of an individual variety. Multilateral methods that are discussed in Chapter 10 (and Chapter 7 of *Consumer Price Index Theory)* are one solution to this problem.

3.83 The selection of the level in the index hierarchy at which the structure and weights are fixed for a period is particularly important. The main advantage of setting the level relatively high is that the actual samples of products and their prices below this level can be adjusted and updated as needed (see Chapter 7). New products can be introduced into the samples, and the weights at the lower level updated using more recent information. There is thus a greater opportunity to keep the index representative through an ongoing review of the sample of representative products. If the level is set relatively low in the index structure, there is less freedom to maintain the representativeness of the index on an ongoing basis, and there will be a greater dependence on the periodic index review and reweighting process. In such circumstances, the arguments for frequent reweighting become stronger.

3.84 Whenever the weighting pattern has been updated, the new index using updated weights should be calculated for an overlapping period with the old one so that the two can be linked. These techniques are discussed in Chapter 9. During the year that follows the weight update, the year over year rates of the higher-level aggregates compiled from the linked series not only reflect changes in prices, but are also impacted by the use of different weights and a different item structure.

Items Requiring Special Treatment

Seasonal Products

3.85 In practice, there are two types of approaches for the treatment of seasonal products:

- A fixed-weight approach, which assigns the same weight for the seasonal product in all months, using an imputed price in the out-of-season months. Seasonal products are treated in the same way as other consumption products.

- A seasonal-weight approach, in which a zero weight is attached to a product which is out of season, and a positive weight is used for the in-season periods when the product is available for pricing. The in-season weights are kept fixed as much as possible and only vary to the extent necessary to reflect changes in the composition of the basket. Moreover, the principle of a fixed basket (that is, fixed weights) should be maintained at least at some level of aggregation. One disadvantage of such an approach is that the monthly changes in the index may be more difficult to interpret as they may reflect not only price changes but also quantity changes.

The treatment of seasonal products is further discussed in Chapter 11. In addition, this topic is examined in Chapter 9 of the publication *Consumer Price Index Theory*.

Internet Purchases

3.86 As internet purchases become increasingly important, these expenditures should be included in the CPI weights according to the conceptual approach that has been adopted. Chapter 11 discusses how internet purchases should be treated either under the national or the domestic concept. Ideally, data on the share of internet purchases for all relevant product categories could be available, so that detailed strata can be defined for this outlet type. The HBS should, in principle, cover internet purchases made by resident households. The survey should be designed so that it is possible to separate internet purchases from other purchases. The estimation of expenditure on internet purchases is of interest to both the HBS and the CPI programs and therefore it would be beneficial to cooperate on this topic. Similarly, the treatment of internet purchases in the national accounts should be carefully examined if this is the primary data source for CPI weights.

3.87 Alternative data sources for measuring e-commerce transactions include bank account data and credit card data. However, excluding business expenditure from these data sets could be problematic and identifying specific products and outlets may not be straightforward. Finally, reports prepared by external organizations that monitor and describe e-commerce markets can also help to estimate weights for internet purchases. The scope, coverage, and data collection methods underlying the statistics presented in such reports must be well understood when combining such figures with those obtained from other sources.

Insurance

3.88 As explained in Chapters 2 and 11, the weights for nonlife insurance could be based on either (1) the gross premiums paid, consisting of the payment for the insurance, or (2) on the implicit service charges payable to the insurance enterprise for arranging the insurance. The implicit service charges for administering the insurance and providing the insurance services are estimated by the gross premiums plus the income from investment of the insurance reserves less the amounts payable to policyholders in settlement of claims. This definition can potentially lead to negative weights for instance if there are irregular and unexpected large fluctuations in claims due to natural disasters or large-scale accidents. To avoid negative weights, an average service charge covering several years could be considered.

3.89 If the weights are based on the gross premiums, expenditure weights should normally exclude goods and services provided for or reimbursed by the insurance company on the basis of claims. If the weights are based on the implicit service charge, expenditure weights include goods and services that households buy and that are reimbursed by insurance companies, and also goods and services that are paid for and provided by insurance companies on the basis of claims. In general, it seems preferable to base the weights for nonlife insurance on the service charges.

Second-Hand Goods

3.90 The prices of used, or second-hand, goods purchased by households are included in the CPI in the same way as the prices of new goods (Chapter 11 discusses this topic in more detail). However, households also sell used goods, such as cars. If the price of a second-hand good rises, a purchasing household is worse off, but a selling household is better off. From a weighting perspective, sales constitute negative expenditures, which implies that price changes for used goods sold by households implicitly carry a negative weight in the CPI. In effect, purchases and sales of second-hand goods between households, whether directly or indirectly through a dealer, cancel out (except for the dealers' margins, as explained in Chapter 2) and carry no weight in the CPI. However, households also buy from, and sell to, other sectors. For the reference population, namely the entire set of households covered by the CPI, the weight to be attached to a particular kind of second-hand good is given by the households' total expenditure on it less the value of the households' revenue from sales to/from outside the household sector, including the rest of the world. There is no reason why these should cancel out on aggregate. For example, many of the second-hand cars purchased by households may be imported from abroad. The difference between total expenditures and total sales is usually described as households' net expenditure. This is the weight to be attached to the second-hand good in question. Table 3.5 illustrates how to develop weights for used goods. In this example, the net weight would be obtained as $(100 + 300) - (100 + 200) = 400 - 300 = 100$.

3.91 Second-hand markets may exist for a whole range of durable and semidurable goods. Except in the case of used cars, it is often very difficult to estimate the net expenditure because most HBSs do not collect the data that would allow for a comparison between expenditure and revenue from sales of individual kinds of second-hand goods. Usually, only the total amount received from the sale of second-hand goods is collected. However, this information gives an idea of the volume and significance of these transactions in the economy.

3.92 In countries where the volume of second-hand purchases is small, second-hand goods (except used cars)

Table 3.5 Estimation of Net Expenditure Weights

Seller Buyer	Households	Other Institutional Sectors
Households	100	300
Other Institutional Sectors	200	Out of Scope

may be ignored when calculating the weights of the index. In countries where second-hand purchases are important, and their prices are believed to change at different rates from those of new goods, separate weights are needed. The information may be obtained, at least for some major durables, from the HBS, if the survey asks about expenditure on second-hand and new goods. Because the amounts spent on purchasing second-hand cars are usually large, they should be included in the CPI basket if the data are available.

3.93 Even if countries include expenditure on second-hand goods in the estimation of CPI weights, second-hand goods may not be covered in the price collection. By excluding second-hand goods from the price collection, it is implicitly assumed that the prices of new and second-hand goods move in the same way. If they are included, the price-determining characteristics of the second-hand good must be kept constant over time so the same good is priced each month. If the goods are different, appropriate quality adjustments must be made.

Owner-Occupied Housing

3.94 If the CPI includes owner-occupied housing under the rental equivalence approach, weights represent the rents that owners would pay for the dwelling that they occupy. The owners could be directly asked what rent they would pay for their dwelling; however, such answers are often found to be unreliable. The preferred option is to rely on observed rent data to impute a rental value for the stock of owner-occupied dwellings. The assumption is that the rent of an owner-occupied dwelling is expected to be equal to the observed rent of a dwelling with similar characteristics. Such an approach is also consistent with the *2008 SNA* (paragraph 6.117) which recommends valuing the output of the housing services produced by owner-occupiers at the estimated rental that a tenant would pay for the same accommodation.

3.95 If the CPI includes owner-occupied housing under the acquisitions approach, the weights are based on the (net) purchases of dwellings plus major repairs. The purchase of a dwelling includes both a structure and a land and location component. Only the value of the structure element should be included in the weights of a CPI that aims at measuring consumption expenditure, whereas the value of the land should in principle be excluded. Moreover, only dwellings acquired for the purpose of own occupation should be covered. In addition, an owner-occupied housing index under the acquisitions approach would include transaction costs and other costs related to the use of the dwelling, in which case weights must also be estimated for these components. Possible data sources for deriving owner-occupied housing weights are statistics on building activity, business statistics in construction, or administrative records of property transactions. Chapter 11 describes in more detail the treatment of owner-occupied housing in the CPI.

Inclusion of Newly Significant Products

3.96 As discussed in Chapter 7, newly significant products that appear over time should be identified. If a new product becomes important with regard to household expenditure, it should be included in the index structure. One option is to wait and introduce the new product at the time of a complete weight update. Alternatively, the current weighting structure could be adjusted, using the techniques described in Chapter 7, to introduce the new products in the CPI in a timely manner. In any case, expenditure weights must be estimated for the new products. Such data may not always be readily available from the HBS. If that is the case, the newly identified products should be incorporated in the HBS as soon as possible. In the meantime, alternative data sources may be used to estimate the weights of the new products so that their inclusion in the CPI is not delayed.

Key Recommendations

- CPI weights represent the expenditure shares for specific goods and services that define the basket.
- CPI weights should be consistent with the decisions made regarding the geographic coverage, the household reference population, the type of consumption expenditure included in the CPI, and the product coverage.
- The objective is to estimate expenditure consistent with the scope of the CPI at a sufficiently detailed product level, possibly stratified by region or by outlet type, so that reliable weights can be attached to the different elementary aggregates that make up the index structure.
- The primary data source for deriving expenditure weights are typically HBSs, but expenditure data may also be directly obtained from the national accounts.
- When using the HBS as the primary source for deriving the weights, the data have to be reviewed and corrected for possible under or overreporting by comparing them with other data sources in order to obtain a representative weighting structure.
- Secondary data sources can be useful to estimate expenditure for certain product categories, to further disaggregate the expenditure at the lower levels, and to correct for over or underreporting.
- The weights should be updated as often as possible, but at least once every five years, to ensure their relevance and the representativity of the index.
- Countries which are experiencing significant economic changes, and thus more rapid changes in consumption patterns, should update their weights even more frequently.
- The lowest level weights are likely to become out of date more quickly than upper-level weights. Therefore, these lower-level weights, for at least some categories, need to be reviewed and updated more frequently than upper-level weights to reflect changes in consumption patterns. The best use of the available statistical information (for example, market research or small annual surveys) should be made for this purpose.
- A regular schedule of updating the weights (at least every five years or as often as possible) should be followed and made available to users.

SAMPLING

4

Introduction

4.1 To construct a perfectly accurate consumer price index (CPI), the price statistician would need to record the price of every variety of all the goods and services that are in the scope of the CPI. Because it is too costly and, in practice, impossible to regularly record all the prices of the universe in a timely manner, sampling techniques are used to select a subset of prices that eventually enter the index compilation. Consequently, a CPI compilation is based on samples.

4.2 Sampling occurs on several different levels in the CPI:

- Geographic (locations) and outlet samples: all places and outlets where a product is sold
- Product samples: all goods and services available for purchase
- Time: the subperiods of the index

4.3 In practice, CPI sampling follows a multistage approach. The universe of products is structured by first selecting the items within the different categories of the expenditure classification. For each item of the CPI classification, one or more representative varieties can then be sampled. For the geographic and outlet samples, specific locations for price collection are selected first. In a second step, outlets are selected within the sampled locations. The specific varieties to be priced are ideally selected within the sampled outlets. Finally, time can be considered as another level of sampling as it must be decided at which moment during the reference month prices are observed.

4.4 Within each of the different sampling stages, either probability or nonprobability sampling methods can be considered, possibly in combination with stratification. If the sampling frames required for probability sampling are not available, the price statistician either creates one or relies on nonprobability sampling techniques. For this reason, nonprobability sampling techniques are commonly used to draw samples for price collection in the CPI. However, the use of some form of probability sampling is generally the preferred option as it avoids the need for arbitrary decisions and ensures unbiased results. In addition, there are practical considerations when organizing the price collection in the field. In practice, different sampling approaches may be adopted for different parts of the CPI basket. It is thus essential that sampling procedures are clearly defined and well documented.

4.5 When sampling designs are planned, the full universe of locations, outlets and outlet types, items, and varieties belonging to the scope of the CPI should be considered. All significant parts of that universe should be appropriately represented. An additional challenge is that representativity is not static but evolves over time. The samples that were initially designed for the price reference period may not be fully representative of the current period. Therefore, samples should be continuously monitored and updated as needed. Chapter 7 describes in more detail the challenges of a dynamic target universe.

4.6 The sample design should support the publication of the detailed subindices that have been agreed for dissemination, such as regional indices or separate subindices for urban and rural areas. Sample designs should be efficient to maximize sampling precision while minimizing the costs for fieldwork and processing. Even without any formal variance estimation (as described in 4.83–4.94), sample allocation should be optimized by taking into account the weight and the magnitude of the price change variance of the subindices.

Sampling Techniques

4.7 In survey sampling theory,[1] there is a distinction between the parameter and the estimator. In the context of a CPI, the parameter is the target price index number that is based on prices and quantities of the products that belong to the universe. The estimator is the price index that is actually compiled using the sampled data as input. The result of the estimator depends on the price index formula that may or may not use weights, and on the sampling scheme that has been adopted for selecting the varieties for which prices are collected. In practice, the parameter is unknown although simulations can be conducted, for example, using scanner data to study the performance of different sampling strategies.

4.8 In assessing the quality of a sample estimator (that is, how well it estimates the parameter), two measures are often considered in the case of probability sampling. The first measure is the bias of the estimator, which is the difference between the universe parameter and the average of the estimator over all possible samples that could be drawn under the specified sample design. An estimator is unbiased if it has zero bias. The second measure is the variance of the estimator with respect to the sampling distribution.

4.9 An estimator is considered accurate if both its bias and variance are small; that is, the estimator is on average very close to the parameter and does not vary significantly from its mean. The mean square error, defined as the sum of the variance and the squared bias, measures the accuracy of the estimator. In addition, samples should be efficient, so that the maximum sampling precision (and minimum variance) can be obtained for the minimum cost with regard to

[1] For a full treatment of the subject, please refer to one of the many textbooks available, for example, Särndal and others (1992) or Cochran (1977).

fieldwork and processing. If bias is a more relevant problem than sampling error, the deterioration in precision caused by small samples can be offset by spending sufficient resources to select and maintain representative samples.

4.10 There are two approaches that can be used to sample units: probability sampling techniques and nonprobability sampling techniques. Probability sampling techniques require that the probability of a unit being selected as part of the sample is known in advance and is strictly positive for each unit. Units can represent the locations and the outlets where households shop or the items and varieties that households buy. Nonprobability sampling techniques do not rely on sampling probabilities. In practice, a combination of probability sampling and nonprobability (or purposive) sampling is used at the various sampling stages of a CPI. These techniques are often applied together with stratification.

Probability Sampling Techniques

4.11 In probability sampling, a sample of n units from the universe of N units is selected by attaching a nonzero inclusion probability π_j to each unit j. The inclusion probabilities p_j for each unit in the sample are assumed to be strictly positive and known in advance. This requires the availability of a sampling frame, that is, a list of all the units eligible to be sampled. A frame may suffer from overcoverage if it includes units that are not in the universe or includes duplicates of units. It may have undercoverage if units in the universe are missing from the frame.

4.12 In simple random sampling (SRS) and systematic sampling, each unit is sampled with equal probability and $\pi_j = n/N$. In SRS (without replacement), a random number is assigned to each unit in the frame and the n highest (or lowest) values are selected. In systematic sampling, the sampling units are selected at equal distances from each other in the frame, with random selection of only the first unit. These techniques are usually recommended in situations where the units are relatively homogeneous.

4.13 In probability proportional to size (PPS) sampling, the inclusion probability $\pi_j = \frac{nx_j}{\sum_{k \in N} x_k}$ is proportional to some auxiliary variable x_j. Units for which the inclusion probability is greater than one are selected with certainty, while the inclusion probabilities for the remaining units are calculated after excluding the large ones. This technique is recommended if the units are of different sizes, so that larger units have a greater probability of selection than smaller units.

4.14 In the context of a CPI, the auxiliary variable is typically the household expenditure on the goods and services covered by the CPI. In practice, this variable is often not available and alternative variables correlated to expenditure must be used, such as retail turnover, population of geographic areas, or number of outlets. The extent to which this assumption about the alternative variables holds true eventually determines the quality of the sampling design.

4.15 In a CPI, the size of a sample is often fixed a priori. It is therefore impractical to let the sample size be randomly fixed by the sampling procedure. Several techniques exist for drawing fixed sample size samples, for example, systematic sampling or simple random sampling, and so on.

4.16 In systematic PPS sampling, the list of units is first ordered randomly and the cumulative total of the auxiliary variable x_j is calculated. Selection of units then takes place using interval sampling with the interval value calculated by dividing the cumulative total $\Sigma_{i \in N} x_i$ by the sample size n. This is done by generating a random starting point between zero and the interval value to select the first unit. The second random number is generated by adding the interval value to the starting point and used to select the second unit. This process of adding the interval value to the previous random number, and selecting the corresponding units, is repeated until the requisite number of units has been sampled. If the size of a unit is larger than the interval value, then it is selected with certainty. These units are then removed from the sampling frame and the process of cumulating the size variable and compiling an interval value is repeated with the remaining units.

4.17 Systematic sampling is best explained using an example. Table 4.1 shows how a sample of three outlets can be drawn from 10 outlets. In a first step, the outlets are listed in a random order (column A). Although turnover, or total gross sales of the establishment, would be the preferred selection variable, it is often not available in the sampling frame. An alternative might be the use of the number of employees as a proxy for turnover. The table includes the cumulative sizes and the inclusion intervals (columns C and D). Taking the cumulated (or total) size measure, which is 90 in this case, and dividing it by the sample size, 3, gives a sampling interval of 30. Next, a random number between 1 and 30 is chosen, say 25. The sample will then consist of the outlets whose inclusion intervals cover the numbers 25, 25 + 30 = 55 and 25 + 2 × 30 = 85 (column E).

4.18 PPS sampling has the advantage of selecting the sample in proportion to the relevant variable. It ensures a sample which reflects the heterogeneity of the population, and the sample does not need to be rebalanced by reweighting. Alternatively, if each unit could be given an equal chance of selection in the sample, then reweighting may be necessary. For example, SRS would give a large outlet the same chance of selection as a small independent shop, despite the enormous differences in turnover, and so reweighting would be needed.

Table 4.1 Systematic Sample of 3 out of 10 Outlets, Based on PPS Sampling

	Number of Employees (x)	Cumulative x	Inclusion Interval under PPS	Included when Starting Point is 25
(a)	(b)	(c)	(d)	(e)
Outlet 1	13	13	0–13	
Outlet 2	2	15	14–15	
Outlet 3	5	20	16–20	
Outlet 4	9	29	21–29	X
Outlet 5	1	30	30	
Outlet 6	25	55	31–55	X
Outlet 7	10	65	56–65	
Outlet 8	6	71	66–71	
Outlet 9	11	82	72–82	
Outlet 10	8	90	83–90	X

4.19 Assuming that the prices used to compile the index have been obtained using a specific probability sampling design, it can then be shown how common price indices are estimators for certain population price indices (see Balk [2005] for details). If the size variable in PPS sampling corresponds to the expenditure on the variety in the base period, then the sample Jevons price index is an approximately unbiased estimator for the population geometric price index. Similarly, if the size variable corresponds to the quantities in the base period, then the sample Dutot price index is an approximately unbiased estimator for the population Laspeyres price index. These results suggest that varieties should be sampled based on expenditures if using a Jevons index whereas for a Dutot index, varieties should be sampled based on sold quantities. Finally, the Carli index is an unbiased estimator for the population Laspeyres price index if the size variable corresponds to the expenditures in the base period (the different index formulas are discussed in Chapters 1 and 8).

4.20 These estimators are "approximately" unbiased in the sense that the bias tends to zero if the sample size increases. It can be shown that the finite sample bias of the Jevons index is always positive. Under SRS, the sample Jevons price index is on average larger than the population Jevons price index. For the Dutot index, the sign of the finite sample bias is undetermined, although its magnitude is often negligible. However, for the Jevons index the bias may be significant if sample sizes are very small. Thus, when using the geometric mean, very small sample sizes should be avoided (see Bradley [2007]). Increasing the sample sizes will not only reduce finite sample bias, but also reduce the variance caused by sampling. As a rule of thumb and unless price change variance is very low, at least eight to ten observations for each elementary aggregate should be selected for the compilation of the Jevons index.

Nonprobability Sampling Techniques

4.21 In many circumstances, detailed sampling frames are not available, and nonprobability sampling techniques are applied, because they do not necessarily rely on sampling frames. Moreover, such techniques allow, to a certain extent, more control over the samples than random approaches. For example, the costs and the feasibility of price collection play a key role when designing samples for a CPI, especially given that the sample has to be priced continuously over the next periods. Examples of nonprobability sampling techniques that are often applied in a CPI context include cutoff sampling, quota sampling, and the representative item method.

Cutoff Sampling

4.22 Cutoff sampling refers to the practice of choosing the n largest sampling units with certainty and giving the remaining units a zero chance of inclusion. To apply cutoff sampling, a sampling frame is required that contains an appropriate variable measuring the size of the unit. Moreover, the quality of that variable has to be judged when performing cutoff sampling. The term "cutoff" refers to the threshold value between the included and the excluded units. Unlike with probability sampling, there is no randomness involved. All units above the threshold are selected with certainty, whereas those below the threshold are excluded.

4.23 The disadvantage of cutoff sampling is that it does not produce unbiased estimators, since the small units may display price movements that systematically differ from those of the larger units. Any estimator resulting from cutoff sampling has zero variance because there is only one sample that can be drawn for a given threshold. With regard to mean square error, cut-off sampling might be a good choice if the variance reduction more than offsets the introduction of a small bias.

4.24 Cutoff sampling can be considered when the size variable is highly skewed. The goal is to select the largest units that are not so numerous and disregard the many small units. This design is also useful when the "below cutoff section" of the universe is considered insignificant and difficult to measure. A CPI practice considered as cutoff sampling occurs when the price collector selects the most sold product in an outlet, within a centrally defined specification. In this case, the sample size is one (in each outlet).

4.25 Table 4.2 shows the three largest outlets that have been selected using cutoff sampling, with the size of the outlet being measured by its number of employees (column B). This cutoff sampling technique allows covering 54 percent of the total number of employees (column D). If the cutoff rule is defined to cover at least 70 percent of the total number of employees, two additional outlets must be selected. Instead of fixing the sample size, the cutoff rule can be defined with regard to the cumulative size variable for a certain threshold. Contrary to PPS sampling, an outlet with a small number of employees will systematically be excluded in cutoff sampling. At the same time, this technique ensures that all the largest units are always covered.

Quota Sampling

4.26 Quota sampling is another nonprobability sampling technique used in the CPI. Many product groups, even rather small ones, are quite heterogeneous in nature, and the price varies according to many subgroups or characteristics. There may be different price movements within such a product group, and a procedure to represent the group by one or a few tightly specified item types may then carry a substantial risk of bias.

Table 4.2 Cutoff Sample of 3 out of 10 Outlets

	Number of Employees (x)	Cumulative x	Cumulative x (percent)	Included in Cutoff Sampling When $n = 3$
(a)	(b)	(c)	(d)	(e)
Outlet 6	25	25	28	X
Outlet 1	13	38	42	X
Outlet 9	11	49	54	X
Outlet 7	10	59	66	
Outlet 4	9	68	76	
Outlet 10	8	76	84	
Outlet 8	6	82	91	
Outlet 3	5	87	97	
Outlet 2	2	89	99	
Outlet 5	1	90	100	

4.27 In quota sampling, the sample selection is made using judgmental procedures with respect to known and relevant characteristics when choosing products to price or the type of outlet to select. The sample is drawn to have the same proportions as the total population or universe to ensure that the sample is representative. Consequently, the sample is self-weighted. Quota sampling is a stratified sampling method with a sample allocation that is proportional to the stratum weights and where the sampling within a stratum is conducted in a judgmental way.

4.28 The following example illustrates the concept of quota sampling. If there is a characteristic that allows dividing a product group into three product types (for example, red delicious apples, granny smith apples, and Honeycrisp apples), each representing 30, 20, and 50 percent of household expenditure, then the sampled prices will also represent the same proportions. If there are 10 prices to be collected, a quota sampling approach recommends that three prices are collected for the first product type, two for the second and five for the third. If the Dutot index is used, then quantities should be used instead of expenditure for defining the importance of the strata.

Representative Item Method

4.29 In the representative item method, one or several item specifications are defined to represent the item. For example, spaghetti may be a representative item for "Pasta." In this example, the price changes for pasta will be measured using the sampled price changes for spaghetti. According to this method, only varieties matching the specification are priced and no varieties falling outside the specifications will enter the index. The sampling of representative items for a CPI is usually purposive or judgmental, because of the lack of adequate sampling frames that formally list all the possible product types.

4.30 If the representative item method is used for sampling products, the number of items must be sufficiently large to properly represent the diversity of products that can be found in a given product category. Prices that belong to the same representative item may be relatively homogeneous, both with regard to price level and price change. What matters is the variance in price changes between the different representative items that could be selected. Sampling variance can be reduced by specifying more representative items in those product categories where the price change variance between the representative items is large.

Stratification

4.31 A common sampling technique used in the CPI is to divide, in advance, the universe into disjoint homogeneous subpopulations or strata. An independent sample of appropriate size is then selected for each stratum using any of the probability or nonprobability sampling techniques previously described in this chapter. Stratified systematic random sampling is a sampling technique in which systematic random sampling is conducted independently within each of the predefined strata.

4.32 Stratification can be applied to all of the different samples relevant for the CPI. In practice, the CPI is typically stratified by geography (for example, region, city, rural, or urban), by type of outlet or by outlet, and by item/product. Samples are set up within each geographic area, for each of the different outlet types, and for each item/product within outlets. For example, suppose that the CPI classification contains the item refrigerators that can be stratified by region. In a given region, refrigerators are primarily sold in larger specialized shop chains and in several small independent shops. In addition, refrigerators can be classified according to their capacity. Such a stratification structure is illustrated in Table 4.3. Within each cell, prices can be sampled using a two-stage approach. In the first step, specialized chains and independent shops that sell this type of goods are selected within the different regions. In the selected outlets, specific refrigerator models that meet the product-type specifications are then identified for continuous pricing.

Table 4.3 Stratification by Region, Outlet Type, and Product Type

Type of Outlet Product		Region 1		Region 2	
		Specialized Chains	Independent Shops	Specialized Chains	Independent Shops
Refrigerator Capacity	**Small Capacity**				
	Large Capacity				

4.33 Formally, if a subcomponent of the CPI is composed of several strata and the subindex for stratum k is labeled I_k, then the subcomponent's estimate is obtained using the strata's weights and indices:

$$I = \frac{\sum_{k \in K} w_k I_k}{\sum_{k \in K} w_k} \tag{4.1}$$

where w_k is the weight of stratum k. The weight of the stratum corresponds to the expenditure of that stratum, and not only to the (smaller) expenditure of the locations, outlets, or varieties that have been sampled within that stratum.

4.34 Ideally, the stratification should be designed to minimize the sampling error. The strata should be constructed so that the variance of the price changes within strata is low, while the variance between the strata can remain large. A low-price change variance within stratum also has the advantage that results obtained using different price indices are likely to be similar. Consequently, the choice of the elementary aggregate price index will have a smaller impact on the final results.

4.35 Stratified sampling avoids selection bias by ensuring that the universe is appropriately represented, as it controls for the fact that prices must be collected for each specified stratum. Without stratification, certain parts of the universe may be completely ignored. In addition, the use of explicit weights, if available, guarantees that the prices are weighted according to the importance of each stratum. In price statistics, stratification thus helps reduce the bias of the estimates.

4.36 Stratification is a useful strategy to make the sample more efficient. The allocation of the number of prices across the strata is further discussed later in this chapter (paragraphs 4.83–4.94). Furthermore, the availability of detailed subindices can be convenient for meeting specific publication needs. The impact of stratification on sample sizes using different elementary aggregation formulas has been analyzed by De Gregorio (2012).

4.37 Although the universe can exhaustively be divided into a set of strata K, there are circumstances where only a sample of these strata $S(K)$ is used in practice for index compilation. Only prices belonging to the sampled strata $S(K)$ will be collected. The strata can be selected purposively. One strategy could be to select only the most important strata, which is equivalent to running a cutoff sampling procedure. The bias that results from this process depends on the weight of the omitted strata and on the difference between the price change of the omitted strata and the sampled prices. If the weight of the omitted strata is small or their price change is similar to the price change of the sampled prices, then the bias may be small.

4.38 If the strata composing the index structure are selected using probability sampling, then the aggregation of the stratum indices should be adjusted using sampling weights. In particular, if expenditure is used as the size variable in PPS sampling, the higher-level estimate is compiled as the simple arithmetic average of the sampled stratum indices. In the example shown in Table 4.1, three outlets were selected using PPS sampling. If outlets 4, 6, and 10 each represent a stratum in the index structure, then the weight associated with each stratum does not correspond to the actual weight of that outlet. Instead, an unbiased estimate is obtained by equally weighting the three stratum indices:

$$I = \frac{30}{90} I_{\text{Outlet\_4}} + \frac{30}{90} I_{\text{Outlet\_6}} + \frac{30}{90} I_{\text{Outlet\_10}} \tag{4.2}$$

4.39 A challenge arises in systematic PPS sampling when the size of a stratum is larger than the interval value. In such a situation, a distinction must be made between the larger strata that are selected with certainty ("take-all" strata) and the other strata that are sampled after the larger units have been removed (the "take-some" strata). The higher-level index is then obtained as a weighted average of two subindices. The first subindex covers all the certainty strata, while the second subindex contains a sample of some of the lower weighted strata. In the first subindex, the actual weights of the certainty strata must be used in the aggregation, as these strata only represent themselves. In the second subindex, the remaining sampled strata are aggregated with equal weights.

Sampling Stages in a Consumer Price Index

4.40 In practice, national statistical offices often adopt four levels of sampling in a CPI: locations, items within different sections of the expenditure classification, outlets within locations, and item varieties.[2] These four steps are discussed in the following paragraphs. The product level is related to the outlet level. At some point, the sample of items must be matched to the sample of outlets to decide which items are priced in which outlets. Time is an additional sampling level that must be considered. If timing is relevant, it may be necessary to incorporate timing elements in the outlet or item specifications.

[2]The order of the sampling stages can differ. For instance, varieties could be selected centrally and then outlets could be selected to price these varieties. Alternatively, outlets could be selected first, and the choice of the specific varieties to be priced is only taken when the price collector visits the outlet.

Sampling of Locations

4.41 The objective of the first sampling stage is to select the locations where prices are going to be collected. A location is an area where outlets that sell products to households can be found. Ideally, a large part of the CPI product basket should be available to purchase within each location. To obtain a representative sample of outlets, it may be necessary to create locations by combining, for example, out-of-town shopping areas that mainly sell non-food items with a neighboring urban area in which food is available. The sampling of locations can be omitted if outlets are directly sampled independently of where they are located.

4.42 To define the list of possible locations, a decision must be made on the geographical scope of the price collection areas. For example, price collection can be limited to the capital city only or to the main cities of a country or of a region. Some countries restrict price collection to urban areas because of the challenges and costs of collecting prices in rural areas. Alternatively, it can be decided to select locations belonging to both urban and rural areas. Under the broadest geographical scope, locations must be sampled to be representative of the national territory as a whole (as further discussed in Chapter 2).

4.43 The sampling of locations is typically conducted using regional stratification. Location selection can then be done separately within each region. For instance, the strata used for sampling can be aligned with the administrative subdivisions of a country and considered the distinction between urban and rural areas. In principle, stratification works best if the locations of a stratum are homogeneous. In that sense, the territory could also be partitioned by grouping together the locations that are situated close to each other or that have similar sociodemographic characteristics. If no regional stratification is used, locations are sampled directly at the national level.

4.44 Within each region, some locations may be selected with certainty, and the selection process is not random. This can be the case of the main cities. Locations can also be selected randomly, using, for example, systematic PPS sampling. To apply this kind of technique, a variable that measures the size of the locations must be available and the number of sampled locations within a region must be fixed in advance. As the information on expenditure made by households in outlets situated in a given location is rarely available, proxy measures must be used. The number of households living in a location can be used as a size variable, although the residence of a household does not necessarily coincide with the place of purchase. Population size can be obtained from population registers or from a recent census. The number of locations to be selected in each region can be determined as the proportion of national expenditure, income, or a corresponding proxy measure, such as regional gross domestic product, in that region, multiplied by the total number of locations to be visited nationally.

4.45 There are operational implications for setting up a new price collection in the sampled locations, and the process described previously may need to be modified for practical considerations. For example, because data collection costs are important, it may not be efficient to send a price collector to a small isolated location where many of the items in the CPI basket are not available for pricing. Location resampling might be needed, although it is likely to be conducted on a less frequent basis than outlet or product resampling. Sample coordination techniques can be used to adjust the initial selection probabilities to increase the likelihood of an overlap between the old and the new sample of locations.

Sampling of Items

4.46 Cutoff sampling can be applied to select the items that comprise the CPI basket. Expenditure data on items are typically obtained from a household budget survey (see Chapter 3 for more information on data sources). However, not all items for which expenditure data are available might be included in the CPI basket. There may be low-expenditure items for which it would not be an efficient use of limited resources to collect prices (although they are within the scope of the CPI). Thresholds can be defined to identify the low-expenditure items that will not be included in the CPI sample.

4.47 In practice, an expenditure share is estimated for all the items that could be included in the basket. If this share is below a given threshold, the item could be excluded. For example, it might be decided to exclude from the index items with an expenditure share lower than 0.1 percent for food items and 0.2 percent for nonfood items. A lower minimum threshold for the food items might be set because the prices of these products tend to display a higher variability and because prices for food products are usually less costly to collect. If an item is excluded, its expenditure may be redistributed to another expenditure group with similar content and price development.

4.48 The cutoff process can be conducted at the national level or separately within a region. The list of items used in each region may differ. This approach ensures that the regional baskets are representative of the consumption structure within each region. Manual adjustments may also be needed so that an item that falls below the threshold can nevertheless be included in the basket. For example, it may not be so costly to collect a few additional prices if these are collected together with prices for more important items. The additional costs may be acceptable given the advantage of achieving wider product coverage.

4.49 The descriptions (or detailed specifications) of the items that are included in the CPI basket can be general or more detailed. This largely depends on how detailed expenditure data were recorded in the household budget survey. If information is available from other sources, a finer stratification can be developed. In any case, the universe of varieties that fall within the scope of an item is often quite large. Consequently, additional sampling is required at this level for the selection of the specific varieties to be priced over time.

4.50 To provide effective control over the sample of prices collected in the field, a list of product types (items) can be drawn up by the national statistical office using specifications. This is what is referred to as the representative item method (as described in 4.29–4.30). The product group is thus represented by a sample of specified product types (items). The selection of representative items at a central level ensures that they are representative of consumer behavior, rather than of one shopping location. Consistent with the principle of a fixed basket, the representative items are usually reviewed periodically at the same time as the weights and chain linking is carried out. The disadvantage of this method is that the national specification may often be unavailable in some locations and does not reflect regional tastes and preferences.

4.51 A representative variety can be defined using either loose or tight specifications. For example, it may be decided to collect prices for "Tea," which is a loose specification, as it encompasses many different tea varieties that could be selected to be priced. Alternatively, the representative variety may be specified tightly, as a specific variety of tea defined by a brand, flavor, and package size. The discussion between loose and tight specifications has implications for the choice of the elementary aggregate formula (see Chapter 8 for more information).

4.52 If specifications are too tight, the price collectors may have difficulty in finding the varieties, and this will lead to fewer price quotes and a deficit in the sample. There is also a risk that tight specifications will miss important parts of the market, and consequently, results can be biased. For these reasons, the representative variety method is more suitable for homogeneous product groups. In heterogeneous groups, it is more likely that important segments of the item universe, with different price movements, will be left out.

4.53 Loose specifications give the price collector some freedom in choosing locally popular items and varieties and to adjust the sample to match local conditions. It will normally lead to greater representativity of the sample, as it will reflect regional tastes and preferences. However, this approach may require training for price collectors on how to select within the outlet a variety to be priced that matches the loose specifications. This requires a more formal process selecting the varieties within an outlet. Even with loose specifications, the variety selected in the outlet must be described in sufficient detail by the price collector to ensure that the same variety is priced over time, and in case of a replacement, a correct quality adjustment can be made.

Sampling of Outlets

4.54 Different data sources can be used as sampling frames for selecting outlets. In the CPI, an outlet should be defined broadly to include any retail channel that sells goods or services to households, including different types of physical shops, online shops, or the offices of providers of utilities even when a physical shop that customers can visit is not available. Outlets to be visited in the field may be selected only in locations that were previously identified as price collection centers.

4.55 Business registers can be a starting point for selecting outlets. Business registers are databases that list the business units resident in a given area and contain information such as location, type of business activity, turnover, and employment. Business registers should be updated regularly for new businesses and for closures. One limitation of business registers is that, in some cases, data are available only at the level of establishment or enterprise, and the information at the local level is not always available or regularly updated. Provided that some size measure is included in the database, such as number of employees, business registers can be used for selecting a PPS sample. Similarly, tax data such as value-added tax records may be used as a data source that has a wide coverage and contains timely information on outlets. Tax records typically refer to a legal unit that can be composed of one or several outlets. With tax data, the selection of random samples can usually be based on gross sales as the measure of size.

4.56 Administrative records kept by local government, business associations, or marketplace managers are another potential data source for outlet sample selection. These records can be used to create sampling frames and might be particularly useful for sampling local markets. Depending on the availability of information on size, these sources might provide a frame for PPS sampling. Business telephone directories usually contain less information, such as the business name, address, and activity, and do not include any size information. Therefore, telephone directories are useful for simple random sampling or systematic sampling, but not for PPS sampling unless additional information is made available, for example, by visiting the outlets.

4.57 Information on outlets can also be obtained from surveys designed for this purpose. For example, the objective of point-of-purchase surveys is to collect information on the place where purchases are made by households and on the amount of these purchases. In some cases, the household budget survey includes information on the outlets or type of outlet from where the households purchased the goods and services recorded. Surveys that include this information could be used as a source of relevant data on outlets for sampling frames. However, as these surveys are based on a sample, they are unlikely to provide an exhaustive list of all outlets and the results obtained may become quickly out of date.

4.58 If the data sources described previously are not available, it is necessary to enumerate the outlets within a selected location to provide supplementary information for the sampling frame or even to construct a sampling frame. This enumeration can be made by price collectors and their supervisors, visiting each location and noting details (for example, name, type of outlet, and items sold) of all retail outlets found. This can be costly, and the price statistician will need to compare the costs and benefits of a more representative sample. To reduce costs, the number of outlets enumerated per location may be limited by enumerating only a subdivision of a location. The ideal size measure of an outlet is turnover. However, a proxy may be used when an estimate of turnover is not available. For instance, the approximate net retail floor space estimated by the outlet enumerators may provide an adequate alternative. Additionally, it is important that the assortment of goods and services sold by the outlet is recorded, to allow matching the outlets with the CPI product basket.

4.59 If none of the formal sampling techniques are feasible, outlets must be selected in a more judgmental way. For example, field staff can identify the largest retail and service outlets where households typically shop for a given type of product. Additional guidance may be provided to the price collector by specifying the type of outlet or by defining the area where outlets are to be selected, to ensure that the overall sample of outlets remains representative of where households shop. This sampling method often involves visits by the price collector to the outlet to gather the necessary information on the outlet's characteristics before deciding which outlets are included in the sample and before the first price collection is conducted. For example, if prices for children's clothes are to be collected, a price collector may visit a clothing shop initially selected from a central list to verify and check whether it sells clothes for children and not just for adults.

4.60 The sampling strategy for outlets typically relies on stratification by outlet type. Within each stratum, outlets are sampled randomly or purposively if no appropriate sampling frame is available. For example, the number of outlets to be sampled in each stratum could be proportional to the weight of that stratum. In any case, all significant outlet types should be covered. If relevant, the internet can also be considered as an outlet type or stratum from which specific websites are selected.

4.61 As similar price trends can be expected in the outlets that belong to the same chain, it may be useful to also stratify by retail chain. For example, the sample design could include a first stratum that contains all the major retail chains as substrata and a second stratum that covers the remaining independent shops. In this case, outlets can be selected separately for each retail chain and from the remaining universe of independent shops. The index should be designed so that the retail chains and other outlet types are properly represented according to their market share.

Sampling of Varieties

4.62 In a final step, the selection of specific varieties within outlets is usually made by the price collector in a purposive way. The objective is to select the most sold variety that fits the item specifications. This process essentially corresponds to a type of cutoff sampling. In addition to being a high-volume seller, the variety is also expected to be available over time so that the same variety can easily be priced during the following periods.

4.63 A compromise must sometimes be made between representativity and comparability. On the one hand, it is important to select varieties with high sales, as this will ensure that the samples are representative of what households are buying. On the other hand, the future availability of the variety must be considered to improve comparability over time by minimizing the need for replacements. However, there is a risk of bias if the choice of varieties is mainly driven by the convenience to collect. Chapter 5 discusses the price collection in more detail.

4.64 With broad item specifications, many products available in an outlet can be selected for inclusion in the CPI sample. A more formal approach may be adopted by designing a process that approximates PPS sampling to the sales of each product.[3] To apply this technique, all possible

[3] This applies if the Jevons index is used for elementary aggregation. If the Dutot index is used, the size variable should be the number of sales and not the total sales revenue.

products or product types (items) must first be enumerated, and selection probabilities are determined for these products based on their sales, for example, using the information on sales obtained directly from the respondents. Alternatively, shelf space can be used to estimate sales proportions in some cases. Even with no information on sales, random sampling can still be conducted by simply assuming that all products have the same selection probability.

4.65 If the data for the sales measure is taken during a very short period, this may coincide with a special promotion or sale with temporarily reduced prices. If a variety with a temporarily reduced price is given a larger probability for selection, and if this price is likely to increase more than average, an overestimating bias may result. It is thus essential that the sampling takes place before the first price collection or that sales values from an earlier period are used. Generally, annual sales values would be the best measure.

4.66 Administrative data sources are sometimes available with detailed expenditure data by product or by product group. Such data sources can help build detailed stratifications and serve as a sampling frame for selecting the individual varieties to be priced.

4.67 If no explicit weights are used in the elementary aggregate compilation, the sample will be implicitly weighted by the number of observations. For example, if prices of the same two varieties are collected in five outlets, then each outlet and variety implicitly have the same weight. The elementary aggregate is often the lowest level for which weights are available. However, efforts can be made to improve the accuracy of this detailed subindex using implicit or explicit weights. The sample can be designed so that the proportions within an elementary aggregate represent those of the universe with respect to the outlet type or outlet, if these aspects are not explicitly weighted in the CPI aggregation structure. Similarly, the sample should be well balanced with respect to product type (item) or item characteristics. For example, if local beer has an approximate market share of 80 percent and imported beer of 20 percent, these proportions can be reflected in the elementary aggregate. Chapter 8 discusses the use of weights within elementary aggregates in more detail.

Sampling in Time

4.68 The timing of price collection is chosen purposively in most cases. The main principle is that the prices of each item should be collected each month at the same time, during the same week or the same day of the month. If there is some price variation within a day, it is important that prices are collected always at the same time of the day. Price collection can be limited to a certain week of the month, for example, during the middle of the month, or it can be spread over several weeks of the month according to some pattern, for example, in different weeks in different regions or for different product groups.

4.69 If prices are known to fluctuate considerably during a month, then an increased price collection frequency should be considered. In this case, it can make sense to collect prices once a week or sometimes once a day instead of once a month, as practical. This could be the case for energy products or for fresh food.

4.70 Some products have a time-dependent component that should be incorporated into the product specifications. For example, for airfares or other transport services, the price can be highly dependent on the day of the week, the time of the flight, and how long in advance the ticket is purchased. Such timing elements should be held constant to ensure the comparability of the collected prices over time. Moreover, the specifications including their time-dependent components should be defined to be representative of consumer behavior.

Central Price Collection

4.71 For some products, prices can be collected centrally by CPI staff. These include those prices obtained from a specific data source or by a survey conducted centrally. The same general principles apply as with price collection in the field in the sense that outlets or respondents must be chosen and specific varieties for regular pricing must be selected. However, there is no operational need to select specific price collection areas in advance, and a broader geographical coverage of price collection can often be achieved. Moreover, it is possible at the head office to design specific sampling strategies adapted to the product or to the data sources at hand. Some examples of central price collection are discussed in the following text.

Scanner Data

4.72 When using scanner data, the product and the outlet sampling levels are closely related. A two-stage sampling approach can be adopted where outlets are sampled first, possibly belonging to the same retail chain or outlet type, and then varieties are selected within the sampled outlets. If price levels are similar between outlets or if data are not available by outlet, varieties can also be sampled at a more aggregated level, for instance at the level of an entire retail chain. Eventually, the compilation methods can be adapted to use all the available data on both prices and quantities, and no sampling is thus involved. Even if scanner data cover “all” transactions, these data do not necessarily cover the entire universe. In principle, the remaining part of the universe should also be covered if it is significant, if it is expected to have different price developments, and if there are sufficient resources to maintain separate price indices not derived from scanner data. Weights must then be used at some level of the index hierarchy so that each part is appropriately represented. Chapter 10 discusses the use of scanner data in detail.

Tariffs

4.73 For many tariffs, there is often a national pricing strategy and the regional dimension discussed previously becomes irrelevant. There may only be a limited number of providers (sometimes only one), and it is straightforward to select either all of them or at least the most important ones, and these can then be explicitly weighted in the index. For tariffs, it is often possible to obtain additional information on products directly from the providers, authorities, regulatory bodies, or other administrative data sources. Consumer profiles are sometimes defined (sampled) to price the tariff structure. Chapter 11 discusses the different price measurement approaches for tariffs.

Rents

4.74 Examples of sampling frames used for rental dwellings are registers of dwellings, lists of addresses, or registers of tenants and landlords. Information may also be available in the microdata of a census of buildings and dwellings. Stratified sampling would be the preferred option to select rents. Typical stratification variables that correlate with rental change are the location, type, and size of the dwelling, the type of rent (social/fixed/regulated rent or market rent), or the type of landlord. Ideally, each stratum should be weighted according to its total rental expenditure and random samples should be drawn within each stratum. If no sampling frame is available and it is too costly to build one, two-stage cluster sampling can be a practical option. The country or the region has first to be divided into detailed geographic subdivisions ("clusters") from which a sample can be drawn. The in-scope rental dwellings of the selected clusters are then enumerated so that a random sample of rents in each selected cluster can eventually be obtained. An alternative approach is to collect rental data directly from real estate agencies. Chapter 11 examines the treatment of housing in a CPI.

Chains with National Pricing Strategies

4.75 Prices can be collected in a single outlet of a larger chain if it is believed that the same price applies in all the other outlets of the same chain across the country. This approach may however be subject to some caveats. First, there is no guarantee that prices are always the same in all the outlets of the same chain. For example, sales or promotions could be outlet-specific. Second, it must be ensured that the varieties selected in one outlet are representative of the consumption habits in the outlets located in the other regions. In any case, the prices must be appropriately weighted in the CPI. If a price quote from a large retail chain is combined with prices from other outlets within an elementary aggregate, an appropriate representation of the retail chain can be achieved through implicit weighting by replicating the price of the retail chain. Alternatively, specific elementary aggregates weighted according to the market shares of the different outlets could be constructed.

Internet

4.76 For prices collected on the internet, a distinction must be made between prices collected online, so that there is no need for a price collector to visit an outlet, or those prices that genuinely represent e-commerce transactions (online or web-based outlets with no physical location). In the latter case, one could still adopt the same sampling strategy as for price collection in the field, by first selecting websites and then selecting specific varieties to be priced. The selected websites are typically organized according to different product categories that can serve as strata for product sampling. Instead of collecting prices for only a few varieties, web scraping techniques can be used to obtain significantly more data in an automated way (see Annex 5.6). Prices collected on the internet can sometimes be highly volatile over time with some websites applying dynamic or personalized pricing strategies. This implies that prices should be collected more often. The number of price quotes collected on a website can be larger than the number of prices collected in the physical outlets because of lower price collection costs, a wider product coverage, or an increased price collection frequency. Chapter 11 discusses the treatment of internet purchases.

Sample Maintenance

4.77 The samples are drawn at a point in time and based on the information available at that moment. However, the situation in the market is seldom static. Products and outlets gain or lose importance over time. New products constantly enter the market while other products may no longer be available. New outlets can open in a certain location and previously popular outlets close. This means that the sample that was set up at an earlier period may not be representative of household expenditure at the current period.

4.78 Over time, the quality of the sample can deteriorate. To avoid this deterioration, it is recommended that samples be continuously reviewed and adjusted as needed (see Chapter 7 for more information on maintaining the sample). If resources do not permit a systematic full review of products and outlets, a rolling review can be set up, where every year a different part of the basket is analyzed. The focus should be on products and outlet locations that are likely to be affected by major developments.

4.79 In practice, feedback received from field staff can be considered to maintain the ongoing representativity of the samples. Price collectors and their supervisors should be encouraged to report if the item specifications used for price collection are no longer in line with the products sold. Through their local knowledge, the staff in charge of price collection may identify new outlets that are becoming popular and should be included in the CPI samples. An increasing number of missing prices can also be an indication that the outlets or the product specifications are no longer appropriate, and action must be taken to update the samples. Some national statistical offices have dedicated product specialists who monitor the markets of complex product groups and can assist with sampling and quality adjustments.

4.80 Replacements are one way of preserving the representativity of the samples over time. In some cases, price collectors find that an outlet at which they have been collecting prices closes or no longer stocks one of the products being priced. Disappearing outlets and varieties within a specific outlet are handled by replacing on a one-to-one basis when the outlet closes or the variety ceases to be sold. A more proactive approach can also be adopted by anticipating the expected disappearance of an outlet or a variety so that the number of forced replacements is kept to a minimum.

4.81 The criteria for selecting replacements will vary. An outlet can be replaced on a like-for-like basis by another outlet of the same type, in the same or similar location, selling the same or similar range of items and varieties. In replacing a variety, two strategies are usually adopted. If the initial selection rule was "most sold" or "probability proportional to (sales) size" then the replacement may follow the same rule with the advantage of maintaining the representativity of the sample. However, the replacement variety may no longer be comparable to the variety that it replaces. In this case, quality-adjustment methods must be applied to ensure the index measures pure price changes (see Chapter 6 for more information on quality adjustments). There is a risk of bias if the differences in quality are not properly adjusted. Alternatively, the replacement may be made based on the variety most similar to the one which disappeared, thereby reducing the need for quality adjustment. When replacements are performed, there is an inherent tension between representativity and comparability.

4.82 The dynamic nature of the target universe can also be addressed through sample rotation involving a full or a partial resampling. Sample rotation is a technique where the length of time that outlets and varieties are included in the price surveys sample is limited. In a given period (for example, every year or every two years), a defined proportion (for example, 20 percent or 25 percent) are rotated out of the sample and replaced with a new sample of outlets and varieties for that proportion thereafter. The process of resampling can be based on any of the methods and sampling frames that are used for initial sample selection. Resampling in the CPI can apply to outlets or even locations. Technically, resampling involves an overlap period where the first period of the new sample overlaps with the last period of the old sample.

Variance Estimation and Optimal Allocation

4.83 A CPI is a statistic with a complex sampling design that involves different stages and that often relies on nonprobability sampling methods. Therefore, estimating the variance of a CPI is not a trivial task. Strictly speaking, variance estimation is only applicable in case of probability sampling, as the sampling mechanism is known. To the extent that samples in a CPI are not probability-based, variance estimates must rely on models in which some type of random sampling is assumed. Different approaches for variance estimation in a CPI have been developed, taking into account national circumstances. It is useful to know the sampling error of a CPI as this can inform the users about the level of precision of the published indices. The interpretation of such error margins depends on the specific approach adopted for variance estimation

4.84 A very general form of a CPI is $I = \sum_k w_k I_k$, where k denotes products, w_k is the expenditure share of this product, and I_k is the product price index. If the estimation of each product index was independent, the variance would be $V(I) = \sum_k w_k^2 V(I_k)$, where $V(I_k)$ denotes the variance of the product index k. However, product indices are not statistically independent. For instance, the price change of different products collected in the same outlet can be related. The sampling errors of the product indices are therefore correlated, which means that this expression probably underestimates the total sampling errors to some extent.

4.85 From an operational point of view, variance estimation is a useful tool for deciding on the optimal allocation of sample prices. Many resources are spent on price collection to produce a CPI. It is therefore worthwhile to devote some effort to allocating these resources in the most efficient way. A better allocation of prices can often minimize the sampling error and consequently improve the quality of the CPI without increasing the resources associated with price collection activities. If a variance and a cost function are known, an optimization program can be defined to minimize the variance given the budget available for price collection. Alternatively, costs can be minimized under the constraint that a minimal variance must be achieved.

4.86 The general approach to distribute the number of observations across strata was established by Neyman. If each stratum has a known weight w_k and samples are drawn randomly and independently in each stratum, then the standard deviation of the individual price changes (not the price levels) within a stratum can be denoted by s_k. In addition, let c_k be the cost to collect one unit in stratum k. If the total sample size is n, the following allocation is optimal:

$$n_k = n \frac{w_k s_k / \sqrt{c_k}}{\sum_k w_k s_k / \sqrt{c_k}} \tag{4.3}$$

4.87 This expression formally shows that the number of observations in a stratum should be proportional to the weight of that stratum times the standard deviation of the price changes and inversely proportional to the square root of the unit cost. The expression can be simplified by assuming that costs are identical in all strata. The underlying idea is that more price observations are needed for those strata with a higher weight and a significant variance in price changes. Additionally, it is sufficient to allocate fewer prices to the strata with a smaller weight and more similar price changes.

4.88 In practice, there are challenges in systematically applying this type of allocation. While stratum weights are in principle available, the estimation of the standard deviation of price changes may be more problematic. One disadvantage of this approach is that it depends on the target price change. For instance, the prices can be compared to the previous month or to the same month of the previous year. The optimal allocation can be different if it is derived for monthly price changes or for annual price changes. Moreover, the standard deviation of price changes of a stratum is not necessarily constant over time.

4.89 Data sources, such as previous CPI surveys, can be used to estimate the standard deviations of the price changes of each stratum. However, there is a risk that an estimation based only on past observed prices is biased. Considering the situation in which a stratum is represented by a unique item with very tight specifications, the prices collected in the different outlets may all change at a similar rate, and this will consequently lead to a low sample price change variance. The true population price change variance may be much larger than the estimated because of the unobserved price change behavior of the varieties that belong to the stratum but are not included in the CPI sample.

4.90 Costs also need to be considered when defining sample sizes. It may be more time-consuming and complex, and, hence, costly, to collect prices for some goods and services than for others. For instance, for products where quality adjustment plays an important role, the price collector can be asked to record, in addition to the price, many technical characteristics. Moreover, some outlets have larger assortments, meaning that more prices can be collected in one outlet, which then reduces the cost per collected price. In practice, the prices could be classified in categories, such as "easy to collect" or "difficult to collect." Such ordinal information could be used to derive an optimal allocation.

Table 4.4 Different Allocation Strategies

Item	Weight (percent)	Price Change Variance	Number of Prices		
			Option 1	Option 2	Option 3
(a)	(b)	(c)	(d)	(e)	(f)
Item 1	10	Medium	20	10 percent × 100 = 10	11
Item 2	40	Medium	20	40	43
Item 3	25	Low	20	25	18
Item 4	20	Medium	20	20	21
Item 5	5	High	20	5	7
Total	**100**		**100**	**100**	**100**

A more advanced quantification of costs would be based on estimates of the average time per collected price by product or product group, while considering the travel time from one outlet to another.

4.91 In Table 4.4, a sample of 100 prices needs to be distributed over five items. A first strategy consists of collecting the same number of prices for each item (option 1). Instead of allocating the same number of price observations to each stratum, an alternative approach consists of linking the number of prices to the weight, collecting more prices in those strata that have a larger weight (option 2). This will improve the sampling error of the subindices that have more impact on the higher-level aggregates because of their weight. In addition, judgments can be made on the magnitude of the variance. This means that the sample sizes should be increased (or decreased) for strata with an expected higher (or lower) price change variance. As an approximation, the Neyman allocation formula is applied by assuming factors of 1 (low), 1.5 (medium), and 2 (high) for the standard deviation. The result of the allocation can be found in the last column (option 3). Because the price change variance is expected to be low for item 3 (as indicated in column C), sample size for this item is decreased whereas the number of prices to be collected for the other items increases. Out of these three options, the third allocation aims at reducing the sampling variance while keeping the total number of prices collected unchanged. Finally, the sample size per stratum should not drop below a fixed threshold to avoid formula bias or to guarantee a sufficient precision if stratum indices are separately published. Totals are shown in bold.

4.92 To design optimal samples, it must be well understood how the different sampling stages contribute to the CPI variance. For example, consider a two-stage sampling design, where outlets are sampled first and then varieties are selected within the sampled outlets. The sampling variance of the price index can be decomposed into a sum of two terms that are linked to these two stages. The first term relates to the variance of the price changes between the outlets, and the second term relates to the variance of the price changes of the varieties that are available within an outlet.

4.93 If the price changes between the outlets are rather homogeneous but the price changes of the different varieties that are sold in an outlet are more diverse, then the preferred strategy is to select a smaller number of outlets and a larger sample of varieties within each outlet. In addition, such a strategy is cost-efficient as it is often less costly to sample an additional price in an already selected outlet than to increase the outlet sample. For example, in some countries, car prices do not vary much across outlets for the same model and specification, but there are many models with different prices. One car retailer could easily provide prices for several models during the same collection period.

4.94 The time dimension must also be considered for price collection. If prices vary a lot over time, it is preferable to collect more prices for the same product during a month. For example, petrol prices normally show little variation among outlets on the same day while prices can vary considerably even over a month. It would thus make sense to have a relatively small sample of outlets but follow prices several times in the same month. The time dimension is also highly relevant for internet purchases. As it is probably less costly to consult websites than to visit physical outlets, it can be feasible to improve the temporal coverage of prices collected on the internet.

Key Recommendations

- When designing samples for the CPI, the index compiler must consider the different sampling stages relevant for a CPI: geographic and outlet, products, and time. All significant parts of that universe should be appropriately represented unless there are excessive costs or estimation problems involved in doing so.
- The CPI aggregation structure is organized according to a product classification, and possibly stratified by region and by outlet type.
- Within each stratum, the collected prices are typically the result of multistage sampling designs. Price collection locations and items are defined beforehand. Outlets that sell the items of interest must then be chosen in the selected locations. The specific varieties to be priced may only be selected when the price collector visits the outlet.
- Either probability or nonprobability sampling techniques can be used. Probability sampling is the preferred option if detailed sampling frames that include data on size (for example, total sales) are available.
- Samples should be reasonably optimized, based on at least a rudimentary analysis of sampling variance. Different options can be considered:
  - Best method would be to multiply each weight by a measure of price change dispersion in the group. Variance and cost considerations together call for allocations where relatively many products are measured per outlet and relatively few outlets are contained in the sample.
  - Second-best method would be to set the sample sizes approximately proportional to the weights of the product groups.

PRICE COLLECTION AND VALIDATION 5

Introduction

5.1 Several factors will determine the choice of which price collection methods a national statistical office (NSO) uses, taking into consideration efficiency, accuracy, and representativity of consumers' purchasing patterns. For example, local price collection is costly but can have the advantage of covering a wide range of locations and items, particularly for food, alcohol, tobacco, and durable goods such as clothing, furniture, and electrical products. On the other hand, central collection, either at the head office or in regional offices, can be cheaper and may be used for products where there are national pricing policies, as for rail fares, or where prices cannot be observed directly in retail outlets, such as for many professional services. With regard to representing consumers' purchasing patterns, the price collection method also needs to reflect methods of shopping. For instance, internet purchases or goods purchased through mail order and catalogs need to be properly reflected in the sample.

5.2 Price collection will therefore require different practical solutions in different countries according to local circumstances. Thus, the most appropriate sampling and survey methods, and the best data sources for price collection will depend on the structure of retailing with regard to the characteristics of outlets, their geographical spread, and the range of goods and services available to purchase, plus the shopping behavior of the households covered by the index. The compiler should always be guided by the principles and objectives of the price index being compiled, as addressed in earlier chapters.

5.3 Price collection is becoming increasingly multimodal with prices being web scraped from the internet or obtained from scanner data, as well as being collected by hand from outlets and by telephone inquiry. Issues of coherence can arise when integrating price data from different sources, with relevant consequences. The internet prices charged by online retailers can differ from the prices charged by traditional outlets. Similarly, the internet prices obtained from a retail chain's website and the associated sales volume can differ from the corresponding in-store prices. The prices collected from each source should be weighted according to the respective values of sales via the different channels to ensure the index properly represents the purchases of the target population. Moreover, products representative of in-store sales may not be representative of internet sales and vice versa. Constructing separate elementary aggregates to represent different outlets or outlet types, and aggregating the elementary aggregates using explicit weights relating to the respective sales can help to ensure a balanced sample. For example, prices from a sample of bakeries (using price collectors), prices for bread from supermarkets (using scanner data), and prices obtained via web scraping have to be aggregated in a correct and coherent way taking into account the weights of the different channels or sources. Ideally, indices per data source should be weighted and prices from different sources should not be mixed; however, in practice, this will depend on the availability of data to develop weights.

5.4 The activity of price collection needs to be carefully planned and a number of organizational options can be followed. The focus of this chapter is on traditional forms of price collection where price surveys are undertaken in outlets, using paper forms, handheld computers, or tablets, and supplemented by prices obtained centrally from postal, email, or telephone inquiry. However, the general principles described in paragraphs 5.15–5.49 apply to all types of price collection.

5.5 A separate section details the collection of prices on the internet (paragraphs 5.194–5.208). The use of scanner data is discussed in Chapter 10, considering the conceptual and practical issues associated with the use of these data.

5.6 The relative advantages of central and local price collection will depend on individual country circumstances. A further option involves the outsourcing of certain elements of price collection. In reviewing these options, this chapter covers the relationship between the field and the head office, and the handling of the flow of information.

Organization Options

Local Price Collection

5.7 Local price collection involves collectors visiting individual outlets to collect prices for several goods and services. This is the predominant method of price collection in most countries, although more countries are now starting to use other methods. The range and number of outlets visited and the types of goods and services priced vary among countries.

5.8 Although the precise method of local price collection varies, each price collector is usually responsible for collecting prices from a certain location or from certain types of outlets. Collectors will visit the same outlets in each collection period to attempt to price the same items. Through this type of arrangement, price collectors can build up effective relationships with retailers and gain specialist knowledge.

5.9 There are several important criteria relating to the conduct of the collection:

(1) Collectors should be appropriately dressed and be polite—they are representing the NSO.

(2) Collectors should carry identification to confirm their role and status.

(3) Collectors should make themselves known to the retailer or store manager when they arrive, and before they begin collecting prices.
(4) Collectors should comply with any request from the outlet staff if it does not invalidate the sample. For instance, if the store is very busy, the collector may comply with a request to return later in the day.
(5) The collection should be carried out as quickly as possible, causing minimal disruption to store business.

Central Price Collection

5.10 Centrally collected prices are obtained from the central offices of major retailing chains with national pricing strategies. Branches of these chains may be excluded from the local collection if data can be collected more effectively centrally. Data suppliers may provide information on paper forms, or by sending spreadsheets to the NSO by email, fax, or on external media such as a flash memory stick. Mail order catalogs can also be treated in the same way. These prices are then combined with those for the same items from the local collection. Prices can also be collected centrally online or by using web scraping or scanner data (see paragraphs 5.194–5.208 and Annex 5.6 and, for scanner data, Chapter 10).

5.11 Price data for services or fees may be collected centrally from organizations such as trade associations or national or local governmental departments. This is often the case for tariffs, for example, for gas and electricity, or for telephone and internet charges, where data from administrative sources on pricing structures and purchasing patterns are required (see Chapter 11).[1] Whenever possible, centrally collected prices are obtained from one central source, although contact with regional or competing companies is needed if there are local variations. Data may be requested in writing, by telephone, or may be delivered automatically because the NSO is on a provider's mailing list. Providers may send a full price list or tariff sheet, from which the relevant prices will be extracted by the consumer price index (CPI) staff, or just the prices of the items specified in the data request. It is good practice to confirm price quotations by some form of written documentation. When collecting prices from the internet, screen prints can be useful as displayed prices can frequently change (see paragraphs 5.194–5.208 relating to collecting prices online). Frequency of inquiry can vary across the range of items depending on when prices are known or expected to change. The most common frequencies are monthly, quarterly, and annual, but there are also instances of collecting as frequently as weekly or even daily. The frequency depends on price volatility. For regulated and fixed prices, collection could occur on the date when the change becomes effective. For instance, this may be the case where tariffs for gas, electricity, and water change once a year on a set date. Internal checking procedures need to be in place for centrally collected prices, because these prices can often represent items with a relatively high expenditure weight. Credibility checking should be carried out to test the reliability of the collected prices, for instance, by comparing whether the price change relative to the previous price looks reasonable compared with historic evidence while taking into account sales prices.

The Principles of Price Collection

5.12 The procedures for price collection should follow the general concepts underlying the CPI and should reflect the expenditure of the target population.

Defining the Price

5.13 Given that the aim of the CPI is to measure price inflation, prices are defined according to what consumers pay in the marketplace (that is, the actual transaction prices of goods and services purchased by the consumer, including all taxes). However, in practice, the advertised price is usually selected because it can be readily observed. Practical difficulties stem from the existence of discounts offered when stock is sold off or when end-of-line, damaged, or special stock is brought in at sale time. In these cases, special procedures apply. Another complication that can arise is bargaining, where a price might not be displayed or where goods and services are purchased on the black market. Procedures to address these situations are discussed in paragraphs 5.24–5.29.

Nontransaction Prices

5.14 There are some exceptions that deviate from the stated aim of measuring actual transaction prices. The most notable example is the treatment of owner-occupied housing services, where alternative conceptual approaches require different measurement methodologies, and the choice of conceptual treatment depends on the main purpose of the index. For some services, the transaction price may be represented by a tariff or daily or hourly rate. More details on owner-occupied housing and tariffs are discussed in Chapter 11.

Catalog and List Prices (Not Mail Order)[2]

5.15 Catalog or list prices provided by the supplier to the retail outlet are in many cases identical to the transaction price. However, the catalog or list price may only be the recommended price and not the actual price the item is sold at. Even where it is supposed to be the actual price charged, retailers may not always comply with the prescribed prices. Although the use of catalog prices is contrary to the principle of recording transaction prices, in practice it can be a cost-effective method of obtaining prices. Therefore, catalog or list prices can be used, but their reliability should be confirmed periodically.

Price Reductions and Related Issues

5.16 Transaction prices may differ from advertised prices, for example, if at time of purchase a discount is

[1] There are a number of common issues associated with the use of administrative sources for the use of listed prices in the CPI, including coverage, definitions, data quality, and resilience of supply. For instance, does the source relate to the definition of the population being measured (transaction prices and sales to private households)? What is the quality of the data source (up to date with no errors)? How resilient is the supply (appropriate gateways available to access the data in an appropriate and reliable form on a regular and timely basis)?

[2] The pricing of goods and services ordered by mail can be conducted by reference to mail order catalogs. The index will need to include posting and packaging costs.

offered. In practice, however, discriminatory discounts, which are available only to a restricted group of households (as opposed to nondiscriminatory discounts that are available to all), are generally excluded on principle. For example, money-off coupons and loyalty rewards for previous expenditure are normally ignored and the nondiscounted price is recorded. Also, it may be difficult to obtain the price paid if it is subject to individual bargaining. The following practices are recommended to address different types of price reductions. Price collectors should make extensive notes on the situations confronted so that decisions on how to treat specific cases can be reviewed and confirmed at the head office. In general, if on the day scheduled for price collection, the price of an item is reduced due to sale or promotion, the reduced price is collected even if the sale or promotion is only for one or two days.

(1) *Discounted prices*: should only be included if generally available to everyone with no conditions attached; otherwise, the nondiscounted or unsubsidized price should be recorded. The general practice is to ignore money-off coupons and loyalty rewards. A judgment needs to be made, however, relating to the interpretation of "generally available." For instance, reduced prices for payment by direct debit may be collected depending on the extent to which consumers have access to, and use, of this service. A judgment is required on the threshold to be set for access, above which the discounted price is included in the index. Alternatively, for tariffs, different payment methods may all be priced individually (for example, separate data collection for payments for electricity by cash, direct debit, and prepayment) and the prices weighted and aggregated to form a single price index for that item.

(2) *Price discrimination*: discounts systematically available only to a restricted group of households should be disregarded because they are discriminatory, unless they are significant and are available either to the vast majority of the population or to identifiable subgroups who qualify for such discounts on the basis of demographic or other characteristics not requiring action by the individuals concerned at the time of purchase. If included, they should be treated as stratification or coverage issues in item sampling. A judgment is required from the compiler. Examples of price discrimination generally included in the CPI may include lower prices offered to senior citizens (for example, discounted travel or haircuts) and discounts for people who receive state benefits. An example where prices are not universally available and judgment is required is when a nominal or token membership fee is required by the retail outlet. In these cases, the take-up of such membership, which is widely available, needs to be considered with regard to thresholds and general spending patterns of the consumers and the conditions placed on membership that may make it restrictive (for example, minimum levels of purchase). See paragraphs 5.24–5.29 for a discussion on price bargaining.

(3) *Sale or special offer prices*: should be recorded if they are temporary reductions on items likely to be available again at normal prices or are stock-clearing sales (for example, January sales or summer sales). However, before designating a price as a "sale" price, special care should be taken to ascertain that there is a genuine sale with price reductions on normal stock. On occasion, stock is continually sold below the recommended retail price or advertised as a special offer even though these prices are available all year. In such cases, prices should not be considered as sale prices, but should still be collected. Special purchases of end-of-season, damaged, or defective goods should not normally be priced, as they are likely not of the same quality as, or comparable with, goods previously priced and are unlikely to be available in the future. If the special offer is limited to the first customers, the item should not be priced, as the offer is not available to everyone. Introductory special offers may be included if they are available to all. However, given the need to price the same "basket" each month, such offers will not be chosen as representative items, unless they have sufficient volume of sales to be considered representative and are introduced at the time of an update of the basket, or when a replacement item needs to be chosen. Discounts on goods close to expiry date should be disregarded or treated as specification or quality changes.

(4) *Bonus offers, extras, and free gifts*: prices for items temporarily bearing extra quantities (for example, 30 percent extra free) should be adjusted to take account of the increased quantity unless it can be determined that the extra quantities involved will not be wanted by most consumers, will not have influenced the decision to purchase, and will not be consumed. Similarly, "2 for the price of 1" offers should be included. The reasoning behind this is that, if the CPI is tracking the price of a specific product, say a 330-milliliter can of a diet soda, and the offer is two cans for the price of one, the consumer will always take the two cans representing a 50 percent discount on a single can. However, an offer of three cans for the price of two would be disregarded because the offer requires the purchase of two cans and the item specification is for a single can. Money-off coupons for future purchases are usually disregarded as these may not be used or wanted. Free items with other purchases (for example, a free gift with every product purchased) are generally disregarded. For example, free gifts such as plastic toys in cereal boxes should be ignored because they are not included in the list for price observations; it is the price to be paid for the cereal in the box that is relevant. Also, such free gifts can be difficult to value. Similarly, receiving a free toothbrush when buying a bottle of mouthwash should be disregarded because it would be difficult to value the free gift and the consumer may only want the mouthwash and not the toothbrush. The treatment of bonus offers, extras, and free gifts is subject to interpretation on a case-by-case basis. Collectors should be aware that temporary "special offer" weight changes (X percent extra free) could become a permanent weight change (for example, cans of alcoholic drinks changing size from 440 milliliters to 500 milliliters) and should feed the information back to the head office as they become aware of it. In this way,

CPI staff can issue new or amended guidance to price collectors about item specifications.

(5) *Stamps*: sometimes purchasers are given special stamps, which can be accumulated and subsequently exchanged for goods and services. If a discount is available as an alternative to such stamps, then the discounted price should be recorded. Otherwise, the stamps should be disregarded.

(6) *Trade-ins*: in general, the price reduction obtained by trading in an old item (for example, a car) compared with the nominal full price should be ignored. This treatment follows convention, as the transaction essentially relates to a second-hand good and only the service charge levied by the outlet in buying and selling the good comes under the scope of the index. In practice, however, the situation is not so clear-cut. For instance, a garage may give a discount that is greater than the retail value of the traded-in car and, therefore, in effect gives a genuine discount on the new car. In many cases, discounts from trade-ins are difficult to evaluate. The trade-in value may be negotiable in each case, and the full nominal price—which is used as the benchmark against which the discount is measured—may not be known. It is therefore generally best to report the list price or asking price.

(7) *Sales taxes*: when a tax is not included in the price of individual items in an outlet, but is added when the customer pays for the item, care must be taken to record the price including tax. To make sure of this, with items for which the price is normally quoted pre-tax, and in areas where a general sales tax is added to the bill, the price collection forms should require the collector to indicate whether or not the price recorded includes the tax, as a price check, so that it can be added where necessary.

(8) *Tips for services*: if a compulsory service charge is included, for example, on a restaurant bill, only the compulsory amount should be included in the price, but not any additional discretionary tips. For services that are free in principle, but that in practice can rarely be obtained without a tip, or where tipping at a standard rate is the common practice, such tips may be added to the specified price. However, there is no agreed-upon convention.

(9) *Regular rebates or refunds*: should only be considered when attributable to the purchase of an individual identifiable product and granted within a time period from the actual purchase, and are expected to have a significant influence on the quantity buyers purchase. For example, money-back deposits on bottles should be deducted from the price if these are a sufficient incentive for returning the bottle, whereas money-back offers on lawn mowers after a five-year period should be disregarded. In all cases, a consistent decision for each item must be applied over time. Decisions about the treatment of rebates are made on an individual basis. They may reflect income rather than expenditure changes and may require different treatment from that used by national accounts.

(10) *Irregular rebates or refunds*: as with regular rebates or refunds, these should only be considered when they apply to the purchase of an individual product and are granted within a time period, and are expected to have a significant influence on the quantities purchasers are willing to buy. Loyalty rebates or coupons associated with previous expenditure at the outlet, to be used for similar or other purchases, should be disregarded as they are conceptually out of scope because they are discriminatory relying on previous purchases. One-off rebates should be disregarded as they do not relate to the specific time period of the consumption and are unlikely to affect levels of consumption. They are viewed more as a source of additional income.

(11) *Credit card and other payment arrangements involving interest, service charges, or extra charges*: charges incurred as a consequence of failing to pay within a specified period of time from the purchase should be disregarded. For example, zero or positive interest loans granted to finance a purchase should be disregarded when determining the price. These charges come under financial services.

(12) *Cash back*: whether to include a cash back offer depends on the circumstances. Some large retailers offer credit card accounts to their customers. In this case, a cash back offer could be considered a form of discount. Each time consumers use the retailer's credit card, they could earn a percentage of the total amount paid in the form of cash back. For example, if the card pays 2 percent cash back and the customer spends £100 in the retail outlet, they will earn £2. Most cash back cards credit the amount earned by the customer onto their statement, thereby reducing their credit card bill. Like loyalty cards, data collectors should collect additional information to determine what proportion of consumers use the retailer's credit card to judge whether the "discount" provided by the cash back offer is widely available or should be considered discriminatory. If deemed widely available, the CPI price should reflect the net purchase price (price less 2 percent cash back). If discriminatory, these offers should be excluded. In other cases, cash back offers are provided by the bank that issues a credit card. The cash back offer provides an incentive for consumers to use a particular credit card for purchases but does not represent a discounted price offered by the retailer and should be excluded. Cash back offers can also be tied to loyalty cards. A percentage of the total amount spent accrues and can be used as a discount on future purchases. These types of cash back offers are excluded because they apply to future purchases and the price paid is not discounted in any way.

(13) *Dual pricing for cash and for credit or debit card purchases*: some outlets may sell goods at different prices depending on whether the item is paid for in cash or if a bank debit or credit card is used. The primary objective of the price collection is to achieve a representative sample and continuity. The price collector should determine the proportions of buyers who pay by the different methods and this should be used to judge what prices should be collected to ensure representativeness. If the price collected on a particular month is based on cash payment, then a price based on

cash payment must be obtained in each of the following months. If a price collected on a particular month is based on the use of a bank debit or credit card, then the prices collected in the following months should be based on the use of a bank debit or credit card. Widely available reductions for cash payments may be included, but care should be taken to ensure representative purchases are measured, treatment is consistent from one period to the next, and practice adheres to the fixed-basket concept. Thus, where relevant, item descriptions should include method of payment and the proportions that are paid by different methods should be kept constant between reviews of the CPI basket.

(14) *Bank-specific credit card offers*: in some countries, banks that issue credit cards will negotiate with retailers to offer customers who use their credit cards a discount on all purchases. For example, a bank can negotiate with a supermarket to offer all customers using their credit card a discount off the total purchase price. Judgments need to be made whether such offers can be defined as generally available. Like discounts associated with loyalty cards, if the majority of consumers use that bank-issued credit card, it could be considered generally available and the discount reflected in the collected prices. However, if it is judged to be discriminatory and not generally available, they should be ignored.

(15) *Foreign currency denominated prices*: the price collector should collect prices of items quoted in foreign currency from outlets selling goods and services in foreign currency, if their exclusion from the CPI basket would undermine the representativeness of the index. The price should then be converted into local currency using an average exchange rate obtained by the head office from the central bank or appropriate dealers in the foreign-exchange market. The price in local currency (obtained after conversion) should be used in the CPI.

(16) *Product with a local and foreign currency price*: in some countries, there are outlets that sell products in local and foreign currency (that is, a purchaser is given an option to pay for an item in local or foreign currency). The local currency price is used when purchases are made in local currency. However, if more purchases are made in foreign currency, the foreign currency price is converted to local currency as in the previous example. To determine whether more purchases are made in local or in foreign currency, the enumerator must ask the outlet staff which currency is being used more frequently for purchasing the item, and this currency should be used for pricing purposes, unless purchases are frequently made in both currencies, in which case the price in both currencies is collected and a weighted average used after conversion to the local currency.

5.17 The appropriate practice to be followed will be determined by individual circumstances, which might vary among different countries. Price collectors should make extensive notes on the situations confronted so that decisions on how to treat specific cases can be quality assured and reviewed at the head office.

Unavoidable Costs That Are Not Part of the Advertised Price

5.18 In some cases, the consumer has no choice but to pay an extra cost, in addition to the advertised price of the product, to obtain the use of the product. In cases where most customers will treat and pay this cost as part of the purchase price, the extra cost should be added to the advertised price to determine the price for CPI purposes.

5.19 A common example of this situation is the sale of large household appliances and furniture. Most consumers would not be able to provide their own transport to carry these products home. As a result, many stores arrange delivery to the customer's home for an additional cost. It can be argued that most customers must pay for the delivery service, and this additional charge should be included as part of the purchase price for CPI purposes. The concept still applies when the transport is provided by another business, if this is part of the transaction. In this case, the transport cost would be priced separately but added to the cost of the appliance when the index is being compiled. However, if the customer arranges for the transportation under a separate contract then the transportation should be priced separately under transport services.

5.20 A similar situation can occur in marketplaces when live poultry is bought for meat. If consumers regularly buy live fowls and then go to other stalls to have the fowls slaughtered, then the two purchases can be combined to calculate the cost of buying poultry meat.

Price Bargaining[3]

5.21 Bargaining relates to a situation where prices are individually negotiated between sellers and purchasers and are not predetermined. In some marketplaces, the prices for a wide range of daily necessities are negotiated. Final transaction prices and quantities will vary from one transaction to another and cannot be determined until the purchase has been made. Similarly, there will be variations between transactions in the quality of the goods being purchased which will impact on the price that is paid. For example, the bargained price for fresh fruit is likely to be lower the longer the fruit is on display. Clearly, these special conditions require special methods to determine purchasers' prices for inclusion in the CPI.

5.22 Where prices are determined by bargaining, standard price survey methods, which consist of collecting prices directly from sellers, can generate erratic price indices that do not reflect actual price movements in a market. The prices that are collected should be "bargained prices" and will depend on the ability, willingness, and power of price collectors to bargain in the same way as genuine purchasers. In addition, prices can vary during the day and from

[3] It can be argued from the viewpoint of the *System of National Accounts* that bargaining is a form of price discrimination. A purchaser is not free to choose the purchase price because the seller can charge different prices for identical goods and services sold under the same circumstances. It follows that "identical" products sold at different prices should be recognized as having the same quality, and their prices must be averaged to obtain a single price relative to calculate price indices. In practice, the variation in transaction price can rarely be associated with identifiable price-related categories of customers. Rather, purchasers may inadvertently buy at a higher price than may be found elsewhere or could have been negotiated.

one day to the next, adding an extra dimension to the concept of representativeness. A number of survey methods and price collection techniques have been developed to overcome the difficulties inherent in measuring prices that have been bargained.

(1) *Survey by purchase of products, simulating a consumer.* The principle is that price collection should be carried out in conditions that simulate as closely as possible situations in which real transactions take place. Price collectors behave like regular consumers by actually purchasing items to be priced and spreading their purchases over the day to ensure representativeness. In each case, the field manager will need to carry out regular checks on quantities and prices obtained by collectors. The following approaches may be taken:

  (1.1) Price collectors buy items to determine the relevant price through bargaining. They should be trained to behave as normal purchasers and strive to get the lowest possible price from selected outlets and sellers. Given the high turnover of sellers in many informal markets, the sample of sellers should be partially renewed on a regular basis to ensure that it remains representative.

  (1.2) Price collectors buy items and, in addition, are given an incentive to get the best price. For example, a price ceiling may be set, and the collector may receive a proportion of the difference between the ceiling and the bargained price. This incentive system guards against potential difficulties caused by the collectors not getting the lowest price because, unlike an ordinary customer, they are not concerned with maximizing value for money and are not constrained by income although there might be a limit on the money available for purchasing.

(2) *Survey of purchasers.* The prices purchasers have paid are collected throughout the day immediately after the purchaser leaves the outlet or market stall, together with a record of the quantity and quality of the product purchased. The extent of the haggling or bargaining should be determined (for example, opening and closing prices) together with an indication of the relevant parameters determining the price. A form of incentive payment for survey participation may be needed where there is reluctance among purchasers to submit to such time-consuming questions. Determining the quantity and quality of the items purchased can be difficult.

  (2.1) For the survey by purchase of products and the survey of purchasers, all CPI basket items subject to bargaining should be covered. The number of prices collected needs to be sufficient to cover all relevant items and to provide a reliable guide to average price. This may be difficult to determine beforehand, although previous price collections should provide some guidance. It is suggested that price collectors engaging in a survey of purchasers are given a form on which to record the number of quotations per stall or shop, as indicated by the various respondents. This can be used to check the number of quotes obtained against the target number set by the head office.

(3) *Survey of trends in wholesale prices.* A limited parallel collection of wholesale prices can be a useful supplement for items where the information obtained from the previous survey techniques is only partially successful, for example, where there is a deficit in the number of observations obtained. Ideally, prices should be obtained from the wholesalers where the relevant retailers get their goods. All factors should be observed that might result in increases in the corresponding retail prices, such as changes in taxes on retail activities, license fees, and the rental for the market stall. On the assumption that these factors remain constant over time, the evolution of wholesale prices may be used as a proxy for the retail prices of relevant items. The price of an item for the current period would be estimated by multiplying the price of the previous period by the corresponding evolution in wholesale price.

5.23 Determination of the prices paid by a purchaser can be challenging where the final price is for a bundle of items, for example, where a stall holder gives the purchaser extra quantities as a bonus for buying a number of goods. If the bonus comprises several categories of items, including the item on which a transaction price was being directly negotiated, then the purchase has to be split into as many subtransactions as item categories. In these cases, a common-sense approach is needed regarding treatment in the CPI. For example, consumers who are living on a subsistence income consume all food purchases and the extra quantities involved will be consumed and should be included when calculating the price paid. Purchasers will have actively bartered an overall price for the total basket of purchases, including any "free" goods thrown in.

5.24 The method for determining the price paid by the purchaser is illustrated in the following example: a purchaser wants to buy five kilograms of carrots and is offered a bonus consisting of 500 grams of carrots, a head of lettuce, and three onions.

5.25 Three transactions can be identified, involving: 5.5 kilograms of carrots, 100 grams of lettuce, and 200 grams of onions. The bonus should be valued at prices at which the seller would have sold the items and the purchaser would have bought them. The assumption made is that prices would have been determined through bargaining on the same conditions as the price of the item that initiated the purchase (carrots). In this example, the opening value of five kilograms of carrots is 15,000 pesos and the closing value 12,000 pesos, whereas the opening values of other food products included in the bonus are 990 pesos for a bunch of 264 grams of lettuce and 4,620 pesos for a pile of onions of 4.4 kilograms. The actual closing price of carrots will be determined as shown in Table 5.1. The actual purchaser's price of carrots is found to be 2.0967 pesos per gram or 2,096.7 pesos per kilo.

5.26 If the price collector does not know the closing price at which lettuce and onions would have been sold by the seller of the carrots, it can be estimated. This is done by collecting opening values and standard quantities from a

Table 5.1 Determining Purchaser Price When Bargaining Takes Place

		Requested Item	Bonus Items		
		Carrots	Carrots	Lettuce	Onions
(a)	**Opening Value of Standard Quantities (local currency units)**	15,000	15,000	990	4,620
(b)	**Standard Quantities (grams)**	5,000	5,000	264	4,400
(c)	**Opening Unit Price of Standard Quantities (local currency units per gram) (a/b)**	3.00	3.00	3.75	1.05
(d)	**Opening Unit Price of Quantities and Bonus Quantities (local currency units per gram) (as per (c))**	3.00	3.00	3.75	1.05
(e)	**Quantities and Bonus Quantities Offered (grams)**	5,000	500	100	200
(f)	**Opening Value of Quantities and Bonus Quantities (local currency units) ((e) at unit price at (d))**	15,000	1,500	375	210
(g)	**Closing Value of Items Received (local currency units) (assumes bargaining ratio for lettuce and onions same as for carrots, that is, 15,000/12,000 = 1.25)**	12,000	1,200	300	168
(h)	**New Price (local currency units per gram) (g/e)**	2.40	2.40	3.00	0.84
(i)	**Bargaining Ratio (D/H) (for example, old price for carrots/ new price for carrots, that is, 15,000/12,000 = 1.25)**	1.25	1.25	1.25	1.25
(j)	**Payment (local currency units)**	12,000			
(k)	**Estimated Closing Value of Bonus (local currency units) (1,200 + 300 + 168 = 1,668)**	1,668			
(l)	**Actual Value of Requested Item (all carrots) (local currency units) (12,000 – 1,668 = 10,332)**	10,332			
(m)	**Quantity Received of Requested Item (grams)**	5,500			
(n)	**Actual Purchaser's Unit Price of Requested Item (local currency units per gram) ((12,000 – 300 – 168)/5,500) = 2.0967)**	2.10			
(o)	**Improved Bargaining Ratio (*d*/*n*), that is, 3/2.10 = 1.43**	1.43			

sample of sellers in the same market or at different outlets in the same area. The average opening price of an item is equal to the sum of opening values of the item divided by the sum of relevant standard quantities. For each bonus item (lettuce and onions), the resulting average opening price will be divided by the bargaining ratio calculated on the item needed (carrots) to estimate a closing price for that bonus item. The value of each bonus item is obtained by multiplying the closing price by the quantity offered. If the packet of bonus items contains an item of the same quality as the requested item, that bonus item will be valued based on the closing value of the requested item.

The Principle of the Fixed Basket

5.27 The important principle underlying price collection is the need to compare prices on a like-to-like basis from one period to the next. This has consequences:

(1) Where there is a choice of variety of product to be priced initially, an important consideration should be whether that variety will be available to price over a reasonably long period. This is in addition to being typical of what is sold to customers. Note that tight specifications are of no use if the described item cannot be found in the outlets.

(2) A record should be kept of additional information needed to ensure the unique identification of the variety priced so that:

(2.1) The same variety continues to be priced in the case of subsequent price collection being carried out by a different person.

(2.2) The identification and adjustment for any quality change can be made when the variety disappears and is replaced by a different one.

Item Specifications

5.28 The recording of item specifications is particularly relevant for traditional forms of price collection where products are sampled and where price collection involves price collectors visiting retail outlets to collect prices or where prices are collected by postal inquiry, email, or telephone most particularly from central sources.

5.29 There are no firm rules, especially regarding the use of loose or tight item specifications: each NSO may choose their preferred methods. Considerations in deciding on item specifications are the following:

(1) Loose specifications leave more discretion to the price collector, so the reliability and training of collectors are factors to consider when deciding whether to use loose or tight specifications.

(2) The specification should be more detailed for heterogeneous items where there is scope for significant difference of varieties, and for items that by nature are highly specified, such as cars and hi-tech goods.

(3) Loose specifications allow the index to more broadly reflect regional differences in tastes and preferences, and account for differences resulting from socioeconomic factors.

(4) Tight specifications allow for the calculation of meaningful average prices.

(5) Average prices are useful to identify outliers and to assess the accuracy of reported prices.

(6) Subject to satisfactory sample design, average prices allow comparisons of price levels, including between regions or urban and rural areas. Tight specifications facilitate the use of CPI prices in the computation of purchasing power parities.

(7) However, specifications should not be so detailed that the item cannot be found in an adequate number of out-

lets. Individual varieties sold differ from outlet to outlet and region to region, and the CPI should reflect these differences. Overly tight specifications do not reflect this diversity and can increase the number of missing prices.

(8) Without tight specifications, average prices have little meaning or use. For example, an average price for a liter of whole milk is more meaningful than an average price for men's shirts.

5.30 Responsibility for deciding whether to use loose or tight specifications and for specifying the items to be priced should normally rest with the head office. In general, loose specifications can be useful for food, beverages, clothing, and personal items. Tight specifications tend to be useful for electronic and other items with high rates of turnover. Specifications should be reviewed on a regular basis to determine whether they continue to be relevant. The following could signal the need to review and revise specifications:

- A large number of missing price quotations
- A large number of substitutions
- A wide variation in the distribution of collected price levels
- An observed distortion in the achieved sample, for example, where an item is stocked only by one retail chain indicating that the item is unlikely to be fully representative of what households buy, or where there is a reduction in the number of brands available possibly indicating a fall in demand

5.31 Practical difficulties stem from the temporal dimension in price collection. Issues such as the timing of entering prices into the index, the treatment of missing prices, seasonality, and the frequency of price collection are temporal issues that need to be addressed to maintain the quality of the index. Aspects relating to the frequency and timing of price collection are addressed in paragraphs 5.35–5.47.

Frequency

5.32 Decisions about the frequency of price collection are governed by several factors. The most important are: the volatility of prices; the characteristics of the market from which the prices are collected; the known regularity of price changes; and the frequency and method of calculation of the CPI. The general principle is that each item should be priced as often as is necessary to ensure that the index reflects a reliable and meaningful measure of price change. Thus, the desired frequency of price collection will vary by product, depending on how frequently the prices to be observed change. For instance, the prices of some products (for example, fees for government services and utilities) might need to be collected only once a year if it is known that prices are reviewed annually at a regular point in time. However, it is advisable for the price collector to occasionally check that the assumption of regular and predictable reviews still holds. In contrast, the prices of products with more volatile prices, such as fresh food, might have to be collected more frequently than the frequency of index calculation and publication. Also, price collection will need to reflect user needs with regard to whether the target index is a point-in-time or period-of-time index.

Period-of-Time or Point-in-Time Price Collection

5.33 Prices for a monthly (quarterly) CPI should aim to reflect the average price of the reference period. To that end, NSOs should strive to calculate an index based on prices covering the whole period (for example, a month). Ideally, price collection would be organized so that prices are collected from different outlets throughout the month. This ensures that the prices used to calculate the index more broadly reflect the average price for the reference month. While resource constraints could restrict price collection to a specific period during the month, effort should be made to maximize the price collection period to include as many days in the month as possible. Regardless of the price collection period, the interval between successive price observations must be held constant, for example, by visiting an outlet during the same fixed time period each month or quarter. If the CPI is used to deflate income, expenditure, or sales, the index should relate to the time period of these money flows. For economic analysis, where the index will be used in conjunction with other economic statistics, most of which relate to a period rather than to a point in time, the CPI should do the same.

5.34 Under the traditional approaches to price measurement, where price collectors visit retail outlets and record prices, spreading price collection over a period of time will result in a more even workload. This avoids some of the operational problems and inefficiencies associated with point-in-time price collection but will involve collecting sufficient price quotations to obtain a reliable average price level for each product over the period.

5.35 From an operational perspective, the uneven workloads associated with point-in-time price collection when using traditional price collection techniques can be inefficient and have a negative impact on price collector performance at peak times. For instance, a sizeable price collection team will be required for a short time in each collection period. This has implications for the recruitment and deployment of price collectors and for management of the fieldwork. Communication and planning between collectors and their supervisors to manage events like absence because of illness must be prompt and effective. Staff at the head office will similarly be confronted with a heavy workload of data checking and editing of price data over a short period of time.

5.36 With the point-in-time approach, major price setters, notably the government, can influence the index according to whether their price changes take effect on a day just before or just after the day for which their price information is obtained, or on the day of collection. Since prices are often collected centrally from such price setters, it should be possible to obtain information from them about the amount and timing of price changes at the end of each month, so that in applying the period-of-time approach, an average price for the whole month can be calculated. For example, if electricity charges are made quarterly and prices increase partway through the three-month period, individual customers' payments could include zero, one, two, or three months at the higher rate depending on when the price change is implemented.

5.37 The point in time or period is chosen to represent a prespecified reference period, normally the calendar month in which the price observations take place. Whether collection is continuous or point-in-time, the interval between successive price observations must be held constant, for example, by visiting an outlet during the same fixed time period each month or quarter.

5.38 The sampling variance will differ according to whether a period or point-in-time index is compiled and the frequency of collection. Regarding the timing and frequency of price collection, the CPI compiler should consider the trade-off between statistical accuracy and cost, particularly when prices are collected by visits to local outlets, as this can be a costly activity. The budget for price collection can limit the available options.

5.39 The timing of the publication of the resulting price indices can be a constraint on the price collection schedule and vice versa. For example, there may be legal constraints on the timing of the publication of indices, such as a requirement to publish at a set time each month. In such cases, prices must be collected to a schedule that allows quality assurance, processing, and aggregation procedures to be completed before the deadline. The quality management of the price collection process is covered in paragraphs 5.78–5.116.

Timing of Price Collection

5.40 The interval between price observations should be uniform for each outlet. Since the length of the month varies, this uniformity must be defined carefully, for instance, not by date but by a formula such as "second Monday in the month."

5.41 Regular timing is important, particularly when inflation is high. Where there is a specific collection day, the most volatile prices should be collected on that specific day rather than on the days around it. Items where prices can be more volatile include fresh fruit and vegetables, fresh meat and fish, and fuels. In the case of food products sold in marketplaces, the time of day as well as the day of the week matters. Prices of fresh fruits, vegetables, meat, and fish can be higher in the mornings when produce is fresh and lower in the evenings, especially if there is limited refrigeration. Thus, the precise timing of price collection is particularly important for fresh produce.

5.42 When inflation is low and stable there will be little difference between the annual inflation rates based on point-in-time and period-of-time collections. For example, there is likely to be very little difference between the annual rate of change in the index from Monday, January 8, 2018 to Monday, January 7, 2019 and the corresponding annual rate of change between the complete months of January 2018 and January 2019. This will not be the case if inflation is high or the inflation rate changes significantly during the year. The difference between January 1 and February 1 and between average January and average February inflation rates may be different, particularly if so-called "sale" periods fall on regular dates each year or are limited by laws. For certain products with high index weights, where price changes are sudden and tend to affect the whole market on about the same day, the choice between point-in-time or period-of-time price collection is especially influential. Examples are fuels, electricity, and telecommunication prices. For these kinds of products, it can be argued that the case for taking an average price for the period is stronger. This ensures a more meaningful measure of price change for the month. The calculation of the average monthly price should relate to the periodicity of the collection, taking into account the appropriate pricing periods. For example, if prices are increased a third of the way through the period, then two-thirds of the average price over the month should reflect the higher pricing. In these cases, different areas or locations should be scheduled for price collection at different times of the month according to a regular pattern to be repeated each month. This makes the use of the collectors' time more efficient and has the advantage of providing a spread of collection dates for many representative items. Individual price observations should be carried out at the same time each month so that the index does not move because of a change in the length of interval between collection dates. Prices may vary by day of the week (for example, depending when is market day) or by time of the day (for example, fish is more expensive in the morning when it is fresher), and prices should be collected on the same day, at the same time, if this is the case.

5.43 Preferably, days of the week and month should be chosen taking into account when purchases are concentrated and where prices and goods in stock are known to be representative of the whole month. In some countries, the results of the household budget survey suggest that most households do the shopping on the day of the market or souk. However, retailers may be less prepared to cooperate when they are busy, so a balance needs to be struck between the ideal timing for collection and the impact on response rates.[4] An entirely fixed interval is impossible because of the varying length of a month and the timing of public or religious holidays. One solution is to take sequences of four and five weeks, so maintaining a relatively stable monthly or quarterly period where price collection takes place on a fixed day or days each month; another is to follow a rule such as collecting prices on the regular market day or on a Wednesday through Friday of the first full week in the month.

5.44 Price collection days (and sometimes the time of collection) need to be set in advance. The NSO should explain the procedures used for setting collection dates and the underlying objectivity of the method to assure the public of the integrity of the index. Any data suppliers who supply prices directly to head office staff need to know the collection date in advance to be able to prepare and supply the necessary price. To enhance transparency, it is recommended practice to include the price collection period in the CPI metadata.

Measuring Hyperinflation or Selected Large Price Changes

5.45 Special arrangements need to be put into place in case of hyperinflation. Hyperinflation is an economic phenomenon that occurs when inflation increases very rapidly. Economists typically consider monthly inflation rates of above 50 percent as hyperinflation episodes. In these circumstances, it becomes even more important that the prices

[4] There is no rule of thumb on what constitutes an acceptable response rate as this will depend on the sample design that has been adopted and the structure of the retail sector (most particularly, the variability of product and item varieties available and their prices, and the range of outlets in which they are stocked).

of individual items in individual outlets are collected at precisely the same time each month, otherwise misleading figures may result. The NSO should consider collecting prices more frequently and, correspondingly, a more frequent compilation of the index. For example, where prices are normally collected on a quarterly basis, it may be sensible to collect them more frequently. If this is not feasible, it may be appropriate to adjust prices proportionately by some relevant indicator, such as a subset of the index, to provide an approximation to a monthly index. An appropriate comparator must be chosen because relative prices can change dramatically in periods of hyperinflation. The same considerations apply to collecting prices online.

5.46 In some circumstances, rapid or frequent price changes may be associated with certain items only and action should be taken accordingly. For example, food prices may rise disproportionately because of a bad harvest and it may be sensible to increase the frequency of the index for food items only, possibly publishing a separate index. Alternatively, a simpler way of dealing with this situation may be to monitor a small number of relevant prices on a regular basis without producing a full price index. Such subindices can be published separately or used to adjust the index as mentioned previously, or to provide background briefing for analytical purposes. These items may be chosen according to their importance for the household budget and whether they are particularly susceptible to big price increases.

The Practical Aspects of Managing Price Collection

5.47 As mentioned in the introduction, the most appropriate sampling and survey procedures will vary depending on the use of the CPI and on national circumstances. This also applies to the practical aspects of price collection. Paragraphs 5.51–5.116 describe aspects of planning and organization and provide indicative guidance on the processes and procedures that contribute to successful price collection in the field.

Practical Procedures for Local Price Collection: Planning and Organization

5.48 The discussion that follows is based on period-of-time pricing rather than point-in-time pricing (see paragraphs 5.36–5.42), but the concepts discussed generally apply to both collection methods.

5.49 The procedures governing the collection of prices have the requirements of obtaining usable prices from the outlets, and the practical problems faced in managing travel to and from the various locations, in transferring data, and in validating the data back in the office. The overall operation can only be achieved by cooperation between the price collectors, their supervisors, and, of course, the retailers selected for the price survey.

5.50 An overview of local price collection is given in Annex 5.1. It is in the form of a flow chart and shows the different situations that confront the price collector and the decisions or referrals to the head office for further action.

Planning the Collection Schedule

5.51 Price collection is a complex process that needs to be effectively managed by the head office. Proper training of price collectors in the concepts and practices of price collection is an essential element in achieving a representative and error-free sample of prices. Price collectors should be given help and practical support when undertaking price collection. The collection of prices should be supported by good documentation. Also, the scheduling of price collection and the drawing up of contingency plans, for example, in the case of price collector illness or other factors outside the control of the price collection team should be in place so that the price collection operation runs smoothly. Effective management of the price collection process should be given the necessary attention and funding. More detailed guidance on good practices is given in the paragraphs that follow.

5.52 The collection schedule should include time for the price collector to travel around all required locations within a reasonable number of working hours in a day. The schedule needs to allow the price collector to perform all the necessary checking of prices, to answer queries from the supervisor or the head office, and where necessary to revisit the outlet. The collection schedule also needs to allow for the transfer of data and forms between the data collectors, regional offices (if applicable), and the head office. If paper forms are being posted or hand-delivered, time must be allowed to ensure that all information reaches its destination by the required deadline. If electronic transmission of data and forms is used, time needs to be allowed to ensure that all the data arrives in the correct format and to address potential problems if the files are corrupted. Plans for recovery in case of technical breakdowns need to be in place.

5.53 Public holidays can occur on days that would otherwise be price collection days. In general, prices due to be collected on the holiday should be collected as close as practicable to that day. This usually means adjusting the regular price collection schedule to the immediately preceding or following few days. Any adjustments to the regular schedule should be made so that prices reflect the normal pattern of buyer–seller behavior. The work schedule for index compilation and publication also needs to be considered.

Dealing with Queries: Inquiry Management System

5.54 Price collection queries need to be dealt with in a timely and efficient manner both because of the tight schedules associated with the compilation of a CPI and because of the difficulty to correct errors in pricing retrospectively given the dynamic nature of retailing where prices and stock can change very quickly without warning. The progress in dealing with queries (for example, verify questionable prices or seek additional details on incomplete specifications) needs to be monitored and the system for monitoring must be simple, in order to be effective and flexible to the needs of the CPI production cycle and to any problems that may arise. An inquiry management system should be able to monitor progress and provide an effective audit trail. Information recorded should include: date price collection form received and from whom; date due; collection date/trip/period (if applicable); current progress (with date); dates when queries were raised and responses sent; and date completed. It is particularly important that decisions are recorded and signed off to provide price collectors with confirmation for their own purposes of verification and as audit trails for quality assurance purposes at the head office. Audit trails are an effective way to ensure that processes were carried out correctly and to support the review of the effectiveness of those processes. The information gathered should also feed into a quality management system for the computation of the CPI (see Chapter 13).

5.55 A simple inquiry management system might use emails to send the query. As these will be seen and read, they satisfy the notification requirement. A template form requiring the entry of simple ticks and dates could be created in a spreadsheet and a new copy provided for every collector each collection period.

5.56 An inquiry management system can be either paper or electronic. The two methods should be matched to the resources and infrastructure available. For instance, messages to and from price collectors to their supervisor might be on paper but messages between a regional office and the head office could be by email.

5.57 Queries about collected prices are a two-way process. The head office may want to question some prices collected and request a check, while price collectors may ask for further guidance on situations arising in the field such as the selection of a suitable replacement for a disappearing good.

Practical Collection Procedures and Questionnaire Design

Design of Price Collection Questionnaire

5.58 Good design of the questionnaire form (or its electronic equivalent) is essential for the successful collection of prices (see Annex 5.2). Price collectors should be given the appropriate direction and find it easy to use, and the format and layout should facilitate the extraction of data (for example, price, item description, or comments) by the head office for effective quality assurance. The price collection form should cover: collection date and collector's name; name or location of the particular outlet; product name and specification of the actual item to be priced; price entry; and collector comments about the product or price movement or changes in the representative item being priced such as package size.

5.59 Whether recording price information obtained from personal visits on paper form or via handheld computer or tablet, the price collector needs to be provided with all the information required to successfully collect prices and, correspondingly, the head office will want from price collectors all the information needed to assure the quality of the prices collected.

5.60 Including the previous period price on the collection form continues to be a topic of debate. There are advantages and disadvantages to including the previous period price on the collection form. The optional inclusion in the form of the price collected in the previous period raises concerns that the price collector may be inclined to automatically record the previous price or be too influenced by it when identifying the item in the outlet to be priced. However, this information is sometimes included to assist the collector in ensuring that the correct item and price are being recorded and, where paper forms are being used, to identify any unusual price movements that need to be investigated. With electronic collection, if the collected price differs from the previous period price, data collectors are prompted to justify or explain the price change. Price collectors are encouraged to add additional information to the "standard" description to facilitate the unique identification of the product to be priced without a reliance on price. Such information might include: brand, make, size, model name and number, reference number, distinctive features, and location in outlet (for example, "bottom shelf at rear of shop").

5.61 Items should appear on the form in the same order in which prices are collected. A correctly ordered list will reduce time-consuming swapping and searching between pages. Even with a handheld computer or tablet, searching and pressing of navigation buttons will be less time-consuming if the item list is ordered to match the layout of the outlet.

5.62 For fruit and vegetables, weight and quantity should be part of the item description, but the amount actually priced should be recorded separately so that a unit price can be calculated. Weight and quantity are needed because the unit price is often lower if larger quantities are purchased. For example, if the price collector prices a bunch of bananas and the item description is one kilo of bananas, the price collector should choose a bunch weighing approximately one kilo, weigh the bunch, and calculate the price per kilo.

5.63 When an index basket is updated, the questionnaire will need to list all items included in the old and the new basket. Where an update of the outlet sample is planned to coincide with the introduction of a new basket, it will be necessary in the chain link period for the price collection to cover both the old sample of locations, outlets, and items and the new sample of locations, outlets, and items.

5.64 An example of a typical price collection form is given in Annex 5.2. This example is of a form used by the collector for recording prices when visiting an outlet, either in paper form or electronic. It is also possible to ask the outlet staff concerned to complete the form themselves and to send it to the NSO, although there are obvious potential problems in the form not being completed correctly. Such a form may therefore serve for reporting as well as for collecting. If the form has space for recording prices over a sequence of months, the collector may keep the form and transcribe the prices each month onto a separate report form, which is then sent to the NSO. Where the form used for collection is also used for reporting, there are two main options: either the form has space for recording prices over a whole sequence of months, and the form is shuttled backward and forward monthly between the collector and the head office, or new forms for collection and reporting are provided each month. In the latter case, it can be useful if the form contains the prices recorded in the previous month alongside the spaces for recording the current month's prices, although this might encourage the price collector or data provider to overly rely on the previously recorded price. The transfer of the prices to another form or system, especially when done manually, may lead to transcription errors and is best avoided. In the example given in Annex 5.2, the previous month's price is shown (see paragraphs 5.185–5.193 on Computer-Assisted Data Collection for a more detailed discussion of the advantages and disadvantages of giving price history). For simplicity, the example assumes all prices entered on the form will include a sales tax.

5.65 Completion of the price collection forms, whether by paper or electronically, should comply with the following guidelines:

(1) All prices should be entered in the collection sheet in full even if there is no price change. This is good practice as it helps to ensure that the correct item is being priced, the price has been recorded correctly, and the price collector has not relied on information given by the outlet staff without checking. For instance, a price may not have changed but the package size might have been reduced, a practice sometimes used to make price increases less transparent, but to the outlet staff, there has been no price change. A price should never be recorded as "no change." All other entry fields on the price collection sheet should have something entered if only to indicate that they were not accidentally missed, for instance, "Not Available (NA)."

(2) If a price is not available a reason must always be supplied. The information given will be useful to the collector's supervisor and the index compilers as well as to the price collector. The price collector may need to ask the outlet staff for an explanation and may also need to choose a replacement, for example, if the outlet staff indicates that the item is no longer stocked.

5.66 No matter which method of local price collection is used, it is essential to provide some procedures to allow the tracking of activities and formal sign-off, confirming that processes have been completed and necessary actions undertaken on data checking and transfer to the head office. Audit trails are essential for work and quality management.

5.67 The price collection form should have space to provide full descriptions of the items being priced. Price collectors should be given a checklist or set of codes to record relevant information on changes relating to outlets, items, or prices. The information needs to be systematically collected. For instance, codes to help with quality adjustment need to reflect those characteristics that most influence price. Prior research, for example, based on the hedonic method (see Chapter 6), can help to predetermine these characteristics.

5.68 Codes for managing the sample of outlets can be helpful and may include:

- *Closed down*: outlet permanently shut or closed down
- *Temporarily unavailable*: outlet temporarily closed, but likely to be open next month
- *Refusal*: owner or staff refuses to cooperate
- *Change of details*: change of ownership or name or change of purpose

Continuity and the Use of Price Collection Codes

5.69 As the index measures pure price changes, the same item should be priced every month to establish a true picture of price change. For example, if a jar of a supermarket's own brand strawberry jam has been selected, that brand and flavor should continue to be collected; if it is out of stock, another brand and flavor should not be used without further investigation to establish whether this is a temporary situation or likely to be permanent. In the latter case, and if another flavor of the same brand, size, and quality is available, then in normal circumstances, this item should be chosen as a "comparable" item and the item description suitably amended.[5] If a different brand, size, or quality product is available then this should be selected as a "new" item, but only where no comparable items are available. The same principles apply to other items such as clothes and fresh fruit and vegetables. With clothes, it is important that color, fabric, country of origin, logos, and size are specified to ensure that the same item is priced each month. For fresh fruit and vegetables, useful attributes to record may be country of origin, class, and variety. For electrical equipment, the specifications and features given in the manufacturer's catalog may be important.

5.70 A detailed description of the items being priced is recorded to assist the price collector and the head office in choosing or confirming the suitability of a replacement for an item that has been withdrawn and in identifying changes in quality. The focus should be on recording price-determining characteristics. If the regular price collector is unable to carry out the normal collection, full and accurate descriptions will also enable a relief collector to carry out the collection without any doubt concerning the correct items to be priced.

Most of the time, the item will be exactly as collected in the previous month, and all that will be recorded is a current price. However, if there is a change or uncertainty in the item, it is necessary for price collectors to use their judgment and to inform the head office, bearing in mind that the head office staff is responsible for making the final decision. A precoded specification is less time-consuming and provides better guidance to the price collector on what information should be reported. The codes should cover situations faced regularly when collecting prices. The codes can be numeric or alphanumeric, and each one should indicate the action taken by the price collector or supervisor and will be associated with corresponding procedures to be followed in the calculation of the index by the head office. The form should include codes such as:

- *Comparable (C)*. The original item is no longer stocked but a similar alternative has been collected that does not differ with regard to major price-determining attributes. The price is likely to be in a similar range although this may not always be the case.
- *Noncomparable (N)*. The original item has been replaced by a new item that is not really comparable but is equally representative of that product group. If possible, the collector should try to find the price of the "new" item in the previous or price reference period.
- *Sale or special offer (S)*. A price decrease because of a genuine sale or special offer. This does not include damaged or out-of-date stock or clearance goods, which should never be included. A price reduction where there is no notice of a sale or special offer is not a "sale"; the item should still be priced, but without the S indicator code.

[5]The replacement should be either (1) as similar as possible to the previous one; (2) the most popular "similar" product in the outlet; or (3) the "similar" product that most likely will be available for future pricing. Unlike approach (1), which leaves the sample "static" with the risk that it will be increasingly out of date and difficult to collect prices for, approaches (2) and (3) have the advantage of introducing an element of sample replenishment.

- *Recovery (R)*. A return to the normal selling price after a sale or special offer. This does not need to be a return to the price prior to the sale or special offer. A referral back to the previous price collected and consultation with the outlet staff will normally be required.
- *Temporarily out of stock (T)*. Guidance will need to be given to the price collector concerning the meaning of "temporarily" (with regard to expected duration, which may vary for different items). If nonseasonal items are missing for three or more months, depending upon country circumstances, enumerators should replace items immediately (for example, fashion clothing, if it is unlikely that the identical item will come back into stock). Typically, "T" indicators should not be used for more than three consecutive months, and in the fourth month, a replacement should be chosen. In food outlets, it is very unusual for items to go permanently out of stock. The collector should always try to check future availability with the retailer.
- *Missing (M)*. Used where the outlet does not stock an item or no longer intends to stock an item and there is no appropriate alternative replacement. In these circumstances, it is recommended that the item is checked at subsequent collections to ensure that a suitable replacement item has not come into stock.
- *Weight (W)*. A permanent weight or quantity change to the product.
- *Query (Q)*. Such a code may be used to supply extra retail information to the head office (some examples are "10 percent extra free," "2 for the price of 1," or a strange price difference that is not covered by one of the other indicators, such as a special edition issue of a magazine at an increased price). Arrangements need to be in place for the head office to respond to these comments and to treat the price quotes accordingly.

5.71 Even if the retailer says there have been no price changes since the previous month, the price collector should confirm prices. This will require some diplomacy, but it is important because the outlet staff may overlook a small number of price increases, or forget when the last increase has occurred. Also, checks need to be made to ensure that there have been no changes in the price-determining characteristics of the item such as package size or weight.

5.72 As noted previously, a price should be recorded only if the exact product being priced is on display and immediately available for sale; however, for certain large items that must normally be ordered, such as furniture or cars, the price should be recorded as long as the retailer confirms that it is available for delivery.

Unit Prices

5.73 Some food items, such as meat, fish, or cheese, are typically sold in variable weights and it is necessary to collect prices per unit of weight. The price per unit of weight should be taken from the package labeling or calculated directly by the collector. Roughly, the same package size and type should be used each month, as the unit price might be lower for larger pack sizes or differ between package types. Other items, such as eggs, are often sold in specified quantities. For these, collectors record prices for the specified quantity, as total and unit prices usually depend on the number bought. If X eggs are to be priced and the price for the number is not quoted directly, the price of one egg can be obtained and multiplied by X to get the required price. However, the price collector must ensure that the unit price does not decrease with quantity: significant changes in weight or quantity are to be avoided. Other examples are herbs, such as mint, or vegetables, such as cabbage leaves, sold in bunches of variable size with no label giving the weight. In this instance, a number of bunches should be weighed and priced to obtain an average price per unit of weight (for example, kilogram). It is necessary to purchase bundles and weigh them at the head office when reliable scales are not available at the outlet or market stall.

5.74 Certain food items, such as fruit or vegetables, are more difficult to price as some outlets might price items per number purchased while others might price by weight. For example, peppers may be priced either by weight or by unit no matter what the size; garlic may be priced per bulb, clove, or by weight; and various types of berries may be priced either by weight or by container, which may differ in size or how full it is. In these instances, care needs to be taken with the product descriptions. The item description given on the price collection form should refer to the pack size, weight, or quantity being priced. Collectors need to be aware of the importance of collecting the same item from one month to another, so that genuine price changes are recorded and not quantity or quality price changes.

Practical Collection Procedures: Quality Management in the Field

5.75 Adequate field procedures are required to ensure that the quality of the price index is not compromised by errors in price collection. Price collection needs to be carefully planned and managed, and effective instructions and training are given to price collectors. In traditional price collection, most prices are collected through price collectors visiting individual outlets. Checks need to be carried out to ensure the accuracy of the data. This section gives guidance on field procedures relating to local price collection and provides an overview of quality management. It focuses on data validation in the field. Chapter 13 provides a broader look at the organization and management issues associated with central price collection and with the complete process of producing a CPI.

Data Validation in the Field

5.76 Data validation should be carried out throughout the entire process of compilation of a CPI, from the collection of individual prices to their aggregation into indices.

5.77 The questionnaires, and the data collection software if handheld computers or tablets are used, should facilitate quality assurance of the collected prices at or close to the time of collection and record the results of the checks made in the field as part of an audit trail.

5.78 Collected prices can be compared to the prices of the same product sold in the same outlet previously collected, and large movements can be checked for accuracy. Preferably, the head office should provide guidance on what are viewed as acceptable ranges for price movements based on previous price movements. If a price has changed significantly or remained unchanged for a very long period, the retailer should be asked to explain why.

5.79 Where resources allow, field supervisors and independent auditors should be deployed to support price collectors in providing accurate prices for input into the CPI. Supervisors should check the validity of the prices and related information recorded by the price collectors, provide assistance, and help when required as part of a collaborative effort. The required level of the validity checks may vary depending on the nature of retailing and the data collection procedures. For example, the use of handheld computers and tablets facilitates real-time data editing and the creation of price collection reports, reducing the chance of errors in price collection.

Data Validation: Field Supervisors

5.80 Checks to ensure that data are complete and correct should be carried out as early as possible in the collection and compilation processes. A return to the outlet to re-input prices becomes increasingly less feasible as time goes on, and there is a greater risk that the prices in the outlets will have changed since the initial collection. The use of handheld computers or tablets by price collectors facilitates much more detailed checking at the time of the initial collection of prices in the outlet than the equivalent paper system (see paragraphs 5.185–5.193 on electronic reporting).

5.81 Field supervisors have a number of important roles: training of data collectors when implementing new procedures or methods; one-on-one training of price collectors during joint field trips to correct any deviations from the procedures and tasks laid down in the price collection documentation; and reviewing the work done by price collectors in previous days to verify the quality and to facilitate the correction of errors.

5.82 In an ideal system, field supervisors will be employed to regularly check that price collectors are adhering to the price collection schedule and are undertaking the required checks at the appropriate time. The supervisor should check that price collectors are completing price collection forms correctly. A sample of collection forms from each collector should be checked where it is not practical for supervisors to check every form. Checks may be made, for example, on whether the price collector has attempted to collect all prices from all outlets, that explanations have been given where prices were not obtained, and adequate descriptions entered where replacements for disappearing products have been priced. The supervisor may also be required to check the accuracy with which data are transferred from data collection forms to the computer. This is an essential task associated with the quality assurance process and needs to be allocated to somebody other than the person who initially inputs the data so that an independent check can be performed.

5.83 Supervisors should also be encouraged to visit outlets and check the individual prices collected by price collectors. These checks can be organized either on a random basis or chosen on the basis of indicative information, such as extreme price variations. A typical audit report will include the percentage error rate and a breakdown of whether the errors are likely to have a high impact (for example, wrong price, wrong item, or item available but listed as temporarily unavailable) or a low impact (for example, incomplete product description or inadequate reason given for price change). The audit report should be followed up by a formal request to the price collector asking for corrective action and confirmation that all necessary follow-up actions have been carried out.

5.84 Field supervisors should check for consistency and credibility in price movements recorded by the collectors under their oversight. For instance, if one location is reporting different price movements from the other locations within the collection region, some explanation or a follow-up price collection will be required to check the accuracy of the prices collected. Preferably, this should be done once data have been transferred into the computer system and have been checked for errors. Tabulations of price changes grouped by product or elementary aggregate should be provided to enable the supervisor to conduct these checks efficiently. This will enable the supervisor to quickly identify extreme or inconsistent movements, which may indicate either errors in collection or unexpected behavior in the market. These checks should be conducted regularly during the price collection period.

Quality Checks in the Head Office: Data Entry Queries and the Role of the Head Office

5.85 Once the price collection has been completed and the prices submitted to the head office, a series of further validation checks can be run. In determining the checks to use, the validation checks carried out in the field should be considered. For example, the use of handheld computers or tablets will increase the potential for validation at the time of price collection and reduce the need for detailed scrutiny at the head office. In addition, it would clearly not be productive or cost-effective to repeat tests already carried out.

5.86 The range of tests carried out on individual price quotes can include:

(1) *Price change.* The price entered is compared with the price for the same product in the same outlet in the previous month and triggers a query where the price difference is outside preset percentage limits. These limits will vary, depending on the item or group of items, and may be determined by analyzing historical evidence of price variation for the product or item concerned. If there is no valid price for the previous month because, for example, the item was out of stock, the check can be made against the price two months or three months before.

(2) *Maximum/minimum prices.* A query is raised if the price entered exceeds a maximum or is below a minimum price for the item of which the particular variety is representative. The range may be derived from the validated maximum and minimum values observed for that item in the previous month expanded by a standard scaling factor. This factor may vary between items, again based on previous experience. Where necessary and possible, the maximum/minimum price should take account of any significant differences in average prices between, for example, regions.

5.87 If a handheld computer or tablet is used (see paragraphs 5.185–5.193), both tests (related to price change and maximum/minimum prices) can be implemented easily to take place at the time of collection; otherwise, they will need to be conducted in the head office as soon as possible after collection and prior to the computation of the index. A failure in either test should prompt the collector to check and correct or confirm the entry, and prompt for an explanatory comment.

5.88 Queries raised may be either dealt with at the head office or sent to the price collector for resolution. For example, scrutiny of a form might show that a significant price difference has arisen because the item priced was a new product replacing another that has been discontinued. In this case, there may be no need to raise a query with the price collector, unless there is evidence to suggest that labeling the item "new product" is incorrect.

5.89 If a price collection error is discovered and is too late in the process of computing a nonrevisable CPI for the collection of the correct price, the head office will need to reject the price and exclude that item from that month's index and the price reference period, or treat it as a missing price and impute a price using the price movements of similar products. Where a CPI is revisable, it can be recompiled and the corrected figure published the following month. In some countries, the CPI is first published as a provisional figure to facilitate the late take-on of data including the situation just described.

5.90 Collectors should be encouraged to give feedback to the head office on their experiences of price collecting. Collectors are a valuable source of information and often give good early feedback on changes in the marketplace and can often warn of size or product changes before the head office is able to obtain this information from other sources such as newspaper advertisements. Collectors' feedback can be used to support observed price movements and to provide supplementary briefing material.

5.91 Feedback can also form the basis of a newsletter for collectors. Collectors' shared experiences can guide other collectors on how to treat different situations or circumstances.

5.92 The periodic routine of collecting prices in the field needs to be carefully planned and monitored, with arrangements in place to reflect local conditions. However, price collectors should send in information when it is due, and late submissions require follow-up.

Quality Checks of Local Price Collection: The Role of Auditors

5.93 One way of monitoring the work being carried out by price collectors and addressing any issues is to employ auditors to occasionally accompany collectors during the field collection or to carry out a retrospective check on the collected data. The function of the auditor is to check the validity of the prices collected and to initiate corrective action that may extend beyond correcting an individual price quote to reviewing and updating instructions to price collectors and to general retraining. The function can cover more than one geographical area, but it does not normally extend to the supervisor's role in managing price collectors and the price collection process. Sometimes the function of the auditor is combined with that of the field supervisor. The observations and comments of auditors are an essential part of quality management.

5.94 The range of tasks that an auditor carries out will vary from one NSO to another. Monitoring the standard of price collection will always be the main focus of the auditor. There are several other areas, however, in which auditors can be called upon to contribute. Auditors may be required to help with the sampling of locations and items and check that proposed collection locations contain an adequate range of outlets, and advise on economic conditions in these locations and on any dangerous areas. Auditors can carry out product reviews. For example, if an item is causing difficulty for price collectors, auditors can speak to collectors and retailers to determine the reasons for these difficulties. Auditors can also advise on changes to basket composition, ensure that products suggested by the head office are available across the country, and suggest item descriptions. Furthermore, auditors can provide reports on price collection in existing locations. For example, the head office may raise a query about an outlet in a location, and the auditors can visit this outlet to find the answer to the question or to persuade a retailer to continue with the survey.

5.95 The main purpose of audits is to ensure that each collector is following the procedures laid down for price collection so that the risk of errors is reduced. However, there are other benefits of strategic importance with regard to continuous quality improvement:

- Raising awareness of quality
- The identification of the scope for introducing improvements to quality, including rectifying weaknesses in procedures, documentation, and price collection skills

Quality Checks of Local Price Collection: Back-Checking

5.96 Another approach to monitoring the standard of price collection is to carry out a back-check (that is, a retrospective check of a proportion of the prices recorded during the collection).

5.97 Back-checks can be used to:

- Assess the standard of competence of individual price collectors
- Audit the overall standard of price collection
- Identify general training needs or the specific needs of an individual
- Highlight any key issues including, for example, problems with documentation or instructions issued by the head office
- Identify areas where collection is problematic; for example, all collectors may have problems in certain types of outlets, prompting the need for more detailed instructions from the head office

5.98 Back-checking should be done by an expert independent of the process (preferably employed by the NSO), such as an auditor. Back-checking is carried out by visiting the selected outlet and recollecting the prices and other relevant information, such as attribute or description codes. This activity should be carried out close to the original collection period to avoid problems of price changes occurring in the interim. Back-checkers should seek permission from the outlet staff beforehand and follow the general criteria of conduct for local collection.

5.99 Performance criteria should be determined to which all back-check results can be compared. These criteria should set, for example, the acceptable number of pricing errors per number of items checked. Well-defined criteria will enable performance of collectors or locations following a back-check.

5.100 A back-check may include a range of tests to identify the following:

- Price difference—if the price is different, the auditor should check with outlet staff if there has been a price change since the original collection took place
- Insufficient item description—incomplete descriptions should be augmented to include all price-determining characteristics
- Wrong item priced—such as incorrect size or brand being chosen
- Items wrongly recorded as missing or temporarily out of stock

5.101 A report should be sent to the head office for scrutiny once the back-check has been completed. The head office will then need to take appropriate action, which may include, for example, retraining the price collector or sending out supplementary instruction.

Quality Checks Conducted Centrally by the Head Office

5.102 Four kinds of regular checks are necessary at the head office:

- Check that the price collectors' reports are sent in when they are due. If this is not done, it is necessary to find the reason and take appropriate action to obtain the reports.
- Confirm that the reports contain what they are supposed to contain (for example, mandatory fields have not been left blank, numeric fields contain numbers, or nonnumeric fields do not contain numbers).
- Review and edit each return. Substitutions may have to be made centrally, or those made by the collectors may have to be approved. Unusual or large price changes may need to be queried. Items priced in multiple units or varying weights may have to be converted to price per standard unit. Missing prices must be dealt with according to standard rules relating to the cause.
- Find and correct errors introduced when keying the numbers into the computer or transcribing them onto worksheets. Errors preferably should be avoided by eliminating the need to transcribe.

5.103 The way the data are organized in worksheets or in the computer may differ from the way they are arranged on receipt. For instance, the data may arrive at the head office organized for price collection purposes by collector, outlet, and item but will be entered on to a spreadsheet designed to reflect the computational needs of CPI compilation. The data in original format should be recorded for reference if any problems with the data are disclosed during processing. This facilitates operational management when dealing with queries. Furthermore, even if the same set of codes are used in price collection and in the processing of collected prices, other codes may have to be used for information that comes in from the collectors in noncoded form.

5.104 The organization of the quality checks conducted centrally by the head office will vary from country to country. In some cases, local or regional supervisors will do some of it; in other cases, it will be more appropriate for it all to be done centrally. Some of these tasks can be done by computer and others manually.

5.105 Procedures should be in place to check that all documents, messages, or files are returned from the field, so that price collectors can be contacted about missing returns. Initial checks should then be carried out to ensure that data are complete and correct. For instance, checks should be run to ensure that unexpected duplicate prices (that is, for the same item, in the same outlet, in the same location) are not taken on, and that the location, outlet, and item identifier codes, which accompany each price, exist and are valid. If any prices fail these checks, a query should be raised with the price collector for clarification. Since some of the checking may require reference back to the price collectors (or to their supervisors or respondents when direct mail questionnaires are used), the timetable for producing the index must allow for this communication to take place.

5.106 In deciding on what checks should take place in the head office, account should be taken of the validation checks carried out in the field. The use of handheld computers or tablets will increase the potential for validation at the time of price collection and reduce the need for detailed scrutiny at the head office. It would clearly not be productive or cost-effective to repeat all the tests already carried out locally, except as a secondary audit or random check that those checks have been completed.

Data Reports

5.107 Reports can help the head office staff identify prices for which the level or change stands out as different from that reported for similar varieties elsewhere, or simply where a change may need to be queried because it lies outside specified limits. Thus, a comparative analysis of other prices collected for an item can be undertaken. A printout can list all prices that either fall well outside the range of prices obtained for that representative item or for which the percentage change from last time falls outside a specified range, and a similar list can be compiled identifying outliers based on the recent price behavior of the same item in the same outlet. The limits used will vary from item to item and can be amended in the light of experience. The CPI compiler can then work through these lists, first ascertaining whether there has been a keying-in error, and then examining whether any explanation furnished by the collector adequately explains the divergent price behavior or whether a query should be sent back to the supervisor or collector. Again, the timetable for CPI compilation should allow for this, and anomalous observations should be discarded where an acceptable explanation or correction cannot be obtained in time.

5.108 Other reports may be produced regularly covering several periods (for example, three monthly) to detect accumulated patterns, thus enabling broader problems to be detected. For example:

- One collector's reports might show many more "outlet closed" remarks than those of other collectors, perhaps indicating either a motivational or training need on the part of that collector, or a change in retail trade patterns in a particular area.

- Variety substitution for a particular representative item might become more numerous than before, suggesting a possible need for revision of the specification or the choice of another representative item.
- Where tight specifications list several brands and models of which one is to be chosen, but a large number of collected prices are for items not specified in the original list, this suggests that the specified brands and models are no longer appropriate and that a review of the list is required.
- The dispersion of price changes for a specific representative item might be much larger than it used to be, raising the question of whether it has been appropriately specified.

5.109 Routine computer-generated reports should enable to detect such problems. Two types of reports are particularly useful: index dispersion reports and price quote reports:

- *Index dispersion report.* This is a list of the current index for each elementary aggregate, the number of valid quotes for each item, and the number of price relatives and their values. The ratios of current to previous valid prices can be compared and queries generated, if these ratios fall out of acceptable ranges based on previous price behaviors and considering any special circumstances such as the introduction of discounted prices in seasonal sales. The index dispersion reports can be used to identify quotes with price relatives that fall outside the range of the main bulk of quotes. These suspect quotes can then be investigated, and appropriate action is taken.
- *Price quote report.* This consists of a range of information on an item that the index dispersion report has highlighted as warranting further investigation. Information listed may include current price, recent previous prices, and base price, together with locations and types of outlet. The report can be used to identify the quotes that require further investigation and to investigate rejected prices.

5.110 While price collectors should examine every price they collect, it is not considered necessary nor feasible for collection supervisors and index compilers to subject every collected price to the same level of scrutiny. It is recommended that, to improve cost-effectiveness, a significance rating should be applied to determine how much time and effort should be expended on examining and, where necessary, editing individual prices.

- In general, prices from elementary aggregates with relatively small price samples should receive more attention from the index compiler. This is because, if the weights of the elementary aggregates are broadly equal, each individual price movement within these elementary aggregates can have a much more significant influence on the index calculation than any individual price movement from within an elementary aggregate with many price quotes.
- Price samples from elementary aggregates with high expenditure weights should also be examined critically as a higher expenditure weight will cause all price movements within the sample to have a greater influence on the CPI.
- The highest risk is associated with elementary aggregates with relatively large weights but few price quotes and with complex index construction methods. This situation is associated with utilities and other services that account for relatively large expenditures and where there may be only one or a few suppliers and prices are based on complex tariffs.

5.111 Some of the techniques discussed in paragraphs 5.116–5.156 work best when applied to large quantities of data and have the advantage of being automated with the intervals identified for closer examination being generated by the prices data. Abnormal individual prices such as sale prices, or price movements such as sale recovery prices, may be excluded from manual and automated procedures for the detection of outliers, particularly in the calculation of upper and lower bounds, as they are not representative of the general trend in prices. Nevertheless, such prices should be checked for accuracy, for instance by reference to previous price history. Automated checking can be applied to seasonal sale prices and prices for seasonal items.

5.112 Automated checking essentially performs the same basic filtering purpose for the identification of outliers as the manual techniques described previously. It is sometimes referred to as statistical checking in contrast with the manual techniques which are sometimes referred to as nonstatistical checking.

Data Validation and Editing

Data Validation and Editing by the Head Office: Automated (Statistical) Checking and the Use of Algorithms

5.113 Data validation methods identify possible errors and outliers for validation. Errors are incorrect prices, while outliers can be defined as price movements that are exceptionally large compared with most movements. The purpose of data validation is to validate and confirm prices flagged as errors or outliers. Any errors should be corrected. Outliers verified as correct should be used in the calculation of the index.

5.114 The main conceptual difference between automated (statistical) checking and manual checking is that the automated technique calculates the limits for acceptable movement based on the data collected. These techniques have the benefit of automatically updating the acceptable limits in line with any overall change in price volatility, as observed when new price data are received and the limits are recalculated. These techniques require a large amount of data to provide reliable results and so are best suited to data handlers and index compilers in regional offices and the head office, where prices data from several collection centers will have been collated and stored, rather than at the local level.

5.115 Automated (statistical) checking compares each price change with changes in the other items from a given price sample. The chosen price sample is usually the sample to which the item being checked belongs, but the sample for testing may be a combination of price samples for similar products. It can also be updated as more prices are received from the field. For each of the methods described in the following text, the price ratios may measure the price change over any time period: for instance, the change from the previous period or the change from the same period in the previous year.

The Use of Median and Quartile Values

5.116 One method of setting the limits to determine whether a movement is a possible error is based on the median and quartile values of the price ratios (R) from the sample. The acceptable limits are set as a predefined multiple of the range between the median and the quartiles. Any observation with a price change outside this range is identified as a possible error. The major benefit of a method like this is that it is not affected by any single outlier value. A numerical example is provided in Annex 5.3.

5.117 The basic approach to estimating sensible upper and lower limits of acceptable price movement relies on the assumption that the observed price changes are normally distributed. Under this assumption, the distance between each of the first and third quartiles (R_{Q1} and R_{Q3}) and the median (R_M) will be the same: call this distance "D_M." Operating under this assumption, the proportion of price changes that are likely to lie outside specified upper (L_U) and lower (L_L) limits can be estimated from a normal distribution table. The limits can be defined as

$$L_U = R_M + C \times D_M; \text{ and} \qquad L_L = R_M - C \times D_M \tag{5.1}$$

where C is a user-defined value.

5.118 As discussed in paragraphs 5.126–5.134, a variation of this basic approach is recommended to allow for the skewed distribution of price changes that can be observed in practice.

5.119 If C is defined as equal to one, then approximately 50 percent of the observations will lie between the upper and lower limits. Using the standardized normal distribution, this is equivalent to setting the limits at plus or minus 0.7 times the standard deviation (σ) from the median. Table 5.2 provides approximate multiples of σ for selected values of C and the associated percentage of the observations that will be flagged as possible errors and outliers. In practice, there are serious shortcomings with this method as described here.

5.120 In normal circumstances, the majority of observations for many products will not show any price movement. Therefore, the values of the quartiles are likely to be very close to the median value. As a result, using small values for C is likely to cause the majority of price movements to be flagged as possible errors and outliers. To demonstrate this effect, in Example 2 in Annex 5.3, 16 additional observations indicating no price movements have been added to the sample of 30 observations used in Example 1. A price sample with at least one-third of the observations showing no movements would not be unusual for many categories of items. If C is set to two, then 60 percent of the actual price movements would be flagged as possible errors, compared with 30 percent in the unadjusted sample.

Table 5.2 Selected Values of *C* and the Proportion of Observations Flagged

C	σ Multiplier	Expected Proportion of Observations Flagged (percent)
1	0.68	50.00
2	1.37	17.00
3	2.07	4.00
4	2.75	0.70
6	4.00	0.14

5.121 The index compiler should experiment with different values of C for different product groups or outlet types to determine appropriate values for local use. It is recommended that a relatively low value of C be used. C need not be an integer and can be expressed with regard to fractions as well.

5.122 The distribution of prices and price movements is rarely normal; rather in most cases, a skewed distribution exists. Thus, the underlying assumption of a normal distribution is not valid, and the use of symmetrical upper and lower limits will result in a skewed distribution of prices flagged up as possible errors or outliers. This is operationally inefficient and the examination of differing proportions of "low" and of "high" prices and price movements could lead to bias.

A Modified Use of Median and Quartile Values

5.123 To use the previous method in practice, three modifications are recommended, as shown in paragraphs 5.127–5.134.

5.124 Based on the simple price ratios, the distances from the median represented by price decreases are not as large as the distances represented by price increases. As an example, consider a case where a product is on special offer at half price. This is represented by a price decrease of 50 percent. However, to return to the original price requires a 100 percent increase. To make the calculation of the distance from the center the same for extreme changes for price decreases and for price increases, the price ratios should be transformed. The transformed distance, S_i, for the ith price observation can be calculated as

$$S_i = 1 - \frac{R_M}{R_i} \quad \text{if } 0 < R_i < R_M \qquad S_i = \frac{R_i}{R_M} - 1 \quad \text{if } R_i \geq R_M \tag{5.2}$$

where

R_M = median.

5.125 The observations with a price ratio lower than R_M have now been transformed into the negative of the increase required to return the price ratio to the value of R_M. Any observations with a price ratio equal to R_M will have a transformed price movement of zero. Observations with a price ratio greater than R_M have been transformed to show changes as though they had increased from R_M. The procedure is then carried out on the set of S_i.

5.126 In situations where the quartiles (R_{Q1} and R_{Q3}) are quite close in value to the median (R_M), many small price movements are likely to be identified as possible errors or outliers. To reduce this problem, items with no price movements may be removed from the calculations. If the acceptance interval is still very narrow, some minimum distance should be set. A starting value is 5 percent for monthly changes but it is up to the CPI compiler to choose, based on past experience.

5.127 The third modification is intended to overcome the problem of using small samples. When using a small sample, the impact of one observation on the distances between the quartiles and the median might be considered too significant. In practice, the sample sizes for many elementary aggregates will be small. To improve the usefulness of this method, the samples from several similar elementary aggregates can be combined. In this regard, elementary aggregates can be considered similar if their prices are believed to exhibit similar behavior.

5.128 The Hidiroglou and Berthelot method, as described in detail in Hidiroglou and Berthelot[6] (1986), can easily be extended according to the description in paragraphs 5.133–5.135. The variable s_i is independent of the price levels. To address the issue that the level of the prices can influence the acceptance interval, s may be transformed into a new variable, E:

$$E_i = s_i \cdot \left(\max\left\{p_i^{t-1}, p_i^t\right\}\right)^U, \; 0 \leq U \leq 1 \qquad (5.3)$$

5.129 E is calculated as s multiplied by the largest of the prices in period t or $t - 1$, raised to the power U. The variable U determines to what degree the price level influences the acceptance interval. The larger U is, the larger the influence of the price level will be. If $U = 0$ the price level plays no role. This method is helpful, if the compiler wishes to pay more attention to a price increase from 1,000 to 1,100 than from 10 to 11.

5.130 A further transformation can be made to ensure a minimum acceptance interval to avoid that too many price changes being identified as possible errors for elementary aggregates (E) with only small price changes. In this case, for each elementary aggregate, the median, E_M, and the first and third quartiles, E_{Q1} and E_{Q3}, of the E_i's are found, and the following values calculated:

$$d_{Q1} = \text{Max } \{E_M - E_{Q1}, |AE_M|\} \qquad (5.4)$$
$$d_{Q3} = \text{Max } \{E_{Q3} - E_M, |AE_M|\}$$

5.131 A is a constant that enters $|AE_M|$ to ensure a minimum acceptance interval. A low value of A raises the probability that $(E_M - E_{Q1})$ or $(E_{Q3} - E_M)$ determines d_{Q1} or d_{Q3}, and vice versa. For instance, if A is set to 0.05, $|AE_M|$ will be quite small so that $(E_M - E_{Q1})$ or $(E_{Q3} - E_M)$ are likely to determine d_{Q1} or d_{Q3}, even if the dispersion of the E_i's is relatively small. If, on the other hand, the dispersion of the E_i's becomes very small, $|AE_M|$ determines d_{Q1} and d_{Q3}. Hence, A can be used to avoid having too many price changes identified as possible errors for elementary aggregates with only small price changes. The acceptance interval is finally defined as

$$\text{Acceptance interval} = \{E_M - C^*d_{Q1}; E_M + C^*d_{Q3}\}, \qquad (5.5)$$

where $(E_M - C^*d_{Q1})$ is the lower bound, and $(E_M + C^*d_{Q3})$ is the upper bound of the interval. C is an extra variable that may be introduced. The larger the C, the larger the acceptance interval, and the fewer extremes and potential errors will be identified.

The Tukey Algorithm

5.132 The Tukey algorithm overcomes the problem of validating data when there are many observations with no price change (that is, where many price relatives are equal to one indicating no price movement). The first step is to sort the sample of price relatives. The highest and lowest 5 percent are flagged for examination as possible errors or outliers and removed from further calculation. All observations with no price movement are also removed from the sample before further calculations are done. The next step is to calculate the arithmetic mean (AM) of the remaining observations (referred to as the Tukey sample). This value is then used as the dividing value to separate the observations into two smaller samples: an upper and a lower set of price ratios. The arithmetic mean of each of these two samples is then calculated as (AM_L, AM_U). The upper and lower Tukey limits (T_U, T_L) are then calculated for the Tukey set as

$$T_U = AM + 2.5(AM_U - AM) \qquad (5.6)$$
$$T_L = AM - 2.5(AM - AM_L)$$

5.133 All observations that are greater than T_U or less than T_L are flagged as possible errors or outliers.

5.134 As this method excludes all observations with no price movement, the calculated limits are unlikely to be close to the mean. Therefore, there will be no need to impose a minimum difference. However, the problem of requiring a reasonably large number of observations in the sample remains. Again, it may be necessary to combine the samples of similar elementary aggregates. Example 3 in Annex 5.3 shows that five observations would have been flagged by this method in comparison to 18 observations by the previous method based on the modified use of median and quartile values (see 5.126–5.134).

5.135 As mentioned before, statistical methods of filtering have an advantage over simple filtering, because the limits are set by the data and can be recalculated over time. The disadvantage is that filtering cannot be done until sufficient quantities of data have been collected, unless the index compiler uses approximations from past experience. The processes can be repeated as additional prices are received. Compilers should aim to set filters so that most of the records flagged as potential errors do turn out to be errors (or outliers requiring explanation). The aim of all these methods of filtering is to indicate which records require examination, not to flag records for automatic deletion from the sample. Each price movement should be checked for credibility and representativeness. Only if the movement is an error or unrepresentative should modification be considered. There should not be a presumption that an outlier is "wrong until proven right," and outliers should not be treated as incorrect prices.

[6]Mike Hidiroglou and Jean-Marie Berthelot. 1986. "Statistical Editing and Imputation for Periodic Business Surveys." *Survey Methodology* 12 (1): 73–83.

Visual Data Validation

5.136 Using plot charts is helpful to spot the outliers on the collected data and focus validation on these (see Figure 5.1 with arrows highlighting outliers). For visual data validation, it is easy to use plot charts that are readily available in spreadsheet software tools or can be programmed on the information technology (IT) system. Visualization can be more convenient than focusing validation to the change of prices, especially when there are extreme price changes such as during sales periods or in the case of fresh fruit and vegetables. If the plot chart is programmed into the IT system, from the outlier it is possible to make a direct link to the observation.

Review of Outliers

5.137 The detection of price observations that are outliers may be conducted through an examination of both price levels and of price movements. The movements will have been verified as being based on correctly collected and recorded data but may not be representative of the behavior of the section of the market that they are meant to represent. This leads to the concern that a different sample would have produced a significantly different and more representative average price movement.

5.138 It is recommended to use resources efficiently on validation and checking of input data and to focus on identifying the most important errors/outliers. The general rule should be to include verified prices. Excluding or modifying prices should be the exception. The aim should be to reflect the reality.

5.139 The tests for outliers are the same as those for identifying potential errors. Outliers can be determined by comparing the price movement relative to defined allowable limits. These may be either predetermined numerically or predefined based on statistical tests.

5.140 If, by exception, outliers are to be modified, they are usually modified to lie on the predefined boundaries of acceptable movement or to be imputed by the movement of a suitable sample of prices. Imputation by the average price change of the product group to which the item belongs yields a similar result as its exclusion (the same result within the elementary aggregate), but such imputations can have operational advantages as they employ protocols already in the calculation system for the imputation of missing prices. An automatic adjustment should generally be avoided, and not be used to reduce volatility in an index, for example, at the elementary aggregate level. The index compiler should consider each case on its individual merits, following agreed guidelines and deciding based on all relevant information. Prices should be modified or discarded only if there is sufficient justification. The CPI protocols followed by the NSO may even forbid the modification or exclusion of outliers.

5.141 Price collectors and their supervisors are responsible for providing as much information as possible about the reasons for extreme price movements or levels and why they accepted the price quote as valid. In addition to checking for better accuracy, supervisors can also be instructed to compare the price movements for equivalent products obtained by all the collectors they supervise.

Figure 5.1 Price Changes in Plot Chart during Sales Season

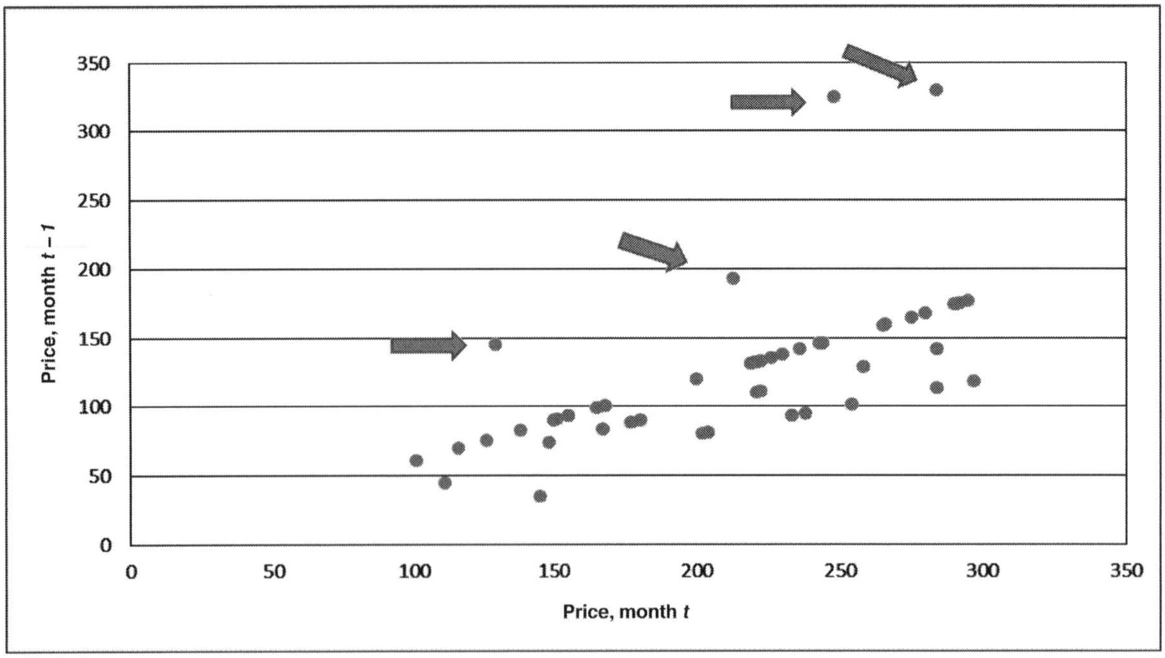

No Price Change

5.142 If the price observations are collected in a way that prompts the respondent with the previously reported price, the respondent may report the same price as a matter of convenience. This can happen even though the price may have changed, or even when the particular product being surveyed is no longer available or has changed its price-determining characteristics. As many item prices do not change frequently, this kind of error is unlikely to be spotted by normal checks. Often the situation comes to light when the contact at the responding outlet changes and the new contact has difficulty in finding something that corresponds to the price previously reported. It is advisable, therefore, to keep a record of the last time a respondent reported a price change.

Missing Prices

5.143 Treatment of missing prices is dealt with in more detail in Chapter 6. This section discusses ways of minimizing the occurrence of missing observations.

5.144 It is important to maintain the relevance of the sample of items priced. As part of the longer-term maintenance of price samples, items and locations for which prices are missing can be examined for common patterns. For instance, if many retailers are missing the same item, there may be a general supply problem. This may be an indication that an item will have to be replaced. If the number of regularly missing items is growing, then the sample might need to be reviewed. If a particular outlet is recorded as having a relatively large number of missing prices it may no longer be appropriate for the particular items assigned to it, or the varieties whose prices are collected in the outlet may need to be reviewed.

5.145 When prices are collected using a questionnaire sent to the outlet, individual respondents generally follow a regular pattern in terms of response. Some will return their price survey promptly, while others will take more time. Price collectors should be encouraged to become familiar with these patterns. If the system for recording the return of these surveys also records the expected return date, then unexpected nonreturns can be flagged even though the final deadline for return of survey forms has not passed. These respondents can be contacted in advance of the final deadline to ensure that the survey form has not been forgotten. Early contact can reduce the number of prices still missing by the deadline. Respondents that provide prices for heavily weighted items can also be monitored and contacted earlier.

Credibility Checking

5.146 Credibility checking tests the reasonableness of the input data and the results obtained. Credibility checking of the results should take place after the checking of the numerical accuracy of the data at or shortly after price collection as described previously. These early checks are the responsibility of the price collectors and their supervisors but also involve outlier detection at the head office. These early checks should discover all straightforward errors like incorrect coding (for example, wrongly attributing a price as a sale price) and the incorrect recording of prices.

5.147 Addressing other potential errors is less straightforward. Results that fail a data check, such as exceeding the predefined movement limits described earlier, may be judged by the index compiler to be valid as a result of referring to other information such as market intelligence. Other potential errors might only be resolved after checking with the respondent, if time allows.

5.148 If it is possible with individual price quotations to resurvey the price or obtain a satisfactory explanation from the respondent, the query can be sent back to the price collector and the data can be flagged as being verified and then subsequently corrected if found to be in error. Even if it is not possible to check with the respondent before the computation deadline, the respondent could be questioned during the next regular visit, as the answer may assist the NSO's understanding of market behavior for the particular product or retail sector. When a satisfactory explanation is not available, the CPI procedures should provide guidelines to aid the compiler in deciding how to treat the questionable price. For instance, the compiler could omit the price, allowing the processing system to impute a price, or modify the price to keep the price change within a predefined limit, but this is best avoided and should be the exception. If prices are modified without verification from the respondent, it is recommended that price collectors be informed of potential problems during the next collection.

5.149 NSOs can minimize problems caused by unusual prices and price movements by training price collectors to recognize these situations, to check prices when first observed, and to collect relevant explanatory information during the initial price collecting visit. Avoiding return visits or calls keeps costs down and reduces the burden placed on respondents.

Checking by Impact or Data Output Checking

5.150 Filtering by impact, or output editing, is based on calculating the impact that an individual price change has on an index to which it contributes. This index can be an elementary aggregate index, the total index, or some other aggregate index. The impact that a price change has on an index is its percentage change times its effective weight. However, the exact calculation of the impact will depend on which formula has been applied for the elementary indices. It is possible to set a maximum value for this impact, so that all price changes that cause an impact greater than this can be flagged for review. The impact of a price change on a higher-level index will also depend on the weight of the elementary index in the aggregate.

5.151 At the lowest level, the appearance and disappearance of products in the sample cause the *effective weight* of an individual price to change substantially. The effective weight is also affected if a price observation is used as an imputation for other missing observations. The evaluation of effective weights in each period is possible, though complicated. To help highlight potential errors, nominal weights, as a percentage of their sum, will usually provide a reasonable approximation. If the impact of 12-month changes is required to highlight potential errors, approximations are the only feasible filters, as the effective weights will vary over the period.

5.152 One advantage of identifying potential errors in this way is that it focuses on the results. Another advantage is that this form of filtering helps the CPI compiler describe the contributions to change in the price indices. Much of this analysis is done after the indices have been calculated, as the CPI staff often wishes to highlight in the statistical press release those indices that contributed most to overall index changes. Sometimes the CPI staff findings that some retail sectors have a relatively high contribution to the overall price change may be considered counterintuitive. The change may also be traced back to an error, but it may be late in the production cycle and jeopardize the scheduled release date. There is thus a case for identifying such unusual contributions early as part of the data editing procedures rather than for analytical purposes. The disadvantage of this method is that in practice the final calculation of an elementary index change may be rejected only after the CPI has been computed.

Price Collector Training

5.153 The training of local price collectors and clear instructions for them are vital elements in ensuring the quality of the prices data and of the CPI. Collectors need to be properly trained, require adequate instructions, and must have easy access to guidance because:

- Price collection is of significant policy relevance.
- Quick judgments often need to be made.
- Collectors often work remotely and on their own.
- Instant communication is not always possible.
- Collectors work in a dynamic environment.
- Errors are difficult to rectify.

5.154 Documents are needed to explain what is to be done, when it should be done, how it should be done, and why it should be done. Reviewing the documentation also provides an opportunity to review the procedures.

5.155 Good documentation as part of an integrated quality management system is addressed in Chapter 13. The current chapter deals specifically with the documentation needs of price collectors and training.

5.156 Training for price collectors should enable them to successfully perform all essential activities and deal with potential difficulties including:

- Persuade new outlets to become price providers
- Understand and recognize occasions when prices provided are unacceptable
- Record relevant information to describe the quality change in a product
- Recognize unusual price movements when checking their collected prices

Training for Price Collectors

5.157 Introductory training should be given to all price collectors so that they gain the necessary skills before collecting prices for the CPI. It can also be a motivational tool.

5.158 A typical training schedule might consist of a one-day training course at the head office (which may include some refresher training for experienced collectors) covering:

- Background to the NSO and the CPI
- Use of the CPI and importance of accurately recording prices
- The general principles of index compilation and price collection
- How local price collection fits into the overall CPI compilation process
- Instructions for retailer recruitment, getting permission to enter outlets, and so on
- *Practical price collection issues*: for example, product identification or descriptions; pricing (for example, item descriptions, definition of price/sale price, rules relating to seasonal items, quantity conversions, quality adjustment—when is an item or product equivalent?)
- The timetable and administrative arrangements

5.159 Practical examples and practice collections should be an integral part of the learning process. For example, there should be an opportunity for:

- Discussions about "equivalent" replacements using photographs and item descriptions
- Practice collections in office
- Supervised practice collection in the field

5.160 Tests and evaluation of individual performance should be an integral part of the training. This could be achieved through:

- Written tests at the end of the training day
- Evaluation by supervisors of practice collections in the field
- Feedback to new collectors, including additional training needs
- Evaluation by collectors of training provided (essential for ensuring training is relevant and effective)

5.161 The evaluation of individual collector performance is essential. Collectors must pass the required standards, against a checklist of tasks, before being allowed to conduct a real collection.

Follow-Up Training and Refresher Training

5.162 The longer-term training is just as important as introductory training to the integrity of price collection, particularly with the evolution of the retail sector and CPI methodology and when CPI baskets are updated. One way of facilitating this is for the price collector's supervisor to:

- Accompany the new price collector on a live price collection.
- Conduct a back-check of the prices collected to identify any problems.
- Produce an evaluation report that will provide a basis for further training of the price collector. The evaluation report can include a scorecard against a checklist of required actions.

5.163 Where resources allow, NSOs should conduct regular accompanied checks and background checks of all price collectors in addition to special checks of performance issues. The information gathered can be used to compile scorecards for individual price collectors, supervisors, and groups of price collectors.

5.164 Regular refresher training workshops should be considered, especially where evidence from the field indicates a need or where price collection procedures and conventions change, or the CPI basket or sample of outlets has been updated. These present an opportunity to: raise awareness of the importance of collecting correct prices; provide formal training on revised guidelines; resolve recurring or recent problems; and provide price collectors with an opportunity to assist each other in managing problem situations encountered in the field, such as dealing with reluctant respondents.

Training of Supervisors and the Head Office Staff

5.165 Supervisors must be at least as well informed as the price collectors. As the supervisor will normally be the first point of contact when a difficult situation is encountered during price collection, they also need a good understanding of the methodology and theory behind the selection of the product sample. Supervisors are part of the management team. Their training should cover:

- Team management
- Performance appraisal (where this is normal office practice)
- Project management

5.166 The head office staff should also be provided with a basic training in price collection. The benefits are threefold:

- It gives the head office staff a better understanding of collectors' needs.
- It helps editing (staff at the head office will know what to look out for).
- It supports disaster recovery (paragraphs 5.175–5.177) or business continuity (the head office staff will be able to undertake price collection in an emergency).

Documentation: Work Instructions

5.167 Accessible, relevant, and up-to-date work instructions are essential for both price collectors and their supervisors. Documentation should cover all aspects of the job and should in large part reflect what has been covered in training. Price collectors should be provided with work instructions on:

- How to approach outlet staff
- How to ask questions to ensure that the required information is obtained
- Appropriate personal behavior and dress codes
- Procedures for recording and passing on collected prices and other relevant information
- Data checking
- Creating collection schedules
- Recognizing when recorded prices appear to be incorrect

5.168 The work instructions for supervisors of price collectors should be in the form of a supplement to the price collectors' work instructions and should cover:

- Checking the quality of the price collectors' work
- Checking the accuracy and completeness of the prices collected
- Official recording of resource use (for example, cars and bicycles for transport and funds for buying goods in markets)
- Official procedures for maintenance of resources (for example, testing the accuracy of scales)
- Creating complementary collection timetables for all collectors within the supervisor's area of responsibility

5.169 Most of the documentation should be prepared by the head office, with input as appropriate from regional offices, fieldwork supervisors, and data collectors. Centrally prepared documentation will help ensure consistent practices in the field including between regions and should be readily available to all collectors and supervisors. The documents can be available in paper or electronic form and should be accessible to the relevant staff.

5.170 All documentation should be kept up to date. Effective documentation control systems should be in place. With paper-based documentation, this could mean keeping the instructions in a loose-leaf folder and issuing individual updates. The amendment pages should include version number and date printed and be kept to a reasonable number for ease of reference. Editorial access should be restricted and password protected. A judgment will need to be made on when a redraft of a chapter or the complete working instructions is justified. Documentation is an essential part of a quality management system.

5.171 An example of a documentation control template is given in Annex 5.4.

Disaster Recovery

5.172 The prices data should be stored on a database with hardware and software that is robust and supported to minimize the business continuity risks associated with running the existing system. But even with a resilient production system, contingency planning and operational continuity in the field and the head office are essential.

5.173 In a world of rapidly changing statistical needs, a statistical system should be able to respond quickly and effectively to changing demands and should have the resilience needed to ensure continuity in the production of statistics. This is not possible if systems are old, inflexible, and extensively tailored to past requirements. Building a modern statistical infrastructure of methods, tools to implement them, and a technical environment to support the statistical processes is a significant component of achieving quality CPI compilation and computation. Contingency plans are needed when the unexpected happens, for example, when there is a systems failure or the price collection team is affected by an unexpected illness. Disaster recovery plans address these risks by, for example, saving regular and frequent backup copies of the prices database on a secondary computer and by having the capacity to collect prices when significant numbers of price collectors are not available. Two strategies have been followed to accommodate a short-term unexpected deficit in the numbers of price collectors:

- The collection of prices from a subsample of outlets chosen to be representative of the full sample, thereby not needing so many price collectors. The price evolution from one period to the subsequent period can then be calculated from the subsample using matched pairs of price observations.
- The training of the head office staff in price collection (for example, as part of their initial training), so that they can provide cover. The head office can also be given responsibility for price collection on a routine basis in a location close to the head office, with individual head office staff allocated the task of price collection on a rotating basis. An added benefit of this is that the head office staff become more familiar with the issues confronted by price collectors.

5.174 In cases where no fieldwork can be performed, for example, where there is an all-out strike and no prices can be collected by visiting outlets, an indicative figure may be possible using data from other sources, such as retailers websites, but only if it can be established that like-for-like comparisons are being made and that the fixed-basket principle is being adhered to.

Other Methods of Price Collection

5.175 This chapter has so far focused in large part on traditional methods of price collection where price collectors visit outlets and record prices on paper forms. It now considers other methods of price collection. As noted at the beginning of the chapter, scanner data are given a separate consideration in Chapter 10.

Electronic Reporting

5.176 Electronic reporting for centrally collected prices and use of handheld computers and tablets for local price collection can introduce greater efficiency into price collection and processing, and provide more scope for effective quality assurance of prices and auditing, but both depend on the introduction of effective quality control procedures. Electronic reporting through electronic point of sale, commonly referred to as scanner data, is another option.

5.177 Centrally collected data can be collected electronically in several ways. Once initial contact has been made with data suppliers, a mutually convenient electronic data collecting procedure can be initiated. Options include:

- Emailing data collection spreadsheets between the NSO and the retailer
- Emailing of price lists at agreed times by retailers
- Touch-tone dialing facilities for data to be supplied in an agreed-upon format
- The use of the internet (supplemented, if necessary, by telephone calls to clarify definitions and availability and whether the prices displayed on the internet are the same as those displayed in the corresponding outlets) (see also paragraphs 5.192–5.206 on collecting prices online and web scraping and Chapter 10 on scanner data)

5.178 The use of electronic websites/portals, where respondents can report prices online, is becoming increasingly common and can also be an excellent channel for communicating with the respondents.

Collection by Telephone

5.179 The prices for certain items, particularly services such as electricians' and plumbers' charges and the cost of home security, may be obtained by telephoning the business or organization concerned. This applies when the outlets provide standard items or services. However, even if prices are obtained by telephone, the outlet should be visited occasionally. This helps to maintain cooperation through personal contact and to ensure that there are no misunderstandings over the prices. This will be more important for some outlets than others. For example, the price of hiring a van may be less certain than the cost of an eye exam.

Computer-Assisted Data Collection (CADC): The Use of Mobile Telephones, Handheld Computers, and Tablets

5.180 A number of NSOs have successfully used mobile telephones, handheld computers, or tablets for local price collection. These technologies are now available at competitive prices and the necessary infrastructures are generally in place to make the use of CADC an attractive option.

5.181 A CADC system can lead to improvements in the quality of CPI data, particularly as increased quality control at the point of data entry helps identify anomalies and ensure that prices are correct. CADC has the potential to significantly improve the quality of the final CPI in the following ways:

- *Price history*. The price collection program might allow for a more comprehensive price history to be available to the price collector, rather than just one previous price included on paper forms. The availability of such data leads to less judgmental editing at the point of data collection and helps ensure the comparability of items, particularly where prices for a particular item are variable. Some price statisticians have argued that machines should be programmed to reveal the price history only after a price quote has been entered so that collectors are not overly influenced when locating the item to be priced or when choosing a replacement item. Others argue that an early sight of the price history is useful information for the price collectors as it assists them in their work.
- *Quality checks in the field*. The price collection program can include several automatic validity checks that can be used to identify where the price entered varies by a certain percentage (positive or negative) from the previous month's price and the average price for that item over a number of months and to flag up where data were not entered in all required fields (price, weight, indicator code). These checks provide a useful marker for when a price needs to be double-checked. In a paper-based system, such checks are carried out in the head office after the data have been collected, and audits can be carried out after the collection period when prices may have changed.
- *Transcription*. There is a major risk of errors when transcribing paper forms. This is not a risk when using CADC, where data can be transferred electronically to the head office.

5.182 The use of CADC also significantly reduces the time taken to make data available electronically at the head office and between data collection and finalization. This can be achieved through:

- *Transcription.* Data collected on paper must be transcribed onto a computer for computation. This process is time-consuming and resource-intensive. When data are collected on handheld computers or tablets, the data can be directly transferred electronically to the servers at the head office potentially in real time.
- *Transmission from regions.* Electronic transmission will allow price collectors or regional offices to directly transmit an electronic data file to the head office thus avoiding the need for postal or courier services or hand delivery forms. This significantly increases the speed of data transmission to the head office and reduces the cost of doing so. In addition, the head offices can look up the latest returns of price data from all regions immediately on receipt and identify early any issues.
- *Quality checks in advance.* As the functionality is available to run certain quality checks in the field that would normally be run in the office after data were transcribed, the time taken for quality checking centrally can be reduced, or, alternatively, extra supplementary checks can be carried out.

5.183 These improvements to the speed of the processing system can facilitate an earlier publication or provide opportunities to spend more time on analysis and interpretation, the production of press releases and associated briefing, or the collection of more prices.

5.184 A CADC system enables certain checks that improve the efficiency of the CPI management. These include:

- *A check that all prices have been collected before the collector leaves the outlet.* An electronic data collection form can easily check whether all prices have been collected and flag when they have not. This mitigates the risk of the price collector inadvertently forgetting to price an item.
- *A check on when prices were imputed.* Electronic data collection can automatically record a date/time when the prices were entered in the machine. This is useful for validation purposes.
- *Indicator codes.* CADC provides the opportunity for additional features to be included in the data collection form. One such feature would be indicator codes (represented by a single letter) that can be used to show when a price collected is for an item on sale, a replacement item, a missing item, a discontinued item, etc. This is a simple tool to enhance the ease of validation and the management of the item list (see paragraph 5.73).

  Having price histories more readily at hand can:

  - Make briefing of price collectors prior to fieldwork more effective, for example, by a better appreciation of when an "outlier" is a legitimate price change and vice versa.
  - Add to the quality assurance processes through assisting with analysis when the index has been compiled and the briefing is being put together. These advantages are particularly relevant when there can be significant regional variations in price levels and trends.

5.185 There is a short-term cost associated with the introduction and implementation of CADC for CPI price collection. Costs include:

- The purchase of equipment.
- Upgrading "back-office" systems to enable interaction with the handheld computers, mobile telephones, or tablets.
- The development of appropriate software for local price collection building on the experience of others. Costs depend on the functionality and sophistication of the program. Some NSOs have developed software for CADC that they may be ready to share.
- Training of field staff and NSO staff on using the new systems, including pilot price collection.

5.186 There will also be longer-term costs associated with maintenance of the system and training of new staff, but the additional expenditure on the latter is likely to not be significant as new staff must be trained whatever system of price collection is used.

5.187 When planning to use handheld computers, mobile telephones, or tablets for local price collection, the decision needs to be made on whether the software is designed specifically for a certain hardware or not. If it is hardware dependent, the life cycle of the software is usually dictated by the life cycle of the hardware. In data transmission, the issue of confidentiality needs to be addressed as well as how to secure the transmission action in practice with regard to reliability. The speed and reliability of any network that is used should be tested from all price collection locations.

5.188 There are several advantages when using CADC, but as with all data collection methods it has risks and limitations. With CADC the first risks are with the devices: the battery might not last the whole day of price collection, especially if price collection is done in extreme conditions, and the data might be lost if the device breaks down during price collection period. Also, the devices have life cycles and if the software is coded to operate on a certain device this may need to be rewritten for a replacement device. This limitation causes costs when the devices come to the end of their life cycle. There are also risks in data transfer, especially if the connections are poor, for example, if for any unpredicted situation the connection fails during downloading the data from CADC to the database. Some of these risks can be avoided using different solutions, like programming the software independently from the device choice.

Collecting Prices Online and Web Scraping

5.189 A distinction should be made between collecting the prices of goods and services purchased online, to reflect the increasing importance of the internet as a channel for making purchases. A strategy to collect prices online through automation has the potential to reduce costs when compared to the resource-demanding process of manual price collection. Prices for online sales can differ from the prices charged at physical outlets—even for the same retailer—and the profile of goods and services purchased online can be different to other purchases. The prices in the

CPI must be representative and accurate. The motivation in adopting different data sources and extraction techniques is important. The motivation for collecting prices online can be twofold—efficiency and to ensure online purchases are properly representative.

5.190 Retailers with an online presence—either as sellers of goods and services online, or as retailers who do not sell online but use the internet to list prices—should be treated like any other retailer and be contacted first by the head office and be invited to participate in the price survey even though this will not involve a physical interface.

Online Collection of Prices

5.191 This section relates to collecting prices online from publicly accessible websites, referring to goods and services also sold in the corresponding physical outlets. It is a way of increasing the efficiency of price collection for a traditional sample of retail outlets and a fixed basket of goods and services. It does not relate to web scraping, the collection of prices for online purchases or the use of scanner data.

5.192 Instead of the traditional way of sending a price collector to a retail outlet, extracting prices online directly from websites will significantly reduce the price collection costs. Similarly, the response burden on data providers will be reduced to close to zero when extracting prices online directly from websites to replace postal or online questionnaires. Collecting prices online is relatively straightforward although care needs to be taken and checks put in place, especially when automated technical solutions are adopted. The prices obtained online must represent the transaction price in the physical outlet. Checks need to be made that the price advertised online is the same as the price advertised on the retailer's website and in the physical outlet and that no overhead associated with buying online, such as delivery charges, are included.[7] Also, online data need to contain sufficient information on characteristics to detect changes in quality. When using online data sources, checks also need to be made that product code numbers, if used to identify the good or service, have not changed between price collection periods and that the codes are unique.

5.193 Collecting prices online, which can be relatively easy and cheap, will not always be a suitable substitute for price collectors.

Collection of Prices for Online Purchases

5.194 Goods and services purchased on the internet need to be properly reflected in the sample of prices used to compile the CPI.

5.195 Elementary product groups should be stratified to reflect products purchased online. Sale information for weighting and the drawing of samples of internet purchases can be taken from HBSs, which should record information about outlet type (including internet purchases), and from information supplied by online retailers and market research companies.

5.196 The sample of items to be priced should be representative of all online purchases and will be different from online collection of prices charged by physical outlets. The prices recorded should represent the full cost of purchase. Online purchases may include standard extras such as delivery charges. Unavoidable charges that are directly connected to the purchase of the priced product and which are not separately invoiced should be included in the price for the purpose of CPI compilation. If the charge is separately invoiced or relates to the purchase of a number of items, then the treatment is less clear-cut. One option is to include these charges under transport services, but issues relating to the Classification of Individual Consumption According to Purpose (COICOP) arise (for more information on COICOP, see Chapter 2). Another option is to follow the approach used for the Harmonised Index of Consumer Prices in European Union countries, where such unavoidable charges that are not part of the basic advertised price may be considered as an inseparable bundle of a good and a service and can be treated as one product (for additional information, see the section on internet purchases in Chapter 11).

Web Scraping

5.197 Web scraping is the process of automated collection of data from the internet through a set of computer software techniques for extracting information from websites (webpages) or using an application programming interface, which is a set of routines, protocols, and tools for building software applications. Web scraping identifies and retrieves relevant data and downloads and organizes them in a suitable format for computing a CPI.

5.198 There are technical measures applied in some websites to avoid web scraping activities. These measures block the scraper Internet Protocol address access to the website or block the response to the scraper http browser agent identification. The action is triggered after identifying an "abnormal" behavior (by analyzing the activity log) or by filtering access from some agents (through the robots.txt server configuration file).[8]

5.199 Anti–web scraping devices by retailers reinforce the need to gain the cooperation of online retailers prior to data scraping to avoid being blocked from data collection. Retailers should always be informed about the nature, extension, and frequency of web scraping actions prior to any web scraping taking place. NSOs should inform and ask permission from retailers and agree to the most suitable web scraping technique with the retailer's management. Additional measures, such as pauses between "scrapes," may be required to maintain access given that the technology employed to block access may be automated. There may also be legal constraints to web scraping.

5.200 When undertaking web scraping, the same considerations apply as with online collection, most particularly whether the aim is to download from publicly accessible websites, the prices of goods and services sold in

[7] Charges relating to a delivery service arranged by the customer for specific items, or for bulk delivery with other items purchased, are legitimate for inclusion in a CPI but should be recorded under a separate heading as indicated in COICOP (2018 COICOP 07.4 Transport services of goods).

[8] Web Robots (also known as Web Wanderers, Crawlers, or Spiders) are programs that traverse the internet automatically. Search engines use them to index the web content. Website owners use the robots.txt file to give instructions about their website to web robots; this is called the Robots Exclusion Protocol. For further information visit http://www.robotstxt.org/robotstxt.html.

physical outlets to increase the efficiency of price collection or whether to download prices paid for online purchases.

5.201 For web scraping to replace traditional price collection, it needs to be demonstrated that prices, both online and in traditional outlets, are the same. While true for some retailers and some products, it is almost certainly not true for all retailers and all products. When prices on the web differ from the prices in outlets, the price collection from a website should be seen as a different outlet type, which should be sampled along with traditional outlets. Traditional price collection would continue along with web scraping. It should be noted that to integrate these prices into a CPI it is necessary to evaluate if there are some extra fees associated with the purchase and that are not included in the prices listed on the website (see paragraphs 5.207–5.209).

5.202 Integration of prices from different data sources needs to consider differences in sampling regimes (for example, the relatively bigger samples facilitated by web scraping) and the relative values of sales. It is one of the reasons why online purchases are often treated as separate elementary aggregates with separate weights.

5.203 Annex 5.6 provides more details on web scraping.

Calculation of Average Price from Different Data Sources in the Elementary Aggregate

5.204 Another aspect to be taken into consideration when combining traditional data sources with web-scraped data refers to the different collection frequencies. Traditional price collection deals with price "snapshots" scheduled in such a way that the price series for a product in an outlet respects both frequency and equidistance with regard to time. In contrast, one of the perceived advantages of web-scraped data is that prices can be collected daily during a certain period, extract the average value and take that as the "snapshot" price for that week. A problem arises when trying to integrate data collected in "continuous daily" frequency into the regular monthly CPI. When using web-scraped data, care must be taken not to apply the raw collected data directly on the calculation of the average monthly price at the elementary aggregate level. Since the number and nature of observations (probably many more than one per month per outlet/period for price obtained by web scraping) are different, they should be transformed into compatible data. This can be accomplished simply by calculating an "outlet monthly price" for the product offer. This average price will then have the same importance as other prices generated by the traditional snapshot approach. The consequences of using directly the online prices will lead to a distorted estimate of inflation, since average prices will be calculated using a disproportionate number of prices that came from online collection, regardless of any relative weight information. Annex 5.5 gives a brief example of these calculations and how a disregard of the differences in the frequency of price collection can lead to an underestimate of inflation. However, the use of an empirical country-based data set is needed for a more accurate evaluation.

5.205 There is a variety of tools to aid the scraping activity. For example, many programs are available in common programming languages (for example, C, Python, or JavaScript), for standalone applications or, most commonly, as add-ins to the browser. In most cases, web scraping tools are primarily designed to fulfill web application testing and verification. For that reason, most of the tools used are implemented as browser add-ins (or plug-ins). This is not the ideal situation with regard to IT architecture.

5.206 When combining prices using traditional price collection techniques with prices obtained from web scraping, allowance needs to be made in the computation of average product prices for the different collection techniques being deployed, especially the frequency of price collection where web scraping is sometimes carried out at a greater frequency than traditional price collection (see Annex 5.5).

Key Recommendations

- Price collection methods and organization decisions will depend upon country-specific circumstances, available resources, and could potentially vary by item.
- Collected prices should reflect actual transaction prices including any tax and reflecting any discounts, sales, or promotions.
- Items should be priced as often as necessary to ensure that the index reflects a reliable and meaningful measure of price change.
- NSOs should strive to calculate an index based on prices covering the whole period (for example, month or quarter).
- The interval between price observations should be uniform for each outlet.
- The price collection period should be made publicly available and any changes announced well in advance.
- Proper training of price collectors is essential. Detailed documentation on data collection procedures and processes should be drafted and made available to data collectors and CPI staff.
- Quality assurance procedures should be defined and implemented to ensure the accuracy of collected prices.
- Data validation techniques are necessary to ensure the accuracy and reliability of the collected prices.
- Outlier detection methods should be defined and implemented. All questionable prices should be verified and errors are corrected as necessary.

Annex 5.1

Consumer Price Index Price Collection Procedures

Figure A5.1 Planning and Organizing Price Collection

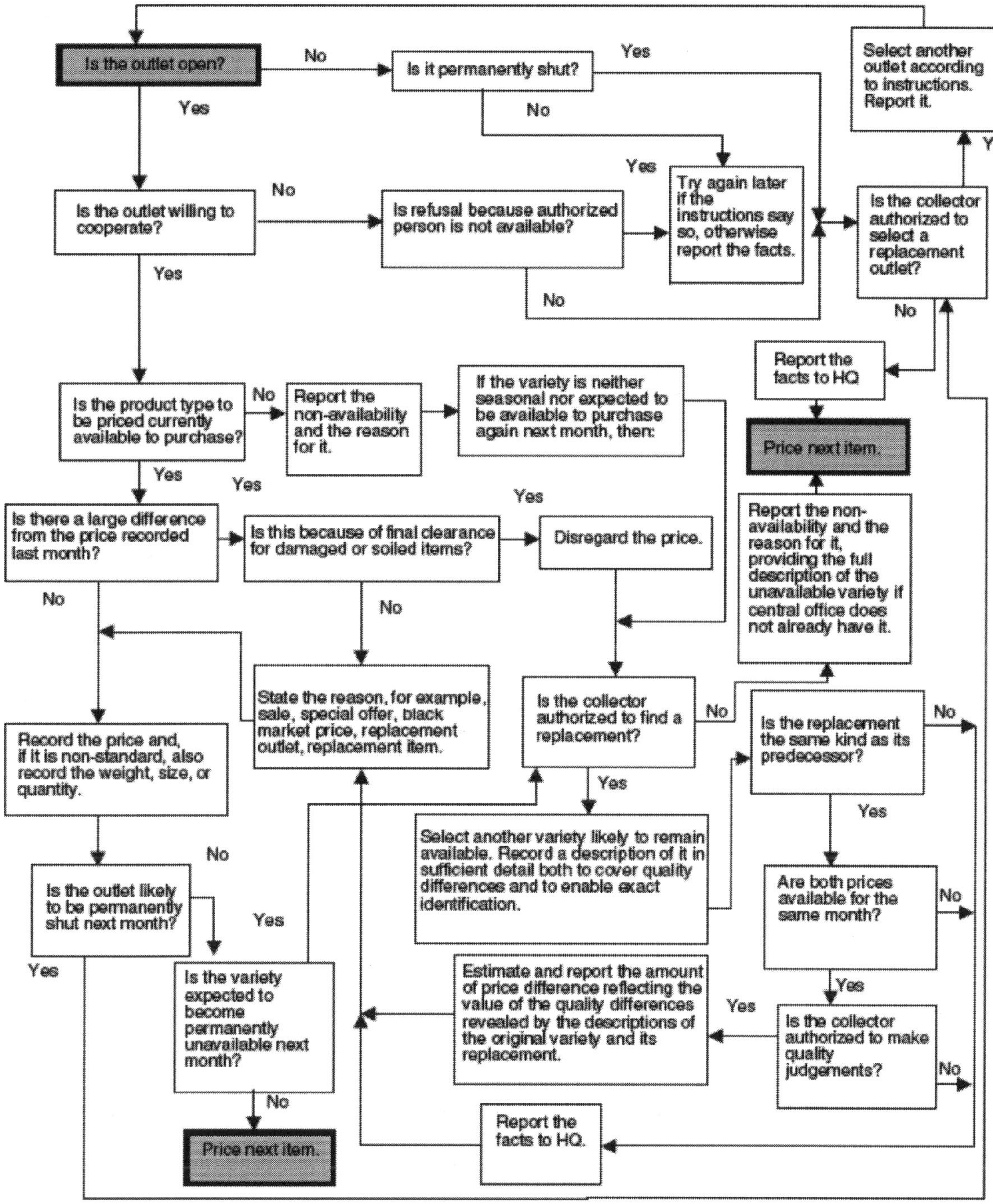

Annex 5.2

Consumer Price Index—Example of a Price Collection Form

Figure A5.2 Price Collection Form

Consumer Price Index: Pricing Form - September 2008 **Confidential**

Collection Period: WEEK 1 **Collection Date:** 1

WOOLWORTHS

Unique Number: 8379435 **Quote** 1 **of** 502

Contact Person: ADRIAAN JOUBERT **Alt. Contact Person:** MARISA LOUW

Contact Number: 015 516 2620 **Alt. Contact Number:** 015 516 2620

Product Group: 1101 BREAD

Product Subgroup: 1101001 (1) LOAF OF WHITE BREAD

Brand Name: Woolworths

Product Name: Sandwich White Bread

Quantity: 1 Loaf **Size:** 700 **Unit Of Size:** Gram

Observations: Transparent Plastic Bag With Blue Lines Has An Woolworths Symbol

Origin: South Africa

Code	Feature	Description	Other Information
IK043	Product presentation	Plastic bag	
MN018	Variety	Sliced	

Specification Changes: **Code** **Feature and Description**

Item Availability: AVAILABLE

Available ☐ **Out Of Season** ☐ **Temp. Unavailable** ☐ **Perm. Unavailable** ☐

Unique Item Season: ALL YEAR **All Year** ☐ **Seasonal** ☐ **If seasonal indicate the seasonal months below:**

Jan ☐ **Feb** ☐ **Mar** ☐ **Apr** ☐ **May** ☐ **Jun** ☐ **Jul** ☐ **Aug** ☐ **Sep** ☐ **Oct** ☐ **Nov** ☐ **Dec** ☐

	2008/08	**2008/09**
Price:	R 7.95	
Type of price:	REGULAR	REGULAR ☐ SALE ☐
Quantity:	1 Loaf	
Size:	700	
Unit of size:	Gram	

LAST REGULAR PRICE	**QUANTITY**	**SIZE**	**UNIT**	**COLLECTION PERIOD**
R 7.95	1 Loaf	700	Gram	2008/08

Previous Months Comments:

Field Message:

Office Use Only
Unit Status Code: ☐

Annex 5.3

Consumer Price Index—Automated Data Checking

Example 1

Example 1 demonstrates the use of median and quartile values to identify outliers. Table A5.1, column A, shows the price ratios for the illustrative sample.

$$S_i = 1 - \frac{R_M}{R_i}, \quad \text{if } 0 < R_i < R_M \qquad \text{(A5.1)}$$

$$S_i = \frac{R_i}{R_M} - 1, \quad \text{if } R_i \geq R_M$$

The first and third quartiles (R_{Q1} and R_{Q3}) and the median (R_M) can be obtained using the quartile function in Microsoft Excel. The average distance of the quartiles from the median (D_M) is defined as

$$D_M = (R_{Q3} - R_{Q1})/2 \qquad \text{(A5.2)}$$

The upper and lower limits are then calculated as

$$L_U = R_M + C \times D_M; \text{ and} \qquad \text{(A5.3)}$$
$$L_L = R_M - C \times D_M$$

Table A5.1 Price Relatives Showing Movement from Previous Period (Example 1)

Price Ratio	S_i	Flagged Using PR Above 1.08723 or Below 0.87628	Flagged Using S_i Above 0.10894 or Below −0.10894
(a)	(b)	(c)	(d)
0.81380	−0.20638	Extreme	Extreme
0.85250	−0.15161	Extreme	Extreme
0.87600	−0.12072	Extreme	Extreme
0.89900	−0.09205	OK	OK
0.90860	−0.08051	OK	OK
0.91350	−0.07471	OK	OK
0.93390	−0.05124	OK	OK
0.94140	−0.04286	OK	OK
0.95530	−0.02769	OK	OK
0.96080	−0.02180	OK	OK
0.96580	−0.01651	OK	OK
0.96680	−0.01546	OK	OK
0.97020	−0.01190	OK	OK
0.97240	−0.00962	OK	OK
0.98170	−0.00005	OK	OK
0.98180	0.00005	OK	OK
0.98430	0.00260	OK	OK
0.98690	0.00525	OK	OK
1.00340	0.02205	OK	OK
1.00500	0.02368	OK	OK
1.00610	0.02480	OK	OK
1.03010	0.04925	OK	OK
1.05710	0.07675	OK	OK
1.08240	0.10252	OK	OK
1.09090	0.11118	Extreme	Extreme
1.09310	0.11342	Extreme	Extreme
1.13000	0.15101	Extreme	Extreme
1.15500	0.17647	Extreme	Extreme
1.22960	0.25246	Extreme	Extreme
1.23040	0.25327	Extreme	Extreme

Table A5.2 Parameters and Derived Limits (Example 1)

Parameter	Series PR	Series S_i
(a)	(b)	(c)
R_{Q1}	0.94488	−0.03907
R_M	0.98175	0
R_{Q3}	1.05035	0.06988
D_M	0.05274	0.05447
C	2	2
L_L	0.87628	−0.10894
L_U	1.08723	0.10894

where the multiplier C is a user-defined value and has been set equal to two to limit the number of observations flagged up as potential errors.

The resulting upper and lower limits are shown in the "Series PR" in column B in Table A5.2.

The price ratio series can be transformed to provide more equal weighting between negative and positive price movements. The transformations are repeated here as

$$S_i = 1 - \frac{R_M}{R_i}, \quad \text{if } 0 < R_i < R_M \qquad \text{(A5.4)}$$

$$S_i = \frac{R_i}{R_M} - 1, \quad \text{if } R_i \geq R_M$$

The transformed observations are shown in the "Series S_i" in column C in Table A5.1. The quartiles, median, and calculated limits for the transformed series are shown in column C in Table A5.2. The increased value for D_M for the transformed sample shows that the transformation has increased the distances for the price decreases while leaving the distances for positive movements the same.

Columns C and D in Table A5.1 show, respectively, the observations that would be flagged for further examination (indicated by the word "extreme") for the original price ratios and the transformed price movements.

Example 2

Example 2 demonstrates the same statistical filtering method as in Example 1, but with 16 additional price ratios added to the sample. All the new price ratios show zero change. The same calculations are done but on a sample of 46 instead of 30 observations. Table A5.3 shows the sample of price ratios and the transformed price movements, as well as the observations flagged for further observations. Table A5.4 shows the parameters and calculated limits.

A comparison of the results from the two examples demonstrates the effect of having a significant number of observations with no price movement. The distance from the median (D_M) is reduced and the number of observations flagged for further examination is significantly increased.

Example 3

Example 3 demonstrates the alternative statistical filtering method, the Tukey algorithm. The enlarged sample from Example 2 is used here to demonstrate the benefit of this method when the sample has a large proportion of price ratios indicating no movement. Table A5.5 presents the intermediate

Table A5.3 Price Relatives Showing Movement from Previous Period (Example 2)

Price Ratio	S_i	Flagged Using PR	Flagged Using S_i
		Above 1.03490 or Below 0.96510	Above 0.03598 or Below −0.03598
(a)	(b)	(c)	(d)
0.81380	−0.22880	Extreme	Extreme
0.85250	−0.17300	Extreme	Extreme
0.87600	−0.14160	Extreme	Extreme
0.89900	−0.11230	Extreme	Extreme
0.90860	−0.10060	Extreme	Extreme
0.91350	−0.09470	Extreme	Extreme
0.93390	−0.07080	Extreme	Extreme
0.94140	−0.06220	Extreme	Extreme
0.95530	−0.04680	Extreme	Extreme
0.96080	−0.04080	Extreme	Extreme
0.96580	−0.03540	OK	OK
0.96680	−0.03430	OK	OK
0.97020	−0.03070	OK	OK
0.97240	−0.02840	OK	OK
0.98170	−0.01860	OK	OK
0.98180	−0.01850	OK	OK
0.98430	−0.01600	OK	OK
0.98690	−0.01330	OK	OK
1.00000	0.00000	OK	OK
1.00000	0.00000	OK	OK
1.00000	0.00000	OK	OK
1.00000	0.00000	OK	OK
1.00000	0.00000	OK	OK
1.00000	0.00000	OK	OK
1.00000	0.00000	OK	OK
1.00000	0.00000	OK	OK
1.00000	0.00000	OK	OK
1.00000	0.00000	OK	OK
1.00000	0.00000	OK	OK
1.00000	0.00000	OK	OK
1.00000	0.00000	OK	OK
1.00000	0.00000	OK	OK
1.00000	0.00000	OK	OK
1.00000	0.00000	OK	OK
1.00340	0.00340	OK	OK
1.00500	0.00500	OK	OK
1.00610	0.00610	OK	OK
1.03010	0.03010	OK	OK
1.05710	0.05710	Extreme	Extreme
1.08240	0.08240	Extreme	Extreme
1.09090	0.09090	Extreme	Extreme
1.09310	0.09310	Extreme	Extreme
1.13000	0.13000	Extreme	Extreme
1.15500	0.15500	Extreme	Extreme
1.22960	0.22960	Extreme	Extreme
1.23040	0.23040	Extreme	Extreme

Table A5.5 Price Relatives Showing Movement from Previous Period (Example 3)

Price Relative	Less 5 Percent Tails and Less Zero Movement	T Lower Set	T Upper Set	Flagged as Extreme
				Above 1.17184 or Below 0.88332
(a)	(b)	(c)	(d)	(e)
0.8138				Extreme
0.8525				Extreme
0.8760	0.8760	0.8760		Extreme
0.8990	0.8990	0.8990		OK
0.9086	0.9086	0.9086		OK
0.9135	0.9135	0.9135		OK
0.9339	0.9339	0.9339		OK
0.9414	0.9414	0.9414		OK
0.9553	0.9553	0.9553		OK
0.9608	0.9608	0.9608		OK
0.9658	0.9658	0.9658		OK
0.9668	0.9668	0.9668		OK
0.9702	0.9702	0.9702		OK
0.9724	0.9724	0.9724		OK
0.9817	0.9817	0.9817		OK
0.9818	0.9818	0.9818		OK
0.9843	0.9843	0.9843		OK
0.9869	0.9869	0.9869		OK
1.0000				OK
1.0000				OK
1.0000				OK
1.0000				OK
1.0000				OK
1.0000				OK
1.0000				OK
1.0000				OK
1.0000				OK
1.0000				OK
1.0000				OK
1.0000				OK
1.0000				OK
1.0000				OK
1.0000				OK
1.0000				OK
1.0034	1.0034		1.0034	OK
1.0050	1.0050		1.0050	OK
1.0061	1.0061		1.0061	OK
1.0301	1.0301		1.0301	OK
1.0571	1.0571		1.0571	OK
1.0824	1.0824		1.0824	OK
1.0909	1.0909		1.0909	OK
1.0931	1.0931		1.0931	OK
1.1300	1.1300		1.1300	OK
1.1550	1.1550		1.1550	OK
1.2296				Extreme
1.2304				Extreme

Table A5.4 Parameters and Derived Limits (Example 2)

Parameter	Series PR	Series Si
(a)	(b)	(c)
R_{Q1}	0.96765	−0.03343
R_M	1.00000	0
R_{Q3}	1.00255	0.00255
D_M	0.01745	0.01799
C	2	2
L_L	0.96510	−0.03598
L_U	1.03490	0.03598

data stages in addition to the basic sample and the indicator flagging extreme observations as possible errors.

The price ratios for the sample are shown in column A. The first step was to remove the highest and lowest 5 percent of price ratios. Five percent of this sample equals 1.5 observations. This was rounded up to two observations so the two highest and the two lowest price ratios were removed. Observations with zero price movement were also removed. The remaining observations are shown in column B. The arithmetic mean (AM) of the remaining set of observations was calculated. This value, along with other parameter calculations is shown in Table A5.6. The arithmetic means of the lower and upper sets of data are then calculated (labeled AM_L and AM_U, respectively). The lower and upper data sets have been presented in columns C and D, respectively, of Table A5.5 purely for explanatory

Table A5.6 Parameters and Derived Limits (Example 3)

Parameter	Value
(a)	(b)
AM	0.99429
AM_L	0.94990
AM_U	1.06531
T_L	0.88332
T_U	1.17184

purposes. The Tukey lower and upper limits are then calculated as

$$T_L = AM - 2.5(AM - AM_L) \quad (A5.5)$$
$$T_U = AM + 2.5(AM_U - AM)$$

The results are shown in Table A5.6.

Using this method, five observations would be selected for further examination—many fewer than the 18 selected in Example 2.

Annex 5.4
Documentation Control Template

The documentation control template is an essential element of documentation, production, and dissemination and control. Documentation control contributes to better quality management as access to nonauthors is restricted to "read only." It provides checks, background (including explanations for changes), and an audit trail. Two further benefits accrue when combined with an electronic system:

- More efficient production of documentation as it helps with initial compilation and updates, and reduces the need to print and circulate paper copies
- Better informed staff because they have immediate electronic access to the latest documentation, including desk instructions, with search facility by subject and author

Figure A5.3 Documentation Control Template

Date Issued	Documentation	Reference	Details of Change	Reason for Change	Name of Issuer
Day/Month/Year	Calculating CPI Food Item Weights (nonseasonal)	2.1	Change in Process with Effect from . . . (date)	CPI Technical Board Has Agreed That in Future Weights Should Be Taken from National Accounts	L. Smith, Statistician, CPI Program
XX/XX/XX	Calculating and Updating Price Index for Telecommunication Services	2.5	Change in Process with Effect from . . . (date)	Methodology Changes in Pricing Structures for Mobile Telephones—New Methodology Agreed by CPI Technical Board. Reflects Changing Market	L. Smith, Statistician, CPI Program
XX/XX/XX	Desk Instructions for Checking and Editing of Prices	3.1	Additional Checks to Be Carried Out Based on Month-on-Month Price Change	Last Audit Indicated Current Checks Inadequate Resulting in Incorrect Prices Entering the CPI	C. Brown, Operations Manager, CPI Program

Annex 5.5

The Calculation of Average Product Price When Combining Prices from Different Price Collection Methods and for Different Price Collection Frequencies

When combining traditional and web scraping price collection methods, there are two options for average product price computation. Web scraping can follow the same calendar collection that is used in traditional collection. With this option, the advantages of web scraping are disregarded. The second option will be to collect prices more frequently with web scraping techniques. This will increase the number of observations used in the computation, potentially providing more reliability to the estimation. In the following simplified example relating to just one item, the price for a specific product A is collected in a sampled local outlet in the framework of traditional price collection twice along the considered time frame of 10 days. The price for the same product is collected on a daily basis using web scraping. These data are collected for two months and the price at day 1 and at day 10 is the same for both outlet/collection types. However, the price averages and the indices will differ according to the way these are computed at the elementary aggregate level.

There are two methods of calculating the average price (geometric mean) at the elementary aggregate level. The assumption is made that there are no expenditure weights (and each observation at a given point in time has the same weight) and prices are collected to be representative of all sales.

- Method 1: compute the geometric mean in two steps: first, an average price is calculated by kind of outlet/collection method; second, a geometric average is calculated with the two average prices per outlet
- Method 2: compute the geometric mean in a single stage using all prices (not recommended)

Taking into consideration the different collection frequencies, method 2 will undervalue price change (noting that in this example prices are falling) since it takes into account a huge number of observations taken every day where the price change is not significant and it is providing more "weight" to the internet outlet with a price series that is more stable than to the local outlet where the price being observed each 10 days is recording a higher change. Due to these differences and the circumstance described, method 1 is recommended since it will provide the same "weight" to both kinds of outlets/collection methods. In summary, the prices can only be averaged in a single step when there is an equal number of price observations generated by each price collection for each item over a given period. Averaging prices in a single step when the frequency of price collection varies between different price collection methods leads to distorted results.

Table A5.7 Combining Prices from Different Price Collection Methods and for Different Price Collection Frequencies

Product A	Month 1										Geometric Mean	
	Day 1	Day 2	Day 3	Day 4	Day 5	Day 6	Day 7	Day 8	Day 9	Day 10		
Local Shop (traditional collection)	500									480	489.898	
Internet Website (web scraping)	500	500	500	497	497	490	489	483	480	480	491.536	
Geometric Mean: Method 1											490.717	
Geometric Mean: Method 2											491.263	
Product A	Month 2										Geometric Mean	Indices
	Day 1	Day 2	Day 3	Day 4	Day 5	Day 6	Day 7	Day 8	Day 9	Day 10		
Local Shop (traditional collection)	450									430	439.886	89.79
Internet Website (web scraping)	450	452	452	448	445	445	445	440	435	430	444.146	90.25
Geometric Mean: Method 1											442.011	90.02
Geometric Mean: Method 2											443.433	90.17

Annex 5.6
Web Scraping

Introduction

The collection of prices is an integral component of the production of a CPI. Several data collection modes are available and used by countries. These include personal visits, online, telephone, administrative data, and transactions data. More recently, with the growth of online retailing, pricing information may be obtained directly from websites. Advances in technology and automated scraping software have enabled large-scale data collection from the internet. This is referred to as web scraping.

Benefits of Web Scraping

Web scraping enables many more products to be priced, and for these products to be priced more often than would be possible using traditional data collection methods. Web scraping provides an opportunity to significantly enhance the sample of products and prices collected by expanding product coverage. Other benefits of web scraping include:

- Automated data collection at a reduced collection cost.
- Enhanced price representativity.
- Increased price collection frequency (that is, daily versus once per month) allows for a more representative price for the period to be obtained. Secondary effects of using an average period price include reduced volatility.
- Faster identification of new and disappearing products.
- Reduced respondent burden.
- Rich source of metadata (that is, product characteristics) that can be extracted, stored, and potentially used for an explicit quality adjustment (for example, hedonics). Such metadata may also complement other data sources such as transactions data.

Limitations of Web Scraping

The lack of expenditure information from web scraping means that products/product groups cannot be weighted by economic importance and limits the types of index formulas that can be used to compile the index. Other potential limitations of web scraping are the following:

- Web scraping is limited to retail outlets that have an online presence (that is, potential for undercoverage).
- Web scraping requires regular IT maintenance. Website changes may cause the web scraping program to fail. Businesses can block Internet Protocol addresses if they detect the web scraping activity and wish to prevent it.
- If performed within the NSO, web scraping requires compilers with intermediate programming knowledge to deal with the regular IT maintenance.
- Web scraping distinct prices for different geographic regions may be difficult if the website detects the physical location of the computer's Internet Protocol address. This may require assumptions that retailers use national pricing for regional price indices.
- Web scraping may be time-consuming for large retailers with many different webpages and products.

The Process of Web Scraping

For those NSOs using web-scraped data for research and production purposes, the process of performing web scraping has focused on two main methods:

- Web scraping performed within the NSO using statistical software[9]
- Web scraping services procured from a third-party/private company[10]

The choice to perform web scraping within the NSO or contracting with an external vendor will depend on the local context in which the NSO operates (for example, budgets, NSO programming capacity, maintenance costs). With respect to those NSOs performing web scraping internally using statistical software, the process of web scraping information from the internet can be broken down into three main steps:

- Confirm if the website allows scraping
- Scrape the website
- Clean the collected data

There are two main ways to determine whether a website is eligible for web scraping. First, staff setting up web scrapers should check the terms and conditions section of a website for "conditions of use." Here, websites will often specify if web scraping is allowed or prohibited. Additionally, a "robots.txt" file can be located within the root directory of a website. These text files contain detailed information and may outline the conditions for web scraping possibly including who is allowed to web scrape, which information is available for scraping, and anything for which scraping is forbidden.

Once it is determined that a website is available for scraping, a scraper is set up for the website. Each website is unique and the optimal scraping strategy may change from one site to the next. The scraper locates the website's category structure and identifies all the relevant categories to be scraped. The programmer defines the parts of the structure to be included and excluded. For example, a website may list all the individual product categories, then additional categories such as "new products" or "all products" which duplicate the products in the individual categories. These additional categories can be excluded by the programmer.

The scraper then proceeds to download all products and prices from the internet. An attempt is made to show as many products on each page as possible by experimenting with URL options on the website prior to setting up the scraper. There are two options available for pulling in the information. First, data may be collected as text that essentially uses scrapers to copy and paste from the website. In this case, the process of cleaning the text is carried out following the scraping. Alternatively, products and prices can be pulled in using designated HTML tags and classes which provide a more targeted approach to extracting and cleaning the data. Another advantage of this approach is that product identifiers

[9] Van Loon and Roels (2018).
[10] Bentley and Krsinich (2017).

Table A5.8 Web Scraping—Typical Data Structure

Date	Retailer	Category	Product ID	Price
July 10, 2019	Retailer ABC	Children's Shirts	Brand XYZ—Short Sleeve Polo Shirt	$45.00
July 10, 2019	Retailer ABC	Children's Shirts	Brand XYZ—S/S Regular Shirt	$55.00
July 10, 2019	Retailer ABC	Children's Shirts	Brand XY—Short Sleeve Regular T-Shirt	$15.00
July 10, 2019	Retailer ABC	Children's Shirts	Brand XYZ—Long Sleeve Regular Shirt	$65.00
July 10, 2019	Retailer ABC	Children's Shirts	Brand XYZ—Short Sleeve Regular Shirt	$35.00

can occasionally be hidden in the HTML so pulling them in using the tags allows these to be added to the product description (as opposed to relying purely on the text description). However, the use of HTML tags is not easy for every website.

For information collected as text, the raw data need to be cleaned post-scraping so that only the set of products and prices remain. A pattern in the data needs to be uncovered and coded to separate the products and prices from the "noise" (including removing all the information prior to and after the list of products). For products which are on sale, multiple prices may be listed. In these instances, the scraper records the sale prices as the current price of the product.

With regard to the available information to construct price indices, Table A5.8 provides a summary of a typical metadata scraped by NSOs. In summary, the data frame will typically include:

- Date: specific day of the scrape (date)
- Retailer: name of the retailer (text)
- Category: retailer's website classifications (text)
- Product ID: text description of product (text)
- Price: specific price of product (numeric)

Practical Considerations

The basic information required to compile a price index includes prices, expenditure information (or reasonable assumptions on substitution if no expenditure information is available), and classifications (for both products and product groups). While web-scraped data (such as the example in Table A5.8) may appear reasonably consistent with these requirements, it is important to ensure the conceptual requirements of the CPI (for example, quality adjustment) are maintained. "Big data (transaction, online, and administrative data) is 'found data' in the sense that measuring CPI inflation is a secondary use of the data—the data were not created with this use in mind."[11]

This subsection describes some of the main challenges identified by NSOs when using web-scraped data, including:

- Classifying web-scraped data
- Options to define individual products
- Index aggregation options

[11] Bentley and Krsinich (2017, 6).

Classification of Web-Scraped Data

The classification of web-scraped data involves similar considerations as described in Chapter 10 for the use of scanner data. Web-scraped data typically have some basic product text and category description that are required to be mapped to a NSO hierarchical classification (for example, COICOP). Approaches considered by NSOs to solve these classification problems include:

- *Text string searches*: Check for the presence or absence of keywords in the description string for classification.
- *Category mapping*: Some of the data sets (or parts thereof) contain retailer categories for each product; if one of these categories sits within a classification, the category can be mapped to the classification.
- *Manual mapping*: A compiler looks at the description string. This is the most feasible option for small data sets.
- *Supervised learning algorithms*: Provide training data (for example, using one or multiple methods previously mentioned) to statistical learning algorithm that identifies patterns between text and training decision for automatic classification.

Options to Define Individual Products

An essential part of price measurement is accounting for quality change and the introduction of new products. The CPI measures the price inflation in a basket of goods and services priced at constant quality. If the quality of a product changes over time, then prices are adjusted so that the index movements reflect pure price change. This has important implications for web scraping.

The appearance and disappearance of products from a CPI sample has the potential to bias the index unless any corresponding changes in the quality of the sample are dealt with appropriately. This poses a problem for the calculation of indices incorporating all (or most) web-scraped prices due to a large number of prices these data sets contain, the high rate of product attrition, and the tendency for products to have unusual price movements near the start and end of their life cycles.

One approach for dealing with this problem is to estimate the price change between two periods using the products available at both time points only, thus excluding the prices of new and disappearing products. The matched-model method (as described in Chapter 6) involves discarding information about new and disappearing products. However, it gains strength from the comprehensive coverage from the census of products represented in the full web-scraped data set. This can be considered as an application of the overlap method, as it is almost certain that sales of new and disappearing products would overlap with the sales of other products that consumers would use as substitutes.

An assumption behind the overlap method is that price differences between products are reflective of quality differences. This assumption seems reasonable in a competitive marketplace and in normal circumstances. However, disappearing products are sometimes sold at discounted prices to clear remaining stock (end of life cycle), and if not linked to a product of comparable quality, may produce a "relaunch" problem and could potentially create a downward bias in the index.[12] This problem has been identified in various price index studies on different types of products including high-technology goods,[13] clothing,[14] and personal care products.[15]

To overcome this problem, several practical strategies have been proposed, primarily focused on extracting characteristics information (for example, brand and shirt type) from text strings to form broader product definitions. Key techniques proposed are the following:

- Use of a broader product category (for example, children's shirts in Table A5.8)
- Text/regular expression functions: used to extract characteristics from semistructured text data (for example, "XYZ" in Table A5.8 extracts the characteristic "brand")
- Approximate (fuzzy) matching functions: used to approximately match text strings using a penalty function
- Supervised learning algorithms:[16] provide training data to statistical learning algorithm that identifies patterns between text and training decision for product classification
- Unsupervised learning algorithms:[17] use characteristics (for example, text string and price) and algorithms to automatically define "clusters" of products

Options to Aggregate Prices

Web-scraped data do not contain quantity or expenditure information. This would naturally restrict the choice of index formula to an unweighted price index formula (for example, Jevons), which is the current choice for many NSOs in the CPI production.

The use of web-scraped data in compiling price indices continues to be the subject of extensive research. Some researchers have experimented with approximating expenditure weights based on data observed from the websites.[18] Using brand and product-type definitions and the number of products as a proxy for quantity data, results demonstrate that the web-scraped data approximate a benchmark index (scanner data) using the Geary–Khamis method. Additional published studies (for example, Metcalfe and others [2016]) experiment with several bilateral and multilateral price index methods. Research findings showed a substantial amount of drift across most bilateral and multilateral indices with granular product definitions for clothing products.

Country Case Study—Web Scraping

As part of a broader project to modernize the CPI, one NSO began collecting prices using web scrapers beginning in May of 2016. Web scrapers are currently programmed and maintained by the NSO staff using Microsoft Excel (Visual Basic for Applications), collecting approximately 500,000 prices per week across more than 50 retailers. Web scraping increases the sample of prices used to compile the index, thus providing a more meaningful measure of price change. From the second quarter of 2017, the NSO began using web-scraped data in the calculation of the CPI. Varieties are selected using the same methods as other forms of price collection (field collection, online collection, or other methods). An average price is calculated for each item over a given period.

Representative and stable products are selected. When transitioning a respondent from using traditional data collectors to web-scraped prices, an attempt is made to link the current field-collected product to the identical product on the website. A determination regarding quality adjustment is made for each product to ensure that the new web-scraped product's base period price is correct.

For each web-scraped product in the sample, the price for a given period (month or quarter) is an arithmetic average of the prices which fall within the specified period. If a product disappears, a replacement product is selected from among the other products within the relevant category from that respondent. A quality adjustment is performed to ensure that only pure price change is shown. The combination of category name, brand/product description, and price history of both the old and new product is sufficient to enable an accurate quality adjustment to be applied.

This NSO has adopted a phased approach to implementing new retailers and price index methods using web-scraped data. With respect to respondents, an assessment is made for each respondent to be transitioned to web-scraped data, taking into account the quality of web-scraped data over a period of time, the correlation between online prices and field-collected prices in each city, and the potential for collection efficiencies and sample improvements. With respect to price index methods, development work continues within the NSO on text mining techniques (to form broader product definitions, especially for clothing) and price index methods (both bilateral and multilateral index methods) that maximize and automate the use of web-scraped data.

[12]Chessa (2016).
[13]Silver and Heravi (2005).
[14]Chessa (2017).
[15]Chessa (2016).
[16]Abe and Shinozaki (2018).
[17]Metcalfe and others (2016).
[18]Chessa and Griffioen (2016).

TEMPORARILY AND PERMANENTLY MISSING PRICES AND QUALITY CHANGE

6

Introduction

6.1 Chapter 6 focuses on the treatment of temporarily and permanently missing varieties and their prices. While Chapter 5 focuses on the collection of data, Chapter 6 highlights the important role of the price collector in the context of the treatment of missing prices and starts by providing an overview of the matched-model method (MMM). While the MMM serves as the underlying method regarding the treatment of missing prices, the chapter describes how the MMM can potentially fail, the consequences of this failure, and how to deal with the effects of such failure on price measurement.

6.2 Temporarily missing prices and the methods used for the treatment of missing varieties are reviewed in this chapter. The concept of quality is defined and discussed. Explicit (direct) and implicit (indirect) methods for quality adjustment are identified and described.

6.3 Some introductory notes are provided on general measurement issues including the use of additive versus multiplicative quality adjustments, price reference versus current period quality adjustment, short-term versus long-term comparisons, and geometric aggregation formula. Finally, this chapter considers the need of price measurement in product markets with a rapid turnover of models,[1] usually in the electronic and high-technology product markets.

Background

6.4 The measurement of changes in the level of consumer prices is complicated by the appearance and disappearance of new and old goods and services, as well as changes in the quality of existing ones. If there were no such complications, a representative sample could be taken of the varieties of goods and services households consumed in a reference period 0, their prices recorded and compared with the prices of the same matched varieties in subsequent periods. In this way, the prices of like would be compared with like. In practice, some complications do exist. Varieties change in quality over time and replacements are of a different quality compared to the original. New and old models of varieties appear and disappear.

6.5 Changes in the quality of varieties should be treated as changes in the volume of the goods or service provided, as opposed to changes in the price. For example, increases over time in the concentration of a detergent (number of washes per one kilogram packet), faster internet service (megabits per second, Mbps), and inclusion of a warranty in the price of a dishwasher, all contribute to effective decreases in price; consumers get more for their money. Similarly, quality decreases, for example, less legroom in economy flights, when prices remain constant, are effective increases in price. A volume change for an individual variety may be comprised of a quantity *and* quality change. The change in the variety's nominal value of consumption expenditure is the product of its price and volume change. It follows that the price change is the change in value divided by the change in volume.

6.6 National statistical offices (NSOs) go to great lengths to ensure measured price changes are not influenced by changes in the quality of items. By measuring the price change of a fixed, constant-quality basket of goods and services, NSOs use the MMM. When updating the basket, price collectors visit selected outlets with broad details of an item and identify the most popular, regularly stocked varieties sold in each of the outlets. Next, they develop a detailed description of the variety including all the price-determining characteristics (for example, brand or size) and record the price. This specification must be sufficiently detailed to include all price-determining characteristics to define a unique, specific variety. The detailed specification allows the price collector to easily identify the variety or model in subsequent periods and record its matched price.

6.7 The measurement of changes in the level of consumer prices using the MMM is appropriate when variety prices are not missing. However, the use of the MMM is complicated by *temporarily unavailable* prices, for example for one, two, or three months, because of a variety being out of stock and not yet replenished. A matched price is unavailable in these intervening months. The treatment of prices of temporarily missing varieties is considered in more detail in paragraphs 6.52–6.72, but typically requires the missing variety's price to be imputed for the month(s) in which it is missing using the price changes of similar goods or services, or price changes drawn from a higher level of aggregation. Actual prices are then compared with imputed prices for the measurement of the consumer price index (CPI).

6.8 If varieties become *permanently unavailable* a replacement variety is required that is preferably comparable with regard to the price-determining characteristics of the missing variety. If the replacement is of a comparable quality (that is, possesses the same price-determining characteristics), its price can be directly compared with the last actual or imputed price for the missing variety. If the replacement is noncomparable, for example, it is of a better quality, the improvement in quality has to be explicitly quantified with regard to its "worth" or its contribution to the price. Using this value, compilers make a price adjustment to reflect the difference in quality allowing the price

[1] The term "model" of a good or service is used in this chapter mainly in the context of high-technology goods such as laptops, household appliances, or cars. This use of the term "model" follows general usage and refers to a specific variety whose characteristics are updated regularly.

of like be compared with like. If a reliable explicit quality adjustment to the price is not possible, for data or resource reasons, implicit methods of quality adjustment are available. Details of explicit and implicit methods of quality adjustment are provided in paragraphs 6.90–6.188, and methods for dealing with new and disappearing goods and services are illustrated in Chapter 8.

6.9 Products that are "strongly" seasonal, that is, missing in particular months when out of season but expected to return in the next season, could also be treated as temporarily missing and imputed. Chapter 11 describes in more detail the different options that can be used for the treatment of seasonal products. Strongly seasonal products include some fresh fruits, vegetables, and clothing. Also considered in Chapter 11 is the treatment of "weakly" seasonal products: available throughout the year but whose prices, sales, and quality fluctuate. The prices of weakly seasonal products are not missing and are treated differently from strongly seasonal ones, as discussed in Chapter 11.

6.10 The matching of models facilitates the measurement of constant-quality price change. When the matching breaks down because of missing prices, temporary imputations are necessary until the variety's temporarily missing price becomes available or a replacement can be introduced, thus helping to update the sample. However, there are product markets where the matching breaks down on a regular basis because of high turnover of models, with new models of different quality compared to the old ones, such as laptop computers. In this case, a failure to match and replace models would lead to a seriously depleted and unrepresentative sample. Yet, a continual process of linking-in new replacement varieties has been found to lead to a bias in CPI measurement. Paragraphs 6.141–6.177 of this chapter outline an alternative approach making use of hedonic regressions.

Potential Errors in the Matched-Model Method

6.11 Three potential sources of error arise from the MMM: missing varieties, representativity of sample space, and new products.

Missing Varieties

6.12 The first source of error in the MMM, and the focus of this chapter, occurs when a variety is no longer available in the outlet. It may be temporarily out of stock, discontinued, or one or more of the price-determining characteristics may have changed. Whatever the reason, the variety is effectively missing in the current period and a price cannot be collected. The variety's price may be missing for other reasons: it may be a seasonal variety or one whose price does not need to be recorded so frequently, or it may be a custom-made good or service, supplied each time to the customer's specification.

6.13 It is necessary to distinguish between varieties that are permanently and temporarily missing. Varieties that are *temporarily* missing are varieties that are not available and not priced in the current period, but that are available and priced in subsequent periods. The treatment of varieties missing because demand and supply are seasonal, as is the case with some fruits and vegetables, is described in Chapter 11.

6.14 The different methods for the treatment of missing prices, and the implied assumptions, are listed in Figure 6.3 and discussed in some detail in paragraphs 6.90–6.234. By definition, the prices of the unavailable varieties cannot be determined and the accuracy of some of the assumptions about their price changes is difficult to establish. The matching of prices of varieties allows for the measurement of price changes unaffected by quality changes. When varieties are replaced with new ones of a different quality, then a quality-adjusted price is required. If the adjustment is inappropriate, there is an error, and if it is inappropriate in a systematic direction, there is a bias. Careful quality-adjustment practices are required to avoid error and bias. Such adjustments are the subject of this chapter.

Sampling Issues

6.15 There are three sampling concerns when using the MMM. First, the MMM and the use of replacements are designed to meet the needs of constant-quality price measurement and while the sample of varieties priced might initially be designed to be representative of price changes of the population of varieties, it is effectively following a static sample of varieties that, over time, can become increasingly unrepresentative. The matching of prices of identical varieties over time, by its nature, is likely to lead to the monitoring of a sample of varieties increasingly unrepresentative of the population. The sample deteriorates over time because the MMM fails to incorporate new models/varieties into the sample, except as replacements to obsolete ones. For example, substantial developments in telecommunication hardware and services, reflected in the growing number of models available, are excluded from the sample covered by the CPI. This omission would not be problematic if the (implicit) quality-adjusted price changes of the excluded varieties were similar to those of the included matched-model sample. However, this is unlikely to be the case. The (quality-adjusted) prices of old models being dropped may be relatively low and the (quality-adjusted) prices of new ones relatively high as part of a sales strategy of dumping old models at relatively low price to make way for the introduction of new models priced relatively high.

6.16 A second sampling concern with the use of the MMM relates to the timing of the substitution and to when a replacement variety is chosen to replace an old one. In general, the prices of varieties continue to be monitored until they are no longer sold. This means that old varieties with limited sales continue to be monitored and included in the sample. Such varieties may show unusual price changes as they approach the end of their life cycle because of the marketing strategies of firms. Firms typically identify gains to be made from different pricing strategies at different times in the life cycle of products, particularly at the introduction and end of their life cycle. The (implicit or explicit) weight of end-of-cycle varieties in the index would thus remain relatively high, being based on their sales share when they were sampled. Furthermore, new unmatched varieties with possibly relatively large sales would be ignored. Consequently, greater weight would be given to the unusual price changes of matched varieties at the end of their life cycle.

6.17 The final sampling concern with the use of the MMM results from the price collector collecting prices until the variety is no longer available, thus forcing a replacement. Data collectors replace the missing discontinued variety with the most popular or typically consumed variety. This improves the coverage and representativity of the sample. But it also makes reliable quality adjustments of prices between the old and new popular varieties more difficult. The differences in quality are likely to be beyond those that can be attributed to price differences in some overlap period, as one variety is in the final stages of its life cycle and the other in its first. Furthermore, the technical differences between the varieties are likely to be of an order that makes it more difficult to provide reliable, explicit estimates of the effect of quality differences on prices. Finally, the (quality-adjusted) price changes of very old and very new varieties are unlikely to meet assumptions of "similar price changes to existing varieties or classes of varieties," as required by the imputation methods. Many of the methods of dealing with quality adjustment for unavailable varieties may be better served if the switch to a replacement variety is made earlier rather than later. Sampling issues are closely linked to quality-adjustment methods. This topic is discussed in Chapter 8.

6.18 This chapter references the need to permanently replace missing varieties to ensure that the sample of varieties does not become unrepresentative. Samples of representative varieties and outlets are generally updated when an index is updated. Where there is a lengthy period between rebasing, the sample can become seriously deteriorated. It is feasible to update/rotate the sample between periods of revising the index and Chapter 7 outlines how this can be done in the context of maintaining the representativity of the sample. Chapter 6 refers to the need for regular updating of the sample which could be achieved through sample rotation.

New Products

6.19 Another potential source of error when using the MMM arises when a new product is introduced into the marketplace. When a really new product is introduced, there is an immediate gain in welfare or utility as demand switches from the old variety to the new variety. For example, the introduction of mobile telephones represented a completely new good that led to an initial gain in utility or welfare to consumers as they switched from the old (landlines) to the new technology. This gain from the introduction of mobile telephones, and subsequently of increasingly smarter telephones, would not be properly brought into the index by waiting until the index was rebased, or by waiting for at least two successive periods of prices for mobile telephones and linking the new price comparison to the old index. Subsequent prices might be constant or even fall. The initial welfare gain would be calculated from a comparison between the price in the period of introduction and the hypothetical price in the *preceding* period, during which supply would be zero. The practical tools for estimating such a hypothetical price are neither well developed nor practical for CPI compilation, as referenced in more detail in Chapter 7. For a CPI built on the concept of a base period and a fixed basket, this situation, strictly speaking, does not represent a problem. The new product was not in the old basket and should be excluded. Although an index properly measuring an old fixed basket would be appropriate in a definitional sense, it would not be representative of what households purchase. Such an index would thus be inappropriate. For a cost of living index concerned with measuring the change in expenditure necessary to maintain a constant level of utility, there is no doubt that it would be conceptually appropriate to include the new product and any welfare gain from its introduction, though as outlined in Chapter 8, this is highly problematic in practice.

Useful Concepts for the Treatment of Missing Prices

Multiplicative versus Additive Adjustment

6.20 Explicit quality adjustments to prices can be made by adding a fixed amount (additive adjustment) or multiplication by a ratio (multiplicative adjustment). For example, consider m, an old variety, and n its replacement; for a price comparison over periods t, $t+1$, and $t+2$, the price of m is only available in periods t and $t+1$ and n only available in periods $t+1$ and $t+2$. The measurement of constant-quality price change between periods t and $t+1$ is based on variety m, p_m^{t+1} / p_m^t, and the price change between periods $t+1$ and $t+2$ on variety n, p_n^{t+2} / p_n^{t+1}. Although not necessary for the compilation of the price index, the previous calculation can be elaborated in an equivalent, though more complex, form that enables the nature of the quality adjustment from m to n to be identified and the multiplicative formulation demonstrated.

6.21 A price relative over periods t, $t+1$, and $t+2$ requires an overlap ratio p_n^{t+1} / p_m^{t+1} to be used as a measure of the relative quality difference between the old variety and its replacement. This ratio could then be *multiplied* by the price of the old variety in period t, p_m^t to obtain the quality-adjusted prices p_n^{*t} as outlined later in equation (6.6), and illustrated in Table 6.1:

6.22 Such multiplicative formulations are generally recommended, as the adjustment is invariant to the absolute value of the price. If the overlap ratio equals, for example, 1.2, the new variety costs 20 percent more than the old. There may be some varieties for which the worth of the constituent parts is not considered to be in proportion to the price. In other words, the constituent parts have their own, intrinsic, absolute, additive worth, which remains constant over time. For example, retailers selling on websites may include free shipping in the price. In some instances, the cost of shipping may remain the same in the short to medium-term irrespective of what happens to the price of the variety (exclusive of shipping). If the price no longer includes free shipping, this fall in quality should be valued as a fixed additive sum.

Table 6.1 Example of a Replacement Variety with Overlap

	t	$t+1$	$t+2$
Old Variety m	p_m^t	p_m^{t+1}	
Replacement Variety n	p_n^{*t}	p_n^{t+1}	p_n^{t+2}

Price Reference versus Current Period Adjustment

6.23 Two variants of the approaches to quality adjustment are to make the adjustment either to the price in the price reference period or to the price in the current period. For example, in the overlap method, described previously, the implicit quality-adjustment coefficient was used to adjust p_m^t to p_n^{*t}. An alternative procedure would have been to multiply the ratio p_m^{t+1} / p_n^{t+1} by the price of the replacement variety p_n^{t+2} to obtain the quality-adjusted price p_m^{*t+2}. The first approach is more straightforward since, once the reference period price has been adjusted, no subsequent adjustments are required. Each new price of a replacement can be compared with the adjusted reference price.

Long-Term versus Short-Term Comparisons

6.24 Much of the analysis of quality adjustments in this Manual is undertaken by comparing prices between two adjacent periods, say, month-on-month period t prices with those in a subsequent period $t + 1$. For long-term comparisons, the price reference period is taken as, for example, period t and the index compiled by comparing prices in period t first with $t + 1$; then t with $t + 2$; t with $t + 3$, and so on. The short-term framework allows long-term comparisons built up as the product of links: t first with $t + 1$; then $t + 1$ with $t + 2$; $t + 2$ with $t + 3$, and so on; built up as a sequence of links joined together by successive multiplication. This chapter focuses on short-term comparisons, for reasons of their inherently better properties and for focus of exposition; In particular, as outlined in paragraphs 6.51–6.71, the short-term approach enables superior imputations to be made for temporarily missing prices and facilitates the incorporation of replacement varieties as and when an old variety's price is permanently missing. The short-term approach is generally recommended.

Treatment of Missing Variety Prices and Quality Adjustment within an Elementary Aggregate: Short-Term Comparisons

6.25 This chapter uses a short-term framework of comparing period-on-period prices rather than a long-term framework of comparing the current period's price with a fixed price reference period. The use of matching is particularly problematic for long-term price comparisons. For long-term price comparisons a selection of representative models in period 0, for example, the year (or a month in) 2020, have their prices compared with those in January 2021; in February, for the 2020-February price relative; in March, for the 2020-March price relative; continuing for what may be, in some countries, several years. The sample is increasingly depleted over time as 2020 varieties become obsolete.

6.26 The short-term approach has several advantages. An illustration of the short-term against the long-term approach is included in Chapter 7. This chapter is concerned with temporarily and permanently missing variety prices. Temporarily missing variety prices return to the sample, as do seasonal ones (as described in Chapter 11), and there is no issue with maintaining the sample. However, permanently missing variety prices need a replacement variety so that, over time, the sample does not become increasingly depleted and degraded. Yet such one-on-one replacement is unlikely to be sufficient to maintain the representativity of the sample, which may be based on variety selection when updating the index (Chapter 9) or sample rotation that may for some countries be many years ago. Since this initiation, many newer varieties/products may have been introduced and old ones become obsolete. Maintaining the representativity of the sample is addressed in Chapter 7 and a related use of web-based and scanner data sources in Chapter 10. The treatment of permanently missing variety prices was set within the context of an elementary aggregate, where weights were neither available nor used. A modified Lowe price index number is used. The formulas are presented in more detail in Chapters 7 and 8 (see paragraphs 8.109–8.116).

6.27 The example in Table 6.3 might be used to illustrate an individual elementary aggregate with geometric mean prices compiled from several outlets. If a variety is temporarily not available, an imputation can be based on a short-term month-on-month price relative, rather than a long-term price that might assume similar price movements over several years. Similarly, for permanently missing prices where imputations are used to form an overlap comparison for the missing variety price and its replacement, assumptions based on similar short-term month-on-month price movements are more reasonable than the less plausible ones based on long-term price movements.

6.28 This mechanism facilitates the inclusion of new specifications when old specifications become obsolete and enables the index to better represent the dynamic changes taking place in consumer choice. A direct comparison between the price of a new replacement variety specification in April 2020 with its old specification in 2019 is likely to be challenging given the quality differences between the two variety specifications over a long period.

6.29 The short-term formula will differ (be improved) from its fixed-base long-term counterpart since the monthly imputations will differ.

6.30 This chapter's work has for the large part been concerned with short-term price relatives compiled within an elementary aggregate, i. The larger picture of weighted aggregation across elementary aggregates is for this context of missing prices and sample representativity, considered in Chapter 7, with illustrative calculations of the aggregation formulas in Chapter 8, and the introduction of new weights in Chapter 9.

Aggregation Formula for Elementary Price Indices

6.31 A ratio of geometric means (that is, the Jevons price index number formula) is used to measure price changes at the unweighted level of the elementary aggregate. Alternative formulas include a ratio of arithmetic means (that is, the Dutot price index number formula) and an arithmetic average of price ratios—the Carli price index number formula. The Jevons price index formula is used here for reasons of its better properties and focus of exposition. Chapter 9 provides detail, an illustration, and the relative merits of the use of the Dutot and Carli price index number formula.

6.32 With scanner and other such data, information on prices, expenditure values, and quality characteristics will often be available for most individual models sold by major outlets.

This availability of data on transaction values allows weights to be used at this detailed level of aggregation and thus the use of weighted price index formulas as outlined in Chapter 9.

The Role of Price Collectors

6.33 Price collectors have a critical role to play in the treatment of missing price observations. They observe and record that a price is missing; whether it is temporarily or permanently missing; if permanently missing, whether a comparable or noncomparable replacement is available, and in the latter case, the price and details of the replacement variety. When selecting a sample of prices, the outlets are visited in a process referred to as initiation. During the initiation phase of price collection, collectors identify the detailed specifications of representative varieties sold. For example, for the general class of "large white bread, unsliced," the more detailed, "large loaf, white, unsliced, Brand A, 800 gm" may be selected and its details entered along with its price for subsequent periodic repricing. Ideally, price collectors should have in their possession a checklist of these specifications when visiting outlets in subsequent periods. The detailed specifications serve many purposes including (1) to help identify the variety to be priced; (2) to review and verify the variety's specification to ensure there have been no changes in the price-determining characteristics; and (3) if the variety is noncomparable, to use the specifications to identify a replacement variety to be priced and record any changes in the price-determining specifications. Initiation activities occur only when it is necessary to select a new variety for pricing.

6.34 The price collector also plays an important role in determining whether the missing price should be treated as temporarily or permanently missing. A variety's price is considered temporarily missing if the same variety is likely to return to the market within a reasonable time period. On finding that the specified variety is not available for immediate sale, the price collector should check with the manager or informed member of outlet staff whether it is temporarily or permanently missing. If temporarily missing, record the expected duration: one, two, or more periods should be recorded along with the reason for it being unavailable and an indication of the likelihood of its return.

6.35 Temporarily missing varieties have their prices imputed; permanently missing ones require a replacement. As these are different issues requiring different treatments, it is important for the price collector to establish whether the unavailability of the variety is temporary or permanent. Consider the case of a monthly CPI. When a price is temporarily missing, it should be imputed using an overall mean imputation, a targeted mean imputation, or a class mean imputation. Some NSOs use a method referred to as carryforward (repeating the last observed price). As stressed in paragraph 6.65, this is not recommended.

6.36 Permanent unavailability occurs when the variety is withdrawn from the market with no prospect of returning. In some instances, it might be absent the next month and confirmed by the outlet manager or informed staff that it is not going to be replaced. With such information the price collector should immediately look to collecting the price and specifications of a replacement variety. In other cases, if a variety is out of stock, for example during three consecutive months, the price collector should be instructed to choose a replacement that matches as closely as possible the missing variety's specification. After being unavailable for three months and with no indication that the variety will return, it is treated as being permanently missing and a replacement variety is sought. There may be particular products or circumstances in which the three-month rule can be relaxed, such as a temporary withdrawal of products for health reasons, national emergencies, or the logistics of restocking where there is a sound basis for a belief that the product will return in the near future, but not within three months.

Table 6.2 Illustrative Variety Codes for Price Collector for Missing Values

Collection Code	Description
T	**Temporarily Missing:** The Variety Is Unavailable but Is Expected to Be Available Again in the Near Future
P	**Permanently Missing:** The Variety Is No Longer Available and Is Unlikely to Return
S	**Seasonally Missing:** The Variety (Product Group) Is Strongly Seasonal and Is out of Season
C	**Comparable Replacement:** A Replacement Variety That Is Comparable to the Old Variety in All Major Aspects
NC	**Noncomparable Replacement:** A Replacement Variety That Is Not Comparable to the Old Variety

6.37 Decisions on the treatment of missing prices are made by CPI staff based on information provided by the price collector and, in some instances, by a follow-up telephone contact or visit to the outlet.

6.38 Variety prices may be missing for products because they are seasonal and out of season. Products that are out of season, but expected to return in the next season, are treated differently from those considered in this chapter, and their treatment is the subject of Chapter 11.

6.39 Data collection codes, such as those illustrated in Table 6.2, should be used to justify or explain each missing price to ensure proper treatment. Metadata should be collected on those products in which, for example, there is a high level of missing prices of different forms and the extent to which the prices are missing. Illustrative variety codes are given in Table 6.2 and NSOs should build on the detail required to meet their specific needs.

The Treatment of Temporarily and Permanently Missing Variety Prices

6.40 To measure aggregate price changes, a representative sample of varieties is selected from a sample of outlets, along with detailed item descriptions that define each variety and its specifications. For each selected variety, detailed item specifications, or descriptions, define a unique, specific variety that will be priced each period. The detailed specifications are included on the repricing form each period and serve as a prompt to help ensure that the same varieties are being priced. Detailed checklists of variety descriptions should be used, as any lack of clarity in the specifications may lead to errors. Attention should also be devoted to ensuring that the specifications used are not just to identify the variety on a subsequent visit, for example its location in the outlet, but contain all pertinent, price-determining characteristics, otherwise it will not be possible to identify if changes in quality have occurred.

6.41 The MMM succeeds in ensuring the prices of like being compared with like. The detailed variety specifications facilitate this process, and the method ensures that the measurement of price change is not influenced by quality changes. However, when a price is missing there is potential for mismeasurement. The treatment of missing prices depends on whether the variety is temporarily missing (that is, the product will be available in the near future) or permanently missing (that is, the variety will not be available in the future). Each month, all imputed prices are used in the calculation of the index. For example, an imputed March price would be compared with the actual price collected in February in order to calculate the price change from February to March. If the variety returns in April, the imputed March price is compared with its actual price collected in April to calculate the March to April price change. All permanently missing prices require a replacement.

6.42 When a variety is missing in a month a number of approaches may be used. Details of each method are provided in separate sections of this chapter. While the terminology may differ between NSOs, the methods include:

- *Imputation.* The price change for the missing variety is assumed to be the same as the price changes of all varieties in the item group, or targeted similar ones. Such imputations can be used for temporarily missing varieties. Permanently missing varieties, however, require a comparable or noncomparable replacement.
- *Direct comparison.* If a variety is permanently missing and a replacement variety is directly comparable, that is, it is so similar it can be assumed to have had more or less the same quality characteristics as the missing one, its price replaces the price of the unavailable variety. Any difference in price level between the new and the old is judged to be price change and not quality change.
- *Explicit quality adjustment.* If a replacement variety is noncomparable (that is, there are identifiable quality differences) estimates of the impact of the quality differences on the price enable quality-adjusted price comparisons to be made between the old and the new varieties.
- *Implicit quality adjustment—overlap.* If a replacement variety is noncomparable and no information is available, or resources are too limited to allow reasonable explicit estimates to be made of the impact of a quality change on the price, the price difference between the old variety and its replacement in the overlap period is then taken to be a measure of the quality differential.

6.43 Specific attention needs to be devoted to products with relatively big weights, where large proportions of varieties are turned over. Some of the methods are not straightforward and require a higher level of expertise and experience. Quality adjustment should be implemented by developing a methodical approach on a product-by-product basis. Such concerns should not be used as excuses for failing to attempt to estimate quality-adjusted prices. Ignoring quality change results in an implicit quality adjustment. This approach assumes that any difference in price is pure price change and not changes because of a difference in quality. Such an implicit approach may not be appropriate and may even be misleading.

6.44 The treatment of missing price quotes is divided into two types, depending on if these are for temporarily or permanently missing variety prices. These two types cannot always be readily identified and treated accordingly. Some form of mechanism or rule is required to enable a transition from temporary to permanently missing variety prices. A price collector, supported by the head office, would regard a variety as permanently unavailable if verified by an informed member of the outlet's staff or, following a three-month period, the variety is no longer available and there is no evidence that it will reappear. A price index suffers from sample depletion if an increasing number of temporary missing prices are imputed over a lengthy period. Once judged to be a "permanently missing" variety type a replacement is found. If noncomparable, a quality adjustment is made, and imputations are no longer necessary.

6.45 It may also be the case that a replacement, comparable or not, is unavailable (for example, for a videocassette player when it became obsolete). The topic of introducing new goods and services and removing obsolete ones is the subject of Chapter 7. Alternatively, a price collector may find the variety to be permanently missing in the outlet visited, and with no comparable or noncomparable replacement, although the variety is sold in other outlets. An informed outlet staff may inform the price collector that the product is no longer being stocked. For example, considering bicycles in a sports shop, a price index for bicycles could be continued by imputing the price change for this outlet using the price change in other outlets as described in paragraphs 6.51–6.71. Such a procedure depletes the sample and in the longer term this should be remedied by a forced outlet replacement, sample rotation, or rebasing (see Chapter 7).

6.46 Adjustments to prices are not a simple matter of applying routine methods to prices in specified product areas, and alternative approaches are suggested in this chapter. Some approaches are more appropriate than others for specific product areas. An understanding of the consumer market, technological features of the producing industry, and alternative data sources will be required for the successful implementation of quality adjustments.

The Treatment of Temporarily Missing Price Observations

Overall Mean Imputation

6.47 The overall mean imputation method uses the price changes of other similar varieties as estimates of the price change of the missing variety. Considering a Jevons elementary price index (that is, a geometric mean of price relatives, equivalent to the ratio for geometric means of prices),[2] the price of the missing variety in the current period, $t + 1$, is imputed by multiplying its price in the immediately preceding period t by the geometric mean of the price relatives of the remaining matched varieties in the product group between these two periods. This method provides the same

[2]Chapter 8 provides further examples of imputations and replacements using the Jevons index, as compared with the Dutot (ratio of arithmetic means) and Carli indices (mean of the ratio of price relatives), and outlines the relative merits of the three indices.

result as simply dropping the variety that is missing from both periods from the calculation. In practice, the series is continued in the database by including the imputed prices; and, as described in Table 6.3, this forms a complete table of the variety prices in outlets A to F. The imputations are based on assumptions of similar price movements.

6.48 In the example in Table 6.3, a product with broad specifications is sold in six outlets, A to F, with different detailed outlet-specific specifications adopted for each outlet. The price reference period is December 2019 with successive prices collected for each outlet's specification in January, February, March, April, May, June, and July 2020. The price collector finds the variety temporarily missing in outlet F's price collection for March 2020, and likely to remain missing for the next month or two, but to return thereafter. In Table 6.3, the figures in bold for prices of March to May 2020 in outlet F represent two alternative imputation methods, as explained in the following paragraphs.

6.49 The Jevons index number formula is shown in equation 6.2 as a direct or long-term index comparing, in its second to last term, the geometric mean of the prices of each matched variety in the current month t with the geometric mean of the prices in the price reference period, hereafter referred as period 0, and in the last term, for the example in Table 6.3, July 2020 with the price reference period (= 100) of December 2019.

$$I_J\left(I^0, I^t\right) = \prod_{i=1}^{nN}\left(\frac{p_i^t}{p_i^0}\right)^{\frac{1}{n}} \equiv \frac{\prod_{i=1}^{N}\left(p_i^{Jul2020}\right)^{\frac{1}{n}}}{\prod_{i=1}^{N}\left(p_i^{Dec2019}\right)^{\frac{1}{n}}} \tag{6.2}$$

where p = price.

6.50 In practice, the use of the Jevons formula in this long-term form is not advised. Instead, a short-term formulation is recommended as the product of month-on-month Jevons indices. The short-term cumulative Jevons index for December 2019 = 100 to July 2020 is

$$I_J\left(I^{Dec2019}, I^{Jul2020}\right) = \frac{\prod_{i=1}^{N}\left(p_i^{Jan2020}\right)^{\frac{1}{n}}}{\prod_{i=1}^{N}\left(p_i^{Dec2019}\right)^{\frac{1}{n}}} \times \frac{\prod_{i=1}^{N}\left(p_i^{Feb2020}\right)^{\frac{1}{n}}}{\prod_{i=1}^{N}\left(p_i^{Jan2019}\right)^{\frac{1}{n}}} \times \frac{\prod_{i=1}^{N}\left(p_i^{Mar2020}\right)^{\frac{1}{n}}}{\prod_{i=1}^{N}\left(p_i^{Feb2019}\right)^{\frac{1}{n}}} \times \ldots \times \frac{\prod_{i=1}^{N}\left(p_i^{Jul2020}\right)^{\frac{1}{n}}}{\prod_{i=1}^{N}\left(p_i^{Jun2019}\right)^{\frac{1}{n}}} \tag{6.3}$$

6.51 The long-term and short-term approaches in equations 6.2 and 6.3 provide the same result as the numerator of each term on the right-hand side of equation 6.3 cancels with the denominator of the next. However, a major advantage of the short-term formulation is that when an individual variety is missing, its price can be imputed using the month-on-month price changes of similar or higher-level aggregates rather than the long-term comparison of the current month to the price reference period, which may be several years ago.

6.52 The right-hand side of equation 6.3 requires monthly geometric mean prices to be calculated for the numerators and denominators for each month-on-month comparison.Table 6.3 shows the geometric means for the price reference period (December 2019, January 2020, and February 2020); missing prices for March, April, and May; and prices returning in June and July. The first task is to impute the missing price for March 2020. This is obtained using the ratio of geometric mean prices for each of the

Table 6.3 Temporarily Missing Price Observations and Imputed Prices

Outlets	Price Reference Period							
	Dec.-19	Jan.-20	Feb.-20	Mar.-20	Apr.-20	May-20	Jun.-20	Jul.-20
A Supermarket	5.25	5.25	5.49	5.49	5.49	5.49	5.49	5.49
B Supermarket	5.10	5.10	5.10	5.25	5.25	5.25	5.25	5.25
C Supermarket	5.20	5.20	5.20	5.20	5.20	5.25	5.25	5.25
D Independent Trader	5.49	5.49	5.49	5.65	5.75	5.80	5.80	6.00
E Independent Trader	5.99	6.50	6.50	6.90	6.90	6.90	6.90	7.00
F Independent Trader	5.99	5.99	5.99	**6.13**	**6.15**	**6.17**	6.25	6.25
Overall Mean Imputation: F Mar:May								
Geometric Mean: A:E			5.54	5.67	5.69	5.71		
Geometric Mean: A:F	5.49	5.57	5.61	5.74	5.76	5.78	5.79	5.84
Short-Term Price Relatives: A:F	1.00000	1.01371	1.00748	1.02377	1.00352	1.00365	1.00198	1.00864
Long-Term Indices as Product of Short Term	100.00	101.37	102.13	104.56	104.92	105.31	105.52	106.38
Targeted Imputation: Independent Traders								
D Independent Trader	5.49	5.49	5.49	5.65	5.75	5.80	5.80	6.00
E Independent Trader	5.99	6.50	6.50	6.90	6.90	6.90	6.90	7.00
F Independent Trader	5.99	5.99	5.99	**6.26**	**6.32**	**6.34**	6.25	6.25
Geometric Mean: A:C & D:F	5.49	5.57	5.61	5.76	5.79	5.81	5.79	5.84
Short-Term Price Relatives: A:F	1.00000	1.01371	1.00718	1.02731	1.00440	1.00377	0.99753	1.00808
Long-Term Indices as Product of Short Term	100.00	101.37	102.13	104.92	105.38	105.78	105.52	106.37

Bold: Imputed values

matched sample of outlets A to E in February and March to provide the short-term price relative:[3]

$$P_J\left(P^{Feb2020}, P^{Mar2020}\right) = \frac{\prod_{i=A}^{E}\left(p_i^{Mar2020}\right)^{\frac{1}{5}}}{\prod_{i=A}^{E}\left(p_i^{Feb2020}\right)^{\frac{1}{5}}}$$

$$= \frac{(5.49\times5.25\times5.20\times5.65\times6.90)^{\frac{1}{5}}}{(5.49\times5.10\times5.20\times5.49\times6.50)^{\frac{1}{5}}}$$

$$= \frac{5.67}{5.54} = 1.02347 \qquad (6.4)$$

This change in the (geometric) mean price for the matched prices A to E is from February to March. The increase of 1.02347 when multiplied by the February price of 5.99 yields an imputed March price of 1.02347 × 5.99 = 6.13.

6.53 The price collector subsequently finds April and May prices for variety F to be temporarily missing. The respective imputed prices are: 1.0353 × 6.13 = 6.15 and 1.00351 × 6.15 = 6.17. The imputed prices are entered in Table 6.3, highlighted in bold, providing a complete table of prices for outlets A to F over the price reference period and subsequent months.

6.54 The short-term month-on-month price relative for all outlets A to F for February to March 2020 is given as follows:

$$P_J\left(P^{Feb2020}, P^{Mar2020}\right) = \frac{\prod_{i=A}^{F}\left(p_i^{Mar2020}\right)^{\frac{1}{6}}}{\prod_{i=A}^{F}\left(p_i^{Feb2020}\right)^{\frac{1}{6}}} = \frac{5.74}{5.61}$$

$$= 1.02317 \qquad (6.5)$$

6.55 The short-term price relatives for outlets A to F calculated from imputed prices, as in equation 6.5, provides the same measure as the price relative calculated from outlets A to E since the price for outlet F is computed from the price change for outlets A to E. Other short-term price relatives are shown in Table 6.3. The long-term price index (December 2019 = 100) to July 2020 is shown in Table 6.4 and in Table 6.3 as the cumulative product of short-term relatives.

Targeted Mean Imputation

6.56 The overall mean imputation is based on assuming that the price change of the temporarily missing variety is similar to the overall price change at a higher level of aggregation. A targeted form of the method would use price movements of an elementary aggregate or an aggregate of similar varieties, that is, varieties expected to have similar short-term price changes. The sample of observations used for the targeting may be specific to a type of outlet and region and cluster of features, for example, "up-market" television sets. It would generally be a subset of varieties within a higher level of aggregation. The decision to target the imputation using similar varieties in the subset or to use a wider subset of the higher level of aggregation will depend in part on the adequacy of the sample size for the subset of similar varieties and the homogeneity of the elementary aggregate at the higher level.

Table 6.4 Overall Mean and Targeted Mean Imputations

	Overall Mean Imputation	Targeted Mean Imputation
	(a)	(b)
Dec.-19	100	100
Jan.-20	100.00 x 1.013712 = 101.37	100.00 x 1.013712 = 101.37
Feb.-20	101.37 x 1.007478 = 102.13	101.37 x 1.007181 = 102.13
Mar.-20	102.13 x 1.023765 = 104.56	102.13 x 1.026738 = 104.92
Apr.-20	104.56 x 1.003515 = 104.92	104.92 x 1.004396 = 105.38
May-20	104.92 x 1.003652 = 105.31	105.38 x 1.003766 = 105.78
Jun.-20	105.31 x 1.001977 = 105.52	105.78 x 0.997531 = 105.52
Jul.-20	105.52 x 1.008081 = 106.37	105.52 x 1.008081 = 106.37

6.57 Column B in Table 6.4 shows imputed prices for the missing variety prices in outlet F for March, April, and May 2020, based on adjusting the preceding period's price by the price movements of the remaining matched pairs of prices at other independent traders, D and E, rather than all outlets, presented in column A for comparison. Changes in the geometric mean price relative as applied to adjust the preceding period's price are:

$$5.99 \times (5.65 \times 6.90)^{1/2}/(5.49 \times 6.50)^{1/2} = 5.99 \times 1.04522 = 6.26 \text{ for March 2020; and}$$

$$6.26 \times (5.75 \times 6.90)^{1/2}/(5.65 \times 6.90)^{1/2} = 6.26 \times 1.00881 = 6.32 \text{ for April 2020; and}$$

$$6.32 \times (5.80 \times 6.90)^{1/2}/(5.75 \times 6.90)^{1/2} = 6.32 \times 1.00434 = 6.34 \text{ for May 2020} \qquad (6.6)$$

6.58 The price index is compiled as the cumulative product of the short-term price relatives, as shown in Tables 6.3 and 6.4, again highlighted in bold.

6.59 The higher levels used at this elementary stage of aggregation are country-specific and follow the country's CPI aggregation structure, as described in Chapter 8 (paragraphs 8.9–8.10) and Figure 8.1. The higher level might be a region and type of outlet. For example, in Figure 8.1, this would be Brand A of whole grain bread sold in supermarkets in the Northern region; if there is an insufficient sample size for Brand A, similar Brands A and B, or all brands, might be used for all types of outlets in the region. Imputation of the missing price by the average change of the available prices may be applied for elementary aggregates where the prices can be expected to move in the same direction. The imputation can be made using all of the remaining prices in the elementary aggregate. This is numerically equivalent to omitting the variety for the immediate period, but it is necessary to make the imputation (see 6.69–6.71).

6.60 An imputed price should always be directly compared with the actual price on the variety's return as this provides a self-correcting measure. For example, if the imputation was not accurate and showed decreases in prices over the period, when in fact the price of the variety sold elsewhere or, if not sold, being held in storage, was increasing, then a direct comparison between the last imputed and the returning actual price would bring the index back to

[3] Geometric means over large samples are more accurately computed as the equivalent: $\exp\left[\frac{1}{N}\left(\sum_{i=1}^{N}\ln p_i^t - \sum_{i=1}^{N}\ln p_i^0\right)\right]$.

its longer-term trend. The long-term price indices in Table 6.3 using an overall imputation for June and July 2020 are 105.42 and 106.37, respectively. These are the same results as those given in Table 6.3 for targeted imputations. Both series have self-corrected the imputations to return to the long-term price changes as properly measured using actual prices in outlet F. The overlap method described in paragraphs 6.90–6.118 links in a replacement variety's price change and can be used for permanently missing varieties. The overlap method does not have this self-correcting feature and should not be used for temporarily missing varieties.

Carryforward Imputation

6.61 Carrying forward the last observed price should be avoided and is acceptable only in the case of fixed or regulated prices. Special care needs to be taken in periods of high inflation or when markets are changing rapidly as a result of a high rate of innovation and product turnover. While simple to apply, carrying forward the last observed price biases the resulting index toward zero change. In addition, when the price of the missing variety is recorded again, there is likely to be a large compensating step change in the index to return to its proper value. The adverse effect on the index will be increasingly severe if the variety remains unpriced for some length of time. In the example in Table 6.3, if carryforward imputation was used the missing prices in March 2020 would be imputed with the February 2020 price of 5.99, as would be the imputed prices in April and May 2020. In June, on the variety's return, there would be a step increase in price from May to June of 5.99 to 6.25. In general, carrying forward is not an acceptable procedure or solution to this problem. Exceptions may be well-established and well-advertised periodic increases of fixed or controlled prices and tariffs.

General Considerations

6.62 As a general principle, temporarily missing prices require an explicit imputation entered into the data compilation. The overall mean imputation should, by default, be based on a higher level of aggregation; however, it also may refer to a variety within a region or type of outlet. The higher level of aggregation may comprise more than one variety, some with different price changes. For example, if the missing price observation is for "canned tuna," where the higher weighted level aggregate is "canned fish" which includes "canned tuna" and "canned salmon," then subject to a sufficient sample size, the imputation should be based on price movements of "canned tuna."

6.63 An overall mean imputation benefits from an automation of its implementation, and the transparency of this methodology contributes to the integrity of the index. By using an overall imputation, NSOs guard themselves against criticisms of influencing the CPI by their choice of "similar varieties," particularly where there are missing prices for heavily weighted elementary aggregates. However, this method should not be used when there are strong a priori or empirical grounds to believe a targeted imputation would improve the results. NSOs should have retrospective monthly price data available at higher levels of aggregation and be able to examine differences in short-term month-on-month price changes between the missing variety's price changes, and price changes of similar varieties and higher levels of aggregation, to choose between an overall or targeted imputation accordingly. In the much-simplified illustration of Table 6.3, price changes of supermarkets are very different from independent traders and a target imputation is illustrated for outlet F using independent traders. Outlet F might also have been imputed using the price index at a higher level of aggregation or even a single outlet's price. Similar principles of aggregation apply.

6.64 Typically, a price collector reports a variety price as temporarily missing; this is then passed to the head office for confirmation and then, perhaps, further at a higher level. If confirmed, a decision is made as to use a targeted or overall imputation. If the overall mean imputation is chosen, an appropriate computer routine is applied which enters the imputed price with a designation as being imputed into the data system. If a targeted imputation is used, the CPI compiler selects the variety rows regarded as likely to have similar price changes, and the imputation is applied accordingly. For quality assurance, the computer routine should record the decisions made and tabulate the number of temporarily missing varieties by elementary aggregate and their treatment.

6.65 Imputations are preferable to simply omitting the missing price observation for the calculation of the index. For example, consider a variety priced at 4 in January, temporarily missing in February, and returning at 6 in March. If the price change between January and February for the remaining varieties in the elementary aggregate was 25 percent (a price relative of 1.25). The imputed variety price for February would be $1.25 \times 4 = 5$. The actual price is not known, but the imputation serves as a benchmark without impairing the 25 percent price index measure based on observed matched prices. The February to March price relative for the missing variety is $6/5 = 1.20$. This is referred to as a self-correcting imputation; it self-corrects in the sense that the long-term February to March calculation would allow the index to return to its appropriate level: $5/4 \times 6/5 = 6/4 = 1.5$. Similar principles apply for the treatment of seasonal products as outlined in Chapter 11. Simply omitting the February price, and basing the February to March price relative on matched prices in these two months, would not have this self-correcting property.

6.66 Omitting a missing variety's price from the calculation is equivalent to an overall imputation using the other matched prices in the elementary aggregate. The entering of an imputed value allows for the flexibility of using a targeted imputation, if desired.

6.67 The designation of an imputed value by a different tab or color clearly shows in the prices database the extent to which imputations are used, the length of their runs, and product codes where they are overused. Summary counts of imputed prices should be monitored by type, product code, frequency, and duration as part of quality assurance. This is particularly important to identify if or where temporarily missing variety prices have continually imputed values well over a three-month run, with the possibility of continuing sample depletion as other variety prices go missing.

The Nature of Quality Change

6.68 Understanding the meaning of quality change requires well-defined conceptual and theoretical background, so that adjustments to prices for quality differences are made against this framework, as described in this section.

6.69 Over time, the quality of what is produced changes. For example, new automobiles typically have an increasing number of options and become more reliable, durable, safe, powerful, and economical. Another example is smartphones, as each new model includes faster processing speeds and power, more memory, improved screen resolution, and other technological advances such as facial recognition. In matching the prices of a sample of models selected in a price reference period with the same models in subsequent periods, the quality mix remains constant to avoid affecting the price measurement with quality differences. However, the resulting sample of models gives less emphasis to newer models that have benefited from more recent technological change and have different price changes given the quality of services they provide.

6.70 Observed changes in prices arise in theory from several sources, including quality changes, changes in tastes and preferences, and changes in the technology of producers. Price differences of similar products are often taken to be measures of differences in quality. However, differences in prices are often observed for varieties of the same quality. This may arise for a number of reasons:

- Some consumers may be unaware of the availability of the same varieties at lower prices, as there may be "search costs" to exploring the market to discover lower priced varieties.
- There may be price discrimination because the seller is able to charge different prices to different categories of consumers, such as movie tickets for children and senior citizens.
- Prices may be sticky with some retailers changing their prices infrequently to avoid the costs of doing so, including adverse customer reaction, or as strategic competitive behavior, such as loss leaders, leading to different retailers changing prices at different times.
- Cases where there are parallel markets, an official market subject to government or official control at which products are rationed and an unofficial unregulated market. The unofficial market may be at a lower price because it avoids taxes and regulations, or at higher price since the official price is a subsidized one, but has limited, possibly varying, quantities available for sale (*System of National Accounts 2008*, paragraphs 15.64–15.75).

6.71 In addition to the changing mix of the characteristics of varieties, there is also the practical problem of not always being able to observe or quantify characteristics such as the style, reliability, ease of use, and safety of what is produced. The same product provided at a different and more convenient location may result in a higher price and be considered to be of a higher quality. Furthermore, different times of the day or periods of the year may also give rise to quality differences, for example, electricity or transport provided at peak times must be treated as being of higher quality than the same amount of electricity or transport provided at off-peak times. The fact that peaks exist shows that purchasers or users attach greater utility to the products at these times and reflect supply-side pressure. Other differences, including the conditions of sale and circumstances or environment in which the products are supplied or delivered, can make an important contribution to differences in quality. For example, a retailer may attract customers by providing free delivery, financing, or better variety, by being more accessible, by offering shorter order times, smaller tailor-made orders, clearer labeling, better support and advice, more convenient car parking, or a wider range of brands, or simply by operating in a more pleasant or fashionable environment. Although these sorts of benefits are not always specified in the variety description, such quality improvements should conceptually not be outside the scope of the index.

6.72 To consider how to adjust prices for quality changes, it is first necessary to define quality. While there may be an intuition as to whether a variety consumed in one period is better than its counterpart in the next, a theoretical framework will help in establishing the basis for such comparisons. For example, a variety of clothing is sampled and, after a few periods, is missing. One option is to replace it with a similar variety, but the most comparable option may have more cloth in it, or have a lining, a different color or buttons, better stitching, or be considered more fashionable. There is a need to put a price estimate on the difference in quality between the old and new varieties so that the price of like can be compared with like. To propose or criticize a quality-adjustment procedure requires some concept of what is ideally required and how it is done in practice.

6.73 In Chapter 4 of *Consumer Price Index Theory*, a cost of living index is defined as the ratio of the minimum expenditure in the base and current period required to achieve a given standard of living or utility. Quality adjustments to prices involve attempting to measure the price change for a product that has exhibited some change in its characteristics from an earlier period that provides a different level of utility to the consumer. Equating of the value of a quality change with the change in utility derived by the consumer, while falling naturally under a cost of living index framework, is not exclusive to it. A cost of goods index can also benefit from regarding quality in this way. While a cost of goods index requires the pricing of a fixed basket of products, some varieties will become unavailable and the replacement varieties selected to maintain the sample may not be of the same quality. A cost of goods index based on a fixed-basket concept has the pragmatic need to adjust for quality differences when a variety becomes unavailable, and in the definition of a fixed-basket index does not preclude differences in utility being used as a guideline. If variety A is better than its old version, variety B, it is because it delivers more utility to the consumer who in turn is willing to pay more.

6.74 The definition of a quality change is based on equating some change in characteristics to a different level of utility provided. For example, consider the case in which a new variety with improved quality is made available, and the consumer has to choose between the old and new varieties in period t. If both varieties were offered to the consumer at the same price, $p^t = 100$, the consumer would naturally prefer the new variety. If the price of the old variety was then progressively reduced until $p'^* = 75$, at which the consumer was indifferent between purchasing the old variety (at $p'^* = 75$) and the new variety (at $p' = 100$), the consumer might select the old variety or the new one and would obtain the same utility from both. Any further decrease below $p'^* = 75$ would cause the consumer to switch back to the old variety.

6.75 The difference between p' and p'^* would be a measure of the additional utility that the consumer placed on the new variety as compared with the old. It would measure the maximum amount that the consumer was prepared to pay for the new variety over and above the price of the old variety. In economic theory, if consumers are indifferent between two purchases, the utility derived from them is the same. The difference between p' and p'^* (75 and 100) must therefore arise from the consumers' valuation of the difference in utility they derive from the two varieties: their quality difference.

6.76 The utility-based framework provides insights into the question of how consumers might choose between varieties of different qualities. Consumers derive more utility from a variety of higher quality than from a variety of lower quality, and thus they prefer it. But this does not explain why consumers buy one variety rather than the other. For this, it is also necessary to know the relative price of one variety with respect to the other, since if the lower-quality variety is cheaper, it may still be purchased ($p'^* \leq 75$ in the previous example) and to determine the price below which the old quality would be purchased.

Permanently Missing Price Observations

6.77 Tables 6.5A–C illustrate the treatment of permanently missing price observations. In these tables, prices are observed for outlets A to E over the seven months of December 2019 to June 2020. For outlet F, the price observations for the variety is reported as permanently missing from May 2020, and the price collector has to find a replacement variety (the prices in bold for May and June are imputed as explained in the following text). The use of replacement varieties maintains the original sample sizes at the last rebasing and the representativity of the varieties selected. Informed outlet staff should be asked to confirm that the missing variety is permanently missing and help identify a best-selling replacement variety, its specifications, and how these specifications differ from those of the old variety. For logistical reasons the selected replacement variety would be expected to have high sales for the foreseeable future. The CPI staff at the head office would confirm or reject the choice of replacement variety.

Comparable Replacement

6.78 The price collector should use the missing variety's specification and identify a comparable variety with the same specifications, for example, a washing machine with the same spin speed, capacity, brand, or equivalent brand. If a comparable replacement exists, its detailed specifications should be confirmed by the price collector against the specifications for the missing variety. Any changes in the specification deemed to be not sufficiently price-determining should be noted for the head office to confirm, for example, color and trim.

6.79 The comparable replacement method requires the price collector to make a judgment that the replacement is of a similar quality to the old variety and any price changes are unaffected by changes resulting from quality differences. In Table 6.5A, there is a comparable variety F1 to replace variety F, also from outlet F. The replacement variety is considered by the price collector and confirmed by the head office as being directly comparable, and its prices in May and June (respectively, 6.20 and 6.25) are entered into the data system as a continuation of the outlet F series. The price index is calculated using short-term price relatives built into a long-term price index. The price index in July 2020 (December 2019 = 100) is 105.52, a 5.52 percent increase over this period. The price index remains as a constant-quality index since in May and June 2020 the prices of like quality varieties continue to be compared with like.

6.80 A common practice of manufacturers of electronic goods, such as televisions, household appliances, computers and computer-related hardware and software, and of automobiles is to have major quality changes in some years but relatively minor ones in other years. A new "comparable" model would have a new model number with a new

Table 6.5A Illustration of Treatment of Comparable Replacements

Outlets		Price Reference Period						
		Dec.-19	Jan.-20	Feb.-20	Mar.-20	Apr.-20	May-20	Jun.-20
A	**Supermarket**	5.25	5.25	5.49	5.49	5.49	5.49	5.49
B	**Supermarket**	5.10	5.10	5.10	5.25	5.25	5.25	5.25
C	**Supermarket**	5.20	5.20	5.20	5.20	5.20	5.25	5.25
D	**Independent Trader**	5.49	5.49	5.49	5.65	5.75	5.80	5.80
E	**Independent Trader**	5.99	6.50	6.50	6.90	6.90	6.90	6.90
F	**Independent Trader**	5.99	5.99	5.99	6.13	6.15	**6.20**	**6.25**
Permanently Missing: F, May, June; F1: Comparable Replacement								
Geometric Mean: A:F		5.49	5.57	5.61	5.74	5.76	5.79	5.79
Short-Term Price Relatives: A:F		1.00000	1.01371	1.00748	1.02370	1.00347	1.00440	1.00134
Long-Term Indices as Product of Short Term		100.00	101.37	102.13	104.55	104.91	105.37	105.52

Values in bold are imputed.

production run, though physically not much has changed. The method of comparable replacement relies on the efficacy of the price collectors and head officer and, in turn, on the completeness of the specifications used as a description of the varieties. NSOs may tend toward designating replacements as comparable since they are concerned with sample sizes being reduced by dropping varieties, and the intensive use of resources to introduce noncomparable replacements or make explicit estimates of quality differences. The use of varieties of a comparable specification has practical advantages. However, if the quality of varieties is improving, the preceding variety will have inferior quality compared to the current one. Continually ignoring small changes in the quality of replacements can lead to an upward bias in the index. The extent of the problem will depend on the proportion of such occurrences, the extent to which comparable replacements are accepted as being so despite quality differences, and the weight attached to those varieties. Chapter 8 includes proposals to monitor types of quality-adjustment methods by product group providing a basis for a strategy for applying explicit adjustments where they are most needed.

Noncomparable Replacements

6.81 Noncomparable replacements result when the price-determining characteristics of the replacement variety are different from those of the old variety. This means that the collected price of the replacement variety cannot be compared directly to the price of the old variety because the difference in these prices reflects not only pure price change, but also differences because of changes in quality. Noncomparable replacements require some form of quality adjustment.

6.82 Methods of quality adjustment for prices are classified into implicit (or indirect) quality-adjustment methods and explicit (or direct) methods. Implicit and explicit methods are discussed in paragraphs 6.90–6.188. Both decompose the price change between the old variety and its replacement into quality and pure price changes.

6.83 Implicit (or indirect) quality-adjustment methods estimate the pure price change component of the price difference between the old and new products based on the price changes observed for similar products. The difference between the estimate of pure price change and the observed price change is considered as change due to quality difference. The most commonly used implicit method is the overlap method. The replacement's price change is linked to the old variety's price change using an overlap period that includes both the old and the replacement variety's price. Where an overlap price for the replacement variety does not exist, it might be imputed.

6.84 Explicit (or direct) quality-adjustment methods directly estimate the value of the quality difference between the old and new product and adjust one of the prices accordingly. Pure price change is then estimated as the difference in the adjusted prices. Explicit methods include quantity adjustments, option/feature costs, and "patched" hedonic regression methods.

6.85 Some of these methods are complex, costly, and difficult to apply. The methods used should as far as possible be based on objective criteria.

Implicit Methods of Quality Adjustment

6.86 This section discusses the following implicit methods for obtaining adjusting for quality differences: overlap method, class mean imputation, and link-to-show-no-change.

Overlap Method

The Use of an Overlap Price

6.87 A numerical illustration of the overlap method is shown in Table 6.5B. In this example, in outlet F there is a preexisting old model F available up to April 2020, and a noncomparable new replacement model, F2, available from May 2020, with the same actual price of 5.25 in both May and June. The prices are lower than would be expected from the prices of F, but this is a noncomparable replacement: it is a replacement variety with a major share and is expected to remain on the market in the foreseeable future.

6.88 The overlap method requires a price for both the old and new models in an overlap period. In the example in Table 6.5B, F exists up to and including April, F2 exists in May, June, and thereafter. The question is how to determine an overlap price in this case. One source of information for this overlap price (of 5.25 in April) is the price collector.

Table 6.5B Illustration of Treatment Using the Overlap Method, Noncomparable Replacements: Actual Preceding Period Price

Outlets		Price Reference Period						
		Dec.-19	Jan.-20	Feb.-20	Mar.-20	Apr.-20	May-20	Jun.-20
A	**Supermarket**	5.25	5.25	5.49	5.49	5.49	5.49	5.49
B	**Supermarket**	5.10	5.10	5.10	5.25	5.25	5.25	5.25
C	**Supermarket**	5.20	5.20	5.20	5.20	5.20	5.25	5.25
D	**Independent Trader**	5.49	5.49	5.49	5.65	5.75	5.80	5.80
E	**Independent Trader**	5.99	6.50	6.50	6.90	6.90	6.90	6.90
F	**Independent Trader**	5.99	5.99	5.99	6.13	6.15		
Permanently Missing: F, May, June; F2: Noncomparable Replacement								
F2	**Noncomparable Replacement**					**5.25**	5.25	5.25
Geometric Mean: April, May, June: A:E,F2						5.61	5.63	5.63
Short-Term Price Relatives		100.00	1.0137	1.0075	1.0237	1.0035	1.0030	1.0000
Long-Term Indices as Product of Short Term		100.00	101.37	102.13	104.55	104.91	105.23	105.23

Values in bold are imputed.

Use the Actual Price of the Replacement in the Preceding Period, If It Exists

6.89 The price collector may have anticipated falling sales of a variety and the switch of consumers to a new model, brand, or variety, and recorded the price for the replacement prior to its adoption, obtaining in this way an overlap price. In the example in Table 6.5B, the price collector would start to record the price of the new variety F2 in April rather than May. Price collectors should be trained to anticipate such changes, to corroborate them with informed outlet staff, and to relay the information to the head office for possible action. In the example, the price collector would have seen diminishing sales and a poorer positioning for display in the outlet for the variety F, and it would have been apparent that it was to be replaced by F2. Outlet staff would confirm that F2 was to effectively replace F as a model aimed at that the same segment of the market, and the price for F2 and its quality characteristics should have been recorded alongside that of F to provide an overlap April price to facilitate the introduction of F2 in May. As a general principle, the replacement of models is best not undertaken when the old model has limited sales and is at the end of its life cycle.

6.90 Alternatively, the price collector may have asked informed outlet staff in May whether the new model was sold in the previous month to obtain an overlap price for April, or if sold in other outlets, whether there is a pricing agreement with the supplier that this outlet would have followed had it been supplied to them, and what would have been the price. The head office should confirm such details by visit or contact with informed staff of outlet F. Table 6.5B shows 5.25 to be entered as an *estimated* price in April 2020 for the new model, to provide an overlap price in April for the old and replacement models, F and F2.

6.91 The price index is measured through and including April 2020 using the prices of the old model: from Table 6.5A, the geometric mean of the prices of the old model in April 2020 is 5.76, and in March it is 5.74, with a short-term price relative of 5.76/5.74 = 1.0035. The price index to April 2020 is the cumulated product of the old index's price relatives: for April 2020, it is 104.91 = 104.55 × 1.0035 (December 2019 = 100).

6.92 In Table 6.5B, the index from May onward no longer uses F, but switches to F2. For this, there is a need for the overlap prices: average prices up to and including April using the old variety F and for May, June, and onward, using the new variety F2. The prices for outlet F in May and June (5.25 in both) are based on F2. The overlap in April for the new model F2 is 5.25. This overlap price is used to calculate the index for May. Using the overlap price, the short-term price relative for April to May in outlet F is 5.25/5.25 = 1.00000. This completes the price table. The geometric means are calculated as before, and their ratios form the short-term price relatives, and, in turn, the cumulative product of the price relatives, starting in December 2019 is the price index, at 105.23 for June 2020 (December 2019 = 100). The index from December to April is calculated using A–F and the index beginning in May onward is based on the prices of A–E and F2.

Imputed Overlap Prices

6.93 In the previous example, the new replacement variety may not have existed in April or the price collector may not have been able to obtain a reliable estimate of its price. In this situation, the overlap price in April can be imputed. The validity of this imputation is critical to the quality-adjustment methodology. In Table 6.5B, there was a price of 6.15 for the old model and 5.25 for the new model for April 2020. As shown in equation 6.6, this method implicitly attributes the price difference in the common April overlap period as an indicator of the quality difference between the old and new models.

6.94 If the new model was not sold in April, an imputation for the May price of the old model can be made to provide an overlap price. The imputation may be an overall mean or a targeted imputation following the principles outlined for temporarily missing variety prices (as described in paragraphs 6.52–6.72 and illustrated in Table 6.3). Table 6.5C illustrates a *forward* imputation of the old model's price to provide an estimate of the price in May 2020 had it existed then. The imputed price is given in Table 6.5C as 6.17. It is calculated by taking the ratio (relative) of the geometric mean of the May prices of outlets A to E to the geometric

Table 6.5C Illustration of Treatment Using the Overlap Method, Noncomparable Replacements: Imputed Succeeding Period Price

Outlets		Price Reference Period						
		Dec.-19	Jan.-20	Feb.-20	Mar.-20	Apr.-20	May-20	Jun.-20
A	**Supermarket**	5.25	5.25	5.49	5.49	5.49	5.49	5.49
B	**Supermarket**	5.10	5.10	5.10	5.25	5.25	5.25	5.25
C	**Supermarket**	5.20	5.20	5.20	5.20	5.20	5.25	5.25
D	**Independent Trader**	5.49	5.49	5.49	5.65	5.75	5.80	5.80
E	**Independent Trader**	5.99	6.50	6.50	6.90	6.90	6.90	6.90
F	**Independent Trader**	5.99	5.99	5.99	6.13	6.15	**6.17**	
Permanently Missing: F, May, June; F3: Noncomparable Replacement								
F3	**Noncomparable Replacement**						5.25	5.25
Geometric Mean: May, June: A:F						5.76	5.78	
Geometric Mean: May, June: A:E,F3							5.63	5.63
Short-Term Price Relatives		100.00	1.0137	1.0075	1.0237	1.0035	1.0037	1.0000
Long-Term Indices as Product of Short Term		100.00	101.37	102.13	104.55	104.91	105.30	105.30

Values in bold are imputed.

mean of the April prices for the same outlets, 5.78/5.76 = 1.0037, and multiplying this by the old variety's price in April. The index in Table 6.5C is calculated by multiplying the short-term May to June price relative for the new replacement F3, 5.63/5.63 = 1.0000, by the value of the long-term index for May, 105.30. The 5.63 are the geometric means of the prices in outlets A to E and that of the replacement F3.

Forward versus Backward Imputation

6.95 In Table 6.5B, the overlap took place in April, while in Table 6.5C, it was in May. In Table 6.5B, an actual price was sought and found for the new (replacement) variety in April. There would be no equivalent May price for the permanently missing old variety. Given that an actual price may be preferred to an imputation based on the price movements of varieties priced in other outlets, the use of a *backward* price to provide an overlap in April can be used. In Table 6.5C, a *forward imputation* is used for the old variety's price in May, which is also an acceptable means of making an imputation. But one could apply a *backward imputation* for the new (replacement) variety's price in April to provide an overlap in April as the one in Table 6.5C. It is relatively straightforward to demonstrate algebraically that the result would be the same if the index is calculated either way. Both methods impute the missing price using the price movements of varieties in the outlets A to E for which prices exist in both April and May. The backward imputation is simply the inverse of the forward one. The ratio of prices in the overlap periods, as shown by equation 6.6, is the implicit measure of the quality differential between the old variety and the replacement variety, will be numerically the same for backward and forward imputations. As a result, either forward or backward imputations can be made.

Class Mean Imputation

6.96 The overall imputation method has many advantages considering the use of resources. It can be automated as a default measure to readily link-in replacement varieties keeping the sample up to date. However, the (forward) imputation assumes that the price movements of existing continuing varieties would be the same as that for the old variety, if it had continued to exist. A backward imputation assumes the price movement of the new (replacement) variety would be the same as existing continuing varieties had the new variety existed in the period prior to its introduction. Such assumptions are unlikely to be valid for high-technology goods being replaced at the end of their life cycle. An alternative imputation procedure designed to mitigate this problem is the class mean imputation which in principle, is more suited to this context of imputing replacement variety prices for permanently missing varieties, as opposed to temporarily missing ones.

6.97. *The class mean imputation method* is a specifically designed targeted imputation used to introduce a replacement when a variety's price is permanently missing. The class mean method of implicit quality adjustment to prices arose from concerns that unusual prices were charged at the start and end of a model's life cycle. Thus, the price movement of continuing varieties appears to be a flawed proxy for the pure price component of the difference between old and replacement varieties. A class mean imputation is mainly considered as a means of quality adjustment where there is a relatively high rate of frequent replacements, such as different models of automobiles launched each year.

6.98 The class mean method is a form of targeted imputation, for the treatment of replacements for permanently missing varieties, in which only the price changes of "comparable" replacements are used to impute the overlap price. The comparable replacements are being limited to those that have exactly the same price-determining characteristics, or those varieties with replacements that have been declared comparable after review or have already been quality-adjusted through one of the "explicit" methods, as described in paragraphs 6.120–6.188. For example, when the arrival of a new model of a particular kind of motor vehicle forces price collectors to find replacements, some of the replacements will be of comparable quality, and others comparable with explicit quality adjustments, but imputed prices for an overlap month will be needed for the remaining ones. Class mean imputation calculates imputed price relatives using only the prices of comparable and, where appropriate, explicitly quality-adjusted varieties or models. In general, it does not use the prices of the varieties or models that were not replaced, because these are likely to be different from those of the new models. The prices of old models tend to fall as they become obsolete, while the new models (represented by the replacements) tend to have a higher price before falling.

6.99 Class mean imputations rely on other explicit quality adjustments and comparable replacements. The other explicit quality adjustments may be from an available option or feature prices and may be limited in nature, covering only some of the differences in product attributes, available for only a small proportion of unrepresentative model or variety changes, and the availability of comparable replacements may be limited. Given a substantial churn in the market and difficulties with such imputations and estimates, an alternative recommended approach is that of hedonic indices, as outlined in paragraphs 6.140–6.176.

6.100 In some cases, sufficiently large samples of comparable substitutes or directly quality-adjusted varieties are unavailable, or the quality adjustments and selection of comparable varieties are not deemed sufficiently reliable. In that case, a targeted imputation may be considered. The targeted mean is less ambitious because it seeks only to capture price changes of similar varieties, irrespective of their point in the life cycle. However, it is an improvement on the overall mean imputation, as long as sufficiently large sample sizes are used.

Assumptions and Concerns on the Use of the Overlap Method

6.101 The accuracy of the estimates obtained with the overlap method depends on the validity of its underlying assumptions, as described in this section. If p_m^t and p_m^{t+1} denote the prices of an old variety m in periods t and $t+1$, and p_n^{t+2} denote the price of a new replacement variety n in period $t+2$, an overlap can be made by imputing a price for the new replacement variety in period $t+1$, p_n^{t+1*}. In the case where variety n replaces m and is of a different quality, the measured price index between periods t and $t+2$ (shown by the right-hand side expression in equation 6.7 is the price change of the old to new variety between these two periods, multiplied by (adjusted for) the price overlap for m to n in period $t + 1$ which the method implicitly takes to be a measure of the quality difference.

6.102 A *forward* imputation is used in the previous example for the price of the old variety in period $t + 1$. Equation 6.7 also shows for this forward imputation that the overlap method depends on the validity of the relative difference in the prices of the old and new varieties in period $t + 1$ as a measure of the quality difference between the varieties, and on the reliability of the imputed price, designated with an asterisk (*), of the old variety m in period $t + 1$, p_m^{t+1*}, as an estimate of p_m^{t+1}.

$$I^{t,t+2} = \frac{p_m^{t+1*}}{p_m^t} \times \frac{p_n^{t+2}}{p_n^{t+1}} = \frac{p_n^{t+2}}{p_m^t} \times \frac{p_m^{t+1*}}{p_n^{t+1}} \qquad (6.7)$$

6.103. Table 6.6 shows an old model m permanently missing from March ($t + 1$) and replaced by a new model n in April ($t + 2$), with an overlap in March ($t + 1$). The price index for February (t) to April ($t + 2$), obtained using the overlap method, is given by the first expression in equation 6.7 as the product of the old model's price change between February and March and the new model's price change between March and April. This is equivalent to the second expression in equation 6.7, which is a direct price comparison between the new and old models between February and April with a quality adjustment as the value of the relative prices in the overlap month March ($t + 1$). The overlap method implicitly values the quality difference as the ratio of the two prices in the overlap period:

$$I^{\text{Feb,Apr}} = \frac{p_m^{\text{Mar*}}}{p_m^{\text{Feb}}} \times \frac{p_n^{\text{Apr}}}{p_n^{\text{Mar}}} = \frac{p_n^{\text{Apr}}}{p_m^{\text{Mar}}} \times \frac{p_m^{\text{Mar*}}}{p_n^{\text{Mar}}}$$
$$= \frac{30}{28} \times \frac{38}{35} = \frac{38}{28} \times \frac{30}{35} = 1.163 \qquad (6.8)$$

6.104 Moreover, for a longer-term price comparison, say January to June, the valuation of the quality difference remains as the price ratio in March, the time of the splice:

$$I^{\text{Feb,Apr}} = \frac{p_m^{\text{Feb}}}{p_m^{\text{Jan}}} \times \frac{p_m^{\text{Mar*}}}{p_m^{\text{Feb}}} \times \left(\frac{p_n^{\text{Apr}}}{p_n^{\text{Mar}}} \times \frac{p_n^{\text{May}}}{p_n^{\text{Apr}}} \times \frac{p_n^{\text{Jun}}}{p_n^{\text{May}}} \right)$$
$$= \frac{p_n^{\text{Jun}}}{p_m^{\text{Jan}}} \times \frac{p_m^{\text{Mar*}}}{p_n^{\text{Mar}}} = \frac{41}{25} \times \frac{30}{35} = 1.4057 \qquad (6.9)$$

6.105 The price of a missing variety is, by definition, not usually observed at the same time period as the price of the replacement variety, since the decision to replace the variety is only made after it has disappeared. Additionally, the list of specifications is not always comprehensive, since the main aim is to identify the variety in the outlet rather than to compare the varieties. However, the replacement variety may have been sold in the previous period and outlet staff may have a record of its price.

6.106 The underlying assumption in this case is that the quality difference in any period is equal to the price difference at the *time of the splice*. The *timing* of the switch from the old variety m to the new variety n is thus crucial. Unfortunately, price collectors usually maintain a variety until the decision to replace it is taken, so the switch may take place at an unusual period of pricing, near the end of variety m's life cycle and the start of variety n's life cycle. This analysis is more formally given in Annex 6.1.

6.107 Relative prices may not always reflect quality differences. For example, a new replacement model or brand of an improved quality may be stocked and sold at the same price as the old model, and the outlet competes in the market in part by changing the quality of what is sold, as opposed to the price. In other cases, retailers may reflect unusual pricing policies aimed at minority segments of the market. For example, the ratio of prices in an overlap period of a generic and a branded pharmaceutical drug may reflect the needs of two different market segments, rather than quality. The overlap method can be used with a careful choice of the overlap period. If possible, the overlap period should be a period before the use of the replacement, since in such periods the pricing may reflect a strategy to drop the old model to make way for the new one.

6.108 The overlap method is based on the law of one price: when a price difference is observed, it must arise from a difference in quality or similar factors for which consumers are willing to pay a premium, such as the timing of the sale, location, convenience, or conditions. Economic theory would dictate that such price differences would not persist, given that markets are made up of rational producers and consumers. However, as outlined in paragraph 6.74, there are many reasons why identical varieties can be sold at different prices, and the law of one price does not hold in practice. These reasons include lack of information caused by search costs, price discrimination, and the existence of parallel markets.

6.109 The overlap method is commonly used as a default procedure for introducing replacements when varieties are permanently missing. NSOs that rebase the CPI less frequently may experience sample deterioration with many varieties becoming permanently missing and, without replacements, the sample becoming increasingly composed of imputed prices. Replacements serve to maintain the sample composition and to update the representativity of the varieties being priced.

6.110 In some cases, only noncomparable replacements (that is, those of a different quality) of varieties with missing prices are available. In these cases, an explicit adjustment to the price to account for the quality difference should be made to compare the prices of the noncomparable

Table 6.6 Introducing a Noncomparable Replacement via an Overlap

Model	January	February	March	April	May	June
Old (m)	25	28	**30**			
New (n)			35	38	40	41

Values in bold are imputed.

Table 6.6A Introducing a Noncomparable Replacement to Illustrate Link-to-Show-No-Change

Model	January	February	March	April	May	June
Old (m)	25	28	**28**			
New (n)			35	38	40	41

Values in bold are imputed.

replacements in one period with the price of the now missing varieties in a previous period. The widely used overlap method has a major advantage of not requiring an explicit quality adjustment. Explicit quality adjustments (described in paragraphs 6.119–6.187) are more resource-intensive than the implicit overlap method. Furthermore, it is recommended that the overlap method be automated with information from the price collector, reported to the head office, and used in a computational routine. The recommendation is that in accepting the use of the overlap method, the CPI compiler should ensure that relative prices at the time of the overlap reflect quality differences. For example, a much-improved new model of a smartphone may be launched at the same price as the old model, and the relative price would not reflect the differences in quality. If the relative price does not reflect quality differences and resources allow, an explicit quality-adjustment method should be used.

6.111 The overlap method is implicitly employed when samples of varieties are rotated. That is, the old sample of varieties is used to compute the category index price change between periods $t-1$ and t, and the new sample is used between t and $t+1$. The "splicing" together of these index movements is justified by the assumption that—on a group-to-group rather than variety-to-variety level—differences in price levels at a common point in time accurately reflect differences in qualities.

6.112 The bias in using the overlap method within an elementary aggregate depends on (1) the ratio of missing to total observations, and (2) the difference between the mean of price changes for existing varieties and the mean of quality-adjusted replacement price changes. As noted previously in paragraph 6.91, imputations can be made either forward or backward. The bias decreases as either of these terms decrease. A formal analysis is given in Annex 6.2.

Link-to-Show-No-Price-Change

6.113 Returning to the example in Table 6.6, reproduced in Table 6.6A, where the new replacement variety is noncomparable (that is, of a different quality), the link-to-show-no-price-change method imputes the price in March for the old model m to be the same as its February price, 28. The new variety is linked-in to show no price change in the period of replacement: February to March. This method is used for the treatment of a noncomparable replacement variety and should not be confused with carrying forward a previous period price for the treatment of temporarily missing prices (described in paragraph 6.65). This method biases the index downward when prices are rising and biases them upward when (true, quality-adjusted) prices are falling. The link-to-show-no-price-change method attributes the price difference between the new and old model in February to quality difference. The new model is of a better quality, valued at being worth an additional 7, from 28 to 35. The (quality-adjusted) price is therefore constant between February and March. The February to April price change is $\frac{28}{28}\times\frac{38}{35}=1.0857$, an 8.57 percent increase in price.

In equation 6.6

$$p_n^{t+1}=p_n^{t^*}\,p_m^{t+1^*}=p_m^t \text{ and } I^{t,t+2}=\frac{p_m^t}{p_m^{t-1}}\times\frac{p_n^{t+2}}{p_n^{t+1}}=\frac{p_n^{t+2}}{p_n^t} \quad (6.10)$$

That is, a (quality-adjusted) price change between February (period t) and April (period $t+2$) is measured as that for the new variety between March ($t+1$) and April ($t+2$).

6.114 The bias is perpetuated through subsequent periods of measurement. For example, the February to June index would still have its price change measured as the product of month-on-month price changes which would include the February to March link that would show no price change.

6.115 The link-to-show-no-price-change method is not recommended. As with carryforward, the method is particularly harmful since it can be readily incorporated into a regular automatic compilation routine and not noticed: the price of the replacement is automatically imputed to form the overlap price and the index compiled.

Explicit Methods of Quality Adjustment

6.116 The methods described previously do not rely on explicit information on the value of the change in quality. This section discusses methods that rely on obtaining an explicit valuation of the quality difference: quantity adjustment; differences in production or option costs; and the hedonic approach.

Quantity Adjustment

6.117 Quantity adjustment is one of the most straightforward explicit quality-adjustment methods. It is applicable when the size of the replacement variety differs from that of the available variety, and any change in quantity is considered a change in quality. In some situations, there is a readily available quantity measure that can be used to compare the varieties. Examples are the number of units in a package (for example, paper plates or vitamin pills) or the size or weight of a container (for example, kilogram of flour or liter of cooking oil). Quantity adjustment to prices can be accomplished by scaling the price of the old or new variety by the ratio of quantities. The index calculation system may do this scaling adjustment automatically, by converting all prices in the category to a price per unit of size, weight, or number. For example, if the weight of a candy bar is 450 grams in the current period and 500 grams in the previous period, but the price remains unchanged, an adjustment is needed so that the index reflects the implicit price increase.

6.118 The specification of a variety is often to a specific size, for example, a one-kilogram packet of flour. If only two-kilogram packets are now sold in a specific outlet, the price collector should choose a representative two-kilogram packet, but mark the new specification as such and, after confirmation by the head office, prices should continue to be collected for the two-kilogram packet. In this example, an adjustment would be needed to ensure that the index reflects only pure price change and not changes resulting from differences in quality (that is, the change in size). This is particularly important where price variances are computed, or use is made of a Dutot price index number formula (that is, an elementary index formula sensitive to the homogeneity of the varieties used).[4]

[4] A Dutot elementary price index number formula is a ratio of arithmetic means of matched prices. More weight is given to price changes with higher prices in the reference period. Thus, if the price of a container in the price reference period doubles, while others remain the same, the implicit weight given to its price change will also double (see Chapter 8).

6.119 When replacing a variety, changes in the size of different varieties sold can be dealt similarly; however, there are some caveats. For example, in the pharmaceutical context, prices of bottles of pills of different sizes differ: a bottle of 100 pills, each having 50 milligrams of a drug, is not the same as a bottle of 50 pills of 100 milligrams, even though both bottles contain 5,000 milligrams of the same drug. If there is a change, for example, to a larger size container, and a *unit* price decrease of 2 percent accompanies this change, then it should not be regarded as a price fall of 2 percent if consumers gain less utility from the larger and more inconvenient containers. In practice, it will be difficult to determine what proportion of the price fall is attributable to quality and what proportion to price. A general recommendation is not to automatically interpret unit price changes arising from packaging size changes as pure price changes, if contrary information is available.

6.120 Consider another example shown in Table 6.7: a branded bag of flour previously available in a 0.5-kilogram bag priced at 1.5 is replaced by a 0.75-kilogram bag priced at 2.25. The main concern here is with rescaling the quantities. The method would use the relative quantities of flour in each bag for the adjustment. The price may have increased by [(2.25/1.5) × 100 = 150] 50 percent but the quality-adjusted price (that is, price adjusted by size) has remained constant [(2.25/0.75) = (1.5/0.5) = 3]; three per kilogram. The approach can be outlined in a more elaborate manner as illustrated by Figure 6.1. The concern here is with the part of the unbroken line between the (price, quantity) coordinates (1.5, 0.5) and (2.25, 0.75), both of which have *unit* prices of 3 (price = 1.5/0.5 and 2.25/0.75). There should be no change in quality-adjusted price. The symbol Δ denotes a change. The slope of the line is β which is Δprice/Dsize = (2.25 − 1.5)/(0.75 − 0.50) = 3 (that is, the change in price arising from a unit [kilogram] change in size). The quality-(size-) adjusted price in period $t-1$ of the old m bag, to make it equivalent to the new bag, n, is

$$\hat{p}_n^{t-1} = p_m^{t-1} + \beta \Delta size = 1.5 + 3(0.75 - 0.5) = 2.25 \quad (6.11)$$

The quality-adjusted price change shows no change, as before:

$$\frac{p_n^t}{\hat{p}_n^{t-1}} = \frac{2.25}{2.25} = 1.00 \quad (6.12)$$

6.121 The approach is outlined in this form so that it can be seen as a special case of the hedonic approach (discussed in paragraphs 6.140–6.176), where the price is related to a number of quality characteristics of which size may be only one.

6.122 Now assume that the 0.5-kilogram bag was not available (missing) and a 0.25-kilogram replacement packet was used, priced at 0.75, as shown by the continuation to the coordinate (0.75, 0.25) of the unbroken line in Figure 6.1 and in Table 6.7; the quality-adjusted prices would again not change. However, if the unit (kilogram) prices were 5, 3, and 3 for the 0.25-, 0.5-, and 0.75-kilogram bags, respectively, as shown in Table 6.7 and in Figure 6.1 (including

Table 6.7 Example of Size, Price, and Unit Price of Bags of Flour

Size (kilograms)	First Price	First Unit Price	Second Price	Second Unit Price
0.25	0.75	3	1.25	5
0.50	1.50	3	1.50	3
0.75	2.25	3	2.25	3

Figure 6.1 Quality Adjustments for Different Sized Varieties

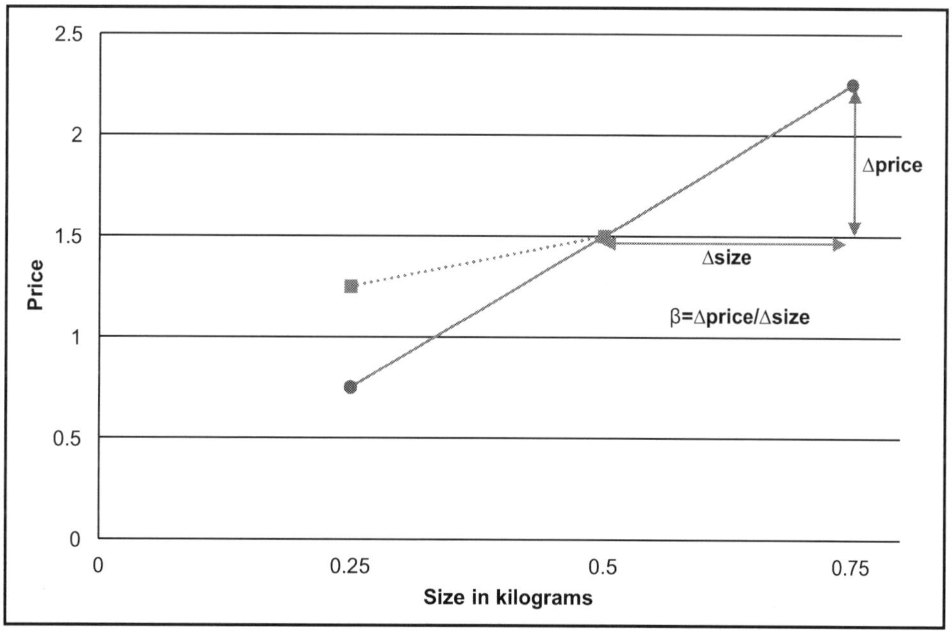

the broken line), then the measure of quality-adjusted price change would depend on whether the 0.5-kilogram bag was replaced by the 0.25-kilogram one (a 67 percent increase) or the 0.75-kilogram one (no change). This result is not satisfactory because the choice of replacement size is arbitrary. The rationale behind the quality-adjustment process is to separate pure price change from changes caused by differences in quality (in this case, quantity changes).

Differences in Feature/Option Costs

6.123 Consider an example of the *price* of an option being used to adjust for quality. Let the prices for a variety in periods $t-1$ and t be 10,000 and 10,500, respectively, but assume the price in period t is for the variety with a new feature, as standard, that previously in period $t-1$ had to be purchased as an "option" for an additional 300. Then between periods $t-1$ and t, the price change including the feature in both periods would be 10,500/10,300 = 1.01942 or 1.942 percent.

6.124 Option costs are useful in situations in which the old and new varieties differ by quantifiable characteristics that can be valued in monetary terms by reference to market prices. The valuation of a quantifiable product feature may be readily available from the comparison of different product prices. This is especially convenient because some goods and services sold on the internet can be identified by their brands and price-determining characteristics.

6.125 Consider the addition of a feature to a product, for example, an automatic icemaker in the door of a refrigerator, and refrigerators for a particular brand may be sold as standard or with a door-installed automatic icemaker. The price collector may always have collected prices on the standard model, but this may no longer be in production, being replaced by a model with an installed automatic icemaker. The cost of the option is thus known from before and a continuing series can be developed by simply adjusting the old price in the price reference period to include the option price. However, this process may have problems. First, the cost of producing an option as standard may be lower than when it was an option, and this saving may be passed on, at least in part, to the consumer. The option cost method would thus understate the price increase. Further, by including an option as standard, the consumer's valuation of it may fall since buyers cannot refuse it, and some consumers may attribute little value to the option. The overall effect would be that the estimate of the option cost, priced for those who choose it, is likely to be higher than the implicit average price consumers would pay for it as standard. Estimates of the effect on price of this discrepancy should in principle be made, though in practice they are difficult to quantify.

6.126 Quality differences are not necessarily positive, for example an airline may charge for a second piece of baggage when previously it did not. Again, there will be an option price available for the additional piece of baggage so that the price of like—two pieces of baggage—is compared with like.

6.127 Option cost adjustments can be seen to be similar to quantity adjustments, except that instead of size being the additional quality feature of the replacement, the added quality can be an individual option/feature. The comparison is $\hat{p}_n^t / p_m^{t-1}$ where $\hat{p}_m^{t-1} = p_m^{t-1} + \beta\Delta z$ for an individual z characteristic where $\Delta z = \left(z_n^t - z_m^{t-1}\right)$. The characteristics may be the size of the memory (RAM) of a computer when a specific model of computer is replaced by a model that is identical except for the amount of RAM it possesses. For example, the webpages of sellers of laptops allow buyers to customize their purchase, an extra four gigabytes of RAM, from eight to twelve gigabytes, for a specific brand and model of a laptop may cost an additional ¥70. Consider that the standard laptop used for CPI measurement has eight gigabytes of memory and costs ¥900 and is not available in the next period. The new standard model in period t has 12 gigabytes but costs the same ¥900, p_n^t. To compare the (constant-quality) price of the new model with the old model in $t-1$, the latter should have its price adjusted to include an extra four gigabytes of RAM. The price of an additional gigabyte of memory for this brand/model in period $t-1$ is 70/4 = 17.5, and its quality-adjusted price in period $t-1$ is $p_m^{t-1} = 900 + 17.5 \times (12-8) = 970$. The period t (unchanged) price of ¥900 is now compared with its comparable period $t-1$ price to yield a constant-quality price change of 900/970 = 0.9278, which is a price fall of 7.22 percent, while the package price is constant.

6.128 The previous description of the calculation is more complex than required: the adjustment is to simply add 70 to the old price, 70 + 900 = 970. However, it serves to demonstrate some limitations of this approach as a special case of the hedonic method, as outlined in the section on hedonic prices.

6.129 This calculation conveniently makes the quality adjustment to the old model's price in period $t-1$ so that the new model's price in future months can be directly compared with the *quality-adjusted* old price for the life of the new specification. However, the required information on the value of the option cost (an extra four gigabytes) may only be available in period t and not be applicable to a period $t-1$ adjustment. NSOs should ideally keep a record of, for example, web customizations of specified varieties along with comparable/noncomparable replacements especially for products with a high degree of technical change and turnover of models and maintain good relations with outlet staff.

6.130 In the previous example, if the relationship between price and RAM is linear, the previous formulation is appropriate. Many webpages give the price of additional RAM as being independent of other features of PCs, and a linear adjustment is appropriate. A linear formulation values the worth of an additional fixed amount of RAM to be the same, irrespective of the amount of RAM the computer possesses or a number of other features.

6.131 The relationship between price and the product features may be nonlinear. Denote the price-determining characteristics as z and assume there are k of them. The change in z is intended to reflect the service flow, but the nonlinearity in the price–z relationship may reflect consumer's decreasing marginal utility to the scale of the provision. In the previous example, the price a customer is willing to pay per gigabyte falls as increasing amounts of gigabytes are purchased. For some features, there will be economies of scale: supplying much more of a feature makes the price fall, possibly substantially; while for others, it may become technically difficult, and more expensive, to compress higher amounts of a feature into the available space. The data should reveal some of this relationship, and caution is needed against applying linear relationships outside of the range in which they are warranted. Further, data should give some insight into the required adjustments for such nonlinear relationships, though this may be better estimated using a regression formulation and nonlinear specification, as considered in the section on hedonic prices.

6.132 The similarity between the quantity adjustment and the option cost approaches is apparent since both relate price to some dimension of quality: the size or the option. The option cost approach can be extended to more than one quality dimension. Both approaches rely on estimates of the change in price resulting from a unit change in the option or size: the β slope estimates. In the case of the quantity adjustment, this was taken from a variety identical to the one being replaced, aside from the fact that it was of a different size. The β slope estimate in this case was perfectly identified from the two pieces of information. It is as if the nature of the experiment controlled for changes in the other quality factors by comparing prices of what is essentially the same thing except for the quantity (size) change.

6.133 This same reasoning applies to option costs. For example, two varieties are identical except for a single feature. Their difference in price allows the value of the feature to be determined. Yet sometimes the value of a feature or option has to be extracted from a much larger data set. This may be because the quality dimension takes a relatively large range of possible numerical values without an immediately obvious consistent valuation. Consider the simple example of only one feature varying for a product, the speed of a computer. It is not a straightforward matter to determine the value of an additional unit of speed. To complicate matters, there may be several quality dimensions to the varieties and not all combinations of these may exist as varieties in the market in one period. Furthermore, the combinations existing in the second period being compared may be quite different from those in the first. Considering these aspects leads to a more general framework, known as the hedonic approach.

Differences in Production Costs

6.134 An alternative approach to quality adjustment is to adjust the price of an old variety by an amount equal to the resource costs of the additional features of the new variety. An important source of such data is the manufacturers. In this approach, the NSO can ask the manufacturer to provide data on direct and indirect production costs for the embodied quality change which would include research and development (R&D) costs, assembly and installation associated with the change, the manufacturer's established markup, the retail margin, and associated indirect taxes. This method is similar to estimating market-equivalent option prices in the absence of market prices. This approach is most practicable in markets where there is a relatively small number of manufacturers, and where updates of models are infrequent and predictable. Additionally, it can only be successfully implemented if there is good communication between manufacturers and the NSO staff. It is particularly suitable when the quality adjustments are also being undertaken to calculate the producer price index and export and import price indices. As an example of the practical use of this approach, an NSO uses production cost estimates to value quality adjustments arising in from model changes in new vehicles. Allowable product changes for the purpose of quality adjustments include reliability, durability, safety, fuel economy, maneuverability, speed, acceleration/deceleration, carrying capacity, and related changes and additional parts required to accommodate the principal change in a component. Only price-determining characteristics are included, and any characteristics or features that do not affect or impact the price are excluded. Also excluded for the CPI, unlike the producer price index, are changes mandated by the government that provide no direct benefit to the purchaser, including modifications to meet air pollution standards. When a new model of a specified automobile is introduced, its changes in quality components are identified, valued, and added to the price of the old model so that the price of the old and new models can be compared on a like-to-like basis.[5]

6.135 A critical feature of this method is its reliance on estimates of the retail margin for the new components. With the option cost approach, a consumer's valuation of the new feature was available. If only production cost data are available, estimates of the retail markup must account for the (average) age of the models under consideration. Markups will decrease as models come to the end of their life cycles. Therefore, retail markups based on models at the start of their life cycle should not be applied to the production costs of models during their life cycle, and particularly at the end. Moreover, estimates of the retail margin of a component may well not be available. A pragmatic practice in one NSO is to use the proportionate retail markup on the vehicle. The proportionate retail markup is calculated based on the price charged by the manufacturer to the dealer for the identical vehicle and the manufacturer's suggested retail delivered price for the equipped vehicle.

Hedonic Approach: Patching

6.136 The hedonic approach is an extension of the two preceding approaches: the feature/option cost and the production cost approach. First, in the hedonic approach, the change in price arising from a unit change in quality (that is, the quantity or option/feature) is estimated from a data set comprising prices and quality characteristic values of a larger number of varieties. Second, the quality characteristic set is extended to cover, in principle, all major characteristics that might determine price, rather than just the quantity or option/feature adjustment.

6.137 The hedonic approach is particularly useful when the market does not reveal the price of the quality characteristics required for the adjustment. Markets reveal prices of varieties, not quality characteristics, and it is useful to consider varieties as tied bundles of characteristics. A sufficiently large data set of varieties with their characteristics and sufficient variability in the mix of characteristics between the varieties allows the hedonic regression to provide estimates of the implicit prices of the characteristics. For example, the

[5] An illustration of the procedure used in the United States is available at: https://www.bls.gov/cpi/quality-adjustment/new-vehicles.pdf.

Figure 6.2 Scatter Diagram of Price against Capacity: Washing Machine Data

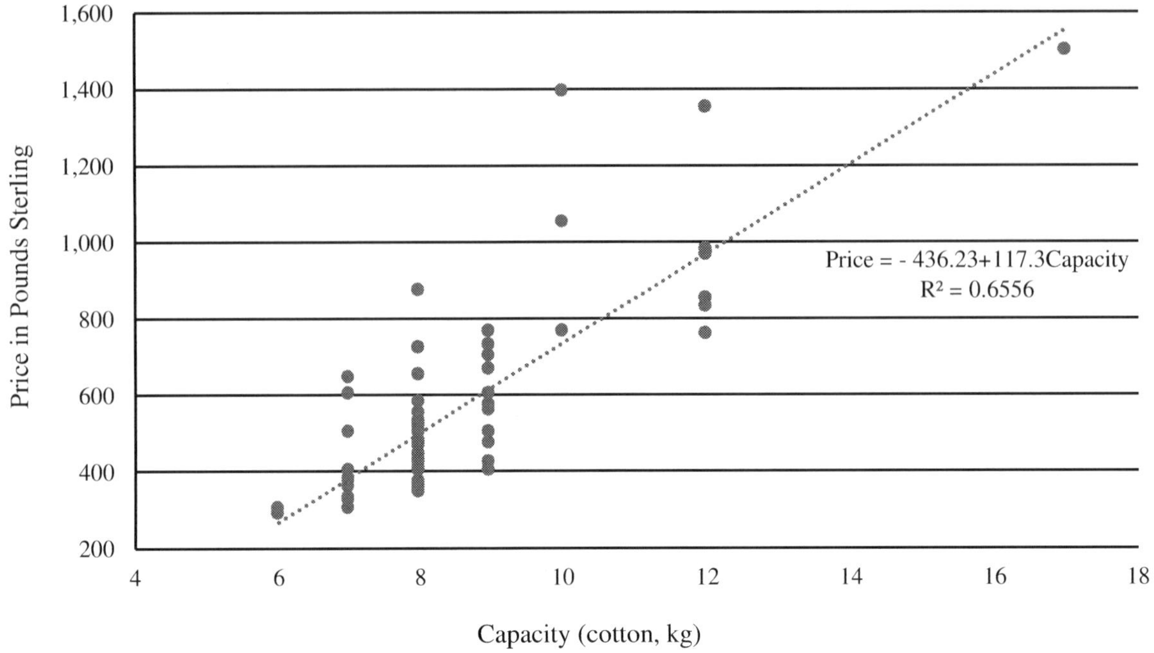

Source: example developed for Manual.

price of (clothes) washing machines will be listed, though a new (replacement) model for a brand may have a (cotton) capacity load size not previously available, say 12 kilograms, instead of the preceding model's 10 kilograms. To make an explicit quality adjustment, the price of the additional two kilograms is required. The regression approach using a data set of many models' prices and characteristics can estimate the price of additional kilogram of capacity from data for models of washing machines on their price, capacity, year (age of model), color, running cost, and so forth.

6.138 Under the MMM, each price collector needs to select a representative variety, record its price and specifications, and reprice the same variety in subsequent periods. The extension required in the hedonic approach is that the prices and price-determining characteristics should be collected for all, or a large sample of models. The method is particularly suitable when there are no immediately apparent comparable replacements and the noncomparable ones vary in their characteristics over more than one variable. A new model of car, household appliance, computer or related hardware and software, or telecommunications equipment, can differ from the old model in many respects, yet there is a single price for each new and old model. This approach is particularly necessary when there is a frequent turnover of models in the market, where new models with quite different values for their characteristics are frequently replacing old ones.

6.139 The requirement that data be collected on the prices and specifications of a large sample, if not all models, is not as demanding as it might appear. Extensive data on prices and characteristics of models of consumer goods and services are generally readily available on websites (for example, many comparing prices and salient characteristics), can be copied with relative ease, and automated using web scraping. Such detailed information is also available as scanner data (see Chapter 10).

6.140. Figure 6.2 is a scatter diagram relating the price (in pounds sterling, £) to the (cotton) capacity (kilogram) of models of washing machines sold in one country (the data are from a well-known consumer magazine). It is apparent that washing machines with larger capacities have higher prices—a positive relationship. It is also apparent from Figure 6.2 that there are several models of washing machine with the same capacity but quite different prices, resulting from the fact that other features differ. For example, 12-kilogram capacity machine prices range from £754 to £1,349.

6.141 To estimate the value given to additional units of capacity, an estimate of the slope of the line that best fits the data is required. The equation of a straight line is $Price = \beta_0 + \beta_1 z_1$.

6.142 The slope $\hat{\beta}_1$ is a measure of the change in *Price* that arises from a one-unit change in the characteristic, z_1, *Capacity*. The ^ (hat) above denotes that it is estimated from the data. The estimated slope is from the equation of a line that best fits the data (that is, that best represents the underlying pattern of the relationship). In Figure 6.2, the equation of the line that best fits the data was derived using an ordinary least squares (OLS) regression. The intercept and slope of the line that best fits the data are estimated as ones that *minimize the sum of the squared differences* between the individual prices and their counterpart prices predicted by the line: the least squares criterion. Tools for regression analysis are available on standard statistical and econometric software, as

Table 6.8 Estimated (Linear) Equation of Price against Capacity: Washing Machine Data

	Coefficients	Standard Error	*t* Stat	*P*-Value
Intercept	−436.229	86.310	−5.054	3.09E−06
Capacity	117.298	9.949	11.789	1.43937E−18

Table 6.9 Illustrative Hedonic Regression Estimates for Washing Machines

	Linear			Log-Linear		
	Coefficient	Std. Error	***p-Value***	Coefficient	Std. Error	***p-Value***
(Intercept)	−206.939	112.3	0.06986+	5.217	0.17	< 2E−16***
Age	−1.579	2.1	0.44971	−0.006	0.00	0.054218+
Capacity	81.024	13.2	5.32E−08***	0.108	0.02	4.86E−07***
Warranty	−138.651	48.7	0.00592**	−0.265	0.07	0.000466***
Steel	144.036	74.0	0.05608+	0.266	0.11	0.017575*
Energy Cost	10.103	3.4	0.00430**	0.019	0.01	0.000353***
LG	−115.816	43.9	0.01044*	−0.220	0.06	0.001167**
Steam	191.196	92.3	0.04233*	0.257	0.14	0.063056+
Hyg_AllergyP	63.627	40.2	0.11842	0.153	0.06	0.012198*
LED Display	49.409	52.9	0.35391	0.166	0.08	0.036833*
$\bar{R}^2$	0.701			0.721		
F-Statistic	20.25			22.22		
***P*-Value**	1.06E−15			2.20E−16		

***,**,*, and + denote statistically significant at 0.1, 1, 5, and 10 percent levels, respectively.

well as spreadsheets.[6] The estimated (linear) equation in this instance is presented in Table 6.8.

$$\text{Price} = -436.229 + 117.298 \quad \text{Capacity} \;\; \bar{R}^2 = 0.65 \quad (6.13)$$

6.143 Formula 6.13 is the estimated regression equation of *Price* on *Capacity*; although there are many other price-determining variables, this regression equation only includes *Capacity*, for illustration. In Table 6.9, the regression model is expanded to include other variables.

6.144 The coefficient on *Capacity* is the estimated slope of the line: the change in price (£117.30) resulting from a one-kilogram change in *Capacity*. This can be used to estimate quality-adjusted price changes for washing machines of different capacities. The value of $\bar{R}^2$ (that is, the adjusted coefficient of determination) is 0.65; this indicates that 65 percent of price variation is explained by variation in *Capacity*. A *t*-statistic to test the null hypothesis of the coefficient being zero was found to be 11.789: recourse to standard tables on *t*-statistics found the null hypothesis was rejected with a *p*-value of 1.43937E−18. The fact that the estimated coefficient differs from zero cannot be attributed to sampling errors at this level of significance. There is a very low probability that the test has wrongly rejected the null hypothesis.

6.145 Hedonic regressions should generally be conducted using a semilogarithmic formulation. The focus is thus on the semilogarithmic form. The estimated (semilogarithmic) regression equation in this instance is

$$\log(\text{Price}) = 4.776 + 0.174 \quad \text{Capacity} \;\; \bar{R}^2 = 0.61 \quad (6.14)$$

[6]The illustrative empirical work in this section was undertaken using R, though it would be equally applicable with any such standard statistical software including EViews, SAS, and STATA.

6.146 The coefficient of 0.174 has a useful direct interpretation: when multiplied by 100, it is the percentage change in price arising from a one unit (kilogram) change in capacity. There is an estimated 17.4 percent change in price for each additional kilogram of capacity.

6.147 The range of prices for a given capacity was noted to be substantial which suggests that other quality characteristics may be involved. Table 6.9 provides the results of a regression equation that relates price to a number of quality characteristics as listed in the Column A.[7] While the results are given for both linear and semilogarithmic regression specifications, the focus here is on the latter functional form.

6.148 A semilogarithmic hedonic multiple regression model is given by

$$\ln p = \beta_0 + z_1\beta_1 + z_2\beta_2 + z_3\beta_3 + \ldots . z_n\beta_n + \varepsilon \quad (6.15)$$

where ε is an error term assumed to have the usual properties to satisfy OLS assumptions (see paragraph 6.171). For this semilogarithmic form, logarithms are taken only of the left-hand side variable (that is, *Price*). Each of the z characteristics enters the regression without having logarithms taken. This has the advantage of allowing dummy variables for having or not having a feature included on the right-hand side.

[7]These include Age (months since model was launched); Capacity (for cottons, kilogram); Warranty (if five years, benchmark: two years); Steel (stainless steel outer); (Annual) Energy Cost, in £; LG (manufactured, benchmarked on Samsung); Steam (wash/refresh); Hygiene/Allergy program; LED display (benchmarked on LCD); and price for 74 models as advertised on November 2017 in *Which?* for three up-market brands: Brand A, Brand B, and Brand C. A much larger general regression model with more variables was first estimated but reduced to this smaller specific model using standard econometric principles and practice. The White (studentized) Breusch–Pagan test for homoscedastic residuals was not rejected at conventional significance levels with a *p*-value of 0.2197.

Such dummy variables assume the value of one if the variety has the feature and zero otherwise. The taking of logarithms of the first equation in 6.15 allows it to be transformed in the second equation to a linear form, and a conventional OLS estimator can then be used to yield estimates of the logarithms of the coefficients. These are given as the coefficients for the semilogarithmic model in Table 6.9. The estimated coefficients in Table 6.9 are based on a multiple regression model: for example, for *Capacity*, the estimated coefficient of 0.108 is of the effect of a unit change in capacity on price, *having controlled for the effect of other variables in the equation.* The scatter diagram in Figure 6.2 clearly shows the inadequacy of relying on a single price-determining variable and this approach can be justified because it addresses this issue. The preceding estimated coefficient of 0.174 was based on only one variable and is different from this improved result.

6.149 When dummy variables are used, the coefficients, when multiplied by 100, are estimates of the percentage change in price, given by $\left(e^{\beta_1}-1\right)\times 100$. For example, from Table 6.9, Brand A models have a $\left(e^{-0.219743}-1\right)\times 100=19.73$ percent lower price than their benchmarked Brand B counterpart, having controlled for other differences in their price-determining characteristics as specified in the regression equation.[8]

6.150 The value $\bar{R}^2=0.721$ is the proportion of variation in (the logarithm of) price explained by the estimated equation.[9] A high value of $\bar{R}^2$ can be misleading for the purpose of quality adjustment, although such values indicate that the explanatory variables account for much of the price variation over a relatively large number of varieties in the period concerned. This, of course, is not the same as implying a high degree of prediction for an adjustment to a replacement variety of a single brand in a subsequent time period. Predicted values depend for their accuracy not just on the fit of the equation, but also on how far the characteristics of the variety whose price is to be predicted are from the means of the sample. The more unusual the variety, the higher the prediction probability interval. Second, the value $\bar{R}^2$ indicates the proportion of variation in prices explained by the estimated equation. It may be that 0.90 is explained while 0.10 is not explained. If the dispersion in prices is very large, this still leaves a large absolute margin of prices unexplained. A high $\bar{R}^2$ is a necessary, though not sufficient, condition for the use of hedonic adjustments.

The Interpretation of Estimated Hedonic Coefficients

6.151 Concerning the interpretation of the coefficients from hedonic regressions, there used to be a mistaken perception that these represented estimates of user value as opposed to resource cost. The former is the relevant concept in constructing a CPI, while for producer price index compilation it is the latter. Yet hedonic coefficients may reflect both user value and resource cost, both supply and demand influences. There is an identification problem, as referred in econometrics; the observed data do not permit the estimation of the underlying demand and supply parameters. What is being estimated is the actual point of intersection of the demand curves of different consumers with varying tastes and the supply curves of different producers with possible varying technologies of production.

6.152 In many cases, the implicit quality adjustment to prices arising from the use of the overlap method may be inappropriate because the implicit assumptions are unlikely to be valid (as described in paragraphs 6.104–6.112). In such instances, the practical needs of reliable economic statistics require explicit quality adjustments. However, the use of the hedonic approach may only be justified when the weight, churn, and extent of the quality adjustment is substantial, due to the cost of implementing the method.

6.153 The proper use of hedonic regressions requires an examination of the coefficients of the estimated equations to ensure their plausibility. It might be argued that the very multitude of distributions of tastes and technologies, along with the interplay of supply and demand, that determine the estimated coefficients, make it unlikely that "reasonable" estimates will arise from such regressions. For example, a firm may cut a profit margin pertaining to a characteristic for reasons related to long-term strategic plans; this may yield a coefficient on a desirable characteristic that may even be negative. This situation does not invalidate the usefulness of examining hedonic coefficients as part of a strategy for evaluating estimated hedonic equations. First, there has been extensive empirical work in this field and the results for individual coefficients are, for the most part, quite reasonable. Over time, individual coefficients can show quite sensible patterns. Unreasonable coefficients on estimated equations are the exception and should be treated with some caution. Second, the CPI compiler should rely more on an estimated equation whose coefficients make sense, and which makes good predictions, than on one which may also predict well but whose coefficients do not make sense. Third, if a coefficient for a characteristic does not make sense, it may be due to multicollinearity, a data problem, and should be examined using, for example, variance inflation factors, to see if this is the case.

The Implementation of a Hedonic Quality Adjustment

6.154 The implementation of hedonic methods to estimate quality adjustments for matched noncomparable replacements can take two forms. The first form is referred to as "patching": undertaking a quality adjustment to the price of the old model to make it comparable with the new model. For many varieties, this can be seen as a one-off process for individual varieties within the lifetime of updating a sample. The second form is the more comprehensive process for rapidly changing high-technology products with substantial changes in quality within relatively short periods.

6.155 "Patching" is the term used in this Manual for introducing noncomparable replacements (that is, replacements of a different quality), using hedonic regression estimates.

[8] There is some bias in these coefficients; and in the (semi)logarithmic equation, half the variance of each coefficient should be added to the coefficient before using it. For the Brand A coefficient, the standard error from Table 6.9 is 0.064687; its variance is $(0.064687)^2=0.00418$: the adjustment is to add 0.00418/2 to −0.219743, giving −0.21765; a lower price of $-\left(e^{-0.21765}-1\right)\times 100=19.56$ percent; see Triplett (2006) for further details.

[9] More formally, where p_i^t is the price of washing machine i in period t, $\bar{R}^2$ is 1 minus the ratio of the variance of the residuals, $\sum_{i=1}^{N}\left(p_i^t-\hat{p}_i^t\right)^2/N$, of the equation to the variance of prices, $\sum_{i=1}^{N}\left(p_i^t-\hat{p}_i^t\right)^2/N$. The bar on the term R^2 denotes that an appropriate adjustment for degrees of freedom is made to this expression, which is necessary when comparing equations with different numbers of explanatory variables.

Table 6.10A Hedonic Regression Imputation of New Variety's Price

Variety/ Period	t	$t+1$	$t+2$	$t+3$	$t+4$
l	p_l^t	p_l^{t+1}	p_l^{t+2}	p_l^{t+3}	p_l^{t+4}
m	p_m^t	p_m^{t+1}	p_m^{t+2}		
n			$\breve{p}_n^{t+2}$	p_n^{t+3}	p_n^{t+4}

Consider varieties *l, m,* and *n* in Table 6.10A where variety *l* is available in all periods, the "old" variety *m* is only available in periods t, $t+1$, and $t+2$, and the replacement variety *n* is only available in period $t+3$ and subsequently. The varieties are defined by their *z* quality characteristics; for example, for variety *m*, in period *t* these are z_m^t and the price of variety *m* is p_m^t. The example assumes that there is no problem with comparing the prices of matched variety *l* with characteristics Z_l, as they have the same quality characteristics, but there is a problem when comparing varieties *m* and *n*. Variety *m*'s replacement *n* is noncomparable, so p_m^{t+2} cannot be directly compared with p_m^{t+3}. An imputed price is required in order to have prices for both the old and new varieties in the same period. This could be achieved by imputing the price of the new variety *n* in period $t+2$ to form an overlap in this period with the actual price of the old variety *m*, in that period, as illustrated in Table 6.5C. This is a *backward* imputation. In this case, as illustrated in Table 6.10A, the overlap period is period $t+2$. However, variety *n* does not have a recorded price in period $t+2$, and it may not have been sold then. The backward hedonic *imputation* approach would predict the price of variety *n* in period $t+2$ using a hedonic regression estimated in period $t+2$ and the characteristics of the new variety *n,* taken from period $t+3$ (that is, the predicted price of variety *n* in period $t+2$, $\hat{p}_n^{t+2}$ —the hat over the price, $\hat{P}$, denotes a predicted value from the regression). The predicted prices are for the characteristics of the replacement variety *n*. This is an estimate of how much the price for the characteristics of the new replacement variety would have been if it had been sold in period $t+2$.

6.156 Where data are not available to support the monthly estimation of regression coefficients, as described in the previous paragraph, an alternative approach would be the hedonic quality-adjustment method.[10]

6.157 For short-term comparisons, an overlap method is used with a price relative for $t+2$ compared with $t+1$ given by p_m^{t+2} / p_m^{t+1}, and for $t+3$ compared with $t+2$ given by $p_n^{t+3} / \breve{p}_n^{t+2}$, and subsequently, without the need for an imputation, by p_n^{t+4} / p_n^{t+3}.

6.158 The simple example outlined before using data on washing machines is used here to illustrate the methodology. Assume that the linear regression equation 6.13 was estimated using period $t+2$ data, the old model *m* had a capacity of 10 kilogram, and the new model *n* in period $t+3$ had a capacity of 12 kilograms. In this case, model *n*'s price in period $t+2$ would be the predicted price, $\breve{p} = 117.3 \times 12 - 436.23 = 971.37$. The ratio of the actual price of model *m* in period $t+2$, for example, £750, to the predicted price in period $t+2$, is the quality adjustment shown for the overlap method in equation 6.6, though for period $t+2$ in this example, $\frac{p_m^{t+2}}{p_n^{t+2^*}}$, that is, $\frac{750}{971.37} = 0.7721$. The models are not comparable. The new model in period $t+2$ is more expensive even when its superior quality, its capacity, has been considered.

6.159 Given the availability of an estimate of the worth of an extra unit of capacity, an alternative approach would be to simply add 2 × 117.3 to the price of *m* in period $t+2$, rather than use predicted prices. Such use of individual coefficients is not recommended. In practice, a hedonic regression will include several explanatory price-determining variables that may be linearly related and thus not strictly independent. For example, larger (higher-capacity) washing machines may also have higher spin speeds or be more likely to have a steam feature. The estimated coefficient of each such multicollinear variable would be imprecise, though the predicted price of a regression equation that includes them would be unbiased.

6.160 With the option cost example, the quality adjustment might be for a single characteristic and an explicit valuation of the price of further units of this characteristic (for example, a gigabyte of storage for a computer, available from another source). Hedonic regressions are used where the market does not reveal the implicit shadow prices of individual characteristics; these shadow prices have to be estimated from price data for many varieties with differing bundled sets of characteristics.

6.161 The hedonic method makes use of short-term month-on-month comparisons. Predicting the price of variety *n* in period $t+2$, if it was sold then, is only for this one-off period as the new variety replaces the old, with a quality adjustment. Variety *n*'s characteristics are held constant for month-on-month comparisons from $t+2$ onward, and variety *m*'s characteristics are held constant for month-on-month comparisons from period *t* up to, and including, period $t+2$.

6.162 Alternatively, a forward imputation might have been used, a procedure similar to that adopted in Table 6.5C. The price of variety *m* might be predicted from a hedonic regression run on period $t+3$ data, $\hat{p}_m^{t+3}$. As with the preceding methodology, a predicted price is only required for the overlap period, after which the replacement variety forms the continuing index. It is not obvious which of the two approaches, predicting prices for *m* or *n*, is preferred. Resources permitting, a geometric mean of the two would be defensible, as would a clear rule from the outset as to the method applied based on some retrospective research on the outcome of using either method for particular product groups.

6.163 Table 6.5C shows that the backward and forward imputation methods yield the same result when the imputation is based, for both methods, on the price movements of varieties available in all periods. However, in this case, the backward prediction is based on a hedonic regression run in period $t+2$ and the forward imputation on a hedonic regression run in period $t+3$. The practical advantage of

[10] Jack Triplett. 2006. *Handbook on Hedonic Indexes and Quality Adjustment in Price Indexes.* Paris: OECD. https://www.oecd-ilibrary.org/science-and-technology/handbook-on-hedonic-indexes-and-quality-adjustments-in-price-indexes_9789264028159-en.

running a hedonic regression in a prior period argues for a *backward* imputation, as in Table 6.10A, as the most feasible procedure.

6.164 A refinement to these approaches is to use predicted values, for varieties *m* and *n,* in the overlap period, p_m^{t+3} / p_m^{t+2}. For this purpose, consider a misspecification problem in the hedonic equation, for example, there may be an interaction effect between a brand dummy and a characteristic. Having a characteristic for a particular brand may be priced higher than all other brands, say a 5 percent premium. The use of $\hat{p}_m^{t+3} / \hat{p}_m^{t+2}$ would be misleading since the actual price in the denominator would incorporate the premium, while the one predicted from the hedonic regression would not. It is stressed that, in adopting this approach, a recorded actual price is being replaced by an imputation. This is not desirable, but neither is the omitted variable (interaction term) bias. The dual imputation approach is preferred whenever there are concerns about the suitability of the regression equation's specification to fully model prices, as would generally be the case.

6.165 A further approach would be to not use a replacement variety. Variety *m*'s characteristics would be held constant in the comparison from period $t + 2$ onward. However, this would require a hedonic regression being run for each subsequent period, $\hat{p}_m^{t+3}$, $\hat{p}_m^{t+4}$. It would also lead to a continuing degradation of the sample as an obsolete old variety *m* would have its characteristics repeatedly priced into the future, rather than being replaced by a new variety. For this reason, this method is not recommended.

6.166 In the previous examples, short-term price comparisons are used and are preferable to long-term ones. A long-term equivalent of Table 6.10A is shown in Table 6.10C. A predicted price for any replacement variety *n* in its month of introduction is estimated for the reference period *t* using a hedonic regression based on that period's data. The regression is estimated using period *t* prices and characteristics, but the predicted prices are for the characteristics of the replacement variety *n* in $t + 3$ and subsequently. It is an estimate of what the characteristics of the new replacement variety would have been priced at had it been sold in period *t*.

6.167 The long-term method has the significant advantage of only requiring a hedonic regression to be estimated in the single reference period. For periods $t + 3$ and $t + 4$, the price relatives are $p_n^{t+3} / \hat{p}_n^t$ and $p_n^{t+4} / \hat{p}_n^t$, respectively. However, as time passes, such comparisons become less meaningful. For example, comparing the actual price this month of a model of a laptop with one predicted 18 months ago using the hedonic approach, would estimate market valuations of each characteristic which is then applied to the characteristic set of a laptop sold now. Indeed, the need for a double imputation becomes more important as time passes by, yet a double imputation requires monthly estimation of hedonic regressions that hinder the advantage of this approach. If hedonic regressions are to be used on this long-term basis, it is important that the regressions are reestimated regularly at a rate that will depend on the rate of the technological innovations, and changes in consumer preference specific to that product. For example, it may be that consumer's valuations of characteristics of washing machines, including spin speed, front-loaders, capacity, or number and types of wash programs, are fairly constant over time, even if the technology is changing rapidly. Frequent, say monthly, updating of estimated hedonic regression equations is not required. Prior empirical studies on the stability over time in hedonic characteristics would be valuable in this respect. As a general principle, short-term hedonic imputations are preferred to long-term ones.

Limitations of the Hedonic Approach

6.168 The limitations and challenges of implementing the hedonic approach should be considered by the NSO:

(1) First, the hedonic approach requires statistical expertise for the estimation and maintenance of the hedonic regression equations. The availability of user-friendly statistical/econometric software with regression tools makes this less problematic. Yet staff must possess sufficient expertise and understanding of statistical regression methodology applied to hedonic regression equations, and the interpretation of the results and diagnostic statistics of regression models.
   - Statistical and econometric software carry a range of diagnostic tests to help judge if the final formulation of the model is satisfactory. These include $\bar{R}^2$ as a measure of the overall explanatory power of the equation, and F-test and t-test statistics that test whether the differences between the estimated coefficients of the explanatory (price-determining) variables are jointly and individually different from zero at specified levels of statistical significance. These statistics make use of the errors from the estimated regression equation.
   - The regression equation can be used to predict prices for each variety by inserting the values of the characteristics of the varieties against the estimated coefficients of the explanatory variables. The differences between the actual prices and these predicted results are the residuals. Statistical/econometric software calculate predicted values and residuals as a routine. A hedonic regression equation estimated using OLS requires assumptions on the nature of the distribution

Table 6.10B Hedonic Regression Imputation of Old Variety's Price

Variety/ Period	t	$t+1$	$t+2$	$t+3$	$t+4$
l	p_l^t	p_l^{t+1}	p_l^{t+2}	p_l^{t+3}	p_l^{t+4}
m	p_m^t	p_m^{t+1}	p_m^{t+2}	$\breve{p}_m^{t+3}$	
n				p_n^{t+3}	p_m^{t+4}

Table 6.10C Hedonic Regression Imputation of New Variety's Price

Variety/ Period	t	$t+1$	$t+2$	$t+3$	$t+4$
l	p_l^t	p_l^{t+1}	p_l^{t+2}	p_l^{t+3}	p_l^{t+4}
m	p_m^t	p_m^{t+1}	p_m^{t+2}		
n	$\breve{p}_n^t$			p_n^{t+3}	p_n^{t+4}

of the residual errors. These include: (1) the error term has a constant variance—if this assumption is violated, the errors are heteroscedastic; consequently, standard tests of statistical significance can be biased and unreliable; (2) that explanatory variable(s) are not correlated with the error term, they are not endogenous—this is particularly important when explanatory price-determining characteristics are omitted from the hedonic regression: if an omitted variable is correlated with an included one, the estimated coefficient on the included one is biased; and (3) the price-determining explanatory independent variables are not truly independent, but correlated with each other—multicollinearity; the coefficient estimates and their tests become sensitive to change in the model and data. While the estimated coefficients are imprecise, the predicted prices in a hedonic regression would be unbiased.

- A full account of all OLS assumptions, consequences, means of detection of violation, and treatment, that may involve use of an alternative to OLS estimators, can be found in any introductory econometrics/statistical text. Modern software provides the appropriate tests for, and means of overcoming, violations of these assumptions and thus, validation of the hedonic model used. It is recommended that the NSO develops and publishes detailed metadata on the hedonic regression model used and its supporting diagnostic statistics to demonstrate the validity of the model and satisfy the need for transparency.

(2) Second, the estimated coefficients require regular updating. Consider that the predicted price is for the new model in a reference period, as presented in Table 6.10C. Although it might seem that there is no need to update the estimated coefficients each period, the valuation of characteristics in the price reference period may be quite out of line with their valuation in the new period. For example, quite dramatic falls in the price of storage and processing speed of computers, among other attributes, make the valuation of additional GBs of a new model, introduced a few years after the hedonic regression was estimated, a less meaningful exercise. Continuing to use the coefficients from some far-off period to adjust prices in the current period is similar to using out-of-date reference period weights. The comparison may be well defined but have little meaning. There is a need to update the hedonic regression estimates if they are considered out of date, because of changing tastes or technology, and to splice the new estimated comparisons onto the old. The regular updating of hedonic estimates when using imputations or adjustments is thus recommended, especially when there is evidence of instability in the parameter estimates of the hedonic regression over time.

(3) Third, the sample of prices and characteristics used for the hedonic adjustments should be suitable for the purpose. If they are taken from a particular outlet or outlet type, trade group, or webpage, and then used to adjust noncomparable prices for varieties sold in quite different outlets, there must at least be an intuition that the marginal price differences for characteristics are similar between the outlets. A similar principle applies for the brands of varieties used in the sample for the hedonic regression. It should be borne in mind that high $\bar{R}^2$ statistics do not alone ensure reliable results. Such high values arise from regressions in periods prior to their application and indicate the proportion of variation in prices across many varieties and brands. They are not a measure of the prediction error for a particular variety, sold in a specific outlet, of a given brand in a subsequent period, though they can be an important part of this.

(4) Fourth, the functional form and choice of variables to include in the model should be considered. Simple functional forms generally work well, though there is a class of more complex flexible-functional forms. These include linear, semilogarithmic (logarithm of the left-hand side), and double-logarithmic (logarithms of both sides) forms. Semilogarithmic models are often employed since many of the price-determining explanatory variables are binary, 1 or 0, depending on whether or not a model has a particular feature (dummy variables). The specification of a model should include all price-determining characteristics. Typically, a study would start with a large number of explanatory variables and a general econometric model of the relationship, while the final model would be more specific, having dropped a number of variables. The dropping of variables would depend on the result of experimenting with different formulations, and analyzing their effects on diagnostic test statistics, including the overall fit of the model and the accordance of signs and magnitudes of coefficients with prior expectations.

(5) Fifth, the resources requirements for hedonic regression should be considered. Hedonic regressions require data on prices and price-determining characteristics for varieties (models) sold. Extensive data sets may be readily available on the internet or from scanner data, containing all pertinent price-determining characteristics, either from the websites of individual retailers or specialist websites comparing prices and features of laptops, household appliances, and many other such goods and services. For example, the data used for the previous example of (patched) hedonic explicit quality adjustments for washing machines was taken from a website and was copied and pasted relatively quickly. Web scraping software can reduce even this workload substantially.

(6) Finally, while data and software may not be problematic, NSO staff resources will be required in devising the specification, estimation, and validation of the estimated hedonic model for each product. Such hedonic models should be estimated regularly prior to their use in the CPI and the results made available as part of the detailed metadata for the purpose of transparency and feedback. In this regard, the resource requirements can be substantial compared with an implicit overlap method. At least at first, hedonic methods should be applied only to products with a relatively high weight and profile for which the implicit assumptions of alternative methods are found to be invalid and badly distort the results, especially if they provide a reputational risk to the NSO.

6.169 Hedonic methods may also improve quality-adjustment procedures in the CPI by indicating which product attributes do *not* appear to have material impacts on the prices. That is, if a replacement variety differs from the old variety only in characteristics that have been rejected as price-determining variables in a hedonic study, this would support a decision to treat the varieties as comparable. Care has to be exercised in such analysis because a feature of multicollinearity in regression estimates is an imprecision of the estimated parameter estimates. This may give rise to statistical tests that do not reject null hypotheses that are false. However, econometric/statistical software provides the tools to explore the nature and extent of multicollinearity; these include variance inflation factors. The results from variance inflation factors provide valuable information on the nature and extent to which different explanatory variables (characteristics) are interrelated and this in turn can help in the selection of replacement varieties. The results from hedonic regressions thus have a role to play in identifying price-determining characteristics and may be useful in the design of quality checklists in price collection.

Choice between Quality-Adjustment Methods

6.170 The choice of the method to be used for quality adjustments is not straightforward. The CPI compiler must consider the technology and market for each product and devise appropriate methods, considering that the methods selected for one product area might not be independent of those selected for other areas. Expertise built up using one method may encourage its use elsewhere, and intensive use of resources for one product may lead to less resource-intensive methods for others. The methods adopted for individual product groups may vary between countries as access to data, relationships with the outlet managers, resources, expertise and features of the production, and market for the product vary. Guidelines on choice of method arise directly from the features of the methods outlined in this chapter. A good understanding of the methods, and their implicit and explicit assumptions, is essential to the choice of an appropriate method.

6.171 Figure 6.3 provides a guide to the decision-making process. Assume that the MMM is being used. If the variety is matched for repricing in a subsequent period, there is no change in the specifications and no quality adjustment is required. This is the simplest procedure. However, there is a caveat: if the variety belongs to a product group where model replacement is rapid, and replacements are noncomparable, the matched sample may become unrepresentative of the universe of transactions. Continued long-term matching would deplete the sample. This is a matter for the frequent rebasing and maintenance of the sample (see Chapter 7).

6.172 Consider a variety found to be *temporarily missing*. If it was a seasonal product, its treatment would follow the principles and practices outlined in Chapter 11. If it was temporarily missing but not a seasonal product, a price imputation is required, and if subsequently determined to be permanently missing (for example, either from information from outlet staff or use of a three-month rule) a replacement needs to be found. *Overall or targeted price imputations* for temporarily missing prices may be used; the carryforward method is not recommended except for controlled or regulated prices.

Figure 6.3 Guide to Treatment of Missing Prices

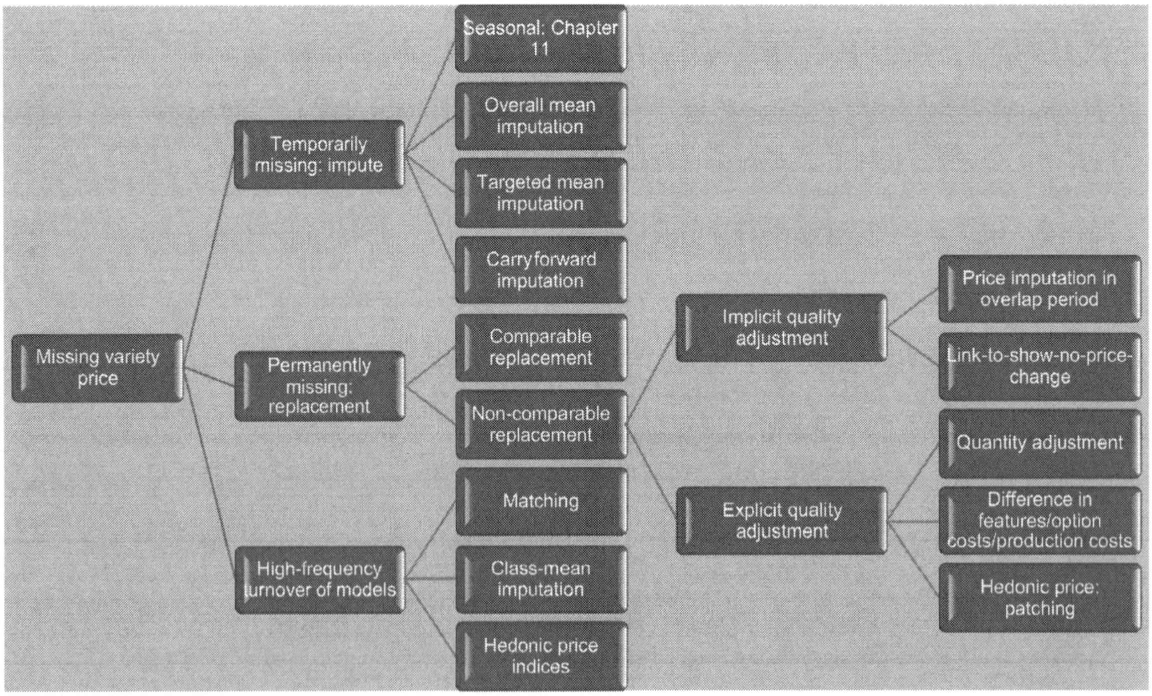

6.173 For *permanently missing* varieties, the selection of a comparable variety is preferred, as is the use of its price as a *comparable replacement* price which is then directly compared with the preceding variety price. This direct price comparison would require that none of the price difference between the comparable replacement and the previous variety is attributable to quality, and confidence that all price-determining factors are included in the specification. In practice, varieties may be considered comparable if there are limited price-determining differences, as might be the case with styling, color, even some more substantial technical changes, including performance and reliability, that may not be immediately apparent to the consumer. A decision on the comparability of a replacement must be made by CPI staff with appropriate information on product differences supplied by the price collector. A comparable replacement variety should also be representative and account for a reasonable proportion of sales. Caution is required when replacing near obsolete varieties with unusual pricing at the end of their life cycles with similar ones that account for relatively low sales, or with ones that have quite substantial sales but are at different points in their cycle. Strategies for ameliorating such effects are discussed in paragraphs 6.182–6.222 and in Chapter 7, including early substitutions before pricing strategies become dissimilar. With comparable replacements, the price of the old variety is directly compared with the price of the comparable replacement in the next period.

6.174 Figure 6.3 considers the case where only *noncomparable replacements* are available. If explicit estimates of the price dimension of the quality differences are unavailable, and no replacement varieties are deemed comparable, *implicit estimates* might be used. One such method is the continued use of *imputations* as they are applied to temporarily missing varieties. Such use is *not recommended* as a default procedure.

6.175 The use of imputations has advantages resource-wise, as it is relatively easy to employ and requires no judgment (unless it is a targeted mean imputation) and is therefore objective. Targeted mean imputation is preferred to overall mean imputation as long as the sample size upon which the target is based is adequate. The bias from using imputations for permanently missing variety prices is directly related to the proportion of missing varieties and the difference between quality-adjusted prices of available matched varieties and the quality-adjusted prices of unavailable ones. The nature and extent of the bias depends on whether short-term or long-term imputations are being used (the former being preferred) and on market conditions. Imputation, in practical terms, produces the same result as deletion of the variety for an elementary aggregate. The inclusion of imputed prices may give the illusion of larger sample sizes. Imputation should by no means be the overall catch-all strategy, and NSOs are strongly advised against its use as a default device that may lead to serious sample degradation.

6.176 Imputations can be used to extend the period of search for a replacement, though the absence of the old variety and the unavailability of a replacement should indicate to the CPI compiler that the weight for that variety might be better attributed to a quite different variety. Such changes naturally take place on updating an index, as described in Chapter 7.

6.177 If the old and replacement varieties are available simultaneously, and if the quality difference cannot be quantified, an implicit approach can be used whereby the price difference between the old and replacement varieties in a period in which they both exist is assumed to be attributable to quality. This *overlap method*, in replacing the old variety by a new one, takes the ratio of prices in a period to be a measure of their quality difference. It is implicitly used when new samples of varieties are taken. The assumption of relative prices equating quality differences at the time of the splice is unlikely to hold if the old and replacement varieties are at different stages in their life cycles and different pricing strategies are used at these stages. For example, there may be deep discounting of the old variety to clear inventories, and price skimming of market segments that will purchase new varieties at relatively high prices. As with comparable replacements, early substitutions are advised so that the overlap is at a time when varieties are at similar stages in their life cycles. It may well be the case, however, that overlap prices are unavailable. In such cases, a range of imputation approaches is available to estimate an overlap price.

6.178 The quality differences between the replacement and missing variety may be explicitly quantified. *Explicit estimates* of quality differences are generally considered to be more reliable, although they are also more resource-intensive, at least initially. Once an appropriate methodology has been developed, it can often be easily replicated. General guidelines are more difficult to provide as the choice depends on the factors already discussed in this chapter, which are likely to make the estimates more reliable in each situation. Central to all of this is the quality of the data upon which the estimates are based. Estimates based on objective data are preferred. A relatively straightforward quality adjustment is when the quantity differs. The standardization of quantity units sold across outlets, for example, to price per kilogram, is relatively straightforward, though a change in the quantity of a variety included in the price—a quantity adjustment—may be more complicated than expected.

6.179 The replacement variety may differ from the old one for *having a different characteristic*. Often it is the *price collector* who is best placed to provide an estimate of the price difference in quality of a noncomparable replacement. For example, if a specified brand of a bottle of tomato ketchup used for pricing is missing in the current period, and a noncomparable replacement of the same brand is available, though the bottle has been restyled to now stand on its head, and the label has been reversed. The price collector might note that other brands have both sizes sold with a 25 percent price margin for the new one. The price collector in selecting a noncomparable replacement might also provide the basis for the head office staff to make an explicit quality adjustment. The head office staff might also make *use of the internet* to identify the percentage markup for a quality characteristic, for example, for additional memory for a computer or Bluetooth technology in an automobile. The *option cost* approach is applicable when a new feature is first sold as an option and then becomes a standard component included in the basic price. This requires that the old and new varieties differ by easily identifiable characteristics that are or have been separately priced as options. The use of production cost estimates critically relies on the availability of suitable estimates for the price-cost margin.

6.180 The use of *hedonic regressions for patching* price changes because of quality differences is most appropriate where data on price and characteristics are available for a range of models and where the characteristics are found to predict and explain price variability well with regard to a priori reasoning and econometric terms. Their use is appropriate where the cost of an option or change in characteristics cannot be separately identified and should be collected from the prices of varieties sold with different specifications in the market. The estimated regression coefficients are the estimate of the contribution to price of a unit change in a characteristic, having controlled for the effects of variations in the quantities of other characteristics. The estimates are particularly suited to valuing changes in the quality of a variety when only a given set of characteristics changes and the valuation is required for changes in these characteristics only. The results from hedonic regressions may be used to target the salient characteristics for variety selection. The synergy between the selection of prices according to characteristics defined as price determining by the hedonic regression, and their subsequent use for quality adjustment, should reap rewards. The method should be applied where there are high ratios of noncomparable replacements, though not a frequent churn, and where the differences between the old and new varieties can be well defined by its characteristics.

6.181 As previously discussed in this chapter, the use of the *link-to-show-no-price-change* method for permanently missing and the *carryforward* method for temporarily missing variety prices are not generally advised for making quality adjustment and imputations.

6.182 While Figure 6.3 is appropriate for the treatment of temporarily and permanently missing prices in the routine compilation of a CPI, there is a context in which a quite different strategy is required. The context is where there is a rapid turnover or "churn" in the models or varieties sold. For example, television sets are sold by several manufacturers each having a range of models with different features. Over time many new phases of technological development have occurred including the cathode ray tube, color televisions, wireless remotes, plasma, LCD televisions, digital, high definition, larger screens, smart functions, 3D, LEDs, ultra HD resolution, OLED, and roll-up OLED. New features and restyling extend the life cycle of each model in each phase. As with automobiles, computers, computer-related hardware and software, telecommunications equipment, or household appliances, the product market is characterized by different manufacturers producing several varieties (models) each of different quality, such as screen size for a computer or television set, aimed at different segments of the market. These will, over time, usually have a rapid turnover in their quality characteristics. The previously outlined methods, if applied to these markets, may lead to a biased CPI. Figure 6.3 notes that *matching, class mean imputations,* and *hedonic price indices* may be used, though there may be severe bias in the use of the former. The next section considers CPI measurement for these product markets.

High Technology and Other Sectors with a Rapid Turnover of Models

6.183 The measurement of price changes of varieties unaffected by quality changes is primarily achieved by matching models; however, when the matching breaks down the implicit or explicit methods can be used. But what should be done in the case of industries where the matching breaks down on a regular basis because of the high turnover in new models of different qualities than the old ones? The matching of prices of identical models over time, by its nature, is likely to lead to a seriously depleted sample. There is both a dynamic universe of all varieties consumed and a static universe of the varieties selected for repricing. For example, if the sample is initiated in December, by the subsequent May, for a long-term price comparison, the static universe will be matching prices of those varieties available in the static universe in both December and May but will omit the unmatched new varieties introduced in January, February, March, April, and May, and the unmatched old ones available in December but unavailable in May. For December to May cumulative month-on-month short-term comparisons, similar considerations apply. Although there will be improved imputations for temporarily missing variety prices and an improved timelier introduction of replacements, the replacements only draw from the dynamic universe of new models on a one-on-one basis. This example refers to a December to January matched price comparison. For many countries, matching may effectively continue for many years until the CPI is updated leaving an extremely degraded sample. Two empirical questions indicate whether there will be any significant bias. First, is sample depletion substantial? Substantial depletion of the sample is a necessary condition for such bias. Second, are the unmatched new and old varieties likely to have quality-adjusted prices that substantially differ from those of the matched varieties in the current and the reference periods?

6.184 The matching of prices of identical models over time may lead to the monitoring of a sample of models that is increasingly unrepresentative of the population of transactions. Some of the old models that existed when the sample was drawn are not available in the current period, and new models that enter the sample are not available in the reference period. It may be that the models that are disappearing have relatively low prices, while the entrants have relatively high ones. By ignoring these prices, a bias, known as sampling bias, is being introduced. Using old low-priced varieties and ignoring new high-priced ones has the effect of biasing the index downward. For some products, the new variety may be introduced at a relatively low price though the old one may continue at a relatively high price, serving a minority segment of the market. In this case, the bias would take the opposite direction. The nature of the bias will depend on the pricing strategies of firms for new and old varieties. Some strategies for the introduction of new models, and implications for CPI measurement, are considered in Annex 6.3.

6.185 This sampling bias exists for most products. However, the concern here is with product markets where the NSOs are finding the frequency of new variety introductions and old variety obsolescence sufficiently high that they may have little confidence in their results. Three procedures will be considered: an extensive use of the matched-model (overlap) technique, class mean imputation, and the use of hedonic price indices (as opposed to the partial, hedonic patching discussed in paragraphs 6.136–6.150).

Matching and the Overlap Method for Markets with Rapid Turnover of Models

6.186 The first approach to address markets with rapid turnover of models is simply a more extensive use of the overlap approach outlined previously for permanently missing prices. In this case, it is adopted for permanently missing varieties that occur frequently, as is usual for changes in models of electronic goods and automobiles. Matching prices of a few representative varieties becomes a less feasible approach in this context. A backward imputation is illustrated in Table 6.11 though, as outlined in the illustration for Table 6.5C, a forward imputation can be equally justified and both methods provide the same results when the imputations are based on the price changes of overlapping matched samples.

6.187 Considering model 1 in Table 6.11, in November there is no overlap price for the new model 1R, so its price is imputed "backward" by using the ratio of geometric means of the December to November prices but only including those for which matched models exist, that is, models 2R, 4R, and 5. These are all constant-quality price comparisons; of like with like. As shown in expression 6.13, its imputed price is 0.974 × 30 = 29.2:

$$\frac{(37\times 30\times 29)^{\frac{1}{3}}}{(40\times 30\times 29)^{\frac{1}{3}}}=\left(\frac{37}{40}\times\frac{30}{30}\times\frac{29}{29}\right)^{\frac{1}{3}}=0.974$$

6.188 The imputed price for the replacement model 2R in June is based on the price changes of matched models 1, 3, and 5 for June and July, that is, $\frac{(25\times 30\times 29)^{\frac{1}{3}}}{(25\times 30\times 29)^{\frac{1}{3}}}=1.00$ and its imputed price: 1.00 × 30 = 30. The imputed prices for 3R in November and 4R in June are 32.15 (rounded to 32.2, for simplicity of exposition) and 30.0, respectively.

6.189 The overall price relatives for each model, and their linked-in replacements, can now be computed as the product of short-term month-on-month price changes, that is, model 1 and its replacement 1R, for January to January, using the overlap month of November:

$$\frac{p_1^{\text{Feb}}}{p_1^{\text{Jan}}}x\frac{p_1^{\text{Mar}}}{p_1^{\text{Feb}}}x\frac{p_1^{\text{Apr}}}{p_1^{\text{Mar}}}\frac{p_1^{\text{May}}}{p_1^{\text{Apr}}}x\frac{p_1^{\text{Jun}}}{p_1^{\text{May}}}x\frac{p_1^{\text{Jul}}}{p_1^{\text{Jun}}}$$

$$x\frac{p_1^{\text{Aug}}}{p_1^{\text{Jul}}}x\frac{p_1^{\text{Sep}}}{p_1^{\text{Aug}}}x\frac{p_1^{\text{Oct}}}{p_1^{\text{Sep}}}x\frac{p_1^{\text{Nov}}}{p_1^{\text{Oct}}}x\frac{p_1^{\text{Dec}}}{p_{1R_{\text{imp}}}^{\text{Nov}}}x\frac{p_{1R}^{\text{Jan}}}{p_{1R}^{\text{Dec}}}$$

$$=\frac{p_1^{\text{Nov}}}{p_1^{\text{Jan}}}x\frac{p_{1R}^{\text{Dec}}}{p_{1R_{\text{imp}}}^{\text{Nov}}}x\frac{p_{1R}^{\text{Jan}}}{p_{1R}^{\text{Dec}}} \qquad (6.16a)$$

$$\frac{25}{25}\times\frac{25}{25}\times\frac{25}{25}\times\frac{25}{25}\times\frac{25}{25}\times\frac{25}{25}\times\frac{25}{25}$$

$$\times\frac{25}{25}\times\frac{25}{25}\times\frac{20}{25}\times\frac{30}{29.2}\times\frac{30}{30}$$

$$=\frac{20}{25}\times\frac{30}{29.2}\times\frac{30}{30}=0.8219 \qquad (6.16b)$$

Table 6.11 Illustration of Rapid Model Turnover

	Jan.	Feb.	Mar.	Apr.	May	Jun.	Jul.	Aug.	Sep.	Oct.	Nov.	Dec.	Jan.
1	25	25	25	25	25	25	25	25	25	25	20		
1R											**29.2**	30	30
2	35	35	35	35	35	32							
2R						**37**	37	37	37	37	37	40	40
3	30	30	30	30	30	30	30	30	30	30	27		
3R											**32.2**	33	33
4	29	29	29	29	29	28							
4R						**30**	30	30	30	30	30	30	30
5	29	29	29	29	29	29	29	29	29	29	29	29	29

Values in bold are imputed.

6.190 The price relative for model 1 from January in the preceding year to January in the current year shows a (1 − 0.8219) × 100 = 17.81 percent price decrease. It is clear from Table 6.11 that the price for model 1 has been constant up to October, and there was a price fall in November, but this was to clear the market for the replacement. There should be a November to December price increase for the old model 1 to the new replacement 1R that reflects that part of the price difference between model 1 and model 1R was not due to quality differences. But the imputation is based on the constant price movements of models 4R and 5 and a coincidental price increase in model 2R; it assumes that short-term price movements of matched pairs will proxy the price change of model 1. However, in this context, the constant price changes of matched models are an inappropriate proxy badly biasing the measured price change downward. At fault are first, the use of the unrepresentative price for model 1 at the end of its life cycle in November, and second, the inappropriate imputation for the replacement variety.

6.191 The January to January price decreases for models 2, 3, and 4, using replacements, and 5 are, respectively, 1.2, 6.3, and 3.4 percent and no change for model 5. With a substantial churn of models, possibly more frequently than annual, the bias from using overlaps can be substantial.

6.192 As an advantage, the method is simply an extension of the linking-in of new products and can be readily applied by an NSO, especially one with limited resources. However, this approach biases the CPI because it bases the imputations on price changes of matched varieties not subject to the price changes that occur on the replacement of a model.

6.193 The overlap method may be subject to bias if applied to where there is substantial churn in the product market and an active policy by the supplier of introducing upgraded replacement models. The nature and extent of the bias depends on the pricing strategy. Table 6.11 illustrates a policy of lower pricing at the end of the life cycle and a higher price at the start. Importantly, the example has no price change for other matched models, from which the imputation was drawn, and thus a biased imputation at this critical overlap period. The bias is substantial and downward. Alternative pricing strategies are given in Annex 6.3 along with their implication for bias from using the overlap matching. It has been demonstrated in empirical studies that the method can introduce substantial bias under quite reasonable conditions. The nature and extent of the bias depend on business pricing strategies that may change over time and are unpredictable, which is a concern for CPI compilation in this important product area. The overlap method is thus not recommended for product markets with a high rate of model churn.

Use of a Class Mean Imputation

6.194 The previous example showed that an imputation based on price movements of other matched models not at the end of their life cycle could introduce a bias. An alternative, though more resource-intensive method, is to base the imputations not on price changes of matched varieties but to use, where possible, explicit quality adjustments for linked-in noncomparable replacement. For example, internet webpages of prices of similar products may show the difference in characteristics and prices of the old models and the replacement models. The replacement may simply have a higher value of some performance characteristic or feature for which the price is available as an option. If enough explicit quality adjustments can be made, imputations might be better made on the basis of only those models that have had explicit quality adjustments to their price.

6.195 The nature of the high frequency of replacements makes the procedure resource-intensive and, in some instances, not viable because of the absence of explicit information on prices of features or options. However, if enough models have an explicit adjustment, an average of their price change could be used to impute the price change of other models being replaced. This is the basis of using class mean imputations. The method requires care that the linking-in of replacement models does not take place at the end of the model's life cycle when pricing might be abnormally low for a variety that relatively few consumers are purchasing. This not only has a detrimental effect on the quality-adjustment methodology, but also on the representativity of the models upon which the prices change measurement is based.

6.196 The class mean imputation method was outlined in paragraphs 6.96–6.100. It is similar in procedure to the overall mean imputation and is a form of targeted imputation. The "target" is measured price changes of replacements for permanently missing products. Only the price changes of "comparable" replacements are used to impute the overlap price, the replacements being limited to those that have exactly the same price-determining characteristics, or those varieties with replacements that have been declared comparable after review and have already been quality-adjusted through one of the "explicit" methods. For example, when the arrival of a new model of a particular kind of automobile forces price collectors to find replacements, some of the replacements will be of comparable quality, while others can be made comparable with explicit quality adjustments, but the remaining ones will need imputed prices for an overlap month

Hedonic Price Indices

6.197 It is important to distinguish between the use of hedonic regressions for patching and their use as *hedonic price indices,* which are measures of quality-adjusted price changes. Patching adjusts individual item prices for quality differences when a noncomparable replacement is used while hedonic price indices are measures of quality-adjusted price changes. Hedonic price indices are suitable when the pace and scale of replacements of varieties are substantial because, first, an extensive use of these overlap quality adjustments may lead to bias and, second, the sampling will be from a static matched/replacement universe likely to be biased. With new models being continually introduced and old ones disappearing, the coverage of a matched sample may deteriorate, and bias may be introduced as the price changes of new/old models differ from those of the matched ones. What is required is a sample to be drawn in each month and price indices constructed; but instead of controlling for quality differences by matching, they will be controlled for in the hedonic regression. Note that all the indices described in the following text use a fresh sample of the data available in each period. If there is a new variety in a period, it is included in the data set and its quality differences controlled for by the regression. Similarly, if old varieties drop out, they are still included in the data for the indices in the periods in which they exist. Paragraphs 6.110–6.115 stress the need for caution in the use of hedonic regressions for quality adjustments.

6.198 Consider a price comparison between two adjacent time periods, periods t and $t + 1$. The models sampled do not have to be matched, they may simply be all recorded models sold in the two periods, and they comprise a different mix of qualities. The hedonic formulation regresses the price of model i, p_i, on the $k = 2, \ldots, K$ characteristics of the varieties z_{ki}. A single regression is estimated on the data in the two time periods compared, the equation also including a dummy variable D^{t+1} being 1 in period $t + 1$, zero otherwise.

The Time Dummy Variable Approach

6.199 A single hedonic regression equation is estimated with observations across models over adjacent time periods, including the reference period 0 and a subsequent period t. The logarithm of prices of individual models is regressed on their characteristics and a dummy variable for time, taking the values of $D_i^1 = 1$ if the model is sold in period 1 and 0 otherwise. A log-linear specification is given by

$$\ln p_i^t = \ln \beta_0^t + \sum_{k=1}^{K} z_{k,i}^t \ln \beta_k^t + \ln \varepsilon_i^t \qquad (6.17)$$

6.200 The δ^t are estimates of the *proportionate* change in price arising from a change between the excluded reference period $t = 0$ and successive periods $t = 1$, T having controlled for changes in the quality characteristics via the term $\Sigma_{k=1}^{K} Z_{k,i}^{0,t} x \widehat{ln\beta}_k$.

6.201 In principle, the index $100 \times \exp\left(\hat{\delta}^t\right)$ requires an adjustment for it to be a consistent (and almost unbiased) approximation of the proportionate impact of the time dummy variable.[11] In practice, the adjustment usually has little effect.

6.202 The method implicitly restricts the coefficients on the quality characteristics to be constant over time: for example, for an adjacent period January and February regression, for $k = 1, \ldots, K$ characteristics and where period 0 and t are January and February, respectively, $\beta_k = \beta_k^{\text{Jan}} = \beta_k^{\text{Feb}}$. The (relative) valuation of a characteristic, for example, for a washing machine with an additional 100 revolutions per minute spin speed, is the same in January as in February.

[11] See Triplett (2006) for more details.

The index, $100 \times \exp\left(\hat{\delta}^{\text{Feb}}\right)$, is an estimate of the quality-adjusted price change for February (January = 100).

The Characteristics/Repricing Approach

6.203 A hedonic regression is run to determine the price-determining characteristics of models, for example in a reference period 0. The average model in period 0 can then be defined as a tied bundle of the averages of each price-determining characteristic. In the previous example for washing machines, these would include: spin speed: 1,375 revolutions per minute; capacity (cotton load): 8.5 kilogram; annual energy cost: £36.5; steam facility: 4 percent; Brand A: 15 percent; warranty period: 5.4 years; and run-time (cotton): 18.8 minutes. These are the $\bar{Z}_k$ averages for each of the k price-determining characteristics.

6.204 The average values of each characteristic are held constant in each period but valued in turn using period 0 and period t hedonic regressions. One form of the (average) *characteristics* approach is as a measure of the price change of a set of average period 0 characteristics valued first, at period t hedonic valuations, and second, at period 0 hedonic valuations. A ratio of the results is a constant (period 0 characteristics) quality price index. The numerator, the period t hedonic valuation, provides an answer to a counterfactual question: what would be the estimated transaction price of a model with period 0 average characteristics, were it on the market in period t?

6.205 A constant-quality *hedonic geometric mean characteristics* price index from a log-linear hedonic regression equation is a ratio of geometric means with average characteristics held constant in the *reference* period 0, $\bar{z}_k^0$:

$$I^{0:t}_{\text{HGMC}:\bar{z}^0} = \frac{\prod_{k=0}^{K}\left(\hat{\beta}_k^t\right)^{\bar{z}_k^0}}{\prod_{k=0}^{K}\left(\hat{\beta}_k^0\right)^{\bar{z}_k^0}} = \frac{\exp\left(\sum_{k=0}^{K}\bar{z}_k^0 \ln \hat{\beta}_k^t\right)}{\exp\left(\sum_{k=0}^{K}\bar{z}_k^0 \ln \hat{\beta}_k^0\right)} \qquad (6.18)$$

where $\bar{z}_k^0 = \frac{1}{N^0}\sum_{i \in N^0} z_{i,k}^0$.

6.206 Equation 6.18 holds the (quality) characteristics constant in period 0, though a similar index could be equally justified by valuing in each period a constant period t average quality set:

$$....I^{0:t}_{\text{HGMC}:\bar{z}^t} = \frac{\prod_{k=0}^{K}\left(\hat{\beta}_k^t\right)^{\bar{z}_k^t}}{\prod_{k=0}^{K}\left(\hat{\beta}_k^0\right)^{\bar{z}_k^t}} = \frac{\exp\left(\sum_{k=0}^{K}\bar{z}_k^t \ln \hat{\beta}_k^t\right)}{\exp\left(\sum_{k=0}^{K}\bar{z}_k^t \ln \hat{\beta}_k^0\right)} \qquad (6.19)$$

where $\bar{z}_k^t = 1\big/_{N^t}\sum_{i \in N^t}^{N^t} z_{i,k}^t$.

$N^0 = N^t$ are the number of matched observations (varieties) in the sample. Neither a period 0 constant-characteristics index nor a period t constant-characteristic quantity basket can be considered to be superior, both acting as bounds for their theoretical counterparts. Some average or compromise solution is required. An index making symmetric use of period 0 and period t characteristics values is intuitive:

$$I^{0:t}_{\text{HGMC}:\bar{z}^T} = \frac{\prod_{k=0}^{K}\left(\hat{\beta}_k^t\right)^{\bar{z}_k^T}}{\prod_{k=0}^{K}\left(\hat{\beta}_k^0\right)^{\bar{z}_k^T}} = \frac{\exp\left(\sum_{k=0}^{K}\bar{z}_k^T \ln \hat{\beta}_k^t\right)}{\exp\left(\sum_{k=0}^{K}\bar{z}_k^T \ln \hat{\beta}_k^0\right)} \qquad (6.20)$$

where $\bar{z}_k^T = \left(\bar{z}_k^0 + \bar{z}_k^t\right)/2$.

6.207 Equations 6.18, 6.19, and 6.20 all use predicted prices in both the denominator and numerator. This follows the recommendation in the following text to use dual imputations. However, this method also entails running hedonic regressions in each period. Yet a fortuitous result is that a feature of the OLS estimator is the mean of actual prices being equal to the mean of predicted prices:

$$\frac{1}{N^0}\sum_{i \in N^0}\ln \hat{p}^0_{i|z_i^0} = \frac{1}{N^0}\sum_{i \in N^0}\ln p_i^0 \text{ and } \frac{1}{N^t}\sum_{i \in N^t}\ln \hat{p}^t_{i|z_i^t} = \frac{1}{N^t}\sum_{i \in N^t}\ln p_i^t$$

Thus, while the numerator of equation 6.18 and denominators of equation 6.19 must be counterfactual—the valuing period 0 (t) average characteristics at period t (0) prices—the denominator of equation 6.18 and numerator of 6.19 can use actual prices, since the means are the same for an OLS estimator. This leads to the important results that equation 6.19 does not require a hedonic regression to be estimated in every current period t, only in the price reference period 0. This is an important result since it aids the practical work of compilers who do not have to estimate a hedonic regression equation in each period, but maybe once every one or two years, depending on the amount of churn in the market and shifting technologies and preferences. The hedonic indices from one regression can be chained to its preceding hedonic indices, and so forth, using successive multiplication.

The Hedonic Imputation Approach

6.208 In contrast to the characteristics approach, the *imputation* approach works at the level of individual varieties/models, rather than the average values of their characteristics. The rationale for the imputation approach lies in the MMM. Consider a set of models transacted in period 0. The objective is to compare their period 0 prices with the prices of the same matched models in period t. In this way, there is no contamination of the measure of price change by changes in the quality mix of models transacted. However, for goods and services with a high model turnover, not all the period 0 models were sold in period t—there is no corresponding period t price in many cases. The solution—in the numerator of equation 6.21—is to predict the period t price of each i period 0 model, $\hat{p}^t_{i|z_i^0}$.

6.209 A constant-quality *hedonic geometric mean imputation* price index from a log-linear hedonic regression equation is a ratio of geometric means with characteristics held constant in the *reference* period 0, $\bar{z}_k^0$:

$$I^{0:t}_{\text{HGMI}:z_i^0} = \frac{\prod_{i \in N^0}\left(\hat{p}^t_{i|z_i^0}\right)^{\frac{1}{N^0}}}{\prod_{i \in N^0}\left(\hat{p}^0_{i|z_i^0}\right)^{\frac{1}{N^0}}} = \frac{\exp\left(1\big/_{N^0}\sum_{i \in N^0}\ln \hat{p}^t_{i|z_i^0}\right)}{\exp\left(1\big/_{N^0}\sum_{i \in N^0}\ln \hat{p}^0_{i|z_i^0}\right)} \qquad (6.21)$$

6.210 Alternatively, the value in the numerator of equation 6.21 is the geometric mean of the period t price for the price-determining characteristics in that period, $Z^t_{i,k}$. This is compared, in the denominator, with the geometric mean of the period 0 predicted price of the same period t price-determining characteristics, $Z^t_{i,k}$. For each model, the quantities of characteristics are held constant in period t, $Z^t_{i,k}$; only the characteristic prices change:

$$I^{0:t}_{HGMI:z^t_i} = \frac{\prod_{i \in N^t} \left(\hat{p}^t_{i|z^t_i}\right)^{\frac{1}{N^t}}}{\prod_{i \in N^t} \left(\hat{p}^0_{i|z^t_i}\right)^{\frac{1}{N^t}}} = \frac{\exp\left(\frac{1}{N^t} \sum_{i \in N^t} \ln \hat{p}^t_{i|z^t_i}\right)}{\exp\left(\frac{1}{N^t} \sum_{i \in Nt} \ln \hat{p}^0_{i|z^t_i}\right)} \tag{6.22}$$

6.211 As with the characteristics approach, a compromise solution of whether period 0 or period t constant characteristics should be used, is to apply an average of the two. However, as with the characteristics approach, equation 6.22 has the advantage of only requiring a single hedonic regression to be estimated in the price reference period 0. If this is used, the regression should be reestimated every year or so, the frequency being determined by the turnover of products.

6.212 The three approaches have different, yet valid, intuitions. As long as the functional form of the aggregator is aligned to the hedonic regression in the manner shown in Table 6.12, the imputation and characteristics approaches yield the same result. This consolidation not only markedly narrows down the choice between approaches, but also validates the measure as one resulting from quite different intuitions.

6.213 For a log-linear functional form of a hedonic regression, the requirements are that (1) for the characteristics approach, $\bar{z}^0_k$ and $\bar{z}^t_k$ are arithmetic means of characteristic's values, the right-hand side of the hedonic regression, and (2) for the imputation approach, the ratio of average predicted prices is a ratio of geometric means, the left-hand side of the regression.

6.214 The important feature of the hedonic indices is that they require no matching of individual models in the periods compared. Matching is required so that the price of a model in period 0 can be compared with that in period t, without a concern that the price change is affected by changes in quality. Such matching restricts the sample and, importantly in this context of a high level of churn in models and where prices change when models change, can lead to bias. This was illustrated in Table 6.11. The price comparison of matched models effectively removes from the sample price changes in the important period of a price comparison when models change. The imputation for November to December for model 1 in Table 6.11 is based on matched prices only. Hedonic indices adjust for quality change not by any meticulous or time-consuming matching and, for that matter, identification of replacements, but by applying a hedonic regression to value constant-quality characteristics.

6.215 Hedonic indices use data on matched and unmatched observations and, again importantly, can naturally be applied to large monthly data sets, such as scanner and web-scraped data, as opposed to a small sample of what may have been in some long-past reference period, a representative variety.

6.216 An advantage of the imputation approach over the dummy variable approach is that explicit weighting systems can be more readily, accurately, and intuitively applied at this elementary level. For example, equation 6.22 may be defined for models i over a set of models of television sets sold in period t. The formula gives equal weight to each model sold. A major improvement would be to apply to each model's quality-adjusted price change the weight of that price change, that is, the individual model's share of transaction expenditure values, for example from scanner data. Silver (2018) outlines the methodology for the imputation approach, in the context of house price indices, to include quasi-superlative and superlative formulations. The weighted imputation approach also has a correspondence to a weighted characteristics approach, and the more intuitive application of weights, if formulated as in Table 6.12.

6.217 Hedonic indices are particularly well suited for large data sets, as web-scraped or scanner data (see Chapter 10), for which there is no matching of varieties. It is at initiation that a price collector selects a representative variety and matches its characteristics in subsequent periods in order to track the price of this same variety. In doing so, the sample of prices collected is highly restricted to what may be a single price. With hedonic indices, it is the varying values of the characteristics of the models that enable a constant-quality price change. There may be data sets in which accurately matched sampled prices form part of the sampled data. In such a case there would be no need for predicted prices to be used for constant-quality price change. The overall measure for this data set would contain: (1) actual price changes for the matched sample; (2) hedonic price changes for the period 0 models not sold in period t (as, for the hedonic imputation approach, in equation 6.21); and (3) hedonic price changes for the period t models not sold in period 0 (as, for the hedonic imputation approach, in equation 6.22). Each of these terms would be weighted by their relative expenditure shares, if available. It is from the measure of all three components that the difference between the MMM and hedonic indices becomes apparent.

Table 6.12 Equivalences of Hedonic Approaches

Hedonic Regression: Functional Form	Characteristics Approach: Form of Average of Characteristics	Imputation Approach: Form of Average of Predicted Prices
Linear	Arithmetic Mean	Arithmetic Mean
Log-Linear	Arithmetic Mean	Geometric Mean
Log–log	Geometric Mean	Geometric Mean

The Difference between Hedonic Indices and Matched Indices

6.218 As already mentioned, an advantage of hedonic indices over matched comparisons was the inclusion by the former of unmatched data. Consider a data set of prices and characteristics over two successive time periods, periods 0 and t. Assume there are m matched models in both periods 0 and t, o old models in period 0, but disappearing thereafter, and n new models appearing in period t, and subsequently, as shown in Table 6.13.

Table 6.13 Difference between Hedonic and Matched Indices

	Period 0	Period t
Matched Models (m)	m	m
Old Model (o)	o	
New Model (n)		n

6.219 A constant-quality, period 0 to t, price index, from a hedonic imputation approach, is made up of three terms:

- *The change in the geometric mean price of the* m *matched models*, with no need for quality adjustment because they are matched.
- *The change in the constant-quality geometric mean price of the old models with actual prices in period 0 and counterfactual ones in period* t. The counterfactual constant-quality price in period t has to be estimated since there is only a price in period 0. A prediction is required of what each old model's price in period 0 would have been had it been sold in period t. A period t hedonic regression is estimated, and a predicted price estimated for each model by inserting its period 0 characteristic Z_k^0 values into the right-hand side of the estimated regression equation. A geometric mean is compiled of these predicted values, $\prod_{i \in o} \left(\hat{p}^t_{i|z_i^0} \right)^{\frac{1}{No}}$, and compared with the period 0 geometric mean, $\prod_{i \in o} \left(p_t^0 \right)^{\frac{1}{No}}$, as in equation 6.19.
- *The change in the constant-quality geometric mean price of the new model in period* t. The counterfactual constant-quality price in period 0 has to be estimated since there is only a price in period t. A prediction is required of what each new model's price in period t would have been had it been sold in period 0. A period 0 hedonic regression is estimated, and a predicted price estimated for each model by inserting its period t characteristics Z_k^t values into the right-hand side of the estimated regression. A geometric mean is compiled of these predicted values, $\prod_{i \in n} \left(\hat{p}^0_{i|z_i^t} \right)^{\frac{1}{Nn}}$, and compared with the period t geometric mean, $\prod_{i \in n} \left(p_i^t \right)^{\frac{1}{No}}$, as in equation 6.20.

6.220 The overall index can be phrased as a weighted average of these three elements with the matched comparison having a weight of $2Nm/(2Nm + No + Nn)$, the old of $No/(2Nm + No + Nn)$, and the new, $Nn/(2Nm + No + Nn)$, though preferably the weights should be expenditure shares rather than the numbers of each model.

6.221 The MMM effectively ignores the last two elements of the bullet points in paragraph 6.222. This procedure would result in no bias if the imputed quality-adjusted price change of new and old varieties were the same as that for matched models. The MMM might be appropriate if the number of new and old models—or their expenditure weights—is small relative to matched models. This would be the case for the hedonic patching of permanently missing model prices outlined previously, but not for this context where there is a high and frequent turnover in models.

6.222 Even if the MMM is used with replacements, something of the dynamic universe of models is brought into the measure, but only insofar as there is one-on-one variety replacement. Furthermore, hedonic indices employ a consistent basis for the explicit quality adjustment for noncomparable replacements.

6.223 The deficiency of the MMM against a hedonic index has been shown previously with regard to the hedonic imputation approach, though similar considerations apply to a time dummy variable approach. Consider an adjacent period time dummy variable hedonic index of the form of equation 6.17, with the index change captured by the coefficient on the dummy variable for time. For example, a sample of models of washing machines for periods t and $t + 1$ would have in the regression the log of price on the left and price-determining characteristics on the right-hand side. On the right-hand side, a dummy variable would also denote whether the observation is drawn from period t or $t + 1$. The hedonic regression includes matched, new, and old models and the quality adjustment is achieved through the term $\sum_{k=1}^{K} z_{k,i}^t \ln \beta_k^t$ in equation 6.17. A matched-model measure of price change would again only measure the price change for the more limited sample of matched models but would not require a quality adjustment. The hedonic dummy variable approach, with its inclusion of unmatched old and new observations, will likely differ from a geometric mean of matched prices changes, the extent of any difference depending, in this unweighted formulation, on the proportions of old and new varieties leaving and entering the sample and on the price changes of old and new varieties relative to those of matched ones. If the market for products is one in which old quality-adjusted prices are unusually low while new quality-adjusted prices are unusually high, then the matched index will understate price changes. Different market behavior will lead to different forms of bias (see Annex 6.3).

Key Recommendations

- All temporarily missing prices should be imputed using one of the imputation methods described in the chapter. Methods include overall mean and target mean imputations.
- The imputation of temporarily missing prices is especially important when using the short-term formulas—modified Lowe and modified Young. Imputations, which are self-correcting, avoid introducing any bias into the index.
- Imputations can be made either forward or backward. The results are equivalent, and the countries can choose which is most appropriate.
- The carryforward method should not be used, except for fixed or controlled prices. This method introduces a downward bias into the index.
- NSOs should define a period during which nonseasonal products can be considered temporarily missing. While this threshold varies from country to country, the most commonly used threshold is three months but can be longer.
- Permanently missing prices require a replacement variety.

- Quality change refers to changes in the price-determining characteristics when one variety replaces another. If these differences are judged to be comparable (that is, they are deemed to be similar), the price of the old and the new variety can be compared directly and any difference in price is reflected as price change. Should the differences be such that the old and the new variety are deemed to be noncomparable, a quality adjustment is needed. Quality adjustments ensure that the index reflects only pure price change and not changes because of differences in quality.
- Explicit or direct quality adjustments are preferred. They include quantity adjustment resulting from changes in size or quantity, changes in option costs, differences in production costs, and hedonics. Quantity adjustments are straightforward, and many countries apply this method for changes in size. The other explicit methods require data and experience making explicit quality adjustments.
- Implicit or indirect quality adjustments are the second-best approach; however, they could be preferred given a lack of data and expertise required for the explicit methods. Implicit methods include overlap pricing and imputation.
- The rapid turnover in the models sold of select products (for example, televisions, computers, telecommunications equipment, or appliances) requires a different strategy. Over time, these products usually have a rapid turnover in their quality characteristics. While the MMM, class mean imputations, and hedonic price indices may be used, the chapter notes that the MMM may lead to significant bias.

Annex 6.1

Overall Mean (or Targeted) Imputation

Consider $i = 1 \ldots m$ varieties in period t and p_i^t as the price of variety i in period t. All varieties continue into period $t + 1$ except for the single variety m which is replaced by variety n. p_n^{t+1} is the price of a replacement variety n in period $t + 1$. Now n replaces m but is of a different quality. There are $(m - 1)$ matched prices between periods t and $t + 1$ and a single replacement price. Let $A(z)$ be the quality adjustment to p_n^{t+1} which equates its quality services or utility to p_m^{t+1}, had it existed, such that the quality-adjusted price $p_m^{*t+1} = A(z)p_n^{t+1}$. For the imputation method to work, the average price change of the $i = 1 \ldots m$ varieties, including the quality-adjusted price p_m^{*t+1}, given on the left-hand side of equation A6.1.1, must equal the average price change from just using the overall mean of the rest of the $i = 1 \ldots m - 1$ varieties, on the right-hand side of equation A6.1.1. The discrepancy or bias from the method is the balancing term Q. It is the implicit adjustment that allows the method to work. The arithmetic formulation given is based on Triplett (2006), though a similar geometric one can be readily formulated. The equation for one unavailable variety is given by

$$\frac{1}{m}\left[\frac{p_m^{*t+1}}{p_m^t}+\sum_{i=1}^{m-1}\frac{p_i^{t+1}}{p_i^t}\right]=\left[\frac{1}{(m-1)}\sum_{i=1}^{m-1}\frac{p_i^{t+1}}{p_i^t}\right]+Q \qquad \text{(A6.1.1)}$$

$$Q=\frac{1}{m}\frac{p_m^{*t+1}}{p_m^t}-\frac{1}{m(m-1)}\sum_{i=1}^{m-1}\frac{p_i^{t+1}}{p_i^t}$$

and for x unavailable varieties by

$$Q=\frac{1}{m}\sum_{i=m-x+1}^{m}\frac{p_m^{*t+1}}{p_m^t}-\frac{x}{m(m-x)}\sum_{i=1}^{m-x}\frac{p_i^{t+1}}{p_i^t} \qquad \text{(A6.1.2)}$$

The relationships are readily visualized if r_1 is defined as the arithmetic mean of price changes of varieties that continue to be recorded and r_2 of quality-adjusted unavailable varieties. For the arithmetic case, where

$$r_1\left[\sum_{i=p}^{m=x}p_i^{t+1}/p_i^t\right]\div(m-x) \text{ and}$$

$$r_2=\left[\sum_{i=m-x+1}^{m}p_i^{*t+1}/p_i^t\right]\div x \qquad \text{(A6.1.3)}$$

then the bias of the arithmetic mean of ratios from substituting equation A6.1.3 in equation A6.1.2 is

$$Q=\frac{x}{m}(r_2-r_1) \qquad \text{(A6.1.4)}$$

which equals zero when $r_1 = r_2$. The bias depends on the ratio of unavailable values and the difference between the mean of price changes for existing varieties and the mean of quality-adjusted replacement price changes. The bias decreases as either (x/m) or the difference between r_1 and r_2 decreases. Furthermore, the method is reliant on a comparison between price changes for existing varieties and quality-adjusted price changes for the replacement or unavailable comparison. This is more likely to be justified than a comparison without the quality adjustment to prices. For example, suppose there were $m = 3$ varieties, each with a price of 100 in period t. Let the $t + 1$ prices be 120 for two varieties, but assume the third, that is, $x = 1$, is unavailable and is replaced by a variety with a price of 140, of which 20 is attributable to quality differences. Then the arithmetic bias as given in equations A6.1.3 and A6.1.4, where $x = 1$ and $m = 3$, is

$$\frac{1}{3}\left[(-20+140)/100-\left(\frac{120}{100}+\frac{120}{100}\right)/2=0\right] \qquad \text{(A6.1.5)}$$

If the bias depended on the unadjusted price of 140 compared with 100, the imputation would be prone to serious error. In this calculation, the direction of the bias is given by $(r_2 - r_1)$ and does not depend on whether the quality is improving or deteriorating, in other words, whether $A(z) < 1$ or $A(z) > 1$. If $A(z) < 1$, a quality improvement, it is still possible that $r_2 < r_1$ and for the bias to be negative.

The analysis is framed with regard to a short-term price change framework. That is, the short-term price changes between the prices in a period and those in the preceding period are used for the imputation. This is different from the long-term imputation where a base price is compared with prices in subsequent months, and where the implicit assumptions are more restrictive.

Table A6.1 provides an illustration in which the (mean) price change of varieties that continue to exist, r_1, can vary for values between 1.0 and 1.5, corresponding to a variation between no price change and a 50 percent increase. The (mean) price change of the quality-adjusted new varieties compared with the varieties they are replacing is assumed not to change (that is, $r_2 = 1.00$). The bias is given for ratios of missing values of 0.01, 0.05, 0.1, 0.25, and 0.5, for both arithmetic means and geometric means. For example, if 50 percent of price quotes are missing and the missing quality-adjusted prices do not change, but the prices of existing varieties increase by 5 percent ($r_1 = 1.05$), then the bias for the geometric mean is represented by the proportional factor 0.9759 (that is, instead of 1.05), the index would be $0.9759 \times 1.05 = 1.0247$. For an arithmetic mean, the bias is −0.025; instead of 1.05, it should be 1.025.

Equation A6.1.4 shows that the ratio x/m and the difference between r_1 and r_2 determine the bias. Table A6.1 shows that the bias can be quite substantial when x/m is relatively large. For example, for $x/m = 0.25$, an inflation rate of 5 percent for existing varieties translates to an index change of 3.73 and 3.75 percent for the geometric and arithmetic formulations, respectively, when $r_2 = 1.00$ (that is, when quality-adjusted prices of unavailable varieties are constant). Instead of being 1.0373 or 1.0375, ignoring the unavailable varieties would give a result of 1.05. Even with 10 percent missing ($x/m = 0.1$), an inflation rate of 5 percent for existing varieties translates to 4.45 and 4.5 percent for the geometric and arithmetic formulations, respectively, when $r_2 = 1.00$.

Table A6.1 Example—Bias from Implicit Quality Adjustment When the (Mean) Price Change of Quality-Adjusted New Varieties Compared with the Varieties They Are Replacing Is Assumed Not to Change (r_2 = 1.00)

r	Geometric Mean					Arithmetic Mean				
1	Ratio of Missing Varieties, *x/m*					Ratio of Missing Varieties, *x/m*				
	0.01	0.05	0.10	0.25	0.50	0.01	0.05	0.10	0.25	0.50
1	1.00000	1.00000	1.00000	1.00000	1.00000	0.00000	0.00000	0.00000	0.00000	0.00000
1.01	0.99990	0.99950	0.99901	0.99752	0.99504	−0.00010	−0.00050	−0.00100	−0.00250	−0.00500
1.02	0.99980	0.99901	0.99802	0.99506	0.99015	−0.00020	−0.00100	−0.00200	−0.00500	−0.01000
1.03	0.99970	0.99852	0.99705	0.99264	0.98533	−0.00030	−0.00150	−0.00300	−0.00750	−0.01500
1.04	0.99961	0.99804	0.99609	0.99024	0.98058	−0.00040	−0.00200	−0.00400	−0.01000	−0.02000
1.05	0.99951	0.99756	0.99513	0.98788	0.97590	−0.00050	−0.00250	−0.00500	−0.01250	−0.02500
1.1	0.99905	0.99525	0.99051	0.97645	0.95346	−0.00100	−0.00500	−0.01000	−0.02500	−0.05000
1.15	0.99860	0.99304	0.98612	0.96566	0.93251	−0.00150	−0.00750	−0.01500	−0.03750	−0.07500
1.2	0.99818	0.99093	0.98193	0.95544	0.91287	−0.00200	−0.01000	−0.02000	−0.05000	−0.10000
1.3	0.99738	0.98697	0.97411	0.93651	0.87706	−0.00300	−0.01500	−0.03000	−0.07500	−0.15000
1.5	0.99595	0.97993	0.96027	0.90360	0.81650	−0.00500	−0.02500	−0.05000	−0.12500	−0.25000

Considering a fairly low ratio of x/m, for example, 0.05, then even when r_2 = 1.00 and r_1 = 1.20, Table A6.1 shows that the corrected rates of inflation should be 18.9 percent and 19 percent for the geometric and arithmetic formulations, respectively. In competitive markets, r_1 and r_2 are unlikely to differ by substantial amounts since r_2 is a price comparison between the new variety and the old variety after adjusting for quality differences. If r_1 and r_2 are the same, then there would be no bias from the method even if x/m = 0.9. There may, however, be more sampling error. It should be borne in mind that it is not appropriate to compare bias between the arithmetic and geometric means, at least in the form they take in Table A6.1. The latter would have a lower mean, rendering comparisons of bias meaningless.

An awareness of the market conditions relating to the products concerned is instructive in understanding likely differences between r_1 and r_2. The concern is when prices vary over the life cycle of the varieties. For instance, at the introduction of a new model, the price change may be quite different from price changes of other existing varieties. Thus, assumptions of similar price changes, even with quality adjustment, might be inappropriate. For example, if new computers enter the market at prices equal to, or lower than, prices of previous models, but with greater speed and capability, an assumption that $r_1 = r_2$ could not be justified. Or if new clothing enters the market at relatively high quality-adjusted prices, while old, end-of-season, or out-of-style clothes are being discounted, there will be bias, as r_1 differs from r_2.

Some of these differences arise because markets are composed of different segments of consumers. Indeed, the very training of consumer marketers involves consideration of developing different market segments and ascribing to each appropriate pricing, product quality, promotion, and place (method of distribution). In addition, consumer marketers are taught to plan the marketing mix for the life cycle of varieties. Such planning allows for different inputs of each of these marketing mix variables at different points in the life cycle. This includes "price skimming" during the period of introduction, when higher prices are charged to skim off the surplus from segments of consumers willing to pay more. The economic theory of price discrimination would also predict such behavior. Thus, the quality-adjusted price change of an old variety compared with a new replacement variety may be higher than price changes of other varieties in the product group. After the introduction of the new variety, its prices may fall relative to others in the group. There may be no law of one price change for differentiated varieties within a market.

There is thus little in economic or marketing theory to support any expectation of similar (quality-adjusted) price changes for new and replacement varieties, as compared to other varieties in the product group. Some knowledge of the realities of the particular market under study would be helpful when considering the suitability of this approach. Two aspects need to be considered in any decision to use the imputation approach. The first is the proportion of replacements; Table A6.1 provides guidance here. The second is the expected difference between r_1 and r_2. It is clear from the previous discussion that there are markets in which they are unlikely to be similar. This is not to say the method should not be used. It is a simple and expedient approach. What arguably should not happen is that it is used by default, without any prior evaluation of expected price changes and the timing of the switch. Furthermore, its use should be targeted, by selecting varieties expected to have similar price changes. The selection of such varieties, however, should take account of the need to include a sufficiently large sample so that the estimate is not subject to undue sampling error.

The manner in which these calculations are undertaken is also worth considering. In its simplest form, the pro forma setting for the calculations (for example, on a spreadsheet), would usually have each variety description and its prices recorded on a monthly basis. The imputed prices of the missing varieties are inserted into the spreadsheet and are highlighted to show that they are imputed. The need to highlight such prices is, first, because they should not be used in subsequent imputations as if they were actual prices. Second, the inclusion of imputed values may give a false impression of a larger sample size than actually exists. Care should be taken in any audit of the number of prices used in the compilation of the index to code such observations as "imputed."

The method described previously is an illustration of a short-term imputation. As discussed in Chapter 8, there is a strong case for using short-term imputations as against long-term ones.

Annex 6.2

Quality Adjustment Using a Replacement and Price Overlap

Consider p_m^t as the price of variety m in period t, p_n^{t+1}, the price of a replacement variety n in period $t+1$; n replaces m but is of a different quality. Let there be overlap prices for m and n in period t and let $A(z^{t+1})$ be the quality adjustment to p_n^{t+1} which equates its quality to p_m^{t+1} such that the quality-adjusted price $p_m^{*t+1} = A(z^{t+1})p_n^{t+1}$. Now the quality adjustment to prices in period $t+1$ is defined as $p_m^{*t+1} = A(z^{t+1})p_n^{t+1}$ which is the adjustment to p_n in period $t+1$ that equates it to p_m in period $t+1$ (had it existed then).

A desired measure of price changes between periods $t-1$ and $t+1$ is thus:

$$\left(p_m^{*t+1} / p_m^{t+1}\right) \tag{A6.2.1}$$

The overlap formulation equals this when:

$$\frac{p^{*t+1}}{p_m^{t-1}} = A\left(z^{t+1}\right)\frac{p_n^{t+1}}{p_m^{t-1}} = \frac{p_n^{t+1}}{p_n^{t}} \times \frac{p_m^{t}}{p_m^{t-1}} \tag{A6.2.2}$$

$$A\left(z^{t+1}\right) = \frac{p_m^t}{p_n^t} \text{ and similarly for future periods of the series}$$

$$A\left(z^{t+1}\right) = \frac{p_m^t}{p_n^t} \text{ for } \frac{p_m^{*t+i}}{p_m^{t-1}} \text{ for } i = 2, \ldots, T$$

But what if the assumption does not hold? What if the relative prices in period t, $P^t = p_m^t \big/ p_n^t$, do not equal $A(z^t)$ in some future period, say $A\left(z^{t+i}\right) = \alpha_i R^t$? If $\alpha_i = \alpha$, the comparisons of prices between future successive periods, say, between $t+3$ and $t+4$, are unaffected, as would be expected, since variety n is effectively being compared with itself:

$$\frac{p_m^{*t+4}}{p_m^{t-1}} / \frac{p_m^{*t+3}}{p_m^{t-1}} = \frac{\alpha R^t\, p_n^{t+4}}{\alpha R^t\, p_n^{t+3}} = \frac{p_n^{t+4}}{p_n^{t+3}} \tag{A6.2.3}$$

However, if differences in the relative prices of the old and replacement varieties vary over time, then:

$$\frac{p_m^{*t+4}}{p_m^{t-1}} / \frac{p_m^{*t+3}}{p_m^{t-1}} = \frac{\alpha_4\, p_n^{t+4}}{\alpha_3\, p_n^{t+3}} \tag{A6.2.4}$$

Note that the quality difference here is not related to the technical specifications or resource costs, but to the relative prices that consumers pay.

Annex 6.3

The Nature and Extent of the Index Number Bias If Only Matched Varieties Are Used

Sample degradation and differences in the (quality-adjusted) prices of unmatched new, unmatched old, and matched models can lead to bias in matched-model price indices that take into account only models available in two consecutive periods. The nature and extent of such bias depends on the frequency with which manufacturers turn over their models and the pricing strategy retailers employ over the life cycle of the models. For example, assuming that matched prices go down, if the quality-adjusted prices of new unmatched models in period $t = 2$ are higher than their matched counterparts in period 2, and if the quality-adjusted prices of old unmatched models in period 1 are lower than their matched counterparts in period 1, then there will be a *larger* fall in the matched-model index between periods 1 and 2 compared with a hedonic index that uses all of the data. Similarly, if the quality-adjusted prices of unmatched new models are *below* matched ones in period 2, and the quality-adjusted prices of old models *above* matched ones in period 1, there will be a *smaller* fall in the matched-model index compared with a hedonic index that uses all of the data. The nature and extent of the matched models index bias thus depends on the pricing strategy adopted for new and old models. Indeed, if hedonic-adjusted prices are consistently above or below average prices for unmatched new *and* old models some of the bias will cancel.

The case for old unmatched models having below average quality-adjusted prices is based on an inventory-clearing argument. For an old model near or at the end of its life cycle retailers want to clear out the remaining inventory from both their warehouses and store shelves so they have room to stock and display the replacement model. They do not wish the old model to cannibalize some of the sales of the new model which may have a higher price (profit) margin. The extent of any such cannibalization will depend on the cross-price elasticities between the new and old models. This inventory-clearing argument is noted in quadrant IV of Figure A6.2.

New and old models may coexist for some time and existing models having their prices *increased* following the introduction of a new model is of interest. Such a pricing strategy can be used by a multiproduct firm that anticipates the introduction of a new model. A *multiproduct* monopolist can increase the prices of existing models because some of the demand for existing models that would usually be lost to competitors, because of the price increase, will now not go to the competitor's products but will go instead to the firm's new model. The new model will cannibalize some of the existing model's sales that would otherwise be lost because of the price increase in the existing model (Figure A6.2, quadrant II). For example, the price of old, branded pharmaceutical drugs can increase after the expiration of a patent and introduction of new generic models. This is due to price discrimination with some market segments remaining with particularly strong preferences for the old models willing to pay higher prices (Figure A6.2, quadrant II). However, it has been argued that any such effect may be outweighed by the need to cut the prices of the existing models to prevent the existing model's sales cannibalizing sales of the new, more profitable model (Figure A6.2, quadrant IV). A study of computer processors and disk drives found that with the introduction of products embodying new technologies the prices for older products decline rapidly to permit the older technology to compete with the newer one for a limited time, but the old technology is eventually driven out.

New models may have *above* average quality-adjusted prices in their period of introduction because firms "price skim" market segments willing to pay a premium for the new model over and above that due to its improved quality (Figure A6.2, quadrant I). Indeed, marketing texts advocate price skimming as one of two "new product" pricing strategies. The alternative strategy is "market-penetration" pricing for which a low initial price is set for a new model to attract a large number of buyers quickly to win market share and take advantage of falling costs because of scale economies. Such pricing may initially be possible because the new model is based on new, lower cost components that can provide a feature set that is comparable to existing models, but at a lower price point. In either event, quality-adjusted prices of new models may have *below* average prices (Figure A6.2, quadrant III).

Figure A6.2 summarizes these positions. The combination of above average prices for new models in quadrant

Figure A6.2 Matched-Model Price Index Bias and Pricing Strategies

	New Unmatched Models	Old Unmatched Models	Pricing	Matched-Model Price Index Bias
Quality-Adjusted Prices **above** Matched-Model Prices	Market Skimming	Multiproduct Monopoly Pricing Strategy; Price Discrimination to Segments with Sticky Downward Pricing; Old Technologies Reduce Prices	I and IV	Upward
	[quadrant I]	*[quadrant II]*	II and III	Downward
Quality-Adjusted Prices **below** Matched-Model Prices	Market-Penetration Pricing; Low Unit Costs, New Producing Technology	Inventory Clearing	I and II	Countervailing
	[quadrant III]	*[quadrant IV]*	III and IV	Countervailing

I and below average prices for old models in quadrant IV leads to an overall net downward bias of the matched-model price index. Similarly, pricing in quadrants II and III leads to matched-model indices that are biased upward. However, pricing in quadrants I and II leads to an indeterminate bias, with countervailing effects from the new and old above average priced models. The outcome from pricing in quadrants III and IV is also indeterminate, with countervailing effects from the new and old below average priced models.

It is possible to say something about the likely pricing strategies of different products. Consider the case of digital cameras compared to film-based cameras. Given the current differential in product costs for the two technologies, and where the two categories are in their respective life cycles, relatively greater effort is likely to be placed on R&D in new models that reduce unit costs for digital cameras compared to R&D in film-based camera models that reduce unit costs. Products in a mature stage of their category life cycle, where R&D development is relatively small and product enhancing, as opposed to cost reducing, may be more likely to have above average quality-adjusted prices for new models.

MAINTAINING THE SAMPLE 7

Introduction

7.1 When a new good or service is produced and consumed, there is a need for it to be included in the index as soon as possible, especially if the good or service will have relatively high sales. New products might have quite different price changes than existing ones, especially at the start of their life cycle. In the initial period of introduction of a new product, producers and retailers often set higher prices than might be attainable once the market settles into a competitive equilibrium. There is a related problem of obsolete products, as the price changes of such products may be unusual. The products will be at the end of their life cycle and may be priced at unusually low prices to clear the way for new models.

Sample Maintenance and Matching

7.2 Matching is designed to avoid price changes being affected by quality changes. As described in Chapter 6, matching refers to comparing like with like. Its adoption constrains the sampling to a static universe of goods and services that exists in the price reference period. Therefore, items or varieties that exist in the reference period, but not in the current period, are not matched, and similarly, those new goods and services existing in the current period but not in the reference one. The challenge is that the products that are not in the matched universe (that is, the new product appearing after the reference period and the old products that disappeared in the current period) may be the ones whose price changes differ substantially from existing matched ones. They may include different technologies and be subject to different (quality-adjusted) strategic price changes. The same method used to maintain a constant-quality sample may give rise to a sample biased away from technological developments. Furthermore, when this sample is used to make imputations (as discussed in Chapter 6) to the price changes of replacement products, it reflects the technology of a sample not representative of current technological changes. The matched-model method similarly constrains the incorporation of new products.

7.3 The problem described in paragraph 7.2 has been outlined with regard to a variety having to "exist" in both periods being compared. The concern for price collection in an outlet is for the price collector to be able to collect a price quote for the period for the comparable, matched variety selected and priced in the previous period. A variety may not be found by the price collector on an outlet shelf in a given month and thus not "exist" in the previous sense, but still be consumed, sold by outlets not sampled or sold by the outlet on a day of the month not sampled. Similarly, a price may be collected but there may be no or limited expenditure on it.

7.4 Consider three universes:

- An intersection universe, which includes only matched products
- A dynamic double universe, which includes all products in the price reference period and all in the current period, although they may be of different qualities
- A replacement universe, which starts with the price reference period universe but also includes one-to-one replacements when a product from the sample in the price reference period is missing in the current period

7.5 A sample of *representative varieties* that comprises only those varieties selected for pricing in the price reference period and having a matched sample provides an estimator of the price change for the *intersection universe.*

7.6 It is difficult to ascertain the extent to which matching from the intersection universe constrains the penetration of the sample into the dynamic double universe, since national statistical offices (NSOs) generally do not collect data for the dynamic double universe. Its extent will, in any event, vary between products. Scanner data have been used to determine the coverage of *intersection* and *replacement* universes for consumer durables, finding the intersection and replacement universes to be highly restricted.

7.7 A first implication of this issue described in the previous paragraph is that for permanently missing varieties, variety replacement is an opportunity to bring in a variety with a relatively large sales value to increase the coverage of the index. However, the selection of variety replacements by price collectors puts coverage of the sample to some extent under the control of the price collectors. Guidelines and training on direct replacements in particular product groups may be needed. Where updating is infrequent, rotating the sample has benefits. Sample rotation, as outlined in paragraphs 7.18–7.24, is equivalent to initiating a new sample, but for specific product groups that maintain the same weights until the next update. A particularly useful method would be to refresh the sample for product groups with a high level of sample churn, though as a rule, more frequent updating is advocated.

Item Replacement or Substitution

7.8 The price collectors often are best placed to select replacement varieties for price collection. They are aware of the price-determining characteristics of the products being produced and purchased, and their terms of sale. The selection of the replacement for price collection might be quite obvious to the price collector, especially if there is only a slight, nominal improvement to the product. For example, the "improved" product can be simply a replacement variety sold instead of the previous one. The replacement could have a different code or model number and will be known to the price collector as simply a different color or packaging. The specification list given to the price collector is a critical prompt to identify when a variety has changed, and it is important that all price-determining characteristics have been included.

7.9 The price collector, supported by the consumer price index (CPI) compilers and prompted by the specification list, takes on the role of identifying whether a variety is of comparable quality or not. If it is judged to be comparable when it is not, the quality difference is taken to be a price difference, and a bias will result if the unrecognized quality changes are in a consistent direction. Informed comparable substitution requires general guidelines on what makes a suitable replacement as well as product-specific information on likely price-determining characteristics. It also requires timely substitution to maximize the probability of an appropriate substitute being available. Chapters 5 and 6 provide further information on the need for and type of training to be provided to price collectors in this regard. The selection of replacement varieties is very much product-specific and guidelines for price collectors should focus on specific product groups and tailored to their needs.

7.10 The results from hedonic regressions can be useful in the selection of varieties and their replacements. The results provide an indication of the major quality factors that make up the good or service, with regard to explaining price variation. The selection of varieties will be more representative and the coefficients from hedonic regressions would be more tailored to the sample because of their subsequent use to estimate quality-adjusted prices.

7.11 Price collectors traditionally are required to find substitute varieties that are as similar as possible to the varieties being replaced. This maximizes the likelihood that the old and replacement variety will be equivalent and minimizes the need to employ some method of quality adjustment. Replacement varieties should be chosen to make the sampled varieties more representative of the dynamic universe. The inclusion of a popular replacement variety to refresh the sample allows for a useful and accurate price comparison and increases the chance of an appropriate quality adjustment. It is of little merit to substitute a new variety with limited sales for a missing variety with limited sales, as the index would become more unrepresentative. If replacements are made for varieties at the end of their life with popular replacements varieties at the start of their life cycle, the quality adjustment will be substantial and substantive. More frequent sample rotation or directed replacements will be warranted for some item areas. The selection of replacement varieties:

- Offers an opportunity to cut back on sample bias in the period of replacement.
- The more frequent the replacement, the less the bias.
- If there is more than one new (replacement) variety in the market, there may still be bias since only the most popular one will be selected, and it may be at a different stage in its life cycle than others and priced differently.
- It is assumed that accurate quality adjustments are made on replacements. The less frequent the replacement, the more difficult this might be, because the latest replacement variety on the market may have more substantial differences in quality than earlier ones.
- If the replacement variety has relatively high sales, is of comparable quality, and at the same stage in its life cycle as the one being replaced, then its selection will minimize bias, but this replacement variety would also be at the end of its life cycle and subject to replacement soon.
- If there is more than one new (replacement) variety and the most comparable one is selected in line with the old technology, it will have low market share and unusual price changes.
- Given the availability of advance market or consumption information, replacements undertaken before obsolescence are likely to increase the sample's share of the market, include varieties more representative of the market, and facilitate quality adjustment.

Outlet Replacement

7.12 The problem of variety substitution is analogous to the problem that arises when an outlet closes. It may be possible to find a comparable outlet not already in the sample, for example, a franchise, in the same chain. It may also be possible to find a noncomparable outlet for which, in principle, an adjustment can be made, for example, for the better quality of service of the new (replacement) outlet. It is not unusual for an outlet to close following the introduction of a new one, and in this case, there is an obvious replacement outlet. However, if the new outlet has comparable prices but a better range of varieties, delivery, and service quality, there is a gain to purchasers from substituting one outlet for the other. Since such facilities have no direct price, it is difficult to provide estimates of the value of such services for an adjustment to be made for the better quality of service. Simply rotating the new outlet into the sample via the overlap method would miss the quality difference, as outlined in Chapter 6. The index thus would have an upward bias, which would be eliminated when rebasing. In such cases, substituting an old outlet for a new one that provides a similar standard of service would be preferable.

Sample Rotation, Chaining, and Hedonic Indices

7.13 For some product groups, the product samples will become quite out of date if left to the next update or revision for the sample to be reinitiated. This is especially so if the rebasing is infrequent. Sample rotation is equivalent to initiating a new sample, but for a product group that maintains the same weights until the next rebasing. Sample rotation is undertaken for specific product groups at different points in time to save on the resources required if all the product groups had their products rotated at the same time. The criteria for choice of product groups to benefit from sample rotation, and the timing of the rotation, should be clearly and openly scheduled in advance according to objective criteria.

7.14 It is important to recognize the interrelationships among the methods for addressing product rotation, product replacement, and quality adjustment. The rotation of CPI product samples is a form of product substitution, although not "forced" by a missing variety price but undertaken for a general group of items/varieties to update the sample. Rotation has the effect of making future forced replacements less likely. The implicit assumptions in its use are equivalent to those for the overlap adjustment method: price differences are an adequate proxy for the value of the quality change between products disappearing from the sample and replacement products. Consider the initiation of a new sample of items. Prices for the old and new samples are collected in the same month and the new index is compiled based on the new sample, with the results being linked to the old.

7.15 As an example, assume that the initiation of a new sample is taking place in January. The prices of an old variety in December and January are, respectively, 10 and 11, a 10 percent increase, and those for the replacement variety in January and February are 16 and 18, respectively, an increase of 12.5 percent. The new variety in January is of a better quality than the old, and this difference in quality is estimated to be worth 16 – 11 = 5; that is, the price difference is assumed to be equal to the value of the quality difference, which is the assumption implicit in the overlap method. If the price of the old variety in December was compared with the quality-adjusted price of the new variety in January under this assumption, the price change would be the same: 10 percent ([16 – 5]/10 = 1.10). However, if the price difference in January was an unsuitable reflection of the quality difference (for example, the old variety was being sold at a low price to clear the market for the new one), then the implicit assumption underlying the overlap method would not hold. In practice, the need to simultaneously replace and update a large number of products requires the assumptions of the overlap method. This process is not error-free, and in cases where the assumptions are likely to be particularly untenable, explicit adjustments should be used, resources permitting (as discussed in Chapter 6).

7.16 Sample rotations to refresh the sample between rebasing are expensive exercises. However, if rebasing is infrequent, this might be appropriate for particular product groups where there is a substantial loss of products. The need for a metadata system to facilitate such decisions is outlined in paragraphs 7.83–7.86. The use of more frequent sample rotation helps the process of quality adjustment in two ways. First, the updated sample will include newer varieties, comparable replacements with substantial sales will be more likely to be available, and noncomparable ones will be of a more similar quality, which will improve the accuracy of explicit quality adjustments. Second, because the sample has been rotated, there will be fewer missing varieties and less need for quality adjustments.

7.17 An extension of more frequent sample rotation is to use a chained formulation in which the sample is reselected each period. The prices of all varieties available in each successive linked comparison are compared: those available, for example, in both January and February are compared for the January to February link, while those available in both February and March are compared for the February to March link. The index for January to March is derived by successive multiplication of the two monthly links. The principles and methods of this chained formulation were outlined in Chapter 6 in the context of products in which there is a rapid turnover of models, and such principles apply in this case. Similarly, the use of hedonic indices and short-term comparisons might be useful in this context (see Chapter 6).

7.18 The chained formulation allows the price changes of a new model to be included in the index as soon as the model can be priced for two successive periods. For example, a new model that appears in period 3 can be introduced into the index in the period 3 to period 4 link. However, the new model's effect on the price index in the initial period of introduction, period 3, is ignored for the period 2 to period 3 link. Similar concerns arise for disappearing models. If the last period a price is observed for a model is period 1, its effect on the price index is lost for the period 1 to period 2 link. This situation, and its resolution, is outlined in Chapter 6 in the context of product groups with a high turnover of differentiated models with identifiable price-determining characteristics. Only subsamples of matched items exist between successive periods and these form biased price comparisons since it is on the dumping of old models that unusually low prices, and on the introduction of new ones that unusually high prices exist. Hedonic price indices allow the price of old model in period 1 to be used in the period 1 to 2 price comparison and the price of the new model in period 3 to be used in the period 2 to 3 price comparison, because it uses the prices of all models in each period, though adjusted for their differences in quality characteristics. In this case, there is no need for the use of the matched-model method.

7.19 Hedonic indices are applicable if a new model/variety is not entirely new—it is an evolutionary product in the sense that it is providing more services than those of the old model. The price can be determined with regard to a different combination of the existing price-determining characteristics.

Incorporation of New Products

New Products and How They Differ from Quality Changes

7.20 A new model of a product may provide more of a currently available set of service flows. Chapter 6 describes how new models often with quality improvements replace existing ones. A number of methods to incorporate the replacement models into the CPI and help to maintain the CPI's representativity were outlined. However, there may be many characteristics of the new model that go beyond the service flow of the existing model.

7.21 The first practical concern with defining a new product's quality changes against the existing model is that the new model cannot be easily linked to the existing model as a continuation of an existing resource base and service flow because of the nature of its "newness." For example, some forms of frozen foods, self-driving and all-electric and hybrid cars, computers, printers, and mobile phones, while extensions of existing products, have dimensions of service that are new. Second, new products can generate a welfare gain to purchasers and surplus to producers when purchased/sold at the time of introduction and the simple introduction of the new product into the index, once two successive price quotes are available, misses this gain.

7.22 Many product markets are defined by a multitude of brands and differentiated offerings along with a rapid turnover in varieties. In some cases, there are core brands and varieties that may be used for CPI price measurement as representative variety. However, the concern remains that the rationale for the introduction of new or differentiated brands and varieties is to be distinct and not exact substitutes for existing ones. If the CPI misses both an increasing variety of offerings and their distinctive quality improvements, the index may misrepresent actual price inflation. However, the magnitude and turnover in offerings in differentiated markets can make the definition and measurement of quality change and "newness" impractical.

7.23 A new product can be identified with regard to the absence of substitutes and the ensuing monopolistic power. For example, some new movies, digital games, and toys may have small cross-elasticities with other movies, games, and toys; their shared service is to provide entertainment and they are only similar in this respect. The same argument may apply to new books or breakfast cereals. There are many new forms of existing products that are not easily substitutable for similar products but can generate consumer utility well above that of the preexisting counterparts and are not always sold at a higher price.

7.24 A more practical classification that will meet the needs of CPI compilation is to consider *evolutionary* and *revolutionary* products. Examples of evolutionary products would be new models of household appliances such as refrigerators and washing machines where improvements in quality are introduced from time to time. Consequently, in theory at least, it should be possible to quality adjust for any differences between a preexisting and an evolutionary product, as outlined in Chapter 6. Where the new model is a one-for-one replacement with the old model, the sample is maintained. However, where there are many new brands/varieties spawned by a new innovation, the one-on-one replacement will not reflect the representativity of the sample. *Revolutionary* products are products that are substantially different from preexisting ones. *Revolutionary* products represent a good or service that:

- Was not included and could not be included in the price index during the initial selection of the current basket and which is later available for possible inclusion in the index
- Cannot be easily linked to the service flow or production technology of existing goods and services (that is, it represents a distinct departure from previously available products to the extent that it is a step change with regard to technology or utility to the customer)
- Has a recognizable and generally accepted new benefit to consumers as a result of becoming available

7.25 The last two points in paragraph 7.24 help to distinguish a *revolutionary* product from an *evolutionary* product. A revolutionary product is an entirely new good or service that is not closely tied to a previously available product. A revolutionary product tends to be a good or service that is expected to satisfy some need in a new way and is unlikely to fit neatly into an existing CPI item category. For example, a mobile phone, although an extension of an existing flow of service (telecommunication), has a new dimension of service (it provides the opportunity to make "mobile" calls away from a fixed telephone) and is a distinct product from existing landline telephone services (it is a step change in technology). It is therefore an example of a revolutionary product.

7.26 Quality adjustments to prices are therefore suitable for evolutionary products, but unsuitable for revolutionary products. The definitions are designed to distinguish between the two types of products not with regard to what is analytically appropriate, but by what is practically meaningful for the needs of CPI compilation and calculation. Practical needs are important in this context, especially because the methods for providing reliable estimates of consumer surplus on a large-scale basis are not practically possible given the substantial resource needs of data and econometric expertise.

Incorporation of New Products: Major Concerns

7.27 There are two major concerns regarding the incorporation of new products into a CPI: their identification and detection, and the related decision on the need and timing for their inclusion. This refers to both the weight and price changes of the new products.

7.28 For example, the levels of expenditure on mobile phones were in some countries at such a significant level that their early inclusion in CPIs became a priority. They shifted from no expenditure to be a quite large proportion of expenditure in their product group in a short time. Furthermore, their price changes were atypical of other goods in their product group. Many new products can command substantial sales and be the subject of distinct pricing strategies at introduction prompted by a need to recuperate research and development expenditure and take advantage of an opportunity to expand market share and make profits, as, for example, with high-technology goods, such as computers, pharmaceuticals, and entertainment gaming devices.

7.29 Waiting for a new product to be established or for the rebasing of an index before incorporating new products may lead to errors in the measurement of price changes if the unusual price movements are ignored at critical stages in the product's life cycle. NSOs should have strategies in place for the early identification of new products and mechanisms for their incorporation either at launch, if preceded by major marketing campaigns, or soon after, if there is evidence of market acceptance. This should form part of the metadata system. Waiting for a new product to achieve market maturity may result in an implicit policy of ignoring the different price movements that accompany their introduction. New product prices may be very close to, or even lower than, the existing ones and serve to expand the new product's market share. There may be something in the "newness" of the technology and production that enables a price reduction for a better product.

Methods for Incorporating New Products

7.30 The methods outlined in paragraphs 7.32–7.52 include those that fall under normal CPI procedures and those that would require exceptional treatment. In the case of normal CPI procedures, the focus will be on *evolutionary products*, and the rebasing of the index, rotating of products, and introduction of new products as replacements for disappearing ones are considered. Much use is made of the overlap method where the price changes of new products are linked/spliced onto the index. Of importance in this context of maintaining the representativity of the sample is a move, where appropriate, away from one-for-one replacements and the introduction of appropriate weights for the new products The overlap method invokes some highly restrictive assumptions, and these will be explored in the context of explicit quality adjustments, all following the principles and practices described in Chapter 6. The case of *revolutionary products* is more problematic from a practical measurement perspective. The focus on paragraphs 7.43–7.52 is less on an understanding of how such new products can be incorporated into the CPI, but is instead on the need for users to be made aware of the conceptual limitations of the resulting measures.

Evolutionary Products

Updating and Chaining the Index

7.31 A new product may be readily incorporated into the index at the time of updating or revising the index. If the new product has, or is likely to have, substantial sales, and is not a replacement for an existing one, or is likely to have a much higher or lower market share than the existing one it is replacing, then new weights are necessary to reflect this. New weights are fully available when updating the index. There will be a delay in the new product's full inclusion, and the extent of the delay will depend on how close its introduction is to the next rebasing, the frequency with which the index is updated, and the time lapse between determining the new expenditure weights from a household budget survey (as described in Chapter 3) and their use in index compilation (see Chapter 9 for more information). However, even if the index was updated annually and chained, it would take until the annual update before weights could be assigned, and even then, there might be a further delay in the sampling and finalizing the survey results for the weights. Annual updating allows for a relatively early introduction of new products and is advised when the weights are not keeping pace with innovations in the product market.

7.32 Updating provides two further opportunities to maintain/refresh the sample:

- The first is to develop a new set of elementary aggregates. Some elementary aggregates may no longer have a sufficiently substantive weight and expected longevity to merit inclusion in the CPI, according to some cutoff criterion, as outlined in Chapter 4, while others may have now passed the cutoff and be expected to continue to gain importance. The formal inclusion of new evolutionary and revolutionary products at this juncture, along with their weights, and removal of "obsolete" elementary aggregates, provides an opportunity for an NSO to formally announce and integrate new products in the CPI along with their weights. The price changes of the new CPI basket are chain linked onto the price changes of the old, as described in Chapter 9.
- The second is the reinitialization of the sample of outlets and representative varieties within outlets, as outlined in Chapter 4. On rebasing, the sample of outlets for the existing elementary aggregates can be revisited with the purpose of introducing new outlets, especially those invoking new retailing technologies, including internet purchases, and remove obsolete outlets. There might also be a need for a reweighting and switching of the sample toward specific locations, for example, because of new metropolitan areas being developed because of new transportation links or job opportunities. Within each outlet, there is the opportunity to reappraise the representative varieties selected for regular pricing and replace them as necessary.

Sample Rotation (Reinitiation)

7.33 In many countries, rebasing is infrequent. Rather than continuing to utilize a sample of varieties that have become increasingly unrepresentative, NSOs may select new samples of outlets and of representative varieties between regularly scheduled index updates. This does not need to be done for all product groups in the same period, with different major groups of the Classification of Individual Consumption According to Purpose (COICOP) having their samples updated periodically, and perhaps with different frequencies, according to needs and resources. During this process, the weights remain constant until the next rebasing. This should involve a reappraisal of the product groups, locations, outlets, and representative varieties within outlets, and the elementary aggregates. This may be undertaken on a phased basis to reduce the workload with more frequent rotations directed to product groups experiencing rapid changes. However, unlike rebasing, there is neither a comprehensive introduction of new weights nor a sampling basis for identifying new locations, outlets, and product selection. A continuing matching of prices of products that are unrepresentative of expenditure patterns is also not desirable. Where resources do not permit a regular rebasing, sample rotation provides a viable mechanism for making some in-roads into maintaining sample representativity, but it is not a complete solution.

Sample Rotation (Reinitiation) in High-Turnover Product Groups and Hedonic Regressions

7.34 In product groups where new products are continuously appearing and old ones disappearing, the sample of products can quickly become outdated and unrepresentative of what consumers are purchasing. The existing sample within a class may cover a broad and representative range of varieties that were available in the market during the price reference period but not be representative of all the varieties currently purchased. In such a case, the sample of varieties within each elementary aggregate can be totally resampled to reflect current spending patterns. One approach to facilitate the sample rotation or reinitiation process uses an overlap. The old and new sample prices are collected in an overlapping period.

7.35 Care should be exercised in the application of this technique for product areas where there is a rapid change in the turnover of models. For example, new generations of electronic goods, such as television sets, might be incorporated into the price index using the overlap method. The new products would have their price change measured when two successive price quotes are available, possibly at the same price at the start of the new model's life cycle, and this would be linked to the price change of the old model it is replacing near the end of its life cycle. The method might miss any effective fall in (quality-adjusted) prices from new technological developments.

7.36 Modern data sources including scanner data and web-scraped data, as outlined in Chapter 10 and Annex 5.6 of Chapter 5, enable a continuous resampling of products with high rates of technological change. They also include price-determining characteristics data. For example, for washing machines, the spin speeds, capacity, dimensions, programs, brand, and many more salient price-determining characteristics are provided alongside the price for each model. In Chapter 6, hedonic regressions were advocated as one option for avoiding the pitfalls of overusing the overlap method.

7.37 It is not necessary for NSOs to wait until a product is obsolete before the new one is introduced. It is quite feasible for NSOs to preempt the obsolescence of the old product and to direct an early substitution. In some product groups, the arrival of a new product is well advertised in advance of the launch, while in others it is feasible for an NSO to have more general procedures for directed substitutions. Without such a strategy and infrequent rotation and rebasing, a country's CPI would be open to serious new product bias (as described in Chapter 12).

Forced Replacement

7.38 It is quite straightforward to extend the principles of replacements outlined in Chapter 6 to more than one representative variety simply by using the weighted (or unweighted) price change of more than one replacement variety. Indeed, existing samples may be supplemented by new varieties even when a replacement is not motivated by a permanently missing variety. A comparison at the elementary aggregate level between, for example, prices in 2020 and prices in June 2021 may be undertaken in two stages: first, by comparing average prices for several matched representative varieties in 2020 with average prices of comparable representative varieties in May 2021; multiplied by, second, a comparison of average prices in May 2021 compared with June 2021. The basket of representative varieties in the May to June 2021 stage may include new representative varieties in addition to the replacements for the ones used in 2020 to May 2021 stage. In introducing such representative varieties there is an implicit weighting, and care has to be exercised to ensure it is meaningful. At the elementary level of aggregation, the Jevons index is the ratio of geometric means, which is equal to the geometric mean of price relatives (for more information see Chapter 6 of the publication *Consumer Price Index Theory*). Equal (implicit) weight is given by the Jevons index to each variety's price relative. Explicit weights may also be used.

Sample Augmentation

7.39 Sample augmentation does not require a representative item to be missing, as was the motivation in Chapter 6. With sample augmentation, new items or varieties are introduced into the index. To illustrate sample augmentation, take the case where a new canned fish, tuna packed in water, has been recently introduced to the retail market and has significant popularity in the shops. This new variety can be added to the existing sample in the elementary aggregate for canned fish as shown in Table 7.1.

7.40 In the example in Table 7.1, period 1 displays the sample currently used. The NSO then decides to add the additional variety (tuna in water) in period 2. But prices for two periods are required before there is a matched pair. The period 2 elementary aggregate index (140.6) is computed using the geometric mean of short-term price relatives for the original five varieties (1.0307) multiplied by the previous period elementary aggregate index (136.4). In period 3 the new variety's price is available in both periods and the elementary aggregate index (143.3) is calculated by taking the geometric mean of short-term price relatives for the six available varieties (1.0190) multiplied by the period 2 price index (140.6). To estimate the period 2 variety level index for "tuna in water," the same value is assigned as the elementary aggregate index (140.6). This implicitly assumes that the price trend for the new variety from the price reference period is the same as that for all the other varieties within the elementary aggregate. If the long-term price relative method is used to calculate the elementary aggregate index, then the base price for tuna in water is estimated by dividing the first price of the new variety (60.00) by the long-term price change (1.406) to get a base price of 42.66. The aggregate index is calculated as the geometric mean of the variety indices.

7.41 The example in Table 7.1 is for augmenting the sample using a single additional variety.

Revolutionary Products

7.42 Revolutionary new products are often high-profile and a failure to properly integrate them into a CPI in a timely manner can damage the credibility of the index.

7.43 For evolutionary products, the sample of products was outdated, and new varieties were selected within existing elementary aggregates. Occasionally, new revolutionary products arise that are not covered within the scope of existing elementary aggregates but fall within the more widely defined COICOP classes. They may be primarily sold by a new outlet, or type of outlet, and there will be no previous products to match them against and make a quality adjustment to prices since, by definition, they are substantially different from preexisting goods. Further, there is no reference period weight to attach to the new outlet and product.

Table 7.1 Example of Sample Augmentation

Variety	Period 1		Period 2			Period 3		
	Price Index	Price	Price	Price Relative	Price Index	Price	Price Relative	Price Index
Canned Mackerel (in oil)	125.0	50.0	51.0	1.0200	127.5	51.0	1.0000	127.5
Canned Anchovies (in oil)	133.3	45.0	47.0	1.0444	139.2	48.0	1.0213	142.2
Canned Tuna (in oil)	150.0	50.0	52.0	1.0400	156.0	52.0	1.0000	156.0
Canned Salmon (in oil)	145.5	55.0	55.0	1.0000	145.5	57.0	1.0364	150.8
Canned Herring (in oil)	130.0	40.0	42.0	1.0500	136.5	43.0	1.0238	139.8
Canned Tuna (in water)	—	—	60.0		140.6	62.0	1.0333	145.3
Elementary Aggregate Index	136.4			1.0307	140.6		1.0190	143.3

7.44 Adding a new elementary aggregate and redistributing the weight for the COICOP class to all the elementary aggregates (or varieties) is a way of including such products. Table 7.2 illustrates how to redistribute the weight.

7.45 As an example, assume that currently desktop computers have a weight of 60 percent and laptops 40 percent, respectively, within subclass 08.1.3.1 (computers, laptops, and tablets) of COICOP 2018 and that the latest information from importers of information processing equipment indicates that sales of desktop computers to households (that is, where sales to businesses have been identified and excluded) now have a market share of 20 percent, laptops 10 percent, and tablets 70 percent. The NSO can use this information to introduce a new elementary aggregate for computers, laptops, and tablets. The weights at the subclass levels, including subclass 08.1.3.1, remain fixed for aggregating to the class-, group-, and division-level indices while the relative weighting of the elementary aggregates within the subclass level are allowed to change as new aggregates are added. Thus, there is a two-tier aggregation system in which the weights at the subclass level remain fixed at the weight reference period level and the weights within the subclasses at the elementary aggregate level are changed when new varieties are added, though are constrained to add to the unchanged subclass weight.

7.46 An overlap approach similar to sample rotation is used in this situation, where a new sample is selected, and an elementary aggregate is added. Prices are collected for both the old and new samples in the same period and the old sample is used for compiling the current period index (period 2) and the new sample for the next period (period 3). This is illustrated in Table 7.2.

7.47 For each of the two elementary aggregates in period 1, a new variety to price in period 2 is selected together with a sample of tablets (that is, the new revolutionary product). In period 2, the old sample is used to calculate the elementary aggregate indices and to compile the subclass-level index. Thus, the indices for computers and laptops are aggregated using the old weights for the elementary indices to derive the period 2 class index ([101.5 × 0.6] + [94.3 × 0.4] = 98.6).

7.48 In period 3, the elementary- and subclass-level indices are compiled using the new sample of products and varieties along with the new set of weights for each component. The computers in period 3 (99.6) are calculated by using the geometric mean price relative for the three new varieties (0.9811) multiplied by the period 2 price index for computers (101.5). The same calculation is used to derive the, period 3, elementary index for laptops (0.9967 × 94.3 = 94.0).

7.49 The new elementary index for tablets has no period 2 index to use so the period 2 subclass-level index (98.6) is used as the tablets index, on the assumption that the elementary index for tablets would have changed by the same percentage, on average, as the other products within the subclass. Note that this value is also used as the starting index for each of the variety indices within tablets. The period 3 tablets elementary index is calculated as 98.0 by using the elementary-level price relative (0.9933) multiplied by 98.6.

7.50 The aggregate index is calculated as the geometric mean of the variety indices. The period 3 subclass-level index is derived using the index for the new elementary aggregates along with the new weights for the elementary indices ([99.6 × 0.2] + [94.0 × 0.1] + [98.0 × 0.7] = 97.9).

7.51 This use of the overlap method is similar to the inclusion of new elementary aggregates on rebasing.

Introducing New Items and Higher-Level Weights in the Consumer Price Index in between Basket Revisions

7.52 The example of adding an elementary aggregate presented in Table 7.2 provides a method of introducing a new revolutionary product index, in this case for tablets within the COICOP subclass 08.1.3.1 (computers, laptops, and tablets). The relevant index now includes the contribution to price change of the tablets item within the subclass. The subclass, however, is likely to be underrepresented within the corresponding class (08.1.3 Information Processing Equipment), group (08.1 Information and Communication Equipment), division (0.8 Information and Communication), and the all-items CPI, because its weight does not reflect the increased expenditure resulting from the introduction of tablets. In most instances, NSOs are hesitant to change the weights for the subclass, class, group, and division until a new set of weights for all items can be obtained from a recent household budget survey. NSOs will typically include the tablet in subclass 08.1.3.1 without changing the weights for higher-level aggregates.

7.53 If the NSO has no plans for conducting a household budget survey in the near future to update weights for the subclass, class, group, and division, there are alternative sources it can consider for updating weights. To update the weights for high-level aggregates, the NSO first needs to estimate weights for each subclass within the class where the new product is added so that these subclass indices can be aggregated to the class level. Likewise, new weights are needed for each class and group to compile the group and division-level indices. In the example for tablets, weights are needed for each of the three microclasses (that is desktop computers, laptops, and tablets). Administrative sources may provide sales revenues from value-added tax data for groups 08.1 and 08.2. Importers of computers, laptops, and tablets may also be able to provide revenue data for group 08.1. Regulatory authorities can be a source for revenue data on internet service fees. Alternatively, the national accounts may have expenditure data already compiled for these groups. The next step is to use the revenue information to calculate relative shares for each group and to use the share weights to aggregate group indices to the division level. Note that the previous procedure will still not be completely satisfactory if it does not incorporate, into division 08, increases or decreases in the overall share of communications expenditures as a result of the revolutionary new product class.

7.54 Table 7.3 contains an example of introducing new weights at the aggregate level when the new items for tablets have been introduced. The new share weights for these three groups in column C sum to 100. The new weights are introduced into the calculation of the index in period 1. The component price indices for period 1 (columns D and E) below the total CPI level are the same, but they are aggregated

Table 7.2 Example of Introducing a New Elementary Aggregate

Computers

Variety	Period 1		Period 2			Weight in Class
	Price Index	Price	Price	Price Relative	Price Index	
Brand A (Model 240 w memory)	110.0	50.00	50.00	1.0000	110.0	
Brand B (Model 960)	105.0	30.00	27.50	0.9167	96.3	
Brand C (Model 520)	104.5	27.50	26.00	0.9455	98.8	
Elementary Aggregate Index	**106.5**			**0.9534**	**101.5**	**0.6**

Computers

Variety	Period 2		Period 3			Weight in Class
	Price Index	Price	Price	Price Relative	Price Index	
Brand A (Model 2000)	101.5	100.00	100.00	1.0000	101.5	
Brand F (Model 1500)	101.5	90.00	85.00	0.9444	95.9	
Brand A (Model 500)	101.5	75.00	75.00	1.0000	101.5	
Elementary Aggregate Index				**0.9811**	**99.6**	**0.2**

Laptops

Variety	Period 1		Period 2			Weight in Class
	Price Index	Price	Price	Price Relative	Price Index	
Brand D (Model 7160)	100.0	2000.00	1950.00	0.9750	97.5	
Brand E (Model 5180)	95.0	1250.00	1200.00	0.9600	91.2	
Elementary Aggregate Index	**97.5**			**0.9675**	**94.3**	**0.4**

Laptops

Variety	Period 2		Period 3			Weight in Class
	Price Index	Price	Price	Price Relative	Price Index	
Brand D (Model 9900)	94.3	2500.00	2500.00	1.0000	94.3	
Brand C (Model 2800)	94.3	1500.00	1490.00	0.9933	93.7	
Elementary Aggregate Index				**0.9967**	**94.0**	**0.1**

Tablets

Variety	Period 2		Period 3			Weight in Class
	Price Index	Price	Price	Price Relative	Price Index	
Brand G (Model 14K25)	98.6	250.00	245.00	0.9800	96.7	
Brand C (Model 2J564)	98.6	180.00	180.00	1.0000	98.6	
Brand H (Model MI7J2369)	98.6	200.00	200.00	1.0000	98.6	
Elementary Aggregate Index				**0.9933**	**98.0**	**0.7**

Subclass Index

	Period 1	Period 2
08.1.3.1 Computers, Laptops, and Tablets	**102.9**	**98.6**

Subclass Index

	Period 2	Period 3
08.1.3.1 Computers, Laptops, and Tablets		**97.9**

See Chapter 8, section on the calculation of higher-level indices for more details (beginning paragraph 8.89).

using different weights. As a result, the index for division 08 (Information and Communication) differs between column D (197.9) and column E (192.0). The all-items CPI also differs because of the different weights—column D (386.6) using the old weights and column E (393.4) using the new weights. As the difference between these values is solely due to weighting effects, the reweighted index value should not be published—it should only be used to calculate the current period price change. Footnotes should be provided to explain the introduction of the new weights.

7.55 To derive the period 2 indices for division 08 and the all-items CPI in column G, the indices are compiled using the new weights and the price relatives between period 1 and period 2 (column F) are calculated. The price relative for division 08 (0.999229) is applied to the period 1 published index for 08 Information and Communication (197.9) to derive the period 2 index (197.8). Likewise, the price relative for the total CPI (0.997954) in column F is applied to the period 1 published index for the all-items CPI (386.6) to derive the period 2 all-items CPI (385.8). These same calculations, using the price change in the reweighted 08 Information and Communication index and total CPI, are repeated for all future periods (see columns H and I in Table 7.3).

Table 7.3 Example of Introducing New Weights for Higher-Level Aggregates

COICOP Code	Old Weights	New Weights	Period 1		Period 1 to Period 2	Period 2	Period 2 to Period 3	Period 3
			Index		Price Relative	Index	Price Relative	Index
			Old Weights	New Weights		New Weights		New Weights
(a)	(b)	(c)	(d)	(e)	(f)	(g)	(h)	(i)
Total CPI	**100.00**		**386.6**			**385.8**		**386.8**
Total CPI Using New Weights		***100.00***		***393.4***	***0.9980***	***392.6***	***1.0026***	***393.6***
01 Food and Nonalcoholic Beverages	67.29	58.23	345.2	345.2		342.5		343.7
02 Alcoholic Beverages and Tobacco	0.54	0.77	453.2	453.2		455.1		454.1
03 Clothing and Footwear	1.37	1.70	376.9	376.9		375.0		376.0
04 Housing, Water, Electricity, Gas, and Other Fuels	7.91	8.45	572.4	572.4		576.8		577.2
05 Furnishings, Household Equipment, and Routine Household Maintenance	2.54	2.71	401.5	401.5		402.0		402.8
06 Health	1.47	2.12	215.1	215.1		217.3		217.3
07 Transport	6.06	8.25	685.9	685.9		687.7		686.5
08 Communication	2.14		197.9			**197.7**		**197.5**
Communication Using New Weights		**4.15**		**192.0**	**0.9992**	**191.9**	**0.9986**	**191.6**
08.1 Information and Communication Equipment	0.47	0.24	201.1	201.1		201.1		201.1
08.2 Software	6.54	37.35	179.8	179.8		177.9		177.5
08.3 Information and Communication Services	92.99	62.41	199.2	199.2		200.1		199.9
09 Recreation and Culture	1.79	2.55	348.2	348.2		349.6		350.3
10 Education	1.43	1.98	433.7	433.7		433.7		435.9
11 Restaurants and Hotels	3.41	5.67	411.2	411.2		413.2		415.5
12 Miscellaneous Services	4.05	3.42	391.3	391.3		393.1		397.8

See Chapter 8, section on the calculation of higher-level indices for more details (beginning paragraph 8.89).

The Overlap Method and the Incorporation of New Products and Outlets into a Consumer Price Index

Evolutionary Products—Similar Service Flows

7.56 The methods previously discussed in this chapter introduce a new product into the CPI as soon as two successive period prices are available. For example, consider the digital economy whereby many purchases of existing goods and services can be made in a manner that may enhance search, choice, and convenience of purchase as well as providing the same good or service at a cheaper price. While much of this can be disputed for many products, there has been a substantial shift in expenditure toward such digital services.

7.57 Consider a simple stylized example of a taxi service accessed by an application on a mobile phone in which the consumer enters the destination, is matched with driver and vehicle, confirms the pick-up and destination, and is automatically charged. Assume, for this stylized example, the taxi service is cheaper, *and the overall quality in all other respects is equal to that of a traditional taxi, at least on aggregate*. The use of the overlap method to replace the existing taxi service with this new replacement would not take account of the effective fall in price experienced by consumers. The overlap method treats the difference in price between the new and old taxi service in the overlap period as an indication of the difference in quality, as described in Chapter 6: the new service is treated as being cheaper because it has a poorer quality, though this is not the case here. The measured CPI would not include the benefit of the fall in price from the consumer switching to the cheaper taxi service.

7.58 Now assume that the new taxi service was incorporated into the CPI not as a replacement, but *within the same elementary aggregate as an additional representative variety—a sample augmentation*. It was recognized that this new service was different from the existing one, but it had its own market niche substantial enough to merit inclusion as a new representative variety. Again, the CPI compiler would wait until prices for the new taxi service were available for two successive periods and, using the overlap method, link the new price index into the existing classification for taxi services. And again, the cheaper taxi service would not be registered in the CPI measurement as a price fall for those who switched to it.

7.59 Alternatively, it might be considered that the new taxi service is so different from the existing one that it falls within a brand-new elementary aggregate, but still within COICOP 2018 code 07.3.2.2—passenger transport by taxi and hired car with driver. The new taxi service would have its own weight and *be incorporated into the index by adding a new elementary aggregate and redistributing the weight*. Again, prices for two successive periods are required and this procedure precludes the CPI from taking into account any effective fall in price arising from the availability of a substitute taxi service that is effectively cheaper.

7.60 An appropriate treatment in this stylized example would be to treat the new taxi provider as a comparable replacement: the assumption is that the same quality of service is maintained. If this assumption is valid, the price fall is captured by the index.

7.61 The inclusion of new products using the overlap method is, as outlined previously, a normal part of CPI compilation being undertaken on rebasing, when new elementary aggregates are introduced and outlets and representative varieties for elementary aggregates within them, are reinitialized. Price changes of the "old" sample are measured up to and including the overlap period, for example, December 2020 for an annually chained CPI, and then from December 2020 to include successive months in 2021, for the new sample. For example, if online purchases were introduced in the CPI in the rebasing from December 2020, the price relatives for December 2020 to January 2021 would include the price changes from online outlets, while that from November to December 2020 would exclude them. If prices in online outlets were cheaper than those in brick-and-mortar stores, the price fall experienced by consumers switching their expenditure from one to the other would not be registered.

7.62 A further example would be from an "outcomes" approach to medical services. Consider that an outcome is to fix a medical problem and a new medical procedure makes this cheaper. The overlap method used the price change of the old procedure up to the introduction of the new, and then links-in the price change of the new. The prices of the old procedure may be constant in the months prior to the new method and the price changes of the new procedure may also be constant when introduced, although at a lower level.

7.63 The underlying measurement flaw is that while the fixed basket is regularly updated to maintain the representativity of the CPI, it fails to reflect price change benefits resulting from switching to these new products.

Revolutionary New Products and Welfare (Utility) Gains

7.64 Revolutionary new products might be introduced on rebasing or, if attracting a high share of expenditure, through sample augmentation. In both instances, the overlap method while including the new product would not effectively capture the benefits experienced by the consumer from its purchase.

7.65 The successful introduction of a revolutionary new product leads to a welfare (utility) gain to consumers reflected in, and evidenced by, a switch in consumer expenditure to the new product. Consumers are better off as a result of their purchase of the new product. There is no preexisting service flow for a quality adjustment to be made. The introduction of the new product through either sample augmentation or a new elementary aggregate when updating using the overlap method misses the welfare gain at the moment of entry of the new good. It is only when two successive prices are available that the revolutionary new product is included, and then it is too late to capture the initial welfare gain. Consider the case of a new good to be introduced into a CPI, in period 3. A conceptually sound approach to its incorporation into the index is to impute its price for period 2, that is, to estimate its (Hicks) reservation (or choke) price. This is the price that would drive the demand for the good down to zero in the period prior to its introduction. The fall in the reservation price in period 2 to the actual price in period 3 might be substantial, though neglected in the CPI measurement. The measured CPI would be biased upward, in this welfare sense. An analogous approach applies to disappearing products, where the reservation price for a product last appearing in period 1, is estimated for period 2. Furthermore, delays in the introduction of the new product into the CPI might generate more bias. Typically, the price of a revolutionary product declines rapidly after introduction, so there would be an upward bias in delaying its introduction, again to the detriment of the credibility of the CPI regarding what may be high-profile products. Exiting products have the opposite welfare effect of new products and excluding the welfare loss of the exiting products would result in a downward biased CPI.

Evolutionary and Revolutionary Products: A Continuum

7.66 Evolutionary new products can be linked, with a quality adjustment, to the preexisting technology. This would be the case, for example, for household appliances, where the spin speed, running cost, reliability, and other price-determining features are improved. This might be as a replacement for an existing representative model with an explicit quality adjustment or integrated into the dynamic sample of models of washing machines sold each month using a database, scanner or web-based, that includes the quality characteristics of the models. Chapters 6 and 10 outline the hedonic methodology and data requirements for integrating such new evolutionary products into a CPI while avoiding the unrealistic assumptions implicit in the use of overlap linking-in of a new model that makes its use likely to misrepresent quality-adjusted price changes, as also outlined in Chapter 6.

7.67 However, evolutionary new products may combine both a continuing service and a "newness." For example, mobile phones could be considered an evolutionary good in the sense that they continued the provision of a communication service previously provided by landlines, but had a substantive revolutionary characteristic on introduction, their wireless mobility, and this defined their revolutionary newness. This service flow was further developed as the mobile phone became a platform for the extensive range of applications it is commonly used for. The introduction of mobile phones into the CPI when updating or through sample augmentation using the overlap method could not be justified as a simple continuation of an existing service. Similarly, color television was a continuation of a black-and-white service flow, but there is no simple metric of "more of the service flow" that could be used to encapsulate the switchover to such a new service feature.

Distinguishing between New Elementary Aggregates and New Products

7.68 New elementary aggregates are introduced on rebasing using the overlap method. The distinction between introducing a new product when updating the index and the introducing a new elementary aggregate should be made. For example, "*charges for undertaking and other funeral services*," under COICOP class 13.9.0, were newly introduced into a CPI on updating. Its inclusion in the CPI would neither be as a new revolutionary product providing a previously unavailable service to consumers nor as an evolutionary product providing a different, usually improved, existing service flow, for example, at a lower price. It is simply an updating of the basket of products consumers typically purchased resulting from an increased expenditure share over and above a threshold cutoff, meriting inclusion. There is neither a switch in consumers' expenditure away from an existing product to a new variant nor a welfare gain from consumers purchasing a revolutionary new product.

How to Respond to Limitations in the Use of the Overlap Method Regarding New Goods

7.69 When updating the CPI, the overlap method can be useful because of its virtues in updating the fixed basket, along with new weights, outlets, products, and representative varieties. However, publicizing the incorporation of a new product, for example, a technological innovation into the CPI using the overlap method may mislead users who may be expecting a fall in prices because of a switch to the new product but find that when introduced into the index, price changes are not reflected as such.[1] The overlap method would not provide a measure that could be explained in this manner. Simple statements to the effect that new goods are being incorporated into the CPI by use of the overlap method through either forced substitution, sample augmentation, sample rotation, or rebasing may damage the credibility of the CPI. An important response is transparency. To explain in the CPI dissemination publication that although the new products are being introduced so that its future successive price changes are reflected in the CPI, the price changes from consumers switching from one to the other will not.

7.70 Given the practical problems in introducing revolutionary new products into the CPI, NSOs may opt to define a CPI to exclude the implicit price falls and welfare gains arising from the introduction of revolutionary new products. "Welfare gains" and "reservation prices" are not considerations employed in the usual interpretation of CPIs. While there are studies on the estimation of such reservation prices, their practical use for CPI compilation is problematic.[2]

7.71 However, this is not to justify the statistical practice of an inability to include welfare gains on practical grounds. A reality of revolutionary new products is that the standard of living increases and this increase, when matched against changes in the nominal income, implies a price fall. When the CPI for the product group concerned does not reflect this fall, a recognition and explanation given in the CPIs metadata and "frequently asked questions" can reinforce the credibility of the CPI. Revolutionary new products, and evolutionary new products whose main innovation is a revolutionary service, should be introduced through sample augmentation and rebasing in a timely manner with adequate explanation as to the limitation of the measure.

7.72 Within the range of evolutionary and revolutionary products, CPI compilers should identify evolutionary new products whose main features are the extension of a preexisting service flow, although they may result from a new technology, and integrate the measures into the existing elementary aggregates using the techniques of explicit quality adjustment outlined in Chapter 6. There should be a recognition of the different aspects of the evolutionary products that would not be taken into account and these would be documented and explained to the user, much in the manner that the shortcomings in the introduction of revolutionary products.

7.73 There may be specific instances where a relatively homogeneous service flow is still provided by the evolutionary product. For example, specific varieties or services may now be sold through online or mobile applications. These may be cheaper and have better search options than would be possible using brick-and-mortar stores. The introduction of such new outlets using an overlap method would not enable the effective price fall to be included in the CPI. There is a different, positive service aspect of buying some items at brick-and-mortar locations that are not available online. It is possible that the service through a brick-and-mortar store is considered superior for some outlets/products. Again, the quality difference would not be reflected by simply linking-in an overlap price change.

7.74 If the purchases were considered homogeneous, a unit value index would appropriately reflect these differences. When there is price variation for the same quality of good or service, the price relatives used for index number calculation should be defined as the ratio of the weighted average price of that good or service in the two periods, the weights being the relative quantities sold at each price, a unit value index. For example, suppose that a certain quantity of a particular good or service is sold at a lower price to a particular category of purchaser without any difference in the nature of the good or service offered, location, timing or conditions of sale, or other factors. A subsequent increase in the proportion sold at the lower price lowers the average price paid by purchasers for quantities of a good or service whose quality is the same and remains unchanged, by assumption.

7.75 If the new good or service has a quality dimension different from the existing one, a judgment must be made as to the advantages of properly including the price fall in the index resulting from the cheaper online purchase, but not taking account of the other quality dimensions, as against simply introducing the outlet using the overlap method and ignoring effective decreases in average prices paid.

7.76 The simple use of the overlap method creates a distinct bias in the CPI as it overstates price inflation in ignoring the switch to cheaper prices. The benefits of the digital economy, in this respect, would be absent from the official statistics. CPI compilers would point to the integration of such outlets into the CPI sample, but this would only conceal the deficiency of the methodology; indeed, it might be argued that based on the CPI data the new online outlets have no impact on consumer prices.

7.77 The unit value's assumption of homogeneity of consumer services in the two types of outlets may be argued to open up a higher level of bias, the nature of which will vary depending on the product considered. Analytical

[1] It may be the case that a price increase is expected with the introduction of the new product, but consumers are aware that the CPI measurement may mitigate this because of the effect of the quality innovation on this price increase.

[2] Erwin Diewert, and Robert Feenstra. 2017. "Estimating the Benefits and Costs of New and Disappearing Products." Discussion Paper Series 17-10, University of British Columbia, Vancouver School of Economics; Erwin Diewert, Kevin J. Fox, and Paul Schreyer. 2017. "The Digital Economy, New Products and Consumer Welfare." Discussion Paper 17-09, University of British Columbia, Vancouver School of Economics; and Marshall Reinsdorf, and Paul Schreyer. 2017. "Measuring Consumer Inflation in a Digital Economy." Paper presented at the Fifth IMF Statistical Forum, Washington, DC, November 16–17. https://www.imf.org/en/News/Seminars/Conferences/2017/05/03/5th-statistical-forum.

frameworks for unit value indices with quality adjustments have been developed with this problem in mind.[3]

7.78 The recommendation is to provide as part of the published metadata detailed information on methods used to maintain the sample. This would include statistics on the use of temporary and permanently missing varieties and their replacements, and the methods employed for their replacement, as outlined in Chapter 6. Specific attention should be given to product areas where there is a high churn or expansion in model turnover and introduction of new products, as outlined in this chapter.

7.79 The metadata should be further extended to include an audit of new products that are believed to have a sufficient impact on the standard of living of households. The broad principles of how such new products are treated and any practical limitations in such treatment should be highlighted. The inclusion of the products should for the large part be focused on traditional criteria such as those product areas with relatively high (up-to-date) expenditure weights and should exclude free products.[4] The exclusion should not just be confined to expenditure weights but draw attention to relatively low-expenditure new products that are considered to be responsible for substantial increases in the standards of living. The document should be a living document updated regularly.

7.80 Impact studies and methodological developments are likely to have a cross-country relevance. Therefore, methodologies, and results, from single-country studies may be applied more generally, or at least cited so that users have some indication of the impact of specific new products. The Expert Group on Consumer Price Indices[5] and the Ottawa Group on Price Indices[6] may provide useful references for developments in such work.

Information Requirements Maintaining the Sample

7.81 Metadata are systematic, descriptive information about data content and organization that help those who operate the statistics production systems to remember what tasks they should perform and how they should perform them. Such data also serve to encourage transparency in the methods used and help ensure that they are understood and continued as staff members leave and others join. In the context of Chapter 6, a variety of methods might be employed for the treatment of missing prices and their replacement including implicit and explicit approaches and, further, the detailed use and nature of these methods for particular product groups may change over time. Metadata may need to be updated regularly. Such a monitoring system should serve to alleviate the monthly degradation of the price reference period sample for each product group. The term "metadata" is used to include this aspect of quality assurance.

7.82 A strategy for the maintenance of the sample must be linked to sample representativity, and it requires building a statistical metadata system. The CPI compilation requires the continual development of market information and the recording and evaluation of the sample development on a product-by-product basis. Such a metadata system relates to the variety of procedures for quality adjustments to prices discussed in Chapter 6 and how their suitability might vary on a case-by-case basis, all of which require documentation.

7.83 Metadata facilitate identifying those product groups where the sample is deteriorating and how it might be replenished. The metadata help counter the degradation of the static sample selected at the last rebasing by monitoring the use of appropriate replacements when variety prices go missing. It also can be used to ensure the static sample remains representative of the universe of transactions and is not biased against the introduction of new varieties and new products.

7.84 The metadata should monitor and document the extent of temporarily and permanently missing prices and methods used for quality-adjusted prices. Price indices for specific products, such as personal computers, may be derived using specific compilation and estimation routines and metadata are required to document such procedures. Because the rationale for the employment of different methods of treating missing variety prices and quality changes is usually specific to the features of the product groups concerned, information is required on such features. For example, data can be maintained on market features, such as the dates for the introduction of new products and the nature of their technological change. Information can also be collected and kept on out-of-sample developments (that is, market developments outside the static sample), such as the obsolescence of existing products and the emergence of new products onto the market. New technologies, products, and a proliferation of new varieties, accompanied by emerging brands, may grow to become responsible for a major part of the market. To increase transparency in the procedures used and allow the effort to be directed where it is most needed:

- NSOs should monitor the incidence of temporarily and permanently missing variety prices at perhaps a two-digit COICOP level, as appropriate, and if the incidence is high for a particular product group, at the three- or four-digit level. The advantage of a top-down approach is that resources are saved by monitoring at the detailed level only those product groups that are problematic.
- The ratios of temporarily missing prices, comparable replacements, and noncomparable replacements to the overall number of variety prices, and the methods for dealing with each of these three circumstances, should also be monitored. Against each product group, the weight of the product concerned should be listed so that a disproportionate effort is not given to relatively low-weighted products.

[3] Such work includes Mick Silver. 2011. "An Index Number Formula Problem: The Aggregation of Broadly Comparable Items." *Journal of Official Statistics* 27 (4): 553–67.

[4] As discussed in Reinsdorf and Schreyer (2017).

[5] The Expert Group on CPI is established by the Conference of European Statisticians. The meetings of the Group take place every second year, jointly organized by the United Nations Economic Commission for Europe and the International Labour Organization. The proceedings of the Expert Group meetings are available from the United Nations Economic Commission for Europe website, www.unece.org/statistics.

[6] The Ottawa Group is a city group set up in 1994 under the auspices of the United Nations Statistical Commission. It is dedicated to methodological work and applied research in CPI and other price statistics, and provides a forum for specialists and practitioners who work for or advise NSOs or international organizations to exchange experiences and thoughts. Information about the Ottawa Group and proceedings from its meetings are available from the Group's website, www.ottawagroup.org.

- The metadata system should be directed to the periodic monitoring, preferably on a monthly/quarterly basis, of the methods used for treating temporarily and permanently missing prices as recommended in Chapter 6.
- Such metadata should extend to the CPI compilers developing market expertise on selected high-profile, heavily weighted product groups where the consumer goods and services provided are sufficiently complex to impose on the measurement system the need for special consideration: product groups such as telecommunications, computers and computer-related hardware and software, electronics, property and rentals, internet purchases, and so forth, as outlined in Chapter 11.

7.85 The metadata might also include:

- Product-specific information, such as the timing of the introduction of new models, pricing policies, especially in months when no changes were made, and popularity of models and brands according to different data sources.
- Information arising from contacts with market research organizations, retailers, manufacturers, and trade associations for products for which replacement levels are high. The development of such contacts may lead, for example, to option cost estimates, which can be easily introduced. Where possible, staff should be encouraged to learn more about specific product groups whose weights are relatively high and where product replacement is common. Contacts with organizations concerning such product groups will allow staff to better judge the validity of the assumptions underlying implicit quality adjustments.
- Product groups likely to be undergoing regular technological change should be identified. The system should attempt to ascertain the pace at which models change and, where possible, the timing.
- Price-determining characteristics for those products undergoing technological change, especially if quality-adjustment procedures used make use of hedonic regressions. Information may be included from market research organizations, responding businesses, wholesalers, trade associations, and other such bodies. This should contribute to the statistical metadata system and be particularly useful in providing subsequent guidelines on product selection.
- An analysis is needed of what have in the past been judged to be "comparable" replacements with regard to the factors that distinguish the replacement and old product. The analysis should identify whether different price collectors are making similar judgments.
- When hedonic regressions are used either for partial patching of missing prices or as indices, information on the specification, estimated parameters, and diagnostic tests of the regression equations should be kept along with notes as to why the final formulation was chosen and used along with the data.
- A strategy for the use of alternative data sources for prices and weights including scanner data, web-based prices, monthly billing statements, and methodologies and software for their use. Such alternative sources are likely to directly benefit the maintenance of the representativity of a sample especially as there is a movement away from the static sample of matched-model method.

7.86 While these metadata reflect best practice, developing such detailed and comprehensive metadata requires significant resources. NSOs should begin developing detailed metadata on the incidence of temporarily and permanently missing prices. Understanding which items and varieties are missing, the duration the prices are missing, and why these prices are missing will serve as the first step for maintaining the sample. As resources permit, a plan to develop additional metadata over time can be developed and implemented.

Key Recommendations

- The samples of outlets, items, and varieties should be reviewed and updated as needed between regular index updates. This ensures that samples remain representative.
- A rotation policy could be implemented for the outlet sample, depending upon the availability of replacement outlets. For example, each year, 20 or 25 percent of the outlet sample is replaced by new outlets. This reduces the respondent burden and allows for the selection of new items and varieties.
- The variety sample should be reviewed on a routine basis as well to ensure that the selected varieties remain the most popular with regard to sales volume.
- New products should be introduced into the index as quickly as possible to ensure the index remains representative.
  - For evolutionary products, the new product replaces the obsolete product and maintains the same weights until the next index update. For example, streaming video services replaces the rental of DVD movies.
  - For revolutionary products, covered by an existing elementary aggregate, the new item can easily be included. If not covered by an existing elementary aggregate and data on sales to households are available, a new elementary aggregate can be developed for the new item. If no sales data are available, the new item can temporarily be included in a related elementary aggregate until the next weight update.
- Detailed metadata should describe methods used to maintain the samples of outlets and varieties. These metadata should include a description of how new products (both evolutionary and revolutionary products) are included in the index.

CALCULATING CONSUMER PRICE INDICES IN PRACTICE

8

Introduction

8.1 The purpose of this chapter is to provide a general description of the ways in which consumer price indices (CPIs) are calculated in practice. The methods used in different countries are not exactly the same, but they have much in common. There is clearly interest from both compilers and users of CPIs in knowing how most national statistical offices (NSOs) actually calculate their CPIs.

8.2 As a result of the greater insights into the properties and behavior of price indices that have been achieved in recent years, it is now recognized that some traditional methods may not necessarily be optimal from a conceptual and theoretical viewpoint. Concerns have also been voiced in a number of countries about possible biases that may be affecting CPIs. These biases and concerns are considered in Chapter 13. The methods used to compile CPIs are inevitably constrained by the resources available, not merely for collecting and processing prices, but also for gathering the expenditure data needed for weighting purposes. In some countries, the methods used may be severely constrained by lack of resources. Nonetheless, there are still methods that should be avoided at all costs because they result in severe bias in the indices.

8.3 The calculation of CPIs usually proceeds in two stages. First, price indices are estimated for the elementary aggregates. These are referred to as the elementary price indices. The elementary aggregate is the lowest level of groups of goods or services for which expenditure weights are assigned and kept constant for a period of one year or more. An elementary aggregate should consist of a relatively homogeneous set of goods or services, with similar end uses and similar expected price movements. More detailed weights to reflect the relative importance of individual price observations within elementary aggregates may be applied and updated more frequently. In the second stage, these elementary price indices are aggregated to obtain higher-level price indices using the expenditure shares of the elementary aggregates as weights. This chapter starts by explaining how the elementary aggregates are constructed, and what economic and statistical criteria need to be taken into consideration in defining the aggregates. The index number formulas most commonly used to calculate the elementary indices are then presented, and their properties and behavior illustrated using numerical examples. The advantages and disadvantages of the various formulas are considered, together with some alternative formulas that might be used instead. The problems created by disappearing and new varieties (that is, one variety with another of similar or different quality) are also explained, as well as the different ways of imputing values for missing prices.

8.4 The chapter also discusses the calculation of higher-level indices. The focus is on the ongoing production of a monthly price index in which the elementary price indices are averaged, or aggregated, to obtain higher-level indices. Price updating of weights, chain linking, and reweighting are discussed in Chapter 9. Data editing procedures are discussed in Chapter 5 on price collection. Statistical tools and methods for index analysis such as contributions to price change appear in Chapters 9 and 14.

8.5 While the purpose of this chapter is the compilation of CPIs at the various levels of aggregation, NSOs must keep in mind that the end goal of producing the indices is to disseminate and publish CPIs of high quality. To this end, the sampling process for selecting the items that are included in the indices and the price observations that are representative of the product varieties in the consumer markets are critically important in determining the quality of the indices at the elementary and aggregate levels. In this regard, the sampling procedures presented in Chapter 4 are very important to attain this end goal.

The Calculation of Price Indices for Elementary Aggregates

8.6 CPIs are typically calculated in two steps. In the first step, the elementary price indices for each of the elementary aggregates are calculated. In the second step, higher-level indices are calculated by taking weighted averages of the elementary price indices. The elementary aggregates and their price indices are the basic building blocks of the CPI.

Construction of Elementary Aggregates

8.7 Elementary aggregates are groups of relatively homogeneous goods and services (that is, similar in characteristics, content, price, or price change). They may cover the whole country or separate regions within the country. Likewise, elementary aggregates may be distinguished for different types of outlets. The nature of the elementary aggregates depends on circumstances and the availability of information, such as detailed expenditure data. Elementary aggregates may therefore be defined differently in different countries. Some key points, however, should be noted:

- Elementary aggregates should consist of groups of goods or services that are as similar as possible, and preferably fairly homogeneous in construction and content.
- Elementary aggregates should consist of varieties that may be expected to have similar price movements. The objective should be to try to minimize the dispersion of price movements within the aggregate.

- Elementary aggregates should be appropriate to serve as strata for sampling purposes in the light of the sampling regime planned for the data collection.

8.8 Each elementary aggregate, whether relating to the whole country or to an individual region or group of outlets, will typically contain a very large number of individual goods or services, or varieties. In practice, only a small number can be selected for pricing. When selecting the varieties, the following considerations need to be made:

- The varieties selected should be ones for which price movements are believed to be representative of most of the products within the elementary aggregate.
- The number of varieties within each elementary aggregate for which prices are collected should be large enough for the estimated price index to be statistically reliable. The minimum number required will vary between elementary aggregates depending on the nature of the products and their price behavior. However, there should be at least eight to ten observations for calculating the elementary index as discussed in Chapter 4.
- The objective is to try to track the price of the same variety over time for as long as the variety continues to be representative. The varieties selected should therefore be ones that are expected to remain on the market for some time, so that like can be compared with like, and problems associated with replacement of varieties be reduced.

The Aggregation Structure

8.9 The aggregation structure for a CPI is illustrated in Figure 8.1. Using a classification of consumers' expenditure such as the Classification of Individual Consumption According to Purpose (COICOP), the entire set of consumption goods and services covered by the overall CPI can be divided into divisions, such as "Food and Nonalcoholic Beverages." Each division is further divided into groups, such as "Food." Groups are divided into classes, such as "Cereals and Cereal Products." Classes are further divided into subclasses, such as "Cereals." Many countries use an even finer classification by further disaggregating below the level of the subclasses. For CPI purposes, each subclass can then be further divided into more homogeneous microclasses,[1] such as "Basmati Rice." The microclass could be the equivalent of the basic headings used in the International Comparison Program,[2] which calculates purchasing power parities between countries. Finally, the microclass may be further subdivided by dividing according to region or type of outlet, as in Figure 8.1. In some cases, a particular microclass cannot be, or does not need to be, further subdivided, in which case the microclass becomes the elementary aggregate. Within each elementary aggregate, one or more products are selected to represent all the products in the elementary aggregate. For example, the elementary aggregate consisting of "Bread" sold in supermarkets in the Northern region covers all types of bread, from which "Wheat Bread" and "Whole Grain Bread" are selected as representative products. Of course, more representative products might be selected in practice. Finally, for each representative product, several specific varieties should be selected for price collection, such as particular brands of wheat bread. Again, the number of sampled varieties selected may vary depending on the nature of the representative product.

Figure 8.1 Illustrative Aggregation Structure of a CPI[3]

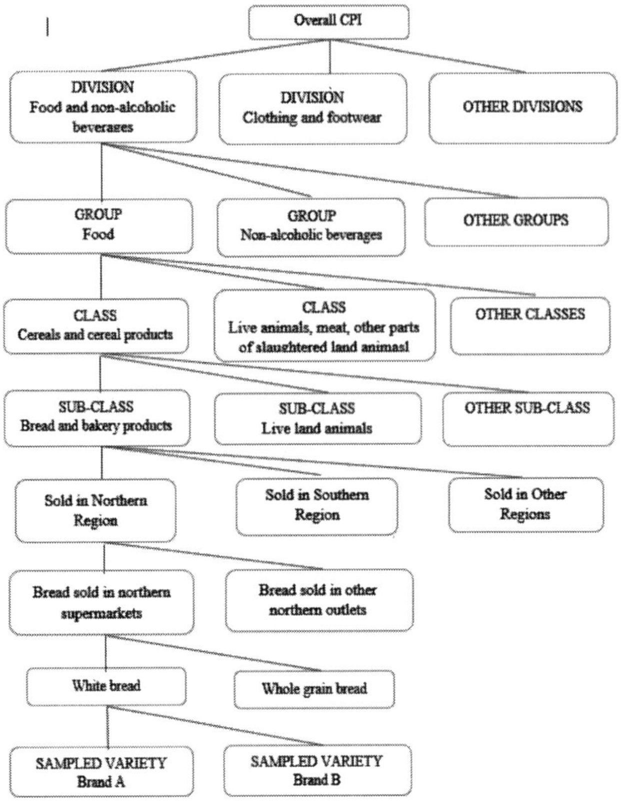

8.10 Methods used to calculate the elementary indices from the individual price observations are discussed in paragraphs 8.15–8.88. Working upward from the elementary price indices, all indices above the elementary aggregate level are higher-level indices that can be calculated from the elementary price indices using the elementary aggregate expenditure as weights. The aggregation structure should be consistent, so that the weight at each level above the elementary aggregate is always equal to the sum of its components. The price index at each higher level of aggregation can be calculated based on the weights and price indices for its components, that is, the lower-level or elementary indices. This applies for indices with fixed weights. If the weight structure is updated and the index series based on the new weights is chain linked, the linked index for the previous year is not consistent in aggregation. The individual elementary price indices not only should be designed to be sufficiently reliable to be published separately, but they should also remain the basic building blocks of all higher-level indices.

[1]In this Manual, levels below the subclass are referred to as microclasses.
[2]Additional information available at https://www.worldbank.org/en/programs/icp.

[3]The Classification of Individual Consumption According to Purpose 2018 structure breakdown includes divisions (food and beverages), group (food), class (cereals and cereal products), and subclass (bread and bakery products).

Weights within Elementary Aggregates

8.11 The ideal index number formula to use for CPI calculations would have weights for each price observation used to compile the elementary price indices, as well as weights for aggregating elementary indices to higher-level price indices. In some countries, this approach has been achieved through comprehensive sampling procedures or the use of scanner data for select item groups (for example, food). Those countries that have weights at this level use fixed-basket indices that are discussed in paragraphs 8.89–8.136. Also, having weights for both the weight reference period and the current period would be ideal to produce one of the preferred target indices for CPI compilation (Fisher, Törnqvist, or Walsh price indices). Several countries that have access to scanner data use the prices and quantities for the individual observations to derive elementary aggregate indices of their CPI.

8.12 In most cases, the price indices for elementary aggregates are calculated without the use of explicit weights. The elementary aggregate is simply the lowest level at which reliable expenditure weighting information is available. In this case, the elementary index must be calculated as an unweighted average of the prices of which it consists. However, even in this case, it should be noted that when the varieties are selected with probabilities proportional to the size of some relevant variables such as sales (as described in Chapter 4), weights are implicitly introduced by the sampling procedure.

8.13 For certain elementary aggregates information about sales of particular varieties, market shares, and regional weights may be used as explicit weights within an elementary aggregate. When possible, weights that reflect the relative importance of the sampled varieties should be used, even if the weights are only approximate.

8.14 For example, assume that the number of suppliers of a certain product such as fuel for cars is limited. The market shares of the suppliers may be known from business survey statistics and can be used as weights in the calculation of an elementary aggregate price index for car fuel. Alternatively, prices for water may be collected from a number of local water supply services where the population in each local region is known. The expenditure weights for each region may then be used to weight the price in each region in order to obtain the elementary aggregate price index for water. The calculation of weighted elementary indices is discussed in more detail in paragraphs 8.75–8.88.

Calculation of Elementary Price Indices

8.15 Various methods and formulas may be used to calculate elementary price indices. This section provides a summary of the methods that have been most commonly used and the advantages and disadvantages that NSOs must evaluate when choosing a formula at the elementary level. Chapter 6 of *Consumer Price Index Theory* provides a more detailed discussion.

8.16 The methods most commonly used are illustrated in a numerical example in Tables 8.1–8.3. In these examples, an elementary aggregate consists of seven varieties of an item that could be collected from several outlets, and it is assumed that prices are collected for all seven varieties in all months, so that there is a complete set of prices. There are no disappearing varieties, no missing prices, and no replacement varieties. This is quite a strong assumption since many of the problems encountered in practice are attributable to breaks in the continuity of the price series for the individual varieties for one reason or another. The treatment of disappearing and replacement varieties is taken up in paragraphs 8.51–8.74. It is also assumed that there are no explicit weights available.

8.17 The properties of the three indices used to compile elementary aggregates (Jevons, Dutot, and Carli) are examined and explained in some detail in Chapter 6 of *Consumer Price Index Theory* where it is shown that the Jevons is preferred in most circumstances when weights are not available. Here, the purpose is to illustrate how they perform in practice, to compare the results obtained by using the different formulas, and to summarize their strengths and weaknesses. These widely used formulas that have been, or still are, in use by NSOs to calculate elementary price indices are illustrated in Tables 8.1–8.3 by using average prices, averages of price relatives, and long-term versus short-term price relative methods. It should be noted, however, that these are not the only possibilities and some alternative formulas are considered later. The first is the Jevons index for $i = 1 \ldots n$ varieties. It is defined as the unweighted geometric mean of the price relatives, which is identical to the ratio of the unweighted geometric mean prices, for the two periods, 0 and t, to be compared:

$$I_J^{0:t} = \prod \left(\frac{p_i^t}{p_i^0} \right)^{\frac{1}{n}} = \frac{\prod \left(p_i^t \right)^{\frac{1}{n}}}{\prod \left(p_i^0 \right)^{\frac{1}{n}}} \tag{8.1}$$

The Jevons price index in 8.1 is calculated by comparing directly the prices of the two periods, 0 and t. Indices that are calculated by comparing the price of the reference period and the current period directly are referred to as direct indices.

8.18 Assuming the time from 0 to t exists for a number of periods, 0, 1, 2, … $t-1$, t, it is possible to calculate the index by first calculating the price indices from period to period, and then multiplying, or chaining, these together to obtain the price index from 0 to t:

$$I_{JC}^{0:t} = \Pi \left(\frac{p_i^t}{p_i^o} \right)^{\frac{1}{n}} = \frac{\Pi \left(p_i^1 \right)^{\frac{1}{n}}}{\Pi \left(p_i^0 \right)^{\frac{1}{n}}} \frac{\Pi \left(p_i^2 \right)^{\frac{1}{n}}}{\Pi \left(p_i^1 \right)^{\frac{1}{n}}} \cdots \frac{\Pi \left(p_i^t \right)^{\frac{1}{n}}}{\Pi \left(p_i^{t-1} \right)^{\frac{1}{n}}}$$

$$= \frac{\Pi \left(p_i^t \right)^{\frac{1}{n}}}{\Pi \left(p_i^0 \right)^{\frac{1}{n}}} = \Pi \left(\frac{p_i^t}{p_i^0} \right)^{\frac{1}{n}} \tag{8.2}$$

A price index calculated by multiplying the period-to-period, or short-term, price indices, is referred to as a chained or chain-linked price index. When calculating the Jevons index in 8.2 the numerators and denominators of periods 1, 2, … , $t-1$ cancel out leaving only the prices of period 0 and t, so that the resulting chained index is identical to the direct version of the index in 8.1.

8.19 The second elementary index formula is the Dutot index, defined as the ratio of unweighted arithmetic mean prices:

$$I_D^{0:t} = \frac{\frac{1}{n} \sum p_i^t}{\frac{1}{n} \sum p_i^0} \tag{8.3}$$

Table 8.1[4] Jevons and Dutot Price Indices Using Averages of Prices

Item A	Base	Jan.	Feb.	Mar.	Apr.	May	Jun.	Jul.
	Prices							
Variety 1	2.36	2.09	1.93	2.59	2.05	2.85	2.59	2.36
Variety 2	5.02	5.38	5.12	5.52	4.08	4.08	5.52	5.02
Variety 3	5.34	5.07	5.09	5.88	6.29	5.86	5.88	5.34
Variety 4	6.00	5.73	4.27	6.00	4.75	5.27	6.60	6.00
Variety 5	6.12	6.39	5.50	6.12	5.86	6.29	6.74	6.12
Variety 6	2.80	2.72	2.82	3.08	2.85	2.05	3.08	2.80
Variety 7	6.21	5.45	6.95	6.21	5.27	4.75	6.84	6.21
Geometric Mean Price	***4.55***	***4.38***	***4.20***	***4.81***	***4.17***	***4.17***	***5.01***	***4.55***
L-T Price Relative	*1.000*	*0.963*	*0.923*	*1.056*	*0.917*	*0.917*	*1.100*	*1.000*
S-T Price Relative		*0.963*	*0.959*	*1.143*	*0.868*	*1.000*	*1.200*	*0.909*
Arithmetic Mean Price	**4.84**	**4.69**	**4.53**	**5.06**	**4.45**	**4.45**	**5.32**	**4.84**
L-T Price Relative	*1.000*	*0.970*	*0.936*	*1.046*	*0.920*	*0.920*	*1.100*	*1.000*
S-T Price Relative		*0.970*	*0.965*	*1.117*	*0.880*	*1.000*	*1.196*	*0.909*
Jevons Index (L-T ratio of geometric mean prices)	**100.0**	**96.3**	**92.4**	**105.6**	**91.7**	**91.7**	**110.0**	**100.0**
Dutot Index (L-T ratio of arithmetic mean prices)	**100.0**	**97.0**	**93.6**	**104.6**	**92.0**	**92.0**	**110.0**	**100.0**
Jevons Index (chained S-T ratio of geometric mean prices)	**100.0**	**96.3**	**92.4**	**105.6**	**91.7**	**91.7**	**110.0**	**100.0**
Dutot Index (chained S-T ratio of arithmetic mean prices)	**100.0**	**97.0**	**93.6**	**104.6**	**92.0**	**92.0**	**110.0**	**100.0**

Table 8.2 Jevons and Carli Price Indices Using Averages of Long-Term Price Relatives

Item A	Base	Jan.	Feb.	Mar.	Apr.	May	Jun.	Jul.
	Long-Term (L-T) Price Relatives							
Variety 1	1.000	0.886	0.818	1.097	0.869	1.208	1.100	1.000
Variety 2	1.000	1.072	1.020	1.100	0.813	0.813	1.100	1.000
Variety 3	1.000	0.949	0.953	1.101	1.178	1.097	1.100	1.000
Variety 4	1.000	0.955	0.712	1.000	0.792	0.878	1.100	1.000
Variety 5	1.000	1.044	0.899	1.000	0.958	1.028	1.100	1.000
Variety 6	1.000	0.971	1.007	1.100	1.018	0.732	1.100	1.000
Variety 7	1.000	0.878	1.119	1.000	0.849	0.765	1.100	1.000
Geometric Mean of L-T Price Relatives	*1.000*	*0.963*	*0.924*	*1.056*	*0.917*	*0.917*	*1.100*	*1.000*
Jevons Index (L-T geometric changes)	**100.0**	**96.3**	**92.4**	**105.6**	**91.7**	**91.7**	**110.0**	**100.0**
Arithmetic Mean of L-T Price Relatives	*1.000*	*0.965*	*0.933*	*1.057*	*0.925*	*0.932*	*1.100*	*1.000*
Carli Index (L-T arithmetic changes)	**100.0**	**96.5**	**93.3**	**105.7**	**92.5**	**93.2**	**110.0**	**100.0**

Table 8.3 Jevons and Carli Price Indices Using Chained Short-Term Price Relatives

Elementary Aggregate A	Jan.	Feb.	Mar.	Apr.	May	Jun.	Jul.
Variety 1	0.886	0.923	1.342	0.792	1.390	0.911	0.909
Variety 2	1.072	0.952	1.078	0.739	1.000	1.353	0.909
Variety 3	0.949	1.004	1.155	1.070	0.932	1.003	0.909
Variety 4	0.955	0.745	1.405	0.792	1.109	1.253	0.909
Variety 5	1.044	0.861	1.113	0.958	1.073	1.070	0.909
Variety 6	0.971	1.037	1.092	0.925	0.719	1.501	0.909
Variety 7	0.878	1.275	0.894	0.849	0.901	1.438	0.909
Geometric Mean of S-T Price Relatives	*0.963*	*0.959*	*1.143*	*0.868*	*1.000*		
Jevons Index (chained S-T geometric changes)	**96.3**	**92.4**	**105.6**	**91.7**	**91.7**	**110.0**	**100.0**
Arithmetic Mean of S-T Aggregate Relatives	*0.965*	*0.971*	*1.154*	*0.875*	*1.018*	*1.219*	*0.909*
Carli Index (chained S-T arithmetic changes)	**96.5**	**93.7**	**108.1**	**94.6**	**96.3**	**117.4**	**106.7**

A chained Dutot price index is calculated as

$$I_{Dc}^{0:t} = \frac{\frac{1}{n}\sum p_i^1}{\frac{1}{n}\sum p_i^0}\,\frac{\frac{1}{n}\sum p_i^2}{\frac{1}{n}\sum p_i^1}\cdots\frac{\frac{1}{n}\sum p_i^t}{\frac{1}{n}\sum p_i^{t-1}} = \frac{\frac{1}{n}\sum p_i^t}{\frac{1}{n}\sum p_i^0} \qquad (8.4)$$

The third is the Carli index, defined as the unweighted arithmetic mean of the price relatives, or price ratios. The direct Carli and the chained Carli, respectively, are calculated as

$$I_C^{0:t} = \frac{1}{n}\sum\left(\frac{p_i^t}{p_i^0}\right) \qquad (8.5)$$

$$I_{Cc}^{0:t} = \frac{1}{n}\sum\left(\frac{p_i^1}{p_i^0}\right)\frac{1}{n}\sum\left(\frac{p_i^2}{p_i^1}\right)\cdots\frac{1}{n}\sum\left(\frac{p_i^t}{p_i^{t-1}}\right) \qquad (8.6)$$

The chained Carli should be avoided because it has a known, and potentially substantial, upward bias.[4]

8.20 Table 8.1 shows the comparison of the Dutot and Jevons indices using the monthly average prices. The first calculation for the Dutot index uses the average prices in the

[4]The results in the following tables are rounded to three decimals for aggregate price relatives and one decimal for price indices. The actual calculations are derived in an Excel spreadsheet.

long-term formula (direct approach) where each month's (t) average is compared to the initial base price (0) (that is, the base price reference period). The Dutot index is also calculated using the short-term relatives (chained approach) where the *month-to-month* changes in average prices are used to move forward the previous month's index level as shown in Table 8.3. The results are the same for both the direct and chained approaches in the Dutot calculations. Similarly, in Table 8.1 the Jevons index uses the geometric average prices in the long-term and short-term formulas to derive the price index levels that are the same for both the long-term and short-term method. The Jevons indices do, however, differ from those calculated using the Dutot formula.

8.21 In Table 8.2, the Jevons and Carli indices are calculated using the averages of long-term price relatives from the price reference period (base price). The results for the Carli indices are different from those of both the Jevons and Dutot indices. The Jevons indices are exactly the same whether calculated using ratio average prices or average of price relatives.

8.22 The properties and behavior of the different index formulas are summarized in paragraphs 8.21–8.48 (see also Chapter 6 of *Consumer Price Index Theory*). First, the differences between the results obtained by using the different formulas tend to increase as the variance of the price relatives, or ratios, increases. The greater the dispersion of the price movements, the more critical the choice of index formula, and method, becomes. If the elementary aggregates are defined in such a way that the price variations within the aggregate are minimized, the results obtained become less sensitive to the choice of formula.

8.23 Certain features displayed by the data in Tables 8.1 and 8.2 are systematic and predictable; they follow from the mathematical properties of the indices. For example, it is well known that an arithmetic mean is always greater than, or equal to, the corresponding geometric mean, the equality holding only in the trivial case in which the numbers being averaged are all the same. The direct Carli indices are therefore all greater than the Jevons indices, except in the price reference period, in June when all prices increased by 10 percent above their base prices, and the end period (July) when all prices return to their base price values. In general, the Dutot may be greater or less than the Jevons but tends to be less than the Carli.

8.24 The Carli and Jevons indices depend only on the price relatives and are unaffected by the price level. The Dutot index, in contrast, is influenced by the price level. In the Dutot index, price changes are implicitly weighted by the price in the base (price reference) period, so that price changes on more expensive products are assigned a higher importance than similar price changes for cheaper products (this can be seen from equation 8.3). In Tables 8.1 and 8.3, this is illustrated in the development of the March index where prices for varieties 4, 5, and 7, which have the highest base prices, are the same as in the price reference month and mitigate the 10 percent price increases of varieties 1, 2, 3, and 6 from the price reference month. The monthly Dutot price index is 104.6 versus 105.6 in the Jevons, and 105.7 in the Carli. Because of the relatively high base prices for varieties 4, 5, and 7, that results in a lower level for the Dutot index.

8.25 Another important property of the indices is that the Jevons and the Dutot indices are transitive, whereas the Carli is not. Transitivity means that the chained monthly indices are identical to the corresponding direct indices. This property is important in practice, because many elementary price indices are in fact calculated as chained indices that link together the month-on-month indices. The intransitivity of the Carli index is illustrated dramatically in Table 8.3 when each of the individual prices in the final month (July) return to the same level as it was in base month (as observed in Table 8.1), but the chained Carli registers an increase of 6.7 percent over the base month. Similarly, in June, although each individual price is exactly 10 percent higher than the base month, the chained Carli registers an increase of 17.4 percent. These results would be regarded as problematic in the case of a direct index, but even in the case of a chained index, the results seem so intuitively unreasonable as to undermine the credibility of the chained Carli. The price movements between April and May illustrate the effects of "price bouncing" in which the same seven prices are observed in both periods but they are switched between the different varieties. The monthly Carli index (short-term and long-term) increases from April to May whereas both the Dutot and the Jevons indices are unchanged.

8.26 One general property of geometric means should be noted when using the Jevons index. If any single observation out of a set of observations is zero, their geometric mean is undefined, whatever the values of the other observations. The Jevons index is sensitive to extreme falls in prices and it may be necessary to impose upper and lower bounds on the individual price ratios of, for example, 10 and 0.1, respectively, when using the Jevons index. This range should be determined after assessing the typical size of price movements and may vary across different product groups. Of course, extreme observations often result from errors, so extreme price movements should be carefully checked. It is not recommended to replace a zero price by an arbitrary low value in the Jevons index as this could lead to unstable results. If the Jevons index is used and the price moves from positive to zero, a practical solution is to split the aggregate into two and estimate weights for each part. The zero subindex multiplied by the positive weight plus the nonzero Jevons subindex multiplied by the remaining weight is well defined, and the price change is taken into account.

8.27 The message emerging from this brief illustration of the behavior of just three possible formulas is that different index numbers and methods can deliver very different results. With the knowledge of these interrelationships, one can infer that the chained Carli formula is not recommended. However, this information in itself is not sufficient to determine which formula should be used, even though it makes it possible to make a more informed and reasoned choice. It is necessary to appeal to other criteria to settle the choice of formula. There are two main approaches that may be used, the axiomatic and the economic approaches, which are presented in paragraphs 8.28–8.41. First, however, it is useful to consider the sampling properties of the elementary indices.

Sampling Properties of Elementary Price Indices

8.28 The interpretation of the elementary price indices is related to the way in which the sample of goods and services is drawn. Hence, if goods and services in the sample are selected with probabilities proportional to the population expenditure shares in the price reference period, then:

- The sample (unweighted) Carli index provides an unbiased estimate of the population Laspeyres price index (see equation 8.11).
- The sample (unweighted) Jevons index provides an unbiased estimate of the population geometric Laspeyres price index (see equation 8.14).

8.29 If goods and services are sampled with probabilities proportional to population quantity shares in the price reference period, the sample (unweighted) Dutot index would provide an estimate of the population Laspeyres price index. However, if the basket for the Laspeyres index contains different kinds of products whose quantities are not additive, the quantity shares, and hence the probabilities, are undefined.

Axiomatic Approach to Elementary Price Indices

8.30 As explained in Chapters 3 and 6 in *Consumer Price Index Theory*, one way to decide upon an appropriate index formula is to require it to satisfy certain specified axioms or tests. The tests throw light on the properties that different kinds of indices have, some of which may not be intuitively obvious. Four basic tests are cited to illustrate the axiomatic approach:

- *Proportionality test.* If all prices are λ times the prices in the price reference period, the index should equal λ. The data for June in Tables 8.1–8.3, when every price is 10 percent higher than in the price reference period, show that all three direct indices satisfy this test. A special case of this test is the *identity test*, which requires that if the price of every variety is the same as in the reference period, the index should be equal to unity, as in the last month (July) in the example.
- *Changes in the units of measurement test (commensurability test)*. The price index should not change if the quantity units in which the products are measured are changed, for example, if the prices are expressed per liter rather than per pint. The Dutot index fails this test, as explained in paragraphs 8.29–8.33, but the Carli and Jevons indices satisfy the test.
- *Time reversal test.* If all the data for the two periods are interchanged, the resulting price index should equal the reciprocal of the original price index. The chained Carli index fails this test, but the Dutot and the Jevons indices both satisfy the test. The failure of the chained Carli to satisfy the test is not immediately obvious from the example but can easily be verified by calculating the index backward from June to the index reference period. In this case, the chained Carli from June backward is 97.0 whereas the reciprocal of the forward chained Carli is (1/1.174) × 100 = 85.2.
- *Transitivity test.* The chained index between two periods should equal the direct index between the same two periods. It can be seen from the example in Tables 8.1–8.3 that the Jevons and the Dutot indices both satisfy this test, whereas the Carli index does not. For example, although the prices in July have returned to the same levels as the index reference period, the chained Carli registers 106.7. This illustrates the fact that the chained Carli may have a significant built-in upward bias.

8.31 Many other axioms or tests can be devised, but the previous ones[5] illustrate the approach and also throw light on some important features of the elementary indices under consideration in this Manual and provide evidence of the preference for the Jevons index.

8.32 The sets of products covered by elementary aggregates are meant to be as homogeneous as possible. If they are not fairly homogeneous, the failure of the Dutot index to satisfy the units of measurement or commensurability test can be a serious disadvantage. Although defined as the ratio of the unweighted arithmetic average prices, the Dutot index may also be interpreted as a weighted arithmetic average of the price relatives in which each relative is weighted by its price in the base price period.[6] This can be seen by rewriting formula 8.3 as

$$I_D^{0:t} = \frac{\frac{1}{n}\sum p_i^0 \left(\frac{p_i^t}{p_i^0}\right)}{\frac{1}{n}\sum p_i^0} \qquad (8.7)$$

However, if the products are not homogeneous, the relative prices of the different varieties may depend quite arbitrarily on the quantity units in which they are measured.

8.33 Consider, for example, salt and pepper, which are found within the same class of Classification of Individual Consumption According to Purpose. Suppose the unit of measurement for pepper is changed from grams to ounces, while leaving the units in which salt is measured (for example, kilos) unchanged. As an ounce of pepper is equal to 28.35 grams, the "price" of pepper increases by over 28 times, which effectively increases the weight given to pepper in the Dutot index by over 28 times. The price of pepper relative to salt is inherently arbitrary, depending entirely on the choice of units in which to measure the two goods. In general, when there are different kinds of products within the elementary aggregate, the use of the Dutot index is not acceptable.

8.34 The use of the Dutot index is acceptable only when the set of varieties covered is homogeneous, or at least nearly homogeneous. For example, it may be acceptable for a set of apple prices even though the apples may be of different varieties, but not for the prices of several different kinds of fruits, such as apples, pineapples, and bananas, some of which may be much more expensive per variety or per kilo than others. Even when the varieties are fairly homogeneous and measured in the same units, the Dutot's implicit weights may still not be satisfactory. More weight is given to the price changes for the more expensive varieties,

[5] Note that an index that satisfies the transitivity test and the identity test automatically also satisfies the time reversal test.

[6] Although the Jevons index is nonlinear, it can be approximated as a weighted average of price relatives, where the weights correspond to the square root of the inverse price relatives (see J. Mehrhoff. 2007. "A Linear Approximation to the Jevons Index." in: y.d. Lippe, P.M.).

but in practice, they may well account for only small shares of the total expenditure within the aggregate. Consumers are unlikely to buy varieties at high prices if the same varieties are available at lower prices.

8.35 It may be concluded that from an axiomatic viewpoint, both the Carli and the Dutot indices, although they have been, and still are, used by some NSOs, have disadvantages. The Carli index fails the time reversal and transitivity tests. In principle, it should not matter whether it is chosen to measure price changes forward or backward in time. It would be expected to give the same answer, but this is not the case for the chained Carli indices that may be subject to a significant upward bias. The Dutot index is meaningful for a set of homogeneous varieties but becomes increasingly arbitrary as the set of products becomes more diverse. On the other hand, the Jevons index satisfies all the tests listed in paragraph 8.28 and emerges as the preferred index when the set of tests is enlarged, as shown previously in paragraphs 8.28–8.29. From an axiomatic point of view, the Jevons index is clearly the index with the best properties.

Economic Approach to Elementary Price Indices

8.36 In the economic approach, the objective is to estimate an economic index, that is, a *cost of living index* (COLI) for the elementary aggregate (see Chapter 6 of *Consumer Price Index Theory*). The varieties for which prices are collected are treated as if they constituted a basket of goods and services purchased by consumers, from which the consumers derive utility. A COLI measures the minimum amount by which consumers would have to change their expenditures in order to keep their utility level unchanged, allowing consumers to make substitutions between the varieties in response to changes in the relative prices of varieties.

8.37 The economic approach is based on several assumptions about consumer behavior, market conditions, and the representativity of the sample. These assumptions do not always hold in reality. At the detailed level of elementary aggregates, special conditions will often prevail and change over time, and the information available about outlets, products, and market conditions may be incomplete. Thus, although the economic approach may be useful in providing a possible economic interpretation of the index, conclusions should be made with caution. In general, in the decision of how to calculate the elementary indices one should be careful not to put too much weight on a strict economic interpretation of the index formula at the expense of the statistical considerations.

8.38 In the absence of information about quantities or expenditure within an elementary aggregate, an economic index can only be estimated when certain special conditions are assumed to prevail. There are two special cases of some interest. The first case is when consumers continue to consume the same *relative* quantities whatever the relative prices. Consumers prefer not to make any substitutions in response to changes in relative prices. The cross-elasticities of demand are zero. The underlying preferences are described in the economics literature as "Leontief." In this first case, the Carli index calculated for a random sample would provide an estimate of the COLI if the varieties are selected with probabilities proportional to the population expenditure shares. If the varieties were selected with probabilities proportional to the population quantity shares (assuming the quantities are additive), the sample Dutot would provide an estimate of the underlying COLI.

8.39 The second case occurs when consumers are assumed to vary the quantities they consume in inverse proportion to the changes in relative prices. The cross-elasticities of demand between the different varieties are all unity, the expenditure shares being the same in both periods. The underlying preferences are described by a "Cobb–Douglas" utility function. With these preferences, the Jevons index calculated for a random sample would provide an unbiased estimate of the COLI, provided that the varieties are selected with probabilities proportional to the population expenditure shares.

8.40 On the basis of the economic approach, the choice between the sample Jevons and the sample Carli rests on which is likely to approximate more closely the underlying COLI: in other words, on whether the (unknown) cross-elasticities of demand are likely to be closer to unity or zero, on average. In practice, the cross-elasticities of demand could take on any value ranging up to plus infinity for an elementary aggregate consisting of a set of strictly homogeneous varieties (that is, perfect substitutes). It should be noted that in the limit when the products really are homogeneous, there is no index number problem, and the price "index" is given by the ratio of the unit values in the two periods. It may be conjectured that the average cross-elasticity is likely to be closer to unity than zero for most elementary aggregates, especially since these should be constructed in such a way as to group together similar varieties that are close substitutes for each other. Thus, in general, the Jevons index is likely to provide a closer approximation to the COLI than the Carli. In this case, the Carli index must be viewed as having an upward bias.

8.41 The use of the Jevons index in the context of the economic approach implies that the quantities are assumed to vary over time in response to changes in relative prices. As a result of the inverse relation of movements in prices and quantities, the expenditure shares are constant over time. Carli and Dutot, on the other hand, keep the quantities fixed while the expenditure shares vary in response to change in relative prices.

8.42 The Jevons index does not imply that expenditure shares remain constant. Obviously, the Jevons index can be calculated whatever changes do or do not occur in the expenditure shares in practice. What the economic approach shows is that if the expenditure shares remain constant (or roughly constant), then the Jevons index can be expected to provide a good estimate of the underlying COLI. Similarly, if the relative quantities remain constant, then the Carli index can be expected to provide a good estimate, but the Carli index does not actually imply that quantities remain fixed.

8.43 It may be concluded that, on the basis of the economic approach as well as the axiomatic approach, the Jevons emerges as the preferred index, although there may be cases in which little or no substitution takes place within the elementary aggregate and the direct Carli or Dutot indices might be used. The chained Carli should be avoided altogether. The Dutot index may be used provided the elementary aggregate consists of homogeneous products. In general, the index compiler should use the Jevons index for the elementary aggregates.

Chained versus Direct Indices for Elementary Aggregates

8.44 In a direct elementary index, the prices of the current period are compared directly with those of the price reference period. In a chained index, prices in each period are compared with those in the previous period, the resulting short-term indices being chained together to obtain the long-term index, as illustrated in Tables 8.1–8.3.

8.45 Provided that prices are recorded for the same set of varieties in every period, as in Table 8.1, any index formula defined as the ratio of the average prices will be transitive: that is, the same result is obtained whether the index is calculated as a direct index or as a chained index. In a chained index, successive numerators and denominators will cancel out, leaving only the average price in the last period divided by the average price in the reference period, which is the same as the direct index. Both the Dutot and the Jevons indices are therefore transitive. As already noted, however, a chained Carli index is not transitive and should not be used because of its upward bias.

8.46 Although the chained and direct versions of the Jevons and Dutot indices are identical when there are no breaks in the series for the individual varieties, they offer different ways of dealing with new and disappearing varieties, missing prices, and quality adjustments. In practice, products continually need to be excluded from the index and new ones included, in which case the direct and the chained indices may differ if the imputations for missing prices are made differently.

8.47 When a replacement variety must be included in a direct index, it will often be necessary to estimate the price of the new variety in the price reference (base) period, which may be some time in the past. The same happens if, as a result of an update of the sample, new varieties are linked into the index. If no information exists on the price of the replacement variety in the price reference period, it will be necessary to estimate it using price ratios calculated for the varieties that remain in the elementary aggregate, a subset of these varieties, or some other indicator. However, the direct approach should only be used for a limited period of time. Otherwise, most of the reference prices would end up being imputed, which would be an undesirable outcome. This effectively rules out the use of the Carli index over a long period of time, as the Carli should only be used in its direct form and not in chained form as previously discussed. This implies that, in practice, the direct Carli may be used only if the overall index is chain linked annually, or biannually.

8.48 In a chained index, if a variety becomes permanently missing, a replacement variety can be linked into the index as part of the ongoing index calculation by including the variety in the monthly index as soon as prices for two successive months are obtained. Similarly, if the sample is updated and new products must be linked into the index, this will require successive old and new prices for the present and the preceding months. For a chained index, the replacement variety for a missing observation would also need to have prices for the current and previous period. However, if the previous price is not available, it will have an impact on the index for two months, since the substitute observation cannot be used until the subsequent month. It also is possible to impute the price of the missing variety in the first missing month so that the next period price can be compared to the imputed price.

8.49 A missing price does not present such a problem in the case of a direct index. In a direct index a single, non-estimated missing observation will only have an impact on the index in the current period. For example, for a comparison between periods 0 and 3, a missing price of the replacement in period 2 means that the chained index excludes the variety for the last link of the index in periods 2 and 3. By comparison, the direct index includes it in period 3 since a direct index will be based on varieties whose prices are available in periods 0 and 3 (unless an imputation is made). In general, however, the use of a chained index can make the estimation of missing prices and the introduction of replacements easier from a computational point of view, whereas it may be inferred that a direct index will limit the usefulness of overlap methods for dealing with missing observations.

8.50 The direct and the chained approaches also produce different by-products that may be used for monitoring price data. For each elementary aggregate, a chained index approach gives the latest monthly price change, which can be useful for both data editing and imputation of missing prices. By the same token, however, a direct index derives average price levels for each elementary aggregate in each period, and this information may be a useful by-product. Nevertheless, because the availability of computing power at a low cost and of spreadsheets allows such by-products to be calculated whether a direct or a chained approach is applied, the choice of formula should not be dictated by considerations regarding by-products.

Consistency in Aggregation

8.51 Consistency in aggregation means that if an index is calculated stepwise by aggregating lower-level indices to obtain indices at progressively higher levels of aggregation, the same overall result should be obtained as if the calculation had been made in one step. For example, aggregating the elementary aggregate indices to the all-items index gives the same result as aggregating the group-level indices to the all-items index. For presentational purposes, this is an advantage. If the elementary aggregates are calculated using one formula and the elementary aggregates are averaged to obtain the higher-level indices using another formula, the resulting CPI is not consistent in aggregation. However, consistency in aggregation is not necessarily the most important criterion, and it is unachievable when the amount of information available on quantities and expenditure is not the same at the different levels of aggregation. In addition, there may be different degrees of substitution within elementary aggregates as compared to the degree of substitution between products in different elementary aggregates.

8.52 The Carli index would be consistent in aggregation with the Laspeyres index if the varieties were to be selected with probabilities proportional to expenditures in the reference period. This is typically not the case. The Dutot and the Jevons indices are not consistent in aggregation with a higher-level Laspeyres. As explained in paragraphs 8.88–8.94, however, the CPIs actually calculated by NSOs are usually not true Laspeyres indices, even though they may be based on fixed baskets of goods and services. If the higher-level index were to be defined as a geometric Laspeyres, consistency in aggregation could be achieved by using the Jevons index for the elementary indices at the lower level, provided that the individual varieties are sampled with probabilities proportional to expenditure. Although unfamiliar, a geometric Laspeyres has desirable properties from an economic point of view and is considered again later.

Missing Price Observations

8.53 The price of a variety may fail to be collected in some period either because the variety is missing temporarily or because it has permanently disappeared. The two classes of missing prices require different treatment as noted in Chapter 6. Temporary unavailability may occur for seasonal varieties (particularly for fruit, vegetables, and clothing), because of supply shortages, or possibly because of some collection difficulty (for example, an outlet was closed or a price collector was ill). The treatment of seasonal varieties raises several particular problems. These are dealt with in Chapter 11.

Treatment of Temporarily Missing Prices

8.54 In the case of temporarily missing observations for nonseasonal varieties, one of four actions may be taken:

- Omit the variety for which the price is missing so that a matched sample is maintained (like is compared with like) even though the sample is depleted
- Carryforward the last observed price
- Impute the missing price by the average price change for the prices that are available in the elementary aggregate
- Impute the missing price by the price change for a particular comparable variety from another similar outlet

8.55 Omitting an observation from the calculation of an elementary index is equivalent to assuming that the price would have moved in the same way as the average change in the prices of the varieties that remain included in the index. Omitting an observation changes the implicit weights attached to the other prices in the elementary aggregate.

8.56 Carrying forward the last observed price is not recommended, except in the case of fixed or regulated prices. Special care needs to be taken in periods of high inflation or when markets are changing rapidly as a result of a high rate of innovation and product turnover. While simple to apply, carrying forward the last observed price biases the resulting index toward zero change. In addition, when the price of the missing variety is recorded again, there is likely to be a compensating step change in the index to return to its proper value. The adverse effect on the index will be increasingly severe if the variety remains unpriced for some length of time. In general, to carryforward is not an acceptable procedure or solution to the problem of missing prices.

8.57 Imputation of the missing price by the average change of the available prices may be applied for elementary aggregates where the prices can be expected to move in the same direction. The imputation can be made using all the remaining prices in the elementary aggregate. As already noted, this is numerically equivalent to omitting the variety for the immediate period, but it is useful to make the imputation so that if the price becomes available again in a later period the sample size is not reduced in that period. In some cases, depending on the homogeneity of the elementary aggregate, it may be preferable to use only a subset of varieties from the elementary aggregate to estimate the missing price. In some instances, this may even be a single comparable variety from a similar type of outlet whose price change can be expected to be similar to the missing one. See Chapter 6 on imputation methods.

8.58 Tables 8.4A and 8.4B illustrate the calculation of the price index for the elementary aggregate where the price for variety 6 is missing in March. The long-term (direct) indices are therefore calculated based on the six varieties with reported prices. The short-term (chained) indices are calculated based on all seven prices from January to February and from April to July. From February to March and from March to April the monthly indices are calculated based on six varieties only.

8.59 The average prices (both arithmetic and geometric) are calculated using the six available prices for the base period, February, March, and April in Table 8.4A. The direct Jevons and Dutot indices use the average of the six prices in March and the base period to derive the March index (104.9 and 104.1, respectively). This calculation uses a matched sample for the prices available in each period (March and the base period) to derive the averages. In April, all seven prices are again available so the direct indices are derived by comparing the averages of the seven prices to their average in the base period.

8.60 For the chained Jevons and Dutot indices that use the short-term price relatives, the average prices for the six varieties available in March are compared to the average prices of the six available varieties in February. The resulting price relatives are multiplied by the February indices to derive the March indices (106.4 for the Jevons and 104.8 for the Dutot). The same holds true for April's compilation—the average of the six prices that were available in both March and April are used to derive the April indices (91.4 for the Jevons and 91.8 for the Dutot).

8.61 For both the Jevons and the Dutot indices, the direct and chained indices now differ from March onward. The first link in the chained index (January to February) is the same as the direct index, so the two indices are identical numerically. The direct index for March completely ignores the price increase of variety 6 between January and February, while this is counted in the chained index. As a result, the direct index is lower than the chained index for March. On the other hand, in April, when all prices are again available, the direct index captures the price development for the

Table 8.4A Jevons and Dutot Elementary Price Indices Using Averages with Missing Prices

	Base	Match	Jan.	Feb.	Mar.	Apr.	May	Jun.	Jul.
Elementary Aggregate A									
Variety 1	2.36	2.36	2.09	1.93	2.59	2.05	2.85	2.59	2.36
Variety 2	5.02	5.02	5.38	5.12	5.52	4.08	4.08	5.52	5.02
Variety 3	5.34	5.34	5.07	5.09	5.88	6.29	5.86	5.88	5.34
Variety 4	6.00	6.00	5.73	4.27	6.00	4.75	5.27	6.60	6.00
Variety 5	6.12	6.12	6.39	5.50	6.12	5.86	6.29	6.74	6.12
Variety 6	2.80		2.72	2.82		2.85	2.05	3.08	2.80
Variety 7	6.21	6.21	5.45	6.95	6.21	5.27	4.75	6.84	6.21
Geometric Mean Price (seven observations)	***4.55***		***4.38***	***4.20***		***4.17***	***4.17***	***5.01***	***4.55***
Geometric Mean Price (six matched observations)		***4.93***		***4.49***	***5.17***	***4.45***			
L-T Aggregate Relative	*1.000*		*0.963*	*0.924*	*1.049*	*0.917*	*0.917*	*1.100*	*1.000*
Jevons Index (direct)	**100.0**		**96.3**	**92.4**	**104.9**	**91.7**	**91.7**	**110.0**	**100.0**
Geometric Mean S–T Aggregate Relatives			**0.963**	**0.959**	**1.152**	**0.859**	**1.000**	**1.200**	**0.909**
Jevons Index (chained averages)	**100.0**		**96.3**	**92.4**	**106.4**	**91.4**	**91.4**	**109.7**	**99.7**
Arithmetic Mean Price (seven observations)	**4.84**		**4.69**	**4.53**		**4.45**	**4.45**	**5.32**	**4.84**
Arithmetic Mean Price (six matched observations)		**5.18**		**4.81**	**5.39**	**4.72**			
L-T Aggregate Relative	*1.000*		*0.970*	*0.936*	*1.041*	*0.920*	*0.920*	*1.100*	*1.000*
Dutot Index (direct)	**100.0**		**97.0**	**93.6**	**104.1**	**92.0**	**92.0**	**110.0**	**100.0**
S–T Aggregate Relatives			*0.970*	*0.965*	*1.120*	*0.876*	*1.000*	*1.196*	*0.909*
Dutot Index (chained averages)	**100.0**		**97.0**	**93.6**	**104.8**	**91.8**	**91.8**	**109.7**	**99.7**

Note: The text in gray refers to six matched observations whereas the text in bold refers to seven matched observations.

Table 8.4B Jevons and Carli Elementary Price Indices Using Relatives with Missing Prices

	Jan.	Feb.	Mar.	Apr.	May	Jun.	Jul.
Elementary Aggregate A							
Variety 1	0.886	0.818	1.097	0.869	1.208	1.100	1.000
Variety 2	1.072	1.020	1.100	0.813	0.813	1.100	1.000
Variety 3	0.949	0.953	1.101	1.178	1.097	1.100	1.000
Variety 4	0.955	0.712	1.000	0.792	0.878	1.100	1.000
Variety 5	1.044	0.899	1.000	0.958	1.028	1.100	1.000
Variety 6	0.971	1.007		1.018	0.732	1.100	1.000
Variety 7	0.878	1.119	1.000	0.849	0.765	1.100	1.000
Geometric Mean Price Relatives (seven observations)	***0.963***	***0.924***		***0.917***	***0.917***	***1.100***	***1.000***
Geometric Average Price Relatives (six observations)			***1.049***				
Jevons Index (mean L-T price relative)	**96.3**	**92.4**	**104.9**	**91.7**	**91.7**	**110.0**	**100.0**
Arithmetic Mean Price Relative (seven observations)	*0.965*	*0.933*		*0.925*	*0.932*	*1.100*	*1.000*
Arithmetic Mean Price Relative (six observations)			*1.050*				
Carli Index (average L-T price relative)	**96.5**	**93.3**	**105.0**	**92.5**	**93.2**	**110.0**	**100.0**
	S-T Price Relatives						
Elementary Aggregate A							
Variety 1	*0.886*	*0.923*	*1.342*	*0.792*	*1.390*	*0.911*	*0.909*
Variety 2	*1.072*	*0.952*	*1.078*	*0.739*	*1.000*	*1.353*	*0.909*
Variety 3	*0.949*	*1.004*	*1.155*	*1.070*	*0.932*	*1.003*	*0.909*
Variety 4	*0.955*	*0.745*	*1.405*	*0.792*	*1.109*	*1.253*	*0.909*
Variety 5	*1.044*	*0.861*	*1.113*	*0.958*	*1.073*	*1.070*	*0.909*
Variety 6	*0.971*	*1.037*			*0.719*	*1.501*	*0.909*
Variety 7	*0.878*	*1.275*	*0.894*	*0.849*	*0.901*	*1.438*	*0.909*
Geometric Mean Aggregate Relatives (seven observations)	**0.963**	**0.959**			**1.000**	**1.200**	**0.909**
Geometric Mean Aggregate Relatives (six matched observations)			*1.153*	*0.859*			
Jevons Index (chained S-T price relatives)	**96.3**	**92.4**	**106.4**	**91.4**	**91.4**	**109.7**	**99.7**
Arithmetic Mean Aggregate Relatives (seven observations)	***0.965***	***0.971***			***1.018***	***1.219***	***0.909***
Arithmetic Mean Aggregate Relatives (six matched observations)			***1.164***	***0.866***			
Carli Index (chained S-T *aggregate* relatives)	**96.5**	**93.7**	**109.1**	**94.5**	**96.2**	**117.3**	**106.6**

Note: The text in gray refers to six matched observations whereas the text in bold refers to seven matched observations.

full sample, whereas the chained index only tracks the long-term development in the six-price sample.

8.62 Table 8.4B shows the compilation of the Jevons and Carli indices using the long-term and short-term average of price relative methods. The long-term Carli index shows similar effects in March and April as those for the Jevons index in missing the long-term price change for variety 6. The short-term Carli, however, shows a significant upward bias as it increased to 106.6 when all the prices return to their base period levels in July.

8.63 As Tables 8.4A and 8.4B demonstrate, the Jevons, Dutot, and Carli direct indices return to 100.0 in the final period when all prices return to their base period levels. The chained versions do not, with the Carli showing a large upward drift by the end month and the Jevons and Dutot with a slight downward drift.

8.64 The problem with the chained index will be resolved if the missing price is imputed using the average short-term change of the other observations in the elementary aggregate. In Table 8.5A, the missing price for variety 6 in March is imputed using the geometric average of the price changes of the remaining varieties from February to March. While the imputation might be calculated using long-term relatives (that is, comparing the prices of the present period with the base period prices), the imputation of missing prices should be made based on the price change from the preceding to the present period, as shown in the table. Imputation based on the average price change from the base period to the present period should not be used as it ignores the information about the price change of the missing variety that has already been included in the index. The treatment of imputations is discussed in more detail in Chapter 6.

8.65 The calculations in Tables 8.5A and 8.5B show that when the missing price for variety 6 is imputed using the short-term price change of the other varieties, the trend of the Jevons, Dutot, and Carli indices reflect the changes for all the observations using the direct and long-term relative methods. For the Jevons and Dutot indices, the chained method gives the same results as the direct method. However, the chained Carli is significantly upward biased demonstrating that this method should not be used for index compilation.

Table 8.5A Jevons and Dutot Elementary Price Indices Using Averages with Imputed Prices

	Base	Match	Jan.	Feb.	Mar.	Apr.	May	Jun.	Jul.
Elementary Aggregate A	*Prices*								
Variety 1	2.36	2.36	2.09	1.93	2.59	2.05	2.85	2.59	2.36
Variety 2	5.02	5.02	5.38	5.12	5.52	4.08	4.08	5.52	5.02
Variety 3	5.34	5.34	5.07	5.09	5.88	6.29	5.86	5.88	5.34
Variety 4	6.00	6.00	5.73	4.27	6.00	4.75	5.27	6.60	6.00
Variety 5	6.12	6.12	6.39	5.50	6.12	5.86	6.29	6.74	6.12
Variety 6	2.80		2.72	2.82	3.25	2.85	2.05	3.08	2.80
Variety 7	6.21	6.21	5.45	6.95	6.21	5.27	4.75	6.84	6.21
Geometric Mean Price (seven observations)	***4.55***		***4.38***	***4.20***	***4.84***	***4.17***	***4.17***	***5.01***	***4.55***
Geometric Mean Price (six observations)		***4.93***		***4.49***	***5.17***				
L-T Aggregate Relative	*1.000*		*0.963*	*0.924*	*1.064*	*0.917*	*0.917*	*1.100*	*1.000*
Jevons Index (direct)	**100.0**		**96.3**	**92.4**	**106.4**	**91.7**	**91.7**	**110.0**	**100.0**
Geometric Mean S-T Aggregate Relative			*0.963*	*0.959*	*1.152*	*0.862*	*1.000*	*1.200*	*0.909*
Jevons Index (chained averages)	**100.0**		**96.3**	**92.4**	**106.4**	**91.7**	**91.7**	**110.0**	**100.0**
Variety 6 (imputed price)	2.80		2.72	2.82	3.16	2.85	2.05	3.08	2.80
Arithmetic Mean Price (seven observations)	**4.84**		**4.69**	**4.53**	**5.07**	**4.45**	**4.45**	**5.32**	**4.84**
Arithmetic Mean Price (six observations)		**5.18**		**4.81**	**5.39**				
L-T Aggregate Relative	*1.000*		*0.970*	*0.936*	*1.048*	*0.920*	*0.920*	*1.100*	*1.000*
Dutot Index (direct)	**100.0**		**97.0**	**93.6**	**104.8**	**92.0**	**92.0**	**110.0**	**100.0**
S–T Aggregate Relatives			*0.970*	*0.965*	*1.120*	*0.878*	*1.000*	*1.196*	*0.909*
Dutot Index (chained averages)	**100.0**		**97.0**	**93.6**	**104.8**	**92.0**	**92.0**	**110.0**	**100.0**

Note: The text in gray refers to six matched observations whereas the text in bold refers to seven matched observations.

Table 8.5B Jevons and Dutot Elementary Price Indices Using Relatives with Imputed Prices

	Jan.	Feb.	Mar.	Apr.	May	Jun.	Jul.
Elementary Aggregate A							
Variety 1	0.888	0.816	1.100	0.869	1.207	1.100	1.000
Variety 2	1.072	1.019	1.100	0.813	0.813	1.100	1.000
Variety 3	0.949	0.953	1.100	1.178	1.097	1.100	1.000
Variety 4	0.955	0.712	1.000	0.792	0.878	1.100	1.000
Variety 5	1.044	0.898	1.000	0.957	1.028	1.100	1.000
Variety 6	0.974	1.008	*1.160*	1.018	0.733	1.100	1.000
Variety 7	0.877	1.118	1.000	0.848	0.765	1.100	1.000
Geometric Mean Price Relatives (seven observations)	***0.963***	***0.924***	***1.064***	***0.917***	***0.917***	***1.100***	***1.000***
Jevons Index (average L-T *price* relatives)	**96.3**	**92.4**	**106.4**	**91.7**	**91.7**	**110.0**	**100.0**
Variety 6 (imputed L-T *price* relative)	*0.963*	*0.924*	***1.173***	*0.917*	*0.917*	*1.100*	*1.000*
Arithmetic Mean Aggregate Relatives (seven observations)	***0.933***	***1.067***	***0.925***	***0.932***	***1.100***	***1.000***	***0.933***
Carli Index (average L-T *price* relatives)	**93.3**	**106.7**	**92.5**	**93.2**	**110.0**	**100.0**	**93.3**
Elementary Aggregate A							
Variety 1	*0.886*	*0.923*	*1.342*	*0.792*	*1.390*	*0.909*	*0.911*
Variety 2	*1.072*	*0.952*	*1.078*	*0.739*	*1.000*	*1.353*	*0.909*
Variety 3	*0.949*	*1.004*	*1.155*	*1.070*	*0.932*	*1.003*	*0.908*
Variety 4	*0.955*	*0.745*	*1.405*	*0.792*	*1.109*	*1.252*	*0.909*
Variety 5	*1.044*	*0.861*	*1.113*	*0.958*	*1.073*	*1.072*	*0.908*
Variety 6	*0.971*	*1.037*	*1.152*	*0.877*	*0.719*	*1.502*	*0.909*
Variety 7	*0.878*	*1.275*	*0.894*	*0.849*	*0.901*	*1.440*	*0.908*
Geometric Mean Price Relatives (seven observations)	***0.963***	***0.959***	***1.152***	***0.862***	***1.000***	***1.200***	***0.909***
Jevons Index (chained S-T *price* relatives)	**96.3**	**92.4**	**106.4**	**91.7**	**91.7**	**110.0**	**100.0**
Variety 6 (imputed S-T price relative)	*0.963*	*0.959*	***1.164***	*0.782*	*1.000*	*1.200*	*0.909*
Arithmetic Mean Aggregate Price Relatives (seven observations)	***0.965***	***0.971***	***1.164***	***0.868***	***1.018***	***1.219***	***0.909***
Carli Index (chained S-T *price* relatives)	**96.5**	**93.7**	**109.2**	**94.7**	**96.4**	**117.5**	**106.8**

Note: The text in gray refers to six matched observations whereas the text in bold refers to seven matched observations.

Treatment of Permanently Disappeared Varieties

8.66 Varieties may disappear permanently for a number of reasons. The variety may disappear from the market because new varieties have been introduced or the outlets from which the price has been collected have stopped selling the product. Where varieties disappear permanently, a replacement variety must be sampled and included in the index. The replacement variety should ideally be one that accounts for a significant proportion of sales, is likely to continue to be sold for some time, and is likely to be representative of the sampled price changes of the market that the old variety covered. In practice when selecting replacement varieties, compromises must be found between representativity, comparability over time, and similarity.

8.67 The timing of the introduction of replacement varieties is important. Many new products are initially sold at high prices that then gradually drop over time, especially as the volume of sales increases. Alternatively, some products may be introduced at artificially low prices to stimulate demand. In such cases, delaying the introduction of a new or replacement variety until a large volume of sales is achieved may miss some systematic price changes that ought to be captured by CPIs. It is desirable to avoid making replacements when sales of the varieties they replace are significantly discounted in order to clear out inventory. In such cases, the disappearing variety's price should be returned to its last nondiscounted price as the new variety is introduced.

8.68 To include the new variety in the index, an imputed price needs to be calculated. The imputation will differ based on the formula used. For the Jevons index, the geometric average of short-term relatives is used, while for the Carli index, the arithmetic average of short-term relatives is used. For the Dutot index, the short-term relative of average prices is used. If a direct index is being calculated from average prices, the imputed price must be included in calculating the average prices in the current month. For the Jevons and Carli indices, the base price can be estimated by using the price ratio of the new variety price to the imputed price of the old variety as the relative quality difference. This ratio is then applied to the base price of the old variety. A different method must be used for estimating the Dutot base price that involves estimating the average base price using the long-term price change of the elementary aggregate.

8.69 Table 8.6 shows an example where variety A disappears after March and variety D is included as a replacement from April onward. Varieties A and D are not available on the market at the same time and their price series do not overlap. The base price estimation in the examples applies to the Jevons and Carli price indices. The methods for the Dutot price index are shown in Table 8.7.

8.70 If a chained index is calculated, the imputation method ensures that the inclusion of the new variety does not, in itself, affect the index and an adjustment of the base price is not necessary. In the case of a chained index, imputing the missing price by the average change of the available prices gives the same result as if the variety is simply omitted from the index calculation. However, by storing the imputed price as an observation, it can be used with a reported price for index calculation in the subsequent month as previously demonstrated in Table 8.5A. Thus, the chained index is compiled by simply chaining the month-to-month price movement between periods $t-1$ and t, based on the matched set of prices in those two periods, onto the value of the chained index for period $t-1$. In the example, no further imputation is required after April, and the subsequent movement of the index is unaffected by the imputed price change between March and April.

8.71 For the Dutot index, the short-term relative of average prices is used to make imputations. In the Dutot example in Table 8.7, the average base price used in the direct calculation must be adjusted for the relative difference between the old sample's average price and the new sample's average price. When using the long-term Dutot index based on an arithmetic mean of prices, the imputation of base price is made using the new sample average price and long-term elementary index to estimate the average base price. The trend of the index is affected by the level of the base prices where the movement of the observation with largest base price has the most importance in the trend of the elementary index. In the Jevons and Carli indices, each observation is equally important, and estimation of the base prices is not affected by the level of the other observations in the sample.

8.72 The adjusted base price in this example is derived by dividing the new average price level by the long-term price change of the elementary index. From another perspective, the adjusted base price is estimated by applying the ratio of the new sample's average price to the old sample's average price to the old base price. This implicitly assumes that the difference in the average prices reflects the difference in quality.

8.73 The situation is somewhat simpler when there is an overlap month in which prices are collected for both the disappearing and the replacement variety. In that case, it is possible to link the price series for the new variety to the price series for the old variety that it replaces. Linking with overlapping prices involves making an implicit adjustment for the difference in quality between the two varieties, as it assumes again that the relative prices of the new and old varieties reflect their relative qualities. For perfect or nearly perfect markets, this may be a valid assumption, but for certain markets and products, it may not be so reasonable. The question of when to use overlapping prices is dealt with in detail in Chapter 6. The overlap method is illustrated in Table 8.8.

8.74 In the example in Table 8.8 overlapping prices are obtained for varieties A and D in March. There is now an overlapping sample for March—one using varieties A, B, C, and the other using varieties B, C, and D. A monthly chain Jevons index of geometric mean prices will be based on the prices of varieties A, B, and C until March, and from April onward on the prices of varieties B, C, and D. The replacement variety is not included until prices for two successive periods are obtained. Thus, the monthly chain index has the advantage that it is not necessary to carry out any explicit imputation of a reference (base) price for the new variety. The same approach applies to the Dutot chain index.

8.75 If a direct index is calculated as the ratio of the arithmetic (geometric) mean prices, the price in the price reference period needs to be adjusted by deflation of the new average in March by the long-term index so that the March index level is maintained and the new sample does not affect the long-term price change through March. If a new reference price of variety D for January was imputed, different

Table 8.6 Replacing Varieties with No Overlapping Prices: Jevons and Carli Price Indices

	January	February	March	April	May
Elementary Aggregate B	*Prices*				
Variety A	6.00	7.00	5.00		
Variety B	3.00	2.00	4.00	5.00	6.00
Variety C	7.00	8.00	9.00	10.00	9.00
Variety D				9.00	8.00
Geometric Mean	**5.01**	**4.82**	**5.65**	**7.66**	**7.56**
Average of L-T Price Relatives		**0.992**	**1.151**	**1.360**	**1.540**
(a) No Imputations for Missing Prices *(price indices calculated directly from monthly averages)*					
Jevons Index—The Ratio of Geometric Mean Prices = Geometric Mean of Price Relatives					
Direct Index	100.0	96.1	112.6	152.9	150.8
Month-to-Month Change		0.961	1.171	1.357	0.986
Chained m/m Index	100.0	96.1	112.6	152.9	150.8
Carli Index—The Arithmetic Average of Price Relatives					
Direct Index	100.0	99.2	115.1	136.0	154.0
Month-to-Month Change		0.992	1.278	1.181	0.996
Chained m/m Index	100.0	99.2	127.0	149.9	149.3

(B) Imputation for Missing Prices

Jevons Index—The Ratio of Geometric Mean Prices = Geometric Mean of Price Relatives

Impute the Price of Variety A in April Using the S-T Relative of Average Prices: 5.00 × [(5 × 10)/(4 × 9)]$^{0.5}$ = ***5.89***
The April Average Price Is Derived as (5.89 × 5 × 10)$^{1/3}$ = 6.65
The April Index Is Derived Using the January Geometric Average Price (6.65/5.01) = 1.327 × 100 = 132.7
A January Base Price Is Set for Variety D to Be Equal to the Base Price of Variety A Adjusted for the Quality Difference = Relative Price Difference Between Varieties D and A in April: 6 × (9/5.89) = 9.17. By Taking the Geometric Average of the Base Prices of B, C, and D, One Then Obtains the adjusted Average of 5.77. The May Average Price Is (6 × 9 × 8)$^{1/3}$ = 7.56
The May Index Is Then Calculated as (7.56/5.77) × 100 = 130.9

	January	February	March	April	May
Elementary Aggregate B	*Prices*				
Variety A	6.00	7.00	5.00	5.89	
Variety B	3.00	2.00	4.00	5.00	6.00
Variety C	7.00	8.00	9.00	10.00	9.00
Variety D	9.17			9.00	8.00
Geometric Mean	5.01	4.82	5.65	6.65	
Adjusted Average	5.77			7.66	7.56
Direct Index	100.0	96.1	112.6	132.7	130.9
The Month-to-Month Changes Are Calculated from the Geometric Mean of Price Changes of Varieties A, B, C from January through April. The Monthly Change in May Is Calculated Using the Geometric Mean of Price Changes for Varieties B, C, D from April to May					
Month-to-Month Change		0.961	1.171	1.178	0.987
Chained m/m Index	100.00	96.1	112.6	132.7	130.9

Carli Index—The Arithmetic Mean of Price Relatives

The April Price of Variety A Is Missing, and the Average S-T Price Relative in April Is Derived from Varieties B and C: (5/4 + 10/9) × 0.5 = 1.181
Impute the Price of Variety A in April as 5.00 × 1.181 = ***5.90*** *, So That L-T Relative Is (5.90/6) = 0.984*
The Average L-T Relative in April Is (0.984 + 1.667 + 1.429)/3 = 1.360 × 100 =136.0, the April Index
A January Base Price Is Set for Variety D to Be Equal to the Base Price of Variety A Adjusted for the Quality Difference = Relative Price Difference between Varieties D and A in April: 6 × (9/5.90) = 9.15. The L-T Relative for Variety D in May Is (8/9.15) = 0.8745. The May Index Is (1/3 × (2.000 + 1.2857 + 0.8745)) = 138.67

	January	February	March	April	May
Elementary Aggregate B	*Prices*				
Variety A	6.00	7.00	5.00	5.90	
Variety B	3.00	2.00	4.00	5.00	6.00
Variety C	7.00	8.00	9.00	10.00	9.00
Variety D	9.15			9.00	8.00
	Price Relatives				
Variety A		1.167	0.833	0.984	
Variety B		0.667	1.333	1.667	2.000
Variety C		1.143	1.286	1.429	1.285
Variety D					0.874
Direct Index	100.00	99.2	115.1	136.0	138.7

results would be obtained because the price changes are implicitly weighted by the relative reference period prices in the Dutot index, which is not the case for the Carli or the Jevons indices. The April and May index change in the Dutot index is lower than the Jevons because the declines in price of varieties C and D have larger implicit weights in the Dutot (39 and 43 percent) versus the Jevons (33 and 33 percent).[7]

[7]The new sample starts in March as the price reference. The Dutot implicit weights are 17.4 percent (4/23), 39.1 percent (9/23), and 43.5 percent (10/23) percent, respectively, for varieties B, C, and D.

Table 8.7 Replacing Varieties with No Overlapping Prices: Dutot Index

	January	February	March	April	May
Elementary Aggregate B	*Prices*				
Variety A	6.00	7.00	5.00		
Variety B	3.00	2.00	4.00	5.00	6.00
Variety C	7.00	8.00	9.00	10.00	9.00
Variety D				9.00	8.00
Arithmetic Average	**5.33**	**5.67**	**6.00**	**8.00**	**7.67**
(a) No Imputations for Missing Prices					
Dutot Index—The Ratio of Arithmetic Mean Prices					
Direct Index	100.00	106.25	112.50	150.00	143.75
Month-to-Month Change		1.0625	1.0588	1.3333	0.9583
Chained m/m Index	100.00	106.25	112.50	150.00	143.75

(b) Imputation for Missing Prices

Dutot Index—The Ratio of Arithmetic Mean Prices

Impute the Price of Variety A in April Using the S-T Relative of Average Prices: 5.00 × (5 + 10)/(4 + 9) = **5.77**

The April Average Price Is Derived as (5.77 + 5 + 10)/3 = 6.92

The April Index Is Derived Using the January Average Price (6.92/5.33) = 1.2981 × 100 = 129.81

A New Imputed Average Price Is Calculated for January by Taking the April Arithmetic Mean Price of Varieties B, C, and D (5+10+9)/3 = 8 and Deflating the Value Using the April L-T Price Change (8/1.2981) = **6.16**

The May Index Is Then Calculated as (7.67/6.16) × 100 = 124.40

	January	February	March	April	May
Elementary Aggregate B	*Prices*				
Variety A	6.00	7.00	5.00	5.77	
Variety B	3.00	2.00	4.00	5.00	6.00
Variety C	7.00	8.00	9.00	10.00	9.00
Variety D				9.00	8.00
Arithmetic Mean	**5.33**	**5.67**	**6.00**	**6.92**	
Adjusted Average	***6.16***			8.00	**7.67**
Direct Index	100.00	106.25	112.50	129.81	124.40
The Month-to-Month Changes Are Calculated from the Average Price for Varieties A, B, C from January through April. The Monthly Change in May Is Calculated on the Average Price for Varieties B, C, D in April and May					
Month-to-Month Change		1.0625	1.0588	1.1538	0.9583
Chained m/m Index	100.00	106.25	112.50	129.81	124.40

Table 8.8. Disappearing and Replacement Varieties with Overlapping Prices

	January	February	March	April	May
Elementary Aggregate B	*Prices*				
Variety A	6.00	7.00	5.00		
Variety B	3.00	2.00	4.00	5.00	6.00
Variety C	7.00	8.00	9.00	10.00	9.00
Variety D			10.00	9.00	8.00
Geometric Average Price A,B,C; *(B,C,D)*	5.01	4.82	5.65 *(7.11)*	*(7.66)*	*(7.56)*
Arithmetic Average Price A,B,C; *(B,C,D)*	5.33	5.67	6.00 *(7.67)*	*(8.00)*	*(7.67)*
Jevons Index—The Ratio of Geometric Mean Prices = Geometric Mean of Price Ratios					
Chain the Monthly Indices Based on Matched Prices					
Month-to-Month Change	1.0000	0.9615	1.1713	*1.0774*	*0.9869*
Chained m/m Index	100.00	96.15	112.62	*121.33*	*119.75*
For the Direct Index, a New Imputed Average Price Is Calculated for January by Taking the Average Price of Varieties B, C, and D in March $(4 \times 9 \times 10)^{1/3}$ *= 7.11 and Deflating by the March L-T Index (1.1262) to Derive the Adjusted Base Price (6.31). This Calculation Maintains the Level of the March Index*					
The Adjusted Base Price Is Used to Compile the April and May Indices					
Direct Index	100.00	96.15	112.62	121.32	119.68
Dutot Index—The Ratio of Arithmetic Mean Prices					
Chain the Monthly Indices Based on Matched Prices					
Month-to-Month Change	1.0000	1.0625	1.0588	*1.0435*	*0.9583*
Chained m/m Index	100.00	106.25	112.50	*117.39*	*112.50*
For the Direct Index, a New Imputed Average Price Is Calculated for January by Taking Average Price of Varieties B, C, and D in March (4 + 9 + 10)/3 = 7.67 and Deflating by the March L-T Relative (1.1250) to Derive the Adjusted Base Price (6.81). This Calculation Maintains the Level of the March Index. This Adjusted Base Price Is Used to Compile the April and May Indices					
Direct index	100.00	106.25	112.50	117.39	112.50
Carli Index—The Arithmetic Mean of Price Relatives					
Variety A	1.0000	1.1667	0.8333		
Variety B	1.0000	0.6667	1.3333	1.6667	2.0000
Variety C	1.0000	1.1429	1.2857	1.4286	1.2857
Variety D	1.0000			1.0357	0.9206
L-T relative		0.9921	1.1508	1.3770	1.4021
Average L-T Relative for Elementary Index in March Is (0.8333 + 1.333 + 1.2857)/3 = 1.1508 × 100 =115.08, the March index					
Impute the Price of Variety D in January as 10.00 /1.1508 = **8.69** *, Keeping the L-T Relative as 1.1508 So That the Introduction of Variety D Does Not Affect the March Index Level. The New L-T Relatives for Variety D in April and May Are 1.3770 (9.00/8.69) and 0.9206 (8.00/8.69)*					
The Average L-T Relative for Varieties B, C, and D Are Used to Calculate the April and May Indices					
Direct Index	100.00	99.21	115.08	137.70	140.21

8.76 If the index is calculated as a direct Carli, the January base period price for variety D must be imputed by dividing the price of variety D in March (10.00) by the long-term index change for March (1.1508). This deflation of the variety D price maintains the index level in March. The long-term relative for replacement variety D in April and May is calculated by dividing the prices by the estimated base price (8.69) of variety D in January.

Calculation of Elementary Price Indices Using Weights

8.77 The Jevons, Dutot, and Carli indices are all calculated without the use of explicit weights. However, as already mentioned, in certain cases weighting information may be available that could be exploited in the calculation of the elementary price indices. Weights within elementary aggregates may be updated independently and possibly more often than the elementary aggregate weights themselves.

8.78 Sources of weights include scanner data for selected divisions, such as food and beverages. Because scanner data include quantities, the relative importance of sampled varieties can be calculated. Weights can also be developed by outlet or outlet type within an elementary aggregate. For example, for bread and bakery products, scanner data could provide data to develop weights for different grocery stores. In some countries, the household budget survey (HBS) includes a question asking respondents to identify the type of outlet where an expenditure on a particular item was made. These data could be used to develop weights for the different outlet types identified. Another potential source of data for developing weights for outlets or outlet type would be estimates of market shares obtained from business or trade groups and marketing firms. A special situation occurs in the case of tariff prices. A tariff is a list of prices for the purchase of a particular kind of good or service under different terms and conditions. One example is electricity, where one price is charged during the daytime while a lower price is charged at night. Similarly, a telephone company may charge a lower price for a call at the weekend than in the rest of the week. Another example may be bus tickets sold at one price to ordinary passengers and at lower prices to children or pensioners. In such cases, one option, depending upon the availability of data, would be to assign weights to the different tariffs or prices in order to calculate the price index for the elementary aggregate. Another option would be to calculate a unit value, as described in paragraph 8.85. However, changes in the tariff structure can be more difficult to capture. The treatment of tariffs is further discussed in Chapter 11.

8.79 The increasing use of electronic points of sale in many countries, in which both prices and quantities are scanned as the purchases are made, means that valuable new sources of information are increasingly available to NSOs. This could lead to significant changes in the ways in which price data are collected and processed for CPI purposes. The treatment of scanner data is examined in Chapter 11.

8.80 If the weight reference period expenditure for all the individual varieties within an elementary aggregate, or estimates thereof, were to be available, the elementary price index could itself be calculated as a fixed-basket price index, or as a geometric price index. The arithmetic index is calculated using a weighted arithmetic average of the price observations:

$$I_{\mathrm{EA}}^{0:t} = \sum w_i^b \cdot \left(\frac{p_i^t}{p_i^0}\right), \quad w_i^b = \frac{p_i^b \cdot q_i^b}{\sum p_i^b \cdot q_i^b} \tag{8.8}$$

where $I_{EA}^{0:t}$ is the elementary aggregate price index

p_i^0 is the base price observed for variety i

w_i^b is the weight for the variety in the weight reference period

8.81 The geometric index is calculated using a weighted geometric average of the price observations:

$$I_{ge}^{0:t} = \prod \left(\frac{p_i^t}{p_i^0}\right)^{w_i^b} \tag{8.9}$$

Table 8.9 Calculation of a Weighted Elementary Index

	Weight	December	January	February	Price Relative Dec.–Feb.
Variety A	0.80	7	7	9	1.2857
Variety B	0.17	20	20	10	0.0500
Variety C	0.03	28	28	12	0.4286
Weighted Arithmetic Mean of Price Relatives					**Index**
((9/7) × 0.8 + (10/20) × 0.17 + (12/28) × 0.03) × 100 =					112.64
Weighted Geometric Mean of Price Relatives					
((9/7)$^{0.8}$ × (10/20)$^{0.17}$ × (12/28)$^{0.03}$) × 100 =					105.95

8.82 Table 8.9 provides an example of calculations of fixed-base elementary aggregate indices. The group consists of three varieties for which prices are collected monthly. The expenditure shares are estimated to be 0.80, 0.17, and 0.03.

8.83 One option is to calculate the index as the weighted arithmetic mean of the price relatives, which gives an index of 112.64. The individual price changes are weighted according to their explicit weights, irrespective of the price levels. The index may also be calculated as the weighted geometric mean of the price relatives, which yields an index of 105.95.

Other Formulas for Elementary Price Indices

8.84 Another type of average is the harmonic mean. In the present context, there are two possible versions: either the harmonic mean of price relatives or the ratio of harmonic mean prices. The harmonic mean of price relatives is defined as

$$I_{\mathrm{HR}}^{0:t} = \frac{1}{\frac{1}{n}\sum \frac{p_i^0}{p_i^t}} \tag{8.10}$$

The ratio of harmonic mean prices is defined as

$$I_{\mathrm{RH}}^{0:t} = \frac{\sum \frac{n}{p_i^0}}{\sum \frac{n}{p_i^t}} \tag{8.11}$$

Formula 8.11, like the Dutot index, fails the commensurability test and would only be an acceptable possibility when the varieties are all fairly homogeneous. Neither formula appears to be used much in practice, perhaps because the harmonic mean is not a familiar concept and would not be easy to explain to users. Nevertheless, at an aggregate level, the widely used Paasche index is a weighted harmonic average.

8.85 The ranking of the three common types of mean is always arithmetic ≥ geometric ≥ harmonic. It is shown in Chapter 6 of *Consumer Price Index Theory* that, in practice, the Carli index (the arithmetic mean of the price ratios) is likely to exceed the Jevons index (the geometric mean) by roughly the same amount that the Jevons exceeds the harmonic mean. The harmonic mean of the price relatives has the same kind of axiomatic properties as the Carli index, but with opposite tendencies and biases. It fails the transitivity, time reversal, and price bouncing tests.

8.86 In recent years, attention has focused on formulas that can take account of the substitution that may take place within an elementary aggregate. As already explained, the Carli and the Jevons indices may be expected to approximate a COLI if the cross-elasticities of substitution are close to 0 and 1, respectively, on average. A more flexible formula that allows for different elasticities of substitution is the unweighted Lloyd–Moulton index:

$$I_{\text{LM}}^{0:t} = \left[\sum \frac{1}{n} \left(\frac{P_i^t}{P_i^0} \right)^{1-\sigma} \right]^{\frac{1}{1-\sigma}} \qquad (8.12)$$

where σ is the elasticity of substitution. The Carli and the Jevons indices can be viewed as special cases of the Lloyd–Moulton in which $\sigma = 0$ and $\sigma = 1$. The advantage of the Lloyd–Moulton formula is that σ is unrestricted. Provided a satisfactory estimate can be made of σ, the resulting elementary price index is likely to approximate the underlying COLI. The Lloyd–Moulton index reduces "substitution bias" when the objective is to estimate the COLI. The difficulty is the need to estimate elasticities of substitution, a task that will require substantial development and maintenance work. The formula is described in more detail in Chapter 4 of *Consumer Price Index Theory*.

Unit Value Indices

8.87 The unit value index is simple in form. The unit value in each period is calculated by dividing total expenditure on some product by the related total quantity. The quantities must be strictly additive in an economic sense, which implies that they should relate to a single homogeneous product. The unit value index is then defined as the ratio of unit values in the current period to that in the reference period. It is not a price index as normally understood, as it is essentially a measure of the change in the average price of a *single* product when that product is sold at different prices to different consumers, perhaps at different times within the same period. Unit values, and unit value indices, should not be calculated for sets of heterogeneous products. Unit value methods are discussed in more detail in Chapters 10 and 11.

Formulas Applicable to Scanner Data

8.88 As noted at the beginning of this chapter, it is preferable to introduce weighting information as it becomes available rather than continuing to rely on simple unweighted indices such as Carli and Jevons. Advances in technology, both in the retail outlets and in the computing power available to NSOs, suggest that traditional elementary price indices may eventually be replaced by superlative indices, at least for some elementary aggregates in some countries. A superlative index is a type of index formula that can be expected to approximate the COLI. An index is said to be exact when it equals the true COLI for consumers whose preferences can be represented by a particular functional form. A superlative index is then defined as an index that is exact for a flexible functional form that can provide a second-order approximation to other twice-differentiable functions around the same point. The Fisher, the Törnqvist, and the Walsh price indices are examples of superlative indices. Superlative indices are generally symmetric indices. The methodology must be kept under review in the light of the resources available.

8.89 Scanner data obtained from electronic points of sale have become an increasingly important source of data for CPI compilation. Their main advantage is that the number of price observations can be enormously increased and that both price and quantity information is available in real time. There are, however, many practical considerations to be taken into account, which are discussed in other chapters of this Manual, particularly in Chapter 10. To date, scanner data has been used for selected components of the CPI, primarily for goods.

8.90 Access to the detailed and comprehensive quantity and expenditure information within an elementary aggregate means that there are no constraints on the type of index number that may be employed. Not only Laspeyres and Paasche but superlative indices such as Fisher and Törnqvist can be calculated. However, the frequent weight and price changes that are prevalent in the scanner data cause several problems with index estimation. Scanner data application and formulas are discussed in more detail in Chapter 10.

The Calculation of Higher-Level Indices

8.91 As shown in Figure 8.1, the elementary indices are the starting point (building blocks) for calculating the CPI. These indices are then aggregated to successively higher levels (for example, city, region, class, or group), to derive the national all-items index. These higher-level indices are derived by aggregations using weights that are generally derived from an HBS, although other sources are presented in Chapter 3. The aggregation formulas can take several forms such as arithmetic and geometric depending on the target index. Fixed-basket indices tend to use arithmetic aggregations while for the superlative indices, the Törnqvist index uses geometric aggregations, the Walsh uses an arithmetic aggregation, and the Fisher is the geometric average of two arithmetic average price indices (Paasche and Laspeyres).

8.92 An NSO must decide on the target index at which to aim. The target index takes into consideration the observable price, quantity, and expenditure data that can be used to calculate the index in practice. The advantages of having a target index are the following:

- Providing reference and guidance for compilation of the CPI
- Ability to quantify the size of any bias, the differences between what is actually measured and what should be measured
- Use in identifying and making improvements to the CPI
- Being able to document the sources and methods used in the CPI and how they approximate the target index compilation

8.93 NSOs must consider what kind of index they would choose to calculate in the ideal hypothetical situation in which they had complete information about prices and quantities in both time periods compared. What is the purpose of the index? Should it measure both inflation and maintaining economic welfare? If so, the best CPI measure could be a COLI, and a superlative index such as a Fisher, Törnqvist, or Walsh would have to serve as the theoretical target. A superlative index may be expected to approximate the underlying COLI.

8.94 In many countries the purpose of the CPI is to measure inflation and to adjust wages, income, or social payments for changes in a fixed basket of goods and services, as discussed in Chapter 2. Thus, the concept of a *basket index* might be preferred, sometimes also referred to as a cost of goods index. A basket index is one that measures the change in the total value of a given basket of goods and services between two time periods. This general category of index is described here as a *Lowe index* (see Chapter 2 of *Consumer Price Index Theory*). It should be noted that, in general, there is no necessity for the basket to be the actual basket in one or other of the two periods compared. If the target index is to be a basket index, the preferred basket might be one that attaches equal importance to the baskets in both periods; for example, the Walsh index. Thus, the same index may emerge as the preferred target in both the cost of goods and the cost of living approaches.

8.95 In Chapters 2–4 of *Consumer Price Index Theory* the superlative indices Fisher, Törnqvist, and Walsh show up as being "best" in all the approaches to index number theory. These three indices, and the Marshall–Edgeworth price index, while not superlative, give very similar results so that for any practical reason it will not make any difference which one is chosen as the preferred target index. In practice, an NSO may prefer to designate a basket index that uses the actual basket in the earlier of the two periods as its target index on grounds of simplicity and practicality. In other words, the Laspeyres index may be the preferred target index. Similarly, if the quantities in both periods are available, the Walsh index, which is also a fixed-basket index, might be the target. The target indices, whether Fisher, Törnqvist, or Walsh, can be calculated retrospectively as additional expenditure estimates become available. The retrospective indices can then be used to assess the performance of the CPI and estimate the potential bias from the target index.

8.96 The theoretical target index is a matter of choice. In practice, it is likely to be either a Laspeyres or some superlative index. Even when the target index is the Laspeyres, there may be a considerable gap between what is actually calculated and what the NSO considers to be its target. Chapters 2–4 of *Consumer Price Index Theory* present the alternatives from a theoretical point of view. It is also shown that some combination of an arithmetic index such as the Laspeyres index and a geometric index such as geometric Laspeyres index may approximate the superlative Fisher and Törnqvist indices.[8] Such an approach may be the ideal solution when both of these indices or their proxies can be produced in real time. What many NSOs tend to do in practice varies; many use the Laspeyres index as their target, but a few have chosen the Fisher, Törnqvist, or Walsh as their targets.

Reference Periods

8.97 It is useful to recall that three kinds of reference periods may be distinguished:

- *Weight reference period.* The period covered by the expenditure data used to calculate the weights. Usually, the weight reference period is a period of 12 consecutive months.
- *Price reference period.* The period whose prices are used as denominators in the index calculation.
- *Index reference period.* The period for which the index is set to 100.

8.98 The three periods are generally different. For example, a CPI might have 2016 as the weight reference year, December 2018 as the price reference month, and the year 2015 as the index reference period. The weights typically refer to a whole year, or even two or three years, whereas the periods for which prices are compared are typically months, quarters, or a year. The weights are usually estimated on the basis of an expenditure survey that was conducted some time before the price reference period. For these reasons, the weight reference period and the price reference period are invariably different periods in practice. The price reference period should immediately precede the introduction of the updated index. For example, if January 2019 is the first month for the updated CPI, the price reference period would be December 2018 or the year 2018, depending on whether December or the full year is used as the price reference period.

8.99 The index reference period is often a year, but it could be a month or some other period. An index series may also be re-referenced to another period by simply dividing the series by the value of the index in that period, without changing the rate of change of the index. For the CPI, the expression "base period" can mean any of the three reference periods and is ambiguous. The expression "base period" should only be used when it is absolutely clear in context exactly which period is referred to.

[8] Janice Lent, and Alan H. Dorfman. 2009. "Using a Weighted Average of Jevons and Laspeyres Indexes to Approximate a Superlative Index." *Journal of Official Statistics* 25 (1): 129–49.

Higher-Level Price Indices as Weighted Averages of Elementary Price Indices

8.100 A higher-level index is an index for some expenditure aggregate above the level of an elementary aggregate, including the overall CPI. The inputs into the calculation of the higher-level indices are the following:

- The elementary aggregate price indices
- The expenditure shares of the elementary aggregates

8.101 The higher-level indices are calculated simply as weighted averages of the elementary price indices. The weights typically remain fixed for a sequence of at least 12 months. Some countries revise the weights at the beginning of each year to try to approximate as closely as possible to current consumption patterns, but many countries continue to use the same weights for several years and the weights may be changed only every five years or so. The use of fixed weights has a considerable practical advantage that the index can make repeated use of the same weights. This saves both time and resources. Revising the weights can be both time-consuming and costly, especially if it requires a new HBS to be carried out. The disadvantage is that as the weights become older, they are less representative of consumer purchasing patterns and usually result in substitution bias in the index.

Examples of Fixed-Basket Price Indices

8.102 When describing their calculation methods, some NSOs note that the Laspeyres price index is used for the calculation of higher-level aggregate indices; however, it is not possible to calculate a Laspeyres index in practice. The Laspeyres price index is defined as

$$I_L^{0:t} = \frac{\sum p_i^t \cdot q_i^0}{\sum p_i^0 \cdot q_i^0} = \sum w_i^0 \cdot \left(\frac{p_i^t}{p_i^0}\right), \quad w_i^0 = \frac{p_i^0 \cdot q_i^0}{\sum p_i^0 \cdot q_i^0} \quad (8.13)$$

where w_i0 indicates the expenditure shares for the individual varieties in the reference period. As the quantities are often unknown, the index usually will have to be calculated by weighting together the individual price relatives by their expenditure share in the price reference period, w_i^0. The expenditure shares are usually derived by consumption expenditure estimates from an HBS. The available weighting data may refer to an earlier period than the price reference period but may still provide a reasonable estimate.

8.103 While NSOs often refer to the Laspeyres formula for compiling their CPI, this is not the case. In fact, the most commonly used formulas for compiling the CPI are either the *Lowe* or *Young* formulas.[9] If the weights are derived from expenditure in period 0, the price reference period, as in equation 8.11, the index is a *Laspeyres* price index. If the weights from an early weight reference period b (that is, $b < 0$) are used directly in the index as expenditure shares in period 0, the index is known as a *Young index*. If the weights are updated for price change from b to 0, which keeps the quantity shares fixed, the index is called a *Lowe index*. This is similar to the attribution given to the more noted Laspeyres index where the $b = 0$ and the *Paasche index* where period t weights are used in a harmonic mean formula. Whether the Lowe or Young index should be used depends on how much price change occurs between the weight and price reference period as well as the target index. This is discussed in more detail in Chapter 9.

8.104 As noted, a more frequent version of equation 8.11 would be that of a Young or a Lowe index, where the weights are derived from an earlier period, $b < 0$. This is often the case because it may take a year or longer to compile the expenditure weights from the HBS before they are available for use in the CPI. The Young index is

$$I_Y^{0:t} = \sum w_i^b \cdot \left(\frac{p_i^t}{p_i^0}\right), \quad w_i^b = \frac{p_i^b \cdot q_i^b}{\sum p_i^b \cdot q_i^b} \quad (8.14)$$

8.105 The Young index is general in the sense that the shares are not restricted to refer to any particular period but may refer to any period or an average of different periods, for example. The Young index is a fixed-weight index where the focus is that the weights should be as representative as possible for the average value shares of the period covered by the index. A fixed-weight index is not necessarily a fixed-basket index (that is, it does not necessarily measure the change in the value of an actual basket such as the Lowe index). The Young index measures the development in the cost of a period 0 set of purchases with period b value proportions between the expenditure components. This does not correspond to the changing value of any actual basket, unless the expenditure shares have remained unchanged from b to 0. In the special case where b equals 0, it reduces to the Laspeyres.

8.106 In the case of the Lowe index the weights from period b are updated for price change between b and 0. The Lowe index is

$$I_{Lo}^{0:t} = \sum w_i^{b:0} \cdot \left(\frac{p_i^t}{p_i^0}\right), \quad w_i^{b:0} = \frac{p_i^0 \cdot q_i^b}{\sum p_i^0 \cdot q_i^b} \quad (8.15)$$

8.107 By price updating, the weights are aligned to the same reference period as the prices. If the NSO decides to price update the weights, the resulting index will be a Lowe index. The Lowe index is a fixed-basket index, which from period to period measures the value of the same (annual) basket of goods and services. Because it uses the fixed basket of an earlier period, the Lowe index is sometimes loosely described as a "Laspeyres-type" index, but this description is unwarranted. A true Laspeyres index requires the basket to be that purchased in the price reference month, whereas in most CPIs the basket refers to a period different from the price reference month. When the weights are annual and the prices are monthly, it is not possible, even retrospectively, to calculate a monthly Laspeyres price index.

Typical Calculation Methods for Higher-Level Indices

8.108 The most common method for calculating higher-level indices in the CPI is not done using individual prices or quantities. Instead, a higher-level index is calculated by averaging the elementary price indices by their predetermined weights. Using weights instead of quantities,

[9] The Young and Lowe indices are named for the nineteenth-century index number pioneers who advocated these indices.

equation (8.11) can be expressed as the following formula for aggregating price indices:

$$I_L^{0:t} = \sum w_j^b I_j^{0:t},\ \sum w_j^b = 1 \qquad (8.16)$$

where $I_L^{0:t}$ denotes the all-items CPI, or any higher-level index, from period *0* to *t*, and w_j^b is the weight attached to each of the elementary price indices where the weights sum to 1. $I_j^{0:t}$ is the corresponding elementary price index. The elementary indices are identified by the subscript *j*.

8.109 The weight reference period (*b*) usually will refer to a year, or an average of several years, that precedes the price refence period (*0*). If the weights are used as they stand, without price-updating, the resulting index will correspond to a Young index. If the weights are price-updated from period b to period 0, the resulting index will correspond to a Lowe price index.

8.110 Provided the elementary aggregate indices are calculated using a transitive formula such as Jevons or Dutot, but not Carli, and that there are no new or disappearing varieties from period *0* to *t*, equation 8.16 is equivalent to

$$I_{MLo}^{0:t} = \sum w_j^{b:0} I_j^{0:t-1} I_j^{t-1:t}, \sum w_j^{b:0} = 1 \qquad (8.17)$$

8.111 The difference is that equation 8.16 is based on the direct elementary indices from 0 to *t*, while (8.17) uses the chained elementary indices. $I_j^{t-1:t}$ is the short-term price index for the elementary aggregate between $t-1$ and *t*. A CPI calculated according to (8.17) in this manual is referred to as a modified Lowe index if the weights are price-updated from the weight reference period to the price reference period. If the weights are used as they stand, the index is referred to as a modified Young index.

8.112 The recommended procedure is to use the short-term price index formulation, instead of basing the aggregation on long-term elementary price indices compiled in a single stage.

8.113 There are two ways that the modified index can be compiled. First, chaining the monthly elementary indices into long-term price indices and compiling the higher-level indices by aggregating the elementary indices using the expenditure shares as weights. Alternatively, the modified index can be compiled by each month multiplying the expenditure weights with the elementary indices to form the long-term weighted relatives up to period $t-1$. These can then be multiplied with the elementary price indices from $t-1$ to *t* and the resulting series are aggregated into higher-level price indices. The two methods give identical results and it is up to countries to decide which to apply.

Some Alternatives to Fixed-Weight Indices

8.114 Monthly CPIs are typically arithmetic weighted averages of the price indices for the elementary aggregates, in which the weights are kept fixed over a number of periods that may range from 12 months to many years (but no more than five). The repeated use of the same weights relating to some past period *b* simplifies calculation procedures and reduces data collection requirements. It is also cheaper to keep using the results from an old HBS than to conduct an expensive new one. Moreover, when the weights are known in advance of the price collection, the index can be calculated immediately after the prices have been collected and processed.

8.115 The longer the same weights are used, however, the less representative they become of current consumption patterns, especially in periods of rapid technological changes when new kinds of goods and services are continually appearing on the market and old ones disappearing. This may undermine the credibility of an index that purports to measure the rate of change in the total cost of a basket of goods and services typically consumed by households. Such a basket needs to be representative not only of the households covered by the index but also of expenditure patterns at the time the price changes occur.

8.116 Similarly, if the objective is to compile a COLI, the continuing use of the same fixed basket is likely to become increasingly unsatisfactory the longer the same basket is used. The longer the same basket is used, the greater the upward bias in the index is likely to become. It is well known that the Laspeyres index has an upward bias compared with a COLI. However, a Lowe index between periods 0 and *t* with weights from an earlier period *b* will tend to exceed the Laspeyres between 0 and *t* by an amount that increases the further back in time period *b* is (see Chapter 2 of *Consumer Price Index Theory*).

8.117 There are several possible ways of minimizing or avoiding the potential biases from the use of fixed-weight indices. These are outlined in the following sections.

Annual Chaining

8.118 One way in which to minimize the potential biases from the use of fixed-weight indices is obviously to keep the weights and the index reference period as up to date as possible by frequent rebasing and chaining. Quite a few countries have adopted this strategy and revise their weights annually. In any case, as noted earlier, it would be impossible to deal with the changing universe of products without some chaining of the price series within the elementary aggregates, even if the weights attached to the elementary aggregates remain fixed. Annual chaining eliminates the need to choose a weight reference period, as the weight reference period is always the previous year ($t-1$), or possibly the preceding year ($t-2$).

8.119 *Annual chaining with current weights.* When the weights are changed annually, it is possible to replace the original weights based on the previous year, or years, by those of the current year, if the index is revised retrospectively as soon as information on the current year's expenditures becomes available. The long-term movements in the CPI are then based on the revised series. This method could provide unbiased or less-biased results.

Other Index Formulas

8.120 When the weights are revised less frequently, say every five years, another possibility would be to use a different index formula for the higher-level indices instead of an arithmetic average of the elementary price indices. An alternative method for aggregating elementary indices would be geometric aggregation. Geometric aggregation is similar to arithmetic aggregation but involves weighting each elementary index by the exponent of its share weight.

8.121 The geometric version of the Laspeyres index is defined as:

$$I_{GL}^{0:t} = \prod \left(\frac{p_i^t}{p_i^0} \right)^{w_i^0} = \frac{\prod \left(p_i^t \right)^{w_i^0}}{\prod \left(p_i^0 \right)^{w_i^0}}, \ \sum w_i^0 = 1 \qquad (8.18)$$

where the weights, w_i^0, are again the expenditure shares in the price reference period. When the weights are all equal, equation (8.18) reduces to the Jevons index. If the expenditure shares do not change much between the weight reference period and the current period, then the geometric Laspeyres index approximates a Törnqvist index. Using equation (8.18) the Geometric Young index, $I_{GY}^{0:t}$, can be derived using the weights w_j^b, and the Geometric Lowe index, $I_{GLo}^{0:t}$, can be derived using the weights $w_j^{b:0}$.

8.122 The geometric version of the Young index is defined as:

$$I_{GY}^{0:t} = \prod \left(I_j^{0:t} \right)^{w_j^b}, \ \sum w_j^b = 1 \qquad (8.19)$$

8.123 The geometric version of the Lowe index is defined as:

$$I_{GLo}^{0:t} = \prod \left(I_j^{0:t} \right)^{w_j^{b:0}}, \ \sum w_j^{b:0} = 1 \qquad (8.20)$$

8.124 Another form of aggregation that yields the same result as equation (8.18) is to convert the elementary indices to natural logarithms and use linear weighting of the logarithms. In this case, the result of the aggregation must be converted from natural logarithm to a real number (the antilog or exponential function). This formula is most suited for compilation purposes using spreadsheets or other similar software.

$$I_{GY}^{0:t} = \exp\left[\sum w_j^b \ln\left(I_j^{0:t} \right) \right] \qquad (8.21)$$

Again, note that if the weight reference period refers to period b, the index is a geometric Young index; if the reference period is 0, the index is a geometric Laspeyres index, and if the reference period is the average of periods 0 and t, it is a Törnqvist index. Recent empirical research discussed in Chapter 2 of *Consumer Price Index Theory* has indicated that taking a geometric-average of an upward biased fixed-weight arithmetic index and a downward biased fixed-weight geometric index may closely approximate the Fisher index. The reason for this close fit is that the possible upward bias in the arithmetic index is offset by a possible downward bias in the geometric index.

Arithmetic versus Geometric Aggregation for Higher-Level Indices

8.125 Given that both arithmetic and geometric aggregation can be used for compiling higher-level indices in the CPI, the question arises as to which is the most appropriate. An index using arithmetic aggregation will normally produce an index level that is greater than one using geometric aggregation for the same data points. The exception is when all prices change at the same rate, so both will give the same result. Chapter 2 of *Consumer Price Index Theory* suggests the following ordering in the levels of price indices: Young or Lowe > Laspeyres > Fisher > geometric Lowe or geometric Young > geometric Laspeyres > Paasche. The Törnqvist and Walsh price indices provide the same results as the Fisher, so that they will place in the same position as the Fisher. There are several factors to consider in the choice of the aggregation method:

- *The country target index.* The target index for the CPI is one factor to consider in deciding on the aggregation method. The CPI can be compiled as a fixed-basket cost of goods index. The target index could be a Laspeyres price index in which the quantity of items purchased is assumed to be fixed. Also, it could be a Walsh or Marshall–Edgeworth index where the fixed weights are averages of the base and current periods. This is a traditional approach for the CPI and the traditional arithmetic aggregation method would be used. The purpose of the index might be a COLI with the Fisher or Törnqvist price index as the target index. In this case, a geometric aggregation could be used. The Walsh index, which uses arithmetic aggregation, represents an equally good estimate of the COLI.
- *Timeliness and availability of source weight data.* Another factor in the aggregation formula decision is the timeliness of the expenditure weights. In most cases, the weights for the current period will take several months to become available and for the most part may only be available following an HBS. If the HBS or other source is conducted on an ongoing basis, a superlative index such as Fisher, Törnqvist, or Walsh can be calculated on a timelier basis, particularly if the CPI can be revised as the new weights become available.
- *Elasticity of substitution.* If the cross-elasticity of substitution is approximately 1, it implies that the expenditure shares are not changing as the relative change in prices is offset by the relative change in quantities purchased. In such a case where the expenditure shares remain unchanged, a geometric Young index would provide a close approximation to a superlative index and geometric aggregation would be justified. If, on the other hand, the cross-elasticity of substitution is close to zero, it implies that there is no change in quantities purchased as relative prices change. In such a case, the Laspeyres, Lowe, or Young price indices that assume quantities (or shares) remain fixed would be appropriate and arithmetic aggregation would be justified.
- *Consistency in aggregation.* To maintain consistency in aggregation, the same type of formula would be used throughout the aggregation process. Thus, if a Dutot or direct Carli index is used at the elementary level, then the arithmetic aggregation of indices should occur at higher levels. If a Jevons index is used at the elementary level, then the corresponding higher-level indices would use geometric aggregation. This criterion should not be the only one used in determining the method of aggregation.
- *Public understanding of the different averaging methods.* For decades the traditional definition for the CPI has been a fixed-basket index of constant quality. Public perception has been directed to understanding the fixed-basket concept where a historical basket is priced at today's prices. This also involves the understanding

of deriving higher-level indices as weighted arithmetic averages of component indices. This concept is widely understood by the public. The use of geometric aggregations and superlative indices has not been widely presented and discussed with the public and thus is not well understood. The result has been that most NSOs produce a fixed-basket index using arithmetic aggregation, although a few have begun producing a superlative version of the CPI, but often with a lag as the new weight data become available.

8.126 Which of these factors are the most important must be decided by the NSOs. To the extent that traditional fixed-basket indices are being produced and the public has a good understanding of these concepts, then NSOs will tend to stick with the traditional, and most commonly used, arithmetic aggregation. As NSOs move to implementing one of the superlative indices as their target index, then geometric aggregation could become more prevalent and public education about the target index and the methods for producing it should become a priority.

Retrospective Superlative Indices

8.127 It is possible to calculate a superlative price index retrospectively. Superlative indices, such as Fisher, Törnqvist, and Walsh, treat both periods symmetrically and require expenditure data for both periods. Although the CPI may have to be a Lowe or Young index when it is first published, it may be possible to estimate a superlative index later when much more information becomes available about consumers' expenditure period by period. In practice, currently one country publishes a Walsh index, while another publishes a Törnqvist index. The publication of revised or supplementary CPIs raises matters of statistical policy, although users readily accept revisions in other fields of economic statistics. Moreover, users are already confronted with more than one CPI in the European Union where the harmonised index for European Union purposes may differ from the national CPI. Thus, the publication of supplementary indices that throw light on the properties of the main index and which may be of considerable interest to some users seems justified and acceptable.

Use of Long-Term and Short-Term Links to Calculate the CPI

8.128 Consider a long-term chain index in which the weights are changed annually. The Walsh index requires weights from the previous and current years. In any given year, the current monthly indices are first calculated using the latest set of available weights, which cannot be those of the current year. However, when the weights for the year in question become available subsequently, the monthly indices can then be recalculated based on the weights for the current year. The resulting series can then be used in the long-term chain index, rather than the original indices first published. Thus, the movements of the long-term chain index from, say, any one December to the following December are based on weights of that same year, the weights being changed each December. This method has been developed by a European NSO.[10]

[10] P. Bäckström, and M. Sammar. 2012. "The Use of Superlative Index Links in the Swedish CPI." Paper presented at the Meeting of the Group of Experts on CPI, Geneva. https://www.unece.org/index.php.

8.129 Assume that each link runs from December to December. The long-term index for month m of year Y with December of year 0 as index reference period is then calculated using the formula:

$$I^{\text{Dec0}:mY} = \left(\prod_{y=1}^{Y-1} I^{\text{Dec}y-1:\text{Dec}y} \right) I^{\text{Dec}Y-1:mY} \tag{8.22}$$

$$= I^{\text{Dec0:Dec1}} I^{\text{Dec1:Dec2}} \ldots I^{\text{Dec}y-2:\text{Dec}Y-1} I^{\text{Dec}Y-1:mY}$$

8.130 In the actual practice of the European NSO, a factor scaling the index from December year 0 to the average of year 0 is multiplied onto the right-hand side of equation 8.22 to have a full year as the reference period. The long-term movement of the index depends on the long-term links only, as the short-term links are successively replaced by their long-term counterparts. For example, let the short-term indices for January to December 2018 be calculated as

$$I^{\text{Dec2018}:m2019} = \sum w_j^{2018(\text{Dec2018})} I_j^{\text{Dec2018}:m2019} \tag{8.23}$$

where $w_j^{18(\text{Dec18})}$ are the weights from 2018 price updated to December 2018, and $P_j^{\text{Dec18}:m19}$ is the price index from December 2018 to month 1 of 2019. In subsequent months (2, 3, …, 12), the price index is calculated with December 2018 as the base. When weights for 2019 become available, this is replaced by the long-term link:

$$I^{\text{Dec2018:Dec2019}} = \sum w_j^{2019(\text{Dec2018})} I_j^{\text{Dec2018:Dec2019}} \tag{8.24}$$

where $w_j^{19(\text{Dec18})}$ are the weights from 2019 price backdated to December 2018. The same set of weights from 2019 price updated to December 2019 is used in the new short-term link for 2020:

$$I^{\text{Dec2019}:m2020} = \sum w_j^{2019(\text{Dec2019})} I_j^{\text{Dec2019}:m2020} \tag{8.25}$$

When weights for 2020 become available, this is replaced by the long-term link:

$$I^{\text{Dec2019:Dec2020}} = \sum w_j^{2020(\text{Dec2019})} I_j^{\text{Dec2019:Dec2010}} \tag{8.26}$$

8.131 Using this method, the movement of the long-term index is determined by contemporaneous weights. The method is conceptually attractive because the weights that are most relevant for most users are those based on consumption patterns at the time the price changes actually take place. The method takes the process of chaining to its logical conclusion, at least assuming the indices are not chained more frequently than once a year. As the method uses weights that are continually revised to ensure that they are representative of current consumer behavior, the resulting index also largely avoids the substitution bias that occurs when the weights are based on the consumption patterns of some period in the past. The method may therefore appeal to NSOs whose objective is to estimate a COLI. This method also provides better deflators for national accounts.

8.132 A North American NSO[11] publishes a chained index using the Törnqvist price index and must use short-term links to calculate the current month index. The weights for the current period are lagged by about a year so that the current calculations are made using a different formula. In this case, the short-term link is estimated using the Lloyd–Moulton price index from equation 8.10, where the estimate of the elasticity of substitution is based on historical patterns.

8.133 Finally, it may be noted that these methods involve some revision of the index first published. In some countries, there is opposition to revising a CPI once it has been first published, although it is standard practice for other economic statistics, including the national accounts, to be revised as more information and more up-to-date information become available.

Calculation of Geographic and National Indices

8.134 CPIs are often calculated for individual geographic areas within a country and then aggregated to provide a national index based on the price movements in the individual areas. The aggregation approach is the same where elementary aggregates are combined using weights for each item index in the geographic area to derive the all-items CPI for the area. The elementary item indices are then aggregated using their area weights to derive the national item index. The formula for aggregation of items across areas to derive a national item index is

$$I_I^{0:t} = \sum_{a=1}^{k} w_{j,a}^{b}\left(I_{j,a}^{0:t}\right) / \sum_{a=1}^{k} w_{j,a}^{b} \qquad (8.27)$$

where $I_I^{0:t}$ is national index for item I from period 0 to t

$I_{j,a}^{0:t}$ is the area index for item j in area a from the period 0 to t

$w_{j,a}^{b}$ is the weight for item j in area a from the weight reference period b

k is the number of areas in the CPI

8.135 The national all-items index can be compiled by the aggregation of items across areas using their area weights:

$$I_N^{0:t} = \sum_{j=1}^{n}\sum_{a=1}^{k} w_{j,a}^{b}\left(I_{i,a}^{0:t}\right) / \sum_{j=1}^{n}\sum_{a=1}^{k} w_{j,a}^{b} \qquad (8.28)$$

where $I_N^{0:t}$ is the national all-items index from the period 0 to t

$I_{j,a}^{0:t}$ is the area index for item j in area a from the period 0 to t

$w_{j,a}^{b}$ is the weight for item j in area a from the weight reference period b

n is the number of items in the CPI

k is the number of areas in the CPI

8.136 The same result is obtained if the national item indices are aggregated using the national item weights:

$$I_N^{0:t} = \sum_{I=1}^{n} w_I^{b}\left(I_I^{0:t}\right) / \sum_{I=1}^{n} w_I^{b} \qquad (8.29)$$

where $I_N^{0:t}$ is the national all-items index from the period 0 to t

$I_I^{0:t}$ is national index for item I from period 0 to t

w_I^{b} is the national weight for item I in the weight reference period (sum of all area weights for that item)

n is the number of items in the CPI

Numerical Examples

8.137 Table 8.10 illustrates the calculation of higher-level indices using arithmetic aggregation where the weight and the price reference periods are identical (that is, $b = 0$). The index consists of five elementary aggregate indices and two intermediate higher-level indices, G and H. The overall index and the higher-level indices are all calculated using (8.29). Thus, for example, the overall index for April can be calculated from the two intermediate higher-level indices for April as

$$I^{\text{Jan:Apr}} = (0.6\times103.91)+(0.4\times101.79)=103.06$$

or directly from the five elementary indices as

$$I^{\text{Jan:Apr}} = (0.2\times108.75)+(0.25\times100)+(0.15\times104) + (0.1\times107.14)+(0.3\times100)=103.06$$

8.138 Table 8.10 illustrates the calculation of higher-level indices using geometric aggregation where the weight and the price reference periods are identical (that is, $b = 0$). The index consists of the same five elementary price indices and two intermediate higher-level indices, G and H. The overall index and the higher-level indices are all calculated using (8.29). Thus, for example, the overall index for April can be calculated from the two intermediate higher-level indices for April as

$$I^{(\text{Jan:Apr})} = [(103.85)^{0.6} + (101.74)^{0.4}] = 103.00$$

or directly from the five elementary indices as

$$I^{\text{Jan:Apr}} = \left[\begin{array}{l}(108.75)^{0.2}+(100)^{0.25}+(104)^{0.15}\\ +(107.14)^{0.1}+(100)^{0.3}\end{array}\right] = 103.00$$

8.139 The calculation of geographic area indices is similar to those for the national index. The items and their weights should be derived for an HBS that covers each area. If the HBS sample does not support independent estimates for each area, NSOs will often use the national item shares in the areas and collect price information for varieties in the areas. Such an approach assumes that there are no significant differences in the purchasing patterns among areas. This is a second-best solution as producing independent consumption estimates for each geographic area is preferred. The assumption of similar purchasing patterns across areas is often flawed. Usually, capital cities have quite different purchasing patterns from those of regional centers.

8.140 Another issue that arises when consumption expenditure weights are not available for the geographic areas

[11] David M. Friedman. 2016. "A New Estimation System for the US CPI—Capabilities and Impacts." Presentation at the Meeting of the Group of Experts on CPI, Geneva. http://www.unece.org/index.php.

Table 8.10 Aggregation of Elementary Price Indices

	Weight	January	February	March	April	May	June
Month-to-Month Elementary Price Indices							
EA *A*		100.00	102.50	104.88	101.16	101.15	100.00
EA *B*		100.00	100.00	91.67	109.09	101.67	108.20
EA *C*		100.00	104.00	96.15	104.00	101.92	103.78
EA *D*		100.00	92.86	107.69	107.14	100.00	102.67
EA *E*		100.00	101.67	100.00	98.36	103.33	106.45
Direct or Chained Monthly Elementary Price Indices with January = 100							
EA *A*	0.20	100.00	102.50	107.50	108.75	110.00	110.00
EA *B*	0.25	100.00	100.00	91.67	100.00	101.67	110.00
EA *C*	0.15	100.00	104.00	100.00	104.00	106.00	110.00
EA *D*	0.10	100.00	92.86	100.00	107.14	107.14	110.00
EA *E*	0.30	100.00	101.67	101.67	100.00	103.33	110.00
Total		100.00	100.89	99.92	103.06	105.03	110.00
Higher-Level Indices (arithmetic)							
$G = A + B + C$	0.6	100.00	101.83	99.03	103.91	105.52	110.00
$H = D + E$	0.4	100.00	99.47	101.25	101.79	104.28	110.00
Total		100.00	100.89	99.92	103.06	105.03	110.00
Higher-Level Indices (geometric)							
$G = A + B + C$	0.6	100.00	101.82	98.79	103.85	105.47	110.00
$H = D + E$	0.4	100.00	99.39	101.25	101.74	104.27	110.00
Total		100.00	100.84	99.77	103.00	104.99	110.00

EA = Elementary aggregate

Table 8.11 Aggregation of Elementary Price Indices (Arithmetic) across Locations

	Weight	January	February	March	April	May	June
Area 1							
EA *A*	0.12	100.00	102.50	107.50	108.75	110.00	110.00
EA *B*	0.15	100.00	100.00	91.67	100.00	101.67	110.00
EA *C*	0.09	100.00	104.00	100.00	104.00	106.00	110.00
EA *D*	0.06	100.00	92.86	100.00	107.14	107.14	110.00
EA *E*	0.18	100.00	101.67	101.67	100.00	103.33	110.00
All Items	**0.60**	*100.00*	*100.89*	*99.92*	*103.06*	*105.03*	*110.00*
Area 2							
EA *A*	0.08	100.00	103.53	108.04	108.21	110.82	110.55
EA *B*	0.10	100.00	101.00	92.13	99.50	102.43	102.17
EA *C*	0.06	100.00	105.04	100.50	103.48	106.79	106.53
EA *D*	0.04	100.00	93.79	100.50	106.61	107.94	107.67
EA *E*	0.12	100.00	102.69	102.18	99.50	104.11	103.85
All Items	**0.40**	*100.00*	*101.90*	*100.42*	*102.55*	*105.82*	*105.55*
National							
EA *A*	0.20	100.00	102.91	107.72	108.53	110.33	110.22
EA *B*	0.25	100.00	100.40	91.85	99.80	101.97	106.87
EA *C*	0.15	100.00	104.42	100.20	103.79	106.32	108.61
EA *D*	0.10	100.00	93.23	100.20	106.93	107.46	109.07
EA *E*	0.30	100.00	102.08	101.87	99.80	103.64	107.54
All Items	***1.00***	***100.00***	***101.29***	***100.12***	***102.86***	***105.34***	***108.22***

EA = Elementary aggregate

is which weights should be used. Often there is a tendency to use weights based on population. Again, population weights have a potential bias because one assumes that they are representative of distribution of consumption expenditure across areas, which is frequently not the case. The second-best solution would be to use area income estimates that should have a closer approximation to consumption than does the population.

8.141 Table 8.11 illustrates the calculation of higher-level indices using arithmetic aggregation where the weight and the price reference periods are identical (that is, $b = 0$). The index consists of five elementary aggregate indices in two geographic areas. The area all-items indices are calculated using equation 8.16 in which the weights are the items' share within the area. The national-level item indices are all calculated using equation 8.20. The national all-items index can be calculated using either equation 8.28 or 8.29. Thus, for example, the area 2 index for April is calculated from the five item-level indices for April as

$$I_a^{\text{Jan:Apr}} = [(0.08\times 108.21)+(0.10\times 99.50)+(0.06\times 103.48) +(0.04\times 106.61)+(0.12\times 99.50)]/0.4 = 102.55$$

The national item index for item A is calculated from the two area indices for item A:

$$I_I^{\text{Jan:Apr}} = \left[(0.12\times 108.75)+(0.08\times 108.21)\right]/\,0.20 = 108.53$$

The national all-items index is calculated using equation 8.15 as

$$I^{\text{Jan:Apr}} = [(0.2\times 108.53)+(0.25\times 99.8)+(0.15\times 103.79) + (0.1\times 106.93)+(0.3\times 99.8)]/\,1.0 = 102.86$$

Key Recommendations

- Elementary aggregates should be constructed to include groups of relatively homogeneous goods and services (that is, similar in characteristics, content, price, or price change).
- Elementary aggregates should be designed to be sufficiently reliable for publication. This promotes greater transparency and enhances user confidence in the data.
- Temporarily missing price observations should be imputed using all available prices or a subset of the available prices. The imputation of temporarily missing prices is especially important when using the modified Lowe or modified Young index. When using these formulas, a price in the previous period is needed. Without imputation, the sample of prices used to calculate the index deteriorates.
- In general, the Jevons formula should be used for the calculation of elementary indices because of its better statistical properties. With the Jevons formula, the results are identical whether the elementary index is calculated using the ratio of average prices or the average of price relatives. This is not the case when using the arithmetic mean.
- The Dutot index should be used only for homogeneous elementary aggregates since the price relatives are implicitly weighted by the price level in the reference period.
- The permanently missing goods or services should be replaced, and appropriate methods used to adjust for any changes because of the difference in quality. This ensures that the index remains representative and reflects only pure price change, not changes due to differences in quality.
- The chained Carli formula for elementary aggregates (arithmetic mean of price relatives) should not be used. The chained Carli has a well-known upward bias.
- It is recommended to calculate the elementary price indices by chaining the short-term (month-to-month) price indices. This short-term formula is preferred because it is more flexible and has a number of advantages, including (1) facilitation of the introduction of new outlets, items, and varieties; (2) imputations of temporarily missing prices should be made using the short-term change; and (3) facilitation of data verification since outliers in short-term changes are more readily identifiable than those in long-term ones.
- Higher-level price indices should be calculated using the short-term index formulation (modified Lowe and modified Young). Two methods for calculating the index using the short-term formula are described in the chapter and either method is acceptable.
- When compiling a national index, elementary aggregates for each region should be summed using their area expenditure weights to derive the national item index.

UPDATING CPI WEIGHTS AND LINKING NEW TO PREVIOUS CPI SERIES

9

Introduction

9.1 Consumer price index (CPI) weights should be updated on a periodic basis (see Chapter 3). The preferred interval is at least once every five years. This chapter discusses the processes and procedures for introducing a new basket and corresponding weights in the CPI as well as approaches for linking the new and previous CPI series following the introduction of new weights. It includes examples of the steps involved in linking CPI series with different price reference periods, methods to keep the current index reference period or shift to a new one and explores whether interim or partial weight updates might be implemented in the period between major surveys such as a Household Budget Survey (HBS).

Calculating a Chain Index

9.2 Assume that a series of fixed weight Young indices has been calculated with period 0 as the price reference period and that in a subsequent period, k, a new set of weights has to be introduced in the index. The new set of weights may, or may not, have been price-updated from the new weight reference period to period k. A chain index is then calculated as:

$$\begin{aligned} I^{0:t} &= I^{0:k}\sum w_j^k I_j^{k:t-1} I_j^{t-1:t} \\ &= I^{0:k}\sum w_j^k I_j^{k:t} \\ &= I^{0:k} I^{k:t} \end{aligned} \quad (9.1)$$

9.3 There are several important features of a chain index:

- The chain index formula allows weights to be updated and facilitates the introduction of new items and sub-indices and the removal of obsolete ones.
- In order to be able to chain the old and the new series, an overlapping period (k) is needed in which the index has to be calculated using both the old and the new set of weights.
- A chain index may have two or more links. In each link, the index may be calculated as a fixed weight index using equation 9.1, or indeed using any other index formula. The chaining period may be a month or a year, provided the weights and indices refer to the same period.
- Chaining is intended to ensure that the individual indices on all levels show the correct development through time.
- Chaining leads to non-additivity so that chained indices at the lower-level cannot be aggregated into indices at higher level using the latest set of weights. If, on the other hand, the index reference period is changed and the index series prior to the chaining period is rescaled to the new index reference period, this series cannot be aggregated to higher-level indices by use of the new weights.

9.4 An example of the calculation of a chain index is presented in Table 9.1. From 2008 to December 2016 the index is calculated with 2008 as weight and price reference period. From December 2016 onwards, a new set of weights is introduced. The weights may refer to the year 2014, for example, and may or may not have been price-updated to December 2016. A new fixed weight index series is then calculated with December 2016 as the price reference month.

Table 9.1 Calculation of a Chain Index

	Weight 2008	2008	Nov. 2016	Dec. 2016	Weight 2016	Dec. 2016	Jan. 2017	Feb. 2017	Mar. 2017
		2008 = 100				*December 2016 = 100*			
1. Elementary price indices									
A	0.20	100.00	120.00	121.00	0.25	100.00	100.00	100.00	102.00
B	0.25	100.00	115.00	117.00	0.20	100.00	102.00	103.00	104.00
C	0.15	100.00	132.00	133.00	0.10	100.00	98.00	98.00	97.00
D	0.10	100.00	142.00	143.00	0.18	100.00	101.00	104.00	104.00
E	0.30	100.00	110.00	124.00	0.27	100.00	103.00	105.00	106.00
Total		100.00	119.75	124.90		100.00	101.19	102.47	103.34
2. Higher-level indices									
G=A+B+C	0.60	100.00	120.92	122.33	0.55	100.00	100.36	100.73	101.82
H=D+E	0.40	100.00	118.00	128.75	0.45	100.00	102.20	104.60	105.20
Total		100.00	119.75	124.90		100.00	101.19	102.47	103.34
3. Chaining of higher-level indices to 2008 = 100									
G=A+B+C	0.60	100.00	120.92	122.33	0.55	122.33	122.78	123.22	124.56
H=D+E	0.40	100.00	118.00	128.75	0.45	128.75	131.58	134.67	135.45
Total		100.00	119.75	124.90		124.90	126.39	127.99	129.07

Finally, the new index series is linked onto the old index with year 2008 = 100 by multiplication to get a continuous index from 2008 to March 2017. The chained higher-level indices in Table 9.1 are calculated as:

$$I^{2008:t} = I^{2008:Dec2016} \sum w_j^{2008(Dec2016)} I_j^{Dec2016:t} \qquad (9.2)$$

9.5 Because of the lack of additivity, the overall chain index for March 2017 (129.07), for example, cannot be calculated as the weighted arithmetic mean of the chained higher-level indices G and H using the weights that was introduced from December 2016.

Updating Weights for Price Change: Pros and Cons

Approaches to Updating Weights

9.6 An issue that National Statistical Offices (NSOs) face in conducting revisions of the CPI is the timeliness of the data on weights and their introduction in the CPI. Typically, a HBS or other expenditure survey collects data during a prior year to the current time period. While the expenditure data from the HBS are the most commonly used source for developing weights, alternative sources can be used. For example, national accounts data. Alternative sources for developing weights are discussed in more detail in Chapter 3. Thus, the period to which the weights refer precedes the current period and the NSO cannot produce one of the target indices that require weights for the current period. When the weights are introduced, the price reference period precedes the current period and the time period over which the weights will be used extends beyond the current period. Thus, there is a continuum for the life cycle of the CPI that begins at a point in the past and continues to a point in the future, as illustrated in Figure 9.1.

9.7 The index must have a period to which the weights refer, the *weight reference period b*, when the expenditure data are collected over a period of months or quarters, usually for a year. The results of the survey are processed, compiled to provide estimates of expenditures by detailed products to establish elementary aggregates, and introduced in the CPI. In addition, the index must have a starting point, the *price reference period 0*, to which future prices will be compared in *current periods t*. The CPI will continue through time to its end point *T* after which a new set of weights, products, and prices will be introduced. Finally, the index must have a *index reference period* which is the period when the index is set to 100.

9.8 When introducing the new weights, NSOs must decide which method to use. There are two main options for updating the CPI weights: (i) price-updating the weights to the price reference period (Lowe index) to keep the implied quantities fixed at the weight reference period levels; or (ii) simply introducing the new weight structure (Young index) which keeps the expenditure shares fixed. This chapter examines what the choice of the updating method should be, using some objective criteria.

9.9 The target index for the CPI can be a Laspeyres price index which is easy to explain to users. It is a fixed quantity basket price index, with quantities held fixed in the price reference period. Alternatively, the target index for the CPI could also be the Fisher, Törnqvist, or Walsh price indices. Chapter 4 in *Consumer Price Index Theory* demonstrates that these three indices produce essentially the same results in practice. The Laspeyres index formula, however, is not generally used in practice. This is because the weight reference period, the period to which the expenditure weights refer, is generally earlier than the price reference period of the CPI. To derive an index that commences from its price reference period but keeps quantity weights fixed based on the earlier weight reference period, many NSOs would price update the earlier weights. In this way, the resulting Lowe index was often referred to as a "Laspeyres-type index." This raises the question of which index currently produced by NSOs would best approximate the target indices: the Lowe index with price-updated weights, or the Young index that simply uses the weights from the weight reference period.

9.10 For example, the European Union Harmonized Index of Consumer Prices (HICP)[1] is defined as a Laspeyres-type index where the weight reference period is year t-1 and the price reference period is December of year t-1. In practice, year t-1 expenditure data are not available, thus weights are derived using preliminary national accounts data referring to year t-2. The observed year t-2 expenditure may, or may not, be price updated between year t-2 and year t-1. The objective is to obtain the best possible estimate of the expenditure shares for the year t-1. If goods and services are perfect complements (i.e. there is no substitution between them and they are consumed in fixed proportions), the best approximation would be the price-updated weights. If goods and services are substitutes at such a rate that expenditure on one product relative to another is independent of the relative prices, the preferred approach would be not to price-update. It is possible to evaluate retrospectively which of the two options performs better by comparing the outcomes with that from using actual expenditure shares when they become available. The degree of substitution may vary across products, so the choice between these two options is not necessarily straightforward. In any case, the estimate of the expenditure shares for the year t-1 are always price-updated to the price reference period, December of year t-1.

9.11

Figure 9.1 The CPI Life Cycle

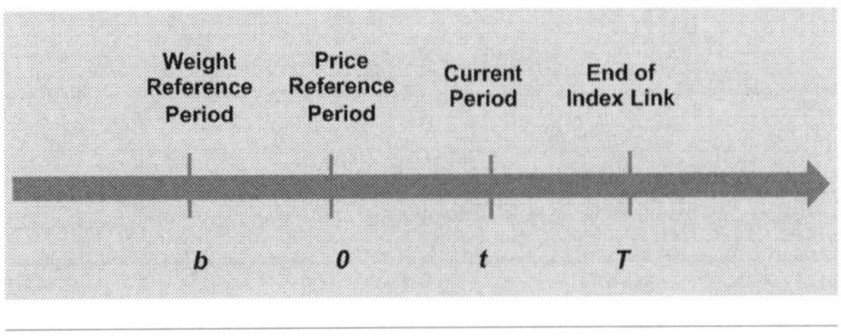

Should NSOs Use the Lowe or the Young Index (To Price Update or Not)?

9.12 In Chapter 3 of *Consumer Price Index Theory* various axioms are used to measure the performance of different price index formulas. From an axiomatic point of view, the Lowe

[1] See also *Harmonized Index of Consumer Prices (HICP) Methodological Manual*, Section 3.5, https://ec.europa.eu/eurostat/web/products-manuals-and-guidelines/-/KS-GQ-17-015

index performs better than the Young index. Of the twelve tests used, the Lowe passes all, while the Young index passes ten, failing the time reversal and the circularity tests. Thus, some NSOs consider the Lowe index preferable to the Young index.

9.13 The recent research cited suggests that price updating weights before introducing them in the CPI may not be the best approach for the CPI based on the performance of the resulting index formula when compared to the preferred target indices. Price-updating the expenditure shares does not imply that the resulting weights are necessarily more up to date. When there is a strong inverse relation between movements of price and quantities, price-updating on its own could produce unreliable results. For example, assume the price of beef increases relative to the price of chicken. If the quantities are held fixed while the prices are updated, the resulting expenditure weights for beef would increase substantially while the expenditure weights for chicken would decrease. In fact, consumers would spend less on beef and spend more on the relative less expensive chicken; however, because the quantities are fixed and the changes in relative expenditure are not reflected by price updating.

9.14 By price updating, the weights are aligned to the same reference period as the prices. If the NSO decides to price update the weights, the resulting index will be a Lowe index. The Lowe index is a fixed basket index, which from period to period measure the value of the same (annual) basket of goods and services.

9.15 Not price-updating the weights results in the calculation of a Young index. The Young index keeps the expenditure shares fixed in the expenditure survey period *b*. The Young index is a *fixed weight index* where focus is that the weights should be as representative as possible for the average value shares of the period covered by the index.

9.16 By keeping the expenditure shares constant from the weight reference period to the price reference period the underlying quantities are assumed to vary in response to changes in relative prices. Hence, if households tend to keep constant expenditure shares by substituting from goods or services with relative price increases to goods or services with relative price decreases, the period *b* expenditure shares will be good estimates of the expenditure shares in the price reference period when the weights are introduced in the index. In turn, if expenditure shares stay unchanged, the Young index will be a good estimate of a target superlative index. However, if quantities tend to remain constant (i.e., the households do not substitute between goods and services in response to relative price changes), the Young index will be biased downwards compared to a superlative target index.

9.17 Whether a Young or Lowe index is the better estimate of a superlative target index depends on whether the original or the price-updated weights are the better estimate of the average expenditure shares from 0 to *t*. Normal consumer behavior suggests that in general some substitution should be expected, so that the Lowe index will tend to be biased upward compared to a superlative target index. As the Young index allows for some substitution from *b* to *0*, while Lowe does not, it may be argued that the traditional Laspeyres bias to some degree is reduced in the Young index as compared to the Lowe index. Thus, to omit price-updating may be one practical way in which to reduce this type of bias.

9.18 Both quantities and expenditure shares change through time and progressively more, the longer the elapse of time between the weight reference period and the period when the weights are introduced in the index. Thus, whether the weights are price-updated or not, they should be reviewed and updated as frequently as possible to reduce potential bias. When rapid changes take place in relative quantities as well as relative prices, NSOs are effectively obliged to change the expenditure weights more often. Price-updating on its own cannot cope with this situation. The weighting basis must be updated with respect to both quantities and prices, which, in effect, implies that new weights have to be included.

Recent Research on Price-updating Expenditure Weights

9.19 Economists make certain assumptions about normal consumer behavior based on observation and economic theory. Both indicate that in response to relative price change consumers will adjust the quantities of goods and services they purchase. When the price of a product rises relative to other similar products, consumers will usually reduce the amount purchased of the product with the relatively higher price increase and purchase more of the similar products with the relatively lower price increases. The opposite phenomenon will occur as relative prices fall—consumers purchase more of the product with the relative decline in prices and less of the products with the relative price increases. This consumer reaction to price movements, known as substitution, is the theory underlying the downward sloping demand curve.

9.20 Given this behavior, Chapter 4 in *Consumer Price Index Theory* outlines why the Laspeyres price index will be an upper bound to the true cost-of-living index (COLI) and the Paasche price index will be a lower bound. It also shows subsequently that the three target indices—Fisher, Törnqvist, and Walsh—are very close approximations to one another and to the true COLI.

9.21 The Lowe index, like Laspeyres, assumes that consumers do not substitute away from items with relatively large price increases; the relative quantities are fixed at the weight reference period (*b*). In practical terms this means that items with relatively large increases in price gain an unduly large expenditure share in period 0 relative to period *b* (where *b* precedes 0). Balk and Diewert (2003), Balk (2010), and Chapter 4 in *Consumer Price Index Theory* show that the Lowe index has an upward substitution bias compared to the true COLI. This bias increases the longer the period between the weight reference period (*b*) and the price reference period (0). Chapter 4 in *Consumer Price Index Theory* also notes that the Lowe index is upwardly biased relative to the Laspeyres index. Thus, price updating the weights results in an index number that is upward biased relative to the target indices, as well as the Laspeyres index.

9.22 The dispersion of price change over the period affects the magnitude of the substitution bias. In the unlikely event that all prices change in the same proportion, there will be no bias from using the Lowe index rather than Laspeyres. The price-updated weights will be the same as the weights in the weight reference period. However, if prices are trending upward with normal consumer substitution behavior, the dispersion in prices is expected to increase and price-updating would have a substantial effect on the weights. This implies the bias in the Lowe index would be larger than if there were little price change. In general, prices tend to trend upward over time and therefore it is clear that price updating weights from period b to 0 will result in an upward bias compared to the target indices (and the Laspeyres index also).

9.23 An alternative approach would be to use the weights from the weight reference period directly. Boldsen Hansen (2006) argues for using the Young index. Keeping the expenditure shares fixed at the weight reference period level means that there has been no change in weights between b and 0. Unchanging weights is consistent with consumer substitution behavior that exhibits unitary elasticity—consumer shifts in reducing the quantities purchased are in the same proportion as the increase in prices.

9.24 Whether the Young index is biased relative to the Laspeyres index will depend on the long-term trend in prices and the elasticity of substitution.[2] In general, the long-term trend in prices for most items has been positive. Given this trend, if the elasticity is lower than one (inelastic), the Young index may have a downward bias compared to the Laspeyres. This occurs because consumers on average do not substitute as much in response to price changes as the Young index implies. They tend to purchase the relatively higher priced items in greater quantities than implied by unitary elasticity. If the elasticity is greater than one (elastic), the Young index may have an upward bias compared to the Laspeyres, because consumers tend to substitute more than assumed. This is presented in more detail in Chapter 2 of *Consumer Price Index Theory*.

9.25 Recent studies of the potential bias in the Young and Lowe indices indicate that measured price changes using the Lowe index generally exceed those of the Young index and both exceed the target indices. Boldsen Hansen (2007) using Danish CPI data, Greenlees and Williams (2010) and Armknecht and Silver (2013) using United States (US) CPI data, Pike *et al* (2009) with New Zealand CPI data, and Huang, Wimalaratne, and Pollard (2016) using Canadian CPI data all verify that the CPI price changes measured using the Lowe exceed those of the Young index, and both are greater than those of the Törnqvist index.

9.26 Armknecht and Silver (2013) also suggests that there are practical solutions that might be used to simulate a target index. This study provides evidence from the methodology proposed by Lent and Dorfman (2009) that using the geometric average of arithmetic indices, such as Young or Lowe, with geometric indices such as geometric Lowe or geometric Young, respectively, can closely approximate the Fisher or Törnqvist indices. NSOs should be able to produce these four indices using the expenditure data available from the HBS. First, the NSO can calculate the Young and Lowe indices with the HBS weights and the price-updated weights. Next, the NSO can calculate the geometric Young and geometric Lowe by using the geometric aggregation formula (e.g., by taking a weighted average of natural logarithms of price relatives and converting the logarithm back to an index number). The NSO can then test which combination of the resulting arithmetic and geometric versions provide the best approximation to the Fisher or Törnqvist indices.

Detailed Methods for Updating Weights

Decide on Price Reference Period for Calculating the Updated CPI

Annual Price Reference Periods

9.27 As the new weights are developed from the HBS or alternative sources for weights such as national accounts data, the NSO must decide on what time period to use for the new price reference period. Often the choice is between a single period of less than a year (month or quarter) that is close to the current period or a yearly average. In either case, the price reference period should immediately precede the introduction of the new index series. For example, an index introduced in January should have a price reference of either the month prior, December, or an average of the previous year.

9.28 For infrequently updated CPIs, a single year is preferred as the price reference period. If a single month (or quarter) is used, the prices of some seasonal products will be unavailable or unusually high or low and a large number of unusual or imputed prices may have to be used for the price reference period. Furthermore, if a single unusual price reference month is to act as the reference period, the initial result of the index change may be a distorted one. Preferably the price reference period for infrequently updated CPIs is a whole year in which seasonal prices would be appropriately represented. In some months there will be no sales, for example, of a seasonal fruit, but an average price for the whole year would still be available for the price reference period. For a homogeneous item specification, say a large Bartlett class I pear grown in California, it is recommended that, data permitting, the average price used in the reference period be a unit value, that is, the sum of the value purchased over the whole year divided by the sum of the quantity purchased as measured in the HBS. The advantage of the unit value is that the resulting average price gives accordingly less weight to prices in months in which there were fewer purchases.

9.29 If the NSO chooses the annual period for the price reference period, it will need annual average prices for all items of the rebased series. Such prices will be collected alongside those of the existing index and in many cases may be for the same specification. The existing index's prices, for example for 2017, will be collected and used for the monthly index compiled and published for 2017, however the prices for the supplementary items/products for the new index should be collected alongside them for the rebased index to commence in January 2018, or soon afterwards, with year 2017 as the index reference period (100). The price collection for the items that belong to the old index but not to the new index can be stopped once the rebased index has been released.

9.30 It is important to stress the practical arrangements required for price collecting the specifications for the new index alongside the old. Many items sold in the same outlets sampled for the existing index will remain the same for the revised index and thus involve no additional workload. There may be some changes to items that replace an old one, for example brown sauce, with a new one, say ketchup, in the same outlet which again requires limited additional resources. However, the very need for the rebase to capture changes in item/variety specifications

[2] Often the Laspeyres price index is the target index for countries' CPI so the comparison is made first to the more standard target then to the superlative index targets (Fisher, Törnqvist, or Young).

and include new outlets in place of old ones—a purpose of the rebasing—will require prices to be collected for some new items in new outlets. Resources have to be committed in advance to plan for this. The sampling of products and broad item specifications and the associated outlet selection provides the basis for determining the new item/variety specifications to be sampled and the old ones replaced.

9.31 Some of the items for the new index will be the same as the old; some will be different, but available in the same outlet; and some will be available in new outlets, with the existing or new items. These provide the prices in the price reference period from which the new index is measured. An average of the existing index for 2017 and the rebased index 2017 = 100 provides the linking factors that enable the new index to be a continuation of the existing index.

9.32 It is usually the case that the overlap year and prices collected for the rebased index are for a period following the weight reference (survey) period. This is because CPI compilers have to wait until the results of the HBS have been compiled and new elementary aggregates determined to know what to price. The purpose of rebasing is to update the products and items priced and this needs to be informed by results from the survey. For example, the HBS may be undertaken in 2015; during 2016 (i) the results would be compiled to yield expenditure shares by product category (and possibly region); (ii) the results are validated/developed using ancillary data as appropriate; (iii) elementary aggregate products are selected (e.g., using cut-off sampling) and their broad specifications developed; (iv) use of centrally-determined prices for selected products are determined (e.g., electricity, water, insurance); and (v) an outlet sample selected for the remaining products. Pricing will commence with an initiation of the sample by visits to the outlets to determine and price the appropriate representative attributes for the selected item. This may commence in January 2017 or later depending on the resources of the NSO. A whole year's price data, say for 2017, will be collected for the new products and their specifications alongside the old. The rebased index will be a Lowe index with a weight reference period of 2015 and a price and index reference period of 2017 = 100.

9.33 NSOs that calculates the elementary indices as chained monthly indices in which prices are compared to previous month's prices, have the advantage of being able to readily introduce replacement items/varieties so the task of collecting specifications for the new index alongside those of the existing one will be less arduous. The long-term price relative method (i.e., the current period price compared to the average price from the price reference period), makes such procedures more difficult because adjustments to base prices are often required.

Monthly (Or Quarterly) Reference Period

9.34 NSOs that use chained CPIs and annually update their weights with a relatively small-time lag between the weight and price reference period should use a single month as the price reference period. For instance, the weights that refer to year y-2 are available and finalized in year y-1 so that they can be introduced in the January index of year y with December year y-1 as the price reference period. There is a continuing flow of price data that may include imputations, and a relatively small number of changes in specifications or products; the major exercise is to bring the new weights to bear on the flow of price data and link this to the existing chain. At the same time, the annual update of the price reference period remains an opportunity for re-sampling in order to ensure that the basket remains representative, and for possibly implementing other methodological improvements.

9.35 For infrequently updated CPIs (i.e., those updated every five years or less frequently), the use of a single-month price reference period is not ideal; however it is often the case that the resources of an NSO are only sufficient to allow for a price reference period of less than a year. Often this is monthly, though it follows from the reasons given in paragraphs 9.28 and 9.29 that six-months is preferred to quarterly, and quarterly to monthly. The principles for using a monthly price reference period are similar to those of an annual one, the issue being to mitigate as much as possible its shortcomings.

9.36 A primary shortcoming of using a monthly reference period is that out-of-season items in the price reference period will have no observed or economically meaningful price. The decision as to which month to use for the price reference month should take account when seasonal items with relatively high weights are in-season. If not in season, an imputed price will have to be used and consideration should be given to the validity of imputation methods for out-of-season items in this context. For example, if the carryfor method is used, the month's imputed price in the price reference period for the out-of-season item may be unduly low. As mentioned above, the short-term price relative method is preferred since it avoids a need for long-run price comparisons with this one-month price reference period.

Developing Update Factors

9.37 While an NSO can maintain the same weights and price reference period, most NSOs choose to use a more current period to introduce the new weight structure. Assume the NSO decides to introduce the new weights from the 2015 HBS in the January 2018 CPI with a price reference date of December 2017, it has two choices for the weights: (a) introduce the 2015 weights directly, or (b) price update the weights to December 2017. As noted, the first choice will result in a Young index while the second will result in a Lowe index.

9.38 Table 9.2 presents the approach for price updating the weights from the 2015 weight reference period to December 2017. A single month is used here for illustrative purposes although, for reasons outlined in paragraphs 9.28 and 9.29, the whole year 2017 could also be used. The NSO begins the rebased CPI using the price data for December 2017 and January 2018. It also produces the old CPI with 2010=100 for December 2017. These data will be used for linking the old and new series as discussed in paragraphs 9.73 to 9.88.

9.39 The first step in updating the weights is to develop the update factors that measure the price change from 2015 to December 2017. This process requires a measure of price

Table 9.2. Updating Weights for Price Change from Weight Reference Period

COICOP Code	Description	Expenditure Share 2015	Avg. CPI 2015	CPI Dec. 2017	Update Factor	Updated Weight	Normalized Weight
(A)	(B)	(C)	(D)	(E)	(F)	(G)	(H)
					Col E/D	Col. FxC	
01	**Food and Non-alcoholic Beverages**	**100.000**				**206.883**	**100.000**
01.1	**FOOD**	**93.306**				**197.80**	**95.61**
01.1.1	**Bread & Cereals**	**21.419**				**40.08**	**19.37**
01.1.101	Rice (white)	1.406	150.7	318.1	2.111	2.969	1.435
01.1.102	Rice (Brown)	3.361	151.7	224.6	1.480	4.975	2.405
01.1.103	Flour	2.578	134.8	320.2	2.375	6.121	2.959
01.1.104	Bread	6.864	127.2	222.4	1.748	12.006	5.803
01.1.105	Biscuits (Salted)	0.813	113.0	140.1	1.240	1.008	0.487
01.1.106	Cakes, Pastry, etc.	1.034	131.2	233.7	1.781	1.842	0.891
01.1.107	Chow mein	1.716	125.1	309.8	2.476	4.247	2.053
01.1.109	Macaroni	1.284	105.8	200.3	1.893	2.429	1.174
01.1.110	Oat flakes	0.450	100.6	225.7	2.244	1.010	0.488
01.1.111	Sago	0.341	103.5	222.9	2.154	0.735	0.355
01.1.112	Tennis Rolls	1.392	126.0	219.6	1.743	2.426	1.173
01.1.113	***Whole Wheat Bread****	0.180	***127.2***	***222.4***	1.749	0.315	0.152
01.1.2	**Meat**	**17.632**				**39.94**	**19.31**
01.1.201	Stew Beef	1.940	110.5	254.8	2.306	4.474	2.162
01.1.205	Chicken (live)	1.038	112.6	229.7	2.040	2.117	1.023
01.1.206	Chicken (frozen)	10.202	110.2	252.5	2.291	23.370	11.296
01.1.207	Pork Leg	0.610	138.8	483.4	3.483	2.123	1.026
01.1.210	***Corned beef****	0.866	***111.9***	***253.7***	2.114	1.832	0.949
01.1.211	Duck	0.217	107.3	148.3	1.382	0.300	0.145
01.1.212	Liver	0.207	115.4	198.6	1.720	0.356	0.172
01.1.213	Mutton	0.271	106.8	256.7	2.404	0.651	0.315
01.1.214	Sausages (pork & chicken)	1.823	120.3	233.0	1.937	3.531	1.707
01.1.215	***Brisket****	0.458	***110.5***	***254.8***	2.306	1.056	0.511
01.1.3	**Fish & Seafood**	**5.982**				**12.66**	**6.12**
...	...	...	...	...	...	...	...

change for the elementary aggregates in the new basket. A large majority of the items in the new basket are the same as in the previous basket and continue in the rebased CPI. Their price change can be measured either by using a matched sample of (geometric) average prices for 2015 compared to those in December 2017 or elementary aggregate price indices over the same period. It is very difficult to have the same set of matched price observations in both periods because product substitutions have most likely occurred over the two-year period. Therefore, NSOs will find it easier to use the elementary aggregate indices already available for the CPI elementary aggregates that continue.

$$Factor_i^{Dec\ 2017} = I_{i,\,2010=100}^{Dec\,2017} \,/\, I_{i,\,2010=100}^{Avg\ 2015} \tag{9.3}$$

9.40 There is an issue, however, for deriving the update factors for the new elementary aggregates in the basket. As previously noted, NSOs will not have price data for the new items from 2015, nor will they have price indices to use for calculating the weight update factors for the new elementary aggregates.[3] In some instances the CPI compiler may have anticipated that certain items were becoming important and most likely would appear in the new basket. For these items, the compiler may have collected prices or started test elementary aggregate indices during 2015. Such cases are the exception rather than the rule, and it is unlikely that all new items in the basket will have prices or indices available in December 2017.

9.41 For the new items, the CPI compiler can identify existing elementary aggregates whose price trends might be reflective of the new elementary aggregates in the basket. Otherwise, the price index for the higher-level class aggregate can be used. In Table 9.2, there are three new items and for each of these the CPI compiler needs to select a representative elementary aggregate price index. As in the previous example, brisket uses the stew beef index as representing its trend. For most other new items, the same approach is taken: whole wheat bread uses the bread index. The only item for which the class index is used is corned beef.

9.42 For each elementary aggregate index in Table 9.2, the 2015 monthly indices were averaged for the calendar year and appear in column D.[4] The December 2017 indices are in column E. The update factors are calculated in column F as the December 2017 index (column E) divided by the 2015 average index (column D). Next, the 2015 weights (column C) are multiplied by the update factors (column F) to derive the updated weights (column G). Finally, the updated weights are normalized (divided by the total of the

[3]A similar issue may arise with changes to the classification system or introduction of new geographical areas into the CPI.

[4]The calculations for updating the weights are only made for the item indices where the new weights are applied. The class and higher-level indices will be calculated using the weights updated to December 2017 in paragraphs 9.47–9.56.

updated weights in the first row of column G and converted to percentages) to sum to 100 (column H).

$$\textit{Updated weight: } w_i^{2015(Dec\ 2017)} = Factor_i^{Dec\ 2017} w_i^{Avg\ 2015}$$

$$\textit{Aggregate updated weight: } w_{agg}^{2015(Dec\ 2017)} = \sum_{i=1}^{k} w_i^{2015(Dec\ 2017)}$$

$$\textit{Percentage shares: } s_i^{Dec\ 2017} = \left(w_i^{2015(Dec\ 2017)} / \sum_{i=1}^{n} w_i^{2015(Dec\ 2017)} \right) \times 100$$

9.43 Note that the update factors are only calculated at the elementary aggregate level and are used only to update the elementary aggregate weights. The higher-level weights are calculated by aggregating the lower-level weights: (i) subclass weights are the sum of the elementary aggregate weights within the subclass, (ii) class weights are the sum of the subclasses within the class, (iii) group weights are the sum of the classes within the group, and (iv) the division weights are the sum of the groups within the division. If the NSO calculates an update factor at the subclass level, it will not get the same result as when summing the elementary aggregate weights. The new aggregated weights reflect the new basket's structure. Using the aggregate indices to calculate update factors at the subclass level or above reflects the structure of the old basket.

9.44 Another important point is that, when price updating the weights, the elementary aggregates that have relatively larger price changes from the weight reference period receive a larger share of the weight and those with relatively lower price changes receive a smaller share. For example, the elementary aggregate with the largest price change is pork leg (update factor of 3.484) and the updated weight is 1.026 versus 0.610 in the weight reference period. The elementary aggregate with the smallest price change is biscuits (update factor of 1.240) and the updated weight is 0.813 verses 0.487 in the weight reference period. In sum, all the elementary aggregates that exceed the average price changes receive greater weight than in the weight reference period while all the elementary aggregates with less than average price changes receive less weight.

Introducing New Weights

9.45 The NSO has three options on introducing the new basket and weights. First, new weights can start with the weight reference period and price reference period being the same (Laspeyres). The second option is to introduce the expenditure weights directly in a new (subsequent) price reference period (Young). The third option is to introduce price-updated weights in a new price reference period (Lowe). Each of these options is demonstrated in paragraphs 9.46 to 9.54.

Introduce New Weights With the Same Weight and Price Reference Periods—Laspeyres Index

9.46 The NSO can use the weight reference period as the price reference period. In addition, the NSO would also need to reset the index reference period of the elementary indices to 100 using the same period as the weight and price reference periods. In Table 9.3 the average price for 2015 (the weight reference period for the HBS) is set to 100 (column D) by dividing all the elementary indices by their 2015 average and expressing them as an index. In columns E, F, and G, the new weights are used to aggregate the rebased elementary indices to higher levels starting with the subclass levels.

$$I_i^{t,2015=100} = I_i^{t,2010=100} / I_i^{2015\ Avg,\ 2010=100} \tag{9.4}$$

At the elementary aggregate level the new weights are applied to derive all higher-level indices, up to the overall CPI.

$$I_{agg}^{t,2015=100} = \sum_{i=1}^{k} w_i^{Avg\ 2015} I_i^{t,2015=100} / \sum_{i=1}^{k} w_i^{Avg\ 2015} \tag{9.5}$$

9.47 The CPI compiler must complete this aggregation for all months from January 2015 through January 2018. Table 9.3 only shows the aggregates for three months—December 2016, December 2017, and January 2018. The revised index series will now be available from 2015 through January 2018.

9.48 The argument for keeping the weight reference period and price reference period the same is that the resulting price index will approximate a true Laspeyres index; however, this procedure is not without problems. Consider for example a weight reference period of 2015 for which the new sample of products/items have prices collected in 2017 with an aim to commence the index in January 2019. Instead of using 2017 as the new overlap index reference period, 2015 = 100 is used. As explained below, this is achieved by backcasting the 2017 prices to 2015, a procedure that may involve some imputations. Nonetheless, if this method is used, what is derived is a Laspeyres index with the same weight and price reference periods. However, the interest in compiling the new rebased index is for indices from January 2016 onward. The period-to-period comparisons use Laspeyres price indices, but the resulting measure will be a Lowe index comparison, not Laspeyres. The ratio of the two Laspeyres indices used in calculating the price change results in a Lowe formula as follows:

$$I_L^{0:t} / I_L^{0:t-1} = \frac{\sum p_i^t q_i^0}{\sum p_i^0 q_i^0} \Big/ \frac{\sum p_i^{t-1} q_i^0}{\sum p_i^0 q_i^0} = \frac{\sum p_i^t q_i^0}{\sum p_i^{t-1} q_i^0} \tag{9.6}$$

where $I_L^{0:t}$ is the Laspeyres price index for period t

$I_L^{0:t-1}$ is the Laspeyres price index for period $t-1$

9.49 The resulting price change does not yield a Laspeyres price index but a Lowe index where the quantities of period 0 are valued at the prices in period t and t–1. A true Laspeyres index would value the fixed quantities of period t-1 at the prices of period t-1 and t (i.e., $\sum p_i^t q_i^{t-1} / \sum p_i^{t-1} q_i^{t-1}$). Thus, going through the process of calculating the Laspeyres index by backcasting still results in comparisons that result in Lowe index price changes.

9.50 The NSO often has difficulty in obtaining price measures for new items that are introduced with the new weights. Because of the time lag between the HBS and the development of the CPI weights, the required price data to use as the reference prices would usually be two to three years old. Retail outlets will find it very difficult to provide accurate prices for the period covered by the weights. This

Table 9.3. Updated CPI with the Same Weight and Price Reference Periods

COICOP Code	Description	Expenditure Share 2015	Avg. CPI 2015	CPI Dec. 2016	CPI Dec. 2017	CPI Jan. 2018
(A)	(B)	(C)	(D)	(E)	(F)	(G)
01	**Food and Non-alcoholic Beverages**	**100.00**	**100.00**	**153.20**	**206.41**	**209.24**
01.1	**FOOD**	**93.31**	**100.0**	**155.7**	**211.5**	**214.4**
01.1.1	**Bread & Cereals**	**21.42**	**100.0**	**143.6**	**187.1**	**189.5**
01.1.101	Rice (white)	1.406	100.0	155.5	211.1	213.2
01.1.102	Rice (Brown)	3.361	100.0	124.0	148.0	150.2
01.1.103	Flour	2.578	100.0	168.7	237.5	242.2
01.1.104	Bread	6.864	100.0	137.5	174.9	176.7
01.1.105	Biscuits (Salted)	0.813	100.0	112.0	123.9	125.8
01.1.106	Cakes, Pastry, etc.	1.034	100.0	139.1	178.1	181.7
01.1.107	Chow Mein	1.716	100.0	173.8	247.6	250.1
01.1.109	Macaroni	1.284	100.0	144.6	189.3	190.2
01.1.110	Oat flakes	0.450	100.0	162.2	224.4	227.8
01.1.111	Sago	0.341	100.0	157.7	215.5	218.7
01.1.112	Tennis Rolls	1.392	100.0	137.2	174.3	176.0
01.1.113	***Whole Wheat Bread****	0.180	***100.0***	***137.5***	***174.9***	***178.4***
01.1.2	**Meat**	**17.63**	**100.0**	**161.6**	**226.5**	**226.9**
01.1.201	Stew Beef	1.940	100.0	165.3	230.6	232.9
01.1.205	Chicken (live)	1.038	100.0	152.0	204.0	207.0
01.1.206	Chicken (frozen)	10.202	100.0	164.5	229.1	233.6
01.1.207	Pork Leg	0.610	100.0	224.2	348.3	351.8
01.1.210	***Corned beef****	0.866	100.0	128.5	226.8	159.3
01.1.211	Duck	0.217	100.0	119.1	138.2	141.0
01.1.212	Liver	0.207	100.0	136.0	172.0	173.8
01.1.213	Mutton	0.271	100.0	170.2	240.4	241.6
01.1.214	Sausages (pork & chicken)	1.823	100.0	146.8	193.7	196.6
01.1.215	***Brisket****	0.458	***100.0***	***165.3***	***230.6***	***234.0***
01.1.3	**Fish & Seafood**	**5.98**	**100.0**	**155.8**	**211.6**	**214.5**
…	…	…	…	…	…	…

can be problematic for an index that uses the long-term price relative method (i.e., the current period price compared to the average price from the price reference period).

9.51 The alternative is to use price indices to measure the change in prices for the time lapse between the weight reference period and the introduction of the new weights. For items that are already in the CPI basket, their index can be re-referenced to the weight reference period. For example, if the current time period is late in 2017 and the weight reference period is 2015, the NSO can use the annual average price index for 2015 to re-reference the series so that the 2015 average is set to 100. Or it could use the prices for the item from 2015 (if they are available) to calculate the 2015 average price and compare current period prices to the 2015 average.

9.52 For new items to the CPI, the NSO will not have the prices or an index for the item. In this case, an index for a related item or for the subclass in which the new item is included may be used to reflect the price change from the weight reference period.

Introduce the New Weights Directly in a New Price Reference Period—Young Index

9.53 The second option is for the NSO to introduce the new weights directly in a new price reference period. As discussed in paragraphs 9.12 to 9.18, this may be the preferred approach if there has been significant price change between the weight reference period and the introduction of the new weights.

9.54 Assume the CPI compiler has decided to introduce the new weights directly in December 2017 to use in the compilation of the January 2018 index (skipping the compilations in columns D to F of Table 9.3). The new price reference period is December 2017. The price relatives for January 2018 are used to estimate the January 2018 elementary index levels and the new weights (from Table 9.4, column C) are used directly with the elementary indices to derive the higher-level aggregates.

9.55 The new index starts with December 2017 = 100 as shown in column D of Table 9.4. The January 2018 elementary indices appear in column E. The 2015 CPI weights are used to aggregate the elementary indices to the subclass, class, group, and division levels as discussed in the previous example.

$$I_i^{t,\,Dec2017=100} = \left(\prod_{j=1}^{m} \frac{I_j^t}{I_i^{Dec2017}} \right) \times 100 \tag{9.7}$$

9.56 The aggregate index changes are different from those in the previous example because the weights reflect that the expenditure shares are kept fixed at their 2015 levels, but not used in the index calculation until December 2017.

$$I_{agg}^{t,\,Dec2017=100} = \sum_{i=1}^{k} w_i^{Avg\ 2015} I_i^{t,\,Dec2017=100} \Big/ \sum_{i=1}^{k} w_i^{Avg\ 2015} \tag{9.8}$$

In Table 9.3, the price change for Food and Non-alcoholic Beverages is 1.37 percent ([209.24 ÷ 206.41] x 100 – 100), compared to 1.36 percent (column E) in Table 9.4.

Introduce the Updated Weights in a New Price Reference Period—Lowe Index

9.57 The third option is for the NSO to introduce the new weights updated for price change between 2015 and December 2017 (Table 9.2, column H) in the new price reference period. The new price reference period is December 2017. The price relatives for January 2018 are used to estimate the January 2018 elementary index levels and the price-updated weights are used with the elementary indices to derive the higher-level aggregates.

9.58 Referring to Table 9.4, the revised index starts with December 2017 = 100 as shown in column D. The price-updated weights from 2015 to December 2017 (column F) are used to aggregate the elementary indices to the subclass, class, group, and division levels as discussed in the previous examples.

$$I_{agg}^{t,\,Dec2017=100} = \sum_{i=1}^{k} w_i^{2015(Dec2017)} I_i^{Dec2017:t} \Big/ \sum_{i=1}^{k} w_i^{2015(Dec2017)} \quad (9.9)$$

The aggregate index changes are the same as those in Table 9.3 because the weights reflect the fact that the quantities (not expenditure) shares are fixed at their 2015 levels. In Table 9.4, the price change for Food and Non-alcoholic Beverages using the price-updated weights is 1.37 percent (column G).

9.59 In the first approach (Table 9.2), the NSO estimated a Laspeyres index with the quantity shares fixed at 2015 levels and the price reference period of 2015. The Laspeyres index requires that the price and weight reference periods are the same. In the third approach (Table 9.4, columns F-G), the NSO compiled a Lowe index using price-updated weights to December 2017 with the same date as the new price reference period. The price changes for these two indices will be the same because they keep the same fixed quantities. As prices change through time, thc expenditures and their shares will change providing greater importance to those items with larger than average price changes. This fact can be seen in Table 9.2. The aggregate price relative between 2015 and December 2017 is 2.069 (206.883 ÷ 100). All items with price changes (update factors in column F) greater than this value have larger final weights (column H) when compared to the 2015 weights (column 3). The Young index produced in the second approach (column E of Table 9.4) holds the expenditure shares fixed and allows for substitution of quantities inversely proportional to price changes. For this example, the Young index has a smaller price change between December 2017 and January 2018 than the Lowe index, as confirmed by several empirical studies cited earlier (see paragraphs 9.19 – 9.26). In general, however, it cannot be said *a priori* if either the Young or the Lowe index is higher.

Decide on the Index Reference Period

9.60 The NSO has the choice of setting a new index reference period or keeping the old index reference period. In the previous examples, new reference periods were set. In the first case, the NSO used the HBS weight reference period of the 2015 annual average as the weight, price, and index reference periods (Laspeyres index). In the second example, a new price and index reference period was established for December 2017 with the weight reference period of 2015

Table 9.4. Updated CPI with a New Price Reference Period

COICOP Code	Description	Expenditure Share 2015	CPI Dec. 2017	CPI Jan. 2018	Expenditure Share Dec 2017	CPI Jan. 2018
(A)	(B)	(C)	(D)	(E)	(F)	(G)
01	**Food and Non-alcoholic Beverages**	**100.00**	**100.0**	**101.36**	**100.00**	**101.37**
01.1	**FOOD**	**93.31**	**100.0**	**101.38**	**95.61**	**101.39**
01.1.1	**Bread & Cereals**	**21.42**	**100.0**	**101.26**	**19.37**	**101.27**
01.1.101	Rice (white)	1.406	100.0	101.00	1.435	101.00
01.1.102	Rice (Brown)	3.361	100.0	101.50	2.405	101.50
01.1.103	Flour	2.578	100.0	102.00	2.959	102.00
01.1.104	Bread	6.864	100.0	101.00	5.803	101.00
01.1.105	Biscuits (Salted)	0.813	100.0	101.50	0.487	101.50
01.1.106	Cakes, Pastry, etc.	1.034	100.0	102.00	0.891	102.00
01.1.107	Chow Mein	1.716	100.0	101.00	2.053	101.00
01.1.109	Macaroni	1.284	100.0	100.50	1.174	100.50
01.1.110	Oat flakes	0.450	100.0	101.50	0.488	101.50
01.1.111	Sago	0.341	100.0	101.50	0.355	101.50
01.1.112	Tennis Rolls	1.392	100.0	101.00	1.173	101.00
01.1.113	***Whole Wheat Bread****	0.180	***100.0***	***102.00***	0.152	***102.00***
01.1.2	**Meat**	**17.63**	**100.0**	**100.17**	**19.31**	**100.16**
01.1.201	Stew Beef	1.940	100.0	101.00	2.162	101.00
01.1.205	Chicken (live)	1.038	100.0	101.50	1.023	101.50
01.1.206	Chicken (frozen)	10.202	100.0	102.00	11.296	102.00
01.1.207	Pork Leg	0.610	100.0	101.00	1.026	101.00
01.1.210	***Corned beef****	0.866	100.0	70.20	0.949	70.20
01.1.211	Duck	0.217	100.0	102.00	0.145	102.00
01.1.212	Liver	0.207	100.0	101.00	0.172	101.00
01.1.213	Mutton	0.271	100.0	100.50	0.315	100.50
01.1.214	Sausages (pork & chicken)	1.823	100.0	101.50	1.707	101.50
01.1.215	***Brisket****	0.458	***100.0***	***101.50***	0.511	***101.50***
01.1.3	**Fish & Seafood**	**5.98**	**100.0**	**101.28**	**6.12**	**101.37**
...	...	...	...	...	...	...

(Lowe index or Young index). The previous index reference period was 2010 and the NSO also has the option to maintain the 2010 index reference period. In such an instance, the weight (2015), price (December 2017), and index (2010) reference periods might all be different.

9.61 Many NSOs change the index reference period to correspond to the price reference period. Often this is the case in countries where CPI revisions have historically occurred on a ten-year cycle or longer. Defining a new index reference period often is notice to users that a new basket and CPI procedures have been put in place. Users may not pay close attention to NSO announcements about the CPI being revised, but when they find the new CPI index level on a different reference period, they take note and inquire about getting historical data or the revised CPI on the old index reference period.

9.62 If the NSO chooses to keep the old index reference period, users may not notice that the CPI has been revised. Most users are concerned with the overall all-items CPI and perhaps some of the major division indices, and do not necessarily use any of the detailed indices at the group or class level. These users may not realize that the CPI has been revised and that some of the detail has changed because new products entering, old products leaving, and, perhaps, an updated classification system or improved methodologies. However, maintaining the old reference period is probably helpful to most users whose only interest is to monitor changes in the overall CPI. Any changes in weights or methodologies should be clearly explained and announced to users well in advance to avoid any confusion. It should be clear to users that a revised index has been disseminated. All relevant metadata should be updated accordingly.

9.63 If the NSO decides to change the index reference period, the old series should be linked to the new series so that users have the appearance of a continuous CPI series. Nonetheless, users should be advised that the new series is not strictly comparable with the old because of the change in basket, weights, and often methodology. If the NSO keeps the old reference period, the new series must be linked to the old series to give users a continuous series. Linking techniques to form a time series for the CPI are presented in paragraphs 9.73 to 9.88.

Formula Used for Estimation

Elementary Aggregate Indices

9.64 The process of updating the weights from the weight reference period until their introduction in the CPI involved using a long-term price relative as the update factor. The period-to-period estimation of the CPI can be accomplished using either a long-term relative approach or a short-term (two-stage or chained) approach. The long-term relative approach is straightforward in that the elementary aggregate index for the period is derived directly as either the ratio of average prices in the current period to the average prices in the price reference period or the average of the long-term price relative for each observation from the price reference period to the current period.

9.65 Chapter 8 of this Manual and Chapter 6 in *Consumer Price Index Theory* strongly urge the NSOs to use geometric averages of prices and price relatives rather than arithmetic averages whenever weights are not available, and identifies several problems with the arithmetic formulas that are avoided when using geometric averages.

Higher-level Indices

9.66 The higher-level price indices are compiled by either aggregating the elementary (item) level price indices or by aggregating the elementary price relatives. For aggregating indices, the NSO uses the item weights from the introduction of the new CPI series. The weights for the Laspeyres and Young indices refer to the weights from the weight reference period, while those for the Lowe index refer to the price reference period. These weights and their elementary (item) indices are used to calculate weighted average price indices for the current period. As noted earlier, the reference period of the weights and the price reference period used in the index formula determine whether the index is Laspeyres, Young, or Lowe.

9.67 As noted above, aggregating price relatives requires a different set of weights each month to derive the higher-level aggregates. The price relatives have a price reference in the previous period. Therefore, the aggregation weights must refer to the previous period. A good rule to remember is that when calculating price movements, the price period in the denominator of the index formula should be the same as the price period implicit in the weights.

9.68 The weight required is one that reflects the price reference period weights that are price-updated to the previous period. These weights may be referred to as cost weights and reflect what the cost would be to purchase the same quantity of the item at the current period's prices. This weight is derived each period by using the price relatives for the current period to bring forward the previous cost weight. These weights and their elementary (item) price relatives are used to calculate weighted average aggregate price relatives for the current period. The aggregate price relative is multiplied by the previous period aggregate index to derive the current aggregate index.

9.69 The NSOs could also use geometric estimators to derive higher-level indices. Using a Geometric Young, Geometric Laspeyres, or a Geometric Lowe formula could help reduce the substitution bias inherent in the use of fixed base indices. They also provide for consistency in aggregation when geometric indices are compiled at the elementary level.

Linking the Previous CPI to the New Price Index Reference Period

9.70 When the NSO introduces a new basket and weights, the new series is not completely comparable to the previous series. Nonetheless, users typically want a CPI time series that covers a long period of time and provides historical context. In order to provide such a series, the NSO will need to link or splice the two series together. For example, if the previous series had an index reference period of 2012 and the new series has a reference period of 2017, there is likely to be a large difference in the index levels. The CPI with 2012 = 100 will have registered price changes over the period from 2012 to the end of December 2017. The new series with 2017 = 100 will show little change comparatively with the new index level close to 100. Thus, it becomes important to have procedures for NSOs to use, in this case, to adjust the old series to reflect the level of the new series. Alternatively, the NSO could use procedures to adjust the new series to the level of the old series. These approaches are presented in paragraphs 9.74 to 9.88.

9.71 The NSO may choose to start the new series using the new price reference period. In Chapter 3 the recommendation is that when a new index is introduced there should be an overlap period for the two indices so that they can be linked together. The overlap period is used to develop adjustment factors that may be applied to the old series to bring it to the same level as the new series.

Price Reference Period is a Single Month (Or Quarter)

9.72 At minimum, a single common period is required as an overlap period between the indices. When updating weights less frequently (e.g., every five years), a single common period is not the ideal method. However, some NSOs update the CPI weights each year so that the time lapse between the weight reference period and the link month is short. The single period link could be used in these instances. The NSO should be aware of possible distortions when introducing methodological changes. If the changes result in a different seasonal pattern of the linking month, this would lead to a permanent shift in the level of the index series. Paragraphs 9.98 to 9.113 provide a detailed discussion on annual weight updates.

9.73 Although not a preferred method, some NSOs update the weights using a single period overlap which is presented here as an example of the linking process. Assume December 2017 is the link period and price reference period when the new weights for 2015 will be introduced. Also, the last weight update occurred in December 2012 when the weights for 2010 were introduced. The new CPI and the old CPI series should be produced for December 2017. If that is the case, the linking of the series is straightforward. In December 2017 each of the new CPI indices has a value of 100. For the previous CPI series, each index will have a value that could be different from the new series. The goal of the linking process is to set the old indices' levels to those of the new index. Since the new indices all have a value of 100 and the NSO wants the old indices to have that same value, the NSO can simply reference the old series to 100 by dividing each item, subclass, class, group, etc. index by its value for December 2017. The NSO can also derive an adjustment factor for each of the new CPI series that users can apply to the new series going forward in time to raise the new series level to that of the old series if the index reference period is to remain the same as that for the old CPI (December 2012 = 100).

9.74 Table 9.5 provides an example of linking the previous and revised CPI using a single period overlap. The table contains the old CPI for a Division (Food and Non-alcoholic Beverages), a Group (Food), two classes (Bread & Cereals and Meat)[5], and 12 items. Column D contains the old CPI

[5]These classes refer to COICOP 1999. In COICOP 2018, these classes have been revised to Cereals and Cereal Products and Meat, Fresh, Chilled, or Frozen.
[6]These classes refer to COICOP 1999. In COICOP 2018, these classes have been revised to Cereals and Cereal Products and Meat, Fresh, Chilled, or Frozen.

Table 9.5. Linking CPI Series Using a Single Period Overlap on a New Index Reference Period[6]

COICOP Code	Description	Expenditure Share 2015	Old CPI for Dec. 2017 Dec. 2012=100	New CPI for Dec. 2017 Dec. 2017=100	Linking Factor Backward (Old Series)	Linking Factor Forward (New Series)
(A)	(B)	(C)	(D)	(E)	(F)	(G)
					Col. E / D	Col. D / E
01	**Food and Non-alcoholic Bev.**	**100.00**	**119.88**	**100.00**	**0.8341**	**1.1988**
01.1	**FOOD**	**94.83**	**119.80**	**100.00**	**0.8347**	**1.1980**
01.1.1	**Bread & Cereals**	**22.41**	**132.49**	**100.00**	**0.7548**	**1.3249**
01.1.101	Rice (white)	5.759	150.7	100.0	0.6636	1.5070
01.1.102	Rice (Brown)	0.381	151.7	100.0	0.6591	1.5173
01.1.103	Flour	4.356	134.8	100.0	0.7416	1.3484
01.1.104	Bread	6.167	127.2	100.0	0.7863	1.2718
01.1.105	Biscuits (Salted)	1.083	113.0	100.0	0.8846	1.1305
01.1.106	Cakes, Pastry, etc.	0.375	131.2	100.0	0.7622	1.3121
01.1.107	Chow Mein	1.370	125.1	100.0	0.7992	1.2513
01.1.109	Macaroni	0.426	105.8	100.0	0.9447	1.0585
01.1.110	Oat flakes	0.751	100.6	100.0	0.9945	1.0056
01.1.111	Sago	0.535	103.5	100.0	0.9664	1.0347
01.1.112	Tennis Rolls	0.589	126.0	100.0	0.7938	1.2598
01.1.113	***Whole Wheat Bread****	0.622	***127.2***	***100.0***	***0.7863***	***1.2718***
01.1.2	**Meat**	**17.358**	**111.87**	**100.00**	**0.8939**	**1.1187**

in the overlap month (December 2017) and column E presents the new index in the overlap month (and new price reference period) so that all series are equal to 100. There are two ways to link the old series to the new series level going backward in time. The first is to re-reference the old series by dividing each old series by the overlap period index (December 2017 value). The second method is to calculate a "linking factor" that can be applied to each of the old series historically. This linking factor is the reciprocal of the December 2017 index level and appears in column F. Multiplying each series by their link factor backward in time has the same effect as dividing by the December 2017 value. These methods are applied to all index series in the old CPI at all levels—Division, Group, Class, Subclass, and Item.

9.75 If the NSO or users want to continue the old series CPI going forward in time, they can produce a set of forward linking factors to use in future months as the new CPI is released. The forward linking factor raises the level of the new CPI series to that of the old series thus keeping the series on the old reference period. The forward linking factors (column G) are simply the ratios of the old index levels (column D) to the price reference index levels (column E).

$$Backward\ Linking\ Factor_i = 1 / Link\ period\ index_i$$

$$Forward\ Linking\ Factor_i = Link\ period\ index_i / 100$$

Price Reference Period is a Yearly Average

9.76 Most NSOs will establish a new price reference period using an annual average from a previous year. The simplest and easiest method is to link the series with data for the month preceding the introduction of the new series (link month). This involves re-referencing the old series at each level to the annual average index for the new price reference period. However, there will be a discontinuity between the index level for the new index and that for the re-referenced index level for the old series in the link month. This reflects the difference in price trends between the old and new series as the new weights are being introduced. Table 9.6 shows the method for linking a new series to the old using a

Table 9.6. Linking Old and New Index Series to a Previous Annual Average[6]

		CPI (2012=100)	Forward Link	CPI (2017=100)	Backward Link	12-month % change	
(A)		(B)	(C)	(D)	(E)	(F)	(G)
Year	Month	All Items	2017=100	All Items	2017=100	old series	new series
2016	Jan	123.2	94.7		94.7		
	Feb	124.7	95.8		95.8		
	Mar	125.1	96.1		96.1		
	Apr	125.6	96.5		96.5		
	May	125.8	96.7		96.7		
	Jun	126.5	97.2		97.2		
	Jul	126.5	97.2		97.2		
	Aug	126.7	97.4		97.4		
	Sep	126.8	97.4		97.4		
	Oct	127.3	97.8		97.8		
	Nov	127.8	98.2		98.2		
	Dec	127.6	98.1		98.1		
	AVG	**126.1**	**96.9**		**96.9**		
2017	Jan	128.1	98.4	98.5		4.0	4.0
	Feb	128.1	98.4	98.5		2.7	2.8
	Mar	128.4	98.7	98.8		2.6	2.8
	Apr	129.4	99.4	99.6		3.0	3.2
	May	129.6	99.6	99.8		3.0	3.2
	Jun	130.2	100.1	100.1		2.9	3.0
	Jul	130.6	100.4	100.3		3.2	3.2
	Aug	131.5	101.1	100.7		3.8	3.4
	Sep	131.5	101.1	100.9		3.7	3.6
	Oct	131.4	101.0	101.1		3.2	3.4
	Nov	131.4	101.0	100.9		2.8	2.7
	Dec	131.4	101.0	100.8		3.0	2.8
	AVG	**130.133**	**100.000**	**100.000**		**3.2**	**3.2**
Link	**Factors**		**1.00172**	**0.768443**			
2018	Jan		101.9	101.7		3.5	3.2
	Feb		102.1	101.9		3.7	3.5
	Mar		101.9	101.7		3.3	2.9
	Apr		102.2	102.0		2.8	2.4
	May		102.2	102.0		2.6	2.2
	Jun		102.8	102.6		2.7	2.5
	Jul		103.0	102.8		2.6	2.5
	Aug		103.0	102.8		1.9	2.1
	Sep		103.4	103.2		2.3	2.3
	Oct		103.6	103.4		2.6	2.3
	Nov		103.7	103.5		2.7	2.6
	Dec		104.7	104.5		3.7	3.7

previous year's annual average index as the new index reference period. There are three steps involved: (i) re-reference the old index series to the new index reference period; (ii) compile the new index series in the link month using the new weight structure; and (iii) link the new series to the old series by using forward linking factors or, if using the short-term price relative method, start the new series indices at the level of the old series in the link month.

Step 1: Calculate the annual average index from the old series for the new index reference period which in this example is 2017. The annual average index for 2017 with 2012 = 100 appears in column B. The new index starts in January 2018 with 2017 = 100 and the link month is December 2017. The old series is then re-referenced to the new reference period by dividing the monthly indices by the 2017 annual average which appears in column B. The link month index for the old series is December 2017.

$$I_{w=2012}^{t,\ 2017=100} = I_{w=2012}^{t,\ 2012=100} / I_{w=2012}^{Avg\ 2017,\ 2012=100} \qquad (9.10)$$

The re-referencing of the old series could also be done by using a backward linking factor that is the reciprocal of the new reference period average for the old index (column B: 1/1.30133 = 0.768443). The backward linking factor is in column D and the backward linked series is in column E (note that column E is identical to the series in column C). Whereas the forward linking factor is based on a single month (monthly overlap), the backward linking factor is based on an entire year (annual overlap).

Step 2: The indices for the new series are compiled for all months of 2017 using the new weights and price reference period. These appear in column D of Table 9.6.

$$I_{w=2017}^{Jan\ 2017,\ 2017=100} = \left(\sum_{i=1}^{n} w_i^{2017}\left(I_i^{Jan\ 2017} / I_i^{Avg\ 2017}\right)\right) \times 100 \qquad (9.11)$$

$$I_{w=2017}^{Dec\ 2017,\ 2017=100} = \left(\sum_{i=1}^{n} w_i^{2017}\left(I_i^{Dec\ 2017} / I_i^{Avg\ 2017}\right)\right) \times 100 \qquad (9.12)$$

Step 3: Because there is a difference in the index levels for the two series in the December 2017 link month, the new series should be linked to the re-referenced old series index level in the link month. This approach maintains a continuous series that will reflect the short-term price movements of the old series up to the link month and the short-term price movements for the new series following the link month. The easier approach is to simply use the link month level of the re-referenced old series as the starting point for the new series.

$$I_{w=2017}^{Jan\ 2018,\ 2017=100} = I_{w=2012}^{Dec\ 2017,\ 2017=100} \times \left(\sum_{i=1}^{n} w_i^{2017,Dec17}\left(I_i^{Jan\ 2018} / I_i^{Dec\ 2017}\right)\right) \qquad (9.13)$$

Where: $w_i^{2017,Dec2017} = w_i^{2017}\left(I_i^{Dec2017} \Big/ I_i^{Avg2017}\right) \Big/ I_{w=2017}^{Dec2017,2017=100}$

From the example, all the indices for December 2017 in the new series will be set to the index levels of the re-referenced old series in column C. This method is consistent with using the short-term price relative compilation procedure. The other approach is to calculate a forward linking factor to apply to each of the new index series every month in the future.

$$I_{w=2017}^{Jan\ 2018,\ 2017=100} = Linking\ factor_i \times \left(\sum_{i=1}^{n} w_i^{2017}\left(I_i^{Jan\ 2018} / I_i^{Dec\ 2017}\right)\right) \qquad (9.14)$$

$$Linking\ factor_i = I_{w=2012}^{Dec\ 2017,\ 2017=100} / I_{w=2017}^{Dec\ 2017,\ 2017=100}$$

The forward linking factor is calculated by dividing the link month index level of the old series (December 2017) by the link month index level of the new series: (131.4/130.133) × 100/100.8 = 1.00172. In the example, the old series link month index is in column C and the new series link month index is in column D. The forward linking factor appears in column C.

9.77 An important point to note when new series are introduced is the calculation of the 12-month (year-over-year) inflation rates. Series with annual overlaps provide two sets of indices to use for the annual inflation rates. The old series will have inflation rates calculated through the link month. In Table 9.6, column F shows the inflation rates that would have been calculated using the old series (note that the inflation rates are the same for the original and rebased series). In the example, the NSO has not published the new series; it has only published the old series on the 2012 = 100 base. The inflation rates during 2018 should then be calculated using the rebased series (2017 = 100 in column D), as appears in column G.

Keeping the Old Index Reference Period

9.78 An alternative method NSOs may pursue is linking the new CPI series to the old CPI series. This approach is similar to linking the new series forward in time to maintain the same index reference period as the old series. The only difference is that the new index on an updated price reference and weight reference period is not released to the public. Instead, linking factors are applied to each index before release. For example, if the NSO kept the index reference period as 2012 = 100 while starting compilation of the new index with 2017 = 100, the forward linking factor in column B of Table 9.7 would be applied to the new index level in column D beginning in January 2018 and continue to be used until the next revision. The forward linking factor is simply the old index series in the new indices' reference period (2017 = 100) expressed as a price relative (column B).

$$I_{w=2017}^{Jan\ 2017:t,\ 2012=100} = Linking\ factor_i \times \left(I_{w=2017}^{Jan\ 2017:t,\ 2017=100}\right) \qquad (9.15)$$

$$Linking\ factor_i = I_{w=2012}^{Avg\ 2017,\ 2012=100} / 100$$

9.79 Each period, the new index series is being tied to the old index levels for item and higher-level aggregates. Because the new index series on a new index reference period is not published, the annual rates of change in column F are all calculated using the published series with 2012=100. If the short-term relative compilation method is used, each index starts with its level in December 2017.

Table 9.7. Linking New Series to an Old Index Reference Period

		CPI (2012=100)	Forward Link	CPI (2017=100)	Backward Link	12-month % change
(A)		(B)	(C)	(D)	(E)	(F)
Year	Month	All Items	2012=100	All Items	2017=100	2012=100
2016	Jan	123.2			94.7	
	Feb	124.7			95.8	
	Mar	125.1			96.1	
	Apr	125.6			96.5	
	May	125.8			96.7	
	Jun	126.5			97.2	
	Jul	126.5			97.2	
	Aug	126.7			97.4	
	Sep	126.8			97.4	
	Oct	127.3			97.8	
	Nov	127.8			98.2	
	Dec	127.6			98.1	
	AVG	**126.1**			**96.9**	
2017	Jan	128.1	128.2	98.5		4.0
	Feb	128.1	128.2	98.5		2.7
	Mar	128.4	128.6	98.8		2.6
	Apr	129.4	129.6	99.6		3.0
	May	129.6	129.9	99.8		3.0
	Jun	130.2	130.3	100.1		2.9
	Jul	130.6	130.5	100.3		3.2
	Aug	131.5	131.0	100.7		3.8
	Sep	131.5	131.3	100.9		3.7
	Oct	131.4	131.6	101.1		3.2
	Nov	131.4	131.3	100.9		2.8
	Dec	131.4	131.2	100.8		3.0
	AVG	**130.133**	**130.133**	**100.000**		**3.2**
Link	**Factors**	**1.301333**		**0.768443**		
2018	Jan		132.4	101.7		3.3
	Feb		132.6	101.9		3.5
	Mar		132.4	101.7		3.1
	Apr		132.8	102.0		2.6
	May		132.8	102.0		2.4
	Jun		133.5	102.6		2.6
	Jul		133.8	102.8		2.5
	Aug		133.8	102.8		1.8
	Sep		134.3	103.2		2.1
	Oct		134.6	103.4		2.4
	Nov		134.7	103.5		2.5
	Dec		136.0	104.5		3.5

Example of Calculating New Series at the First Level of Aggregation

9.80 As another example, assume the NSO keeps the 2012 = 100 reference period while introducing the new CPI with 2017 = 100, but the revision starts at the lowest level of aggregation. In this case, the NSO will have to revise elementary price indices with the first pricing period in 2017. Assuming the CPI series is monthly, each monthly elementary aggregate index (first level of aggregation) in 2017 must be divided by the 2017 annual average to re-reference the indices to 2017 = 100. The re-referenced item indices (elementary aggregates) are aggregated using the new weights to derive the higher-level indices.

$$I_i^{m,\,2017=100} = I_i^{m,\,2017} \,/\, I_i^{Avg\ 2017} \quad (9.16)$$

$$I_{w=2017}^{m,\,2017=100} = \sum_{i=1}^{m}\left(w_i^{2017} I_{i,}^{m,\,2017=100}\right) / \sum_{i=1}^{m} w_i^{2017} \quad (9.17)$$

9.81 This aggregation results in a class index that is different from the one obtained by simply re-referencing the old CPI class index. In addition, the new CPI monthly class indices adjusted to the 2012 index reference period will be different because the new weights have changed the levels of the monthly indices.

9.82 The example in the first box of Table 9.8 shows the monthly item and subclass indices for Oils and Fats (COICOP 2018 01.1.5) in 2017 on the old reference period (2012 = 100). It also has the annual averages[7] for 2017 and

[7] Standard international practice for calculating annual average indices is to use a simple arithmetic average of the monthly indices. While geometric averaging could be used, the results can be different when aggregate indices are calculated using arithmetic aggregation. If geometric aggregation were used at the higher level, then geometric annual averages should be used. Consistency in aggregation is important for calculating the annual averages.

the re-referenced monthly indices for the class index in column G (i.e., dividing the monthly class indices by the annual average of 111.8).

9.83 In the second box of Table 9.8 the monthly item indices for the four items in the class are re-referenced to 2017 = 100 and these indices are aggregated (columns B-E) to the class level (column F) using the new weights for 2017. Note that the new class indices with 2017 = 100 in column F of the second box are different from those in column G7 of the first box. The reason for this is that the higher-level indices are compiled using different weights and index levels than those in the old CPI.

9.84 The class indices in column G of the second box represent the new CPI on the weight and price reference for 2017. If the NSO was introducing the new series, then the indices beginning in January 2018 would be linked to the December 2017 index level in column G as shown in Table 9.6. The NSO, however, is keeping the old 2012 index reference period. So it will need to use the forward linking factors to adjust the new CPI levels to the same level as the old CPI. As noted previously in the discussion of Table 9.7, the forward linking factor is the old index level in the overlap period (2017 average) expressed as a price relative (i.e., divided by 100) which is 1.118 (111.8 ÷ 100). This factor is applied to the monthly class level indices in column G of the second box to tie them to the old index levels that appear in column H. Note that these values are different from the values in column G of the first box, again because the new indices are compiled using different weights and index levels than those in the old CPI.

Aggregation Across Linked Series

9.85 When the new series is introduced there is a break in the comparability of the historical indices. The new and previous series are no longer strictly comparable because of the change in weights, item structures, and, in the case of re-referencing the indices, the level of the indices. Each old series is re-referenced to the new index reference period. The re-referenced series will no longer yield the same results as before the rebasing when aggregated. This is demonstrated in column H of Table 9.8. In the first box of column H the new CPI series for the item indices are aggregated using the old item weights. There are differences between the rebased old series (column G) and the re-aggregated new series using old weights (column H) in April, May, September, and December demonstrating the effects of the weight differences. In the second box of Table 9.8, column H, the old item indices are aggregated using the new weights. There are differences in every month reflecting the effects of both the weight changes and the index level differences. Had there been a new item added to the class, for example lard, this could also account for a difference.

Table 9.8 Aggregating new CPI Series using an Annual Period Overlap

2017	Butter, fresh (item)	Margarine (item)	Peanut butter (item)	Vegetable Oil (item) 2012=100	Old CPI Oils & Fats (class)	Old CPI Class index rebase to 2017=100	Old CPI aggregate item indices using rebased series
(A)	(B)	(C)	(D)	(E)	(F)	(G)	(H)
Item weights (2012)	0.307	2.669	1.155	2.600	**6.731**		
January	108.2	105.8	108.3	119.4	**111.6**	**99.8**	**99.8**
February	110.5	101.5	98.0	114.5	**106.3**	**95.1**	**95.1**
March	112.8	103.6	100.1	116.9	**108.6**	**97.1**	**97.1**
April	107.1	105.8	97.0	119.4	**109.6**	**98.0**	**97.9**
May	113.9	100.4	103.2	113.3	**106.5**	**95.2**	**95.3**
June	115.1	106.8	104.2	120.6	**112.1**	**100.2**	**100.2**
July	112.8	107.9	102.1	121.8	**112.5**	**100.6**	**100.6**
August	113.9	107.9	102.1	120.6	**112.1**	**100.2**	**100.2**
September	120.8	106.8	103.2	127.8	**114.9**	**102.8**	**102.6**
October	115.1	113.2	109.4	126.6	**117.8**	**105.4**	**105.4**
November	117.4	110.0	104.2	124.2	**114.8**	**102.7**	**102.7**
December	119.6	112.2	106.3	121.8	**115.2**	**103.0**	**103.1**
Average	**113.9**	**106.8**	**103.2**	**120.6**	**111.8**	**100.0**	**100.0**
Re-referenced indices	(2017 =	100)			**New CPI**	**Linked CPI**	**Old base with**
Item weights (2017)	0.269	1.435	1.194	2.674	**5.573**	**2012=100**	**new weights**
January	95.0	99.0	105.0	99.0	**100.1**	**111.9**	**113.0**
February	97.0	95.0	95.0	95.0	**95.1**	**106.3**	**107.4**
March	99.0	97.0	97.0	97.0	**97.1**	**108.6**	**109.7**
April	94.0	99.0	94.0	99.0	**97.7**	**109.2**	**110.5**
May	100.0	94.0	100.0	94.0	**95.6**	**106.9**	**107.9**
June	101.0	100.0	101.0	100.0	**100.3**	**112.1**	**113.3**
July	99.0	101.0	99.0	101.0	**100.5**	**112.4**	**113.6**
August	100.0	101.0	99.0	100.0	**100.0**	**111.9**	**113.0**
September	106.0	100.0	100.0	106.0	**103.2**	**115.4**	**116.8**
October	101.0	106.0	106.0	105.0	**105.3**	**117.7**	**118.9**
November	103.0	103.0	101.0	103.0	**102.6**	**114.7**	**115.9**
December	105.0	105.0	103.0	101.0	**102.7**	**114.8**	**115.9**
Average	**100.0**	**100.0**	**100.0**	**100.0**	**100.0**	**111.8**	**113.0**

Frequency of Weight Updates

Data Sources for More Frequent Weight Updates

9.86 The primary source for more frequent updating of the CPI would be the HBS; however, in some countries, national accounts data are used as the source for developing new index weights. Countries that have a continuous HBS conducted every quarter or every year can use the data from the HBS to verify any significant shifts in the CPI basket and the weights. The NSO can develop a concordance between the HBS and the CPI basket and review the changes in the basket and weight shares on a regular basis. As the shares shift, the NSO could update the CPI basket as discussed in Chapter 3, paragraph 3.80:

> *Even if weights are updated only every five years, it is desirable to review the weights in between to ensure that they remain sufficiently reliable and representative. The review, which may be limited to weights at the elementary index level and their major components, should examine whether there are indications that important changes may have taken place in the consumption pattern since the weight reference period.*

9.87 There is no specific guidance on what constitutes an important change, but the CPI compiler should look at all changes in shares that exceed ±0.5 percent on an annual basis. Such shifts may indicate significant economic changes in the pattern of consumer purchases.

9.88 If HBSs are conducted on a two- or three-year cycle, the CPI compiler should give serious consideration to updating the weights as the latest HBS results become available. In fact, many countries update their CPI weights every year or every two years to minimize the substitution bias that is problematic with fixed-base indices. Such frequent updating of the weights keeps the CPI basket more representative of consumer purchases.

9.89 As discussed in Chapter 3, other sources for more frequent updating are the national accounts where data on household final consumption expenditure are often available on an annual basis. A retail sales survey could also provide indications of changes in purchasing patterns for goods and services sold at retail outlets.

9.90 The shortcoming of these two data sources is that they do not have the detail that is found in the HBS. Typically, these sources may have data at the COICOP class, group, or even division levels. In such cases, a full reweighting at the item level will not be possible. The NSO will need to decide if it wants to introduce new weights at the higher level, such as the class, group, or division levels, while maintaining the weighting pattern fixed at the lower levels. The introduction of weights for the higher-level aggregates is referred to as "partial reweighting" or "partial weight updates". More generally, this is also an illustration how national accounts and HBS data can be combined in practice in order to derive CPI weights.

9.91 Table 9.9 presents an example of partial weight updates. Assuming that the CPI compiler was able to use data from the national accounts and retail sales survey to derive a new weight distribution at the class level, column D

Table 9.9 Partial Weight Updates at the COICOP Class Level

COICOP Code	Description	Expenditure Share 2015	High-Level Shares 2017	Allocation with 2015 Shares	Updated Shares 2017 base	Allocation with updated 2015 Shares	Updated Shares 2017 base
(A)	(B)	(C)	(D)	(E)	(F)	(G)	(H)
01	**Food and Non-alcoholic Bev.**	**100.00**	**100.00**		**100.00**		**100.00**
01.1	**FOOD**	**93.31**	**91.90**		**91.90**		**91.90**
01.1.1	**Bread & Cereals**	**21.42**	**21.90**		**21.90**		**21.90**
01.1.101	Rice (white)	1.406		0.06567	1.438	0.07406	1.622
01.1.102	Rice (Brown)	3.361		0.15692	3.437	0.12411	2.718
01.1.103	Flour	2.578		0.12036	2.636	0.15272	3.345
01.1.104	Bread	6.864		0.32048	7.019	0.29953	6.560
01.1.105	Biscuits (Salted)	0.813		0.03795	0.831	0.02514	0.551
01.1.106	Cakes, Pastry, etc.	1.034		0.04829	1.058	0.04596	1.007
01.1.107	Chow Mein	1.716		0.08009	1.754	0.10596	2.321
01.1.109	Macaroni	1.284		0.05993	1.312	0.06061	1.327
01.1.110	Oat flakes	0.450		0.02101	0.460	0.02519	0.552
01.1.111	Sago	0.341		0.01592	0.349	0.01833	0.401
01.1.112	Tennis Rolls	1.392		0.06498	1.423	0.06053	1.326
01.1.113	***Whole Wheat Bread****	0.180		0.00840	0.184	0.00785	0.172
01.1.2	**Meat**	**17.63**	**16.50**		**16.50**		**16.50**
01.1.201	Stew Beef	1.940		0.11004	1.816	0.11237	1.854
01.1.205	Chicken (live)	1.038		0.05885	0.971	0.05317	0.877
01.1.206	Chicken (frozen)	10.202		0.57862	9.547	0.58705	9.686
01.1.207	Pork Leg	0.610		0.03457	0.570	0.05334	0.880
01.1.210	***Corned beef****	0.866		0.04913	0.811	0.04601	0.759
01.1.211	Duck	0.217		0.01232	0.203	0.00754	0.124
01.1.212	Liver	0.207		0.01174	0.194	0.00894	0.148
01.1.213	Mutton	0.271		0.01536	0.253	0.01636	0.270
01.1.214	Sausages (pork & chicken)	1.823		0.10339	1.706	0.08869	1.463
01.1.215	***Brisket****	0.458		0.02598	0.429	0.02653	0.438
01.1.3	**Fish & Seafood**	**5.98**	**6.70**		**6.70**		**6.70**

contains the compiler derived share weights. The weights at the item level are not available so the compiler chooses to keep the same allocation of the original weights at the item level. This approach assumes the shares will not have changed at the item level and is consistent with a Young index. Column E contains the item allocation share for each class. These are calculated by taking the 2015 expenditure shares for each item (column C) and dividing them by the class share (column C). The item allocation share in column E for each item is multiplied by the new class share to derive the updated item shares in column F. The compiler can use these updated shares in the CPI to revise the weights.

9.92 Another alternative that the NSO could choose for allocating the weights is to use shares derived from the weights updated for price change from the original period when the weights were introduced. This approach assumes the weights have changed because of price change but the quantities have remained the same. It is consistent with a Lowe index. Column G contains the item allocation share for each class using the updated weights.

$$\hat{s}_i^{2017} = S_c^{2017}\left(s_i^{2015}\right) \Big/ \sum_{i=1}^{m} s_i^{2015} \tag{9.18}$$

These are calculated by taking the 2017 cost weights for each item (not shown in Table 9.9) and dividing it by the class cost weight for 2017.

$$S_c^{2017} = w_c^{2017} \Big/ \sum_{c=1}^{k} w_c^{2017} \tag{9.19}$$

9.93 The item allocation share in column G for each item is multiplied by the new class share to derive the updated item shares in column H. The NSO can use these updated shares based on the 2017 cost weights in the CPI to revise the weights.

9.94 The NSO can use either method depending on the type of index they are compiling—Young, Lowe, or Laspeyres. Once the new weights at the item level are available, the NSO can introduce them using the methods described in paragraphs 9.45 to 9.54. The resulting revised indices should be linked to the previous series using the methods described in the previous section on linking the previous CPI to the new index reference period (paragraphs 9.70 – 9.85).

Annual Updating and Linking

9.95 If data are available for updating the weights on an annual basis, the updating procedures for the NSO to use are the same as those already presented. The primary difference is that the process is done every year versus every five to ten years. The NSO must determine when introducing the new weights what the new price reference period will be and the date for the weight update. The weight reference period is still annual (e.g., 2015) so the price reference period could be the annual average for 2017 or December 2017. If this is the case, the NSO will most likely decide not to update the index reference period, and they will use procedures for keeping the same index base (e.g., 2010 = 100) described in paragraphs 9.82 to 9.83.

9.96 If the NSO chooses to update the weights annually with the most recent weight data, it usually does it at the beginning of the year. It also will use the last pricing period of the previous year as the price reference period.[8] The NSO must decide whether to price update the weights to the price reference period or simply introduce them with the new price reference period. In this example, the NSO would need to update the weights from the 2015 annual average to December 2017. The same procedures described for Tables 9.7 and 9.8 apply: (i) re-reference the old series (e.g., with December 2016 = 100) to the new reference (overlap) period (e.g., December 2017); (ii) convert the old index levels in the link month to price relatives by dividing each by 100 to derive the forward linking factors; and (iii) use the linking factor for tying the new series to the old series level going forward in time.

9.97 If this linking process continues for multiple years, the linking factors for each year must be derived from the indices on the fixed index reference period or made cumulative by chaining the annual series through time. With the annual linking, there are a series of one-year links going forward in time. Each annual link starts an index with a new price and index reference period of 100. For the first weight introduction, the annual index starts with 100; for the second, it too will start with 100 as will the third. If the linking factors are calculated at the end of each new annual index, they will only tie the index level to that of the previous annual index. For example, the NSO introduced a new set of weights with a price and index reference period of December 2015 at the end of January 2016. In January 2017, new weights are introduced with December 2016 = 100. In order to keep the previous index reference period of December 2015 = 100, forward linking factors are needed and compiled using the index values for the overlap period in December 2016. These reflect the index level of the previous index period, December 2015. When yet another set of weights are introduced in January 2018 with December 2017 = 100, the linking factors for the overlap period will refer to the index with December 2016 = 100. In this situation, in order to adjust the new index level to that with December 2015 =100, the linking factors for December 2016 and December 2017 must each be used (chained) to get the correct index levels. The series of one-year indices must be chained together because each only represents the change over a yearly period. To get the long-term change, these annual changes need to be made cumulative.[9]

9.98 The aggregation to the higher-levels must always be based on the initial indices using the most recent weights that have not yet been multiplied by the linking factors. The chain-linked indices will not be consistent in aggregation. The published indices may have a reference period of 2015 = 100 but they are initially compiled on a more recent reference period (e.g., December of the previous year). The linking factors are then applied to the new index to adjust to the level of the chain-linked indices. Because there are differences in the index levels, aggregations using the new weights on the chain-linked indices give different results.

[8] The new weights can be introduced in any time period. Normally, the price reference period will either be the date of the weight reference period, a calendar year, or the period prior to the introductory period.

[9] The alternative approach to using linking factors, as discussed earlier, is to apply the short-term price relatives each month to update the previous month's indices.

For users to derive the correct indices for their own special aggregations, they must first unchain the published indices by dividing them with the chain-linked index of the link month before they can be aggregated with the weights that are applied during that year.

9.99 Because of the introduction of new weights every year, the annual rates will not only capture changes in prices but also changes in the weight structure. In such a situation, the contribution of each item to the all-items annual rate of change is ill-defined and different approaches have been proposed for measuring contributions or impacts (paragraphs 9.108 to 9.118 describe how to calculate contributions to change).[10] If the weights are introduced in January with the previous December month having the role of the new price reference period, the distortion on the annual rates caused by the different weights vanishes in the December month of that year.

9.100 When a methodological change is introduced together with the annual weight updates, annual rates of change can sometimes be affected by the fact that indices 12 months apart are calculated according to different methods. The samples that can be renewed together with the weight update may also have different seasonal patterns than the samples that were priced in the previous year. Different seasonal patterns in the samples, combined with linking over a single month, could lead to distortions in the annual rates of the chain-linked index due to a permanent shift in the index level. Generally, this is the case when the index values of the old and new sample strongly differ in the linking month. Some form of parallel calculations may be needed in order to measure the impact of such changes. Ideally, the NSO should test alternative linking approaches in order to minimize any statistical distortions in the index series.

9.101 The resulting annually chained indices can in principle be presented in any index reference period. The index reference period corresponds to the period for which the index is set to 100. A price index expressed for instance as 2010 = 100 can be re-referenced or re-scaled to 2015 = 100 by simply dividing the 2010 indices by the arithmetic average of the 2010 indices for the 12 months of 2015. Apart from rounding errors, re-referencing should have no impact on monthly or annual rates of change. The index reference period may correspond to the first price reference period used in the series. Another option would be to update the index reference period from time to time, say every 10 years, or when major methodological changes are taking place. When the index reference period is changed, it may be useful to continue providing the results in the old reference period because some users may still need the index levels expressed in the old reference period.

9.102 Table 9.10 demonstrates the process for linking annual indices for multiple periods. The new index reference period in January 2015 was December 2014 = 100

[10]The contribution to change must be broken down into two components. The first component is the change from the relevant month in the previous year to the link month using the old weights and added to this is the (second component) change from the link month to the relevant month in the current year using the new weights.

Table 9.10 Linking Annual Indices for Multiple Periods with Chained Linking Factors

COICOP Code	Description	CPI Dec. 2014=100	CPI Dec. 2015 with Dec. 2014=100	Linking Factor Forward (2016 Series)	CPI Dec. 2016 with Dec. 2015=100	CPI Dec. 2016 with Dec. 2014=100	Linking Factor Forward (2017 Series)	CPI Dec. 2017 with Dec. 2016=100	CPI Dec. 2017 with Dec. 2014=100
(A)	(B)	(C)	(D)	(E)	(F)	(G)	(H)	(I)	(J)
01	**Food and Non-alcoholic Bev.**	**100.00**	**108.99**	**1.089859**	**103.69**	**113.01**	**1.130084**	**104.33**	**117.90**
01.1	**FOOD**	**100.00**	**108.91**	**1.089085**	**106.29**	**115.76**	**1.157578**	**106.87**	**123.71**
01.1.1	**Bread & Cereals**	**100.00**	**120.45**	**1.204490**	**103.75**	**124.96**	**1.249616**	**115.37**	**144.16**
01.1.101	Rice (white)	100.0	137.0	1.370003	135.4	185.4	1.854301	171.19	317.44
01.1.102	Rice (Brown)	100.0	137.9	1.379356	95.6	131.8	1.318197	121.70	160.42
01.1.103	Flour	100.0	122.6	1.225822	136.2	167.0	1.670136	154.19	257.52
01.1.104	Bread	100.0	115.6	1.156216	94.7	109.4	1.094450	101.04	110.58
01.1.105	Biscuits (Salted)	100.0	102.8	1.027706	59.6	61.3	0.612767	56.57	34.67
01.1.106	Cakes, Pastry, etc.	100.0	119.3	1.192797	99.4	118.6	1.186214	109.51	129.91
01.1.107	Chow Mein	100.0	113.8	1.137564	131.8	150.0	1.499635	138.45	207.62
01.1.109	Macaroni	100.0	96.2	0.962266	85.3	82.0	0.820352	75.74	62.13
01.1.110	Oat flakes	100.0	91.4	0.914144	96.0	87.8	0.877843	81.04	71.14
01.1.111	Sago	100.0	94.1	0.940671	94.9	89.2	0.892387	82.39	73.52
01.1.112	Tennis Rolls	100.0	114.5	1.145302	93.4	107.0	1.070218	98.80	105.74
01.1.113	*Whole Wheat Bread**	*100.0*	*115.6*	*1.156216*	*94.7*	*109.4*	*1.094450*	*101.04*	*110.58*
01.1.2	**Meat**	**100.00**	**101.70**	**1.016968**	**108.42**	**110.26**	**1.102645**	**101.80**	**112.25**
01.1.201	Stew Beef	100.0	100.5	1.004750	108.4	109.0	1.089502	100.58	109.59
01.1.205	Chicken (live)	100.0	102.3	1.023498	97.7	100.0	1.000247	92.34	92.37
01.1.206	Chicken (frozen)	100.0	100.2	1.002088	107.4	107.7	1.076706	99.40	107.03
01.1.207	Pork Leg	100.0	126.2	1.261643	205.7	259.5	2.595448	239.62	621.91
01.1.210	Corned beef	*100.0*	*101.7*	*1.016968*	*100.7*	*102.4*	*1.023703*	*94.51*	*96.75*
01.1.211	Duck	100.0	97.5	0.975450	63.1	61.5	0.615484	56.82	34.97
01.1.212	Liver	100.0	104.9	1.049449	84.5	88.7	0.886868	81.88	72.61
01.1.213	Mutton	100.0	97.1	0.970904	109.2	106.1	1.060580	97.91	103.85
01.1.214	Sausages (pork & chicken)	100.0	109.3	1.093397	99.1	108.4	1.083866	100.06	108.46
01.1.215	*Brisket**	*100.0*	*100.5*	*1.004750*	*108.4*	*109.0*	*1.089502*	*100.58*	*109.59*
01.1.3	**Fish & Seafood**	**100.00**	**96.93**	**0.969334**	**96.98**	**94.00**	**0.940030**	**86.78**	**81.58**

(column C). The NSO proceeded to update the weights in January 2016, January 2017, and January 2018, while maintaining the original index reference period of December 2014. In January 2015, new weights were introduced from 2013 and the new price reference period was set to December 2014 = 100. This is also the overlap month, so the indices are converted to long-term relatives and serve as the linking factors (column E) to tie to the next year's indices. In January 2016 weights were introduced from 2014 and the new price reference period was set to December 2015 = 100. The link factors from the previous year (column E) are applied to the new index levels for December 2015 (column F) to derive the current year index levels (column G) with December 2015 = 100. These indices are then converted to linking factors to use with the 2016 indices (column H). The same actions were taken in January 2017 with new weights from 2015 and a new index using December 2016 = 100. The previous year linking factors (column H) were applied to the December 2017 index (column I) to derive the index for December 2017 with December 2014 = 100 (column J).

9.103 The index levels in columns F and I reflect the levels of each index referencing the previous December (2015 and 2016, respectively). They are not calculated on the December 2014 reference period. This is accomplished by linking each of these periods together successively. As can be seen in Table 9.9, the chaining of the linking factors is similar to chaining the annual indices of the three-year period (December 2014 to December 2016). For example, the December 2017 index for the Food Group (COICOP 1999 01.1) of 123.71 is the product of chaining the price changes (indices converted to price relatives) for the three years (1.089085 × 1.0629 × 1.0687) to the December 2014 reference period index of 100.

Calculating Cntributions to Change

9.104 Contributions to change help explain those groups of goods and services that contribute most to inflation. These data are useful to better understand the sources of inflation and can contribute to greater transparency. Whether the weights are fixed for a period of time or updated annually, different formulas would apply.

Fixed Weight Indices

9.105 The formula used to calculate the contributions from the aggregates to the total index is as follows:

$$C_i^t = \frac{w_i^{t_0} * \left(I_i^t - I_i^{t-m}\right)}{I_{TOT}^{t-m}} \qquad (9.20)$$

where

C_i^t: contribution of aggregate i in period t

$w_i^{t_0}$: weight of aggregate i in period t_0

I_i^t: index of aggregate i in period t

I_i^{t-m}: index of aggregate i in period t-m

I_{TOT}^{t-m}: total index in period t-m

9.106 The addition of individual contributions is equal to the published rate of change. It should be noted that this formula may only be applied if the weights remain constant. When the weights change, in the case of a chained index, the additivity of individual contributions does not provide exactly the published rate of change. However, estimates are possible as shown in the section that follows on annual weight updates. When the comparison period t-m to t crosses over a link period k, then the contribution must be calculated separately for each period (t-m to k and k to t) and combined.

Annual Weight Updates[11,12]

9.107 When expenditure weights are annually updated, price indices spanning more than a year are chain-linked and the formula to compute contributions to inflation between month *m* of year *(y-1)* and month *m* of year *y* needs to be modified. The annual inflation rate denoted by $\pi TOTy,m$ can thus be decomposed as follows, assuming that each year the new weights are introduced with the December to January link:

$$\pi_{TOT}^{y,m} \equiv \frac{I_{TOT}^{y,m} y,m - I_{TOT}^{y-1,m}}{I_{TOT}^{y-1,m}}$$

$$= \frac{I_{TOT}^{y-1,12}}{I_{TOT}^{y-1,m}} \sum_j \left[w_j^{y-1,12} \frac{I_j^{y,m}}{I_j^{y-1,12}} \right] - \frac{I_{TOT}^{y-2,12}}{I_{TOT}^{y-1,m}} \sum_j \left[w_j^{y-2,12} \frac{I_j^{y-1,m}}{I_j^{y-2,12}} \right]$$

$$= \frac{I_{TOT}^{y-1,12}}{I_{TOT}^{y-1,m}} \sum_j \left[W_j^{y-1,12} \left(\frac{I_{TOT}^{y-1,12}}{I_j^{y-1,12}} \right) - 1 \right] + \underbrace{\frac{I_{TOT}^{y-1,12}}{I_{TOT}^{y-1,m}}}_{= \frac{I_{TOT}^{y-2,12}}{I_{TOT}^{y-1,m}} \sum_j \left[W_j^{y-2,12} \frac{I_j^{y-1,12}}{I_j^{y-2,12}} \right]}$$

$$- \frac{I_{TOT}^{y-2,12}}{I_{TOT}^{y-1,m}} \sum_j \left[W_j^{y-2,12} \frac{I_j^{y-1,m}}{I_j^{y-2,12}} \right]$$

$$= \frac{I_{TOT}^{y-1,12}}{I_{TOT}^{y-1,m}} \sum_j \left[W_j^{y-1,12} \left(\frac{I_j^{y,m}}{I_j^{y-1,12}} \right) \right] + \frac{I_{TOT}^{y-2,12}}{I_{TOT}^{y-1,m}} \sum_j W_j^{y-2,12} \left(\frac{I_j^{y-1,12} - I_j^{y-1,m}}{I_j^{y-2,12}} \right) \qquad (9.21)$$

9.108 The contribution of component *j* to the overall annual rate of inflation in month *m* of year *y* can be written as follows. By construction, these contributions sum to overall inflation.

$$Contrib_j^{y,m} = \left[\left(\underbrace{\frac{I_{TOT}^{y-1,12}}{I_{TOT}^{y-1,m}}}_{(1)} * \underbrace{W_j^{y-1,12}}_{(2)} \right) * \left(\underbrace{\frac{I_j^{y,m} - I_j^{y-1,12}}{I_j^{y-1,12}}}_{(3)} \right) \right] + \left(\underbrace{\frac{I_{TOT}^{y-2,12}}{I_{TOT}^{y-1,m}}}_{(4)} * \underbrace{W_j^{y-2,12}}_{(5)} \right) * \left(\underbrace{\frac{I_j^{y-1,12} - I_j^{y-1,m}}{I_j^{y-2,12}}}_{(6)} \right) \qquad (9.22)$$

[11]For detailed methodology, see http://www.oecd.org/sdd/prices-ppp/OECD-calculation-contributions-annual-inflation.pdf

[12]See also *Harmonized Index of Consumer Prices (HICP) Methodological Manual*, Section 8.5.3, https://ec.europa.eu/eurostat/web/products-manuals-and-guidelines/-/KS-GQ-17-015

Notations:
$W_{jy}-1,12$ is the expenditure weight corresponding to COICOP component j in December of year *(y-1)* and used for the link from December of year *(y-1)* until December of year y;
I_{TOT}, is the overall price index in month m of year y;
I_j, is the price index of component j in month m of year y;

9.109 The first part of the above formula (terms 1 to 3) considers price developments that occurred between December of year *(y-1)* and month m of year y, whereas its second part (terms 4 to 6) takes into account price developments that occurred between month m of year *(y-1)* and December of year *(y-1)*. This cut in December of year *(y-1)* is introduced due to the change in expenditure weights that is introduced after this month.

9.110 Note that when m = 12 (December), the second part of the formula is equal to zero and the first part simplifies as follows, which leads to the same contribution formula as in the fixed basket case when $y^0 = y - 1$ and $m^0 = 12$:

$$Contrib_j^{y,12} = \underbrace{W_j^{y-1,12}}_{(2)} * \underbrace{\frac{I_j^{y,12} - I_j^{y-1,12}}{I_j^{y-1,12}}}_{\equiv \pi_j^{y,12}:(3)} \qquad (9.23)$$

9.111 Alternative approaches to calculating the contributions to change are possible. First, when the weights are fixed, the relative change of the index from t-m to t can then be written as:

$$\frac{I^{0:t}}{I^{0:t-m}} - 1 = \frac{\sum w_j^b I_j^{0:t-m} I_j^{t-m:t}}{\sum w_j^b I_j^{0:t-m}} - 1 \qquad (9.24)$$

Hence, a sub-index, j, from t-m to t enters the higher-level index with a weight of:

$$\frac{w_j^b I_j^{0:t-m}}{\sum w_j^b I_j^{0:t-m}} = \frac{w_j^b I_j^{0:t-m}}{I^{0:t-m}} \qquad (9.25)$$

The effect on the higher-level index of a change in a sub-index can then be calculated as:

$$Effect = \frac{w_j^b I_j^{0:t-m}}{I^{0:t-m}} \left(\frac{I_j^{0:t}}{I_j^{0:t-m}} - 1 \right) = \frac{w_j^b}{I^{0:t-m}} \left(I_j^{0:t} - I_j^{0:t-m} \right) \qquad (9.26)$$

With $m = 1$, the formula **9.27** gives the effect of a monthly change; with $m = 12$, it gives the effect of the change over the past 12 months.

9.112 If the weights have been updated, then a sub-index, j, from t-m enters the higher-level index with a weight of:

$$\frac{w_j^k I_j^{k:t-m}}{I^{k:t-m}} = \frac{w_j^k \left(I_j^{0:t-m} / I_j^{0:k} \right)}{\left(I^{0:t-m} / I^{0:k} \right)} \qquad (9.27)$$

9.113 The effect on the higher-level index of a change in a sub-index then is:

$$Effect = \frac{w_j^k}{I^{k:t-m}} \left(I_j^{k:t} - I_j^{k:t-m} \right) = \frac{w_j^k}{\left(I^{0:t-m} / I^{0:k} \right)} \left(\frac{I_j^{0:t} - I_j^{0:t-m}}{I_j^{0:k}} \right) \qquad (9.28)$$

It is assumed that t-m lies in the same link (i.e. t-m refers to a period later than k). If the effect of a sub-index on a higher-level index is to be calculated across a chain, the calculation needs to be carried out in two steps: one with the old series up to the link period, and one from the link period to period t.

9.114 The calculation of the effect of a change in a sub-index on a higher-level index is illustrated in Table 9.11. The index is calculated in one link so that equation 9.26 may be applied for the decomposition. For instance, the effect in percentage points of the increase for housing from January 2018 to January 2019 can be calculated as 0.25/118.6 × (120.0 – 110.0) = 2.11 percentage points. This means that, of the increase of 10.03 per cent in the all-items index, 2.11 percentage points can be attributed to the increase in the index for housing.

Introducing New Classification Systems

9.115 Chapter 2 recommends that countries adopt the United Nations' COICOP. Many countries that have been using a national product classification system will want to introduce the COICOP at the time of their next CPI revision in order to meet the recommendations of this Manual. The introduction of COICOP may cause a break with the old classification system. For example, COICOP 2018 classifies household final consumption expenditure into 13 Divisions

Table 9.11 Decomposition of Index Changes

	Weight	Index			Change in % from Jan. 18 to Jan. 19	Effect (contribution)	
		2015	Jan. 18	Jan. 19		% points of total change	% of total change
Food	0.30	100.0	120.0	130.0	8.33	2.53	25.21
Clothing	0.10	100.0	130.0	145.0	11.54	1.26	12.61
Housing	0.25	100.0	110.0	120.0	9.09	2.11	21.01
Transport	0.20	100.0	125.0	130.0	4.00	0.84	8.40
Miscellaneous	0.15	100.0	114.0	140.0	22.81	3.29	32.77
Items	1.00	100.0	118.6	130.5	10.03	10.03	100.00

as shown in Annex 2. Countries who have not adopted COICOP often have classifications with 9 or 10 Divisions. Both classification systems will cover the detailed items, but they are often classified in different Divisions. One common area of difference is food eaten at restaurants, cafes, canteens, and kiosks. COICOP includes these expenditures in Division 11 Restaurants and Accommodation Services, while the national classification may include these in Division 01 Food and Non-Alcoholic Beverages.

9.116 When the NSO is ready to introduce the revised CPI using the COICOP, there will be a difference in the old and new classification structures for the published indices. Some Divisions such as Clothing and Footwear and Health may be the same. Others such as Furnishings, Household Equipment, and Routine Household Maintenance (where televisions and video equipment are moved to Entertainment).will have differences in the detailed components

9.117 In most instances, the old CPI includes the same detailed components as the COICOP, but the components appear in different divisions. If this is the case, it may be a straightforward task to develop a concordance between the old classification and the COICOP. The old index series at the detailed level can be recompiled using the old series weights to reflect the COICOP structure at the 13 Division level. The recompiled old series can then be linked with the new COICOP series to form a time series going back to the point of the previous revision. For example, assume the last revision was on a 2010 =100 reference period and introduced in January 2013. These series can be recompiled to form COICOP Division level indices for January 2013 through December 2017. The new COICOP series is introduced in January 2018 with 2015 = 100 reference period. The old series can be linked to the new series at the Division and Total CPI levels using 2015 = 100 as the overlap period. The old series can be re-referenced to the 2015 annual average = 100 if a new reference base is introduced.

9.118 Alternatively, if the NSO decides to keep the 2010 =100 reference period, the changes in the revised CPI can be applied to the old index series at the COICOP Division level. In this latter instance, the new series must be compiled for both December 2017 and January 2018 on the 2015 = 100 reference period and the monthly price relative for January 2018 is applied to the recompiled old series at the Division and Total CPI levels on the 2010 = 100 reference period. This process is carried out each month going forward in time. Note that the new weights are applied to the revised index levels with 2015 = 100. They are not applied and are not relevant for the old series with 2010 = 100. The new weights refer to the CPI structure in 2015, not the structure from 2010.

9.119 It is important for the NSO to advise users about changes that are made to the CPI, particularly when a revision takes place. When the NSO updates the index reference period, users will generally take note of the change and ask about the difference between the old and revised series. The NSO should provide users with the information about all the changes taking place including new weights, new item structure, and improvements in methods and procedures. Users also need to be aware that the series are not strictly comparable. Some items may have been dropped from coverage and others added. For example, radios, tape recorders, and stereo systems may no longer be important items in the basket and may be replaced with Bluetooth speakers and other audio media. In addition, electronic items such as tablets and e-readers may be added. In some instances, owner-occupied housing may now be represented whereas only rental units were included previously.

9.120 When the NSO does not change the index reference period (i.e., keeps the old reference period), it is less obvious to users that a change has taken place. This is particularly true when it has been several years since the last CPI revision. If the weights are updated annually, users may be aware of the change in weighting; however, when revisions only take place every five to ten years, the NSO needs to make extra efforts to ensure that users are aware of changes and discontinuities in series.

Expanding CPI Geographic Coverage

9.121 Many countries have CPIs with limited geographic coverage—capital city, two or three of the largest areas, large and medium-sized cities—when they are first developed. Over time as the CPI becomes more important in economic planning and inflation monitoring, and population centers expand, efforts are made to expand the CPI to cover more geographic areas including all urban and rural areas. Generally, this expansion takes place by increasing the coverage of the HBS so that representative baskets can be developed for more geographic areas.[13] As new geographic areas are added to the CPI, the comparability between the previous index and the revised index becomes questionable. In these cases, linking the aggregate indices to the previous measures needs to be done with caution and users advised about the differences in coverage.

9.122 In some countries, NSOs first produce a CPI for the capital city only and, as resources become available for subsequent CPI revision, they expand to cover more areas. As the revised CPI is introduced, estimates should be provided for both the capital city and for the new areas in addition to the all-items index. In such a case, the capital city index for the revised CPI can be linked to the previous capital city index with meaningful results in that the geographic coverage has not changed even though the structure of consumer spending patterns may differ.

9.123 However, linking the revised CPI with expanded geographic coverage (perhaps with two or more new areas) needs to be done with caution. The NSO assumes when it produces such a linked series that the historical price changes for the new coverage would be the same as that for old coverage. The NSO can evaluate the differences in the baskets among the new areas with that for the old area to determine how similar or different the baskets and price trends might be. If there are significant differences between the areas (e.g., the capital city may have substantially more weight for housing, clothing, and education, and substantially less for food and transport than the new areas), then

[13] In some cases, the expansion may take place by using an existing basket such as that for the capital city or urban areas in conjunction with broader data collection in targeted geographic locations. In such instances it is assumed the basket is very similar across areas as described in Chapter 3.

the NSO should not link the aggregate old and new series. Rather, they should continue to produce the CPI series for comparable geographic areas and link these series to form a time series. The new geographic areas and the new aggregate CPI should be published separately as new series and not linked with old series.

9.124 At the same time, if the CPI already had broad coverage such as all urban areas and the weight structure included all urban areas, then the aggregate series for the all-urban CPI might be linked together as the city sample is expanded. For example, the previous CPI could have included five urban areas (but their weights represented all urban areas) and now the number of urban areas in the city sample is expanded to include eight urban areas whose weights also cover all urban areas. In this instance, the NSO could still derive meaningful comparisons for price change for all urban areas by linking the all urban index for the old series with that for the new series using the larger sample. The basket has changed so the series are not strictly comparable, but the new, larger sample would have more precision because of the increased sample size compared to the old. If city indices were also produced, those with the same geographic coverage could be linked to form a time series.

9.125 If the NSO went one step further and included total national coverage by adding a sample of rural areas to the CPI, it would need to do an analysis of the differences in the baskets and price trends before linking the old urban series to the new national coverage. In this instance the NSO would not link the urban and national series together; the national series should start as a new CPI with broader coverage.

Key Recommendations

- NSOs should update the basket, update the weights, and link the revised CPI to the previous series to form a continues time series of data.
- Reduce the lag between the weight reference period and the price reference period.
- NSOs should carefully consider the advantages and disadvantages of price updating the weights, based on the target of the CPI and its primary uses.
- If a CPI is updated less frequently, a one-year price reference period is preferred.
- If a CPI is updated on a more frequent basis (annually, biannually), a one-month price reference period is used.
- If resource constraints do not allow for a one-year price reference period, a quarterly price reference period would be the second-best option and a monthly price reference period the third best option.
- A one-year index reference period is preferred for all CPIs.
- When using a one year overlap to link indices, the new index compiled as an overlap series for linking purposes should be used internally and not disseminated. When calculating the 12-month (year on year) change, the change should be calculated on the published linked index and not the internally compiled new index used for linking.

SCANNER DATA

10

Introduction

10.1 The environment in which statistical agencies operate is changing. New opportunities to access and interrogate big data are becoming available, increasing the potential to provide new insights and possibilities for the compilation of consumer price indices (CPIs). The statistical landscape is becoming more complex, expectations of decision makers are growing, and national statistical offices (NSOs) are being challenged to deliver the best possible statistical program in more efficient and innovative ways.

10.2 The launch of barcode scanner technology during the 1970s, and its growth in the twentieth century, enabled retailers to capture detailed information on transactions at the point of sale. Scanner data are high in volume and contain information about individual transactions, including date, quantities and values, and detailed product characteristics. The data provided to NSOs are typically aggregated across consumers and across time (week or month). It is a rich data source that can potentially be used to improve the accuracy of the CPI and reduce the costs of physically collecting data; however, it may increase the costs for data analysis and processing. Also, scanner data give opportunities for improved quality in other aspects, such as publishing more detail and new data products.

10.3 This chapter discusses the opportunities and challenges presented when using scanner data to compile the CPI and aims to provide guidance to NSOs on different practices for the treatment of scanner data. It outlines several practical considerations regarding the acquisition of scanner data sets, the assessment and preparation of the data, and implementation issues. New methods that have been developed to construct price indices from scanner data, so-called multilateral methods, are presented. This chapter concludes with a discussion of the assessment of the new methods and the empirical results, communication with users and stakeholders, and publication and dissemination of the "new" price indices.

10.4 Given the dynamic nature of using scanner data for CPI compilation, this chapter provides an overview of country practices. Work on the treatment of scanner data continues, especially with regard to developing elementary aggregate formulas appropriate for compiling an index using scanner data. The treatment of scanner data has been included on the CPI research agenda for further discussion and development.

Practical Considerations

Introduction

10.5 The availability of scanner data provides opportunities to improve the CPI. Scanner data sets typically contain complete coverage of items sold by a retailer at all their locations and include both quantities sold and revenue received by the retailer for these items. This information has the potential to: improve the accuracy of the prices used to compile the CPI by calculating unit values for homogeneous products (see paragraphs 10.26–10.61); improve the samples of items priced, with the potential to use a census of items for the product categories and outlets covered by the scanner data, for example, the product categories in the data provided by a particular supermarket chain; and use quantity or revenue information to weight items according to their economic importance. Scanner data will typically not cover the entire universe that is in scope of the CPI. For example, in most countries, scanner data do not cover services, rents, automobiles, restaurants, or cafes. In addition, this information may only be available for large retail chains but not for small independent stores or other types of outlets.

10.6 While scanner data sets present opportunities to improve the accuracy of the CPI, there are also challenges that need to be addressed before NSOs can use scanner data to compile the CPI.

Obtaining Scanner Data Sets

10.7 Scanner data have existed for several decades and their value in the compilation of official statistics has become more and more evident over time. One challenge faced by NSOs is obtaining the scanner data sets. Two main options are available. NSOs may seek the supply of scanner data sets directly from retail businesses or from third-party data providers. Both options present benefits and challenges.

10.8 Several NSOs have successfully negotiated the supply of scanner data directly from retail businesses and used these data in the compilation of their CPI. Direct collection of data sets from the retail business by NSOs has potential benefits. These include the ability to negotiate:

- The supply of the data set at no (or minimal) cost
- The scope of items included in the data set
- The level of item aggregation to ensure homogeneous information
- The temporal coverage and detail (day, week, or month)
- An agreed timetable for the supply of the data set to meet CPI processing requirements
- A contact officer within the retail business who is familiar with the data set to answer NSO data queries

10.9 Negotiating the supply of scanner data sets directly with retail businesses presents challenges as well. The primary challenge is that the bilateral negotiation of scanner data sets concerns data that may be regarded as confidential because they contain information on turnover and quantities at items level. Another factor is the legal and institutional setting that governs the relationship between NSOs and retailers. In some countries, it may be necessary that the (statistical) law stipulates which data are to be supplied, whereas in other countries a verbal agreement between the parties is sufficient. Experiences in countries using scanner data suggest these negotiations will take at least six months to complete. The negotiations relate to a wide range of topics: from information technology (IT) systems and reporting formats to confidentiality concerns. An agreement reached between the NSO and retail business is typically formalized in a memorandum of understanding (or similar) which documents the roles and obligations of each party and aims to ensure an ongoing supply of scanner data to the NSO according to the agreed timetable.

10.10 An alternate approach to obtaining scanner data sets directly from retail businesses is to obtain these data sets from intermediaries or market research companies. Market research companies possess scanner data sets obtained by some NSOs for CPI assessment and compilation purposes (Krsinich 2015). Market research companies have no legal obligation to provide scanner data; however, for a fee they may be willing to provide older scanner data that would allow the NSO to explore and become more familiar with the data. A better understanding of these data may clarify the requirements before starting negotiations with retailers or market research companies. The primary benefit of this approach is the ability to negotiate the supply of multiple data sets relating to a diverse set of products with a single or small number of data providers.

10.11 The experience of NSOs using scanner data sets to compile their CPI suggests that obtaining data sets directly from retail businesses is preferred. However, obtaining scanner data sets from market research companies is beneficial in those cases where securing data sets directly from retail businesses is not possible or resources are not available to negotiate bilateral data supply agreements. Accessing scanner data from market research companies, in most cases, requires resources to purchase these data.

Assessing and Preparing Scanner Data for Use

10.12 If the NSO is successful in securing access to scanner data sets, these data sets should then be turned into information that can be effectively and efficiently used to compile the CPI. NSOs need to overcome several challenges to achieve these objectives.

Developing an IT System

10.13 Scanner data are by their very nature *big* data. The size of the files depends on the characteristics of the underlying data. For instance, files with daily data by outlet will be more voluminous than files with weekly data aggregated at the retail chain level. The use of this information by the NSO requires an IT/computing system that can acquire, store, and process the large scanner data sets if the information is to be used to compile the CPI. The IT system needs to be able to acquire and process data sets that have different classification structures, formats, and contents. This is because retail businesses (and third-party data providers) normally develop unique systems for their own internal reporting purposes. These data sets can be used to minimize the burden on retailers and enhance the timely delivery of data to the NSO. IT system development requires human and financial resources. Several NSOs have documented the challenges presented by the need to develop an IT system. The solution is dependent on individual NSO circumstances. NSO resources will be required for an IT system if the NSO is to utilize scanner data to compile the CPI, irrespective of the data provider.

10.14 Given these large investments, it is important for the NSOs to gain experience with test data (for example, from market research companies) and engage with other NSOs with experience. The system needs to be designed to last some time, while at the same time being able to adapt to evolving methodological developments and being scalable to cater for the large volume of data received from an increasing number of data providers. It is recommended that, regardless of the methods that are implemented to produce the CPI, the system remains easily adaptable to newer calculation methods as they evolve.

Classifying Scanner Data

10.15 Scanner data sets generally include product classifications that are unique to the individual retailer. The NSO will most likely receive data sets that contain different product classifications which need to be mapped to a single CPI classification. The classification of scanner data sets may require significant NSO resources. The largest investment of resources is needed when the data sets are first received by the NSO. However, there is a need for ongoing classification resources as new products enter the data set.

10.16 Classifying scanner data items to the CPI classification has been addressed by NSOs in various ways, many of them using the classification of the individual retailer. Such classifications provide important information and can be very useful if they are at the same (or more) level of detail than the lowest level of the Classification of Individual Consumption According to Purpose (COICOP) If the correspondence is 1:1 or *n*:1 (retailer:COICOP), then scanner data can be mapped automatically. In other cases, scanner data either need to be classified by the NSO or the data are excluded. From time to time, the retailer may also change its classification. The IT system and the classification process should be designed to be flexible so that changes in retailer classifications can be handled in a timely manner.

10.17 NSOs have attempted to find a solution given their circumstances. Some countries have classified scanner data items to the CPI classification by purchasing market research metadata (Müller 2010). One European NSO uses the most detailed classification provided by the retailers and then checks if the mapping is correct and makes appropriate changes if required (van der Grient and de Haan 2010). Some NSOs have, for various reasons, undertaken the entire classification of scanner data items to their CPI classification internally (Howard and others 2015).

10.18 Several NSOs have been exploring the use of machine learning algorithms for classifying scanner data (see Van Loon and Roels 2018). These methods use an input data set either of prelabeled items (supervised learning) or of unlabeled items (unsupervised learning) to predict the correct taxonomy label for each item. The resulting model can then be used to classify new data sets. Machine learning methods are particularly promising where there is a mismatch between the product classifications used by retailers and the classification used for CPI compilation. As with all classification methods, ongoing maintenance is required to ensure that items with new features that have not previously been identified are classified appropriately.

10.19 The challenge of classifying scanner data items to the CPI classification primarily arises when scanner data sets have been secured directly from retail businesses. Obtaining scanner data sets from market research companies may enable the NSO to negotiate the supply of scanner data that have already been classified according to the CPI classification. This is viewed by some NSOs as a particular advantage of obtaining scanner data from market research companies.

10.20 The reliability of the classification system needs to be continuously monitored. Errors that are made at this stage will be reflected in the resulting subindices that may then be compiled based on wrongly classified items.

Quality Assurance of the Scanner Data Sets

10.21 Compared with traditional price collection in outlets, scanner data sets are a new data source to compile the CPI. As is the case with any change in data source, the compilers of statistical series should undertake a range of checks to ensure the new data source provides the foundation from which to produce fit-for-purpose statistics.

10.22 The checks should become routine and performed automatically each production run. Because scanner data sets are new, it is important that NSOs gain some experience with them before using these data in production. The experience gained will facilitate setting the values for the checks.

10.23 These scanner data checks can be classified as either *global* checks or *detailed* checks. *Global* checks occur when the data enter the production process and are part of the acceptance procedure. *Detailed* checks typically occur toward the end of the production process.

10.24 *Global* checks relate to broad quality measures generally applied at the time the NSO receives the data set. These checks ensure the data set is broadly consistent with data sets received by the NSO from the same data provider in previous periods. The checks may relate to the format of the data set, the total number of items within the data set, and the total revenue by outlet. These global checks should highlight significant errors with the data set.

10.25 *Detailed* checks are generally applied at the variety or item group level. These checks aim to highlight significant changes in the quantities sold, revenue, and the prices of the items within the data set. These detailed checks have traditionally been referred to as micro-editing of price data. Unexpected changes in the development of prices, turnover, or quantities will trigger these checks. Processing scanner data means processing much larger sets of data and it may require a different approach than processing traditionally collected data.

10.26 Both the *global* and *detailed* checks should be automated to generate reports for analysis by NSO staff. These checks may require contact with the data provider, as well as comparing the data with alternate price information sources (for example, flyers and online prices). The final compiled indices should be reviewed and validated to ensure plausibility.

Implementation—From Confrontation to New Methods

The Benefits and Challenges of Using Scanner Data

10.27 The use of information contained in scanner data sets to compile the CPI can represent a significant change to the data collection practices and the price index methods traditionally employed by NSOs. This suggests that these changes need to be carefully managed, both with regard to the impact on the statistical program as well as communication with users, key stakeholders, and staff. NSO staff need to understand how to manage these data because scanner data sets are so much larger than the traditional CPI data sets. Traditionally, the influence of each price could be traced, and often needed to be visible. In dealing with scanner data, such attention to detail may not be feasible, and these data may require a more top-down approach. Communication with users and key stakeholders is important. It is important for data users to fully understand how scanner data are used in the compilation process. This enhances transparency and user confidence.

10.28 Scanner data potentially enhance the accuracy of the CPI in several ways and provide significantly more data at lower cost. The scanner data sets can be used to (1) compare and validate price data; (2) replace field-collected prices (including a better treatment of sales, promotions, and discounts); (3) expand pricing samples; (4) expand the period over which prices are collected; (5) weight items at the lowest levels of the CPI to reflect their economic importance; and (6) implement new improved index calculation methods and enable process automation. Each of these enhancements is explained in the following text.

Using Scanner Data Sets for Data Validation and Quality Assurance

10.29 The availability of scanner data provides NSOs with the opportunity to validate or quality assure the data used to construct the CPI. Scanner data sets contain variety quantities sold and revenue received by the retailer for these varieties for some period of time, usually a week or a month. This information enables NSOs to calculate a price for an individual variety by dividing a variety's revenue by the quantity sold. This price, referred to as a *unit value,* represents the average price experienced by consumers over a period of time. Note, however, that revenue data may not align perfectly with the purpose and concept of the national CPI because it may include expenditure by nonresident households, businesses, or even government (Fenwick 2014).

10.30 For a homogeneous item, the unit value more accurately reflects prices paid by consumers over the whole period than point-in-time pricing (Balk 1998). Unit values contain discounts and the effects of these discounts on the quantity of varieties sold. The period for which unit values are calculated is important with regard to the accuracy of the unit value. Diewert and others (2016) argue that unit value prices used for constructing the CPI should be for the same period as the index to be constructed, rather than for a subperiod.

10.31 It is acknowledged that NSOs may use a subperiod of the reference period due to data supply timeliness and publication deadlines. The bias and variance this introduces can be assessed by comparing indices compiled using a subperiod of data with indices compiled using the full reference period (Krsinich 2015).

10.32 Price analysts can compare the prices collected in the field to those calculated from the scanner data sets. This analysis provides insight into any biases introduced to the CPI from point-in-time pricing compared with unit values. An analysis of the variety's revenue and quantities sold can be used by the NSO price analysts to highlight where CPI samples could be improved.

Using Scanner Data Sets to Replace Field-Collected Prices

10.33 In most countries, the majority of the prices used to compile the CPI are collected by visits to sampled retail businesses. These visits are made by NSO field officers who observe point-in-time prices as well as discuss discounts, special offers, and volume-selling items with the respondent. The field officers record this information during the visit, often in handheld electronic devices. The regular visits to outlets enable the NSO field officers to actively monitor market developments and observe quality change.

10.34 Replacing field-collected prices by prices (unit values) from scanner data generally results in NSO resource savings, because NSO field officers are no longer required to visit businesses where prices were collected. The potential for NSO resource savings is influenced by the size of the field officer reductions and the increase in resources required by the NSO to manage and process scanner data sets.

10.35 Unit values should relate to a single homogeneous variety whose specification remains constant over time because changes in the composition of varieties sold and the quality of these varieties should not be reflected as price changes. These requirements present some challenges when replacing field-collected prices with information from scanner data sets. Negotiation between the NSO and data provider is needed to ensure access to data at the appropriate level of item aggregation (or disaggregation) required to support the production of unit values for use in compiling the CPI. The direct supply of product characteristics can facilitate the classification of items. Such information, if available, could then be used to perform explicit quality adjustment.

10.36 Several NSOs have experience in producing unit value data from scanner data sets. At the most detailed level, items in scanner data sets are typically identified by barcode or the corresponding Global Trade Item Number (GTIN) or its subvariants, the Universal Product Code, and the European Article Number. While standardized identifiers such as GTIN allow for the tracking of items across different retailers, they may be too detailed, differentiating varieties by characteristics, such as packaging, which are considered irrelevant to consumers (Dalen 2017). Item churn will then be overestimated and there is a potential problem of relaunches which may impede the calculation of the CPI. For example, when using GTIN as the item identifier, the price change of a homogeneous variety whose GTIN changes at the same time will not be measured. In some countries, the use of stock keeping unit (SKU) rather than GTIN has proven to be successful (Howard and others 2015).

10.37 An essential part of price measurement is accounting for quality change and the introduction of new items. This has been achieved by NSOs when field officers visit retail outlets with the aim of measuring price change for identical or equivalent items in successive periods and identifying new items. As the characteristics of varieties are altered, the NSO field officers collect descriptive information that enables the effects of a change in quality to be separated from the price change, so that the CPI measures only pure price change.

10.38 Accounting for quality change is particularly challenging when using scanner data. Scanner data sets tend to exhibit a high level of churn in the varieties available from month to month. There are new models (and versions of models) of items becoming available in the market and old models dropping out of the market as they become obsolete. Calculating quality-adjusted prices is therefore difficult.

Using Scanner Data Sets to Update Pricing Samples

10.39 The collection of point-in-time prices by NSO field price collectors visiting retail outlets is resource-intensive. A census of items cannot practically be priced each period resulting in the need for some sort of sampling approach. For example, sampled products may be selected for inclusion in the CPI basket by NSO field price collectors who discuss with the respondent which items are volume sellers or examine the shelf space of the products and make judgments about their relative importance. NSO field staff then aim to select a representative basket of items for pricing. This is a purposive sampling approach.

10.40 Nonprobability or purposive sampling has traditionally been used because sampling frames for items purchased were not available and detailed quantity or revenue data to measure the economic importance of the items was lacking (see Chapter 4 for further information on sampling). Nonprobability or purposive sampling can lead to biases when the selected items are not representative of the product population.

10.41 This traditional approach to sampling can be replaced by more scientific sampling methods due to the availability of scanner data. Since scanner data typically is a census of products, scanner data sets can be used as a sampling frame for updating pricing samples. A pricing sample is usually two-dimensional; it is a combination of a sample of outlets and a sample of items/product varieties. If all the stores from a retail chain are covered, the scanner data set can be used as a sampling frame for both the outlet and item dimension (see also Chapters 4 and 5). For example, a two-stage sampling approach could be adopted by first selecting outlets and then selecting items within the sampled outlets.

10.42 Revenue shares for each product (or product/outlet combination) can be used to determine the significance of each product within a product group. Products are then selected for inclusion in the CPI "basket" based on revenue share either through sampling proportional to revenue or cutoff sampling (de Haan and others 1999).

10.43 Over time, however, products in the sample can lose relevance or even cease to exist. In these situations, a replacement product is needed to maintain the relevance of the sample. Relevance tests can be used to highlight those items in the samples that have become unsuitable, and also highlight and rank suitable items as replacements.

10.44 The main principle behind these relevance tests is that the products should have a stable revenue share (that is, consistent revenue share compared to other products), within the CPI product group. These product groups are referred to as the elementary aggregate. The stable revenue share is important as items can have large sales when introduced into the market due to novelty or introductory sales prices, have insignificant revenue thereafter, and hence not be representative of the broader market.

10.45 To mitigate these problems, possible replacement products' revenue must have been stable and significant for a specified period (for example, three to six months) before they can be considered for inclusion in the price samples. CPI analysts can then manually review all items which are flagged for replacement and select items from a list ranked according to average monthly revenue share over the previous six months.

10.46 Many food and household items will have varieties of the same base item which have similar if not identical price evolution. A specific brand of canned tuna, for example, is available in many flavors and CPI compilers will be aware that prices for the different flavors from the same brand will behave similarly, going on sale at the same time and changing price at the same time. Having a single flavor in the sample will hence represent the price movement for a much more significant portion of the market than that single flavor's revenues would suggest.

10.47 The sampling process used to ensure product samples are representative is usually manually driven, requiring the CPI analysts to select a replacement from this ranked list of potential products that pass certain eligibility criteria. This scanner data sampling approach requires additional CPI analyst resources which, ideally, are offset by the reduced field collection resources.

Using Scanner Data to Update Index Structures and to Apply Weights

10.48 Variety samples have traditionally been small. When the additional CPI analyst resources are indeed offset by the reduced field collection resources, the NSO could decide to expand the variety samples without changing the price index formula at the elementary aggregate level or the sampling procedure.

10.49 It may be worthwhile, however, to reconsider the index structure and the sampling procedure when the NSO obtains scanner data directly from retail chains. Traditionally, an elementary aggregate index is compiled from prices collected at outlets that belong to different retail chains (or independent stores). When the NSO wants to use much more price information from a retail chain than before, it seems preferable to treat elementary aggregate[1]-chain combinations as separate strata in the index compilation process.

10.50 If the NSO chooses to use the classification system provided by the retailer, it will be necessary to expand the index structure below the elementary aggregate level with separate elementary price indices for each retail chain. This raises several issues. The first issue is whether the stores belonging to the chain in question should be viewed as separate outlets. If this is the case, unit values for the sampled items should be calculated at the store level. On the other hand, when the service levels are similar across stores belonging to a retail chain, it may be useful to calculate unit values at the chain level (Ivancic and Fox 2013). In this case, the retail chain scanner data directly represent all the stores of that chain. When using chain-level data, one must ensure that each retail chain is weighted in the final index. Some retail chains operate different types of stores with different assortments of products and price levels. In this case, a stratification can be introduced that distinguishes between the types of stores belonging to a retail chain. Some NSOs do not have a choice if they receive scanner data at the chain level.

10.51 A regional disaggregation of the scanner data may be needed if regional CPIs are compiled. The chains, stores, products, and prices included in the resulting indices should be representative for the respective region(s). Alternatively, scanner data can be directly exploited at the national level. It has then to be determined whether the resulting scanner data price indices, which are representative for the country as a whole, can also be used to compile the regional CPIs.

10.52 The next issue to be considered by the NSO is to what extent existing sampling procedures should be improved. Suppose the NSO formerly used sampling of items proportional to revenue from the scanner data. This procedure can also be used to sample items from chain-specific elementary price indices, where items are either defined (and unit values calculated) at the outlet level or the chain level. If the NSO wants to significantly increase the sample sizes to make use of a substantial part of the price information contained in the scanner data set, sampling procedures need to be reconsidered.

10.53 Another issue is how to integrate the chain-specific elementary price indices from scanner data with price information from other sources. Because these elementary price indices are different from the elementary price indices in the traditional index structure, the scanner data price indices have to be aggregated up to a level—perhaps the lowest level of product aggregation the NSO publishes price indices—where they can be combined with price indices from other sources. If a retailer-specific classification is used, it must be as detailed as the lowest level of product aggregation that the NSO publishes. If not, the data need to be reclassified accordingly. In other words, two aggregation steps are required: aggregation of the chain-specific elementary price indices up to some higher-level product category, and aggregation of the resulting scanner data indices with price indices at that level pertaining to other retail chains and independent stores.

10.54 The revenue data provides the opportunity for NSOs to weight price indices more frequently using more timely data. This can be achieved in various ways, depending on the availability to the NSO of scanner data for multiple chains. It is suggested that the weights to combine the price indices from scanner data be updated annually, using product revenue data from the previous 12 months. Combining the scanner data indices with the price indices compiled

[1]The elementary aggregate refers to the lowest level for which expenditure weights are available. Because scanner data contains detailed and timely quantity information, the elementary price indices are stratum indices that are aggregated to obtain the higher-level indices in the CPI classification structure.

from other sources requires expenditure data for the latter indices, which may be difficult to come by or estimate.

10.55 With the household budget survey, detailed data by item (or item/outlet combination) are not available. The majority of NSOs therefore apply unweighted price index methods at the lowest levels of the CPI: the prices or price changes of the items sampled from an elementary aggregate are combined without explicitly weighting the items according to their economic importance. In most cases, the Jevons index formula is used by NSOs.

10.56 Scanner data sets contain revenue data at the most detailed variety level. These data can be used to sample varieties proportional to their revenue, as mentioned previously, but this raises a few issues. The inclusion probabilities serve as implicit weights. That is, the elementary price index will be an implicitly weighted index, and the inclusion probabilities should correspond with the target/population index aimed at (Balk 2005). Moreover, the revenue distribution within an item category as observed in scanner data is often highly skewed. Consequently, sampling proportional to revenue is likely to select some high-revenue varieties with a probability of one, and the high-revenue items in this "self-selecting" subsample should be explicitly weighted—without explicit or implicit[2] weighting of these items the (unweighted) sample-based Jevons index cannot be an unbiased estimator of a weighted geometric target index.

10.57 It is preferable to reflect the items' economic importance explicitly via a weighted index number formula rather than implicitly via the inclusion probabilities in an unweighted index.

Using Scanner Data Sets to Implement New CPI Compilation Methods

10.58 The approaches outlined previously enable the NSO to continue using sample-based methods to compile their CPI. Improvements to the accuracy of the CPI will be achieved because the prices (unit values) are more representative of those actually paid by consumers. Also, the varieties sampled reflect volume sellers, and the weights used to produce aggregate measures of price change are based on more timely information and can be updated more frequently.

10.59 The major challenge faced by NSOs implementing these approaches relates to the increase in resources needed. Maintaining a sample-based approach, especially when the variety samples are extended, requires significant manual intervention, primarily because variety turnover can be large. When one European country first introduced scanner data for supermarkets into the CPI, a Lowe index was used (Schut and others 2002). The idea was to mimic traditional methods and processes on a sample of about 10,000 items (barcodes) from each supermarket chain. This approach was very demanding with regard to the manual selection of items to replace disappearing items and with regard to quality adjustments when deemed necessary.

10.60 Ideally, acknowledging practical constraints, an NSO would use all the available information in scanner data sets rather than taking samples. Manually processing a census of varieties from scanner data sets is prohibitively expensive, however, and cannot be undertaken to meet the CPI production timeframes. Automating CPI compilation processes is required.

10.61 Also, when using a census of varieties, not a sample, a weighted index number formula is preferred. Again, variety turnover poses a significant problem. To maximize the number of matches in the data, chaining at high frequency will be needed. This can lead to a significant drift in the index. Multilateral price index number methods, which are drift-free by construction, are currently considered a suitable method to handle a census of items and varieties from scanner data; however, work continues on how best to apply multilateral methods to compile elementary aggregates using scanner data. The scanner data offer many opportunities for new research and developments.

Multilateral Price Index Methods

Introduction

10.62 Scanner data can be implemented in the CPI using traditional sample-based methods. Prices formerly observed by price collectors visiting outlets can be replaced by unit values from scanner data without changing the sampling design or the price index number formula used. If the NSO decides to use all the available data rather than taking samples, the preferred approach, multilateral price index number methods are most suitable. Multilateral methods were originally developed to compare price levels across countries, but they can be adapted to price comparisons over time. These methods are particularly useful for scanner data, where item turnover is often high and promotional sales occur frequently.

10.63 The most important multilateral price index number methods are described in the following text; for a comprehensive discussion, see Chapter 7 of *Consumer Price Index Theory*. After defining the variety, a short overview of traditional bilateral price indices and chaining is provided.

Defining the Variety

10.64 Before applying any index calculation method, the individual variety to be priced must be defined. The basic principle is to compare like with like and to track the price of the same variety over time. The article code level usually represents the most detailed level of homogeneity in the data. In addition to this product dimension, one must also consider the outlet and the time dimensions. Often, the same article sold at different moments of time, in the same or similar outlets can be considered to define a variety which is sufficiently homogeneous so that an average transaction price (unit value) can be calculated for the variety.

10.65 In some cases, the article codes such as GTINs are stable and long-lived. Some countries have access to retailers' product codes, for instance, an internal SKU code that is already more aggregated than the GTIN code. However, in other cases, these article codes level may be too detailed for price index calculation. In some product categories, such as clothing and footwear, the article codes frequently appear and disappear making it difficult to match them across time and therefore price changes are not adequately measured.

[2] Implicit weights result when samples are selected using probabilities proportional to size sampling methods.

The different strategies to cope with the article code changes are described in the paragraphs that follow.[3]

10.66 One approach is to group together different individual articles with similar characteristics. NSOs can choose to define the variety more broadly or more narrowly. It is important to create groupings so that consumers are more or less indifferent between the different individual articles within these groupings. Calculating unit values at this level not only makes it possible to capture substitution effects between comparable articles but also facilitates the inclusion of new articles entering the market. NSOs face trade-offs in balancing these groupings. If a grouping is too broad, this can lead to unit value bias (and high volatility) as the individual articles are not strictly comparable. On the other hand, defining the grouping too narrowly may lead to a lack of matching between outgoing and new or returning articles. Decisions made at this stage can significantly impact the price indices that are eventually obtained. This could be especially relevant for technology products, especially models with high turnover (see Chapter 6 for more details). If feasible, the sensitivity of the definitions of the groupings on the results should be tested.

10.67 The practical construction of these groupings can be challenging. NSOs require information about article characteristics, including brand and size, as well as internal classification codes used by retailers. Some retailers may only provide characteristics in a specific text string while others may have several different variables that describe the characteristics of the different articles. Characteristics gathered in one single variable (text string) require some form of text mining to make it useful for classification. Not all characteristics are equally important and affect the price in the same degree. The clustering of individual articles should be defined by the most important price-determining characteristics.

10.68 Another approach would be to impute the prices for the new and disappearing articles in the periods when they are not available. Prices could, for instance, be imputed with the help of a hedonic function. Instead of using the characteristics of the articles to form the groupings, this information is now used to estimate missing prices. However, such a strategy is only appropriate for index number formulas, such as the Törnqvist or the Gini, Eltetö, Köves, and Szulc (GEKS)–Törnqvist, which are responsive to imputations for missing prices.

Bilateral Price Indices and Chaining

10.69 Suppose first that the set of varieties sold is fixed over time (that is, that the price statistician is dealing with a *static universe*). This fixed set of items is denoted by S and its size by N. The sample period consists of $(T+1)$ time periods $t=0,...,T$. The prices (unit values) of item $i \in S$ $(i=1,...,N)$ in periods 0 and t $(t=1,...,T)$ are denoted by p_i^0 and p_i^t; q_i^0 and q_i^t are the corresponding quantities sold. The aim is to construct price indices that compare period 0, the starting period of the time series, with each period t.

[3]A similar problem can also be encountered with web-scraped data (see Chapter 5, Annex 5.6).

10.70 In the situation with no expenditure information, Chapter 8 of this Manual recommends the use of the *Jevons price index*, the unweighted geometric mean of price relatives:

$$I_J^{0:t} = \prod_{i \in S} \left(\frac{p_i^t}{p_i^0} \right)^{\frac{1}{n}} = \frac{\prod_{i \in S} \left(p_i^t \right)^{\frac{1}{n}}}{\prod_{i \in S} \left(p_i^0 \right)^{\frac{1}{n}}} \qquad (10.1)$$

10.71 The NSO traditionally draws a sample of items from the entire universe S to reduce CPI production cost. Without access to scanner data, S is unknown and a detailed sampling frame is lacking. Most CPI samples have therefore been drawn purposively, with the risk of introducing bias in the index.

10.72 Since scanner data contains expenditure information for a census of items, the construction of superlative price indices is possible on the entire set S. The focus here is on the Törnqvist rather than the Fisher index or other superlative index formulas. While the Fisher and Törnqvist produce very similar results, the Törnqvist index allows for simpler expressions. The Törnqvist price index is given by

$$I_T^{0:t} = \prod_{i \in S} \left(\frac{p_i^t}{p_i^0} \right)^{\frac{s_i^0 + s_i^t}{2}} \qquad (10.2)$$

where $s_i^0 = p_i^0 q_i^0 / \sum_{i \in S} p_i^0 q_i^0$ and $s_i^t = p_i^t q_i^t / \sum_{i \in S} p_i^t q_i^t$ denote the expenditure shares in periods 0 and t.

10.73 In a *dynamic universe*, there are new and disappearing items so that not all items can be matched over time. The sets of items in periods t $(t=0,...,T)$ are denoted by S^t with size N^t. To maximize the number of matches in the data, chaining matched-model superlative price indices seems useful, for example, chaining period-on-period Törnqvist price indices:

$$I_T^{t-1:t} = \prod_{i \in S_M^{t-1,t}} \left(\frac{p_i^t}{p_i^{t-1}} \right)^{\frac{s_{i,M}^{t-1} + s_{i,M}^t}{2}} \qquad (10.3)$$

where S_{iM}^{t-1} and S_{iM}^t are the expenditure shares in the two periods with respect to the set $S_{iM}^{t-1,t} = S^{t-1} \cap S^t$ of matched items that are available in both period $t-1$ and period t.

10.74 However, empirical work showed that high-frequency chaining of weighted price indices, including superlative price indices, can lead to strong *chain drift*. In case of promotional sales with reduced prices, the quantities purchased often increase substantially. But when the prices return to their original level, the quantities purchased of storable goods may not return to their "normal" level. This type of asymmetric behavior can cause chain drift in superlative price indices, which is typically downward. Ivancic (2007), using market research scanner data on goods sold in supermarkets, found a downward drift in chained Fisher price indices (see also Ivancic and others 2009, 2011). Drift in chained matched-model superlative price indices has been documented for durable goods as well. Here, the drift is likely due to seasonal fluctuations in prices and quantities. De Haan and Krsinich (2014), using scanner data, found a downward drift in chained Törnqvist price indices for

Table 10.1 A Numerical Example of Chain Drift

Period	P1	P2	Q1	Q2	Share 1 (percent)	Share 2 (percent)	Average Share in t and $t-1$ for Item 1 (percent)	Average Share in t and $t-1$ for Item 2 (percent)	Period-to-Period Törnqvist	Chained Törnqvist
1	3	4	12	10	47.4	52.6				100.00
2	3	2	12	30	37.5	62.5	42.4	57.6	67.10	67.10
3	1	4	40	5	66.7	33.3	52.1	47.9	78.66	52.78
4	3	4	5	10	27.3	72.7	47.0	53.0	167.53	88.42
5	3	4	12	10	47.4	52.6	37.3	62.7	100.00	88.42
6	3	2	12	30	37.5	62.5	42.4	57.6	67.10	59.33
7	1	4	40	5	66.7	33.3	52.1	47.9	78.66	46.67
8	3	4	5	10	27.3	72.7	47.0	53.0	167.53	78.18
9	3	4	12	10	47.4	52.6	37.3	62.7	100.00	78.18

consumer electronics goods sold. Silver and Heravi (2005) presented evidence of downward bias in chained Fisher indices using scanner data on televisions.

10.75 Table 10.1 shows a numerical example of downward drift in the chained Törnqvist price index. There are two items and nine periods distinguished. The "regular" prices of items 1 and 2 are 3.00 and 4.00, respectively, but the price of item 1 is temporarily reduced in periods 3 and 7, while the price of item 2 is reduced in periods 2 and 6. Notice that in the last period (period 9) the prices and quantities are exactly the same as those in the first period. Nevertheless, the period-on-period chained Törnqvist price index ends up at 78.18, thus measuring a price decline of almost 22 percent. For the multilateral indices, the index equals one (as will the direct Törnqvist). This downward drift for the period-on-period chained Törnqvist stems from the fact that because the quantities do not immediately return to their "normal" level after the discount, the price change from the normal price to the reduced price has a bigger weight than the following price change from the reduced price back to the normal price.

10.76 One way to avoid chain drift due to promotional sales for storable goods would be not to weight the items and to construct a time series by chaining period-on-period matched-model Jevons price indices:

$$I_J^{t-1:t} = \prod_{i \in S_M^{t-1,t}} \left(\frac{p_i^t}{p_i^{t-1}} \right)^{\frac{1}{N_M^{t-1,t}}} \quad (10.4)$$

where $N_M^{t-1,t}$ is the number of matched items between periods $t - 1$ and t. This is not to say that the use of the chained matched-model Jevons index is without problems. For instance, clearance sales can put downward pressure on the index. In order to mitigate this problem, a dump filter can be implemented. The filter removes an item if both the price and the quantities sold of an item fall sharply. A downward drift may also arise for fashion goods, such as clothing, that exit the sample at low clearance prices and never return. Clothing requires special treatment as noted in Chapter 11.

10.77 The lack of weighting is problematic as well. Item expenditures are usually highly skewed, and so the many low-expenditure items will be given the same weight as the few high-expenditure items. A crude form of implicit weighting can be attained by simply excluding low-expenditure items (that is, by giving them an inclusion probability of zero), for example, using a threshold based on the items' average expenditure shares in adjacent months. This approach, sometimes referred to as the "dynamic approach" (see Eurostat 2017), has been implemented by several European countries (for example, see van der Grient and de Haan 2010, 2011). This method reduces the risk of chain drift because weights are used implicitly for the sampling of items, but not explicitly in the index calculations. This method has the advantage that it relies on the usual bilateral index methods while at the same time making the best use of the information contained in the scanner data sets. The method is therefore easy to explain to users. Yet, this is not an optimal situation. A more advanced solution would be to explicitly weight the items and construct weighted multilateral price indices.

Multilateral Methods

10.78 Multilateral methods produce transitive price indices. For price comparisons across time, this means the indices are independent of the choice of base period, can be written in chained form, and are therefore free from chain drift. Multilateral methods have in common that price indices are constructed simultaneously for the entire sample period.

10.79 Two types of multilateral methods can be defined. The first type starts from matched-model price comparisons between any pair of time periods across the entire sample period and then "transitivizes" this set of bilateral price indices. The best-known method is GEKS (Eltetö and Köves 1964; Gini 1931; Szulc 1964). An alternate method is based on spanning trees (Hill 1999a, 1999b), where a spanning tree is a supplier of paths between countries. For a certain spanning tree, the bilateral indices are chain linked to construct price comparisons between any pair of countries or, adapted to our context, time periods. It is not clear, however, what the theoretical and practical advantages are over the easier-to-construct GEKS indices. The second type of multilateral method attains transitivity in another way, which will be explained in the following text, and includes the Geary–Khamis method (Geary 1958; Khamis 1972) and the Country Product Dummy method (Summers 1973).

GEKS Method

10.80 The GEKS index between period 0 and period t is calculated as the geometric average of the ratios of the matched-model bilateral price indices $I^{0,j}$ and $I^{0,k}$, constructed with the same index number formula, where each period l is taken as the base. Provided that the bilateral indices satisfy the time reversal test, the GEKS index can be written as (de Haan and Van der Grient 2011; Ivancic and others 2011):

$$I_{\mathrm{GEKS}}^{0:t} = \prod_{l=0}^{T}\left(\frac{I^{0,l}}{I^{t,l}}\right)^{\frac{1}{T+1}} = \prod_{l=0}^{T}\left(I^{0,l} \times I^{l,t}\right)^{\frac{1}{T+1}} \quad (10.5)$$

10.81 The time reversal test requires that when the base period and the comparison period are reversed, the result should be equal to the reciprocal of the original index. In its standard form, the GEKS method uses bilateral Fisher indices, which satisfy the test, but other choices are possible, including bilateral Törnqvist indices. GEKS–Törnqvist indices are also referred to as Caves, Christensen, and Diewert indices.

Geary–Khamis Method

10.82 The Geary–Khamis (GK) method, when applied to comparisons over time, gives rise to the following price index:

$$I_{GK}^{0:t} = \frac{\dfrac{\sum_{i\in S^t} p_i^t q_i^t}{\sum_{i\in S^t} \widehat{p}_i\, q_i^t}}{\dfrac{\sum_{i\in S^0} p_i^0 q_i^0}{\sum_{i\in S^0} \widehat{p}_i\, q_i^0}} = \frac{\left[\sum_{i\in S^t} s_i^t \left(\dfrac{p_i^t}{\widehat{p}_i}\right)^{-1}\right]^{-1}}{\left[\sum_{i\in S^0} s_i^0 \left(\dfrac{p_i^0}{\widehat{p}_i}\right)^{-1}\right]^{-1}} \quad (10.6)$$

10.83 The numerator of equation 10.6 is a price index (using period t quantities) with "reference prices" $\widehat{p}_i$ that are fixed across the sample period. The index should be equal to one in the starting period 0, so it will be necessary to normalize the index by dividing by its period 0 value, which is the denominator of equation 10.6. The reference prices are given by

$$\widehat{p}_i = \frac{\sum_{\tau\in S_i} q_i^\tau \left(\dfrac{p_i^\tau}{I_{GK}^{\tau\ 0,tau}}\right)}{\sum_{\tau\in S_i} q_i^\tau} \quad (10.7)$$

where S_i is the set of time periods in which item i is actually sold and for which prices are available. Equation 10.7 shows that $\widehat{p}_i$ equals a weighted arithmetic average of the deflated observed prices, with each period's share in the total number of sales of the item across the entire sample period serving as weights.

10.84 Since the GK index acts as the deflator in equation 10.7, equations 10.6 and 10.7 define a system of equations which must be solved simultaneously. This can be done iteratively (which may be simpler to implement), but there are other ways to solve the system (Balk 2008).

Time Product Dummy Method

10.85 This is a regression-based approach. Assuming n different items are observed in the entire sample period $0,\dots,T$ (most of which will typically not be sold in every time period), the time product dummy (TPD) regression model for the pooled data is

$$\ln p_i^t = \alpha + \sum_{t=1}^{T} \delta^t D_i^t + \sum_{i=1}^{N-1} \gamma_i D_i + \varepsilon_i^t, \quad (10.8)$$

where D_i is a dummy variable that has the value of one if the observation relates to item i and zero otherwise, and D_i^t is a dummy variable with the value one if the observation relates to period t and zero otherwise; dummies for item n and period 0 are excluded to identify the model.

10.86 Diewert (2005) proposed to estimate model (10.8) by Weighted Least Squares regression with the items' expenditure shares in each period serving as weights. Exponentiating the estimated time dummy parameter $\hat{\delta}^t$ yields the TPD index between periods 0 and t; $I_{TPD}^{0,t} = \exp\left(\hat{\delta}^t\right)$. The weighted TPD method can be written as a system of equations that is similar to the geometric GK-style system defined by (10.6) and (10.7), and thus, the TPD can be solved iteratively as well as via direct regression methods (Rao 2005):

$$I_{\mathrm{TPD}}^{0:t} = \frac{\prod_{i\in S^t}\left(\dfrac{p_i^t}{\exp\left(\hat{\gamma}_i\right)}\right)^{s_i^t}}{\prod_{i\in S^0}\left(\dfrac{p_i^0}{\exp\left(\hat{\gamma}_i\right)}\right)^{s_i^0}} \quad (10.9)$$

$$\exp\left(\hat{\gamma}_i\right) = \prod_{\tau\in S_i}\left(\frac{p_i^\tau}{I_{TPD}^{0,t}}\right)^{\frac{s_i^\tau}{\sum_{\tau\in S_i} s_i^\tau}} \quad (10.10)$$

10.87 Equation 10.10 shows that the exponentiated item fixed effect estimates $\hat{\gamma}_i$, or reference prices, are equal to the expenditure-share weighted geometric averages of the deflated prices with the TPD index serving as deflator. Both GK and TPD explicitly arrive at reference prices. In the case of GK, this means that the index is consistent with national accounts, as it is additively decomposable. TPD, being a geometric index, is not.

10.88 Notice that the TPD index (10.9) can be viewed as a normalized geometric Paasche index with imputed period 0 prices based on the reference prices (10.10). Similarly, the GK index (10.6) can be viewed as a normalized (ordinary) Paasche index with imputed period 0 prices based on the reference prices (10.7).

Lack of Matching and Quality Adjustment

Implicit Quality Adjustment

10.89 Like GEKS, GK and TPD are matched-model methods in the sense that items with a single observation in the entire sample period do not affect the index. Items contribute to aggregate price change only when *price relatives* can be calculated from the prices observed in both periods compared, unless information on characteristics would be available to perform explicit quality adjustments. One implication of the matched-model method is that items introduced in the most recent period T are ignored.

10.90 Implicit quality adjustment can also be illustrated by using an alternate interpretation of the GK index. Dividing the value index of the product category by the ratio of "quality-adjusted quantities" defines a *quality-adjusted unit value index* (de Haan 2004, 2015):

$$I_{\text{QAUV}}^{0:t}=\frac{\dfrac{\sum_{i\in S^t}p_i^tq_i^t}{\sum_{i\in S^0}p_i^0q_i^0}}{\dfrac{\sum_{i\in S^t}\lambda_{i/b}q_i^t}{\sum_{i\in S^0}\lambda_{i/b}q_i^0}}=\frac{\dfrac{\sum_{i\in S^t}p_i^tq_i^t}{\sum_{i\in S^t}\lambda_{i/b}q_i^t}}{\dfrac{\sum_{i\in S^0}p_i^0q_i^0}{\sum_{i\in S^0}\lambda_{i/b}q_i^0}}=\frac{\left[\sum_{i\in S^t}s_i^t\left(\dfrac{p_i^t}{\lambda_{i/b}}\right)^{-1}\right]^{-1}}{\left[\sum_{i\in S^0}s_i^0\left(\dfrac{p_i^0}{\lambda_{i/b}}\right)^{-1}\right]^{-1}} \qquad (10.11)$$

10.91 If $\lambda_{i/b}=1$ for all i, equation 10.11 simplifies to the ordinary unit value index. The quality-adjustment factors $\lambda_{i/b}$ aim to express the quantities purchased of each item i with regard to quantities of an arbitrary item b. The ratios $p_i^t/\lambda_{i/b}$ and $p_i^0/\lambda_{i/b}$ in the second expression of (10.11) are quality-adjusted prices. In the static universe case (with no new and disappearing items), if the quality-adjustment factor of an item corresponds to its base price, the quality-adjusted unit value index turns into the Paasche price index. Von Auer (2014) argued that many conventional price indices can be viewed as, what he called, a generalized unit value index.

10.92 A comparison of equations 10.6 and 10.11 shows that the GK index can be viewed as a quality-adjusted unit value index where the quality-adjustment factors are measured by the reference prices in equation 10.7. Similarly, the TPD index in 10.9 can be viewed as its geometric counterpart where the quality-adjustment factors are measured by the reference prices (10.10). Whether the reference prices in the GK and TPD indices properly reflect quality differences is likely to depend on the market circumstances.

Explicit Quality Adjustment

10.93 Data on item characteristics permitting, *explicit quality adjustment* is preferred, in particular through hedonic regression methods. A useful starting point is the multilateral time dummy hedonic (TDH) model:

$$\ln p_i^t=\alpha+\sum_{t=1}^{T}\delta^tD_i^t+\sum_{k=1}^{K}\beta_kz_{ik}+\varepsilon_i^t \qquad (10.12)$$

where z_{ik} is the quantity of characteristic k ($k=1,\ldots,K$) for item i. Notice that, as pointed out by Aizcorbe and others (2003) and Krsinich (2016), the TPD model (10.8) arises from the TDH model (10.12) by replacing the hedonic effects $\exp(\sum_{k=1}^{K}\beta_kz_{ik})$ by item-specific fixed effects $\exp(\gamma_i)$. Similar to the estimation of the TPD model, it is assumed that equation 10.12 is estimated by expenditure-share weighted regression on the pooled data of all time periods $t=0,\ldots,T$.

10.94 The resulting weighted TDH index, $I_{\text{TDH}}^{0,t}=\exp(\hat{\delta}^t)$, can be expressed in a similar way as the TPD index (10.9), with the estimated hedonic effects $\exp(\sum_{k=1}^{K}\breve{\beta}_kz_{ik})$ instead of the estimated item fixed effects $\exp(\breve{\gamma}_i)$ now acting as reference prices. The formula $\exp(\sum_{k=1}^{K}\breve{\beta}_k(z_{ik}-z_{bk}))$ can also be used to estimate the quality-adjustment factors $\lambda_{i/b}$ in equation 10.11. The resulting explicitly quality-adjusted unit value index—or "hedonic variant" of the GK index—is expected to be very close to the TDH index (de Haan and Krsinich 2018).

10.95 De Haan and others (2016) compared the TPD and TDH methods. They argued that the TPD model suffers from overfitting because it has too many parameters and "distorts the regression residuals towards zero." Under certain pricing strategies of retailers, such as price skimming (new items) and dumping (old items), the TPD index can be quite different from the TDH index. Similarly, the GK index can be quite different from its hedonic counterpart, the quality-adjusted unit value index.

10.96 If relaunches of homogeneous items with different barcodes or SKUs are a major cause of a low matching rate, then defining items by their characteristics rather than barcode or SKU could be an option (Chessa 2016). However, scanner data sets provided by retailers typically include rather broad item descriptions, from which it may only be possible to extract a few characteristics, such as package size and brand name. In that case, the prices, calculated as unit values across all the barcodes of SKUs that belong to the various "groups," can suffer from unit value bias.

10.97 Unlike TPD and GK, GEKS does not aim at implicitly adjusting for quality change. A potential advantage of GEKS over TPD and GK, however, is that the "missing prices" of the unmatched new and disappearing items can be imputed. It is therefore possible to estimate explicitly quality-adjusted GEKS indices by replacing the bilateral matched-model Törnqvist price indices by bilateral hedonic imputation Törnqvist indices, for example, as proposed by de Haan and Krsinich (2014) or de Haan (2019). This means there is no need to define the items by their characteristics; barcode or SKU will suffice to distinguish between items. The hedonic imputations for the unmatched items adjust for quality changes and also deal with the relaunch problem. De Haan (2019) suggests using the same characteristics information in the hedonic regressions that would be used to define the "groups" for dealing with relaunches in the TPD and GK methods.

10.98 Missing information on important characteristics makes the use of hedonic quality adjustment, or explicit quality adjustment in general, problematic as this can lead to an omitted variables bias. Also, as mentioned previously, it may give rise to unit value bias in the "group approach." A few NSOs have been exploring the use of web scraping to observe quality characteristics from retailers' or manufacturers' websites to enrich scanner data sets. Scanner data obtained from a market research company may already contain detailed information on item characteristics. One NSO, for example, produces quality-adjusted GEKS price indices for consumer electronics products based on scanner data sets from one market research company that include many item characteristics (Krsinich 2015). All these methods are rather data-intensive as they require prices, turnover, and price-determining characteristics at a detailed level.

Revisions in Multilateral Indices

10.99 When new data become available, previously estimated multilateral indices change when new data are processed. This is problematic as the CPI is not revisable. Also, as time passes, recent price movements will be increasingly affected by prices and price changes in the distant past. In the context of the GEKS index, this is known as a *loss of characteristicity.* Different methods have been proposed to extend a multilateral time series without revising published index numbers (and mitigate the loss of characteristicity). The methods can be characterized by a number of choices: window adjustment (rolling window or extending window), the link period, and the index in the link period (Chessa 2019).

10.100 *Rolling window methods* estimate multilateral indices on a rolling window with fixed length, say $T + 1$, which is shifted forward each period. Table 10.2 illustrates a rolling time window of 13 periods. The multilateral index compiled in period 13 covers periods 1–13. The multilateral index compiled in period 14 covers periods 2–14 and so on. The results of the latest window are then linked onto a previously calculated index. For example, movement splice links the most recent period-to-period index change onto the index of the previous period (that is the latest published index). In Table 10.2, the *movement splice* index of period 14 is obtained by linking onto period 13 the price change between periods 13 and 14 derived from the corresponding multilateral index.

10.101 An alternative to *movement splice* is a *window splice*, which links the full period index change onto the latest calculated index of T periods ago. The movement splice was proposed by Ivancic and others (2011) for the GEKS method, and the window splice was proposed by Krsinich (2016) for the TPD method. However, each splicing method can be combined with any multilateral method. These splicing methods link index changes onto a single link period. Diewert and Fox (2017) proposed a *mean splice* by taking the geometric mean of the price indices obtained from using every possible link period. This makes the result independent of the choice of link period.

10.102 Chessa (2019) pointed out that there are in fact two main options for splicing methods (apart from movement splicing, which has the index published in the previous period as the only link option). Successive window shifts generate a sequence of recalculated or "revised" indices alongside the initially published index in the same period. Both the recalculated and published indices are candidates for the index on which a new index series can be linked. In empirical research, and in applications by two NSOs, the first option has been applied. The second option (that is, linking onto the published index numbers) has been recently suggested by Chessa (2019). Linking onto the published index numbers has advantages. For example, year-on-year rates (inflation figures) calculated from shifted windows will also be the published figures if the link period corresponds to the period which is 12 months ago. This increases the transparency of splicing methods. Moreover, each year-on-year rate is derived from a transitive index series and is in that sense free from chain drift. This is not the case when splicing on the latest recalculated index which can therefore still lead to some drift (see Chessa 2019).

10.103 The choice of window length is a point of concern. Ivancic and others (2011) advocated a 13-month (or five-quarter) window as this is the shortest window that can deal with strongly seasonal goods. However, recent research suggests that indices for strongly seasonal items can be significantly improved with a 25-month (or nine-quarter) window (Chessa 2020). It is possible to construct weighted GEKS indices which consider the reliability of the bilateral price indices (Rao 2001b). Melser (2018) proposed a weighted GEKS method where the weights depend on the degree of matching of the items, for example, with regard to expenditure shares. Here, the choice of window length is less important since bilateral indices with a lower degree of matching will be down weighted.

10.104 The annually chained *direct extension method* (Chessa 2016) constructs multilateral index series of, say, 13 months, starting in, for example, December and ending in December of the next year, and chain links them in December of each year to obtain a long-term time series. The length of the estimation window for the short-term indices is extended each month—the index for January in the short-term series is estimated on two months of data (which is a bilateral rather than multilateral comparison), and so forth, until in December 13 months of data is used.

10.105 A potential weakness of the direct extension method is that the price indices for the first couple of months of each year are based on sparse data and expected to be volatile. Also, December acts as the short-term index reference period and is given special importance. If, for some reason, December is an unusual month, the results may be adversely affected. To mitigate these problems, Lamboray

Table 10.2 Movement Splice Linking with Rolling Window of 13 Months

Period	1	2	3	4	5	...	11	12	13	14	15
First Compilation Round in Period 13	100	100.7	100.6	101.6	102.7	...	104.3	106	103.8		
Second* Compilation Round in Period 14		100	100.2	101.1	102.2	...	103.8	105.5	103.3	104.6	
Third Compilation Round in Period 15			100	101	102	...	103.5	105.3	103.2	104.4	104.1
Published Index (movement splice)	100	100.5	100.6	101.6	102.7	...	104.3	106	103.8	**105.1**	**104.8**

The splicing starts in period 14 (shown in bold). The published indices for periods 1–13 are obtained at the first compilation round. The published index in period 14 is obtained by applying the change between period 13 and period 14 indices of the second compilation round to the published index of period 13 (103 8 × 104.6/103 3 = 105.1). The published index in period 15 is obtained by applying the change between period 14 and period 15 indices of the third compilation round to the published index of period 14(105 1 × 104 1/104 4 = 104 8).

(2017) suggested combining the annually chained direct extension method with a rolling window approach.

Implementation of Multilateral Methods

Assessing Multilateral Methods

10.106 The implementation of new data sources and methods in any statistical series requires careful consideration of the statistical impacts as well as the benefits and costs. Only a handful of NSOs have implemented multilateral price indices in the CPI.

10.107 A suggested criteria to assess multilateral methods should consider a broad concept of statistical quality. A possible framework could include seven dimensions of statistical quality:

- Institutional environment—pertains to the institutional and organizational context in which a statistical producer operates
- Relevance—pertains to how well a statistic meets user needs
- Timeliness—pertains to how quickly and frequently the statistic is published
- Accuracy—pertains to how well a statistic measures the desired concept
- Coherence—pertains to how consistent the statistic is with sources of related information
- Interpretability—pertains to the information available to provide insight into the statistic
- Accessibility—pertains to ease of access to the statistic

10.108 Of note, multilateral methods are more complicated than standard bilateral indices and present communication challenges for NSOs. High value should be placed on transparency to explain the statistics published, and describing and justifying the methods used. This is of critical importance for the trust in the published CPI. Two aspects of interpretability need consideration: first, to what extent the methods themselves are easy for index practitioners and users to understand; and second, whether it is easy to understand the price movements each index produces, especially which products have the greatest influence on these movements and why.

10.109 This framework can be used by an NSO to determine the benefits and challenges of using multilateral index methods considering country-specific circumstances.

10.110 Multilateral index methods to compile the CPI can also be assessed from a theoretical perspective. The assessment can use approaches previously applied to bilateral and spatial indices. The bilateral price indices are assessed both from axiomatic/test approaches (Chapter 3 of *Consumer Price Index Theory*) and economic approaches (Chapters 4 and 5 of *Consumer Price Index Theory*). Similar approaches to assessing multilateral indices in a spatial context have been developed and presented in several papers, especially Diewert (1999b) and Balk (2001).

10.111 A description of the theoretical assessments of multilateral price index methods in the present temporal context using the axiomatic/test and economic theory approaches is available (ABS 2016a; Zhang and others 2019). This assessment can be used as a basis for NSOs to undertake similar assessments in their local context. A comprehensive discussion of the various multilateral methods using the economic approach to index number theory can be found in Chapter 7 of *Consumer Price Index Theory*; see also Diewert and Fox (2017). The most important result is that GEKS deals appropriately with substitution effects whereas GK and TPD are appropriate only under restrictive assumptions about consumer preferences. However, in practice, GK and TPD generate very similar results. Another NSO developed a generic processing method based on the GK (see Chessa 2016). In a first step, the method was only implemented for mobile phones before being applied to more products and retailers in the following years.

10.112 In addition, expert peer review of the proposed multilateral methods may be appropriate in circumstances where CPI users may expect NSOs to demonstrate broader endorsement of the proposed changes.

Calculating Indices

Operational Choices

10.113 The matched-model property of (nonhedonic) multilateral indices implies that without any manual intervention, the results depend on the *choice of item identifier*. For example, when using the barcode as item identifier, the price change of a homogeneous item whose barcode changes at the same time—a "relaunch"—will not be measured. As mentioned earlier, the use of SKU codes mitigates the problem since SKU generally consists of multiple barcodes for similar items and is more stable than barcode. Nevertheless, even SKU may be too detailed.

10.114 If a relatively small number of observable attributes with discrete values suffice to define homogeneous items, items could be defined by cross-classifying the sets of categorical variables for each attribute and prices calculated as unit values across all the barcodes/SKUs. Most likely there will still be new and disappearing items (cells) across the sample period. To maximize the degree of matching without introducing chain drift, a multilateral method could be applied (Chessa 2016). A potential issue is that the available characteristics information may be limited, especially when the characteristics are extracted from variety descriptions in scanner data, which are often rather broad. In this case, unit value bias is likely to arise. Also, if the characteristics information is deemed sufficient, it may be better to construct hedonic indices.

10.115 While taking a (cutoff) sample that ignores items, however defined, with small expenditure shares would in many cases not significantly affect the results, it is not necessary when using a weighted multilateral method. Most of the issues discussed earlier in this chapter, such as the choice of calculating unit values at the store or at the chain level, and the need to have an index structure that facilitates the use of scanner data, apply here as well.

Producing Empirical Results

10.116 The purpose of producing empirical results of multilateral methods is twofold: examining the performance of various methods in local contexts as well as demonstrating to CPI users the likely impacts of moving from *current* CPI data sources and methods to new approaches. Ideally, these multilateral methods should be examined against each other, as well as in comparison to the official CPI. These comparisons should be undertaken at the lowest level of the published CPI and at various aggregation levels, including the all-items CPI. For some empirical evidence on multilateral price index methods, see Chapter 5 of ABS (2016a), Chapter 3 of ABS (2017), and Chessa and others (2017).

10.117 Several insights can be obtained from producing empirical results. Often these insights further reinforce the theoretical arguments for utilizing multilateral index methods to compile the CPI. This may include the impact of using contemporaneous information for weighting purposes that capture consumer behavior, including substitution, over time. The empirical results should be communicated to CPI users and stakeholders.

Communicating with Users and Stakeholders

10.118 The use of scanner data to compile the CPI potentially represents quite a significant change to the data sources and methods employed by NSOs. These changes need to be carefully communicated to CPI users and stakeholders. A suggested set of activities includes:

- Publishing information papers that outline the proposed new methods and data sources
- Conducting face-to-face meetings with key stakeholders (for example, central banks, treasury, and finance ministries) and other interested parties, including members of the public
- Using media releases and briefing of economic journalists to help inform the public of proposed changes
- Encouraging stakeholders and the public to provide submissions to the NSO for consideration
- Engaging with leading academics both to review the proposed changes and to encourage their support

10.119 Following this consultation, which could take a couple of years, the NSO should publish a position paper that both responds to the topics raised as part of the consultation process and articulates how the NSO will proceed with the use of scanner data to compile the CPI, including the rationale and empirical results that support this approach. The position paper should clearly state the data sources and methods to be employed and provide a timetable for the implementation of changes.

Publication and Dissemination

10.120 Following the publication of the position paper, it is suggested the NSO compile the CPI using both current and new data sources and methods in parallel for a period of approximately six months. This transition period allows the NSO to refine processes and procedures to compile the CPI using the new methods, as well as to compare the empirical results of the two approaches. This transition period is often the first opportunity for the NSO to use the new data sources and methods in real time following the CPI processing and publication timetable. It is at the NSO's discretion whether the results of the parallel processing are made public.

10.121 The first period for which the new data sources and methods are used to compile the CPI should be announced well in advance and should include detailed metadata for the media and other key data users. This will ensure that the methodological changes implemented to the CPI are well understood. Further information relating to the CPI dissemination can be found in Chapter 14 of this Manual.

SELECTED SPECIAL CASES

11

Introduction

11.1 Certain products have proven to be challenging for consumer price index (CPI) compilers with regard to developing weights and collecting prices. Chapter 11 focuses on selected special cases and provides detailed advice for some of the more challenging products and issues facing compilers. These include the treatment of seasonal products, internet purchases, housing, second-hand goods, own-account production, tariffs, telecommunications, transport services, health, education, social protection, and financial services.

11.2 Wherever possible, the chapter identifies the preferred approach for the treatment of each special case. However, at this time there is no preferred approach for the treatment of owner-occupied housing, and the section on this topic provides an overview of the different methods for its treatment and describes the advantages and disadvantages of each method.

Seasonal Products

Introduction

11.3 Seasonal products are those products that are either not available in the market during certain seasons or periods of the year or are available throughout the year but with regular fluctuations in their quantities and prices that are linked to the season or time of the year.

11.4 Climate, traditions, and institutional arrangements are the main causes of regular variations in the supply and demand for products. Fresh fruit and vegetables often have particularly marked seasonal purchasing and consumption patterns, and certain fruit and vegetables may not be available at all at certain times of the year. Other products that can display some seasonality include other fresh foods, clothing, water, electricity, and fuels. The list of seasonal products is not uniform across countries. For example, oranges may be available for purchase year-round in some countries, but only at certain times of the year or at a premium price in other countries. Similarly, seasonality can vary between different regions within the same country. Certain religious and other festivals can also be associated with goods or services whose consumption is limited wholly or partially to the festival period, such as Christmas trees, or products that are in high demand or especially produced, such as certain gifts given at the end of Ramadan.

11.5 In the compilation of a CPI, a useful distinction can be made between "strongly" seasonal products, that are available only part of the year when "in season," and "weakly" seasonal ones, that are available throughout the year but their prices and availability for purchase fluctuate significantly with the time of the year. Weakly seasonal products generally do not require any direct intervention by the index compiler. The seasonally fluctuating prices of weakly seasonal products will typically be captured in the index although they are not without problems for CPI users. For instance, when the weakly seasonal product is "out of season," its price may be unusually high or low and the annual basket will reflect these unusual price fluctuations, leading to seasonal fluctuations in the overall index. This volatility can cause "statistical noise" with the analysis and understanding of inflation. For some purposes, users want a CPI that measures the underlying price change and not these seasonal fluctuations. Measures of "core inflation" address these issues (see Chapters 12 and 14). It is the strongly seasonal products that pose the bigger problem for the index compiler. If a price is available in only one of two periods being compared, then it is not possible to calculate a price relative for the product.

11.6 There are two preferred approaches for the treatment of strongly seasonal products. Ignoring the issue and excluding all the challenging products from a CPI is not a solution in the context of an index whose purpose is to reflect changes in all consumer prices. If these products have some importance in the index basket then there is no justification for ignoring them.

11.7 This section describes the alternative ways of dealing with strongly seasonal products. Essentially, there are two methods: a *fixed-weight approach* that uses the annual weight for the seasonal product in all months using an imputed price in the out-of-season months, and a *seasonal-weight approach* where the weight is zero for out-of-season months and the annual weight is used for in-season months. The 2003 International Labor Organization Resolution states that *the way these (strongly seasonal) products are dealt with should be determined by the main purpose of the indices, national circumstances, and the practicalities of compilation.* For instance, the relative importance given to measuring month-on-month inflation and how the alternative methods of treatment perform in practice may inform a decision on which method to use.

11.8 There is no completely satisfactory way of dealing with strongly seasonal products. Index number theory can provide reasonably effective solutions where the focus is on comparing prices in one month with prices in the same month a year earlier. But the estimate of month-on-month inflation can vary, depending on the approach used, making the analysis of short-term inflation trends difficult. For example, since under the *fixed-weight approach* the absence of price quotes in particular months means that no month-on-month price ratio can be compiled without imputing a price, the result will depend on the method of imputation. Alternatively, a zero weight can be attached to the missing product, as in the *seasonal-weight approach,* but the resulting monthly variations in the composition of the CPI basket hinder month-on-month comparisons of inflation. In general, very large seasonal fluctuations in volumes combined with large systematic changes in prices can make month-on-month price index comparisons behave rather poorly.

11.9 The difficulties for CPI compilation that are raised by the existence of strongly seasonal items, and their seasonal unavailability can be tackled by choosing one of two main approaches:

- *The fixed-weight approach (also referred to as the strict annual weights method)*. Allocating fixed annual weights, on the assumption that seasonal products are to be treated in the same way as all other products. Prices will need to be imputed in the out-of-season period either from the last observed price or from what is considered the "typical" or "normal" price. The main imputation methods are overall mean imputation or class mean imputation (see Chapter 6 for more details on imputation methods).
- *The seasonal-weight approach.*[1] Allocating seasonal weights according to the consumption pattern found in the weight reference period. Items are given a zero weight in the out-of-season period, and the expenditure on other selected items is adjusted so that the basket weights sum to 100.

11.10 The methods are discussed in more detail in paragraphs 11.13–11.38. A common predicament is the determination of the in-season and out-of-season periods. A conservative approach is recommended in determining the in-season period to avoid abnormal prices from entering the index, for instance, high prices being charged for the first supply appearing in the outlets of a fresh crop (for example, summer fruit) where quantities may be low and demand and prices high. The chances of this happening are minimized in the fixed-weight approach by imputing from what is considered a "typical" or "normal" price. There is no universally accepted standard definition of what constitutes a "typical" or "normal" price. In the European Union (EU) context, in the Harmonised Index of Consumer Prices (HICP), the average price in the previous season or the regular price observed before the sales period is used. The aim is to prevent exceptional prices from having an impact on the indices during the full out-of-season period.

11.11 Even though existing index number theory cannot deal satisfactorily with seasonal products in the context of constructing month-on-month indices of consumer prices, it can better deal with seasonal products if the focus is changed from month-on-month CPIs to CPIs that compare the prices of one month with the prices of the same month in a previous year, that are individual annual inflation rates.

11.12 The use of seasonal adjustment techniques to extract the seasonal components of a CPI for analysis are not covered in this chapter and should be used only for analytical purposes (for more information, see Chapter 14). It should also be noted that, in general, the imputation of missing prices does not eliminate seasonal fluctuations in prices. The CPI should reflect actual prices paid by consumers and these fluctuations should be included.

[1] Referred to in EU HICP as the class-confined seasonal weights method.

Fixed-Weight Approach

11.13 The fixed-weight approach, where the weights remain constant over all months of the year and that imputes a price when the product is out of season and not available for price collection, is theoretically consistent with the concept of a fixed basket. However, it raises the issue of the choice of imputation method for the unobservable out-of-season prices. The most commonly used approach is to impute a price using the last available observed price (that is reliable) and multiplying this last available price by the amount of price inflation for the most similar or "comparable" group of items that has taken place since the time of this last available observed price. For instance, a similar item or group of varieties that is in season might be used. The missing prices can be estimated using the monthly rate of change in the prices of the set of products within the same class of the Classification of Individual Consumption According to Purpose (COICOP) or using an appropriate subset. Measured inflation of higher-level aggregates is likely to be influenced to a large extent by factors that are not so relevant for the seasonal product. Using products from the same COICOP subclass, class, or group also enhances comparability with the seasonal-weight approach, thus increasing statistical integrity.

11.14 The basis for the imputation could be an elementary index that uses Dutot or Jevons averaging, depending on the formula used for the CPI at the elementary aggregate level, or it could even be the all-items CPI (that is, at the aggregate level) if there is no similar group of items.

11.15 The use of the carryforward method (repeating the last collected price) is discouraged. Using the carryforward method may introduce bias into the index, as month-on-month changes would be zero (as described in Chapter 6).

11.16 The main drawback of the fixed-weight approach is that the annual fixed weights will not be representative of the monthly consumption pattern. For example, oranges might be available for sale only in some months, but the fixed-weight approach assumes that they are sold throughout the year and introduces artificial prices that do not exist in the market but are based on the price movements of a comparable product, such as bananas, that in reality may be of limited comparability. The limited comparability of the comparable product can lead to an extreme fluctuation in the oranges subindex when oranges return to the market and are available again for direct pricing. In practice, the fixed-weight approach normally gives reasonably smooth 12-month rates of change. The imputation of prices by reference to the most similar group of products or items normally reflects reasonably well the price inflation expectation when the product returns to the market and thus is often considered appropriate for the medium- and long-term measurement of inflation. However, the use of carryforward prices can, of course, bias the month-on-month changes to zero.

11.17 For clothing, in the first month, the seasonal item is missing; the price should be returned to the last "normal" price. The "normal" price refers to the last collected price before the seasonal discount or sale period. In the second month, the imputation should be made on this last "normal" price. Imputing the sale or discounted price can introduce a downward bias in the clothing index. For other seasonal items, such as fresh fruits and vegetables, it may also be preferable to return the final in-season price to a "normal" price before beginning the imputation. Alternatively, the imputation could be made on the last available price beginning with the first month the seasonal item is missing. Imputation methods are described in the section that follows.[2]

11.18 The advantage of the fixed-weight approach where missing prices are imputed is that it is easy to explain and implement and keeps the annual fixed-basket methodology more or less intact.

11.19 An additional recommendation is that the method applied to deal with seasonal products should ideally be "self-correcting." For example, if the item after the out-of-season period reappears at the same price as it left the market, then the method should ensure that this will take the index back to 100; similarly, if the price reappears 10 percent higher, it should take the index to 110.

Imputation of Prices under the Fixed-Weight Approach: Overall Mean or Class Mean Imputation

11.20 The principle behind imputation is that it makes use of the best available information to provide an unbiased estimate of price and price movement. There are essentially three choices:

- Overall mean imputation. Impute the missing price by reference to the average price change for the prices that are available in the elementary aggregate. This assumes that the price change of the missing variety, if it had been available in the outlet, would have been equal to the average change in prices in the elementary aggregate. This may be a reasonable assumption if the elementary aggregate is relatively homogeneous. This method of imputation is equivalent to omitting the variety from the elementary index, no matter whether a Jevons, Carli, or Dutot method of aggregation is used at the elementary aggregate level. This imputation method, as well as the next one, is discussed in Chapter 6.
- Targeted mean imputation. Impute the missing price by reference to the average price change for the price of a "comparable" item from a similar outlet. This represents a more precise match between the missing variety and the varieties or item supplying an imputed price. It is normally preferable to impute using the average price change in the elementary aggregate unless the imputations are unreliable because of small sample sizes.
- Counter seasonal imputation. Impute by using only the prices of seasonal products in the COICOP subclass, class, or group. The reasoning underlying counterseasonal imputation is that both in-season and out-of-season products serve similar purposes, although in different conditions. In contrast, nonseasonal products within the same COICOP subclass, class, or group may have different uses. For instance, formal ball gowns are available all year round to serve a specific purpose, so it is argued that they cannot be substituted by either a summer or winter dress. However, warm and lightweight clothes have the same purpose of protecting the body and are substitutable according to the temperature conditions.

11.21 There are many examples of consumption products that are available seasonally. The example in Tables 11.1 and 11.2 illustrates the method of imputing prices for out-of-season products based on price movements of related in-season products. In this example, there are two seasonal products but only one is available during each collection period. In addition, there are occasions when neither is available. The two products are children's summer nightwear and children's winter nightwear. As both products serve the same purpose, they are substitutes for each other within their respective seasons. This allows the compiler to assume that the price movements of the available product would be suitable to impute price movements for the unavailable product. This assumption would also hold in situations where both products are available in the same pricing period (that is, the seasons overlap for a short time). There would simply be no need to impute any prices during these periods.

11.22 A well-constructed CPI structure would have products that could be considered substitutable or very similar in nature as neighboring components. This allows the index structure to determine the appropriate price movements to be used in computing price movements for unavailable seasonal products.

11.23 Table 11.1 shows the price relatives for a monthly index for most of a year; in this case, the short-term monthly price relatives noting the same can be applied using long-term price relatives. Only the structure for one small portion of the entire CPI structure is displayed. There are four elementary aggregates shown: *Underwear*, *Socks*, *Summer nightwear*, and *Winter nightwear*. The prices that have been collected and for which short-term price relatives can normally be calculated from actual nonimputed prices are the figures not in italics. *Underwear* and *Socks* are available (and priced) all year round. Both seasonal elementary aggregates (*Summer* and *Winter nightwear*) are grouped together under an aggregate component (sub-index) labeled *Nightwear*. No other elementary aggregates are included in this aggregate component. Consequently, the structure implies that each seasonal nightwear elementary aggregate is the best index from which to impute price movements for the other. Price relatives calculated from prices imputed in this situation are in italics. When there are no prices available for either of the two seasonal products, other components must provide suitable price movements to be used in the imputation process. If the structure has been organized to group comparable components as neighbors, then the best components for providing appropriate price movements are likely to be similar to the component of the seasonal elementary aggregates. In this example, the components *Underwear* and *Socks* are judged to be similar to *Nightwear*. Therefore, a weighted average of the price movements of *Underwear* and *Socks* will be considered as the best imputation of an appropriate price movement for both *Summer nightwear* and *Winter nightwear*. Price relatives calculated from prices imputed in this situation have been shaded in bold italics.

[2] Paul A. Armknecht, and Fenella Maitland-Smith. 1999. "Price Imputation and Other Techniques for Dealing with Missing Observations, Seasonality and Quality Change in Price Indices." Working Paper No. 99/78, International Monetary Fund, Washington, DC. http://www.imf.org/external/pubs/ft/wp/1999/wp9978.pdf.

Table 11.1 Short-Term Price Relatives Based on Monthly Indices for Four Selected Elementary Aggregates

CPI Structure	2019							
	Feb.	Mar.	Apr.	May	Jun.	Jul.	Aug.	Sep.
Children's Clothing								
Subindex: Underwear, Nightwear, and Socks								
Elementary Aggregates:								
Underwear	1.010	1.000	1.050	1.005	1.010	1.000	1.030	1.020
Socks	1.000	1.005	1.000	1.030	1.020	1.005	1.000	0.999
Nightwear								
Winter Nightwear	*1.010*	*0.970*	***1.036***	*1.100*	*1.050*	*0.980*	*0.950*	***1.014***
Summer Nightwear	*1.010*	*0.970*	***1.036***	*1.100*	*1.050*	*0.980*	*0.950*	***1.014***

Table 11.2 Monthly Price Indices Using Imputed Prices for Missing Values of Winter and Summer Nightwear

CPI Structure	Weights (base period)	2019								
		Jan.	Feb.	Mar.	Apr.	May	Jun.	Jul.	Aug.	Sep.
Children's Clothing										
Subindex: Underwear, Nightwear, and Socks	1000	**118.3**	**119.2**	**118.3**	**122.6**	**127.1**	**130.2**	**129.5**	**129.4**	**131.3**
Elementary Aggregates:										
Underwear	500	119.0	120.2	120.2	126.2	126.8	128.1	128.1	131.9	134.6
Socks	200	120.0	120.0	120.6	120.6	124.2	126.7	127.3	127.3	127.2
Lower-Level Index: Nightwear	300	116.0	117.2	113.6	117.8	129.5	136.0	133.3	126.6	128.4
Elementary Aggregates:										
Winter Nightwear	*150*	*116.0*	*117.2*	*113.6*	***117.7***	*129.5*	*136.0*	*133.3*	*126.6*	***128.3***
Summer Nightwear	*150*	*116.0*	*117.2*	*113.6*	***117.7***	*129.5*	*136.0*	*133.3*	*126.6*	***128.4***

11.24 The example commences with pricing conducted in February. As this is the winter season (in the Northern Hemisphere), no prices are available for *Summer nightwear*. Under this method, the price movement for *Summer nightwear* is imputed to be the same as for *Winter nightwear*. The same situation occurs in March.

11.25 However, in April no prices were collected for either summer or winter nightwear items. Price movements in the components judged to be most similar to the aggregate nightwear component must be used to impute a price movement for all nightwear items. To first aggregate the indices (or long-term relatives), then base the imputation on month-on-month change of the aggregate index of those two components. In other words, calculate the indices of Table 11.2 first, adding a line for a subindex of underwear and socks, then use the month-on-month change of the subindex for underwear and socks to impute the relative for missing nightwear.

11.26 In May, summer nightwear was again available and so prices were collected. The price relatives for the summer nightwear items are calculated from the collected prices. The price movements for summer nightwear items in May are measured as the change from the imputed prices for April to the actual prices collected in May. This method does, therefore, self-correct if the imputed prices do start to diverge from the "true" level.

11.27 While this example has shown price imputation occurring at the elementary aggregate level, this has been done for simplicity in presenting the method. It can be thought of as an example where there is just one price observation in each of the elementary aggregates. In practice, most CPI systems would impute price movements for individual items in the price samples within an elementary aggregate using the same figures for the imputation. Index calculations would then proceed as normal. The resulting indices are given in Table 11.2. The figures in italics are based on imputed prices as in Table 11.1.

11.28 This method can also be applied to other products, such as fresh fruit and vegetables, as long as the CPI has an appropriate structure. For instance, seasonal fruits should be imputed from price movements of other in-season fruits, and seasonal vegetables should be imputed from other in-season vegetables.

Seasonal-Weight Approach

11.29 The seasonal-weight approach gives a zero weight to an item when out of season and reverts to the annual fixed weights when the product is in season and available for pricing. It is usually applied within a COICOP subclass for which the weight is held constant. When the out-of-season item is assigned a zero weight, the upper-level weight is redistributed proportionally to the available in-season items. For example, take the seasonal food category that covers fresh fruit and vegetables. Only the item weights within fresh fruit and vegetables can vary between zero and the annual fixed weight, though the section weights are fixed so that, at least at the upper levels, the principle of the fixed basket is maintained.

11.30 The underlying assumption is that total expenditure on the relevant COICOP subclass (often synonymous with an elementary aggregate) does not vary between different times of the year, the main tendency being for expenditure to switch between similar items only (for example, consumers will tend to buy other fruits if oranges are not available).

11.31 The seasonal-weight approach has the advantage of minimizing the practice of price imputation, as prices will not be imputed in those months when the product is not available for purchase. Prices are observed only in months where weights are not zero. For products that have prices observed in two consecutive months, the monthly changes of the product price indices are computed using matched samples. When a product has a positive weight after the weight has been zero for some months, the product index is compiled by matching the price observation in the first month of the new season with the observations from the last month of the previous season and applying the relative change to the last index of the previous season to give the price index for the first month of the new season.

11.32 The seasonal-weight approach has two key disadvantages:

- It is conceptually inconsistent with a fixed-basket index.
- Month-on-month price changes reflect not only changes in price relatives but also changes in the weights (from zero to the fixed annual weights approach). This makes it difficult to interpret month-on-month changes in the price index.

11.33 In addition, concerns have been expressed about the variability in the precise timing of the seasons from one year to the next, meaning that the imputation of prices is not totally avoided. For instance, if unusual weather conditions delay the appearance in the market of oranges, then prices would need to be imputed for those months that oranges are unavailable but where a nonzero weight has been allocated.

11.34 It is strongly recommended that the set of products defined as seasonal should not vary from year to year, unless strongly justified on the grounds of necessity to keep the sample representative.

Fixed or Seasonal Weights?

11.35 Comparing the fixed- and seasonal-weight approaches, the two approaches provide similar results. The imputation of prices based on the price movements of similar products—the fixed-weight approach—is a form of reweighting where more weight is given to the price movements of products that are available for pricing.

11.36 An "ideal" solution to the treatment of seasonal items does not exist, particularly where the existence of seasonal products (especially strongly seasonal products) means that it is impossible to compute a completely satisfactory month-on-month index that accurately measures month-on-month price change.

11.37 If the focus of the CPI is the accurate measurement of annual price inflation, then the challenges associated with strongly seasonal products are minimized (although changes in seasonal patterns from one year to the next continue be problematic).[3]

11.38 The advantages and disadvantages of each method should be considered and, if possible, the impact on measured inflation assessed for reasonableness before a particular method is implemented. The use of the index will also be an important consideration. For example, if the main purpose of the index is for indexation of payments and salaries, then the fact that the seasonal-weight approach means that the month-on-month price change will reflect not only changes in price relatives but also changes in consumption baskets may be considered a significant disadvantage (that is, users might question the meaning of comparing the price of this month's basket with the price of last month's basket that might be very different). More generally, if the user focus is on month-on-month change, then the seasonal-weight approach is recommended, despite the problems of interpretation, as the annual weights attached to each month-on-month price relative under the fixed-weight approach can be misleading. If user focus is on long-term index changes, then the use of an annual basket and annual expenditure shares is the most appropriate.

Monthly Approach: Maximum Overlap—Not an Alternative

11.39 The maximum overlap approach deals directly with the seasonality problem, but strictly speaking is not an alternative to the fixed or seasonal weight options for dealing with particular products. Rather it is a method of index construction that overcomes the challenges of seasonal products by considering only those observations present in both compared months. In this case, it would seem reasonable at first glance to prefer a chained index, that compares prices in adjacent months, because a fixed-base index could fail to effectively follow closely market developments. This is because of the dynamics in the retail market resulting from seasonality, the introduction of new products, and the disappearance of older ones. The expenditure shares for month $m + 1$ are calculated excluding the products not priced in that month.

11.40 The main disadvantage of the maximum overlap price index is that it can have a significant downward bias because of the chained nature of the index. Seasonal products tend to enter the market at relatively high prices, which drop in the subsequent months. The initial high prices are not always captured by the maximum overlap index. When these products first become available, they come into the market at relatively high prices and then, in subsequent months, their prices drop substantially. The effects of these initially high prices (compared to the relatively low prices that prevailed in the last month that the products were available in the previous year) are not captured by the maximum overlap month-on-month indices, so the resulting indices build up a significant downward bias. The downward bias is most pronounced in the Paasche indices that use the quantities or volumes of the current month. Those quantities are relatively large compared to the initial month when the products become available, reflecting the effects of lower prices when the quantity in the market increases.

11.41 The maximum overlap method is not recommended when there are particularly large price variations. The month-on-month maximum overlap method is generally not recommended because of the possible chain drift bias. However, it can be checked if there is a problem with the use of the method in practice by comparing the product

[3]The focus on annual price inflation leads to the possibility of a further solution—the construction of 12 year-on-year monthly Lowe indices (or geometric Young indices or four quarter-over-quarter indices), using seasonal baskets that are appropriate for each month or quarter. From a practical point of view, annual household budget surveys (HBSs) would have to be augmented to cover seasonal products in more detail and this would entail higher costs.

of 12 consecutive month-on-month maximum overlap indices with the corresponding direct year-on-year comparison. If the product of the 12 links is reasonably close to the corresponding year-on-year index, then the month-on-month overlap method can be used.

Implementation Problems

The Identification of Seasonal Items in the Basket and the Corresponding Length of the Seasonal Cycle

11.42 The most important characteristics that can be associated with a strongly seasonal product are: it is not available for purchase during certain months (or the quantity available for purchase is negligible); there is a significant variation in demand during the year; and there are corresponding large fluctuations in price. The variations in supply and demand, mean that prices cannot be observed during the out-of-season months. Seasonal products are associated with variations both in availability of products and in demand and this can lead to pronounced variations in stocks in outlets, expenditure levels, and prices. Any period of nonavailability for pricing in outlets should have some typical annual cyclical pattern. If for some reason a product becomes unavailable in a month where it would normally be available and sold at a normal price, this does not make it a seasonal product. The out-of-season period of a product includes the months in that no prices are observed or used in the compilation for that product, because it is not available for pricing or only available in small quantities in very few outlets at abnormal prices. The inclusion of abnormally high "start-of-season" prices collected from relatively few outlets can potentially introduce a downward bias in the index for both the fixed-weight and seasonal-weight approaches. It may also cause difficulties for price collectors trying to find the products.

The Geographical Dimension

11.43 The seasonal availability of products may vary between regions within a large country. There may also be a difference in supply (and demand) between markets in rural and urban areas, or between market stalls and more upmarket outlets catering to higher incomes. For example, some prices may be collectable in the capital city even though the product is generally not available elsewhere. Where this is the case, different seasonal cycles may be applied, particularly if the differences are marked and regional or urban/rural subindices are being computed. The decision should take account of the extent of the differences and the needs of users.

Lack of Well-Defined Seasons

11.44 In practice, seasonal products do not always appear and disappear in the same month every year. This presents a problem both for year-on-year monthly comparisons of monthly indices, and for year-on-year comparisons of quarterly indices, but is particularly pronounced for the former. The consequence of neglecting the importance of carefully predefined seasons can contribute to a method, failing to correctly reflect the price changes in the price index in the short term, particularly the seasonal-weight approach. Decisions made regarding the relevance of prices that could have been observed but were not (and have not been included in the index or the imputation of missing prices) can affect the stability of the price index. Thus, the fact that seasonal patterns change and the need to confront whether to accept this or force data into a predetermined seasonal pattern poses a dilemma to CPI compilers. It is particularly important that when data are published, the national statistical office (NSO) should provide background explanations for both the monthly changes and the 12-month rate of change, and whether this is influenced by a change in the timing of sales and in what direction and by what magnitude.

Domestic Products Being Replaced with Imported Products When Out of Season

11.45 When domestically produced, the product description is especially important. The CPI compiler will need to make a judgment on whether an imported apple is of the same quality as a domestic one and if so whether it can be treated as an equivalent or "comparable" fruit. This judgment should be based not just on the variety of apple, its general condition, and flavor, but also on whether the market perceives it to be the same and treats it as the same.

11.46 To correctly define those months that the price index of the seasonal product will be calculated from observed prices, particularly in the situation where the methodology requires a fixed seasonal pattern, the NSO should examine in detail the historical data on prices and availability for each product and undertake a sensitivity analysis to identify working rules for determining the inclusion and exclusion of products in the index in specific months. These working rules include:

- The data on availability are needed to decide whether it is likely that in any specific month the product will keep returning to the market every year.
- The price data will show how the inclusion of the product in the index for the first month that the product returns to the market may contribute to the volatility of the index. For example, if the entry price is particularly high (for example, more than 250 percent higher than the product's last actual price), then it would be reasonable to consider not including the product for that month, especially as it is improbable that the product was widely purchased at such a high price.
- Strongly seasonal products enter the market at high prices that decline toward the end of the season but can go up sharply before exiting the market. This will also have an impact that may vary depending on the calculation approach used.

Common Seasonal Products and Their Treatment

Fruits and Vegetables

11.47 The prices of seasonal fruits and vegetables are strongly dependent on supply conditions, such as weather, and are thus liable to show extreme price movements and shifts in seasons, as well as seasonal unavailability. However, changes in specification or quality are not common and therefore do not cause the same challenges as are experienced when dealing with, for example, seasonal clothing (see paragraphs 11.49–11.51).

Clothing

11.48 The treatment of seasonal clothing can be challenging, especially because fashion is involved. In many countries, the price patterns of clothing are the result not just of seasonal availability (for example, winter coats or bathing suits) but, especially for fashion goods, of discounts in seasonal sales. In addition, the problem of extreme price movements is combined not only with seasonal unavailability, but by annual changes in the products because of the effect of fashion. New stocks of clothes that arrive in the outlets at the beginning of their season may have styles that are different from those that disappeared at the end of the previous season, so there is the question of whether the new styles are different in quality from the old styles. In addition, prices generally fall over the course of the season: prices at the end of a season are often discounted as outlets clear their stocks in readiness for the next season. For seasonal items, comparisons must be made between the new replacement products and the old products that disappeared at the end of the previous season, maybe six months earlier. Dealing with these issues can be challenging:

- *Specification changes*. Since it can be difficult to make like-to-like observations for many categories of clothing, the rules for judging whether a replacement is comparable to an original item may need to be less rigid or strict. For example, this season's high-fashion coat can be viewed as comparable to last season's model, unless there are obvious differences in important characteristics such as textile replacing leather. For high-fashion items, only changes in compositional and material characteristics, if significant, should be treated as quality changes (see Chapter 6). The primary characteristic of most high-fashion items is the product brand, which incorporates the fashion element. Keeping the same or an equivalent brand is often the key to measuring the fashion element.
- *Discounted end-of-season prices*. In the case of a product showing temporary discounts or promotions, where it seems likely that the price will return to its normal level after a short period, then the discounted price should be included, and no special method is needed to handle it. If, however, the discounting is seasonal in nature and intended to help the outlet clear stocks of old styles, then the issue is more problematic because, unless specific procedures are applied to ensure a return to normal prices, the index will be subject to a systematic downward bias. The exclusion of such situations is an important consideration in defining the in-season period. Products that have flaws or are irregular should not be included.

11.49 As a result of the complications discussed in the previous paragraphs, some NSOs employ the following procedures during the period covering the time when a seasonal clothing item is not available. This adopts the fixed-weight approach and imputes missing prices by applying price movements, using the overall mean or the targeted mean (see Chapter 6) to the last available normal price.

- In the first month that the item or variety is unavailable, record the price at its "normal" level; in other words, in the first month impute the last available normal price.
- Impute a price during the period of unavailability, for the second and subsequent months, by applying the monthly movements for clothing items for which prices are available to the last normal price.
- When the normal season resumes, select a replacement as similar as possible to the variety that was priced during the previous season and compare its price directly to the final imputed price of the old variety. It is important that the index reflects the full extent of the price difference between the last month that a price was imputed and the first month of the new season. If the replacement has a different level of quality, then the price should be adjusted using one of the quality-adjustment methods presented in Chapter 6.
- Continue price collection using this new variety for the new season.

Chapter 5 includes further guidance on the treatment of sale prices.

Intractable Problems and Serious Challenges

11.50 In the context of constructing a month-on-month index that accurately reflects consumer price inflation, there is no fully effective method of dealing with large monthly fluctuations in prices and quantities generated by strong seasonality. The fixed- and seasonal-weight approaches yield the same results. If the user focus is on month-on-month change, then it has been argued that the seasonal-weight approach is probably the preferred method, as it avoids the problem associated with the fixed-weight approach where the annual weights attached to each month-on-month price relative can be misleading, but the fixed basket has been compromised. From a presentational point of view, indices showing the 12-month inflation rate assist in trend analysis but do not easily identify changes in the monthly trends. Additionally, month-on-month indices using maximum overlap are prone to downward bias.

11.51 It should be noted that when estimating the contribution of a subcomponent to the change in the all-items CPI, the way this is calculated is different for a seasonal component. This is dealt with in Chapters 9 and 14.

Internet Purchases

Introduction

11.52 The traditional concept of consumers visiting outlets to purchase goods and services has been changing over recent years. The importance of internet purchases has been growing significantly. Conceptually, the CPI should broadly represent the expenditure patterns of the reference population; therefore, online purchases should be included in the CPI to maintain the relevance of the index by properly representing consumer purchasing habits.

11.53 Internet purchases are a form of electronic commerce that allows consumers to directly buy goods or services from a seller over the internet using a web browser. Consumers find a product of interest by visiting the website of the retailer directly or by searching among alternative vendors using a shopping search engine that displays the product's availability and price at different e-retailers.

11.54 In principle, internet purchases also include in-app purchases,[4] purchases via social media, and other similar avenues that provide a mobile, desktop, and internet-based sharing application. These services can be extended to allow the consumer to get the product name and price information for items in a photo. By clicking on a specific item, consumers are taken to its product page, and if they click the "Shop Now" button, they are taken to the brand's website to complete their purchase. While these services have been excluded because of the practical difficulties of identifying these forms of purchase and estimating the volume and value of purchases, there is a need to collect information from households on how they make purchases on the internet. The household budget survey (HBS) can be used to collect these data.

11.55 The growth of internet purchases facilitates more efficient price collection as collecting prices online can be relatively easy and cheap compared to sending price collectors to outlets. However, identifying and measuring online purchases to develop weights and augment outlet samples can be a challenge.

11.56 The practical measurement challenges of including internet purchases in the CPI share some common issues with other types of shopping. Whether internet purchases are any different from any other form of retailing is debatable. Perhaps the main distinction from more traditional forms of shopping is the practicality of measurement, that is, estimating the expenditure weights and collecting price observations proportional to sales.

11.57 As mentioned in Chapter 5, prices for goods and services sold by web-based outlets can be collected in the same way as the online collection of prices from the websites of outlets with a corresponding physical location. The sample of items to be priced should be representative of online purchases and may have different prices from the ones charged online by physical outlets. The prices recorded should represent the full cost of purchase, including any tax and surcharges. Online purchases may include delivery charges. For CPI compilation, charges that are directly connected to the purchase of the priced product and that are not separately invoiced should be included in the price. If the charge is separately invoiced or relates to the purchase of a number of items, then it should be included under transport services.

11.58 This chapter explores the conceptual issues and challenges as well as the practicalities of incorporating internet purchases into the CPI. The underlying principles of measurement are the same as with collecting prices from physical outlets.

Coherence and Data Integration

11.59 Internet purchases can be made through retailers that have both an online and physical presence (multichannel retailers) or just an online presence (web-based retailers). For multichannel retailers, there may not be a need to price both methods of purchasing if there is no difference in price, terms and conditions of purchase, or product availability. For the online presence of the outlet, the collection of delivery charges and credit card surcharges might need to be addressed. When the prices are the same, CPI price collection could simply switch from collecting prices in store to collecting prices online to save on collection costs. Where prices and price movements are similar in both modes of collection, the different market shares of online versus in store will not play a role in the calculation of average price movements. The fundamental question is whether prices online do in fact match the prices in the physical outlet. If not, online purchases should be treated as a distinct outlet type requiring separate and proper representation in the CPI.

11.60 A study by Cavallo (2017) undertook a comparison of online versus offline prices in large multichannel retailers across 10 countries. The findings indicate that the price levels, in general, were identical in approximately 72 percent of the cases across sampled countries; however, for clothing and electronics, identical prices were found in 83 percent and 92 percent of the cases, respectively. Based on these findings, there is scope for the internet to be used as an alternative mode for price collection when the same prices are available online and in the traditional physical outlet. However, when using the internet for price collection the NSO should confirm that the online prices do in fact match the in-store prices and that the strong correlation between movements of in-store and online prices continues. The relationship between in-store and online prices can change over time, so this should be monitored.

11.61 The simplest method for determining whether a website matches in-store prices is to concurrently price in-store and online items for a few periods to confirm that both the price and price change are the same. Another option would be to meet with the respondent in the outlet and discuss whether the prices online are similar to those in the physical outlet. If prices and price changes are considered different and the expenditure is considered representative and significant across both purchase channels then ideally both modes of purchase should be priced.

11.62 From a more strategic viewpoint, the NSO should decide if internet purchases in general should be considered as purchases from a distinctive type of outlet, in which case they should be fully integrated into the structure of the elementary aggregates and into the CPI outlet and item samples. It would follow that internet purchases should be treated as a separate stratum for sample selection and elementary aggregation.

Estimating Expenditure Weights for Internet Purchases and Selecting Samples

11.63 The requirement that a broadly representative basket of goods and services is used to compile the CPI and that the same basket is repriced month after month can be particularly challenging for internet prices. This is especially so when having to account for changes in the characteristics of products, and their disappearance from a website from one month to the next, along with the appearance of new or updated items and varieties. Internet purchases represent a share of the data universe available for the products that are to be sampled and, as such, represent a particular outlet type. Online outlet and product selection are based on the same criteria and methods used for traditional collection,

[4] In-app purchasing refers to the buying of goods and services from inside an application on a mobile device, such as a smartphone or tablet.

drawing on information on modes of purchase for different products as recorded in an HBS and on sales information supplied by, for instance, the online retailers. The sales information should exclude sales to businesses and should conform with the geographical concept followed by the CPI (see paragraphs 11.65–11.72); however, as this can be difficult to separately identify from sales data supplied by retailers, information from HBS is often preferred, despite the fact that it is sample-based and can be out of date. HBS data can be updated using commercial information on trends in internet purchases, but care must be taken to ensure consistency of weights to reflect expenditure patterns in the weight reference period.

Geographical Coverage

11.64 Internet purchases can be made from either domestic websites or foreign websites. The treatment of these transactions can cause challenges for producing a CPI and is dependent on the geographical coverage of the CPI. The CPI follows either the national or domestic concept, as described in Chapter 2. The concept followed determines from a geographical perspective what expenditure is included in the weights and what goods and services are priced.

The National versus the Domestic Concept

11.65 The *national* concept means that the CPI should cover all expenditure (and prices) relating to the resident households of the country, regardless of where the expenditure takes place. The national concept aligns with the *System of National Accounts* (SNA).[5] The weights for expenditure abroad can be computed from the HBS, at least in theory, but measuring prices paid abroad can pose significant practical and operational problems especially for purchases from physical outlets as opposed to purchases made online.

11.66 The *domestic* concept means that the CPI should cover all the expenditure made by households within the economic territory of the country, including the nonbusiness expenditure made by foreign visitors. It excludes the expenditure abroad of the resident households.

11.67 As discussed in Chapter 2, the treatment of purchases made online requires special consideration. In principle, the domestic and national concepts could provide guidance on how to treat the expenditure made on goods and services, including digital downloads, purchased online. In many cases, however, internet-based outlets may be based (registered) abroad and this expenditure would be considered cross-border shopping. For those countries following the national concept, the approach is clear. Strictly speaking, under the domestic concept, this expenditure would not be included because it would be defined as expenditure abroad; in practice, this requires a broader interpretation. The nature of internet purchases, therefore, requires a different way of thinking and special consideration, especially with regard to the domestic concept. Additionally, internet purchases continue to grow in importance.

11.68 Many countries have carefully considered how to include the expenditure (and prices) made on goods and services via the internet. For the purchase of goods, the expenditure and prices should be reflected in the country where the goods are delivered.

11.69 Services purchased on the internet can be more problematic for CPI compilation because there are both tangible and digital services. Tangible services would include traditional services such as transportation, hotels, entrance to cultural/sporting events, or education. Digital services would include telecommunications, broadcasting (for example, streaming or downloading music, movies, or television content), and other services (for example, software). If the service is consumed in the economic territory where the household is resident, it should be included in the CPI; however, if the service is consumed outside of the economic territory of the country, it would be excluded. For example, if a household reserves a hotel room that will be used and paid for in another country, it would be considered out of scope. For digital services, because the service is being consumed within the economic territory of a country, the expenditure and prices should be included in the country where the household resides.

11.70 The estimation of expenditure weights can be a more challenging measurement issue. When expenditure or alternative sources of data are not readily available, but internet purchases are known to be substantial, an NSO could investigate augmenting the CPI basket using an estimated weight until the precise weight can be established. By doing this, the relevance of the CPI basket is better maintained.

11.71 For item and variety selection, online retailers often identify their top-selling products on their websites. This can help with identifying those products to price; however, the bestseller or most popular item lists may be skewed by the web-based retailer to sell specific items. CPI staff should carefully review these lists to identify those items that represent the most popular or best seller.

Determining the Location of the Online Retailer and of the Transaction

11.72 The location of the purchaser, the location of the website, and the location of the transaction may be spread across different countries. Several alternative locations may be considered in determining whether an online transaction complies with the national or domestic concept:

- Purchaser's domicile at the time of the order
- Address where the product is delivered to
- Purchaser's address
- Billing address
- The location where the product is consumed
- Country where tax, most particularly value-added tax (VAT) or goods and services tax (GST), is paid

11.73 As noted previously, internet purchases force a broader interpretation of the domestic concept. In this case, a pragmatic approach needs to be adopted rather than

[5] Another issue raised by the increasing use of the internet for purchases is the distinction between goods and services. The Impact of Globalisation on National Accounts (UNECE 2015) includes a chapter on e-commerce. The chapter includes a table (Table 13.1) on whether to classify different types of internet purchases as goods or services according to the *2008 SNA* concepts and the Sixth Edition of the IMF's *Balance of Payments and International Investment Position Manual*. In the discussions about the problems in measuring globalization the issue of having suitable price indices for deflation of flows of goods and services is often mentioned as a major challenge.

establishing and adhering to rules and regulations designed to maintain strict consistency with national accounts. For this reason, alternative workable approaches are sometimes used. Feldman and Sandberg (2012) suggest using the address where the product is delivered to as a practical solution. The country of delivery is where the consumer and the product come together. If the purchaser's country is not listed as the standard location for the delivery of purchases from the website, then it may be assumed that the seller's location is in another country. Following this approach, downloads of music, e-books, or software should be classified as domestic purchases as these are normally delivered instantaneously to the user. Although, conceptually this deviates from the concept of a foreign internet purchase, as it will most likely capture purchases from some foreign-based websites, practically it is considered by some as the next best alternative. However, it can lead to inconsistencies between a CPI and the coverage of both the national accounts and of the balance of payments. The approach adopted by Eurostat for the EU HICP uses administrative rules relating to taxation as the basis for determining how to treat internet purchases.[6] Eurostat's recommendations on the treatment in the EU of cross-border internet purchases borrow from the VAT rules as applied to all member states. The VAT rules consider the fact that an increasing number of products are electronic (for example, an e-book), rather than a physical good or service in the traditional sense. The rules make a distinction between goods, digital services, and other services. For goods ordered on the internet, the place of delivery determines the VAT rate, and usually, this will be the country of residence of the purchaser. For digital services, the VAT rate is determined by the country where the purchaser normally resides. For nondigital services, even if booked online, such as flights and package holidays, the VAT is determined by the country where the tangible service is provided. The recommendations also cover purchases ordered over the telephone or by mail order catalog that are treated in the same way as internet purchases because of the similarities between different forms of *remote* purchase.

11.74 In the EU, the scope of the HICP follows the *domestic concept*, as it covers all household final monetary consumption expenditure (as defined on the EU Regulations on HICP and described in Chapter 2) in the economic territory, regardless of the nationality or normal residence of the consumer.

11.75 According to Eurostat, applying the VAT rules to CPI compilation concerning internet purchases results in the following:

- The expenditure and the prices for goods purchased through the internet are recorded in the HICP of the country where the product is delivered.
- The expenditure and the prices for tangible services purchased through the internet are recorded in the HICP of the country where the service is provided.
- The expenditure and the prices for digital services (for example, communication, broadcasting, or electronic services) are recorded in the HICP of the country where the consumer usually resides.
- The price to be recorded should be the full price, including any compulsory additional costs, provided that these costs can be attributed solely to the purchase of the product concerned.

Price Collection

11.76 With regard to price collection and the maintenance of a fixed basket, collecting prices online poses similar, but more difficult to resolve, challenges to collecting prices in physical outlets, such as nonavailability of products and the issues of substitution and quality adjustment, as well as the treatment of delivery charges.[7] The standard principles of price collection apply. Under traditional price collection, if a product is sold out or is no longer available, the price collector can speak to the outlet staff and choose a replacement item and make any necessary quality adjustments. With internet price collection, it is unlikely that there will be an opportunity for interaction with the retailer, and the availability of an item can often only be determined by attempting a purchase. Moreover, if an item is unavailable it can be difficult to determine online whether it is permanently or temporarily unavailable and, in the former case, the detailed product information needed to select a replacement and make any necessary quality adjustment is generally not accessible given the limited information that is contained on a retailer's website. NSOs should investigate potential websites for online price collection to ensure that there are a sufficient number of products and enough product detail to price consistently and to constant quality. For example, for products like clothing, websites should contain enough characteristics, such as brand, material, style, and cut, to facilitate the selection of a suitable replacement for an article of clothing that is discontinued and, where necessary, to perform a quality adjustment.

11.77 Platform websites pose additional challenges for the collection of prices. Many websites sell products directly to consumers, while others serve more as a virtual marketplace selling products from a variety of different web-based and online retailers. If the website sells products directly to consumers, it should be treated as an outlet for purposes of price collection. If the website is more of a virtual marketplace, the individual retailers can be regarded as separate outlets. This would be similar to how physical shopping malls are treated in the CPI. A shopping mall is not treated as a single outlet; rather the individual retailers within a shopping mall are treated as separate outlets. A platform website serving as a virtual marketplace can be treated in the same way.

Treatment of Additional Costs for Internet Purchases

11.78 Often, when purchasing goods and services on the internet, there are additional costs associated with buying

[6] http://ec.europa.eu/eurostat/documents/272892/7048317/HICP-recommendation-on-internet+purchases-December-2016/.

[7] As mentioned in Chapter 5, delivery charges should be included in the cost of the online purchase where these are not separately invoiced and where they are inseparable from the purchase.

that product. These costs can include, for example, delivery charges or credit card fees. In some cases, these are separately invoiced and in other cases, they are not. It can also be noted that some additional costs only become apparent at the point of purchase. It can be argued that if the cost is inescapable to the consumer, that is, if ownership of the product cannot be transferred unless these costs are incurred by the household, then it should be included in the CPI as part of the transaction. The delivery charges may vary according to the geographical location of the purchaser and this variation will need to be included in the national CPI and in a regional or city CPI. The approach can also be applied when the delivery is provided by another business, if this is part of the transaction. In this case, the cost of transport would be priced separately and included under transportation services for purposes of index compilation.

11.79 *Delivery charges*. COICOP 2018 classifies delivery charges separately from the purchase price. This will allow the CPI to more accurately reflect the appropriate price change. In COICOP 1999, delivery charges are included in the price paid for the product. If the delivery fee changed, this would be reflected as a price change for the item. For example, if the price of a table was $500 in period t1 and remained unchanged in period t2 at $500, and the delivery fees increased from $50 to $70, under COICOP 1999, the final price would show a change from $550 to $570 because the CPI compiler includes the delivery fee in the price of the item. Consequently, even though the price of the item has not changed, the index is showing a movement that relates not to the product itself but to a transport service.[8]

11.80 *Credit card fees* should be captured if it is an inescapable cost of buying the item and incurred by most households buying that product. Some websites charge multiple fees for the use of different credit cards. If this is the case, markup rates (percent charged to use a specific credit card) should be obtained where possible to weight the different fees; otherwise, an estimate could be derived by taking an average of the different fees. For example, if an airline charged a fee of 1.3 percent for the use of a credit card and 0.6 percent for the use of a debit card, and it was estimated that the take-up rates were 70 percent and 30 percent, respectively, the compiler would calculate a weighted percentage fee of 1.09 percent. Alternatively, if no take-up rates are available the compiler could average the two card fees together generating 0.95 percent. This rate can then be applied to the price of the airline ticket.

Housing

Introduction

11.81 This section first describes the treatment of owner-occupied housing services costs and then of the costs borne by tenants. The treatment of owner-occupied housing services costs in the CPI depends on the agreed-upon conceptual approach and the practical constraints relating to data availability. The treatment of rented accommodation is more straightforward, and the costs borne by tenants are often used to impute owner-occupied housing services costs.

Owner-Occupied Housing Services

11.82 The treatment of owner-occupied housing services costs in CPIs is arguably one of the most difficult issues faced by CPI compilers. Depending on the proportion of the reference population that are owner-occupiers, the alternative conceptual treatments can have a significant impact on the CPI, affecting both weights and, especially in the short term, measured inflation.

11.83 Ideally, the approach chosen should align with the conceptual basis that best satisfies the main use of the CPI. However, the data requirements may be such that it is not feasible to adopt the preferred treatment. Also, the CPI may be multipurpose and it may be difficult to ascertain the main use of the index. The dual use of CPIs as both macroeconomic indicators and for indexation purposes (as described in Chapter 2) can lead to clear tensions in designing an appropriate treatment for owner-occupied housing services costs that suits all needs. In these circumstances, it may be necessary to adopt a treatment that is not entirely consistent with the approach adopted for other items in the CPI. National house market structures and practical measurement issues are also important considerations in determining which approach to apply in practice.

11.84 The inclusion of owner-occupied housing services costs will improve the representativeness and relevance of a CPI. When used in an international context, for example, to measure economic convergence, the inclusion of owner-occupied housing services costs should, in principle, enhance the comparability of CPIs across countries. However, for this purpose two major concerns have been expressed. First, given the relatively high weight for owner-occupied housing in most countries, including owner-occupied housing services costs could impact the inflation rate and its volatility. Second, it could add to cross-country divergence in inflation rates and may make it more difficult for a country to meet inflation convergence criteria set for a block of countries, because of differences between the relative importance of each country's owner-occupied housing market and divergences in the respective movement in house prices across countries.

11.85 Depending on the methodological approach used, data on owner-occupied housing services costs may not be as timely as other data for the CPI, and the compilation of representative owner-occupied housing services costs indices might only be feasible on a quarterly basis. Both aspects will have an impact on the underlying statistical quality and usability of the CPI.

11.86 Once a decision has been made to include owner-occupied housing services costs in the CPI, all the previous considerations need to be taken into account by an NSO in deciding which approach to adopt. The criteria for choosing which approach will include: alignment with user needs and the main purpose of the CPI; consistency with the rest of the CPI; alignment with international practices (although in the case of housing services costs there is no single

[8]Although this classification is different from the SNA, which defines the "purchaser's price" to include any transport charges paid separately by the purchaser to take delivery at the required time and place (*2008 SNA*, paragraph 6.64) when this is not feasible many countries' national accounts deviate from this approach and include delivery charges under transport services rather than allocating the cost to the price of the product.

agreed methodology); public acceptance; and practicality of implementation.

The Different Conceptual Approaches

The Use Approach: Valuing the Flow of Services

11.87 The general objective of the use approach is to measure the change over time in the value of the flow of shelter services consumed by owner-occupiers. Detailed approaches fall under one of two headings: user cost and rental equivalence.

11.88 The *user cost approach* attempts to measure the changes in the cost to owner-occupiers of using the dwelling. In the weight reference period, these costs comprise two elements: recurring actual costs, such as those for repairs and maintenance, and property taxes; and the opportunity cost of investing in the dwelling rather than use the amount invested for some other purpose. At its simplest, and where houses are purchased outright, this opportunity cost is represented by the rate of return available on alternative assets. More usually, house purchase will be at least partially financed through mortgage borrowing. In this case, the opportunity cost can be viewed as an average of interest rates on mortgages and the alternative assets, weighted by the proportion of the purchase price borrowed and paid outright, respectively.

11.89 Estimation of the base period weights for recurring actual costs, such as expenditure on repairs and maintenance, is generally obtainable from the HBS. However, care must be taken to distinguish between routine repairs and maintenance that maintain a dwelling in its original condition, and alterations and additions, that represent significant functional improvements in the dwelling (for example, converting an attic into a room or building an extension). Alterations and additions are outside the user cost approach. In practice, distinguishing between major repairs and maintenance, on the one hand, and alterations and additions, on the other hand, may prove difficult when relying on information gathered from an HBS. In contrast, the construction of price measures for these items generally presents few difficulties.

11.90 Estimation of the base period weight for opportunity costs is more complex and will require modeling. One simplistic approach is to assume that all owner-occupiers purchased their dwellings outright at the beginning of the period and sold them at the end. During the period their opportunity costs comprise the amount of interest forgone (that is, the amount of interest they might have earned by investing this amount elsewhere), transaction costs, and depreciation. Offsetting these costs would be any capital gains earned on the sale of the dwellings. Construction of the required measures of price change is also quite complex and, particularly for the depreciation element, a good deal of imputation is required, including allowing for dwelling purchases partly financed by mortgage borrowing. A typical formula for user cost (UC) is

$$\mathrm{UC} = rM + iE + D + \mathrm{RC} - K \qquad (11.1)$$

where M and E represent mortgage debt and equity in the home, and r and i represent mortgage interest rates and the rate of riskless return available on alternative assets, respectively. D is depreciation, RC other recurring costs, and K capital gains.[9] From an aggregate perspective, this implies computing the proportion of homeowners who have a mortgage and the average size of mortgage and apply to this the mortgage rate. The other rate in the user cost formula must be a riskless nominal interest rate that is applicable to capital.

11.91 In general, NSOs do not use the full user cost approach. This partly reflects the conceptual and methodological complexity of the measure, which may also make it difficult to obtain widespread public understanding and support for the approach. For this reason, the methodology is not discussed in detail in this Manual. It is, however, worth noting that both the weights and the ongoing measures of price change are significantly influenced by the relative rate of change in house prices. Since the user cost formula is typically dominated by capital gains and interest rates, the user cost weight can be negative (implying a negative price for user cost) if house price inflation exceeds nominal interest rates.

11.92 In practice, it is possible to avoid some of these difficulties by adopting a variant or a narrower definition of user cost. For example, some countries have adopted a variant of the user cost approach focusing on gross mortgage interest payments and depreciation, in part, because these items are readily recognizable as key costs by homeowners. The mortgage interest may be viewed as the cost of retaining housing shelter today, while the depreciation element represents current expenditure that would be required to offset the deterioration and obsolescence in dwellings that would otherwise occur over time. Methodologies for calculating actual average mortgage interest payments for index households are described in the section on the payments approach to owner-occupied housing services costs (paragraphs 11.128–11.141).

11.93 The use of mortgage interest payments in the user cost approach and the payments approach, as described in paragraphs 11.128–11.141, may pose conceptual and practical difficulties for some users depending on the stated purpose of the CPI. For almost all items in the CPI basket, an increase in price represents an increase in living costs for the target household population in aggregate. However, this is not necessarily the case for mortgage interest payments. An increase in interest rates generally benefits savers, which would include a considerable share of the target population. An increase in savings interest rates will leave this share of the target population commensurately better off. For pensioners in particular, who tend to be savers rather than borrowers, indexation of pension entitlements to a CPI that is based in part on mortgage interest charges may perplex the general public.[10] Explaining to those financially affected when interest rates fall why mortgage interest payments are in the scope of the CPI whereas savings interest is out of scope may prove difficult. A more fundamental concern,

[9] An alternative to this approach would be to use ex ante or forecasted costs for a suitable period. Randal Verbrugge. 2008. "The Puzzling Divergence of Rents and User Costs, 1980–2004." Review of Income and Wealth, Series 54, Number 4, Bureau of Labor Statistics, Washington, DC, discusses various methodologies.

[10] In general, the primary purpose of indexation of payments is to hold payment recipient's purchasing power constant rather than eliminate the effects of financial shocks on payments.

from a macroeconomic perspective, is that including mortgage interest rates in a CPI diminishes its relevance and usefulness for monetary policy purposes, as interest rates are one of the main macroeconomic levers for controlling inflation.

11.94 A way of overcoming the issue of indexation for savers and borrowers under a user cost approach is to compile population subgroup indices alongside the official CPI. The population subgroups can be derived through income, wealth, or stages of the life cycle, and can be weighted using HBS data. A separate index for that portion of the population receiving indexed pension entitlements can be created excluding mortgage interest charges thereby removing the payments that are not relevant for that subgroup of the population. Such disaggregated estimates can assist in the formulation of policy. More generally, it is open to countries to compile supplementary CPIs aimed at measuring the inflation experience of different segments of the population. Many would argue that, if a certain subgroup of the population is to be compensated for increases in the living costs, then, in principle, expenditure weights should be constructed for this subgroup accepting that this reenforces the continuation of the current expenditure patterns of the subgroup.[11]

11.95 Depreciation is a gradual process and so is best represented by the amount that needs to be estimated each year as opposed to actual expenditure (that will typically be large but infrequent). The base period weight for depreciation may be estimated from the current market value of the owner-occupied housing stock excluding land values, multiplied by an average rate of depreciation. The latter may be derived from national accounts estimates of housing capital consumption. Imputed this way, the appropriate price indicator should ideally be an index of house prices, excluding land, rather than an index of the costs of renovation work. Discussions on how this could be achieved are included in paragraphs 11.128–11.141.

11.96 The *rental equivalence approach* attempts to measure the change in the price of the housing services consumed by owner-occupiers by estimating the market value of those services. In other words, it is based on estimating how much owner-occupiers would have to pay to rent their dwelling. Under this approach, it would be inappropriate to also include those input costs normally borne by landlords such as dwelling insurance, major repair and maintenance, and property taxes, as this would involve an element of double counting. The rental equivalence approach is recommended in the *2008 SNA* (*2008 SNA* paragraphs 6.117 and 15.141) for measuring housing services to be included in the household final consumption expenditure estimates and is also used in constructing international comparisons of living standards. The price indicator for imputed rents can be sourced from either a readily available price series for rents weighted to reflect the current composition of the stock of owner-occupied housing, that can then be applied to the rental equivalents in the weight and price reference periods, or from acquiring on a regular basis from an expert such as a real estate agent or broker, the current equivalent rents for a sample of houses with different characteristics that are representative of the owner-occupied housing stock.[12]

11.97 The rental equivalence approach is considered as a viable option by many countries, but there is a requirement to have a transparent rental market and reliable information on rents by type of accommodation, location, and other rent-determining factors. A number of countries use this approach for conceptual and practical reasons. For many developing economies, newly constructed dwellings (sometimes self-builds) on family-owned land, or older dwellings that have been significantly upgraded, make up a significant proportion of the housing stock. Differences in quality between newly constructed dwellings can be significant and housing mobility may be low resulting in limited markets for the sale of dwellings. This can be further complicated by a lack of formal transfers of ownership or of transparent property rights. The lack of this information, normally readily available in more developed economies, makes the rental equivalence approach a practical option for incorporating owner-occupied housing services costs in a CPI for developing economies. Many developed economies also use this approach in their CPIs, for instance, if their purpose is to compile a cost of living index (COLI), or their aim is to more closely align with the national accounts.

11.98 Deriving the weight for rental equivalence requires estimating how much owner-occupiers would have paid in the weighting base period to rent their dwellings. This is not something that owner-occupiers can normally be expected to estimate and reliably reported in an HBS. However, in principle, it can be estimated by matching the dwellings of owner-occupiers with comparable dwellings that are being rented and applying those rents to the owner-occupied dwellings. In practice, this raises a number of problems, particularly in countries where the overall size of the private rental market is small or where rented housing is of a different type from owner-occupied housing with regard to general quality, age, size, and location. Direct imputation from actual rents may also be inappropriate if the rental market is subject to price control.[13]

11.99 In those countries where the reference population for the CPI corresponds to all resident households, greater collaboration with the national accounts helps address estimation problems such as sample sizes, lower-level weights, and specific market variations. The corresponding price series for the rents of owner-occupiers can be derived from an actual rent index, except where such rents are subject to price control. Depending on both the relative significance of owner-occupiers to renters and the composition of the

[11] The HBS provides data about household characteristics such as income and number of members. This is useful for ensuring that the expenditure corresponds to those of the CPI reference population and can also be used for producing CPIs for different population subgroups. Depending on its design, the HBS may provide information on the types of outlet where purchases are made and on the varieties purchased. This information can be used to construct elementary aggregates at a finer level of detail and to improve the sample design for outlets and items for price collection to reflect the differences by population in the varieties of goods and services purchased and the types of outlets used.

[12] The use of a private sector data source should be done with care as the methodology employed by the private entity could be potentially predisposed to bias and less appropriate than one produced by an independent authority.

[13] In addition, it is also argued that owner-occupiers may be considered to derive significant additional utility from features such as security of tenure and the ability to modify the dwelling, implying a need to make additional adjustments to the initial imputations.

housing stock with regard to dwelling characteristics, any existing rent surveys may need to be modified to meet the requirements of an owners' equivalent rent series. If the total value of owners' equivalent rent is significantly larger than actual rents, the absolute size of the existing price sample may be insufficient. If the characteristics of owner-occupied dwellings differ significantly from the overall rental market, the existing rent survey may also require stratifying more finely (for example, by type and size of dwelling, and by location) if the sample size is large enough to do so. The price measures for the different strata can then be given different weights when calculating the actual rents and the owners' equivalent rent series.

11.100 While it may be acceptable to include subsidized and controlled prices in the actual rent series, these should not be used in calculating the owners' equivalent rent series. Given the increased significance of rent prices in the overall index, it may also be necessary to pay greater attention to the measurement of price change for individual properties when tenancies change. As a change in tenancy often presents landlords with an opportunity to refurbish properties and to increase rents regardless of any refurbishment, the practice of regarding the total price change as quality change should be avoided. For these reasons, a stock-based index is most appropriate under the user cost approach. A flow-based rental index compiled from new rental agreements may behave quite differently from a stock-based rental index. A stock-based rental index is generally more stable and, as such, is more representative of the owner-occupied sector which, by definition, enjoys security of tenure. Furthermore, the rent series may need to be quality-adjusted to take account of ongoing depreciation to housing structures, depending on the treatment in the CPI of owner-occupiers' repair and maintenance costs.

11.101 Whereas the rental equivalence approach has the advantage of relative simplicity, requiring only more than a suitable rental price index and appropriate weights, it is a method based on notional or imputed prices rather than actual transaction prices. This could be viewed both as a significant conceptual departure from how other items are treated in a CPI and as an overreliance on imputed rather than actual prices.

11.102 Double counting can also be an issue when the rental equivalence approach is used. If expenditure on repairs, maintenance, local property taxes, water charges, and so on are included in rents, these costs should not be included elsewhere in the index. It is also important that HBSs determine if the renter household receives any additional services, such as electricity or use of facilities outside the housing unit, such as off-street parking. It is also important to learn if the household must pay any additional costs, such as taxes, that the owner of the dwelling does not pay. The value of any supplementary items provided and the cost of any items borne by the tenant should be allocated to their proper CPI category. For example, the dwelling may have water supplied at cost by the landlord: in this case, CPIs may either leave landlord-supplied water in the rent or move an estimated value for it from the rent index to an index for water, but this must be done consistently in the weights and the rent survey. Leaving supplementary items in the rent avoids the need to adjust the weight but leaves the potential problem that if the landlord ceases to provide them, the CPI compiler will need to adjust the values of the rents collected in the rent survey.

The Payments Approach

11.103 The scope for a payment index is defined by reference to actual expenditure made by households to gain access to consumer goods and services. Thus, the payments approach covers the expenditure actually incurred in occupying a dwelling. The set of expenditure specific to owner-occupiers in the weight reference period includes:[14]

- Down payments or deposits on newly purchased dwellings
- Legal and real estate agency fees payable on property transfers
- Repayments of mortgage principal
- Mortgage interest payments
- Alterations and additions to the dwelling
- Insurance of the dwelling
- Repair and maintenance of the dwelling
- Property rates and taxes

11.104 While it is conceivable to include all these items in the index, it is generally agreed that at least some represent capital transactions that ought to be excluded from a CPI. For example, while down payments and repayments of the mortgage principal result in a running down of household cash reserves, they also result in the creation of a real asset (at least part of a dwelling) or in the reduction of a liability (the amount of mortgage debt outstanding). Similarly, any cash expenditure on alterations and additions result in a running down of cash reserves offset by increases in dwelling values. In other words, those transactions that result in no net change to household balance sheets should be excluded.

11.105 The remaining items can be regarded as current expenditure that does not result in any offsetting adjustments to household balance sheets. It is therefore considered appropriate that these items be included in a payments-based CPI. By defining a payments index in this way, the aggregate payments equal a household's source of funds. A household's total source of funds comprises income after tax (for example, wages, transfers, property income, and insurance claims) and net savings (as a balancing item). It is for this reason that a payments-based CPI is commonly considered to be the best construct for assessing changes in net money income over time.

11.106 It is sometimes argued that the payments approach is more consistent with the traditional approach to CPI compilation, this is a carryover from a time when the CPI was mostly used as a compensation tool. It is more easily understood by the public and measures costs directly, thereby avoiding imputation.

11.107 There are also disadvantages to using the payments approach. The items of direct expenditure by purchasers of property include mortgage interest payments,[15]

[14]This is not the recommended approach used in the national accounts, and some of the items listed are not included in household final consumption expenditure.

[15]In the national accounts, the payment of interest is not included in household final consumption expenditure (except the part that is considered FISIM), but is counted as an interest payment in the household primary income account.

repayment of capital, and large repairs (associated with depreciation from wear and tear as properties get older). All of these expenditure items are generally considered out of the scope of a CPI because they represent capital formation. A CPI should only relate to final consumption expenditure and should exclude financial transactions and investment. The acquisition of a house will normally represent a substantial capital asset over a period of time, a point that emerges when comparing the position of owner-occupiers with tenants who rent. It can therefore be argued that the capital element of mortgage repayments should be regarded as an investment or saving rather than final consumption expenditure and should therefore be excluded from the index.

11.108 When using the payments approach, the question arises over whether the weight and price indicator should be net of any tax allowances for mortgage interest payments. It is recommended that, in accordance with the principle that a CPI should be based on the amounts actually paid, the weight and price indicator should both be based on payments after tax relief.

11.109 The adoption of the payments approach is that it requires a large volume of data that may not be available to the compiler. Mortgage interest payments will be affected by changes in both interest rates and house prices in different ways. Changes in interest rates will affect all of those buying a house apart from those on fixed-interest loans, while changes in house prices will affect only those buying a house in the current period. Thus, a price indicator consisting of the current interest applied to a standard-sized mortgage to a standard-sized house would not be appropriate. An appropriate indicator involves two components: the rate of interest and the average amount of mortgage debt outstanding. To calculate the average outstanding debt at any point in time can be problematic as it consists of a large number of individual debts, some from mortgages taken out recently and others from mortgages taken out some time ago at historic prices and with some of the debt paid back. It is unlikely that all countries will have the necessary data to apply this method.

11.110 It can be argued that the main disadvantage of the payments approach is that it includes a major (explicit) cost of owning a home, namely mortgage interest, but it does not include a major offsetting (implicit or imputed) benefit, namely possible price appreciation or capital gains on the home. The neglect of this benefit is particularly troublesome when there is moderate or high inflation in the economy: the observed mortgage interest cost can increase compared with other costs and give a very misleading picture of the homeowner's true long-term costs of living in the home (because the offsetting benefit is neglected). But the counterargument is that the capital gains of owning a house that appreciates in value are of limited relevance when people must bear such costs from current income, and the value of the underlying asset can only be materialized if the home is sold and the proceeds are not used to purchase another property for own occupation. This is, perhaps, a case where the measurement approach that is adopted will vary depending on the use and purpose of the CPI.

11.111 Estimation of gross expenditure on the items listed in paragraph 11.104 in the weight reference period is readily achievable using HBS data, as the items are generally reportable by households. The construction of price indices for real estate agency fees and insurance is discussed in paragraphs 11.378–11.384 and 11.385–11.403, respectively. Indices for repair and maintenance, and property rates and taxes, are not considered particularly problematic and so are not discussed in this chapter. The remainder of this section addresses the construction of price measures for mortgage interest charges.

11.112 The construction of price indices for mortgage interest charges is complex. The degree of complexity will vary from country to country depending on the operation of domestic financial markets and the existence of any income tax provisions applying to mortgage interest payments. What follows therefore is a description of an overall objective for producing the required index in the most straightforward cases. The methodology will need to be modified to account for additional complexities that may be encountered in some countries.

11.113 The general approach to construct price indices for mortgage interest charges may be summarized, briefly, as follows. Under a fixed-basket approach, the objective of the index is to measure the change over time in the interest that would be payable on a set of mortgages equivalent to those existing in the weight reference period. This base stock of mortgages will vary widely in age, from those taken up in the weight reference period to those taken up many years previously. In compiling a fixed-base index, the distribution of mortgages by age must be held constant.

11.114 The amount of interest payable on a mortgage is determined by applying some rate of interest, expressed as a percentage, to the monetary value of debt. Therefore, changes in mortgage interest charges over time can, in principle, be measured by periodically collecting information on a representative selection of mortgage interest rates, using these to derive an average interest rate, and then applying this to an appropriate debt figure. At least for standard variable rate mortgages, interest due on the revalued stock of base period mortgages may be derived simply with reference to current mortgage interest rates.

11.115 The main challenge in constructing a price index for mortgage interest charges is determining the appropriate debt figure in each of the comparison periods. Since the real value of any monetary amount of debt varies over time according to changes in the purchasing power of money, it is not appropriate to use the actual base period monetary value of debt in calculations for subsequent periods. Rather, it is necessary first to update that monetary value in each comparison period so that it remains constant in real terms (that is, so that the quantities underpinning the base period amount are held constant).

11.116 To update the monetary value of debt, it is necessary to form at least a theoretical view of the quantities underpinning the amount of debt in the base period. The amount of mortgage debt outstanding for a single household in the base period depends on the original house purchase price and loan-to-value ratio, and on the rate of repayment of principal since the house was purchased. An equivalent value of debt can be calculated in subsequent comparison periods by holding constant the age of the debt, the original value of the debt (as some fixed proportion of the total value of the dwelling when the mortgage was initially entered into), and the rate of repayment of the principal (as some proportion of the original debt), and applying these factors to house prices for periods corresponding to the age of the debt.

11.117 To illustrate how the update of the monetary value of debt can be done in practice, suppose a household purchased a dwelling five years earlier than base period for \$100,000 and financed 50 percent by mortgage. If, between the time of purchase and the base period, the household repaid 20 percent of this debt, then the outstanding debt on which base period interest charges were calculated would have been \$40,000. Considering a subsequent comparison period and supposing that it is known that house prices doubled between the period when the household was originally purchased and the period five years prior to the comparison period, then the equivalent amount of outstanding debt in the comparison period would be calculated by first taking 50 percent of the revalued house price (of \$200,000) to give \$100,000, and then reducing this by the principal repayment rate (of 20 percent) to give \$80,000.

11.118 Under the assumptions described in paragraph 11.117, the comparison period value of outstanding debt may be estimated directly from the base period value of outstanding debt based on house price movements between five years prior to the base period and five years prior to the comparison period. In other words, while preservation of original debt/equity ratios and rates of repayment of principal help in understanding the approach, estimates of these variables are not strictly required to calculate the required comparison period debt. All that is required is the value of the outstanding debt in the base period, the age of that debt and a suitable measure of changes in dwelling prices.

11.119 Supposing that all mortgages are of the variable rate type, and that average nominal interest rates rose from 5 percent in the base period to 7.5 percent in the comparison period, interest payments in the two periods can be calculated as \$2,000 and \$6,000, respectively, and so the mortgage interest payments index for the comparison period is 300.0. An identical result may be found directly from index number series for debt and nominal interest rates. The mortgage interest charges index equals the debt index multiplied by the nominal interest rate index divided by 100. In this example, the debt index equals 200.0 and the nominal interest rate index equals 150.0. Therefore, the mortgage interest rate index equals (200.0 × 150.0)/100 or 300.0.[16]

11.120 While the single-household example shown previously is useful in explaining the basic concepts, it is necessary to devise a methodology that can be employed to calculate a mortgage interest charges index for the overall reference population. The main complication when moving from the single-household to the many-household case is the fact that the age of the debt will vary across households. Given the importance of revaluing base period debt to maintain a constant age, this is no trivial matter. While it is conceivable that information on the age of mortgage debt could be collected in HBSs, the additional respondent burden and the generally small number of households reporting mortgages often serve to make estimates from this source unreliable. Another option is to approach a sample of providers of mortgages (for example, banks or building societies) for an age profile of their current mortgage portfolio. This type of data is normally available from financial institutions and is generally reliable.

Table 11.3 Calculation of a Mortgage Interest Charges Series

Year	Quarter	Debt Index	Nominal Interest Rates Index	Mortgage Interest Charges Index
		(a)	(b)	(c) = (a) × (b)/100
Y0	Q1	100.0	100.0	100.0
	Q2	100.7	98.5	99.2
	Q3	101.4	100.8	102.2
	Q4	101.9	101.5	103.4

11.121 To calculate mortgage interest charges, a nominal mortgage interest rate index series is applied to the aggregate level of outstanding debt. A nominal mortgage interest rate index series is obtained by calculating average quarterly interest rates on variable rate mortgages from a sample of lending institutions (starting in period Y0:Q1) and presenting them in index number form. The nominal interest rate series can then be combined with the debt series to calculate the final mortgage interest rate charges series, as illustrated in Table 11.3.

11.122 The construction of equivalent indices for fixed-interest mortgages is more complicated since an interest charges index needs to be calculated separately for each age cohort of debt to reflect the fact that interest payable today, for example, on a loan four years old, depends on the interest rate prevailing four years ago. This requires the compilation of a nominal fixed-interest rate index extending back as far as the dwelling price series. To the extent that the interest rates charged on fixed-interest loans also depend on the duration of the loan, calculation of the nominal fixed-interest rate series is also more complex. The additional complexity of these indices may make the construction of a mortgage interest charges index impractical for countries where fixed-interest rate mortgages predominate.

11.123 The construction of the index for mortgage interest payments is based on the assumption that the purpose of the mortgage is to finance the purchase of the dwelling (hence revaluation of debt by changes in dwelling prices). However, it is increasingly common, particularly in developed economies, for households to draw down on the equity they have in their home. That is, households may take new or additional mortgages, or withdraw part of the principal already paid to finance other activities, for example, to purchase a large consumer durable such as a car or a boat, to go on holiday, or to purchase stocks and bonds. If these alternative uses of the funds made available by way of mortgages are significant, it may be appropriate to regard at least some proportion of mortgage interest charges as the cost of a general financial service rather than a housing cost. For that proportion of the debt deemed to be used for other purposes, it would be more appropriate to use a general index of price inflation for debt revaluation purposes.

11.124 Despite being a relatively simple method of representing owner-occupied housing services costs, the payments approach is open to conceptual challenge. As

[16]This simple example illustrates the very important point that percentages (for example, interest rates or taxes) are not prices and cannot be used as if they were. Percentages must be applied to some monetary value to determine a monetary price.

Figure 11.1 The Acquisitions Approach for Owner-Occupied Housing

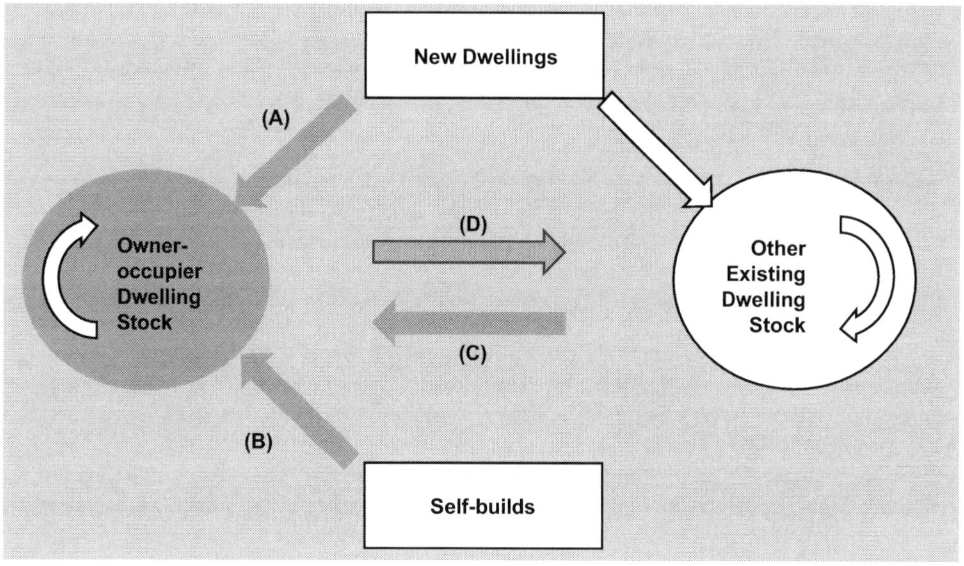

discussed in the user cost approach, including mortgage interest payments could be problematic for monetary policy purposes. However, another issue is that if both house prices and mortgage interest rates remain unchanged for a period, the mortgage interest charges index does not usually remain unchanged for the same period. This is because the mortgage debt index will continue to change, as changing house prices prior to the stable period continue to work their way through the various debt age cohorts. Conceptually, this may prove unsatisfactory to many users, who generally expect CPIs to reflect current interest rate movements only.

The Acquisitions Approach

11.125 The scope for an acquisition index is defined as all consumer goods and services acquired by households for own consumption. Those countries that compile their CPIs on an acquisitions basis have generally concluded that the principal purpose of their CPI is to provide a measure of price inflation for the whole household sector. Based on the view that price inflation is a phenomenon peculiar to the operation of markets, the domain is also normally restricted to those consumer goods and services acquired in monetary transactions. Consumer goods and services provided at no cost to households by governments and nonprofit institutions serving households (NPISHs) are excluded (as discussed in Chapter 2).

11.126 The expenditure of owner-occupiers of housing that could be included in an acquisitions index are the following:[17]

- Net purchases of dwellings (that is, purchases less sales by the reference population)
- Direct construction of new dwellings
- Alterations and additions to existing dwellings
- Legal and real estate agency fees payable on property transfers
- Repair and maintenance of dwellings
- Insurance of dwellings
- Property rates and taxes

11.127 The construction of price indices for real estate agency fees and insurance is discussed in paragraphs 11.378–11.384 and 11.385–11.403, respectively. Indices for repair and maintenance, and property rates and taxes are not considered particularly problematic and are not discussed in this chapter. Paragraphs 11.141–11.145 address the issues involved in constructing measures for dwelling purchase, construction, and alterations and additions. The advantages of the acquisitions approach compared to the user cost and payments approaches are discussed in paragraphs 11.88 and 11.103

11.128 As CPIs are constructed to measure price change for a group of households in aggregate (that is, the reference or target population), like for other second-hand goods a net expenditure should be used for those transactions that take place between those households. In the case of an index covering all private households, the weight should only reflect net additions to the household sector owner-occupied housing stock. In practice, net additions will mainly comprise those dwellings purchased from businesses (that is, newly constructed dwellings, company houses, or rental dwellings) and those purchased from or transferred from the government sector plus any purchases, for owner-occupation, of rental dwellings from reference population households. If the CPI is constructed for some subgroup of the population (for example, wage and salary earners), the weight should also include purchases from other household types.

11.129 The acquisition approach can be represented in Figure 11.1. The circle on the left represents the existing owner-occupied dwelling stock. The circle on the right represents all other existing dwelling stock (that is, rented

[17]This is not the recommended approach used in national accounts, and some of these items are not included in household final consumption expenditure.

dwellings and vacant dwellings). The rectangle on top represents newly constructed dwellings. The rectangle on the bottom represents self-builds. The flows of properties from one sector to another are represented by arrows. There are also internal flows within the existing owner-occupied dwelling stock (as one owner-occupier buys an existing dwelling from another) and within the other existing dwelling stock.

11.130 In CPI compilation, a normal procedure is to account expenditure that is used in weighting in "net" terms. For most products, the reference population makes purchases, not sales; however, for some product groups, sales are significant. This happens with the purchase of dwellings, where it would be necessary to net out the sales from the purchases. These same principles apply to all second-hand goods.

11.131 According to the net acquisition approach, sales of dwellings between households have a negative weight and purchases have a positive weight. Any sale or purchase between households has no impact unless an intermediary, such as a real estate agent is involved. Thus, it is the net acquisition cost approach that is followed. Under the net acquisitions approach, only four flows are considered, depicted by A, B, C, and D in Figure 11.1. A is the flow of new dwellings to the owner-occupied sector (that is, the expenditure owner-occupiers make to acquire new dwellings). B is the flow of self-builds to the owner-occupied sector (by definition, self-builds must flow to this sector only). C is the flow of existing dwelling stock to the owner-occupied sector. And D is the counterflow of existing dwellings from the owner-occupied sector to the nonowner-occupied sector. Under the net acquisitions approach, the net expenditure by owner-occupiers on dwelling acquisitions is given by the following formula (note that this refers to the dwelling purchase component only, and other costs, such as major renovations and transfer costs, are not included):

$$\text{Acquisition} = A + B + C - D \qquad (11.2)$$

11.132 In many countries, the flows C and D will be similar and will largely cancel each other out. Thus, the owner-occupied housing net acquisition weight will largely be determined by A and B, the purchase of new dwellings and self-builds. In exceptional circumstances, for example, after a particularly severe downturn in the property cycle, it may be that the rate of owner-occupied acquisition of new and existing dwellings becomes very low. If there is a net flow of existing dwellings from the owner-occupied sector to the nonoccupied sector (that is, if $D > C$), then the owner-occupied housing net acquisition weight may fall to zero (negative weights are not permissible). Conversely, if there is a construction boom, A and B may grow very large. Property boom and bust cycles will therefore have considerable effect on the owner-occupied housing weight under the net acquisitions approach, with implications for the stability of the CPI.

11.133 In the national accounts, acquisition less disposal of housing is recorded as gross fixed capital formation, which would suggest purchases of dwellings should be excluded from household final consumption expenditure. While this is unambiguously the case for housing purchased for rental, the case is less clear-cut when it comes to the treatment of owner-occupied housing in the CPI. Housing represents both an asset and a source of shelter services. Although households recognize the likelihood of making capital gains when they purchase housing and invariably regard their dwelling as an asset, they also commonly cite the primary motivation for the purchase of a dwelling as being to gain access to a service (that is, shelter and security of tenure). From the households' perspective, therefore, the costs borne by owner-occupiers in respect of their principal dwelling represent a mix of investment and consumption expenditure, and the total exclusion of these costs from an acquisitions-based CPI would be counterintuitive and could lead to criticism by the population at large. This is particularly so in those countries where the rental sector is relatively small, with limited opportunities for substitution between owner-occupation and renting. In these circumstances it might be argued that the consumption element dominates.

11.134 The challenge confronting CPI compilers is how to separate these two elements (that is, investment and consumption expenditure) so as to include only the consumption of housing services in the CPI. Although there is no single agreed-upon technique, one approach is to regard the cost of the land as representing the investment element and the cost of the structure as representing the consumption element. The rationale for this is that, while the structure may deteriorate over time and hence be "consumed," the land generally remains at constant quality. As the land (or location element) accounts for most of the variation in observable prices for otherwise identical dwellings sold at the same point in time, the exclusion of land values may also be seen as an attempt to exclude asset price inflation from the CPI. Measures of asset price inflation are, of course, useful in their own right. The conceptual simplicity of this approach appeals to some NSOs as a suitable method for compiling owner-occupied house price indices.

11.135 Derivation of weight reference period expenditure on the net acquisition of dwellings (excluding land), the construction of new dwellings, and alterations and additions to existing dwellings pose some problems. Although HBSs may yield reliable estimates of the amount households spend on alterations and additions and on construction of dwellings, it is unlikely that they will provide reliable estimates of net expenditure on existing dwellings exclusive of the value of the land.

11.136 An alternative approach to derive weights for the expenditure on the net acquisition of dwellings is to combine data from population censuses and housing and building activity surveys. Population censuses normally collect information on housing tenure, from which average annual growth in the number of owner-occupied households represents a good proxy for net additions to the housing stock. Building activity surveys are also conducted in most countries, providing data on the total value of dwellings constructed. These data can be used to estimate the average value of new dwellings, which can then be applied to the estimated volumes derived from the population census. The suitability of this approach would need to be assessed by each country and may be complicated if the CPI relates only to some subset of the total population, for example, by excluding the very rich who will purchase expensive homes.

11.137 A price index is required to measure the change in price over time in existing dwelling structures, newly constructed dwellings, and alterations and additions. As the appropriate price for existing dwelling structures is current replacement cost, an index measuring changes in prices of newly constructed dwellings is also appropriate for this purpose. Given that the prices for both newly constructed dwellings, and alterations and additions are, in principle, determined by costs of building materials, labor costs, and builders' profits, it may also be satisfactory to construct a single price sample for all elements. The requirement for a separate price sample for alterations and additions will depend on the relative significance of this activity and whether the material and labor components differ significantly from those for a complete dwelling (for example, if alterations and additions are predominantly to kitchens and bathrooms). In all cases, it is important that the price indices are adjusted for the mix of these components to eliminate price variations that reflect changes in the characteristics of newly constructed dwellings.

11.138 The type of dwelling constructed in each country will significantly influence the complexity and cost of compiling appropriate price measures. If each newly constructed dwelling is essentially unique (that is, individually designed to meet site or other requirements) it will be necessary to adopt "model pricing." This approach requires the selection of a sample of building firms, the identification of samples of recently constructed dwellings, and the collection of prices for constructing identical dwellings in subsequent periods (exclusive of site preparation costs that will vary from site to site). This is likely to entail significant costs for the respondents. Moreover, care needs to be taken to ensure that the supplied prices truly reflect all prevailing market conditions. That is, prices need to reflect the amount builders could realistically expect to be able to charge in the current market rather than the prices they would like to be able to charge based on conditions prevailing in some prior period.

11.139 It should be noted that in many countries, purchasing a new or existing dwelling can have tax implications. The transaction may be liable for "stamp duty" and "taxes on transfers" or a related registration fee. In this case, the national tax authorities may be able to provide comprehensive information on both the number and the value of new and existing dwelling purchases. If detailed dwelling characteristic information is available, including the exact location, the floor area of the dwelling, and the plot size of the land, it may be possible to decompose each individual dwelling price into implicit structure and land prices, using hedonic methods (described in Chapter 6), to arrive at aggregate owner-occupied expenditure on new and, where relevant, existing dwellings, that exclude land price. If this level of detailed information is not available in the transaction data, it may still prove possible to estimate the aggregate expenditure on dwellings (excluding land) from combining the transaction numbers with standardized building costs (typically building costs per square meter) that may be available from construction representative bodies, chartered surveyors, building insurers, or other third parties.

11.140 Whereas having price indices for new dwellings, exclusive of the land cost, is ideal under the net acquisition approach, in practice this is not always possible. Sufficient information to compile satisfactory dwelling construction price indices is not always available. In this situation, house price indices that include the land component may be a necessary compromise.

Practical Options for Measuring Owner-Occupied Housing under an Acquisitions Approach

11.141 In some countries, a significant proportion of newly constructed dwellings are of the type referred to as "project homes." These are dwellings that builders construct on a regular basis from a suite of standard designs maintained for this purpose. This practice is most feasible in countries where a significant proportion of new dwelling construction takes place in new developments (that is, land recently developed or redeveloped specifically for residential housing). If project home construction is significant in scale, then it is possible to select a sample of these project homes for pricing over time, safe in the knowledge that the prices provided will be actual transaction prices (in this case priced net of any site preparation costs to ensure the fixed-basket approach is adhered to). Even if project homes do not account for most new dwellings constructed, they may still provide a representative measure of overall price change.

11.142 In pricing project homes, it is necessary to monitor the selected sample to ensure that the selected plans remain representative and to detect changes in quality arising from modifications in design and changes to basic inclusions. Whenever a change is made to the plans, the change in overall quality needs to be estimated. For physically measurable characteristics, such as a small increase in the overall size of the dwelling, it may be assumed that the change in quality is proportional to the change in the relevant quantity. Other changes, such as the addition of insulation, the inclusion of a free driveway, and so on, will need to be valued, preferably with regard to the current value to the consumer. These could be estimated by obtaining information on the amounts that consumers would have to pay if the items were provided separately (the option cost method). An alternative is to ask the builder if a cash rebate is available in lieu of the additional features. Where plans are modified to meet changed legal requirements, the consumer has no choice in purchase, and it may be acceptable to classify the full change in price as pure price movement (even though there may be some discernible change in quality).

11.143 In some countries, attached and semidetached dwellings such as apartments, flats, and townhouses, make up a significant share of additions to dwelling stock and the price index needs to be mix-adjusted to adhere to the principle of a fixed basket. As mentioned previously, measuring owner-occupied housing excluding land and to constant quality can be a challenge, and a matched-model approach may not be possible because of the heterogeneous nature of the buildings being constructed. In these instances, the component cost approach or hedonic models may be viable alternatives depending on the type and amount of data available. A component costs approach is most commonly used in producer price indices and entails the aggregation of a basket of representative items used to construct the type of dwelling being measured. The assumption with this measure is that price change is predominately influenced by changes in the price or cost of goods and services used to construct the dwelling. Depending on the state of the owner-occupied

Table 11.4 Relationship between the Choice of Owner-Occupied Housing (OOH) Approach and CPI Purposes

Approaches to OOH	Primary Purpose of CPI	OOH Price Definition	Notes
User Cost	Measures the Change Through Time of the Total Value of All Goods and Services That Are Actually Consumed by Households	Opportunity Cost Associated with the Use of a Dwelling by a Household for Own Occupancy	Approach Consistent with a COLI. Uses Imputed Prices/ Rental Equivalence. Can Be Difficult to Implement in Practice
Rental Equivalence	Measures the Change Through Time of the Total Value of All Goods and Services That Are Actually Consumed by Households	Implicit Cost That Owner-Occupier Households Would Have to Pay to Rent Their Dwelling	Approach More Consistent with a COLI. Approach Is Recommended in *2008 SNA*. Uses Imputed Prices. Requires a Suitable Private Rental Index
Payments	Measures the Change Through Time of the Total Payments for All Goods and Services by Households	Cash Outlays Associated with Owner-Occupied Dwellings	More Appropriate for the Evaluation of Money Income. Consistent with a COLI. No Imputed Prices
(Net) Acquisition	Measures the Change Through Time of the Total Expenditure by Households for Acquiring and Goods and Services for Consumption	Acquisition and Maintenance Cost of a Dwelling, Usually on a Net to the Sector Basis	Approach More Suitable for Measuring Monetary Inflation. Consistent with Treatment of Other CPI Items. No Imputed Prices. Prone to Volatility in the Housing Market

housing market, this may not always be representative of consumer final prices and adjustments in the index compilation method may need to occur, for example, for changes in profit margins. If undertaking a component cost approach, it is important to ensure the selected components continue to reflect current building standards, materials, and estimates for both builder and developer profit margins.

11.144 As mentioned before, there is no single agreed-upon approach that is internationally recommended or applied for the treatment of owner-occupied housing services. Rather, there are four approaches that have gained recognition, each with its own conceptual basis. While the Manual refers to four approaches, in fact, there are three main approaches as rental equivalence approximates the user cost approach and would be considered a variant of this approach. These four approaches are summarized in Table 11.2. The precise approach to adopt in any given country depends very much on the primary purpose of the CPI and on practical issues such as data availability.

11.145 In general terms, the most prevalent approaches for the treatment of owner-occupied housing services are the rental equivalence approach and the net acquisitions approach. The former is relatively straightforward to apply where there is a suitable rental market. The latter, although more complex, is consistent with the treatment of most other goods and services in the CPI and is not directly affected by methods of financing for house purchases.

Rented Accommodation

11.146 Unlike owner-occupiers, renters buy shelter services from others who own the dwellings that the renters occupy. Consequently, there is a market transaction to observe and the cost of rented accommodation is, in principle, relatively easy to observe in the market.

Weights

11.147 Obtaining the weight for renter-occupied housing in the CPI basket is relatively straightforward. HBSs typically collect data from households at their place of residence. The surveys obtain the rents from those residences that are renter-occupied, and the NSOs estimate the annual expenditure on rents using standard methods. The HBS should also inquire whether the household rents other housing in addition to its main residence, perhaps near to a job or in a holiday location.

11.148 It is important that the HBS determines if any additional services are included in the rent. This is to ensure that no double counting takes place and that a consistent approach is taken on where the expenditure is accounted for in the CPI.

11.149 Data should also be collected on the HBS on whether common expenses are charged. Common expenses include payment for common area lighting, cleaning, building porters, maintaining elevators, and other services. These payments are paid monthly along with the rent. In most cases, it is not possible to separate what portion of the payment goes for lighting or cleaning or to pay a building porter. Because these fees are mandatory, many countries regard them as part of the rent index. Data are needed to develop separate weights for actual rent and the common fees.

Prices—Rent Surveys

11.150 The rent to be recorded is the amount that the household pays, including taxes and excluding any subsidies. If the rent is subsidized or taxed, the amount the household pays will not be the same as what the landlord receives. Although information on rents may be collected from any knowledgeable respondent, the ideal respondent is the dwelling's occupants. The goal is to collect an actual rent paid. Collecting rent data from a landlord, or the landlord's representative, can be challenging in some countries because the landlord may not report the actual rent paid by the tenant out of fear the data will be used for taxation purposes. To respect the fixed-basket principle of the CPI, an effort should be made to continue collecting prices from the same dwelling units over time. Despite the perceived difficulties, a longitudinal survey of rental units will often be the best solution to ensure that the proper rents are collected.[18]

[18] With longitudinal studies, the same units are observed at regular intervals over long periods of time.

11.151 Alternatively, it may be possible to collect rents from an existing continuous household survey, such as a labor force survey. In this case, a specific module on rent can be distributed to those tenants who participate in the main survey. The respondent should be knowledgeable about the rent paid. For example, some occupants may not be the ones who actually pay the rent and may be unsuitable as respondents. The important feature of any such survey is that it provides rents at multiple time intervals but, because people may move, it will not necessarily follow the rents of a fixed set of housing units. In these circumstances, the rent data should be stratified by rent-determining characteristics so that the average rent increase for a house with preassigned characteristics, or for a fixed basket of house types, can be determined.

11.152 If rents change rather infrequently, it may be more efficient to use a relatively large sample that is divided into representative subsamples to collect the rents less frequently than every month from each household. The CPI requires monthly data on rent. Given the nature of rental contracts and the reality that rent does not change every month, the panel survey approach satisfies the monthly data needs of the CPI and minimizes respondent burden.

11.153 Where a survey of rental dwellings is undertaken, a sample can be drawn from any frame that contains the residential units of an area. This may be the population census (if it has a shelter component), postal lists, or street directories.

11.154 If the population census can provide information on the average rent or dwelling value by geographic area, sampling of the areas by probability proportional to rent will increase the final sample's representativeness. Where a sampling frame is not readily available, a grid can be placed on a map of the area and a sample of cells in the grid can be selected. The grid method can also be used as a second stage of sampling after selecting larger areas using available information on rents. Several countries, including developing countries, have used satellite images of the selected areas to obtain an accurate view of the housing in the cells or target areas. Ideally, all the dwellings in the selected cells should be enumerated and from this, a random sample should be selected for the price collector to visit to determine if they are tenant-occupied and, if so, to obtain their rents and initiate them into the sample. The initial selection of target areas for enumeration should be small enough to be manageable and relatively homogeneous; and, on the other hand, should be large enough to allow for an initial sample selection that takes into consideration nonresponse and the fact that some dwellings will be owner-occupied. Where an enumeration exercise is not possible, for example, because of the cost, judgmental or purposive sampling may be used but, in this case, it is particularly important that the individual cells on the grid are relatively homogeneous (that is, that there is little variation in the type, size, and quality of the dwellings) to minimize the potential for drawing an unrepresentative sample.

Calculating the Rent Index When Data Collection Is Less Frequent than Monthly

11.155 As previously mentioned, spreading price observations by pricing the rent for a particular dwelling less frequently than monthly (that is, pricing a subsample of rents each month) is a strategy used for increasing the sample without necessarily having to allocate more resources to the collection exercise. Ideally, a panel survey is used to collect rent on a monthly basis. Many countries divide the sample into six panels and collect rent from each household twice each year. Another option may be to divide the sample into 12 representative panels and collect rent prices from each household one time each year.

11.156 Where rent changes are not obtained monthly for the full sample of dwellings, the monthly rent index from months t to $t-1$, $\Delta_{\text{Rent}}^{t-1\to t}$, can be derived from a subsample of rental units for that month. To obtain the full estimates of rent change over longer periods, the values from the different monthly subsamples are chained together in succession.

11.157 To calculate the monthly rent index with a subsample of units, $\Delta_{Rent}^{t-1\to t}$, the same set of rental units is priced at intervals m months apart. The monthly change obtained at time t is the mth root of the sum of the weighted sample rents in period t to the sum for the same dwellings in period $t-m$:

$$\Delta_{Rent}^{t-1:t} = \sqrt[m]{\frac{\sum_i \left[w_i \times r_i^t\right]}{\sum_i \left[w_i \times r_i^{t-m}\right]}} \quad (11.3)$$

where

$\Delta_{Rent}^{t-1:t}$ is the change in rents from period $t-1$ to period t

r_i^t is the rent of sample dwelling i in period t

r_i^{t-m} is the rent of sample dwelling i in period $t-m$ (the last time a rent for that dwelling was collected)

w_i is the optional weight of sample rented dwelling i

11.158 Sample weights may be ignored for simplicity if the sampled rental dwellings represent roughly the same number of rental dwellings in the sampling frame. Equivalently, the weights in the formula 11.3 can be set to "1" in most cases, and this will provide a mechanism to handle nonresponse and sampling anomalies appropriately.

11.159 Geometric, rather than arithmetic, averages can be taken in formula 11.3 to avoid the defects of the Dutot index that it is not invariant to changes in the units of measurement of the dwellings or, in the present context, very expensive dwellings will get a large implicit weight. Alternatively, expensive dwellings can be treated as outliers and be excluded from the calculation.

Accounting for Missing Observations

11.160 When a dwelling fails to respond because of a temporary failure to collect the information (for example, the data collector was not able to contact the respondent), but data relating to the other dwellings were collected that month, the collected dwellings should be given the weight of the missing unit. For example, if there are three assigned dwellings in a cell each with a weight of 1 (because they are equally weighted) and two are collected and one is not, the rent of the missing dwelling can be imputed from the two that are collected as follows:

$$\hat{r}_{\text{missing}}^t = r_{\text{missing}}^{t-m} \times \frac{r_{\text{collected1}}^t + r_{\text{collected2}}^t}{r_{\text{collected1}}^{t-m} + r_{\text{collected2}}^{t-m}} \quad (11.4)$$

11.161 If all observations in an elementary aggregate are missing (for example, because of a data collection problem), they can be omitted entirely from the calculation for that month; however, their rents must be estimated to be used the next period. If a rental dwelling is a nonresponse in period t, its imputed rent for period t is as follows:

$$\hat{r}^{t}_{missing} = r^{t-m}_{missing} \times \left(\Delta^{t-1:t}_{Rent}\right)^{m} \qquad (11.5)$$

This imputed rent is not used until period $t + m$. Notice that it cannot be computed until after period t, when the value for $\Delta^{t-1:t}_{Rent}$ is known.

11.162 If dwellings become unsuitable for inclusion in the CPI (for example, they become uninhabitable because of a fire) they can be dropped from the sample (if unlikely to be repaired) or, if there is reason to believe they will be repaired and returned to use, they can be treated as nonresponse.

11.163 Dwellings that cease to be rental dwellings (for example, they become owner-occupied or are converted to nonhousing use) should be dropped from the sample, but it is good practice to find a replacement dwelling nearby, if feasible. Until the replacement dwelling can be used in the index, the old dwelling should be treated as a nonresponse.

11.164 Geometric imputation is more desirable if a Jevons index is being constructed at the elementary level, as geometric imputation is consistent with the Jevons formula. The use of geometric weighting also avoids the problem previously referred to of large expensive houses dominating the calculation.

Updating the Sample

11.165 The rent sample, like all CPI surveys, needs to be kept up to date. This is especially important to ensure that the sample reflects new construction of rental dwellings. An entirely new sample can be drawn, run in parallel with the old one, after which the old one can be dropped. The new sample should be based on a new sampling frame. Deploying an entirely new sample at one time can be quite expensive. An alternative is to replace part of the sample each year. If the rent sample uses several panels, the usual way to do this is to rotate out one or more panels per year and replace them with equally representative panels. For example, the January/July panel can be replaced one year and the April/October one the next year. The new area cells would be selected and assigned to panels all at one time, but the data collection work would then be limited to one panel at a time. Rents for the old and new panels need to be collected at the same time so that the new panel is spliced in using the overlap method: the CPI uses the old panel for the last time while collecting the initial rents for the new panel.

11.166 The index is a chaining of the rent change values:

$$I^{t}_{\text{Rent}} = I^{t-1}_{\text{Rent}} \times \Delta^{t-1 \to t}_{\text{Rent}} \qquad (11.6)$$

Depreciation, Major Home Improvements, and Quality Change

11.167 Sample rental dwellings can change between visits from CPI data collectors. Sample dwellings that undergo dramatic changes, either improvements or deteriorations, are best dropped from the sample, at least temporarily. More subtle changes affect all dwellings: they get older and depreciate. Regular maintenance (for example, replacing the roof) offsets this phenomenon to some extent at least. Some countries make an explicit quality adjustment to observed rents to take account of the fact that a rental dwelling that is older has depreciated and hence is generally not as desirable as it once was. However, an older property does not necessarily become less desirable especially when it is properly maintained (for example, a "heritage property"). In the case where the money is spent on a property for the repairs needed for the property to avoid physical deterioration[19] as it gets older, care should be taken not to double count these ongoing and long-term maintenance costs associated with physical deterioration as they will often be reflected in the overall level of rents charged. Only those costs of repairs and maintenance that the tenant is responsible for paying should be included in the CPI and these can be obtained through the regular CPI survey of prices as with any other household expenditure. A study of rental agreements between landlord and tenant should provide the information needed to identify whether the dwelling is depreciating, and which maintenance costs should be covered by the price survey.

11.168 Empirical estimates of the net physical deterioration of dwellings generally, including those of owner-occupiers, mostly indicate that it can be small, at least in the short term, so that where physical deterioration is not measured either directly or indirectly, ignoring it should not be too problematic for users of a CPI who are interested in inflation trends in the short term. The compiler should nevertheless be aware of this phenomenon.

11.169 As mentioned earlier, for owner-occupied dwellings there is no internationally accepted method of treatment of the quality change associated with physical deterioration or the cost of major repairs.

Second-Hand Goods

Introduction

11.170 The 2003 International Labor Organization Resolution on CPIs states that the expenditure weights for second-hand goods should be based either on the net expenditure of the reference population on such goods or on the gross expenditure, depending on the purpose of the index. A CPI is generally understood to be a price index that measures the changes in the prices of consumption goods and services acquired and should use weights consistent with this concept. Chapter 2 reiterates that second-hand goods are in the scope of a CPI and introduce the "net expenditure" concept (that is, total purchases less sales) for weights. The latter is in line with the concept of household final consumption expenditure as defined in the *2008 SNA*.

11.171 The use of gross expenditure as weights for changes in the prices of second-hand goods is inconsistent with the SNA.[20] The SNA states that sales of second-hand

[19]The *2008 SNA* distinguishes between physical deterioration and depreciation (*2008 SNA*, paragraph 6.240). Physical deterioration is one of the reasons for depreciation or consumption of fixed capital (the decline in value of fixed asset during the accounting period), but the two are not synonymous.

[20]The SNA does not directly treat consumer durables as fixed assets or their acquisition as gross fixed capital formation (*2008 SNA*, paragraphs 10.32–10.37). The one exception is dwellings. However, through a recognition that consumer durables are goods that can be used repeatedly or continuously over time, the SNA does indirectly recognize them as durable goods, despite their purchase being treated as consumption. By implication, durables are subject to the SNA guidelines relating to expenditure on gross fixed capital formation. These guidelines explicitly define the latter as acquisitions less disposals of fixed assets (*2008 SNA*, paragraphs 10.38–10.42).

goods (that is, partly used durables) have to be accounted for and are treated as negative expenditure to be consistent with the treatment of the original purchases (*2008 SNA*, paragraph 10.38). Furthermore, the use of gross expenditure weights and the inclusion of disposals also would be inconsistent with an index based on acquisitions and could clearly overstate, potentially by a substantial amount, the resources that are devoted by households to acquiring second-hand goods. It is therefore not appropriate for either a COLI or a non-COLI (for example, a cost of goods index).[21]

11.172 In nearly all cases, net weights should be used in the CPI compilation.[22] Regarding the weights, the following list details four different scenarios for the net expenditure concept:

- *Directly from another household.* The net expenditure is zero as the transaction is between households. It follows that these purchases should be excluded from a CPI.
- *From another household via a dealer.* In this case, dealers purchase second-hand goods from households and resell them. Theoretically, these purchases should be included with a "net" weight reflecting the difference between the buying and the selling price that is deemed to represent the service the dealer is giving the buyer.
- *Directly from another sector (that is, from an establishment, government, NPISH, or from abroad).* The appropriate net weight is household purchases from these other sectors less any sales to them.
- *From an enterprise or from abroad via a dealer.* Following the same principles as applied previously, the appropriate net weight consists of household purchases from dealers minus household sales to dealers plus the aggregate value of dealers' margins on the products that they buy from and resell to households.[23]

11.173 For both a COLI and a cost of goods index the wording can be simplified and "household" transactions in second-hand goods can be divided into three groups:[24]

- *Transactions between households.* The net expenditure is zero. The changes in the prices of the goods concerned carry no weight and have no effect on a CPI.
- *Purchases by households from units in other sectors including the rest of the world.* The price changes are weighted by the values of the purchases or expenditure incurred.
- *Sales by households to units in other sectors including the rest of the world.* The price changes are given negative weights equal to the values of the receipts from the sales.

11.174 One consequence of using gross expenditure for weights for second-hand goods will be that the weights carried by second-hand goods in the index would be greater than if net expenditure were to be used, and too large compared with other goods and services, as it would overstate in relative terms the amount of household resources taken up by transactions in second-hand goods. If the price of a second-hand good increased, the index would reflect the purchasing household being worse off but not the selling household being better off. Similarly, from a national accounts' perspective, there is no justification for including acquisitions but arbitrarily excluding disposals. Such a procedure would be illogical and inconsistent with the SNA. Thus, putting aside some highly specialized uses, in general, there does not appear to be a circumstance in which use of gross expenditure can be justified in a mainstream price index for household consumption, especially one intended to be used to adjust rates of compensation for changes in the cost of living.

11.175 From the previous discussion, guidelines for the measurement of second-hand goods in a price index can be derived with practical implications that are most pronounced for durable second-hand goods, such as houses, where the treatment is dependent on whether a use, payments, or acquisition approach is adopted in the CPI. For further details relating to owner-occupied housing services, see paragraphs 11.89–11.149 relating to the alternative treatments of owner-occupied housing. Where the second-hand good is semidurable, such as for second-hand clothes and cars, its treatment is not practically affected by whether the use, payments, or acquisition approach is adopted.

11.176 Some goods such as cars may be sold by households to dealers who subsequently resell them at a higher price to other households. This implies that households' net expenditure on goods that are purchased indirectly from other households via a dealer should be positive. It can be argued that the net expenditure should be treated as purchases of intermediate services provided by the dealers and not as purchases of second-hand goods. The weight carried in the CPI is the same whichever interpretation is adopted although the estimated price changes might be different.

11.177 Weights are generally derived from HBSs that should cover second-hand goods and be designed to generate the information required to separate the weights of second-hand items from new items. Explicit weighting is recommended even when based on approximate estimates of expenditure. Administrative records of, for example, the value of imported second-hand cars and of changes in second-hand car registrations, may provide an alternative source of information to compute approximate weights when adequate information is not available from the HBS. Weights can be estimated "top-down" by taking total sales and making an approximate distribution between old and

[21] A cost of goods index measures the percentage change in expenditure a household requires to purchase a fixed basket of goods and services. As its name implies, it seeks to measure the change in cost. In contrast, a COLI measures the percentage change in expenditure needed to maintain a household's standard of living. As its name implies, its objective is to measure the change in the cost of living.

[22] There is one important exception that occurs when the user cost approach is used for the measurement of owner-occupied housing costs. The loan costs associated with house purchase enter the index regardless of whether a newly built house is being purchased or a house from another owner-occupier. But under an acquisition approach owner-occupied housing would be based on a net acquisition cost basis, that is, the cost of purchasing all newly built houses or converted dwellings or existing dwellings newly acquired by the household sector (for example, private purchases of houses previously owned by the government) less disposals of houses (for example, demolitions or sales of private houses to government).

[23] This category covers, for instance, both imports and domestic sales of former company cars.

[24] The payment for the services of estate agents and other intermediaries such as housing agents, auctioneers, and salesroom operators come under COICOP 2018 13.9.0.9 (Other Services, not elsewhere classified).

new goods or "bottom-up" by computing separate estimates and summing them.

11.178 There are several practical difficulties in pricing second-hand goods. These exist whether using the traditional approach of sending price collectors to outlets or pricing second-hand goods online. First, it can be difficult to determine what prices are actually paid, since bargaining is more common with second-hand goods than new ones, for instance reflecting concerns about the condition of the item. Second, two sampling problems are particularly challenging:

- The initial selection of a representative sample
- Following the prices of a fixed basket of items

Initial Sample Selection

Items

11.179 The factors that need to be considered when choosing a representative sample of a specific second-hand good include:

- The items chosen must be generally available and easy to find by price collectors.
- The item description must be sufficiently detailed for the item to be easily identified both initially and on repeated visits to physical and online or web-based outlets to provide sufficient guidance when a replacement needs to be chosen.
- The item must be representative of the second-hand market.

11.180 For most second-hand goods the selection of precisely which items to be priced is likely to be purposive. To facilitate this, the CPI compiler will need to identify not only which characteristics physically differentiate the items, but also which factors have a significant impact on price, including, most particularly, the age and condition of the good concerned. The latter may need to be deduced by observation based on a number of price-determining characteristics. For instance, with clothing there may be noticeable thinning of the material. The attributes may be determined in part indirectly, for instance in the case of a car by reference to its age. These should make up part of the item description and be used when selecting an item to price each month.

11.181 Specifications should be kept up to date to reflect the second-hand market so that problems relating to sample depletion and "forced" replacements are minimized. Forced replacements are to be avoided, particularly for cars, as explicit forms of quality adjustment are problematic for second-hand goods. For example, option costing, which is commonly employed for new cars, cannot be applied to second-hand cars, and hedonic regression techniques require a rich data source. In these circumstances, expert judgment is often used to inform quality adjustment for differences in technical specifications, mileage, or condition of vehicle.

Outlets

11.182 The outlet needs to be representative of where second-hand goods are purchased, whether from shops, fixed markets, street traders, or online. It also must be chosen considering the need for continuity, so price collectors are able to collect as far as possible from the same retailers each month. It is likely that selecting the locations for price collection and the sample of actual outlets selling second-hand goods will be judgmental. From a practical perspective there are two main approaches:

- Periodically conducting a full enumeration of the relevant outlets selling second-hand goods at a specific location and then selecting one at random for price collection each month. The difficulty with this approach is that it is not only resource-intensive but also may not be efficient in circumstances where it is unlikely that the item priced in an outlet at the previous price collection will still be available the following month as it is likely to have been sold. By definition, second-hand goods are unique. In addition, it is not a practical option when outlets are moveable, which can often be the case for street traders selling second-hand semidurable goods (for example, unbranded clothing).
- A form of quota sampling where the price collector visits a preselected location, for instance a market that is known to sell goods in a midprice and quality range, taking a "random" walk around the stalls until a second-hand item meeting the required description is found. This may be the preferred method, especially under the circumstances described previously and is a departure from the conventional CPI practice where the same outlet is visited each month and the same good is priced. Outlets and other points of sale for specific types of second-hand goods, such as clothing, can often be identified by their specific location on a market day. Choosing the appropriate day of the week for the collection of prices from street traders is also important because they may change their position (and prices) on different days.

11.183 In practice, a mixture of the two approaches described previously might be desirable and possible. Under both approaches, stratification by outlet type, for example, shop, market stall, street trader, and online, is recommended to keep the sample representative.

Following the Prices of a Basket of Items

11.184 In ideal circumstances, after initial selection and pricing in an outlet, the identical item should be priced each month. In practice, this is almost impossible to achieve for second-hand goods because, for instance, the identical T-shirt is unlikely to be on sale in two consecutive price collection periods as it is likely to have been sold in the intervening period. In addition, the price collectors are unlikely to be able to identify and know whether they are pricing exactly the same good. A more practical approach, and a departure from normal price collection practice, is to reselect an item each month, in this case a T-shirt, that most resembles the one priced in the previous month. The selection of the new item is based on the price-determining characteristics previously identified. To facilitate this approach, the price collectors will need a checklist of characteristics for each item requiring a price quotation. This can be completed during each price collection and a price adjustment made at the head office when there is a deviation from the stated price-determining characteristics. Advice from the retailer can be sought to assist this process. An example of a price collection form is given in Annex 11.1 for a man's branded T-shirt.

Quality Adjustment

11.185 An overdetailed checklist of characteristics should be avoided, as it can result in difficulties in locating products matching the exact definitions because of sellers not being able to guarantee that the second-hand goods that they acquire for resale will not vary from one period to another. This may in turn require a large number of quality adjustments as replacement items have to be constantly chosen. Where a matching item cannot be located, price collectors should be asked to collect the price of a product that most closely meets the specifications. The CPI compiler will then need to make a quality adjustment to the price to reflect the value of the difference (if any) between the specified item and its replacement. The option most suited to second-hand goods is expert judgment. This relies on product experts, often in consultation with outlet staff, determining the value of a change in specification. This role is often undertaken by price collectors.

11.186 When there is a planned change of model, for instance in pricing second-hand automobiles, the use of overlap pricing is often seen as a way of making quality adjustments, as the prices of both old and replacement models can be collected in the overlap month. Their price ratios can be presumed to reflect the market value of relative quality when linking price quotes for different models. This removes any need for explicit quality adjustment. But the compiler should beware the possibility of computing a flat index as a result of a high turnover in models rather than any real stagnation in the second-hand prices. Chapter 6 provides more guidance about quality adjustment.

Alternative Approaches

11.187 Given the potential for finding challenging practical sampling problems associated with collecting prices of second-hand goods, some NSOs do not collect prices directly but instead adopt one of two possible alternative approaches, depending on circumstances and the goods involved. One approach is to ask a dealer in second-hand goods to complete a questionnaire with the current price that they would expect to achieve. This is sometimes done for clothing, for instance, where market traders purchase bundles of second-hand clothes from suppliers (normally from other market traders who act as wholesalers). It is then assumed that retail prices will move in parallel to wholesale prices. Another approach is to assume that the price trends for second-hand goods are the same as those of the corresponding new goods obtained from the main CPI price collection. The latter is most likely to be the practice where purchases of second-hand goods have been historically much less important than purchases of new goods. Both cases use other price movements as a proxy for the price movements of the corresponding second-hand goods.

Wholesalers' Prices

11.188 Under this approach, the prices collected for second-hand goods are wholesale prices and these are used as a proxy for consumer prices. Wholesalers are selected to be representative of the types of wholesalers who are likely to supply the retail outlets that are used by the reference population covered by the CPI, taking into account, for instance, the geographical coverage and the type of retail outlet, including the income bracket of its customers. The product descriptions of the second-hand goods that are priced are normally more oriented to the wholesale rather than retail market to be easier for the wholesaler to complete the form. For example, the wholesaler may be asked to give the indicative prices (that is, the current price they have been getting or expects to get) for a "bale" of "average quality" T-shirts with designer logos. In this case, "bales" are the standard quantity purchased wholesale that will contain some good, average, and low-quality T-shirts mounting to a bale being of "average quality" overall. It is then assumed that retail prices move in line with these wholesale prices. An example of the type of questionnaire sent to wholesalers is given in Annex 11.2.

Prices of New Goods

11.189 The use of new goods as a proxy for old should be kept regularly under review to identify anything that might challenge the historic price relationship, for instance, where new safety regulations or environmental laws reduce the value of second-hand cars compared with new ones.

11.190 If the price trend of the corresponding new good is used as a proxy, then the expenditure weight used in compiling the index must reflect expenditure on both new and second-hand goods. One approach is to include the weight of the second-hand good with that of the new good. Another is to keep the second-hand item separate with its own weight, compute an index, and then combine it with the price index for the new good. The latter approach is more transparent.

Own-Account Production

Introduction

11.191 Households can engage in various kinds of productive activities that may be either aimed at the market or intended to produce goods or services for own consumption (*2008 SNA*, paragraphs 1.41–1.42). When households engage in production for the market, the associated business transactions are all outside the scope of a CPI. Expenditure incurred for business purposes are excluded, even though they involve purchases of goods and services that might have been used instead to satisfy the personal needs and wants of members of the household. In practice, households also produce goods and services directly for their own consumption and this can account for a significant proportion of a country's household final consumption expenditure. For example, households grow vegetables, fruit, and flowers or other crops for their own use, and owner-occupiers produce housing services for their own consumption. Goods and services produced by households for their own consumption are called own-account production. According to the SNA (*2008 SNA*, paragraphs 6.27), all services produced for own consumption are excluded from the production boundary, except services produced by employing paid domestic or household staff and the housing services produced by owner-occupiers. This means that only those services produced by employing paid domestic staff and the housing services produced by owner-occupiers would be included in the CPI. Excluded services produced for own consumption include, for example, the preparation of meals, the care of children, the sick or the elderly, the cleaning and maintenance of durables and dwellings, or the transportation of household members.

11.192 Many of the goods or services purchased by households do not provide utility directly but are used as inputs into the production of other goods and services that do provide utility: for example, raw foodstuffs, fertilizers, cleaning materials, paints, electricity, coal, oil, or petrol.

11.193 For purchased final consumption goods and services, the measurement of prices is not a problem as the price is determined at the time of purchase. However, for those goods and services produced and consumed by households, there is a problem because no purchases are involved and there are no direct prices to measure or associated expenditure for the construction of weights. For example, conceptually, the purchase of seeds and fertilizer to grow vegetables and fruits that are then consumed is, in principle, *intermediate* consumption whereas a CPI is based on *final* consumption. This is sometimes referred to as the own-account production dilemma. The CPI compiler has two options: measure output prices indirectly or measure some (but not all) input prices and use them as a proxy for the prices of goods and services consumed. The *2008 SNA* recommends the indirect measurement. Although this seems a simple and conceptually acceptable solution, exceptions may be made for one or two kinds of household production that are particularly important and whose outputs can readily be identified: most particularly, *subsistence agriculture and housing services* produced for own consumption.

Background

11.194 How goods and services produced for own consumption are treated in the CPI depends on the scope and use of index. Assuming for the purpose of illustration that in principle a CPI should cover final consumption by households (that is, not restricted to monetary transactions). The scope and purpose of the index and implications for the treatment of own-account production are considered beginning with paragraph 11.191.

11.195 A distinction can be made between:

- *Intermediate consumption.* In the context of household own-account production, this refers to the goods and services that households use in the process of producing other goods and services. They are not part of the final consumption of households.
- *Final consumption.* This refers to goods and services produced for direct consumption where utility is derived by the household through the act of consumption.
  - Goods and services to be used repeatedly in production over extended periods (more than one year), provide benefits to the owner over the lifetime of the goods. These goods are called fixed assets (*2008 SNA*, paragraph 10.33) and, in general, are recorded as *gross fixed capital formation.* For example, a house will normally provide shelter for many years. Similarly, a stove may provide cooking services for decades. A house is treated as gross fixed capital formation in the SNA and there are four primary approaches used for the treatment of owner-occupied housing in the CPI depending on the different conceptual approach adopted (that is, use, payments, or acquisition). However, other durable goods (for example, stoves, washing machines, or cars that are commonly referred to as "consumer durables") are treated in both the CPI and the SNA as though they are fully consumed at the time they are purchased rather than being depreciated over time, so their price is included in the CPI in the period in which they are purchased.
  - In practice, in the context of own-account production, it can be difficult to draw a clear distinction between intermediate and final consumption, as the same goods and services may be used for either purpose. There are numerous examples. Basic constituents of foods, such as flour, cooking oils, raw meat, and vegetables, may be processed into bread, cakes, or meals, with the assistance of other inputs including fuels, the services provided by consumer durables, such as refrigerators and cookers, and the labor of members of the household. Inputs of materials, equipment, and labor are used to clean, maintain, and repair dwellings. Inputs of seeds, fertilizers, insecticides, equipment, and labor are used to produce vegetables or flowers, and so on. Some of the production activities taking place within households' activities, for example, gardening or cooking, may provide satisfaction in themselves. Others, such as cleaning, may be regarded as chores that reduce utility. In any case, the goods or services used as inputs into these productive activities do not provide utility in themselves.
  - Utility is derived from consuming the outputs from household production undertaken for own consumption. It is necessary, therefore, to decide whether a CPI should try to measure the changes in the prices of the outputs or the prices of the inputs. In principle, it seems desirable to measure the output prices, but there are objections to this procedure.
  - On a conceptual level, it is difficult to decide what are the real final outputs from many of the different household production activities, such as growing vegetables or raising livestock. Even if they could be satisfactorily identified conceptually, they would have to be measured and priced. There are no prices to be observed, as there are no monetary transactions. Prices would have to be imputed for them and such prices would be not only hypothetical but inevitably very speculative. Their use in CPIs is not a realistic possibility in general and almost certainly would not be acceptable to most users who are primarily interested in the market prices paid by households.
  - The practical alternative is to treat the goods and services acquired by households on the market for use as inputs into the various kinds of household production activities as if they were themselves final consumption goods and services. They provide utility *indirectly* on the assumption that they are used exclusively to produce goods and services that are directly consumed by households.
  - There are two important areas of own-account production that warrant special consideration: *subsistence*

agriculture and *housing services* produced for own consumption.

- In the national accounts, an attempt is made to record the value of *subsistence agriculture*, which is the agricultural output produced for own consumption (*2008 SNA*, paragraphs 24.47–24.49). In some countries, subsistence agriculture may account for a large part of the production and consumption of agricultural produce. The national accounts require such outputs to be valued at their market prices (*2008 SNA*, paragraph 6.124). A CPI may record either the actual input prices or the imputed output prices, but not both. If the imputed output prices for subsistence agriculture are included in a CPI, the prices of the purchased inputs should be excluded. This could remove from the index most of the market transactions made by such households. Expenditure on inputs may constitute the principal contact that the households have with the market and through which they experience the effects of inflation. It therefore seems preferable to record the actual prices of the inputs and not the imputed prices of the outputs in CPIs.
- The treatment of *owner-occupied housing services* is particularly challenging as described in paragraphs 11.102–11.161.

The Scope and Choice of Index

11.196 While the general purpose of a CPI is to measure changes in the prices of consumption goods and services, the precise scope of a CPI with regard to the goods and services and households covered should be determined by what is intended to be the main use of the index. Considering the household coverage and the item scope of the CPI, subsistence households generally have a weak connection to the formal economy, as a major part of their consumption is from their own or bartered production. However, indices designed for the indexation of wages or state benefits would exclude subsistence households from their scope. For simplicity of the following discussion, the latter indices will be referred to as "compensation indices." Indices designed to measure price changes covering all monetary transactions will include purchases by subsistence households but will not include production for own consumption. These can be referred to as "monetary transactions indices." There is a third type of index that includes production for own consumption within its scope. These can be referred to as "general consumption indices."

11.197 For countries where production for own consumption represents a major part of total household final consumption, the three types of index will behave differently when the prices of basic food, imported manufactured goods, and farm inputs diverge. In such circumstances, an index that excludes subsistence households will not be representative of the whole population as it is designed to be representative of the price experience of a more limited group of households. Similarly, the monetary transactions index and the general consumption index will give divergent results. Each index provides a different picture of what is happening within the economy. The first does not attempt to be representative of the whole population and the remaining two indices attempt to be representative of all households but in different ways.

11.198 To understand the differences in the indices referred in paragraphs 11.195 and 11.196, consider, for example, that drought affects a country with a high proportion of subsistence households. Assume nonsubsistence households are included within the scope of the compensation index and have no subsistence consumption. These households are also affected by the drought but to a lesser extent. Assume that the price of basic food products increases sharply, that there is relatively little change in the prices of imported manufactured goods, and that the prices of farm inputs fall because of a sharp fall in demand from subsistence farmers.[25] In this example, the compensation index will rise because basic food products cost more, but the rise will be moderated because the price of imported manufactured goods has not increased to the same extent. The rise in the monetary transactions index will be moderated further because of the fall in the price of farm inputs. The general consumption index will show the greatest increase because the weight given to basic food products will be much higher, reflecting production for consumption, and no weight will be given to farm inputs.

11.199 Which index in this example is "correct"? If properly constructed, all three are "correct" in the sense that each addresses a user's need. They are different simply because they serve different purposes and have different uses. The general consumption index would give the best picture of how the drought was affecting the whole of the country. The fact that the price of farm inputs had fallen would not reflect the problem faced by subsistence farmers who had to find ways of providing food for their families and were unable to benefit from the fall in farm input prices. The monetary transactions index would give the most relevant measure, for the country as a whole, of the change in prices of goods exchanged within the market. For the purposes of monetary policy, the general consumption index would overstate the level of inflation but for the purposes of understanding, the impact of the drought on the price of consumption products it would not. The converse is true of the monetary transactions index. The compensation index would not reflect the full impact of the drought on all households, but it would reflect the impact of the drought on indexation households. The general consumption index would overstate the impact of the drought on indexation households and the monetary transactions index would understate the impact; both would be biased if used in the context of indexation.

11.200 Each NSO needs to decide which of the three types of index is appropriate in its own national circumstances. In countries with well-developed price statistics systems, the NSO could consider compiling alternative indices to meet different user needs. They would need to educate users about their respective uses. In most countries, the NSO opts for one general-purpose index. If the primary use of the index is to use in monetary policy decisions and serve as a macroeconomic measure of inflation, it is not appropriate to

[25] Many different scenarios could be considered. This example is designed to show that all three index types are sensitive to the treatment of subsistence households and subsistence consumption. If there are changes in the relative prices of the selected product groups, the choice of index type will affect the outcome. Each index will present different results concerning the impact of the drought on households, particularly subsistence households.

include production for own consumption. If the primary use of the index is to index wages and government payments, production for own consumption should be excluded. In both cases, only monetary transactions should be included in the index. It should be noted that the housing services produced by owner-occupiers are treated differently (as described in paragraphs 11.98–11.104).

11.201 A number of countries compile and disseminate a monetary transaction index as the headline measure of price change but also compile an alternative index that includes production for own consumption in the weights. Such an index would be for analytical purposes and would meet the needs of poverty economists.

Construction of a "General Consumption" Index

11.202 To include subsistence households and consumption in a general consumption index it is necessary to construct appropriate consumption weights and to decide how subsistence consumption will be priced. Both aspects are described in paragraphs 11.207–11.209.

11.203 In general, the available data source for consumption weights will be an HBS or a survey of subsistence households. To measure consumption, households are asked to record the quantities consumed of own-account produced goods. To obtain a value weight a "price" is applied to the product. Usually, this will be the price of the product in a relevant market. Most countries with significant subsistence production will prepare estimates of the value of consumption classified by product. This will be prepared for use in poverty analysis and possibly also for use in compiling the national accounts. When preparing weights for a general consumption index these estimates of consumption should be combined with estimates of purchases of the same products by nonsubsistence households to obtain the total consumption weight for each product. It is important to exclude weights for any market purchases of items used as inputs into subsistence production, for example, fertilizer, tools, and herbicides. These products are excluded but only in respect of households for which subsistence production is estimated. For all other households, they are included in the weights and classified within recreational expenditure (COICOP 09.3.1).[26]

11.204 The price of basic food products may vary, particularly between urban and rural areas. This reflects availability, demand, transport costs, and other factors. The most appropriate price to apply to subsistence consumption would be the price in a market near to where the consumption takes place. Typically, this would include many rural areas. If a country collects basic foods products prices in both urban and rural areas, the most appropriate price would be an average of the rural prices weighted to reflect the distribution of subsistence agriculture. In practice, a simple average of rural prices might provide a reliable estimate, particularly if the selection of rural outlets is approximately self-weighted.

11.205 Similar pricing considerations apply to the prices used when compiling the results of a household survey used to estimate subsistence consumption. CPI compilers can assist the household survey compilers with these estimates. If the CPI compilers are producing a general consumption index, they should ensure that the prices used to value consumption are consistent with the prices used in construction of the price index.

Construction of a "Monetary" Transactions Index

11.206 One of the main challenges in including subsistence households in a monetary transactions index is to construct appropriate expenditure weights. This is because this index uses purchases of inputs used in producing subsistence outputs as a proxy for subsistence consumption. Additional price information is only required for input items that are unique to subsistence households. If items are purchased by nonsubsistence households and are already priced for CPI purposes, this price information can be used for the subsistence inputs component of the monetary transactions index, such as spades, seeds, or fertilizer.

11.207 In general, the available data source of weights for inputs into subsistence production will be a household survey, such as a general HBS or a survey of subsistence households. When preparing weights for a monetary transactions index these estimates of consumption should be combined with estimates of purchases of the same products by nonsubsistence households to obtain the total expenditure weight for each product. It is important to exclude weights for subsistence consumption that may have been computed as part of the household survey. Subsistence consumption is excluded because the weight for inputs used in subsistence production is included in this index as a proxy for subsistence consumption and to include that consumption would involve double counting.

Construction of a "Compensation" Index

11.208 If the NSO decides to compile a "compensation index" it is unnecessary to construct subsistence consumption weights and to decide how subsistence consumption should be priced because an index designed for the indexation of wages or benefits will generally exclude subsistence households, or more precisely subsistence consumption, from its scope.

Own-Account Household Services (Excluding Owner-Occupied Housing Services)

11.209 Services produced by households include such things as the preparation of meals, the care of children, the sick and the elderly, the cleaning and maintenance of dwellings, and the transport of household members. The actual outputs of the services are excluded from the scope of the CPI and no attempt should be made to impute expenditure to them. Home-cooked meals are a service output produced within the household, and it is recommended that there should be no imputation of expenditure in respect of the preparation of these meals. Similarly, it is recommended that there should be no imputation of expenditure to other services produced within the household such as when parents transport their children to school or care for a sick child.

[26]For nonsubsistence households, garden produce may be treated as a recreational output rather than the result of a production process, depending on the motivation and circumstances of production. Using this treatment, purchases such as tools or fertilizers are gardening or recreational expenses and not inputs into the production of food. For some households the line between subsistence production and recreational activity will be unclear. NSOs should adopt practical rules based on national circumstances for making this distinction. For example, urban food production for own consumption may be treated as recreational and rural food production for own consumption may be treated as subsistence production.

These treatments are consistent with the SNA.[27] Although it may be conceptually more appropriate to regard the outputs of household production as consumption rather than the inputs, data in respect of the outputs of these areas of household production would require many assumptions and imputations and would be of little practical use and so are excluded from the CPI and the SNA production boundary.

11.210 A long-term bias can result if households increase their purchases of services and decrease their production for own consumption and this is not addressed when updating the weights. For example, if households purchase more takeaway or restaurant food instead of preparing food for their own consumption, over time the relative expenditure on takeaway and restaurant food will increase and the relative expenditure on food ingredients will decrease. If long-term labor costs increase more rapidly than basic food prices, there will be a long-term downward bias to the index (and conversely if they increase less rapidly) unless the impact of this change in behavior is reflected in a revision of the weights for both own-account production associated purchases and other household purchases. This is because labor costs have a greater impact on takeaway and restaurant food prices than on food ingredient prices. Although the household contributes labor when producing household services, this is not included in the index because it is outside of the production boundary. Expenditure weights should be reviewed on a regular basis (for more information on weights, see Chapter 3).

Tariffs

11.211 A tariff is a list of prices for the purchase of a particular kind of good or service under different terms and conditions. For example, one price may be charged for electricity during the day and a lower price may be charged at night, or a higher price may be charged the more electricity is consumed. Similarly, a telephone company may charge a lower price for a call on weekends than in the rest of the week. Another example may be bus tickets sold at one price to general passengers and at a lower price to children and pensioners. Construction of the corresponding price index should adhere to the core principles that price collection should be undertaken consistently over time and in a way that represents consumer purchasing patterns, and that the selection of representative items, in this case the different tariffs charged, should represent consumer behavior and be weighted by consumer expenditure patterns. It follows that it is appropriate to assign weights to the different tariffs or prices to calculate the price index for the elementary aggregate. This section provides advice on the measurement and inclusion of tariff prices in a CPI and gives illustrative examples of the more common types of tariffs.

[27]The SNA includes all production of goods for own use within the production boundary, as the decision whether goods are to be sold or retained for own use can only be made after they have been produced. However, it excludes all production of services for own final consumption within households, except for the services produced by employing paid domestic staff and the own-account production of housing services by owner-occupiers. The services are excluded because the decision to consume them within the household is made even before the service is provided (*2008 SNA*, paragraph 1.42).

Introduction

11.212 Tariffs cover a large and diverse range of pricing structures. For example, the EU definition states that a tariff is a list of preestablished prices and conditions for the purchase and consumption of one and the same good or service, or of similar goods and services, that has been centrally fixed by the supplier, by the government, or by agreement to exert influence on the consumption patterns by means of appropriately differentiated prices and conditions according to characteristics of consumers, the level, the structure, or the timing of the consumption. A tariff price can be defined as a price within a tariff that applies to a component element or unit of consumption of the good or service in question. At its most basic, a tariff consists of a list of prices based on detailed specifications of the goods or services that are priced individually but can only be bought as part of the package.

11.213 Added complications can exist where goods and services providers adopt a range of strategies to differentiate their goods and services to attract and retain customers. For example, to appeal directly to different types of customers, suppliers of telecommunication services may bundle services in different ways or adopt tariff pricing. This is often accompanied by regular changes in the contracts offered to potential customers to encourage the take-up of services. Such contracts are often fixed-term with prices fixed for the period of the contract and a penalty clause if the contract is terminated early. A more detailed discussion of tariff pricing in the telecommunications sector is included in paragraphs 11.256–11.284. There may exist in the market many tariff pricing programs. Some of the more common include:

- *Peak-load pricing* (also known as "congestion" pricing). This occurs when producers charge higher fees during periods of greater demand, usually because of the higher production costs caused by capacity constraints. Peak-load pricing thus helps in balancing capacity usage over a period that decreases the need for firms to invest in costly infrastructure expansions. Such pricing practices are often found in the areas of toll roads and bridges, ferry services, electricity, long-distance phone calls, and home delivery of goods.
- *Two-part tariffs*. These occur when consumers are charged both an entry (or lump-sum) fee and a per unit charge. A fee is charged up front for the right to use (or buy) the product, and an additional fee is charged for each unit that the household consumes. Examples where two-part tariff pricing is often applied are the following:
  - Amusement parks that charge an entry fee in addition to a fee for each ride
  - "Membership" discount programs or shopping clubs that require the purchase of a membership card to access the point of sale and then the consumer pays a lower price for the products purchased
  - Landline telephone services where there is a fee to use the service ("line rental") and also a fee per call (the line rental covers the cost of providing the service and the "per minute" or metered charge, covers the cost of placing the call on the network)
  - Taxi fares where a variable fare based on distance traveled is added to the base "fixed" initial charge that is not dependent on mileage

- *Block pricing*. This occurs when prices vary according to the volume consumed. Electric utilities, for example, often charge a per kilowatt-hour (kW h) price up to X units consumed and then charge a different price for the remaining units.
- *Special group discounts*. This occurs when members of certain segments of the population such as students and seniors may be charged a lower price for the good or service compared to the general population. Bus fares and haircuts are good examples of services where these group discounts are applied.

11.214 In some countries, private and public firms have come to rely increasingly on tariff-type pricing as a tool for generating additional revenues or for public policy purposes. For example, publicly administered electric or water utilities may charge a lower tariff for the first units of electricity consumed up to a certain level (the first block), followed by a higher tariff for subsequent units consumed (the second block). It is argued that such an increasing block tariff strategy is often used to promote better and greater access by lower-income households to what is considered a vital service. Similarly, other companies charge more for the first block than the second as an encouragement to increase usage. More generally, private sellers can often increase their profits by charging a higher price for a product to some consumers and a lower price to others, but this depends on whether the customer base can be successfully segmented.

11.215 Tariff-type pricing programs can be applied to a wide range of products. The extent of the practice will vary according to the country. In cases such as electricity, the expenditure weight can be relatively high, and so it is important to measure accurately the price change for such products. The CPI compiler will need to have available data on the tariff prices and weights that reflect the structure of the consumption of the product according to the characteristics of the consumers, the level, the structure, or the timing of the consumption.

Main Measurement Issues

11.216 In some cases, tariff-type pricing programs are affected by price index problems associated with services. These include:

- Charges for services can be subject to such complex pricing schedules that it is difficult to select the appropriate prices for inclusion in the price index.
- Identification or specification of individual products or units of consumption can be difficult, particularly when they are offered as bundled packages consisting of several types of microexpenditure that may be priced separately but are typically only available as a part of a package.
- Services are often provided under long-term contractual arrangements and these may include different types of "customer loyalty" rebates, clauses for the minimum duration of contracts, surcharges for the provision of services not foreseen in the contract, and so on. Loyalty rebates or coupons are usually ignored because of difficulties of measurement (see Chapter 5).
- There are often difficulties in accounting for substitution between different providers of the same type of service, and in accounting for quality differences in the services provided.
- Accounting for customers moving from one tariff to another under the same service provider might be difficult. For instance, when a mobile telephone company offers several different pricing packages targeted at different patterns of usage, current customers may undertake periodic reviews during which they may decide to move to a more advantageous tariff for their level of usage while staying with the same provider.

Price Measurement Methods

11.217 There are four basic approaches to measure tariff pricing in the CPI: matched samples, unit values, consumer profiles, and the sample of bills approach. The minimum information required includes all tariff prices and weights that reflect the structure of the consumption of the product according to the characteristics of the consumers, the level, the structure, or the timing of the consumption.

Matched Samples

11.218 *Matched samples* are used when a full tariff list or an element of the tariff structure is treated as a product specification and repriced in subsequent periods. This mirrors the traditional CPI methodology of matched pairs. The simplest form of traditional matching methodology would be to take the tariff price lists of some major companies and follow the changes in the entire pricing program, preferably with accurate weighting information for the different elements of the price list. This option may be feasible in markets of limited competition where the pricing structures are quite stable. There are practical challenges associated with ensuring that the same product specification is priced each month (that is, that the matched pairs methodology is adhered to). There is usually limited data about the customer base. In practice, the product to be priced using a full price list usually has to be priced in a rather simple manner without much differentiation on the basis of customers' characteristics, and for the sake of simplicity, some variations in tariff are sometimes ignored.

11.219 Another version of matching methodology is to select some elements of a tariff as representative items and reprice them in subsequent periods. For each representative item, detailed specifications combined with information supplied by the provider are constructed. For instance, for airfares, this could be for each airline carrier, a nonrefundable and nonchangeable airline fare from one prespecified location to another, with predetermined outbound and inbound dates chosen by time of day and day of the week, including all surcharges.

11.220 The representative tariff element has the advantage that it can be applied to different service providers, at least in principle. It becomes possible to incorporate new service providers into the index without significant difficulties. However, the choice of only a few items as representative may limit the validity of the approach. Neither of the matching approaches is suitable for situations where there are major changes in the structures of tariffs.

Unit Values

11.221 The *unit value approach*, in this case, the overall average price of one unit, for example, of electricity, for customers of a particular supplier is used for monitoring prices instead of following individual elements of the tariff. The unit value approach can be used when contents of the tariff-based service are homogeneous (for example, kilowatt-hour of electricity) and the method should be used only in such cases. The unit value is calculated using overall revenue and quantity data at a higher level that does not distinguish between different tariffs or customers. It attributes all the differences between different packages to price alone, assuming that quality differences between different pricing approaches are zero or insignificant. This may not be the case where, for example, the reliability of continuity of supply varies between suppliers. The advantages of this approach are that it can be easier to compute; more fully reflects changes in customer profiles and usage; and better reflects changes in discounts and promotions.

Consumer Profiles

11.222 The *prespecified consumer profiles approach* defines the product independently of a single producer's or supplier's tariff structure. Instead, a more general formulation of the consumer's behavior is constructed based on information (for example, sales information provided by the industry as a whole) that can be used to define a range of typical consumers irrespective of supplier. Different suppliers' services are priced through these typical consumers. A unit value price is calculated for each consumer profile and then this unit value is recalculated over time. The advantage of this approach is that it does not require an actual sample of bills, only the details of the different tariffs and some information on usage by typical customers. Also, the CPI compiler could potentially define consumer profiles by class of household, for example, prices for household with lower and higher income could be computed.

Sample of Bills Approach

11.223 The *sample of bills approach* is a more refined version of the consumer profile approach where a level of service activity from an actual sample of customers is priced each month, rather than defining profiles representative of the average monthly activities of a range of customers. This can be done, for example, by selecting a sample of customers from each category of customer, to reflect the structures of the tariffs of the corresponding service providers. For instance, a sample of customers and their bills might be drawn from low-, medium-, and high-volume consumers of the product. The resulting index measures the cost of the current billing period's consumption (normally over a month or a quarter) at prices charged in the index period compared with prices charged in the price reference period. The sample of bills approach has a number of differences compared with the consumer profile approach, most particularly:

- It takes into account seasonal variations in consumption, for example, a greater volume of international telephone calls during public holidays and festivals.
- It reflects actual customer behavior by reference to bills.
- It detects price changes not associated with tariff changes, such as reduced unit charges when a minimum threshold of consumption is reached.

There can be an inherent time lag because of bills being issued after the index for the relevant time period has been compiled.

11.224 In each of the previous approaches, the resulting calculation should be based on prices and weights that reflect the structure of the consumption of the goods or services according to the predetermined characteristics of the consumers and the level, the structure, or the timing of the consumption. The corresponding checklist of price-relevant characteristics for tariff-based expenditure may include:

- The time-pattern of use of the service. The patterns of use may be measured over one day, one week, or even one year.
- The volume of use of the service, for example, where pricing programs differentiate between small and large customers.
- The past behavior of the customer. Particularly in insurance services where previous claims or medical histories may have an impact on the price paid.
- The expected future behavior of a group of customers, leading to price differentiation between, for example, males and females or for different socioeconomic groups. This is particularly prevalent in insurance services where companies analyze claims information by personal characteristics.
- Income-dependent prices, most prevalent in public sector tariff structures.

11.225 The bundling of different services, where a supplier might provide, for example, a mobile telephone plus free calls at certain off-peak times, or telephone and digital services, needs to be considered in sampling procedures where such practices are common.

11.226 There are numerous combinations of the previous factors that can be used to create different tariff structures and the structure of tariffs can undergo regular change. The CPI compiler will need to thoroughly research the topic and monitor the market to ensure that all relevant price differentials are picked up.

Examples of Price Measurement Methods

11.227 Examples of the different methods of incorporating tariff prices in a CPI are described in paragraphs 11.228–11.235. Quality adjustment is addressed in paragraphs 11.236–11.247.

Matched Samples

11.228 The example given in Table 11.5 is based on telecommunications services (telecommunications services are addressed in more detail in paragraphs 11.249–11.275).

11.229 The example in Table 11.5 considers that there is just one service provider for national calls and three for international calls. It is assumed that in the price reference period the overall unit price is 1.9200.

11.230 Table 11.5 illustrates several issues pertinent to the different approaches to the measurement of tariff prices and the need to review and verify all calculations. For example, if the overall weighted average price is used to calculate the index, then the average fixed-weight price increase from the price reference period to current period is 11.5 percent

Table 11.5 Matched Models: Landline Telephones

	Expenditure Weights	Quantity Weights	Tariff (unit price $): Base Period	Tariff (unit price $): Period *t*	Change in Unit Tariff Price (percent in brackets)
National Calls					
Local	**50.00**				
Peak	30.00	33.53	1.20	1.30	+0.10 (8.3)
Off-Peak	20.00	33.53	0.80	0.80	0.0 (0.0)
Long-Distance	**20.00**				
Peak	5.00	3.19	2.10	2.50	+0.40 (19.0)
Off-Peak	15.00	22.37	0.90	1.10	+0.20 (22.2)
International Calls	***30.00***				
To Cape Town (service provider A)	10.00	3.84	3.50	3.50	0.0 (0.0)
To Singapore (service provider B)	10.00	3.19	4.20	4.40	+0.20 (4.8)
To Washington (service provider C)	10.00	0.35	3.90	5.10	+1.20 (30.8)
Weighted Average Tariff Price (revenue weights)	**100.00**	**100.00**	**1.92**	**2.14**	**+0.22 (11.5)**
Weighted Average Tariff Price (quantity weights)			**1.22**	**1.32**	**+0.10 (8.3)**

if revenue weights are applied and 8.3 percent if quantity weights are applied. The use of quantity weights is correct, whereas the use of revenue weights should be avoided. The fixed-weight increase is 12.2 percent if the average of the price relatives is used (that is, Carli index), which is known for its upward bias. This provides a good example of why a Carli index should not be used in the computation of the CPI. If a geometric mean (that is, Jevons index) is applied, the increase is 11.6 percent. It also illustrates the importance of analyzing tariffs at a detailed level given the fact that different elements of the tariff can be subject to very different price changes. Thus, the use of overall unit values, without some form of stratification, and where weights are contemporary and not fixed could result in volatile average unit value/price changes.

Unit Values

11.231 For example, in telecommunications services, the unit price for national long-distance calls is derived as the total revenue received from such calls, divided by the number of call minutes. The advantage of the unit value approach is that, since there is no sampling, the coverage of the services is complete and there is no need to specify representative items or different user categories. On the other hand, the compilation of unit values typically requires close collaboration with the service providers. The CPI compiler will need to persuade the providers of the importance of providing this commercially sensitive information on a confidential basis. The NSO will need to assure that the information will only be used for compiling the CPI, will be kept secure, and will not be disclosed to a third party. In this case, stratification continues to be important, for instance by whether a call is local or long-distance and made off-peak or at peak times. Effective stratification is particularly critical in the compilation process if the effect of mixing quality and quantity is to be minimized.

Consumer Profiles

11.232 For marketing purposes, companies often classify their customers based on their consumption habits. Table 11.6 shows a typical range of representative consumer profiles for mobile telephones. Information on different consumer profiles may be obtained from service providers that use consumer profiling when planning their product pricing strategies. This type of information should generally be more readily available as it is less sensitive than actual revenue data. It can provide data for the unit value approach or for detailed weights in the matching methodology. National regulatory authorities may also be able to provide detailed customer use profiles on a confidential basis.

11.233 The use of consumer profiles is quite straightforward in principle. Once the profiles have been identified, each service plan selected for pricing is priced and repriced based on the (fictional) bills that these virtual customers would receive. Costs to each customer group can be estimated with reference to several plans using sales information to determine the relative importance of the different plans on offer and the corresponding consumer groups being targeted. The overall index is then derived in the usual way by weighting together the average unit costs for these user profiles according to the relative importance of each consumer profile (representing a category of consumer) in expenditure terms.

11.234 A potential disadvantage with the consumer profiles method is that if a new plan that is different and cheaper is introduced in the following year, but the old plan continues to be priced, then the fall in unit value prices will not be reflected in the index. A new plan could offer higher or lower average prices and the CPI would miss the price change going from year one to year two. This problem could be addressed by updating the weights used when introducing the new plan. Also, the consumer profile approach is sometimes based on the plan that would be cheapest for the consumer. This assumes consumers minimize their costs, have full knowledge of the options, and can move to the cheaper plan without any barriers such as a contract that ties the customer into a particular tariff for a minimum length of time.

The Sample of Bills Approach

11.235 With this approach, a sample of actual bills is selected and used to collect prices. Each month, the billing details are used to collect a price. This is in principle very similar to the consumer profiles approach but may be more difficult to apply in practice because it is more data-intensive and requires access to personal and commercially sensitive information.

Table 11.6 Consumer Profiles: Mobile Telephones

Specification	Unit	Low Usage Customer	Medium Usage Customer	High Usage Customer
Total Usage (per billing period) Excluding Text Messages	**Minutes**	**14**	**24**	**59**
Calls				
Within Same Mobile Network				
Peak	Number*	5 (35)	10 (35)	15 (40)
Off-Peak	Number*	10 (55)	10 (65)	20 (80)
To Different Mobile Network				
Peak	Number*	0 (0)	5 (20)	15 (25)
Off-Peak	Number*	5 (20)	10 (30)	20 (40)
To Landline				
Peak	Number*	0 (0)	0 (0)	5 (20)
Off-Peak	Number*	5 (3)	5 (8)	5 (13)
Other Services				
Text Messages	Number	5	10	30
Data	Mb	500 Mb	2 GB	10 GB

* In brackets, average call length in seconds.
Mb, Megabyte; GB, Gigabyte.

Quality Adjustment

11.236 The practical options to account for quality change and new products are different for different tariff strategies.

Matched Samples

11.237 The detection of quality changes depends on the degree of detail in the product specifications at the lowest level of the index. This is because the matched-model method will not take account of price changes outside the specifications, for example, those related to the total volume of the service used. In the matched sample approach, the quality change situation is similar to the situation of disappearing products (that is, some prespecified element of the tariff is no longer available for pricing). A replacement should be selected for the disappearing element of the tariff and the elements compared directly (where applicable) or treated as entirely new products. An example follows for public transport bus fares.

Public Bus Transport in City X

- *Old tariff element.* Bus fare from city center X to suburb Y, on a Saturday, 10:30 p.m. (night tariff, last connection)
- *New tariff element.* Bus fare from city center X to suburb Y, on a Saturday, 9:30 p.m. (night tariff, last connection)

The basis for the direct comparison is the index compiler's judgment that from the consumers' point of view the change in timing is not a significant change.

11.238 Concerning the example in paragraph 11.236, the CPI compiler could also reason that the quality of the service has changed and an allowance for that should be made in the index. But in drawing this conclusion and making a quality adjustment the CPI compiler should not use a subjective judgment or personal view. In this example, some travelers may consider this change in tariff and time as a reduction in quality of service, if last cinema sessions finish at 9:45 p.m. mean that a bus journey is replaced by an expensive taxi journey home, but other users of the bus may welcome the earlier timing because most restaurants close at 9:15 p.m. and they can now avoid waiting for a bus, in the cold, until 10:30 p.m. For them, it is a quality improvement. If possible, the CPI compiler should solicit the views of users for an indication of whether the change is considered to be for the better or for the worse. An indication of subsequent changes in passenger numbers may confirm whether the initial assessment was correct but even this involves some judgment. The decision to use direct comparison, without quality adjustment, is always to a certain extent judgmental and should therefore be based on explicit lines of reasoning so that it is transparent and can be justified.

Unit Values

11.239 The unit value approach regards quality differences related to different pricing programs as implicit price differences. The detection of quality change depends on the degree of detail in the specification of the unit of consumption. Unit values perform best when there is a high degree of homogeneity among the items within a product category. To prevent quality differences from affecting the price index, the specifications of the units of consumption should be as detailed as the available data permit to maximize homogeneity.

11.240 In Table 11.7, relating to bus fares for children the previous tariff categories have to be transformed into the new ones. For customers aged from 12 to 16, there was a price rise of 60 percent (from \$5 to \$8) while for 16-year-olds there was a price decrease of 20 percent (from \$10 to \$8). The proportion of customers falling in these categories (that is, the previous consumption patterns) should be used to calculate the average price change, or in the absence of

Table 11.7 Bus Fares: Old and New Tariffs

	Current Ticket Prices (\$)	New Ticket Prices (\$)
Children	5–15 Years = \$5	5–11 Years = \$5
Teenagers		12–16 Years = \$8
Adults	16 and above = \$10	17 and above = \$10

such information, the CPI compiler might assume about the proportions based on the available information, including revenue information from the bus company.

Consumer Profiles

11.241 The key issue when dealing with quality changes in the context of consumer profiles is the choice of which consumer profiles should be priced through the period of tariff change and change in goods or services provider. An example of a profile is based on a situation where broadband internet service providers increase the download speed substantially (that is, an increase in quality), while keeping prices constant. It can even be the case that an increase in download speed can be accompanied by a price reduction. In Table 11.8, it is assumed that the differentiating factors of an internet-provided broadband connection are limited to the download speed and that this is reflected by different tariffs. It therefore follows that the increase in speed is a quality enhancement, in the marketplace this feature is clearly a price-determining characteristic. As a result of the increased speed, page loading times will be faster and consumers will typically experience improved streaming services such as videos and movies. Most times, only under more intensive applications (for example, downloading large files such as movies) will the difference in bandwidth be noticeable for consumers. But this case may not hold in the future with improvements to the internet infrastructure.

11.242 The assumption may be made that the product versions provided are also, in effect, descriptions of consumer profiles, in this case essentially making the consumer profile approach equivalent to the unit value (or unit price) approach. This applies as long as the usage is such that the average price paid equals the unit price in both periods. This assumption should be tested.

11.243 The key point is that a unit price for the "volume of use" is calculated for each class of consumer, that is, in essence, a form of stratification. Implicit in the unit value approach is a specific form of quality adjustment—namely, a quantity adjustment.

11.244 Table 11.9 presents a simplified example where there are just two speeds (low and high) and where only the download speeds, expressed in megabits per second (Mbs), change. Treating the two speeds as separate elementary aggregates, the price per megabits per second both in the price reference period and in the next period can be calculated. In column G, these unit values (prices) are expressed with regard to indices with the price reference period equaling 100. Using standard fixed-based index methodology, an expenditure weighted average of each elementary aggregate index is taken to obtain the overall index for internet services. The expenditure weights are, respectively, 0.75 and 0.25 for low- and high-speed services. Although these weights are likely not available from the HBS, they could be obtained from administrative sources such as the regulators, the service providers, or market-based intelligence. The quality-adjusted index so derived in the next period is 76.7, which corresponds to a price fall of 23.3 percent. If the average of the price relatives (the Carli index) was wrongly taken, the fall in the index would have been predictably greater at 26.5 percent. If no quality (or quantity) adjustment had been applied, the price index for internet services in the next period would have been 105.4 that is obtained by using only the observed package prices in the calculation of the index (in period 1: 55.95 and 74.95, and in period 2: 60.00 and 74.95). By using the unit value as the price when computing the index, the improvement in the internet service that consumers now have access to is accounted for in the index, which is the preferred treatment in this case.

Table 11.8 Internet Services

Service Level (slow, medium, or fast speed)	Current Speed in kbit/s (down/up)	New Speed in kbit/s (down/up)	Difference in Speed (percent) (down/up)	Current Price ($)	New Price ($)
Slow	256/64	384/96	50/50	34.90	34.90
Medium	768/128	1024/160	33/25	52.25	52.25
Fast	1536/256	2048/320	33/25	86.10	79.95

kbit/s, Kilobit per second.

New Goods and Service Providers and New Products

11.245 From the consumer's point of view, many tariff-priced goods or services are relatively uniform. Electricity delivered to the consumer is almost homogeneous, the main difference being the reliability of supply. The same may hold true for other goods or services, like telephone services

Table 11.9 Changes in the Tariff for Internet Prices

	Share of Expenditure	Download Speed in Mbs	Transfer Allowance in GB	Price for Package in $	Price per Mbs in $	Index
(a)	(b)	(c)	(d)	(e)	(f)	(g)
Base Period						
Low Speed	0.75	30	150	55.95 (100)	1.87	100.0
High Speed	0.25	120	Unlimited	74.95 (100)	0.62	100.0
Weighted Average Price					**1.55 (100)**	**100.0**
Next Period						
Low Speed	0.75	45	150	60.00 (107.24)	1.33	71.5
High Speed	0.25	130	Unlimited	74.95 (100.00)	0.58	92.3
Weighted Average Price					**1.14 (73.58)**	
Expenditure Weighted Average of the Two Elementary Aggregates						**76.686**

Mbs, Megabytes; GB, Gigabyte.

or internet services, despite the service provider's attempts to differentiate their products and make their pricing structures less transparent. Therefore, different suppliers of tariff-priced goods or services could be considered as providing the same type of goods or services and treated as substitutes for each other.

11.246 Changes in the market mix of a clearly homogeneous product from different tariff structures and suppliers should be incorporated in the index. Index construction will require information about the market share of different producers and the various pricing plans. As a general principle, for homogeneous goods or services the price impact of a new good or service provider should be shown in the index, that is, the target price measure for homogeneous goods or services is the unit price in the overall market for the good or service, quality adjusted as necessary.

11.247 In some tariff-priced parts of the retail market, new service elements are frequently introduced (for example, multimedia messages or email on mobile telephones). These should be introduced into the pricing programs or consumer profiles by chaining, once they have significant market share.

Classifications

11.248 COICOP, as well as other national classification systems, is not constructed with a stratification structure that is sufficiently detailed to reflect the various tariffs for those products that are subject to such pricing practices. For example, electricity under the COICOP hierarchy appears as a subclass (five-digit COICOP) in its own right (COICOP 2018 04.5.1.0) and according to its description includes associated expenditure such as hire of meters, reading of meters, or standing charges. A finer breakdown is not given in COICOP. However, when sellers of a product, such as electricity, use tariff pricing, the accuracy of the CPI can be improved if the price index for this product is constructed in a way that reflects as accurately as possible the market realities. In other words, a subclass-level price index should be composed of a number of subindices, each one corresponding to its particular tariff price. This may require the use of a specially designed classification for the purpose of stratification within an elementary aggregate.

Telecommunications

Introduction

11.249 Telecommunications services represent a specific case of tariff pricing (detailed information on tariffs is available in paragraphs 11.211–11.248), but the tariffs tend to be less transparent, more complex, and dynamic with frequent updates of the tariff structures and prices.

11.250 The global telecommunications sector is subject to rapid change. Technological innovation has led to a proliferation of new services that has resulted in suppliers adopting a range of new strategies to differentiate their services to attract and retain customers. In this context, characteristics of significance to CPI compilers include:

- Fewer linear pricing schedules and the adoption of different pricing structures across providers
- The increasing tendency to offer contracts that bundle services in different ways to appeal to different types of consumers
- Rapid changes in the contracts offered to consumers as an effective means of encouraging the take-up of the ever-increasing range of services

11.251 Increasingly, telecommunication companies offer services via plans that require customers to enter into longer-term contractual arrangements with the providers. Two broad types of plans are typically offered. The first type of plan has no fixed duration and makes allowance for the provider to change pricing structures with advance notice to the consumer. The second type of plan, increasingly more popular, provides a fixed-term contract (generally of one to two years) with prices fixed for the duration of the contract, and with scope for annual updates by an agreed-upon measure of inflation that should be accounted for in the price index. The type of contract can influence the approach to measurement. For instance, experience suggests that a consumer profile approach can work best for computing a price index for customers on a prepaid tariff subject to the relevant information being available, otherwise an alternative could be a matched sample. Similarly, where customers are on a fixed-term contract, other approaches may be adopted. One method selects for pricing the appropriate package from each service provider and assumes a rational consumer who has perfect market information and uses this to purchase an appropriate package at the lowest price. Each user profile is assumed to switch freely between packages, picking up the cheapest available each month but constrained by the reality that customers are generally unable to move service providers without financial penalty. Thus, assuming an annual contract, each month only a twelfth of customers can move service provider. In some cases, moving to a different tariff offered by the same service provider prior to the end of the contract also is subject to a penalty.[28] It is often desirable to compute separate indices for the different types of tariffs and combine these using sales weights.

11.252 If NSOs follow traditional sampling approaches for fixed-term contracts and select price schedules according to some price reference period set of plans, and follow them until they expire, no price changes will be observed (likewise if plans expire and replacements are linked to show no change). The marketplace reality, by contrast, is that average prices for telecommunication services have declined significantly in many countries in recent years. Thus, perhaps the biggest challenge is the quality adjustment when there is a change of service provider. For instance, where one service provider is more reliable than another. This is generally ignored as being unmeasurable.

11.253 The lack of a harmonized method across NSOs demonstrates the complexities of this sector. It is recognized that current best practice approaches have difficulty in accounting for substitutions across providers and in adequately accounting for changes in the quality of the services provided.

11.254 With the telecommunications sector under continuous change, statistical practices should be constantly reviewed. NSOs that are considering the construction of

[28] For more information, see Adrian Ball and David Fenwick. 2004. "Costing Mobile Telephone Calls: The Use of Constrained User Profiles." Paper presented at the Eighth Meeting of the International Working Group on Price Indices, Ottawa Group, Helsinki, August 23–25.

telecommunications indices for the first time, or are reviewing their current practices, are advised to seek out the most recent research in this field. Notwithstanding, this chapter seeks to provide a general description of four approaches that are currently used by NSOs to measure changes in the prices of telecommunication services. The approaches are the following:

- Matched samples
- Unit values
- Customer profiles
- Sample of bills

11.255 The choice of approach will depend largely on the market conditions prevailing in individual countries, the sophistication of the index compilation system in use, and the extent of access to accurate and timely telecommunication services data. Depending on these factors, it may be appropriate to use different approaches for different telecommunication services, or even for the different services of specific providers.

Matched Samples—Representative Items

11.256 Matched samples are used when a full tariff list or an element of the tariff structure is treated as a product specification and repriced in subsequent periods. The use of matched samples mirrors traditional techniques adopted elsewhere in the CPI. The total expenditure of reference group households on telecommunication services in the weight reference period is derived from sources such as HBSs. A sample of service providers is contacted to obtain information on revenue by types of services (for example, line rental, local calls, international calls, handset sales or rentals, connection fees, voicemail services, or internet charges) and a number of these are selected as representative items of the different tariff elements, or all are taken, with weights derived from the revenue data.

Table 11.10 An Illustrative Index Structure for Telecommunication Services (representative item approach)

Fixed-Line Services		
	Telephone Connection Costs	
	Telephone Line Rental	
	Local Calls	
		Peak
		Off-Peak
	Long-Distance National Calls	
		Peak
		Off-Peak
	International Calls	
		Peak
		Off-Peak
Mobile Telephones		
	Connection Costs	
	Handset Purchase or Rental	
	National Calls	
	International Calls	
Payphones		
	Local Calls	
Internet Services		
	Connection Fees	
	Usage Fees	

Note: Peak and off-peak are defined times. For example, peak may be between 9 a.m. and 6 p.m. on weekdays and off-peak any other time.

11.257 For each representative item, detailed specifications (for example, a telephone call from location A to location B, at time X, of duration Y minutes) are developed to sufficiently represent the range of specific services purchased by consumers within each representative item or tariff element. This specification is held constant from period to period, and movements in the indices for representative items are computed, based on the movements in the prices of this matched sample. Table 11.10 illustrates this approach. The detailed application will depend on the tariff structure. For instance, in some countries, there will be a regional dimension.

11.258 The list of representative items (that is, the lowest level in the structure) should be sufficient to be representative of price behavior as a whole, taking account of the published tariffs. As with other parts of the CPI basket, expenditure on those services not selected for pricing should be distributed over the other services within that general class for deriving weights. For example, the expenditure on any fixed- or landline services not selected for pricing should be distributed over those fixed-line services selected.

11.259 Compared to suppliers of goods, service providers have a great capacity to tailor both the services and the prices they charge, for example, based on the time at which the service is provided. A five-minute telephone call at 9 a.m. can be regarded as a different product from an equivalent call made at 9 p.m., and service providers are able to charge different prices for these calls. Representative items therefore need to be described in enough detail to capture all the price-determining characteristics.

11.260 Given the ease with which providers can adjust the differential aspects of their pricing schedules (for example, the time span designated as peak and the duration of a call before a different rate applies), it is necessary to use a sufficient number of varied specifications to capture these aspects reliably. It is not enough to simply describe a call as peak or off-peak, or from zone 1 to zone 2 without defining the call in more detail. Examples of the types of specifications that may be applicable for two representative items—international calls (fixed line) and usage fees (internet services)—are provided in Table 11.11.

Table 11.11 Examples of Specifications of Telecommunication Services

Representative Item	**Examples of Specifications**
International Calls (fixed line)	**Peak: Plan A:** Call to Athens at 8 a.m. on a Friday, Duration 10 Minutes
	Off-peak: Plan B: Call to London at 9 p.m. on a Saturday, Duration 5 Minutes
	Peak: Plan A: Call to New York at 11 a.m. on a Wednesday, Duration 20 Minutes
	Off-Peak: Plan B: Call to Paris at 7 p.m. on a Sunday, Duration 15 Minutes
Usage Fees (internet)	**Plan A:** Broadband Connection, Unlimited Downloads, Speed 38 Mb
	Plan B: Fiber Broadband, Unlimited Downloads, Speed 300 Mb
	Plan C: Mobile Broadband, 24-Month Contract, 32 GB per Month

Note: Peak and off-peak are defined times. For example, peak may be between the hours of 9 a.m. and 6 p.m. on weekdays and off-peak any other time.

GB, Gigabyte.

11.261 In Table 11.11, it is assumed that the origin of both the telephone calls and internet access is also identified. All minutes consumed are domestic. It should also be noted that the nature of internet access generally precludes pricing on the basis of access, and hence the timing of access cannot be as tightly defined as for international telephone calls: instead, all specifications are for total monthly usage.

11.262 The most challenging aspect of the matched samples approach is obtaining the data needed to establish the representative items and to identify suitable specifications, as this will require detailed information from service providers. Once implemented, most price information should be readily available from published fee schedules, minimizing the burden on respondents between reviews of the specifications. However, much reliance will be placed on the service provider to supply the corresponding expenditure information.

11.263 The dynamic nature of the telecommunication sector and the common use of the pricing mechanism to change consumer behavior are likely to require that the specifications be updated frequently. A major practical challenge associated with the matched samples approach is ensuring that exactly the same product specification is priced each month and that the matched samples methodology is adhered to. When a variety disappears (that is, a specific plan is no longer offered), all efforts must be made to find a suitable comparison variety. Where varieties are replaced, it is possible to argue that, because different plans involve different conditions of sale, they are fundamentally different products. It is equally reasonable to question whether the entire price difference between plans is because of quality differences, particularly in light of the evidence of ever-increasing volumes and reductions in unit values. The difficulty lies in quantifying the quality differences.

Unit Values—Representative Items

11.264 The unit value approach is used when the overall price or, more precisely, the revenue generated by one unit (for example, a long-distance telephone call for customers of a specific supplier) is used to monitor prices. Unlike the matched samples approach, individual specifications are not priced. The unit value approach can be applied instead of the matched samples approach when the quality of the service is homogeneous between providers with the advantage that it is less resource-intensive. The indicative price for each representative item is calculated from revenue and quantity data collected from the service provider. For example, the price for national long-distance calls can be derived as the total revenue received from such calls divided by the number of call minutes. Similarly, in the case of monthly line rental fees, the price can be calculated as the total revenue from line rental divided by the total number of subscribers.

11.265 Compared to the matched samples approach, the unit value approach attributes all the difference between plans, and time and duration of calls to price (that is, the quality difference is assumed to be zero). The unit value approach is also seen as providing a method for accounting for price change when the items are subject to a proliferation of discount programs or promotions (for example, $2 to call anywhere for any duration for the next week). While the approach avoids some of the customer sampling choices inherent in some other methodologies, the compilation does rest on analysis of aggregate company data and so is likely to be less timely than methodologies based on prepublished prices. However, care needs to be exercised to ensure that the measure is not affected by undesirable compositional changes. A unit value index should only be constructed for truly homogeneous items. This points to a requirement for defining the representative items at a relatively fine level of disaggregation. For example, international calls may need to be further subdivided by destination to avoid changes in unit values arising purely from shifts in the numbers of calls made to different destinations. Thus, unit values need to be calculated at a sufficient level of detail to minimize the effect of changes in customer usage being reflected in the index.

11.266 Although the unit value approach appears to address at least some of the known deficiencies of the matched sample approach, it is likely to exhibit period-to-period volatility because of compositional shifts, for example, because of seasonal variations in usage patterns. There are also several respondent and data quality aspects that need to be considered. The unit value approach imposes a greater data burden on service providers, who often regard revenue and quantity data as highly sensitive. To be effective, the service providers also need to be able to furnish data relating only to households (that is, they should be able to separate out revenue and quantities relating to businesses) and the revenue information needs to conform to the requirements of the index. For example, some service providers may record certain discounts as a marketing expense, rather than a reduction in revenue as is required for the unit value index.

Customer Profiles

11.267 For marketing purposes, telecommunication companies often classify their customers according to their volume of service use. Although the number of categories can vary, a common approach is to use a three-way classification: low-volume, medium-volume, and high-volume customers. Service providers analyze customer usage patterns by category when developing new plans targeted specifically at each group. National regulatory authorities may also be able to provide detailed customer use profiles on a confidential basis.

11.268 NSOs can take a similar approach to the telecommunications companies for the construction of price indices by devising profiles that reflect the average usage patterns for each category of consumer. Costs faced by these average consumers in each period can then be estimated by reference to the rates set out in the plan that is currently most commonly applicable to each customer category. Variations on this general theme include estimation of costs based on the plan that would deliver the cheapest overall cost, individually, to each of the representative consumer profiles (based on the simplifying assumption of cost-minimizing consumer behavior with perfect knowledge). This has the advantage of providing a clear basis for choosing a comparable replacement if an existing package ceases to be available. Alternatively, costs to each customer group may be estimated with reference to several plans, where sales information indicates that this is a closer approximation to reality. The overall index is derived by weighting together

Table 11.12 Example of a User Profile for Mobile Phone Services

Specification	Unit	Low Usage Customer	Medium Usage Customer	High Usage Customer
Total Usage (per billing period) Excluding Text Messages	Minutes	14	24	59
Calls				
Within Same Mobile Network				
Peak	Number*	5 (35)	10 (35)	15 (40)
Off-Peak	Number*	10 (55)	10 (65)	20 (80)
To Different Mobile Network				
Peak	Number*	0 (0)	5 (20)	15 (25)
Off-Peak	Number*	5 (20)	10 (30)	20 (40)
To Landline				
Peak	Number*	0 (0)	0 (0)	5 (20)
Off-Peak	Number*	5 (3)	5 (8)	5 (13)
Other Services				
Text Messages	Number*	5 (20)	10 (25)	30 (35)

*In brackets, average call length in seconds.

the results from these user profiles according to information about the relative importance of each category of consumer.

11.269 In constructing the aggregate index, these calculations are likely to be made for a representative sample of service providers, using the information on their overall market share for sampling or weighting purposes, if available. Information on the distribution of customer profiles by service provider may not be available or at least may be very costly to obtain. Table 11.12 gives an example of a profile for mobile telephone calls. This approach can be extended to include internet usage.

11.270 Consistent with the fixed-basket approach, the activity of consumers (with regard to numbers and types of calls, numbers of texts, and amount of internet data used) is held constant between comparison periods. Prices may change when not fixed by contract or when plans are replaced. CPI compilers may also allow tariffs to change in response to a changing mix of plans within customer categories. This approach assumes that tariff changes fundamentally represent price change rather than quality change, but eliminates the cruder compositional effects associated with the unit value approach that does not take account of customer profiles.

11.271 The success in the use of the unit value approach is determined by the degree to which the profiles truly reflect consumer behavior and therefore a great effort needs to be put into their development. The construction of the customer profiles will require a high degree of cooperation from service providers or regulators and, given the known volume changes, they will require updating at regular intervals, possibly more frequently than other items in the CPI basket. Data on plan usage by customer category for each index compilation period (a month or quarter) may also be required if compilers decide to allow for such effects.

Sample of Bills

11.272 This method is a more refined application of the customer profile approach. A fixed level of service activity from an actual sample of customers is priced each month rather than defining profiles representative of the average monthly activities of customers. A sample of customers should be selected from each category of customer (that is, low-, medium-, and high-volume customers) and, ideally, the bills (or activity statements) should cover a full year's activity.

11.273 The perceived advantages of this approach compared to the customer profile approach are the following:

- It is able to take account of any within-year variations in customer behavior (for example, a higher incidence of international calls associated with religious or cultural events of significance). But it can be argued that this contravenes the principle of the fixed basket.
- It better reflects the diversity of consumer behavior by identifying actual activities (that is, calls actually made by a sample of consumers) and potentially captures out of contract activity charges (for example, exceeding allowances).
- It accommodates within each bill any instances of annual charges.
- It allows for the detection and recording of other sources of price change associated with customers' overall relationship with the service provider (for example, where overall discounts are provided when aggregate monthly spending exceeds certain values, or where an aggregate discount is provided if customers acquire bundles of services from a single provider, such as landline phone plus internet).

11.274 Calculation of the index still requires monthly information on the relative significance of various plans by customer category. With the sample of bills repriced each period, the resulting index measures the cost of a full year's consumption at the prices prevailing in each index period compared to the same cost at base prices. This assumes that the quality difference between old and new plans is zero for households changing plans. Because of the generally larger number of bills (compared with the number of available profiles), price changes can be reflected more gradually, as the proportion of bills priced using each plan can better mirror the changing population distribution.

11.275 As with the consumer profiles approach, it is important that the sample of bills is updated regularly to reflect changes in consumption patterns and the take-up of new services such as call-waiting, voicemail, and text messaging. Although, with adequate sampling, the sample of bill approach is likely to provide a better measure of the aggregate rate of price change for telecommunication services as a whole, it may not be best suited to the calculation of separate indices for the components of those services (depending on whether overall or bottom-line discounts are offered). The approach is also data-intensive, requiring many calculations each period and thus a relatively advanced data processing system capable of handling and manipulating large amounts of data. It can also suffer from a lack of timeliness.

Transport Services

Introduction

11.276 Transport services cover a wide range of modes of transport from airplanes, trains, buses and ferries, taxis and motorbike taxis, to private cars. The example given in paragraph 11.282 focuses on air travel.

11.277 Transport, as defined by COICOP 2018 Division 07 covers the purchase of vehicles (COICOP 2018 7.1), the operation of personal transport equipment (COICOP 2018 7.2), passenger transport services (COICOP 2018 7.3), and transport services of goods (COICOP 2018 7.4).

11.278 The current chapter does not cover the purchase of vehicles or the operation of personal transport equipment (COICOP 2018 7.1 and 7.2), rather it relates to transport services provided by and purchased from third parties as defined by COICOP 2018 7.3 and 7.4. The latter includes bus and train fares, taxi fares, and the purchase of air and ferry tickets.

11.279 There are common elements between this section and the one on tariffs. Most particularly, the section on tariffs uses examples of tariffs relating to public buses to illustrate the application of the matched samples and unit value approaches.

11.280 Some public transport services may be paid for in full or in part by government or NPISH and are provided free or at a nominal price to households, and are considered social transfers in kind in the SNA. The standard convention is that the price entering the CPI should be the subsidized price.

Public Transportation

11.281 Elementary aggregates should distinguish between different modes of transport as reflected in the structure of COICOP (purchases of transport services are generally classified by mode of transport in COICOP). The computation of prices should reflect the different tickets available for purchase from different channels. In the case of airlines, different prices may apply to online bookings compared with bookings made through an agent, and to advanced nonrefundable purchases compared with, for example, a fully flexible fare purchased close to or on the day of travel.

11.282 Let P be the total cost of providing a trip from A to B and let Q be the number of trips carried by the transport system from A to B during the period under consideration. Suppose the household sector pays only sP of this price and the quantity is Q. Obtaining the prices for inclusion in the elementary aggregate normally requires a method of sampling that takes account of complex fare structures.

11.283 The index for airline and other public transport services should use the prices of a sample of specific trips rather than revenue per kilometer or per passenger-kilometer. If the CPI has strata for different geographic locations that are typical in large countries, points of origin (for example, airports, train stations, or motor coach stops) should be chosen in each location, and trips selected within origins or destinations in those locations. There are generally multiple classes of service. In addition, transport fares may vary by day of the week, time of day, time of year in response to variations in demand, and how long in advance the ticket is purchased. The selected trips should reflect this variety but hold these variables constant.

11.284 For airfares, the sample should be stratified by domestic, short-haul, and long-haul flights as scheduling and service providers between these categories can vary widely.

11.285 Once chosen in the price reference period, the route, the departure and arrival times, and the ticket type and class of travel should remain the same throughout the year. While some flexibility should be allowed to accommodate changing schedules for specific routes, if specifications diverge too much from the price reference period, the replacement ticket should be considered noncomparable and a new base price imputed based on the movement of prices for routes in the same category. This is the standard form of implicit quality adjustment.

11.286 For sample selection of routes and providers and for weighting between routes and travel subcategories (for example, long-haul or domestic), expenditure data from appropriate surveys or administrative sources should be used. Where this is unavailable, passenger numbers and average prices can be used to calculate expenditure data. Note that the coverage of routes depends on whether the CPI covers the national or domestic concept (as defined in Chapter 2) and, if purchased online, the location of the transaction and service delivery. For instance, if a ticket is purchased online from a foreign carrier it can be argued that the purchase should be attributed to the country where the consumption first commences. This is because the consumer needs to be present at the location of the service provider for consumption to commence, and the place of consumption normally determines where the sales tax, such as VAT, is actually paid. If this reasoning is followed, then such transactions for the booking of flights totally outside the country of residence will be excluded from a CPI following the domestic concept. Paragraphs 11.65–11.71 discuss the treatment of internet purchases and the domestic concept.

11.287 Providers of transport services often practice some form of price discrimination so that different groups of travelers will be charged with different fares or prices for essentially the same service. Examples include special discount fares for students or retired people, or trips booked for weekend departure or return, and a 30-day advance booking. Since these can change frequently, CPIs usually ignore minor changes in the requirements for a discount fare.

11.288 The recommended approach to differential and complex fare structures that is most likely to ensure like-for-like comparisons is to price the cost of a journey on a specific day of the month (for example, the fourth Tuesday) between two points, pricing a ticket for transportation purchased at a fixed time in advance, and with fixed terms and conditions. This should be done for various fare classes, for example, a full economy fare (if purchased in significant quantities for personal travel) and a typical discounted economy fare that may include travel restrictions such as for a stated date and time and not being refundable. Prices can be downloaded by staff at the head office from reservation systems available on the internet, although sometimes the full cost is not shown without going through the procedures for purchase.

11.289 When selecting the sample, the NSO should also consider how far in advance of the date of travel a ticket price is collected. In airfares, for example, ticket prices can increase the closer the booking is made to the departure time, because the number of available seats for a specific route becomes limited. However, in other cases, there can be last-minute discounts to fill empty seats. Further stratification of the sample should be considered to account for this, for example, by collecting prices for the same departure time and date but collecting separate prices for booking the ticket so many months, weeks, or days in advance, depending on the nature of transport service being priced. Taking airfares as an example, once the routes, ticket types, and departure date have been selected, price collection for this sample could be repeated six, three, and one month in advance to capture the changing price as the departure date approaches.

11.290 Changes in transport schedules can cause price changes. For example, an airline might cancel its noon flight, forcing passengers to take the evening flight that is priced higher because that is a time of peak demand, unless a competitor airline can be found that offers a noon flight. If the CPI was following the price of the noon flight, it must now price the evening flight if the customer has no choice but to use it, or price a noon flight available from an alternative comparable airline if available. The replacement journey should be treated as comparable and the full price change should be reflected in the index if it is assumed that there has been no change in the quality of the service being provided. But the latter might be a strong assumption, for instance, if an evening flight is inconvenient because it means traveling the day before and staying in a hotel to attend a morning appointment the following day. In the latter case, the noon flight might best be treated as a missing item or the evening flight selected as a noncomparable replacement and a new base price calculated for it.

11.291 Data challenges can be encountered when selecting representative items, estimating weights, and pricing selected flights especially with the emergence of online booking. In the case of air transport, the main data sources alternative to HBS for both sampling and weights estimation are airports, the airlines, national civil aviation authorities that often collect detailed data covering the entire country, or market research companies and trade organizations that collect data. The data most likely to be available for the sampling of flights will generally relate to the total number of passenger flights taken and is likely to include business travelers. Nonetheless, such data will be better than using a subjective approach and assumptions can be made, such as assuming that all business and first-class bookings are for business purposes. Normally, expenditure data on last-minute deals can be gathered either through the HBS or, more likely, through an ad hoc survey of travel service providers, if not available from other sources.

11.292 Transport ticket prices should feed into the index at the time of travel, not at the time they were booked. For example, a ticket price for a December flight should feed into the December index even if the price relates to a purchase in the previous October.

Health, Education, and Social Protection Services

Introduction

11.293 Health, education, and social protection cover a wide range of services. Transactions that involve an expenditure by a household in the health, education, and social protection services fields are in scope and should be covered by the CPI if it is to be consistent with the SNA concept of household final consumption expenditure. In many countries, various government units or NPISH[29] will finance and pay for the full or partial provision of a significant proportion of goods and services in the health, education, and social protection sectors.

11.294 The preferred approach regarding the treatment of health, education, and social protection services in the CPI is as follows:

- Only expenditure by households that is a direct result of purchase of individual goods or services is within the scope of CPI. These prices should be net of direct reimbursements. Reimbursements refer to payments to households by government units, social security administrations, or NPISHs that are made as direct consequences of purchases of individually specified goods and services, initially paid for by households.
- Mandatory payments are excluded from the scope of the index (for example, employee's contributions to social security programs). These are collected to finance social security programs and these payments do not directly relate to the provision of goods or services. Reimbursements that do not directly relate to goods or services are also not in the scope of the CPI.

11.295 It should be noted that, in compiling a CPI, a number of situations may be encountered. For example, with childcare systems where the government partially subsidizes the full cost of providing the service, it is the net (or purchaser) price paid by the household that is covered by the CPI and should be included under the proper elementary aggregate (or elementary product group) entry in the classification system. This is regardless of whether the childcare service is privately or publicly run. But if these services are provided by the households themselves, they are regarded as own production and not included in the SNA production boundary, as no monetary transaction is involved even though the government might give the household money in the form of a social security payment. This approach is consistent with the conceptual basis of the national accounts.

11.296 Goods and services acquired by households and that the government or NPISH provide a social benefit either through a full or partial reimbursement should be measured net of direct reimbursements. For example, individuals who are part of a particular socioeconomic group may be eligible for a full or partial refund for dental care: if the refund covers the full cost of the dental service, then the expenditure weight would be zero and no prices would need to be monitored for the purpose of the CPI.

11.297 Where individual goods and services are provided at no charge to individual households by governments or NPISH, these transfers are regarded as social transfers in kind and costs are included in government or NPISH

[29]NPISH make up an institutional sector in the context of national accounts consisting of nonprofit institutions which are not mainly financed and controlled by government and which provide goods or services to households for free or at prices that are not economically significant (*2008 SNA*, paragraph 4.93). NPISH are private, nonmarket producers which are separate legal entities. Their main resources, apart from those derived from occasional sales, are derived from voluntary contributions in cash or in kind from households in their capacity as consumers, from payments made by general governments, and from property income.

expenditure.[30] Examples include food stamps, social benefits to households prescription drugs, and job training programs. These social transfers in kind can contribute substantially to the standard of living of the individual households that receive them.

11.298 Depending on national circumstances, it could be that the public authorities have decided to partly or fully finance the provision of certain goods and services. Regardless of the practice, those expenditures incurred by government or NPISH to finance social transfers in kind are outside the scope of a CPI (although it can be argued that it is desirable to take them into account when estimating a comprehensive COLI extending beyond purchases by the household sector). However, when the consumer pays part of the cost associated with the provision of such goods and services, this element is within the scope of the CPI: although there is a social transfer, this expenditure may account for a large part of a household's final consumption expenditure. For example, take a rental unit for which the monthly cost of providing the rental service is $800 and where, after the government transfer, the actual rent paid by the tenant is $500. While the $300 transfer is excluded from the scope of the CPI, the rent of $500 paid by the tenant is a legitimate consumption expenditure that should be included in the CPI.

11.299 Users' expenditure on all relevant goods and services should be included in the CPI to properly reflect changes in prices and to support the addition of related services in cases where governments and NPISH introduce charges for services that were previously provided at no charge, or vice versa.

11.300 In practice, there are many possible combinations of payment and reimbursement systems and there can be a complex mix of publicly financed social security programs, employee or worker financed social security programs, and social security programs financed by households. The CPI compiler should investigate such programs in sufficient depth to facilitate a well-informed decision on their treatment in the CPI. Thus, the nature of the health, education, and social protection sectors is a challenge for price index compilation. The index methodologies used by the NSO need to be built around the national circumstances.

11.301 The procedures used in the treatment of tariffs, as described in paragraphs 11.211–11.248, are often applicable for pricing programs encountered in health, education, and social protection services.

11.302 Detailed in-depth research will be needed to identify and measure newly introduced significant charges. Additionally, some of the goods and services included in health, education, and social protection are difficult to measure at constant quality. The social security systems can also cause complications. The CPI compiler is advised to keep in close contact with data users to obtain the information that is necessary to make informed decisions about which charges should be included in the index and how they should be measured, and to gain access to relevant sources of data and advanced notice of any changes.

[30] Social transfers in kind consist of individual goods and services provided to individual households by government units (including social security funds) and NPISHs (*2008 SNA*, paragraph 8.141), whether purchased on the market or produced as nonmarket output by government units or NPISHs.

Health Services (Doctors and Dentists)

11.303 The treatment of health services in the compilation of individual countries' CPIs will depend on the institutional arrangements for providing them. Government-provided free medical care is out of scope, but many countries adhere to some form of two-tier health care system whereby some health care services are provided, often for a fee, by a private system that coexists with the public system or where medical services are financed partially by the government but the consumer pays part. In both cases, fees paid by the users are in scope. Employer-provided medical care is beyond the scope of the CPI, because a monetary transaction does not take place and it is treated in the national accounts as remuneration in kind.

11.304 Although health is a broad term, for the construction of an elementary aggregate in a CPI, it generally refers to medical care provided by medical professionals, para-professionals, or medical institutions. COICOP divides the health care sector into classes according to the type of medical care provider (for example, doctors or hospitals). This facilitates sampling, price collection, and index construction.

11.305 The weights are the amounts consumers spend on each type of provider. In countries where the government provides a substantial portion of medical care free of charge, the relative importance of medical care in the CPI is less than its total expenditure share (by households, government, and NPISH), as measured by the national accounts.

11.306 The COICOP categories are based on purpose. Some critics state a preference for categorizing according to types of medical condition and are of the view that the CPI should measure the cost of treating a disease or of obtaining a fixed outcome after treatment rather than the medical service or treatment that, in their terms, is an input. But it should be noted that this medical condition approach, which would define elementary aggregates for categories of medical conditions, is not sufficiently developed to be recommended at this time.

Sampling

11.307 The general CPI approach is to select samples of providers within each COICOP category (for example, doctors in Medical Services, or dentists in Dental Services), and then choose one or more representative service items for each sampled provider. The principle of using loose specification when sampling and tight specification when pricing is followed. When first visiting a doctor or other medical provider, the price collector should find what services are provided or what medical procedures are performed and select a representative sample with guidance from the provider. The price collector should describe them as completely as possible, and then continue pricing them for as long as possible or until they are no longer part of the sample that constitutes the CPI basket. One approach to the initial sample selection of services or medical procedures is for the price collector to ask the medical practitioner or dentist what was provided recently to a typical patient with a representative medical condition or to ask the respondent to describe a simple service they recently performed. When returning to obtain prices in the following periods, the price collector should collect the price for that identical service, even if the doctor or dentist has

Figure 11.2 Loose Specification Sampling and Tight Specification Pricing

Sampling	Collection	Replacement
Agree Service to be Priced with Medical Practitioner (for example, prosthetic replacement of hip joint)	Collect Price of That Exact Service Across Months	Identify Replacement Procedure If Original Service No Longer Provided (for example, prosthetic replacement of knee joint)

not performed it recently. However, if the respondent has not performed it, for example, for a year or indicates they will no longer perform that particular procedure, the price collector should find a replacement procedure, preferably for the same medical purpose. The head office should then decide if it can be treated as a comparable item (see Figure 11.2). There is less need to price many types of medical services from the same doctor, when it is known that price movements among various medical services move closely together.

Pricing

11.308 There are two approaches to pricing that align with the view taken on whether an input or medical condition approach is followed. The traditional input approach treats medical items as consumption items, without regard to their effectiveness in preventing, curing, or ameliorating an illness or injury. The approach prices a selection of medical items, such as an annual check-up by a doctor or a particular surgical procedure, such as an operation in a hospital or clinic, and follows the cost over time.

11.309 The alternative approach, the treatment approach, is a partial response to increasing criticism that the input approach ignores medical advances and does not consider that the patient generally looks to buy a cure to a medical condition rather than a specific course of treatment. Under the treatment approach, the CPI compiler or price collector first selects a specific medical condition by selecting a disease or injury that a patient recently received treatment and then follows the price of treating that condition regardless of medical procedures or medicines used. For example, if treating the disease or injury initially requires five visits to the doctor, the CPI price is the cost of five visits. However, if subsequently the doctor reports a new way of treating the condition that requires only two visits, then from that point the cost of two visits is included in the CPI.

11.310 Only expenditure by households that is a direct result of purchase of individual goods or services is within the scope of CPI. It follows that the prices entering the index should be net of direct reimbursements. Mandatory payments, such as employees' contributions to social security programs, are out of the scope of a CPI. These are collected to finance social security programs and do not directly relate to the provision of goods or services. Reimbursements made where the recipient can spend the amount received on something unrelated to the treatment that is the subject of the reimbursement are also excluded.

11.311 Both approaches, the input and the treatment approach, may involve quality adjusting the prices where a change of treatment or course of medication results in a change in outcome. For instance, if in the previous example the reduction to two visits to the doctor is associated with a shorter course of treatment and with the patient being in less pain and suffering fewer adverse side effects, then the quality-adjusted price should see a steeper price reduction because of the better treatment. As quantifying this change in quality is generally not straightforward, implicit methods of quality adjustment are usually applied.

Coverage of Medical Insurance

11.312 The existence of medical insurance adds complexity to the situation and there is a lack of consensus regarding measurement in a CPI. Some consumers buy medical care directly from medical care providers, while others buy medical insurance that pays for some or all their medical care. It is useful to review exactly what kind of product the consumer is purchasing. Medical insurance may be considered a way of prepaying for likely future medical expenses, a way of reducing the risk of catastrophic expenses (that is, giving peace of mind), and a way of reducing the total expected cost of medical care because insurance companies have market power in determining prices that individual consumers lack. The view taken about what is being purchased, which may be a mix of the previous ones, has implications for measurement. For example, the use of net premiums for weights fits better, conceptually, with insurance being purchased for peace of mind.

11.313 In many countries, the government provides health insurance either for free or through compulsory or voluntary contributions. This is generally out of scope for the CPI regardless of how the government funds it and is excluded from the CPI weights and pricing samples. Compulsory or voluntary contributions to public health insurance are not covered in household final consumption expenditure as these are categorized as social contributions and treated as transfers. Health care that is covered by private insurance (or not covered by any health insurance at all) is part of the coverage of a CPI. Only the cost of insurance paid directly by the consumer is in the scope of the CPI.

11.314 In constructing expenditure weights, care should be taken to avoid the double counting of expenditure. Consumers may pay insurance premiums and then either pay the costs (that is, the medical bills) that the insurance company reimburses in full or partially, or the insurance company directly reimburses the providers (for example, the doctor or the hospital).

11.315 In the paragraphs on property insurance services (11.385–11.404) three alternative treatments of insurance are identified that can similarly be applied to health insurance:

- Gross insurance premiums/net (medical) expenditure
- Net insurance premiums/gross (medical) expenditure
- Gross insurance premiums/gross expenditure

11.316 If applied to health insurance, the first alternative (that is, gross insurance premiums/net [medical] expenditure) results in a relatively large weight for medical insurance and small weights for medical care categories. The second alternative (that is, net insurance premiums/gross [medical] expenditure) reverses this. The third alternative (that is, gross premiums/gross expenditure) double counts consumer expenditure and should not be used.

11.317 The gross premiums method is not recommended for CPI compilation, but is supported by some economists. Under this method, there is an elementary aggregate for health insurance with a weight that is based on consumers' total expenditure on health insurance premiums during the reference period. The expenditure weights of the other medical care elementary aggregates (for example, for doctors or hospitals) must be reduced by the amount of insurance payments consumers received in the same period. These elementary aggregates represent what consumers pay directly for medical care. The total expenditure weight is the same regardless of whether the insurer reimburses the provider or if the consumer pays the provider and is later reimbursed. The CPI prices for these elementary aggregates are what providers receive from consumers, not from insurance companies. It can be argued that, compared with the net premium approach, the use of gross premiums is more consistent with the concept of prepaying for likely future medical expenses and is therefore better able to cope with a situation where some consumers purchase medical services directly and others purchase the same medical services through an insurance company.

11.318 The main difficulty with the gross premiums method is constructing a price relative for gross premiums, which ideally would be a measure of the change in the premiums of a sample of constant-quality insurance policies. However, in practice, insurance companies change the detail of their policies from year to year, with new rules and requirements and changes in what they cover; some of this is in response to the appearance of new medical techniques. It is extremely difficult to track and adjust for these changes, but without doing so a premium index is likely to be biased upward.

11.319 For the reason stated previously, the "net" premiums method is the most common approach implemented in a CPI. In this case, the CPI weight of the insurance elementary aggregate is gross premiums paid minus reimbursements paid out by insurers. The CPI weight comprises the insurance companies' operating expenses and their profit, which will be much smaller than the gross turnover. The net approach distributes part of the expenditure for health insurance premiums that consumers report in the HBS to the other medical care elementary aggregates such as doctors, dentists, or pharmaceutical products. This is usually done using insurance industry data on the insurance companies' income received from premiums and the companies' payments to doctors, hospitals, clinics, drug stores, and any other providers. To do this, the CPI compiler computes the share of payments to each type of provider and allocates medical insurance premiums to other medical care elementary aggregates in proportion to these shares. Health insurance companies retain a small portion of the premiums not paid out as benefits to cover overheads and profits. The CPI can treat this as a separate elementary aggregate for health insurance to purchase "peace of mind" or just allocate it to the medical care categories using the same proportions. Many consider this option to be conceptually more appropriate. Table 11.13 provides an example for the calculation of weights.

11.320 The CPI price movement over time can be the same as in the direct approach. Under the assumption that there is proper control for changes in quality of insurance plans and average utilization and patient risk are kept constant over a long period, the change in the premiums of a sample of insurance policies can be used as a proxy for a measure of the change in the insurance companies' overheads and profit per capita (that is, the change in the cost of providing the insurance service).

11.321 The price relative for the net insurance premiums aggregate can be developed in the same way as under the gross premiums method, using a sample of insurance policies. The problem of holding the policies constant over time remains, but this is less troublesome because the weight is much smaller. Alternatively, a measure of the change in the insurance companies' net earnings (premiums less payouts) can be used. This may be volatile and net earnings could be negative in some years, and so NSOs using this approach often take an average figure over several years. In addition, such a measure requires data that insurance companies may be reluctant to make available and it takes no account of any change in the volume of insurance services provided. For example, earnings may rise because the insurance companies are taking new business and not because either individual gross or net premiums are rising.

Weights

11.322 In the first row of Table 11.13, the HBS reports that consumers spent on average (from their own pockets—government-provided benefits are not in scope) a total of $1,800 on medical care, which includes $1,000 on insurance and the rest on direct payments to medical providers. Under a gross premium approach, these are the weights for insurance and medical care categories, which is standard CPI weights: expenditure reported in the HBS of what consumers paid directly.

11.323 To obtain weights for a "net premiums" approach more data are required. The second row of Table 11.13 presents the insurance industry's spending on medical care: the insurance companies spent $900 in benefits and retained $100 to cover their costs and their profits. Using this industry data to construct CPI weights yields a small aggregate for net insurance premiums, as shown in the third row.

Education

11.324 The scope of the CPI is limited to payments actually made by consumers. Consequently, fully publicly funded education is out of the scope of the CPI. However, there can be some minor ancillary fees for materials or services, such as pens and paper, and sports activities that students must pay for, and these should be included in the index. Out-of-pocket educational expenses for tuition and

Table 11.13 CPI Weights: Medical Insurance and Medical Care Elementary Aggregates

	Total	Health Insurance Premiums	Hospitals	Doctors	Drugs
HBS Data	**1,800**	1,000	300	300	200
Insurance Industry Data	**900**		500	300	100
CPI Weights with Net Insurance	**1,800**	100	800	600	300

related costs also are treated as standard consumption items. The main issue is determining the main expenditure category for their inclusion.

11.325 The goods and services included in the Education Services category (COICOP 2018 division 10) cover educational services provided by the main channels of education. These include:

- Education by radio or television broadcasting or over the internet
- Educational programs, generally for adults, that do not require any special prior knowledge or instruction (these can include vocational training and cultural development)
- Literacy programs for students too old for primary school including out-of-school secondary education for adults and young people and out-of-school postsecondary non-tertiary education for adults and young people

11.326 COICOP 2018 division 10 does not include:

- Expenditure on educational materials, such as books (COICOP 2018 09.7.1) and stationery (COICOP 2018 09.7.4), or education support services, such as health care services (COICOP 2018 06), transport services (COICOP 2018 07.3), catering services (COICOP 2018 11.1.2), and accommodation services (COICOP 2018 11.2.0)
- Driving lessons (COICOP 2018 07.2.4); recreational training courses such as sport or bridge lessons given by independent teachers (COICOP 2018 09.4.6)

11.327 In many countries, the government partially finances education services, particularly higher education, and students pay a portion of the cost of their education and this portion is in the CPI's scope. The tuition fees faced by students are not always the full cost of education, and in these cases, the CPI weight should not and does not represent the full cost of providing education to the population, just the cost to the individual of acquiring the education services. Changes to the amount of the government transfer can lead to changes in the tuition charged to students and the index should reflect any resulting change in the fees. If a student goes to a private school, where there is no government support, the total advertised price P for fees should be reflected in the CPI weights and in the price collected, as this is what it costs the household to educate the student. In the case of government support, let s be the share of this total advertised price that is borne by the household (that is, the household is presented with a bill showing a net price of sP), then the appropriate price for the CPI and for the construction of weights is sP. In this way, the proportion of the cost borne by the household will feed through into the calculation of the CPI; that is, the CPI will reflect the actual fees paid by the household that, in this case, will be less than the basic advertised price.

11.328 Weights for educational services can be difficult to obtain. Information from the HBS can be unreliable since sample sizes and relatively low response can result in large sampling errors. Additionally, national accounts data are often not available at the level of detail needed to develop CPI weights. The level of detail in accounting is often varied and may not allow the division of the costs to the level of detail required for index compilation, for example, separating out university tuition fees from other education costs or breaking university tuition fees down into subcategories by type of course (for example, postgraduate or undergraduate). Therefore, a better source of detailed weighting information may be the public institutions in charge of the educational programs, for example, administrative data from government departments or regulatory bodies.

Pricing

11.329 The typical item to be priced will be the cost of a term or semester at a sample of schools. A school term is usually longer than one month, that is, the calculation frequency for most CPIs. Standard practice in this case is to collect prices only in months when the terms begin, and to use that same price in the intervening months. The pricing months can vary depending on the country or the school. For example, if a school has two semesters, one starting in September and the other in January, then tuition fees should be priced in these months only. In other months, the price is carried forward and the same price is used for the remaining months of the term. The index and the associated inflation rate may display step changes, changing only in the months when the terms begin.

11.330 The recommended approach is to use student profiles to price the cost of education for a selection of typical students who are chosen to reflect different levels of fees and base-weighted to reflect their distribution in the particular educational institute that is being priced. These profiles should aim to reflect the range of courses on offer, for example, covering full-time and part-time undergraduate courses in arts, sciences, and medicine; postgraduate research; and teacher training courses. Where the fee structure is simple, it may be sufficient to simply collect prices for the posted or advertised tuition fees directly from the institution or its website. In practice, any discounted tuition fees can be ignored where it is known or can be assumed that they change at the same rate as the full fees and that the proportion of students benefiting from them remains constant over time. However, any assumptions would need to be checked on a regular basis as there is an inherent risk of introducing an element of bias in the index if differential changes in fee structures or changes in the student population are missed. The approach should be used with care. Similarly, the use of average revenue (total tuition fees divided by the number of students) is generally not an appropriate way to price tuition fees that include price differentials, as changes in the composition of the students attending the college, and the courses they attend, can affect the average fee even when no price change takes place.

11.331 In some countries, it is common for students to travel abroad for their higher education. In such cases, expenditure paid by residents for tuition at foreign institutions may be deemed to be in scope for the national CPI depending on the geographical coverage of the index and whether the expenditure was incurred in the domestic territory of the country of residence or abroad (as discussed in Chapter 2). Where such costs are included, changes in the education or tuition index from the destination countries can be used to construct the price relatives for the education component, adjusted to the national currency using the exchange rate applying in the reference month.

Scholarships and Other Forms of Discounting

11.332 Schools and universities often reduce the tuition fees for some students. Tuition fee reductions offered in exchange for work (for example, teaching assistants or participants in sports teams) should not be reflected in the index as they are a form of income.

11.333 The treatment in the CPI of scholarships awarded to particularly talented students or tuition assistance in the form of financial aid to students from certain socioeconomic backgrounds, such as low-income households, depends on the method of payment:

- Those that are paid directly to students to assist them in bearing the cost of the full fee but that the students can use, if they wish, to finance something else are transfer payments that should not be reflected in the CPI.
- Where the scholarship or subsidy results in students being subject to reduced fees (that is, they are billed for a reduced amount), it is the reduced fee that should be priced for the CPI.

Social Protection

11.334 According to COICOP 2018, social protection covers nonmedical assistance and support services provided to persons who are elderly, disabled, having occupational injuries and diseases, survivors, unemployed, destitute, homeless, low-income earners, indigenous people, immigrants, refugees, alcohol and substance abusers, and so on. It also covers assistance and support services provided to families and children.

11.335 As with health and education, the purchaser price of goods and services in the social protection sector is the amount to be paid by consumers, net of reimbursements.

11.336 Suppose that in country A, the entity offering childcare services charged a price of £20 per hour at period $t-1$; and at period t, the price of the services increases to £21 per hour. Children typically spend 50 hours per month in the kindergarten so that the generated revenue for the entity for the service goes from £1,000 per child to £1,050. But in recognition of the greater financial burden on the household, the hourly support offered by the public authorities is increased from £8 at period $t-1$ to £10 at period t. The net price paid by the household per hour falls from £12 to £11 (= £21 − £10).

11.337 In the case of country B, the exact same changes apply except that here the authorities provide an income tax transfer instead of a price subsidy. As a result of the increased price, the household now receives an increase in its childcare grant from 400 pesos at period $t-1$ to 500 pesos at period t.

11.338 Note that regardless of the approach used for reducing the burden from the higher price of the service, the net cost to the household of consuming the childcare service (a drop from \$600 to \$550) is the same for both countries.[31] However, the impact on inflation as measured by the CPI differs depending on the approach used for supporting childcare services. The index in country A falls by 8.33 percent whereas the corresponding index in country B increases by 5 percent. The reimbursement given in country B is classified as a social transfer so there is no direct applicable price reduction. It should also be noted that the expenditure weights differ according to the approach used for reducing the burden. In country A, this value is £600 in year $t-1$, and in country B, the equivalent value is 1,000 pesos. These are the amounts that would be reported by a household in an HBS.

[31]For country A, the immediate out-of-pocket expenditure is the net price paid times the hours of the service which are consumed (\$12 × 50 = \$600 at period $t-1$).

Table 11.14 The Effects of a Subsidy and Tax Credit on a CPI

	Country A		Country B	
	$t-1$	t	$t-1$	t
Gross Price for Childcare Services (\$/hour)	20.00	21.00	20.00	21.00
Usage in Hours Per Month	50.00	50.00	50.00	50.00
Income for Childcare Provider (\$/month)	1,000.00	1,050.00	1,000.00	1,050.00
Government Subsidy (\$/hour)	8.00	10.00	n/a	n/a
Income Tax Transfer Per Month (\$/month)	n/a	n/a	400.00	500.00
Net Price Paid by Households (\$/hour)	12.00	11.00	20.00	21.00
Net Expenditure Determining Weight (\$/month)	600.00	550.00	1,000.00	1,050.00
Net Cost (\$/month)	600.00	550.00	600.00	550.00
CPI ($t-1$ = 100)	100.00	91.67	100.00	105.00

n/a, Not applicable.

Financial Services

Introduction

11.339 The construction of price indices for financial services is by nature challenging, as there is no consensus about which financial services ought to be included in the CPI or how they should be measured. The discussion in this section attempts to present what is feasible from a practical perspective.

11.340 Common examples of financial services acquired by households include: financial advice; currency exchange; services associated with deposit and loan facilities; services provided by fund managers, life insurance offices, and superannuation funds; stockbroking services; and real estate agency services. The range of financial services appropriate to be covered in a CPI, and the way to measure them, depend on the principal use of the CPI and hence on whether an acquisitions, use, or payments approach is employed.

11.341 Financial services covered in this section come under COICOP 2018 12.2. This group covers actual charges for the financial services of banks, post offices, saving banks, money changers, and similar financial institutions; fees and service charges of brokers, investment counselors, tax consultants, and the like; and administrative charges of private pension funds and the like. Also included in COICOP 2018 12.2 are financial intermediation services indirectly measured (FISIM) but in practice these are sometimes excluded from a CPI (see later discussion). Insurance is not covered under financial services as it comes under COICOP 12.1. This group includes service charges for insurance as classified by type of insurance, namely, life insurance and nonlife insurance (that is, insurance in connection with the dwelling, health, transport, and so on).[32] A discussion on medical insurance is included in paragraphs 11.312–11.323, and mortgage arrangement and application fees are discussed in paragraphs 11.81–11.146.

11.342 If a payments approach is used, the gross interest payable on mortgages is often included as a cost of owner-occupied housing services. For consistency, this might suggest that the CPI should also cover consumer credit charges, measured in a similar way to mortgage interest charges, as well as gross outlays on direct fees and charges paid in respect of other financial services. In practice, and as noted in the section on housing services costs, the treatment of housing services sometimes differs in concept from other interest charges in national CPIs, partly reflecting mixed objectives for the overall index combined with public perceptions of what should be included in a CPI and the importance of housing services costs in household budgets.

11.343 On the assumption that households acquire all their financial services from the private sector, and that these services are not generally supported by government or provided by NPISH, the acquisitions and use approaches take similar views of the measurement of financial services. With regard to coverage, however, some proponents of the use approach take a more restrictive view of which services should be included by limiting the scope to only those financial services that are acquired to directly facilitate current household final consumption.

11.344 Under the more restrictive view of coverage, it is argued that the use of some financial services is more associated with capital or investment activity. This implies that such activities should be considered outside the scope of CPIs intended to measure changes in consumer prices. Proponents of this view often draw upon national accounts practices as the starting point. For example, the *2008 SNA* classifies expenses associated with the transfer of real estate (for example, real estate agents' commissions, legal fees, and government taxes and charges) as part of gross fixed capital formation (*2008 SNA*, paragraphs 10.48–10.52). Although harmonization is desirable, in some countries some CPI concepts do not precisely follow the national accounts concepts.

11.345 Practices relating to financial services vary. In principle a CPI should include the prices of all goods and services included in household final consumption expenditure. Nonconsumption expenditure such as financial transactions, transfers, and purchases of financial assets are excluded. According to the *2008 SNA* all insurance services are within the scope of household final consumption expenditure and are to be included by the amount of the implicit service charge (*2008 SNA*, paragraph 9.64). However, the practice is more complicated, confounded by conceptual and measurement issues.

11.346 For example, the EU HICP and the CPIs compiled in some countries exclude life insurance services, for practical reasons and because some life insurance services (notably those that are fixed term and with profit) can be a form of tax-efficient saving. The premiums paid for life insurance (COICOP 2018 12.1.1), including pension-funding services, are partly to be regarded as savings. Life insurance services are thus excluded from the HICP, as it is not feasible in practice to separate the implicit service charge from the investment component. In accordance with CPI conventions, nonlife insurance services are, however, included in the HICP. Public insurance connected with health (ECOICOP[33] 12.5.3.1) is generally considered outside the scope of a CPI, including the HICP, as compulsory contributions under social security programs are not included in household final consumption expenditure.

11.347 The HICP also excludes FISIM (COICOP 12.2.1), which comprises those parts of financial services that are charged for by way of the interest margin of financial institutions. It is excluded because it is difficult to measure the transaction. On the other hand, those financial services that attract explicit charges, for example, annual charges for credit cards (excluding interest charges), bank charges for money transfers, and explicit currency exchange commissions, are included in the HICP. The HICP mentioned in this section is one example of how financial services can be treated in a CPI.

11.348 One broad definition that could be adopted for the coverage of financial services within the CPI is all those services acquired by households in relation to the acquisition, holding, and disposal of financial and real assets, including advisory services, except those acquired for business purposes. This definition serves two purposes: first, it distinguishes between the services facilitating the transfer and holding of assets and the assets themselves; second, it makes no distinction between whether the underlying asset is a tangible asset or a financial asset.

11.349 The degree of complexity involved in placing a value on financial services acquired by households and in constructing the companion price indices varies by service. The following examples illustrate the issues. It should be noted in regard of the example on deposit and loan facilities that the complexity involved in measuring FISIM and an aversion to the overuse of imputed prices in a CPI have led to many compilers to follow the HICP example by not including these services in a CPI.

Currency Exchange

11.350 For weighting purposes, the estimation of the weight reference period expenditure incurred by households in exchanging domestic currency for currencies of other countries is not entirely straightforward. In practice, the amounts reported by HBSs can be biased downward because of forgetful underreporting of currency exchange transactions by households. The national accounts can often provide a more accurate source for weighting data.

[32] Life insurance are generally excluded from the coverage of a CPI as the premiums paid for life insurance (COICOP 2018 12.1.1), including pension-funding services, are regarded as savings. Also, there are measurement issues associated with the difficulty of separately identifying the implicit service charge of the insurance element from the implicit service charge of the investment component.

[33] ECOICOP refers to the European Classification of Individual Consumption According to Purpose.

11.351 Construction of the price index for currency exchange services is in general more complex. The service for which a price is required is that of facilitating the exchange of domestic currency for other currency (the acquisition of an asset—foreign currency). The price for the service is often specified as some percentage of the domestic currency value of the transaction plus a fixed per transaction charge. The percentage margins may change only rarely, with service providers relying on the nominal value of the transactions increasing over time to deliver increases in fee receipts. The price required for index construction purposes is the monetary value of the margin (that is, the amount determined by applying the percentage rate to the value of the currency transaction) plus the fixed charge. To measure price change over time, the CPI compiler needs to form a view about the quantity underpinning the original transaction. Further feasible forms of charging, other than percentage plus fixed fees, occur for currency exchange services, such as fees following a step function or a spread between service providers' selling and buying rates (that is, an implicit rather than an explicit fee). The following description pertains to the issues in the case of percentage fees (plus fixed fee) for currency exchange.

11.352 The purchase of foreign currency can be viewed as facilitating the purchase of some desired quantity of foreign goods and services (for example, purchased during traveling abroad, or for the direct import of a product). The service price in comparison periods would be expressed as the amount payable on the conversion of a sum of domestic currency corresponding to that sum of foreign currency required to purchase the same quantities of foreign goods and services purchased in the price reference period. Thus, the fixed basket relates to the purchase of a fixed good or service in a foreign currency.

11.353 To follow the principle of a fixed basket, the original foreign currency amount should be indexed forward using changes in foreign prices, and then converted to domestic currency at the prevailing exchange rate, with the prevailing percentage margin applied to this new amount, plus any fixed charge, to produce the current price. This current price would be compared to the base price to derive the measure of price change. Although the ideal measure for indexing forward the foreign currency amount would be an index specifically targeting those foreign goods and services purchased by households wanting to exchange currency, this is unlikely to be feasible. A practical alternative is to use the published all-items CPI for the relevant foreign countries. A further approximate simplification for the revaluation by indexing forward is to use the CPI of the country of residence; this can be defended as following potential expenditure for consumption forgone (see paragraphs 11.371–11.375).

11.354 If a single margin (percentage rate) does not apply to all transactions (for example, different rates apply to different size transactions), then the price measure should be constructed by reference to a representative sample of price reference period transactions. The value margin for each transaction in the current period in the domestic currency should be determined by the current domestic currency value of each transaction and the current period percentage margin applying to each. This captures any price change resulting from the value of an underlying transaction moving from one price band to another.

Stockbroking Services

11.355 Stockbrokers buy or sell shares or other securities on behalf of clients (for example, the purchase of a parcel of shares in a publicly listed company; in most countries this has to be arranged through a licensed stockbroker). The service provided consists of arranging for a transaction to take place on the conditions specified by the client (that is, a certain block of shares that is being bought or sold). The total amount paid by the purchaser generally comprises three elements: an amount for the shares (the asset), a fee for the brokerage service, and some form of transaction tax (stamp duty).

11.356 The tax should be considered part of the cost of acquiring the shares, as opposed to being part of the price of the security. The tax should be included along with the brokerage cost in the CPI. This is consistent with both the intention of the tax and the more commonly accepted basis for the valuation of the shares. It also aligns with the comparable treatment of taxes on banking services. Allowing for current tax schedules is feasible as they are publicly available.

11.357 Working from the premise that stockbrokers' fees can likely follow a step function, as opposed to a linear function, a price measure would be constructed as follows. First, a representative sample of transactions (domestic currency values) is selected and the fees and the tax payable are calculated according to the respective schedules. A representative unit of transaction should be the charge to be paid by consumers in exchange for trading a set basket of securities (defined in value terms) that are representative of the base or reference period. The fees and taxes payable in subsequent periods are calculated by first indexing forward the values of the sample transactions and then applying current fee and tax schedules to the revalued transactions. This method raises two main questions: first, what is the most appropriate index for revaluing the transactions; and, second, how should the current schedule of fees be determined.

11.358 The quantity underlying share transactions can be regarded as forgone consumption, or the quantity of goods and services that could have been purchased instead. The value of a constant set of quantities of consumption forgone in successive comparison periods thus will vary with consumer prices. In this case, one choice for a revaluation index is the CPI, based on current month's or quarter's preliminary estimates, or the previous month's or quarter's published CPI. However, it could be argued that the use of a single period's movement in the CPI has the potential to show the prices of stockbroking services as moving in a way not reflecting reality. This could occur if the current or previous period's CPI was influenced notably by some unusual price change (for example, an oil price shock or change to health care arrangements). As an alternative, a 12-month moving average CPI might be employed, consistent with a price reference period comprising a full year's activity.

11.359 Hypothetically, it might be argued from a conceptual viewpoint that the set of shares could be revalued in subsequent periods in line with movements in equity prices. According to this view, the price of equities would be seen as an important influence on the actual costs of storing forgone consumption in much the same way as fee and tax schedules specific to equity purchases are allowed to enter the calculations described previously. The strong argument against this treatment is that it assumes that households have a desire to acquire equities per se, rather than using them as an advantageous vehicle to store forgone consumption. Moreover, the introduction of equity prices within the price index is likely to impart additional short-term irrelevant volatility to the CPI, although not significantly so given the relatively small weight for brokerage fees in a CPI.

11.360 Competition in the stockbroking industry means that there is unlikely to be a common fee schedule. If individual brokers adhere reasonably closely to an in-house fee schedule, obtaining copies of these schedules should be relatively simple. On the other hand, if no such fee schedules exist, then a survey of stockbrokers may be required to collect information on a sample of trades (value of trade and fee charged) and this information used to derive a current period fee schedule.

11.361 In the case of sales of shares, the underlying transaction represents the exchange of one asset for another (shares for cash). Quantities underlying sales can be viewed similarly to share purchases (that is, some current period basket of consumption goods and services). In practice, households presumably review their investment strategies occasionally to store their deferred consumption in asset forms they may expect to offer security or prospect for growth. A symmetrical treatment of the purchase and sale of shares is a natural approach. Unless different fees or taxes apply to sales, there is no need to distinguish between the two in constructing the index.

Investment Funds

11.362 Investment funds often apply an annual management charge defined as a given percentage of the current asset value. For example, the charge can have the form that 1.50 percent of the asset value is deducted annually from the latter. This charge can be applied either instead of or in addition to charges applied to the buying or selling of fund shares. In the CPI, the annual management charge proportional to asset value can be treated in a similar way as a charge for currency exchange proportional to the transaction value. Funds can be discontinued from time to time and in the price collection they should then be replaced with similar funds to ensure that the index reflects actual price developments. The underlying transaction for annual management charges can be defined as the annual management of fund shares worth a given amount in monetary terms in the price reference period. The underlying transaction is revalued periodically by the CPI. The use of the CPI is motivated by the fact that the user functionality of the service deteriorates with inflation, which makes the monetary value of the assets handled less useful to the consumer. The updating with the CPI adjusts for this change in user functionality. A stock price index such the FTSE 100, DAX, or Dow Jones indices should not be used as these do not keep the user functionality of the service constant. Namely, the more the investment is worth, the greater is the user functionality of the service managing it. Also, stock price indices follow asset price values that can be volatile and asset price movements would dominate the modeling of the service charge.

Deposit and Loan Facilities

11.363 Accounting for the costs of services provided by financial intermediaries represents a step up in complexity in CPI compilation. Even where a prior decision has been made to include such facilities within the scope of the CPI, the service being provided is challenging to visualize comprehensively, and the prices comprise elements that are not directly observable.

11.364 The *2008 SNA* (paragraphs 6.163–6.169 and A4.33) recommends that the value of financial intermediation services output produced by an enterprise should be valued as the following sum:

- For financial assets involved in financial intermediation, such as loans, the value of services provided by the enterprise to the borrower per monetary unit on account is the margin between the rate payable by the borrower and a reference rate; plus
- For financial liabilities involved in financial intermediation, such as deposits, the value of services provided by the enterprise to the lender or depositor per monetary unit on account is the margin between the reference rate and the rate payable by the enterprise to the lender; plus
- The value of actual or explicit financial intermediation service charges levied

11.365 The Organisation for Economic Co-operation and Development has been instrumental in developments in the national account's treatment in this area.[34] In concept, the *2008 SNA* describes the reference rate as the risk-free or pure interest rate. The value of the service provided to a borrower is the difference between the actual amount of interest paid by the borrower and the lower amount that would have been paid had the reference rate applied. The converse applies for depositors. In practice, it is difficult to effectively identify the reference rate, and in particular to avoid volatility in or even negative measures of the value of such services (as would occur if the reference rate lay above the lending rate or below the deposit rate). As a matter of practical expediency, an average of borrowing and lending rates may be used, with preference for the midpoint. Given the complexities involved, expenditure on financial intermediation required for index weighting purposes cannot be collected from households in expenditure surveys and thus must be estimated by collecting data from financial institutions or a regulatory authority.

11.366 Concerns have been expressed about the use of a midpoint reference rate as a measure of the risk-free rate of interest. There are, however, some doubts about whether

[34]The SNA uses the concept of FISIM to put a value on financial services that are not explicitly priced. However, measurement is often narrowly defined around the traditional deposit/loan business, thereby leaving out other financial instruments that may be carriers of financial services with implicit prices. An extension of the notion of FISIM relates the use of output indirectly measured to obtain as complete as possible a measure of the services produced by financial corporations. Not doing so may underestimate value added. Nevertheless, considerations have recognized current practice of computing FISIM on deposits and loans only as a workable and useful way of estimating the value of financial services, although these calculations are not necessarily an exhaustive measure of the value of indirectly measured financial services. See, for example, the report of the OECD Task Force on Financial Services (Banking Services) in National Accounts, 2002, particularly Conclusion 5 of Section 14.2.

the conceptual ideal is for some "risk-free" interest rate, or whether a more appropriate concept might be the interest rate that would have been struck in the absence of financial intermediaries (that is, the rate that would have been struck by depositors dealing directly with borrowers). Such a rate would have incorporated the lenders' knowledge of risk. Taking the midpoint of the borrowing and lending rates would appear to be a good means of estimating this market-clearing rate.

11.367 When planning the construction of the index number, it is useful to start by considering the case of a traditional bank providing a single loan product and a single deposit product; the example will then be extended to a typical bank. Much of a bank's income is derived through an interest margin on lending rates over deposit rates.

11.368 The base period weighting value of the financial service (and so household final consumption of such services) therefore is estimated by applying a margin (the absolute difference between the reference rate and the rate of interest charged to borrowers or paid to depositors) to an aggregate balance (loan or deposit). In line with the suggested treatment of other financial transactions, the construction of accompanying price measures should allow for the indexation forward of price reference period balances, applying comparison period margins to calculate a money value. The price index is then calculated as the ratio of comparison period and price reference period money values.

11.369 Again, the issue of choosing an appropriate revaluation index needs to be addressed as with currency exchange. While the base period flows of deposits and withdrawals can readily be conceptualized as foregone consumption at base period prices, how should the balances (stocks) reflecting an accumulation of flows over a number of years, be viewed? If an age profile for balances were available, accumulated consumption forgone could be computed as a moving average of the CPI. The more practical alternative is to view base period balances as representing some set of quantities of final consumption goods and services at base period prices, in which case the 12-month moving average CPI can be used. This is consistent with the idea that households review temporal consumption or investment decisions (and so accumulated financial balances) on a regular basis, in this case annually.

11.370 The traditional bank is not currently so frequent in some countries and generally financial institutions now derive income from a combination of implicit charges (margins) and explicit fees, with the trend having been for a move toward more use of explicit fees and relatively less use of margins. In this case a challenge is to construct measures of price change that reflect the total price of the service and therefore capture any offsets between margins and direct fees. As with stockbroking services, there may also be taxes levied on financial transactions or balances and these should also be included in the price. Frost (2001), for example, provides a description of practical aspects of constructing price indices for deposit and loan facilities.

11.371 Given the options for financial intermediaries to shift charges between the explicit or direct (fee) and implicit or indirect (margin) elements, there are risks in choosing measures of margins (that is, FISIM in the SNA) independently of direct fees and taxes. Rather, the approach should be to construct price measures for specific relatively homogeneous products that can then be weighted together to provide a measure for deposit and loan facilities, in aggregate, and taking account of both the explicit and implicit elements in total price. This represents a similar strategy to that adopted throughout the CPI. For example, the index for motor vehicles is constructed by pricing a sample of individual vehicles and weighting these price measures to derive an aggregate, instead of, for example, attempting to directly construct an index for the supplier or producer of a range of vehicles.

11.372 A basic process to treat the services of financial intermediaries in the CPI is, first, to select a sample of representative products from each sampled institution; second, to select a sample of customers for each product; and third, to estimate the total base period value of the service for each product by element (margin, direct fees, and taxes). These values can be viewed as being equivalent to prices for some quantity. Comparison period prices are derived by moving forward the base period value aggregates as follows:

- *Margin*—index forward the base period balance and apply the comparison period margin (the difference between the comparison period reference rate and the product yield). In practice, the price movement is given as the product of the indexation factor and the ratio of margins.
- *Fees*—index forward the transaction values for each sampled account (or profile) and apply the comparison period fee structure. The ratio of new aggregate fees to base fees is used to move the fee value aggregate. The aggregate fees in the base and comparison periods can be constructed as either arithmetic or geometric averages of the fees calculated for the individual customers.
- *Taxes*—as for fees but use tax schedules instead of fee schedules.

11.373 Annex 11.3 contains an example of the calculation of a price index for a single deposit product.

11.374 Since step-function pricing and taxing schedules (for example, fees that are only payable after some number of transactions or if balances fall below some level) are prevalent in financial services, samples of detailed customer accounts with all the necessary charging variables identified will be required. These samples should cover a full year's activity. If it is not possible to sample actual accounts, customer profiles may be developed as a fallback option.

11.375 To minimize problems associated with nonresponse and changing industry structures, a separate reference rate should be constructed for each sampled service provider. The reference rate should be calculated in respect of all loans and deposits (including those to businesses). Furthermore, to avoid problems that may arise in the timing of accounting entries (for example, revisions or interest income on credit cards), monthly yields, reference rates, and margins should be constructed by reference to three-month moving averages of the reported underlying balances and interest flows.

Credit and Debit Card Fees When Abroad

11.376 The use of credit and debit cards while abroad to purchase goods and services, or to withdraw cash, is usually subject to explicit fees and charges. The fees levied on the use of the card abroad are not part of the price of the good or service purchased as consumers have the option of paying in cash. However, ideally it should be considered that as the fees that consumers are charged for using their cards abroad are levied by the service provider (bank or credit card company) in the country of residence and not in the country where the purchase occurred, these charges should be allocated to the country of residence. By contrast the situation is different for internet purchases as the credit or debit card charges are unavoidable because paying by cash is not an option, thus being part of the price for the good or service bought on the internet.

11.377 The underlying transactions for using credit and debit cards abroad typically include:

- The service fee charged to the consumer's account for using an automated teller machine (ATM) outside the country of residence to withdraw an amount of local currency equivalent of a given amount in the currency of the consumer's residence, in the price reference period.
- The service fee charged to the consumer's account when purchasing abroad a good or service of a given value in the currency of the consumer's residence, in the price reference period. The value in real terms of the underlying transactions should be kept constant by monthly price updating using the CPI for revaluation, until the next annual basket update. It may be noted that keeping the real value of the reference transaction constant implies that the value in nominal terms varies.
- Prepaid cards for, for instance, toll charges for bridges and motorways are allocated to the COICOP division of the good or service being purchased. The transaction price is the corresponding cost of, for example, one crossing of the bridge.

Real Estate Agency Services

11.378 The services provided by real estate agencies in the acquisition and disposal of properties can be treated in various ways. The transfer costs involved in the acquisition of a dwelling (legal fees, real estate agency fees, and taxes) can be included in both a *payments* and an *acquisitions* CPI. They can be classified as either a cost of homeownership or as a distinctly separate financial service. Although all transfer costs should be included in such measures, the following discussion focuses on real estate agents' fees for simplicity. Price measures for the other elements are calculated using similar procedures. In all cases, the general approach is to estimate the current cost of the various services relative to, and as they would apply to, some fixed basket of activity in the base period. Consistent with some of the areas already discussed, this involves indexing forward the weight reference period expenditure on which the fees are charged (to preserve the underlying quantity) via some appropriate price index, and then estimating the fees payable in the comparison period.

11.379 Real estate agents typically state their fees as some percentage of the price settled for the dwelling. In common with other services for which charges are determined as a margin, this needs to be converted to a domestic currency price in cases where the sale price is stated in a foreign currency. If the percentage margin is known, the agents' price for any given transaction (sale/purchase of a dwelling for a known price) can be computed by multiplying the value of the dwelling by the percentage margin, and the index can be constructed on the basis of estimates of both components.

11.380 The method chosen for estimating the percentage margin will depend on an assessment of the variation in margins across and within individual agencies. In the most straightforward case, firms may operate with a single percentage margin applicable to all transactions regardless of value. In other words, at any point in time the percentage margins charged may vary by agency, but not by value of transaction within agency. In this case, what is required is an estimate, in each comparison period, of the average percentage margin charged by agencies. This can be achieved by collecting the percentage margins, exclusive of any taxes levied on agents' fees such as VAT or GST, from a sample of agencies and deriving an average.

11.381 Percentage margins charged by individual agencies sometimes vary with transaction price (typically declining with higher prices of dwellings). Where tariffs do vary within agencies, a more sophisticated estimation procedure may be needed. Using data from a sample of transactions from a sample of agents, the relationship between the value of transaction and the percentage margin can be derived through econometric analysis. Empirical analysis may be useful to determine the functional form for this relationship. In one country, for example, research has shown that ordinary least squares regression can be used to estimate this relationship and that the following functional form can be adequate:

$$R = a + b_1(1/p) + b_2(1/p)^2 \qquad (11.7)$$

where R denotes the commission rate, p denotes the house price, a is a constant, and b_1 and b_2 are parameters to be estimated.

11.382 Estimation of the current period value of transactions to which the percentage margin applies depends on whether real estate agency fees are classified as (1) a cost of housing or as (2) a separate financial service. In the former case, the value of the current period transaction, relative to the value of the price reference period transaction, would follow changes in house prices. In the latter case, the purchase of a dwelling is regarded as forgone consumption, and the current period value would follow changes in the CPI.

11.383 If a single percentage margin is assumed to operate, then only a single current period transaction value is needed, namely, an estimate of the average value of price reference period transactions at comparison period prices. For example, if real estate agency fees are classified as a housing cost, then the base period price is calculated by applying the average price reference period percentage margin to the average house price in the price reference period, with any VAT or GST then added. The comparison period price is calculated by revaluing the average base period house price by indexing forward, and then applying the average comparison period percentage margin and adding GST or VAT.

11.384 If a single percentage margin is not assumed to operate, then a sample of representative base period transactions is needed. The monetary value of the margin on each representative transaction is then calculated from published tariffs or from an estimated functional relationship, such as that described previously. Comparison period prices are likewise estimated by first revaluing by indexing forward for each of the base period representative transactions, and then applying the same model.

Property Insurance Services

11.385 The construction of reliable price indices for insurance can be challenging. This section is restricted to a discussion of property insurance, as this type of insurance can be assumed to operate in similar ways across countries. It provides only an illustration of the issues to be met, with each sector raising specific conceptual and measurement difficulties. The separation of the service charges relating to the insurance and investment elements within a single premium poses particular problems.

11.386 For the purposes of this discussion, property insurance is defined to include:

- Dwelling insurance
- Household contents insurance
- Motor vehicle insurance

11.387 The common feature of these types of insurance policies is that for a fee (premium), households receive financial compensation if a nominated event results in damage to, or loss of, specified property. The alternative to purchasing insurance is for the household to self-insure. For households, the service received relieves the risk of financial loss. The appropriate treatment of property insurance with respect to scope, weighting structure, and pricing in the CPI partly depends on whether the CPI is constructed to follow the acquisitions, use, or payments approach.

Payments Approach

11.388 Under the payments approach, each of the previous policy types is in the scope of the CPI. In thinking about how property insurance should be included in the CPI, it is appropriate to consider both the gross premiums payable and the claims receivable by households for inclusion in weights. The definitions of gross premiums payable and claims receivable are straightforward. It is possible, however, to treat claims receivable in various ways that will have an impact on either the weight assigned to insurance or the weight assigned to consumption products insured. Spending on insurance can be weighted on either a gross basis (that is, valued using gross premiums payable) or on a net basis (that is, valued using gross premiums payable less claims receivable). Similarly, damage to property insured may also be weighted gross or net (in the latter case, excluding purchases explicitly financed by insurance claims receivable). Taken together, this suggests three basically plausible alternative treatments in the weighting structure:

- Gross premiums, net expenditure
- Net premiums, gross expenditure
- Gross premiums, gross expenditure

11.389 With respect to *gross premiums, net expenditure*, it may be argued that calculating expenditure net of purchases financed by insurance claims avoids double counting of that portion of gross premiums that funds the claims. But there are some problems with this approach. First, it is assumed that all proceeds from insurance claims are used to purchase replacement products or to repair damaged property. Second, in some cases, claims receivable may be to compensate for damage to the property of agents beyond the scope of the index (for example, businesses, government or even other households where the CPI reference group covers only some subset of households). Households may also choose to use the proceeds for entirely different purposes. Thus, the estimation of the net expenditure weights is likely to involve some partly arbitrary choices. More generally, because money is fungible (that is, one sum of money can be replaced by another as money can be used to purchase a variety of goods and services), attempts to restrict coverage only to that expenditure made from selected sources of funds is a questionable practice. Finally, the potential distortion of weights for the products concerned might possibly reduce the usefulness of subindices for other purposes.

11.390 Considering the second option, *net premiums, gross expenditure*, within a payments index, this approach is based on the view that claims receivable should be regarded as negative expenditure on insurance. This may be viewed as an attempt to avoid a double counting of expenditure on products financed by claims receivable and already included in gross expenditure on other consumption products elsewhere in the index. The net premiums approach is in some ways less problematic than the net expenditure approach, as the impact is restricted to the weights for insurance and does not affect weights for replacement product expenditure financed out of claims. It may, however, be argued that the net premiums approach is inconsistent with approaches adopted for other products in a payments index—in particular, with mortgage interest and consumer credit charges, where weights are based on gross payments. Any allowance for interest receipts would yield negative weights when households are net savers overall.

11.391 The net premiums approach effectively measures the value of the insurance service and can be appropriate for indices constructed according to both the acquisitions and use approaches, as well as for a payments-based index considered here. It also tends to be favored for medical insurance although with such finely balanced arguments it is difficult to be prescriptive.

11.392 The use of *gross premiums, gross expenditure* is based on the view that the claims receivable by households represent one of the sources of funds from which expenditure are made. This is the main justification for using gross expenditure. The *gross premiums, gross expenditure* method is the most appealing approach for a payments index, as it recognizes the fungible nature of money for purchasing goods and services and provides a consistent means of identifying both the product coverage of the index and the relative weights by reference only to the actual outlays of households.

Use Approach

11.393 Under the *use approach*, dwelling insurance can be seen as out of the scope of the CPI as conceptually it is an input cost of the notional landlord, which is reflected in the imputed rent. The weights should relate to the value of the insurance service consumed by households. This is defined as being equal to gross insurance premiums payable by households, plus premium supplements, less provisions for claims, and less changes in actuarial reserves.

11.394 It is not possible to estimate the nominal value of the net insurance service from HBSs alone. For weighting purposes, a feasible approach is to obtain data from a sample of insurance providers, or from a regulatory authority, facilitating estimation of the ratio of net insurance services to gross premiums, and to apply this ratio to the estimated value of gross premiums obtained, for example, from the HBSs. However, it has not been possible to devise a corresponding price measure that is conceptually sound and can be accurately observed frequently enough from insurance companies' accounts. For this reason, those countries that have adopted the net concept for weighting purposes are using movements in gross insurance premiums as a proxy price measure.

Acquisitions Approach

11.395 Under the *acquisitions approach*, all three policy types (as listed earlier) are in the scope of the CPI. Because the objective is to measure price inflation for the household sector, the expenditure required for weighting purposes should reflect the insurance companies' contribution to the inflation process, which equates to the value of the insurance service as per the use approach.

Pricing Gross Insurance Premiums

11.396 The gross insurance premium payable by households in any one period is determined by the conditions of the policy, the administration costs and profit objectives of the insurance provider, the risk of a claim being made, and any relevant taxes. For any single policy, the principal quality-determining characteristics (generally specified in the conditions of the policy) can be summarized as being:

- The type of property being covered (for example, dwelling, motor vehicle)
- The type of cover provided (for example, physical damage, liability)
- The nature of the compensation (for example, replacement cost, current market value)
- Any limits on the amount claimable
- The location of the property
- Amount of any excess payable by the insured
- Risks (or events) covered

11.397 Although it is clear that pricing to constant quality requires these conditions to be held fixed, there is also a question about whether the risk of a claim being made should be held constant. In other words, if the incidence of, for example, vehicle theft increases, should an increase in the premium paid be regarded as a quality improvement or a price change? If, on the one hand, it is argued that as the consumers' decisions to insure are based on their assessment of the likelihood of suffering a loss compared to the premium charged, the risk factors should be held constant. On the other hand, it may be argued that, once insured, the consumer expects to be compensated for any loss irrespective of changes in risk. From the perspective of the consumer, any increase in risk represents an increase in the insurer's cost base (which may or may not be passed on to the consumer by way of a price change). Obtaining reliable data to make quality adjustments in response to changes in risk is problematic, so in practice most indices reflect changes in risk as a price change.

11.398 In pricing insurance policies, the approach should be to select a sample of policies representative of those policies held in the base period and to reprice these in subsequent periods. Taking dwelling insurance as an example, base period insurance policies would be taken out to insure dwellings of various values and types (for example, detached versus terraced house; timber or brick-built) in different locations. The price samples should therefore consist of specifications that aim to cover, in aggregate, as many combinations of these variables as is reasonable. While the conditions of the policy, the dwelling type, and location should be held constant over time, the value of the dwelling should be updated each period to reflect changes in house prices and in rebuilding costs (that is, the underlying real quantity needs to be preserved). It is important to note that, as the premiums will be related in some way to the value of the insured property, the price index for insurance can change without there being any change in premium schedules.

11.399 Efforts should be made to identify any changes in the conditions applying to selected policies in order to facilitate appropriate quality adjustments. Examples would include cessation of coverage for specific conditions and changing the excess (or deductible) paid by the consumer when a claim is made. Estimates of the value of such changes may be based on the insurance company's own assessments of their likely impact on the value of total claims payable. If it is assumed that the change in the aggregate value of claims can be equated to the change in service to the consumer (compared to the service that would have been provided prior to policy renewal), then an appropriate adjustment can be made to the premium to provide a (quality-adjusted) movement in price. For example, consider the case where the excess on a policy is doubled and advice from the company is that this will result in a 3 percent drop in the aggregate value of claims payable. This could be considered as equivalent to a 3 percent increase in price.

11.400 In some cases, clients reap the benefits of a "no claims" bonus where the premium is lower if no insurance claim has been made over a period of years. Measuring the cost of a fixed basket of goods and services implies that the price relatives should follow the price evolution of identical products; that is, the product specification should remain constant. The price changes recorded should reflect *pure price changes*; that is, the specifications of the insurance premiums should be held constant while reflecting in the price reference period the presence of "no claims" bonuses.

11.401 A combination of, for example, motor insurance and dwellings insurance or health and travel insurance may be offered as a package at a cheaper price than separate purchases. Bundled products are generally required, if feasible in practice, to be separated and classified under the appropriate COICOP subclasses or classes within the same or different COICOP groups or divisions. However, COICOP, while showing its awareness of the problem of bundling, does not normally provide clear guidance on their classification. Outlays covering two or more purposes are dealt with on a case-by-case basis with the aim of obtaining a purpose breakdown that is as precise as possible and consistent with practical considerations of data availability.

Using Gross Premiums as a Proxy for the Net Insurance Service

11.402 The net insurance service charge captures the administration costs and profits of the insurance provider along with any taxes and represents the amount paid for "peace of mind." A problem arises from the fact that taxes on insurance are normally levied on the gross premiums. Namely, if the gross insurance premiums are subject to a high tax rate, then the taxes will account for an even higher proportion of the net insurance service charge. Using the gross insurance premium inclusive of taxes as the price measure understates the effect, in relation to the service charge, of any increase in tax rates. This can be illustrated by the example in Table 11.15.

Table 11.15 Illustration of the Impact of Taxes on Measures of Insurance Services ($)

Period	Premiums Before Tax	Tax	Gross Premiums	Claims	Insurance Service
1	100.00	5.00	105.00	60.00	45.00
2	100.00	20.00	120.00	60.00	60.00

11.403 For the sake of simplicity, the example in Table 11.15 assumes that there are no premium supplements and no actuarial reserves. Then the insurance service charge is given by gross premiums less provisions for claims. Suppose the only change between two periods is a change in the tax rate, from 5 to 20 percent of gross premiums. Then the values in the following table are likely to be observed. Under this scenario, it turns out that the insurance service charge has increased from $45 to $60 (an increase of 33.3 percent); yet gross premiums have only increased by 14.3 percent.

11.404 Given that changes in the tax rates on gross insurance premiums are often subject to significant variation, this can result in a volatile index. It is not a trivial problem. A practical solution is to decompose insurance service into two components: insurance service before tax (or net of tax) and tax on insurance services. The price measure for the first is constructed by reference to movements in gross premiums net of tax, and the price measure for the second is given by changes in taxes on gross premiums.

Annex 11.1

Example of Price Collection Checklist for Second-Hand Clothing

Figure 11A.1 Price Collection Checklist for Second-Hand Clothing

Category: Second-hand Clothing	
Product Name: Men's Branded T-Shirt	
Product Code: 123.321	
Preferred Quantity and Unit of Measurement:	1 Unit
Product Description: o Product Presentation: No Package o Quantity: 1 Unit o Fiber Type: Cotton 100% o Units per package: One o Type: T-Shirt o Brand/label category: Well known. Indicate. Not brand imitation. o Sleeve Length: Short sleeve o Fabric design: Single color o Neck style: Round neck	

Collector:	....	
Date:	....	
Market:	....	
Product Detail ***(ok or specify as appropriate)*:**		
Brand:		
Quality:	Perfect	
	Minor Wear and Tear (e.g., some fraying at edges)	
	Major Wear and Tear (e.g., some holes or major repairs)	
Fabric design:	Small logo	
	Large printed design	
	Multi-colored fabric (e.g., stripes)	
Neck Style:	Round	
	V-neck	
Outlet Type:	Licensed outlet	
	Temporary stall	
	Street vendor	
Other Comments:		

Annex 11.2
Example Price Collection Letter to Retailer

Figure 11A.2 Price Collection Letter to Retailer

Bureau of Statistics
P.O Box 1

Date XX/XX/XX

B. Graham
Dealer, Second-Hand Clothes
Market A

SECOND-HAND CLOTHING PRICE INDEX

Every month the Bureau of Statistics collects clothing prices for the purpose of constructing a Second-hand Clothing Price Index and for this purpose we would request you to advise us on the following prices as at XXXXX.

We would remind you that it is important for you to let us know if the size of the bundles or the quality of the content has changed from the previous month. Any such changes should be recorded in the remarks' column.

ITEM	TYPE	PREVIOUS PRICE PER BALE	CURRENT PRICE PER BALE	REMARKS
1. Shirt	Brand 1 (an international logo)	300		
	Brand 2 (a national brand)	350		
2. T-Shirt	Brand 1 (an international logo)	210		
	Brand 2 (a national brand)	200		
3. Women's Dress (Cotton)	Brand 1	400		
	Brand 2	425		
4. Men's Trousers (Cotton)	Brand 1	350		
	Brand 2	350		

Annex 11.3

Calculation of a Price Index for a Deposit Product

(1) Base period sample account. Only a single month's data is used in this example (Table 11A.1). In practice, many accounts would be sampled with each account containing data for a full year.

Table 11A.1 Calculation of a Price Index for a Deposit Product: Base Period Sample Account

Date	Debit (D) or Credit (C)	Transaction	Transaction Value ($)	Tax ($)	Balance ($)
02-Jan.	D	Over-the-Counter Withdrawal	107.05	0.70	348.48
12-Jan.	C	Deposit	4,000.00	2.40	4,346.08
13-Jan.	D	EFTPOS[1] Transaction	50.62	0.30	4,295.16
13-Jan.	D	Over-the-Counter Withdrawal	371.00	0.70	3,923.46
14-Jan.	D	Own ATM[2] Cash	300.00	0.70	3,622.76
14-Jan.	D	Own ATM Cash	100.00	0.70	3,522.06
16-Jan.	D	Own ATM Cash	100.00	0.70	3,421.36
16-Jan.	D	Over-the-Counter Withdrawal	371.00	0.70	3,049.66
16-Jan.	D	Check	90.00	0.30	2,959.36
19-Jan.	D	Own ATM Cash	100.00	0.70	2,858.66
19-Jan.	D	Own ATM Cash	100.00	0.70	2,757.96
19-Jan.	C	Deposit	4,000.00	2.40	6,755.56
19-Jan.	D	Check	740.00	1.50	6,014.06
20-Jan.	D	EFTPOS Transaction	76.42	0.30	5,937.34
21-Jan.	D	Other ATM Cash	20.00	0.30	5,917.04
21-Jan.	D	Check	100.00	0.70	5,816.34
22-Jan.	D	Check	43.40	0.30	5,772.64
22-Jan.	D	Check	302.00	0.70	5,469.94
22-Jan.	D	Check	37.00	0.30	5,432.64
23-Jan.	D	Over-the-Counter Withdrawal	371.00	0.70	5,060.94
23-Jan.	D	Check	72.00	0.30	4,988.64
27-Jan.	D	Own ATM Cash	150.00	0.70	4,837.94
27-Jan.	D	Check	73.50	0.30	4,764.14
27-Jan.	D	Check	260.00	0.70	4,503.44
27-Jan.	D	EFTPOS Transaction	51.45	0.30	4,451.69
28-Jan.	D	Over-the-Counter Withdrawal	19.95	0.30	4,431.44
28-Jan.	D	Check	150.00	0.70	4,280.74
29-Jan.	D	Check	140.00	0.70	4,140.04
30-Jan.	D	Over-the-Counter Withdrawal	371.00	0.70	3,768.34
30-Jan.	D	Check	8.00	0.30	3,760.04
30-Jan.	D	Check	60.00	0.30	3,699.74
Total Taxes:				**21.10**	
Fees					
		Activity	Total Number	Number Charged	Amount ($)
		Over-the-Counter Withdrawal	6	2	6.00
		EFTPOS Transaction	3	0	0.00
		Own ATM Cash	6	0	0.00
		Own ATM Cash	1	1	1.20
		Check	13	3	3.00
		Deposit	2	2	0.00
Total Fees:					**10.20**

1 EFTPOS, Electronic funds transfer point of sale.
2 ATM, Automatic teller machine.

Source: Woolford (2001).

(2) Fee schedule. Table 11A.2 is a summary of the information typically available from financial institutions. For each period, the table includes the number of free transactions and the per transaction charge for additional transactions. A zero number of free transactions indicates that no transactions are free and a zero charge indicates that all transactions are free.

Table 11A.2 Calculation of a Price Index for a Deposit Product: Fee Schedule

Description	Base Period		Current Period	
	Number Free	Charge ($)	Number Free	Charge ($)
Over-the-Counter Withdrawal	4	3.00	4	3.00
EFTPOS Transaction	10	0.50	9	0.50
Own ATM Cash	10	0.50	9	0.50
Other ATM Cash	0	1.20	0	1.20
Check	10	1.00	9	1.00
Deposit	0	0.00	0	0.00

Source: Woolford (2001).

(3) Tax schedule. Tables 11A.3 and 11A.4 present an example of the types of taxes applied to a bank account. For example, the debits tax is levied on all debit transactions to eligible accounts, with the amount charged being set for ranges of transaction values (that is, using a step function). Financial institutions' duty is levied on all deposits, the amount being determined as a percentage of the value of the deposit.

(4) Interest data. Table 11A.5 presents, in summary form, the balances and annualized interest flows derived by taking moving averages of data reported by financial institutions. Interest rates and margins are calculated from the balances and flows.

Table 11A.3 Calculation of a Price Index for a Deposit Product: Bank Accounts Debit Tax

Transaction Value ($)		Tax ($)	
Min.	Max.	Base Period	Current Period
0	1	0.00	0.00
1	100	0.30	0.30
100	500	0.70	0.70
500	5,000	1.50	1.50
5,000	10,000	3.00	3.00
10,000+		4.00	4.00

Source: Woolford (2001).

Table 11A.4 Calculation of a Price Index for a Deposit Product: Financial Institutions Duty (percent)

Base Period	Current Period
0.06	0.06

Source: Woolford (2001).

Table 11A.5 Calculation of a Price Index for a Deposit Product: Interest Data

	Base Period				Current Period			
	Balance ($ million)	Interest ($ million)	Interest rate (percent)	Margin (percent)	Balance ($ million)	Interest ($ million)	Interest rate (percent)	Margin (percent)
Deposit Products								
Personal	22,000.00	740.00	3.364	2.494	23,600.00	775.00	3.284	2.397
Current Accounts	*6,000.00*	*68.00*	*1.133*	*4.724*	*6,600.00*	*75.00*	*1.136*	*4.545*
Other accounts	*16,000.00*	*672.00*	*4.200*	*1.657*	*17,000.00*	*700.00*	*4.118*	*1.563*
Business Accounts	25,000.00	920.00	3.680	2.177	28,000.00	1,000.00	3.571	2.110
Total Deposit Accounts	47,000.00	1,660.00	3.532	2.326	51,600.00	1,775.00	3.440	2.241
Loan Products								
Personal	42,000.00	3,188.00	7.591	1.733	46,000.00	3,400.00	7.391	1.710
Business	28,000.00	2,540.00	9.071	3.214	31,000.00	2,700.00	8.710	3.029
Total Loan Accounts	70,000.00	5,728.00	8.183	2.326	77,000.00	6,100.00	7.922	2.241
Reference Rate			**5.857**				**5.681**	

Source: Woolford (2001).

(5) CPI data. Table 11A.6 presents data required to derive the indexation factor. This example follows the Australian practice of a quarterly CPI. If a monthly CPI is produced, 12-term moving averages would be required.

(6) Projected current period sample account. Table 11A.7 shows that the opening balance and transaction values are derived by applying the indexation factor to the base period amounts. The tax payable is determined by reference to the data in Table 11A.3. Fees payable are determined by reference to the data in Table 11A.2.

Table 11A.6 Calculation of a Price Index for a Deposit Product: CPI Data

	$t-5$	$t-4$	$t-3$	$t-2$	$t-1$
All Groups	117.5	121.2	123.4	127.6	129.1
Four-Term Moving Average				122.4	125.3
Indexation Factor (movement)					**1.0237**

Source: Woolford (2001).

Table 11A.7 Calculation of a Price Index for a Deposit Product: Projected Current Period Sample Account

Date	Debit (D) or Credit (C)	Transaction	Transaction Value ($)	Tax ($)	Balance ($)
02-Jan.	D	Over-the-Counter Withdrawal	109.59	0.70	356.75
12-Jan.	C	Deposit	4,094.75	2.46	4,449.05
13-Jan.	D	EFTPOS Transaction	51.82	0.30	4,396.93
13-Jan.	D	Over-the-Counter Withdrawal	379.79	0.70	4,016.44
14-Jan.	D	Own ATM Cash	307.11	0.70	3,708.63
14-Jan.	D	Own ATM Cash	102.37	0.70	3,605.56
16-Jan.	D	Own ATM Cash	102.37	0.70	3,502.50
16-Jan.	D	Over-the-Counter Withdrawal	379.79	0.70	3,122.01
16-Jan.	D	Check	92.13	0.30	3,029.57
19-Jan.	D	Own ATM Cash	102.37	0.70	2,926.51
19-Jan.	D	Own ATM Cash	102.37	0.70	2,823.44
19-Jan.	C	Deposit	4,094.75	2.46	6,915.73
19-Jan.	D	Check	757.53	1.50	6,156.70
20-Jan.	D	EFTPOS Transaction	78.23	0.30	6,078.17
21-Jan.	D	Other ATM Cash	20.47	0.30	6,057.40
21-Jan.	D	Check	102.37	0.70	5,954.33
22-Jan.	D	Check	44.43	0.30	5,909.60
22-Jan.	D	Check	309.15	0.70	5,599.75
22-Jan.	D	Check	37.88	0.30	5,561.57
23-Jan.	D	Over-the-Counter Withdrawal	379.79	0.70	5,181.08
23-Jan.	D	Check	73.71	0.30	5,107.08
27-Jan.	D	Own ATM Cash	153.55	0.70	4,952.83
27-Jan.	D	Check	75.24	0.30	4,877.28
27-Jan.	D	Check	266.16	0.70	4,610.43
27-Jan.	D	EFTPOS Transaction	52.67	0.30	4,557.46
28-Jan.	D	Over-the-Counter Withdrawal	20.42	0.30	4,536.73
28-Jan.	D	Check	153.55	0.70	4,382.48
29-Jan.	D	Check	143.32	0.70	4,238.46
30-Jan.	D	Over-the-Counter Withdrawal	379.79	0.70	3,857.98
30-Jan.	D	Check	8.19	0.30	3,849.49
30-Jan.	D	Check	61.42	0.30	3,787.77
Total Taxes:				**21.21**	
Fees					
		Activity	Total Number	Number Charged	Amount ($)
		Over-the-Counter Withdrawal	6	2	6.00
		EFTPOS Transaction	3	0	0.00
		Own ATM Cash	6	0	0.00
		Own ATM Cash	1	1	1.20
		Check	13	4	4.00
		Deposit	2	2	0.00
Total Fees					**11.20**

Source: Woolford (2001).

(*7*) *Indices for current accounts*. Table 11A.8 brings the results together. The current period value aggregates are derived as follows. For margins, the base period aggregate is multiplied by the product of the indexation factor (5) and the ratio of the current and base period margins for current accounts (4). For fees, the base period aggregate is multiplied by the ratio of total fees payable on the sample account in the current period (6) and the base period (1). For taxes, the same procedure is followed as for fees.

Table 11A.8 Calculation of a Price Index for a Deposit Product: Indices for Current Accounts

Component	Base Period		Current Period	
	Value Aggregate ($)	Index	Value Aggregate ($)	Index
Margins	28,344	100.00	27,913	98.50
Fees	11,904	100.00	13,071	109.80
Taxes	14,739	100.00	14,818	100.50
Total	**54,987**	**100.00**	**55,803**	**101.50**

Source: Woolford (2001).

ERRORS AND BIAS

12

Introduction

12.1 The consumer price index (CPI), like all other statistics, may be subject to general error that may occur during any stage of the estimation process but also errors that are unique to the CPI (for example, substitution bias and quality change bias). This chapter first describes the general types of potential errors and the sources of sampling and nonsampling error that arise in estimating a population CPI from a sample of observed prices, and then reviews the arguments made in numerous studies that attribute bias to CPIs as a result of not properly addressing the treatment of quality change, consumer substitution, and other factors. It should be emphasized that many of the underlying issues discussed in this chapter are dealt with in much greater detail elsewhere in the Manual.

12.2 The CPI is subject to various types of errors and biases that affect the precision and accuracy of the CPI estimates. Several potential sources of errors and bias have been identified in the CPI and addressed, though the debate continues over to what extent and in what direction bias may still exist and the ways in which its accuracy can continue to be increased.

Types of Errors

12.3 One of the main objectives of a sample survey is to compute estimates of population characteristics. Such estimates will never be exactly equal to the population characteristics. There will always be some error, and the precision and accuracy of the estimate is affected by both sampling and nonsampling error. Table 12.1 gives a taxonomy of the different types of errors.[1] Two broad categories can be distinguished: sampling errors and nonsampling errors.

Sampling Error

12.4 *Sampling errors* are due to the fact that an estimated CPI is based on samples and not on a complete enumeration of the populations involved. Sampling errors vanish if observations cover the complete population. As mentioned in previous chapters, national statistical offices (NSOs) usually adopt a fixed-weight price index as the object of estimation. A fixed-weight index is a weighted average of partial indices of product groups, with weights being expenditure shares. The estimation procedures that most NSOs apply to a CPI involve different kinds of samples. The most important kinds are the following:

- For each product group, a sample of items to calculate the partial price index of the product group
- For each item, a sample of outlets to calculate the elementary price index of the item from individual price observations
- For each product group, a sample of a day or a time span of the month when the data collection has to be carried out (concerning this issue, the introduction of scanner data, which in general cover more than one week of a month, in CPI compilation could reduce the potential errors arising in the traditional data collection for this dimension of sampling)
- A sample of households needed for the estimation of the average expenditure shares of the item groups (some countries use alternative sources of data, such as national accounts, instead of a household budget survey [HBS] to obtain the expenditure shares, as described in Chapter 3)

Sampling error can be introduced at any of the stages of the sample selection process. The potential for sampling error is greater in the selection of outlets and even more so for products because there is no comprehensive frame from which to select units for sampling.

12.5 The sampling error can be split into a selection error and an estimation error. A *selection error* occurs when the actual selection probabilities deviate from the selection probabilities as specified in the sample design. The *estimation error* denotes the effect caused by using a sample based on a random selection procedure. Every new selection of a sample will result in different elements, and thus in a possibly different value of the estimator.

Nonsampling Error

12.6 CPI surveys involve many operations, all of which are potential sources of nonsampling error. The *nonsampling errors* arise from the survey process, regardless of whether the data are collected from the entire universe or

Table 12.1 A Taxonomy of Errors in a CPI

Total Error:			
	Sampling Error		
		Selection Error	
		Estimation Error	
	Nonsampling Error		
		Observation Error	
			Overcoverage
			Response Error
			Processing Error
		Nonobservation Error	
			Undercoverage
			Nonresponse

[1] See also Balk and Kersten (1986) and Dalén (1995) for overviews of the various sources of stochastic and nonstochastic errors experienced in calculating a CPI.

from a sample of the population. They can be subdivided into observation errors and nonobservation errors. *Observation errors* are the errors made during the process of obtaining and recording the basic observations or responses. The most general categories of observation errors are overcoverage, response error, and processing error.

12.7 *Overcoverage* means that some elements are included in the survey that do not belong to the target population or target universe. For outlets, NSOs usually have inadequate sampling frames. For example, in some countries, a business register is used as the sampling frame for outlets, where outlets are classified according to the main activity. The register thus usually exhibits extensive overcoverage, because it contains numerous outlets which are out of scope from the CPI perspective (for example, firms that sell to businesses rather than to households). In addition, there is usually no detailed information on all the items sold by an outlet, so it is possible that a sampled outlet may turn out not to sell a particular item at all.

12.8 *Response error* results from the collection of incorrect, inconsistent, or incomplete data. Response error may arise because of the collection of data from inappropriate respondents, deliberate distortion of responses, interviewer effects, misrecording of responses, pricing of wrong items, misunderstanding or misapplication of data collection procedures, misunderstanding of the questions or survey needs, and lack of cooperation from respondents. In price surveys, where the main price collection method is by price collectors who regularly visit outlets, they may collect prices of unwanted items.

12.9 *Processing error* occurs after the survey data are collected, during the processes that convert reported data to published estimates and consistent machine-readable information. Each of the processing steps, such as coding, data entry, transfer, and editing (control and correction), can generate errors. For example, at the outlets, the price collectors write down the prices on paper forms or use dedicated software on a tablet or handheld computer. In the first case (paper-and-pencil data collection), after the collectors have returned home, a computer is used as the input and means of transmission for the price information. This way of processing prices is susceptible to errors. The second case (computer-assisted data collection) is less risky because it has built-in validation checks, but it could be susceptible to errors for other reasons such as the lack of adequate controls during the recording of prices. Processing error also fails to identify true errors during regular micro- and macro-editing. Even when errors are discovered, they can be corrected improperly because of inadequate imputation and quality-adjustment procedures. The occurrence of processing errors is strongly influenced by survey planning, and to some extent the survey's resources (for example, staff and budget, devices, and training) and constraints (for example, elapsed time between data collection and publication).

12.10 *Nonobservation errors* are made when the intended measurements cannot be carried out. The most general categories of nonobservation errors are undercoverage and nonresponse error. *Undercoverage* occurs when elements in the target population are not included in the sampling frame used for sample selection. The source of undercoverage error is the sampling frame itself. For instance, it is likely that there are delays in updating the outlet frame to include new in-scope units or to exclude mail order firms and nonfood market stalls from their outlet sampling frame. Undercoverage means that some outlets where relevant items are purchased cannot be contacted.

12.11 *Nonresponse* is another category of nonobservation error. Nonresponse errors may arise from the failure to obtain the required information in a timely manner from some of the units selected in the sample. A distinction can be drawn between total and partial (or item) nonresponse. Total nonresponse occurs when selected outlets cannot be contacted or refuse to participate in the price survey. Another instance of total nonresponse occurs when mail or electronic questionnaires and collection forms are returned by the respondent and the price collector, respectively, after the deadline for processing has passed. Partial (item) nonresponse occurs when a responding unit does not complete the information on an item or items on the survey questionnaire, or the responses obtained are unusable. Mail or electronic questionnaires and collection forms that are only partially filled in, scanner data with missing information concerning specific outlets or Global Trade Item Numbers (GTINs) in the sample, and web-scraped prices where some information is not downloaded from the internet are examples of partial nonresponse. If the price changes of the nonresponding outlets differ from those of the responding outlets, the quality of the price change estimates will be affected.

12.12 Another source of errors is the failure to measure the price actually paid. This failure may be caused, for example, by the use of list prices (for example, for cars) and by the presence of discounts, coupons, or bargaining, which are typically not accounted for or difficult to measure. In many countries, the discounting of prices is becoming more common and the importance of discounted prices is increasing. Another source of error is due to the tendency of price collectors to choose an excessive proportion of regularly priced varieties in the price reference period, whereas the proportion of sales prices increases later and becomes proportional to their real share later in the year.

Measuring Error

Estimation of Variance

12.13 The variance estimator depends on both the chosen estimator of a CPI and the sampling design. The 2012 International Labor Organization Survey of country practices[2] gives an overview of the sampling methods that were applied in the compilation of CPIs by NSOs. It found that only one out of three NSOs use some sort of probability techniques for location selection, 1 in 5 for outlet selection, and only 1 in 10 uses probability sampling for item selection. In the absence of probability techniques, so-called judgmental and cutoff selection methods are applied.

12.14 In view of the complexity of the sample designs in compiling a CPI (where the samples of locations, outlets, items, and varieties are just partially connected), an integrated approach to variance estimation can be problematic. Therefore, it appears to be difficult to present a single formula for measuring the variance of a CPI, which captures all

[2] https://www.ilo.org/stat/Areasofwork/WCMS_180241/lang--en/index.htm.

sources of sampling error. It is, however, feasible to develop partial (or conditional) measures, in which only the effect of a single source of variability is quantified. For instance, Balk and Kersten (1986) calculated the variance of a CPI resulting from the sampling variability of the HBS, conditional on the assumption that the partial price indices are known with certainty. Ideally, all the conditional sampling errors should be put together in a unified framework to assess the relative importance of the various sources of error. Under rather restrictive assumptions, Balk (1989a) derived an integrated framework for the overall sampling error of a CPI.

12.15 There are various procedures for estimating the sampling variance arising from a probability sampling design. For instance, assuming a cross-classified sampling design in which samples of items and outlets are drawn independently from a two-dimensional population, with probabilities proportional to size (PPS) in both dimensions, a variance formula can be derived. Where an overall estimate of the sampling variance cannot be made, at the very least, a basic analysis should be conducted.

12.16 The main problem with nonprobability sampling is that there is no theoretically acceptable way of knowing whether the dispersion in the sample data accurately reflects the dispersion in the population. It is then necessary to rely on approximation techniques for variance estimation. One such technique is quasi-randomization (see Särndal and others [1992, 574]), in which assumptions are made about the probabilities of sampling items and outlets. The problem with this method is that it is difficult to find a probability model that adequately approximates the method actually used for outlet and item selection. Another possibility is to use a replication method, such as the method of random groups, balanced half-samples, jackknife, or bootstrap. This is a completely nonparametric class of methods to estimate sampling distributions and standard errors. Each replication method works by drawing a large number of subsamples from the given sample. From each subsample, the parameter of interest can be estimated. Under rather weak conditions, it can be shown that the distribution of the resulting estimates approximates the sampling distribution of the original estimator. For more details on the replication methods, see Särndal and others (1992, 418–445).

Qualitative Assessment of Nonsampling Errors

12.17 As estimating the quantitative impact of the nonsampling errors is more difficult, a qualitative assessment should be provided. For instance, the coverage of the sampling frames as a proxy of the target populations can be described and provided (including gaps, duplications, and definitional problems). The percentage of the target outlet samples from which responses or usable price data were obtained (that is, the response rates) can be provided. Any known difference in the prices of responding outlets and nonresponding outlets can be described, as can an indication of the method of imputation or estimation used to compensate for nonresponse. Other examples of qualitative measures of nonsampling errors are indicators such as implicit quality indices, which compare indices with and without prices adjusted for quality changes. Similarly, the effects of editing can be measured by comparing the CPI estimates based on edited and nonedited data sets. As processing errors tend not to be well-reported or well-documented, they are seldom treated in the survey research literature. The occurrence of processing errors can be reduced through survey process improvements. Several categories of nonsampling errors provide the bulk of the bias issues discussed in paragraphs 12.30–12.73.

Procedures to Minimize Errors

12.18 The *estimation error* can be controlled and minimized by means of the sampling design. For example, by increasing the sample size, or by taking selection probabilities proportional to some well-chosen auxiliary variable, the error in the estimated CPI can be reduced. The choice of an adequate sampling design for the CPI is an extremely complex matter (see Dorfman and others [2006]). The target population is the set of all goods and services that are acquired, used, or paid for by households from outlets in a particular period. A proper probability sampling procedure selects a sample by a random mechanism in which each good or service in the population has a known probability of selection. In combination with a Horvitz–Thompson estimator,[3] such a probability sampling design will produce an index that is (approximately) unbiased and precise.

12.19 The probability sampling designs used extensively in survey practice are simple random sampling and PPS sampling, with or without some form of stratification (more details are provided in Chapter 4). The advantage of simple random sampling is its simplicity; it gives each population element the same probability of being included in the sample. PPS sampling has the advantage that the more important elements have a larger chance of being sampled than the less important ones. For instance, in one European NSO, the outlets are selected with probabilities proportional to some proxy for size, namely their number of employees. Unequal probability designs can lead to a substantial variance reduction in comparison with equal probability designs. In stratified sampling, the population is divided into nonoverlapping subpopulations called strata. For instance, in another European NSO, the population of outlets is split into two outlet types (chain and independent) to form different strata by region. In each stratum, a sample is selected by PPS sampling or simple random sampling. One of the reasons why stratification is so popular is that, if strata are well constructed, it results in low variance of the price changes within a stratum. Stratification is a useful strategy to make the sample more efficient.

12.20 Because appropriate sampling frames are generally not available, samples are frequently obtained by nonprobability methods. Judgmental (or purposive) sampling is one form of nonrandom selection. In this case, someone with knowledge on where households make expenditure (for example, data collector) selects certain "typical" locations and outlets where data are to be collected. With their knowledge, a fairly good sample might result. A more sophisticated nonprobability method is quota sampling. In quota sampling, the population is first divided into certain strata. For each stratum, the number (quota) of locations and outlets to be included in the sample is fixed. Next, the price

[3] D. G. Horvitz, and D. J. Thompson. 1952. "A Generalization of Sampling without Replacement from a Finite Universe." *Journal of the American Statistical Association* 47: 663–85. JSTOR 2280784

collector in the field simply fills the quotas, which means in the case of outlet sampling that the selection of the outlets is ultimately based on the judgment of the price collectors. Another nonprobability method is cutoff sampling, which means that a part of the target population is deliberately excluded from the sample selection process. This procedure is used when the distribution of the value of some auxiliary variable is highly skewed. For instance, a large part of the population may consist of small outlets whose contribution to total sales is modest. A decision may then be taken to exclude from the sampling frame the outlets with the lowest sales. Because the selection is nonrandom, nonprobability methods usually lead to biased estimates. Empirical results of research presented in de Haan and others (1997) nevertheless show that nonprobability selection methods do not necessarily perform worse, with regard to the mean square error, than probability sampling techniques.

12.21 Provided that the sampling design is given, the sampling variance of an estimated (all-items) CPI can in general be lowered by:

- Enlarging the samples of items and outlets
- The application of suitable stratifications to the various populations (for example, grouping items with respect to similarity of price changes)

12.22 It is important to allocate optimally the available resources both between and within the different CPI samples, since badly allocated samples may lead to unnecessarily high sampling errors. Dalén and Ohlsson (1995) show that the error resulting from item sampling is relatively high compared with the error resulting from outlet sampling. In this case, it is worthwhile increasing the sample size of items and reducing the sample size of outlets. Beisteiner (2008) stresses the importance of allocating resources to those areas where the effect on the quality of the all-items CPI is maximized, especially to goods and services with a high relative expenditure weight and to goods and services with high dispersion of prices. The paper presents a "ready-to-use" formula, the Neyman formula, for the allocation of the sample, which optimizes the precision of the CPI for given resources, as discussed in Chapter 4.

12.23 A systematic analysis of sampling errors offers possibilities for improving efficiency or reducing cost. The problem of optimum sample allocation is usually formulated as the determination of the sizes of the samples of items and outlets, and their distribution over the strata that minimizes the sampling error of an all-items CPI, subject to the available budget.

12.24 The accuracy of the CPI could be improved by making use of scanner data, which collect more prices for more varieties on more days of the month than traditional data collection methods. Bradley (1996) discusses the potential for scanner data to reduce the sampling error of the corresponding official CPI component index. The use of scanner data also has a positive effect on the time dimension of sampling, covering a time span much longer than the one covered by the traditional data collection. In Chapter 10, it is argued that scanner data should cover the whole period for which CPI is constructed, rather than a subperiod. In some cases, the use of scanner data removes the need for sampling as a census of products can be used.

12.25 As already mentioned, a business register can be subject to overcoverage when used as a sampling frame for outlets. Often, they include outlets that are no longer in business or have changed the activity. Other sources, described in more detail in Chapter 4, can be used as a sampling frame. In the absence of any reliable source of data that can be used as a sampling frame, it is recommended to set up an appropriate sampling frame by enumeration of the main outlets within each sampled location. Such enumeration yields a list of all outlets in a location together with the item groups that belong to their assortments. When formal sampling techniques cannot be applied, outlets can be selected using judgmental methods. For example, a more judgmental approach to organizing an outlet sampling frame is to ask the price collectors—who may be assumed to know the local situation well—to make a list of outlets where purchases are made by households. It is important that information about the quality of the sampling frame, with regard to overcoverage or undercoverage, and its completeness for the target population is known.

12.26 The populations of items (and varieties) and outlets are continually changing through time. The composition of most item groups is not constant over time, because items disappear from the market and new ones appear. The outlet population also changes over time: outlets close, temporarily or permanently; new outlets open; and the importance of some outlets diminishes or increases. The samples of items (and varieties) and outlets should be reviewed and updated periodically to maintain their representativity with respect to the current expenditure patterns of the households. In many countries, these are reviewed and updated every year.

12.27 *Measurement errors* by price collectors can be reduced by providing them with handheld computers or tablets for data entry that have integrated validation checks. In this way, the validation and editing of observed prices can be executed at the point of price collection (that is, in the outlet) by comparing the currently observed price quote with the previously observed one (by setting a limit on the percentage price change) and with the price quotes obtained from other outlets (by setting suitable upper and lower limits). Details are provided in Chapter 5 on the use of handheld computers and tablets for price collection. Although using pricing forms that contain information on the previous period's price can reduce response variance, it may also cause response bias and delay in reporting price change. Before introducing handheld computers and tablets, proper usability testing and training for price collectors are required to avoid them being a source of error.

12.28 It is useful to appoint data collection supervisors to conduct quality assurance checks on the price collectors. It is also a good idea to organize regular meetings where price collectors and CPI compilers from the head office can share their experiences. In this way, the compilers will keep in touch with the conditions in the field and may take the opportunity to provide more information about frequently made price collection errors and new representative products.

12.29 It is important to check the collected price data for *processing errors* and, where possible, to correct these errors. This activity is called data editing. The first stage of editing includes the review and validation of individual observations. When the resources to spend on data editing must be minimized, while at the same time maintaining a high level of data quality, selective editing and a broad review of the compiled data are possibilities. Selective editing is a form of traditional micro-editing in which the number of edits is kept to a minimum. Only those edits that have an impact on the survey results are carried out. A review of the compiled indices offers a top-down approach. The edits are carried out on aggregated data (for example, the price index numbers of an item group) instead of individual records (for example, price observations). A review of individual records is then carried out only if the top-down review raises suspicion. Attention should particularly be paid to outliers among the observations (more information on data editing and the use of algorithms is provided in Chapter 5; a comprehensive description of statistical data editing procedures is given in De Waal and others [2011]).

12.30 *Nonresponse* reduces sample size, results in increased variance, and usually introduces selection bias. Nonresponse rates, or missing observations, are often viewed as a proxy for the quality of a survey. While nonresponse rates are important, imputation rates alone provide no indication of nonresponse bias. There are three methods for the treatment of missing price observations. First, the corresponding price can be excluded from the data set of previous period prices, so that the set of previous period prices is "matched" with the set of current prices. Second, this matching can be achieved by using an imputed (or artificial) price for the missing one. The imputed price can be calculated by either carrying forward the previous price observation or by extrapolating the previous price observation using the change of other price observations for the same item. Third, there is the possibility to reweight the sample to minimize the effect of nonresponse error. The objective of reweighting is to inflate the weight given to the prices of the responding outlets. This compensates for those prices that are lost by nonresponse (for details, including advantages and disadvantages of each approach, see Chapter 6).

Types of Bias

12.31 Bias is defined as a systematic tendency for the calculated CPI to diverge from some ideal or preferred index, resulting from the method of data collection or processing, or the index formula used. This section reviews several categories of systematic error, either in pricing or in index construction, that potentially can lead to bias in the all-items CPI. The emphasis here is on the categorization of different types of bias, along with some consideration of their likely size, but also on methods to reduce or eliminate these categories of bias. The question might arise of why such a discussion is necessary, since such issues as quality change, and the appropriate methods for handling them in the CPI, are dealt with at both a conceptual and operational level in other chapters (see Chapter 8 of the publication *Consumer Price Indices Theory*).

12.32 The reason why this chapter addresses the topic of CPI bias is the great surge in interest in price measurement problems during the mid-1990s. Especially in the United States (US), the view became widespread that the CPI was subject to systematic upward biases because of the failure to deal adequately with product substitution by consumers, product quality improvements, and the introduction of new goods and services. Moreover, it was recognized, first, that the existence of such upward bias would have fundamental implications for the measurement of recent trends in output and productivity, and second, that the elimination of upward bias could substantially improve the government budget situation through reduced government expenditure and increased tax revenue (see, for example, Eldridge [1999] and Duggan and Gillingham [1999]). These findings led to a series of papers and reports on CPI measurement problems, often accompanied by point estimates of aggregate bias.

12.33 One of the most prominent examples of these quantitative studies of bias is that by the Advisory Commission to Study the CPI (US Senate 1996).[4] Responses and estimates by statistical agencies include those provided by Abraham and others (1998), US Bureau of Labor Statistics (1998), Ducharme (1997), Edwards (1997), Fenwick (1997), Johnson and others (2006), Lequiller (1997), Moulton (1996b), and Moulton and Moses (1997). Research undertaken has shown that it is difficult to both quantify and assess the direction of potential bias, and that the extent, the direction, and even the existence of bias remain something that will depend upon the specific circumstances of each set of CPI estimates and cannot always be determined with certainty.

12.34 Two points are worth making at the outset with respect to measuring bias in CPIs. First, the issue has usually been addressed in the context of the cost of living index (COLI). That is, the CPI bias has been defined as the difference between the rate of increase in the CPI and the rate of increase in a true COLI. Many discussions on bias have taken as given that the COLI should be the CPI's measurement objective. Somewhat different conclusions might be reached if the index objective was taken to be a fixed-basket price index. Notably, the gains in consumer welfare from a widening array of new products, or the ability of consumers to substitute away from items with increasing relative prices, might be deemed irrelevant and an index that ignored those factors might not be judged biased on that account.

12.35 The second point is that CPI bias is not amenable to estimation with the same level of rigor as that used in CPI variance estimation. Since the COLI or other ideal target index is unobserved, analysts have been forced to rely in part on conjectures and on generalizations from fragmentary empirical evidence to quantify the extent of bias. The notable exception is with respect to substitution bias, when indices using superlative formulas can be computed using the same underlying price and expenditure data and compared with historical CPI data to estimate the upward bias from use of the traditional formulas.

12.36 Several different taxonomies of bias have appeared in the literature mentioned previously. It is sufficient, however, to employ four categories roughly corresponding to those set forth in the best-known study, namely the *Final report of the Advisory Commission to Study the CPI* (the Boskin Commission), established by the US Senate Finance Committee in 1995. These categories are upper-level substitution bias; elementary aggregate bias; quality change and new goods bias; and new outlet bias.

12.37 These categories can be further broken down into two subgroups according to whether they refer to errors in

[4]Others include Congressional Budget Office (1994), Crawford (1998), Cunningham (1996), Dalén (1999a), Diewert (1996c), Lebow and others (1994), Lebow and Rudd (2003), Shapiro and Wilcox (1997b), Shiratsuka (1999), White (1999), and Wynne and Sigalla (1994).

individual price measurements or errors in computing index series. Quality change bias and new goods bias arise because of failures to measure adequately the value to consumers of individual goods and services that appear in (or disappear from) the marketplace. It should be recognized that discussions of "new goods" problems apply equally to all products, whether goods or services. At a conceptual level, it can be difficult to distinguish these two biases from each other. Operationally, however, quality change bias pertains to the procedures for comparing new products or models with the older products they replace in the CPI samples. In general, new goods bias can be thought of as applying to entirely new types of products, or products that would not enter samples routinely through forced replacement. New outlet bias, sometimes referred to as outlet substitution bias, is similar to new goods bias but is focused on the appearance of new types of outlets or marketing methods that offer goods and services at lower prices or higher quality.

12.38 The other categories of bias refer to the procedures for constructing index values from component series. As noted throughout this Manual, CPI compilation can be thought of as taking place in two steps, or at two levels. At the lower level, individual price quotations are combined; at the upper level, these elementary indices are aggregated together. Corresponding to these two levels are two forms of potential bias. Elementary aggregate bias involves the averaging formulas used to combine price quotations into elementary indices. Upper-level substitution bias applies to the formulas used to combine those elementary aggregates into higher-level indices. These components of potential bias, and the means used to measure them, are discussed in more detail in paragraphs 12.38–12.72.

Components of Bias

Upper-Level Substitution Bias

12.39 Upper-level substitution bias is perhaps the most widely accepted source of CPI bias, and the kind with which economists are most familiar from literature on price index theory and practice. Simply stated, it arises when CPIs employ the Laspeyres formula, which is well known to provide an upper bound on a COLI under certain assumptions about consumer behavior (see Chapter 4 of the publication *Consumer Price Index Theory*), or a similar method that uses a fixed-base or -basket index, like the Lowe and Young formulas. The assumption in the definition of the Laspeyres-type price index is that substitution among goods is zero, which is against one of the cornerstones in the theory of consumer demand. Quantitative measures of upper-level substitution bias can be generated by comparing Laspeyres-type price indices to Fisher ideal, Törnqvist, or other superlative indices. Under certain assumptions about, for example, constant preferences, these will stand as relatively precise bias estimates.

12.40 Genereux (1983) and Aizcorbe and Jackman (1993) provide such index comparisons and estimates of upper-level substitution bias using actual CPI series for Canada and the United States, respectively. Other early studies by Braithwait (1980) and Manser and McDonald (1988) estimate the substitution bias in US national account indices. Instead of superlative indices, the Braithwait study uses estimated exact COLIs based on demand system estimation. A similar estimate for the Netherlands is provided by Balk (1990). In these studies, and in the more recent analyses of US CPI data by Shapiro and Wilcox (1997a) and Cage and others (2003), the existence of an upward bias from the Laspeyres formula is demonstrated consistently. The biases in the annual index changes in individual years are relatively small, typically 0.3 percentage points or less, and depend empirically on such factors as the distance from the Laspeyres base period, the level of index detail at which the alternative formulas are applied, and whether the superlative index is of the fixed base or chained variety.

12.41 The major differences between Laspeyres and superlative indices rise from the variation in the relative prices over the period being compared, and from the shift in quantities consumed toward those index categories that have fallen in relative price. This leads to several conclusions:

- If index movements are characterized by continuing, uniform drift in relative prices over time, with accompanying drifts in consumption, the size of the annual Laspeyres bias will tend to increase with the distance from the base period. The estimates of the upper-level substitution bias presented in Australian Bureau of Statistics (2017) show that average annual substitution bias is 0.11 one year after a reweight of the CPI, increasing to 0.20 in the sixth year. Greenlees (1997) notes that there is little evidence for this phenomenon in the United States; see also Szulc (1983).
- Under the same circumstances, reducing the expenditure weight chaining interval will work to reduce the upper-level substitution bias in the Laspeyres-type CPI. The more frequent chaining will increase the weight given to indices that are falling in relative price, thereby reducing the rate of CPI growth. Conversely, if there is "bouncing" in relative index movements, frequent chaining can lead to an upward "chain drift" in a Laspeyres index.
- Upper-level substitution bias will tend to be larger during periods of higher inflation, if these periods also have greater relative price variation. However, little empirical evidence exists on this point.

12.42 The concept of upper-level substitution bias has been derived and discussed in the context of COLI theory, but an equivalent bias may be defined from the perspective of the fixed-basket price index. If the Fisher ideal or other superlative index is judged preferable based on its symmetric treatment of base period and current period expenditure patterns, then the difference between that index and a Laspeyres could be interpreted as a measure of representativity bias. A similar argument could be applied with respect to lower-level substitution bias within elementary index aggregates.

12.43 Lebow and Rudd (2003) have defined and estimated another category of bias related to upper-level aggregation. They concluded that the HBS weights used in the United States CPI were subject to error because of, for example, underreporting of alcohol and tobacco expenditures. This will lead to a weighting bias if the errors in relative weight are correlated with component index changes (sources for and problems with expenditure weight estimation are discussed in detail in Chapter 3).

Elementary Aggregate Bias

12.44 Elementary aggregate bias arises from the use of an inappropriate method for aggregating price quotations at the lowest level of aggregation. An elementary index in the CPI is biased if its expectation differs from its measurement objective. This bias can take two forms: formula bias or lower-level substitution bias. The index suffers from formula bias if, as a result of the properties of the formula, the result produced is biased relative to what would have been the result if a price change of a fixed basket could have been estimated. The index suffers from lower-level substitution bias if it does not reflect product substitution by consumers among the items contained in that elementary aggregate. Lower-level substitution error is only relevant where the measurement objective is a COLI. Thus, given any elementary index formula, the two forms of bias can be distinguished according to the objective of the elementary index.

12.45 Chapter 8 of this Manual and Chapter 6 of the publication *Consumer Price Index Theory* discuss the characteristics and provide detail, an illustration, and the relative merits of the use of different elementary index number formulas. A key finding is that the Carli formula or the arithmetic average of price ratios is unsuitable for a CPI because it is liable to lead to substantial drift in the results, especially when used in its chained form. Therefore, the recommendation is that the Carli formula should not be used, especially in its chained form. The problems with elementary aggregate bias and the methods chosen to address them are discussed, for example, by Reinsdorf (1998), Reinsdorf and Moulton (1997), and Moulton (1996b).

12.46 The ratio of arithmetic mean (Dutot) and geometric mean (Jevons) formulas eliminate formula bias as defined here. Their expectations differ, however, when item prices do not change at a uniform rate. The differences provide one way of evaluating the potential importance of lower-level substitution bias. The geometric mean formula is exact for a COLI if consumers follow the Cobb–Douglas behavioral model (that is, assuming that consumers adjust the relative quantities they consume inversely in proportion to the changes in relative prices so that expenditure shares remain constant), whereas the formula based on the ratio of arithmetic means corresponds to zero-substitution behavior. Thus, if the goal is to approximate a COLI, the geometric mean formula is judged preferable.

12.47 Scanner data provide new opportunities for measuring and addressing elementary aggregate bias. The availability of both prices and quantity information in scanner data remove the need for an unweighted index formula, at least for those items where unit values are available, and allows the calculation of elementary indices by employing superlative formulas. By using scanner data, Gabor and Vermeulen (2015) compute product category level elementary price indices using nine different index formulas (Carli, Dutot, Jevons, Laspeyres, Paasche, Fisher, Lowe, Geometric Lowe, and expenditure weighted Jevons) and compare the resulting indices with the Fisher index. The main findings are that across product groups mean levels of annual elementary index bias vary between −0.53 and 0.55 percentage points depending on the index.

12.48 Haan and Heymerik (2009) have identified a problem associated with the use of scanner data, especially when bilateral superlative price indices are used. The high-frequency chaining, used to handle the high attrition rate of items, can create drift in the index series when prices and quantities change or bounce arising from sales. Therefore, new methods have been developed for price measurement based on scanner data. The approach proposed in Ivancic and others (2009) that provides drift-free, superlative-type indices through adapting multilateral index number theory seems to provide a solution to this problem. The methods proposed, however, pose some practical challenges and require some more evidence before becoming widely accepted. For an overview of methods for price measurement using scanner data, see Chessa and others (2017) and Chapter 10 on scanner data.

12.49 The method used by the NSO for sampling items within a category will determine the effectiveness of formula choice in dealing with lower-level substitution bias. For example, if only a single representative item is chosen to represent the category, the index formula will fail to reflect the consumer response to any relative price change in the universe of items. Therefore, a larger sample of representative items should yield a smaller sampling variance for a given elementary index. More generally, the geometric mean formula index suffers from an upward bias in very small samples (fewer than five observations), so lower-level substitution bias may be underestimated in empirical comparisons of the geometric mean to other index formulas. White (1999) discusses the relationship between sampling error and bias estimates. McClelland and Reinsdorf (1999) also study the impact of small sample sizes on the index and conclude that it has the effect of raising the expected values of an index based on nonlinear formulas, especially the geometric mean formulas. More extensive use of scanner data may mitigate the problem of small sample given that sample sizes in a typical scanner data set are large. In some cases, the use of scanner data may remove the need for sampling.

12.50 The impact of formula choice can be estimated with some degree of precision over a given historical period. Any corresponding bias, however, can be estimated only by assuming that the geometric mean or other functional form successfully approximates the index's measurement objective.

12.51 As implied by the previous discussion, the importance of elementary aggregate bias will vary by country, depending on the particular index formulas used, the degree of heterogeneity within index strata, and the sampling methods employed. Also, as with upper-level substitution bias, elementary aggregate bias will vary with the overall level of inflation in the economy if absolute and relative price changes are correlated.

12.52 The performance of any formula for elementary aggregate calculation will also be affected by the methods used by the NSO to handle special situations, such as seasonal products and other products that are temporarily unavailable. Armknecht and Maitland-Smith (1999) discuss how the failure to impute missing prices can lead to bias in the modified Laspeyres and other index formulas.

Quality Change and New Goods Bias

12.53 Discussion of potential CPI biases arising from inadequate quality adjustment has a long history. For example, the Stigler Committee report on US price statistics (Price Statistics Review Committee, 1961) indicated that *if a poll were taken of professional economists and statisticians, in all probability they would designate (and by a wide majority) the failure of the price indices to take full account of quality changes as the most important defect of these indices*. In most studies of bias, unmeasured or mismeasured quality change is also the largest contributor to the total estimated bias. Just as quality adjustment is widely recognized as an extremely difficult process, it is correspondingly difficult to measure any quality change bias.

12.54 Unlike substitution bias, which can be estimated by comparison of alternative formulas, quality change bias must be analyzed on a product-by-product basis. Products and their associated index components will experience widely varying rates of quality change over time. Moreover, the methods used for quality adjustment will also vary. Whereas the linking method (link to show no change) may dominate with regard to frequency of use, important index components may employ production cost, hedonic adjustment, or the other methods described in Chapter 6 of this Manual and Chapter 8 of the publication *Consumer Price Index Theory*.

12.55 A crucial point to recognize is that the direction of overall quality change does not imply the direction of any quality change bias. Nonexperts sometimes assume that little or no quality adjustment is carried out in the CPI, and that it therefore must overestimate price change in view of the many demonstrable improvements over time in the quality of goods and services. Rather, for any component index, the issue is whether the direct or indirect method chosen for quality adjustment overestimates or underestimates the relative quality of replacement items in the CPI sample. The resulting bias can be either positive or negative.

12.56 Empirical evidence on quality change bias has been based largely on extrapolation from individual studies of particular products. These individual studies may involve, for example, comparisons of hedonic regression indices to the corresponding CPI series or estimates of the value of some product improvement that is ignored in CPI calculations. Although the majority of such studies have suggested upward rather than downward bias, the reliance on fragmentary evidence has led to criticism by observers who point to evidence of quality declines that have not been subjected to systematic analysis.

12.57 Overall quality trends can also be a matter of subjective valuation, especially for services. New technology has led to unambiguous improvements in the quality of many consumer durables and other goods. By contrast, in service sectors such as mail delivery, public transport, and medical care, it can be difficult to evaluate changes in quality. Airline travel, for example, has become safer and faster but perhaps less comfortable and reliable in recent decades, and the lack of cross-sectional variation in these characteristics makes the use of hedonic quality adjustment problematic.

12.58 Digitalization of the economy, if not properly captured, could also be a source of bias. Reinsdorf and Schreyer (2017) identify three possible sources of distortion that the digital economy can cause, one of which is *incomplete adjustment for quality change, that is, the treatment of new, and typically improved, varieties of existing digital products; the treatment of new digital products that replace existing nondigital products; and improved variety selection of digital and nondigital products* yield overestimation of inflation. By using the weights in an average consumption basket for the Organisation of Economic Co-operation and Development (OECD) member countries from the OECD purchasing power parities program,[5] the inflation was overestimated by 0.28 percentage points because of possible underadjustment for quality changes in digital products such as computers, information and communication technology equipment, and telecommunication services.

12.59 New goods bias, like elementary aggregate bias, can be divided conceptually into two components. The first concerns the failure to bring new products into the CPI sample with sufficient speed. This can lead to upward bias if those new products later experience large price reductions that are not reflected in the index. The second component is the welfare gain that consumers experience when a new product appears; however, this may not be viewed as a bias if the CPI measurement objective is a cost of goods index and not a COLI.

12.60 As discussed in Chapter 6, "new goods" can be replacements for disappearing items, for example, cloud storage areas replacing physical storage devices; new varieties of an existing product that widen the range of consumer choice, such as nonalcoholic beers and ethnic restaurants; or products that represent entirely new categories of consumption, such as multitask robots for cooking or smartphones.

12.61 Like quality change bias, new goods bias has sometimes been estimated primarily by generalization from individual product evidence. A frequent approach has been to measure the price change for a product or category during a period prior to its entry into the CPI sample. Studies by Hausman (1997, 1999) on breakfast cereals and mobile phones provided quantitative measures of the consumer surplus gain from the new products, but this complex econometric approach has not been applied widely. Some of the Boskin Commission's estimates of new product bias, notably those for food, were necessarily based on conjecture.

12.62 Also, like quality change bias, new goods bias could be negative if the range of products decreases, if valuable consumer goods disappear from the market, or if the index fails to capture phases of rapid price increase for items. Most observers, however, seem to agree on the direction of bias as upward, and that the uncertainty concerns the magnitude. The extent of the new goods bias depends on the importance of the new products with regard to the proportion of consumer expenditure spent on new products not yet introduced in the CPI basket, and the extent of the price decline from the initial price.

12.63 One of the risks of downward bias in the CPI is associated with producers that reduce the package size of household goods keeping the price stable ("shrinkflation") or repacking the old product. This phenomenon is strictly linked with the minor changes in product packaging or product characteristics (so-called product relaunches). These should be properly handled, through the use of a unit value approach, in particular in scanner data, because the product relaunched in most of the cases presents a new Global Trade

[5] https://www.oecd.org/sdd/prices-ppp/.

Item Number but it is directly comparable with the product before the relaunch. When scanner data are used in CPI and large amounts of data are processed on a weekly basis, it is not possible to observe and report all changes incurred in the size or in the characteristics of the product and assess the comparability of the previous and the replacing product. Therefore, automatic procedures have to be carefully implemented to link different Global Trade Item Numbers in contiguous months and correctly estimate the price change, avoiding the risk of bias that usually is downward.

New Outlet Bias

12.64 Conceptually, new outlet bias is identical to new goods bias. It arises because of the failure to reflect either price changes in new outlets not yet sampled, or the welfare gain to consumers when the new outlets appear. The explanation for its existence as a separate bias category is twofold. The first reason is historical: new outlet bias was identified by Reinsdorf (1993) as a potentially major explanation for anomalous movements in the US CPI. Second, the methods used to sample and compare outlets differ from those used with products, and the problems in controlling new outlet bias are somewhat different.

12.65 A failure to maintain a current outlet sample can introduce bias because the new outlets are distinctive in their pricing or service policy. Reinsdorf (1993) and, more recently, Hausman and Leibtag (2004, 2005) focus on the growth of discount stores. It should be noted, however, that the problem could also be geographical in nature; it is important to employ outlet sampling frames that reflect new as well as traditional shopping locations, although the widespread and increasing weight of online outlets have changed the dimension of this issue.

12.66 One way that new products enter the CPI sample is through forced replacement, when exiting or less successful products disappear from shelves. Outlet disappearance is less frequent, and NSO procedures may not provide for automatic replacement. Moreover, when a new outlet enters the sample there are no standard procedures for comparing data at the new and old outlets. Thus, the index will not incorporate any effects of, for example, lower price or inferior service quality at the new outlet.

12.67 Reinsdorf (1993) estimated the degree of new outlet bias by comparing average prices at outlets entering and disappearing from US CPI samples. There has been little or no empirical work, however, on the measurement or consumer valuation of outlet quality such as product variety, location, car parking, and customer services. As a consequence, there is little evidence on how to evaluate the accuracy of new outlet bias estimates.

12.68 Greenlees and McClelland (2012) confirm the potential importance of new outlets bias in the CPI. This study provides new and detailed evidence on the impact of the appearance and growth of new types of outlets on the CPI. Using price data collected by the US Bureau of Labor Statistics for 2002–2007, the authors observed a continuous increase in the market share of discount department stores and warehouse club stores, and significantly lower prices in these stores than at large grocery stores. The increasing shares of lower-priced store categories reduced the average prices collected by the Bureau of Labor Statistics. Changes in the distribution of outlets within categories also led to a substantial decline in average prices. Hausman (2004) also documents the growing role of discount outlets and provides a specific example of outlet bias.

12.69 Like with new goods bias, most studies seem to agree on the direction of bias as upward. The extent of the new outlet bias depends on (1) the components of the CPI basket that are likely to be affected, (2) the change in market share of new outlets for these items, and (3) the percentage difference in quality-adjusted prices between new outlets and old outlets. Estimates of the size of outlet substitution bias must take into account the fact that the market price of an item depends on both the quality of the item and the quality of the outlet where it is purchased, based on such factors as the level of service and the convenience of the location.

Summary of Bias Estimates

12.70 The 1996 Boskin Commission report gave a range of estimates for the total upward US CPI bias of 0.8–1.6 percentage points, with the point estimate being 1.1 percentage points. This total reflects the straightforward summation of the component bias estimates. As reported in US General Accounting Office (2000), however, changes in CPI methods subsequent to 1996 led the Boskin Commission members to reduce their estimates of total bias. Lacking evidence to the contrary, additivity of biases has been assumed in most such studies. Shapiro and Wilcox (1997b) provide probability distributions and correlations of their component bias estimates, yielding an overall confidence interval for the total bias. Most detailed studies of bias also conclude that the CPI bias is in an upward direction, although there have been numerous criticisms of that conclusion. For example, Brown and Stockburger (2006) estimated that the hedonic quality-adjustment methods in apparel have had both upward and downward impacts at different points in time and for different categories of clothing in the United States.

12.71 In general, NSOs cannot compute or publish CPI bias estimates on a regular basis. Many of the same obstacles that prevent the elimination of bias also stand in the way of estimating bias. These include the lack of complete data on product-level consumer preferences and expenditure behavior, and the inability to observe and value all differences in quality among items in the market. Without such information, it is impossible to calculate a true COLI, and similarly impossible to measure the divergence between its rate of growth and the growth rate of the CPI.

12.72 NSOs have been reluctant to provide their own estimates of CPI bias. In some cases, they have accepted the existence of substitution bias, recognizing that the use of a Laspeyres formula implies that the CPI usually will overstate price change relative to a COLI estimated by a superlative index such as the Fisher. NSOs have, however, been reluctant to draw even qualitative conclusions from the fragmentary and speculative evidence on quality change, new goods, and new outlet bias.

12.73 The CPI bias may appear to a different extent in different countries. Hanousek and Filer (2001) show that bias was especially high in countries in transition and during the period of high inflation. They argue that the substitution bias increases with the increase of the variance of relative price changes. They argue that bias arising from substitution increases in line with the level of inflation, because, as the rate of inflation increases, so does the variance of relative price changes.

Procedures to Minimize Bias

12.74 Although it is almost impossible to eliminate sources of bias, measures can be taken to minimize them. These include:

i. Use appropriate formulas in compiling elementary aggregate indices, in particular use of the geometric mean (Jevons) formula where appropriate or the ratio of arithmetic prices (Dutot) formula.
ii. Review and update weights and CPI baskets frequently, but at least once every five years. Given that a significant part of the total measurement bias in the CPI may be caused by the fixed nature of the CPI basket, the item-substitution bias and some of the new products bias could be reduced by increasing the frequency at which weights are updated. For some categories, it may be necessary to update the weights more frequently as such weights are likely to become out of date more quickly than higher-level weights. In periods of high inflation, the weights should be updated even more frequently. Scanner data may help in this, at least for some areas such as food.
iii. Use a superlative index formula rather than the Laspeyres, if current period weighting data can be obtained on time. Where Lowe or Young indices are used, the upper-level substitution bias can be reduced by more frequent updating of expenditure weights, implementing them with minimal time lag. Other options might be to use formulas that allow substitution or assumptions about substitution between elementary aggregates to be entered.
iv. Closely monitor and update outlet samples to reflect changes in the outlets from which households purchase. For example, there is clearly a need to plan for the inclusion in CPIs of purchases from outlets operating exclusively online, but also from discount outlets, factory outlets, or others whose importance has been increasing.
v. Include new goods in the CPI as soon as possible. For a fixed-weight index such as Laspeyres, there would also be a need to update the fixed weights to allow for the inclusion of new goods if they are substituting for all goods in general, or to adjust the weights within an item group if the new goods are substituting for specific items. For example, one could argue that MP3 players were a new good, but as they were substituting for portable cassette and CD players, they could be introduced into the item grouping for portable cassette and CD players, and weights between these items adjusted accordingly.
vi. Ensure that the most appropriate quality-adjustment methods are applied.
vii. Make greater use of the scanner data to deal with quality change, substitution, and new products. Scanner data contain detailed and timely information on the prices and quantities of all consumer transactions. The role for scanner data cannot be understated, given its ability to track market trends and detect the emergence of new products on the market, helping to reduce the lag in introducing new goods into the CPI basket. The use of scanner data also makes it possible to compile superlative price indices at detailed aggregation levels since prices and quantities are available.

Key Recommendations

- In order to ensure public confidence in a CPI, a detailed and up-to-date description of the methods and data sources should be published. The document should include, among other things, the objectives and scope of the index, details of the weights, and a discussion of the accuracy of the index.
- A description of the sources and magnitude of the sampling and nonsampling errors (for example, coverage or nonresponse rates) in a CPI should be published to provide users with valuable information on the limitations that might apply to their uses of the index.[6]
- Resources should be allocated to those areas where the effect on the quality of the all-items CPI is maximized, especially to goods and services with a high relative expenditure weight and to those with high dispersion of prices.
- To reduce the index's potential for giving a misleading picture, it is in general essential:
    - To update weights and baskets regularly
    - To employ unbiased elementary aggregate formulae
    - To make appropriate adjustments for quality change
    - To allow adequately and correctly for new products
    - To take proper account of substitution issues
    - To undertake quality control of the entire compilation process

12.75 Improving precision and accuracy of the CPI will take both time and resources. Resources should be allocated to those areas where the effect on the quality of the all-items CPI is maximized, especially to goods and services with a high relative expenditure weight and to those with high dispersion of prices. Further uses of scanner data can help NSOs deal with the quality changes, outlet substitution, and new goods bias problems. An investigation into factors affecting consumer choice and an expanded HBS would help identify consumer preferences for different outlet types and to improve accurate price measurement in areas where quality change is rapid. Opportunities presented by technology, such as the use of computer-assisted techniques, scanning, and web scraping techniques, can minimize processing errors.

[6]Examples of handbooks of CPI methods are those published by the US Bureau of Labor Statistics (2015) and Australian Bureau of Statistics (2018, Chapter 11), which devote a section to the varieties and sources of possible error in the index.

DATA QUALITY MANAGEMENT AND REPORTING 13

Introduction

13.1 Consumer price indices (CPI) are one of the most important statistical indicators produced on a regular basis by national statistical offices (NSOs). Besides informing economic policy, they are used for indexation of social security benefits, pensions, salaries and wages, and also for escalation clauses in private contracts, as mentioned in Chapter 2. Given the considerable financial consequences that any errors in the CPI can have on the government budget over the long term, as well as other financial implications related to wages and other uses as an escalator, accuracy and reliability are particularly paramount for a CPI.

13.2 This chapter addresses the issue of quality management and reporting. It gives an overview of the processes and procedures that can be used for quality control of the CPI production process and the quality indicators that can be used to measure the extent to which the computed index meets the prescribed concepts and methodologies that underlie and define the target index. It begins by providing an overview in the context of the International Monetary Fund (IMF) Data Quality Assessment Framework (DQAF) and then describes various quality management systems and key aspects and processes of quality management in the ongoing production of a CPI.

13.3 The CPI should be produced in accordance with the United Nations *Fundamental Principles of Official Statistics*.[1] The International Labour Organization (ILO) *guidelines concerning dissemination practices for labor statistics* should also be respected.[2]

13.4 The IMF DQAF identifies quality-related features of governance of statistical systems, processes, and products. It is rooted in the United Nations *Fundamental Principles of Official Statistics* and grew out of the IMF's Data Standards Initiatives[3] on data dissemination, including the Special Data Dissemination Standard (SDDS) and the Enhanced General Data Dissemination System (e-GDDS). The DQAF provides a structure for assessing existing practices against internationally accepted standards, guidelines, or good practices. It has proved to be useful to NSOs in undertaking self-assessments of the quality of their CPIs that can be the basis for internal planning, justification of additional resources, and evaluation of whether they are fulfilling their obligations to compute a fit-for-purpose CPI, as well as in guiding data users in evaluating data for policy analysis, forecasts, and economic performance.

13.5 The DQAF covers various quality aspects of data governance, collection, processing, and dissemination. It is organized around five dimensions and a set of prerequisites for the assessment of data quality. The five dimensions of data quality include: (1) assurances of integrity (institutional integrity, transparency, and ethical standards); (2) methodological soundness (concepts and definitions, scope, and classifications); (3) accuracy and reliability (adequate data sources and statistical techniques); (4) serviceability (periodicity, consistency, and revisions policy); and (5) accessibility (data and metadata accessibility, and assistance to users). Each dimension comprises three to five elements that are associated with a set of good practices and several relevant indicators. The focus of this chapter is on methodological soundness and, more particularly, accuracy and reliability. The DQAF for a CPI is described in the section that follows.

Data Quality Assessment Framework (DQAF) for a Consumer Price Index

13.6 A conceptually based and systematically executed approach to data quality assessment is essential to achieve a high-quality CPI. The IMF DQAF for a CPI[4] provides a flexible structure specifically for the qualitative assessment of a CPI in a country context. The DQAF for CPI covers the various quality aspects of data collection, processing, and dissemination.

13.7 The Framework is organized in a cascading structure that progresses from abstract principles to more concrete details.

13.8 The methodological soundness of a CPI is assessed against the guidelines outlined in the *System of National Accounts 2008* (*2008 SNA*), this Manual, and the 2003 resolution concerning CPIs adopted by the International Conference of Labor Statisticians (ILO 2003). ILO 2003 outlines the basic principles for the compilation of CPIs. The concepts and definitions from the *2008 SNA* are used as guidelines for coverage and valuation, and the methods and procedures from this Manual are used as guidelines for compiling the CPI. The DQAF lists four elements to be assessed: concepts and definition, scope, classification/sectorization, and basis for recording.

13.9 The accuracy and reliability of a CPI are assessed against whether the source data and statistical techniques are sound and statistical outputs sufficiently portray reality. This dimension covers five elements to be assessed: (1) source data, (2) assessment of source data, (3) statistical techniques, (4) assessment and validation of intermediate data and statistical outputs, and (5) revision studies. The

[1] http://unstats.un.org/unsd/dnss/gp/fundprinciples.aspx.
[2] Sixteenth International Conference of Labour Statisticians, 1998.
[3] https://dsbb.imf.org/.
[4] https://dsbb.imf.org/content/pdfs/dqrs_cpi.pdf.

considerations are wide-ranging. For example, with respect to source data it is assessed if the sample and the estimation procedures are soundly designed to represent the survey universe. This covers both (1) sampling and whether scientific random sampling techniques and cutoff sampling are used to select geographic areas, items, outlets, and varieties, and (2) where sampling frames are not adequate to support statistical sampling, judgmental sampling is used as a second-best procedure with well-defined, published criteria for selection. Similarly, for statistical techniques the assessment is based on a wide range of indicators relating to whether the statistical techniques used conform to sound statistical procedures. These procedures include specific issues that arise in compiling the CPI, such as the treatment of quality change for matched samples, the alternative methods of index construction, and of measurement of owner-occupier housing costs. Concerning index construction, sound statistical procedures require that the arithmetic mean of price relatives (Carli) is not used to calculate the elementary (item) level indices because of its bias that the ratio of arithmetic mean prices (Dutot) is used only for homogeneous items, and that the geometric mean of price relatives (equivalent to the ratio of geometric means) is adopted as the preferred measure. Further explanation is given in Annex 13.1.

13.10 The DQAF for the CPI is very comprehensive with regard to its inclusions. For example, under the subheading Sound Statistical Techniques, it also requires assessment of the statistical methods used to handle missing prices and the introduction of new products that are within the scope of the CPI. Thus, the compiler is asked to confirm that prices for temporarily missing products are appropriately handled (for example, a price is imputed based on the month-on-month price changes of a higher group, or a more targeted subgroup when judged, and prior data show that it is more suitable); the imputed price is posted in the database; and a limit is established and adhered to as to how long (for example, three months) prices for temporarily missing items are imputed or otherwise handled. For seasonal products the compiler is asked to ensure that prices are imputed using the higher group price change or a more targeted subgroup when judged (based on prior data) that it is more suitable, sample sizes permitting.

Quality Management

13.11 For most NSOs, data production will be an area that represents a high risk, given the complexity of the process from price collection to index computation and the financial implications of an error in the index. This is so regardless of the institutional arrangements and formal processes in place for auditing. It follows that a priority area in the quality management of a CPI is quality control of the production process.

13.12 A general theme in statistical production is customer focus and the effective dissemination of relevant, accurate, and timely statistics. Thus, a high level of understanding of customer needs and a coherent statistical and quality framework is required. User needs can be interviewed either formally through negotiation of contractual obligations for the provision and dissemination of data that may be legally binding or less formally through contacting customers or through customer surveys. The overall objectives underpinning user engagement and communication are to identify and where possible address user needs (for example, the publication of a family of indices or CPIs at a subnational level), and to build user understanding and confidence in the CPI.

13.13 In addition, quality management should include effective customer education on the use of CPI data. In these terms, success can be measured not only by the achievement of a high level of satisfaction among well-informed users but also by their proper use of statistics. The accessibility to users of relevant metadata has an important role.

13.14 In many countries, issues relating to the governance of the NSO are set down in a framework or statistical law. This defines the functions and responsibilities of the NSO, or other related agencies with a role in official statistics, and generally guides and directs the work of the office. For instance, an objective that may be stated in the framework document "to improve the quality and relevance of service to customers—in both government and the wider user community"—provides a powerful statement to guide and support NSOs.

13.15 This recognition of the importance of quality can be further endorsed by a published vision statement of the NSO as a key supplier of official, timely, and high-quality information. Such a vision statement can be encapsulated by publishing objectives in an annual report. These objectives can include improving quality and relevance, thereby increasing public confidence in the integrity and validity of statistical outputs.

Quality Management Systems

13.16 A quality management system is a formalized system that documents processes, procedures, and responsibilities for achieving quality products, policies, and objectives. A quality management system helps coordinate and direct the NSOs' activities to meet customer and organization requirements, to comply with regulatory requirements, and to improve its effectiveness and efficiency on a continuous basis.

13.17 Several internationally recognized systems are available to help NSOs improve quality management:

- *Total quality management.* Total quality management (TQM) is a management philosophy that promotes an effective culture of quality in an organization to fulfill operational objectives efficiently and effectively, including:
  - Clearly defined organizational goals
  - Strong customer focus
  - Strategic quality planning
  - Process orientation
  - Employee empowerment
  - Information sharing
  - Continuous quality improvement

TQM requires a commitment by all relevant parts of a production system to define their starting points, procedures, and final results. Revilla (2004) describes four dimensions of TQM: consumer satisfaction; constant improvement; fact-based management; and people-based management.

13.18 TQM has a broad focus ranging from an individual statistical product and its production to the entire system of statistics production and to other core processes, and from there on to the entire management system, personnel, partnerships, and resources. By systematic management of these aspects, one can create an operating system that emphasizes quality and thereby also improves the quality of end products.

- *Benchmarking.* Benchmarking is a process of comparing with others and learning and improving with their experience. Areas that can be considered when benchmarking a CPI collection may include:
  - Timelines, accuracy, and coverage of collection
  - Benefits of index methodologies for various items (for example, seasonal items)
  - Frequency of collection and publication
  - Cost of collection per unit of item

  A number of general observations can be made about benchmarking:
  - Initial discussions between benchmarking partners, prior to the process, can provide a useful tool for the identification of potential issues through informal self-evaluation.
  - The benchmarking is not restricted to performance indicators that may be available. In addition to reviewing issues that are directly measurable, the discussion can extend to topics such as why different NSOs adopt different approaches to some aspects of index construction.
  - Benefits often continue to accrue beyond the benchmarking exercise from, for example, the work on follow-up action points. Correspondingly, the further exploration in greater detail of issues raised during the initial benchmarking can result in further improvement. The general experience is that work becomes more focused on specific issues as the benchmarking progresses and the issues of concern become more apparent.
  - Longer-term benefits also include the subsequent opportunity for networking.
  - Financial and management information compiled specifically for benchmarking can also be useful management information in its own right.
  - Performance indicators are a necessary ingredient of the process of continuous improvement and are not just short-term management tools.
  - A number of general factors can be identified that contribute to successful benchmarking. In particular, benchmarking is dependent on trust and mutual respect between the parties involved.
- *European Foundation for Quality Management Excellence Model.* The Excellence Model constructed by the European Foundation for Quality Management (EFQM) is a diagnostic tool for self-assessment. The model has been widely used by governmental organizations across Europe to improve quality and performance. It may be described as a tool that drives the philosophy of TQM.

The EFQM Excellence Model focuses on general business areas and assesses performance against two sets of criteria. The first consists of five criteria covering what the business area does (the enablers: leadership, people, policy and strategy, partnership and resources, and process), and the second consists of four criteria on what the business area achieves (the results: people results; customer results; society results; and key performance results). Evidence based on feedback from focus groups, questionnaires, and personal interviews is used to score performance, and a resulting action plan for improvement is introduced, which is then included in the business plan.

13.19 Underlying the EFQM Excellence Model is the realization that business excellence—as measured through customer satisfaction—is achieved through effective leadership that drives policy and strategy, allocates resources compatible with that policy, and manages human resources in such a way as to enable them to manage the processes.

13.20 In the case of an NSO, where some procedures are governed by statute or regulation, the use of the EFQM Excellence Model enables continuous improvement to be taken forward across a range of processes and functions. To work effectively and to contribute to the production of a high-quality CPI, the Excellence Model needs the commitment of senior managers, who must be responsible for leading any self-assessment. However, unlike ISO 9001, where assessment is carried out by qualified auditors often from outside the work area (see Section E), the EFQM Excellence Model relies on input from internal staff.

- *Generic Statistical Business Process Model.* The Generic Statistical Business Process Model (GSBPM) describes and defines a set of business processes needed to produce official statistics. It provides a standard framework and harmonized terminology to help statistical organizations to modernize their statistical production processes, as well as to share methods and components. The GSBPM can also be used for integrating data and metadata standards, as a template for processing documentation, for harmonizing statistical computing infrastructures, and to providing a framework for quality assessment and improvement. The GSBPM is intended to apply to all activities undertaken by producers of official statistics, at both the national and international levels, that result in data outputs. It is designed to be independent of the data source, so it can be used for the description and quality assessment of processes based on surveys, censuses, administrative records, and other nonstatistical or mixed sources.

While the GSBPM includes several overarching statistical processes, quality and metadata management are two of the key elements of the model. The data quality management process includes quality assessment and control mechanisms. It recognizes the importance of evaluation and feedback throughout the statistical business process. The GSBPM processes and generates metadata within each phase, and therefore there is a strong requirement for a metadata management system to ensure that the appropriate metadata retain their links to the data throughout the GSBPM. Both processes guide NSOs to improve data quality management and the dissemination of metadata to enhance user confidence in statistical outputs.

- *ISO 9001.* ISO 9001 sets out the criteria for a quality management system that can be applied to any field of activity including the computation of a CPI. This standard is based on a number of quality management principles including a strong customer focus, the motivation and implications with respect to management, the process approach, and continuous improvement. The International Standard ISO 9001 is an international quality standard for management systems. ISO 9001 notes that a quality system is a common sense, well-documented business management system that is applicable to all business sectors. It helps to ensure consistency and improvement of working practices, including the goods and services produced. Users of ISO 9001 add value to their activities and improve their performance continually by focusing on the major processes within the organization. There is a closer alignment of the quality management system with the needs of the organization and the process reflects the way an organization runs its business activities. By meeting the ISO 9001 standard, an organization will come more into line with TQM and the EFQM Excellence Model.

13.21 A coordinated use of these and other quality management techniques at a strategic level in fields of statistics supports the dissemination of better data to meet user needs.

Prototype of a Quality Management System

13.22 A prototype of a quality management system for the monthly collection of prices and compilation of the CPI is given in Figure 13.1. It covers all aspects of CPI data collection and compilation including the auditing of prices, validation of the production cycle, and an annual review process that focuses on strategic and longer-term issues. This review is strongly encouraged because it allows to learn from past experiences and to identify and take forward actions that will improve the future quality of the CPI.

13.23 A conscious decision needs to be made on whether to include in the main quality management system periodic review processes (for example, chain linking, or the updating of the CPI basket), and technical development work (for example, introduction of better sampling techniques, or methods of quality adjustment for replacement goods).

13.24 Each aspect of a quality management system should be seen as interdependent and an integral part of the whole. For instance, a good quality CPI depends both on the accuracy and reliability of the source data and on the methodological soundness of the index computation, and the computation of the index relies on the delivery of an accurate, accessible, and timely database. The precise outline of such a system will depend on the detailed arrangements and approach to price collection. For instance, Figure 13.1 allows for the possibility that some prices data are collected directly from the headquarters of large supermarkets or other chain stores (sometimes referred to as central price collection) and that some price indices are calculated using price and sales information provided by a central authority, such as for energy prices or telecommunications, or are based on special methodologies requiring tailor-made

Figure 13.1 An Example of a Quality Management System for CPI Data Collection

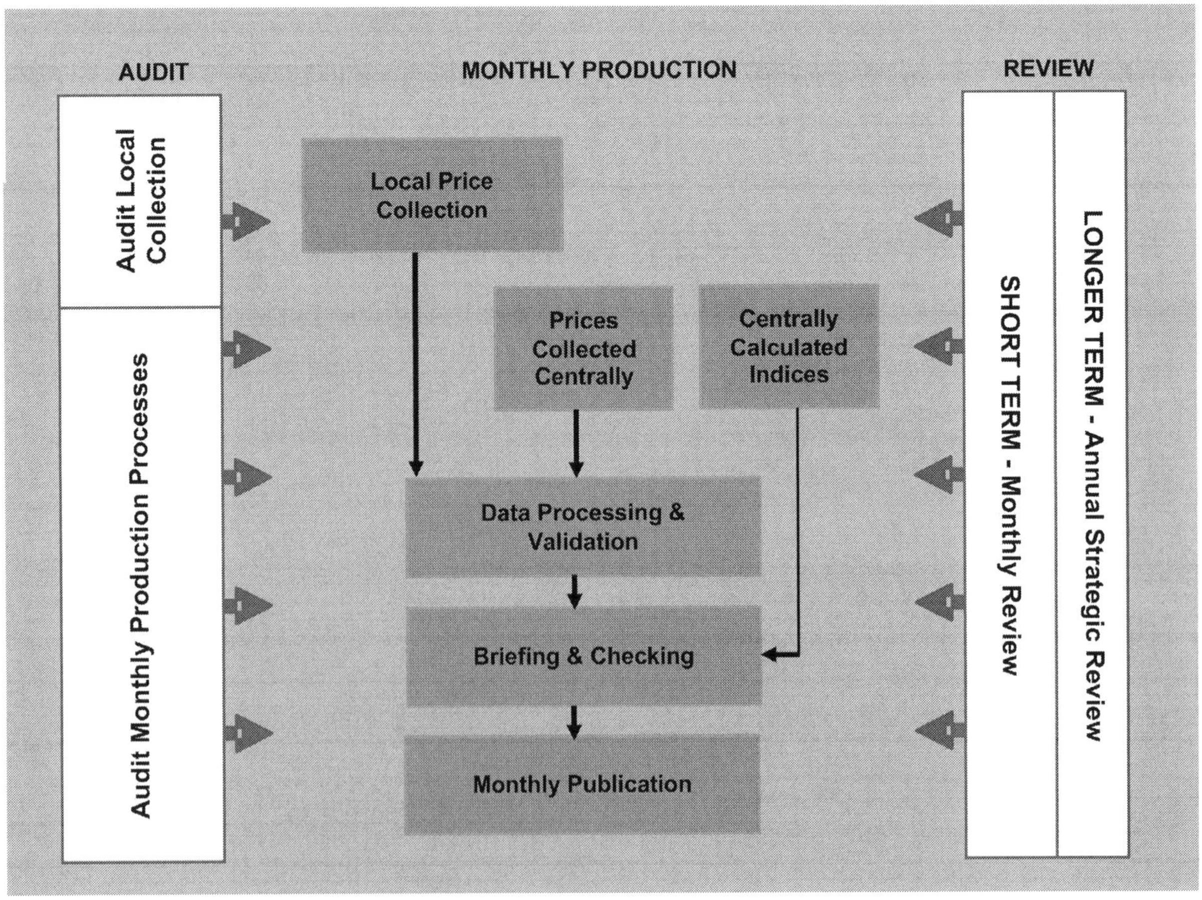

index calculations such as for owner-occupier housing costs (sometimes referred, generically, as centrally calculated indices).

Documentation

Overview

13.25 Good documentation is crucial. Documents are needed to explain what, when, how, and why the different CPI tasks should take place. Preparing such documents provides a useful opportunity to assure the quality of current procedures used to collect prices and compile the index. It also provides an opportunity to review and improve these procedures. Once in place, documentation serves two purposes in the context of producing the index. First, it enables another person to take over the work if the responsible person is not available or leaves. Second, it provides a quality check to ensure that the procedures that should be carried out are indeed being carried out in practice. More generally, documentation can provide a useful reference for CPI users. Figure 13.2 shows a typical structure for documentation relating to a CPI.

- *Level 1—The Quality Manual*. This document defines the quality policy and gives a general description of the system. It also describes the organization of staff involved in producing the CPI, the division of responsibilities for the management of all aspects of the production cycle, and the general structure of the lower levels of documentation.
- *Level 2—Procedures*. These are a set of mandatory procedures, covering all aspects of the production cycle. They explain in broad detail the different parts of the monthly processing cycle and outline the responsibilities of the staff involved.
- *Level 3—Work Instructions*. The work instructions give full details on exactly how a task should be carried out.
- *Level 4—Reference Documents*. These include all CPI metadata, such as a technical manual. The CPI Technical Manual describes the procedures used to produce the CPI and the price indices derived from it. It is aimed at users of the CPI who want to know how the data are collected and analyzed and what formulas are used in the calculation, together with other methodological detail.

13.26 The first three documents are intended for internal use only as they refer to internal processes and procedures. The CPI Technical Manual and other reference documents should be made available to all users on the NSO website and in hardcopy upon request.

Documentation Control

13.27 All documents in the quality management system should be subject to document control. Document control procedures should ensure that all staff have access to the most recent version when carrying out their work. In some NSOs, this is done by storing documents such as the Quality Manual, Procedures, and Work Instructions electronically in a database managed by a document control custodian and using numbered and dated versions to identify the latest copy.

13.28 An electronic system of documentation storage and control is recommended where the necessary technical infrastructure exists. Electronic systems have four benefits over a manual system:

Figure 13.2 Documentation

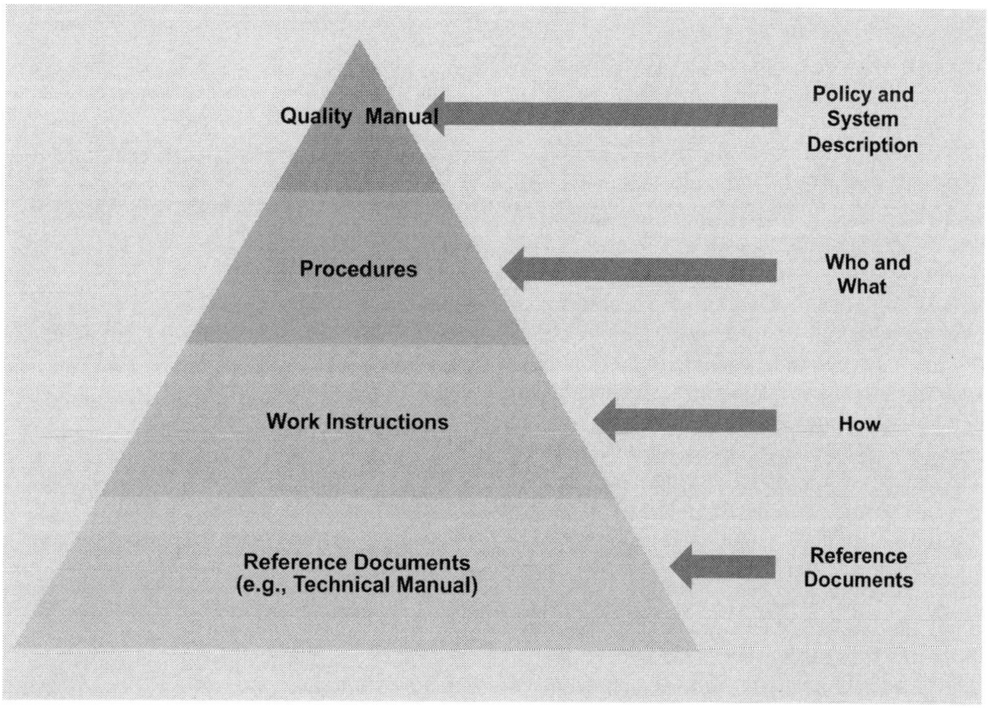

- *More efficient production* of documentation as it helps with initial compilation and reduces the need to print and circulate paper copies
- *Better informed staff* because they have immediate electronic access to the latest documentation
- *Better quality control* to allow authors, with the involvement of the document control custodian, to readily amend, date stamp, and reference number updates, and limit access of nonauthors to "read only"
- *Better search facility*, for example, if staff are looking for cross-references to a particular subject such as chain linking or weights

13.29 Where an NSO does not have the necessary information technology infrastructure or capacity to operate an electronic system, it is still important that a document control custodian is appointed with the task and authority to keep a record of the most up-to-date paper documentation. The same principles of good documentation control illustrated in Figure 13.2 apply whether the documents are stored electronically or are kept in paper folders. A form for a document control template is given in Annex 13.2.

Internal and External Audits of Production Processes

Overview

13.30 In the context of a CPI, an audit is a systematic and independent examination of the agreed-upon processes undertaken to compile the index. An audit evaluates performance against the objective of producing a reliable, accurate, and timely CPI that adheres to the defined scope and definition. Quality audits are performed to verify conformance to standards and best practice through a review of objective evidence but they can also be used to verify the effectiveness of the quality management system. Recommendations with action points are given in the audit report and should systematically be followed up. The advantage of internal and external audits compared with a less formal approach is that they are standardized, systematic, and transparent.

13.31 The auditing function is represented by the left-hand column of Figure 13.1. Note that the auditing of price collection is specifically addressed in Chapter 5. It is strongly advised that internal audits of the entire production process should be carried out regularly according to a systematic timetable. Audits should cover all aspects of the monthly and annual processing cycle to ensure that the management systems are fully implemented. The purpose of each audit should be to verify that operational procedures and controls comply with the documented procedures and to determine their effectiveness in delivering a CPI that is fit for purpose. Thus, an audit should aim not only to ensure that the index compilers adhere to the agreed-upon procedures but also that the procedures are improved where found lacking or insufficient.

13.32 Internal audits should be conducted by staff having appropriate training and experience, ideally by people who are sufficiently detached from routine operations to take an independent and objective view unhindered by close involvement in the production and compilation of the CPI. Too much familiarity can lead to unwarranted assumptions about the appropriateness of the procedures and the extent to which they are followed.

13.33 To achieve external accreditation, such as ISO 9001, requires the organization to undergo an external audit periodically by the appropriate accreditation body. The advantages of obtaining external accreditation are that:

- It provides a routine and regular review of production procedures and ensures proper documentation and quality control.
- It provides the efficiencies associated with a ready-made standard for documentation and quality control and the added confidence associated with a well-tested system. It minimizes risks of errors by adding effective controls including a framework for the initiation, evaluation, and implementation of change.
- It increases public confidence in the CPI, for instance as an index produced in accordance with internationally recognized standards for quality management.
- It provides a basis for more effective training of experienced staff and the induction of new staff.

13.34 Where external accreditation is not an option, internal audits can provide the same level of objectivity and discipline. Another option is an external audit carried out by CPI compilers from another NSO.

The Role of an Audit Team and the Responsibilities of Its Members

13.35 It is recommended that an audit team be assembled that consists of a quality manager and an internal auditor, each with a distinct, well-defined, and complementary role. Where this is not possible because of resource constraints, the two roles can be combined, or the roles can be undertaken in conjunction with other responsibilities. In some NSOs, the role of auditing is undertaken by a methodology branch or by an external government body. Whatever arrangement is adopted, it is important that sufficient staff qualified in auditing are available to carry out these audit functions.

13.36 The quality manager should be responsible for:

- Producing an audit schedule, managing it, and ensuring it is updated as necessary
- Agreeing and specifying the objectives and scope of the audit
- Managing implementation of the audits specified in the schedule
- Ensuring the auditor is properly trained
- Ensuring that, where possible, the auditor is independent of the function being audited
- Ensuring review reports are written
- Ensuring audit action points are implemented

13.37 The quality manager should prepare a schedule of audits covering all aspects of the CPI production processes. This schedule should take account of:

- The importance and complexity of the different stages involved in the compilation of the CPI

- The results and concerns arising from previous audits and any issues that have arisen since
- The time since the previous audit

13.38 The internal auditor should be responsible for:

- Undertaking any necessary preaudit investigation that will help determine the audit schedule and the focus and scope of assessment
- Conducting the audit
- Producing and circulating the audit reports
- Updating documentation where necessary
- Taking responsibility for monitoring and following up actions from the audits

Objectives of an Audit

13.39 The objectives of an audit need to be clearly defined and agreed on before it starts. The precise objectives will depend on local circumstances but may be stated in general terms as follows:

- To assess compliance with documented procedures
- To provide assurance to senior management that the agreed-upon quality management system is being implemented and is effective and relevant
- To identify improvements required and any necessary corrective actions and preventive measures
- To ensure the procedures are adequate

Auditing Procedures and Techniques

13.40 The success of an audit relies not only on clear objective setting and well-trained auditors but also on the use of effective auditing procedures and techniques, including a review of documentation and the carrying out of structured interviews with index compilers.

13.41 It is recommended that audits should incorporate the following procedures as standard:

- Before the audit:
  - Review documentation for completeness and ensure that is it up to date and indexed properly (where applicable, check that updates are signed off correctly, and that minutes, action points, and other documentation are correctly filed)
  - Trace action points from previous audits and any other form of review that has taken place (for example, compilation procedures)
  - Prepare checklists to help facilitate the structured interviews
- During the audit:
  - Conduct structured interviews
  - Ask to be shown documentary evidence (for example, spreadsheets or signatures on spreadsheets) to support staff responses to questions
  - Identify issues as they arise and advise the index compiler
- After the audit:
  - Produce a report, with recommendations
  - Provide compilers with the opportunity to comment and then agree on an action plan
  - Try and resolve any disagreements and, where appropriate, include the index compilers comments in the report
  - Note opportunities for improvement to current procedures as well as noncompliance with them
- Annex 13.3 provides an example of a pro forma audit schedule.

Audit Report

13.42 It is recommended that similar issues identified in several areas should be grouped under the same heading and documented as one audit observation. Clear and succinct headings should be used for each issue identified and a short description should be given of what was found. Observations can either be made in order of the most significant ones first or they can follow a logical sequence, generally the order in which the work activities underlying the compilation of the index are carried out.

13.43 For each audit observation, suitable corrective action should be recommended together with a statement of who is responsible for carrying out the corrective action and the date when the action should be complete. It is important to check that action points are carried through and that this is recorded with any further issues that arise.

Risk Assessment

13.44 In order to prioritize follow-up actions, it is recommended practice for the NSO to attribute an overall score to the risk associated with each issue arising from the audit.

13.45 The issues arising from an audit may be categorized as follows:

- *Low Risk* if the issues that have been identified are unlikely to arise and, if they did, that they would not result in major difficulties for the published CPI
- *High Risk* if there is a significant chance that, unless addressed, the issue could lead to an error in the index; that is, the error will be of high impact and there is a significant chance of it happening
- The results of all other audits should be considered of *Medium Risk*

13.46 If judged appropriate, the quality manager may issue an instruction for a follow-up audit. The proposed date for this audit should be added to the schedule for follow-up audits and progress checks, and the actual date of the audit should be added to the schedule of internal audits. Whenever possible, the follow-up audit should be carried out by the same auditor who undertook the initial audit. Annex 13.4 gives an example of a template for an audit report and the recording of follow-up actions.

Review Systems

13.47 The review system is represented by the right-hand side of Figure 13.1. A review system not only provides a check on current operational procedures but also helps to inform decisions on the introduction of longer-term improvements so that the quality management system continues to be up to date and relevant, and to ensure that business risks are kept to the necessary minimum. For this reason, NSOs are encouraged to put in place monitoring arrangements to track performance, supplemented by both short-term and longer-term review procedures.

Monitoring Performance

13.48 The process of producing a CPI should rely on an agreed-upon set of objectives that, where possible, are supplemented by measurable targets.

13.49 Targets for the delivery of a CPI may cover both quality (data and statistical methodology) and timeliness, and may encompass both the data collection and compilation processes and the quality of the final output. The NSO will need to decide which are the most relevant targets for the CPI. Possible targets for monitoring monthly performance with regard to the process of compiling the CPI and maintaining its relevance can include:

- *Timeliness*. The targets ensure that process delivery meets the agreed-upon schedule. For example, the targets may monitor whether the prices data was entered on to the computer and edited to the agreed-upon timetable, or whether index compilation took place on time so as not to potentially compromise publication.
- *Accuracy*. The targets may include the proportion of prices that are found to be incorrect, the number of prices collected compared with the target sample, or errors in the compilation of elementary aggregates. Accuracy and timeliness are interconnected. It is important that the quality of the index is not compromised by, for example, not allowing sufficient time for data editing and for checking of the index calculation prior to publication.
- *Delivery*. The targets may include the delivery of planned reviews of specific subindices and methodological reviews.

13.50 Quality measures should be set for each stage of the compilation process. These measures, which should be as quantitative as possible, should be evaluated against predetermined targets on an ongoing basis. Problems should be flagged during the production process allowing immediate corrective action to be taken if necessary.

Short-Term Monthly Reviews

13.51 It is good practice to hold an internal meeting of the CPI production team at the end of each month focused on quality and operational issues that have arisen during the most recent production cycle. The meetings can be an informal gathering of the team to exchange experiences and raise issues for resolution, or a more structured general session where management presents a monthly performance report and team members have the opportunity to react or raise particular concerns. The format will reflect local circumstances, including the size of the team producing the CPI and the management arrangements. Depending on the issues that arise, it may be useful to follow up these meetings by smaller ad hoc groups of staff brought together to tackle specific issues. Seminars and presentations may also be given.

13.52 Monthly reports on errors observed at data collection, data entry, editing, coding, and data cleaning stages, together with any compilation issues, should be circulated to relevant members of staff with a view to acting to minimize such errors in the future.

13.53 The monthly review meeting should also include a forward look at issues arising over the next cycle, so that appropriate working arrangements and solutions can be put in place. Thus, the focus should be both on learning from experience, for example, to avoid repeating problems, and on anticipating future issues for forward planning. Action points should be recorded, and individuals identified to follow them up. Recommendations to senior management should also be recorded as appropriate.

13.54 The monthly review should also be used as a basis for continuous improvement processes. As an example, data collectors can be encouraged to analyze the root causes of pricing errors and to develop individual development plans to correct these.

Longer-Term Annual Reviews

13.55 A longer-term element of a quality review system takes a higher-level strategic look at objectives and should be conducted through the annual planning cycle, where such a cycle exists, and should address both the quality of outputs assessed against user needs and the processes by which quality is achieved. Ideally, the quality review system should be laid down in an annual Quality Management Action Plan annexed to the main CPI work program.

13.56 The objectives of an annual review and the activities to be covered need to be stated with clarity. For example:

- The overall aim may be to successfully complete the following processes:
  - The reweight of the CPI
  - The update of the basket of goods and services
  - The compilation of the item list
  - The update of the new items list on the computer system
  - The rewrite of existing computer programs to incorporate the new items
- The objective would be to:
  - Improve the quality and accuracy of the CPI
  - Ensure that the CPI reflects consumer expenditure patterns
  - Enable data collection to be more effective and efficient
  - Ensure a standardized approach for introducing improvements
- To achieve this, the review may cover three main areas:
  - Locally collected prices
  - Centrally collected prices
  - Weights

Quality Reporting and Improving the Consumer Price Index: Frameworks

13.57 This section discusses quality reporting and reviews different quality frameworks that provide guidance on reporting mechanisms; they can assist NSOs to determine whether the quality of the CPIs produced meets the needs of users and how to develop a program for improvement. Quality reports should cover not only metadata about the basic characteristics of the CPI, but also wider issues such as its quality, statistical integrity, accessibility, and dissemination.

13.58 Examples of quality frameworks include the IMF e-GDDS, SDDS,[5] and the IMF DQAF. All frameworks, apart from Eurostat's quality reporting framework for the European Union Harmonised Index of Consumer Prices and the IMF's DQAF (that covers different areas of statistics), are generic in nature and not specific to CPIs.

13.59 The IMF DQAF (discussed in paragraphs 13.6–13.10) provides a flexible structure for the qualitative assessment of a CPI that can be used in a variety of contexts, including self-assessments performed by data producing agencies. Reporting arrangements will depend on the governance structure that is in place and this can vary across countries. In general, the expectation should be that quality reports should be made public with opportunity given to users to react.

13.60 The IMF's e-GDDS provides a framework for developing a clear roadmap to achieving higher data dissemination standards at a pace consistent with evolving statistical capacity. It focuses on the publication of data through a standardized platform to improve efficiency in data sharing, while identifying critical gaps to help prioritize technical assistance and donor support. IMF member countries that participate in the e-GDDS agree to:

- Commit to using the e-GDDS as a framework for statistical development
- Designate a country coordinator
- Prepare descriptions of current statistical production and dissemination practices and plans for their improvement for posting on the Dissemination Standards Bulletin Board (DSBB)[6]

13.61 The IMF's SDDS is a global benchmark for disseminating macroeconomic statistics to the public. Countries that subscribe to the SDDS agree to follow good practices in four areas: coverage, periodicity, and timeliness of data; public access to those data; data integrity; and data quality. Subscribing countries commit to:

- Disseminating the data required by the SDDS punctually and with the prescribed periodicity and timeliness on a national webpage, the National Summary Data Page, which is hyperlinked to the DSBB (provide to the IMF an advance release calendar containing release dates for the current month and at least the following three months for each prescribed category of data for posting on the DSBB)
- Provide detailed information about their statistical practices, or metadata, for dissemination on the DSBB (the metadata follow the rigorous format of the DQAF)
- Certify the accuracy of the metadata on an annual basis
- Use standardized electronic reporting procedures to monitor more effectively their observance of the SDDS

13.62 Using one of the internationally recognized quality frameworks for reporting on the CPI is recommended because it has several advantages. These include:

- It has the authority associated with an internationally agreed-upon framework and benefits from the experience of different countries.
- It allows comparisons on a like-for-like basis with CPIs produced by other countries.
- It is readily available.
- It fulfills the reporting obligations to international organizations.
- It provides the basis for reporting to users.
- It provides a benchmark for future developments, particularly when carried out in conjunction with a checklist.

13.63 Annex 13.5 gives an example of a model quality report document based on the reporting framework for the Harmonised Index of Consumer Prices. Quality is defined as "fitness for use" with regard to user needs and extends beyond the statistical accuracy of the index to its definition and coverage, effective dissemination, and the transparency of the statistical system.

13.64 The general principles underlying the publication of quality reports on the CPI, as with all official statistics, are that:

- The reports should be easy to access and use by all interested parties.
- The contents should be sufficiently detailed to allow users to assess fitness for particular purposes. Qualitative (and where possible quantitative) measures of quality should be included to help users to understand better the strengths and the limitations of the CPI and associated series, and the corresponding implications for interpretation and appropriate use.
- Quality measures and detailed technical information should be supplemented by guidance on interpretation to help users assess fitness for purpose.
- Clear statements should be given on the degree of compliance with agreed-upon definitions, methods, and practice, including both those determined nationally and those laid down in the 2003 ILO Resolution on CPIs,[7] and any known reasons for deviations.

[5]The IMF has taken steps to enhance member country transparency and openness, including setting voluntary standards for dissemination of economic and financial data. The SDDS was established in 1996 to guide IMF members that have, or might seek, access to international capital markets in providing their economic and financial data to the public. The GDDS was established in 1997 for member countries with less developed statistical systems as a framework for evaluating their needs for data improvement and setting priorities. In 2012 the SDDS Plus was created as an upper tier of the IMF's Data Standards Initiatives to help address data gaps identified during the global financial crisis. In 2015 the enhanced GDDS (e-GDDS) replaced the GDDS. Details can be found on https://www.imf.org/en/About/Factsheets/Sheets/2016/07/27/15/45/Standards-for-Data-Dissemination.

[6]The IMF's Dissemination Standards Bulletin Board (DSBB) provides access to SDDS Plus, SDDS, e-GDDS, and the Data Quality Reference Sites. The Data Quality Reference Sites have been created to foster a common understanding of data quality. It provides access to contributions in the field and includes a selection of articles and other sources related to data quality issues.

[7]http://www.ilo.org/global/statistics-and-databases/standards-and-guidelines/resolutions-adopted-by-international-conferences-of-labour-statisticians/lang--en/index.htm.

- Where possible, the presentation of information on quality will be tailored to meet the needs of different types of users, with more comprehensive information being prepared for expert users. This may indicate separate quality reports directed at different user groups.
- Producers should systematically review at regular intervals the documentation relating to the CPI and update it to reflect up-to-date methods and processes.

13.65 For operational purposes relating to internal work programs, a quality report can be usefully supplemented by a more detailed checklist of issues arising and the corresponding corrective actions that need to be taken.

Work Programs: Programming, Planning, and Reporting

13.66 The general principles underlying a programming, planning, and reporting system include clear and transparent governance arrangements relating to:

- The allocation of responsibilities for monitoring and reporting on the production and dissemination of the CPI and on its development
- The setting of protocols relating to the scope and definition of the CPI and the methodological detail that supports the previous point
- Putting in place and managing the routine operational arrangements

13.67 Transparency is built on the free flow of relevant nonconfidential information directly accessible to users of the CPI—enough information for users to understand, interpret, and properly use the index. Transparency generates trust.

13.68 The operational arrangements should be consistent with the governance arrangements and should:

- Incorporate an effective process for consulting with users
- Provide a mechanism for regularly reporting (for example, annually), to users and other relevant parties on the answers to three questions:
  - What has been done to maintain the integrity of the CPI over the past year?
  - What are the outstanding shortcomings and issues?
  - What does the NSO intend to do during the next year to address these questions?

Annex 13.1

Data Quality Assessment Framework (DQAF) for the Consumer Price Index

The DQAF dimensions and respective elements are the following:

0. *Prerequisites of quality*. Although not itself a dimension of quality, this group of "pointers to quality" includes elements and indicators that have an overarching role as prerequisites, or institutional preconditions, for quality of statistics. Note that the focus is on the agency, such as an NSO, central bank, or a ministry/department. These prerequisites cover the following elements:
   - Legal and institutional environment
   - Resources available for the statistical program
   - Relevance
   - Other quality management
1. *Assurances of integrity*. This dimension relates to the adherence to the principle of objectivity in the collection, compilation, and dissemination of statistics. The dimension encompasses institutional arrangements that ensure professionalism in statistical policies and practices, transparency, and ethical standards. The three elements for this dimension of quality are the following:
   - Institutional integrity (statistical policies and practices are guided by professional principles)
   - Transparency (the terms and conditions under which statistics are collected, processed, and disseminated are available to the public and meet international best practice)
   - Ethical standards (guidelines supporting appropriate staff behavior to sustain a strong culture for maintaining ethical standards that discourage political interference, are in place and are well known to the staff)
2. *Methodological soundness*. This dimension covers the idea that the methodological basis for the production of statistics should be sound and can be attained by following internationally accepted standards, guidelines, or good practices. This dimension is necessarily data set-specific, reflecting different methodologies for different data sets. This dimension has four elements, namely:
   - Concepts and definitions
   - Scope
   - Classification/sectorization
   - Basis for recording
3. *Accuracy and reliability*. This dimension covers the idea that statistical outputs sufficiently portray the reality of the economy. This dimension is also data specific, reflecting the sources used and their processing. The five elements of this dimension cover the following:
   - Source data
   - Assessment of source data
   - Statistical techniques
   - Assessment and validation of intermediate data and statistical outputs
   - Revision studies
4. *Serviceability*. This dimension relates to the need that statistics are disseminated with an appropriate periodicity in a timely fashion, are consistent internally and with other major data sets, and follow a regular revision policy. The three elements for this dimension are as follows:
   - Periodicity and timeliness
   - Consistency
   - Revision policy and practice
5. *Accessibility*. This dimension relates to the need for data and metadata to be presented in a clear and understandable manner on an easily available and impartial basis that metadata are up to date and pertinent, and that a prompt and knowledgeable support service is available. This dimension has three elements, namely:
   - Data accessibility
   - Metadata accessibility
   - Assistance to users

The methodological soundness dimension of quality has four elements—concepts and definitions, scope, classifications and sectorization, and basis for recording—each of which is associated with best practice and indicators. For instance, for concepts and definitions, the good practice is that the *concepts and definitions used are in accord with internationally accepted statistical frameworks*. Similarly, for scope the good practice is that the *scope is in accord with internationally accepted standards, guidelines, or good practice*. The indicators for the latter include that the household transactions included in the CPI are selected components of the following *2008 SNA* aggregates: household final consumption expenditure, and fixed capital formation in residential structures, as applicable.

Annex 13.2

Documentation Control Template

Figure 13A.1 Documentation Control Template

Date Issued	Documentation	Reference	Details of Change	Reason for Change	Name of Issuer
Day/ Month/ Year	**Calculating CPI Food Item Weights (nonseasonal)**	2.1	Change in Process with Effect from. . . (date)	CPI Technical Board Has Agreed That in Future Weights Should Be Taken from National Accounts	L. Smith, Statistician, CPI Program
XX/XX/XX	**Calculating and Updating Price Index for Telecommunication Services**	2.5	Change in Process with Effect from. . . (date)	Methodology Changes in Pricing Structures for Mobile Telephones—New Methodology Agreed by CPI Technical Board. Reflects Changing Market	L. Smith, Statistician, CPI Program
XX/XX/XX	**Desk Instructions for Checking and Editing of Prices**	3.1	Additional Checks to Be Carried out Based on Month-on-Month Price Change	Last Audit Indicated Current Checks Inadequate Resulting in Incorrect Prices Entering the CPI	C. Brown, Operations Manager, CPI Program

Annex 13.3

Pro Forma for an Audit Schedule

Figure 13A.2 Pro Forma for an Audit Schedule

Process and Document to Be Audited	Ref	Scheduled Audit		Last Audit				
		Date Audit Due	Audit Allocated To	Last Auditor	Date of Audit	Risk Assessment (High, Medium, or Low)	Follow-Up Required? (Y/N)	Target Date
Calculating CPI Food Item Weights (nonseasonal)	2.1	January	J. Graham	B. Jones	XX/XX/XX	High	N	N/A
Calculating and Updating Price Index for Telecommunication Services	2.5	January	L. Smith	J. Graham	XX/XX/XX	Medium	Y	April
Desk Instructions for Checking and Editing of Prices	3.1	January	B. Jones	L. Smith	XX/XX/XX	Low	Y	April

Annex 13.4

Audit Report Template

Figure 13A.3 Audit Report Template

AUDIT REPORT – CONSUMER PRICE INDEX

Audit No: 50 **Date:** XX/XX/XX **Document Ref:** 2.1

Process Audited: *Calculating CPI food item weights (non-seasonal)*

Owner: *CPI Compiler (name)*

OBSERVATIONS/FINDINGS

1. *The CPI Technical Board has agreed that, in the future, weights should be taken from National Accounts – this will lead to various changes to the processes.*

2. *The process document needs updating in order to reflect changes in methods.*

3. *It was agreed that the initial detailed instructions should be written at the same time as carrying out the process.*

ACTION REQUIRED	DUE:	TAKEN:
1. *Changes made to the process documentation to reflect new methods.*	*XX/XX/XX*	*XX/XX/XX*
2. *Follow-up Audit.*	*XX/XX/XX*	*XX/XX/XX*

RECCOMMENDATIONS FOR FUTURE QUALITY IMPROVEMENTS
1
2
3

Auditor: J. Graham **Audit Date:** *XX/XX/XX*

FOLLOW UP AUDIT – DETAILS OF ACTION TAKEN
1
2
3

Auditor: **Audit Date:** *XX/XX/XX*

Annex 13.5

Model Quality Report Document for the Consumer Price Index

Figure 13A.4 Model Quality Report Document for the CPI

	Sub-Headings: Specific Topics for Inclusion	Illustrative Range of Issues to be Discussed
DATA	Coverage	Population (e.g., treatment of institutional households, wealthy/poor households)
		Basket of goods and services (any exclusions, e.g., owner-occupied housing, informal markets)
		Expenditure (e.g., household final consumption expenditure, treatment of foreign visitors, expenditure of resident population abroad, own-account production)
	Periodicity	Weekly (all or some prices only)
		Monthly (all or some prices only)
		Quarterly or half-yearly (all or some prices only)
		Point in time or spread over month
	Timeliness	Time-lag between price collection and index publication
	Range of published indices and other residual statistics	Lower level sub-indices, special indices (e.g., excluding volatile prices such as petrol), regional price-level comparisons
ACCESS	Public access	Pre-announcement of publication date
		Simultaneous release to all
	Dissemination format	Electronic/paper
	Pre-release access	Protocols on any pre-release arrangements
INTEGRITY	Transparency	Protocols on compilation and dissemination of CPI are published and readily accessible
		Protocols comply with UN Fundamental Principles
	Revisions	Statement of revisions policy, revisions clearly marked
		Advance notice given of methodological changes, numerical impact given
QUALITY	Publication of information needed by users to assess quality	Dissemination of documentation on methodology
		Confidence intervals calculated and disseminated with other information on quality/accuracy of CPI

PUBLICATION, DISSEMINATION, AND USER RELATIONS

14

Introduction

14.1 The consumer price index (CPI) represents a key indicator of economic performance in most countries, as described in Chapter 2. Where statistics are categorized according to their potential impact, the CPI is always prioritized. It follows therefore that it must be published, and otherwise disseminated, according to the policies, codes of practice, and standards set for such data. In addition to having information on price movement at the total level, users often require information on the weights, methodology, and price movements at a more disaggregated level.

14.2 The CPI should therefore be:

- Released as soon as possible
- Made available to all users at the same time (exceptions must be communicated in a transparent way; for example, if the central bank receives the results a few days before they are published on account of its monetary policy tasks, this should be mentioned in the press release)
- Released according to preannounced release calendars
- Released separately from ministerial comment
- Made available in convenient form to users
- Accompanied by methodological explanation
- Backed up by CPI compilers and economists who can answer questions and provide further information

14.3 Above all, the CPI should comply with the *Fundamental Principles of Official Statistics*[1] (United Nations [UN], A/RES/68/261 from 29 January 2014). These principles are published in several languages on the websites of the United Nations and the United Nations Economic Commission for Europe. They refer to dissemination and to all aspects of statistical work. These and other standards are discussed in paragraphs 14.40–14.42.

Time-Series Presentation of Level and Change

14.4 The presentation of the CPI data to users (for example, on press releases disseminated by the national statistical office [NSO]) commonly focuses on the percentage change over 12 months (price movement between the current month and the same month one year earlier). The 12-month comparison provides an indication of price changes over a reasonably long time frame, by reference to periods that may be expected to be similar year to year. Thus, seasonal factors are unlikely to be influential. It is also usual to compare this annual change with the annual change shown one month previously. The illustrative presentation in Figure 14.1 provides an example of this.

14.5 The data release should also focus on the month-on-previous-month change or highlight quarter-on-quarter changes. These provide an indication of price change over a short time frame, which would highlight those products with volatile prices, such as fuels. To avoid any confusion in interpreting the results, it is very important to precisely specify to which period the published inflation relates.

14.6 The index reference period (a month or a longer period, as described in Chapter 8) refers to a period in the past where the index equals 100. All subsequent months/periods then have index numbers that reflect the relative change over time since the index reference period. Indeed, it is that index that is used as the basic figure from which the other changes are calculated. The index reference period generally coincides with a routine update, but some countries choose to retain the old index reference period when updating weights. When implementing changes to compilation methods, re-referencing (setting the index back to 100) signals to users that a new index has been published. The reference period should be defined in all publications and in the methodological explanation.

14.7 Indices and rates of change are usually shown only to one decimal place in the press release, and in this case, figures would be rounded. Rounding may lead to inconsistencies. For example, if the unrounded index of $t-1$ is 101.1459, and the unrounded index of the following month t is 102.7591, the rate of change compiled with unrounded indices will be 1.6 percent while the rate of change compiled with rounded indices will be 1.7 percent. As long as this inconsistency can be explained (use full precision to calculate the rate of change), it is not a problem. An option could be to make available to users both rounded and unrounded figures: in the press release, the figures are rounded to one decimal, but national statistical offices (NSOs) often publish data on the website at or near full precision for analytical and research purposes. To avoid this inconsistency, it is also possible to compile the published rate of change with rounded indices to one or two decimals. This is the case for the European Union (EU) Harmonised Indices of Consumer Prices (HICPs) where the rate of change is compiled with two decimals rounded indices.

14.8 Care must be taken to differentiate between percentages and index points. If in one month the index is, for example, 200 and in the following month 201, then the change can be described as one index point (above the period when the index was set at 100) or as a half percentage point (where the previous month is taken as 100 percent). Both are valid, even if it is more common to refer to change as a percentage.

14.9 The CPI is, by definition, an index and therefore not a level or a series of absolute changes in prices. Nevertheless,

[1] https://unstats.un.org/unsd/dnss/gp/fundprinciples.aspx.

in the process of compiling the CPI, average prices can be calculated for categories of products. It is thus possible to publish some average prices for groups of goods or services, and to show the upper and lower bands of the prices from which the averages have been calculated. These averages may be useful for some users, such as researchers. Average prices should only be published for tightly defined, homogeneous item groups that are relatively similar (in quality) and for which the variation coefficient is acceptable. It is also important to make it clear to users that average prices are a by-product of CPI compilation and are not used to calculate price changes.

14.10 The previous discussion refers not only to the all-items CPI, but also to a more disaggregated level such as regions of a country, population subgroups (for example, pensioners), or to related or alternative measures of price change. Related or alternative measures, and subaggregate indices, are discussed in paragraphs 14.23–14.34.

Seasonal Adjustment and Smoothing of the Index

14.11 The treatment of seasonal products and the estimation of seasonal effects are discussed in Chapter 11 of this Manual and Chapter 4 of the publication *Consumer Price Index Theory*. This chapter discusses the dissemination of adjusted or smoothed series.

14.12 Many series of economic statistics are disseminated seasonally adjusted, as well as unadjusted. CPIs, however, are not normally seasonally adjusted, although some countries do produce a seasonally adjusted CPI. Seasonally adjusted CPIs are purely analytical and do not replace the headline unadjusted index. Seasonal factors, for any series, are frequently recalculated using the most recent data, so seasonally adjusted series can be changed retrospectively, but unadjusted CPIs are not normally revised.

14.13 In comparing one month with the same month a year earlier, it is assumed that seasonal patterns are much the same from one year to the next. There may be, however, exceptional months when the usual seasonal pattern is advanced or delayed. Such exceptional circumstances should be noted in the monthly release as one of the likely causes of a change in the CPI or in one of its components. Even if seasonal patterns are much the same from one year to the next, there may be months when relevant calendar effects differ from one year to the next due to moving holidays such as Ramadan or Easter. Seasonal expenditure patterns can be observed around these holidays which could be considered seasonal in nature.

14.14 Changes over periods of less than a year are subject to seasonality. To differentiate seasonal patterns from other factors, it is necessary to make estimates of seasonal effects and to note them as factors that have contributed to changes in the index. For this purpose, it is necessary to clearly identify seasonal products. The NSO also may possibly calculate complementary indices, for example, a CPI that only contains seasonal products and a CPI without seasonal products.

14.15 Although the CPI is not usually seasonally adjusted, some variants of the CPI (for analytical purposes) may be seasonally adjusted. These variants should be explained to the users and can be revised in retrospect if necessary. Seasonal adjustment usually leads to smoother series than the original unadjusted series. There are other ways of smoothing monthly series, for example using three-month moving averages.

14.16 NSOs do not usually smooth the CPI series in their published presentations. In general, consumer price changes are not so erratic from month to month as to disguise price trends. If there is an erratic change, the producers of the index can usually explain the reasons for it. In any case, if seasonally adjusted or smoothed series are published, it is important to also publish the unadjusted series, so that the effect of the adjustment process is clear to users who may wish to know what has happened to prices and whether or not the changes can be ascribed to seasonal factors. Similarly, a full explanation should be given for the reasons why a particular seasonal adjustment procedure has been followed.

Analysis of Contributions to Change

14.17 Contributions to change help explain what groups of goods and services contributes most to inflation. These data are useful to better understand the sources of inflation and can increase transparency.

14.18 The CPI is an aggregate of many different goods and services with prices changing at different rates, some of which may be going up while others are going down. The weights of these products or groups of products are different, resulting in a varying impact on the all-items index. If the weight of a group of products is high and its price trend strong, the impact on the overall inflation rate will therefore also be high. Many users of the index want to know which goods or services have contributed most to changes in the total, and which prices may be out of step with general price trends.

14.19 The CPI compilers are well placed to provide analyses of the contributions to the overall price change, at the same time as the index is published. Sufficient detail should be made available so that users can understand what has happened to various groups of prices. In addition, to assist journalists and others working under time constraints, the CPI compiler should indicate the goods and services or group of products whose changes in price are the main contributors to the all-items CPI, and also goods and services whose changes in price are the most different from the aggregate. The statistics can be presented in the form of tables and charts so that the trends may be compared. Similarly, compilers should indicate any reasons for price changes that may not be immediately obvious but are nevertheless discernible from the published figures. For example, if there has been a sharp price rise or fall one year earlier, then it will affect the current year-on-year change, regardless of what is currently happening to prices.

14.20 The formulas used to calculate the contributions to change are described in Chapter 9.

Economic Commentary and Interpretation of the Index

14.21 In undertaking an analysis of the CPI results, CPI compilers must be objective so that users of the data may differentiate clearly between the figures and their interpretation. It is therefore essential that care is taken to avoid expressing any judgment of the impact of current policy on price changes or the possible implications of price changes for future policies. Whether the figures should be seen as good or bad news is for the users to decide for themselves. The NSO's role is to provide objective information so that users can form their own judgment from the perspective of their own economic or political views.

14.22 There are several ways of avoiding any apparent or real lapses in the analysis. The first, and perhaps the most important, is to publish the figures independently of any ministerial or other political comment. Another is to be consistent in the way in which the figures are presented; that is, the data should be presented in much the same format every month (see paragraphs 14.35–14.39). For example, tables and charts should cover the same periods every month and use the same baselines.

Presentation of Related or Alternative Measures

Core Inflation

14.23 For the purpose of economic analysis, it is desirable to construct measures of "core" or "underlying" inflation that exclude movements in the inflation rate that are attributable to transient factors. In other words, measures of core or underlying inflation seek to measure the persistent or generalized trend of inflation. For example, central banks use measures of the general trend of inflation when setting monetary policy, and for this reason, economists and statisticians are increasingly interested in developing measures of underlying inflation.

14.24 Several methods can be used to derive a measure of core or underlying inflation. Most measures of underlying inflation focus on reducing or eliminating the influence of exceptionally volatile prices, or of exceptionally large individual price changes. The most traditional approach is to exclude particular components of the CPI on a discretionary basis. The items to be excluded would be based on the compiler's knowledge of the volatility of particular items, depending on the country's economic conditions. Items commonly excluded under this approach are fresh meat, fruit, and vegetables, and fuels and other energy products. Many countries also exclude imported goods, government charges, and government-controlled prices. In some countries, a calculation is made to exclude the effect of indirect taxes such as the value-added tax. Of course, care must be taken not to exclude so many items that the remainder becomes only a small and unrepresentative component of the total. The chosen method for producing underlying inflation should be described in the metadata and publication.

14.25 Other methods of deriving an underlying measure of inflation include smoothing techniques, for example, annualizing three-month average inflation. A more complex method is to exclude outliers (that is, those items with the highest or lowest increases).

Alternative and Subaggregate Indices

14.26 While publishing alternative aggregations of the CPI meets data user needs, this can also create confusion for other data users. Users can be confused over what is the headline, or official, rate of inflation and how these alternative measures compare to the headline index. NSOs must clearly explain the methods used and define the purpose of compiling these alternative indices. It must be clear to users how these indices can be used and why the NSO has published this alternative aggregation.

14.27 Countries commonly calculate price indices for hundreds of products (for example, bread or footwear), based on thousands of individual price records. The number of possible subaggregates is therefore very large. The choice of disseminated subaggregates is left to NSOs, according to the users' needs.

14.28 One kind of subaggregation is the grouping of items or products that, when taken together, comprise the all-items index. An important consideration here is the relationship of the products within the subgroups. For example, an index may be presented for food and, under the heading of food, indices may be presented for subgroups such as cereals or vegetables.

14.29 Subaggregates from different divisions of the Classification of Individual Consumption According to Purpose (COICOP) can be combined to compile special aggregates. For example, a special index for education can be compiled using weights and indices from different groups. Tuition and fees are part of Education Services (Division 10 of COICOP 2018), while school uniforms are part of Clothing and Footwear (Division 03); textbooks and school supplies are part of Recreation, Sport, and Culture (Division 09); and school transport is under Transport (Division 07). An alternative index for education gives users a more complete picture of price change for education. Other examples would be to compile the CPI with and without production for own consumption in the weights. This analytical series meets the needs of poverty economists and analysts. Other examples include CPIs compiled by income group or for the elderly.

14.30 Other forms of subaggregate indices include the dissemination of regional indices. For those countries that compile a national index based on regional indices, the detailed regional indices should be disseminated. As with the national index, the monthly release should include data at a more aggregate level with detailed indices published on the NSO website. Data should be disseminated to the lowest level possible, ideally down to the elementary aggregate level.

14.31 One of the first considerations in presenting such subaggregate data for related products is consistency. There should be a set of subaggregates for which indices are calculated and presented each period. Users commonly attach great importance to being able to continue their analysis for the most recent period.

14.32 Another consideration is international standardization of the division of the index into groups of goods and services, which enables comparison between countries. Some countries also have their own subaggregate groupings which may precede the current international standard. The generally accepted international standard for the presentation of subaggregates is COICOP, as discussed in Chapter 2. It is used, for example, in the EU HICPs. Because COICOP defines groups of items by the general purpose for which they are used (for example, "transport" or "housing and household services"), it combines goods and services within the same subgroups. Where the national CPI is subaggregated by divisions other than the international standard, it is advisable either to present a breakdown also by COICOP or at least to show how the national classification compares to the international standard.

14.33 Another common type of subaggregate index is an index that excludes certain items. The core or underlying inflation index discussed in paragraphs 14.23–14.25 is an example. Some countries publish, in addition to the all-items CPI, an index or indices that exclude certain expenditures (for example, a CPI without fuels) or merge the products differently (for example, a CPI for durable goods or a CPI for public services).

14.34 In the presentation of all related or alternative measures, their definitions (for example, methodology or differences with the all-items CPI) should be made clear. It is also advisable to give the reasons for their publication. Most importantly, it should not be suggested that the subaggregate index is more meaningful than the CPI.

Press Release, Bulletin, and Methodological Statement

14.35 The model presentation of a CPI in Figure 14.1 is an example of a press release for a fictitious country. Other formats are possible. For example, the presentation might include a seasonally adjusted index for analytical purposes. As indicated in the model, the presentation should contain the following information:

- Details of issuing office
- Date and time of release
- Percentage change in current month over the same month one year earlier
- Comparison with change in the previous month
- Information on the product groups which contributed to the change and on any significant component price
- Reference to where more information (for example, detailed results or metadata) can be found
- Date for next release and link to advance release calendar

Note that no judgments are offered on policy or economic reasons for the price change, and no judgment is given on whether the change is good or bad.

14.36 The format of the press release should be the same from month to month. Using a consistent format is

Figure 14.1 Example of an Illustrative CPI Press Release

Office of [name of country] Statistics

Friday 19 January 2018, for release at 11.00 a.m.

CONSUMER PRICE INDEX (CPI)

DECEMBER 2017: PRESS RELEASE

In December 2017, the all items index increased 2.0 percent more as compared to December 2016. This 12-month change was lower than the 12-month change recorded in November (2.5 percent) but higher than in October (1.3 percent).

Compared with the previous month, the CPI fell by 0.3 percent, reaching 105.9 points (2015=100).

Percentage change over 12 months in the consumer price index, for the last five years

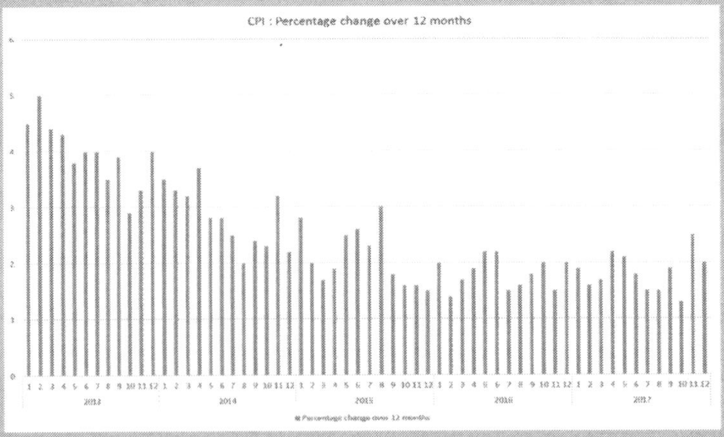

Main contributions to the overall 2.0 percent increase

The largest increase was in the prices of clothing and footwear, with smaller increases in recreation and culture. Within the energy group of prices, there was a significant increase in gas tariffs. There were falls in the prices of furnishings and household goods. The changes in product groups are shown in the table on page x of this release.

Issued by the Office of Xxxxx Statistics address xxxxxx

Press enquiries 1 111 1111 Public Enquiries 2 222 2222 (name of a contact is helpful).
This press release was made available before release date to the following institution(s): *[name of institutions]*.
Background notes on the CPI are given in the annex to this note.
More notes and more details are given in our website at XXX.

Figure 14.2 Model Note on Methodology—To Be Included in Press Releases on CPI or on the Official Website

What is the consumer price index (CPI) measuring and how is it done?

The CPI measures inflation, the average change in the prices of goods and services consumed by households.

Prices are collected each month from shops and other suppliers of goods and services. The pattern of household expenditure on these goods and services (the weights) is derived from a regular household budget (or expenditure) survey. The prices and spending patterns are then combined to calculate the price indices for groups of goods and services and for the all-items index.

The all-items index and its component indices are published each month in our CPI Bulletin. The Bulletin also contains more information on the methodology used in calculating the CPI. A small booklet is also available. For a detailed account of the methodology used in calculating the CPI, please see the CPI technical manual. For more information on these publications, and how they may be obtained, please refer to our website at www.ous.gov or contact the telephone numbers given on the front of this press release.

important to avoid appearing to choose a different format to indicate a preferred trend. Using the same format also allows for rationalization.

14.37 Additional content (in the paper or digital version available on the NSO website) of the press release should provide information on the indices from which the percentage changes are calculated. Similar indices should also be published for major groups of goods and services. Charts may also be used to illustrate, for example, which prices have contributed most or least to the all-items CPI.

14.38 If any other consumer price variant is also being published, then the differences between the indices should be briefly explained, including any methodological differences. Variants that require explanation include, for example, a national index based on the EU HICPs methodology, any regional indices, or versions of the CPI that exclude particular components of consumer expenditure. The press release should include a short note on methodology, similar to that given in Figure 14.2 or a link to the official website where the methodology is described. A more detailed explanation could be given in a handbook.

14.39 Whether released in paper or digitally, the format of the press release remains the same. The only difference is the mode of dissemination. Countries continue to move to a digital format and disseminate the monthly press release in a digital format on the NSO website and via email to those requesting or subscribing to the monthly release. Some countries release the data electronically on the website, but also continue to officially release the data via a press conference using the traditional paper format.

International Standards Concerning the Dissemination of Consumer Price Indices

14.40 There are many international standards that apply, in general terms or specifically, to the CPI. The introduction to this chapter lists some of the broad principles that are reflected in many of the international standards in some form. One very general standard, but by its nature a fundamental one, is the UN *Fundamental Principles of Official Statistics*. It refers not just to dissemination but to all aspects of statistical work.

14.41 The International Monetary Fund (IMF) standards are particularly pertinent in regard to dissemination. As discussed in Chapter 13, two standards refer to statistics including the CPI, the Enhanced General Data Dissemination System (e-GDDS) and the Special Data Dissemination Standard (SDDS and SDDS Plus). The e-GDDS provides a general framework, with some specific indicators defined as "core" and others defined as "encouraged." The Special Data Dissemination Standard is based on the GDDS framework but is more demanding and applies to countries that choose to subscribe to it in writing to the IMF Board. Detailed information on both standards is available on the IMF website.[2]

14.42 Under the heading of *quality*, the e-GDDS refers to the need to provide information on sources and methods, as well as on component details and checking procedures. Under the heading of *integrity*, it refers to declared standards of confidentiality, internal government access before data release, identification of ministerial commentary, and information on revision and advance notice of changes in methodology. Under the heading *access by the public*, it refers to the need for preannounced release dates and simultaneous access for all users. In the tables of data categories, it refers to the CPI as a core indicator that should be issued monthly, within one to two months of the reference period. All these standards are reflected in the present Manual. The International Labour Organization has also published *Guidelines concerning dissemination practices for labor statistics* (ILO 1998), which are available on the International Labour Organization website.[3]

Timing of Dissemination of the Consumer Price Index

14.43 The CPI should be released as soon as possible following the reference month, but it is equally important to release the index following a strict timetable. This timetable of release dates should be published as far in advance as possible. Having a fixed release date, published well in advance, is important for three main reasons. First, it reduces the scope for manipulation of the release date for political expediency. Second, it instills confidence in users that the release date is as soon as possible and has not been delayed (or brought forward) for purely political reasons. A

[2] https://dsbb.imf.org/.

[3] https://www.ilo.org/global/statistics-and-databases/standards-and-guidelines/guidelines-adopted-by-international-conferences-of-labour-statisticians/WCMS_087614/lang--en/index.htm.

third advantage is that users know when to expect the data and can be prepared to use them.

Timeliness of Release versus Data Accuracy

14.44 The IMF's e-GDDS, discussed in paragraphs 14.41 and 14.42, recommends that the CPI be released each month within one to two months of the reference period. It is usual, in practice, for most countries to release the CPI in the middle of the month after the month to which the index refers. This is possible because, in many cases, the data are collected mainly over a limited period in the middle of the month to which the latest data refer. Thus, the CPI compilers have some time to check and analyze the data and to prepare the tables and charts in which the data will be disseminated.

14.45 The accuracy of the index is particularly relevant because of the importance of the CPI, as discussed in more detail in Chapter 2. Also, partly because data are collected according to a strict schedule by price collectors it is rare for data to be reported after the CPI is published, and partly because of the way in which the index is used in contracts, it is very rarely revised. This represents a major difference between the CPI and other economic or socioeconomic statistics.

14.46 It follows that, although timeliness is important, the dissemination timetable must allow time for the data to be properly prepared and thoroughly checked. After the release date, in most cases, a revision to the CPI would not be permissible, except in the case of a seasonally adjusted CPI. The HICPs of the EU are an exception as they are revised from time to time. If any series is revised, then of course the changes must be fully described and explained when the new data are released. If there is any methodological change, this is usually known in advance. Users should be informed before any such change occurs.

14.47 Best practice suggests that NSOs develop a revision policy for the CPI. Should an error be discovered that exceeds a defined threshold, the CPI would be revised. This revision policy allows for the correction of errors and enhances transparency. Users should be made aware of the revision policy in the metadata.

14.48 A possible compromise between accuracy and timeliness can be the publication of flash estimates. A flash estimate is an early estimate of inflation computed from preliminary data at a given time, released at the end of the current month or at the very beginning of the following month, giving users a provisional figure very quickly. A flash estimate is always followed by the official publication of the results, once the data are complete and all controls and analyses have been carried out. For example, Eurostat publishes flash estimates for the euro area.

Access to Data

14.49 For a number of countries, the internet has become the main dissemination medium, usually via the NSO website. For the data producer, distribution costs are relatively small. No printing or mailing costs are involved. As soon as the data are disseminated online, they are available to all users simultaneously. Disseminating a large amount of data on the NSO website costs little more than disseminating a smaller amount.

14.50 Ideally, the CPI, accompanied by any essential metadata, should be released simultaneously to the press and other users. One way in which some NSOs are doing this is by making the press release available confidentially to the journalists shortly before the official release time (maybe half an hour), providing them with the printed press release. Then, when the data are released, the journalists are permitted to release their reports or stories to the public. Care must be taken to ensure that the CPI is available to all users at the same time, regardless of the dissemination medium used.

14.51 With the CPI as with other statistics, users should be allowed access to as much data as possible for two main reasons. First, some users find the detailed data very useful in their analysis. Second, access to the data inspires confidence in the data.

14.52 Data should be disseminated to the lowest level possible, ideally the elementary aggregate level. Whether to publish a particular elementary aggregate may depend upon confidentiality issues, as addressed in paragraph 14.55.

14.53 In general, the CPI and its major components are deemed to be of such wide importance that they are made available for free through press releases and on the NSO website. While the goal should be to meet data user needs, special analyses made at the request of particular users may incur costs outside of the normal monthly production and processing budget. Some countries will charge for special analysis requests to defray the additional cost of preparing the data.

Confidentiality

14.54 Although, in general, as much data as possible should be made available to users, there are reasons why confidentiality is important in some instances. First, some data are supplied by retailers and others on the understanding that the data will be used only for the purpose of aggregation with other data and will not be released in any other form. This can be especially important where the data are given voluntarily, as they often are. For example, in the case when a single respondent provides data for a given elementary aggregate, publishing data at the elementary aggregate level would identify the data provider. To avoid any issues, some countries will obtain written permission from the respondent authorizing the dissemination of the elementary aggregate even though such publication would reveal the identity of the data provider. Second, some elementary aggregates may be compiled based on a small number of prices and could be deemed as not being sufficiently representative for publication purposes. Samples should be selected in such a way as to support the dissemination of all elementary aggregates.

Presentation of Methodology

14.55 When the CPI is published each month, users want to see the main figures and to use them. Users do not generally want to be burdened with explanations concerning the methodology underlying the data. Nevertheless, methodological explanations must be accessible to those who may want them, and in forms which are comprehensible to users with different levels of expertise and interest. Any significant changes in methodology must be fully explained and notified as far in advance as possible of the change being made.

14.56 In addition to a brief statement in press releases (see paragraphs 14.35–14.39), methodological explanations should be available on at least two levels. Nonexperts should be able to refer to a booklet that explains the history, principles, and practice underlying the CPI and any alternative measures which may also be available. A more thorough explanation of sources and methods should also be readily available for those users who are sufficiently interested and, for example, for compilers who may be working on the production of the CPI for the first time. The information must also be kept up to date despite the pressures to devote time to the output at the expense of documentation. The ready availability of a full explanation of sources and methods is essential to confidence and trust in the CPI.

14.57 Developing frequently asked questions (FAQs) provides another level of information on the methodology for users. FAQs provide concise responses to explain key methodological questions and define important concepts. Overly technical language and explanations should be avoided. FAQs should be written in plain language understandable by all users. FAQs should be posted on the NSO website and can be used to summarize index compilation methods at the end of a press release.

Explaining Index Quality

14.58 Some users may regard the CPI results with suspicion, as noted in Chapter 2. Metadata usually refers to the "average consumer" or "average household," but each consumer and household has different expenditure patterns from the expenditure patterns of others and may notice changes in one set of prices but not in others. More importantly, perhaps, there is criticism of the index because of suspicion that it does not keep track of newer types of goods and services, changes in the quality of products, or newer types of retail outlets. See Chapter 2, paragraphs 2.47–2.49, for more details on inflation perceptions.

14.59 It is important for CPI compilers to be willing to discuss these issues and to explain how the compilation methods used address these issues. The producers of the index must be open about their methods and the extent to which they can overcome the potential or real problems that have been identified. It follows that the NSO should publish explanations concerning the quality aspects, whether or not the quality of the index is currently being questioned.

14.60 Some countries develop personal inflation calculators that make data more relevant to individual users. A personal inflation calculator allows a user to define their own individual basket. Users are asked either to input expenditure details for a group of items (monthly, annually, etc.) or to define specific items and the proportion of expenditure made on each item. Based on these inputs, a personal inflation rate is compiled and presented.[4]

[4] https://www.cbs.nl/en-gb/visualisaties/personal-inflation-calculator; https://www.geostat.ge/personalinflation/; https://service.destatis.de/inflationsrechner/InflationCalculator.svg.

User Consultation

Different Uses of Consumer Price Indices

14.61 It is important to explain the different uses of the CPI to potential data users (CPI uses are discussed in Chapter 2). To this end, it is important to explain how the CPI is constructed and to provide details of its sources and methods. It is also important to make readily available explanations of alternative indices or subindices, indicating how their uses differ from the uses of the CPI.

14.62 If there are different uses for CPIs, there are also different users. It is useful to identify the different users to provide them the relevant information. The basic user would be interested in knowing general results on an occasional basis, while the central bank or an academic would be interested in detailed results over a longer period. The identification and classification of CPI users are useful to better respond to their expectations.

Role of Advisory Committees

14.63 For a statistical series as important as the CPI, it is essential to organize an advisory committee, or a set of committees, representing users and producers. There are many contentious issues in the construction of the CPI. In many countries, there have been fierce arguments about, for example, which components should be included and excluded. The role of an advisory committee is to consider and advise on best practice and methodologies. An equally important role of an advisory committee is to enhance the credibility of the CPI.

14.64 In those countries where advisory committees have not been the norm, there may be a fear on the part of the CPI compiler that including nongovernmental participants may raise expectations beyond what the NSO can deliver, thereby increasing dissatisfaction among the general public. In fact, the inclusion of nongovernmental users can lead to a greater understanding of the realities and the practical constraints to meeting theoretical needs. This is the usual experience of NSOs that already have advisory bodies that include representatives of all the major constituencies, both inside and outside government. It is therefore important that the advisory committee should include academics, employers, trade union representatives, and others who have an interest in the index from differing points of view. It is also important that the reports of the advisory committee are made available to the public in full and without undue delay.

Key Recommendations

- NSOs should disseminate two key measures—the 12-month (current month to the same month in the previous year) and the month-on-month change (current to the previous month).
- Disseminate contributions to change so users better understand what items have contributed most to inflation in a given period.
- Written analysis or commentary should be neutral and focus only on describing important or unusual movements in a given period.
- Provide alternative aggregations of CPI data to better meet data user needs.

- Develop and disseminate detailed metadata describing CPI compilation methods. The release should include a short methodology note, and a more detailed description should be available on the NSO website.
- A calendar of release dates should be disseminated at least one year in advance. Once the release date has been established, data should be released without delay.
- CPI data should be released simultaneously to all users.
- Detailed data should be disseminated on the NSO website. These include detailed weights, indices, and changes (monthly and annual).
- Data should be published down to the elementary aggregate level. Every effort should be made to design samples that support the detailed dissemination of data.
- To enhance transparency and increase user confidence, NSOs should explain data quality issues and provide details on the methods used to minimize these biases.
- User groups should be consulted and informed when making updates or revisions to the CPI. Advisory groups can be a useful means of maintaining contact with key data users.

A GLOSSARY OF MAIN TERMS

Acquisitions approach	An approach to consumer price indices (CPIs) in which consumption is identified with the consumption of goods and services acquired by a household in some period (as distinct from those wholly or partially used up for purposes of consumption). Depending on the intended scope of the CPI, acquisitions may include not only goods and services purchased but also those acquired by own-account production or as social transfers in kind from government or nonprofit institutions.
Additivity	At current prices, the value of an aggregate is identical to the sum of the values of its components. Additivity requires this identity to be preserved for the extrapolated values of the aggregate and its components when their current values in some period are extrapolated using a set of interrelated quantity indices; or, alternatively, when the current values of an aggregate and its components in some period are deflated using a set of interrelated price indices.
Aggregate	A set of transactions relating to a specified flow of goods and services, such as the total purchases made by resident households on consumer goods and services in some period. The term "aggregate" is also used to mean the value of the designated set of transactions.
Aggregation	The process of combining, or adding, different sets of transactions to obtain larger sets of transactions. The larger set is described as having a higher *level* of aggregation than the sets of which it is composed. The term "aggregation" is also used to mean the process of adding the values of the lower-level aggregates to obtain higher-level aggregates. In the case of price indices, it means the process by which price indices for lower-level aggregates are averaged, or otherwise combined, to obtain price indices for higher-level aggregates.
Axiomatic, or test approach	The approach to index number theory that determines the choice of index number formula on the basis of its mathematical properties. A list of tests is drawn up, each test requiring an index to possess a certain property or satisfy a certain axiom. An index number may then be chosen based on the number of tests satisfied. Not all tests may be considered to be equally important and the failure to satisfy one or two key tests may be considered sufficient grounds for rejecting an index.
Average of price relatives	See *Carli index*.
Base period	The base period is usually understood to mean the period with which all the other periods are compared. The term, however, has different meanings in different contexts. Three types of base periods may be distinguished: • *The price reference period*—the period that provides the prices to which the prices in other periods are compared. The prices of the price reference period appear in the denominators of the price relatives, or price ratios, used to calculate the index. The price reference period is typically designated as period 0. • *The weight reference period*—the period, usually one or more years, of which the expenditures serve as weights for the index. When the expenditures are *hybrid* (that is, the quantities of one period are valued at the prices of some other period), the weight reference period is the period to which the quantities refer. The weight reference period is typically designated as period *b* in this Manual. • *The index reference period*—the period for which the value of the index is set equal to 100. It should be noted that, in practice, the duration of the weight reference period for a CPI is typically a year, or even two or more years, whereas the CPI is calculated monthly or quarterly, the duration of the price reference period being a month, quarter, or year. The weight and price reference periods seldom coincide in practice, at least when a CPI is first calculated, although the price and index reference periods frequently coincide.
Basket	A specified set of goods and services and their quantities. In a CPI context, the set may comprise the actual quantities of consumption goods or services acquired or used by households in some period, or may be made up of hypothetical quantities.
Basket price index	A price index that measures the proportionate change between periods *0* and *t* in the total value of a specified basket of goods and services: that is, $\sum p^t q / \sum p^0 q$, where the term *q* is the quantities of the specified goods and services. See *Lowe index*.
Bias	A systematic tendency for the calculated CPI to diverge from some ideal or preferred index, resulting from the method of data collection or processing, or the index formula used. See *Cost of living bias* and *Representativity bias*.
Bilateral indices	A type of index that measures the aggregate price change between two periods based on prices observed in these two periods only. Depending on the index formula, the underlying quantities purchased or expenditures can be from the price reference period (for example, Laspeyres), the current period (for example, Paasche), the price reference and the current periods (for example, Fisher, Walsh, Törnqvist), or any other past period (for example, Lowe, Young).

Bouncing	A situation in which the set of prices for the second period is simply a reordering of the set of prices for the first period, the price relatives thus being obtained by matching each price in the first period with another price from the same set of prices.
Carli price index	An elementary price index defined as a simple, or unweighted, arithmetic average of the sample price relatives.
Carryforward	A situation in which a missing price in some period is imputed as being equal to the last price observed for that item.
Central product classification	An internationally agreed-upon classification of goods and services based on the physical characteristics of goods or on the nature of the services rendered.
Chain index	An index number series for a long sequence of periods obtained by linking together index numbers spanning shorter sequences of periods. See *Linking*; see also *equation 6 of Appendix 6 to the Manual.*
Chaining/chain linking	The construction of a continuous price series by multiplying together price indices that have been constructed using different weight reference periods. The resulting index is referred to as a "chain index."
Characteristics	The physical and economic attributes of a good or service that serve to identify it and enable it to be classified. Some characteristics will help determine price and are commonly referred to as price-determining characteristics.
Circularity (transitivity)	An index number property such that, if ${}_jI_k$ denotes a particular kind of price index that measures the change between periods *j* and *k*, then ${}_jI_l \equiv {}_jI_k \cdot {}_kI_l$ where the indices ${}_jI_l$ and ${}_kI_l$ are of the same type. When an index is transitive, the index that compares periods *j* and *l* indirectly through period *k* is identical with the index that compares *j* and *l* directly. One test that might be required under the axiomatic approach is that the index number should be transitive.
COICOP	The Classification of Individual Consumption by Purpose. It is the internationally preferred classification for CPIs, household budget surveys, and the International Comparison Program.
Commensurability	See *Invariance to changes in the units of measurement test.*
Commodity reversal test	A test that might be used under the axiomatic approach that requires that, for a given set of products, the price index should remain unchanged when the ordering of the products is changed.
Component	A subset of the goods and services that make up some defined aggregate.
Conditional cost of living index	A conditional cost of living index measures the change in the cost of maintaining a given utility level, or standard of living, on the assumption that all the factors, *except the prices covered by the index*, that influence the consumer's utility or welfare (for example, the state of the physical environment) remain constant. See *Cost of living index.*
Consistency in aggregation	An index is said to be consistent in aggregation when the index for some aggregate has the same value whether it is calculated directly in a single operation, without distinguishing its components, or whether it is calculated in two or more steps by first calculating separate indices, or subindices, for its components, or subcomponents, and then aggregating them, the same formula being used at each step.
Consumer price index (CPI)	An official indicator constructed to measure the changes over time in the general level of prices for consumer goods and services that households acquire, use, or pay for consumption. Its exact definition may vary from country to country.
Consumption	Consumption of goods and services is the act of completely using up the goods and services in a process of production or for the direct satisfaction of human needs or wants. The activity of consumption consists of the use of goods and services for the satisfaction of individual or collective human needs or wants. Additionally, • *Intermediate consumption* consists of the value of the goods and services consumed as inputs by a process of production, excluding fixed assets whose consumption is recorded as consumption of fixed capital; it is excluded from CPIs. • *Final consumption* consists of goods and services used by individual households or the community to satisfy their individual or collective needs or wants. The *System of National Accounts 2008* (*2008 SNA*) also defines individual and collective consumption goods and services: • An *individual consumption good or service* is one that is acquired by a household and used to satisfy the needs or wants of members of that household. • A *collective consumption service* is a service provided simultaneously to all members of the community or to all members of a particular section of the community, such as all households living in a particular region; it is excluded from CPIs. See *Household final consumption expenditure.*
Consumption of own production	Goods or services that are consumed by the same household that produces them. The housing services consumed by owner-occupiers fall within this category. If goods and services produced and consumed within the same household are to be included in CPIs, prices must be estimated for them. Their inclusion or exclusion depends on the intended scope of the CPI. It should be noted that activities undertaken by households that produce services for their own use are outside of the scope of the *System of National Accounts* (SNA) production boundary, except for services provided by owner-occupied dwellings and services produced by employing paid domestic staff. The own-account production of all goods that are retained by their producers for their own final consumption or gross capital formation is included in the SNA production boundary.

Continuity	The property whereby the price index is a continuous function of its price and quantity vectors.
Cost of living bias	An alternative term used to describe *Substitution bias*.
Cost of living index	An index that measures the change between two periods in the minimum expenditures that *would* be required to achieve a constant standard of living (that is level of utility or economic well-being). As consumers may be expected to change the quantities they consume in response to changes in relative prices (*see Substitution effect*), the cost of living index is not a basket index. The quantities and expenditures made in one or other, or possibly both, periods cannot usually be observed in a timely manner. Cost of living indices cannot be directly calculated but may be approximated by superlative indices. See *Conditional cost of living index*.
Coverage	The set of goods and services of which the prices are actually included in the index. For practical reasons, coverage may have to be less than the ideal scope of the index, that is, the set of goods and services that the compilers of the index would prefer to include if it were feasible.
Current period, or comparison period	In principle, the current period should refer to the most recent period for which the index has been compiled or is being compiled. The term is widely used, however, to mean the comparison period; that is, the period that is compared with the base period, usually the price reference or index reference period. It is also widely used simply to mean the later of the two periods being compared. The exact meaning is usually clear in the context.
Current prices	The actual prices prevailing in the period in question.
Current value	The actual value of some aggregate in the period in question: the quantities in the period multiplied by the prices of the same period.
Cutoff sampling	A sampling procedure in which a predetermined threshold is established with all units in the universe at or above the threshold being included in the sample, and all units below the threshold being excluded. The threshold is usually specified with regard to the size of some relevant variable, the largest sampling units being included and the rest given a zero chance of inclusion.
Deflation	The division of the current value of some aggregate by a price index (described as a deflator) in order to revalue its quantities at the prices of the price reference period.
Democratic index	A form of CPI in which the expenditure proportions of each household are given equal weight in the calculation of the index, irrespectively of the size of its expenditures. See *Plutocratic index*.
Discount	A deduction from the list or advertised price of a good or a service that is available to specific customers under specific conditions. Examples include cash discounts, prompt payment discounts, volume discounts, trade discounts, and advertising discounts.
Divisia index	A price or quantity index that treats both prices and quantities as continuous functions of time. By differentiating with respect to time, the rate of change in the value of the aggregate in question is partitioned into two components, one of which is the price index and the other the quantity index. In practice, the indices cannot be calculated directly, but it may be possible to approximate them by chain indices in which indices measuring the changes between consecutive periods are linked together.
Domain	An alternative term for the scope of an index. See *Scope*.
Domestic concept	The use of weights covering all consumption expenditure on the national territory, regardless of the nationality or normal residence of the consumer. See *National concept*.
Drift	A chain index is said to drift if it does not return to unity when prices in the current period return to their levels in the base period. Chain indices are liable to drift when prices fluctuate over the periods they cover.
Drobisch price index	The arithmetic average of the Laspeyres price index and the Paasche price index.
Durable consumer good	A consumer good that can be used repeatedly or continuously for purposes of consumption over a period of one year or more.
Dutot index	An elementary price index defined as the ratio of the unweighted arithmetic averages of the prices in the two periods compared.
Economic approach	The economic approach to index number theory assumes that the quantities are functions of the prices, the observed data being generated as solutions to various economic optimization problems. In the CPI context, the economic approach usually requires the CPI to be some kind of cost of living index.
Edgeworth price index	A basket price index in which the quantities in the basket are simple arithmetic averages of the quantities consumed in the two periods.
Editing	The process of scrutinizing and checking the prices reported by price collectors. Some checks may be carried out by computers using statistical programs written for the purpose.
Elasticity of substitution	A measure of the extent to which one product is substituted for another in response to relative price changes. A zero elasticity of substitution means that there is no substitution.
Elementary aggregate	The lowest level of groups of goods or services for which expenditure weights are assigned and held constant for a period of one year or more. An elementary aggregate should consist of relatively homogeneous set of goods or services, with similar end-uses and similar expected price movements. More detailed weights to reflect the relative importance of individual price observations within elementary aggregates may be applied and updated more frequently. The elementary aggregates are the building blocks for the calculation of the higher-level indices.

Elementary price index	In general, an elementary index is a price index for an elementary aggregate, but it can also refer to a price index for a more detailed level below the elementary aggregate. Expenditure weights cannot usually be assigned to the price relatives for the sampled products within an elementary aggregate, although other kinds of weighting may be explicitly or implicitly introduced into the calculation of elementary indices. For example, scanner data could be used to develop a more detailed weighting program within an elementary aggregate. Three examples of unweighted elementary index number formulae are the Carli, the Dutot, and the Jevons.
Expenditure weights	See *Weights*.
Explicit (or direct) quality adjustment	A direct estimate of the value of the quality difference between the old and new product used to adjust one of the prices accordingly. Pure price change is then estimated as the difference in the adjusted prices. See *Implicit quality adjustment*.
Factor reversal test	Suppose the prices and quantities in a price index are interchanged to yield a quantity index of exactly the same functional form as the price index. Under the axiomatic approach, the factor reversal test requires that the product of this quantity index and the original price index should be identical to the proportionate change in the value of the aggregate in question.
Fisher price index	The geometric average of the Laspeyres price index and the Paasche price index. It is a symmetric index and a superlative index.
Fixed-basket indices	A time series of basket indices that all use the same basket; *see equation 4 of Appendix 6 to the Manual*. In a CPI context, the fixed basket usually consists of the total quantities of goods and services consumed by the designated set of households over a period of a year or more.
Fixed-weight indices	An abbreviated description for a series of weighted averages of price relatives that all use the same weights; see *equation 13 of Appendix 6 to the Manual*. The weights are usually either actual or hybrid expenditure shares.
Geometric Laspeyres index	A weighted geometric average of the price relatives using the expenditure shares of the price reference period as weights. Also called Logarithmic Laspeyres index.
Goods	Physical, produced objects for which a demand exists, over which ownership rights can be established and for which ownership can be transferred between institutional units by engaging in transactions on the market.
Hedonic method	A regression model in which the market prices of different products are expressed as a function of their characteristics. Nonnumerical characteristics are represented by dummy variables. Each regression coefficient is treated as an estimate of the marginal contribution of that characteristic to the total price. The estimates may be used to predict the price of a new product for which the mix of characteristics is different from that of any product already on the market. The hedonic method can therefore be used to estimate the effects of quality changes on prices.
Higher-level index	An aggregate index as distinct from an elementary index.
Household budget surveys	Sample surveys of households in which the households are asked to provide data on, or estimates of, the value of the goods and services acquired, paid, and used for consumption as well as other purposes over a given period of time. Also referred to household income and expenditure surveys.
Household final consumption expenditure	It consists of the expenditure, including expenditure whose value must be estimated indirectly, incurred by resident households on individual consumption goods and services, including those sold at prices that are not economically significant and including consumption goods and services acquired abroad. They exclude expenditures incurred by governments or nonprofit institutions on goods or services provided to households as free social transfers in kind.
Households	A household is a group of persons who share the same living accommodation, who pool some, or all, of their income and wealth and who consume certain types of goods and services collectively, mainly housing and food. Most countries choose to exclude groups of persons living in large institutional households (barracks, retirement homes, and so on) from the scope of their CPIs.
Hybrid values or expenditures	Hypothetical values, or expenditures, in which the quantities are valued at a different set of prices from those at which they were actually bought or sold: for example, when the quantities purchased in an earlier period, such as b, are valued at the prices prevailing in a later period, such as 0.
Hybrid weights	Weights defined as *hybrid value*, or *hybrid expenditure*, shares.
Identity test	A test under the axiomatic approach that requires that, if each and every price remains unchanged between the two periods, the price index must equal unity.
Implicit (or indirect) quality adjustment	Estimating the pure price change component of the price difference between the old and new products based on the price changes observed for similar products. The difference between the estimate of pure price change and the observed price change is considered as change due to quality difference. See *Explicit quality adjustment*.
Imputed price[1]	The price assigned to a variety for which the price is missing in a particular period. The term "imputed price" may also refer to the price assigned to an variety that is not sold on the market, such as a good or service produced for own consumption, including housing services produced by owner-occupiers, or one received as payment in kind or as a free transfer from a government or nonprofit institution.

[1]This definition differs from that used by the 2008 SNA.

Indexation	The periodic adjustment of the money values of some regular scheduled payments based on the movement of the CPI or some other price index. The payments may be wages or salaries, social security or other pensions, other social security benefits, rents, interest payments, and so on.
Index reference period	The period for which the value of the index is set at 100.
Institutional unit	An economic entity that is capable, in its own right, of owning assets, incurring liabilities, and engaging in economic activities and transactions with other entities. Households are institutional units. Other kinds of units include enterprises and governments.
Institutional households	A group of individuals staying in an institution for long periods of time, such as retirement homes, military accommodation, and boarding schools, and sharing resources. Such people are treated as belonging to private "institutional" households.
Invariance to changes in the units of measurement test	A test under the axiomatic approach that requires that the price index does not change when the units of quantity to which the prices refer are changed: for example, when the price of some drink is quoted per liter rather than per pint. This test is also described as the commensurability test.
Invariance to proportional change in current or base quantities test	A test under the axiomatic approach that requires that the price index remains unchanged when all the base period quantities, or all the current period quantities, are multiplied by a positive scalar.
Inverse proportionality in base year prices test	A test that may be invoked under the axiomatic approach that requires that, if all the base period prices are multiplied by the positive scalar l, the new price index is $1/l$ times the old price index.
Item or product rotation	The deliberate replacement of a sampled item, or product, for which prices are being collected, by another product before the replaced product has disappeared from the market or individual outlet. It is designed to keep the sample of products up to date and reduce the need for forced replacements caused by the disappearance of products.
Jevons price index	An elementary price index defined as the unweighted geometric average of the sample price relatives.
Laspeyres price index	A basket index in which the basket is composed of the actual quantities of goods and services in the earlier of the two periods compared, the price reference period; see *equation 3 of Appendix 6 to the Manual.* It can also be expressed as a weighted arithmetic average of the price relatives that uses the expenditure shares in the earlier period as weights; see *equations 7–10 of Appendix 6 to the Manual.* The earlier period serves as both the weight reference period and the price reference period.
Linking	Splicing together two consecutive sequences of price observations, or price indices, that overlap in one or more periods. When the two sequences overlap by a single period, the usual procedure is simply to rescale one or the other sequence so that the value in the overlap period is the same in both sequences and the spliced sequences form one continuous series. See *equation 6 of Appendix 6 to the Manual.*
Lowe index	A price index that measures the proportionate change between periods 0 and t in the total value of a specified basket of goods and services; that is, $\sum p^t q / \sum p^0 q$, where the term q is the specified quantities. The basket does not necessarily have to consist of the actual quantities in some period. See *Appendix 6 to the Manual.* This type of index is described in the Manual as a Lowe index after the index number pioneer who first proposed this general type of index. The class of indices covered by this definition is very broad and includes, by appropriate specification of the terms q, the Laspeyres, Paasche, Edgeworth, and Walsh indices. Lowe indices are widely used for CPI purposes, the quantities in the basket typically being those of some weight reference period b, which precedes the price reference period 0.
Lower-level index	An elementary index as distinct from an aggregate index.
Matched products or models	The practice of pricing exactly the same product in two or more consecutive periods. It is designed to ensure that the observed price changes are not affected by the quality change. The change in price between two perfectly matched products is described as a pure price change.
Model	A specific variety whose characteristics are regularly updated. See *Variety.*
Mean value test for prices	A test under the axiomatic approach, which requires that the price index should lie between the smallest price relative and the largest price relative.
Modified Lowe index	A version of the Lowe index that compiles the index based on short-term price changes rather than long-term changes. This approach makes it easier for national statistical offices to introduce replacement varieties in the sample when a sampled variety disappears. The short-term approach also facilitates quality adjustments because only the current and previous period prices are needed in order to introduce a new variety into the index. See *Lowe index.*
Modified Young index	A version of the Young index that compiles the index based on short-term price changes rather than long-term changes. This approach makes it easier for national statistical offices to introduce replacement varieties in the sample when a sample variety disappears. The short-term approach also facilitates quality adjustments because only the current and previous period prices are needed in order to introduce a new variety in the index. See *Young index.*

Multilateral indices	A type of index that measures the aggregate price change between two periods based on prices observed in multiple periods including the two comparison periods. Multilateral indices were developed for price comparisons across countries (purchasing power parities) and have been adapted to compare prices over time. For price comparisons over time, multilateral index formulas are mainly used with scanner data. In this context, their main advantage is to avoid chain drift. The most common multilateral index formulas in CPIs are the Gini–Eltetö–Köves–Szulc, the Geary–Khamis, and the time product dummy. *See Chapter 10 for further details.*
National concept	The use of weights covering the expenditure of residents of a country, regardless of whether the expenditure is made within or outside of the country. See *Domestic concept.*
Nonprobability sampling	The deliberate (that is, nonrandom) selection of a sample of outlets and products on the basis of the knowledge or judgment of the person responsible. Also known as purposive sampling and judgmental sampling.
Outlier	A term that is generally used to describe any extreme value in a set of survey data. In a CPI context, it is used for an extreme value of price or price relative that requires further investigation or that has been verified as being correct.
Owner-occupied housing	Dwellings owned by the households that live in them. The dwellings are fixed assets that their owners use to produce housing services for their own consumption, these services being usually included within the scope of the CPI. The value of the services provided may be imputed by the rents payable on the market for equivalent accommodation or by user costs. See *Rental equivalence* and *User cost*. In the *System of National Accounts* (SNA) framework, the production of housing services for their own final consumption by owner-occupiers has always been included within the production boundary in national accounts, although it constitutes an exception to the general exclusion of own-account service production.
Paasche price index	A basket index in which the basket is composed of the actual quantities of goods and services in the later of the two periods compared. The later period serves as the weight reference period and the earlier period as the price reference period. The Paasche index can also be expressed as a weighted harmonic average of the price relatives that uses the actual expenditure shares in the later period as weights. See *equations 7–11 of Appendix 6 to the Manual.*
Plutocratic index	A form of CPI in which the weights are based on total aggregated expenditure values rather than average household expenditure proportions.
Price reference period	The period of which the prices appear in the denominators of the price relatives. See *Base period.*
Price relative	The ratio of the price of a variety in one period to the price of that same variety in some other period.
Price updating	A procedure whereby the quantities in an earlier period are revalued at the prices of a later period. The resulting expenditures are hybrid. In practice, the price-updated expenditures may be obtained by multiplying the original expenditures by price relatives or price indices.
Probability proportional to size sampling	A sampling procedure whereby each unit in the universe has a probability of selection proportional to the size of some known variable, such as the value of the sales of an outlet.
Probability sampling	The random selection of a sample of units, such as outlets or products, in such a way that each unit in the universe has a known nonzero probability of selection.
Proportionality in current prices test	A test under the axiomatic approach that requires that, if all current period prices are multiplied by the positive scalar λ, the new price index is λ times the old price index.
Purchaser's price	The purchaser's price is the amount paid by the purchaser, excluding any value-added tax or similar tax deductible by the purchaser, in order to take delivery of a unit of a good or service at the time and place required by the purchaser. The purchaser's price of a good includes any transport charges paid separately by the purchaser to take delivery at the required time and place.
Pure price change	The change in the price of the same variety; or the change in the price after adjusting for any change in quality.
Quality adjustment	An adjustment to the price of a variety of which the characteristics have changed over time. Quality adjustments are designed to remove the part of the observed price that is due to differences in the price-determining characteristics. In a CPI context, the adjustment is needed when the price of a replacement variety must be compared with the price of the variety it replaces. In practice, the required adjustment can only be estimated. Different methods of estimation, including hedonic methods, may be used in different circumstances. See *Explicit quality adjustment* and *Implicit quality adjustment.*
Quantity relative	The ratio of the quantity of a product in one period to the quantity of that same product in some other period.
Quantity weights	A term sometimes used to describe the quantities in the basket. However, expenditures rather than quantities act as weights for price relatives. See *Weights.*
Quota sampling	Sample selection using judgmental procedures with respect to known characteristics such as product group or outlet type. The sample is drawn so as to contain the same proportions as in the total population of products, items, or outlets.
Ratio of averages	See *Dutot index.*
Rebasing	It refers to changing the weight reference period, price reference period, or index reference period. The weight reference period, price reference period, and index reference period may be changed separately or at the same time.

Reference population	The set of households included within the scope of the index.
Rental equivalence	The estimation of the imputed rents payable by owner-occupiers on the basis of the rents payable on the market for accommodation of the same type.
Replacement variety	A variety chosen to replace a variety for which prices have been collected previously, either because the previous variety has disappeared altogether or because it accounts for a diminishing share of the sales of the outlet, or the expenditures within the elementary aggregate.
Representative variety	A variety, or category of varieties, that accounts for a significant proportion of the total expenditures within an elementary aggregate, and for which the average price change is expected to be close to the average for all varieties within the aggregate.
Representativity bias	Bias in a basket index that results from the use of quantities that are not representative of the two periods compared; that is, that systematically diverge from the average quantities consumed in the two periods. For example, representativity bias may result from the use of an old, out-of-date basket which deviates systematically from the baskets in both the periods compared. In practice, representativity bias tends to be similar to substitution bias, as it is attributable to the same economic factors.
Reweighting	Replacing the weights used in an index by a new set of weights.
Revision	Often refers to changing index weights and implementing new calculation or compilation methodologies.
Sample augmentation	Maintaining and adding to the sample of outlets, items, and varieties in the survey panel to ensure that they continue to be representative of the population of outlets. A fixed sample of outlets tends to be depleted over time, as outlets cease trading or stop responding. Including new outlets also tends to facilitate the inclusion of new products in the CPI.
Sampled price	The price collected for a sampled product in a specific outlet at a specific time, sometimes described as a price quote.
Sample rotation	Limiting the length of time that outlets and products are included in the price surveys by dropping a proportion of them, or possibly all of them, after a certain period of time and selecting a new sample of outlets and products. Rotation is designed to keep the sample up to date.
Sampling frame	A list of the units in the universe from which a sample of units can be selected. The list may contain information about the units, which may be used for probability proportional to size sampling. Examples of lists that may be used for retail outlets are business registers, telephone directories ("yellow pages"), local authority records, or trade directories. Such lists may not cover all the units in the designated universe and may also include units that do not form part of that universe.
Scanner data	Detailed data on sales of products obtained by scanning the bar codes for individual varieties at electronic points of sale in retail outlets. The data can provide detailed information about quantities, characteristics, and values of varieties sold, as well as their prices. Scanner data constitute a rapidly expanding source of data with considerable potential for CPI purposes.
Scope	The set of products for which the index is intended to measure the price changes. The scope of a CPI will generally be defined with regard to a designated set of consumption goods and services purchased by a designated set of households. In practice, certain goods and services or households may have to be excluded because it is too difficult, time-consuming, or costly to collect the relevant data on expenditures or prices: for example, illegal expenditures. The coverage of an index denotes the actual set of products included, as distinct from the intended scope of the index.
Seasonal products	They are products that either are not available on the market during certain seasons or periods of the year or are available throughout the year but with regular fluctuations in their quantities and prices that are linked to the season or time of the year.
Services	They are the result of a production activity that changes the conditions of the consuming units or facilitates the exchange of products or financial assets.
Specification	A description or list of the characteristics that can be used to identify an individual sampled variety to be priced. A tight specification is a fairly precise description of an item intended to narrow the range of varieties from which a price collector might choose, possibly reducing it to a unique variety, such as a particular brand of television set identified by a specific code number. A loose specification is a generic description of a range of items that allows the price collector some discretion as to which particular variety or model to select for pricing, such as color television sets of a particular size.
Stochastic approach	The approach to index number theory that treats the observed price relatives as if they were a random sample drawn from a defined universe for which the mean can be interpreted as the general rate of inflation. The sample mean provides an estimate of the rate of inflation.
Substitute	A product of which the characteristics are similar to those of another product and that can be used to meet the same kinds of consumer needs or wants.
Substitution	The replacement of products by substitutes, typically in response to changes in relative prices. Rational utility-maximizing consumers, as price takers, typically react to changes in relative prices by reducing, at least marginally, their consumption of goods and services that have become relatively dearer and increasing their consumption of substitutes that have become relatively cheaper. Substitution results in a negative correlation between the quantity and price relatives.

Substitution bias	This is generally understood to be the bias that results when a basket index is used to estimate a cost of living index, because a basket index cannot take account of the effects on the cost of living of the substitutions made by consumers in response to changes in relative prices. In general, the earlier the period of which the basket is used, the greater the upward bias in the index; see *Representativity bias*.
Substitution effect	The effect of substitution on the value of an index.
Superlative index	A type of index formula that can be expected to approximate to the cost of living index. An index is said to be exact when it equals the true cost of living index for consumers whose preferences can be represented by a particular functional form. A superlative index is then defined as an index that is exact for a flexible functional form that can provide a second-order approximation to other twice-differentiable functions around the same point. The Fisher, the Törnqvist, and the Walsh price indices are examples of superlative indices. Superlative indices are generally symmetric indices.
Symmetric index	An index that treats both periods symmetrically by attaching equal importance to the price and expenditure data in both periods. The price and expenditure data for both periods enter into the index formula in a symmetric way.
System of National Accounts (SNA)	A coherent, consistent, and integrated set of macroeconomic accounts, balance sheets, and tables based on a set of internationally agreed-upon concepts, definitions, classifications, and accounting rules. Distribution and use of income accounts and household final consumption expenditure form part of the SNA. The expenditure data are some of the sources that are used to estimate expenditure weights for CPI purposes.
Time reversal	An index number property such that, if ${}_jI_k$ denotes a particular kind of price index formula that measures the change from period *j* to period *k*, then ${}_jI_k \equiv 1 / {}_kI_j$ where ${}_kI_j$ measures the change from period *k* to period *j*. When an index has this property, the change is the same whether it is measured forward from the first to the second period or backward from the second to the first period. An index may be required to satisfy the time reversal test under the axiomatic approach.
Törnqvist price index	A symmetric index defined as the weighted geometric average of the price relatives in which the weights are simple arithmetic averages of the expenditure shares in the two periods. It is a superlative index. Also known as the Törnqvist–Theil price index.
Transitivity	See *Circularity*.
Unit value or average value	The unit value of a set of homogeneous products is the total value of the purchases/sales divided by the sum of the quantities. It is therefore a quantity-weighted average of the different prices at which the product is purchased/sold. Unit values may change over time as a result of a change in the mix of the products sold at different prices, even if the prices do not change.
Updating	Changing the index weights. See *Revision* and *Rebasing*.
User cost	The cost incurred over a period of time by the owner of a fixed asset or consumer durable as a consequence of using it to provide a flow of capital or consumption services. User cost consists mainly of the depreciation of the asset or durable (measured at current prices and not at historic cost) plus the capital, or interest, cost.
Uses approach	An approach to CPIs in which the consumption in some period is identified with the consumption goods and services actually used up by a household to satisfy their needs and wants (as distinct from the consumption goods and services acquired). In this approach, the consumption of consumer durables in a given period is measured by the values of the flows of services provided by the stocks of durables owned by households. These values may be estimated by the user costs.
Value	Price times quantity. The value of the expenditures on a set of homogeneous products can be factored uniquely into its price and quantity components. Similarly, the change over time in the value of a set of homogeneous products can be factored uniquely into the change in the unit value and the change in the total quantities. There are, however, many different ways of factoring the change over time in the value of a set of heterogeneous products into its price and quantity components, a phenomenon that gives rise to the index number problem.
Variety	The individual product for which prices are collected during the collection period. It includes the detailed specification of the product or item observed.
Walsh price index	A basket index in which the quantities are geometric averages of the quantities in the two periods; see *Appendix 6 to the Manual*. It is a symmetric index and a superlative index.
Weight reference period	The period of which the expenditure shares serve as the weights for a Young index, or of which the quantities make up the basket for a Lowe index. There may be no weight reference period when the expenditure shares for the two periods are averaged, as in the Törnqvist index, or when the quantities are averaged, as in the Walsh index. See *Base period*.
Weighted arithmetic average index	An index defined as a weighted arithmetic average of the price relatives: namely, $\sum w\left(p^t / p^0\right)$, where the weights *w* sum to unity.
Weights	A set of numbers summing to unity that are used to calculate averages. In a CPI context, the weights are generally actual or hybrid expenditure shares that sum to unity by definition. They are used to average price relatives or elementary price indices; see *Appendix 6 to the Manual*. Quantities of different kinds of products are not commensurate and not additive. They cannot be used to average elementary price indices. The quantities that make up a basket should therefore not be described as quantity weights.
Young index	A Young index is a weighted arithmetic average of the price relatives, $\sum w\left(p^t / p^0\right)$, in which the terms *w* refer to the actual expenditure shares of period *b*, the weight reference period; that is, $w = s^b = p^b q^b / \sum p^b q^b$. It is a weighted version of the Carli index.

Appendix 1

The Harmonised Index of Consumer Prices (European Union)

Introduction

The Harmonised Index of Consumer Prices (HICP) is a specific inflation measure that is developed within the European Union (EU) to result in indices that can be directly compared and aggregated across countries. The HICP is the outcome of major harmonization work by the statistical office of the EU (Eurostat) and the EU countries.

The HICP is a cost of goods index; that is, it measures the changing cost of a fixed basket of products over time. The production of the HICP and its methodology are governed by EU law, which gives the common definitions and concepts to follow. The key HICP aggregates are the euro area index, covering the countries whose currency is the euro, the EU index, and the national HICP for each of the EU countries. Eurostat publishes also HICPs for countries that are not part of the EU, which produce the data on voluntary basis. The national statistical offices produce the national HICP, while Eurostat produces the country-group aggregates.

The HICP serves two main purposes:

- For quantifying the price stability in the European Central Bank's monetary policy strategy. Maintaining price stability is the primary objective of the European Central Bank and the national central banks of the euro area, as set out in the Treaty on the Functioning of the European Union. The ECB's Governing Council has defined price stability as a year-on-year increase in the HICP for the euro area of below 2 percent. The Governing Council has clarified that, in the pursuit of price stability, it aims to maintain inflation rates below, but close to, 2 percent over the medium term.
- For assessing the price stability criterion, which is one of the convergence criteria used to evaluate if a country can join the euro area.

In addition to these specific EU uses, the HICP may be used, like other consumer price indices, for economic analysis and for indexing for example contracts and wages. The HICP has been produced and published since March 1997.

Concepts and Definitions

Household Final Monetary Consumption Expenditure

In general, the concepts, definitions, and conventions adopted in the HICP are as far as possible consistent with those used in the United Nations *System of National Accounts 2008* (*2008 SNA*) and its EU version, the *European System of Accounts 2010* (ESA 2010). Among these concepts is that of household final consumption expenditure. For the HICP this has been adapted to refer to the part that occurs in monetary transactions only. This household final monetary consumption expenditure (HFMCE) is thus a narrower concept than household final consumption expenditure, which includes both monetary and nonmonetary transactions. The HFMCE is a fundamental concept for the HICP. It delineates the scope of the HICP, namely that it includes only expenditure on consumption products by the household sector. And that it excludes all capital expenditure, such as the purchase of land or financial assets like stocks and shares, as well as all imputed transactions, own production, and barter.

Coverage

The domestic concept is used to define the *geographic coverage* of the HICP. This takes into account all HFMCE within the economic territory of a country, whether made by resident or nonresident households. Consumption expenditure incurred by residents when they are outside the country of residence is excluded from the HICP, while expenditure incurred by visitors from other countries is included. Bearing in mind the principal use of the HICP as an indicator for monetary policy purposes, there are two main reasons for using the domestic concept for the coverage of the HICP:

- By confining expenditure to that incurred within an economic territory, the resulting HICPs cover only those price changes which national/euro area monetary policies can directly influence.
- Consistent aggregation of national HICPs: if a European aggregate HICP (for example, for the euro area) is compared with another country or economic bloc, it must be certain to represent the whole of consumer price inflation within the euro area and none of it must be double-counted.

Using the domestic concept ensures that these conditions are met. An alternative to the domestic concept is the national concept, where all expenditure incurred by residents of a country, whether nationals or nonnationals, is measured, regardless of whether it is incurred inside or outside the economic territory. It should be noted that both the domestic and national concepts at the world level would produce theoretically the same results with regard to aggregate expenditure. However, at the EU and euro area levels they would not, due to the expenditure of EU/euro area residents outside the EU and the expenditure of non-EU residents within the EU. In practical terms, this makes the domestic concept the easier one to implement, as the national concept would require detailed information on residents' expenditure and prices paid outside the economic territory.

The HICP *product coverage* is based on the concept of HFMCE and the 1999 version of the Classification of Individual Consumption According to Purpose (COICOP) to which an additional level of (five-digit) subclasses has been added. Some categories of COICOP are excluded either in principle or on practical grounds from the HICP coverage:

02.3	Narcotics
04.2	Imputed rentals for housing
09.4.3	Games of chance
12.2	Prostitution
12.5.1	Life insurance
12.6.1	Financial intermediation services indirectly measured

In principle, "narcotics" and "prostitution" belong to HFMCE but they are not covered in the HICP for practical reasons. "Games of chance" also falls within the scope of the HFMCE. However, they are excluded from the HICP because no harmonized method for their treatment has yet been agreed upon.

"Owner-occupied housing" costs are excluded from the HICP product coverage because no available method is both conceptually consistent with the HICP and able to provide timely data with monthly frequency. The rental equivalence approach is currently considered noncompatible with the HICP on conceptual grounds as that method uses imputations and not actual monetary transactions. Eurostat has instead established a separate index of owner-occupied housing costs using the net acquisition approach. This index meets the requirement of monetary transactions, but can be criticized for including assets (land and dwellings). This is one of the reasons for not including this index into the HICP. In addition, it is apparent that net acquisition-based owner-occupied housing price indices cannot currently be produced monthly and timely in the EU countries. Eurostat is continuing the methodological work required for the integration of an owner-occupied housing price index into the HICP.

The HICP also excludes financial intermediation services indirectly measured consumed by households (that is, those parts of financial services for which an explicit (monetary) charge cannot be identified) because it is considered as an imputed transaction. Note that financial services that have explicit charges, for example, annual charges for credit cards (excluding interest charges), bank charges for money transfers, or currency exchange commissions, are included in the HICP.

Insurance services are within the scope of the HFMCE. However, "life insurance" is excluded from the HICP coverage. Premiums paid for life insurance, including pension-funding services, are regarded as savings and thus are not part of the HICP. "Life insurance" is excluded because it is not possible to separate out the implicit service charge for the insurance component from the implicit service charge for the investment component. Nonlife insurance services are, however, included in the HICP. Although for the HICP weights nonlife insurance services are measured with regard to implicit service charge, it is actually the gross insurance premiums that enter the index compilations, for practical reasons.

Weights

The HICP *weights* for published subindices are updated every year. The weights should represent the expenditure in the previous year and take account of preliminary national accounts data on the HFMCE. In practice, this means that compilers should estimate new subindex weights using the latest available data from the national accounts, normally preliminary estimates relating to the calendar year $t - 2$ (where t is the current year).

To obtain weights for lower levels of aggregation down to the most detailed product level, when national accounts do not provide data, other data sources such as household budget surveys, administrative data, retail sales, market research data, and data derived from scanner data can also be used. The observed year $t - 2$ expenditure may, or may not, be price updated between year $t - 2$ and year $t - 1$. The objective is to obtain the best possible estimate of the expenditure shares for the year $t - 1$. If goods and services are perfect complements (that is, there is no substitution between them and they are consumed in fixed proportions), the best approximation would be the price-updated weights. If goods and services are substitutes at such a rate that expenditure on one product relative to another is independent of the relative prices, the preferred approach would be not to price update. EU countries must carry out an annual review of weights to determine if there have been any important and sustained market developments, for example, the appearance of new significant products, and adjust the weights if necessary. These representative annual weights need to be adjusted with an appropriate price change to reflect the prices of December of the year $t - 1$.

Sampling

The HICP is a *sample* statistic that represents the change in prices, on average, over the target universe, which consists of all the transactions that fall within the scope of the HICP in the two periods being compared. Given the differences in the national markets and populations of the EU countries, it would not be possible to impose a uniform sampling structure across all countries. Nevertheless, certain minimum standards must be followed. Countries are required to ensure that:

- Each COICOP subclass contains a sufficient number of elementary aggregates to represent the diversity of products within the category.
- The number of prices recorded within each elementary aggregate is sufficient to represent the price movements in the population.
- All product categories that form a significant part of total consumption expenditure (at least one part per thousand) must be covered in the sample.

The HICP sample must be designed in such a way as to ensure that it is representative of all transactions: the result is a target sample, which must be maintained to ensure that it remains valid in the face of continual market changes.

Prices

The *prices* used in the HICP should be purchasers' prices, which are the prices actually paid by households. Product-related taxes such as the value-added tax and other sales taxes and excise duties are included and any subsidies deducted. Discounts such as sales prices should be taken into account. Interest payments or service charges added under credit arrangements, and any extra charges incurred as a result of failing to pay within the period specified at the time of purchase, are disregarded. Purchaser prices also include all unavoidable additional costs such as booking and delivery charges, which are typically associated with internet purchases. However, it is not always possible to observe the actual transaction price; so, in practice, it is usual to record the offer price or shelf price.

The HICP follows the acquisition approach to the recording of prices. In this approach, the acquisition is deemed to take place when the purchaser incurs a liability to the seller. In practical terms, for goods it is generally assumed that they are consumed at the time they are purchased, so prices for goods enter the HICP in the month that they are observed. However, many services (for example, flights or package holidays) are either purchased in advance of when they are consumed or they are consumed over a period of time (for example, season tickets for transport and sporting services). The prices of services are therefore recorded in the HICP in the first month that consumption of the service can commence.

Quality Adjustment

The HICP is designed to be a measure of *pure price change* for goods and services falling within its scope. This implies that the index should be calculated from identical or almost identical goods and services; that is, the priced products should remain of similar specification or quality over time. When a product offer in the sample is no longer available or no longer popular, it needs to be replaced, with possibly a quality adjustment, to keep the sample representative. Replacement product offers should be either the same or similar enough with regard to their characteristics that consumers perceive them to be equivalent. Where, from the consumer perspective, a replacement product offer is not seen as equivalent (that is, its characteristics differ from the replaced product offer), it is necessary to apply some type of quality adjustment to the price comparison.

Index Formulas

The HICP uses different formulas for aggregating prices and price indices. In order to compile an elementary price index, either unweighted or weighted index formulas (for example, multilateral methods) can be used depending on whether detailed weights are available. At the level of the elementary aggregate and above weights are available. At those levels, the HICP uses a *Laspeyres-type formula*. The HICP is a Laspeyres-type index obtained by annual chain linking 13-month (December to December) indices. December of each year is the overlap or link month in which the new and old basket of products are priced.

In the HICP, the weight reference period is defined as the year $t - 1$ and the price reference period is a month (December month of the previous year). Thus, in the HICP it is necessary to revalue the weights at the prices of the price reference period. This procedure is applied in order to take into account the relative price changes, which have occurred between the weight reference period and the price reference period.

Release, Timeliness, and Revisions

The HICP is produced and published each month according to a preannounced schedule—in general between 16 and 18 days after the end of the reference month. Each month, Eurostat also publishes an HICP flash estimate for the euro area and countries within that area. The flash estimate gives an early indication of what the HICP inflation is likely to be in the month in question. It is released on the last working day of the reference month, or shortly after.

The current index reference period of the HICP is 2015, and it is changed every 10 years unless there is a major methodological change that requires re-referencing.

HICPs are in principle revisable, but only in limited circumstances. In general, revisions have to be made if errors are found after the initial publication, and may also be made if the HICP is published as provisional and if new or improved basic information becomes available that is needed to improve its accuracy.

HICP Methodological Manual

The HICP methodological manual explains the agreed and preferred methods to be applied for the compilation of the HICP in detail. It also gives examples of good practice, provides index compilers with a practical guide, and serves as compendium of the HICP.[1]

[1]Eurostat. 2018. *Harmonised Index of Consumer Prices (HICP) Methodological Manual, 2018 Edition.* Luxembourg: European Commission. https://ec.europa.eu/eurostat/en/web/products-manuals-and-guidelines/-/KS-GQ-17-015.

Appendix 2

Classification of Individual Consumption According to Purpose 1999 (COICOP 1999)

Introduction

Classification of Individual Consumption According to Purpose (COICOP) 2018 has been endorsed by the United Nations Statistical Commission; however, many countries continue to use COICOP 1999. Countries should begin making plans to implement COICOP 2018 as part of their next consumer price index update and revision. While for some countries the next update may be within the next couple of years, for others, it will be longer. This appendix provides detailed explanations and breakdowns for COICOP 1999.

The objectives of this appendix are: (1) to maintain this reference for those countries who have not yet adopted COICOP 2018; (2) to allow countries the opportunity to better understand the differences between COICOP 2018 and COICOP 1999; and (3) to facilitate planning for the implementation of the new classification standard.

COICOP: Breakdown of Individual Consumption Expenditure of Households by Division and Group

01 Food and Nonalcoholic Beverages

01.1 Food

The food products classified here are those purchased for consumption at home. The group excludes food products sold for immediate consumption away from the home by hotels, restaurants, cafés, bars, kiosks, street vendors, automatic vending machines, and so on (11.1.1); cooked dishes prepared by restaurants for consumption off their premises (11.1.1); cooked dishes prepared by catering contractors whether collected by the customer or delivered to the customer's home (11.1.1); and products sold specifically as pet foods (09.3.4).

01.1.1 Bread and Cereals (ND)[1]

Rice in all forms
Maize, wheat, barley, oats, rye, and other cereals in the form of grain, flour, or meal
Bread and other bakery products (crispbread, rusks, toasted bread, biscuits, gingerbread, wafers, waffles, crumpets, muffins, croissants, cakes, tarts, pies, quiches, pizzas, and so on)
Mixes and dough for the preparation of bakery products
Pasta products in all forms; couscous
Cereal preparations (cornflakes, oatflakes, and so on), and other cereal products (malt, malt flour, malt extract, potato starch, tapioca, sago, and other starches)

Includes: farinaceous-based products prepared with meat, fish, seafood, cheese, vegetables, or fruit.

Excludes: meat pies (01.1.2); fish pies (01.1.3); and sweet corn (01.1.7).

01.1.2 Meat (ND)

Fresh, chilled, or frozen meat of:
- Bovine animals, swine, sheep, and goat
- Horse, mule, donkey, camel, and the like
- Poultry (chicken, duck, goose, turkey, and guinea fowl)
- Hare, rabbit, and game (antelope, deer, boar, pheasant, grouse, pigeon, quail, and so on)

Fresh, chilled, or frozen edible offal
Dried, salted, or smoked meat, and edible offal (sausages, salami, bacon, ham, pâté, and so on)
Other preserved or processed meat and meat-based preparations (canned meat, meat extracts, meat juices, meat pies, and so on)

Includes: meat and edible offal of marine mammals (seals, walruses, whales, and so on) and exotic animals (kangaroo, ostrich, alligator, and so on); animals and poultry purchased live for consumption as food.

Excludes: land and sea snails (01.1.3); lard and other edible animal fats (01.1.5); and soups, broths, and stocks containing meat (01.1.9).

01.1.3 Fish and Seafood (ND)

Fresh, chilled, or frozen fish
Fresh, chilled, or frozen seafood (crustaceans, molluscs and other shellfish, and sea snails)
Dried, smoked, or salted fish, and seafood
Other preserved or processed fish and seafood and fish and seafood-based preparations (canned fish and seafood, caviar, and other hard roes, fish pies, and so on)

Includes: land crabs, land snails, and frogs; fish and seafood purchased live for consumption as food.

Excludes: soups, broths, and stocks containing fish and seafood (01.1.9).

01.1.4 Milk, Cheese, and Eggs (ND)

Raw milk; pasteurized or sterilized milk
Condensed, evaporated, or powdered milk
Yogurt, cream, milk-based desserts, milk-based beverages, and other similar milk-based products
Cheese and curd
Eggs and egg products made wholly from eggs

Includes: milk, cream, and yogurt containing sugar, cocoa, fruit, or flavorings; dairy products not based on milk such as soya milk.

Excludes: butter and butter products (01.1.5).

01.1.5 Oils and Fats (ND)

Butter and butter products (butter oil, ghee, and so on)
Margarine (including "diet" margarine) and other vegetable fats (including peanut butter)

[1]Note: ND, SD, D, and S denote nondurable goods, semidurable goods, durable goods, and services, respectively.

Edible oils (olive oil, corn oil, sunflower seed oil, cottonseed oil, soybean oil, groundnut oil, walnut oil, and so on)
Edible animal fats (lard and so on)

Excludes: cod or halibut liver oil (06.1.1).

01.1.6 Fruit (ND)

Fresh, chilled, or frozen fruit
Dried fruit, fruit peel, fruit kernels, nuts, and edible seeds
Preserved fruit and fruit-based products

Includes: melons and watermelons.

Excludes: vegetables cultivated for their fruit such as aubergines, cucumbers, and tomatoes (01.1.7); jams, marmalades, compotes, jellies, fruit purées, and pastes (01.1.8); parts of plants preserved in sugar (01.1.8); and fruit juices and syrups (01.2.2).

01.1.7 Vegetables (ND)

Fresh, chilled, frozen, or dried vegetables cultivated for their leaves or stalks (asparagus, broccoli, cauliflower, endives, fennel, spinach, and so on), for their fruit (aubergines, cucumbers, courgettes, green peppers, pumpkins, tomatoes, and so on), and for their roots (beetroots, carrots, onions, parsnips, radishes, turnips, and so on)
Fresh or chilled potatoes and other tuber vegetables (manioc, arrowroot, cassava, sweet potatoes, and so on)
Preserved or processed vegetables and vegetable-based products
Products of tuber vegetables (flours, meals, flakes, purées, chips, and crisps) including frozen preparations such as chipped potatoes

Includes: olives; garlic; pulses; sweet corn; sea fennel and other edible seaweed; mushrooms and other edible fungi.

Excludes: potato starch, tapioca, sago, and other starches (01.1.1); soups, broths, and stocks containing vegetables (01.1.9); culinary herbs (parsley, rosemary, thyme, and so on) and spices (pepper, pimento, ginger, and so on) (01.1.9); and vegetable juices (01.2.2).

01.1.8 Sugar, Jam, Honey, Chocolate, and Confectionery (ND)

Cane or beet sugar, unrefined or refined, powdered, crystallized, or in lumps
Jams, marmalades, compotes, jellies, fruit purées, and pastes, natural, and artificial honey, maple syrup, molasses, and parts of plants preserved in sugar
Chocolate in bars or slabs, chewing gum, sweets, toffees, pastilles, and other confectionery products
Cocoa-based foods and cocoa-based dessert preparations
Edible ice, ice cream, and sorbet

Includes: artificial sugar substitutes.

Excludes: cocoa and chocolate-based powder (01.2.1).

01.1.9 Food Products N.E.C. (ND)

Salt, spices (pepper, pimento, ginger, and so on), culinary herbs (parsley, rosemary, thyme, and so on), sauces, condiments, seasonings (mustard, mayonnaise, ketchup, soy sauce, and so on), vinegar
Prepared baking powders, baker's yeast, dessert preparations, soups, broths, stocks, culinary ingredients, and so on
Homogenized baby food and dietary preparations irrespective of the composition

Excludes: milk-based desserts (01.1.4); soya milk (01.1.4); artificial sugar substitutes (01.1.8); and cocoa-based dessert preparations (01.1.8).

01.2 Nonalcoholic Beverages

The nonalcoholic beverages classified here are those purchased for consumption at home. The group excludes nonalcoholic beverages sold for immediate consumption away from the home by hotels, restaurants, cafés, bars, kiosks, street vendors, automatic vending machines, and so on (11.1.1).

01.2.1 Coffee, Tea, and Cocoa (ND)

Coffee, whether or not decaffeinated, roasted or ground, including instant coffee
Tea, maté, and other plant products for infusions
Cocoa, whether or not sweetened, and chocolate-based powder

Includes: cocoa-based beverage preparations; coffee and tea substitutes; and extracts and essences of coffee and tea.

Excludes: chocolate in bars or slabs (01.1.8); cocoa-based food; and cocoa-based dessert preparations (01.1.8).

01.2.2 Mineral Waters, Soft Drinks, and Fruit and Vegetable Juices (ND)

Mineral or spring waters; all drinking water sold in containers
Soft drinks such as sodas, lemonades, and colas
Fruit and vegetable juices
Syrups and concentrates for the preparation of beverages

Excludes: nonalcoholic beverages which are generally alcoholic such as nonalcoholic beer (02.1).

02 Alcoholic Beverages, Tobacco, and Narcotics

02.1 Alcoholic Beverages

The alcoholic beverages classified here are those purchased for consumption at home. The group excludes alcoholic beverages sold for immediate consumption away from the home by hotels, restaurants, cafés, bars, kiosks, street vendors, automatic vending machines, and so on (11.1.1).

The beverages classified here include low or nonalcoholic beverages which are generally alcoholic such as nonalcoholic beer.

02.1.1 Spirits (ND)

Eaux-de-vie, liqueurs, and other spirits

Includes: mead; aperitifs other than wine-based aperitifs (02.1.2).

02.1.2 Wine (ND)

Wine, cider, and perry, including sake
Wine-based aperitifs, fortified wines, champagne, and other sparkling wines

02.1.3 Beer (ND)

All kinds of beer such as ale, lager, and porter

Includes: low-alcoholic beer and nonalcoholic beer; shandy.

02.2 Tobacco

This group covers all purchases of tobacco by households, including purchases of tobacco in restaurants, cafés, bars, service stations, and so on.

02.2.0 Tobacco (ND)

Cigarettes; cigarette tobacco and cigarette papers
Cigars, pipe tobacco, chewing tobacco, or snuff

Excludes: other smokers' articles (12.3.2).

02.3 Narcotics

02.3.0 Narcotics (ND)

Marijuana, opium, cocaine, and their derivatives
Other vegetable-based narcotics such as cola nuts, betel leaves, and betel nuts
Other narcotics including chemicals and man-made drugs

03 Clothing and Footwear

03.1 Clothing

03.1.1 Clothing Materials (SD)

Clothing materials of natural fibers, of man-made fibers, and of their mixtures

Excludes: furnishing fabrics (05.2.0).

03.1.2 Garments (SD)

Garments for men, women, children (3–13 years) and infants (0–2 years), either ready-to-wear or made-to-measure, in all materials (including leather, furs, plastics, and rubber), for everyday wear, for sport or for work:
Capes, overcoats, raincoats, anoraks, parkas, blousons, jackets, trousers, waistcoats, suits, costumes, dresses, skirts, and so on
Shirts, blouses, pullovers, sweaters, cardigans, shorts, swimsuits, tracksuits, jogging suits, sweatshirts, T-shirts, leotards, and so on
Vests, underpants, socks, stockpiles, tights, petticoats, brassières, knickers, slips, girdles, corsets, body stockpiles, and so on
Pajamas, nightshirts, nightdresses, housecoats, dressing gowns, bathrobes, and so on
Baby clothes and babies' booties made of fabric.

Excludes: articles of medical hosiery such as elasticated stockpiles (06.1.2); babies' napkins (12.1.3).

03.1.3 Other Articles of Clothing and Clothing Accessories (SD)

Ties, handkerchiefs, scarves, squares, gloves, mittens, muffs, belts, braces, aprons, smocks, bibs, sleeve protectors, hats, caps, berets, bonnets, and so on
Sewing threads, knitting yarns, and accessories for making clothing such as buckles, buttons, press studs, zip fasteners, ribbons, laces, trimmings, and so on

Includes: gardening gloves and working gloves; crash helmets for motorcycles and bicycles.

Excludes: gloves and other articles made of rubber (05.6.1); pins, safety pins, sewing needles, knitting needles, thimbles (05.6.1); protective headgear for sports (09.3.2); other protective gear for sports such as life jackets, boxing gloves, body padding, belts, supports, and so on (09.3.2); paper handkerchiefs (12.1.3); watches, jewelry, cuff links, tiepins (12.3.1); walking sticks and canes, umbrellas and parasols, fans, and keyrings (12.3.2).

03.1.4 Cleaning, Repair, and Hire of Clothing (S)

Dry-cleaning, laundering, and dyeing of garments
Darning, mending, repair, and altering of garments
Hire of garments

Includes: total value of the repair service (that is, both the cost of labor and the cost of materials are covered).

Excludes: materials, threads, accessories, and so on purchased by households with the intention of undertaking the repairs themselves (03.1.1) or (03.1.3); repair of household linen and other household textiles (05.2.0); dry-cleaning, laundering, dyeing, and hiring of household linen, and other household textiles (05.6.2).

03.2 Footwear

03.2.1 Shoes and Other Footwear (SD)

All footwear for men, women, children (3–13 years), and infants (0–2 years) including sports footwear suitable for everyday or leisure wear (shoes for jogging, cross-training, tennis, basketball, boating, and so on)

Includes: gaiters, leggings, and similar articles; shoelaces; parts of footwear, such as heels, soles, and so on, purchased by households with the intention of repairing footwear themselves.

Excludes: babies' booties made of fabric (03.1.2); shoe trees, shoehorns and polishes, creams, and other shoe-cleaning articles (05.6.1); orthopedic footwear (06.1.3); game-specific footwear (ski boots, football boots, golfing shoes, and other such footwear fitted with ice skates, rollers, spikes, studs, and so on) (09.3.2); and shin guards, cricket pads, and other such protective apparel for sport (09.3.2).

03.2.2 Repair and Hire of Footwear (S)

Repair of footwear; shoe-cleaning services
Hire of footwear

Includes: total value of the repair service (that is, both the cost of labor and the cost of materials are covered).

Excludes: parts of footwear, such as heels, soles, and so on, purchased by households with the intention of undertaking the repair themselves (03.2.1); polishes, creams, and other shoe-cleaning articles (05.6.1); and repair (09.3.2) or hire (09.4.1) of game-specific footwear (ski boots, football boots, golfing shoes, and other such footwear fitted with ice skates, rollers, spikes, studs, and so on).

04 Housing, Water, Electricity, Gas, and Other Fuels

04.1 Actual Rentals for Housing

Rentals normally include payment for the use of the land on which the property stands, the dwelling occupied, the fixtures and fittings for heating, plumbing, lighting, and so on, and, in the case of a dwelling let furnished, the furniture.

Rentals also include payment for the use of a garage to provide parking in connection with the dwelling. The garage does not have to be physically contiguous to the dwelling, nor does it have to be leased from the same landlord.

Rentals do not include payment for the use of garages or parking spaces not providing parking in connection with the dwelling (07.2.4). Nor do they include charges for water supply (04.4.1); refuse collection (04.4.2) and sewage collection (04.4.3); coproprietor charges for caretaking, gardening, stairwell cleaning, heating and lighting, maintenance of lifts and refuse disposal chutes, and so on in multi-occupied buildings (04.4.4); charges for electricity (04.5.1) and gas (04.5.2); and charges for heating and hot water supplied by district heating plants (04.5.5).

04.1.1 Actual Rentals Paid by Tenants (S)

Rentals actually paid by tenants or subtenants occupying unfurnished or furnished premises as their main residence

Includes: payments by households occupying a room in a hotel or boarding house as their main residence.

Excludes: accommodation services of educational establishments and hostels (11.2.0) and of retirement homes for elderly persons (12.4.0).

04.1.2 Other Actual Rentals (S)

Rentals actually paid for secondary residences

Excludes: accommodation services of holiday villages and holiday centers (11.2.0).

04.2 Imputed Rentals for Housing

For coverage see note to (04.1).

04.2.1 Imputed Rentals of Owner-Occupiers (S)

Imputed rentals of owners occupying their main residence

04.2.2 Other Imputed Rentals (S)

Imputed rentals for secondary residences

Imputed rentals of households paying a reduced rental or housed free

04.3 Maintenance and Repair of the Dwelling

Maintenance and repair of dwellings are distinguished by two features: first, they are activities that have to be undertaken regularly in order to maintain the dwelling in good working order; second, they do not change the dwelling's performance, capacity or expected service life.

There are two types of maintenance and repair of dwellings: those which are minor, such as interior decoration and repairs to fittings, and which are commonly carried out by both tenants and owners; and those which are major, such as replastering walls or repairing roofs, and which are carried out by owners only.

Only expenditures which tenants and owner-occupiers incur on materials and services for minor maintenance and repair are part of individual consumption expenditure of households. Expenditures which owner-occupiers incur on materials and services for major maintenance and repair are not part of individual consumption expenditure of households.

Purchases of materials made by tenants or owner-occupiers with the intention of undertaking the maintenance or repair themselves should be shown under (04.3.1). If tenants or owner-occupiers pay an enterprise to carry out the maintenance or repair, the total value of the service, including the costs of the materials used, should be shown under (04.3.2).

04.3.1 Materials for the Maintenance and Repair of the Dwelling (ND)

Products and materials, such as paints and varnishes, renderings, wallpapers, fabric wall coverings, window panes, plaster, cement, putty, wallpaper pastes, and so on, purchased for minor maintenance and repair of the dwelling

Includes: small plumbing items (pipes, taps, joints, and so on), surfacing materials (floorboards, ceramic tiles, and so on), and brushes and scrapers for paint, varnish, and wallpaper.

Excludes: fitted carpets and linoleum (05.1.2); hand tools, door fittings, power sockets, wiring flex, and lamp bulbs (05.5.2); brooms, scrubbing brushes, dusting brushes, and cleaning products (05.6.1); products, materials, and fixtures used for major maintenance and repair (intermediate consumption) or for extension and conversion of the dwelling (capital formation).

04.3.2 Services for the Maintenance and Repair of the Dwelling (S)

Services of plumbers, electricians, carpenters, glaziers, painters, decorators, floor polishers, and so on engaged for minor maintenance and repair of the dwelling

Includes: total value of the service (that is, both the cost of labor and the cost of materials are covered).

Excludes: separate purchases of materials made by households with the intention of undertaking the maintenance or repair themselves (04.3.1); services engaged for major maintenance and repair (intermediate consumption) or for extension and conversion of the dwelling (capital formation).

04.4 Water Supply and Miscellaneous Services Relating to the Dwelling

04.4.1 Water Supply (ND)

Water supply

Includes: associated expenditure such as hire of meters, reading of meters, standing charges, and so on.

Excludes: drinking water sold in bottles or containers (01.2.2); hot water or steam purchased from district heating plants (04.5.5).

04.4.2 Refuse Collection (S)

Refuse collection and disposal

04.4.3 Sewage Collection (S)

Sewage collection and disposal

04.4.4 Other Services Relating to the Dwelling N.E.C. (S)

Coproprietor charges for caretaking, gardening, stairwell cleaning, heating and lighting, maintenance of lifts and refuse disposal chutes, and so on in multi-occupied buildings
Security services
Snow removal and chimney sweeping

Excludes: household services such as window cleaning, disinfecting, fumigation, and pest extermination (05.6.2); bodyguards (12.7.0).

04.5 Electricity, Gas, and Other Fuels

04.5.1 Electricity (ND)

Electricity

Includes: associated expenditure such as hire of meters, reading of meters, standing charges, and so on.

04.5.2 Gas (ND)

Town gas and natural gas
Liquefied hydrocarbons (butane, propane, and so on)

Includes: associated expenditure such as hire of meters, reading of meters, storage containers, standing charges, and so on.

04.5.3 Liquid Fuels (ND)

Domestic heating and lighting oils

04.5.4 Solid Fuels (ND)

Coal, coke, briquettes, firewood, charcoal, peat, and the like

04.5.5 Heat Energy (ND)

Hot water and steam purchased from district heating plants

Includes: associated expenditure such as hire of meters, reading of meters, standing charges, and so on; ice used for cooling and refrigeration purposes.

05 Furnishings, Household Equipment, and Routine Household Maintenance

05.1 Furniture and Furnishings, Carpets, and Other Floor Coverings

05.1.1 Furniture and Furnishings (D)

Beds, sofas, couches, tables, chairs, cupboards, chests of drawers, and bookshelves
Lighting equipment such as ceiling lights, standard lamps, globe lights, and bedside lamps
Pictures, sculptures, engravings, tapestries, and other art objects including reproductions of works of art and other ornaments
Screens, folding partitions, and other furniture and fixtures

Includes: delivery and installation when applicable; base mattresses, mattresses, tatamis; bathroom cabinets; baby furniture such as cradles, high chairs, and playpens; blinds; camping and garden furniture; and mirrors, candleholders, and candlesticks.

Excludes: bedding and sunshades (05.2.0); safes (05.3.1); ornamental glass and ceramic articles (05.4.0); clocks (12.3.1); wall thermometers and barometers (12.3.2); carry-cots and pushchairs (12.3.2); and works of art and antique furniture acquired primarily as stores of value (capital formation).

05.1.2 Carpets and Other Floor Coverings (D)

Loose carpets, fitted carpets, linoleum, and other such floor coverings

Includes: laying of floor coverings

Excludes: bathroom mats, rush mats, and doormats (05.2.0); antique floor coverings acquired primarily as stores of value (capital formation).

05.1.3 Repair of Furniture, Furnishings, and Floor Coverings (S)

Repair of furniture, furnishings, and floor coverings

Includes: total value of the service (that is, both the cost of labor and the cost of materials are covered); restoration of works of art, antique furniture, and antique floor coverings other than those acquired primarily as stores of value (capital formation).

Excludes: separate purchases of materials made by households with the intention of undertaking the repair themselves (05.1.1) or (05.1.2); dry-cleaning of carpets (05.6.2).

05.2 Household Textiles

05.2.0 Household Textiles (SD)

Furnishing fabrics, curtain material, curtains, double curtains, awnings, door curtains, and fabric blinds
Bedding such as futons, pillows, bolsters, and hammocks
Bed linen such as sheets, pillowcases, blankets, traveling rugs, plaids, eiderdowns, counterpanes, and mosquito nets
Table linen and bathroom linen such as tablecloths, table napkins, towels, and face cloths
Other household textiles such as shopping bags, laundry bags, shoe bags, covers for clothes and furniture, flags, sunshades, and so on
Repair of such articles

Includes: cloth bought by the piece; oilcloth; bathroom mats, rush mats, and doormats.

Excludes: fabric wall coverings (04.3.1); tapestries (05.1.1); floor coverings such as carpets and fitted carpets (05.1.2); electric blankets (05.3.2); covers for motor cars, motorcycles, and so on (07.2.1); and air mattresses and sleeping bags (09.3.2).

05.3 Household Appliances

05.3.1 Major Household Appliances Whether Electric or Not (D)

Refrigerators, freezers, and fridge freezers
Washing machines, dryers, drying cabinets, dishwashers, ironing, and pressing machines

Cookers, spit roasters, hobs, ranges, ovens, and microwave ovens
Air-conditioners, humidifiers, space heaters, water heaters, ventilators, and extractor hoods
Vacuum cleaners, steam-cleaning machines, carpet shampooing machines, and machines for scrubbing, waxing, and polishing floors
Other major household appliances such as safes, sewing machines, knitting machines, water softeners, and so on

Includes: delivery and installation of the appliances when applicable.

Excludes: such appliances that are built into the structure of the building (capital formation).

05.3.2 Small Electric Household Appliances (SD)

Coffee mills, coffee makers, juice extractors, can openers, food mixers, deep fryers, meat grills, knives, toasters, ice cream makers, sorbet makers, yogurt makers, hotplates, irons, kettles, fans, electric blankets, and so on

Excludes: small nonelectric household articles and kitchen utensils (05.4.0); household scales (05.4.0); personal weighing machines and baby scales (12.1.3).

05.3.3 Repair of Household Appliances (S)

Repair of household appliances

Includes: total value of the service (that is, both the cost of labor and the cost of materials are covered); charges for the leasing or rental of major household appliances.

Excludes: separate purchases of materials made by households with the intention of undertaking the repair themselves (05.3.1) or (05.3.2).

05.4 Glassware, Tableware, and Household Utensils

05.4.0 Glassware, Tableware, and Household Utensils (SD)

Glassware, crystal ware, ceramic ware, and chinaware of the kind used for table, kitchen, bathroom, toilet, office, and indoor decoration
Cutlery, flatware, and silverware
Nonelectric kitchen utensils of all materials such as saucepans, stewpots, pressure cookers, frying pans, coffee mills, purée makers, mincers, hotplates, household scales, and other such mechanical devices
Nonelectric household articles of all materials such as containers for bread, coffee, spices, and so on, waste bins, waste-paper baskets, laundry baskets, portable money boxes and strongboxes, towel rails, bottle racks, irons and ironing boards, letter boxes, feeding bottles, thermos flasks, and iceboxes
Repair of such articles

Excludes: lighting equipment (05.1.1); electric household appliances (05.3.1) or (05.3.2); cardboard tableware (05.6.1); personal weighing machines and baby scales (12.1.3); ashtrays (12.3.2).

05.5 Tools and Equipment for House and Garden

05.5.1 Major Tools and Equipment (D)

Motorized tools and equipment such as electric drills, saws, sanders and hedge cutters, garden tractors, lawnmowers, cultivators, chainsaws, and water pumps
Repair of such articles

Includes: charges for the leasing or rental of do-it-yourself machinery and equipment.

05.5.2 Small Tools and Miscellaneous Accessories (SD)

Hand tools such as saws, hammers, screwdrivers, wrenches, spanners, pliers, trimming knives, rasps, and files
Garden tools such as wheelbarrows, watering cans, hoses, spades, shovels, rakes, forks, scythes, sickles, and secateurs
Ladders and steps
Door fittings (hinges, handles, and locks), fittings for radiators and fireplaces, and other metal articles for the house (curtain rails, carpet rods, hooks, and so on) or for the garden (chains, grids, stakes, and hoop segments for fencing and bordering)
Small electric accessories such as power sockets, switches, wiring flex, electric bulbs, fluorescent lighting tubes, torches, flashlights, hand lamps, electric batteries for general use, bells, and alarms
Repair of such articles

05.6 Goods and Services for Routine Household Maintenance

05.6.1 Nondurable Household Goods (ND)

Cleaning and maintenance products such as soaps, washing powders, washing liquids, scouring powders, detergents, disinfectant bleaches, softeners, conditioners, window-cleaning products, waxes, polishes, dyes, unblocking agents, disinfectants, insecticides, pesticides, fungicides, and distilled water
Articles for cleaning such as brooms, scrubbing brushes, dustpans and dust brushes, dusters, tea towels, floorcloths, household sponges, scourers, steel wool, and chamois leathers
Paper products such as filters, tablecloths and table napkins, kitchen paper, vacuum cleaner bags, and cardboard tableware, including aluminum foil and plastic bin liners
Other nondurable household articles such as matches, candles, lamp wicks, methylated spirits, clothes-pegs, clothes hangers, pins, safety pins, sewing needles, knitting needles, thimbles, nails, screws, nuts and bolts, tacks, washers, glues and adhesive tapes for household use, string, twine, and rubber gloves

Includes: polishes, creams, and other shoe-cleaning articles; fire extinguishers for households.

Excludes: brushes and scrapers for paint, varnish, and wallpaper (04.3.1); fire extinguishers for transport equipment (07.2.1); products specifically for the cleaning and maintenance of transport equipment such as paints, chrome cleaners, sealing compounds, and bodywork polishes (07.2.1); horticultural products for the upkeep of ornamental gardens (09.3.3); paper handkerchiefs, toilet paper, toilet soaps, toilet sponges, and other products for personal hygiene (12.1.3); cigarette, cigar, and pipe lighters, and lighter fuel (12.3.2).

05.6.2 Domestic Services and Household Services (S)

Domestic services supplied by paid staff employed in private services such as butlers, cooks, maids, drivers, gardeners, governesses, secretaries, tutors, and au pairs
Similar services, including babysitting and housework, supplied by enterprises or self-employed persons
Household services such as window cleaning, disinfecting, fumigation, and pest extermination
Dry-cleaning, laundering, and dyeing of household linen, household textiles, and carpets
Hire of furniture, furnishings, carpets, household equipment, and household linen

Excludes: dry-cleaning, laundering, and dyeing of garments (03.1.4); refuse collection (04.4.2); sewerage collection (04.4.3); coproprietor charges for caretaking, gardening, stairwell cleaning, heating and lighting, maintenance of lifts and refuse disposal chutes, and so on in multi-occupied buildings (04.4.4); security services (04.4.4); snow removal and chimney sweeping (04.4.4); removal and storage services (07.3.6); services of wet-nurses, crèches, day care centers, and other child-minding facilities (12.4.0); and bodyguards (12.7.0).

06 Health

This division also includes health services purchased from school and university health centers.

06.1 Medical Products, Appliances, and Equipment

This group covers medicaments, prostheses, medical appliances and equipment, and other health-related products purchased by individuals or households, either with or without a prescription, usually from dispensing chemists, pharmacists, or medical equipment suppliers. They are intended for consumption or use outside a health facility or institution. Such products supplied directly to outpatients by medical, dental, and paramedical practitioners or to inpatients by hospitals and the like are included in outpatient services (06.2) or hospital services (06.3).

06.1.1 Pharmaceutical Products (ND)

Medicinal preparations, medicinal drugs, patent medicines, serums and vaccines, vitamins and minerals, cod liver oil and halibut liver oil, and oral contraceptives

Excludes: veterinary products (09.3.4); articles for personal hygiene such as medicinal soaps (12.1.3).

06.1.2 Other Medical Products (ND)

Clinical thermometers, adhesive and nonadhesive bandages, hypodermic syringes, first aid kits, hot-water bottles and ice bags, medical hosiery items such as elasticated stockpiles and knee supports, pregnancy tests, condoms, and other mechanical contraceptive devices

06.1.3 Therapeutic Appliances and Equipment (D)

Corrective eyeglasses and contact lenses, hearing aids, glass eyes, artificial limbs and other prosthetic devices, orthopedic braces and supports, orthopedic footwear, surgical belts, trusses and supports, neck braces, medical massage equipment and health lamps, powered and unpowered wheelchairs and invalid carriages, "special" beds, crutches, electronic and other devices for monitoring blood pressure, and so on
Repair of such articles

Includes: dentures but not fitting costs.

Excludes: hire of therapeutic equipment (06.2.3); protective goggles, belts, and supports for sport (09.3.2); and sunglasses not fitted with corrective lenses (12.3.2).

06.2 Outpatient Services

This group covers medical, dental, and paramedical services delivered to outpatients by medical, dental, and paramedical practitioners and auxiliaries. The services may be delivered at home, in individual or group consulting facilities, dispensaries or the outpatient clinics of hospitals, and the like.

Outpatient services include the medicaments, prostheses, medical appliances and equipment, and other health-related products supplied directly to outpatients by medical, dental, and paramedical practitioners and auxiliaries.

Medical, dental, and paramedical services provided to inpatients by hospitals and the like are included in hospital services (06.3).

06.2.1 Medical Services (S)

Consultations of physicians in general or specialist practice

Includes: services of orthodontic specialists.

Excludes: services of medical analysis laboratories and X-ray centers (06.2.3); services of practitioners of traditional medicine (06.2.3).

06.2.2 Dental Services (S)

Services of dentists, oral hygienists, and other dental auxiliaries

Includes: fitting costs of dentures.

Excludes: dentures (06.1.3); services of orthodontic specialists (06.2.1); and services of medical analysis laboratories and X-ray centers (06.2.3).

06.2.3 Paramedical Services (S)

Services of medical analysis laboratories and X-ray centers
Services of freelance nurses and midwives
Services of freelance acupuncturists, chiropractors, optometrists, physiotherapists, speech therapists, and so on
Medically prescribed corrective-gymnastic therapy
Outpatient thermal bath or seawater treatments
Ambulance services
Hire of therapeutic equipment

Includes: services of practitioners of traditional medicine.

06.3 Hospital Services

Hospitalization is defined as occurring when a patient is accommodated in a hospital for the duration of the treatment. Hospital day care and home-based hospital treatment are included as are hospices for terminally ill persons.

This group covers the services of general and specialist hospitals, the services of medical centers, maternity centers, nursing homes, and convalescent homes which chiefly provide inpatient health care, the services of institutions serving old people in which medical monitoring is an essential component and the services of rehabilitation centers providing inpatient health care and rehabilitative therapy where the objective is to treat the patient rather than to provide long-term support.

Hospitals are defined as institutions which offer inpatient care under the direct supervision of qualified medical doctors. Medical centers, maternity centers, nursing homes, and convalescent homes also provide inpatient care but their services are supervised and frequently delivered by staff of lower qualification than medical doctors.

This group does not cover the services of facilities, such as surgeries, clinics, and dispensaries, devoted exclusively to outpatient care (06.2). Nor does it include the services of retirement homes for elderly persons, institutions for disabled persons, and rehabilitation centers providing primarily long-term support (12.4).

06.3.0 Hospital Services (S)

Hospital services comprise the provision of the following services to hospital inpatients:

- Basic services: administration; accommodation; food and drink; supervision and care by nonspecialist staff (nursing auxiliaries); first aid and resuscitation; ambulance transport; provision of medicines and other pharmaceutical products; and provision of therapeutic appliances and equipment
- Medical services: services of physicians in general or specialist practice, of surgeons, and of dentists; medical analyses and X-rays; and paramedical services such as those of nurses, midwives, chiropractors, optometrists, physiotherapists, speech therapists, and so on.

07 Transport

07.1 Purchase of Vehicles

Purchases of recreational vehicles such as camper vans, caravans, trailers, airplanes, and boats are covered by (09.2.1).

07.1.1 Motor Cars (D)

Motor cars, passenger vans, station wagons, estate cars, and the like with either two-wheel drive or four-wheel drive

Excludes: invalid carriages (06.1.3); camper vans (09.2.1); and golf carts (09.2.1).

07.1.2 Motor Cycles (D)

Motorcycles of all types, scooters, and powered bicycles

Includes: sidecars; snowmobiles.

Excludes: invalid carriages (06.1.3); golf carts (09.2.1).

07.1.3 Bicycles (D)

Bicycles and tricycles of all types

Includes: rickshaws.

Excludes: toy bicycles and tricycles (09.3.1).

07.1.4 Animal-Drawn Vehicles (D)

Animal-drawn vehicles

Includes: animals required to draw the vehicles and related equipment (yokes, collars, harnesses, bridles, reins, and so on).

Excludes: horses and ponies, horse- or pony-drawn vehicles, and related equipment purchased for recreational purposes (09.2.1).

07.2 Operation of Personal Transport Equipment

Purchases of spare parts, accessories, or lubricants made by households with the intention of undertaking the maintenance, repair, or intervention themselves should be shown under (07.2.1) or (07.2.2). If households pay an enterprise to carry out the maintenance, repair, or fitting, the total value of the service, including the costs of the materials used, should be shown under (07.2.3).

07.2.1 Spare Parts and Accessories for Personal Transport Equipment (SD)

Tires (new, used, or retreaded), inner tubes, spark plugs, batteries, shock absorbers, filters, pumps, and other spare parts or accessories for personal transport equipment

Includes: fire extinguishers for transport equipment; products specifically for the cleaning and maintenance of transport equipment such as paints, chrome cleaners, sealing compounds, and bodywork polishes; and covers for motor cars, motorcycles, and so on.

Excludes: crash helmets for motorcycles and bicycles (03.1.3); nonspecific products for cleaning and maintenance such as distilled water, household sponges, chamois leathers, detergents, and so on (05.6.1); charges for the fitting of spare parts and accessories and for the painting, washing, and polishing of bodywork (07.2.3); radiotelephones (08.2.0); car radios (09.1.1); and baby seats for cars (12.3.2).

07.2.2 Fuels and Lubricants for Personal Transport Equipment (ND)

Petrol and other fuels such as diesel, liquid petroleum gas, alcohol, and two-stroke mixtures

Lubricants, brake and transmission fluids, coolants, and additives

Includes: fuel for major tools and equipment covered under (05.5.1) and recreational vehicles covered under (09.2.1).

Excludes: charges for oil changes and greasing (07.2.3).

07.2.3 Maintenance and Repair of Personal Transport Equipment (S)

Services purchased for the maintenance and repair of personal transport equipment such as fitting of parts and accessories, wheel balancing, technical inspection, breakdown services, oil changes, greasing, and washing

Includes: total value of the service (that is both the cost of labor and the cost of materials are covered).

Excludes: separate purchases of spare parts, accessories, or lubricants made by households with the intention of undertaking the maintenance or repair themselves (07.2.1) or (07.2.2); roadworthiness tests (07.2.4).

07.2.4 Other Services in Respect of Personal Transport Equipment (S)

Hire of garages or parking spaces not providing parking in connection with the dwelling
Toll facilities (bridges, tunnels, shuttle ferries, motorways) and parking meters
Driving lessons, driving tests, and driving licenses
Roadworthiness tests
Hire of personal transport equipment without drivers

Excludes: hire of a car with driver (07.3.2); service charges for insurance in respect of personal transport equipment (12.5.4).

07.3 Transport Services

Purchases of transport services are generally classified by mode of transport. When a ticket covers two or more modes of transport—for example, intraurban bus and underground or interurban train and ferry—and the expenditure cannot be apportioned between them, then such purchases should be classified in 07.3.5.

Costs of meals, snacks, drinks, refreshments, or accommodation services have to be included if covered by the fare and not separately priced. If separately priced, these costs have to be classified in Division 11.

School transport services are included, but ambulance services are excluded (06.2.3).

07.3.1 Passenger Transport by Railway (S)

Transport of individuals and groups of persons and luggage by train, tram, and underground

Includes: transport of private vehicles.
Excludes: funicular transport (07.3.6).

07.3.2 Passenger Transport by Road (S)

Transport of individuals and groups of persons and luggage by bus, coach, taxi, and hired car with driver

07.3.3 Passenger Transport by Air (S)

Transport of individuals and groups of persons and luggage by airplane and helicopter

07.3.4 Passenger Transport by Sea and Inland Waterway (S)

Transport of individuals and groups of persons and luggage by ship, boat, ferry, hovercraft, and hydrofoil

Includes: transport of private vehicles.

07.3.5 Combined Passenger Transport (S)

Transport of individuals and groups of persons and luggage by two or more modes of transport when the expenditure cannot be apportioned between them

Includes: transport of private vehicles.
Excludes: package holidays (09.6.0).

07.3.6 Other Purchased Transport Services (S)

Funicular, cable car, and chairlift transport
Removal and storage services
Services of porters and left-luggage and luggage-forwarding offices
Travel agents' commissions, if separately priced

Excludes: cable car and chairlift transport at ski resorts and holiday centers (09.4.1).

08 Communication

08.1 Postal Services

08.1.0 Postal Services (S)

Payments for the delivery of letters, postcards, and parcels
Private mail and parcel delivery

Includes: all purchases of new postage stamps, prefranked postcards, and aerograms.
Excludes: purchase of used or canceled postage stamps (09.3.1); financial services of post offices (12.6.2).

08.2 Telephone and Telefax Equipment

08.2.0 Telephone and Telefax Equipment (D)

Purchases of telephones, radiotelephones, telefax machines, telephone-answering machines, and telephone loudspeakers
Repair of such equipment

Excludes: telefax and telephone-answering facilities provided by personal computers (09.1.3).

08.3 Telephone and Telefax Services

08.3.0 Telephone and Telefax Services (S)

Installation and subscription costs of personal telephone equipment
Telephone calls from a private line or from a public line (public telephone box, post office cabin, and so on); telephone calls from hotels, cafés, restaurants, and the like
Telegraphy, telex, and telefax services
Information transmission services; internet connection services
Hire of telephones, telefax machines, telephone-answering machines, and telephone loudspeakers

Includes: radiotelephony, radiotelegraphy, and radiotelex services.

09 Recreation and Culture

09.1 Audiovisual, Photographic, and Information Processing Equipment

09.1.1 Equipment for the Reception, Recording, and Reproduction of Sound and Pictures (D)

Television sets, video cassette players and recorders, and television aerials of all types
Radio sets, car radios, radio clocks, two-way radios, amateur radio receivers, and transmitters
Gramophones, tape players and recorders, cassette players and recorders, CD players, personal stereos, stereo systems and their constituent units (turntables, tuners,

amplifiers, speakers, and so on), microphones, and earphones

Excludes: video cameras, camcorders, and sound-recording cameras (09.1.2).

09.1.2 Photographic and Cinematographic Equipment and Optical Instruments (D)

Still cameras, movie cameras and sound-recording cameras, video cameras and camcorders, film and slide projectors, enlargers and film processing equipment, and accessories (screens, viewers, lenses, flash attachments, filters, exposure meters, and so on)
Binoculars, microscopes, telescopes, and compasses

09.1.3 Information Processing Equipment (D)

Personal computers, visual display units, printers, and miscellaneous accessories accompanying them; computer software packages such as operating systems, applications, languages, and so on
Calculators, including pocket calculators
Typewriters and word processors

Includes: telefax and telephone-answering facilities provided by personal computers.

Excludes: prerecorded diskettes and CD-ROMs containing books, dictionaries, encyclopedias, foreign language trainers, multimedia presentations, and so on in the form of software (09.1.4); video game software (09.3.1); video game computers that plug into a television set (09.3.1); typewriter ribbons (09.5.4); toner and ink cartridges (09.5.4); and slide rules (09.5.4).

09.1.4 Recording Media (SD)

Records and compact discs
Prerecorded tapes, cassettes, video cassettes, diskettes and CD-ROMs for tape recorders, cassette recorders, video recorders, and personal computers
Unrecorded tapes, cassettes, video cassettes, diskettes and CD-ROMs for tape recorders, cassette recorders, video recorders, and personal computers
Unexposed films, cartridges, and disks for photographic and cinematographic use

Includes: prerecorded tapes and compact discs of novels, plays, poetry, and so on; prerecorded diskettes and CD-ROMs containing books, dictionaries, encyclopedias, foreign language trainers, multimedia presentations, and so on in the form of software; photographic supplies such as paper and flashbulbs; and unexposed film the price of which includes the cost of processing without separately identifying it.

Excludes: batteries (05.5.2); computer software packages such as operating systems, applications, languages, and so on (09.1.3); video game software, video game cassettes, and video game CD-ROMs (09.3.1); and development of films and printing of photographs (09.4.2).

09.1.5 Repair of Audiovisual, Photographic, and Information Processing Equipment (S)

Repair of audiovisual, photographic, and information processing equipment

Includes: total value of the service (that is, both the cost of labor and the cost of materials are covered).

Excludes: separate purchases of materials made by households with the intention of undertaking the repair themselves (09.1.1), (09.1.2), or (09.1.3).

09.2 Other Major Durables for Recreation and Culture

09.2.1 Major Durables for Outdoor Recreation (D)

Camper vans, caravans, and trailers
Airplanes, microlight aircraft, gliders, hang gliders, and hot-air balloons
Boats, outboard motors, sails, rigging, and superstructures
Horses and ponies, horse- or pony-drawn vehicles, and related equipment (harnesses, bridles, reins, saddles, and so on)
Major items for games and sport such as canoes, kayaks, windsurfing boards, sea-diving equipment, and golf carts

Includes: fitting out of boats, camper vans, caravans, and so on.

Excludes: horses and ponies, horse- or pony-drawn vehicles, and related equipment purchased for personal transport (07.1.4); inflatable boats, rafts, and swimming pools for children and the beach (09.3.2).

09.2.2 Musical Instruments and Major Durables for Indoor Recreation (D)

Musical instruments of all sizes, including electronic musical instruments, such as pianos, organs, violins, guitars, drums, trumpets, clarinets, flutes, recorders, harmonicas, and so on
Billiard tables, ping-pong tables, pinball machines, gaming machines, and so on

Excludes: toys (09.3.1).

09.2.3 Maintenance and Repair of Other Major Durables for Recreation and Culture (S)

Maintenance and repair of other major durables for recreation and culture

Includes: total value of the service (that is, both the cost of labor and the cost of materials are covered); laying up for winter of boats, camper vans, caravans, and so on; hangar services for private planes; marina services for boats; and veterinary and other services (stabling, feeding, farriery, and so on) for horses and ponies purchased for recreational purposes.

Excludes: fuel for recreational vehicles (07.2.2); separate purchases of materials made by households with the intention of undertaking the maintenance or repair themselves (09.2.1) or (09.2.2); and veterinary and other services for pets (09.3.5).

09.3 Other Recreational Items and Equipment, Gardens, and Pets

09.3.1 Games, Toys, and Hobbies (SD)

Card games, parlor games, chess sets, and the like
Toys of all kinds including dolls, soft toys, toy cars and trains, toy bicycles and tricycles, toy construction sets, puzzles, plasticine, electronic games, masks, disguises,

jokes, novelties, fireworks and rockets, festoons, and Christmas tree decorations

Stamp-collecting requisites (used or canceled postage stamps, stamp albums, and so on), other items for collections (coins, medals, minerals, zoological and botanical specimens, and so on), and other tools and articles n.e.c. for hobbies

Includes: video game software; video game computers that plug into a television set; video game cassettes, and video game CD-ROMs.

Excludes: collectors' items falling into the category of works of art or antiques (05.1.1); unused postage stamps (08.1.0); Christmas trees (09.3.3); and children's scrapbooks (09.5.1).

09.3.2 Equipment for Sport, Camping, and Open-Air Recreation (SD)

Gymnastic, physical education, and sport equipment such as balls, shuttlecocks, nets, rackets, bats, skis, golf clubs, foils, sabers, poles, weights, discuses, javelins, dumbbells, chest expanders, and other body-building equipment

Parachutes and other skydiving equipment

Firearms and ammunition for hunting, sport, and personal protection

Fishing rods and other equipment for fishing

Equipment for beach and open-air games, such as bowls, croquet, frisbee, volleyball, and inflatable boats, rafts, and swimming pools

Camping equipment such as tents and accessories, sleeping bags, backpacks, air mattresses and inflating pumps, camping stoves, and barbecues

Repair of such articles

Includes: game-specific footwear (ski boots, football boots, golfing shoes, and other such footwear fitted with ice-skates, rollers, spikes, studs, and so on); protective headgear for sports; other protective gear for sports such as life jackets, boxing gloves, body padding, shin guards, goggles, belts, supports, and so on.

Excludes: crash helmets for motorcycles and bicycles (03.1.3); camping and garden furniture (05.1.1).

09.3.3 Gardens, Plants, and Flowers (ND)

Natural or artificial flowers and foliage, plants, shrubs, bulbs, tubers, seeds, fertilizers, composts, garden peat, turf for lawns, specially treated soils for ornamental gardens, horticultural preparations, pots, and pot holders

Includes: natural and artificial Christmas trees; delivery charges for flowers and plants.

Excludes: gardening gloves (03.1.3); gardening services (04.4.4) or (05.6.2); gardening equipment (05.5.1); gardening tools (05.5.2); and insecticides and pesticides for household use (05.6.1).

09.3.4 Pets and Related Products (ND)

Pets, pet foods, veterinary and grooming products for pets, collars, leashes, kennels, birdcages, fish tanks, cat litter, and so on

Excludes: horses and ponies (07.1.4) or (09.2.1); veterinary services (09.3.5).

09.3.5 Veterinary and Other Services for Pets (S)

Veterinary and other services for pets such as grooming, boarding, tattooing, and training

Excludes: veterinary and other services (stabling, farriery, and so on) for horses and ponies purchased for recreational purposes (09.2.3).

09.4 Recreational and Cultural Services

09.4.1 Recreational and Sporting Services (S)

Services provided by:

Sports stadiums, horse-racing courses, motor-racing circuits, velodromes, and so on

Skating rinks, swimming pools, golf courses, gymnasia, fitness centers, tennis courts, squash courts, and bowling alleys

Fairgrounds and amusement parks

Roundabouts, seesaws, and other playground facilities for children

Pinball machines and other games for adults other than games of chance

Ski slopes, ski lifts, and the like

Hire of equipment and accessories for sport and recreation, such as airplanes, boats, horses, skiing, and camping equipment

Out-of-school individual or group lessons in bridge, chess, aerobics, dancing, music, skating, skiing, swimming, or other pastimes

Services of mountain guides, tour guides, and so on

Navigational aid services for boating

Includes: hire of game-specific footwear (ski boots, football boots, golfing shoes, and other such footwear fitted with ice skates, rollers, spikes, studs, and so on).

Excludes: cable car and chairlift transport not at ski resorts or holiday centers (07.3.6).

09.4.2 Cultural Services (S)

Services provided by:

Cinemas, theatres, opera houses, concert halls, music halls, circuses, and sound and light shows

Museums, libraries, art galleries, and exhibitions

Historic monuments, national parks, zoological and botanical gardens, and aquaria

Hire of equipment and accessories for culture, such as television sets, video cassettes, and so on

Television and radio broadcasting, in particular license fees for television equipment and subscriptions to television networks

Services of photographers such as film developing, print processing, enlarging, portrait photography, wedding photography, and so on

Includes: services of musicians, clowns, performers for private entertainments.

09.4.3 Games of Chance (S)

Service charges for lotteries, bookmakers, totalizators, casinos, and other gambling establishments, gaming machines, bingo halls, scratch cards, sweepstakes, and so on (service charge is defined as the difference between the amounts paid for lottery tickets or placed in bets and the amounts paid out to winners)

09.5 Newspapers, Books, and Stationery

09.5.1 Books (SD)

Books, including atlases, dictionaries, encyclopedias, textbooks, guidebooks, and musical scores

Includes: scrapbooks and albums for children; bookbinding.

Excludes: prerecorded tapes and compact discs of novels, plays, poetry, and so on (09.1.4); prerecorded diskettes and CD-ROMs containing books, dictionaries, encyclopedias, foreign language trainers, and so on in the form of software (09.1.4); and stamp albums (09.3.1).

09.5.2 Newspapers and Periodicals (ND)

Newspapers, magazines, and other periodicals

09.5.3 Miscellaneous Printed Matter (ND)

Catalogs and advertising material
Posters, plain or picture postcards, calendars
Greeting cards and visiting cards, announcement, and message cards
Maps and globes

Excludes: prefranked postcards and aerograms (08.1.0); stamp albums (09.3.1).

09.5.4 Stationery and Drawing Materials (ND)

Writing pads, envelopes, account books, notebooks, diaries, and so on
Pens, pencils, fountain pens, ballpoint pens, felt-tip pens, inks, erasers, pencil sharpeners, and so on
Stencils, carbon paper, typewriter ribbons, inking pads, correcting fluids, and so on
Paper punches, paper cutters, paper scissors, office glues and adhesives, staplers and staples, paper clips, drawing pins, and so on
Drawing and painting materials such as canvas, paper, card, paints, crayons, pastels, and brushes

Includes: toner and ink cartridges; educational materials such as exercise books, slide rules, geometry instruments, slates, chalks, and pencil boxes.

Excludes: pocket calculators (09.1.3).

09.6 Package Holidays

09.6.0 Package Holidays (S)

All-inclusive holidays or tours which provide for travel, food, accommodation, guides, and so on

Includes: half-day and one-day excursion tours; pilgrimages.

10 Education

This division covers educational services only. It does not include expenditures on educational materials, such as books (09.5.1) and stationery (09.5.4), or education support services, such as health care services (06), transport services (07.3), catering services (11.1.2), and accommodation services (11.2.0).

It includes education by radio or television broadcasting.

The breakdown of educational services is based upon the level categories of the 1997 International Standard Classification of Education (ISCED97) of the United Nations Educational, Scientific and Cultural Organization.

10.1 Preprimary and Primary Education

10.1.0 Preprimary and Primary Education (S)

Levels 0 and 1 of ISCED97: preprimary and primary education

Includes: literacy programs for students too old for primary school.

10.2 Secondary Education

10.2.0 Secondary Education (S)

Levels 2 and 3 of ISCED97: lower-secondary and upper-secondary education

Includes: out-of-school secondary education for adults and young people.

10.3 Postsecondary Nontertiary Education

10.3.0 Postsecondary Nontertiary Education (S)

Level 4 of ISCED97: postsecondary nontertiary education

Includes: out-of-school postsecondary nontertiary education for adults and young people.

10.4 Tertiary Education

10.4.0 Tertiary Education (S)

Levels 5 and 6 of ISCED97: first stage and second stage of tertiary education

10.5 Education Not Definable by Level

10.5.0 Education Not Definable by Level (S)

Educational programs, generally for adults, which do not require any special prior instruction, in particular vocational training and cultural development

Excludes: driving lessons (07.2.4); recreational training courses such as sport or bridge lessons given by independent teachers (09.4.1).

11 Restaurants and Hotels

11.1 Catering Services

11.1.1 Restaurants, Cafés, and the Like (S)

Catering services (meals, snacks, drinks, and refreshments) provided by restaurants, cafés, buffets, bars, tearooms, and so on, including those provided:

In places providing recreational, cultural, sporting or entertainment services: theatres, cinemas, sports stadiums, swimming pools, sports complexes, museums, art galleries, nightclubs, dancing establishments, and so on
On public transport (coaches, trains, boats, airplanes, and so on) when priced separately

Also included are the following:

The sale of food products and beverages for immediate consumption by kiosks, street vendors, and the like, including food products and beverages dispensed ready for consumption by automatic vending machines
The sale of cooked dishes by restaurants for consumption off their premises
The sale of cooked dishes by catering contractors whether collected by the customer or delivered to the customer's home.

Includes: tips.
Excludes: tobacco purchases (02.2.0); telephone calls (08.3.0).

11.1.2 Canteens (S)

Catering services of works canteens, office canteens and canteens in schools, universities, and other educational establishments

Includes: university refectories, military messes, and wardrooms.
Excludes: food and drink provided to hospital inpatients (06.3.0).

11.2 Accommodation Services

11.2.0 Accommodation Services (S)

Accommodation services of:
Hotels, boarding houses, motels, inns, and establishments offering "bed and breakfast"
Holiday villages and holiday centers, camping and caravan sites, youth hostels, and mountain chalets
Boarding schools, universities, and other educational establishments
Public transport (trains, boats, and so on) when priced separately
Hostels for young workers or immigrants.

Includes: tips, porters.
Excludes: payments of households occupying a room in a hotel or boarding house as their main residence (04.1.1); rentals paid by households for a secondary residence for the duration of a holiday (04.1.2); telephone calls (08.3.0); catering services in such establishments except for breakfast or other meals included in the price of the accommodation (11.1.1); and housing in orphanages, homes for disabled or maladjusted persons (12.4.0).

12 Miscellaneous Goods and Services

12.1 Personal Care

12.1.1 Hairdressing Salons and Personal Grooming Establishments (S)

Services of hairdressing salons, barbers, beauty shops, manicures, pedicures, Turkish baths, saunas, solariums, nonmedical massages, and so on

Includes: bodycare, depilation, and the like.
Excludes: spas (06.2.3) or (06.3.0); fitness centers (09.4.1).

12.1.2 Electric Appliances for Personal Care (SD)

Electric razors and hair trimmers, handheld and hood hairdryers, curling tongs and styling combs, sunlamps, vibrators, electric toothbrushes and other electric appliances for dental hygiene, and so on
Repair of such appliances

12.1.3 Other Appliances, Articles, and Products for Personal Care (ND)

Nonelectric appliances: razors and hair trimmers and blades therefor, scissors, nail files, combs, shaving brushes, hairbrushes, toothbrushes, nail brushes, hairpins, curlers, personal weighing machines, baby scales, and so on
Articles for personal hygiene: toilet soap, medicinal soap, cleansing oil and milk, shaving soap, shaving cream and foam, toothpaste, and so on
Beauty products: lipstick, nail varnish, makeup and makeup removal products (including powder compacts, brushes, and powder puffs), hair lacquers and lotions, pre-shave and after-shave products, sunbathing products, hair removers, perfumes and toilet waters, personal deodorants, bath products, and so on
Other products: toilet paper, paper handkerchiefs, paper towels, sanitary towels, cotton wool, cotton tops, babies' napkins, toilet sponges, and so on

Excludes: handkerchiefs made of fabric (03.1.3).

12.2 Prostitution

12.2.0 Prostitution (S)

Services provided by prostitutes and the like

12.3 Personal Effects N.E.C.

12.3.1 Jewelry, Clocks, and Watches (D)

Precious stones and metals and jewelry fashioned out of such stones and metals
Costume jewelry, cuff links, and tiepins
Clocks, watches, stopwatches, alarm clocks, travel clocks
Repair of such articles

Excludes: ornaments (05.1.1) or (05.4.0); radio clocks (09.1.1); precious stones and metals and jewelry fashioned out of such stones and metals acquired primarily as stores of value (capital formation).

12.3.2 Other Personal Effects (SD)

Travel goods and other carriers of personal effects: suitcases, trunks, travel bags, attaché cases, satchels, handbags, wallets, purses, and so on
Articles for babies: baby carriages, pushchairs, carrycots, recliners, car beds and seats, back carriers, front carriers, reins and harnesses, and so on
Articles for smokers: pipes, lighters, cigarette cases, cigar cutters, ashtrays, and so on
Miscellaneous personal articles: sunglasses, walking sticks and canes, umbrellas and parasols, fans, keyrings, and so on
Funerary articles: coffins, gravestones, urns, and so on
Repair of such articles

Includes: lighter fuel; wall thermometers and barometers.
Excludes: baby furniture (05.1.1); shopping bags (05.2.0); and feeding bottles (05.4.0).

12.4 Social Protection

Social protection as defined here covers assistance and support services provided to persons who are elderly, disabled, having occupational injuries and diseases, survivors, unemployed, destitute, homeless, low-income earners, indigenous people, immigrants, refugees, alcohol and substance abusers, and so on. It also covers assistance and support services provided to families and children.

12.4.0 Social Protection (S)

Such services include residential care, home help, day care, and rehabilitation. More specifically, this class covers payments by households for:

Retirement homes for elderly persons, residences for disabled persons, rehabilitation centers providing long-term support for patients rather than health care and rehabilitative therapy, and schools for disabled persons where the main aim is to help students overcome their disability

Help to maintain elderly and disabled persons at home (home-cleaning services, meal programs, day care centers, day care services, and holiday care services)

Wet-nurses, crèches, play schools, and other child-minding facilities

Counseling, guidance, arbitration, fostering, and adoption services for families.

12.5 Insurance

Service charges for insurance are classified by type of insurance, namely, life insurance and nonlife insurance (that is, insurance in connection with the dwelling, health, transport, and so on). Service charges for multirisk insurance covering several risks should be classified on the basis of the cost of the principal risk if it is not possible to allocate the service charges to the various risks covered.

Service charge is defined as the difference between claims due and premiums earned and premium supplement.

12.5.1 Life Insurance (S)

Service charges for life assurance, death benefit assurance, education assurance, and so on

12.5.2 Insurance Connected with the Dwelling (S)

Service charges paid by owner-occupiers and by tenants for the kinds of insurance typically taken out by tenants against fire, theft, water damage, and so on

Excludes: service charges paid by owner-occupiers for the kinds of insurance typically taken out by landlords (intermediate consumption).

12.5.3 Insurance Connected with Health (S)

Service charges for private sickness and accident insurance

12.5.4 Insurance Connected with Transport (S)

Service charges for insurance in respect of personal transport equipment

Service charges for travel insurance and luggage insurance

12.5.5 Other Insurance (S)

Service charges for other insurance such as civil liability for injury or damage to third parties or their property

Excludes: civil liability or damage to third parties or their property arising from the operation of personal transport equipment (12.5.4).

12.6 Financial Services N.E.C.

12.6.1 FISIM (S)

Financial intermediation services indirectly measured

12.6.2 Other Financial Services N.E.C. (S)

Actual charges for the financial services of banks, post offices, saving banks, money changers, and similar financial institutions

Fees and service charges of brokers, investment counselors, tax consultants, and the like

Administrative charges of private pension funds and the like

12.7 Other Services N.E.C.

12.7.0 Other Services N.E.C. (S)

Fees for legal services, employment agencies, and so on

Charges for undertaking and other funeral services

Payment for the services of estate agents, housing agents, auctioneers, salesroom operators, and other intermediaries

Payment for photocopies and other reproductions of documents

Fees for the issue of birth, marriage, and death certificates, and other administrative documents

Payment for newspaper notices and advertisements

Payment for the services of graphologists, astrologers, private detectives, bodyguards, matrimonial agencies and marriage guidance counselors, public writers, miscellaneous concessions (seats, toilets, and cloakrooms), and so on

Appendix 3

Classification of Individual Consumption According to Purpose 2018 (COICOP 2018)[1]

Introduction

The Classification of Individual Consumption According to Purpose (COICOP) serves as the international reference classification of household expenditure. COICOP provides a framework of homogeneous categories of goods and services, which are considered a function or purpose of household consumption expenditure. COICOP functions as an integral part of the *System of National Accounts* (SNA), but it is also used in several other statistical areas, such as the household budget survey or the consumer price index.

This appendix presents descriptions and explanations of the COICOP revision endorsed in 2018 (COICOP 2018) by the 49th Session of the United Nations Statistical Commission. COICOP 2018 provides more detail than the previous version (COICOP 1999), responding to users' need for more detail, and addresses several other issues that prompted the revision of the classification. COICOP 2018 reflects the significant changes in goods and services in some areas, improves the links of COICOP to other classifications, and addresses emerging statistical and policy needs of several international organizations.

COICOP: Breakdown of Individual Consumption Expenditure of Households by Division and Group

01 Food and Nonalcoholic Beverages

Division 01 covers food and nonalcoholic beverages purchased by the household mainly for consumption or preparation at home. It excludes food and nonalcoholic beverages that are provided as part of a food serving service (Division 11).

Services for food processing for own consumption are also included in this division.

Food is composed of all edible goods that are purchased and consumed by the household with the purpose of nourishing. It includes: cereals and cereal products; meat; fish and other seafood; milk, other dairy products, and eggs; oils and fats; fruit and nuts; vegetables, tubers, plantains, cooking bananas, and pulses; sugar, confectionery, and desserts; salt, sauces and condiments, spices and culinary herbs, and seeds.

Division 01 also includes ready-made food that can be eaten as it is or requires heating. Nonalcoholic beverages include drinks that do not contain any alcohol.

[1]As of this draft, COICOP 2018 has not yet been finalized. While only minor edits are expected, additional changes could be identified.

01.1 Food

Food purchased by the household mainly for consumption or preparation at home. It excludes food that is provided as part of a food serving service.

Food is composed of all edible goods that are purchased and consumed by the household with the purpose of nourishing. It includes cereals and cereal products; meat; fish and other seafood; milk, other dairy products, and eggs; oils and fats; fruit and nuts; vegetables, tubers, plantains, cooking bananas, and pulses; sugar, confectionery, and desserts; salt, sauces and condiments, spices and culinary herbs, and seeds.

Includes:

- Products that need to be cooked and further prepared as well as ready-made food

Excludes:

- *Service of local delivery of food or drinks when separately invoiced (07.4.9.2)*
- *Products for animal feeding (09.3.2.2)*
- *Food provided by food serving services (Division 11)*

01.1.1 Cereals and Cereal Products (ND)

01.1.1.1 Cereals (ND)

Dried grains of cereals, whether or not precooked, but not further processed.

Includes:

- Wheat
- Rice, including parboiled rice
- Sorghum
- Barley
- Millet
- Quinoa
- Maize
- Other cereals

Includes also:

- Teff
- Rye
- Oats
- Triticale
- Buckwheat
- Canary seed
- Quihuicha or Inca wheat
- Canagua or coaihua
- Adlay or Job's tears
- Mixed cereal grains, in the form of dried grains, but not further processed

Excludes:

- *Flour of cereals (01.1.1.2)*
- *Breakfast cereals (01.1.1.4)*
- *Ready-made preparations based on cereals, such as ready-made soups based on cereals (01.1.9.1)*
- *Baby rice cereals and other baby cereals (01.1.9.2)*
- *Seeds for planting (09.3.1.2)*

01.1.1.2 Flour of Cereals (ND)

Includes:

- Flour of cereals mentioned in subclass 01.1.1.1

Excludes:

- *Flour as baby food, baby rice cereals, and other baby cereals (01.1.9.2)*

01.1.1.3 Bread and Bakery Products (ND)

Includes:

- Bread and bread rolls
- Crispbread, rusks, toasted bread, crackers
- Tortillas
- Injera
- Pizza bases without topping, whether precooked or not
- Gingerbread and the like
- Sweet biscuits (cookies)
- Waffles and wafers
- Ice cream cones
- Crumpets, muffins, croissants, cakes, sweet tarts, sweet pies, and other pastry goods and cakes

Excludes:

- *Pizza (with topping), quiche, meat, or fish pies (01.1.9.1)*

01.1.1.4 Breakfast Cereals (ND)

Includes:

- Cornflakes, oatmeal and oat flakes, muesli, granola, and puffed cereals including puffed rice cakes
- Breakfast cereals with nuts or dried fruit

Excludes:

- *Popcorn (1.1.1.9)*

01.1.1.5 Macaroni, Noodles, Couscous, and Similar Pasta Products (ND)

Includes:

- Pasta uncooked, whether stuffed or not, and couscous
- Uncooked dumplings, ravioli, and similar
- Bulgur

Excludes:

- *Prepared dishes containing stuffed pasta; prepared couscous dishes (01.1.9.1)*

01.1.1.9 Other Cereal and Grain Mill Products (ND)

Includes:

- Mixes and doughs for the preparation of bakery products
- Popcorn
- Granola bars
- Malt; malt extract
- Chips and crisps of cereals

Includes also:

- Seitan and other meat substitutes made from cereals

Excludes:

- *Soy meat and burgers, veggie burgers, tofu, tempeh, and other meat substitutes made from vegetables and nuts; potato starch, tapioca, sago, and other starches (01.1.7.9)*
- *Ready-made preparations based on cereals, such as ready-made soups based on cereals (01.1.9.1)*

01.1.2 Live Animals, Meat, and Other Parts of Slaughtered Land Animals (ND)

01.1.2.1 Live Land Animals (ND)

Live land animals, both domestic and wild, for food purpose.
Includes:

- Cattle (cow, veal, common zebu or humped ox, watussi ox, gaur, gayal, banteng, Tibetan yak)
- Buffaloes (Indian or water buffaloes, Asiatic buffalo or arni, Celebese anoa or pigmy buffaloes, African buffaloes, such as the dwarf buffaloes and the large Caffrarian buffaloes, the American bison or "buffalo" and the European bison, the "beefalo" [a cross between a bison and a domestic beef animal])
- Pigs
- Goats, lambs, and sheep
- Poultry (chicken, ducks, geese, turkeys, and guinea fowl)
- Horses, donkeys, and other equines
- Camels, dromedaries, alpaca, llama, guanaco, vicuña, and other camelids
- Seals, walruses, whales, and other marine mammals
- Antelopes, deer, boars, kangaroos
- Ostriches, emus, rhea, pheasant, grouse, pigeon, quail, and other birds
- Snakes, alligators, and other reptiles
- Spiders, scorpions, and other insects and worms
- Terrestrial snails
- Frogs

Excludes:

- *Live fish (01.1.3.1)*
- *Other live seafood (01.1.3.4)*
- *Live animals for transport (07.1.4.0)*

01.1.2.2 Meat, Fresh, Chilled, or Frozen (ND)

Meat of all animals, both domestic and wild, fresh, chilled, or frozen.
Includes:

- Meat of cattle (cow, veal, common zebu or humped ox, watussi ox, gaur, gayal, banteng, Tibetan yak)
- Meat of buffaloes (Indian or water buffaloes, Asiatic buffalo or arni, Celebese anoa or pigmy buffaloes, African buffaloes, such as the dwarf buffaloes and the large Caffrarian buffaloes, the American bison or "buffalo" and the European bison, the "beefalo" [a cross between a bison and a domestic beef animal])
- Meat of pigs
- Meat of goats, lambs, and sheep

- Meat of poultry (chicken, ducks, geese, turkeys, and guinea fowl)
- Meat of horses, donkeys, and other equines
- Meat of camels, dromedaries, alpaca, llama, guanaco, vicuña, and other camelids
- Meat of seals, walruses, whales, and other marine mammals
- Meat of antelopes, deer, boars, and kangaroos
- Meat of ostriches, emus, rhea, pheasant, grouse, pigeon, quail, and other birds
- Meat of snakes, alligators, and other reptiles
- Meat of spiders, scorpions, and other insects and worms
- Meat of terrestrial snails
- Meat of frogs

Includes also:

- Minced meat of animals mentioned previously

01.1.2.3 Meat, Dried, Salted, in Brine or Smoked (ND)

Meat of all animals dried, salted, in brine or smoked.
Includes:

- Bacon, ham, salami

Excludes:

- *Pâté (01.1.2.5)*

01.1.2.4 Offal, Blood, and Other Parts of Slaughtered Animals, Fresh, Chilled, or Frozen, Dried, Salted, in Brine or Smoked (ND)

Offal and other parts of slaughtered animals fresh, chilled or frozen, dried, salted, in brine or smoked.
Includes:

- Bones
- Pork heads, tails, and ears; chicken feet

Excludes:

- *Offal, blood, and other parts of slaughtered animals' preparations (01.1.2.5)*

01.1.2.5 Meat, Offal, Blood, and Other Parts of Slaughtered Animals Preparations (ND)

Meat, offal or blood preparations, whether frozen or not.
Includes:

- Sausages and similar products of meat, offal, or blood
- Marinated meat
- Canned meat, meat extracts, meat juices
- Minced meat, if mixed meat from more than one kind of animal's minced meat
- All kind of pâté, including liver pâté
- Breaded meat
- Other preparations of meat, meat offal, or blood

01.1.3 Fish and Other Seafood (ND)

Fish and other seafood, such as crustaceans, molluscs, and other aquatic invertebrates, as whole or part of (that is cuts, fillets, meat, minced or not), including livers, roes, fins, meal, and other offal.

Excludes:

- *Marine mammals, frogs, and terrestrial snails (01.1.2.1, 01.1.2.2, 01.1.2.3)*
- *Seaweeds and other aquatic plants (01.1.7.4)*

01.1.3.1 Fish, Live, Fresh, Chilled, or Frozen (ND)

Fish, live, fresh, chilled, or frozen.
Includes:

- Fish live for food purpose
- Fish fresh, chilled, or frozen
- Fish fillets and meat, minced or not, fresh, chilled, or frozen

Excludes:

- *Livers, roes, fins, and other offal (01.1.3.7)*

01.1.3.2 Fish, Dried, Salted, in Brine or Smoked (ND)

Fish, dried, salted or in brine; smoked.
Includes:

- Fish fillets and meat dried, salted or in brine; smoked

Excludes:

- *Livers, roes, fins, and other offal (01.1.3.7)*

01.1.3.3 Fish Preparations (ND)

Prepared foodstuffs made of fish whether frozen or not.
Includes:

- Fillets merely covered with batter or bread crumbs, whether or not frozen
- Crabmeat and surimi

Excludes:

- *Caviar and caviar substitutes and prepared and preserved shark fins; livers, roes, fins, and other offal (01.1.3.7)*

01.1.3.4 Other Seafood, Live, Fresh, Chilled, or Frozen (ND)

Includes:

- Crabs, lobsters, crayfish, krill, sea spider, shrimps and prawns, and other crustaceans, live, fresh, chilled, or frozen
- Cuttlefish, squid, octopus, sea snails, abalone and bivalves, such as oysters, scallops, mussels, clams, cockles and ark shells, and other molluscs, live, fresh, chilled, or frozen
- Sea urchins, sea cucumbers (bêches-de-mer) and jellyfish, and other aquatic invertebrates, live, fresh, chilled, or frozen

Excludes:

- *Terrestrial molluscs, including terrestrial snails, live, fresh, chilled, or frozen (01.1.2.1, 01.1.2.2, 01.1.2.3)*
- *Seaweeds and other edible aquatic plants (01.1.7.4)*

01.1.3.5 Other Seafood, Dried, Salted, in Brine or Smoked (ND)

Other seafood as defined in 01.1.3.4, dried, salted or in brine; smoked.

01.1.3.6 Other Seafood Preparations (ND)

Prepared foodstuffs made of other seafood as defined in 01.1.3.4 whether frozen or not.

01.1.3.7 Livers, Roes, and Offal of Fish and of Other Seafood in All Forms (ND)

Includes:

- Livers, roes, fins, maws, meal, and other offal in all product forms, that is, fresh, chilled, frozen, dried, salted, in brine or smoked, prepared or preserved

Excludes:

- *Seaweeds and other aquatic plants (01.1.7.4)*

01.1.4 Milk, Other Dairy Products, and Eggs (ND)

01.1.4.1 Raw and Whole Milk (ND)

Raw and whole milk of cattle and buffalo, sheep and goat, camels and other animals, fresh, pasteurized, sterilized (UHT), and reconstituted.

Excludes:

- *Curdled, fermented, or acidified milk and cream (01.1.4.6)*

01.1.4.2 Skimmed Milk (ND)

Skimmed and semiskimmed milk of cattle and buffalo, sheep and goat, camels, and other animals.

01.1.4.3 Other Milk and Cream (ND)

Includes:

- Powdered, whole or skimmed milk
- Evaporated and condensed milk
- Fresh, clotted, thickened, and whipped cream

Includes also:

- Baked milk

Excludes:

- *Beverages flavored with cocoa, coffee, or other substances (01.1.4.7)*
- *Condensed, evaporated or powdered milk as baby food (01.1.9.2)*

01.1.4.4 Nonanimal Milk (ND)

Milk from nonanimal origin.

Includes:

- Almond milk
- Coconut milk drink
- Oat milk
- Rice milk
- Soy milk
- Other milk from vegetables and nuts

Excludes:

- *Coconut milk for cooking (01.1.9.3)*

01.1.4.5 Cheese (ND)

All kinds of cheese (fresh hard, semihard, blue cheese, cottage cheese) and curd both from animal and nonanimal milk.

Excludes:

- *Tofu (01.1.7.9)*

01.1.4.6 Yogurt and Similar Products (ND)

Includes:

- Yogurt
- Buttermilk
- Curdled milk and cream
- Kefir and other fermented or acidified milk and cream whether or not concentrated or containing added sugar or other sweetening matter or flavored or containing added fruit, nuts, or cocoa
- Yogurt from nonanimal milk (for example, coconut yogurt, soy yogurt)

Excludes:

- *Frozen yogurt (01.1.8.6)*

01.1.4.7 Milk-Based Dessert and Beverages (ND)

Includes:

- Milk-based desserts from the milk of animal and nonanimal origin
- Beverages based on milk of animal and nonanimal origin flavored with cocoa, coffee, or other substances

Includes also:

- Puddings based on milk of animal and nonanimal origin; panna cotta; crème brûlée; and crema catalana

Excludes:

- *Lemon curd and similar (01.1.8.3)*

01.1.4.8 Eggs (ND)

Includes:

- Eggs of hen and other birds in shell, fresh
- Eggs of other animals, including turtle eggs, in shell, fresh
- Eggs in shell or not, preserved or cooked
- Eggs yolks, fresh or preserved
- Eggs albumin

Excludes:

- *Fish roes (01.1.3.7)*
- *Omelets, crepes, and other ready-made food products based on eggs (01.1.9.1)*

01.1.4.9 Other Dairy Products (ND)

Includes:

- Whey and casein
- Cream concentrated or containing added sugar or other sweetening matter; cream powder
- Other products consisting of milk constituents, milk protein concentrates, and products obtained from whey

Excludes:

- *Butter and other fats and oils derived from milk (01.1.5.2)*
- *Ice cream (01.1.8.6)*

01.1.5 Oils and Fats (ND)

01.1.5.1 Vegetable Oils (ND)

All oil of vegetable origin, including oil extracted from fruit, nuts, and other crops.
Includes:

- Sunflower-seed and safflower oil
- Palm oil; olive oil
- Soya bean oil
- Groundnut oil
- Rapeseed, colza, and mustard oil
- Corn oil
- Cotton oil
- Other oils of vegetable origin

Includes also:

- Coconut oil
- Avocado oil
- Rice bran oil

01.1.5.2 Butter and Other Fats and Oils Derived from Milk (ND)

Includes:

- Butter
- Butter oil
- Ghee

01.1.5.3 Margarine and Similar Preparations (ND)

Includes:

- Margarine
- Diet margarine

Excludes:

- *Peanut butter (01.1.8.4)*

01.1.5.9 Other Animal Oils and Fats (ND)

Includes:

- Pig fat and lard, also including leaves or other spices
- Fat from cattle, buffalos, sheep, goats, and poultry
- Greaves fat and oleo stock
- Fats and oils of fish

Excludes:

- *Cod or halibut liver oil (06.1.1.1)*

01.1.6 Fruits and Nuts (ND)

01.1.6.1 Dates, Figs, and Tropical Fruits, Fresh (ND)

Includes:

- Dates
- Figs
- Avocados
- Bananas
- Mangoes, guavas, and mangosteens
- Papayas
- Pineapples
- Coconut
- Breadfruits
- Other tropical and subtropical fruit, fresh

Excludes:

- *Plantains and cooking bananas (01.1.7.5)*

01.1.6.2 Citrus Fruits, Fresh (ND)

Includes:

- Oranges
- Pomelos and grapefruit
- Lemons and limes
- Tangerines
- Mandarins and clementines
- Other citrus fruits, fresh

01.1.6.3 Stone Fruits and Pome Fruits, Fresh (ND)

Includes:

- Apples
- Pears and quinces
- Apricots
- Cherries and sour cherries
- Peaches and nectarines
- Plums and sloes
- Other pome fruits and stone fruits, fresh

01.1.6.4 Berries, Fresh (ND)

Includes:

- Currants and gooseberries
- Raspberries
- Blackberries
- Mulberries and loganberries
- Strawberries
- Other berries fresh

01.1.6.5 Other Fruits, Fresh (ND)

Includes:

- Grapes
- Kiwi fruit
- Cantaloupes and other melons
- Watermelons
- Pomegranates
- Other fruits, fresh, n.e.c.

01.1.6.6 Frozen Fruit (ND)

Fruit, uncooked or cooked, frozen, whether or not containing added sugar or other sweetening matter.

01.1.6.7 Fruit, Dried, and Dehydrated (ND)

Includes:

- Raisins
- Prunes
- Dried apricots

- Dried coconut
- Other dried fruits

Excludes:

- *Fruit flour (01.1.6.9)*

01.1.6.8 Nuts, in Shell or Shelled (ND)

Includes:

- Almonds
- Cashew nuts
- Chestnuts
- Hazelnuts
- Pistachios
- Walnuts
- Brazil nuts
- Groundnuts
- Other nuts in shell or shelled

01.1.6.9 Fruit and Nuts Ground and Other Preparations (ND)

Fruit and nuts preparations whether frozen or not.
Includes:

- Fruit flour
- Nuts, groundnuts, and other seeds, roasted, salted, or otherwise prepared
- Canned fruit
- Homogenized fruit preparations
- Fruit pickles

Excludes:

- *Jams, fruit jellies, marmalades, and fruit purée and pastes (01.1.8.3)*
- *Nut purée, nut butter, and nut pastes (01.1.8.4)*
- *Homogenized preparations as baby food (01.1.9.2)*

01.1.7 Vegetables, Tubers, Plantains, Cooking Bananas, and Pulses (ND)

01.1.7.1 Leafy or Stem Vegetables, Fresh or Chilled (ND)

Includes:

- Asparagus
- Cabbages
- Cauliflowers and broccoli
- Lettuce and chicory
- Spinach
- Artichokes
- Other leafy or stem vegetables, fresh or chilled

01.1.7.2 Fruit-Bearing Vegetables, Fresh or Chilled (ND)

Includes:

- Chilies and peppers
- Cucumbers and gherkins
- Eggplants (aubergines)
- Tomatoes
- Pumpkins
- Squash and gourds
- Other fruit-bearing vegetables, fresh or chilled

01.1.7.3 Green Leguminous Vegetables, Fresh or Chilled (ND)

Includes:

- Beans
- Peas
- Broad beans and horse beans green
- Soya beans
- Other green leguminous vegetables, fresh or chilled

01.1.7.4 Other Vegetables, Fresh or Chilled (ND)

Includes:

- Carrots and turnips
- Garlic
- Onions
- Leeks and other alliaceous vegetables
- Other root, bulb, and tuberous vegetables, fresh or chilled
- Mushrooms and truffles
- Seaweeds and other aquatic plants
- Olives
- Other vegetables, fresh or chilled n.e.c.
- Mixtures of vegetables, fresh or chilled

01.1.7.5 Tubers, Plantains, and Cooking Bananas (ND)

Includes:

- All types of potatoes including sweet potatoes
- Cassava; manioc and yucca
- Yams
- Taro
- Yautia, also known as malanga, new cocoyam, ocumo, tannia
- Plantains and cooking bananas

Includes also:

- Arrowroots, lotus roots, salep, Jerusalem artichokes, topinambur, and *Tacca*

Excludes:

- *Dessert bananas (01.1.6.1)*

01.1.7.6 Pulses (ND)

Dried leguminous vegetables.
Includes:

- Common beans and other beans
- Broad beans and horse beans, also known as fava beans
- Chickpeas
- Lentil
- Peas
- Cowpeas
- Pigeon peas
- Bambara beans
- Mixtures of pulses

01.1.7.7 Other Vegetables, Tubers, Plantains, and Cooking Bananas, Dried and Dehydrated (ND)

Vegetables, other than leguminous, tubers, plantains, and cooking bananas dried and dehydrated.

Includes:

- Dried soybeans
- Dried potatoes
- Dehydrated garlic and onions

Excludes:

- *Vegetable flours (01.1.7.9)*

01.1.7.8 Vegetables, Tubers, Plantains, and Cooking Bananas, Frozen (ND)

Includes:

- Frozen vegetables in 01.1.7.1–01.1.7.4
- Frozen tubers
- Frozen plantains and cooking bananas

Excludes:

- *Frozen preparations, such as frozen, chipped potatoes (01.1.7.9)*

01.1.7.9 Vegetables, Tubers, Plantains, Cooking Bananas and Pulses Ground, and Other Preparations (ND)

Vegetables, tubers, plantains, cooking bananas, and pulses preparations, whether frozen or not.

Includes:

- Flours of vegetables, pulses, tubers, plantains, and cooking bananas
- Canned vegetables
- Preserved olives, vegetable flakes, vegetable purée, vegetable chips, and crisps
- Frozen, chipped potatoes
- Vegetable concentrates
- Homogenized preparations
- Vegetable pickles

Includes also:

- Soy meat and burgers, veggie burgers, tofu, tempeh, and other meat substitutes made from vegetables and nuts
- Kocho (flatbread made of plant stem)
- Potato starch, tapioca, sago, and other starches

Excludes:

- *Ready-made vegetables prepared, frozen or not, including other ingredients, such as cheese or meat/fish; ready-made soups (01.1.9.1)*
- *Homogenized preparations as baby food (01.1.9.2)*
- *Culinary herbs and spices (01.1.9.4)*
- *Broths and stocks containing vegetables (01.1.9.9)*
- *Vegetable juices (01.2.1.0)*

01.1.8 Sugar, Confectionery, and Desserts (ND)

01.1.8.1 Cane and Beet Sugar (ND)

Includes:

- Cane or beet sugar, raw or refined, powdered, crystallized or in lumps

01.1.8.2 Other Sugar and Sugar Substitutes (ND)

Includes:

- Sugar other than cane and beet (for example, coconut sugar)
- Stevia
- Glucose and glucose syrup; fructose and fructose syrup
- Lactose and lactose syrup
- Invert sugar
- Artificial honey, saccharin, and other artificial sweeteners
- Refined cane or beet sugar, in solid form, containing added flavoring or coloring matter
- Maple sugar and maple syrup; caramel; molasses; sugars and sugar syrups n.e.c.

01.1.8.3 Jams, Fruit Jellies, Marmalades, Fruit Purée and Pastes, and Honey (ND)

Includes:

- Honey, jams, marmalades, compotes, jellies, and fruit purées and pastes

Includes also:

- Lemon curd and other fruit curd

01.1.8.4 Nut Purée, Nut Butter, and Nut Pastes (ND)

Includes:

- Peanut butter
- Other nut butter, such as almond butter, cashew butter, hazelnut butter, macadamia nut butter, pecan butter, pistachio butter, and walnut butter

01.1.8.5 Chocolate, Cocoa, and Cocoa-Based Food Products (ND)

Includes:

- Cocoa (including cocoa beans) and cocoa powder for all purposes
- Chocolate in bars or slabs, including white chocolate
- Chocolate and cocoa-based foods and cocoa-based dessert
- Chocolate and cocoa-based creams or spreads
- Chocolate-covered marshmallows and chocolate-covered jelly if the product is composed of a majority of chocolate

Excludes:

- *Cocoa and chocolate-based drinks (01.2.4.0)*

01.1.8.6 Ice, Ice Cream, and Sorbet (ND)

Includes:

- Ice cubes for drinks
- Ice cream and kulfi
- Sorbet
- Frozen yogurt
- Ice pop

Includes also:

- Tofu ice cream

Excludes:

- *Ice for cooling (04.5.5.0)*

01.1.8.9 Other Sugar Confectionery and Desserts N.E.C. (ND)

Includes:

- Desserts n.e.c.
- Vegetables, fruit, nuts, fruit peel, and other parts of plants, preserved by sugar
- Chewing gum, toffees, lollies, candies, and pastilles
- Other confectionary products

Excludes:

- *Sugar confectionery based on cocoa and chocolate (01.1.8.5)*

01.1.9 Ready-Made Food and Other Food Products N.E.C. (ND)

01.1.9.1 Ready-Made Food (ND)

Prepared food and meals that can be eaten as is or after heating but that do not require cooking. They contain mixed ingredients and can be fresh, frozen, or dehydrated/instant. They can include sauces and dressing which, especially when food is fresh, can be provided in separate bags. Disposable fork, knife, spoon, or chopsticks are sometimes also included in the package.

Includes:

- Precooked dishes containing stuffed pasta, rice, and other cereals, such as couscous dishes, including vegetables, meat, fish, cheese, or other ingredients; ready to eat dumplings, ravioli, noodles, and similar with sauce
- Ready-made meals and dishes based on precooked meat, meat substitutes, and fish
- TV dinners
- Composed salads and other prepared dishes and meals based on vegetables, pulses, and potatoes also including other ingredients, such as meat, fish, and cheese
- Sandwiches, pizzas, quiches, meat, or fish pies, frozen or not
- Omelets, crepes, and other food products based on eggs when precooked and served as a main dish
- Ready-made soups including dehydrated and instant soups and stews
- Other prepared ready-made dishes and meals n.e.c.

Excludes:

- *Bread and bakery products (01.1.1.3)*
- *Macaroni, noodles, couscous, and similar pasta products uncooked, whether stuffed or not (01.1.1.5)*
- *Cheese (01.1.4.5) and yogurt (01.1.4.6)*
- *Cakes (0.1.1.1.3), ice cream (0.1.1.8.6), and other desserts n.e.c. (01.1.8.9)*
- *Frozen, chipped potatoes (01.1.7.9)*

01.1.9.2 Baby Food (ND)

Food that is for baby use exclusively.

Includes:

- Baby formula (powdered, condensed, and evaporated milk for baby use)
- Baby rice cereals and flour for baby meals
- Homogenized baby food

Excludes:

- *Cereals and flour not intended for baby use exclusively (01.1.1.1, 01.1.1.2)*
- *Powdered milk not intended for baby use exclusively (01.1.4.3)*
- *Yogurt for children (01.1.4.6)*
- *Homogenized fruit and vegetable preparations not intended for baby use exclusively (01.1.6.9; 0.1.1.7.9)*

01.1.9.3 Salt, Condiments, and Sauces (ND)

Includes:

- Salt, sauces, condiments and seasonings (mustard, mayonnaise, ketchup, soy sauce, and so on), and vinegar

Includes also:

- Coconut milk for cooking

Excludes:

- *Coconut milk drink (01.1.4.4)*
- *Fruit and vegetable pickles (01.1.7.9)*

01.1.9.4 Spices, Culinary Herbs, and Seeds (ND)

Includes:

- Pepper, pimento, ginger, and other spices
- Parsley, rosemary, thyme, and other culinary herbs
- Poppy seed, sesame seed, linseed, and other seeds

Excludes:

- *Vegetable oils (01.1.5.1)*
- *Seeds for plating (09.3.1.2)*

01.1.9.9 Other Food Products N.E.C. (ND)

Includes:

- Sugar cane consumed for extracting juice or as a snack
- Prepared baking powders and yeasts, broth, stocks, bouillon cubes, soup bases, agar-agar, instant dessert preparations
- Nutritional supplements and fortified food products

01.2 Nonalcoholic Beverages

Nonalcoholic beverages purchased by the household, regardless of where these are consumed excluding beverages that are provided as part of a food and beverage serving service. (Division 11)

Includes:

- Beverages that do not contain any alcohol

Excludes:

- *Nonalcoholic beverages for immediate consumption provided by a serving service (11.1.1)*
- *Milk (01.1.4.1, 01.1.4.2, 01.1.4.3, 01.1.4.4)*

01.2.1 Fruit and Vegetable Juices (ND)

Includes:

- Fruit and vegetable juices unfermented and not containing added alcohol, whether or not containing added sugar or other sweetening matter

- Concentrated juices and frozen juices
- Powdered juices

Excludes:

- *Sparkling juices (01.2.6.0)*

01.2.1.0 Fruit and Vegetable Juices (ND)

Includes:

- Fruit and vegetable juices unfermented and not containing added alcohol, whether or not containing added sugar or other sweetening matter
- Concentrated juices and frozen juices
- Powdered juices

Excludes:

- *Sparkling juices (01.2.6.0)*

01.2.2 Coffee and Coffee Substitutes (ND)

Includes:

- Coffee, whether or not decaffeinated, roasted or ground, including instant coffee
- Coffee substitutes
- Extracts, essences, and concentrates of coffee
- Coffee-based beverage preparations

Includes also:

- Roasted chicory and other roasted coffee substitutes, and extracts, essences, and concentrates thereof

Excludes:

- *Milk flavored with coffee (01.1.4.7)*

01.2.2.0 Coffee and Coffee Substitutes (ND)

Includes:

- Coffee, whether or not decaffeinated, roasted or ground, including instant coffee
- Coffee substitutes
- Extracts, essences, and concentrates of coffee
- Coffee-based beverage preparations

Includes also:

- Roasted chicory and other roasted coffee substitutes, and extracts, essences, and concentrates thereof

Excludes:

- *Milk flavored with coffee (01.1.4.7)*

01.2.3 Tea, Maté, and Other Plant Products for Infusion (ND)

Includes:

- Green tea (not fermented), black tea (fermented) and partly fermented tea, maté, and other plant products for infusion
- Tea substitutes and extracts and essences of tea

Includes also:

- Fruit and herbal tea
- Rooibos tea
- Instant tea
- Iced tea

01.2.3.0 Tea, Maté, and Other Plant Products for Infusion (ND)

Includes:

- Green tea (not fermented), black tea (fermented) and partly fermented tea, maté, and other plant products for infusion
- Tea substitutes and extracts and essences of tea

Includes also:

- Fruit and herbal tea
- Rooibos tea
- Instant tea
- Iced tea

01.2.4 Cocoa Drinks (ND)

Includes:

- Cocoa and chocolate-based drinks

Excludes:

- *Milk flavored with chocolate or cacao (01.1.4.7)*
- *Cocoa powder for all purposes; chocolate in bars or slabs; cocoa-based food and cocoa-based dessert preparations (01.1.8.5)*

01.2.4.0 Cocoa Drinks (ND)

Includes:

- Cocoa and chocolate-based drinks

Excludes:

- *Milk flavored with chocolate or cacao (01.1.4.7)*
- *Cocoa powder for all purposes; chocolate in bars or slabs; cocoa-based food and cocoa-based dessert preparations (01.1.8.5)*

01.2.5 Water (ND)

Mineral or spring waters, still or sparkling, not added with other ingredients.

Excludes:

- *Flavored water (01.2.9.0)*

01.2.5.0 Water (ND)

Mineral or spring waters, still or sparkling, not added with other ingredients.

Excludes:

- *Flavored water (01.2.9.0)*

01.2.6 Soft Drinks (ND)

Includes:

- Soft drinks, such as sodas, lemonades, and colas
- Sparkling juices

Excludes:

- *Sparkling water (01.2.5.0)*
- *Flavored water (01.2.9.0)*

01.2.6.0 Soft Drinks (ND)

Includes:

- Soft drinks, such as sodas, lemonades, and colas
- Sparkling juices

Excludes:

- *Sparkling water (01.2.5.0)*
- *Flavored water (01.2.9.0)*

01.2.9 Other Nonalcoholic Beverages (ND)
Includes:

- Flavored water
- Energy drinks, energy supplement, and protein powder for drink preparation
- Birch juice and sap, aloe vera juice, and drinks
- Syrups and concentrates for the preparation of beverages
- Other nonalcoholic beverages

01.2.9.0 Other Nonalcoholic Beverages (ND)
Includes:

- Flavored water
- Energy drinks, energy supplement, and protein powder for drink preparation
- Birch juice and sap, aloe vera juice, and drinks
- Syrups and concentrates for the preparation of beverages
- Other nonalcoholic beverages

01.3 Services for Processing Primary Goods for Food and Nonalcoholic Beverages

Services purchased for the processing of primary products provided by households to produce food and nonalcoholic beverages for own final consumption by households.

01.3.0 Services for Processing Primary Goods for Food and Nonalcoholic Beverages (S)
Services purchased for the processing of primary products provided by households to produce food and nonalcoholic beverages for own final consumption by households.

Includes:

- Grinding of cereals for flour production
- Oil pressing
- Fruit/vegetable crushing and pressing services for the production of juices

Excludes:

- *Food processing for business purpose (not in the scope of COICOP)*
- *Fruit/vegetable crushing and pressing services for the production of alcoholic beverages (02.2.1.0)*

01.3.0.0 Services for Processing Primary Goods for Food and Nonalcoholic Beverages (S)

Services purchased for the processing of primary products provided by households to produce food and nonalcoholic beverages for own final consumption by households.

Includes:

- Grinding of cereals for flour production
- Oil pressing
- Fruit/vegetable crushing and pressing services for the production of juices

Excludes:

- *Food processing for business purpose (not in the scope of COICOP)*
- *Fruit/vegetable crushing and pressing services for the production of alcoholic beverages (02.2.1.0)*

02 Alcoholic Beverages, Tobacco, and Narcotics

Division 02 covers the purchase of alcoholic beverages and of tobacco products and narcotics, regardless of where these are consumed but not provided as part of a food and beverage serving service.

It also includes low and nonalcoholic beverages, which are generally alcoholic, such as nonalcoholic beer. Services for the production of alcohol for own consumption are also included in this division.

Division 02 excludes alcoholic beverages purchased for immediate consumption in hotels, restaurants, cafes, bars, kiosks, street vendors, automatic vending machines, and so on (11.1.1).

02.1 Alcoholic Beverages

The beverages classified here include low or nonalcoholic beverages which generally contain some alcohol.

02.1.1 Spirits and Liquors (ND)
Includes:

- Eaux-de-vie, liqueurs, and other spirits with high alcohol content
- Mead
- Pomace brandy, such as pisco, grappa, marc, and so on
- Aperitifs other than wine-based aperitifs

Excludes:

- *Wine-based aperitifs (02.1.2.1, 02.1.2.2)*

02.1.1.0 Spirits and Liquors (ND)
Includes:

- Eaux-de-vie, liqueurs, and other spirits with high alcohol content
- Mead
- Pomace brandy, such as pisco, grappa, marc, and so on
- Aperitifs other than wine-based aperitifs

Excludes:

- *Wine-based aperitifs (02.1.2.1, 02.1.2.2)*

02.1.2 Wine (ND)
Includes:

- Wine, cider, and perry, including sake
- Wine-based aperitifs, fortified wines, champagne, and other sparkling wines
- Ice wine
- Low and nonalcoholic wine
- Wine-based aperitifs

02.1.2.1 Wine from Grapes (ND)
Includes:

- Wine from grapes
- Fortified wines, such as vermouth, sherry, port wine

- Champagne and other sparkling wines from grapes
- Ice wine
- Low and nonalcoholic wine
- Wine-based aperitifs

02.1.2.2 Wine from Other Sources (ND)

Includes:

- Cider and perry, including sake

02.1.3 Beer (ND)

Includes:

- All kinds of beer, such as ale, lager, stout, and porter
- Low-alcoholic beer and nonalcoholic beer

02.1.3.0 Beer (ND)

Includes:

- All kinds of beer, such as ale, lager, stout, and porter
- Low-alcoholic beer and nonalcoholic beer

02.1.9 Other Alcoholic Beverages (ND)

Includes:

- Mixed alcoholic-based drinks, such as soda water or mineral water-based mixed alcoholic drinks (alcopops)
- Shandy, cola beer, radler

02.1.9.0 Other Alcoholic Beverages (ND)

Includes:

- Mixed alcoholic-based drinks, such as soda water or mineral water-based mixed alcoholic drinks (alcopops)
- Shandy, cola beer, Radler

02.2 Alcohol Production Services

Services purchased for the processing of primary products provided by households to produce alcohol for own final consumption by households.

02.2.1 Alcohol Production Services (S)

Services purchased for the processing of primary products provided by households to produce alcohol for own final consumption by households.

Includes:

- Fruit/vegetable crushing and pressing services for the production of alcoholic beverages
- Distilling and fermentation services
- Brewing services
- Aging and bottling services

02.2.1.0 Alcohol Production Services (S)

Services purchased for the processing of primary products provided by households to produce alcohol for own final consumption by households.

Includes:

- Fruit/vegetable crushing and pressing services for the production of alcoholic beverages
- Distilling and fermentation services
- Brewing services
- Aging and bottling services

02.3 Tobacco

This group covers all purchases of tobacco and tobacco products by households, including purchases of tobacco in restaurants, cafés, bars, service stations, and so on due to these venues not adding value, or a service, to the tobacco products sold. The consumption of tobacco through shisha or hookah pipes in these venues, such as restaurants, cafés, or bars, is included in Division 11 as the venue does provide a service. Electronic cigarette refills are included in this group—even though they do not contain tobacco—as they are a substitute for smoking tobacco products.

02.3.0 Tobacco (ND)

Includes:

- Cigarettes, cigarette tobacco, and tobacco leaf
- Cigarette papers and single-use filters that are consumed with the cigarette
- Cigars, pipe tobacco, chewing tobacco or snuff
- Refills for electronic cigarettes with or without nicotine
- Tobacco that is consumed with a shisha or hookah pipes if consumed at home
- Tobacco that is purchased in bars and restaurants, provided that a service charge is not applied

Excludes:

- *Tobacco that is consumed with a shisha or hookah pipes in restaurants, cafés, shisha lounges (11.1.1)*
- *Other smokers' articles; electronic cigarette devices (13.2.9.1)*

02.3.0.1 Cigarettes (ND)

Includes:

- Cigarettes
- Cigarettes that are purchased in bars and restaurants, provided that a service charge is not applied

02.3.0.2 Cigars (ND)

Includes:

- Cigars

02.3.0.9 Other Tobacco Products (ND)

Includes:

- Pipe tobacco, chewing tobacco, hookah blends, snus or snuff
- Cigarette tobacco and tobacco leaf
- Cigarette papers and single-use filters that are consumed with the cigarette
- Refills for electronic cigarettes with or without nicotine
- Tobacco that is consumed with a shisha or hookah pipes if consumed at home

Excludes:

- *Tobacco that is consumed with a shisha or hookah pipes in restaurants, cafés, shisha lounges (11.1.1)*

- *Other smokers' articles; electronic cigarette devices (13.2.9.1)*

02.4 Narcotics
This group covers all narcotics purchased by households, both legal and illegal.

02.4.0 Narcotics (ND)
Includes:

- Marijuana, opium, cocaine, and their derivatives
- Other vegetable-based narcotics, such as cola nuts, kava, chat, betel leaves, psilocybin mushroom, and betel nuts
- Other narcotics including chemicals and man-made drugs

Excludes:

- *Prepared joints and pipes containing marijuana, hashish or similar purchased in coffee shops for immediate consumption (11.1.1.1)*
- *Narcotics for medicinal purpose (06.1.1)*

02.4.0.0 Narcotics (ND)
Includes:

- Marijuana, opium, cocaine, and their derivatives
- Other vegetable-based narcotics, such as cola nuts, kava, chat, betel leaves, psilocybin mushroom, and betel nuts
- Other narcotics including chemicals and man-made drugs

Excludes:

- *Prepared joints and pipes containing marijuana, hashish or similar purchased in coffee shops for immediate consumption (11.1.1)*
- *Narcotics for medicinal purpose (06.1.1.1)*

03 Clothing and Footwear
Division 03 covers all clothing materials, garments, articles and accessories, footwear, and related services including cleaning, repair, and hire of clothing and footwear. The purchase of second-hand clothing and footwear should be included in the same classes as the new articles as the purpose is the same. Unisex garments and footwear should be classified according to the gender of the person wearing them.

Division 03 excludes sport—and game-specific sports—and footwear (09.2.2.1).

03.1 Clothing
The clothing classified in this group covers materials purchased to be transformed into clothing, garments and accessories, and services related to clothing.

Made-to-measure refers to the service of providing custom-fitted clothing when the retailer supplies all of the materials and is included in 03.1.2 Garments as the cost of the garment usually outweighs the cost of the service. Tailoring refers to creating clothing garments where the main material is supplied by the customer and is classified in 03.1.4. Cleaning, repair, tailoring, and hire of clothing as the service is the higher expenditure.

03.1.1 Clothing Materials (SD)
Includes:

- Clothing materials of natural fibers, of man-made fibers and of their mixtures
- Leather, fur, fusible webbing, wadding, and felt filling for making wearing apparel

Excludes:

- *Furnishing fabrics (05.2.1.1)*

03.1.1.0 Clothing Materials (SD)
Includes:

- Clothing materials of natural fibers, of man-made fibers, and of their mixtures
- Leather, fur, fusible webbing, wadding, and felt filling for making wearing apparel

Excludes:

- *Furnishing fabrics (05.2.1.1)*

03.1.2 Garments (SD)
Includes:

- Garments for men or boys, women or girls, and infants, either ready-to-wear or made-to-measure, in all materials (including leather, furs, plastics, and rubber), for everyday wear, for sport, or for work
- Capes, overcoats, raincoats, anoraks, parkas, blousons, jackets, trousers, waistcoats, suits, costumes, dresses, skirts, and so on
- Shirts, blouses, pullovers, sweaters, cardigans, shorts, swimsuits, tracksuits, jogging suits, sweatshirts, T-shirts, leotards, and so on
- Vests, underpants, socks, stockpiles, tights, petticoats, brassières, knickers, slips, girdles, corsets, body stockpiles, and so on
- Pajamas, nightshirts, nightdresses, housecoats, dressing gowns, bathrobes, and so on
- Traditional garments

Excludes:

- *Tailoring services when the customer supplies the material (03.1.4.2)*
- *Articles of medical hosiery, such as elasticated stockpiles (06.1.2.2)*
- *Babies' napkins (13.2.9.1)*

03.1.2.1 Garments for Men or Boys (SD)
Includes:

- Garments for men or boys, either ready-to-wear or made-to-measure, in all materials (including leather, furs, plastics, and rubber), for everyday wear, for sport, or for work
- Capes, overcoats, raincoats, anoraks, parkas, jackets, trousers, waistcoats, suits, costumes, and so on
- Shirts, pullovers, sweaters, cardigans, shorts, swimsuits, tracksuits, jogging suits, sweatshirts, T-shirts, leotards, and so on
- Traditional garments

- Vests, underpants, socks, and so on
- Pajamas, dressing gowns, bathrobes, and so on

Excludes:

- *Garments for infants (0 to under 2 years) (03.1.2.3)*
- *Tailoring services when the customer supplies the material (03.1.4.2)*

03.1.2.2 Garments for Women or Girls (SD)

Includes:

- Garments for women or girls, either ready-to-wear or made-to-measure, in all materials (including leather, furs, plastics, and rubber), for everyday wear, for sport, or for work
- Capes, overcoats, raincoats, anoraks, parkas, blousons, jackets, trousers, waistcoats, suits, costumes, dresses, skirts, and so on
- Shirts, blouses, pullovers, sweaters, cardigans, shorts, swimsuits, tracksuits, jogging suits, sweatshirts, T-shirts, leotards, and so on
- Traditional garments
- Vests, underpants, socks, stockpiles, tights, petticoats, brassières, knickers, slips, girdles, corsets, body stockpiles, and so on
- Pajamas, nightshirts, nightdresses, housecoats, dressing gowns, bathrobes, and so on

Excludes:

- *Garments for infants (0 to under 2 years) (03.1.2.3)*
- *Tailoring services when the customer supplies the material (03.1.4.2)*

03.1.2.3 Garments for Infants (0 to under 2 Years) (SD)

Includes:

- Garments for infants and babies (0 to under 2 years), either ready-to-wear or made-to-measure, in all materials
- Raincoats, anoraks, parkas, blousons, jackets, trousers, waistcoats, suits, costumes, dresses, skirts, and so on
- Vests, underpants, socks, stockpiles, tights, and so on
- Pajamas, nightshirts, nightdresses, dressing gowns, bathrobes, and so on

Excludes:

- *Tailoring services when the customer supplies the material (03.1.4.2)*

03.1.2.4 School Uniforms (SD)

Includes:

- School uniforms

03.1.3 Other Articles of Clothing and Clothing Accessories (SD)

Includes:

- Ties, handkerchiefs, scarves, gloves, mittens, muffs, belts, braces, aprons, smocks, bibs, sleeve protectors, hats, caps, berets, bonnets, and so on
- Sewing threads, knitting yarns, and accessories for making clothing, such as buckles, buttons, press studs, zip fasteners, ribbons, laces, trimmings, and so on

Includes also:

- *Working gloves*

Excludes:

- Pins, safety pins, sewing needles, knitting needles, thimbles; rubber gloves and other articles made of rubber; gardening gloves (05.6.1.9)
- Protective headgear for sports; other protective gear for sports, such as life jackets, boxing and other sporting gloves, body padding, belts, supports, and so on (09.2.2.1)
- Paper handkerchiefs (13.1.2.0)
- Watches, jewelry, cuff links, tiepins (13.2.1.1)
- Walking sticks and canes, umbrellas and parasols, fans, and keyrings (13.2.9.1)

03.1.3.1 Other Articles of Clothing (SD)

Includes:

- Ties, handkerchiefs, scarves, gloves, mittens, muffs, belts, braces, aprons, smocks, bibs, sleeve protectors, hats, caps, berets, bonnets, and so on

Includes also:

- Working gloves

Excludes:

- *Pins, safety pins, sewing needles, knitting needles, thimbles; rubber gloves and other articles made of rubber; and gardening gloves (05.6.1.9)*
- *Protective headgear for sports; other protective gear for sports, such as life jackets, boxing and other sporting gloves, body padding, belts, supports, and so on (09.2.2.1)*
- *Paper handkerchiefs (13.1.2.0)*
- *Watches, jewelry, cuff links, tiepins (13.2.1.1)*
- *Walking sticks and canes, umbrellas and parasols, fans, keyrings (13.2.9.1)*

03.1.3.2 Clothing Accessories (SD)

Includes:

- Sewing threads, knitting yarns, and accessories for making clothing, such as buckles, buttons, press studs, zip fasteners, ribbons, laces, trimmings, and so on

03.1.4 Cleaning, Repair, Tailoring, and Hire of Clothing (S)

The cost of materials is included only if the materials are not separately invoiced.

Includes:

- Dry-cleaning, laundering, and dyeing of garments
- Darning, mending, repair, and altering of garments
- Tailoring services when the customer supplies the material
- Hire of garments

Excludes:

- *Materials, threads, and other accessories purchased by households with the intention of undertaking the repairs themselves (03.1.1.0, 03.1.3.2)*

- *Made-to-measure clothing (03.1.2.1, 03.1.2.2, 03.1.2.3, 03.1.2.4)*
- *Repair of household linen and other household textiles (05.2.2.0)*
- *Dry-cleaning, laundering, dyeing and hire of household linen, and other household textiles (05.6.2.9)*

03.1.4.1 Cleaning of Clothing (S)

Includes:

- Dry-cleaning, laundering, and dyeing of garments

Excludes:

- Dry-cleaning, laundering, dyeing, and hire of household linen, and other household textiles (05.6.2.9)

03.1.4.2 Repair, Tailoring, and Hire of Clothing (S)

The cost of materials is included only if the materials are not separately invoiced.

Includes:

- Darning, mending, repair, and altering of garments
- Tailoring services when the customer supplies the material
- Hire of garments

Excludes:

- *Materials, threads, and other accessories purchased by households with the intention of undertaking the repairs themselves (03.1.1.0, 03.1.3.2)*
- *Made-to measure clothing (03.1.2.1, 03.1.2.2, 03.1.2.3, 03.1.2.4)*
- *Repair of household linen and other household textiles (05.2.2.0)*

03.2 Footwear

This group covers all general footwear, split by footwear for men, footwear for women, and footwear for infants and children, and footwear-related services. Sport-specific footwear is classified in Division 09 Recreation and Culture.

03.2.1 Shoes and Other Footwear (SD)

Includes:

- All footwear for men, women, infants, and children either ready-to-wear or made-to-measure including sports footwear suitable for everyday or leisure wear (shoes for jogging, cross-training, tennis, basketball, boating, and so on)
- Gaiters and similar articles; shoelaces; parts of footwear, such as heels, soles, and so on, purchased by households with the intention of repairing footwear themselves

Excludes:

- *Polishes, creams, and other shoe-cleaning articles (05.6.1.1)*
- *Orthopedic footwear (06.1.3.3)*
- *Game-specific footwear (ski boots, football boots, golfing shoes, and other such footwear fitted with ice skates, rollers, spikes, studs, and so on); shin guards, cricket pads, and other such protective apparel for sport (09.2.2.1)*

03.2.1.1 Footwear for Men (SD)

Includes:

- All footwear for men either ready-to-wear or made-to-measure

Includes also:

- Gaiters and similar articles
- Shoelaces
- Parts of footwear, such as heels, soles, and so on, purchased by households with the intention of repairing footwear themselves
- Sports footwear suitable for everyday or leisure wear (shoes for jogging, cross-training, tennis, basketball, boating, and so on)

Excludes:

- *Cleaning, repair, and hire of footwear (03.2.2.0)*
- *Polishes, creams, and other shoe-cleaning articles (05.6.1.1)*
- *Orthopedic footwear (06.1.3.3)*
- *Game-specific footwear (ski boots, football boots, golfing shoes, and other such footwear fitted with ice skates, rollers, spikes, studs, and so on); shin guards, cricket pads, and other such protective apparel for sport (09.2.2.1)*

03.2.1.2 Footwear for Women (SD)

Includes:

- All footwear for women either ready-to-wear or made-to-measure

Includes also:

- Gaiters and similar articles
- Shoelaces
- Parts of footwear, such as heels, soles, and so on, purchased by households with the intention of repairing footwear themselves
- Sports footwear suitable for everyday or leisure wear (shoes for jogging, cross-training, tennis, basketball, boating, and so on)

Excludes:

- *Cleaning, repair, and hire of footwear (03.2.2.0)*
- *Polishes, creams, and other shoe-cleaning articles (05.6.1.1)*
- *Orthopedic footwear (06.1.3.3)*
- *Game-specific footwear (ski boots, football boots, golfing shoes, and other such footwear fitted with ice skates, rollers, spikes, studs, and so on); shin guards, cricket pads, and other such protective apparel for sport (09.2.2.1)*

03.2.1.3 Footwear for Infants and Children (SD)

Includes:

- All footwear for infants and children (under 13 years) either ready-to-wear or made-to-measure

Includes also:

- Gaiters and similar articles
- Shoelaces

- Parts of footwear, such as heels, soles, and so on, purchased by households with the intention of repairing footwear themselves
- Sports footwear suitable for everyday or leisure wear (shoes for jogging cross-training, tennis, basketball, boating, and so on)
- Baby's booties made of fabric or sheepskin

Excludes:

- *Cleaning, repair, and hire of footwear (03.2.2.0)*
- *Polishes, creams, and other shoe-cleaning articles (05.6.1.1)*
- *Orthopedic footwear (06.1.3.3)*
- *Game-specific footwear (ski boots, football boots, golfing shoes, and other such footwear fitted with ice skates, rollers, spikes, studs, and so on); shin guards, cricket pads, and other such protective apparel for sport (09.2.2.1)*

03.2.2 Cleaning, Repair, and Hire of Footwear (S)

The cost of materials is included only if the materials are not separately invoiced.

Includes:

- Repair of footwear
- Shoe-cleaning services
- Dyeing of shoes
- Hire of footwear

Excludes:

- *Parts of footwear, such as heels, soles, and so on, purchased by households with the intention of undertaking the repair themselves (03.2.1)*
- *Polishes, creams, and other shoe-cleaning articles (05.6.1.1)*
- *Hire and repair of game-specific footwear (ski boots, football boots, golfing shoes, and other such footwear fitted with ice skates, rollers, spikes, studs, and so on) (09.4.4.0)*

03.2.2.0 Cleaning, Repair, and Hire of Footwear (S)

The cost of materials is included only if the materials are not separately invoiced.

Includes:

- Repair of footwear
- Shoe-cleaning services
- Dyeing of shoes
- Hire of footwear

Excludes:

- *Parts of footwear, such as heels, soles, and so on, purchased by households with the intention of undertaking the repair themselves (03.2.1)*
- *Polishes, creams, and other shoe-cleaning articles (05.6.1.1)*
- *Hire and repair of game-specific footwear (ski boots, football boots, golfing shoes, and other such footwear fitted with ice skates, rollers, spikes, studs, and so on) (09.4.4.0)*

04 Housing, Water, Electricity, Gas, and Other Fuels

The "Housing, water, electricity, gas, and other fuels" division comprises goods and services for the use of the house or dwelling, its maintenance and repair, the supply of water and miscellaneous services related to the dwelling, and energy used for heating or cooling. Actual rentals and imputed rentals (according to national accounts [*SNA 2008*]) for main or secondary residences are classified in groups 04.1 and 04.2, respectively.

Maintenance, repair, and security of the dwelling include materials for repair purchased with the intention of undertaking the repair and maintenance themselves, as well as the repair services purchased from enterprises. It should be noted that only expenditures on materials and services for minor repairs are covered by 04.3. Expenditures on materials and services for major maintenance and repair are not part of individual consumption expenditures of households and are thus out of the scope of the classification. This refers especially to owner-occupiers; tenants will not make such expenditures on major maintenance and repair at all as they are not the owner of the dwelling.

04.1 Actual Rentals for Housing

Rentals normally include payment for the use of the land on which the property stands, the dwelling occupied, the fixtures and fittings for heating, plumbing, lighting, and so on, and, in the case of a dwelling let furnished, the furniture.

Rentals also include payment for the use of a garage to provide parking in connection with the dwelling.

The garage does not have to be physically contiguous to the dwelling, nor does it have to be leased from the same landlord.

Rentals do not include payment for the use of garages or parking spaces not providing parking in connection with the dwelling (07.2.4). Nor do they include charges for water supply (04.4.1), refuse collection (04.4.2), and sewage collection (04.4.3); coproprietor charges for caretaking, gardening, stairwell cleaning, heating and lighting, maintenance of lifts and refuse disposal chutes, and so on in multi-occupied buildings (04.4.4); charges for electricity (04.5.1) and gas (04.5.2); and charges for heating and hot water supplied by district heating plants (04.5.5).

Each household has a principal dwelling (sometimes also designated as main or primary home), usually defined with reference to time spent there, whose location defines the country of residence and place of usual residence of this household and of all its members. All other dwellings (owned or leased by the household) are considered secondary dwellings.

Includes:

- Rentals actually paid by tenants or subtenants occupying unfurnished or furnished premises as their main residence

Includes also:

- Payments by households occupying a room in a hotel or boarding house as their main residence

Excludes:

- *Garage rentals to provide parking and storage in connection with the dwelling (04.1.2.2)*

- *Accommodation services of educational establishments and hostels (11.2.0.9)*
- *Retirement homes for elderly persons (13.3.0.2)*

04.1.1 Actual Rentals Paid by Tenants for Main Residence (S)

Includes:

- Rentals actually paid by tenants or subtenants occupying unfurnished or furnished premises as their main residence

Includes also:

- Payments by households occupying a room in a hotel or boarding house as their main residence

Excludes:

- *Garage rentals to provide parking and storage in connection with the dwelling (04.1.2.2)*
- *Accommodation services of educational establishments and hostels (11.2.0.9)*
- *Retirement homes for elderly persons (13.3.0.2)*

04.1.1.0 Actual Rentals Paid by Tenants for Main Residence (S)

Includes:

- Rentals actually paid by tenants or subtenants occupying unfurnished or furnished premises as their main residence

Includes also:

- Payments by households occupying a room in a hotel or boarding house as their main residence

Excludes:

- *Garage rentals to provide parking and storage in connection with the dwelling (04.1.2.2)*
- *Accommodation services of educational establishments and hostels (11.2.0.9)*
- *Retirement homes for elderly persons (13.3.0.2)*

04.1.2 Other Actual Rentals (S)

Includes:

- Rentals actually paid for secondary residences
- Rentals of self-storage units
- Garage rentals

Excludes:

- *Accommodation services of holiday villages and holiday centers (11.2.0.2)*

04.1.2.1 Actual Rentals Paid by Tenants for Secondary Residences (S)

Includes:

- Rentals actually paid for secondary residences

Excludes:

- *Accommodation services of holiday villages and holiday centers (11.2.0.2)*

04.1.2.2 Garage Rentals and Other Rentals Paid by Tenants (S)

Rentals also include payment for the use of a garage to provide parking and storage in connection with the dwelling. The garage or storage does not have to be physically contiguous to the dwelling, nor does it have to be leased from the same landlord.

Includes:

- Garage rentals in connection with the dwelling
- Rentals of self-storage units

Excludes:

- *Payment for the use of garages or parking spaces not providing parking in connection with the dwelling (07.2.4.1)*
- *(Long-term) storage of furniture and other personal effects (07.4.9.1)*

04.2 Imputed Rentals for Housing

Persons who own the dwellings in which they live are treated as owning unincorporated enterprises that produce housing services that are consumed by the household to which the owner belongs. The housing services produced are deemed to be equal in value to the rentals that would be paid on the market for accommodation of the same size, quality, and type. The imputed values of the housing services are recorded as final consumption expenditures of the owners. Imputed rentals normally include value for the use of the land on which the property stands, the dwelling occupied, and the fixtures and fittings for heating, plumbing, lighting, and so on.

Imputed rentals also include the use of a garage to provide parking in connection with the dwelling. The garage does not have to be physically contiguous to the dwelling.

Imputed rentals do not include payment for the use of garages or parking spaces not providing parking in connection with the dwelling (07.2.4). Nor do they include charges for water supply (04.4.1), refuse collection (04.4.2), and sewage collection (04.4.3); coproprietor charges for caretaking, gardening, stairwell cleaning, heating and lighting, maintenance of lifts and refuse disposal chutes, and so on in multi-occupied buildings (04.4.4); charges for electricity (04.5.1) and gas (04.5.2); and charges for heating and hot water supplied by district heating plants (04.5.5).

04.2.1 Imputed Rentals of Owner-Occupiers for Main Residence (S)

Includes:

- Imputed rentals of owners occupying their main residence

04.2.1.0 Imputed Rentals of Owner-Occupiers for Main Residence (S)

Includes:

- Imputed rentals of owners occupying their main residence

04.2.2 Other Imputed Rentals (S)

Includes:

- Imputed rentals for secondary residences
- Imputed garage rentals in connection with the dwelling
- Imputed rentals of storage units

04.2.2.0 Other Imputed Rentals (S)

Includes:

- Imputed rentals for secondary residences
- Imputed garage rentals in connection with the dwelling
- Imputed rentals of storage units

04.3 Maintenance, Repair, and Security of the Dwelling

Maintenance and repair of dwellings are distinguished by two features: first, they are activities that have to be undertaken regularly in order to maintain the dwelling in good working order; second, they do not change the dwelling's performance, capacity, or expected service life.

There are two types of maintenance and repair of dwellings: those which are minor, such as interior decoration and repairs to fittings, and which are commonly carried out by both tenants and owners; and those which are major, such as replastering walls or repairing roofs, and which are carried out by owners only.

Only expenditures which tenants and owner-occupiers incur on materials and services for minor maintenance and repair are part of individual consumption expenditure of households.

Expenditures which owner-occupiers incur on materials and services for major maintenance and repair are not part of individual consumption expenditure of households.

Purchases of materials made by tenants or owner-occupiers with the intention of undertaking the maintenance or repair themselves should be shown under (04.3.1). If tenants or owner-occupiers pay an enterprise to carry out the maintenance or repair, the total value of the service, including the costs of the materials used, should be shown under (04.3.2) unless the materials are separately invoiced.

04.3.1 Materials for the Maintenance and Repair of the Dwelling (ND)

Includes:

- Products and materials, such as paints and varnishes, renderings, wallpapers, fabric wall coverings, window panes, plaster, cement, putty, wallpaper pastes, and so on, purchased for minor maintenance and repair of the dwelling
- Small plumbing items (pipes, taps, joints, and so on), surfacing materials (floorboards, ceramic tiles, and so on) and brushes and scrapers for paint, varnish, and wallpaper
- Fitted carpets and linoleum
- Door fittings, power sockets, wiring flex
- Small equipment for surveillance/security for the individual dwelling
- Door phone for dwelling
- Fire extinguishers

Excludes:

- *Hand tools (05.5.2.1)*
- *Lamp bulbs (05.5.2.2)*
- *Brooms, scrubbing brushes, dusting brushes, and cleaning products (05.6.1.1)*
- *Products, materials, and fixtures used for major maintenance and repair (intermediate consumption) or for extension and conversion of the dwelling (capital formation)*

04.3.1.1 Materials for the Maintenance Repair of the Dwelling (ND)

Includes:

- Products and materials, such as paints and varnishes, renderings, wallpapers, fabric wall coverings, window panes, plaster, cement, putty, wallpaper pastes, and so on, purchased for minor maintenance and repair of the dwelling
- Small plumbing items (pipes, taps, joints, and so on), surfacing materials (floorboards, ceramic tiles, and so on) and brushes and scrapers for paint, varnish, and wallpaper
- Fitted carpets and linoleum
- Door fittings, power sockets, wiring flex

Excludes:

- *Hand tools (05.5.2.1)*
- *Lamp bulbs (05.5.2.2)*
- *Brooms, scrubbing brushes, dusting brushes, and cleaning products (05.6.1.1)*
- *Products, materials, and fixtures used for major maintenance and repair (intermediate consumption) or for extension and conversion of the dwelling (capital formation)*

04.3.1.2 Security Equipment (SD)

Includes:

- Small equipment for surveillance/security for the individual dwelling (smoke detector, security alarms, security/surveillance cameras)
- Door phone for dwelling
- Fire extinguishers

04.3.2 Services for the Maintenance, Repair, and Security of the Dwelling (S)

The cost of materials is included only if the materials are not separately invoiced.

Includes:

- Services of plumbers, electricians, carpenters, glaziers, painters, decorators, floor polishers, and so on engaged for minor maintenance and repair of the dwelling
- Locksmith services
- Service of laying fitted carpets and linoleum
- Security services

Excludes:

- *Separate purchases of materials made by households with the intention of undertaking the maintenance or repair themselves (04.3.1.1)*
- *Locksmith services for cars (07.2.3.0)*
- *Bodyguards (13.9.0.9)*
- *Services engaged for major maintenance and repair (intermediate consumption) or for extension and conversion of the dwelling (capital formation)*

04.3.2.0 Services for the Maintenance, Repair, and Security of the Dwelling (S)

The cost of materials is included only if the materials are not separately invoiced.

Includes:

- Services of plumbers, electricians, carpenters, glaziers, painters, decorators, floor polishers, and so on engaged for minor maintenance and repair of the dwelling
- Locksmith services
- Service of laying fitted carpets and linoleum
- Security services

Excludes:

- *Separate purchases of materials made by households with the intention of undertaking the maintenance or repair themselves (04.3.1.1)*
- *Locksmith services for cars (07.2.3.0)*
- *Bodyguards (13.9.0.9)*
- *Services engaged for major maintenance and repair (intermediate consumption) or for extension and conversion of the dwelling (capital formation)*

04.4 Water Supply and Miscellaneous Services Relating to the Dwelling

04.4.1 Water Supply (ND)

Includes:

- Water supply

Includes also:

- Associated expenditure, such as rental of meters, reading of meters, standing charges, and so on

Excludes:

- *Drinking water sold in bottles or containers (01.2.5.0)*
- *Hot water or steam purchased from district heating plants (04.5.5.0)*

04.4.1.1 Water Supply through Network Systems (ND)

Includes:

- All charges usually included in the bills paid by households, including meters installations and rentals, volumetric or fix charge for water consumption through mains, except steam, and hot water (on a fee and contract basis)

Includes also:

- Associated expenditure, such as rental of meters, reading of meters, standing charges, and so on

Excludes:

- *Drinking water sold in bottles or containers (01.2.5.0)*
- *Hot water or steam purchased from district heating plants (04.5.5.0)*

04.4.1.2 Water Supply through Basic Systems (ND)

Includes:

- Services paid at a public stand post/fountain and to a water vendor (for example, by tanker truck, cart)

Excludes:

- *Drinking water sold in bottles or containers (01.2.5.0)*

04.4.2 Refuse Collection (S)

Includes:

- Refuse collection and disposal
- Fees for recycling paid by households

04.4.2.0 Refuse Collection (S)

Includes:

- Refuse collection and disposal
- Fees for recycling paid by households

04.4.3 Sewage Collection (S)

Sewer systems, also known as sanitary sewer systems, are (most often) an underground carriage system (most usually waterborne) specifically for transporting sewage from houses and commercial buildings and industries, through pipes or other conduits to treatment facilities or disposal sites. They are part of an overall system called a sewerage or sewage system.

Sewage may be treated to reduce water pollution before discharge to surface waters. Sanitary sewers serving mixed urban agglomerations (including commercial and industrial areas) carry "municipal wastewater" which comprises a mix from all sources including in some cases, surface runoff, and stormwater.

"Separate" sewer systems are designed to transport sewage alone. In municipalities served by sewers, separate storm drains may convey surface runoff directly to surface waters. "Separate" sewers are distinguished from "combined sewers," which combine sewage with stormwater runoff in the same conduit. Sanitary sewer systems are often preferred because they avoid the production of large volumes of combined wastewater flows. However, in certain circumstances, they may be preferred and reduce costs.

Basic sanitation systems are improved sanitation facilities where excreta are contained or disposed of onsite. These are generally where fecal (and other) material is collected in a pit or septic tanks or are composting toilets. Their purpose is to hygienically separate human excreta from human contact.

Includes:

- Sewage collection, emptying cesspools and disposal

04.4.3.1 Sewage Collection through Sewer Systems (S)

Includes:

- Services paid to the sanitation or water provider or municipality for the collection, transport, and disposal of sewage through sewer systems

04.4.3.2 Sewage Collection through Basic Sanitation Systems (S)

Includes:

- Services paid to empty and evacuate liquid waste (excreta and wastewater) from onsite
- Sanitation systems (pit latrines, septic tanks, and soak pits) and clean them

- Payments for using communal/commercial collective toilets

04.4.4 Other Services Relating to the Dwelling N.E.C. (S)
Includes:

- Coproprietor charges for caretaking, gardening, stairwell cleaning, heating and lighting, maintenance of lifts and refuse disposal chutes, pool cleaning, and so on in multi-occupied buildings
- Road and sidewalk cleaning and chimney sweeping
- Measuring background radiation and content of harmful substances in dwellings
- Landscaping and cleaning of grounds surrounding the dwelling
- Snow removal

Excludes:

- *Household services, such as window cleaning, disinfecting, fumigation, and pest extermination (05.6.2.9)*
- *Bodyguards (13.9.0.9)*

04.4.4.1 Maintenance Charges in Multi-Occupied Buildings (S)
Includes:

- Coproprietor charges for caretaking, gardening, stairwell cleaning, heating and lighting, maintenance of lifts and refuse disposal chutes, pool cleaning, and so on, in multi-occupied buildings

Excludes:

- *Household services, such as window cleaning, disinfecting, fumigation, and pest extermination (05.6.2.9)*
- *Bodyguards (13.9.0.9)*

04.4.4.9 Other Services Related to Dwelling (S)
Includes:

- Road and sidewalk cleaning and chimney sweeping
- Measuring background radiation and content of harmful substances in dwellings
- Landscaping and cleaning of grounds surrounding the dwelling
- Snow removal

04.5 Electricity, Gas, and Other Fuels

04.5.1 Electricity (ND)
Includes:

- Electricity from all sources (coal, solar, hydro, and so on)

Includes also:

- Associated expenditure, such as rental of meters, reading of meters, standing charges, and so on
- Charges for self-produced energy (in some countries, households producing more electricity than what they consume are charged storage costs if they feed the surplus electricity back into the electricity supply grid)

04.5.1.0 Electricity (ND)
Includes:

- Electricity from all sources (coal, solar, hydro, and so on)

Includes also:

- Associated expenditure, such as rental of meters, reading of meters, standing charges, and so on
- Charges for self-produced energy (in some countries, households producing more electricity than what they consume are charged storage costs if they feed the surplus electricity back into the electricity supply grid)

04.5.2 Gas (ND)
Includes:

- Town gas and natural gas
- Liquefied hydrocarbons (butane, propane, and so on)

Includes also:

- Associated expenditure, such as rental of meters, reading of meters, rental or purchase of storage containers, standing charges, and so on

04.5.2.1 Natural Gas through Networks (ND)
Includes:

- Natural gas and town gas delivered through gas networks
- Associated expenditure, such as rental of meters, reading of meters, standing charges, and so on

04.5.2.2 Liquefied Hydrocarbons (ND)
Includes:

- Liquefied hydrocarbons (butane, propane, and so on) delivered in storage containers
- Associated expenditure, such as rental or purchase of storage containers, standing charges, and so on

Excludes:

- *Delivery fees of liquefied hydrocarbons (butane, propane, and so on) when charged separately (07.4.9.2)*
- *Camping gas in cylinder less than 50 kilograms (09.2.2.2)*

04.5.3 Liquid Fuels (ND)
Includes:

- Domestic heating, lighting, and cooking fuel oils
- Biofuels for domestic use
- Alcohol for fireplaces

Excludes:

- *Liquid fuels for transportation (07.2.2.1, 07.2.2.2, 07.2.2.3)*

04.5.3.0 Liquid Fuels (ND)
Includes:

- Domestic heating, lighting, and cooking fuel oils
- Biofuels for domestic use
- Alcohol for fireplaces

Excludes:

- *Liquid fuels for transportation (07.2.2.1, 07.2.2.2, 07.2.2.3)*

04.5.4 Solid Fuels (ND)
Includes:

- Coal, coke, briquettes, firewood, charcoal, peat, and the like, biomass (wheat, nutshell, and so on) and dry animal dung

04.5.4.1 Coal, Coal Briquettes, and Peat (ND)
Includes:

- Coal
- Coal briquettes
- Peat
- Peat briquettes

04.5.4.2 Wood Fuel, Including Pellets and Briquettes (ND)
Includes:

- Fuelwood, in logs, in billets, in twigs, in faggots, or in similar forms
- Wood in chips or particles
- Nonagglomerated sawdust and wood waste and scrap
- Sawdust and wood waste and scrap agglomerated in briquettes, pellets, or similar forms

04.5.4.3 Charcoal (ND)
Whether or not agglomerated, in the form of blocks, sticks or in granules or powder, or agglomerated with tar or other substances in briquettes, tablets, balls, and so on.
Includes:

- Wood and bamboo charcoal
- Shell or nut charcoal
- Charcoal briquettes

Includes also:

- Charcoal briquettes for barbecue

04.5.4.9 Other Solid Fuels (ND)
Includes:

- Coke
- Other briquettes
- Other biomass n.e.c., such as waste from agricultural production (for example, wheat and nutshells) and dry animal dung

04.5.5 Other Energy for Heating and Cooling (ND)
Includes:

- Hot water and steam purchased from district heating plants
- Ice used for cooling and refrigeration purposes

Includes also:

- Associated expenditure, such as rental of meters, reading of meters, standing charges, and so on

Excludes:

- *Ice cubes (01.1.8.6)*

04.5.5.0 Other Energy for Heating and Cooling (ND)
Includes:

- Hot water and steam purchased from district heating plants
- Ice used for cooling and refrigeration purposes

Includes also:

- Associated expenditure, such as rental of meters, reading of meters, standing charges, and so on

Excludes:

- *Ice cubes (01.1.8.6)*

05 Furnishings, Household Equipment, and Routine Household Maintenance

Division 05 covers a wide range of products for the equipment of the house or dwelling and the household durables, semidurables, and nondurables as well as some kind of household services. Division 05 includes all kinds of furniture, including lighting equipment, household textiles, glassware, tableware, and household utensils, major and smaller electric household appliances, tools and equipment for house and garden, and goods for the routine household maintenance.

Division 05 also includes repair, installation, and rental services of the goods classified in Division 05.

Domestic services by paid staff in private service, supplied by enterprises or self-employed persons are also included. Furthermore, window cleaning and disinfecting services, as well as dry-cleaning and laundering of household textiles and carpets, are classified in Division 05.

05.1 Furniture, Furnishings, and Loose Carpets

05.1.1 Furniture, Furnishings, and Loose Carpets (D)
Includes:

- Sofas, couches, tables, chairs, cupboards, chests of drawers and bookshelves, hanger stands, and coat stands
- Bunk bed, baby furniture, such as cradles, highchairs, and playpens
- Beds, mattresses, base mattresses (tatamis), wardrobes, and bedside tables
- Kitchen tables and chairs, cupboards, and surfaces
- Furniture primarily for bathroom use
- Furniture primarily for garden use
- Wrought iron benches and tables, arbors
- Small garden houses to store garden tools and machines
- Camping furniture
- Lighting equipment, such as ceiling lights, standard lamps, globe lights and bedside lamps, light, and LED strings

Includes also:

- Inflatable sofas, armchairs, and beds
- Pieces of furniture specifically made for the customer
- Rugs (loose) carpets

- Pictures, sculptures, engravings, tapestries, and other art objects including reproductions of works of art and other ornaments
- Statuettes and other decorative articles of porcelain and crystal glass
- Wall clocks, alarm clocks, travel clocks
- Screens, folding partitions, nontextile blinds, mirrors, candleholders, and candlesticks
- Decorative materials for gardens
- Leather and fur for upholstery and room decorating

Excludes:

- *Decorative materials for gardens (05.1.1.4)*
- *Repair and hire of household, garden, and camping furniture and lighting equipment (05.1.2.0)*
- *Bedding (bed linen) and sunshades (05.2.1.2, 05.2.1.9)*
- *Safes (05.3.1.9)*
- *Ornamental glass and ceramic articles (05.4.0.1)*
- *Light bulbs, tubes, LEDs (05.5.2.2)*
- *Delivery and installation of loose carpets and other furniture and furnishings if charged separately (07.4.9.2)*
- *Light strings for Christmas tree (09.2.1.3)*
- *Camping equipment (09.2.2.2)*
- *Carrycots and pushchairs/strollers; wall thermometers and barometers (13.2.9.1)*
- *Works of art and antique furniture acquired primarily as stores of value (capital formation)*

05.1.1.1 Household Furniture (D)

Includes:

- Sofas, couches, tables, chairs, cupboards, chests of drawers and bookshelves, hanger stands, and coat stands
- Bunk bed, baby furniture, such as cradles, highchairs, and playpens
- Beds, mattresses, base-mattresses (tatamis), wardrobes, and bedside tables
- Kitchen tables and chairs, cupboards, and surfaces
- Furniture primarily for bathroom use

Includes also:

- Inflatable sofas, armchairs, and beds
- Pieces of furniture specifically made for the customer

Excludes:

- *Repair and hire of household furniture (05.1.2.0)*
- *Antique furniture acquired primarily as stores of value (capital formation)*

05.1.1.2 Garden and Camping Furniture (D)

Includes:

- Furniture primarily for gardens use
- Wrought iron benches and tables, arbors
- Small garden houses to store garden tools and machines
- Camping furniture

Includes also:

- Pieces of furniture specifically made for the customer

Excludes:

- *Decorative materials for gardens (05.1.1.4)*
- *Repair and hire of garden and camping furniture (05.1.2.0)*
- *Camping equipment (09.2.2.2)*

05.1.1.3 Lighting Equipment (D)

Includes:

- Lighting equipment, such as ceiling lights, standard lamps, globe lights and bedside lamps, light, and LED strings

Excludes:

- *Repair and hire of lighting equipment (05.1.2.0)*
- *Light bulbs, tubes, LEDs (05.5.2.2)*
- *Light strings for Christmas tree (09.2.1.3)*

05.1.1.4 Furnishings, Loose Carpets, and Rugs (D)

Includes:

- Rugs (loose) carpets
- Pictures, sculptures, engravings, tapestries, and other art objects including reproductions of works of art and other ornaments
- Statuettes and other decorative articles of porcelain and crystal glass
- Wall clocks, alarm clocks, and travel clocks
- Screens, folding partitions, nontextile blinds, mirrors, candleholders, and candlesticks
- Decorative materials for gardens
- Leather and fur for upholstery and room decorating

Excludes:

- *Fitted carpets and linoleum (04.3.1.1)*
- *Repair and hire of loose carpets and other furniture and furnishings (05.1.2.0)*
- *Bedding (bed linen) and sunshades (05.2.1.2, 05.2.1.9)*
- *Safes (05.3.1.9)*
- *Ornamental glass and ceramic articles (05.4.0.1)*
- *Charges for the delivery of furniture (when charged separately) (07.4.9.2)*
- *Carrycots and pushchairs/strollers; wall thermometers and barometers (13.2.9.1)*
- *Works of art acquired primarily as stores of value (capital formation)*

05.1.2 Repair, Installation, and Hire of Furniture; Furnishings; and Loose Carpets (S)

The cost of materials is included only if the materials are not separately invoiced.

Includes:

- Repair of furniture, furnishings, and loose carpets
- Restoration of works of art, antique furniture, and antique floor coverings other than those acquired primarily as stores of value (capital formation)

- Charges for the hire of furniture, furnishings, and loose carpets
- Charges for the installation of furniture (when charged separately)

Excludes:

- *Laying and repair of fitted carpets, linoleum, and other such floor coverings (04.3.2.0)*
- *Separate purchases of materials made by households with the intention of undertaking the repair themselves (05.1.1)*
- *Dry-cleaning and shampooing of carpets (05.6.2.9)*

05.1.2.0 Repair, Installation, and Hire of Furniture; Furnishings; and Loose Carpets (S)

The cost of materials is included only if the materials are not separately invoiced.

Includes:

- Repair of furniture, furnishings, and loose carpets
- Restoration of works of art, antique furniture, and antique floor coverings other than those acquired primarily as stores of value (capital formation)
- Charges for the hire of furniture, furnishings, and loose carpets
- Charges for the installation of furniture (when charged separately)

Excludes:

- *Laying and repair of fitted carpets, linoleum, and other such floor coverings (04.3.2.0)*
- *Separate purchases of materials made by households with the intention of undertaking the repair themselves (05.1.1)*
- *Dry-cleaning and shampooing of carpets (05.6.2.9)*

05.2 Household Textiles

05.2.1 Household Textiles (SD)

Includes:

- Furnishing fabrics, curtain material, curtains, double curtains, awnings, door curtains, and fabric blinds
- Bedding, such as futons, pillows, bolsters, and hammocks
- Bed linen, such as sheets, pillowcases, blankets, traveling rugs, plaids, eiderdowns, counterpanes, and mosquito nets
- Table linen and bathroom linen, such as tablecloths, table napkins, towels, and face cloths
- Other household textiles, such as shopping bags, laundry bags, shoe bags, covers for clothes and furniture, flags, sunshades, and so on
- Oilcloth; bathroom mats, rush mats, and doormats, material costs of made-to-measure household textiles

Includes also:

- Feather and other fillers for pillows

Excludes:

- *Fabric wall coverings (04.3.1.1)*
- *Floor coverings, such as loose carpets; tapestries (05.1.1.4)*
- *Repair and sewing services of household textiles (05.2.2.0)*
- *Electric blankets (05.3.2.9)*
- *Covers for motor cars, motorcycles, and so on (07.2.1.3)*
- *Air mattresses and sleeping bags (09.2.2.2)*

05.2.1.1 Furnishing Fabrics and Curtains (SD)

Includes:

- Furnishing fabrics, curtain material, curtains, double curtains, awnings, door curtains, and fabric blinds

Excludes:

- *Repair and sewing services of curtains (05.2.2.0)*

05.2.1.2 Bed Linen (SD)

Includes:

- Bed linen, such as sheets, pillowcases, blankets, traveling rugs, plaids, eiderdowns, counterpanes, and mosquito nets

Excludes:

- *Repair and sewing services of bed linen (05.2.2.0)*
- *Electric blankets (05.3.2.9)*
- *Air mattresses and sleeping bags (09.2.2.2)*

05.2.1.3 Table Linen and Bathroom Linen (SD)

Includes:

- Table linen and bathroom linen, such as tablecloths, table napkins, towels, and face cloths

Excludes:

- *Repair and sewing services of table linen and bathroom linen (05.2.2.0)*

05.2.1.9 Other Household Textiles (SD)

Includes:

- Other household textiles, such as shopping bags, laundry bags, shoe bags, covers for clothes and furniture, flags, sunshades, and so on
- Bedding, such as futons, pillows, bolsters, and hammocks
- Oilcloth
- Bathroom mats, rush mats, and doormats

Includes also:

- Feather and other fillers for pillows

Excludes:

- *Fabric wall coverings (04.3.1.1)*
- *Floor coverings, such as loose carpets; tapestries (05.1.1.4)*
- *Repair and sewing services of other household textiles (05.2.2.0)*
- *Covers for motor cars, motorcycles, and so on (07.2.1.3)*

05.2.2 Repair, Hire, and Sewing Services of Household Textiles (S)

The cost of materials is included only if the materials are not separately invoiced.

Includes:

- Repair of household textiles
- Sewing services of household textiles
- Charges for the hire of household textiles

05.2.2.0 Repair, Hire, and Sewing Services of Household Textiles (S)

The cost of materials is included only if the materials are not separately invoiced.

Includes:

- Repair of household textiles
- Sewing services of household textiles
- Charges for the hire of household textiles

05.3 Household Appliances

05.3.1 Major Household Appliances, Whether Electric or Not (D)

Includes:

- Refrigerators and dual temperature refrigerators
- Dishwashers
- Electric/gas/oil/ceramic/induction panels, hobs, spit roasters, electric/gas/convection ovens, combined cookers, and microwave ovens
- Extractor hoods

Includes also:

- Delivery and installation of the appliances when applicable and when not charged separately
- Separate purchases of parts/materials made by households with the intention of undertaking the repair themselves
- Washing machines, dryers, drum dryers, drying cabinets, drying radiators
- Ironing machines and electric mangles
- Air-conditioners, humidifiers, space heaters, water heaters, and ventilators
- Vacuum cleaners, steam-cleaning machines, carpet shampooing machines, and machines for scrubbing, waxing, and polishing floors
- Other major household appliances, such as safes, sewing machines, knitting machines, water softeners, and so on

Excludes:

- *Repair or hire of major household appliances (05.3.3.0)*
- *Such appliances that are built into the structure of the building (capital formation)*

05.3.1.1 Major Kitchen Appliances (D)

Includes:

- Refrigerators and dual temperature refrigerators
- Dishwashers
- Electric/gas/oil/ceramic/induction panels, hobs, spit roasters, electric/gas/convection ovens, combined cookers, and microwave ovens
- Extractor hoods

Excludes:

- *Repair or hire of major kitchen appliances (05.3.3.0)*

05.3.1.2 Major Laundry Appliances (D)

Includes:

- Washing machines, dryers, drum dryers, drying cabinets, and drying radiators
- Ironing machines and electric mangles

Excludes:

- *Repair or hire of laundry appliances (05.3.3.0)*

05.3.1.3 Heaters, Air-Conditioners (D)

Includes:

- Air-conditioners, humidifiers, space heaters, water heaters, and ventilators

Excludes:

- *Repair or hire of these appliances (05.3.3.0)*

05.3.1.4 Cleaning Equipment (D)

Includes:

- Vacuum cleaners, steam-cleaning machines, carpet shampooing machines, and machines for scrubbing, waxing, and polishing floors

Excludes:

- *Repair or hire of cleaning equipment (05.3.3.0)*

05.3.1.9 Other Major Household Appliances (D)

Includes:

- Other major household appliances, such as safes, sewing machines, knitting machines, water softeners, and so on

Excludes:

- *Repair or hire of major household appliances (05.3.3.0)*

05.3.2 Small Electric Household Appliances (SD)

Includes:

- Multifunction machine, food mixers, blenders, and blenders with heating elements
- Slicing machines
- Rice cookers, slow cookers
- Toasters
- Sandwich grills
- Meat and fish grills
- Deep fryers
- Ice cream makers
- Sorbet makers
- Yogurt makers
- Hotplates
- Can openers
- Electric knives
- Coffee machines
- Tea makers
- Water boilers
- Kettles
- Coffee mills
- Juice extractors
- Electric irons
- Fans
- Electric blankets

Excludes:

- *Ironing machines (05.3.1.2)*
- *Repair or hire of small electric household appliances (05.3.3.0)*
- *Small nonelectric household articles and kitchen utensils; household scales (05.4.0.3)*
- *Baby scales (06.1.2.1)*
- *Personal weighing machines (13.1.2.0)*

05.3.2.1 Small Electric Appliances for Cooking and Processing of Food (SD)

Includes:

- Multifunction machine, food mixers, blenders, and blenders with heating elements
- Slicing machines
- Rice cookers, slow cookers
- Toasters
- Sandwich grills
- Meat and fish grills
- Deep fryers
- Ice cream makers
- Sorbet makers
- Yogurt makers
- Hotplates
- Can openers
- Electric knives

Excludes:

- *Repair or hire of food processing appliances (05.3.3.0)*

05.3.2.2 Small Electric Appliances for Preparing Beverages (SD)

Includes:

- Coffee machines
- Tea makers
- Water boilers
- Kettles
- Coffee mills
- Sparkling water makers
- Juice extractors

Excludes:

- *Repair or hire of coffee machines, tea makers, and similar appliances (05.3.3.0)*

05.3.2.9 Other Small Electric Household Appliances (SD)

Includes:

- Electric irons
- Fans
- Electric blankets

Excludes:

- *Ironing machines (05.3.1.2)*
- *Repair or hire of irons (05.3.3.0)*
- *Small nonelectric household articles and kitchen utensils (05.4.0.3)*
- *Household scales (05.4.0.3)*
- *Personal weighing machines (13.1.2.0)*
- *Baby scales (06.1.2.1)*

05.3.3 Repair, Installation, and Hire of Household Appliances (S)

The cost of materials is included only if the materials are not separately invoiced.

Includes:

- Repair of household appliances
- Charges for the hire of major household appliance
- Charges for the installation of household appliances (if charged separately)

Excludes:

- *Separate purchases of materials made by households with the intention of undertaking the repair themselves (05.3.1)*

05.3.3.0 Repair, Installation, and Hire of Household Appliances (S)

The cost of materials is included only if the materials are not separately invoiced.

Includes:

- Repair of household appliances
- Charges for the hire of major household appliance
- Charges for the installation of household appliances (if charged separately)

Excludes:

- *Separate purchases of materials made by households with the intention of undertaking the repair themselves (05.3.1)*

05.4 Glassware, Tableware, and Household Utensils

05.4.0 Glassware, Tableware, and Household Utensils (SD)

Includes:

- Glassware, crystal ware, ceramic ware, and chinaware of the kind used for table, kitchen, bathroom, toilet, office, and indoor decoration
- Cutlery, flatware, and silverware
- Nonelectric kitchen utensils of all materials, such as saucepans, stew pots, pressure cookers, frying pans, coffee mills, sparkling water makers, purée makers, mincers, hotplates, household scales, and other such mechanical devices
- Nonelectric household articles of all materials, such as containers for bread, coffee, spices, and so on, waste bins, waste-paper baskets, laundry baskets, portable money boxes and strongboxes, towel rails, bottle racks, irons and ironing boards, letter boxes, feeding bottles, thermos flasks, and iceboxes
- Repair and hire of glassware, tableware, and household utensils

Excludes:

- *Lighting equipment (05.1.1.3)*
- *Cardboard tableware (05.6.1.9)*
- *Personal weighing machines (13.1.2.0)*
- *Baby scales (06.1.2.1)*
- *Ashtrays (13.2.9.1)*

05.4.0.1 Glassware, Crystal Ware, Ceramic Ware, and Chinaware (SD)

Includes:

- Glassware, crystal ware, ceramic ware, and chinaware of the kind used for table, kitchen, bathroom, toilet, office, and indoor decoration

Excludes:

- *Repair or hire of glassware, crystal ware, ceramic ware, and chinaware (05.4.0.4)*

05.4.0.2 Cutlery, Flatware, and Silverware (SD)

Includes:

- Cutlery, flatware, and silverware

Excludes:

- *Repair or hire of such cutlery, flatware, and silverware (05.4.0.4)*

05.4.0.3 Nonelectric Kitchen Utensils and Articles (SD)

Includes:

- Nonelectric kitchen utensils of all materials, such as saucepans, stew pots, pressure cookers, frying pans, coffee mills, sparkling water makers, purée makers, mincers, hotplates, household scales, and other such mechanical devices
- Nonelectric household articles of all materials, such as containers for bread, coffee, spices, and so on, waste bins, waste-paper baskets, laundry baskets, portable money boxes and strongboxes, towel rails, bottle racks, irons and ironing boards, letter boxes, feeding bottles, thermos flasks, and iceboxes

Excludes:

- *Lighting equipment (05.1.1.3)*
- *Repair or hire of nonelectric kitchen utensils and articles (05.4.0.4)*
- *Cardboard tableware (05.6.1.9)*
- *Baby scales (06.1.2.1)*
- *Personal weighing machines (13.1.2.0)*
- *Ashtrays (13.2.9.1)*

05.4.0.4 Repair and Hire of Glassware, Tableware, and Household Utensils (S)

The cost of materials is included only if the materials are not separately invoiced.

Includes:

- Repair and hire of glassware, crystal ware, ceramic ware and chinaware, cutlery, flatware and silverware, and nonelectric kitchen utensils and articles

05.5 Tools and Equipment for House and Garden

05.5.1 Motorized Tools and Equipment (D)

Includes:

- Electric drills, percussion drill, electric saws, electric sanders
- Garden tractors, chain saws, lawn mowers, clipper for lawn, hedge cutters, and cultivators
- Water pumps
- Electric screwdrivers

Excludes:

- *Repair or hire of motorized major tools and equipment (05.5.3.0)*

05.5.1.0 Motorized Tools and Equipment (D)

Includes:

- Electric drills, percussion drill, electric saws, electric sanders
- Garden tractors, chain saws, lawn mowers, clipper for lawn, hedge cutters, and cultivators
- Water pumps
- Electric screwdrivers

Excludes:

- *Repair or hire of motorized major tools and equipment (05.5.3.0)*

05.5.2 Nonmotorized Tools and Miscellaneous Accessories (SD)

Includes:

- Hand tools, such as saws, hammers, screwdrivers, wrenches, spanners, pliers, trimming knives, rasps, and files
- Garden tools, such as wheelbarrows, watering cans, hoses, spades, shovels, rakes, forks, scythes, sickles, and secateurs
- Ladders and steps
- Fittings for radiators and fireplaces, other metal articles for the house (curtain rails, curtain rods of wood or plastics, string curtain rods, carpet rods, hooks, and so on) or for the garden (chains, grids, stakes, and hoop segments for fencing and bordering)
- Small electric accessories, such as switches, electric bulbs, fluorescent lighting tubes, torches, flashlights, hand lamps, and electric batteries for general use

Excludes:

- *Door fittings, power sockets, switches, and wiring flex (04.3.1.1)*
- *Repair or hire of miscellaneous small tool accessories (05.5.3.0)*
- *Batteries for information and communication appliances (08.1.9.2)*
- *Batteries for photographic and cinematographic equipment (09.1.1.2)*

05.5.2.1 Nonmotorized Tools (SD)

Includes:

- Saws, hammers, screwdriver, wrenches, spanners, pliers, trimming knives, rasps, and files

- Power shears, wheelbarrows, watering cans, hoses, spades, shovels, rakes, forks, scythes, sickles, and secateurs
- Ladders and steps

Excludes:

- *Repair or hire of nonmotorized small tools (05.5.3.0)*

05.5.2.2 Miscellaneous Accessories (SD)

Includes:

- Fittings for radiators and fireplaces, other metal articles for the house (curtain rails, curtain rods of wood or plastics, string curtain rods, carpet rods, hooks, and so on) or for the garden (chains, grids, stakes, and hoop segments for fencing and bordering)
- Small electric accessories, such as electric bulbs, fluorescent lighting tubes, torches, flashlights, hand lamps, and electric batteries for general use

Excludes:

- *Door fittings, power sockets, switches, and wiring flex (04.3.1.1)*
- *Repair or hire of miscellaneous small tool accessories (05.5.3.0)*
- *Batteries for information and communication appliances (08.1.9.2)*
- *Batteries for photographic and cinematographic equipment (09.1.1.2)*

05.5.3 Repair and Hire of Motorized and Nonmotorized Tools and Equipment (S)

The cost of materials is included only if the materials are not separately invoiced.

Includes:

- Repair and hire of motorized tools and equipment
- Repair and hire of nonmotorized tools and miscellaneous accessories

05.5.3.0 Repair and Hire of Motorized and Nonmotorized Tools and Equipment (S)

The cost of materials is included only if the materials are not separately invoiced.

Includes:

- Repair and hire of motorized tools and equipment
- Repair and hire of nonmotorized small tools and miscellaneous accessories

05.6 Goods and Services for Routine Household Maintenance

05.6.1 Nondurable Household Goods (ND)

Includes:

- Detergents, hand and machine dishwashing detergent, scouring powders, disinfectant bleaches, softeners, conditioners, and stain remover
- General-purpose cleanser, window-cleaning products, unblocking agents, and disinfectants
- Floor wax, polishes
- Polishes, creams, and other shoe-cleaning articles (shoe brush)
- Insecticides, fungicides, and distilled water
- Dustpans and dust brushes, dusters
- Cloths, floor cloths, and chamois leathers
- Dish brush, household sponges, scourers, and steel wool
- Filters, tablecloths and table napkins, kitchen paper, baking parchment roll, kitchen film, aluminum foil, and doily
- Disposable plates, cups, and cutlery
- Vacuum cleaner bags
- Candles, lamp wicks, methylated spirits, plastic bag, and garbage bag
- Matches, clothes-pegs, clothes hangers, pins, safety pins, sewing needles, knitting needles, thimbles, nails, screws, nuts and bolts, tacks, washers, glues and adhesive tapes for household use, string, twine, and rubber gloves
- Pool cleaning chemicals and water treatment chemicals

Excludes:

- *Brushes and scrapers for paint, varnish, and wallpaper (04.3.1.1)*
- *Products specifically for the cleaning and maintenance of transport equipment, such as paints, chrome cleaners, sealing compounds, and bodywork polishes (07.2.1.3)*
- *Horticultural products for the upkeep of ornamental gardens (09.3.1.1)*
- *Paper handkerchiefs, toilet paper, toilet soaps, toilet sponges, and other products for personal hygiene (13.1.2.0)*
- *Cigarette, cigar, and pipe lighters and lighter fuel (13.2.9.1)*

05.6.1.1 Cleaning and Maintenance Products (ND)

Includes:

- Detergents, hand and machine dishwashing detergent, scouring powders, disinfectant bleaches, softeners, conditioners, and stain remover
- General-purpose cleanser, window-cleaning products, unblocking agents, and disinfectants
- Floor wax, polishes
- Polishes, creams, and other shoe-cleaning articles (shoe brush)
- Dustpans and dust brushes, dusters
- Cloths, floor cloths, and chamois leathers
- Dish brush, household sponges, scourers, and steel wool
- Vacuum cleaner bags
- Pool cleaning chemicals and water treatment chemicals

Excludes:

- *Brushes and scrapers for paint, varnish, and wallpaper (04.3.1.1)*
- *Products specifically for the cleaning and maintenance of transport equipment, such as paints, chrome cleaners, sealing compounds, and bodywork polishes (07.2.1.3)*
- *Horticultural products for the upkeep of ornamental gardens (09.3.1.1)*

05.6.1.9 Other Nondurable Household Goods (ND)

Includes:

- Insecticides, fungicides, and distilled water
- Filters, tablecloths and table napkins, kitchen paper, baking parchment roll, kitchen film, aluminum foil, and doily
- Disposable plates, cups, and cutlery
- Candles, lamp wicks, methylated spirits, plastic bags, and garbage bags
- Matches, clothes-pegs, clothes hangers, pins, safety pins, sewing needles, knitting needles, thimbles, nails, screws, nuts and bolts, tacks, washers, glues and adhesive tapes for household use, string, twine and rubber gloves, and gardening gloves

Excludes:

- *Paper handkerchiefs, toilet paper, toilet soaps, toilet sponges, and other products for personal hygiene (13.1.2.0)*
- *Cigarette, cigar, and pipe lighters and lighter fuel (13.2.9.1)*

05.6.2 Domestic Services and Household Services (S)

Domestic services (05.6.2.1) are services provided by personnel employed by households (such as butlers, maids, cooks, nannies, governesses, cleaners, au pairs, and gardeners) who receive a compensation or wage for their services. Domestic services also include services such as babysitting, gardening, and cleaning supplied by enterprises and self-employed persons. Other household services (05.6.2.9) are services provided by enterprises and self-employed persons that are not routinely provided by staff employed by households, such as carpet cleaning, pest extermination, and disinfection.

Includes:

- Domestic services supplied by paid staff employed in private services, such as butlers, cooks, maids, drivers, gardeners, governesses, and au pairs or nannies
- Similar services, including babysitting and housework, supplied by enterprises or self-employed persons
- Household services, such as window cleaning, disinfecting, fumigation, and pest extermination
- Dry-cleaning, laundering, and dyeing of household linen, household textiles, and carpets
- Shampooing of carpets
- Pest extermination, disinfection
- Maintaining flat in the absence of owner

Includes also:

- Housemaids that iron household linen and clothes in the family residence

Excludes:

- *Dry-cleaning, laundering, and dyeing of garments (03.1.4.1)*
- *Refuse collection (04.4.2.0)*
- *Security services (04.3.2.0)*
- *Sewerage collection (04.4.3.0)*
- *Coproprietor charges for caretaking, gardening, stairwell cleaning, heating and lighting, maintenance of lifts and refuse disposal chutes, and so on in multi-occupied buildings (04.4.4.1)*
- *Snow removal and chimney sweeping (04.4.4.9)*
- *Removal and storage services (07.4.9.1)*
- *Child-minding with an educational component (10.1.0.1)*
- *Child-minding outside home (13.3.0.1)*
- *Bodyguards (13.9.0.9)*

05.6.2.1 Domestic Services by Paid Staff (S)

Includes:

- Domestic services supplied by paid staff employed in private services, such as butlers, cooks, maids, drivers, gardeners, governesses, and au pairs or nannies

Includes also:

- Housemaids that iron household linen and clothes in the family residence

Excludes:

- *Child-minding with an educational component (10.1.0.1)*
- *Child-minding outside home (13.3.0.1)*

05.6.2.9 Other Household Services (S)

Includes:

- Dry-cleaning of household linen and textiles
- Carpet cleaning
- Laundering and dyeing of household textiles
- Other services supplied by enterprises or self-employed persons
- Pest extermination, disinfection
- Maintaining flat in the absence of owner

Excludes:

- *Dry-cleaning, laundering, and dyeing of garments (03.1.4.1)*
- *Refuse collection (04.4.2.0)*
- *Security services (04.3.2.0)*
- *Sewerage collection (04.4.3.0)*
- *Coproprietor charges for caretaking, gardening, stairwell cleaning, heating and lighting, maintenance of lifts and refuse disposal chutes, and so on in multi-occupied buildings (04.4.4.1)*
- *Snow removal and chimney sweeping (04.4.4.9)*
- *Removal and storage services (07.4.9.1)*
- *Bodyguards (13.9.0.9)*

06 Health

Division 06 comprises four main categories, one of which concerns health products, while the three other concern health services. Specifically, health services provided during an overnight stay (06.3); services that do not require an overnight stay (06.2); and diagnostic imaging services, medical laboratory services, patient emergency transportation and emergency rescue services (06.4). Medicines and health products (06.1) cover all products that are separately invoiced from health services except when administered under the direct supervision of a health care professional during an overnight stay (06.3).

Services and products included in Division 06 are those that can only be used in response to a health need. These services and products aim at preventing the occurrence of illnesses and diseases (for example, through vaccination); cure from illnesses, diseases, and injuries; relieving symptoms of illnesses, diseases, and injuries; reduce the severity of illnesses, diseases, and injuries; protect against exacerbation and complication of illnesses, diseases, and injuries; and restoring the health status or maintaining/preventing the deterioration of a health condition.

It also includes services provided by health care professional purely for aesthetic beautification purposes (for example, cosmetic surgery; dental work to whiten teeth).

Division 06 excludes food believed to be highly beneficial to health, especially food grown organically as well as foods or food ingredients that have been shown to affect specific functions or system of the body (Division 01).

06.1 Medicines and Health Products

Includes:

- Medicines, vaccines, pharmaceutical preparations, medical devices, assistive products, and other health-related products used for the prevention, diagnosis, and treatment of illnesses, diseases, and injuries, and purchased by individuals or households, either with or without a prescription, usually from pharmacies, health facilities, or medical/assistive equipment suppliers and from reliable internet sources. They are intended for consumption or use outside a health facility or institution.

Excludes:

- *Nutritional supplements and fortified food products (01.1.9.9)*
- *Medicines and health products supplied directly by a health care provider to outpatients (no overnight stay) or inpatients (overnight stay) for consumption outside a health facility or institution are to be classified as outpatient services (06.2) or inpatient services (06.3) if not separately identifiable from the service*
- *Services fees to dispense medicines charged by a health practitioner during an outpatient service (06.2) or an inpatient service (06.3) if not separately identifiable from the service*
- *Veterinary products (09.4.5.0)*
- *Products for personal hygiene or personal care including beauty products and creams (13.1) (for example, aromatherapy products and slimming and beauty enhancing creams)*

06.1.1 Medicines (ND)

Includes:

- Medicines, vaccines, and other pharmaceutical preparations (all medicines, including branded and generic products, and pharmaceutical preparations used to treat diseases; vaccines, hormones, oral contraceptives, and other pharmaceutical products used to prevent, to diagnose or to treat the diseases; vitamins and minerals; fluids required for dialysis, as well as gases used in health care, such as oxygen, when the patient purchases them directly)
- Herbal medicines and homeopathic products

Includes also:

- Service fees to dispense medicines charged by the pharmacists

Excludes:

- *Nutritional supplements and fortified food products (01.1.9.9)*
- *Medicines and health products supplied directly by a health care provider to outpatients (no overnight stay) or inpatients (overnight stay) for consumption outside a health facility or institution are to be classified as outpatient services (06.2) or inpatient services (06.3) if not separately identifiable from the service*
- *Service fees to dispense medicines charged by a health practitioner during an outpatient service (06.2) or an inpatient service (06.3) if not separately identifiable from the service*
- *Veterinary products (09.4.5.0)*
- *Products for personal hygiene or personal care including beauty products and creams (13.1) (for example, aromatherapy products and slimming and beauty enhancing creams)*

06.1.1.1 Medicines, Vaccines, and Other Pharmaceutical Preparations (ND)

Includes:

- All medicines, including branded and generic products to treat illnesses, diseases, and injuries
- Pharmaceutical preparations used to treat illnesses, diseases, and injuries (for example, extemporaneous ointments, syrups, capsules, or other galenical substances prepared on prescription)
- Vaccines, hormones, oral contraceptives, and other pharmaceutical products used to prevent, diagnose, or treat illnesses and diseases
- Vitamins and minerals
- Fluids required for dialysis, as well as gases used in health care, such as oxygen, when the patient purchases them directly

Includes also:

- Service fees to dispense medicines charged by the pharmacists

Excludes:

- *Nutritional supplements and fortified food products (01.1.9.9)*
- *Medicines and health products supplied directly by a health care provider to outpatients (no overnight stay) or inpatients (overnight stay) for consumption outside a health facility or institution are to be classified as outpatient services (06.2) or inpatient services (06.3) if not separately identifiable from the service*

- *Service fees to dispense medicines charged by a health practitioner during an outpatient service (06.2) or an inpatient service (06.3) if not separately identifiable from the service*
- *Veterinary products (09.4.5.0)*
- *Products for personal hygiene or personal care including beauty products and creams (13.1) (for example, aromatherapy products and slimming and beauty enhancing creams)*

06.1.1.2 Herbal Medicines and Homeopathic Products (ND)

Includes:

- Herbal medicines include herbs, herbal materials, herbal preparations, and finished herbal products, which contain as active ingredients parts of plants, or other plant materials, or combinations generally used in traditional medicine or complementary medicine
- Homeopathic products include any medicine prepared in accordance with a homeopathic manufacturing procedure described by a pharmacopeia in official use or other officially recognized documents (a homeopathic medicine may contain a number of homeopathic preparations)

Excludes:

- *Herbal medicines and homeopathic products supplied directly by a health care provider to outpatients (no overnight stay) or inpatients (overnight stay) for consumption or use outside a health facility are to be classified with outpatient services (06.2) or inpatient services (06.3) if not separately identifiable from the service.*

06.1.2 Medical Products (ND)

Includes:

- Diagnostic equipment for self-test or over-the-counter sale for personal use outside a health facility or institution
- Pregnancy tests; thermometers, glucose meters, blood pressure meters, and other point of care tests, baby scales, and so on
- Condoms and other mechanical contraceptive devices (does not include oral contraceptives), masks, medicinal stockpiles (for example, compression stockpiles), medicinal gloves, insecticide-treated mosquito nets, and so on
- Inhalers, syringes, humidifiers, nebulizers, hot bags, ice packs, first aid kits, bandages, and so on

Includes also:

- All internet purchases of medical products for personal use

Excludes:

- *Diagnostic products for use inside a health facility or institution (06.3)*
- *Scales (13.1.2.0)*

06.1.2.1 Medical Diagnostic Products (ND)

Includes:

- Diagnostic equipment for self-test or over-the-counter sale for personal use outside a health facility or institution
- Pregnancy tests; thermometers, glucose meters, blood pressure meters, and other point of care tests, baby scales, and so on

Includes also:

- All internet purchases of medical products for personal use

Excludes:

- *Diagnostic products for use inside a health facility or institution (06.3)*
- *Scales (13.1.2.0)*

06.1.2.2 Prevention and Protective Devices (ND)

Includes:

- Condoms and other mechanical contraceptive devices (does not include oral contraceptives), masks, medicinal stockpiles (for example, compression stockpiles), medicinal gloves, insecticide-treated mosquito nets, and so on

06.1.2.3 Treatment Devices for Personal Use (ND)

Includes:

- Inhalers, syringes, humidifiers, nebulizers, hot bags, ice packs, first aid kits, bandages, and so on

06.1.3 Assistive Products (D)

Includes:

- Assistive products for vision, hearing, and communication; mobility and daily living, such as spectacles (corrective eyeglasses and contact lenses), wheelchairs, hearing aids, walking frames, and artificial legs

Excludes:

- *Sunglasses; earplugs (13.2.9.1)*
- *Glasses for the protection against potential eye damage due to the practice of a sport (09.2.2.1)*

06.1.3.1 Assistive Products for Vision (D)

This comprises all external products whose primary purpose is to maintain or improve an individual's vision, to compensate for an impairment/a loss of intrinsic visual, and to reduce the consequences of gradual functional visual decline.

Includes:

- Corrective eyeglasses (spectacles for low vision, short distance, long distance)
- White canes
- Ocular prosthesis (for example, glass eyes) or contact lenses

Excludes:

- *Dental implants and dentures are to be included in 06.3.1.0 when an overnight stay is required and in 06.2.2. when not*
- *Walking sticks and canes for recreational purposes (hiking/tracking); glasses for the protection against potential eye damage due to the practice of a sport (09.2.2.1)*
- *Sunglasses (13.2.9.1)*

06.1.3.2 Assistive Products for Hearing and Communication (D)

This comprises all external products whose primary purpose is to maintain or improve an individual's hearing and communication, to compensate for an impairment/a loss of intrinsic hearing and communication capacity, and to reduce the consequences of gradual functional hearing/communication decline.

Includes:

- Digital hearing aids

Includes also:

- Cleaning, adjustment, and batteries if not separately identifiable from the product

06.1.3.3 Assistive Products for Mobility and Daily Living (D)

This comprises all assistive products to maintain or improve an individual's mobility and daily living; to compensate for an impairment/a loss of intrinsic mobility or the inability to perform daily activities; and to reduce the consequences of gradual functional mobility and decline in the ability to perform daily activities.

Includes:

- Therapeutic footwear (diabetic/neuropathic/orthopedic); trusses and supports
- Orthoses (brace, splint, or other artificial external device serving to support the leg, spine, neck, hand)
- Prostheses (leg/hand including implants); spinal belts/braces including neck braces or cervical collars
- Crutches
- Rollators/walking/standing frames
- Wheelchairs with or without cushions (powered/manual)
- Walkers; walking sticks and canes for mobility
- Chairs for shower/bath/toilet; handrails/grab bars
- Incontinence products, absorbent including diapers for the aging population
- Pressure relief mattresses and special beds
- Portable ramps

Excludes:

- *Dental implants and dentures are to be included in 06.3.1.0 when an overnight stay is required and in 06.2.2. when not*
- *Walking sticks and canes for recreational purposes (hiking/tracking) (09.2.2.1)*

06.1.4 Repair, Rental, and Maintenance of Medical and Assistive Products (S)

Includes:

- Cleaning repair, rental, and maintenance of medical diagnostic products for personal use and assistive products for vision, hearing, mobility, and daily living (for example, rental of medical alarms for in-home use)

06.1.4.0 Repair, Rental, and Maintenance of Medical and Assistive Products (S)

Includes:

- Cleaning repair, rental, and maintenance of medical diagnostic products for personal use and assistive products for vision, hearing, mobility, and daily living (for example, rental of medical alarms for in-home use)

06.2 Outpatient Care Services

This group covers all preventive, dental, curative, rehabilitative, and long-term care services not provided during an overnight stay. The admission criteria are irrelevant as well as the setting where the outpatient care occurs or the type of provider. As such, outpatient services may be delivered in a hospital setting or outside a hospital setting including at home or even on the street by any type of health care provider. Outpatient services include all medicines and health products supplied directly by a health care provider for consumption or use outside a health facility/institution if not separately identifiable from the service.

It also includes respite care as well as services to maintain people in their private homes that are integrated into a package of medical outpatient care services.

Excludes:

- *The vaccine itself when separately invoiced from the preventive service (06.1.1.1)*
- *Dental, curative, rehabilitative, and long-term care services provided overnight (06.3)*
- *Control and follow-up services after symptoms appeared with overnight care are to be included in 06.3*
- *Laboratory and imaging services separately identifiable from the preventive service (06.4)*
- *Nonmedical services to maintain people in their private homes that are not integrated into a package of medical care (13.3.0.2)*

06.2.1 Preventive Care Services (S)

Preventive services aim at avoiding illnesses and diseases, and detecting diseases (for example, via screening). The main distinction between preventive services and other outpatient services is the criterion "before symptoms appear."

Includes:

- Immunization/vaccination services
- Family planning and counseling
- Healthy condition monitoring services (prenatal care and postnatal care services)
- General and routine check-ups other than dental
- Child growth and development check-ups
- Early disease detection services, before symptoms appear (including screening, diagnostic tests, and medical examinations directed to detect communicable and noncommunicable diseases before symptoms appear)

Includes also:

- Laboratory and imaging services needed to provide preventive services when jointly invoiced with the time and skills of the personnel

Excludes:

- *The vaccine itself when separately invoiced from the preventive service (06.1.1.1)*
- *Dental, curative, rehabilitative, and long-term care services provided overnight (06.3)*

- *Control and follow-up services after symptoms appeared with overnight care are to be included in 06.3*
- *Laboratory and imaging services separately identifiable from the preventive service (06.4)*
- *Nonmedical services to maintain people in their private homes that are not integrated into a package of medical care (13.3.0.2)*

06.2.1.1 Immunization Services (S)

The expenditure involved in the consultation, for both the time and skills of the personnel and the purchase of the vaccine itself when jointly invoiced with the service should be accounted for.

Illustrative examples are immunization for:

Polio, rabies, rubella, tetanus, varicella (chicken pox), and yellow fever
Influenza
Measles
Meningococcal infections, mumps, pertussis (whooping cough), and pneumococcal infections
Diphtheria, hepatitis, herpes zoster, and HPV

Includes:

- Immunization/vaccination services for maternal and childcare
- Travel and tourism vaccination as well as any other compulsory or voluntary immunization/vaccination service

Excludes:

- *The vaccine itself when separately invoiced from the service (06.1.1.1)*

06.2.1.9 Other Preventive Services (S)

Includes:

- Family planning and counseling (including genetic counseling)
- Prenatal and postnatal care services
- General routine check-up services including child growth and development
- Identification of genetic abnormalities
- Screening, diagnostic tests, and medical examinations directed to detect communicable and noncommunicable diseases (for example, malaria, tuberculosis, breast cancer, prostate cancer, cervical cancer, colorectal cancer, diabetes, HIV/AIDS, and any other communicable or noncommunicable disease) before symptoms appear
- Any other medical service provided before symptoms appear

Includes also:

- Laboratory and imaging services needed to provide preventive services jointly invoiced with the time and skills of the personnel (for example, mammogram)

Excludes:

- *Control and follow-up services after symptoms appeared without overnight care (06.2.2 or 06.2.3)*
- *Dental routine preventive check-up (06.2.2.1)*
- *Control and follow-up services after symptoms appeared with overnight care (06.3)*
- *Laboratory and imaging services separately identifiable from the preventive service (06.4)*

06.2.2 Outpatient Dental Services (S)

Includes:

- Services of dentists, dental practitioners, endodontist, dental surgeons; oral and maxillofacial surgeons; oral pathologists; orthodontists; pedodontists; periodontists; prosthodontists; oral hygienists and other dental auxiliaries that do not require an overnight stay

Includes also:

- Services of dentists for aesthetic reasons

Excludes:

- *All health products (pharmaceutical, medical, assistive, therapeutic) needed to deliver outpatient dental services separately invoiced from the provider's service fee (06.1)*
- *Services of medical analysis laboratories and imaging centers separately identifiable from the dental services received (06.4.1.0)*

06.2.2.1 Dental Preventive Services (S)

Includes:

- Routine preventive dental check-ups

06.2.2.9 Other Outpatient Dental Services (S)

Includes:

- All other dental services that do not require an overnight stay (excluding preventive dental services)
- All cost concerning dentures (including the fitting costs)

Includes also:

- Services of dentists for aesthetic reasons

Excludes:

- *All health products (pharmaceutical, medical, assistive, therapeutic) needed to deliver outpatient dental services separately invoiced from the provider's service fee (06.1)*
- *Services of medical analysis laboratories and imaging centers separately identifiable from the dental services received (06.4.1.0)*

06.2.3 Other Outpatient Care Services (Excluding Preventive and Dental) (S)

Include all medical services other than preventive and dental that do not require an overnight stay aimed at relieving symptoms of illnesses, diseases, and injuries (06.2.3.1); reduce the severity of illnesses, diseases, and injuries (06.2.3.1); protect against exacerbation and complication of illnesses, diseases, and injuries (06.2.3.1); restoring health status (06.2.3.1); and maintaining the level of health available or preventing the deterioration of a health condition (06.2.3.2).

The admission criteria, the type of provider, as well as the setting where these curative, rehabilitative, long-term care outpatient care services occur are irrelevant as long as no overnight care is involved.

Includes:

- Services at hospitals or in a hospital setting without an overnight stay (excluding preventive 06.2.1 and dental 06.2.2)
- Medical day care services, that is, services delivered in a hospital setting (sometimes in medical day care centers) to a patient who is formally admitted as long as it does not involve an overnight stay
- Home-based hospital treatment (for example, dialysis 06.2.3.2); medical services delivered at home (for example, palliative care 06.2.3.2); medical and nursing services to maintain people in their private home (including the elderly and people with disabilities 06.2.3.2); and nursing care delivered at home including care aimed at retarding or reducing deterioration or maintaining functionality (for example, nasogastric feeding) or for the management of chronic diseases (06.2.3.2)
- Services delivered in individual (for example, private office) or group consulting facilities (excluding preventive services 06.2.1 and dental 06.2.2) by any type of provider (doctors, specialists, nurses, and other health care practitioners)
- Medical services delivered on the street (for example, injections) as well as any other outpatient service delivered outside a hospital setting

Includes also:

- All health products (pharmaceutical, medical, assistive, and therapeutic), diagnostic imaging services, and medical laboratory services needed to deliver outpatient services not separately identifiable from the provider's service fee (doctor/specialist/nurse/other health care practitioner)

Excludes:

- *Medicines and health products (medical, assistive, therapeutic) separately invoiced from the provider's service fee (doctor/specialist/nurse and other health care practitioner) (06.1)*
- *Preventive services (06.2.1)*
- *Outpatient dental services (06.2.2)*
- *Diagnostic imaging services and medical laboratory services separately identifiable from the provider's service fee (doctor/specialist/nurse and other health care practitioner) (06.4.1.0)*
- *Patient emergency transportation services and emergency rescue (06.4.2.0)*

06.2.3.1 Outpatient Curative and Rehabilitative Services (Excluding Dental Services) (S)

Comprises curative and rehabilitative services that do not require an overnight stay.

Curative care comprises health care contacts during which the principal intent is to relieve symptoms of illness or injury, to reduce the severity of an illness or injury, or to protect against exacerbation and complication of an illness and injury that could threaten the life or normal function. Curative services aim at bringing the person back to their original status before the cure was needed.

Rehabilitation aims to achieve and maintain optimal functioning. In some cases, after rehabilitation, a patient can be better than before or only avoid deterioration.

Includes:

- All components of the curative care of illness or the treatment of injury; the surgery performed; diagnostic and therapeutic procedures; and obstetric services as long as it does not involve an overnight stay.
- Curative and rehabilitative care regardless of the type of provider: (specialized) physician and other health professionals (for example, nurses and midwives).
- Curative and rehabilitative services provided in any setting: in hospitals without an overnight stay; in individual (for example, private office) or group consulting facilities; at home or any other setting outside the hospital including on the street.
- Physical, psychological, and speech therapy. As such, it includes services of chiropractors; physiotherapists and physical therapists; speech therapists; audiologists; inhalation or respiratory therapists, and so on. All health products (pharmaceutical, medical, assistive, therapeutic) needed to deliver curative outpatient services not separately invoiced from the provider's service fee.
- All health products (pharmaceutical, medical, assistive, therapeutic) needed to deliver curative/rehabilitative outpatient services invoiced from the provider's service fee (doctor/specialist/nurse/other health care practitioner).

Excludes:

- *Medicines and health products (medical, assistive, therapeutic) separately invoiced from the provider's service fee (doctor/specialist/nurse and other health care practitioner) (06.1)*
- *Preventive services (06.2.1)*
- *Outpatient dental services (06.2.2)*
- *Diagnostic imaging services and medical laboratory services separately identifiable from the provider's service fee (doctor/specialist/nurse and other health care practitioner) (06.4.1.0)*
- *Patient emergency transportation services and emergency rescue (06.4.2.0)*

06.2.3.2 Outpatient Long-Term Care Services (S)

Outpatient long-term care services do not aim at curing an illness or rehabilitating an individual, but to prevent deterioration of a health condition and remain at the level of health available. Some medical activities and nursing are inherent parts of this status quo. Individuals getting such type of outpatient long-term care might include, for example, the elderly with limited capacity to perform daily activities, physically disabled members of the households, and those with chronic conditions.

In some cases, outpatient long-term care services are part of a package of services including social assistance and social transfer. Where possible only the medical component should go into Division 06 (the social protection part should go to Division 13). If it is not possible to distinguish both the choice of the division should be based upon the extent to which the package of services predominantly includes a social protection component (Division 13) or medical component (Division 06).

Includes:

- Services of medical day care centers; medical day care services for the elderly and people with disabilities
- Home-based long-term care hospital treatment without an overnight stay (for example, dialysis)
- Medical and nursing services to maintain people in their private home (including the elderly and people with disabilities)
- Nursing care delivered at home including care aimed at retarding or reducing deterioration or maintaining functionality (for example, nasogastric feeding) or for the management of chronic diseases (for example, provision of the prescribed psychiatric medication)
- Nonmedical services to maintain people in their private homes that are integrated into a package of care and jointly invoiced
- All health products (pharmaceutical, medical, assistive, therapeutic), diagnostic imaging services, and medical laboratory services needed to deliver outpatient services jointly invoiced with the provider's service fee (doctor/specialist/nurse/other health care practitioner)

Excludes:

- *Medicines and health products (medical, assistive, therapeutic) separately invoiced from the provider's service fee (doctor/specialist/nurse and other health care practitioner) (06.1)*
- *Diagnostic imaging services and medical laboratory services separately invoiced from the provider's service fee (doctor/specialist/nurse and other health care practitioner) (06.4.1.0)*
- *Patient emergency transportation services and emergency rescue (06.4.2.0)*
- *Social assistance services relate to care that enables a person to live independently in a house or apartment, community activities and occupational support given on a continuing or recurrent basis to individuals, such as activities whose primary purpose is social and leisure (13.3.0.3)*

06.3 Inpatient Care Services

The overnight stay criterion is the main distinction between outpatient care services (06.2) and inpatient care services (06.3). The type of provider is irrelevant. This may be a hospital, nursing care facility, or facilities classified as ambulatory care providers but which perform occasional procedures requiring overnight accommodation.

It can also include health facilities within any type of establishment that accommodates patients justifying an overnight stay. Tuberculosis hospitals and sanatoriums are often organized to include accommodation along with medical treatment, which is the predominant purpose during a stay in such facilities.

Includes:

- Inpatient care services comprises treatment and care (including dental) that requires an overnight stay
- All medical services needed to deliver inpatient care services during the overnight stay even if separately invoiced (for example, lab tests, diagnostic imaging services)
- Medicines and health products (medical, assistive, therapeutic) needed to deliver inpatient services during the overnight stay even if separately invoiced

Includes also:

- Expenditures related to the "accommodation costs" for the patient (for example, cooking, cleaning, accommodation) and associated with the hosting of patients' relatives if indispensable and associated with the overnight stay (both types of costs are to be added if separately invoiced)
- Beauty treatments carried out in hospitals (for example, cosmetic surgery for other purposes than reconstructive surgery)

Excludes:

- *Hospital day care (with or without admission but no overnight stay) and home-based hospital treatment (06.2)*
- *Services received in hospitals or hospital setting without an overnight stay (06.2) including services of facilities, such as surgeries, clinics, and dispensaries, devoted exclusively to outpatient care (06.2)*
- *Emergency patient transportation and rescue services (06.4.2.0)*
- *Services of nonmedical retirement homes for elderly persons, nonmedical institutions for disabled persons and nonmedical rehabilitation centers providing primarily long-term social support; retirement villages without inpatient medical services (13.3.0.2)*

06.3.1 Inpatient Curative and Rehabilitative Services (S)

Comprises curative, dental, and rehabilitative care that requires an overnight stay. Inpatient curative care comprises health care contacts that require an overnight stay during which the principal intent is to relieve symptoms of illness or injury, to reduce the severity of an illness or injury, or to protect against exacerbation and complication of an illness and injury that could threaten the life or normal function. Inpatient rehabilitation services that require an overnight stay aiming at achieving and maintaining optimal functioning.

Includes:

- Curative/rehabilitative inpatient care services comprise treatment and care (including dental) that requires an overnight stay from any type of provider (for example, a hospital, nursing care facility, or facilities classified as ambulatory care providers but which perform occasional procedures requiring overnight accommodation; services of alcoholism or drug addiction rehabilitation facilities [other than licensed hospitals]; services of mental health convalescent homes or hospitals and any other health facility within any type of establishment that accommodates patients justifying an overnight stay)
- All medical services needed to deliver inpatient care services during the overnight stay even if separately invoiced (for example, lab tests, diagnostic imaging services)
- Medicines and health products (medical, assistive, therapeutic) needed to deliver inpatient services during the overnight stay even if separately invoiced

Includes also:

- Expenditures related to the "accommodation costs" for the patient (for example, cooking, cleaning, accommodation) and associated with the hosting of patients' relatives if indispensable and associated with the overnight stay (both types of costs are to be added if separately invoiced)

- Beauty treatments carried out in hospitals (for example, cosmetic surgery for other purposes than reconstructive surgery)

Excludes:

- *Hospital day care (with or without admission but no overnight stay) and home-based hospital treatment (06.2)*
- *Services received in hospitals or hospital setting without an overnight stay (06.2) including services of facilities, such as surgeries, clinics, and dispensaries, devoted exclusively to outpatient care (06.2)*
- *Emergency patient transportation and rescue services (06.4.2.0)*
- *Services of nonmedical retirement homes for elderly persons, nonmedical institutions for disabled persons, and nonmedical rehabilitation centers providing primarily long-term social support; retirement villages without inpatient medical services (13.3.0.2)*

06.3.1.0 Inpatient Curative and Rehabilitative Services (S)

Comprises curative, dental, and rehabilitative care that requires an overnight stay. Inpatient curative care comprises health care contacts that require an overnight stay during which the principal intent is to relieve symptoms of illness or injury, to reduce the severity of an illness or injury, or to protect against exacerbation and complication of an illness and injury that could threaten the life or normal function. Inpatient rehabilitation services that require an overnight stay aiming at achieving and maintaining optimal functioning.

Includes:

- Curative/rehabilitative inpatient care services comprise treatment and care (including dental) that requires an overnight stay from any type of provider (for example, a hospital, nursing care facility, or facilities classified as ambulatory care providers but which perform occasional procedures requiring overnight accommodation; services of alcoholism or drug addiction rehabilitation facilities [other than licensed hospitals]; services of mental health convalescent homes or hospitals and any other health facility within any type of establishment that accommodates patients justifying an overnight stay)
- All medical services needed to deliver inpatient care services during the overnight stay even if separately invoiced (for example, lab tests, diagnostic imaging services)
- Medicines and health products (medical, assistive, therapeutic) needed to deliver inpatient services during the overnight stay even if separately invoiced

Includes also:

- Expenditures related to the "accommodation costs" for the patient (for example, cooking, cleaning, accommodation) and associated with the hosting of patients' relatives if indispensable and associated with the overnight stay (both types of costs are to be added if separately invoiced)
- Beauty treatments carried out in hospitals (for example, cosmetic surgery for other purposes than reconstructive surgery)

Excludes:

- *Hospital day care (with or without admission but no overnight stay) and home-based hospital treatment (06.2)*
- *Services received in hospitals or hospital setting without an overnight stay (06.2) including services of facilities, such as surgeries, clinics, and dispensaries, devoted exclusively to outpatient care (06.2)*
- *Emergency patient transportation and rescue services (06.4.2.0)*
- *Services of nonmedical retirement homes for elderly persons, nonmedical institutions for disabled persons, and nonmedical rehabilitation centers providing primarily long-term social support; retirement villages without inpatient medical services (13.3.0.2)*

06.3.2 Inpatient Long-Term Care Services (S)

Comprises long-term care services that require an overnight stay.

Inpatient long-term care services do not aim at curing an illness or rehabilitating an individual, but to prevent deterioration of a health condition and remain at the level of health available. Some medical and nursing activities that require an overnight stay are inherent parts of this status quo.

Individuals getting such type of inpatient long-term care might include, for example, the elderly with limited capacity to perform daily activities, physically disabled members of the households, and those with chronic conditions.

Includes:

- Services of medical convalescent homes or convalescent hospitals; services of homes for the elderly with nursing care; inpatient care hospices; services of palliative care establishments for the terminally ill; services of nursing homes; rest homes with nursing care; services of skilled nursing facilities; services of teaching nursing homes; services of residential mental retardation facilities; and mental health and substance abuse facilities for chronic patient (for example, those with dementia)
- Services of medical retirement homes for the elderly and medical residence for people with disabilities
- All medical services needed to deliver inpatient care services during the overnight stay (for example, lab tests, diagnostic imaging services)
- Medicines and health products (medical, assistive, therapeutic) needed to deliver inpatient services during the overnight stay

Includes also:

- Expenditures related to the "hotel costs" for the patient (for example, cooking, cleaning, accommodation) and associated with the hosting of patients' relatives if indispensable and associated with the overnight stay (both types of costs are to be added if separately invoiced)

Excludes:

- *Social protection services (13.3)*
- *Nonmedical retirement homes for elderly persons and nonmedical residences for disabled persons (13.3.0.2)*

06.3.2.0 Inpatient Long-Term Care Services (S)

Comprises long-term care services that require an overnight stay.

Inpatient long-term care services do not aim at curing an illness or rehabilitating an individual, but to prevent deterioration of a health condition and remain at the level of health available. Some medical and nursing activities that require an overnight stay are inherent parts of this status quo.

Individuals getting such type of inpatient long-term care might include, for example, the elderly with limited capacity to perform daily activities, physically disabled members of the households, and those with chronic conditions.

Includes:

- Services of medical convalescent homes or convalescent hospitals; services of homes for the elderly with nursing care; inpatient care hospices; services of palliative care establishments for the terminally ill; services of nursing homes; rest homes with nursing care; services of skilled nursing facilities; services of teaching nursing homes; services of residential mental retardation facilities; and mental health and substance abuse facilities for chronic patient (for example, those with dementia)
- Services of medical retirement homes for the elderly and medical residence for people with disabilities
- All medical services needed to deliver inpatient care services during the overnight stay (for example, lab tests, diagnostic imaging services)
- Medicines and health products (medical, assistive, therapeutic) needed to deliver inpatient services during the overnight stay

Includes also:

- Expenditures related to the "hotel costs" for the patient (for example, cooking, cleaning, and accommodation) and associated with the hosting of patients' relatives if indispensable and associated with the overnight stay (both types of costs are to be added if separately invoiced)

Excludes:

- *Social protection services (13.3)*
- *Nonmedical retirement homes for elderly persons and nonmedical residences for disabled persons (13.3.0.2)*

06.4 Other Health Services

Includes:

- Diagnostic imaging services and medical laboratory services
- Patient emergency transportation services and emergency rescue

06.4.1 Diagnostic Imaging Services and Medical Laboratory Services (S)

Includes:

- Services of medical analysis laboratories (for example, urine/blood tests)
- Diagnostic imaging services including all diagnostic imaging methods (that is computerized tomography, magnetic resonance imaging, and sonography); imaging diagnosis comprises a variety of services that employ imaging technology, such as X-rays and radiation for the diagnosis and monitoring of patients

Excludes:

- *Diagnostic imaging services and medical laboratory services not separately identifiable from outpatient preventive services (06.2.1)*
- *Dental services (06.2.2)*

06.4.1.0 Diagnostic Imaging Services and Medical Laboratory Services (S)

Includes:

- Services of medical analysis laboratories (for example, urine/blood tests)
- Diagnostic imaging services including all diagnostic imaging methods (that is computerized tomography, magnetic resonance imaging, sonography); imaging diagnosis comprises a variety of services that employ imaging technology, such as X-rays and radiation for the diagnosis and monitoring of patients

Excludes:

- *Diagnostic imaging services and medical laboratory services not separately identifiable from outpatient preventive services (06.2.1)*
- *Dental services (06.2.2)*

06.4.2 Patient Emergency Transportation Services and Emergency Rescue (S)

Includes:

- Ambulance services for individuals with or without emergency rescue
- Individual's transportation by airplane and vehicles for medical emergency reasons whether or not they have been specially adjusted for a medical purpose

Includes also:

- Memberships for emergency transport services

06.4.2.0 Patient Emergency Transportation Services and Emergency Rescue (S)

Includes:

- Ambulance services for individuals with or without emergency rescue
- Individual's transportation by airplane and vehicles for medical emergency reasons whether or not they have been specially adjusted for a medical purpose

Includes also:

- Memberships for emergency transport services

07 Transport

Division 07 distinguishes four main categories of goods and services for the purpose of transportation: purchase of vehicles, goods and services for the operation of the personal transport equipment, the transport services provided by the market, and the transport services of goods.

The purchase of vehicles covers motor cars, motorcycles, bicycles, and animal-drawn vehicles. Due to the high share of second-hand motor vehicles in private consumption expenditures, separate subclasses for new and for second-hand motor cars are distinguished.

The second group concerning the operation of personal transport equipment cover parts and accessories for personal transport equipment, fuels and lubricants, and the repair and maintenance of personal transport equipment. This group also includes expenditures for parking spaces in garages or in public places, expenditures for tolls, and expenditures to acquire a driving certificate.

Passenger transport services are structured by the mode of transport. However, due to the fact that transport tickets may cover more than one mode of transport, a class for the combined passenger transport was created (07.3.6).

The fourth group covers postal and courier services, removal and storage services, and the delivery services of any kind of goods when charged separately.

Division 07 does not cover purchases of recreational vehicles, such as camper vans, caravans, trailers, airplanes, and boats (09.1.2).

07.1 Purchase of Vehicles

Includes:

- Purchase of vehicles used for transport

Excludes:

- *Purchases of recreational vehicles, such as camper vans, caravans, trailers, airplanes, and boats (09.1.2.1, 09.1.2.2, 09.1.2.3)*

07.1.1 Motor Cars (D)

Includes:

- Motor cars, passenger vans, station wagons, estate cars, and the like with either two-wheel drive or four-wheel drive

Includes also:

- Racing motor vehicles and vehicles for shows

Excludes:

- *Invalid carriages (06.1.3.3)*
- *Camper vans (09.1.2.1)*
- *Golf carts (09.1.2.9)*

07.1.1.1 New Motor Cars (D)

Includes:

- New motor cars, passenger vans, station wagons, estate cars, and the like with either two-wheel drive or four-wheel drive

Includes also:

- Racing motor vehicles and vehicles for shows

Excludes:

- *Invalid carriages (06.1.3.3)*
- *Camper vans (09.1.2.1)*
- *Golf carts (09.1.2.9)*

07.1.1.2 Second-Hand Motor Cars (D)

Includes:

- Used or second-hand motor cars, passenger vans, station wagons, estate cars, and the like with either two-wheel drive or four-wheel drive

Includes also:

- Second-hand racing motor vehicles and vehicles for shows

Excludes:

- *Invalid carriages (06.1.3.3)*
- *Camper vans (09.1.2.1)*
- *Golf carts (09.1.2.9)*

07.1.2 Motorcycles (D)

Includes:

- Motorcycles of all types, motor scooters, and motorized bicycles with combustion engines

Includes also:

- Sidecars
- Used or second-hand motorcycles

07.1.2.0 Motorcycles (D)

Includes:

- Motorcycles of all types, scooters, and motorized bicycles with combustion engines

Includes also:

- Sidecars
- Used or second-hand motorcycles

07.1.3 Bicycles (D)

Includes:

- Bicycles and tricycles of all types
- Rickshaws
- E-bikes, pedelecs

Excludes:

- *Motorized bicycles with combustion engines (07.1.2.0)*
- *Toy bicycles and tricycles (09.2.1.2)*

07.1.3.0 Bicycles (D)

Includes:

- Bicycles and tricycles of all types
- Rickshaws
- E-bikes, pedelecs

Excludes:

- *Motorized bicycles with combustion engines (07.1.2.0)*
- *Toy bicycles and tricycles (09.2.1.2)*

07.1.4 Animal-Drawn Vehicles (D)

Includes:

- Animal-drawn vehicles
- Animals required to draw the vehicles and related equipment (yokes, collars, harnesses, bridles, reins, and so on)

Excludes:

- *Horses and ponies, horse- or pony-drawn vehicles, and related equipment purchased for recreational purposes (09.1.2.4)*

07.1.4.0 Animal-Drawn Vehicles (D)

Includes:

- Animal-drawn vehicles
- Animals required to draw the vehicles and related equipment (yokes, collars, harnesses, bridles, reins, and so on)

Excludes:

- *Horses and ponies, horse- or pony-drawn vehicles, and related equipment purchased for recreational purposes (09.1.2.4)*

07.2 Operation of Personal Transport Equipment

Purchases of parts, accessories, or lubricants made by households with the intention of undertaking the maintenance; repair or intervention themselves should be shown under (07.2.1) or (07.2.2). If households pay an enterprise to carry out the maintenance, repair, or fitting, the total value of the service, including the costs of the materials used, should be shown under (07.2.3).

07.2.1 Parts and Accessories for Personal Transport Equipment (SD)

Includes:

- Tires (new, used, or retreaded), inner tubes, spark plugs, batteries, shock absorbers, filters, pumps, and other replacement parts or accessories for personal transport equipment, crash helmets for motorcycles and bicycles
- Hubcaps, if bought separately
- Baby and children seats for cars
- Fire extinguishers for transport equipment; products specifically for the cleaning and maintenance of transport equipment, such as paints, chrome cleaners, sealing compounds, and bodywork polishes; covers for motor cars, motorcycles, and so on
- Dash cameras

Includes also:

- Crash helmets with cameras incorporated

Excludes:

- *Nonspecific products for cleaning and maintenance, such as distilled water, household sponges, chamois leathers, detergents, and so on (05.6.1.1)*
- *Charges for the fitting of parts and accessories and for the painting, washing, and polishing of bodywork (07.2.3.0)*
- *Car radios (08.1.4.0)*

07.2.1.1 Tires (SD)

Includes:

- New, used, or retreaded, including inner tubes for car, bicycles, motorcycles, and so on

07.2.1.2 Parts for Personal Transport Equipment (SD)

Includes:

- Spark plugs, batteries, shock absorbers, filters, pumps, and other parts for personal transport equipment
- Rims

Excludes:

- *Charges for the fitting of parts and accessories and for the painting, washing, and polishing of bodywork (07.2.3.0)*

07.2.1.3 Accessories for Personal Transport Equipment (SD)

Includes:

- GPS (satellite positioning) equipment for personal transport
- Accessories for personal transport equipment but bought separately
- Fire extinguishers for transport equipment
- Products specifically for the cleaning and maintenance of transport equipment, such as paints, chrome cleaners, sealing compounds, and bodywork polishes; covers for motor cars, motorcycles, and so on
- Hubcaps, if bought separately
- Crash helmets for motorcycles and bicycles
- Baby and child seats for cars, motorcycles, and bicycles
- Dash cameras

Includes also:

- Crash helmets with cameras incorporated

Excludes:

- Nonspecific products for cleaning and maintenance, such as distilled water, household sponges, chamois leathers, detergents, and so on (05.6.1.1)
- Car radios (08.1.4.0)

07.2.2 Fuels and Lubricants for Personal Transport Equipment (ND)

Includes:

- Petrol and other fuels, such as diesel, liquid petroleum gas, alcohol, and two-stroke mixtures
- Lubricants, brake and transmission fluids, coolants, and additives
- Electricity as fuel for cars when separately priced from other electricity
- Hydrogen
- Fuel for major tools and equipment covered under 05.5.1 and recreational vehicles covered under 09.1.2

Excludes:

- *Charges for service of oil changes and greasing (07.2.3.0)*

07.2.2.1 Diesel (ND)

Includes:

- Diesel

07.2.2.2 Petrol (ND)

Includes:

- Petrol/gasoline

Includes also:

- Petrol blends, such as petrol with 10 percent ethanol

Excludes:

- *Two-stroke mixtures (07.2.2.3)*

07.2.2.3 Other Fuels for Personal Transport Equipment (ND)

Includes:

- Liquid petroleum gas, natural gas (compressed natural gas, liquefied natural gas), alcohol, biofuels (ethanol, methanol), methane, and two-stroke mixtures
- Electricity as fuel for cars when separately priced from other electricity
- Hydrogen

07.2.2.4 Lubricants (ND)

Includes:

- Lubricants, brake and transmission fluids, coolants, and additives

Excludes:

- *Charges for oil change and greasing service (07.2.3.0)*

07.2.3 Maintenance and Repair of Personal Transport Equipment (S)

The cost of materials is included only if the materials are not separately invoiced.

Includes:

- Services purchased for the maintenance and repair of personal transport equipment, such as fitting of parts and accessories, wheel balancing, breakdown services, oil changes, greasing, and washing
- Installation of car cameras
- Locksmith services for cars

Excludes:

- *Separate purchases of parts, accessories, or lubricants made by households with the intention of undertaking the maintenance or repair themselves (07.2.1, 07.2.2.4)*
- *Roadworthiness tests (07.2.4.3)*

07.2.3.0 Maintenance and Repair of Personal Transport Equipment (S)

The cost of materials is included only if the materials are not separately invoiced.

Includes:

- Services purchased for the maintenance and repair of personal transport equipment, such as fitting of parts and accessories, wheel balancing, breakdown services, oil changes, greasing, and washing
- Installation of car cameras
- Locksmith services for cars

Excludes:

- *Separate purchases of parts, accessories, or lubricants made by households with the intention of undertaking the maintenance or repair themselves (07.2.1, 07.2.2.4)*
- *Roadworthiness tests (07.2.4.3)*

07.2.4 Other Services in Respect of Personal Transport Equipment (S)

Includes:

- Rental of garages or parking spaces not providing parking in connection with the dwelling
- Rental of municipal street parking
- Parking meters
- Charges for parking places in parking garages, such as those in shopping centers hired for a few hours or less (including valet service)

Includes also:

- Parking permits for designated areas (for example, residents parking permits)
- Tolls (bridges, tunnels, shuttle ferries, and motorways) and parking meters
- Charges for hire or purchase of electronic tags and toll devices
- Driving lessons, driving tests, and driving licenses
- Roadworthiness tests
- Hire of personal transport equipment without drivers

Excludes:

- *Rental of a garage or parking space to provide parking in connection with the dwelling (04.1.2.2)*
- *Hire of a car with driver; payments for private arrangements of sharing a means of transport (carpooling, dynamic ridesharing) (07.3.2.2)*
- *Service charges for insurance in respect of personal transport equipment (12.1.4.1)*

07.2.4.1 Services for Parking (S)

Includes:

- Rental of garages or parking spaces not providing parking in connection with the dwelling
- Rental of municipal street parking
- Parking meters
- Charges for parking places in parking garages, such as those in shopping centers hired for a few hours or less (including valet service)

Includes also:

- Parking permits for designated areas (for example, residents parking permits)

Excludes:

- *Rental of a garage or parking space to provide parking in connection with the dwelling (04.1.2.2)*

07.2.4.2 Toll Facilities (S)

Includes:

- Tolls (bridges, tunnels, shuttle ferries, and motorways)
- Charges for hire or purchase of electronic tags and toll devices

07.2.4.3 Driving Lessons, Tests, Licenses, and Road Worthiness Tests (S)

Includes:

- Driving lessons, tests, licenses
- Roadworthiness tests and pollution control tests

Includes also:

- Ownership transfer charges for vehicles
- Driving lessons, test, licenses for recreation transport vehicles (mobile homes, boats, and planes)

07.2.4.4 Hire of Personal Transport Equipment Without Driver (S)

Includes:

- Hire of personal transport equipment without driver (for example, car hire)
- Fees for the participation in "car-sharing" or "bike-sharing" programs

Excludes:

- *Payments for private arrangements of sharing a means of transport (carpooling, dynamic ridesharing) (07.3.2.2)*
- *Service charges for insurance in respect of personal transport equipment (12.1.4.1)*

07.3 Passenger Transport Services

Purchases of transport services are generally classified by mode of transport. When a ticket covers two or more modes of transport—for example, intraurban bus and underground or interurban train and ferry—and the expenditure cannot be apportioned between them, then such purchases should be classified in 07.3.5.0.

Costs of meals, snacks, drinks, refreshments, or accommodation services have to be included if covered by the fare and not separately priced. If separately priced, these costs have to be classified in Division 11.

School transport services are included, but ambulance services are excluded (06.4.2.0).

07.3.1 Passenger Transport by Railway (S)

Includes:

- Transport of individuals and groups of persons and accompanied luggage by train, high-speed trains, maglevs, light-rail, tram, and underground
- Accompanied transport of private vehicles

Excludes:

- *Funicular transport (07.3.6.0)*

07.3.1.1 Passenger Transport by Train (S)

Includes:

- Transport of individuals and groups of persons and accompanied luggage by train, high-speed trains, maglevs

Excludes:

- *Funicular transport (07.3.6.0)*

07.3.1.2 Passenger Transport by Rapid Transit and Tram (S)

Includes:

- Transport of individuals and groups of persons and accompanied luggage by rapid transit (electric railways that operate on an exclusive right-of-way, which cannot be accessed by pedestrians or other vehicles of any sort, and which is often grade separated in tunnels or on elevated railways), light-rail, underground, rubber-tired metros, and people movers
- Transport of individuals and groups of persons and accompanied luggage by tram

07.3.2 Passenger Transport by Road (S)

Includes:

- Transport of individuals and groups of persons and accompanied luggage by bus, trolleybus, and coach
- Transport of individuals and groups of persons and accompanied luggage by share taxis (mode of transport which falls between both taxicabs and buses; these vehicles for hire are typically smaller than buses and usually take passengers on a fixed or semifixed route without timetables; they may stop anywhere to pick up or drop off their passengers; often found in developing countries, the vehicles used as share taxis range from four-seat cars to minibuses; and they are often owner-operated)
- Transport of individuals and groups of persons and accompanied luggage by taxi and hired vehicle with driver
- Transport of individuals and groups of persons and accompanied luggage through private arrangements, such as carpooling and ridesharing
- Local school bus charter services, with driver
- Scheduled interurban or intercity school bus charter services
- Transportation services of pupils by school bus between their homes and school and between schools, including in rural areas
- Transport of individuals and groups of persons and accompanied luggage by animal-drawn vehicles with driver

Includes also:

- Tuk-tuks, rickshaws, and motorcycles as taxis

07.3.2.1 Passenger Transport by Bus and Coach (S)

Includes:

- Transport of individuals and groups of persons and accompanied luggage by bus, trolleybus, and coach
- Transport of individuals and groups of persons and accompanied luggage by share taxis (mode of transport which falls between both taxicabs and buses; these vehicles for hire are typically smaller than buses and usually take passengers on a fixed or semifixed route without timetables; they may stop anywhere to pick up or drop off their passengers; often found in developing countries, the

vehicles used as share taxis range from four-seat cars to minibuses; and they are often owner-operated)

07.3.2.2 Passenger Transport by Taxi and Hired Car with Driver (S)

Includes:

- Transport of individuals and groups of persons and accompanied luggage by taxi and hired vehicle with driver
- Transport of individuals and groups of persons and accompanied luggage through private arrangements, such as carpooling and ridesharing

07.3.2.3 Passenger Transport for Students to and from School (S)

Includes:

- Local school bus charter services, with driver
- Scheduled interurban or intercity school bus charter services
- Transportation services of pupils by school bus between their homes and school and between schools, including in rural areas

07.3.2.9 Other Passenger Transport by Road (S)

Includes:

- Transport of individuals and groups of persons and accompanied luggage by animal-drawn vehicles with driver

Includes also:

- Tuk-tuks, rickshaws, and motorcycles as taxis

Excludes:

- *Bus with driver (07.3.2.1)*

07.3.3 Passenger Transport by Air (S)

Includes:

- Transport of individuals and groups of persons and luggage by airplane and helicopter. It includes also passenger drones and multicopters

07.3.3.1 Passenger Transport by Air, Domestic (S)

Includes:

- Domestic scheduled and chartered air passenger transportation services
- Domestic transport of individuals and groups of persons and accompanied luggage by airplane and helicopter
- Domestic air passenger transport by drones and multicopters

07.3.3.2 Passenger Transport by Air, International (S)

Includes:

- Transportation of passengers by air on an international scheduled and chartered flight

07.3.4 Passenger Transport by Sea and Inland Waterway (S)

Includes:

- Transport of individuals and groups of persons and accompanied luggage by ship, boat, ferry, hovercraft, and hydrofoil
- Accompanied transport of private vehicles
- Water taxis

07.3.4.0 Passenger Transport by Sea and Inland Waterway (S)

Includes:

- Transport of individuals and groups of persons and accompanied luggage by ship, boat, ferry, hovercraft, and hydrofoil
- Accompanied transport of private vehicles
- Water taxis

07.3.5 Combined Passenger Transport (S)

Includes:

- Transport of individuals and groups of persons and accompanied luggage by two or more modes of transport when the expenditure cannot be apportioned between them
- Multiple modes of transport (for example, bus, tram, subway, and ferry) available on the one ticket

Includes also:

- Accompanied transport of private vehicles (for example, train ticket that includes transport of private vehicles)

Excludes:

- *Package holidays (09.8.0.0)*

07.3.5.0 Combined Passenger Transport (S)

Includes:

- Transport of individuals and groups of persons and accompanied luggage by two or more modes of transport when the expenditure cannot be apportioned between them
- Multiple modes of transport (for example, bus, tram, subway, and ferry) available on the one ticket

Includes also:

- Accompanied transport of private vehicles (for example, train ticket that includes transport of private vehicles)

Excludes:

- *Package holidays (09.8.0.0)*

07.3.6 Other Purchased Transport Services (S)

Includes:

- Funicular, elevator, cable car, and chairlift transport
- Services of porters and left-luggage (services to store travelers' luggage for limited amount of time) and luggage-forwarding offices
- Travel agents' commissions, if separately priced
- Transporter bridges, elevators, incline elevators

Excludes:

- *Cable car and chairlift transport at ski resorts and holiday centers (09.4.6.2)*

07.3.6.0 Other Purchased Transport Services (S)

Includes:

- Funicular, elevator, cable car, and chairlift transport
- Services of porters and left-luggage (services to store travelers' luggage for limited amount of time) and luggage-forwarding offices
- Travel agents' commissions, if separately priced
- Transporter bridges, elevators, incline elevators

Excludes:

- *Cable car and chairlift transport at ski resorts and holiday centers (09.4.6.2)*

07.4 Transport Services of Goods

07.4.1 Postal and Courier Services (S)

Includes:

- New postage stamps and other prefranked postal matter (for example, prefranked postcards, envelopes, and so on)
- Courier services for letters
- Parcels delivery services (incoming and outcoming—parcels sent and delivery of parcels at home)
- Courier services for small parcels
- Parcel delivery services of goods purchased online
- Removal services of furniture
- Storage services of furniture
- Services of delivery of goods, such as furniture, supermarket shopping when charged separately
- Local delivery of purchased items, such as take-out meals, groceries, and prescription drugs
- Delivery services generally made immediately after the item is purchased or scheduled within a short time

Excludes:

- *Self-storage units (04.1.2.2)*
- *Installation of goods (furniture, electric devices, and so on) when separately charged (05.1.2.0 or 05.3.3.0)*
- *Services of porters and left-luggage and luggage-forwarding offices (07.3.6.0)*
- *Services of delivery of goods, such as furniture, supermarket shopping when charged separately (07.4.9.2)*
- *Not prefranked postcards, envelopes, and other not prefranked postal matter (09.7.3.0)*

07.4.1.1 Letter Handling Services (S)

Includes:

- New postage stamps and other prefranked postal matter (for example, prefranked postcards, envelopes, and so on)
- Courier services for letters

Excludes:

- *Not prefranked postcards, envelopes, and other not prefranked postal matter (09.7.3.0)*

07.4.1.2 Courier and Parcel Delivery Services (S)

Includes:

- Parcel delivery services (incoming and outgoing—parcels sent and delivery of parcels to a home)
- Courier services for small parcels
- Parcel delivery services of goods purchased online

Excludes:

- *Services of delivery of goods, such as furniture, supermarket shopping when charged separately (07.4.9.2)*

07.4.9 Other Transport of Goods (S)

Includes:

- Removal services of furniture
- Storage services of furniture
- Services of delivery of goods, such as furniture, supermarket shopping when charged separately
- Local delivery of purchased items, such as take-out meals, groceries, and prescription drugs
- Delivery services generally made immediately after the item is purchased or scheduled within a short time

Excludes:

- *Self-storage units (04.1.2.2)*
- *Installation of goods (furniture, electric devices, and so on) when separately charged (05.1.2.0 or 05.3.3.0)*
- *Services of porters and left-luggage and luggage-forwarding offices (07.3.6.0)*

07.4.9.1 Removal and Storage Services (S)

Includes:

- Removal services of furniture
- Storage services of furniture

Excludes:

- *Self-storage units (04.1.2.2)*
- *Services of porters and left-luggage and luggage-forwarding offices (07.3.6.0)*

07.4.9.2 Delivery of Goods (S)

Includes:

- Services of delivery of goods, such as furniture, supermarket shopping when charged separately
- Local delivery of purchased items, such as take-out meals, groceries, and prescription drugs
- Delivery services generally made immediately after the item is purchased or scheduled within a short time

Excludes:

- *Installation of goods (furniture, electric devices, and so on) when separately charged (05.1.2.0 or 05.3.3.0)*

08 Information and Communication

Division 08 covers three main groups of goods and services: information and communication equipment, including equipment for the reception, recording, and reproduction of sound and vision; software; and information and communication services. Information and communication services include telephone other communication services, internet access services, TV and radio licenses, and fee and subscription services, including streaming services of film and music.

Division 08 also includes repair, maintenance, and hire of information and communication equipment.

08.1 Information and Communication Equipment

08.1.1 Fixed Telephone Equipment (D)

Includes:

- Telephones, radiotelephones, telefax machines, telephone-answering machines, and telephone loudspeakers

Excludes:

- *Telefax and telephone-answering facilities provided by personal computers (08.1.3.1)*

08.1.1.0 Fixed Telephone Equipment (D)

Includes:

- Telephones, radiotelephones, telefax machines, telephone-answering machines, and telephone loudspeakers

Excludes:

- *Telefax and telephone-answering facilities provided by personal computers (08.1.3.1)*

08.1.2 Mobile Telephone Equipment (D)

Includes:

- Mobile telephone handsets, including devices with several functions
- Smartphones

08.1.2.0 Mobile Telephone Equipment (D)

Includes:

- Mobile telephone handsets, including devices with several functions
- Smartphones

08.1.3 Information Processing Equipment (D)

Includes:

- Personal computers, printers, scanners, monitors, projectors, virtual reality head mounts, modems, routers, network switches, and the like, keyboards, mice, digitizers
- Tablets
- Calculators, including pocket calculators
- Typewriters and word processors (device)
- Toner and ink cartridges, laser printer drums, and typewriter ribbons

Includes also:

- Telefax and telephone-answering facilities provided by personal computers

Excludes:

- *Computer software packages, such as operating systems, applications, languages, and so on (08.2.0.0)*
- *Video game software; video game computers and consoles (09.2.1.1)*
- *Removable media containing books, dictionaries, encyclopedias, foreign language trainers, multimedia presentations, and so on in the form of software (09.7.1)*

08.1.3.1 Computers, Laptops, and Tablets (D)

Includes:

- Desktop computers and laptops
- Tablets

Includes also:

- Telefax and telephone-answering facilities provided by personal computers

Excludes:

- *Computer software packages, such as operating systems, applications, languages, and so on (08.2.0.0)*
- *Video game software; video game computers and consoles (09.2.1.1)*
- *Removable media containing books, dictionaries, encyclopedias, foreign language trainers, multimedia presentations, and so on in the form of software (09.7.1)*

08.1.3.2 Peripheral Equipment and Its Consumable Components (D)

Includes:

- Printers, scanners, monitors, projectors, virtual reality head mounts, modems, routers, network switches, and the like, keyboards, mice, digitizers
- Typewriters and word processors (device)
- Toner and ink cartridges, laser printer drums, and typewriter ribbons
- Calculators, including pocket calculators
- Web cameras

08.1.4 Equipment for the Reception, Recording, and Reproduction of Sound and Vision (D)

Includes:

- Television sets, video cassette players and recorders, digital video recorders, DVD players, Blu-ray players, Ultra HD Blu-ray players, streaming boxes, television aerials of all types
- Radio receivers (radio sets, digital radio sets, internet radio sets, satellite radio sets, car radios, radio clocks, two-way radios, amateur radio receivers, and transmitters)
- Portable and nonportable CD players
- Portable and nonportable sound players
- Stereo equipment and CD radio cassette recorder
- Turntables, tuners, amplifiers, cassette decks, microphones and speakers, disc jockey equipment, and karaoke systems
- Car stereos, video systems for cars
- Set-top boxes, satellite receivers, IPTV receivers, and television converter boxes
- Digital media players
- Headphone, earplugs, and wireless/Bluetooth headsets

08.1.4.0 Equipment for the Reception, Recording, and Reproduction of Sound and Vision (D)

Includes:

- Television sets, video cassette players and recorders, digital video recorders, DVD players, Blu-ray players, Ultra HD Blu-ray players, streaming boxes, and television aerials of all types
- Radio receivers (radio sets, digital radio sets, internet radio sets, satellite radio sets, car radios, radio clocks, two-way radios, amateur radio receivers, and transmitters)
- Portable and nonportable CD players
- Portable and nonportable sound players
- Stereo equipment and CD radio cassette recorder
- Turntables, tuners, amplifiers, cassette decks, microphones and speakers, disc jockey equipment, and karaoke systems
- Car stereos, video systems for cars
- Set-top boxes, satellite receivers, IPTV receivers, and television converter boxes
- Digital media players
- Headphone, earplugs, and wireless/Bluetooth headsets

08.1.5 Unrecorded Recording Media (SD)

Includes:

- CDs (R and RW)
- DVDs (R and RW)
- Blu-ray discs (R and RE)
- Video cassettes
- Audio tapes, cassettes, DAT
- External hard drives and solid state disks, network attached storage
- USB keys/flash drives
- SD cards, compact flash, and so on
- Magnetic data tapes
- Other magnetic recording media
- Other optical recording media
- Other recording media (phase-change recording media, holographic recording media, molecular recording media)

Excludes:

- *Recorded recording media (09.5.2.0, 09.7.1)*

08.1.5.0 Unrecorded Recording Media (SD)

Includes:

- CDs (R and RW)
- DVDs (R and RW)
- Blu-ray discs (R and RE)
- Video cassettes
- Audio tapes, cassettes, DAT
- External hard drives and solid state disks, network attached storage
- USB keys/flash drives
- SD cards, compact flash, and so on
- Magnetic data tapes
- Other magnetic recording media
- Other optical recording media
- Other recording media (phase-change recording media, holographic recording media, molecular recording media)

Excludes:

- *Recorded recording media (09.5.2.0, 09.7.1)*

08.1.9 Other Information and Communication Equipment and Accessories (D)

Includes:

- Walkie-talkies
- Baby monitors
- Smartwatches
- Fitness trackers, and other wearable devices, such as, for example, smart glasses that do not work without a smartphone or tablet
- E-book readers
- Chargers, batteries, cables, power banks, docking stations, covers, cases, cradles, and mounts
- Disk drives, processors, main boards, and hard drives

08.1.9.1 Other Information and Communication Equipment (D)

Includes:

- Walkie-talkies
- Baby monitors
- Smartwatches
- Fitness trackers, and other wearable devices, such as smart glasses that do not work without a smartphone or tablet
- E-book readers

08.1.9.2 Other Information and Communication Accessories (SD)

Includes:

- Chargers, batteries for information and communication equipment, cables, power banks, docking stations, covers, cases, cradles, and mounts
- Disk drives, processors, main boards, and hard drives

08.2 Software Excluding Games

08.2.0 Software (S)

Includes:

- Computer software packages, such as operating systems, applications, programming languages, and so on

Includes also:

- Software subscriptions and use of online software
- Apps

Excludes:

- *Video game software (09.2.1.1)*
- *Removable media containing books, dictionaries, encyclopedias, foreign language trainers, multimedia presentations, and so on in the form of software (09.7.1.1)*

08.2.0.0 Software (S)

Includes:

- Computer software packages, such as operating systems, applications, programming languages, and so on

Includes also:

- Software subscriptions and use of online software
- Apps

Excludes:

- *Video game software (09.2.1.1)*
- *Removable media containing books, dictionaries, encyclopedias, foreign language trainers, multimedia presentations, and so on in the form of software (09.7.1.1)*

08.3 Information and Communication Services

08.3.1 Fixed Communication Services (S)

Includes:

- Installation and subscription costs of personal telephone equipment
- Telephone calls from a private line or from a public line (public telephone box, post office cabin, and so on)
- Local, regional, national, and international calls
- Telephone calls from hotels, cafés, restaurants, and the like

08.3.1.0 Fixed Communication Services (S)

Includes:

- Installation and subscription costs of personal telephone equipment
- Telephone calls from a private line or from a public line (public telephone box, post office cabin, and so on)
- Local, regional, national, and international calls
- Telephone calls from hotels, cafés, restaurants, and the like

08.3.2 Mobile Communication Services (S)

Includes:

- National calls, including voice and video calls
- International calls, including voice and video calls
- Messages, including voice, written (short message service), and image (multimedia message service) messages, and subscription fees for other messengers
- Additional calling features, such as voicemail and call display, whether sold separately or bundled with the mobile local service plan
- Voice and messaging cell phone plans that also include limited data
- Mobile phone voice, text, and data plans
- Other mobile telephone services

Includes also:

- Costs of telephone equipment if included in subscription costs
- Mobile phones included in a package, that is, prepaid or postpaid packages, generally tied to a specific operator for a certain period of time if not separately priced

08.3.2.0 Mobile Communication Services (S)

Includes:

- National calls, including voice and video calls
- International calls, including voice and video calls
- Messages, including voice, written (short message service), and image (multimedia message service) messages, and subscription fees for other messengers
- Additional calling features, such as voicemail and call display, whether sold separately or bundled with the mobile local service plan
- Voice and messaging cell phone plans that also include limited data
- Mobile phone voice, text, and data plans
- Other mobile telephone services

Includes also:

- Costs of telephone equipment if included in subscription costs
- Mobile phones included in a package, that is, prepaid or postpaid packages, generally tied to a specific operator for a certain period of time if not separately priced

08.3.3 Internet Access Provision Services and Net Storage Services (S)

Includes:

- Internet access services provided by operators of wired, wireless, or satellite infrastructure
- Cloud storage, file hosting, and web hosting services
- Subscriptions for email services

Includes also:

- Activation and installation fees and monthly rate

08.3.3.0 Internet Access Provision Services and Net Storage Services (S)

Includes:

- Internet access services provided by operators of wired, wireless, or satellite infrastructure
- Cloud storage, file hosting, and web hosting services
- Subscriptions for email services

Includes also:

- Activation and installation fees and monthly rate

08.3.4 Bundled Telecommunication Services (S)

Includes:

- Telephony/internet/television packages
- Any combination of telecommunication package

08.3.4.0 Bundled Telecommunication Services (S)

Includes:

- Telephony/internet/television packages
- Any combination of telecommunication package

08.3.5 Repair and Rental of Information and Communication Equipment (S)

The cost of materials is included only if the materials are not separately invoiced.

Includes:

- Repair of all information and communication equipment
- Rental of telephones, telefax machines, telephone-answering machines, and telephone loudspeakers
- Rental of wireless telephone equipment
- Rental of internet access provision equipment
- Rental of telegraphy, telex, telefax, radiotelephony, radiotelegraphy, and radiotelex equipment

08.3.5.0 Repair and Rental of Information and Communication Equipment (S)

The cost of materials is included only if the materials are not separately invoiced.

Includes:

- Repair of all information and communication equipment
- Rental of telephones, telefax machines, telephone-answering machines, and telephone loudspeakers
- Rental of wireless telephone equipment
- Rental of internet access provision equipment
- Rental of telegraphy, telex, telefax, radiotelephony, radiotelegraphy, and radiotelex equipment

08.3.9 Other Information and Communication Services (S)

Includes:

- Telegraphy, telex, and telefax services
- Voice over Internet Protocol provision (nomadic use)
- TV and radio licenses
- Subscription to cable TV, satellite TV, IPTV, and Pay-TV
- Streaming services
- Online videorecorder services (web-based DVR services)
- Video-on-demand services
- Rental or subscription of CDs, videotapes, DVDs, Blu-ray discs, and software (excluding game software)

Includes also:

- Radiotelephony, radiotelegraphy, and radiotelex services
- Software installation services
- Rental/lease fees for a decoder, TV set-top boxes, and so on

Excludes:

- *Rental or subscription of video game software and online games (09.4.3.1)*
- *Audiovisual content purchased online for immediate downloading (09.5.2.0)*

08.3.9.1 TV and Radio Licenses and Fees (S)

Includes:

- TV and radio licenses

08.3.9.2 Subscription to Audiovisual Content, Streaming Services, and Rentals of Audiovisual Content (S)

Includes:

- Streaming services (film and music)
- Rental, download or subscription of CDs, videotapes, DVDs, Blu-ray discs, and software (excluding game software)
- Subscription to cable TV, satellite TV, IPTV, and Pay-TV
- Online videorecorder services (web-based DVR services)
- Video-on-demand services
- Subscription to TV via decoder and rental of decoders

Excludes:

- *Rental or subscription of video game software and online games (09.2.1.1)*
- *Audiovisual content purchased online for immediate downloading (09.5.2.0)*

08.3.9.9 Other Information and Communication Services (S)

Includes:

- Telegraphy, telex, and telefax services
- Radiotelephony, radiotelegraphy, and radiotelex services
- Voice over Internet Protocol provision (nomadic use)
- Rental/lease fees for a decoder
- Software installation services

09 Recreation, Sport, and Culture

Division 09 covers a wide range of goods and services for recreation, sport, and culture, and it is structured into eight groups. The first group covers recreation durables: photographic equipment, other major durables for recreation, such as camper vans, boats, yachts, airplanes, and the like. Division 09.2 covers nonmajor durable recreational goods, such as games and toys, including video game computers, celebration articles, equipment for sport, camping, and open-air recreation. The third group covers garden products and plants and flowers and purchases of pets and expenditures for pets, excluding veterinary services. Recreational services cover rental, maintenance, and repair of goods classified in Division 09, veterinary and other services for pets, recreational and leisure services, such as amusement parks, games of chance and expenditures for sporting services, both expenditures for practising sports as well as expenditures for attendance of sports events.

Division 09.5 covers cultural goods, such as musical instruments and audiovisual media, followed by cultural services (cinema, theatre, concert, museum, and other cultural sites, and photographic services). Whether books or newspapers are in printed or electronic form is irrelevant for classifying them under 09.7.

The last group (09.8) covers package holidays, which as a bundle include all kinds of services, such as transportation, accommodation, food provision, tour guide, and so on. Expenditures for package holidays cannot be split into its components and thus a separate classification category was created. The length of the package holiday and whether the holiday destination is within the home country or outside does not matter.

09.1 Recreational Durables

09.1.1 Photographic and Cinematographic Equipment and Optical Instruments (D)

Includes:

- Still cameras, movie cameras and sound-recording cameras, film and slide projectors, enlargers, and film processing equipment

- Video cameras, including camcorders, action cameras
- Screens, viewers, lenses (including zoom lenses), lenses, flash attachments, filters, exposure meters, and so on
- Photographic developer and photographic paper
- Binoculars, microscopes, telescopes, and compasses

Includes also:

- Separate material purchased by households with the intention of undertaking the repairs themselves
- Batteries and chargers for cameras and other photographic and cinematographic equipment

Excludes:

- *Dash cameras (07.2.1.3)*
- *Webcams (08.1.3.2)*

09.1.1.1 Cameras (D)

Includes:

- Still cameras, movie cameras and sound-recording cameras, film and slide projectors, enlargers, and film processing equipment
- Video cameras, including camcorders, action cameras

Includes also:

- Separate material purchased by households with the intention of undertaking the repairs themselves

Excludes:

- *Dash cameras (07.2.1.3)*
- *Webcams (08.1.3.2)*

09.1.1.2 Accessories for Photographic and Cinematographic Equipment (D)

Includes:

- Screens, viewers, lenses (including zoom lenses), lenses, flash attachments, filters, exposure meters, and so on
- Photographic developer and photographic paper

Includes also:

- Separate material purchased by households with the intention of undertaking the repairs themselves
- Camera-specific batteries and chargers

09.1.1.3 Optical Instruments (D)

Includes:

- Binoculars, microscopes, telescopes, and compasses

09.1.2 Major Durables for Recreation (D)

Includes:

- Camper vans, caravans, and trailers
- Airplanes, microlight aircraft, gliders, hang gliders, and hot-air balloons
- Boats, yachts, outboard motors, sails, rigging, and superstructures
- Vessels for recreation, sailboats, sailboards, and water sport boards
- Canoes, kayaks, and windsurfing boards
- Sea-diving equipment
- Horses and ponies, horse- or pony-drawn vehicles, camels, and dromedaries, purchased for recreational purposes and related equipment (harnesses, bridles, reins, saddles, and so on)
- Golf carts
- Large steel-frame swimming pools for the garden
- Billiard tables, ping-pong tables, pinball machines, gaming machines, and so on
- Bicycles with four wheels
- Other major durables for recreation n.e.c.

Includes also:

- Separate material purchased by households with the intention of undertaking the repairs themselves

Excludes:

- *Horses and ponies, horse- or pony-drawn vehicles, camels and dromedaries, and related equipment purchased for personal transport (07.1.4.0)*
- *Inflatable boats, rafts, and swimming pools for children and the beach (09.2.2.2)*

09.1.2.1 Camper Vans, Caravans, and Trailers (D)

Includes:

- Camper vans, caravans, and trailers

09.1.2.2 Airplanes, Microlight Aircraft, Gliders, Hang Gliders, and Hot-Air Balloons (D)

Includes:

- Airplanes, microlight aircraft, gliders, hang gliders, and hot-air balloons

09.1.2.3 Boats, Yachts, Outboard Motors, and Other Water Sports Equipment (D)

Includes:

- Boats, yachts, outboard motors, sails, jet sky, rigging, and superstructures
- Vessels for recreation, sailboats, sailboards, and water sport boards
- Canoes, kayaks, and windsurfing boards
- Sea-diving equipment

Excludes:

- *Inflatable boats, rafts, and swimming pools for children (09.2.2.2)*

09.1.2.4 Horses, Ponies, Camel and Dromedaries, and Accessories (D)

Includes:

- Horses and ponies, horse- or pony-drawn vehicles, camels and dromedaries, purchased for recreational purposes and related equipment (harnesses, bridles, reins, saddles, and so on)

Excludes:

- *Horses and ponies, horse- or pony-drawn vehicles, camels and dromedaries, and related equipment purchased for personal transport (07.1.4.0)*

09.1.2.9 Other Major Durables for Recreation (D)

Includes:

- Golf carts
- Snowmobiles
- Large steel-frame swimming pools for the garden
- Billiard tables, ping-pong tables, pinball machines, gaming machines, and so on
- Bicycles with four wheels
- Other major durables for recreation n.e.c.

Excludes:

- *Inflatable boats, rafts, and swimming pools for children and the beach (09.2.2.2)*

09.2 Other Recreational Goods

09.2.1 Games, Toys, and Hobbies (SD)

Includes:

- Card games, board games, parlor games, chess sets, and the like
- Video game software, video game computers that plug into a television set, video game cassettes, video game CD-ROMs, and video game downloads
- Game apps
- Gamepads, joysticks, racing wheels, and other accessories for video gaming
- Electronic games
- Toys of all kinds including dolls, soft toys, toy cars and trains, toy bicycles and tricycles, toy construction sets, puzzles, modeling clay, electronic games, masks, disguises, jokes, novelties, fireworks and rockets, festoons, and holiday decorations
- Stamp-collecting requisites (used or canceled postage stamps, stamp albums, and so on), other items for collections (coins, medals, minerals, zoological and botanical specimens, and so on), and other tools and articles n.e.c. for hobbies

Includes also:

- Separate purchases of materials made by households, with the intention of undertaking the maintenance and repair themselves

Excludes:

- *Collectors' items falling into the category of works of art or antiques (05.1.1.1 or capital formation if acquired primarily as stores of value)*
- *Video game subscriptions and rentals (09.4.3.1)*
- *Children's scrapbooks (09.7.1.9)*

09.2.1.1 Video Game Computers, Game Consoles, Game Apps, and Software (SD)

Includes:

- Video game computers
- Video game consoles
- Gamepads, joysticks, racing wheels, and other accessories for video gaming
- Electronic games
- Video game software (for game consoles, computers, tablets, smartphones, download, and on any media, including CD-ROMs, cartridges, DVDs, Blu-ray discs, flash drives, and so on)
- Game apps

Excludes:

- *Video game subscriptions and rentals (09.4.3.1)*

09.2.1.2 Other Games, Toys, and Hobbies (SD)

Includes:

- Traditional games, for example, card games, parlor games, board games, chess sets
- Dolls
- Toy cars, including toy trains, toy bicycles, and tricycles
- Soft toys, teddy bears, and so on
- Toy construction sets
- Puzzles
- Modeling clay
- Masks
- Disguises
- Jokes
- Models/replicas of planes, boats, trains, and so on
- Hobby-stamp-collecting requisites (used or canceled postage stamps, stamp albums, and so on)
- Other items for collections (coins, medals, minerals, zoological and botanical specimens, and so on) and other tools and articles n.e.c. for hobby purposes

Excludes:

- *Collectors' items falling into the category of works of art or antiques (05.1.1.1 or capital formation if acquired primarily as stores of value)*
- *Children's scrapbooks (09.7.1.9)*

09.2.1.3 Celebration Articles (ND)

Includes:

- Fireworks and rockets
- Festoons
- Christmas trees
- Holiday decorations (for Christmas, Easter, Hanukkah, Eid, Diwali, and similar)

09.2.2 Equipment for Sport, Camping, and Open-Air Recreation (SD)

Includes:

- Gymnastic, physical education, and sport equipment, such as balls, shuttlecocks, nets, rackets, bats, skis, golf clubs, foils, sabers, poles, weights, discuses, javelins, dumbbells, chest expanders, and other body-building equipment
- Parachutes, paragliders, and other skydiving equipment
- Firearms and ammunition for hunting, sport, and personal protection

- Fishing rods and other equipment for fishing
- Equipment for beach and open-air games, such as bowls, croquet, flying disks, volleyball, and inflatable boats, rafts, and swimming pools
- Inflatable boats, rafts, and swimming pools for children
- Skateboards, kickboards, smart balance wheels, and hoverboards
- Camping equipment, such as tents and accessories, sleeping bags, backpacks, air mattresses and inflating pumps, camping stoves, and barbecues

Includes also:

- Game-specific footwear (ski boots, football boots, golfing shoes, and other such footwear fitted with ice skates, rollers, spikes, studs, and so on); protective headgear for sports; other protective gear for sports, such as life jackets, boxing gloves, body padding, shin guards, goggles, belts, supports, and so on
- Separate purchases of materials made by households with the intention of undertaking the maintenance or repair themselves
- GPS (satellite positioning) equipment for boats or hiking

Excludes:

- *Garden and camping furniture (05.1.1.2)*
- *Crash helmets for motorcycles and bicycles (07.2.1.3)*
- *Repair of equipment for sport (09.4.4.0)*

09.2.2.1 Equipment for Sport (SD)

Includes:

- Gymnastic, physical education, and sport equipment, such as balls, shuttlecocks, nets, rackets, bats, skis, golf clubs, discuses, and javelins
- Parachutes, paragliders, and other skydiving equipment
- Firearms and ammunition for hunting, sport, and personal protection
- Fishing rods and other equipment for fishing
- Skateboards, kickboards, smart balance wheels, and hoverboards

Includes also:

- Game-specific footwear (ski boots, football boots, golfing shoes, and other such footwear fitted with ice skates, rollers, spikes, studs, and so on)
- Game-specific sportswear (ski suits and so on)
- Protective headgear for sports
- Other protective gear for sports, such as life jackets, boxing gloves, sport gloves, body padding, shin guards, pads, goggles, belts, supports, and helmets, for example, for skateboarding, inline skating, and ice hockey

Excludes:

- *Repair of equipment for sport (09.4.4.0)*

09.2.2.2 Equipment for Camping and Open-Air Recreation (SD)

Includes:

- Equipment for beach and open-air games, such as bowls, croquet, flying disks, volleyball and inflatable boats, rafts, and swimming pools
- Tents, sleeping bags, backpacks, air mattresses and inflating pumps, camping stoves, barbecues, and other accessories related to camping

Excludes:

- *Camping furniture (05.1.1.2)*
- *Repair of equipment for camping and open-air recreation (09.4.4.0)*

09.3 Garden Products and Pets

09.3.1 Garden Products, Plants, and Flowers (ND)

Includes:

- Soil, peat and fertilizers, pesticides, and composts
- Turf for lawns, specially treated soils for ornamental gardens, horticultural preparations
- Pots and pot holders
- Decorations and ornaments for gardens (which are not plants)
- Indoor plants, including natural or artificial
- Outdoor plants
- Seeds, bulbs, and tubers for planting
- Shrubs
- Indoor flowers (natural or artificial in vase or not)
- Outdoor flowers
- Flower seeds and bulbs
- Natural or artificial flowers and wreaths for decoration of burial places
- Cut flowers
- Delivery charges for flowers and plants if not separately priced

Excludes:

- *Gardening services (04.4.4.9, 05.6.2.1)*
- *Gardening equipment (05.5.1.0)*
- *Gardening tools (05.5.2.1)*
- *Insecticides and pesticides for household use; gardening gloves (05.6.1.9)*
- *Delivery charges for flowers and plants if separately priced (07.4.9.2)*
- *Christmas trees (09.2.1.3)*

09.3.1.1 Garden Products (ND)

Includes:

- Soil, peat and fertilizers, pesticides, and composts
- Turf for lawns, specially treated soils for ornamental gardens, horticultural preparations
- Pots and pot holders
- Decorations and ornaments for gardens (which are not plants)

Excludes:

- *Gardening services (04.4.4.9, 05.6.2.1)*
- *Gardening equipment (05.5.1.0)*
- *Gardening tools (05.5.2.1)*
- *Insecticides and pesticides for household use; gardening gloves (05.6.1.9)*

09.3.1.2 Plants, Seeds, and Flowers (ND)

Includes:

- Indoor plants, including natural or artificial
- Outdoor plants
- Seeds, bulbs, and tubers for planting
- Shrubs
- Indoor flowers (natural or artificial in vase or not)
- Outdoor flowers
- Flower seeds and bulbs
- Natural or artificial flowers and wreaths for decoration of burial places
- Cut flowers

Excludes:

- *Soil, peat, and fertilizers (09.3.1.1)*
- *Christmas trees (09.2.1.3)*

09.3.2 Pets and Related Products (ND)

Includes:

- Pets, pet foods, veterinary and grooming products for pets, collars, leashes, kennels, birdcages, fish tanks, cat litter, and so on

Includes also:

- Feed and veterinary products for animals used for transportation, own consumption or recreation

Excludes:

- *Horses and ponies, camels, and dromedaries, for transport (07.1.4.0)*
- *Horses and ponies, camels, and dromedaries, for recreation (09.1.2.4)*
- *Veterinary and other services for pets (09.4.5.0)*

09.3.2.1 Purchase of Pets (ND)

Includes:

- Purchase of pets

Excludes:

- *Horses and ponies, camels, and dromedaries, for transport (07.1.4.0)*
- *Horses and ponies, camels, and dromedaries, for recreation (09.1.2.4)*

09.3.2.2 Products for Pets and Other Household Animals (ND)

Includes:

- Pet foods, veterinary and grooming products for pets, collars, leashes, kennels, birdcages, fish tanks, cat litter, and so on

Includes also:

- Feed and veterinary products for animals used for transportation, own consumption or recreation

Excludes:

- *Veterinary and other services for pets and other household animals (09.4.5.0)*

09.4 Recreational Services

09.4.1 Hire and Repair of Photographic and Cinematographic Equipment and Optical Instruments (S)

The cost of materials is included only if the materials are not separately invoiced.

Includes:

- Hire of photographic and cinematographic equipment and optical instruments
- Repair of photographic and cinematographic equipment and optical instruments

Excludes:

- *Separate purchases of materials made by households with the intention of undertaking the repair themselves (09.1.1.2)*

09.4.1.0 Hire and Repair of Photographic and Cinematographic Equipment and Optical Instruments (S)

The cost of materials is included only if the materials are not separately invoiced.

Includes:

- Hire of photographic and cinematographic equipment and optical instruments
- Repair of photographic and cinematographic equipment and optical instruments

Excludes:

- *Separate purchases of materials made by households with the intention of undertaking the repair themselves (09.1.1.2)*

09.4.2 Hire, Maintenance, and Repair of Major Durables for Recreation (S)

The cost of materials is included only if the materials are not separately invoiced.

Includes:

- Maintenance and repair of major durables for recreation as described in 09.1.2
- Laying up for winter of boats, yachts, camper vans, caravans, and so on; hangar services for private planes; and marina services for boats
- Hire of major durables for recreation as described in 09.1.2.2, 09.1.2.3, and 09.1.2.9

Excludes:

- *Fuel for recreational vehicles (07.2.2.1, 07.2.2.2, 07.2.2.3)*
- *Separate purchases of materials made by households with the intention of undertaking the maintenance or repair themselves (09.1.2.1)*

09.4.2.1 Hire, Maintenance, and Repair of Camper Vans and Caravans (S)

The cost of materials is included only if the materials are not separately invoiced.

Includes:

- Hire of camper vans and caravans
- Maintenance and repair of camper vans and caravans
- Laying up for winter of camper vans and caravans

Excludes:

- *Fuel for recreational vehicles (07.2.2.1, 07.2.2.2, 07.2.2.3)*
- *Separate purchases of materials made by households with the intention of undertaking the maintenance or repair themselves (09.1.2.1)*

09.4.2.2 Hire, Maintenance, and Repair of Other Major Durables for Recreation (S)

The cost of materials is included only if the materials are not separately invoiced.

Includes:

- Hire of major durables for recreation as described in 09.1.2.2, 09.1.2.3, and 09.1.2.9
- Laying up for winter of boats, yachts, and so on; hangar services for private planes; and marina services for boats

Excludes:

- *Fuel for recreational vehicles (07.2.2.1, 07.2.2.2, 07.2.2.3)*
- *Separate purchases of materials made by households with the intention of undertaking the maintenance or repair themselves (09.1.2.1)*

09.4.3 Hire and Repair of Games, Toys, and Hobbies (S)

The cost of materials is included only if the materials are not separately invoiced.

Includes:

- Rental and subscriptions of video game consoles and apps or software
- Repair of video game consoles, toys, and hobby articles

09.4.3.1 Rental of Game Software and Subscription to Online Games (S)

Includes:

- Rental of game software (games on CDs, DVDs, Blu-ray discs, and so on)
- Subscription to play online games (or streaming)

09.4.3.2 Rental and Repair of Games, Toys, and Hobbies (S)

The cost of materials is included only if the materials are not separately invoiced.

Includes:

- Hire and repair of video game consoles and other equipment to play games
- Hire and repair of toys and hobby articles
- Hire of toys and games

09.4.4 Hire and Repair of Equipment for Sport, Camping, and Open-Air Recreation (S)

The cost of materials is included only if the materials are not separately invoiced.

Includes:

- Hire and repair of equipment for sport, camping, and open-air recreation
- Hire of beach umbrellas and deckchairs

09.4.4.0 Hire and Repair of Equipment for Sport, Camping, and Open-Air Recreation (S)

The cost of materials is included only if the materials are not separately invoiced.

Includes:

- Hire and repair of equipment for sport, camping, and open-air recreation
- Hire of beach umbrellas and deckchairs

09.4.5 Veterinary and Other Services for Pets (S)

Includes:

- Veterinary and other services for pets, such as grooming, boarding, tattooing, and training
- Pet boarding services or pet day care services

Includes also:

- Veterinary and hosting services for animals used for transportation

Excludes:

- *Products for pets (09.3.2.2)*

09.4.5.0 Veterinary and Other Services for Pets (S)

Includes:

- Veterinary and other services for pets, such as grooming, tattooing, and training
- Pet boarding services or pet day care services

Includes also:

- Veterinary and hosting services for animals used for transportation

Excludes:

- *Products for pets (09.3.2.2)*

09.4.6 Recreational and Sporting Services (S)

Includes:

Services provided by:

- Sports stadiums, horse-racing courses, motor-racing circuits, velodromes, and so on
- Skating rinks, swimming pools, golf courses, gymnasia, fitness centers, tennis courts, squash courts, and bowling alleys
- Fairgrounds and amusement parks
- Roundabouts, seesaws, and other playground facilities for children
- Pinball machines and other games for adults other than games of chance
- Arcade games
- Ski slopes, ski lifts, and the like
- Out-of-school individual or group lessons in bridge, chess, aerobics, skating, skiing, swimming, or other pastimes
- Membership fees for sports clubs and fitness centers
- Services of mountain guides, tour guides, and so on
- Navigational aid services for boating

- Water parks
- Arcade games
- Services of mountain guides, tour guides, and so on
- Entrance fees for dancing establishments, nightclubs
- Fees for taking part in sports competitions
- Fees for sports title and category certificates

Includes also:

- Hire of game-specific footwear (ski boots, football boots, golfing shoes, and other such footwear fitted with ice skates, rollers, spikes, studs, and so on)
- Paid fishing
- Membership fees of fishermen's and hunters' clubs

Excludes:

- *Cable car and chairlift transport not at ski resorts or holiday centers (07.3.6.0)*

09.4.6.1 Recreational and Leisure Services (S)

Includes:

Services provided by:

- Fairgrounds and amusement parks
- Roundabouts, seesaws, and other playground facilities for children
- Out-of-school individual or group lessons in bridge, chess, sewing, cooking, and so on
- Pin-ball machines and other games for adults other than games of chance
- Water parks
- Arcade games
- Services of mountain guides, tour guides, and so on
- Entrance fees for dancing establishments, nightclubs

09.4.6.2 Sporting Services—Practice (S)

Includes:

- Skating rinks, swimming pools, golf courses, gymnasia, fitness centers, tennis courts, squash courts, and bowling alleys
- Ski slopes, ski lifts, and the like
- Cable car and chairlift transport at ski resorts and holiday centers
- Out-of-school individual or group lessons in aerobics, skating, skiing, swimming, or other sports
- Memberships fees for sports clubs and fitness centers
- Navigational aid services for boating
- Fees for taking part in sports competitions
- Fees for sports title and category certificates

Includes also:

- Hire of game-specific footwear (ski boots, football boots, golfing shoes, and other such footwear fitted with ice skates, rollers, spikes, studs, and so on)
- Hunting licenses
- Paid fishing
- Membership fees of fishermen's and hunters' clubs

Excludes:

- *Cable car and chairlift transport not at ski resorts or holiday centers (07.3.6.0)*

09.4.6.3 Sporting Services—Attendance (S)

Includes:

- Admissions (tickets) to attend live sporting events like football games, hockey games, ice skating competitions, ski competitions, soccer games, tennis matches, horse-racing courses, motor-racing circuits, velodromes, and so on

09.4.7 Games of Chance (S)

Includes:

- Service charges for lotteries, bookmakers, totalizators, casinos, and other gambling establishments, gaming machines, bingo halls, scratch cards, sweepstakes, and so on
- Online games of chance

09.4.7.0 Games of Chance (S)

Includes:

- Service charges for lotteries, bookmakers, totalizators, casinos, and other gambling establishments, gaming machines, bingo halls, scratch cards, sweepstakes, and so on
- Online games of chance

09.5 Cultural Goods

09.5.1 Musical Instruments (D)

Includes:

- Musical instruments of all sizes, including electronic musical instruments, such as pianos, organs, violins, guitars, drums, trumpets, clarinets, flutes, recorders, harmonicas, and so on

Includes also:

- Spare parts of musical instruments

Excludes:

- *Toy instruments (09.2.1.2)*

09.5.1.0 Musical Instruments (D)

Includes:

- Musical instruments of all sizes, including electronic musical instruments, such as pianos, organs, violins, guitars, drums, trumpets, clarinets, flutes, recorders, harmonicas, and so on

Includes also:

- Spare parts of musical instruments

Excludes:

- *Toy instruments (09.2.1.2)*

09.5.2 Audiovisual Media (SD)

Includes:

- Recorded tapes, CD-ROMs, DVDs, Blu-ray discs, gramophone records, and flash drives, for reproduction of sound and picture material
- Downloads of music and films

Excludes:

- *Software (08.2.0.0)*
- *Video games and game apps and software (09.2.1.1)*
- *Recorded tapes and CDs, DVDs, Blu-ray, flash drives of books, novels, plays, poetry, dictionaries, encyclopedias, and so on (09.7.1)*

09.5.2.0 Audiovisual Media (SD)

Includes:

- Recorded tapes, CD-ROMs, DVDs, Blu-ray discs, gramophone records, and flash drives, for reproduction of sound and picture material
- Downloads of music and films

Excludes:

- *Software (08.2.0.0)*
- *Video games and game apps and software (09.2.1.1)*
- *Recorded tapes and CDs, DVDs, Blu-ray discs, flash drives of books, novels, plays, poetry, dictionaries, encyclopedias, and so on (09.7.1)*

09.6 Cultural Services

09.6.1 Cinemas, Theatres, and Concerts (S)

Includes:

- Cinemas
- Theatres, opera houses
- Concert and music venues
- Circuses, sound and light shows, and other

Includes also:

- Services of musicians, clowns, performers for private entertainments
- Music, dancing, and artistic performance
- Art and music festivals

09.6.1.0 Cinemas, Theatres, and Concerts (S)

Includes:

- Cinemas
- Theatres, opera houses
- Concert and music venues
- Circuses, sound and light shows, and other

Includes also:

- Services of musicians, clowns, performers for private entertainments
- Music, dancing, and artistic performance
- Art and music festivals

09.6.2 Museums, Libraries, and Cultural Sites (S)

Includes:

- Museums, art galleries, and exhibitions, including historical monuments and archeological sites
- Libraries
- Historic monuments, national parks, zoological and botanical gardens, and aquaria

09.6.2.0 Museums, Libraries, and Cultural Sites (S)

Includes:

- Museums, art galleries, exhibitions, including historical monuments and archeological sites
- Libraries
- Historic monuments, national parks, zoological and botanical gardens, and aquaria

09.6.3 Photographic Services (S)

Includes:

- Services of photographers, such as film developing, print processing, enlarging, portrait photography, event photography and video (for example, for weddings), and so on

Includes also:

- Photographic services provided by nonspecialized shops (for example, supermarkets, consumer electronic stores, and so on) and purchased by internet

09.6.3.0 Photographic Services (S)

Includes:

- Services of photographers, such as film developing, print processing, enlarging, portrait photography, event photography and video (for example, for weddings), and so on

Includes also:

- Photographic services provided by nonspecialized shops (for example, supermarkets, consumer electronic stores, and so on) and purchased by internet

09.6.9 Other Cultural Services (S)

Includes:

- Services of rental and repair of musical instruments
- Binding services
- Photography, music, dancing, and artistic classes (in classroom or via e-learning)

Includes also:

- Rental of premises for rehearsals of amateur music groups, weddings, and other celebrations

Excludes:

- *Formal education of music, dancing, and art (Division 10 according to the level)*

09.6.9.0 Other Cultural Services (S)

Includes:

- Services of rental and repair of musical instruments
- Binding services
- Photography, music, dancing, and artistic classes (in classroom or via e-learning)

Includes also:

- Rental of premises for rehearsals of amateur music groups, weddings, and other celebrations

Excludes:

- *Formal education of music, dancing, and art (Division 10 according to the level)*

09.7 Newspapers, Books, and Stationery

09.7.1 Books (SD)

Includes:

- Books educational or not, including atlases, dictionaries, encyclopedias, guidebooks, and musical scores
- Recorded tapes and CDs, DVDs, Blu-ray discs, flash drives of educational books novels, plays, poetry, and so on
- All electronic forms of books (e-books and audio books)
- Removable media containing books, dictionaries, encyclopedias, foreign language trainers, multimedia presentations, and so on in the form of software
- Scrapbooks and albums for children

Includes also:

- All electronic forms of educational books (e-books and audio books)

Excludes:

- *Stamp albums (09.2.1.2)*

09.7.1.1 Educational and Text Books (SD)

Includes:

- Formal education text books (school/academic manuals, and so on)
- Recorded tapes and CDs, DVDs, Blu-ray discs, flash drives of educational books
- Download of educational books
- Removable media containing books, dictionaries, encyclopedias, foreign language trainers, in the form of software

Includes also:

- All electronic forms of educational books (e-books and audio books)

09.7.1.9 Other Books (SD)

Includes:

- Fiction and nonfiction books
- Children's books, scrapbooks and albums for children, and coloring books for children
- Art books
- Travel guides
- Recorded tapes and CDs, DVDs, Blu-ray discs, flash drives of books, novels, plays, poetry, and so on
- Download of noneducational books

Includes also:

- All electronic forms of books (e-books and audio books); scrapbooks and albums for children

Excludes:

- *Stamp albums (09.2.1.2)*

09.7.2 Newspapers and Periodicals (ND)

Includes:

- Newspapers, magazines, and other periodicals

Includes also:

- All electronic forms of newspapers and periodicals

09.7.2.1 Newspapers (ND)

Includes:

- Newspaper bought in kiosks
- Subscription for newspapers (home delivery)
- Internet subscription for newspapers

Includes also:

- All electronic forms of newspapers

09.7.2.2 Magazines and Periodicals (ND)

Includes:

- Lifestyle magazines
- Children magazines
- Hobbies, leisure magazines
- Business, political magazines
- TV magazines
- Subscription for magazines and periodicals (home delivery)
- Internet subscription for magazines and periodicals

Includes also:

- All electronic forms of magazines and periodicals

09.7.3 Miscellaneous Printed Matter (ND)

Includes:

- Catalogs and advertising material
- Posters, plain or picture postcards, calendars
- Greeting cards and visiting cards, announcement, and message cards
- Maps and globes

Includes also:

- GPS maps bought separately

Excludes:

- *Prefranked postcards and aerogrammes (07.4.1.1)*
- *Stamp albums (09.2.1.2)*

09.7.3.0 Miscellaneous Printed Matter (ND)

Includes:

- Catalogs and advertising material
- Posters, plain or picture postcards, calendars
- Greeting cards and visiting cards, announcement, and message cards
- Maps and globes

Includes also:

- GPS maps bought separately

Excludes:

- *Prefranked postcards and aerogrammes (07.4.1.1)*
- *Stamp albums (09.2.1.2)*

09.7.4 Stationery and Drawing Materials (ND)

Includes:

- Writing pads, envelopes, account books, diaries, and so on
- Drawing paper
- Educational materials, such as exercise books
- Wrapping paper
- Pens, pencils, fountain pens, ballpoint pens, felt-tip pens, inks, erasers, pencil sharpeners, and so on
- Stencils, carbon paper, inking pads, correcting fluids, and so on
- Paper punches, paper cutters, paper scissors, office glues and adhesives, staplers and staples, paper clips, drawing pins, and so on
- Drawing and painting materials, such as canvas, card, paints, crayons, pastels, and brushes

Includes also:

- Slide rules, geometry instruments, slates, chalks, and pencil boxes

Excludes:

- *Pocket calculators (08.1.3.2)*

09.7.4.0 Stationery and Drawing Materials (ND)

Includes:

- Writing pads, envelopes, account books, diaries, and so on
- Drawing paper
- Educational materials, such as exercise books
- Wrapping paper
- Pens, pencils, fountain pens, ballpoint pens, felt-tip pens, inks, erasers, pencil sharpeners, and so on
- Stencils, carbon paper, inking pads, correcting fluids, and so on
- Paper punches, paper cutters, paper scissors, office glues and adhesives, staplers and staples, paper clips, drawing pins, and so on
- Drawing and painting materials, such as canvas, card, paints, crayons, pastels, and brushes

Includes also:

- Slide rules, geometry instruments, slates, chalks, and pencil boxes

Excludes:

- *Pocket calculators (08.1.3.2)*

09.8 Package Holidays

09.8.0 Package Holidays (S)

Includes:

- All-inclusive holidays or tours which provide for travel, food, accommodation, guides, and so on
- Excursion tours including transport and guide

09.8.0.0 Package Holidays (S)

Includes:

- All-inclusive holidays or tours which provide for travel, food, accommodation, guides, and so on
- Excursion tours including transport and guide

10 Education Services

Division 10 covers educational services only. The focus of groups 10.1–10.4 is on formal education (that leads to certificate or diploma). It includes education by radio or television broadcasting as well as e-learning and correspondence courses. It includes admission and registration fees as well as tuition fees.

It also includes other education-related fees like camps/field trips, course fees, diploma fees, examination fees, graduation fees, laboratory fees, physical education fee, and so on.

The breakdown of educational services is based upon the level categories of the 2011 revision of the International Standard Classification of Education (ISCED 2011) of the United Nations Educational, Scientific and Cultural Organization.

This division does not include expenditures on other education-related goods and services, such as:

- School uniforms (03.1.2.3)
- Education support services, such as health care services (06)
- Transport services except in the case of excursions which are part of the normal school program (07.3.2.3)
- Textbooks and academic journals (09.7.1.1)
- Stationery (09.7.4.0)
- Catering services (11.1.2.1)
- Accommodation services (11.2.0.3)

10.1 Early Childhood and Primary Education

10.1.0 Early Childhood and Primary Education (S)

Includes:

- Levels 0 and 1 of ISCED 2011 Early childhood and primary education
- Literacy programs for students too old for primary school
- Education services for children with special educational needs

Includes also:

- Excursions which are part of the normal school program (travel and accommodation costs)

Excludes:

- *Childcare services without educational program (13.3.0.1)*

10.1.0.1 Early Childhood Education (S)

Includes:

- ISCED 2011 level 0: early childhood education is designed primarily to support children's early cognitive, physical, social, and emotional development and introduce very young children to organized instruction outside of the family context. Programs are designed for children below the entry age to primary education and are typically center- or school-based. This education may also be provided in hospitals or in special schools or training centers; special education services for children with special educational needs.

- Special education services for children with special educational needs.

Includes also:

- Excursions which are part of the normal school program (travel and accommodation costs)

Excludes:

- *Childcare services without educational program (13.3.0.1)*

10.1.0.2 Primary Education (S)

Includes:

- ISCED 2011 level 1: primary education usually begins at age five, six, or seven and generally lasts for four to seven years. Programs are normally designed to provide students with fundamental skills in reading, writing, and mathematics and establish a solid foundation for learning and understanding core areas of knowledge and personal and social development. Organized instruction for children with special needs should also be included and literacy or basic skills programs within or outside the school system which are similar in content to program in primary education.
- Literacy programs for students too old for primary school.
- Excursions which are part of the normal school program (travel and accommodation costs).
- Education services for children with special educational needs.

10.2 Secondary Education

10.2.0 Secondary Education (S)

Includes:

- Levels 2 and 3 of ISCED 2011: lower-secondary and upper-secondary education. Secondary education is designed to lay the foundation for lifelong learning and human development and to provide the skills and knowledge needed either for further studies at postsecondary and tertiary levels or for entry to the labor market, or both.

Programs are increasingly subject-oriented and specialized. Different study options or streams are offered, including vocational education and training. Organized instruction for young people with special needs is also covered:

- Secondary education for adults and young people including second chance or reintegration; programs
- Out-of-school secondary education for adults and young people
- Education services for adolescents with special educational needs

Includes also:

- Excursions or student exchanges which are part of the normal school program (travel and accommodation costs)

10.2.0.0 Secondary Education (S)

Includes:

- Levels 2 and 3 of ISCED 2011: lower-secondary and upper-secondary education. Secondary education is designed to lay the foundation for lifelong learning and human development and to provide the skills and knowledge needed either for further studies at postsecondary and tertiary levels or for entry to the labor market, or both. Programs are increasingly subject-oriented and specialized. Different study options or streams are offered, including vocational education and training. Organized instruction for young people with special needs is also covered.
- Secondary education for adults and young people including second chance or reintegration; programs.
- Out-of-school secondary education for adults and young people.
- Education services for adolescents with special educational needs.

Includes also:

- Excursions or student exchanges which are part of the normal school program (travel and accommodation costs)

10.3 Postsecondary Nontertiary Education

10.3.0 Postsecondary Nontertiary Education (S)

Includes:

- Level 4 of ISCED 2011: postsecondary nontertiary education provides learning experiences building on secondary education, preparing for labor market entry as well as tertiary education. It aims at the individual acquisition of knowledge, skills, and competencies lower than the level of complexity characteristic of tertiary education. Postsecondary nontertiary education is typically designed to provide individuals who completed upper-secondary education without qualifications required for progression to tertiary education and for individuals seeking specific types of employment when their secondary qualification does not grant such access. For example, graduates from general secondary programs may choose to complete a nontertiary vocational qualification; or graduates from vocational secondary programs may choose to increase their level of qualifications or specialize further. Usually, programs at this level are designed for direct labor market entry. General programs designed to give access to or improved access to tertiary education can also exist.
- Out-of-school postsecondary nontertiary education for adults and young people.
- Education services for young people and adults with special educational needs.

Includes also:

- Excursions or student exchanges which are part of the normal school program (travel and accommodation costs)

10.3.0.0 Postsecondary Nontertiary Education (S)

Includes:

- Level 4 of ISCED 2011: postsecondary nontertiary education provides learning experiences building on secondary

education, preparing for labor market entry as well as tertiary education. It aims at the individual acquisition of knowledge, skills, and competencies lower than the level of complexity characteristic of tertiary education. Postsecondary nontertiary education is typically designed to provide individuals who completed upper-secondary education without qualifications required for progression to tertiary education and for individuals seeking specific types of employment when their secondary qualification does not grant such access. For example, graduates from general secondary programs may choose to complete a nontertiary vocational qualification; or graduates from vocational secondary programs may choose to increase their level of qualifications or specialize further. Usually, programs at this level are designed for direct labor market entry. General programs designed to give access to or improved access to tertiary education can also exist.
- Out-of-school postsecondary nontertiary education for adults and young people.
- Education services for young people and adults with special educational needs.

Includes also:

- Excursions or student exchanges which are part of the normal school program (travel and accommodation costs)

10.4 Tertiary Education

10.4.0 Tertiary Education (S)

Includes:

- Levels 5, 6, 7, and 8 of ISCED 2011: tertiary education builds on secondary education and provides learning activities in specialized fields of education. It aims at a high level of complexity and specialization. It includes both academic education and advanced vocational or professional education. At the highest levels, programs lead to an advanced research qualification based on advanced study and original research.

Includes also:

- Excursions or student exchanges which are part of the normal school program (travel and accommodation costs)
- University admission tests
- E-learning courses

10.4.0.0 Tertiary Education (S)

Includes:

- Levels 5, 6, 7, and 8 of ISCED 2011: tertiary education builds on secondary education and provides learning activities in specialized fields of education. It aims at a high level of complexity and specialization. It includes both academic education and advanced vocational or professional education. At the highest levels, programs lead to an advanced research qualification based on advanced study and original research.

Includes also:

- Excursions or student exchanges which are part of the normal school program (travel and accommodation costs)
- University admission tests
- E-learning courses

10.5 Education Not Defined by Level

10.5.0 Education Not Defined by Level (S)

Includes:

- Independent tutors (private lessons), tutor centers, homework help centers, and the like
- Short educational courses, generally for adults, which do not require any special prior instruction, in particular cultural development or some types of vocational training
- Language immersion courses and international travel for learning languages
- Languages courses in classroom or online
- Language proficiency tests
- Courses in the use of computers and specific software
- Exam preparation courses
- Online tutoring

Excludes:

- *Driving lessons (07.2.4.3)*
- *Recreational training courses, such as sport or bridge lessons given by independent teachers (09.4.6.1)*
- *Removable media containing foreign language trainers (09.7.1.1)*

10.5.0.1 Tutoring (S)

Includes:

- Independent tutors (private lessons to support formal education), tutor centers, homework help centers, and the like
- Exam preparation courses
- Online tutoring

10.5.0.9 Other Education Not Defined by Level (S)

Includes:

- Educational programs, generally for adults, which do not require any special prior instruction, in particular vocational training or cultural development
- Language immersion courses and international travels with educational purposes (for example, languages)
- Languages courses in classroom, online, in form of software or audio tapes
- Language proficiency tests
- Information technology courses (for example, learning how to use a specific software)

Excludes:

- *Driving lessons (07.2.4.3)*
- *Recreational training courses, such as sport or bridge lessons given by independent teachers (09.4.6.1)*
- *Removable media containing foreign language trainers (09.7.1.1)*

11 Restaurants and Accommodation Services

Division 11 covers food and beverage serving services provided by restaurants, cafés, and similar facilities, either with full, limited, or self-service, or by canteens, cafeterias, or refectories at work or school, and other educational establishment's premises. The distinction between full service and limited service relates to the range of the food and beverage serving services: a service by waiters to the individual customer seated at tables will be qualified to be a full service.

Accommodation in this division includes services for visitors and other travelers away from their principal or secondary residence. When not separately invoiced, it also includes food and beverage services and other serving services, such as housekeeping, parking, laundry, swimming pools and exercise rooms, recreational facilities, and conference and convention facilities.

Excludes:

- *Permanent principal or secondary residence accommodation (Division 04)*

11.1 Food and Beverage Serving Services

11.1.1 Restaurants, Cafés, and the Like (S)

Food and beverages services provided by restaurants, cafés, and similar eating facilities either providing full, limited, or self-service.

Includes also:

- Tobacco that is consumed with a shisha or hookah pipes in restaurants, cafés, or shisha lounges
- Narcotics purchased in coffee shops, if service charge is applied
- Tips

Excludes:

- *Food products and beverages dispensed by automatic vending machines not as a delivery service provided restaurants, cafés, buffets, bars, tearooms, and similar facilities (01.1.9.1)*
- *Tobacco purchases (02.3.0)*
- *Food and beverage services on public transport, if not separately invoiced (07.3)*
- *Food and beverage provided by supermarkets and markets and consumed at their premises (related products in Division 01)*
- *Food and beverages delivery services, if separately invoiced (07.4.9.2)*
- *Dancing establishments and nightclubs entrance fees (09.4.6.1)*
- *Food and beverage services in places providing recreational, cultural, sporting or entertainment services, if not separately invoiced (09.4.6, 09.6.1.0, 09.6.2.0, 09.6.9.0)*
- *Food and beverage services provided in package holidays, if not separately invoiced (09.8.0.0)*
- *Food and beverage services provided by hotels or other lodging places, if not separately invoiced from accommodation (11.2)*

11.1.1.1 Restaurants, Cafés, and the Like—With Full Service (S)

Food and beverages services provided by restaurants, cafés, and similar eating facilities providing full service consisting of waiter service to individual customers seated at tables, with or without entertainment.

Includes:

- Food and beverages provided by full-service facilities mainly serving drinks: cafés, buffets, bars, tearooms, and similar
- Food and beverages provided by full-service restaurants, cafés, and the like and consumed off their premises; food and beverages provided by full-service restaurants, cafés, and the like and home-delivered
- Food and beverage full services in hotels or other accommodation places, if separately invoiced from accommodation
- Food and beverage full services in places providing recreational, cultural, sporting, or entertainment services (theatres, cinemas, sports stadiums, swimming pools, sports complexes, museums, art galleries, nightclubs, dancing establishments, and similar facilities) if separately invoiced
- Tobacco that is consumed with a shisha or hookah pipes in restaurants, cafés, or shisha lounges
- Narcotics purchased in coffee shops, if service charge is applied
- Tips

Excludes:

- *Tobacco purchases (02.3.0)*
- *Food and beverage services on public transport, if not separately invoiced (07.3)*
- *Food and beverage provided by supermarkets and markets and consumed at their premises (related products in Division 01)*
- *Food and beverages delivery, if separately invoiced (07.4.9.2)*
- *Food and beverage services in places providing recreational, cultural, sporting, or entertainment services, if not separately invoiced (09.4.6, 09.6.1.0, 09.6.2.0, 09.6.9.0)*
- *Entrance fees for dancing establishments, nightclubs (09.4.6.1)*
- *Food and beverage services provided in package holidays, if not separately invoiced (09.8.0.0)*
- *Food and beverage services in hotels or other lodging places, if not separately invoiced from accommodation (11.2)*

11.1.1.2 Restaurants, Cafés, and the Like—With Limited Service (S)

Food and beverages serving services provided by limited and self-service facilities that are without waiter service and with or without seating.

Includes:

- Food and beverage services provided by self-service restaurants

- Food and beverages provided by refreshment stands, fish and chip stands, and fast-food outlets without seating and takeaway facilities
- Food products and beverages prepared on the premises and dispensed through automatic vending machines as a delivery service in a self-service restaurant or similar (for example, automat restaurants)
- Food and beverage for immediate consumption provided by kiosks, food stalls, street vendors, and the like

Includes also:

- Ice cream parlors and cake serving places
- Food and beverages provided by catering contractors whether collected by the customer or delivered to the customer's home
- Food and beverage services on public transport (coaches, trains, boats, airplanes, and so on), if separately invoiced
- Tobacco that is consumed with a shisha or hookah pipes in restaurants, cafés, or shisha lounges
- Narcotics purchased in coffee shops, if service charge is applied
- Tips

Excludes:

- *Food products and beverages dispensed by automatic vending machines not as a delivery service provided restaurants, cafés, buffets, bars, tearooms, and similar facilities (01.1.9.1)*
- *Tobacco purchases (02.3.0)*
- *Food and beverage services on public transport, if not separately invoiced (07.3)*
- *Food and beverage provided by supermarkets and markets and consumed at their premises (related products in Division 01)*
- *Food and beverages delivery, if separately invoiced (07.4.9.2)*
- *Food and beverage services in places providing recreational, cultural, sporting, or entertainment services, if not separately invoiced (09.4.6, 09.6.1.0, 09.6.2.0, 09.6.9.0)*
- *Entrance fees for dancing establishments, nightclubs (09.4.6.1)*
- *Food and beverage services provided in package holidays, if not separately invoiced (09.8.0.0)*
- *Food and beverage services in hotels or other lodging places, if not separately invoiced from accommodation (11.2)*

11.1.2 Canteens, Cafeterias, and Refectories (S)

Food and beverages provided by canteens, cafeterias, or refectories, that is, restaurants, cafés, and the like at work/office premises, in schools, universities, and other educational establishments, to hospital inpatients, if separately invoiced.

Includes:

- University refectories, military messes, and wardrooms

Excludes:

- *Food and beverages provided by schools, university, and other educational establishments, if not separately invoiced (10.1–10.5)*
- *Food and beverages provided to hospital inpatients if not separately invoiced (06.3)*

11.1.2.1 Canteens, Cafeterias, and Refectories of Universities, Schools, and Kindergartens (S)

Food and beverages provided by canteens, cafeterias, or refectories, that is, restaurants, cafés, and the like at in schools, universities, and other educational establishments.

Includes:

- Kindergarten canteens
- School canteens
- University refectories

Excludes:

- *Food and beverages provided by schools, university, and other educational establishments, if not separately invoiced (10.1–10.5)*

11.1.2.9 Other Canteens, Cafeterias, and Refectories (S)

Food and beverages provided by canteens, cafeterias, or refectories, that is, restaurants, cafés, and the like at work/office premises, to hospital inpatients, if separately invoiced.

Includes:

- Military messes and wardrooms

Excludes:

- *Food and beverages provided to hospital inpatients if not separately invoiced (06.3)*

11.2 Accommodation Services

11.2.0 Accommodation Services (S)

Accommodation services for visitors and other travelers away from their permanent principal or secondary residence. It includes other services, when not separately invoiced, such as food and beverage services, housekeeping, parking, laundry, swimming pools and exercise rooms, recreational facilities, and conference and convention facilities.

Includes:

- Resorts, hotels, hotels letting rooms by the hour, motels, inns, and pensions
- Accommodation services provided by private, holiday homes, guesthouses and boarding houses as secondary residence, and other "bed and breakfast" units
- Time-share units
- Holiday villages and holiday centers, camping, and onsite (nonmobile) caravans and boats
- Youth hostels and mountain refuges
- Bungalows, chalets, housekeeping cottages, and cabins
- Student residences, school, and other educational establishments dormitories, when separately invoiced; hostels and other accommodations for workers
- Railway sleeping cars and other public transport, when separately invoiced
- Website fees for people to list, find, and rent lodging
- Travel agency fees for accommodation if priced separately
- Tips for bellmen, bellhops, hotel porters, and maids

Excludes:

- *Payments of households occupying a room in a hotel or boarding house as their main residence (04.1.1.0)*
- *Rentals paid by households for a secondary residence or time-share residence (04.1.2)*
- *Telephone calls (08.3.1.0)*
- *Package holidays (09.8.0.0)*
- *Breakfast, meals, and other food and beverages provided in accommodation and similar establishments, when separately invoiced (11.1.1)*
- *Housing in orphanages, homes for disabled or maladjusted persons (13.3.0.2)*

11.2.0.1 Hotels, Motels, Inns, and Similar Accommodation Services (S)

Includes:

- Accommodation services in resorts, hotels, and motels
- Accommodation services in inns, pensions, and similar establishments
- Short-term accommodation services provided by private, holiday homes, guesthouses and boarding houses as secondary residence, and other "bed and breakfast" units
- Time-share units

Includes also:

- Hotels letting rooms by the hour

Excludes:

- *Payments of households occupying a room in a hotel or boarding house as their main residence (04.1.1.0)*
- *Rentals paid by households for a secondary residence or time-share residence (04.1.2)*
- *Telephone calls (08.3.1.0)*
- *Package holidays (09.8.0.0)*
- *Breakfast, meals, and other food and beverages provided in accommodation and similar establishments, when separately invoiced (11.1.1)*

11.2.0.2 Holiday Centers, Camping Sites, Youth Hostels, and Similar Accommodation Services (S)

Includes:

- Holiday villages and holiday centers
- Camping sites, onsite (nonmobile) caravans and boats, camping grounds, recreational vehicle, and trailer parks
- Youth hostels and mountain refuges
- Bungalows, chalets, housekeeping cottages, and cabins

Excludes:

- *Payments of households occupying a room in holiday centers, camping sites, youth hostels, and similar accommodation as their main or secondary residence (04.1.1.0)*
- *Telephone calls (08.3.1.0)*
- *Breakfast, meals, and other food and beverages provided in accommodation and similar establishments, when separately invoiced (11.1.1)*

11.2.0.3 Accommodation Services of Boarding Schools, Universities, and Other Educational Establishments (S)

Includes:

- Student residences, school, and other educational establishments dormitories, when separately invoiced

Excludes:

- *Housing in orphanages, homes for disabled or maladjusted persons (13.3.0.1, 13.3.0.2)*

11.2.0.9 Other Accommodation Services (S)

Includes:

- Hostels and other accommodations for workers
- Railway sleeping cars and other public transport, when separately invoiced
- Website fees for people to list, find, and rent lodging
- Travel agency fees for accommodation if priced separately

Excludes:

- *Telephone calls (08.3.1.0)*
- *Breakfast, meals, and other food and beverages provided in accommodation and similar establishments, when separately invoiced (11.1.1)*
- *Housing in orphanages, homes for disabled or maladjusted persons (13.3.0.3)*

12 Insurance and Financial Services

Division 12 covers insurance and financial services. Insurance and financial services are provided by financial corporations. These may be paid for explicitly or implicitly. Some transactions in financial assets may also involve both explicit and implicit charges. Implicit charges are not always as evident as the way in which charges are made for most goods and services and are typically calculated using a number of observable transactions. Examples of implicit charges arise from the financial services provided in association with interest charges on loans and deposits, the acquisition and disposal of financial assets and liabilities in financial markets, and insurance and pension programs. The imputed values of expenditure on insurance and financial services are not directly observable from household income and expenditure surveys.

Insurance services are subdivided by type of insurance. Financial services are subdivided by financial intermediation services indirectly measured and by the other forms of actual and indirect charges and remittance fees for financial services. For the definition and the measurement of the insurance and financial services, specific national accounts concepts (*2008 SNA*) do apply.

12.1 Insurance

Service charges for insurance are classified by type of insurance, namely, life insurance and nonlife insurance (that is, insurance in connection with the dwelling, health, transport, and so on). Service charges for multi-risk insurance covering several risks should be classified on the basis of the cost of the principal risk if it is not possible to allocate the service charges to the various risks covered.

The basic method for measuring the service charge for nonlife insurance is total premiums earned plus investment income earned from investing the premiums less adjusted claims incurred.

The basic method for measuring the service charge for life insurance is premiums earned plus investment income earned from investing the premiums less benefits due less increases (plus decreases) in life insurance technical reserves.

12.1.1 Life and Accident Insurance (S)

Includes:

- Service charges for life insurance, annuities, death benefit insurance, education insurance, and so on

12.1.1.0 Life and Accident Insurance (S)

Includes:

- Service charges for life insurance, annuities, death benefit insurance, education insurance, and so on

Includes also:

- Service charges for funeral insurance
- Service charges for accident insurance

12.1.2 Insurance Connected with Health (S)

Includes:

- Service charges for direct sickness insurance
- Service charges for social health insurance
- Service charges for disability insurance
- Service charges for critical illness insurance
- Service charges for long-term care insurance
- Service charges for supplementary health insurance
- Service charges for supplementary prescription drug insurance
- Service charges for travel health insurance

Includes also:

- Service charges for medical transport (for example, ambulance) insurance

12.1.2.0 Insurance Connected with Health (S)

Includes:

- Service charges for direct sickness insurance
- Service charges for social health insurance
- Service charges for disability insurance
- Service charges for critical illness insurance
- Service charges for long-term care insurance
- Service charges for supplementary health insurance
- Service charges for supplementary prescription drug insurance
- Service charges for travel health insurance

Includes also:

- Service charges for medical transport (for example, ambulance) insurance

12.1.3 Insurance Connected with the Dwelling (S)

Includes:

- Service charges paid by owner-occupiers and by tenants for the kinds of insurance typically taken out by tenants against fire, theft, water damage, and so on
- Service charges for household contents insurance

Excludes:

- *Service charges paid by owner-occupiers for the kinds of insurance typically taken out by landlords (intermediate consumption)*

12.1.3.0 Insurance Connected with the Dwelling (S)

Includes:

- Service charges paid by owner-occupiers and by tenants for the kinds of insurance typically taken out by tenants against fire, theft, water damage, and so on
- Service charges paid by owner-occupiers and by tenants for household contents insurance

Excludes:

- *Service charges paid by owner-occupiers for the kinds of insurance typically taken out by landlords (intermediate consumption)*

12.1.4 Insurance Connected with Transport (S)

Includes:

- Service charges for insurance in respect of personal transport equipment
- Service charges for travel insurance (for change of travel plans, travel cancellation, and so on) and luggage insurance

12.1.4.1 Personal Transport Insurance (S)

Includes:

- Service charges for car insurance
- Service charges for insurance in respect of personal transport equipment
- Service charges for insurances covering civil liability or damage to third parties or their property arising from the operation of personal transport equipment

Includes also:

- Service charges for insurance in respect of bikes, motorcycles, boats, yachts, sailboats, airplanes, and so on

12.1.4.2 Travel Insurance (S)

Includes:

- Service charges for travel insurance (for change of travel plans, travel cancellation, and so on) and luggage insurance

Excludes:

- *Travel health insurance (12.1.2.0)*

12.1.9 Other Insurance (S)

Includes:

- Service charges for other insurance, such as civil liability for injury or damage to third parties or their property

- Service charges for standardized guarantees
- Service charges for legal insurance
- Service charges for pet medical insurance

Excludes:

- *Civil liability or damage to third parties or their property arising from the operation of personal transport equipment (12.1.4.1)*

12.1.9.0 Other Insurance (S)

Includes:

- Service charges for other insurance, such as civil liability for injury or damage to third parties or their property
- Service charges for standardized guarantees
- Service charges for legal insurance
- Service charges for pet medical insurance

Excludes:

- *Civil liability or damage to third parties or their property arising from the operation of personal transport equipment (12.1.4.1)*

12.2 Financial Services

Financial services are subdivided by financial intermediation services indirectly measured and by the other forms of actual and implicit charges and remittance fees for financial services.

12.2.1 Financial Intermediation Services Indirectly Measured (S)

Financial intermediation services indirectly measured is calculated as the difference between the actual bank interest receivable and the SNA interest receivable by financial corporations on the loans they issue, and the difference between SNA interest payable and the actual bank interest payable by financial corporations on the deposits of their customers.
Includes:

- Financial intermediation services indirectly measured of deposit-taking corporations

Includes also:

- Implicit financial services provided by moneylenders, credit card issuers, finance associates of retailers who may be responsible for providing loans, pawnshops and corporations involved in lending (for example, in providing student loans and import/export loans)

12.2.1.0 Financial Intermediation Services Indirectly Measured (S)

Includes:

- Financial intermediation services indirectly measured of deposit-taking corporations

Includes also:

- Implicit financial services provided by moneylenders, credit card issuers, finance associates of retailers who may be responsible for providing loans, pawnshops and corporations involved in lending (for example, in providing student loans and import/export loans)

12.2.2 Explicit Charges by Deposit-Taking Corporations (S)

Includes:

- Explicit charges for the financial services of deposit-taking corporations, such as commercial banks, credit unions, cooperative banks, savings banks, post banks, and postal savings banks

Excludes:

- *Remittances fees (12.2.9.1)*

12.2.2.0 Explicit Charges by Deposit-Taking Corporations (S)

Includes:

- Actual charges for the financial services of deposit-taking corporations, such as commercial banks, credit unions, cooperative banks, savings banks, post banks, and postal savings banks

Excludes:

- *Remittances fees (12.2.9.1)*

12.2.9 Other Financial Services N.E.C. (S)

Includes:

- Actual and implicit charges for the financial services of money changers and other financial institutions
- Fees and service charges and implicit charges of money market funds, nonmoney market investment funds, brokers, and the like
- Administrative charges and implicit charges of pension funds and the like
- Remittance fees

12.2.9.1 Remittances Fees (S)

Includes:

- Remittances fees for financial services provided by financial auxiliaries, such as money transfer agents and the like

12.2.9.9 Other Financial Services N.E.C. (S)

Includes:

- Actual and implicit charges for the financial services of money changers and other financial institutions
- Fees and service charges and implicit charges of money market funds, nonmoney market investment funds, brokers, and the like
- Administrative and implicit charges of pension funds and the like
- Other financial services n.e.c.

13 Personal Care, Social Protection, and Miscellaneous Goods

Division 13 covers goods and services for personal care, jewelry and watches, services of social protection, and all other services for households, which are not classified elsewhere. Goods and services for personal care cover electric and nonelectric appliances for personal care as well as hairdressing services. Goods of personal effects cover jewelry and watches, celebration and devotional articles, and travel goods and articles.

Social protection services cover childcare, nonmedical retirement homes for elderly persons and disabled persons, services to maintain people in their private homes, and related service. Group 13.9 covers all the other services for households, which are not classified elsewhere, such as fees for legal and administrative services, fees for real estate agencies, charges for undertaking, and payment for various personal services (for example, graphologists, bodyguards, matrimonial agencies, and so on).

This group also includes religious services.

13.1 Personal Care

13.1.1 Electric Appliances for Personal Care (SD)

Includes:

- Electric razors, hair trimmers and epilators, hand-held and hood hairdryers, straightening irons, curling tongs and styling combs, sunlamps, vibrators, electric toothbrushes, other electric appliances for dental hygiene, and so on
- Repair of such appliances

13.1.1.1 Electric Appliances for Personal Care (SD)

Includes:

- Electric razors, hair trimmers and epilators, hand-held and hood hairdryers, straightening irons, curling tongs and styling combs, sunlamps, vibrators, electric toothbrushes and other electric appliances for dental hygiene, and so on

Excludes:

- *Repair of electric appliances for personal care (13.1.1.2)*

13.1.1.2 Repair of Electric Appliances for Personal Care (S)

The cost of materials is included only if the materials are not separately invoiced.

Includes:

- Repair of electric appliances for personal care

13.1.2 Other Appliances, Articles, and Products for Personal Care (ND)

Includes:

- Nonelectric appliances: shavers, razors and hair trimmers and blades therefor, scissors, nail files, combs, shaving brushes, hairbrushes, toothbrushes, nail brushes, hairpins, curlers, personal weighing machines, scales, and so on
- Articles for personal hygiene: toilet soap, medicinal soap, cleansing oil and milk, shaving soap, shaving cream and foam, toothpaste, epilation wax, paper handkerchiefs, and so on
- Beauty products: lipstick, nail varnish, makeup and makeup removal products (including powder compacts, brushes, and powder puffs), hair lacquers and lotions, pre-shave and after-shave products, sunbathing products and sunscreens, hair removers, perfumes and toilet waters, personal deodorants, bath products, and so on

Excludes:

- *Handkerchiefs made of fabric (03.1.3.1)*

13.1.2.0 Other Appliances, Articles, and Products for Personal Care (ND)

Includes:

- Nonelectric appliances: shavers, razors and hair trimmers and blades therefor, scissors, nail files, combs, shaving brushes, hairbrushes, toothbrushes, nail brushes, hairpins, curlers, personal weighing machines, scales, and so on
- Articles for personal hygiene: toilet soap, medicinal soap, cleansing oil and milk, shaving soap, shaving cream and foam, toothpaste, epilation wax, paper handkerchiefs, and so on
- Beauty products: lipstick, nail varnish, makeup and makeup removal products (including powder compacts, brushes, and powder puffs), hair lacquers and lotions, pre-shave and after-shave products, sunbathing products and sunscreens, hair removers, perfumes and toilet waters, personal deodorants, bath products, and so on

Excludes:

- *Handkerchiefs made of fabric (03.1.3.1)*

13.1.3 Hairdressing Salons and Personal Grooming Establishments (S)

Includes:

- Services of hairdressing salons, barbers, beauty shops, manicures, pedicures, Turkish baths, saunas, solariums, nonmedical massages, and so on
- Body care, depilation, and the like, diet clubs, tattoo, and piercing services
- Cosmetic surgery for other purposes than reconstructive surgery

Excludes:

- *Spas for medical purpose (06.2, 06.3)*
- *Animals tattooing (09.4.5.0)*
- *Fitness centers (09.4.6.2)*

13.1.3.1 Hairdressing (S)

Includes:

- Services of hairdressing salons or barbers for women, men, and children

13.1.3.2 Personal Grooming Treatments (S)

Includes:

- Facial beauty treatments, depilation, solarium, pedicure, body care, manicure, thalassotherapy, Turkish baths, saunas, nonmedical massages, and so on
- Diet clubs, tattoo, and piercing services

Excludes:

- *Spas for medical purpose (06.2, 06.3)*
- *Animals tattooing (09.4.5.0)*
- *Fitness centers (09.4.6.2)*

13.2 Personal Effects N.E.C.

13.2.1 Jewelry and Watches (D)

Includes:

- Precious stones and metals and jewelry fashioned out of such stones and metals
- Costume jewelry, cuff links, and tiepins
- Watches, stopwatches
- Repair, remodeling, and hire of jewelry and watches

Excludes:

- *Wall clocks, alarm clocks, travel clocks (05.1.1.4)*
- *Ornaments (05.1.1.4, 05.4.0.1)*
- *Radio clocks (08.1.4.0)*
- *Smartwatches (08.1.9.1)*
- *Precious stones and metals and jewelry fashioned out of such stones and metals acquired primarily as stores of value (capital formation)*

13.2.1.1 Jewelry and Watches (D)

Includes:

- Precious stones and metals and jewelry fashioned out of such stones and metals
- Costume jewelry, cuff links, and tiepins
- Watches, stopwatches

Excludes:

- *Wall clocks, alarm clocks, travel clocks (05.1.1.4)*
- *Ornaments (05.1.1.4, 05.4.0.1)*
- *Radio clocks (08.1.4.0)*
- *Smartwatches (08.1.9.1)*
- *Precious stones and metals and jewelry fashioned out of such stones and metals acquired primarily as stores of value (capital formation)*

13.2.1.2 Repair and Hire of Jewelry, Clocks, and Watches (S)

The cost of materials is included only if the materials are not separately invoiced.

Includes:

- Repair of jewelry, clocks, and watches
- Remodeling of jewelry
- Hire of jewelry, clocks, and watches

13.2.2 Devotional Articles and Articles for Religious and Ritual Celebrations (SD)

Includes:

- Religious and ritual articles like crucifixes and rosaries, figurines, pictures, votive candles, amulets, strips of paper with prayers, menorah chandeliers, advent wreaths, and others
- Articles to be used in religious celebrations and rituals

Excludes:

- *Christmas trees, holiday decorations (for Christmas, Easter, Hanukkah, Eid, Diwali, and similar) (09.2.1.3)*
- *Religious books (09.7.1.9)*

13.2.2.0 Devotional Articles and Articles for Religious and Ritual Celebrations (SD)

Includes:

- Religious and ritual articles like crucifixes and rosaries, figurines, pictures, votive candles, amulets, strips of paper with prayers, menorah chandeliers, advent wreaths, and others
- Articles to be used in religious and ritual celebrations

Excludes:

- *Christmas trees, holiday decorations (for Christmas, Easter, Hanukkah, Eid, Diwali, and similar) (09.2.1.3)*
- *Religious books (09.7.1.9)*

13.2.9 Other Personal Effects (SD)

Includes:

- Travel goods and other carriers of personal effects: suitcases, trunks, travel bags, attaché cases, satchels, handbags, wallets, purses, and so on
- Articles for babies: baby carriages, pushchairs, carrycots, recliners, back carriers, front carriers, harnesses for babies, and so on
- Articles for smokers: pipes, lighters, cigarette cases, cigar cutters, ashtrays, electronic cigarettes devices, and so on
- Miscellaneous personal articles: sunglasses, protective glasses, walking sticks and canes, umbrellas and parasols, fans, keyrings, pill organizers, earplugs, and so on
- Funerary articles: coffins, gravestones, urns, and so on
- Lighter fuel; wall thermometers and barometers
- Repair and hire of other personal effects

Excludes:

- *Baby furniture (05.1.1.1)*
- *Shopping bags (05.2.1.9)*
- *Feeding bottles (05.4.0.3)*
- *Walking sticks and canes used for medical reasons (06.1.3.3)*
- *Car seats for babies (07.2.1.3)*

13.2.9.1 Travel Goods and Articles for Babies and Other Personal Effects N.E.C. (SD)

Includes:

- Travel goods and other carriers of personal effects: suitcases, trunks, travel bags, attaché cases, satchels, handbags, wallets, purses, and so on
- Articles for babies: baby carriages, pushchairs, carrycots, recliners, back carriers, front carriers, harnesses for babies, and so on
- Articles for smokers: pipes, lighters, cigarette cases, cigar cutters, ashtrays, electronic cigarettes devices, and so on
- Miscellaneous personal articles: sunglasses, protective glasses, walking sticks and canes, umbrellas and parasols, fans, keyrings, pill organizers, earplugs, and so on
- Funerary articles: coffins, gravestones, urns, and so on
- Lighter fuel, wall thermometers, and barometers

Excludes:

- *Baby furniture (05.1.1.1)*
- *Shopping bags (05.2.1.9)*
- *Feeding bottles (05.4.0.3)*
- *Walking sticks and canes used for medical reasons (06.1.3.3)*
- *Car seats for babies (07.2.1.3)*

13.2.9.2 Repair or Hire of Other Personal Effects (S)

The cost of materials is included only if the materials are not separately invoiced.

Includes:

- Repair of other personal effects
- Hire of other personal effects

13.3 Social Protection

Social protection as defined here covers nonmedical assistance and support services provided to persons who are elderly, disabled, having occupational injuries and diseases, survivors, unemployed, destitute, homeless, low-income earners, indigenous people, immigrants, refugees, alcohol and substance abusers, and so on.

It also covers assistance and support services provided to families and children.

13.3.0 Social Protection (S)

Social protection services include residential care, home help, and day care. More specifically, this class covers payments by households for:

- Nonmedical retirement homes for elderly persons, nonmedical residences for disabled persons, rehabilitation centers providing nonmedical long-term support for individuals rather than health care and rehabilitative therapy, schools for disabled persons where the main aim is to help students overcome their disability
- Nonmedical help to maintain elderly and disabled persons at home (home-cleaning services, meal programs, nonmedical day care centers, day care services, and holiday care services)
- Child-minding outside the home, nurseries, day care facilities wet-nurses, crèches, kindergartens (other than educational), play schools, and other child-minding facilities
- Counseling, guidance, arbitration, fostering, and adoption services for families

Excludes:

- *Social assistance and other social care services that are integrated into a package of care along with medical services are to be included in 06.2.3 if medical services do not require an overnight stay and 06.3.2 if they do. For example, services of medical convalescent homes or convalescent hospitals; services of homes for the elderly with nursing care; inpatient care hospices; services of palliative care establishments for the terminally ill; services of nursing homes; rest homes with nursing care; services of skilled nursing facilities; services of teaching nursing homes; services of residential mental retardation facilities; mental health and substance abuse facilities for chronic patient (for example, those with dementia); and services of alcoholism or drug addiction rehabilitation facilities (other than licensed hospitals).*
- *Services of mental health convalescent homes or hospitals (06.3.2.0).*
- *Babysitters and so on (05.6.2.1).*
- *Educational kindergartens (10.1.0.1).*

13.3.0.1 Childcare Services (S)

Includes:

- Child-minding outside the home
- Nurseries, day care facilities, wet-nurses, crèches, and other child-minding facilities for babies
- After school centers

Excludes:

- *Babysitters and so on (05.6.2.1)*
- *Educational kindergartens (10.1.0.1)*

13.3.0.2 Nonmedical Retirement Homes for Elderly Persons and Residences for Disabled Persons (S)

Includes:

- Nonmedical retirement homes for elderly persons
- Nonmedical residences for disabled persons

Excludes:

- *Social assistance and other social care services that are integrated into a package of care along with medical services are to be included in 06.2.3 if medical services do not require an overnight stay and 06.3.2 if they do. For example, services of medical convalescent homes or convalescent hospitals; services of homes for the elderly with nursing care; inpatient care hospices; services of palliative care establishments for the terminally ill; services of nursing homes; rest homes with nursing care; services of skilled nursing facilities; services of teaching nursing homes; services of residential mental retardation facilities; mental health and substance abuse facilities for chronic patient (for example, those with dementia); and services of alcoholism or drug addiction rehabilitation facilities (other than licensed hospitals).*
- *Services of mental health convalescent homes or hospitals (06.3.2.0).*

13.3.0.3 Services to Maintain People in Their Private Homes (S)

Includes:

- Help to maintain elderly and disabled persons at home (home-cleaning services, meal programs, day care centers, day care services, and holiday care services)

13.3.0.9 Other Social Protection Services (S)

Includes:

- Schools for disabled persons where the main aim is to help students overcome their disability
- Guidance, arbitration, fostering, and adoption services for families

13.9 Other Services N.E.C.

13.9.0 Other Services N.E.C. (S)

Includes:

- Fees for legal services, employment agencies, and so on
- Payment for the services of lawyers, notaries, accountants, and so on
- Charges for undertaking and other funeral services
- Payment for the services of estate agents, housing agents, auctioneers, salesroom operators, and other intermediaries
- Payment for photocopies and other reproductions of documents
- Fees for the issue of birth, marriage, and death certificates, and other administrative documents
- Expenditures for religious services, for example, requiems, baptizing, marriage services
- Expenditure for nonreligious services and events, such as coming of age celebrations in Latin American "Quince" or debutante balls
- Payment for newspaper notices and advertisements
- Payment for the services of graphologists, astrologers, palmists, private detectives, bodyguards, matrimonial agencies and marriage guidance counselors, public writers, miscellaneous concessions (seats, toilets, cloakrooms), and so on
- Services provided by prostitutes and the like
- Firearms licenses

Excludes:

- *Food or beverages consumed in brothels if charged separately (11.1.1, 11.1.2)*

13.9.0.1 Prostitution (S)

Includes:

- Services provided by prostitutes or sex workers and the like

Excludes:

- *Food or beverages consumed in brothels if charged separately (11.1.1, 11.1.2)*

13.9.0.2 Religious Services (S)

Includes:

- Expenditures for religious services, for example, requiems, baptizing, marriage services

13.9.0.9 Other Services N.E.C. (S)

Includes:

- Fees for legal services, employment agencies, and so on
- Payment for the services of lawyers, accountants, and so on
- Expenditure for nonreligious services and events, such as coming of age celebrations in Latin American "quince" or debutante balls
- Charges for undertaking and other funeral services
- Payment for the services of estate agents, housing agents, auctioneers, salesroom operators, and other intermediaries
- Payment for photocopies, printing services, and other reproductions of documents
- Fees for the issue of birth, marriage, and death certificates, and other administrative documents
- Payment for newspaper notices and advertisements
- Payment for the services of graphologists, astrologers, palmists, private detectives, bodyguards, matrimonial agencies and marriage guidance counselors, public writers, miscellaneous concessions (seats, toilets, cloakrooms), and so on
- Firearms licenses

Appendix 4

Resolution Concerning Consumer Price Indices Adopted by the Seventeenth International Conference of Labour Statisticians, 2003

Preamble[1]

The Seventeenth International Conference of Labour Statisticians

Having been convened at Geneva by the Governing Body of the International Labour Organization and having met from 24 November to 3 December 2003

Recalling the resolution adopted by the Fourteenth International Conference of Labour Statisticians concerning consumer price indices and recognizing the continuing validity of the basic principles recommended therein and, in particular, the fact that the consumer price index (CPI) is designed primarily to measure the changes over time in the general level of prices of goods and services that a reference population acquires, uses, or pays for

Recognizing the need to modify and broaden the existing standards in the light of recent methodological and computational developments to enhance the usefulness of the international standards in the provision of technical guidelines to all countries

Recognizing the usefulness of such standards in enhancing the international comparability of the statistics

Recognizing that the CPI is used for a wide variety of purposes and that governments should be encouraged to identify the (priority) purposes a CPI is to serve, to provide adequate resources for its compilation, and to guarantee the professional independence of its compilers

Recognizing that the (priority) objectives and uses of a CPI differ among countries and that, therefore, a single standard could not be applied universally

Recognizing that the CPI needs to be credible to observers and users, both national and international, and that better understanding of the principles and procedures used to compile the index will enhance the users' confidence in the index

Agrees that the principles and methods used in constructing a CPI should be based on the guidelines and methods that are generally accepted as constituting good statistical practices

Adopts, this third day of December 2003, the following resolution which replaces the previous one adopted in 1987

[1] All annexes referred to in the footnotes are the annexes to the resolution.

The Nature and Meaning of a Consumer Price Index

1. The CPI is a current social and economic indicator that is constructed to measure changes over time in the general level of prices of consumer goods and services that households acquire, use, or pay for consumption.
2. The index aims to measure the change in consumer prices over time. This may be done by measuring the cost of purchasing a fixed basket of consumer goods and services of constant quality and similar characteristics, with the products in the basket being selected to be representative of households' expenditure during a year or other specified period. Such an index is called a fixed-basket price index.
3. The index may also aim to measure the effects of price changes on the cost of achieving a constant standard of living (that is level of utility or welfare). This concept is called a cost of living index (COLI). A fixed-basket price index, or another appropriate design, may be employed as an approximation to a COLI.

The Uses of a Consumer Price Index

4. The CPI is used for a wide variety of purposes, the two most common ones being (1) to adjust wages as well as social security and other benefits to compensate, partly or completely, for changes in the cost of living or in consumer prices; and (2) to provide an average measure of price inflation for the household sector as a whole, for use as a macroeconomic indicator. CPI subindices are also used to deflate components of household final consumption expenditure in the national accounts and the value of retail sales to obtain estimates of changes in their volume.
5. CPIs are also used for other purposes, such as monitoring the overall rate of price inflation for all sectors of the economy, the adjustment of government fees and charges, the adjustment of payments in commercial contracts, and for formulating and assessing fiscal and monetary policies and trade and exchange rate policies. In these types of cases, the CPI is used as more appropriate measures do not exist at present, or because other characteristics of the CPI (for example, high profile, wide acceptance, predictable publication schedule, and so on) are seen to outweigh any conceptual or technical deficiencies.
6. Given that the CPI may be used for many purposes, it is unlikely that one index can perform equally satisfactorily in all applications. It may therefore be appropriate to construct a number of alternative price indices for specific purposes, if the requirements of the users justify the extra expense. Each index should be properly defined and named to avoid confusion and a "headline." CPI measure should be explicitly identified.
7. Where only one index is compiled, it is the main use that should determine the type of index compiled, the range of goods and services covered, its geographic coverage, the households it relates to, as well as to the concept of

price and the formula used. If there are several major uses, it is likely that compromises may have to be made with regard to how the CPI is constructed. Users should be informed of the compromises made and of the limitations of such an index.

Scope of the Index

8. The scope of the index depends on the main use for which it is intended and should be defined with regard to the type of households, geographic areas, and the categories of consumer goods and services acquired, used, or paid for by the reference population.
9. If the primary use of the CPI is for adjusting money incomes, a relevant group of households, such as wage and salary earners, may be the appropriate target population. For this use, all consumption expenditures by these households, at home and abroad, may be covered. If the primary use of the CPI is to measure inflation in the domestic economy, it may be appropriate to cover consumption expenditures made within the country, rather than the expenditures of households resident within the country.
10. In general, the reference population for a national index should be defined very widely. If any income groups, types of households or particular geographic areas are excluded, for example, for cost or practical considerations, then this should be explicitly stated.
11. The geographic scope refers to the geographic coverage of price collection and of consumption expenditures of the reference population and both should be defined as widely as possible, and preferably consistently. If price collection is restricted to particular areas due to resource constraints, then this should be specified. The geographic coverage of the consumption expenditure may be defined either as covering consumption expenditure of the resident population (resident consumption) or consumption expenditure within the country (domestic consumption).
12. Significant differences in the expenditure patterns and price movements between specific population groups or regions may exist, and care should be taken to ensure that they are represented in the index. Separate indices for these population groups or regions may be computed if there is sufficient demand to justify the additional cost.
13. In accordance with its main purpose, the CPI should conceptually cover all types of consumer goods and services of significance to the reference population, without any omission of those that may not be legally available or may be considered socially undesirable. Where appropriate, special aggregates may be constructed to assist those users who may wish to exclude certain categories of goods or services for particular applications or for analysis. Whenever certain goods or services have been excluded from the index, this should be clearly documented.
14. Goods and services purchased for business purposes, expenditures on assets such as works of art, financial investment (as distinct from financial services), and payments of income taxes, social security contributions, and fines are not considered to be consumer goods or services and should be excluded from the coverage of the index. Some countries regard expenditures on the purchase of houses entirely as a capital investment and, as such, exclude them from the index.

Acquisition, Use, or Payment

15. In determining the scope of the index, the time of recording, and valuation of consumption, it is important to consider whether the purposes for which the index is used are best satisfied by defining consumption with regard to "acquisition," "use," or "payment."[2] The "acquisition" approach is often used when the primary purpose of the index is to serve as a macroeconomic indicator. The "payment" approach is often used when the primary purpose of the index is for the adjustment of compensation or income. Where the aim of the index is to measure changes in the cost of living, the "use" approach may be most suitable. The decision regarding the approach to follow for a particular group of products should in principle be based on the purpose of the index, as well as on the costs and the acceptability of the decision to the users who should be informed of the approach followed for different products. Because of the practical difficulties in uniformly defining consumption and estimating the flow of services provided by other durable goods with regard to "use," it may be necessary to adopt a mixed approach, for example, "use" for owner-occupied housing and "acquisition" or "payment" basis for other consumer durables.
16. The differences between the three approaches are most pronounced in dealing with products for which the times of acquisition, use, and payment do not coincide, such as owner-occupied housing, durable goods, and products acquired on credit.
17. The most complex and important of the products mentioned previously is owner-occupied housing. In most countries, a significant proportion of households are owner-occupiers of their housing, with the housing being characterized by a long useful life and a high purchase outlay (price). Under the "acquisition" approach, the value of the new dwellings acquired in the weight reference period may be used for deriving the weight (and the full price of the dwelling is included in the CPI at the time of acquisition, regardless of when the consumption is taking place). Under the "payment" approach, the weights reflect the amounts actually paid out for housing (and the prices enter the CPI in the period(s) when the prices are paid). Under the "use" approach the weights are based on the value of the flow of housing services consumed during the weight reference period estimated using an implicit or notional cost (and prices or estimated opportunity costs enter the CPI when the consumption is taking place).
18. Own-account consumption, remuneration in kind, and goods and services provided without charge or subsi-

[2]See Annex 1.

dized by governments and nonprofit institutions serving households may be important in some countries where the purpose of the index is best satisfied by defining consumption with regard to "use" or "acquisition" (under the payment approach these are out of scope). The inclusion of these products will require special valuation and pricing techniques.

Basket and Weights

19. Decisions on the composition of the basket and the weights follow directly from the scope, as well as from the choice between the "acquisition," "use," or "payment" approaches.
20. Once defined, the expenditures that fall within the scope of the index should be grouped into similar categories in a hierarchical classification system, for example, divisions/groups/classes, for compilation as well as analytical purposes. There should be consistency between the classification used for index compilation and the one used for household expenditure statistics. The CPI classification should meet the needs of users for special subindices. For the purposes of international comparisons, the classification should also be reconcilable with the most recent version of the United Nations *Classification of Individual Consumption According to Purpose*, at least at its division level.[3]
21. In order to facilitate the analysis and interpretation of the results of the index, it may be desirable to classify goods and services according to various supplementary classifications, for example, source of origin, durability, and seasonality. Calculation of the CPI by using various classifications should generate the same overall results as the original index.
22. The classification should also provide a framework for the allocation of expenditure weights. Expenditures at the lowest level of the classification system, expressed as a proportion of the total expenditure, determine the weights to be used at this level. When the weights are to remain fixed for several years, the objective should be to adopt weights that are representative of the contemporary household behavior.
23. The two main sources for deriving the weights are the results from household expenditure surveys and national accounts estimates on household consumption expenditure. The results from a household expenditure survey are appropriate for an index defined to cover the consumption expenditures of reference population groups resident within the country, while national account estimates are suitable for an index defined to cover consumption expenditures within the country. The decision about what source or sources to use and how they should be used depends on the main purpose of the index and on the availability and quality of appropriate data.
24. The information from the main source (household expenditure surveys or national accounts) should be supplemented with all other available information on the expenditure pattern. Sources of such information that can be used for disaggregating the expenditures are surveys of sales in retail outlets, point-of-purchase surveys, surveys of production, export and import data, and administrative sources. Based on these data the weights for certain products may be further disaggregated by region and type of outlet. Where the data obtained from different sources relate to different periods, it is important to ensure, before weights are allocated, that expenditures are adjusted so that they have the same reference period.
25. Where the weight reference period differs significantly from the price reference period, the weights should be price updated to take account of price changes between the weight reference period and price reference period. Where it is likely that price-updated weights are less representative of the consumption pattern in the price reference period this procedure may be omitted.
26. Weights should be reviewed and if appropriate revised as often as accurate and reliable data are available for this to be done, but at least once every five years. Revisions are important to reduce the impact on the index of product substitutions and to ensure the basket of goods and services and their weights remain representative.[4] For some categories, it may be necessary to update the weights more frequently as such weights are likely to become out of date more quickly than higher-level weights. In periods of high inflation, the weights should be updated frequently.
27. When a new basket (structure or weights) replaces the old, a continuous CPI series should be created by linking[5] together the index numbers based on the new basket of goods and services to those based on the earlier basket. The particular procedure used to link index number series will depend on the particular index compilation technique used. The objective is to ensure that the technique used to introduce a new basket does not, of itself, alter the level of the index.
28. Completely new types of goods and services (that is goods and services that cannot be classified to any of the existing elementary aggregates) should normally be considered for inclusion only during one of the periodic review and reweighting exercises. A new model or variety of an existing product that can be fitted within an existing elementary aggregate should be included at the time it is assessed as having a significant and sustainable market share. If a quality change is detected an appropriate quality adjustment should be made.[6]
29. Some products such as seasonal products, insurance, second-hand goods, expenditure abroad, interest, own production, expenditures on purchase and construction of dwellings, and so on, may need special treatment when constructing their weights. The way these products are dealt with should be determined by the main purpose of the index, national circumstances, and the practicalities of compilation.

[3] See Annex 4.

[4] See Annex 1.
[5] See Annex 2.
[6] See Annex 2.

30. Seasonal products should be included in the basket. It is possible to use (1) a fixed-weight approach which uses the same weight for the seasonal product in all months using an imputed price in the out-of-season months; or (2) a variable weights approach where a changing weight is attached to the product in various months. The decision on the approach should be based on national circumstances.
31. The expenditure weights for second-hand goods should be based either on the net expenditure of the reference population on such goods or the gross expenditure, depending on the purpose of the index.
32. When consumption from own production is within the scope of the index, the weights should be based on the value of quantities consumed from own production. Valuation of consumption from own production should be made on the basis of prices prevailing on the market, unless there is some reason to conclude that market prices are not relevant or cannot be reliably observed, or there is no interest in using hypothetically imputed prices. In this case, the expenditures and prices for the inputs into the production of these goods and services could be used instead. The third option is to valuate it by using quality-adjusted market prices.

Sampling for Price Collection

33. A CPI is an estimate based on a sample of households to estimate weights, and a sample of zones within regions, a sample of outlets, a sample of goods and services, and a sample of time periods for price observation.
34. The sample size and sample selection methods for both outlets and the goods and services for which price movements over time are to be observed should ensure that the prices collected are representative and sufficient to meet the requirements for the accuracy of the index, but also that the collection process is cost-effective. The sample of prices should reflect the importance, with regard to relative expenditures, of the goods and services available for purchase by consumers in the reference period, the number, types, and geographic spread of outlets that are relevant for each good and service, and the dispersion of prices and price changes across outlets.
35. Probability sampling techniques are the preferred methods, in principle, as they permit sound statistical inference and control over the representativity of the sample. In addition, they permit estimation of sampling variation (errors). However, they may be costly to implement and can result in the selection of products that are very difficult to price to constant quality.
36. In cases where appropriate sampling frames are lacking and it is too costly to obtain them, samples of outlets and products have to be obtained by nonprobability methods. Statisticians should use available information and apply their best judgment to ensure that representative samples are selected. The possibility of applying cutoff or detailed quota sampling[7] strategy may be considered, especially where the sample size is small. A mixture of probability and nonprobability sampling techniques may be used.
37. Efficient and representative sampling, whether random or purposive, requires comprehensive and up-to-date sampling frames for outlets and products. Sample selection can be done by the head office from centrally held sampling frames, in the field by price collectors, or by a mixture of the two. In the first case, price collectors should be given precise instructions on which outlets to visit and which products to price. In the second case, price collectors should be given detailed and unambiguous guidelines on the local sampling procedures to be adopted. Statistical business registers, business telephone directories, results from the point-of-purchase surveys or from surveys of sales in different types of outlets, and lists of internet sellers may be used as sampling frames for the central selection of outlets. Catalogs or other product lists drawn up by major manufacturers, wholesalers, or trade associations, or lists of products that are specific to individual outlets such as large supermarkets might be used as the sampling frame for selection of products. Data scanned by barcode readers at the cashier's desk (electronic databases) can be particularly helpful in the selection of goods and services.
38. The sample of outlets and of goods and services should be reviewed periodically and updated where necessary to maintain its representativeness.

Index Calculation

39. The compilation of a CPI consists of collecting and processing price and expenditure data according to specified concepts, definitions, methods, and practices. The detailed procedures that are applied will depend on particular circumstances.
40. CPIs are calculated in steps. In the first step, the elementary aggregate indices are calculated. In the subsequent steps, higher-level indices are calculated by aggregating the elementary aggregate indices.

Elementary Aggregate Indices

41. The elementary aggregate is the smallest and relatively homogeneous set of goods or services for which expenditure data are defined (used) for CPI purposes. It is the only aggregate for which an index number is constructed without any explicit expenditure weights, although other kinds of weights might be explicitly or implicitly introduced into the calculation. The set of goods or services covered by an elementary aggregate should be similar in their end-uses and are expected to have similar price movements. They may be defined not only with regard to their characteristics but also with regard to the type of location and outlet in which they are sold. The degree of homogeneity achieved in practice will depend on the availability of corresponding expenditure data.
42. An elementary index is a price index for an elementary aggregate. As expenditure weights usually

[7] See Annex 1.

cannot be attached to the prices or price relatives for the sampled products within the elementary aggregate, an elementary index is usually calculated as an unweighted average of the prices or price relatives. When some information on weights is available, this should be taken into account when compiling the elementary indices.

43. There are several ways in which the prices, or the price relatives, might be averaged. The three most commonly used formulae are the ratio of arithmetic mean prices, the geometric mean, and the arithmetic mean of price relatives. The choice of formula depends on the purpose of the index, the sample design, and the mathematical properties of the formula. It is possible to use different formulae for different elementary aggregates within the same CPI. It is recommended that the geometric mean formula be used, particularly where there is a need to reflect substitution within the elementary aggregate or where the dispersion in prices or price changes within the elementary aggregate is large. The geometric mean has many advantages because of its mathematical properties. The ratio of arithmetic mean prices may be used for elementary aggregates that are homogeneous and where consumers have only limited opportunity to substitute or where substitution is not to be reflected in the index. The arithmetic mean of price relative formula should be avoided in its chained form, as it is known to result in biased estimates of the elementary indices.

44. The elementary index may be computed by using either a chained or direct form of the formula chosen. The use of a chained form may make the estimation of missing prices and the introduction of replacement products easier.

Upper-Level Indices

45. These price indices are constructed as weighted averages of elementary aggregate indices. Several types of formulae can be used to average the elementary aggregate indices. In order to compile a timely index, the practical option is to use a formula that relies on the weights relating to some past period. One such formula is the Laspeyres-type index, the formula used by most national statistical agencies.

46. For some purposes, it may be appropriate to calculate the index retrospectively by using an index number formula that employs both base period weights and current period weights, such as the Fisher, Törnqvist, or Walsh index. Comparing the difference between the index of this type and the Laspeyres-type index can give some indication of the combined impact of income changes, preference changes, and substitution effects over the period in question, providing important information for producers and users of the CPI.

47. Where the change in an upper-level index between two consecutive periods such as $t - 1$ and t is calculated as the weighted average of the individual indices between $t - 1$ and t, care should be taken to ensure that the weights are updated to take account of the price changes between the price reference period 0 and the preceding period $t - 1$. Failure to do so may result in a biased index.

Price Observations

48. The number and quality of the prices collected are critical determinants of the reliability of the index, along with the specifications of the products priced. Standard methods for collecting and processing price information should be developed and procedures put in place for collecting them systematically and accurately at regular intervals. Price collectors should be well trained and well supervised, and should be provided with a comprehensive manual explaining the procedures they have to follow.

Collection

49. An important consideration is whether the index or parts of the index should relate to monthly (or quarterly) average prices or to prices for a specific period of time (for example, a single day or week in a month). This decision is related to a number of issues, which include the use of an index, the practicalities of carrying out price collection, and the pattern of price movements. When point-in-time pricing is adopted, prices should be collected over a very small number of days each month (or quarter). The interval between price observations should be uniform for each product. Since the length of the month (or quarter) varies, this uniformity needs to be defined carefully. When the aim is monthly (or quarterly) average prices, the prices collected should be representative of the period to which they refer.

50. Attention should also be paid to the time of day selected for price observation. For example, in the case of perishable goods, price observations may need to be collected at the same time on the same day of the week and not just before closing time, when stocks may be low or sold cheaply to minimize wastage.

51. Price collection should be carried out in such a way as to be representative of all geographical areas within the scope of the index. Special care should be taken where significant differences in price movements between areas may be expected.

52. Prices should be collected in all types of outlets that are important, including internet sellers, open-air markets and informal markets, and in free markets as well as price-controlled markets. Where more than one type of outlet is important for a particular type of product, this should be reflected in the initial sample design and an appropriately weighted average should be used in the calculation of the index.

53. Specifications should be provided detailing the variety and size of the products for which price information is to be collected. These should be precise enough to identify all the price-determining characteristics that are necessary to ensure that, as far as possible, the same goods and services are priced in successive periods in the same outlet. The specifications should

include, for example, make, model, size, terms of payment, conditions of delivery, type of guarantees, and type of outlet. This information could be used in the procedures used for replacement and for quality adjustment.

54. Prices to be collected are actual transaction prices, including indirect taxes and nonconditional discounts, which would be paid, agreed, or costed (accepted) by the reference population. Where prices are not displayed or have to be negotiated, where quantity units are poorly defined or where actual purchase prices may deviate from listed or fixed prices, it may be necessary for the price collectors to purchase products in order to determine the transaction prices. A budget may be provided for any such purchases. When this is not possible, consideration may be given to interviewing customers about the prices actually paid. Tips for services, where compulsory, should be treated as part of the price paid.

55. Exceptional prices charged for stale, shop-soiled, damaged, or otherwise imperfect goods sold at clearance prices should be excluded, unless the sale of such products is a permanent and widespread phenomenon. Sale prices, discounts, cut prices, and special offers should be included when applicable to all customers without there being significant limits to the quantities that can be purchased by each customer.

56. In periods of price control or rationing, where limited supplies are available at prices which are held at a low level by measures such as subsidies to the sellers, government procurement, price control, and so on, such prices as well as those charged on any significant unrestricted markets should be collected. The different price observations should be combined in a way that uses the best information available with respect to the actual prices paid and the relative importance of the different types of sales.

57. For each type of product, different alternatives for collecting prices should be carefully investigated, to ensure that the price observations could be made reliably and effectively. Means of collection could include visits to outlets with paper forms or hand-held devices, interviews with customers, computer-assisted telephone interviews, mail-out questionnaires, brochures, price lists provided by large or monopoly suppliers of services, scanner data, and prices posted on the internet. For each alternative, the possible cost advantages need to be balanced against an assessment of the reliability and timeliness of each of the alternatives.

58. Where centrally regulated or centrally fixed prices are collected from the regulatory authorities, checks should be made to ascertain whether the goods and services in question are actually sold and whether these prices are in fact paid. For goods and services where the prices paid are determined by combinations of subscription fees and piece rates (for example, for newspapers, journals, public transport, electricity, and telecommunications) care must be taken to ensure that a representative range of price offers is observed. Care must also be taken to ensure that prices charged to different types of consumers are observed, for example, those linked to the age of the purchaser or to memberships of particular associations.

59. The collected price information should be reviewed for comparability and consistency with previous observations, the presence of replacements, unusual or large price changes, and to ensure that price conversions of goods priced in multiple units or varying quantities are properly calculated. Extremely large or unusual price changes should be examined to determine whether they are genuine price changes or are due to changes in quality. Procedures should be put in place for checking the reliability of all price observations. This could include a program of direct pricing and selective repricing of some products shortly after the initial observation was made.

60. Consistent procedures should be established for dealing with missing price observations because of, for example, inability to contact the seller, nonresponse, observation rejected as unreliable, or products temporarily unavailable. Prices of nonseasonal products that are temporarily unavailable should be estimated until they reappear or are replaced, by using appropriate estimation procedures, for example, imputation on the basis of price changes of similar nonmissing products. Carrying forward the last observed price should be avoided, especially in periods of high inflation.

Replacements

61. Replacement of a product will be necessary when it disappears permanently. Replacement should be made within the first three months (quarter) of the product becoming unavailable. It may also be necessary when the product is no longer available or sold in significant quantities or under normal sale conditions. Clear and precise rules should be developed for selecting the replacement product. Depending on the frequency of sampling and the potential for accurate quality adjustment, the most commonly used alternatives are to select (1) the most similar to the replaced variety, (2) the most popular variety among those that belong to the same elementary aggregate, and (3) the variety most likely to be available in the future. Precise procedures should be laid down for price adjustments with respect to the difference in characteristics when replacements are necessary, so that the impact of changes in quality is excluded from the observed price.

62. Replacement of an outlet may be motivated if prices cannot be obtained, for example, because it has closed permanently, because of a decline in representativeness or because the outlet no longer cooperates. Clear rules should be established on when to discontinue price observations from a selected outlet, on the criteria for selecting a replacement, as well as on the adjustments that may be required to price observations or weights. Such rules should be consistent with the objectives of the index and with the way in which the outlet sample has been determined.

63. Deletion of an entire elementary aggregate will be necessary if all products in that elementary aggregate disappear from most or all outlets and it is not possible to locate a sufficient number of price observations to continue to compile a reliable index for this elementary aggregate. In such situations, it is necessary to redistribute the weight assigned to the elementary aggregate among the other elementary aggregates included in the next level of aggregation.

Quality Changes

64. The same product should be priced in each period as long as it is representative. However, in practice, products that can be observed at different time periods may differ with respect to package sizes, weights, volumes, features, and terms of sale, as well as other characteristics. Thus, it is necessary to monitor the characteristics of the products being priced to ensure that the impact of any differences in price-relevant or utility-relevant characteristics can be excluded from the estimated price change.

65. Identifying changes in quality or utility is relatively more difficult for complex durable goods and services. It is necessary, therefore, to collect a considerable amount of information on the relevant characteristics of the products for which prices are collected. The most important information can be obtained in the course of collecting prices. Other sources of information on price-relevant or utility-relevant characteristics can be producers, importers, or wholesalers of the goods included and the study of articles and advertisements in trade publications.

66. When a quality change is detected, an adjustment must be made to the price, so that the index reflects as nearly as possible the pure price change. If this is not done, the index will either record a price change that has not taken place or fail to record a price change that did happen. The choice of method for such adjustments will depend on the particular goods and services involved. Great care needs to be exercised because the accuracy of the resulting index depends on the quality of this process. To assume automatically that all price change is a reflection of the change in quality should be avoided, as should the automatic assumption that products with different qualities are essentially equivalent.

67. The methods for estimating quality-adjusted prices[8] may be:

    (1) *Explicit (or direct) quality-adjustment methods* that directly estimate the value of the quality difference between the old and new product and adjust one of the prices accordingly. Pure price change is then implicitly estimated as the difference in the adjusted prices.

    (2) *Implicit (or indirect) quality-adjustment methods* which estimate the pure price change component of the price difference between the old and new products based on the price changes observed for similar products. The difference between the estimate of pure price change and the observed price change is considered as change due to quality difference.

    Some of these methods are complex, costly, and difficult to apply. The methods used should as far as possible be based on objective criteria.

Accuracy

68. As with all statistics, CPI estimates are subject to errors that may arise from a variety of sources.[9] Compilers of CPIs need to be aware of the possible sources of error and to take steps during the design of the index, its construction, and compilation processes to minimize their impact, for which adequate resources should be allocated.

69. The following are some well-known sources of potential error, either in pricing or in index construction, that over time can lead to errors in the overall CPI: incorrect selection of products and incorrect observation and recording of their prices, incorrect selection of outlets and timing of price collection, failure to observe and adjust correctly for quality changes, appearance of new goods and outlets, failure to adjust for product and outlet substitution or loss of representativity, and the use of inappropriate formulae for computing elementary aggregate and upper-level indices.

70. To reduce the index's potential for giving a misleading picture, it is in general essential to update weights and baskets regularly, to employ unbiased elementary aggregate formulae, to make appropriate adjustments for quality change, to allow adequately and correctly for new products, and to take proper account of substitution issues as well as quality control of the entire compilation process.

Dissemination

71. The CPI estimate should be computed and publicly released as quickly as possible after the end of the period to which it refers and according to a preannounced timetable. It should be made available to all users at the same time, in a convenient form, and should be accompanied by a short methodological explanation. Rules relating to its release should be made publicly available and strictly observed. In particular, they should include details of who has prerelease access to the results, why, under what conditions, and how long before the official release time.

72. The general CPI should be compiled and released monthly. Where there is no strong user demand for a monthly series or countries do not have the necessary resources, the CPI may be prepared and released quarterly. Depending on national circumstances, subindices

[8] See Annex 2.

[9] See Annex 3.

may be released with a frequency that corresponds to users' needs.

73. When it is found that published index estimates have been seriously distorted because of errors or mistakes made in their compilation, corrections should be made and published. Such corrections should be made as soon as possible after detection according to publicly available policy for correction. Where the CPI is widely used for adjustment purposes for wages and contracts, retrospective revisions should be avoided to the extent possible.

74. The publication of the CPI results should show the index level from the index reference period. It is also useful to present derived indices, such as the one that shows changes in the major aggregates between (1) the current month and the previous month, (2) the current month and the same month of the previous year, and (3) the average of the latest 12 months and the average of the previous 12 months. The indices should be presented in both seasonally adjusted and unadjusted terms, if seasonally adjusted data are available.

75. Comments and interpretation of the index should accompany its publication to assist users. An analysis of the contributions of various products or group of products to the overall change and an explanation of any unusual factors affecting the price changes of the major contributors to the overall change should be included.

76. Indices for the major expenditure groups should also be compiled and released. Consideration should be given to compiling indices for the divisions and groups of the Classification of Individual Consumption According to Purpose.[10] Nine subindices for different regions or population groups, and alternative indices designed for analytical purposes, may be compiled and publicly released if there is a demand from users, they are judged to be reliable, and their preparation is cost-effective.

77. The index reference period may be chosen to coincide with the latest weight reference period or it could be established to coincide with the base period of other statistical series. It should be changed as frequently as necessary to ensure that the index numbers remain easy to present and understand.

78. Average prices and price ranges for important and reasonably homogeneous products may be estimated and published in order to support the research and analytical needs of users.

79. Countries should report national CPI results and methodological information to the International Labour Office as soon as possible after their national release.

80. Comparing national CPI movements across countries is difficult because of the different measurement approaches used by countries for certain products, particularly housing and financial services. The exclusion of housing (actual rents and either imputed rents or acquisition of new houses, and maintenance and repair of dwellings) and financial services from the all-items index will make the resulting estimates of price change for the remaining products more comparable across countries. Therefore, in addition to the all-items index, countries should, if possible, compile and provide for dissemination to the international community an index that excludes housing and financial services. It should be emphasized, though, that even for the remaining products in scope, there can still be difficulties when making international comparisons of changes in consumer prices.

Consultations and Integrity

81. The compiling agency should have the professional independence, competence, and resources necessary to support a high-quality CPI program. The United Nations *Fundamental Principles of Official Statistics*[11] and the International Labour Organization *Guidelines Concerning Dissemination Practices for Labour Statistics*[12] should be respected.

82. The agency responsible for the index should consult representatives of users on issues of importance for the CPI, particularly during preparations for any changes to the methodology used in compiling the CPI. One way of organizing such consultations is through the establishment of advisory committee(s) on which social partners, as well as other users and independent experts, might be represented.

83. In order to ensure public confidence in the index, a full description of the data collection procedures and the index methodology should be prepared and made widely available. Reference to this description should be made when the CPI is published. The documentation should include an explanation of the main objectives of the index, details of the weights, the index number formulae used, and a discussion of the accuracy of the index estimates. The precise identities of the outlets and goods and services used for price collection should not be revealed.

84. Users should be informed in advance of any changes that are going to be made to the scope, weights, or methodology used to estimate the CPI.

85. Technical guidance on the compilation of consumer price indices is provided in the *Consumer Price Index Manual: Theory and Practice*.[13] This manual should be updated periodically in order to reflect current best practices.

[10] See Annex 4.

[11] United Nations Economic and Social Council (1994).

[12] Sixteenth International Conference of Labour Statisticians (1998).

[13] International Labour Organization, International Monetary Fund, Organisation for Economic Co-operation and Development, Eurostat, UN Economic Commission for Europe, and World Bank (2004).

Annex 1
Terminology and Definitions

(1) "Consumer goods" are goods or services that are used by households for the satisfaction of individual needs or wants.

(2) "Consumption expenditures" are expenditure on consumer goods and services and can be defined with regard to "acquisition,"[1] "use," or "payment":

- "Acquisition" indicates that it is the total value of the goods and services acquired during a given period that should be taken into account, irrespective of whether they were wholly paid for or used during the period. This approach could be extended to include the estimated values of own-account production and social transfers in kind received from government or nonprofit institutions. The prices enter the CPI in the period when consumers accept or agree prices, as distinct from the time payment is made.
- "Use" indicates that it is the total value of all goods and services actually consumed during a given period that should be taken into account; for durable goods this approach requires valuing the services provided by these goods during the period. The prices (opportunity costs) enter the CPI in the period of consumption.
- "Payment" indicates that it is the total payment made for goods and services during a given period that should be taken into account, without regard to whether they were delivered or used during the period. The prices enter the CPI in the period or periods when the payment is made.

(3) "Scope of the index" refers to the population groups, geographic areas, products, and outlets for which the index is constructed.

(4) "Coverage" of the index is the set of goods and services represented in the index. For practical reasons, coverage may have to be less than what corresponds to the defined scope of the index.

(5) "Reference population" refers to that specific population group for which the index has been constructed.

(6) "Weights" are the aggregate consumption expenditures on any set of goods and services expressed as a proportion of the total consumption expenditures on all goods and services within the scope of the index in the weight reference period. They are a set of numbers summing up to unity.

(7) "Price updating of weights" is a procedure that is used to bring the expenditure weights in line with the index or price reference period. The price-updated weights are calculated by multiplying the weights from the weight reference period by elementary indices measuring the price changes between weight reference and price reference period and rescaling to sum to unity.

(8) "Index reference period" is the period for which the value of the index is set at 100.

(9) "Price reference period" is the period whose prices are compared with the prices in the current period, the period whose prices appear in the denominators of the price relatives.

[1]This definition differs from the one adopted by the Fourteenth ICLS (1987).

(10) The "weight reference period" is the period, usually a year, whose estimates of the volume of consumption and its components are used to calculate the weights.

(11) "Probability sampling" is the selection of a sample of units, such as outlets or products, in such a way that each unit in the universe has a known nonzero probability of selection.

(12) "Cutoff sampling" is a sampling procedure in which a predetermined threshold is established with all units in the relevant population at or above the threshold being eligible for inclusion in the sample and all units below the threshold being excluded. The threshold is usually specified with regard to the size of some relevant variable (such as some percentage of total sales), the largest sampling units being included and the rest excluded.

(13) "Quota sampling" is a nonprobability method where the population is divided into certain strata. For each stratum, the number ("quota") of elements to be included in the sample is specified. The price collector simply "fills the quotas," which means, in the case of outlet sampling, that the selection of the outlets is based on the judgment of the price collectors and the specified criteria.

(14) "Imputed expenditures" are the expenditures assigned to a product that has not been purchased, such as a product that has been produced by the household for its own consumption (including housing services produced by owner-occupiers) or a product received as payment in kind or as a free transfer from government or nonprofit institutions.

(15) "Imputed price" refers to the estimated price of a product whose price during a particular period has not been observed and is therefore missing. It is also the price assigned to a product for which the expenditures have been imputed, see (14).

(16) "Outlet" indicates a shop, market stall, service establishment, internet seller, or other place where goods and services are sold or provided to consumers for nonbusiness use.

(17) "Linking" means joining together two consecutive sequences of price observations, or price indices, that overlap in one or more periods, by rescaling one of them so that the value in the overlap period is the same in both sequences, thus combining them into a single continuous series.

(18) "Price" is defined as the value of one unit of a product, for which the quantities are perfectly homogeneous not only in a physical sense but also in respect of a number of other characteristics.

(19) "Pure price change" is that change in the price of a good or service which is not due to any change in its quality. When the quality does change, the pure price change is the price change remaining after eliminating the estimated contribution of the change in quality to the observed price change.

(20) "Quality adjustment" refers to the process of adjusting the observed prices of a product to remove the effect of any changes in the quality of that product over time so that pure price change may be identified.

(21) "Consumer substitution" occurs when, faced with changes in relative price, consumers buy more of the good that has become relatively cheaper and less of the good that has become relatively more expensive. It may occur between varieties of the same product or between different expenditure categories.

Annex 2
Quality-Adjustment Methods

Implicit Quality-Adjustment Methods

1. The "overlap" method assumes that the entire price difference at a common point in time between the disappearing product and its replacement is due to a difference in quality.
2. The "overall mean imputation" method first calculates the average price change for an aggregate without the disappearing product and its replacement, and then uses that rate of price change to impute a price change for the disappearing product. It assumes that the pure price difference between the disappearing product and its replacement is equal to the average price changes for continuing (nonmissing) products.
3. The "class mean imputation" method is a variant of the overall mean imputation method. The only difference is in the source of the imputed rate of price change to period $t + 1$ for the disappearing product. Rather than using the average index change for all the nonmissing products in the aggregate, the imputed rate of price change is estimated using only those price changes of the products that were judged essentially equivalent or were directly quality adjusted.

Explicit Quality-Adjustment Methods

4. The "expert's adjustment" method relies on the judgment of one or more industry experts, commodity specialists, price statisticians or price collectors on the value of any quality difference between the old and replacement product. None, some, or all of the price difference may be attributed to the improved quality.
5. The "differences in production costs" approach relies on the information provided by the manufacturers on the production costs of new features of the replacements (new models), to which retail markups and associated indirect taxes are then added. This approach is most practicable in markets with a relatively small number of producers, with infrequent and predictable model updates. However, it should be used with caution as it is possible for new production techniques to reduce costs while simultaneously improving quality.
6. The "quantity adjustment" method is applicable to products for which the replacement product is of a different size to the previously available one. It should only be used if the differences in quantities do not have an impact on the quality of the good.
7. The "option cost" method adjusts the price of the replacements for the value of the new observable characteristics. An example of this is the addition of a feature that earlier has been a priced option as standard to a new automobile model.
8. A "hedonic" regression method estimates the price of a product as a function of the characteristics it possesses. The relationship between the prices and all relevant and observable price-determining characteristics is first estimated and then results are used in the estimation of the index.

Annex 3
Types of Errors

- "Quality change error" is the error that can occur as a result of the index's failure to make proper allowance for changes in the quality of goods and services.
- "New goods error" is the failure to reflect either price changes in new products not yet sampled, or given a COLI objective, the welfare gain to consumers when those products appear.
- "Outlet substitution error" can occur when consumers shift their purchases among outlets for the same product without proper reflection of this shift in the data collection for the index.
- "New outlets error" is conceptually identical to new goods error. It arises because of the failure to reflect either price changes in new outlets not yet sampled, or the welfare gain to consumers when the new outlets appear.
- "Upper-level substitution error" arises when the index does not reflect consumer substitution among the basic categories of consumption owing to the use of an inappropriate method for aggregating elementary aggregates in the construction of the overall index value. Only relevant to a COLI, although an equivalent (representativity error) may be defined from the perspective of the pure price index.
- "Elementary index error" arises from the use of an inappropriate method for aggregating price quotations at the very lowest level of aggregation. The elementary index error can take two forms: formula error and lower-level substitution error. The index suffers from formula error if, as a result of the properties of the formula, the result produced is biased relative to what would have been the result if a pure price change could have been estimated. The index suffers from lower-level substitution error if it does not reflect consumer substitution among the products contained in the elementary aggregate.
- "Selection error" arises when the sample of price observations is not fully representative of the intended population of outlets or products. The first four types of errors listed previously can be seen as special cases of this type of error.

Annex 4

Classification of Individual Consumption According to Purpose[1]

(BREAKDOWN OF INDIVIDUAL CONSUMPTION EXPENDITURE OF HOUSEHOLDS BY DIVISION AND GROUP)

01 Food and nonalcoholic beverages
- 01.1 Food
- 01.2 Nonalcoholic beverages

02 Alcoholic beverages, tobacco, and narcotics
- 02.1 Alcoholic beverages
- 02.2 Tobacco
- 02.3 Narcotics

03 Clothing and footwear
- 03.1 Clothing
- 03.2 Footwear

04 Housing, water, electricity, gas, and other fuels
- 04.1 Actual rentals for housing
- 04.2 Imputed rentals for housing
- 04.3 Maintenance and repair of the dwelling
- 04.4 Water supply and miscellaneous services related to the dwelling
- 04.5 Electricity, gas, and other fuels

05 Furnishings, household equipment, and routine household maintenance
- 05.1 Furniture and furnishings, carpets, and other floor coverings
- 05.2 Household textiles
- 05.3 Household appliances
- 05.4 Glassware, tableware, and household utensils
- 05.5 Tools and equipment for house and garden
- 05.6 Goods and services for routine household maintenance

06 Health
- 06.1 Medical products, appliances, and equipment
- 06.2 Outpatient services
- 06.3 Hospital services

07 Transport
- 07.1 Purchase of vehicles
- 07.2 Operation of personal transport equipment
- 07.3 Transport services

08 Communication
- 08.1 Postal services
- 08.2 Telephone and telefax equipment
- 08.3 Telephone and telefax services

09 Recreation and Culture
- 09.1 Audiovisual, photographic, and information processing equipment
- 09.2 Other major durables for recreation and culture
- 09.3 Other recreational products and equipment, gardens, and pets
- 09.4 Recreational and cultural services
- 09.5 Newspapers, books, and stationery
- 09.6 Package holidays

10 Education
- 10.1 Preprimary and primary education
- 10.2 Secondary education
- 10.3 Postsecondary nontertiary education
- 10.4 Tertiary education
- 10.5 Education not definable by level

11 Restaurants and hotels
- 11.1 Catering services
- 11.2 Accommodation services

12 Miscellaneous goods and services
- 12.1 Personal care
- 12.2 Prostitution
- 12.3 Personal effects n.e.c.
- 12.4 Social protection
- 12.5 Insurance
- 12.6 Financial services n.e.c.
- 12.7 Other services n.e.c.

[1] See Appendix 2 to the Manual for explanatory notes.

Appendix 5

Spatial Comparisons of Consumer Prices, Purchasing Power Parities, and the International Comparison Program

Introduction

This annex deals with the topic of comparing price levels across different areas or regions within a country, as well as across countries. Even though international price comparisons are required to handle differences in currencies in different countries, the index number problems involved in price comparisons across countries mirror those encountered in comparisons over time. There is a large body of literature on cross-country comparisons of prices and real income generated through the International Comparison Program (ICP).

The ICP is a worldwide statistical initiative led by the World Bank under the auspices of the United Nations Statistical Commission. The ICP estimates purchasing power parities (PPPs) of countries through a partnership with international, regional, and national agencies.

PPPs are price indices that serve both as currency convertors and spatial price deflators. PPPs convert different currencies to a common currency and, in the process of conversion, equalize their purchasing power by eliminating the differences in price levels between countries. In their simplest form, PPPs are price relatives that show the ratio of the prices in national currencies of the same good or service in different countries.

PPPs are used to generate the price and volume indices needed for economic research and policy analysis that involves intercountry comparisons of gross domestic product and its expenditure components. The volume indices can be used to compare the size of economies and their levels of material well-being, consumption, investment, government expenditure, and overall productivity. The price indices can be used to compare price levels, price structures, price convergence, and competitiveness. In addition, PPPs are employed for several administrative purposes.

The ICP was launched in the late 1960s as a joint venture of the United Nations Statistical Division and the International Comparisons Unit of the University of Pennsylvania. The first experimental comparison was conducted in 1970, covering 10 countries. Since then, several rounds of comparisons have been conducted covering a varying number of countries, combined with significant advancements in the PPP estimation methodology.

Recognizing the needs for more frequent and reliable PPP estimates, the United Nations Statistical Commission agreed, at its 47th Session in 2016, that the ICP should become a permanent element of the global statistical program, conducted more frequently with shorter intervals between successive rounds and further aligned with regular national statistical programs.

While not providing an exhaustive account of the related problems and relevant aggregation methods, this annex aims to achieve a degree of completeness in the coverage of the problem of consumer price comparisons in the Manual by adding the spatial and international dimensions to the temporal comparisons dealt with in various chapters. The annex also attempts to identify possible avenues for a closer integration between spatial and temporal comparisons of consumer prices.

The main objectives of the annex are: (1) to provide a brief summary of the index number problems encountered in the process of international and interarea price comparisons and to highlight the need for the development and use of specialized aggregation methods; (2) to describe selected aggregation methods used in deriving PPPs and spatial measures of price levels; (3) to examine the relationship between the ICP and PPPs, for cross-country comparisons, with the consumer price index (CPI); and (4) to explore the feasibility of integrating the ICP activities with the streamlined activities of national statistical offices for the compilation of the CPI.

The annex is also designed to provide an introduction for the CPI compilers in various national statistical offices to the issues and methods involved in spatial comparisons of consumer prices. The annex outlines some of the principal differences in the approaches to spatial comparisons. Countries embarking on interarea or regional consumer price comparisons, as well as those countries that may participate in the ICP in the near future, may find the contents of the annex useful.

Differences between Temporal and Spatial Comparisons

There are several major qualitative differences in the nature of price comparisons involved in the standard CPI comparisons over time and price comparisons over space involving regions or countries. These differences highlight the need for specialized methods for aggregating price data in deriving summary measures of price levels, as well as specific types of data requirements associated with cross-country and interarea comparisons.

The foremost difference is the absence of a natural ordering of price and quantity observations in the context of cross-country or interarea comparisons. The CPI framework and methods are devised to measure changes over time. Therefore, the price observations appear in a chronological order. The presence of a natural ordering over time of price observations makes it possible to examine the feasibility and relative merits of the fixed and chain index numbers. In contrast, in the context of constructing price comparisons across countries, or across regions within a country, it is impossible to arrive at any kind of natural ordering.

The multilateral nature of spatial comparisons is a distinguishing feature of price comparisons across regions and countries. When price levels of goods and services across different countries are compared, it is essential that such comparisons are undertaken for every pair of countries being considered. This multilateral nature of comparisons creates several problems. First, the number of comparisons (one for each pair) can be quite large, and presentation and use of such results may be quite unwieldy. For example, if a particular comparison exercise involves 100 countries, then it requires $100 \times 99/2 = 4{,}950$ $\left(\binom{n}{k} = \frac{n!}{k!(n-k)!}\right)$, (where

n is the number of countries and $k = 2$) separate binary comparisons involving distinct pairs of countries. Second, results from such a large tableau of binary comparisons require a degree of consistency. This requirement translates into the "transitivity" condition described in the following text.

The uses and applications of interarea price comparisons may differ significantly from general consumer price indices. The CPI is probably the most significant economic statistic produced in any country. It is not only used as a general measure of price changes over time, but often in assessing and calibrating monetary policy. Despite the conceptual similarities in price comparisons over time and across space, spatial price comparisons are useful in comparisons of standards of living and well-being in different regions in a country or across countries. Such comparisons are essential in assessing development and in ensuring more balanced growth in different regions. There is considerable demand for measures of CPI across different cities and different states and regions (rural versus urban) within countries. However, there are very few countries where interarea price level comparisons are readily available.

International comparisons of prices, in the form of PPPs from the ICP, are used by international organizations and individual researchers in assessing the growth and productivity performance of countries, and also in making meaningful comparisons of various national income aggregates across different countries. PPPs are also essential in assessing the nature and extent of global poverty and its distribution across countries and regions of the world.

In recognition of the major analytical differences between the standard CPI comparisons over time and spatial (between countries or between regions in a country) comparisons of consumer prices and PPPs, considerable research efforts have focused on the development of the data and methods necessary for spatial comparisons of prices. A brief summary of the results of this research is given in the following text.

Data Requirements for Spatial (Interarea) Comparisons

The basic data requirements for spatial comparisons are very similar to the data required for standard CPI calculation. The main components are the data on prices of a large range of products representative of the consumption baskets of households and information on weights associated with various product categories reflecting the importance attached to different products. Within the CPI, it is common practice to collect price quotations from different outlets scattered throughout the country. The selection of the outlets and areas from which prices are collected is based on complex multistage sampling designs. The expenditure weights are based on a classification of goods and services using a standard system such as the Classification of Individual Consumption According to Purpose or a similar national classification. The lowest level of product classification at which expenditure weights are available is used in identifying the elementary indices and higher-level indices at progressively higher levels of aggregation, leading ultimately to the total household expenditure level.

Spatial comparisons pose several problems with regard to identifying products that are to be priced from different areas, regions, or countries involved in a comparison exercise. This problem is less severe when areas with similar economic structures or homogeneous consumption patterns are being compared. However, when comparisons are made between two heterogeneous countries, say the United States and India, there will be major differences in the consumption baskets at the detailed item level, even though the expenditure categories may be identical. This problem is somewhat similar to the treatment of disappearing and new goods in the context of the CPI, but is more serious when cross-country comparisons are being attempted.

Quality mismatches are likely to be smaller in the case of temporal comparisons, but can be a serious problem when comparisons across countries are attempted. The ICP follows the principle of identity (that is, comparing like with like) in dealing with the problem of quality differences across countries. A comprehensive list of products with detailed product specifications is developed at the planning stages of any cross-country comparison exercise. These items are priced in different countries from various outlets distributed across the country, a procedure very similar to that used in the CPI. Development of the product list is, however, a difficult step, with the degree of difficulty depending upon the size and heterogeneity of the group of countries involved. The use of a product listing, based on the identity principle, can have serious implications for the representativeness of the product list of the consumption baskets in different countries. At the same time, the requirement of comparing like with like leads to multiple gaps in the price matrix, as many countries cannot price all the items on the list. A more detailed account of the problems and recommended solutions can be found in *Measuring the Real Size of the World Economy* (2013) and *ICP Operational Guide* (2013).

For purposes of making interarea comparisons of consumer prices, it is necessary to obtain expenditure data specific to each area or country included in the comparisons.

Thus, spatial comparisons of consumer prices pose specific problems because of the nonoverlapping nature of the consumption baskets, potential major differences in the quality of items priced in different regions and countries, and the difficulties to fill data gaps in expenditure patterns.

Aggregation Methods for Spatial Comparisons

This section briefly describes the types of aggregation methods that are commonly used in spatial comparisons of prices. Though most of these methods have been developed in the context of the ICP, and are equally valid for interarea or regional comparisons, the following discussion uses countries as spatial entities. This section is further divided into three parts. The first deals with the notation and conceptual framework necessary to deal with multilateral spatial comparisons. The second describes the construction of elementary indices for aggregation of prices when no quantity or expenditure information is available. Finally, a small selection of index number methods used in spatial price comparisons is presented.

Notation and Conceptual Framework

Consider the case involving comparisons across M countries, and price and quantity data on N products. These products refer to goods and services that are priced in all the countries. If the products refer to items below the elementary level at which no quantity or expenditure share data are available, only the price data is used. At this stage, all the problems relating to nonoverlapping product lists are set aside so that the main focus is just on the aggregation issues. Let $pj = [\ p_1j,\ \ldots\ p_Nj\ ]$ and $qj = [\ q_1j,\ \ldots\ q_Nj\ ]$ represent the price and quantity vectors from country j ($j = 1,2, \ldots, M$). All the prices are expressed in the respective national currency units. As in the case of the CPI computation, the problem is one of decomposing the differences in the value aggregates

$$V^j = \sum_{i=1}^{N} p_i^j q_i^j \tag{A5.1}$$

into measures of price and real expenditure components.

Since there are M sets of price and quantity vectors and, therefore, $M(M-1)/2$ binary comparisons between all distinct pairs of countries, a simpler notation is used in this annex in the place of the notation generally used in the Manual. Let I_{jk} denote the price index number for country k with country j as the base. If j and k are, respectively, the United States and India, and if $I_{jk} = 22.50$, then the index is interpreted to mean that 22.50 Indian rupees have the same purchasing power as one US dollar for the goods and services covered in computing the index. Thus, the index can be interpreted as the PPP between the currencies of j and k. This interpretation is consistent with the meaning accorded to the CPI. Since currency denominations are involved here, a proper measure of relative price level differences can be obtained if the PPP is compared to the exchange rate prevailing at the time when comparisons are made. In the case of subnational comparisons, the PPPs would be the price level differences.

Because of the multilateral nature of spatial comparisons, when M countries are involved, it is necessary to provide comparisons between all pairs of countries. Thus, it becomes necessary to compute each and every entry in the following matrix of binary comparisons:

$$I = \begin{bmatrix} I_{11} & I_{12} & \cdot & I_{1M} \\ I_{21} & I_{22} & \cdot & I_{2M} \\ \cdot & \cdot & \cdot & \cdot \\ I_{M1} & I_{M2} & \cdot & I_{MM} \end{bmatrix} \tag{A5.2}$$

Several points concerning the matrix, I, are worth noting. First, the matrix can be large if the number of countries (or areas) involved is large. Second, the results recorded in the matrix need to be internally consistent. All the index number issues and various approaches discussed in the Manual apply directly to each binary comparison involving two countries. Diewert (1986, 1999b) provides a summary of the microeconomic theoretical and test approaches to cross-country comparisons. Thus, it is possible to apply Fisher, Törnqvist, Walsh, or other index number formulae described in the Manual.

To ensure meaningful interpretation of the results from multilateral cross-country comparisons, the index number methods applied need to satisfy a number of basic requirements, only the most important of which are discussed in the following text. Diewert (2013) provides a complete list of these requirements.

Transitivity. An index number formula I_{jk} is said to satisfy the transitivity property if and only if for all choices of j,k and ℓ (j,k, $\ell = 1, 2, \ldots, M$), the index satisfies

$$I_{jk} = I_{jl} \times I_{lk} \tag{A5.3}$$

Equation A5.3 requires that the application of a formula to make a direct comparison, I_{jk}, should result in the same numerical measure as an indirect comparison between j and k through a link country ℓ. Note that the transitivity property ensures internal consistency of index numbers in the matrix given in equation A5.2. It guarantees that the PPP for two currencies, say A and B, is the same whether it is derived through a direct comparison of A and B or through an indirect comparison that compares A with C and C with B, which are then combined to provide an indirect PPP for A and B. This requirement arises mainly from the spatial nature of the comparisons where no natural ordering of the countries involved could be imposed without a value judgment. Most of the commonly used index number procedures do not satisfy this requirement.

Base invariance. An index number formula is said to be base invariant if a comparison between a given pair of countries (j,k) is invariant to the order in which the countries are listed. This implies that multilateral comparisons should be invariant to all possible permutations of the data set. For example, consider a set of transitive comparisons derived using a particular country (say the United States) as a base country: under this program, price comparison between any pair of countries, say A and B, is effected through the United States which serves as a link country. Therefore,

$$\text{PPP}_{A,B} = \text{PPP}_{A,\text{USA}} \times \text{PPP}_{\text{USA},B} \tag{A5.4}$$

This program is inadmissible under the base invariance criterion since the choice of the base country clearly affects the PPP of currencies of countries A and B. Further, the United States is accorded a special status, in the form of a link country, in deriving transitive multilateral comparisons.

Characteristicity. This is a requirement outlined in Drechsler (1973). This property requires that any set of multilateral comparisons satisfying the transitivity property should retain the essential features of the binary comparisons constructed without the transitivity requirement. Since condition (A5.3) implies that a transitive comparison between a pair of countries j and k is necessarily influenced by the price and quantity data for all the other countries, the characteristicity property requires that distortions resulting from adherence to the transitivity property should be kept at a minimum. The Gini–Eltetö–Köves–Szulc (GEKS) method for multilateral comparisons, discussed in the following text, is specifically designed with the characheristicity in mind.

Additivity or matrix consistency. Another desirable property in spatial comparisons is *additivity* or *matrix consistency*. This property ensures that the additive nature of national accounts within a country, expressed in national currency units, is maintained within the international comparison framework. Basically, additivity means that for any country the real expenditures components should add up to the total real expenditures. Additivity would enable researchers to examine the structure of the real expenditures. However, additivity imposes certain theoretical restrictions and therefore is not always preferred as a property to be maintained in international comparisons. Indices such as the Geary–Khamis (GK) or Iklé–Dikhanov–Balk (IDB) maintain additivity. In intracountry comparisons, those indices seem less problematic as the price and expenditure structures vary much less within a country than between countries.

Index Number Methods for Spatial Comparisons

Spatial price comparisons, similar to temporal indices, use index number methods for aggregating price and quantity data at two different levels. The first is the basic heading level (the elementary aggregation). This is normally the lowest level of aggregation at which expenditure data and weights are available. The basic headings usually consist of a fairly homogeneous group of items that are priced in different outlets in the countries. The subsequent levels of aggregation lead to indices for higher expenditure categories, up to the level of total expenditures.

Aggregation at the Basic Heading Level (Elementary Index)

Two commonly used index number methods and their versions are described in the following text. These procedures explicitly allow for the possibility that price data may not be available for all items in the product list constructed for a given international comparison exercise. Such a situation occurs also in the case of temporal comparisons, though it is usually limited to either disappearing or new goods.

The Jevons–Gini–Eltetö–Köves–Szulc (Jevons–GEKS) Method. The original GEKS method proposed in Eltetö and Köves (1964) and Szulc (1964) is generally used in aggregating price data above the basic heading level. However, the GEKS procedure can be used as an elementary aggregator as well (that is, at the basic heading level). At this stage, binary comparisons have to be constructed using price relatives of those products for which prices are available in both countries, without applying expenditure weights. The Jevons–GEKS method uses the Jevons index as its basic element. The Jevons index can be described as follows. If *S(j)* and *S(k)* are the sets of products priced in countries *j* and *k*, respectively, and n_{jk} is the number of products that are priced in both countries, then the binary elementary index uses the following formula:

$$I_{jk} = \Pi_{i\in S(j)\cap S(k)} \left[\frac{p_i^{\,k}}{p_i^{\,j}}\right]^{1/n_{jk}} \qquad \text{(A5.5)}$$

Obviously, these binary indices are not transitive, since each index is based on prices of a different set of products. The GEKS procedure is then applied to derive a transitive set of indices. The resulting multilateral index is given by

$$I_{jk}^{\,\text{EKS}} = \Pi_{\ell=1}^{M}\left[I_{j\ell} I_{\ell k}\right]^{1/M} \qquad \text{(A5.6)}$$

The elementary index number formula in A5.5 is similar to the formula used in the construction of the CPI. The principal difference results from the fact there is a need for transitivity at all stages of aggregation. The properties of these indices are discussed in Chapter 7 of the publication *Consumer Price Index Theory*.

The Eurostat and the Organisation for Economic Co-operation and Development used a somewhat modified variant of the binary indices shown in equation A5.5, referred to as Jevons–GEKS*. Although this elementary index still does not use expenditure weights below the basic heading level, it incorporates information about importance of products in one or both of the countries. The procedure takes explicit account of those products which are "starred," indicating that the item is important or representative in a given country. The Jevons–GEKS* method uses the same formula (A5.6), but the binary elementary index (A5.5) is replaced by

$$I_{js} = \left\{ \prod_{i\in M(s)} \left[\frac{p_i^{\,s}}{p_i^{\,j}}\right]^{\frac{1}{n(s)}} \prod_{i\in M(j)} \left[\frac{p_i^{\,s}}{p_i^{\,j}}\right]^{\frac{1}{n(j)}} \right\}^{\frac{1}{2}} \qquad \text{(A5.7)}$$

where *n*(*s*) and *n*(*j*) are, respectively, the number of "starred" items in countries *s* and *j*; *M*(*s*) and *M*(*j*) are, respectively, the sets of products that are "starred" (considered representative) in countries *s* and *j*.

In theory, equation A5.7 can have an advantage over (A5.5) due to its considering "representativity" of the products priced in different countries. However, much will depend on how consistent the definition of representativity is across various countries and within basic headings (see more in a discussion on the country–product–representativity–dummy method in the following text).

Today the Eurostat–Organisation for Economic Co-operation and Development program uses a modification of the method, called Jevons–GEKS*(S), due to Sergeev (2003). The method uses an elementary binary index that has three components which are based on (1) items representative in country *s* and not in country *j*, (2) items representative in country *j* and not in country *s*, and (3) items representative in both countries. Then the binary elementary index is computed as a weighted geometric mean with the weights proportional to the number of items in different components, with double weight assigned for the third component based on items representative in both countries:

$$I_{js} = \prod_{i\in M(s^*)} \left[\frac{p_i^{\,s}}{p_i^{\,j}}\right]^{w_1} \prod_{i\in M(j^*)} \left[\frac{p_i^{\,s}}{p_i^{\,j}}\right]^{w_2} \prod_{i\in M(s,j)} \left[\frac{p_i^{\,s}}{p_i^{\,j}}\right]^{w_3} \qquad \text{(A5.7a)}$$

where *M*(*s**) and *M*(*j**) are the sets of priced products that are "starred" (considered representative) only in countries *s* and *j*, respectively, and not in other countries, and *M(s,j)* is the set of products that is representative in both countries s and j.

Finally, equation A5.6 is applied to achieve transitivity.

In both methods, the Jevons–GEKS* and Jevons–GEKS*(S), products that are unrepresentative in both countries do not influence the respective binary index. At the same time, both methods' binary indices may be distorted because they rely on products that are representative in one country but not in the other. The Eurostat-OECD addresses this issue by endeavoring to equalize the number of representative items in each country.

The Country–Product–Dummy (CPD) Method. The CPD method was originally proposed by Summers (1973) as a tool to deal with missing price observations. The method is a simple statistical device that can be used in deriving the PPPs for a particular basic heading by simply regressing the logarithm of observed prices against a set of dummy variables, defined with respect to products and countries.

The CPD procedure can be written as

$$lnp_{cp} = y_{cp} = x_{cp}\beta + \varepsilon_{cp} \quad \text{(A5.8)}$$

where P_{cp} is the price of product p in country c; Dc_j and Dp_i are country and product dummy variables; Np and Nc are the numbers of products and countries, respectively; and

$$x_{cp} = \left[Dc_2 \ldots Dc_{Nc} Dp_1 Dp_2 \ldots Dp_{Np}\right]$$
$$\beta = \left[\alpha_2 \ldots \alpha_{Nc} \gamma_1 \gamma_2 \ldots \gamma_{Np}\right]^T \quad \text{(A5.8a)}$$

In matrix notation, by stacking individual observations, this can be written as

$$\boldsymbol{y} = \boldsymbol{X\beta} + \varepsilon \quad \text{(A5.9)}$$

Note that the first country dummy is dropped from the system because matrix X is of rank ($Np + Nc - 1$). In fact, any variable can be dropped from the system; dropping the first country's dummy simply makes it the base country.

The solution is given (under the conditions of independently and identically distributed random disturbances) by

$$\hat{\beta} = \left(\boldsymbol{X}^T \boldsymbol{X}\right)^{-1} \boldsymbol{X}^T \boldsymbol{y} \quad \text{(A5.10)}$$

Once this regression equation is estimated, the PPP for the currency of country j with country 1 as base can be obtained by

$$\text{PPP}_j = \exp\left(\alpha_j\right) \quad \text{(A5.11)}$$

Then the desired index at the basic heading level is given by

$$I_{jk} = \frac{\text{PPP}_k}{\text{PPP}_j}. \quad \text{(A5.12)}$$

The Country–Product–Representativity–Dummy Method. The CPD model offers a number of generalizations that can explicitly account for a number of data-related problems. One of them was due to Cuthbert (1988), who suggested incorporating the representativity dummy variable into equation A5.8. The rationale was to introduce pseudoweights to account for higher sales of more typical items.

Matrix **X** becomes in this case:

$$x'_{cp} = \left[Dc_2 \ldots Dc_{Nc}\ Dp_1 \ldots Dp_{Np} R_{cp}\right]$$
$$\beta' = \left[\alpha'_2 \ldots \alpha'_{Nc}\ \gamma'_1 \ldots \gamma'_{Np}\ \rho\right]^T \quad \text{(A5.13a)}$$
$$\boldsymbol{y} = \boldsymbol{X}'\boldsymbol{\beta}' + \varepsilon \quad \text{(A5.13b)}$$

where R_{cp} stands for representativity dummy and ρ is its respective regression coefficient.

However, using actual ICP data, it was found that the efficiency of the index depended significantly on the consistency of representativity definitions across countries (just as in the case of Jevons–GEKS* and Jevons–GEKS*(S)). This led to the random nature of the representativity coefficients in many cases, instead of strongly negative coefficients. This does not mean that the index is less efficient than the regular CPD, just that the representativity data quality has to be increased in order to achieve higher efficiency.

The Country–Product–Dummy Weighted Method. Diewert (2004a) suggested using product weights in formula (A5.10). Essentially, this variant uses weights 3 for representative and 1 for nonrepresentative products. The weights were somewhat arbitrary, and, again the index efficiency in this case will depend on the quality of representativity/importance data. Other CPD versions are possible too, for example, the country–product–representativity–dummy with weights, CPD with data frequency adjustments, and so on

It is worth noting that in the case of a full price matrix, both the CPD and Jevons–GEKS indices degenerate into the simple geometric mean of price relatives. An important consideration is the efficiency of the elementary indices. Dikhanov (2005) considered multiple Jevons–GEKS and CPD variants and using Monte Carlo simulations had two findings. One is that Jevons–GEKS variants were less stable and had higher failure rate, especially, when used as defined previously, without any modifications—the modifications that were employed to decrease failure rate could introduce various biases. The other is that the CPD variants used with weights/representativity were the most efficient indices.

Aggregation above the Basic Heading Level

This section presents a small selection of the range of aggregation methods used in the context of spatial comparisons. For a more comprehensive overview see, for example, *Measuring the Real Size of the World Economy* (World Bank 2013).

This level of aggregation in ICP (above the basic heading level) is similar to the stage where elementary indices are aggregated to derive the all-items CPI (above CPI items). It is important to note that as the basic heading level is the lowest level with expenditure weights; it corresponds to the CPI item level, the lowest level with expenditure weights in CPI. In addition, the multilateral nature of spatial comparisons necessitates a different approach to index numbers than in temporal comparisons.

A number of index number methods for aggregation above the basic heading level have been developed but, in the interest of brevity, only the principal methods used in the context of international comparisons are discussed here. The Geary–Khamis (GK), Iklé–Dikhanov–Balk (IDB), and GEKS methods were all used in the ICP, at one time or another. In addition, the weighted CPD and Minimum Spanning Tree approach are discussed as well.

The GEKS Method. The GEKS system is a simple method of generating transitive multilateral index numbers from a system of binary index numbers, with the property that the resulting multilateral indices deviate the least (according to a specific criterion) from the binary indices. Since the seminal paper by Drechsler (1973), it has been well recognized that (transitive) multilateral systems necessarily deviate from their binary counterparts and therefore result in a loss of "characteristicity." The GEKS system is designed to minimize such loss of characteristicity. The original GEKS system uses the Fisher binary indices; however, any other binary index can be used in conjunction with the GEKS method of multilateralization. Thus, for any pair of countries j and k, if F_{jk} represents the Fisher binary index, then

$$\text{GEKS}_{jk} = \prod_{\ell=1}^{M} \left[F_{j\ell} \cdot F_{\ell k} \right]^{1/M} \qquad \text{(A5.14)}$$

provides the GEKS index.

There are several notable features of the GEKS technique. First, it is based on the premise that direct binary comparisons, derived using any chosen formula, provide the best comparison between pairs of countries. Second, even though the GEKS index in equation A5.11 is defined using the Fisher index, this approach can be applied in conjunction with any other index number formula. For example, the Fisher index in equation A5.11 may be replaced by another superlative index, such as the Törnqvist index (see Caves and others 1982b). Third, the GEKS index in equation A5.11 is the multilateral index that deviates the least from the matrix of nontransitive binary indices, when the deviations are measured using a logarithmic distance function. Finally, the GEKS index can be presented as a simple geometric mean of all (direct and indirect) comparisons between j and k through all possible link countries.

The simple unweighted nature of the GEKS index has attracted attention in recent years. Since different binary comparisons have different levels of reliability, measured using various criteria, it is necessary to reflect these differences in defining weighted GEKS index numbers. Rao and Timmer (2000), Rao and others (2000), and Rao (2001b) provide illustrations of how weighted GEKS indices can be generated in order to account for various data-related problems.

The Geary–Khamis (GK) Method. The GK method was originally proposed by Geary (1958) and subsequently developed by Khamis (1970, 1972, and 1984). The GK method has been the principal aggregation method in earlier ICP phases.

The GK method provides a way of calculating PPPs of currencies of different countries from the observed price and quantity data (applied at the basic heading level). The concept of PPP is applicable even when the currency unit is the same in several areas of a country. The GK method simultaneously determines the international average prices of different countries. Let P_i denote the international average price of ith product. The GK method is defined through the following system of interrelated equations, defined for each country j and each product i:

$$P_i = \frac{\sum_{j=1}^{M} p_i^j q_i^j / \text{PPP}_j}{\sum_{j=1}^{M} q_i^j} \quad \text{and } \text{PPP}_j = \frac{\sum_{i=1}^{N} p_i^j q_i^j}{\sum_{i=1}^{N} P_i q_i^j} \qquad \text{(A5.15)}$$

These simultaneous equations are then solved to yield numerical values of PPPs and Ps, after selecting one of the currencies as a numeraire. Once the PPPs are solved, the spatial price index numbers are simply defined as

$$I_{jk} = \frac{PPP_k}{PPP_j} \qquad \text{(A5.16)}$$

One of the main reasons for the continued use of the GK method is "additivity." Additivity requires that aggregates, such as real domestic product, derived by converting national aggregates using PPPs, should be equal to aggregates derived through valuation of quantities at international prices. Thus, additivity requires

$$\sum_{i=1}^{n} p_i^j q_i^j / PPP_j = \sum_{i=1}^{n} P_i q_i^j \qquad \text{(A5.17)}$$

This requirement is satisfied automatically by the PPPs and Ps derived from the GK system defined in equation A5.12. The GK system is also useful in analyzing the structure of real gross domestic product and shares of different components across different countries. This system provides a framework within which internationally comparable national accounts could be constructed. When country outputs are valued at the international reference prices, values are additive across both countries and products. However, additive multilateral methods are not consistent with economic comparisons of utility across countries if the number of countries in the comparison is greater than two (see Diewert in Chapter 5 of *Measuring the Size of the World Economy*, 2013). In addition, larger countries will have a larger effect on the international prices than the smaller ones which in practice leads to an overestimation of poorer countries' gross domestic product (the so-called Gerschenkron effect).

The Iklé–Dikhanov–Balk (IDB) Method. The IDB method was originally intimated by Iklé (1972) but in a very indirect way, so its properties remained unknown. It was subsequently further developed into its current form by Dikhanov (1994), and Balk (1996a) provided the first existence proof.

The IDB method is defined through the following system of interrelated equations, defined for each country j and each product i:

$$P_i = \left(\frac{\sum_{j=1}^{M} \text{PPP}_j / p_i^j \times s_i^j}{\sum_{j=1}^{M} s_i^j} \right)^{-1} \quad \text{and } \text{PPP}_j = \frac{\sum_{i=1}^{N} p_i^j q_i^j}{\sum_{i=1}^{N} P_i q_i^j} \qquad \text{(A5.18a)}$$

where $s_i^j = \dfrac{p_i^j q_i^j}{\sum_{i=1}^{N} p_i^j q_i^j}$.

These equations are similar to the GK equations but now the weights involve country expenditure shares, and countries have more equal influence on forming the international prices. In effect, the index becomes more "democratic" in nature, not unlike the GEKS. Deaton and Heston (2010) show that the IDB-generated PPPs are much closer to the GEKS than the GK PPPs. Dikhanov (1994) shows that the GK becomes the IDB when all the countries have identical volumes.

Weighted Country–Product–Dummy (CPD) Method. It is possible to generalize the CPD method discussed previously in the context of aggregation at the basic heading level. Rao (1995) has generalized the CPD method by incorporating quantity and value data directly into the CPD method described in equation A5.8. The method minimizes a weighted residual sum of squares, with each observation weighted according to the expenditure share of the product in each country. The resulting equation becomes

$$\sqrt{w_{ij}}\, lnp_{ij} = \pi_1\sqrt{w_{ij}}D_1 + \pi_2\sqrt{w_{ij}}D_2 + ... + \pi_M\sqrt{w_{ij}}D_M + \eta_1\sqrt{w_{ij}}D_1^* + ... + \eta_n\sqrt{w_{ij}}D_n^* + v_{ij} \quad \text{(A5.19)}$$

where $w_{ij} = \dfrac{p_{ij}q_{ij}}{\sum_{i=1}^{N} p_{ij}q_{ij}}$ is the value share of the *i*th basic heading in the *j*th country.

Rao (1995) has shown that the weighted CPD method may be considered as a bridge between the GK approach to international comparisons and the standard stochastic approach to index numbers.

Minimum Spanning Tree Method for Making Multilateral Comparisons

This approach advocates spatial chaining of binary comparisons where links are identified using a procedure based on some measure of distance of binary comparisons involved. Recall that the standard GEKS treats each country's associated set of Fisher indices as equally robust, and thus an averaging of the parities would be appropriate.

Using the graphical theoretical concept of minimum spanning trees, Hill (1999c, 1999d) proposed a method of deriving a system of transitive multilateral comparisons from a matrix of binary comparisons. The Hill approach is based on the fact that direct binary comparisons may not always be the best.

For any pair of countries *j* and *k*, Hill suggests a measure of distance (indicating the reliability of the binary comparison) using the Laspeyres–Paasche spread defined as

$$D(j,k) = \left| \ln\left(\frac{L(j,k}{P(j,k)} \right) \right| \quad \text{(A5.20)}$$

where $L(j,k)$ and $P(j,k)$ are, respectively, binary Laspeyres and Paasche price index numbers. Note that the same distance function emerges if price index numbers are replaced by quantity index numbers. $D(j,k)$ is equal to zero if the price structures or quantity structures are identical in countries, *j* and *k*. Thus, this distance function serves as an indicator of similarity of price and quantity structures in these countries.

Other distance (similarity) measures are possible. Diewert (2009), for example, suggests the weighted log quadratic measure, with weights being the country's expenditure shares. Using a matrix of distances calculated for all pairs of countries, Hill (1999c, 1999d) suggests that a minimum spanning tree (MST) be extracted and used in constructing chained links between all pairs of countries. The MST has the property that a chained comparison between any pair of countries has the least distance, and therefore can be considered as the most reliable. It also has the property that the sum of the distances between all the links, in the MST, is the least when compared to all possible tree configurations.

Once the MST is identified, a transitive comparison between a given pair of countries in a particular exercise is constructed using binary indices calculated using a chosen formula, such as the Fisher or Törnqvist index, and the links indicated in the MST. Since the MST provides a unique chain of links between any two countries, comparisons are uniquely defined. The spanning trees are, however, sensitive to the countries included, and the types of measures used in assessing the degree of reliability or comparability of any two countries. In addition, the path of bilateral links between countries generated by the method could be rather unstable and could change drastically from one comparison to next.

Fixity and Interregional Linking in International Comparisons

Any discussion on the methods presented previously, both at and above the basic heading level, would be incomplete, however, without addressing fixity and interregional linking. The need for fixity arises from the regional nature of actual ICP exercises, where individual ICP regions conduct their own comparisons which are later linked into the global comparison, as well as from the regions' desire to preserve intraregional volume relatives within the global comparison. Thus, fixity ensures that regional results get replicated exactly within the global comparison. The fixity principle also allows for a certain independence of the regional computations, in both timing and methods.

The fixity principle necessitates interregional linking to bind the regional results, both at and above the basic heading level. This issue is discussed here only briefly. A fuller treatment is given in Chapters 4 and 6 of *Measuring the Real Size of the World Economy* (2013).

Obviously, only the items common across regions can be used in linking. To this end, every region was required to collect a certain number of common "core" items.

Thus, as the first step, the regional basic heading PPPs are estimated independently for each region. The basic principle of linking the regions at the basic heading level is to convert countries' average item prices into regional currencies using the countries' respective regional basic heading PPPs; then use one of the standard CPD models described previously to estimate interregional linking factors, treating each country's average price as an observation in the CPD regression. Upon linking, the countries' regional PPPs were multiplied by the interregional linking factors to arrive at the global linked set of basic heading PPPs with fixity.

The linking above the basic heading level is carried out using the *country aggregation with redistribution* method. In simple terms, the linking procedure consists of four steps: (1) at every level above basic heading, regional country volumes are estimated independently for each region; thus volume for country j within region r is denoted V_r^j; (2) a full unrestricted GEKS is carried out with every country included in the global comparison, and country volumes within the global comparison are obtained; thus volume for country j in the global comparison is written as V^j; (3) each region's total is estimated by adding up that region's country volumes from the global comparison $V_r = \sum_{j \in C(r)} V^j$, where $C(r)$ is the set of countries in region r; (4) these regional totals are redistributed among individual countries within the regions using the regional country volumes from step (1), the resulting country volumes in the global comparison with fixity are written as: $V_{\text{world}}^j = V_r * V_r^j / \sum_{j \in C(r)} V_r^j$.

Integration of the Consumer Price Index and International Comparison Program

This section provides a brief overview of potential synergies and benefits that could result from the integration of CPI and ICP activities. In addition, it introduces the concept of subnational PPPs and their relation to CPI and ICP.

Benefits from Consumer Price Index and International Comparison Program Integration

PPPs and CPIs serve different analytical purposes and address different dimensions of prices: spatial and temporal. Because of these conceptual differences, PPPs and CPIs have generally been constructed under different production infrastructures.

Despite these differences, harmonization and integration of ICP and CPI activities may provide countries with some potential benefits. One of the most obvious commonalities between CPIs and PPPs is that both require basic price data for household goods and services. This common feature opens the door to potential cost savings by countries from having a joint CPI-ICP data collection process. Savings in data collection are only one of many positive prospects from greater CPI and ICP integration. For instance, cost savings may also result from using a shared data curation and validation process, to name a few possibilities.

A brief compilation of potential benefits from CPI and ICP integration is provided in the following text. These benefits are seen from the point of view of a national statistical office already carrying out CPI-related work. While going through them, note that potential benefits do not exist in isolation, but result from the interaction, dependencies, or relationships they form with other elements that influence the overall quality of a statistical system. This leads to cost savings, accompanied by improvements in efficiency, among other areas.

Cost savings. Shared CPI-ICP data collection and processing operations may result in cost savings in areas such as price collection, data curation, quality assurance procedures, information and technology, and staff training.

Procedural and methodological spillovers. Knowledge of ICP methods can stimulate countries into adopting ICP concepts and practices for national purposes. For example, if analyzing price level differences within a country is of interest, the ICP may provide useful insights into the dynamics of spatial price comparisons. Similarly, ICP concepts such as the structured product description, which add rigor to item definitions by listing price-determining characteristics, may provide a valuable basis for designing more efficient price collection forms.

Scaling opportunities. Increased synergies between ICP and CPI product and outlet frames may allow countries to more easily extend their CPI's geographical and outlet coverage. Since the ICP normally requires coverage which reflects the average level of prices in the entire country, ICP information on product availability and outlets may serve as building blocks for the design of a more extensive CPI. For instance, it may help expand the CPI to cover all urban areas in cases where the CPI only covers the capital city.

It is important to note that the extent to which countries will benefit from CPI and ICP integration will vary depending on national circumstances. It will also depend on the depth of the level of the integration process, with increased harmonization being a common precursor to integration. Nonetheless, the breadth and depth of the potential benefits of bringing CPI and ICP further together are even greater in the current context of a permanent and more frequent ICP.

Subnational PPPs

Subnational PPPs are PPPs compiled within a country. They are similar to ICP PPPs in that they both compare price levels between geographical areas. In the case of subnational PPPs, comparability over time is an occasional feature. The link between CPI and ICP is perhaps most prominent and well established within the framework of subnational PPPs.

The general approach to constructing subnational PPPs can be summarized in three steps:

(1) Organizing the required price and expenditure data
(2) Determining overlapping items across geographical regions
(3) Estimating subnational PPPs through interregional aggregation

Because steps (1) and (2) generally present the biggest challenges, they will be the focus of interest. Step (3) on estimation involves extending the aggregation procedures for international spatial comparisons (presented earlier) to a subnational setting, so it presents no additional difficulties. The aggregation problem becomes more intractable when there is a need to account for the temporal dimension. This occurs when a set of subnational PPPs compares not only price differences across geographical regions of the same country, but also over time. This space–time analysis requires a temporally consistent spatial index for aggregation, which can be achieved, for example, by treating each region in each time period under consideration as a separate entity in standard multilateral aggregation (Dikhanov and others 2011). Thus estimated indices would provide regional

PPPs already linked over time and space. Other approaches are possible, for example, by aggregating regions in each time period independently, and then linking each time period's total using national price measures such as CPI. This two-stage approach to producing time and space consistent estimates would be equivalent to applying fixity not unlike the approach in the current ICP where different regions are linked without changes to their respective regional results.

Constructing subnational PPPs requires price and expenditure data. Prices are required for a set of goods and services that are comparable across the geographical areas of the country being studied. Expenditures are needed at the product group level and disaggregated by geographic location.

Expenditure values can be sourced from representative national household budget surveys, or from the country's regional economic accounts. Since regional accounts are uncommon, expenditure values are generally sourced from the most recent nationally representative household budget survey. Price data, in turn, may be sourced from the CPI collected prices, ICP collected prices, or from specially designed intracountry regional price surveys. The most attractive would be to utilize CPI price information, since this option typically requires no additional price data collection.

The challenge of compiling subnational PPPs is in obtaining price data at the level of disaggregation and detail required. Price data for subnational PPPs require obtaining price observations for *identical* item specifications (varieties) across geographical regions. The idea is to follow the ICP principle of comparing like with like. It is where ICP concepts come into play as a means to add rigor and facilitate the subnational PPP approach. Concepts such as structured product descriptions, for defining item characteristics, or the "core items" approach, for ensuring the pricing of common items across regions, help ensure that the required item variety overlap exists across geographical regions. In this sense, ICP concepts help improve the consistency of the subnational PPP procedure.

Because subnational PPPs have multiple uses at the country level, many countries, especially large ones, have expressed interest in them. Indeed, subnational PPPs can serve as inputs for welfare studies that compare well-being across geographical regions within a country, or in fiscal studies of public transfers between a country's geographical regions. Subnational PPPs may also be used for regional cost of living adjustments when determining wages of public officials working in different locations across a given country.

To meet the growing demand for information on this topic, research on subnational PPPs will also be carried out under the umbrella of the ICP Research Agenda. The task force working on CPI-ICP integration will be studying subnational PPPs in detail and will formulate guidelines on the use of CPI or ICP products list and prices to compute subnational PPPs.

Appendix 6

Some Basic Index Number Formulas and Terminology

1. Throughout this appendix, the sums are understood to be running over all varieties n.

A *basket* price index is an index of the form

$$\frac{\sum p_n^t q_n}{\sum p_n^0 q_n} \quad \text{(A6.1)}$$

which compares the prices of period t with those of (an earlier) price reference period 0, using a certain specified quantity basket. The basket does not have to consist of the actual quantities in any particular period. This general type of index is called a Lowe price index after the index number pioneer who first proposed this general type of index. The family of Lowe indices includes some well-known indices as special cases:

- When $q_n = q_n^0$, one gets the Laspeyres index.
- When $q_n = q_n^t$, one gets the Paasche index.
- When $q_n = \left(q_n^0 + q_n^1\right)/2$, one gets the Marshall–Edgeworth index.
- When $q_n = \left(q_n^0 q_n^t\right)^{1/2}$, one gets the Walsh index. In practice, national statistical offices frequently work with a Lowe index in which $q_n = q_n^b$, where b denotes some weight reference period that is typically prior to 0.

2. A useful feature of a Lowe index for period t relative to period 0 is that it can be decomposed, or factored, into the product of two or more indices of the same type: for instance, as the product of an index for period $t-1$ relative to period 0 and an index for period t relative to period $t-1$. Formally,

$$\frac{\sum p_n^t q_n}{\sum p_n^0 q_n} = \frac{\sum p_n^{t-1} q_n}{\sum p_n^0 q_n} \frac{\sum p_n^t q_n}{\sum p_n^{t-1} q_n} \quad \text{(A6.2)}$$

In particular, when $q_n = q_n^0$, expression (2) turns into

$$\frac{\sum p_n^t q_n^0}{\sum p_n^0 q_n^0} = \frac{\sum p_n^{t-1} q_n^0}{\sum p_n^0 q_n^0} \frac{\sum p_n^t q_n^0}{\sum p_n^{t-1} q_n^0} \quad \text{(A6.3)}$$

The left-hand side of expression (3) is a direct Laspeyres index. Note that only the first of the indices that make up the right-hand side is itself a Laspeyres index, the second being a Lowe index for period t relative to period $t-1$ that uses the quantity basket of period 0 (not $t-1$). Some national statistical offices describe the index on the right-hand side of expression (3) as a modified Laspeyres index.

3. In a time-series context, say when t runs from 1 to T, the series

$$\frac{\sum p_n^1 q_n}{\sum p_n^0 q_n}, \frac{\sum p_n^2 q_n}{\sum p_n^0 q_n}, \ldots, \frac{\sum p_n^T q_n}{\sum p_n^0 q_n} \quad \text{(A6.4)}$$

is termed a series of *fixed-basket* price indices. In particular, when $q_n = q_n^0$, a series of Laspeyres indices are found.

4. At period T, one could change to a new quantity basket q' and calculate from this period onward:

$$\frac{\sum p_n^{T+1} q_n'}{\sum p_n^T q_n'}, \frac{\sum p_n^{T+2} q_n'}{\sum p_n^T q_n'}, \frac{\sum p_n^{T+3} q_n'}{\sum p_n^T q_n'} \quad \text{(A6.5)}$$

To relate the prices of periods $T+1$, $T+2$, $T+3$, ... to those of period 0, chain linking can be used to transform the series (5) into a series of the form:

$$\frac{\sum p_n^T q_n}{\sum p_n^0 q_n} \frac{\sum p_n^{T+1} q_n'}{\sum p_n^T q_n'}, \frac{\sum p_n^T q_n}{\sum p_n^0 q_n} \frac{\sum p_n^{T+2} q_n'}{\sum p_n^T q_n'}, \frac{\sum p_n^T q_n}{\sum p_n^0 q_n} \frac{\sum p_n^{T+3} q_n'}{\sum p_n^T q_n'}, \ldots \quad \text{(A6.6)}$$

This could be termed a series of *chain-linked fixed-basket* price indices. In particular, when $q_n = q_n^0$ and $q_n' = q_n^T$, a series of chain-linked Laspeyres indices are found. Since the basket is changed at period T, the adjective fixed applies literally only over a certain number of time intervals. The basket is fixed from period 1 to period T and is again fixed from period $T+1$ onward. When the time intervals during which the basket is kept fixed are of the same length, such as one, two, or five years, this feature can be made explicit by describing the index as an annual, biannual, or five-yearly chain-linked fixed-basket price index.

5. A *weighted arithmetic-average* price index (so-called to distinguish it from a geometric or other kind of average) is an index of the form:

$$\sum w_n \left(p_n^t / p_n^0\right) \quad \text{(A6.7)}$$

which compares the prices of period t with those of period 0, using a certain set of expenditure weights adding up to 1. In particular, when the weights are the period b value shares

$$w_n = s_n^b \equiv p_n^b q_n^b / \sum p_n^b q_n^b \quad \text{(A6.8)}$$

the Young index is obtained.

Note that any basket price index (1) can be expressed in the form (7), since

$$\frac{\sum p_n^t q_n}{\sum p_n^0 q_n} = \sum \frac{p_n^0 q_n}{\sum p_n^0 q_n} \frac{p_n^t}{p_n^0} \quad \text{(A6.9)}$$

When the weights are the period 0 value shares,

$$w_n = s_n^0 \equiv p_n^0 q_n^0 / \sum p_n^0 q_n^0 \quad \text{(A6.10)}$$

expression (7) turns into the Laspeyres index. When

$$w_n = p_n^0 q_n^t / \sum p_n^0 q_n^t \quad \text{(A6.11)}$$

that is, hybrid period (*0, t*) value shares, one can get the Paasche index.

One could also think of setting

$$w_n = s_n^b \left(p_n^0 / p_n^b\right) / \sum s_n^b \left(p_n^0 / p_n^b\right) = p_n^0 q_n^b / \sum p_n^0 q_n^b \quad \text{(A6.12)}$$

that is, price-updated period b value shares.

Note that hybrid value shares, such as given by expressions (11) or (12), are not observable but must be constructed.

6. In a time-series context, when t runs from 1 to T, the series

$$\sum w_n\left(p_n^1 / p_n^0\right), \sum w_n\left(p_n^2 / p_n^0\right), \ldots, \sum w_n\left(p_n^T / p_n^0\right) \quad \text{(A6.13)}$$

is termed a series of *fixed-weighted arithmetic-average price* indices. In particular, when the weights are equal to the period 0 expenditure shares, a series of Laspeyres indices are found, and when the weights are equal to the price-updated period b expenditure shares, a series of Lowe indices are found in which the quantities in the basket are those of period b.

7. In period T, one could change to a new set of weights w', and calculate from this period onward

$$\sum w_n'\left(p_n^{T+1} / p_n^T\right), \sum w_n'\left(p_n^{T+2} / p_n^T\right), \sum w_n'\left(p_n^{T+3} / p_n^T\right), \ldots \quad \text{(A6.14)}$$

or, using chain linking to relate the prices of periods $T+1, T+2, T+3, \ldots$ to those of period 0,

$$\sum w_n\left(p_n^T / p_n^0\right) \sum w_n'\left(p_n^{T+1} / p_n^T\right), \sum w_n\left(p_n^T / p_n^0\right) \sum w_n'\left(p_n^{T+2} / p_n^T\right) \quad \text{(A6.15)}$$

This could be termed a series of *chain-linked fixed-weighted arithmetic-average* price indices. In particular, when $w_n = s_n^0$ and $w_n' = s_n^T$, a series of chain-linked Laspeyres indices are found. When $w_n = s_n^b\left(p_n^0 / p_n^b\right) / \sum s_n^b\left(p_n^0 / p_n^b\right)$ and $w_n' = s_n^{b'}\left(p_n^T / p_n^{b'}\right) / \sum s_n^{b'}\left(p_n^T / p_n^{b'}\right)$ for some later period b', a series of chain-linked Lowe indices are found.

8. Again, since the weights are changed at period T, the adjective fixed applies literally only over a certain number of time intervals. The weights are fixed from period 1 to period T and are again fixed from period $T + 1$ onward. When the time intervals during which the weights are kept fixed are of the same length, this feature can be made explicit by adding a temporal adjective, such as annual, biannual, or five-yearly.

Appendix 7
Consumer Price Index Research Agenda

The consumer price index (CPI) research agenda lists topics where more work and research are needed to develop guidance and good practices for CPI compilation and meeting existing and emerging user needs.

The research agenda includes conceptual and methodological issues as well as practical measurement and implementation challenges. Different concepts and methods may be applied when developing the CPI, including decisions on index coverage, incorporating different goods and services, and measuring their price development over time. There is a significant need for analytical work and sharing of practical experiences to define and develop best practices for those compilation areas where there is no consensus on which method should be recommended. For example, there is a need to develop clear guidance on the methods used to make quality adjustments and how to use scanner data to compile the CPI.

Countries face ongoing measurement and implementation challenges. These are associated with practical problems implementing best practices due to a lack of data sources, inappropriate methods, or resource constraints. The emerging and rapidly evolving technology and the availability of new electronic data sources such as scanner data and web data also pose particular challenges to countries.

The CPI research topics are listed in the following section grouped under data sources, expenditure weights, index compilation methods, services, and synergies between CPIs, purchasing power parities (PPPs), and the national accounts. The organization of the topics does not reflect their importance. Many of the CPI research topics are linked to the three priority areas of work of the research agenda of the *System of National Accounts* (SNA): digitalization, economic well-being and sustainability, and globalization. These provide major challenges to official statistics, including the CPI, and are therefore listed at the end of the CPI research agenda, highlighting possible challenges involved for the CPI.

Countries, organizations, and researchers are encouraged to contribute to developing further guidance by undertaking work on the research topics and sharing experiences and good practices in these areas. The research topics also aim to guide future work of the Expert Group on Consumer Price Indices, jointly organized by the United Nations Economic Commission for Europe and the International Labour Organization and the Ottawa Group on Price Indices. The Intersecretariat Working Group on Price Statistics[1] has agreed to take the lead to ensure these issues are addressed.

[1]The Intersecretariat Working Group on Price Statistics works to develop international standards and recommendations in price statistics, document best practice guidelines, and support their implementation. The member organizations of the Intersecretariat Working Group on Price Statistics are the Statistical Office of the European Union (Eurostat), the International Labour Organization, the International Monetary Fund, the Organisation for Economic Co-operation and Development, the United Nations Economic Commission for Europe, and the World Bank.

Consumer Price Index Research Topics

Data Sources

Scanner Data

Scanner data may lead to more and better official price statistics, efficiency gains, and reduced response burden. Scanner data can complement and, in some instances, replace traditional approaches to collecting data for compiling the CPI. The use of scanner data challenges traditional interpretations and applications of concepts and raises both methodological and practical issues related to CPI production. Areas where more work is needed include: improving calculation methods for price indices based on scanner data; combining scanner data and data obtained from traditional methods; aggregating scanner data into higher-level indices; using scanner data for sampling purposes and estimating weights; classifying scanner data; dealing with quality changes (for example, implicit versus explicit quality adjustments); clarifying the treatment of seasonal products; and comparing price indices based on scanner data with price indices based on traditional sources. A growing number of national statistical offices (NSOs) have implemented scanner data in the routine production of the CPI, and the practical experience gained can be used to assist those NSOs who want to begin using scanner data. Practical experience can be shared on assessing the quality of scanner data, information technology and software issues, costs and benefits of using scanner data, and organizational and legal issues (such as access to data, or cooperation with scanner data providers). Research and testing are required on expanding the use of scanner data to include other goods, such as electronics and other items with high model turnover, and services. The development of methodologies and frameworks around scanner data is needed, for instance, to ensure consistency in coverage or in the treatment of replacements. There is also no generally agreed quality assurance framework developed, particularly for scanner data. Scanner data offer opportunities to both countries with developed statistical systems and countries with less developed statistical systems.

Web Prices

Internet purchases continue to grow in importance. Traditional outlets have established an online presence, and there are a growing number of internet-based outlets. There is a need to expand price collection and the outlet sample to include these new types of outlets in the CPI. First, for those outlets that have both an online and physical presence, there is a need to determine whether the prices charged and the price changes are the same or different. Second, there is a need to identify and sample the web-based outlets and the goods and services available. Weights consistent with the scope of the CPI need to be estimated for the web-based outlets. A particular important issue emerges when products from physical outlets are replaced by products purchased on the internet. In such cases, there is a need to decide if price differences should be treated as genuine price changes, and included in the CPI, or as a change in quality, and hence not included as price changes in the CPI. Experiences with the collection of data from internet-based outlets should be shared to help develop guidance.

Issues to be addressed when collecting prices on the web include calculation formulas for the CPI; analysis of the performance over time of price indices using prices from the internet and comparing with indices based on traditional sources; maintenance of the sample; treatment of replacements and quality changes; classification of the data; and combination with other data sources used in the CPI. There have been discussions around using and weighting various data sources. Obtaining expenditure weights for web-based prices continues to be a challenge, and there is no obvious way of obtaining this information. More research and practical experience in this area would be useful.

Web Scraping

Web scraping has huge potential for CPI compilation with regard to real-time access to a large amount of information, but also raises technical and potential legal issues and challenges. The drivers for the change toward web scraping include competition from other providers of alternative measures of price changes, the possibility of producing timelier and more frequent CPIs, more efficient production, and reduction of costs. There is a need for exchanging software experiences associated with web scraping and other methods for collecting or harvesting data. While there are advantages to web scraping, it also poses a number of issues that NSOs should be aware of, including the practical and legal issues concerning access to internet price data; how to ensure good cooperation with the owners of these data; and vulnerability, including becoming too dependent on one or a few owners of data and ways to deal with this and reduce possible risks. Countries may develop in-house software or buy this from a provider of software for web scraping. Both ways have their advantages and disadvantages that countries must consider.

Administrative Data

In addition to scanner data and web prices, future work on data sources should also address the use of administrative data sources. Depending on national circumstances, data on different goods and services may be available from administrative sources, for example in the areas of transport, housing, social protection, health, and education. Sharing of experiences and good practices will be helpful to further investigate the potentials of administrative data for compilation of the CPI.

Credit Card and Bank Data

As economies move away from cash transactions, it may be possible in the future to access household transaction records from banks, credit card companies, or providers of payment apps for mobile telephones (often referred to as mobile money). For this information to be useful for statistical purposes, each transaction would need to have an identifying product code associated with it. At present, only rough descriptions of the purchases are available, but this more limited information would still be useful to construct household expenditure data by major category of expenditure. While the use of credit card and other payment information involves issues concerning access to the data and confidentiality, this is a promising future source for household data on purchases.

Expenditure Weights

Plutocratic versus Democratic Weighting

Some NSOs have initiated projects to produce democratic indices. Other NSOs have attempted to compare the evolution of prices as they affect the average household and the average consumption. More clarity regarding the conceptual basis of such an index and calculation methods, but also interpretation and use of democratic indices, is needed.

Price Updating of Expenditure Weights

It is left to the NSO to decide whether to price update the expenditure weights. Since price updating may have a significant influence on the overall CPI this may negatively affect the international comparability of CPIs. It would be useful to discuss empirical studies that assess the magnitude of the effect of price updating and to identify whether clearer guidance could be developed.

Index Compilation

Calculating Elementary Price Indices

The expenditure weights of the elementary aggregate and the elementary price indices are the building blocks of the CPI. In the absence of weighting information, most countries compile the elementary price indices as unweighted averages of the individual prices (or price ratios) that belong to the elementary aggregate. However, with the growing availability of data sources, it may be possible to obtain information that can be used when aggregating individual price observations into elementary price indices. Weighting information may be derived from a variety of sources and may be used for groups of observations. For example, weights may be available for particular product groups within an elementary index, for certain outlets or outlet chains, or for individual observations. Applying such detailed weights has the potential to improve the statistical quality of the elementary price indices. It would be useful to share practical experiences on applying weights for the calculation of elementary indices, including on data sources and index calculation formulas.

Quality Adjustment

Quality adjustment is a cross-cutting issue that continues to pose challenges. Quality-adjustment issues have been noted previously, but there is a general need to provide better guidance on the treatment of quality changes. In particular, NSOs continue to struggle with measuring quality changes for clothing, cars, telecommunication equipment, multipurpose information technology devices, computers, and, in general, products with high churn. Sharing of practical experiences implementing methods and best practices is needed.

Seasonal Products

The treatment of seasonal products continues to confound compilers. There is a need for research and discussion to improve how seasonal items are treated in the CPI. It may also be useful to further discuss and compare different versions of fixed weights and variable weights approaches with the objective to develop clearer guidelines on the treatment of seasonal products.

The Use of Target Price Indices for the Consumer Price Index

It is useful to have a measurable target index for the CPI. The target index can be used as guidance for deciding calculation methods and practices for the regular CPI and for measuring potential bias. Empirical research can address issues including identifying potential target indices (for example, Walsh, Fisher, Törnqvist, or Constant Elasticity of Substitution [CES]) and how to apply these formulas in practice.

Formula for Calculating Higher-Level Price Indices

Arithmetic aggregation is used by almost all countries for calculation of higher-level price indices. Is this the best solution? What are the alternatives, with regard to geometric aggregation or aggregation by other types of averages or by use of indices that apply explicit estimates of substitution elasticities, such as the CES/Lloyd–Moulton price index?

The Use of Long-Term and Short-Term Links

The long-term/short-term link approach has been used in Sweden for many years and has now also been adopted by the United States. This method facilitates calculating the long-term links of the CPI by the use of superlative index number formulas. The use of long-term and short-term links was mentioned in the paper *Estimating the Benefits and Costs of New and Disappearing Products* (Diewert and Feenstra 2017)[2] as the best way to get around the problem of dated weighting information. A growing number of countries will begin to explore this approach. Research, discussion, and practical experiences can be shared to identify the advantages and disadvantages of this method.

Retrospective Calculations of Superlative Price Indices

Retrospective calculations of superlative price indices are very useful for analytical purposes and to serve as a benchmark to assess the quality of the CPI and quantify potential bias. A limited number of NSOs have begun to compile superlative price indices. A sharing of experience can be used to develop best practices.

Consumer Price Indices for Different Groups and Geographic Areas

CPIs for different population groups or geographic areas may be required to meet specific user needs, for instance, indices used for compensation purposes for specific population groups (for example, wage earners in urban areas, receivers of retirement benefits, and so on) or for other political or analytical purposes. Since such indices may be produced as part of the regular CPI, this would increase the efficiency of the resources used to produce CPIs. Issues in the compilation of CPIs for specific income and population groups and geographic areas include sources and methods for developing weights, sample of outlets and items/varieties collecting prices, or defining the scope of the index. Discussions should also address communication and dissemination issues and user relations: How to identify and meet user needs, and how to deal with reactions from users?

Classification of Individual Consumption According to Purpose (COICOP) 2018

The update of COICOP has significant implications for compilers. Guidance on how to proceed with implementing the COICOP 2018 while preserving a historic time series of data would be helpful.

Uncertainty Measures

It is important to inform users about the accuracy and the reliability of a CPI and to guide CPI compilers in allocating resources for CPI compilation in the most efficient way. Often complex and nonprobability sampling programs are used to obtain prices from multiple data sources. In such a context, there is no generally agreed approach for estimating sampling errors. Further studies and practical approaches to measure uncertainty and to assess errors in a CPI are therefore needed.

Services

Measuring Services in the Consumer Price Index

Defining and pricing services continue to create challenges for CPI compilers. Additional research and sharing of practical experiences on how to define and price various services are needed to better identify best practices and develop guidance. Key issues include how to identify suitable units of services that can be priced over time, use of input or output measures (for example, using the hourly salary of the service provider or following the prices of a basket of representative services provided), and how to adjust for changes in the quality of services. Digital platform services also have grown significantly and raise questions on how these should be incorporated into the CPI. Timeliness is also an issue. Digital platform services have emerged quickly and often NSOs incorporate these services into the CPI with a considerable delay. The treatment of telecommunication services in the CPI continues to create issues for compilers. All these issues raise user concerns that the CPI becomes less representative and reliable. Where relevant, work on services should be coordinated with the Voorburg Group on Service Statistics.

Insurance and Financial Services

Insurance and financial services continue to pose measurement issues for the CPI. With the update of the Classification of Individual Consumption According to Purpose (COICOP) to the 2018 version (COICOP 2018), a separate division (Division 12) was created for insurance and financial services. The net versus gross approaches have not been fully reconciled. There are also problems of choosing appropriate deflators for the payment of premiums. More discussion and research are needed to guide compilers on the appropriate measurement of these services.

Owner-Occupied Housing (OOH)

The measurement of OOH and its inclusion in the CPI continues to present a major challenge that requires discussion to formulate clearer guidance. The inclusion of OOH, representing a large share of household consumption, also

[2] https://www.unece.org/fileadmin/DAM/stats/documents/ece/ces/ge.22/2018/University_of_British_Columbia.pdf.

involves conceptual and measurement issues. Country-specific circumstances can create problems with different approaches for the measurement of OOH (for example, small and concentrated rental markets). Informal housing is another issue. Further empirical work representing a wide range of countries with different housing market types and access to different data sources would be very beneficial.

Synergies Between Consumer Price Indices, Purchasing Power Parities (PPPs), and National Accounts

CPIs and PPPs serve different purposes. CPIs measure price changes over time, generally month to month, primarily at a national level. PPPs, on the other hand, measure price differences across space, generally countries, at a given point in time. The temporal and spatial focus of CPIs and PPPs has resulted in different production infrastructures for the two indices. However, there are important synergies to be captured through the integration of data collection and other processing activities, especially given the implementation of the rolling survey approach in the International Comparison Programme. Both CPIs and PPPs require basic price data for final consumption goods and services, so economies of scale may be realized through a joint data collection process, as well as common data processing and quality assurance procedures. Examples of relevant topics include but are not limited to: country experiences with establishing synergies between PPP and CPI data collection activities; harmonization of classification programs for PPPs and CPIs; establishing overlap in PPP and CPI product lists; establishing common data processing and quality assurance processes; and applications in subnational price comparisons.

Moreover, CPI compilers, PPP compilers, and national accountants often face similar challenges when it comes to distinguishing pure price differences from differences in quantity and quality. These problems have been exacerbated by recent developments related to the digitalization of our economies, such as the rapid evolution in the design of new products, the combination of goods and services, new business models, and changes from high street shopping to online purchases. It is important for CPI compilers, PPP compilers, and national accountants to join forces and develop consistent methodologies on all these aspects.

Links to the SNA Research Agenda

On a broader level, the CPI research topics are linked to the SNA research agenda, which includes three priority areas of work: digitalization, well-being and sustainability, and globalization. These are briefly described in the following text, and possible challenges involved for the CPI are mentioned.

Digitalization

Digitalization influences the way households can acquire and consume goods and services. Digital goods or services may replace existing ones or constitute new goods and services that were not available earlier. Digitalization, therefore, raises challenges on how to identify and incorporate digital goods or services in the CPI and how to price such goods or services over time. The Organisation for Economic Co-operation and Development Statistics Working Paper, "Measuring Consumer Inflation in a Digital Economy" (Reinsdorf and Schreyer 2019),[3] discusses in detail the problems in measuring the welfare effects of the digital economy, including the effects of services provided for free (or at least without any direct payment) on the internet. According to this working paper, there is a significant need to identify how CPIs can better reflect and incorporate digital goods and services, and work is needed to clarify the conceptual issues and develop methods that better measure the digital economy in the CPI. These issues include, but are not limited to, defining and identifying the goods and services, including different types of internet purchases, services for free, and shared economy services.

Well-Being and Sustainability

Measures of well-being attract much interest from policymakers, media, and the public. Ongoing research has focused on how time allocation information is needed to better measure household welfare change (Stiglitz and others, *Report on the Measurement of Economic Performance and Social Progress*, 2009).[4] As described previously, the Reinsdorf and Schreyer working paper not only focuses on the welfare effects of the digital economy but also outlines key problems in using the CPI in measuring economic well-being in general. The paper identifies three reasons why the CPI will overestimate the cost of living and hence underestimate progress in real welfare: (1) insufficient adjustment for quality changes; (2) delayed inclusion of truly new products; and (3) disregarding the appearance and use of free products. Solving these issues involves addressing both conceptual and practical measurement issues. In a cost of living index context, the theoretically correct way of including truly new products and products offered for free would be the use of estimated "reservation" or "shadow" prices. This can be done in theory and in research studies. However, for the regular production of the monthly CPI, this is usually not feasible and other approaches must be implemented. According to Reinsdorf and Schreyer, the welfare effects would be difficult to measure, and established measures of gross domestic product and CPI should not be extended to include estimates of welfare effects. The authors conclude that if the aim is to measure welfare, it would be better to develop special measures for this purpose. The issue of a CPI for measuring economic well-being is not restricted to the effects of digitalization, but also includes further discussion on the coverage of the CPI and the treatment of different types of goods and services provided for free, potentially including public goods and services such as education, health, safety, or parks. The issue relates to the discussion of cost of goods indices versus cost of living indices, and conditional versus unconditional cost of living indices, where additional experiences and guidance would be useful. It may be useful to invite experts from other areas of official statistics to discuss measuring welfare and economic well-being.

[3] https://www.oecd-ilibrary.org/docserver/1d002364-en.pdf.

[4] https://ec.europa.eu/eurostat/documents/118025/118123/Fitoussi+Commission+report.

Globalization

In the discussions about the problems in measuring globalization, the issue of having suitable price indices (producer price indices, export and import price indices, or CPIs) for the deflation of international flows of goods and services is often mentioned as a major challenge. Work could include conceptual clarifications as well as practical studies and development of guidelines on measurement. There will be a need to coordinate and align with the SNA and the Balance of Payments standards, for instance on how to classify different types of internet purchases as goods or services.

BIBLIOGRAPHY

Abe, N., and K. Shinozaki. 2018. "Compilation of Experimental Price Indexes Using Big Data and Machine Learning: A Comparative Analysis and Validity Verification." Paper presented at the UNECE/ILO Meeting of the Group of Experts on Consumer Price Indices, Geneva, May 7–9. https://www.unece.org.

Abraham, K. G., J. S. Greenlees, and B. R. Moulton. 1998. "Working to Improve the Consumer Price Index." *Journal of Economic Perspectives* 12 (1): 27–36.

Aczél, J. 1987. *A Short Course on Functional Equations*. Dordrecht: Reidel Publishing Co.

Advisory Commission to Study the Consumer Price Index. 1995. *Toward a More Accurate Measure of the Cost of Living*. Interim Report to the Senate Finance Committee, September 15. Washington, DC.

Aizcorbe, A. M., and P. C. Jackman. 1993. "The Commodity Substitution Effect in CPI Data, 1982–91." *Monthly Labor Review* 116 (12): 25–33.

Aizcorbe, A., C. Corrado, and M. Doms. 2001. *Constructing Price and Quantity Indexes for High Technology Goods*. Industrial Output Section, Division of Research and Statistics. Washington, DC: Board of Governors of the Federal Reserve System.

Aizcorbe, A., C. Corrado, and M. Doms. 2003. "When Do Matched-Model and Hedonic Techniques Yield Similar Price Measures?" Working Paper 2003–14, Federal Reserve Bank of San Francisco, San Francisco, CA.

Alterman, W. F., W. E. Diewert, and R. C. Feenstra. 1999. *International Trade Price Indexes and Seasonal Commodities*. Washington, DC: Bureau of Labor Statistics.

Anderson, R. G., B. E. Jones, and T. Nesmith. 1997. "Building New Monetary Services Indexes: Concepts, Data and Methods." *Federal Reserve Bank of St. Louis Review* 79 (1): 53–83.

Arguea, N. M., C. Haseo, and G. A. Taylor. 1994. "Estimating Consumer Preferences Using Market Data: An Application to U.S. Automobile Demand." *Journal of Applied Econometrics* 9: 1–18.

Armknecht, P. A. 1996. "Improving the Efficiency of the U.S. CPI." Working Paper No. 96/103, International Monetary Fund, Washington, DC.

Armknecht, P. A. 2016. "Fixed Basket Methods for Compiling Consumer Price Indexes." Meeting of the Group of Experts on Consumer Price Indices, Geneva, Switzerland, May 2–4, 2016. http://www.unece.org/index.php.

Armknecht, P. A., and D. Weyback. 1989. "Adjustments for Quality Change in the U.S. Consumer Price Index." *Journal of Official Statistics* 5 (2): 107–23.

Armknecht, P. A., and F. Maitland-Smith. 1999. "Price Imputation and Other Techniques for Dealing with Missing Observations, Seasonality and Quality Change in Price Indices." Working Paper No. 99/78, International Monetary Fund, Washington, DC. http://www.imf.org/external/pubs/ft/wp/1999/wp9978.pdf

Armknecht, P. A., and M. Silver. 2014. "Post-Laspeyres: The Case for a New Formula for Compiling Consumer Price Indexes." *The Review of Income and Wealth* 60 (2): 225–44.

Armknecht, P. A., W. F. Lane, and K. J. Stewart. (1997) 2003. "New Products and the U.S. Consumer Price Index." In *Scanner Data and Price Indexes, NBER Studies in Income and Wealth*, edited by R. C. Feenstra and M. D. Shapiro. Chicago, IL: University of Chicago Press, pp. 375–91.

Arrow, K. J., H. B. Chenery, B. S. Minhas, and R. M. Solow. 1961. "Capital–Labor Substitution and Economic Efficiency." *Review of Economics and Statistics* 63: 225–50.

Astin, J. 1999. "The European Union Harmonized Indices of Consumer Prices (HICP)." In *Proceedings of the Ottawa Group Fifth Meeting*, Reykjavik, Iceland, August 25–27, edited by R. Gudnason and T. Gylfadottir. Reykjavík: Statistics Iceland; also published in *Statistical Journal of the United Nations ECE* 16: 123–35. http://www.statcan.ca/secure/english/ottawagroup/.

Astin, J. 2001. "New Uses of PPPs within the European Union." Paper presented at the Joint World Bank–OECD Seminar on Purchasing Power Parities: Recent Advances in Methods and Applications, Washington, DC, January 30–February 2.

Aten, B., R. Summers, and A. Heston. 2001. "An Explanation of Stability in Country Price Structures: Implications for Spatial–Temporal Comparisons." Paper presented at the Joint World Bank–OECD Seminar on Purchasing Power Parities: Recent Advances in Methods and Applications, Washington, DC, January 30–February 2.

Australian Bureau of Statistics. 1997. "An Analytical Framework for Price Indexes in Australia." Information Paper, Catalogue No. 6421.0. http://www.abs.gov.au.

Australian Bureau of Statistics. 2003. "Australian Consumer Price Index: Concepts, Sources and Methods." Catalogue No. 6461.0. http://www.abs.gov.au/.

Australian Bureau of Statistics. 2009. "Consumer Price Index: Concepts, Sources and Methods." Catalogue No. 6461.0, ABS, Canberra. http://www.abs.gov.au/ausstats/abs@.nsf/mf/6461.0.

Australian Bureau of Statistics. 2013. "Feature Article: The Use of Transactions Data to Compile the Australian Consumer Price Index." Catalogue No. 6401.0, ABS, Canberra. http://www.abs.gov.au/.

Australian Bureau of Statistics. 2015. "Enhancing the Australian CPI: A Roadmap." Catalogue No. 6401.0.60.001, ABS, Canberra. http://www.abs.gov.au/.

Australian Bureau of Statistics. 2016a. "Making Greater Use of Transactions Data to Compile the Consumer Price Index." Information Paper 6401.0.60.003, ABS, Canberra. http://www.abs.gov.au/.

Australian Bureau of Statistics. 2016b. "Measuring Price Change of Attached Dwellings in the CPI." Feature Article, ABS, Canberra. http://www.abs.gov.au.

Australian Bureau of Statistics. 2017a. "An Implementation Plan to Maximise the Use of Transactions Data in the CPI." Information Paper 6401.0.60.004, ABS, Canberra. http://www.abs.gov.au/.

Australian Bureau of Statistics. 2017b. "Introduction of the 17th Series Australian Consumer Price Index." Information Paper 6470.0.55.001, ABS, Canberra. http://www.abs.gov.au/AUSSTATS/abs@.nsf/DetailsPage/6470.0.55.0012017.

Bäckström, Peter, and Muhanad Sammar. 2012. "The Use of Superlative Index Links in the Swedish CPI." Paper presented at the meeting of the Group of Experts on CPI, Geneva. https://www.unece.org/index.php.

Bailey, M. J., R. F. Muth, and H. O. Nourse. 1963. "A Regression Method for Real Estate Price Construction." *Journal of the American Statistical Association* 58: 933–42.

Baker, D. 1998. "Does the CPI Overstate Inflation? An Analysis of the Boskin Commission Report." In *Getting Prices Right*, edited by D. Baker. Washington, DC: Economic Policy Institute, pp. 79–155.

Baldwin, A. 1990. "Seasonal Baskets in Consumer Price Indexes." *Journal of Official Statistics* 6 (3): 251–73.

Baldwin, A., A. Nakamura, and M. Prudhomme. 2010. "An Empirical Analysis of the Different Concepts for Owned Accommodation in the Canadian CPI: The Case of Ottawa, 1996–2005." Paper presented at the UNECE/ILO Meeting of the Group of Experts on Consumer Price Indices, Geneva, May 10–12. https://www.unece.org.

Balk, B. M. 1980a. "Seasonal Products in Agriculture and Horticulture and Methods for Computing Price Indices." *Statistical Studies No. 24*. The Hague: Netherlands Central Bureau of Statistics.

Balk, B. M. 1980b. "Seasonal Commodities and the Construction of Annual and Monthly Price Indexes." *Statistische Hefte* 21: 110–6.

Balk, B. M. 1980c. "A Method for Constructing Price Indices for Seasonal Commodities." *The Journal of the Royal Statistical Society Series A* 143: 68–75.

Balk, B. M. 1981. "A Simple Method for Constructing Price Indices for Seasonal Commodities." *Statistische Hefte* 22: 72–8.

Balk, B. M. 1983. "Does There Exist a Relation between Inflation and Relative Price Change Variability? The Effect of the Aggregation Level." *Economic Letters* 13: 173–180.

Balk, B. M. 1985. "A Simple Characterization of Fisher's Price Index." *Statistische Hefte* 26: 59–63.

Balk, B. M. 1989a. "Changing Consumer Preferences and the Cost of Living Index: Theory and Nonparametric Expressions." *Zeitschrift für Nationalökonomie* 50 (2): 157–69.

Balk, B. M. 1989b. "On Calculating the Precision of Consumer Price Indices." *Contributed Papers 47th Session of the ISI*. Paris: International Statistical Institute.

Balk, B. M. 1990. "On Calculating Cost-of-Living Index Numbers for Arbitrary Income Levels." *Econometrica* 58 (1): 75–92.

Balk, B. M. 1994. "On the First Step in the Calculation of a Consumer Price Index." Paper presented at First Meeting of the International Working Group on Price Indices, Ottawa, October 31–November 4. http://www.ottawagroup.org.

Balk, B. M. 1995. "Axiomatic Price Index Theory: A Survey." *International Statistical Review* 63: 69–93.

Balk, B. M. 1996a. "A Comparison of Ten Methods for Multilateral International Price and Volume Comparisons." *Journal of Official Statistics* 12: 199–222.

Balk, B. M. 1996b. "Consistency in Aggregation and Stuvel Indices." *The Review of Income and Wealth* 42: 353–63.

Balk, B. M. 1998a. *Industrial Price, Quantity and Productivity Indices*. Boston, MA: Kluwer Academic Publishers.

Balk, B. M. 1998b. "On the Use of Unit Value Indices as Consumer Price Subindices." Paper presented at the Fourth Meeting of the International Working Group on Price Indices, Washington, DC, April 22–24. http://www.ottawagroup.org.

Balk, B. M. 2000a. "Divisia Price and Quantity Indexes 75 Years After." Draft Paper, Department of Statistical Methods, Statistics Netherlands, Voorburg.

Balk, B. M. 2000b. "On Curing the CPI's Substitution and New Goods Bias." Research Paper 0005, Department of Statistical Methods, Statistics Netherlands, Voorburg.

Balk, B. M. 2001. *Aggregation Methods in International Comparisons: What Have We Learned?* Report Series Research in Management ERS-2001-41-MKT, Erasmus Research Institute of Management. Rotterdam: Erasmus University.

Balk, B. M. 2005. "Price Indexes for Elementary Aggregates: The Sampling Approach." *Journal of Official Statistics* 21: 675–99.

Balk, B. M. 2008. *Price and Quantity Index Numbers*. Cambridge: University Press.

Balk, B. M. 2008. *Price and Quantity Index Numbers: Models for Measuring Aggregate Change and Difference*. New York: Cambridge University Press.

Balk, B. M. 2010. "Lowe and Cobb-Douglas Consumer Price Indexes and Their Substitution Bias." *Jahrbücher für Nationalökonomie und Statistik* (*The Journal of Economics and Statistics*) 230 (6): 726–40.

Balk, B. M., and H. M. P. Kersten. 1986. "On the Precision of Consumer Price Indices Caused by the Sampling Variability of Budget Surveys." *Journal of Economic and Social Measurement* 14: 19–35.

Balk, B. M., and W. E. Diewert. 2001. "A Characterization of the Törnqvist Price Index." *Economics Letters* 73: 279–81.

Ball, A., and D. Fenwick. 2004. "Costing Mobile Telephone Calls: The Use of Constrained User Profiles." Paper presented at the Eighth Meeting of the International Working Group on Price Indices, Helsinki, August 23–25. http://www.ottawagroup.org.

Bartik, T. J. 1988. "Measuring the Benefits of Land Improvements in Hedonic Models." *Land Economics* 64 (2): 172–83.

Bas, C. 2018. "Different Approaches and Methods for Strong Seasonal Items in the CPI." Paper presented at the UNECE/ILO Meeting of the Group of Experts on Consumer Price Indices, Geneva, May 7–9. https://www.unece.org.

Bascher, J., and T. Lacroix. 1999. "Dishwashers and PCs in the French CPI: Hedonic Modeling, from Design to Practice." Paper presented at the Fifth Meeting of the International Working Group on Price Indices, Reykjavik, August 25–27. http://www.ottawagroup.org.

Baxter, M. (ed.). 1998. *The Retail Prices Index. Technical Manual*. London: Office for National Statistics, UK.

Bean, L. H., and O. C. Stine. 1924. "Four Types of Index Numbers of Farm Prices." *Journal of the American Statistical Association* 19: 30–5.

Becker, G. S. 1965. "A Theory of the Allocation of Time." *Economic Journal* 75: 493–517.

Beck-MacNeil, R. 2018. "Pricing the Internet—The Internet Access Services Component of the Canadian CPI." Statistics Canada. Paper presented at the UNECE/ILO Meeting of the Group of Experts on Consumer Price Indices, Geneva, May 7–9. https://www.unece.org.

Beidelman, C. 1973. *Valuation of Used Capital Assets*. Sarasota, FL: American Accounting Association.

Beidelman, C. 1976. "Economic Depreciation in a Capital Goods Industry." *National Tax Journal* 29: 379–90.

Beisteiner, A. 2008. "Optimal Allocation of Prices in Practice—Using the Neumann Formula as Tool." Paper presented at the UNECE/ILO Meeting of the Group of Experts on Consumer Price Indices, Geneva, May 8–9. https://www.unece.org.

Bentley, A., and F. Krsinich. 2017. "Towards a Big Data CPI for New Zealand." Paper presented at the Fifteen Meeting of the International Working Group on Price Indices, Eltville am Rhein, May 10–12. http://www.ottawagroup.org.

Bernardini, A., C. De Vitiis, A. Guandalini, F. Inglese, and M. D. Terribili. 2016. "Measuring Inflation Through Different Sampling Designs Implemented on Scanner Data." Paper presented at Meeting of the Group of Experts on Consumer Price Indices, Geneva, Switzerland, May 2–4.

Berndt, E. R. 1991. *The Practice of Econometrics: Classic and Contemporary*. Reading, MA: Addison-Wesley.

Berndt, E. R., D. Ling, and M. K. Kyle. 2003. "The Long Shadow of Patent Expiration: Generic Entry and Rx to OTC Switches." In *Scanner Data and Price Indexes, NBER Studies in Income and Wealth*, edited by M. Shapiro and R. C. Feenstra. Chicago, IL: University of Chicago Press, pp. 229–73.

Berndt, E. R., L. T. Bui, D. H. Lucking-Reiley, and G. L. Urban. 1997. "The Roles of Marketing, Product Quality and Price Competition in the Growth and Composition of the U.S. Anti-Ulcer Drug Industry." In *The Economics of New Goods, NBER Studies in Income and Wealth*, edited by T. Bresnahan and R. J. Gordon. Chicago and London: University of Chicago Press, pp. 232–77.

Berndt, E. R., Z. Griliches, and N. J. Rappaport. 1995. "Econometric Estimates of Price Indexes for Personal Computers in the 1990s." *Journal of Econometrics* 68: 243–68.

Berry, S., J. Levinsohn, and A. Pakes. 1995. "Automobile Prices in Market Equilibrium." *Econometrica* 63 (4): 841–90; also published as NBER Working Paper No. W4264, July 1996. http://www.nber.org.

Beuerlein, I. 2001. "The German Consumer Price Index for Telecommunication Services: A User Profile Approach for Mobile Technology and Internet Access." Paper presented at the Sixth Meeting of the International Working Group on Price Indices, Canberra, April 2–6. http://www.ottawagroup.org/.

Bhardwaj, H., T. Flower, P. Lee, and M. Mayhew. 2017. *Research Indices Using Web Scraped Price Data*. August 2017 Update, UK Office for National Statistics, London.

Bird, D., R. Breton, C. Payne, and A. Restieaux. 2014. *Initial Report on Experiences with Scanner Data in ONS*. Report, Office for National Statistics, Newport, UK.

Bode, B., and van J. Dalén. 2001. "Quality-Corrected Price Indexes of New Passenger Cars in the Netherlands, 1990–1999." Paper presented at the Sixth Meeting of the International Working Group on Price Indices, Canberra, April 2–6. http://www.ottawagroup.org.

Boettcher, I. 2015. "Automatic Data Collection on the Internet (Web Scraping)." Statistic Austria. Paper presented at the Fourteen Meeting of the International Working Group on Price Indices, Tokyo, May 20–22. http://www.ottawagroup.org.

Böhm-Bawerk, E. V. 1891. *The Positive Theory of Capital*. Translated from the original German edition of 1888 by W. Smart. New York: G. E. Stechert.

Bortkiewicz, L. V. 1923. "Zweck und Struktur einer Preisindexzahl." *Nordisk Statistisk Tidsskrift* 2: 369–408.

Boskin, M. J. (Chair), E. R. Dullberger, R. J. Gordon, Z. Griliches, and D. W. Jorgenson. 1996. *Final Report of the Commission to Study the Consumer Price Index, U.S. Senate, Committee on Finance*. Washington, DC: U.S. Government Printing Office.

Boskin, M. J. (Chair), E. R. Dullberger, R. J. Gordon, Z. Griliches, and D. W. Jorgenson. 1998. "Consumer Prices in the Consumer Price Index and the Cost of Living." *Journal of Economic Perspectives* 12 (1): 3–26.

Böttcher, I., and S. Sergeev. 2014. "Austrian Scanner Data Project—Report Multipurpose Consumer Price Statistics: The Use of Scanner Data." Paper presented at the UNECE/ILO Meeting of the Group of Experts on Consumer Price Indices, Geneva, May 26–8. https://www.unece.org.

Bowley, A. L. 1899. "Wages, Nominal and Real." In *Dictionary of Political Economy*, Volume 3, edited by R. H. I. Palgrave. London: Macmillan, pp. 640–51.

Bowley, A. L. 1901. *Elements of Statistics*. Westminster: Orchard House.

Bowley, A. L. 1919. "The Measurement of Changes in the Cost of Living." *Journal of the Royal Statistical Society* 82: 343–61.

Bradley, R. 1995. "The Use of Scanner Data as a Means to Reduce the Mean Squared Error in the CPI." Working paper, U.S. Department of Labor, Bureau of Labor Statistics, Washington, DC.

Bradley, R. 2007. "Analytical Bias Reduction for Small Samples in the U.S. Consumer Price Index." *Journal of Business & Economic Statistics* 25: 337–46.

Bradley, R., B. Cook, S. E. Leaver, and B. R. Moulton. 1997. "An Overview of Research on Potential Uses of Scanner Data in the U.S. CPI." Paper presented at the Third Meeting of the International Working Group on Price Indices, Voorburg, April 16–18. http://www.ottawagroup.org.

Braithwait, S. D. 1980. "The Substitution Bias of the Laspeyres Price Index: An Analysis Using Estimated Cost-of-Living Indexes." *American Economic Review* 70 (1): 64–77.

Brand, M., C. Vermeulen, D. Fischbach, and Y. Carpy. 2017. "Swiss Residential Property Price Index: The Use of Geolocalised Information for Quality Adjustment in Location." Paper presented at the Fifteenth Meeting of the International Working Group on Price Indices, Eltville, May 10–12. http://www.ottawagroup.org.

Bresnahan, T. F. 1997. "Comment." In *The Economics of New Goods, NBER Studies in Income and Wealth*, edited by T. F. Bresnahan and R. J. Gordon. Chicago, IL: University of Chicago Press, pp. 237–47.

Breton, R., G. Clews, L. Metcalfe, N. Milliken, C. Payne, J. Winton, and A. Woods. 2016. "Research Indices Using Web Scraped Data." Paper presented at the UNECE/ILO Meeting of the Group of Experts on Consumer Price Indices, Geneva, May 2–4. https://www.unece.org.

Brown, C., and A. Stockburger. 2006. "Item Replacement and Quality Change in Apparel Price Indexes." *Monthly Labor Review* (December): 35–45. https://www.bls.gov/opub/mlr/2006/12/art3full.pdf.

Burnett-Isaacs, K. 2015. "Using Hedonics to Create Land and Structure Indexes for the Ottawa Condominium Market." Paper presented at the Fourteen Meeting of the International Working Group on Price Indices, Tokyo, May 20–22. http://www.ottawagroup.org.

Cage, R., J. S. Greenlees, and P. Jackman. 2003. "Introducing the Chained Consumer Price Index." In *International Working Group on Price Indices (Ottawa Group): Proceedings of the Seventh Meeting*, edited by Thierry Lacroix. Paris: INSEE, pp. 213–46.

Canning, J. B. 1929. *The Economics of Accountancy*. New York: The Ronald Press Co.

Carli, G.-R. 1804. "Del valore e della proporzione dei metallic monetati." In *Scrittori classici italiani di economia politica*, Vol. 13. Milano: G. G. Destefanis, pp. 297–366; originally published in 1764.

Carruthers, A. G., D. J. Sellwood, and P. W. Ward. 1980. "Recent Developments in the Retail Prices Index." *The Statistician* 29: 1–32.

Cassel, E., and R. Mendelsohn. 1985. "On the Choice of Functional Forms for Hedonic Price Equations: Comment." *Journal of Urban Economics* 18 (September): 135–42.

Castles, I. 1997. *The OECD–EUROSTAT PPP Program: Review of Practice and Procedures*. Paris: OECD.

Cavallo, A. 2016. "Are Online and Offline Prices Similar? Evidence from Large Multi-Channel Retailers." Massachusetts Institute of Technology. Paper presented at the UNECE/ILO Meeting of the Group of Experts on Consumer Price Indices, Geneva, May 2–4. https://www.unece.org.

Cavallo, A., and R. Rigobon. 2016. "The Billion Dollar Project. Using Online Data for Measurement and Research." MIT & NBER. Paper presented at the UNECE/ILO Meeting of the Group of Experts on Consumer Price Indices, Geneva, May 2–4. https://www.unece.org.

Cavallo, A., and R. Rigobon. 2016. "The Billion Prices Project: Using Online Prices for Measurement and Research." *Journal of Economic Perspectives* 30 (2): 151–78.

Caves, D. W., L. R. Christensen, and W. E. Diewert. 1982a. "The Economic Theory of Index Numbers and the Measurement of Input, Output and Productivity." *Econometrica* 50: 1393–414.

Caves, D. W., L. R. Christensen, and W. E. Diewert. 1982b. "Multilateral Comparisons of Output, Input and Productivity Using Superlative Index Numbers." *Economic Journal* 92: 73–86.

Cecchetti, S. G. 1997. "Measuring Inflation for Central Bankers." *Federal Reserve Bank of St. Louis Review* 79: 143–55.

Chessa, A. G. 2017. "Comparisons of QU-GK Indices for Different Lengths of the Time Window and Updating Methods." Paper prepared for the Second Meeting on Multilateral Methods Organised by Eurostat, Luxembourg, March 14–15, Statistics Netherlands.

Chessa, A. G. 2020. "A Comparison of Multilateral Index Extension Methods on Transaction Data of Seasonal Items." Paper presented at the meeting of the Ottawa Group, Rio de Janeiro, May 8–10, 2019.

Chessa, A. G., and R. Griffioen. 2016. "A New Methodology for Processing Scanner Data in the Dutch CPI." *Eurona* 1: 49–69.

Chessa, A. G., J. Verburg, and L. Willenborg. 2017. "A Comparison of Price Index Methods for Scanner Data." Paper presented at the Fifteen Meeting of the International Working Group on Price Indices, Eltville am Rhein, May 10–12. http://www.ottawagroup.org.

Christensen, L. R., and D. W. Jorgenson. 1969. "The Measurement of U.S. Real Capital Input, 1929–1967." *Review of Income and Wealth* 15 (4): 293–320.

Christensen, L. R., D. W. Jorgenson, and L. J. Lau. 1971. "Conjugate Duality and the Transcendental Logarithmic Production Function." *Econometrica* 39: 255–56.

Church, A. H. 1901. "The Proper Distribution of Establishment Charges, Part III." *The Engineering Magazine* 21: 904–12.

Clements, K. W., and H. Y. Izan. 1981. "A Note on Estimating Divisia Index Numbers." *International Economic Review* 22: 745–47.

Clements, K. W., and H. Y. Izan. 1987. "The Measurement of Inflation: A Stochastic Approach." *Journal of Business and Economic Statistics* 5: 339–50.

Cobb, C., and P. H. Douglas. 1928. "A Theory of Production." *American Economic Review* 18: 39–165.

Cochran, W. G. 1977. *Sampling Techniques*, 3rd edition. New York: Wiley.

Cockburn, I. M., and A. H. Anis. 1998. "Hedonic Analysis and Arthritic Drugs." Working Paper 6574, National Bureau of Economic Research, Cambridge, MA.

Coggeshall, F. 1887. "The Arithmetic, Geometric and Harmonic Means." *Quarterly Journal of Economics* 1: 83–6.

Combris, P., S. Lecocqs, and M. Visser. 1997. "Estimation of a Hedonic Price Equation for Bordeaux Wine: Does Quality Matter?" *Economic Journal* 107 (441): 390–402.

Commission of the European Communities (Eurostat), International Monetary Fund, Organisation for Economic Co-operation and Development, United Nations, and World Bank. 1993. *System of National Accounts 1993*. Brussels/Luxembourg, New York, Paris, Washington, DC: United Nations.

Congressional Budget Office (CBO). 1994. "Is the Growth of the CPI a Biased Measure of Changes in the Cost of Living?" CBO Paper, October, Washington, DC.

Crawford, A. 1998. "Measurement Biases in the Canadian CPI: An Update." *Bank of Canada Review* (Spring): 39–56.

Cropper, M. L., L. L. Deck, and K. E. McConnell. 1988. "On the Choice of Functional Form for Hedonic Price Functions." *Review of Economics and Statistics* 70 (4): 668–75.

Crump, N. 1924. "The Interrelation and Distribution of Prices and Their Incidence upon Price Stabilization." *Journal of the Royal Statistical Society* 87: 167–206.

Cunningham, A. W. F. 1996. "Measurement Bias in Price Indices: An Application to the UK's RPI, Bank of England." Working Paper 47, Bank of England, London.

Curry, B., P. Morgan, and M. Silver. 2001. "Hedonic Regressions: Misspecification and Neural Networks." *Applied Economics* 33: 659–71.

Czinkota, M. R., and I. Ronkainen. 1997. "International Business and Trade in the Next Decade: Report from a Delphi Study." *Journal of International Business Studies* 28 (4): 827–44.

Dalén, J. 1992. "Computing Elementary Aggregates in the Swedish Consumer Price Index." *Journal of Official Statistics* 8: 129–47.

Dalén, J. 1994. "Sensitivity Analyses for Harmonizing European Consumer Price Indices." Paper presented at the First Meeting of the International Working Group on Price Indices, Ottawa, October 31–November 4. http://www.ottawagroup.org.

Dalén, J. 1995. "Quantifying Errors in the Swedish Consumer Price Index." *Journal of Official Statistics* 13 (3): 347–56.

Dalén, J. 1997. "Experiments with Swedish Scanner Data." Paper presented at the Third Meeting of the International Working Group on Price Indices, Voorburg, April 16–18. http://www.ottawagroup.org.

Dalén, J. 1998a. "On the Statistical Objective of a Laspeyres Price Index." Paper presented at the Fourth Meeting of the International Working Group on Price Indices, Washington, DC, April 22–24. http://www.ottawagroup.org.

Dalén, J. 1998b. "Studies on the Comparability of Consumer Price Indices." *International Statistical Review* 66 (1): 83–113.

Dalén, J. 1999a. "On Reliability, Uncertainty and Bias in Consumer Price Indexes." In *Proceedings of the Measurement of Inflation Conference*, edited by M. Silver and D. Fenwick. Cardiff: Cardiff University, pp. 184–90.

Dalén, J. 2017. "Unit Values and Aggregation in Scanner Data—Towards a Best Practice." Paper presented at the Fifteen Meeting of the International Working Group on Price Indices, Eltville am Rhein, May 10–12. http://www.ottawagroup.org.

Dalén, J., and E. Ohlsson. 1995. "Variance Estimation in the Swedish Consumer Price Index." *Journal of Business and Economic Statistics* 13 (3): 347–56.

Dalton, K. V., J. S. Greenlees, and K. J. Stewart. 1998. "Incorporating a Geometric Mean Formula into the CPI." *Monthly Labor Review* 121 (10): 3–7.

Davies, G. R. 1924. "The Problem of a Standard Index Number Formula." *Journal of the American Statistical Association* 19: 180–88.

Davies, G.R. 1932. "Index Numbers in Mathematical Economics." *Journal of the American Statistical Association* 27: 58–64.

De Gregorio, C. 2012. "Sample Size for the Estimate of Consumer Price Subindices with Alternative Statistical Designs." Rivista di statistica ufficiale N° 1/2012.

De Haan, J. 2001. "Generalised Fisher Price Indexes and the Use of Scanner Data in the CPI." Unpublished paper, Statistics Netherlands, Voorburg.

De Haan, J. 2003. "Time Dummy Approaches to Hedonic Price Measurement." Paper presented at the Seventh Meeting of the International Working Group on Price Indices, Paris, May 27–29. http://www.insee.fr/.

De Haan, J. 2004. "Estimating Quality-Adjusted Unit Value Indexes: Evidence from Scanner Data." Paper presented at the SSHRC International Conference on Index Number Theory and the Measurement of Prices and Productivity, June 30–July 3, Vancouver, Canada.

De Haan, J. 2015. "A Framework for Large Scale Use of Scanner Data in the Dutch CPI." Paper presented at the Fourteen Meeting of the International Working Group on Price Indices, Tokyo, May 20–22. http://www.ottawagroup.org.

De Haan, J. 2018. "Scanner Data in the CPI: The Imputation CCDI Index Revisited." Paper presented at the 18th EMG Workshop, November 29–30, UNSW, Sydney, Australia.

De Haan, J., and F. Krsinich. 2014. "Scanner Data and the Treatment of Quality Change in Nonrevisable Price Indexes." *Journal of Business & Economic Statistics* 32: 341–58.

De Haan, J., and F. Krsinich. 2018. "Time Dummy Hedonic and Quality-Adjusted Unit Value Indexes: Do They Really Differ?" *Review of Income and Wealth* 64: 757–76.

De Haan, J., and H. A. van der Grient. 2011. "Eliminating Chain Drift in Price Indexes Based on Scanner Data." *Journal of Econometrics* 161: 36–46.

De Haan, J., and H. van der Grient. 2009. "Eliminating Chain Drift in Price Indexes Based on Scanner Data." Statistics Netherlands. https://www.unece.org/fileadmin/DAM/stats/documents/ece/ces/ge.22/2010/zip.8.e.pdf.

De Haan, J., E. Opperdoes, and C. Schut. 1999. "Item Selection in the Consumer Price Index: Cut-Off versus Probability Sampling." *Survey Methodology* 25 (1): 31–41.

De Haan, J., R. Hendriks, and M. Scholz. 2016. "A Comparison of Weighted Time-Product Dummy and Time Dummy Hedonic Indexes." Graz Economics Papers 2016-13, Department of Economics, University of Graz, Austria.

De Waal, T., J. Pannekoek, and S. Scholtus. 2011. *Handbook of Statistical Data Editing and Imputation*. Hoboken, NJ: John Wiley & Sons. https://leseprobe.buch.de/images-adb/5c/b5/5cb50a55-cc80-4e75-821b-591e49dc38bb.pdf.

Deaton, A. 1998. "Getting Prices Right: What Should Be Done?" *Journal of Economic Perspectives* 12 (1): 37–46.

Denny, M. 1974. "The Relationship between Functional Forms for the Production System." *Canadian Journal of Economics* 7: 21–31.

Diewert, W. E. (1983a) 1990. "The Theory of the Cost of Living Index and the Measurement of Welfare Change." In *Price Level Measurement*, edited by W. E. Diewert and C. Montmarquette. Ottawa: Statistics Canada, pp. 163–233; reprinted in *Price Level Measurement*, edited by W. E. Diewert. Amsterdam: North-Holland, pp. 79–147.

Diewert, W. E. 1974a. "Applications of Duality Theory." In *Frontiers of Quantitative Economics*, Vol. II, edited by M. D. Intriligator and D. A. Kendrick. Amsterdam: North-Holland, pp. 106–71.

Diewert, W. E. 1974b. "Intertemporal Consumer Theory and the Demand for Durables." *Econometrica* 42: 497–516.

Diewert, W. E. 1976. "Exact and Superlative Index Numbers." *Journal of Econometrics* 4: 114–45.

Diewert, W. E. 1978. "Superlative Index Numbers and Consistency in Aggregation." *Econometrica* 46: 883–900.

Diewert, W. E. 1980. "Aggregation Problems in the Measurement of Capital." In *The Measurement of Capital, NBER Studies in Income and Wealth*, edited by D. Usher. Chicago, IL: University of Chicago Press, pp. 433–528.

Diewert, W. E. 1983a. "The Theory of the Output Price Index and the Measurement of Real Output Change." In *Price Level Measurement*, edited by W. E. Diewert and C. Montmarquette. Ottawa: Statistics Canada, pp. 1049–113.

Diewert, W. E. 1983b. "The Treatment of Seasonality in a Cost of Living Index." In *Price Level Measurement*, edited by W. E. Diewert and C. Montmarquette. Ottawa: Statistics Canada, pp. 1019–45.

Diewert, W. E. 1986. "Microeconomic Approaches to the Theory of International Comparisons, Technical." Working Paper No. 53. National Bureau of Economic Research, Cambridge, MA.

Diewert, W. E. 1992a. "Fisher Ideal Output, Input and Productivity Indexes Revisited." *Journal of Productivity Analysis* 3: 211–48.

Diewert, W. E. 1992b. "Exact and Superlative Welfare Change Indicators." *Economic Inquiry* 30: 565–82.

Diewert, W. E. 1993a. "The Early History of Price Index Research." In *Essays in Index Number Theory*, Vol. 1, Contributions to Economic Analysis 217, edited by W. E. Diewert and A. O. Nakamura. Amsterdam: North-Holland, pp. 33–65.

Diewert, W. E. 1993b. "Duality Approaches to Microeconomic Theory." In *Essays in Index Number Theory*, Vol. 1, Contributions to Economic Analysis 217, edited by W. E. Diewert and A. O. Nakamura. Amsterdam: North-Holland, pp. 105–75.

Diewert, W. E. 1993c. "Symmetric Means and Choice under Uncertainty." In *Essays in Index Number Theory*, Vol. 1, Contributions to Economic Analysis 217, edited by W. E. Diewert and A. O. Nakamura. Amsterdam: North-Holland, pp. 355–433.

Diewert, W. E. 1993d. "Overview of Volume 1." In *Essays in Index Number Theory*, Vol. 1, Contributions to Economic Analysis 217, edited by W. E. Diewert and A. O. Nakamura. Amsterdam: North-Holland, pp. 1–31.

Diewert, W. E. 1995a. "Axiomatic and Economic Approaches to Elementary Price Indexes." Discussion Paper No. 95–01, Department of Economics, University of British Columbia, Vancouver. http://www.econ.ubc.ca.

Diewert, W. E. 1995b. "On the Stochastic Approach to Index Numbers." Discussion Paper No. 95–31, Department of Economics, University of British Columbia, Vancouver. http://www.econ.ubc.ca.

Diewert, W. E. 1996a. "Price and Volume Measures in the National Accounts." In *The New System of National Economic Accounts*, edited by J. Kendrick. Norwell, MA: Kluwer Academic Publishers, pp. 237–85.

Diewert, W. E. 1996b. "Seasonal Commodities, High Inflation and Index Number Theory." Discussion Paper 96–06, Department of Economics, University of British Columbia, Vancouver.

Diewert, W. E. 1996c. "Sources of Bias in Consumer Price Indexes." Discussion Paper No. 96/4, School of Economics, University of New South Wales, Sydney.

Diewert, W. E. 1997. "Commentary on Mathew D. Shapiro and David W. Wilcox: Alternative Strategies for Aggregating Price in the CPI." *The Federal Reserve Bank of St. Louis Review* 79 (3): 127–37.

Diewert, W. E. 1998a. "Index Number Issues in the Consumer Price Index." *The Journal of Economic Perspectives* 12 (1): 47–58.

Diewert, W. E. 1998b. "High Inflation, Seasonal Commodities and Annual Index Numbers." *Macroeconomic Dynamics* 2: 456–71.

Diewert, W. E. 1999a. "Index Number Approaches to Seasonal Adjustment." *Macroeconomic Dynamics* 3: 48–68.

Diewert, W. E. 1999b. "Axiomatic and Economic Approaches to Multilateral Comparisons." In *International and Interarea Comparisons of Income, Output and Prices*, edited by A. Heston and R. E. Lipsey. Chicago, IL: University of Chicago Press, pp. 13–87.

Diewert, W. E. 2000. "Notes on Producing an Annual Superlative Index Using Monthly Price Data." Discussion Paper No. 00-08, Department of Economics, University of British Columbia, Vancouver. http://www.econ.ubc.ca.

Diewert, W. E. 2001. "The Consumer Price Index and Index Number Purpose." *Journal of Economic and Social Measurement* 27: 167–248.

Diewert, W. E. 2002a. "The Quadratic Approximation Lemma and Decompositions of Superlative Indexes." *Journal of Economic and Social Measurement* 28: 63–88.

Diewert, W. E. 2002b. "Similarity and Dissimilarity Indexes: An Axiomatic Approach." Discussion Paper No. 02-10, Department of Economics, University of British Columbia, Vancouver. http://www.econ.ubc.ca.

Diewert, W. E. 2002c. "Harmonized Indexes of Consumer Prices: Their Conceptual Foundations." *Swiss Journal of Economics and Statistics* 138 (4): 547–637.

Diewert, W. E. 2002d. "Notes on Hedonic Producer Price Indexes." Unpublished Paper, Department of Economics, University of British Columbia, Vancouver.

Diewert, W. E. 2002e. "Hedonic Regressions: A Review of Some Unresolved Issues." Unpublished Paper, Department of Economics, University of British Columbia, Vancouver.

Diewert, W. E. 2003a. "Hedonic Regressions: A Consumer Theory Approach." In *Scanner Data and Price Indexes, NBER Studies in Income and Wealth*, edited by R. C. Feenstra and M. D. Shapiro. Chicago, IL: The University of Chicago Press, pp. 317–48.

Diewert, W. E. 2003b. "Measuring Capital." NBER Working Paper W9526, National Bureau of Economic Research, Cambridge, MA.

Diewert, W. E. 2004a. "On the Stochastic Approach to Linking the Regions in the ICP." Discussion Paper No. 04-16, Department of Economics, The University of British Columbia, Vancouver, Canada.

Diewert, W. E. 2004b. "The Treatment of Owner Occupied Housing and Other Durables in a Consumer Price Index." Paper presented at the Eighth Meeting of the International Working Group on Price Indices, Helsinki, August 23–25. http://www.ottawagroup.org.

Diewert, W. E. 2011. "Alternative Approaches to Measuring House Price Inflation." Paper presented at the Twelfth Meeting of the International Working Group on Price Indices, Wellington, May 4–6. http://www.ottawagroup.org.

Diewert, W. E., and D. A. Lawrence. 2000. "Progress in Measuring the Price and Quantity of Capital." In *Econometrics Volume 2: Econometrics and the Cost of Capital: Essays in Honor of Dale W. Jorgenson*, edited by L. J. Lau. Cambridge, MA: The MIT Press, pp. 273–326.

Diewert, W. E., and K. J. Fox. 2017. "Substitution Bias in Multilateral Methods for CPI Construction Using Scanner Data."

Discussion Paper 17-02, Vancouver School of Economics, University of British Columbia, Vancouver, BC.

Diewert, W. E., and R. Feenstra. 2017. "Estimating the Benefits and Costs of New and Disappearing Products." Discussion Paper Series 17-10, Vancouver School of Economics, University of British Columbia, Vancouver, BC.

Diewert, W. E., D. Fixler, and K. Zieschang. 2011. "The Measurement of Banking Services in the System of National Accounts." Paper presented at the Twelfth Meeting of the International Working Group on Price Indices, Wellington, May 4–6. http://www.ottawagroup.org.

Diewert, W. E., K. J. Fox, and J. de Haan. 2016. "A Newly Identified Source of Potential CPI Bias: Weekly versus Monthly Unit Value Price Indexes." *Economics Letters* 141, 169–72.

Diewert, W. E., K. J. Fox, and P. Schreyer. 2017. "The Digital Economy, New Products and Consumer Welfare." Discussion Paper 17-09, Vancouver School of Economics, University of British Columbia, Vancouver, BC.

Dikhanov, Y. 1997. "The Sensitivity of PPP-Based Income Estimates to Choice of Aggregation Procedures." Unpublished Paper, International Economics Department, World Bank, Washington, DC.

Dippo, C. S., and C. A. Jacobs. 1983. "Area Sampling Redesign for the Consumer Price Index." In *Proceedings of the Survey Research Methods Section*. Alexandria, VA: American Statistical Association, pp. 118–23.

Divisia, F. 1926. *L'indice monétaire et la théorie de la monnaie*. Paris: Société anonyme du Recueil Sirey.

Dorfman, A. H., J. Lent, S. G. Leaver, and E. Wegman. 2006. "On Sample Survey Designs for Consumer Price Indexes." *Survey Methodology* 32: 197–216.

Drechsler, L. 1973. "Weighting of Index Numbers in Multilateral International Comparisons." *Review of Income and Wealth* 19: 17–34.

Drobisch, M. W. 1871a. "Ueber die Berechnung der Veränderungen der Waarenpreise und des Geldwerths." *Jahrbücher für Nationalökonomie und Statistik* 16: 143–56.

Drobisch, M. W. 1871b. "Ueber einige Einwürfe gegen die in diesen Jahrbüchern veröffentlichte neue Methode, die Veränderungen der Waarenpreise und des Geldwerths zu berechten." *Jahrbücher für Nationalökonomie und Statistik* 16: 416–27.

Ducharme, L. M. 1997. "The Canadian Consumer Price Index and the Bias Issue: Present and Future Outlooks." In *Bias in the CPI: Experiences from Five OECD Countries*, Prices Division Analytical Series, No. 10, edited by L. M. Ducharme. Ottawa: Statistics Canada, pp. 13–24.

Duggan, J. E., and R. Gillingham. 1999. "The Effect of Errors in the CPI on Social Security Finances." *Journal of Business and Economic Statistics* 17 (2): 161–69.

Dulberger, E. R. 1989. "The Application of an Hedonic Model to a Quality-Adjusted Price Index for Computer Processors." In *Technology and Capital Formation*, edited by D. Jorgenson and R. Landau. Cambridge, MA: MIT Press.

Dulberger, E. R. 1993. "Sources of Price Decline in Computer Processors: Selected Electronic Components." In *Price Measurement and Their Uses, NBER Studies in Income and Wealth*, edited by M. Foss, M. E. Manser, and A. H. Young. Chicago, IL: University of Chicago Press, pp. 103–24.

Dutot, C. 1738. *Réflections politiques sur les finances et le commerce*, Vol. 1. La Haye: Les frères Vaillant et N. Prevost.

Dwyer, L., P. Forsyth, and D. S. Prasada Rao. 2001. "PPPs and the Price Competitiveness of International Tourism Destinations." Paper presented at the Joint World Bank–OECD Seminar on Purchasing Power Parities: Recent Advances in Methods and Applications, Washington, DC, January 30–February 2.

Edgeworth, F. Y. 1888. "Some New Methods of Measuring Variation in General Prices." *Journal of the Royal Statistical Society* 51: 346–68.

Edgeworth, F. Y. 1923. "The Doctrine of Index Numbers According to Mr. Correa Walsh." *The Economic Journal* 11: 343–51.

Edgeworth, F. Y. 1925. *Papers Relating to Political Economy*, Vol. 1. New York: Burt Franklin.

Edwards, R. 1997. "Measuring Inflation in Australia." In *Bias in the CPI: Experiences from Five OECD Countries*, Prices Division Analytical Series, No. 10, edited by L. M. Ducharme. Ottawa: Statistics Canada, pp. 5–12.

EFQM. 2019. "European Foundation for Quality Management Excellence Model." European Foundation for Quality Management, Brussels. http://www.efqm.org.

Ehemann, C., A. J. Katz, and B. R. Moulton. 2002. "The Chain Additivity Issue and the U.S. National Accounts." *Journal of Economic and Social Measurement* 28: 37–49.

Eichhorn, W. 1978. *Functional Equations in Economics*. Reading, MA: Addison-Wesley Publishing Company.

Eichhorn, W., and J. Voeller. 1976. *Theory of the Price Index, Lecture Notes in Economics and Mathematical Systems*, Vol. 140. Berlin: Springer-Verlag.

Eldridge, L. P. 1999. "How Price Indexes Affect BLS Productivity Measures." *Monthly Labor Review* 122 (2): 35–46.

Eltetö, O., and P. Koves. 1964. "On an Index Number Computation Problem in International Comparison." *Statisztikai Szemle* 42: 507–18 (in Czech).

Epple, D. 1987. "Hedonic Prices and Implicit Markets: Estimating Demand and Supply Functions for Differentiated Products." *Journal of Political Economy* 95: 59–80.

European Commission, International Monetary Fund, Organisation for Economic Co-operation and Development, United Nations, and World Bank. 2009. *System of National Accounts 2008*. New York: United Nations.

Eurostat. 1993. Classification of Products by Activity in the European Economic Community (CPA) (Luxembourg).

Eurostat. 2013. *Compendium of HICP Reference Documents, Methodologies & Working Papers, Economy and Finance*. Luxembourg: Publications Office of the European Union. https://ec.europa.eu/eurostat/documents/3859598/5926625/KS-RA-13-017-EN.PDF/.

Eurostat. 2016a. *Handbook on Price and Volume Measures in National Accounts, Manuals and Guidelines, Economy and Finance*. Luxembourg: Publications Office of the European Union. https://ec.europa.eu/eurostat/documents/3859598/7152852/KS-GQ-14-005-EN-N.pdf.

Eurostat. 2016b. *The Treatment of Cross-Border Internet Purchases in the HICP*. Directorate C: National Accounts, Prices and Key Indicators, Unit C-4: Price statistics, Purchasing Power Parities, Housing Statistics. Luxembourg: Publications Office of the European Union. http://ec.europa.eu/eurostat/documents/272892/7048317/HICP-recommendation-on-internet+purchases-December-2016/.

Eurostat. 2017a. *Practical Guide for Processing Supermarket Scanner Data*. Brussels, Belgium: Eurostat.

Eurostat. 2017b. *Technical Manual on Owner-Occupied Housing and House Price Indices*. Brussels, Belgium: Eurostat. https://ec.europa.eu/eurostat/documents/7590317/0/Technical-Manual-OOH-HPI-2017/.

Eurostat. 2018. *Harmonised Index of Consumer Prices (HICP) Methodological Manual, 2018 Edition*. Luxembourg: European Commission. https://ec.europa.eu/eurostat/en/web/products-manuals-and-guidelines/-/KS-GQ-17-015.

Feenstra, R. C. 1994. "New Product Varieties and the Measurement of International Prices." *American Economic Review* 34: 157–77.

Feenstra, R. C. 1995. "Exact Hedonic Price Indices." *Review of Economics and Statistics* 77: 634–54.

Feenstra, R. C., and W. E. Diewert. 2001. "Imputation and Price Indexes: Theory and Evidence from the International Price Program." Working Paper No. 335, Bureau of Labor Statistics, Washington, DC. http://www.bls.gov.

Feenstra, R. C., and M. D. Shapiro. 2003. "High Frequency Substitution and the Measurement of Price Indexes." In *Scanner Data and Price Indexes, NBER Studies in Income and Wealth*, edited by R. C. Feenstra and M. D. Shapiro. Chicago, IL: The University of Chicago Press, pp. 123–46.

Feenstra, R. C., and C. R. Shiells. 1997. "Bias in U.S. Import Prices and Demand." In *The Economics of New Goods, NBER Studies in Income and Wealth*, edited by T. F. Bresnahan and R. J. Gordon. Chicago, IL: University of Chicago, pp. 249–76.

Feldmann, B., and L. Sandberg. 2012. "Internet Purchases—A Challenge for the HICP." Paper presented at the UNECE/ILO Meeting of the Group of Experts on Consumer Price Indices, Geneva, May 30–June 1. https://www.unece.org.

Fenwick, D. 1997. "The Boskin Report from a United Kingdom Perspective." In *Bias in the CPI: Experiences from Five OECD Countries*, Prices Division Analytical Series, No. 10, edited by L. M. Ducharme. Ottawa: Statistics Canada, pp. 45–52.

Fenwick, D. 2006. "Real World Quality Measures." Paper presented at the Ninth Meeting of the International Working Group on Price Indices, London, May 14–16. http://www.ottawagroup.org.

Fenwick, D. 2008. "Collection and Processing of Price Data: The Role of the Tukey Algorithm in Validation Procedures for Prices Data in a Consumer Prices Index." UK Office for National Statistics. Paper presented at the UNECE/ILO Meeting of the Group of Experts on Consumer Price Indices, Geneva, May 8–9. https://www.unece.org.

Fenwick, D. 2014. "Exploiting New Technologies and New Data Sources—The Opportunities and Challenges Associated with Scanner Data." Paper presented at the UNECE/ILO Meeting of the Group of Experts on Consumer Price Indices, Geneva, May 26–28. https://www.unece.org.

Fenwick, D., A. Ball, M. Silver, and P. H. Morgan. 2003. "Price Collection and Quality Assurance of Item Sampling in the Retail Price Index: How Can Scanner Data Help?" In *Scanner Data and Price Indexes, NBER Studies in Income and Wealth*, edited by M. Shapiro and R. Feenstra. Chicago, IL: University of Chicago Press, pp. 67–87.

Fenwick, D., A. Brueton, and A. Ball. 2003. "Internet Retail Channels in Price Indices: The Challenges Involved in Including Non-traditional Retailers in the UK Retail Prices Index." Paper presented at meeting of the Ottawa Group, Rio de Janeiro, May 8–10, 2019.

Fenwick, D., and B. Whitestone. 2001. *The Use of Handheld Computers for the Collection of CPI Price Data*. London: Office for National Statistics (UK).

Ferger, W. F. 1931. "The Nature and Use of the Harmonic Mean." *Journal of the American Statistical Association* 26: 36–40.

Ferger, W. F. 1936. "Distinctive Concepts of Price and Purchasing Power Index Numbers." *Journal of the American Statistical Association* 31: 258–72.

Ferrari, G., G. Gozzi, and M. Riani. 1996. "Comparing GEKS and EPD Approaches for Calculating PPPs at the Basic Heading level." In *Eurostat: Improving the Quality of Price Indices: CPI and PPP*. Luxembourg: Eurostat.

Ferrari, G., and M. Riani. 1998. "On Purchasing Power Parities Calculation at the Basic Heading Level." *Statistica* LVIII: 91–108.

Filer, R., and J. Hanousek. 2002. "Survey-Based Estimates of Biases in Consumer Price Indices during Transition: Evidence from Romania." *Journal of Comparative Economics* 30 (3): 476–87.

Fisher, F. M., and K. Shell. 1972. "The Pure Theory of the National Output Deflator." In *The Economic Theory of Price Indexes*. New York: Academic Press, pp. 49–113.

Fisher, I. 1897. "The Role of Capital in Economic Theory." *Economic Journal* 7: 511–37.

Fisher, I. 1911. *The Purchasing Power of Money*. London: Macmillan.

Fisher, I. 1921. "The Best Form of Index Number." *Journal of the American Statistical Association* 17: 533–37.

Fisher, I. 1922. *The Making of Index Numbers*. Boston, MA: Houghton-Mifflin.

Fisher, W. C. 1913. "The Tabular Standard in Massachusetts History." *Quarterly Journal of Economics* 27: 417–51.

Fixler, D., J. Greenlees, and W. Lane. 2001. "Telecommunications Indexes in the U.S. Consumer Price Index." Paper presented at the Sixth Meeting of the International Working Group on Price Indices, Canberra, April 2–6. http://www.ottawagroup.org.

Fixler, D., and K. D. Zieschang. 1992. "Incorporating Ancillary Measures of Processes and Quality Change into a Superlative Productivity Index." *Journal of Productivity Analysis* 2: 245–67.

Fixler, D., and K. D. Zieshang. 2001. "Price Indices for Financial Services." Paper presented at the Sixth Meeting of the International Working Group on Price Indices, Canberra, April 2–6. http://www.ottawagroup.org.

Flux, A. W. 1921. "The Measurement of Price Change." *Journal of the Royal Statistical Society* 84: 167–99.

Forsyth, F. G., and R. F. Fowler. 1981. "The Theory and Practice of Chain Price Index Numbers." *Journal of the Royal Statistical Society A* 144 (2): 224–47.

Friedman, David M. 2016. "A New Estimation System for the US CPI—Capabilities and Impacts." Presentation at the Meeting of the Group of Experts on CPI, Geneva. http://www.unece.org/index.php.

Frisch, R. 1930. "Necessary and Sufficient Conditions Regarding the Form of an Index Number Which Shall Meet Certain of Fisher's Tests." *Journal of the American Statistical Association* 25: 397–406.

Frisch, R. 1936. "Annual Survey of General Economic Theory: The Problem of Index Numbers." *Econometrica* 4: 1–38.

Frost, S. 2001. "The Construction of Price Indices for Deposit and Loan Facilities." Paper presented at the Sixth Meeting of the International Working Group on Price Indices, Canberra, April 2–6. www.ottawagroup.org/.

Frost, S. 2003. "Experimental Price Indexes for Financial Services." Australian Bureau of Statistics, UNECE Expert Working Group on Consumer Price Indices, Paper presented at the UNECE/ILO Meeting of the Group of Experts on Consumer Price Indices, Geneva, December 4–5. https://www.unece.org.

Funke, H., G. Hacker, and J. Voeller. 1979. "Fisher's Circular Test Reconsidered." *Schweizerische Zeitschrift für Volkswirtshaft und Statistik* 115: 677–87.

Funke, H., and J. Voeller. 1978. "A Note on the Characterization of Fisher's Ideal Index." In *Theory and Applications of Economic Indices*, edited by W. Eichhorn, R. Henn, O. Opitz, and R. W. Shephard. Würzburg: Physica-Verlag, pp. 177–81.

Gabor, E., and P. Vermeulen. 2015. "New Evidence on Elementary Index Bias." Paper presented at the Fourteen Meeting of the International Working Group on Price Indices, Tokyo, May 20–22. http://www.ottawagroup.org.

Garcke, E., and J. M. Fells. 1893. *Factory Accounts: Their Principles and Practice, Fourth Edition* (First Edition 1887). London: Crosby, Lockwood and Son.

Geary, R. C. 1958. "A Note on the Comparison of Exchange Rates and Purchasing Power Between Countries." *Journal of the Royal Statistical Society (Series A)* 121: 97–9.

Genereux, P. A. 1983. "Working Group on Price Indices." INSEE, Paris, May 27–29. http://www.insee.fr.

Gini, C. 1931. "On the Circular Test of Index Numbers." *International Review of Statistics* 9: 3–25.

Greenlees, J. 1997. "Expenditure Weight Updates and Measured Inflation." Paper presented at the Third Meeting of the International Working Group on Price Indices, Voorburg, April 16–18.

Greenlees, J. S. 2011. "Improving the Preliminary Values of the Chained CPI-U." *Journal of Economic and Social Measurement* 31 (1–2): 1–18.

Greenlees, J., and R. McClelland. 2012. "New Evidence on Outlet Substitution Effects in Consumer Price Index Data." *Review of Economics and Statistics* 93 (2): 632–46.

Greenlees, J., and E. Williams. 2010. "Reconsideration of Weighting and Updating Procedures in the U.S. CPI."*Jahrbücher für Nationalökonomie und Statistik* (*The Journal of Economics and Statistics*) 230 (6): 741–58.

Griffioen, R., and O. Ten Bosch. 2016. "On the Use of Internet Data for the Dutch CPI." Statistics Netherlands. Paper presented at the UNECE/ILO Meeting of the Group of Experts on Consumer Price Indices, Geneva, May 2–4. https://www.unece.org.

Griliches, Z. 1988. *Technology, Education and Productivity: Early Papers with Notes to Subsequent Literature*. New York: Basil Blackwell.

Griliches, Z. 1990. "Hedonic Price Indices and the Measurement of Capital and Productivity: Some Historical Reflections." In *Fifty Years of Economic Measurement: The Jubilee of the Conference on Research in Income and Wealth, NBER Studies in Income and Wealth*, edited by E. R. Berndt and J. E. Triplett. Chicago, IL: University of Chicago Press, pp. 185–206.

Guðnason. 2001. "Telecommunications Services in the CPI—A Quantity Approach." Paper presented at the Sixth Meeting of the International Working Group on Price Indices, Canberra, April 2–6. http://www.ottawagroup.org.

Guðnason. 2003. "How Do We Measure Inflation? Some Measurement Problems." Paper presented at the Seventh Meeting of the International Working Group on Price Indices, May 27–29, Paris. http://www.insee.fr.

Hansen, Carsten Bolden. 2007. "Recalculations of the Danish CPI 1996–2006." Proceedings of the Tenth Meeting of the International Working (Ottawa) Group on Price Indexes, Ottawa, Canada, October 9–12. www.ottawagroup.org.

Hardy, G. H., J. E. Littlewood, and G. Pólya. 1934. *Inequalities*. Cambridge: Cambridge University Press.

Harper, M. J., E. R. Berndt, and D. O. Wood. 1989. "Rates of Return and Capital Aggregation Using Alternative Rental Prices." In *Technology and Capital Formation*, edited by D. W. Jorgenson and R. Landau. Cambridge, MA: The MIT Press, pp. 331–72.

Haschka, P. 2003. "Simple Methods of Explicit QA for Services in Complex Pricing Schemes." Paper presented at the Seventh Meeting of the International Working Group on Price Indices, May 27–29, Paris. http://www.insee.fr.

Hausman, J. A. 1997. "Valuation of New Goods under Perfect and Imperfect Conditions." In *The Economics of New Goods, NBER Studies in Income and Wealth*, edited by T. F. Bresnahan and R. J. Gordon. Chicago, IL: University of Chicago Press, pp. 209–37.

Hausman, J. A. 1999. "Cellular Telephone, New Products, and the CPI." *Journal of Business and Economic Statistics* 17 (2): 188–94.

Hausman, J. A. 2002. "Sources of Bias and Solutions to Bias in the CPI." Working Paper 9298, National Bureau of Economic Research, Cambridge, MA.

Hausman, J. A. 2005. "Consumer Benefits From Increased Competition in Shopping Outlets: Measuring the Effect of Wal-Mart." Working Paper 11809, National Bureau of Economic Research, Cambridge, MA.

Hausman, J. A., and E. Leibtag. 2004. "CPI Bias from Supercenters: Does the BLS Know that Wal-Mart Exists?" Working Paper 10712, National Bureau of Economic Research, Cambridge, MA.

Hawkes, W. J. 1997. "Reconciliation of Consumer Price Index Trends in Average Prices for Quasi-homogeneous Goods Using Scanning Data." Paper presented at the Third Meeting of the International Working Group on Price Indices, Voorburg, April 16–18. http://www.ottawagroup.org.

Hawkes, W. J., and F. W. Piotrowski. 2003. "Using Scanner Data to Improve the Quality of Measurement in the Consumer Price Index." In *Scanner Data and Price Indexes, NBER Studies in Income and Wealth*, edited by R. C. Feenstra and M. D. Shapiro. Chicago, IL: University of Chicago Press, pp. 17–38.

Haworth, M. F., D. Fenwick, and R. Beaven. 1997. "Recent Developments in the UK Retail Prices Index: Quality Management." Paper presented at the Third Meeting of the International Working Group on Price Indices, Voorburg, April 16–18. http://www.ottawagroup.org.

Hicks, J. R. 1940. "The Valuation of the Social Income." *Economica* 7: 105–24.

Hicks, J. R. 1941–42. "Consumers' Surplus and Index Numbers." *The Review of Economic Studies* 9: 126–37.

Hicks, J. R. 1946. *Value and Capital*, 2nd edition. Oxford: Clarendon Press.

Hidiroglou, M. A., and J.-M. Berthelot. 1986. "Statistical Editing and Imputation for Periodic Business Surveys." *Survey Methodology* 12 (1): 73–83.

Hill, R. J. 1995. "Purchasing Power Methods of Making International Comparisons." Ph.D. dissertation, University of British Columbia, Vancouver.

Hill, R. J. 1999a. "Comparing Price Levels across Countries Using Minimum Spanning Trees." *The Review of Economics and Statistics* 81: 135–42.

Hill, R. J. 1999b. "Comparing Price Levels across Countries using Spanning Trees." In: *International and Inter-Area Comparisons of Income, Output and Prices*, edited by A. Heston and R. E. Lipsey, Studies in Income and Wealth, Vol. 61. Chicago, IL: University of Chicago Press.

Hill, R. J. 1999c. "International Comparisons using Spanning Trees." In *International and Interarea Comparisons of Income, Output and Prices, NBER Studies in Income and Wealth*, edited by A. Heston and R. E. Lipsey. Chicago, IL: University of Chicago Press, pp. 109–20.

Hill, R. J. 1999d. "Chained PPPs and Minimum Spanning Trees." In *International and Interarea Comparisons of Income, Output and Prices, NBER Studies in Income and Wealth*, edited by A. Heston and R. E. Lipsey. Chicago, IL: Chicago University Press, pp. 327–64.

Hill, R. J. 1999e. "Comparing Price Levels Across Countries Using Minimum Spanning Trees." *The Review of Economics and Statistics* 81: 135–42.

Hill, R. J. 2001. "Measuring Inflation and Growth Using Spanning Trees." *International Economic Review* 42: 167–85.

Hill, R. J. 2002. "Superlative Index Numbers: Not All of Them Are Super." Discussion Paper No. 2002/04, School of Economics, University of New South Wales, Sydney.

Hill, T. P. 1988. "Recent Developments in Index Number Theory and Practice." *OECD Economic Studies* 10: 123–48.

Hill, T. P. 1996. *Inflation Accounting: A Manual on National Accounting under Conditions of High Inflation*. Paris: OECD.

Hill, T. P. 1998. "The Measurement of Inflation and Changes in the Cost of Living." *Statistical Journal of the United Nations ECE* 15: 37–51.

Hill, T. P. 1999. "COL Indexes and Inflation Indexes." Paper tabled at the Fifth Meeting of the International Working Group on Price Indices, Reykjavik, August 25–27. http://www.ottawagroup.org.

Hill, T. P. 2006. "Household Production, Consumption and CPIs." Paper presented at the Ninth Meeting of the International Working Group on Price Indices, London, May 14–16. http://www.ottawagroup.org.

Hillinger, C. 2002. "A General Theory of Price and Quantity Aggregation and Welfare Measurement." CISifo Working Paper No. 818, University of Munich, Munich.

Hoffmann, J. 1998. "Problems of Inflation Measurement in Germany." Discussion Paper 1/98, Economic Research Group of the Deutsche Bundesbank, Deutsche Bundesbank, Frankfurt.

Hoffmann, J. 1999. "The Treatment of Quality Changes in the German Consumer Price Index." Paper presented at the Fifth

Meeting of the International Working Group on Price Indices, Reykjavik, August 25–27. http://www.ottawagroup.org.

Hoffmann, J., and C. Kurz. 2002. "Rent Indices for Housing in West Germany: 1985 to 1998." Discussion Paper 01/02, Economic Research Centre of the Deutsche Bundesbank, Deutsche Bundesbank, Frankfurt.

Holdway, M. 1999. "An Alternative Methodology: Valuing Quality Changes for Microprocessors in the PPI." Unpublished Paper, Bureau of Labor Statistics, Washington, DC.

Horvitz, D. G., and D. J. Thompson. 1952. "A Generalization of Sampling without Replacement from a Finite Universe." *Journal of the American Statistical Association* 47: 663–85.

Hotelling, H. 1925. "A General Mathematical Theory of Depreciation." *Journal of the American Statistical Association* 20: 340–53.

Houthakker, H. S. 1952. "Compensated Changes in Quantities and Qualities Consumed." *Review of Economic Studies* 19: 155–64.

Hoven, L. 1999. "Some Observations on Quality Adjustment in the Netherlands." Unpublished Paper, Department of Consumer Prices, Statistics Netherland, Voorburg.

Howard, A., K. Dunford, J. Jones, M. van Kints, K. Naylor, and R. Tarnow-Mordi. 2015. "Using Transactions Data to Enhance the Australian CPI." Paper presented at the Fourteen Meeting of the International Working Group on Price Indices, Tokyo, May 20–22. http://www.ottawagroup.org.

Hulten, C. R. 1973. "Divisia Index Numbers." *Econometrica* 41: 1017–26.

Hulten, C. R. 1990. "The Measurement of Capital." In *Fifty Years of Economic Measurement: The Jubilee of the Conference on Research in Income and Wealth, NBER Studies in Income and Wealth*, edited by E. R. Berndt and J. E. Triplett. Chicago, IL: University of Chicago Press, pp. 119–58.

Hulten, C. R. 1996. "Capital and Wealth in the Revised SNA." In *The New System of National Accounts*, edited by J. W. Kendrick. New York: Kluwer Academic Publishers, pp. 149–81.

Hulten, C. R. 1996. "Issues in the Measurement of Economic Depreciation: Introductory Remarks." *Economic Inquiry* 34: 10–23.

Hulten, C. R., and F. C. Wykoff. 1981a. "The Estimation of Economic Depreciation Using Vintage Asset Prices." *Journal of Econometrics* 15: 367–96.

Hulten, C. R., and F. C. Wykoff. 1981b. "The Measurement of Economic Depreciation." In *Depreciation, Inflation and the Taxation of Income from Capital*, edited by C. R. Hulten. Washington, DC: The Urban Institute Press, pp. 81–125.

Imai, S., E. Diewert, and C. Shimizu. 2015. "Consumer Price Index Biases—Elementary Index Biases vs. Sampling Biases." Paper presented at the 14th Meeting of the International Working Group on Price Indices (the Ottawa Group), Tokyo, Japan, May 20–22.

International Labour Organization (ILO). 1987. *Report of the Fourteenth International Conference of Labour Statisticians*. Geneva: ILO.

International Labour Organization (ILO). 1990. *ISCO-88: International Standard Classification of Occupations*. Geneva: ILO.

International Labour Organization (ILO). 1998. "Guidelines Concerning Dissemination Practices for Labour Statistics." In *Report of the Sixteenth International Conference of Labour Statisticians*. Geneva: ILO. http://www.ilo.org/public/english/bureau/stat/standards/guidelines/index.htm.

International Labour Organization (ILO). 2003. *Report III to the Seventeenth International Conference of Labour Statisticians*. Geneva: ILO.

International Labour Organization, International Monetary Fund, Organisation for Economic Co-operation and Development, Eurostat, UN Economic Commission for Europe, and the World Bank. 2004. *Producer Price Index Manual*. Brussels/Luxembourg; Geneva; Washington, DC: International Monetary Fund.

International Labour Organization, International Monetary Fund, Organisation for Economic Co-operation and Development, UN Economic Commission for Europe, Eurostat, and the World Bank. 2004. *Consumer Price Index Manual: Theory and Practice*. Geneva: International Labour Office.

International Monetary Fund (IMF). 2013. "General Data Dissemination System (GDDS)." Washington, DC. http://dsbb.imf.org/Applications/web/gdds/gddshome/.

International Monetary Fund (IMF). 2013. "Special Data Dissemination Standard (SDDS)." Washington, DC. http://dsbb.imf.org/Applications/web/sddshome.

International Monetary Fund (IMF). 1993. *Balance of Payments Manual*, 5th edition. Washington, DC.

International Monetary Fund (IMF). 2001. *Government Finance Statistics Manual*. Washington, DC.

International Monetary Fund (IMF). 2009. *Balance of Payments and International Investment Position Manual*, 6th edition. Washington, DC.

International Monetary Fund (IMF). 2014. *Government Finance Statistics Manual*. Washington, DC.

International Standards Organization. 1994. *ISO 9000*. Geneva: International Standards Organization. http://iso.ch.

International Standards Organization. 2000. *ISO 900*. Geneva: International Standards Organization. http://iso.ch.

Ioannidis, C., and M. Silver. 1999. "Estimating Hedonic Indices: An Application to UK Television Sets." *Journal of Economics. Zeitschrift für Nationalökonomie* 69 (1): 71–94.

Ivancic, L. 2007. "Scanner Data and the Construction of Price Indices." PhD thesis, University of New South Wales, Sydney, Australia.

Ivancic, L., W. E. Diewert, and K. J. Fox. 2009. "Scanner Data, Time Aggregation and the Construction of Price Indexes." Discussion Paper No. 09-09, Department of Economics, University of British Columbia, Vancouver, Canada.

Ivancic, L., W. E. Diewert, and K. J. Fox. 2011. "Scanner Data, Time Aggregation and the Construction of Price Indexes." *Journal of Econometrics* 161: 24–35.

Ivancic, L., and K. J. Fox. 2013. "Understanding Price Variation across Stores and Supermarket Chains: Some Implications for CPI Aggregation Methods." *Review of Income and Wealth* 59: 629–47.

Jaluzot, L., and P. Sillard. 2016. "Échantillonnage des agglomérations de l'IPC pour la base 2015." Document de travail F160, INSEE.

Jensen, J. L. W. V. 1906. "Sur les fonctions convexes et les inégalités entre les valeurs moyennes." *Acta Mathematica* 8: 94–6.

Jevons, W. S. (1863) 1884. "A Serious Fall in the Price of Gold Ascertained and Its Social Effects Set Forth." Reprinted in *Investigations in Currency and Finance*. London: Macmillan and Co., pp. 13–118.

Jevons, W. S. 1865. "The Variation of Prices and the Value of the Currency since 1782." *Journal of the Statistical Society of London* 28: 294–320; reprinted in *Investigations in Currency and Finance* (London: Macmillan and Co., 1884), pp. 119–50.

Jevons, W. S. 1884. "A Serious Fall in the Value of Gold Ascertained and Its Social Effects Set Forth. 1863." In *Investigations in Currency and Finance*. London: Macmillan and Co., pp. 13–118.

Johannessen, R. 2004. "Owner Occupied Housing in the Norwegian CPI." Paper presented at the Eighth Meeting of the International Working Group on Price Indices, Helsinki, August 23–25. http://www.ottawagroup.org.

Johansen, I., and R. Nygaard. 2012. "Various Data Collection Methods in the Norwegian CPI." Statistics Norway. Paper presented at the UNECE/ILO Meeting of the Group of Experts on Consumer Price Indices, Geneva, May 30–June 1. https://www.unece.org.

Johnson, D. S., S. B. Reed, and K. J. Stewart. 2006. "Price Measurement in the United States: A Decade after the Boskin Report." *Monthly Labor Review* 129: 10–9.

Johnson, P. 2015. "UK Consumer Price Statistics: A Review." UK Statistics Authority, London. https://www.statisticsauthority.gov.uk/archive/reports---correspondence/current-reviews/uk-consumer-price-statistics---a-review.pdf.

Jorgenson, D. W. 1989. "Capital as a Factor of Production." In *Technology and Capital Formation*, edited by D. W. Jorgenson and R. Landau. Cambridge, MA: The MIT Press, pp. 1–35.

Jorgenson, D. W. 1996. "Empirical Studies of Depreciation." *Economic Inquiry* 34: 24–42.

Jorgenson, D. W., and Z. Griliches. 1967. "The Explanation of Productivity Change." *Review of Economic Studies* 34: 249–83.

Karanka, J., R. O'Neill, N. Weaden, R. Sanderson, C. Jenkins, and D. Bird. 2013. "Developing a Definitive Measure of House Prices in the UK." Paper presented at the Thirteenth Meeting of the International Working Group on Price Indices, Copenhagen, May 1–3. http://www.ottawagroup.org.

Katz, A. J. 1983. "Valuing the Services of Consumer Durables." *The Review of Income and Wealth* 29: 405–27.

Kennedy, P. 1998. *A Guide to Econometrics*. Oxford: Blackwell Publishers.

Keynes, J. M. 1930. *A Treatise on Money in Two Volumes: 1: The Pure Theory of Money*. London: Macmillan.

Khamis, S. H. 1970. "Properties and Conditions for the Existence of a New Type if Index Numbers." *Sankhya, Series B* 32: 81–98.

Khamis, S. H. 1972. "A New System of Index Numbers for National and International Purposes." *Journal of the Royal Statistical Society, Series A* 135: 96–121.

Khamis, S. H. 1984. "On Aggregation Methods for International Comparisons." *Review of Income and Wealth* 30 (2): 185–205.

Knibbs, Sir G. H. 1924. "The Nature of an Unequivocal Price Index and Quantity Index." *Journal of the American Statistical Association* 19: 42–60; 196–205.

Kokoski, M. F., B. R. Moulton, and K. D. Zieschang. 1999. "Interarea Price Comparisons for Heterogeneous Goods and Several Levels of Commodity Aggregation." In *International and Interarea Comparisons of Income, Output and Prices, NBER Studies in Income and Wealth*, edited by A. Heston and R. E. Lipsey. Chicago, IL: University of Chicago Press, pp. 123–66.

Kokoski, M. F., K. Waehrer, and P. Rozaklis. 2001. "Using Hedonic Methods for Quality Adjustment in the CPI: The Consumer Audio Products Component." Working Paper 344, Bureau of Labor Statistics, Washington, DC.

Konüs, A. A. 1924. "The Problem of the True Index of the Cost of Living." *The Economic Bulletin of the Institute of Economic Conjuncture* (in Russian), 9–10: 64–71; also published in English in 1939 in *Econometrica* 7: 10–29.

Konüs, A. A., and S. S. Byushgens. 1926. "K probleme pokupatelnoi cili deneg." *Voprosi Konyunkturi* 2: 151–72.

Koskimäki, T., and M. Ylä-Jarkko. 2003. "Segmented Markets and CPI Elementary Classifications." Paper presented at the Seventh Meeting of the International Working Group on Price Indices, Paris, May 27–29. http:// www.insee.fr/.

Koskimäki, T., and Y. Vartia. 2001. "Beyond Matched Pairs and Griliches Type Hedonic Methods for Controlling Quality Changes in CPI Subindices." Paper presented at the Sixth Meeting of the International Working Group on Price Indices, Canberra, April 2–6. http://www.ottawagroup.org.

Kotler, P. 1991. *Marketing Management*, 7th edition. Englewood Cliffs, NJ: Prentice Hall.

Kravis, I. B., A. W. Heston, and R. Summers. 1982. *World Product and Income: International Comparisons of Real Gross Domestic Product*. Baltimore, MD: Johns Hopkins University Press.

Krsinich, F. 2015. "Implementation of Consumer Electronics Scanner Data in the New Zealand CPI." Paper presented at the Fourteen Meeting of the International Working Group on Price Indices, Tokyo, May 20–22. http://www.ottawagroup.org.

Krsinich, F. 2015. "Price Indexes from Online Data Using the Fixed-Effects Window-Splice (FEWS) index." Statistics New Zealand. Paper presented at the Fourteen Meeting of the International Working Group on Price Indices, Tokyo, May 20–22. http://www.ottawagroup.org.

Krsinich, F. 2016. "The FEWS Index: Fixed Effects with a Window Splice." *Journal of Official Statistics* 32: 375–404.

Krueger, A. B., and A. Siskind. 1998. "Using Survey Data to Assess Bias in the Consumer Price Index." *Monthly Labor Review* 121 (4): 24–33.

Lamboray, C. 2017. "The Geary Khamis Index and the Lehr Index: How Much Do They Differ?" Paper presented at the Fifteen Meeting of the International Working Group on Price Indices, Eltville am Rhein, May 10–12. http://www.ottawagroup.org.

Lancaster, K. J. 1966. "A New Approach to Consumer Theory." *Journal of Political Economy* 74 (2): 132–56.

Lancaster, K. J. 1971. *Consumer Demand: A New Approach*. New York: Columbia University Press.

Lane, W. 2001. "Addressing the New Goods Problem in the Consumer Price Index." Paper presented at the Sixth Meeting of the International Working Group on Price Indices, Canberra, April 2–6. http://www.ottawa.org.

Laspeyres, E. 1871. "Die Berechnung einer mittleren Waarenpreissteigerung." *Jahrbücher für Nationalökonomie und Statistik* 16: 296–314.

Lau, L. J. 1979. "On Exact Index Numbers." *Review of Economics and Statistics* 61: 73–82.

Le Gallo, F., and F. Magnien. 2003. "Measuring Price Change in Mobile-Telephony Services: An Arduous Task." INSEE, Paper presented at the Seventh Meeting of the International Working Group on Price Indices, Paris, May 27–29. http://www.ottawagroup.org.

Leaver, S. G., and D. Swanson. 1992. "Estimating Variances for the U.S. Consumer Price Index for 1987–1991." In *Proceedings of the Survey Research Methods Section*. Alexandria, VA: American Statistical Association, pp. 740–45.

Lebow, D. E., J. M. Roberts, and D. J. Stockton. 1994. "Monetary Policy and the 'Price Level'." Unpublished Paper, Board of Governors of the Federal Reserve System, Washington, DC.

Lebow, D. E., and J. B. Rudd. 2003. "Measurement Error in the Consumer Price Index: Where Do We Stand?" *Journal of Economic Literature* 41: 159–201.

Lehr, J. 1885. *Beiträge zur Statistik der Preise*. Frankfurt: J. D. Sauerlander.

Lent, J., and A. H. Dorfman. 2009. "Using a Weighted Average of Jevons and Laspeyres Indexes to Approximate a Superlative Index." *Journal of Official Statistics* 25(1): 129–49.

Leontief, W. 1936. "Composite Commodities and the Problem of Index Numbers." *Econometrica* 4: 39–59.

Lequiller, F. 1997. "Does the French Consumer Price Index Overstate Inflation?" In *Bias in the CPI: Experiences from Five OECD Countries*, Prices Division Analytical Series, No. 10, edited by L. M. Ducharme. Ottawa: Statistics Canada, pp. 25–43.

Levy, F., H. Beamish, R. J. Murnane, and D. Aurtor. 1999. "Computerization and Skills: Example from a Car Dealership, Brookings Program on Output and Productivity Measurement in the Services Sector." Workshop on Measuring the Output of Business Services, May 14, Brookings Institution, Washington, DC.

Ley, E. 2003. "Comment." In *Scanner Data and Price Indexes, NBER Studies in Income and Wealth*, edited by R. C. Feenstra and M. D. Shapiro. Chicago, IL: University of Chicago Press, pp. 379–82.

Liegey Jr., P. R. 1992. "Adjusting Apparel Indices in the CPI for Quality Differences." In *Price Measurements and Their Uses, NBER Studies in Income and Wealth*, edited by M. F. Foss, M. Manser, and A. Young. Chicago, IL: University of Chicago Press.

Liegey Jr., P. R. 1994. "Apparel Price Indexes: Effects of Hedonic Adjustments." *Monthly Labor Review* 117: 38–45.

Liegey Jr., P. R. 2000. "Hedonic Quality Adjustment Methods for Microwave Ovens in the U.S. CPI." Methodology Paper, Bureau of Labor Statistics, Washington, DC.

Linacre, S. 2004. "Experimental Price Indexes for Financial Services, 1998 to 2003." Information Paper 6413.0, Australian Bureau of Statistics, Canberra, Australia.

Linder, F. 1996. *Reducing Bias in the Estimation of Consumer Price Indices by Using Integrated Data*. Research Report, Statistics Netherlands, Voorburg.

Lloyd, P. J. 1975. "Substitution Effects and Biases in Nontrue Price Indices." *American Economic Review* 65: 301–13.

Lowe, J. 1823. *The Present State of England in Regard to Agriculture, Trade and Finance*, 2nd edition. London: Longman, Hurst, Rees, Orme and Brown.

Lowe, R. 1996. "The Type and Extent of Quality Changes in the Canadian CPI." In *Proceedings of the Second Meeting of the International Working Group on Price Indices*, edited by J. Dalén. Stockholm: Statistics Sweden, pp. 231–49. http://www.ottawagroup.org.

Lowe, R. 1999. "The Use of the Regression Approach to Quality Change for Durables in Canada." Paper presented at the Fifth Meeting of the International Working Group on Price Indices, Reykjavik, August 25–27. http://www.ottawagroup.org.

Maddala, G. S. 1988. *Introduction to Econometrics*. New York: Macmillan.

Malmquist, S. 1953. "Index Numbers and Indifference Surfaces." *Trabajos de Estadistica* 4: 209–42.

Malpezzi, S., L. Ozanne, and T. Thibodeau. 1987. "Microeconomic Estimates of Housing Depreciation." *Land Economics* 63: 372–85.

Manser, M. E., and R. J. McDonald. 1988. "An Analysis of Substitution Bias in Measuring Inflation, 1959–85." *Econometrica* 56 (4): 909–30.

Marshall, A. 1887. "Remedies for Fluctuations of General Prices." *Contemporary Review* 51: 355–75.

Marshall, A. 1898. *Principles of Economics*, 4th edition. London: The Macmillan Co.

Matheson, E. 1910. *The Depreciation of Factories and Their Valuation*, 4th edition. London: E. & F. N. Spon.

McClelland, R., and M. Reinsdorf. 1999. "Small Sample Bias in Geometric Mean and Seasoned CPI Component Indexes." Economic Working Paper, Bureau of Labor Statistics, Washington, DC.

McCracken, P. M., J. Tobin, and others. 1999. *Measuring Prices in a Dynamic Economy: Re-Examining the CPI*. New York: The Conference Board.

Melser, D. 2018. "Scanner Data Price Indexes: Addressing Some Unresolved Issues." *Journal of Business & Economic Statistics* 36: 516–22.

Mendelsohn, R. 1984. "Estimating the Structural Equations of Implicit Market and Household Production Functions." *Review of Economics and Statistics* 66 (4): 673–77.

Mendershausen, H. 1937. "Annual Survey of Statistical Technique: Methods of Computing and Eliminating Changing Seasonal Fluctuations." *Econometrica* 5: 234–62.

Merkel, F. K. 2000. "Addressing New Item Bias in the Producer Price Indexes: a PPI Quality Improvement Initiative." Unpublished Paper, Bureau of Labor Statistics, Washington, DC.

Metcalfe, E., T. Flower, T. Lewis, M. Mayhew, and E. Rowland. 2016. *Research Indices Using Web Scraped Data: Clustering Large Datasets into Price Indices (CLIP)*. London: Office of National Statistics (ONS).

J. Mehrhoff. 2007. "A Linear Approximation to the Jevons Index." in: y.d. Lippe, P.M.

Mitchell, W. C. 1927. *Business Cycles*. New York: National Bureau of Economic Research.

Moulton, B. R. 1996a. *Constant Elasticity Cost-of-Living Index in Share Relative Form*. Washington, DC: Bureau of Labor Statistics.

Moulton, B. R. 1996b. "Bias in the Consumer Price Index: What Is the Evidence?" *Journal of Economic Perspectives* 10 (4): 159–77.

Moulton, B. R. 2001. "The Expanding Role of Hedonic Methods in the Official Statistics of the United States." In *Proceedings of a Symposium on Hedonic Methods*. Wiesbaden: Deutches Bundesbank and German Federal Statistical Office.

Moulton, B. R., and E. P. Seskin. 1999. "A Preview of the 1999 Comprehensive Revision of the National Income and Product Accounts." *Survey of Current Business* 79: 6–17.

Moulton, B. R., and K. E. Moses. 1997. "Addressing the Quality Change Issue in the Consumer Price Index." *Brooking Papers on Economic Activity* 1: 305–66.

Moulton, B. R., T. LaFleur, and K. E. Moses. 1999. "Research on Improved Quality Adjustment in the CPI: The Case of Televisions." In *Proceedings of the Fourth Meeting of the International Working Group on Price Indices*, edited by W. Lane. Washington, DC: Bureau of Labor Statistics, pp. 77–99. http://www.ottawagroup.org.

Mudgett, B. D. 1955. "The Measurement of Seasonal Movements in Price and Quantity Indexes." *Journal of the American Statistical Association* 50: 93–8.

Muellbauer, J. 1974. "Household Production Theory, Quality, and the 'Hedonic Technique.'" *The American Economic Review* 64 (6): 977–94.

Müller, R. 2010. "Scanner Data in the Swiss CPI: An Alternative to Price Collection in the Field." Paper presented at the UNECE/ILO Meeting of the Group of Experts on Consumer Price Indices, Geneva, May 10–12. https://www.unece.org.

Murray, J., and N. Sarantis. 1999. "Price–Quality Relationships and Hedonic Price Indexes for Cars in the United Kingdom." *International Journal of the Economics of Business* 6 (1): 1–23.

Muth, R. F. 1966. "Household Production and Consumer Demand Functions." *Econometrica* 34: 699–708.

Nevo, A. 2001. "New Products, Quality Changes, and Welfare Measures Computed from Estimated Demand Systems." NBER Working Paper W8425, National Bureau of Economic Research, Cambridge, MA.

Norberg, A. 1999. "Quality Adjustment: The Case of Clothing." In *Proceedings of the Measurement of Inflation Conference*, edited by M. Silver and D. Fenwick. Cardiff: Cardiff University. http://www.cardiff.ac.uk.

Norberg, A., K. Strandberg, and O. Ståhl. 2018. *En modell för resursallokering inom KPI*. Stockholm, Sweden: Statistics Sweden.

Nordhaus, W. D. 1998. "Quality Change in Price Indexes." *Journal of Economic Perspectives* 12 (1): 59–68.

Nygaard, R. 2015. "The Use of Online Prices in the Norwegian Consumer Price Index." Statistics Norway. Paper presented at the Fourteen Meeting of the International Working Group on Price Indices, Tokyo, May 20–22. http://www.ottawagroup.org.

Obst, Carl. 2000. "A Review of Bias in the CPI." *Statistical Journal of the United Nations ECE* 17: 37–58.

Office for National Statistics (UK). 1998. *The Retail Prices Index: A Technical Manual*. London: Office for National Statistics. http://www.statistics.gov.uk.

Office for National Statistics (UK). 2014. "Consumer Price Indices Technical Manual." London: Office for National Statistics. http://www.statistics.gov.uk.

Oi, W. Y. 1997. "The Welfare Implications of Invention." In *The Economics of New Goods, NBER Studies in Income and Wealth*. Chicago, IL: University of Chicago Press, pp. 109–41.

Okamoto, M. 2001. "Mid-Year Basket Index as a Practical Approximation to a Superlative Index." Paper presented at the Sixth Meeting of the International Working Group on Price Indices, Canberra, April 2–6. http://www.ottawagroup.org.

Opperdoes, E. 2001. "Some Empirical Experiments with CES Functions." Unpublished Paper, Statistics Netherlands, Voorburg.

Organisation for Economic Co-operation and Development (OECD). 1997. "Synthesis Paper on Shortcomings of the

Consumer Price Index Measure of Inflation for Economic Policy Purposes." Paper prepared for Working Party No. 1 on Macroeconomic and Structural Policy Analysis, ECO/CPE/WP1 (97)12, September, Paris.

Organisation for Economic Co-operation and Development (OECD). 1998. "FISM, A Note by the OECD Secretariat." Prepared for the Joint OECD/ESCAP Meeting on National Accounts—1993 System of National Accounts: Five Years On, Bangkok, May 4–8.

Organisation for Economic Co-operation and Development (OECD). 1999. *Purchasing Power Parities and Real Expenditures*. Paris: OECD.

Organisation for Economic Co-operation and Development (OECD). 2001a. *Measuring Productivity: Measurement of Aggregate and Industry-Level Productivity Growth*. Paris: OECD.

Organisation for Economic Co-operation and Development (OECD). 2001b. *Measuring Capital: Measurement of Capital Stocks, Consumption of Fixed Capital and Capital Services*. Paris: OECD.

Osgood, W. F. 1925. *Advanced Calculus*. New York: Macmillan.

Paasche, H. 1874. "Über die Preisentwicklung der letzten Jahre nach den Hamburger Borsennotirungen." *Jahrbücher für Nationalökonomie und Statistik* 12: 168–78.

Pakes, A. 2001. "A Reconsideration of Hedonic Price Indices with an Application to PC's." Working Paper 8715, National Bureau of Economic Research, Cambridge, MA, revised November 2001.

Palgrave, R. H. I. 1886. "Currency and Standard of Value in England, France and India and the Rates of Exchange between These Countries." Memorandum submitted to the Royal Commission on Depression of Trade and Industry, Third Report, Appendix B, pp. 312–90.

Parker, P. 1992. "Price Elasticity Dynamics over the Adoption Life Cycle." *Journal of Marketing Research* XXIX: 358–67.

Pierson, N. G. 1895. "Index Numbers and Appreciation of Gold." *Economic Journal* 5: 329–35.

Pierson, N. G. 1896. "Further Considerations on Index-Numbers." *Economic Journal* 6: 127–31.

Pigou, A. C. 1920. *The Economics of Welfare*. London: Macmillan.

Pike, C., B. Nimmo, and L. Mariposa. 2009. "New Zealand 2006 and 2008 Consumers Price Index Review: Price Updating." Room Document, Eleventh Meeting of the International Working (Ottawa) Group on Price Indexes, Neuchatel, Switzerland, May. http://www.ottawagroup.org/.

Pollak, R. A. 1975. "Subindexes of the Cost of Living." *International Economic Review* 16: 135–60.

Pollak, R. A. 1980. "Group Cost-of-Living Indexes." *American Economic Review* 70: 273–78.

Pollak, R. A. 1981. "The Social Cost-of-Living Index." *Journal of Public Economics* 15: 311–36.

Pollak, R. A. 1989. "The Treatment of the Environment in the Cost-of-Living Index." In *The Theory of the Cost-of-Living Index*, edited by R. A. Pollak. Oxford: Oxford University Press, pp. 181–85.

Pollak, R. A. (1983) 1989, 1990. "The Theory of the Cost-of-Living Index." In *Price Level Measurement*, edited by W. E. Diewert and C. Montmarquette. Ottawa: Statistics Canada, pp. 87–161; reprinted in *The Theory of the Cost-of-Living Index*, edited by R. A. Pollak. Oxford: Oxford University Press, pp. 3–52; also reprinted in *Price Level Measurement*, edited by W. E. Diewert. Amsterdam: North-Holland, pp. 5–77.

Pollak, R. A. 1998. "The Consumer Price Index: A Research Agenda and Three Proposals." *Journal of Economic Perspectives* 12 (1): 69–78.

Popkin, J. 1997. "Improving the CPI: The Record and Suggested Next Steps." *Business Economics* 32 (3): 42–7.

Prais, S. J. 1959. "Whose Cost of Living?" *The Review of Economic Studies* 26: 126–34.

Prennushi, G. 2001. "PPPs and Global Poverty: Strengths and Weaknesses." Paper presented at the Joint World Bank–OECD Seminar on Purchasing Power Parities: Recent Advances in Methods and Applications, Washington, DC, January 30–February 2.

Price Statistics Review Committee. 1961. *The Price Statistics of the Federal Government*. New York: National Bureau of Economic Research.

Rao, D. S. Prasada. 1990. "A System of Log-Change Index Numbers for Multilateral Comparisons." In *Comparisons of Prices and Real Products in Latin America*, edited by J. Salazar Carrillo and D. S. Prasada Rao. Amsterdam: North Holland.

Rao, D. S. Prasada. 1995. "On the Equivalence of the Generalized Country Product-Dummy (CPD) Method and the Rao-System for Multilateral Comparisons." Working Paper No. 5, Centre for International Comparisons, University of Pennsylvania, Philadelphia, PA.

Rao, D. S. Prasada. 1997. "Aggregation Methods for International Comparison of Purchasing Power Parities and Real Income: Analytical Issues and Some Recent Developments." In *Proceedings of the International Statistical Institute, 51st Session*. The Hague: International Statistical Institute, pp. 197–200.

Rao, D. S. Prasada. 2001a. "Integration of CPI and ICP: Methodological Issues, Feasibility and Recommendations." Paper presented at the Joint World Bank–OECD Seminar on Purchasing Power Parities: Recent Advances in Methods and Applications, Washington, DC, January 30–February 2.

Rao, D. S. Prasada. 2001b. "Weighted EKS and Generalized Country Product Dummy Methods for Aggregation at Basic Heading Level and Above Basic Heading Level." Paper presented at the Joint World Bank–OECD Seminar on Purchasing Power Parities: Recent Advances in Methods and Applications, Washington, DC, January 30–February 2.

Rao, D. S. Prasada. 2005. "On the Equivalence of Weighted Country-Product Dummy (CPD) Method and the Rao-System for Multilateral Price Comparisons." *Review of Income and Wealth* 51: 571–80.

Rao, D. S. Prasada, and K. S. Banerjee. 1984. "A Multilateral Index Number System Based on the Factorial Approach." *Statistische Hefte* 27: 297–313.

Rao, D. S. Prasada, C. J. O'Donnell, and E. Ball. 2000. "Transitive Multilateral Comparisons of Agricultural Output and Productivity Using Minimum Spanning Trees and Generalized EKS Methods." Paper presented at the Workshop on Agricultural Productivity: Data, Methods, and Measures, March 9–10, Washington, DC

Rao, D. S. Prasada, and M. Timmer. 2000. "Multilateralisation of Manufacturing Sector Comparisons: Issues, Methods and Empirical Results." Research Memorandum No. GD 47, Groningen Growth and Development Centre, Groningen.

Rasmussen, D. W., and T. W. Zuehlke. 1990. "On the Choice of Functional Form for Hedonic Price Functions." *The Review of Economics and Statistics* 72: 668–75.

Reese, M. 2000. "Hedonic Quality Adjustment Methods for College Textbooks for the U.S. CPI." Methodology Paper, Bureau of Labor Statistics, Cambridge, MA. http://www.bls.gov.

Reinsdorf, M. B. 1993. "The Effect of Outlet Price Differentials on the U.S. Consumer Price Index." In *Price Measurement and Their Uses, NBER Studies in Income and Wealth*, edited by M. F. Foss, M. E. Manser, and A. H. Young. Chicago, IL: University of Chicago Press, pp. 227–54.

Reinsdorf, M. B. 1994. "Price Dispersion, Seller Substitution and the U.S. CPI." Working Paper 252, Bureau of Labor Statistics, Washington, DC.

Reinsdorf, M. B. 1996. "Constructing Basic Component Indexes for the U.S. CPI from Scanner Data: a Test Using Data on Coffee." Working Paper 277, Bureau of Labor Statistics, Washington, DC.

Reinsdorf, M. B. 1998. "Divisia Indices and the Representative Consumer Problem." Paper presented at the Fourth Meeting of

the International Working Group on Price Indices, Washington, DC, April 22–24. http://www.ottawagroup.org.
Reinsdorf, M. B. 2003. personal communication, September 9.
Reinsdorf, M. B., W. E. Diewert, and C. Ehemann. 2002. "Additive Decompositions for the Fisher, Törnqvist and Geometric Mean Indexes." *Journal of Economic and Social Measurement* 28: 51–61.
Reinsdorf, M. B., P. Liegey, and K. Stewart. 1996. "New Ways of Handling Quality Change in the U.S. Consumer Price Index." Working Paper 276, Bureau of Labor Statistics, Washington, DC.
Reinsdorf, M. B., and B. R. Moulton. 1997. "The Construction of Basic Components of Cost-of-Living Indexes." In *The Economics of New Goods, NBER Studies in Income and Wealth*, edited by T. F. Bresnahan and R. J. Gordon. Chicago, IL: University of Chicago Press.
Reinsdorf, M. B., Quirós, G., and STA Group. 2018. *Measuring the Digital Economy*. IMF Staff Report, International Monetary Fund, Washington, DC. https://www.imf.org/en/Publications/Policy-Papers/Issues/2018/04/03/022818-measuring-the-digital-economy.
Reinsdorf, M. B., and P. Schreyer. 2017. "Measuring Consumer Inflation in a Digital Economy." Paper presented at the Fifth IMF Statistical Forum, Washington, DC, November 16–17. https://www.imf.org/en/News/Seminars/Conferences/2017/05/03/5th-statistical-forum.
Ribe, M. 2003. "Financial Services in Swedish Price Indices." Paper presented at the Seventh Meeting of the International Working Group on Price Indices, Paris, May 27–29. http://www.ottawagroup.org.
Richardson, D. H. 2003. "Scanner Indexes for the Consumer Price Index." In *Scanner Data and Price Indexes, NBER Studies in Income and Wealth*, edited by R. C. Feenstra and M. D. Shapiro. Chicago, IL: The University of Chicago Press, pp. 39–65.
Rosen, S. 1974. "Hedonic Prices and Implicit Markets: Product Differentiation and Pure Competition." *Journal of Political Economy* 82: 34–49.
Rothwell, D. P. 1958. "Use of Varying Seasonal Weights in Price Index Construction." *Journal of the American Statistical Association* 53: 66–77.
Ryten, J. 1998. *The Evaluation of the International Comparison Project (ICP)*. International Monetary Fund, Washington, DC.
Samuelson, P. A. 1953. "Prices of Factors and Goods in General Equilibrium." *Review of Economic Studies* 21: 1–20.
Samuelson, P. A., and S. Swamy. 1974. "Invariant Economic Index Numbers and Canonical Duality: Survey and Synthesis." *American Economic Review* 64: 566–93.
Särndal, C.-E., B. Swensson, and J. Wretman. 1992. *Model Assisted Survey Sampling*. New York: Springer-Verlag.
Schlömilch, O. 1858. "Über Mittelgrössen verschiedener Ordnungen." *Zeitschrift für Mathematik und Physik* 3: 308–10.
Schultz, B. J. (Szulc). 1996. "Treatment of Changes in Product Quality in Consumer Price Indices." In *Proceedings of the Second Meeting of the International Working Group on Price Indices*, edited by J. Dalén. Stockholm: Statistics Sweden, pp. 209–29. http://www.ottawagroup.org.
Schultz, B. J. (Szulc). 1999. "Effects of Using Various Macro-Index Formulae in Longitudinal Price and Comparisons: Empirical Studies." In *Proceedings of the Fourth Meeting of the International Working Group on Price Indices*, edited by W. Lane. Washington, DC: Bureau of Labor Statistics, pp. 236–49. http://www.ottawagroup.org.
Schultze, C. L., and C. Mackie. (eds.). 2002. *At What Price? Conceptualizing and Measuring Cost-of-Living and Price Indices*. Washington, DC: National Academy Press.
Schut, C., and others. 2002. *The Use of Scanner Data from Supermarkets in the Consumer Price Index* [in Dutch]. Statistics Netherlands, Voorburg, The Netherlands.
Scrope, G. P. 1833. *Principles of Political Economy*. London: Longman, Rees, Orme, Brown, Green and Longman.
Sellwood, D. 2001. "Improving Quality Adjustment in Practice." Paper presented at the Sixth Meeting of the International Working Group on Price Indices, Canberra, April 2–6. http://www.ottawagroup.org.
Selvanathan, E. A., and D. S. Prasada Rao. 1994. *Index Numbers: A Stochastic Approach*. Ann Arbor, MI: University of Michigan Press.
Shapiro, M. D., and D. W. Wilcox. 1997a. "Alternative Strategies for Aggregating Prices in the CPI." *Federal Reserve Bank of St. Louis Review* 79 (3): 113–25.
Shapiro, M. D., and D. W. Wilcox. 1997b. "Mismeasurement in the Consumer Price Index: An Evaluation." Working Paper No. W5590, National Bureau of Economic Research, Cambridge, MA. http:// www.nber.org.
Shephard, R. W. 1953. *Cost and Production Functions*. Princeton, NJ: Princeton University Press.
Shephard, R.W. 1970. *Theory of Cost and Production Functions*. Princeton, NJ: Princeton University Press.
Shepler, N. 2000. "Developing a Hedonic Regression Model for Refrigerators in the U.S. CPI." Methodology Paper, Bureau of Labor Statistics, Washington, DC. http://www.bls.gov/cpi/cpirfr.htm.
Shinozaki, K. 2017. "Web-Scraped Prices Comparison Method Adopted for the PPI in Japan." Bank of Japan. Paper presented at the Fifteen Meeting of the International Working Group on Price Indices, Eltville am Rhein, May 10–12. http://www.ottawagroup.org.
Shinozaki, K. 2018. "Compilation of Experimental Price Indexes Using Big Data and Machine Learning: A Comparative Analysis and Validity Verification." Paper presented at the UNECE/ILO Meeting of the Group of Experts on Consumer Price Indices, Geneva, May 7–9. https://www.unece.org.
Shiratsuka, S. 1999. "Measurement Errors in the Japanese Consumer Price Index." *Monetary and Economic Studies* 17 (3): 69–102.
Sidgwick, H. 1883. *The Principles of Political Economy*. London: Macmillan.
Silver, M. 1995. "Elementary Aggregates, Micro-Indices and Scanner Data: Some Issues in the Compilation of Consumer Price Indices." *Review of Income and Wealth* 41: 427–38.
Silver, M. 1999. "An Evaluation of the Use of Hedonic Regressions for Basic Components of Consumer Price Indices." *Review of Income and Wealth* 45 (1): 41–56.
Silver, M. 2002. "The Use of Weights in Hedonic Regressions: The Measurement of Quality Adjusted Price Changes." Unpublished Paper, Cardiff Business School, Cardiff University, Cardiff.
Silver, M. 2011. "An Index Number Formula Problem: The Aggregation of Broadly Comparable Items." *Journal of Official Statistics* 27 (4): 553–67.
Silver, M. 2018. "How to Measure Property Price Indices Better." *Eurostat Review of National Accounts and Macroeconomic Indicators (EURONA)*, 1/2018: 35–66.
Silver, M., and S. Heravi. 2001a. "Scanner Data and the Measurement of Inflation." *The Economic Journal* 111 (June): F384–F405.
Silver, M., and S. Heravi. 2001b. "Hedonic Price Indices and the Matched Models Approach." Unpublished Paper, Cardiff Business School, Cardiff University, Cardiff.
Silver, M., and S. Heravi. 2002. "Why the CPI Matched Models Method May Fail Us." Working Paper 144, European Central Bank, Frankfurt.
Silver, M., and S. Heravi. 2003. "The Measurement of Quality Adjusted Price Changes." In *Scanner Data and Price Indexes, NBER Studies in Income and Wealth*, edited by R. C. Feenstra and M. D. Shapiro. Chicago, IL: University of Chicago Press, pp. 277–316.
Silver, M., and S. Heravi. 2005. "A Failure in the Measurement of Inflation: Results from a Hedonic and Matched Experiment

Using Scanner Data." *Journal of Business & Economic Statistics* 23: 269–81.

Silver, M., and S. Heravi. 2007. "Why Elementary Price Index Number Formulas Differ: Price Dispersion and Product Heterogeneity." *Journal of Econometrics* 140(2): 874–83.

Solomons, D. 1961. "Economic and Accounting Concepts of Income." *The Accounting Review* 36: 374–83.

Solow, R. M. 1957. "Technical Change and the Aggregate Production Function." *Review of Economics and Statistics* 39: 312–20.

Statistics Sweden. 2001. *Swedish Consumer Price Index: A Handbook of Methods*. Stockholm: Statistics Sweden.

Stiglitz, J. E., Sen, A., and Fitoussi, J. P., 2009. *Report by the Commission on the Measurement of Economic Performance and Social Progress*. Commission on the Measurement of Economic Performance and Social Progress.

Stoevska, V., and E. Namukasa. 2012. "Methodologies of Compiling Consumer Price Indices." 2012 ILO Survey of Country Practices. https://www.ilo.org/ilostat-files/SSM/SSM1_NEW/CPI%20Summary%20report%202013.pdf.

Stone, R. 1956. *Quantity and Price Indexes in the National Accounts*. Paris: OECD.

Summers, R. 1973. "International Price Comparisons Based Upon Incomplete Data." *Review of Income and Wealth* 19 (1): 1–16.

Sundgren, B. 1993. "Statistical Metainformation Systems Pragmatics, Semantics, and Syntatctics." *Statistical Journal of the United Nations Economic Commission for Europe* 10 (2): 121–42.

Szulc, B. J. (Schultz). 1964. "Index Numbers of Multilateral Regional Comparisons" (in Polish). *Przeglad Statysticzny* 3: 239–54.

Szulc, B. J. (Schultz). 1983. "Linking Price Index Numbers." In *Price Level Measurement*, edited by W. E. Diewert and C. Montmarquette. Ottawa: Statistics Canada, pp. 537–66.

Szulc, B. J. (Schultz). 1987. "Price Indices below the Basic Aggregation Level." *Bulletin of Labour Statistics* 2: 9–16.

Tauchen, H., and A. D. Witte. 2001. "Estimating Hedonic Models; Implications of the Theory." Technical Working Paper No. 271. National Bureau of Economic Research, Cambridge, MA. http://www.nber.org.

Teekens, R., and J. Koerts. 1972. "Some Statistical Implications of the Log Transformations of Multiplicative Models." *Econometrica* 40 (5): 793–819.

Tellis, G. J. 1988. "The Price Elasticity of Selective Demand: A Meta-Analysis of Econometric Models of Sales." *Journal of Marketing Research* 25: 167–77.

Theil, H. 1954. *Linear Aggregation of Economic Relations*. Amsterdam: North-Holland.

Theil, H. 1967. *Economics and Information Theory*. Amsterdam: North-Holland.

Törnqvist, L. 1936. "The Bank of Finland's Consumption Price Index." *Bank of Finland Monthly Bulletin* 10: 1–8.

Törnqvist, L., and E. Törnqvist. (1937) 1981. "Vilket är förhållandet mellan finska markens och svenska kronans köpkraft?" *Ekonomiska Samfundets Tidskrift* 39: 1–39; reprinted in *Collected Scientific Papers of Leo Törnqvist* (Helsinki: The Research Institute of the Finnish Economy), pp. 121–160.

Trajtenberg, M. 1989. *Economic Analysis of Product Innovation: The Case of CT Scanners*. Cambridge, MA: Harvard University Press.

Triplett, J. E. 1981. "Reconciling the CPI and the PCE Deflator." *Monthly Labor Review* (September):3–15.

Triplett, J. E. 1983. "Concepts of Quality in Input and Output Price Measures: A Resolution of the User-Value Resource-Cost Debate." In *The U.S. National Income and Product Accounts: Selected Topics, NBER Studies in Income and Wealth*, edited by M. F. Foss. Chicago, IL: University of Chicago Press, pp. 269–311.

Triplett, J. E. 1987. "Hedonic Functions and Hedonic Indices." In *The New Palgrave: A Dictionary of Economics*, Vol. 2, edited by J. Eatwell, M. Milgate, and P. Newman. London: Macmillan, pp. 630–34.

Triplett, J. E. 1990. "Hedonic Methods in Statistical Agency Environments: An Intellectual Biopsy." In *Fifty Years of Economic Measurement: The Jubilee of the Conference on Research in Income and Wealth, NBER Studies in Income and Wealth*, edited by E. R. Berndt and J. E. Triplett. Chicago, IL: University of Chicago Press, pp. 207–38.

Triplett, J. E. 1997. "Current Status of the Debate on the Consumer Price Index in the U.S." In *Bias in the CPI: Experiences from Five OECD Countries*, Prices Division Analytical Series, No. 10, edited by L. M. Ducharme. Ottawa: Statistics Canada, pp. 53–60.

Triplett, J. E. 1999. "The Solow Productivity Paradox: What Do Computers Do to Productivity?" *Canadian Journal of Economics* 32(2): 309–34.

Triplett, J. E. 2001. "Should the Cost-of-Living Index Provide the Conceptual Framework for a Consumer Price Index?" *The Economic Journal* 111: F311–F334.

Triplett, J. E. 2002. *Handbook on Quality Adjustment of Price Indexes for Information and Communication Technology Products*. Draft, OECD Directorate for Science, Technology and Industry. Paris: OECD.

Triplett, J. E. 2003. "Using Scanner Data in Consumer Price Indexes: Some Neglected Conceptual Considerations." In *Scanner Data and Price Indexes, NBER Studies in Income and Wealth*, edited by R. C. Feenstra and M. D. Shapiro. Chicago, IL: University of Chicago Press, pp. 151–62.

Triplett, J. E. 2006. *Handbook on Hedonic Indexes and Quality Adjustments in Price Indexes: Special Application to Information Technology Products*. Paris: OECD Publishing.

Trivedi, P. K. 1981. "Some Discrete Approximations to Divisia Integral Indices." *International Economic Review* 22: 71–7.

Turvey, R. 1979. "The Treatment of Seasonal Items in Consumer Price Indices." In *Bulletin of Labour Statistics*, Fourth Quarter. Geneva: ILO, pp. 13–33.

Turvey, R. 1995. "Three Kinds of Monthly CPI." Paper presented at the Second Meeting of the International Working Group on Price Indices, Stockholm, November 15–17. http://www.ottawagroup.org.

Turvey, R. 1996. "Elementary Aggregate (Micro) Indexes." Paper presented at the Eurostat Seminar on Improving the Quality of Price Indices: CPI and PPP, Florence, December 18–20, 1995.

Turvey, R. 1998. "New Outlets and New Products." In *Proceedings of the Third Meeting of the International Working Group on Price Indices*, edited by B. Balk. Voorburg: Statistics Netherlands, pp. 97–110.

Turvey, R. 1999. "Incorporating New Models into a CPI: PCs as an Example." In *Proceedings of the Measurement of Inflation Conference*, edited by M. Silver and D. Fenwick. Luxembourg, London, Cardiff: Eurostat, Office for National Statistics, Cardiff University. http://www.cardiff.ac.uk.

Turvey, R. 2000. "True Cost of Living Indexes." In *Proceedings of the Fifth Meeting of the International Working Group on Price Indices*, edited by R. Gudnason and D. Gylfadóttir. Reykjavik: Statistics Iceland. http://www.ottawagroup.org.

Turvey, R., and others. 1989. *Consumer Price Indices: An ILO Manual*. Geneva: ILO.

U.S. Bureau of Labor Statistics. 1983. "Changing the Home Ownership Component of the Consumer Price Index to Rental Equivalence." In *CPI Detailed Report*. Washington, DC: U.S. Bureau of Labor Statistics.

U.S. Bureau of Labor Statistics. 1997. *BLS Handbook of Methods*, Bulletin 2490. Washington, DC: U.S. Bureau of Labor Statistics.

U.S. Bureau of Labor Statistics. 1998. "Measurement Issues in the Consumer Price Index." *Statistical Journal of the United Nations ECE* 15: 1–36.

U.S. Bureau of Labor Statistics. 2001. "Direct Pricing of Health Insurance in the Consumer Price Index." Ottawa Group, 2001.

Paper presented at the Sixth Meeting of the International Working Group on Price Indices, Canberra, April 2–6. http://www.ottawagroup.org.

U.S. Bureau of Labor Statistics. 2015. *Handbook of Methods, Consumer Price Indexes*. Washington, DC: U.S. Bureau of Labor Statistics. https://www.bls.gov/opub/hom/pdf/homch17.pdf.

U.S. General Accounting Office. 2000. "Consumer Price Index: Update of Boskin Commission's Estimate of Bias." Report GAO/GGD-00–50, U.S. General Accounting Office, Washington, DC.

U.S. Senate, Committee on Finance. 1996. *Final Report of the Advisory Commission to Study the Consumer Price Index, Print 104–72, 104 Cong., 2nd Session*. Washington, DC: Government Printing Office.

United Nations Economic Commission for Europe, International Labour Office, International Monetary Fund, Organisation for Economic Development and Co-operation, Statistical Office of the European Communities, The World Bank, and the (UK) Office for National Statistics. 2009. *Practical Guide to Producing Consumer Price Indices*. Geneva and New York: United Nations. http://www.unece.org/index.php.

United Nations. 1990. "International Standard Industrial Classification of All Economic Activities." Statistical Papers Series M, No. 4, Rev. 3, United Nations, New York.

United Nations. 1992. *Handbook of the International Comparison Program*, Series F, No. 62. New York: United Nations.

United Nations. 1994. *Fundamental Principles of Official Statistics, Adopted by the UN Statistical Commission*. UN Economic and Social Council, 1994, Report of the Special Session of the Statistical Commission, New York, April 11–15, 1994, E/1994/29. New York: United Nations.

United Nations. 1998a. "Principles and Recommendations for Population and Housing Censuses." Revision 1, Statistical Papers Series M, No. 67/Rev. 1, Sales No. E.98.XVII.8, United Nations, New York.

United Nations. 1998b. "Central Product Classification. CPC." Version 1.0, Statistical Papers Series M, No. 77, Ver. 1.0, United Nations, New York.

United Nations. 1999. "Classifications of Expenditure According to Purpose." Statistical Papers Series M, No. 84, United Nations, New York.

United Nations. 2002. *International Standard Industrial Classification of All Economic Activities, ISIC, Revision 3.1*. New York: United Nations Statistical Division.

Van der Grient, H. A., and J. de Haan. 2010. "The Use of Supermarket Scanner Data in the Dutch CPI." Paper presented at the UNECE/ILO Workshop on Scanner Data, May 10, Geneva, Switzerland.

Van der Grient, H., and J. de Haan. 2011. "Scanner Data Price Indexes: The 'Dutch' Method versus Rolling Year GEKS." Paper presented at the Twelfth Meeting of the International Working Group on Price Indices, Wellington, May 4–6. http://www.ottawagroup.org.

Van Haren, G., F. Kleima, and J. de Haan. 2006. "The CPI and the New Dutch Health Care System." Paper presented at the Ninth Meeting of the International Working Group on Price Indices, London, May 14–16. http://www.ottawagroup.org.

Van Ijzeren, J. 1987. "Bias in International Index Numbers: a Mathematical Elucidation." Dissertation for the Hungarian Academy of Sciences, Koninklijke Bibliotheek, The Hague.

Van Loon, K., and D. Roels. 2018. "Integrating Big Data in the Belgium CPI." Belgium STATBEL. Paper presented at the UNECE/ILO Meeting of the Group of Experts on Consumer Price Indices, Geneva, May 7–9. https://www.unece.org.

Van Mulligen, P. H. 2003. "Quality Aspects in Price Indices and International Comparisons: Applications of the Hedonic Method." Ph.D. thesis, University of Groningen, Groningen. http://www.cbs.nl/en/publications/articles/general/theses/theses.htm.

Vartia, Y. O. 1976. *Relative Changes and Index Numbers*. Helsinki: The Research Institute of the Finnish Economy.

Vartia, Y. O. 1978. "Fisher's Five-Tined Fork and Other Quantum Theories of Index Numbers." In *Theory and Applications of Economic Indices*, edited by W. Eichhorn, R. Henn, O. Opitz, and R. W. Shephard. Würzburg: Physica-Verlag, pp. 271–95.

Verbrugge, R. 2008. "The Puzzling Divergence of Rents and User Costs, 1980–2004." Review of Income and Wealth, Series 54, Number 4, Bureau of Labor Statistics, Washington, DC.

Viglino, L. 2003. "Insurance and Quality Adjustment: Excess and Option-cost Method." Paper presented at the Seventh Meeting of the International Working Group on Price Indices, Paris, May 27–29. http://www.ottawagroup.org.

Ville, J. 1946. "The Existence-Conditions of a Total Utility Function" (in French). Translated in 1951 in *The Review of Economic Studies* 19: 123–8.

Vogt, A. 1977. "Zum Indexproblem: Geometrische Darstellung sowie eine neue Formel." *Schweizerische Zeitschrift für Volkswirtschaft und Statistik* 113: 73–88.

Vogt, A. 1978. "Divisia Indices on Different Paths." In *Theory and Applications of Economic Indices*, edited by W. Eichhorn, R. Henn, O. Opitz, and R. W. Shephard. Würzburg: Physica-Verlag, pp. 297–305.

Vogt, A. 1980. "Der Zeit und der Faktorumkehrtest als 'Finders of Tests.'" *Statistische Hefte* 21: 66–71.

Vogt, A., and J. Barta. 1997. *The Making of Tests for Index Numbers*. Heidelberg: Physica-Verlag.

Von Auer, L. 2001. "An Axiomatic Checkup for Price Indices." Working Paper No. 1/2001, Faculty of Economics and Management, Otto von Guericke University, Magdeburg.

Von Auer, L. 2002. "Spurious Inflation: The Legacy of Laspeyres and Others." *The Quarterly Review of Economics and Finance* 42: 529–42.

Von Auer, L. 2014. "The Generalized Unit Value Index Family." *Review of Income and Wealth* 60: 843–61.

Von der Lippe, P. 2001. *Chain Indices: A Study in Price Index Theory*, Publication Series Spectrum of Federal Statistics, Vol. 16. Wiesbaden: Statistisches Bundesamt.

Walras, L. 1954. *Elements of Pure Economics*. Translated from French by W. Jaffe. London: George Allen and Unwin; first published in 1874.

Walschots, J. 2011. "The Treatment of Internet Purchases in Consumer Price Statistics, Harmonising Their Treatment in the HICP (European Commission, Eurostat)." Paper presented at the Twelfth Meeting of the International Working Group on Price Indices, Wellington, May 4–6. http://www.ottawagroup.org.

Walsh, C. M. 1901. *The Measurement of General Exchange Value*. New York: Macmillan and Co.

Walsh, C. M. 1921a. *The Problem of Estimation*. London: P. S. King & Son.

Walsh, C. M. 1921b. "Discussion." *Journal of the American Statistical Association* 17: 537–44.

Walsh, C. M. 1932. "Index Numbers." In *Encyclopedia of the Social Sciences*, Vol. 7, edited by E. R. A. Seligman. New York: The Macmillan Co., pp. 652–8.

Ward, M. 2001. "True Comparisons in Real and Money Terms." Paper presented at the Joint World Bank–OECD Seminar on Purchasing Power Parities: Recent Advances in Methods and Applications, Washington, DC, January 30–February 2.

Westergaard, H. 1890. *Die Grundzüge der Theorie der Statistik*. Jena: Fischer.

White, A. G. 1999. "Measurement Biases in Consumer Price Indexes." *International Statistical Review* 67 (3): 301–25.

White, A. G. 2000. "Outlet Types and the Canadian Consumer Price Index." *Canadian Journal of Economics* 33: 488–505.

Wold, H. 1944. "A Synthesis of Pure Demand Analysis, Part 3." *Skandinavisk Aktuarietidskrift* 27: 69–120.

Wold, H. 1953. *Demand Analysis*. New York: John Wiley.

Wooldridge, J. M. 1996. "Estimating Systems of Equations with Different Instruments for Different Equations." *Journal of Econometrics* 74: 387–405.

Woolford, K. 1999. "Measuring Inflation: A Framework Based on Domestic Final Purchases." In *Proceedings of the Measurement of Inflation Conference*, edited by M. Silver and D. Fenwick. Cardiff: Cardiff University, pp. 534–43.

Woolford, K. 2001. "Financial Services in the Consumer Price Index." Paper presented at the Sixth Meeting of the International Working Group on Price Indices, Canberra, April 2–6. http://www.ottawagroup.org.

Wynne, M. A. 1997. "Commentary." *Federal Reserve Bank of St. Louis Review* 79 (3): 161–7.

Wynne, M. A. 1999. "Core Inflation: A Review of Some Conceptual Issues." Research Department Working Paper 99-03, Federal Reserve Bank of Dallas, Dallas, TX.

Wynne, M. A., and F. D. Sigalla. 1994. "The Consumer Price Index." *Federal Reserve Bank of Dallas Economic Review*, Second Quarter. Dallas: Federal Reserve Bank of Dallas, pp. 1–22.

Young, A. 1812. *An Inquiry into the Progressive Value of Money in England as Marked by the Price of Agricultural Products*. Piccadilly: Hatchard.

Yule, G. U. 1921. "Discussion of Mr. Flux's Paper." *Journal of the Royal Statistical Society* 84: 199–202.

Zarnowitz, V. 1961. "Index Numbers and the Seasonality of Quantities and Prices." In *The Price Statistics of the Federal Government*, G. J. Stigler (Chair). New York: National Bureau of Economic Research, pp. 233–304.

Zhang, L., I. Johansen, and R. Nygaard. 2019. "Tests for Price Indices in a Dynamic Item Universe." *Journal of Official Statistics*, 35 (3): 683–97.

Zieschang, K. D. 1988. "The Characteristics Approach to the Problem of New and Disappearing Goods in Price Indexes." Working Paper No. 183, Bureau of Labor Statistics, Washington, DC.

Zieschang, K. D., P. A. Armnecht, and D. Smith. 2001. "Integrated InterArea and International Price Comparisons with Consumer Price Index Compilation." Paper presented at the Joint World Bank–OECD Seminar on Purchasing Power Parities: Recent Advances in Methods and Applications, Washington, DC, January 30–February 2.

INDEX